THE GOSPEL
ACCORDING TO LUKE I–IX

VOLUME 28

The ANCHOR BIBLE is a fresh approach to the world's greatest classic. Its object is to make the Bible accessible to the modern reader; its method is to arrive at the meaning of biblical literature through exact translation and extended exposition, and to reconstruct the ancient setting of the biblical story, as well as the circumstances of its transcription and the characteristics of its transcribers.

THE ANCHOR BIBLE is a project of international and interfaith scope: Protestant, Catholic, and Jewish scholars from many countries contribute individual volumes. The project is not sponsored by any ecclesiastical organization and is not intended to reflect any particular theological doctrine. Prepared under our joint supervision, THE ANCHOR BIBLE is an effort to make available all the significant historical and linguistic knowledge which bears on the interpretation of the biblical record.

THE ANCHOR BIBLE is aimed at the general reader with no special formal training in biblical studies; yet, it is written with most exacting standards of scholarship, reflecting the highest technical accomplishment.

This project marks the beginning of a new era of co-operation among scholars in biblical research, thus forming a common body of knowledge to be shared by all.

William Foxwell Albright
David Noel Freedman
GENERAL EDITORS

THE ANCHOR BIBLE

The Gospel According to

LUKE
(I–IX)

Introduction, Translation, and Notes

by

JOSEPH A. FITZMYER, S.J.

DOUBLEDAY & COMPANY, INC.
GARDEN CITY, NEW YORK

NIHIL OBSTAT
Joseph N. Tylenda, S.J., *Censor Deputatus*

IMPRIMI POTEST
V. Rev. Joseph P. Whelan, S.J., *Provincial*
Maryland Province, Society of Jesus

IMPRIMATUR
Rev. Msgr. John F. Donoghue, *Vicar General*
Archdiocese of Washington
27 December 1979

The *nihil obstat* and *imprimatur* are official declarations that a book or pamphlet is free of doctrinal or moral error. No implication is contained therein that those who have granted the *nihil obstat* and *imprimatur* agree with the content, opinions, or statements expressed.

Library of Congress Cataloging in Publication Data
Bible. N.T. Luke I-IX. English. Fitzmyer. 1981.
The gospel according to Luke I-IX.

(The Anchor Bible; v. 28)
Bibliography: p. 271
1. Bible. N.T. Luke—Commentaries. I. Fitzmyer,
Joseph A. II. Title. III. Series: Anchor Bible;
v. 28.
BS192.2.A1 1964.G3 vol. 28 [BS2593] 220.7′7s [226′.4077]
ISBN: 0-385-00515-6
Library of Congress Catalog Card Number 80–702

PREFACE

This commentary on the Lucan Gospel has been written with the aim of explaining its meaning for twentieth-century readers. During the nineteen centuries since the Gospel was first composed many persons have turned their hand to commenting on it. One feels, therefore, somewhat like Luke himself who composed the prologue to his Gospel with a similar awareness: that many others had already tried to do a similar job before him. If I too have decided, after studying everything carefully, to try my hand at it, it is less easy to say in a few words wherein the distinctive character of this commentary lies. Instead, I shall simply say what I have tried to do in commenting on the Lucan text.

I have tried to keep in mind that the Lucan Gospel is only one part of the two-volume work which comes from this author. Consequently, constant reference is made to Acts as well as the rest of the Gospel in commenting on any given passage.

I make no apology for the solution to the Synoptic problem that I use in this commentary, a modified form of the Two-Source Theory. The reasons for this decision will be found in the proper place in the Introduction. In each passage I have tried to discuss its Synoptic relationship, whether it is derived from "Mk" (short for "the Marcan source," which is the canonical Mark), from "Q" (short for the *Quelle* or "source" of the Double Tradition in Matthew and Luke), or from "L" (short for Luke's private source, written or oral). I have also tried to distinguish between Lucan "redaction" and Lucan "composition." By the former I mean the modification of preexistent source-material inherited by Luke; this is often evident from his distinctive language and style. By the latter is meant Luke's freely composed formulations.

Having set forth the Synoptic relationship of the passage, I have always tried to explain its form-critical character, i.e. what sort of a literary form is one reading in the passage.

These two questions, the Synoptic relationship and the form-critical character, are, however, only preliminary and serve only to clear the air for the discussion of the *meaning* of the passage as a unit in its relation to the Gospel-part in which it is found and to the Gospel as a whole. The attempt to arrive at its meaning may require a discussion of the passage's structure, theological preoccupation, and essential message. All of these aspects of the passage are treated in a section called "COMMENT," which is then followed by "NOTES," in which minor problems raised by individual words or phrases, textual criticism, philological analysis, or history are treated in detail. Both the "COMMENT" and the "NOTES" contribute to the understanding of the passage as a unit; of the two the former is the more important, and for this reason it precedes in this commentary.

In the Introduction to the commentary one will find a discussion of the usual questions: general bibliography on the Lucan Gospel, the current state of Lucan studies, the authorship, date, and destination of the Gospel, its composition, style, language, and outline. An important part of the Introduction, however, is a sketch of Lucan theology; this has been included because it is not possible to treat adequately in the discussion of individual passages the more comprehensive theological themes of the Lucan writings. Such discussion could often become repetitious, and so an attempt has been made to set forth briefly the major aspects of Lucan theology, to which reference in a given passage can always be made. The addition of this sketch reveals that my attempt in writing this commentary is not to limit it to historical-critical exegesis. This sort of interpretation of Scripture has long since won its place in the sun, but it has to be combined with a sense of the theological interest and purpose of the writer.

Attention is also called here to a fundamental distinction that is employed throughout this commentary on the Lucan Gospel. Various stages of the gospel tradition are invoked at times to explain one aspect or other of the Lucan story of Jesus. Stage I of the gospel tradition is concerned with what the historical Jesus of Nazareth did and said; Stage II with what was preached and proclaimed about him after the resurrection; and Stage III with what NT writers decided to put in writing concerning him. What immediately confronts the reader of the Lucan Gospel is a form of Stage III of that tradition. It is the result of literary composition, based on material inherited by the author from Stages I and II and fashioned by him into a synthesis, an interpretation of the Christ-event. Stage III should not be confused with Stage I. The primary concern of this commentary is to interpret the Lucan form of Stage III: how has Luke presented Jesus in his two-volume work, especially in its first part, the Gospel. At times questions about Stage I will arise—inevitably—and an attempt will be made to handle them; but it should be noted at the outset that such questions are secondary to the aim of this commentary.

In the course of my comments or notes I shall often refer to the Old Testament, and my readers should realize that I am using this shorthand way of referring to both the protocanonical and deuterocanonical books of the Christian Bible. In references to the Psalter, I follow the numbering of the Hebrew text, even when the Greek form of some psalms is being discussed.

Finally, it is my pleasant task to express my gratitude to various persons who have helped me in many ways during the composition of this commentary. In particular, Francis T. Gignac, S.J., who at one point read through my translation of Luke and made many valuable suggestions; the Georgetown Jesuit Community, which allowed me to take a leave of absence from teaching for a semester in order to bring this volume to completion; Henry J. Bertels, S.J., and William J. Sheehan, C.S.B., for much library assistance; David Noel Freedman, the general editor of the Anchor Bible series, and Michael Patrick O'Connor, his assistant, for many critical comments and suggestions which have improved the text of my commentary; Robert W. Hewetson, copy editor; and Eve F. Roshevsky, of Doubleday & Company, Inc., who has overseen the publication of this volume.

JOSEPH A. FITZMYER, S.J.
Department of Biblical Studies
School of Religious Studies
The Catholic University of America
Washington, DC 20064

Matris patrisque
piae memoriae

CONTENTS

TRANSLATION AND COMMENTARY

THE PROLOGUE

I. THE INFANCY NARRATIVE

II. THE PREPARATION FOR THE PUBLIC MINISTRY OF JESUS

PRINCIPAL ABBREVIATIONS

AAGA[3]	M. Black, *An Aramaic Approach to the Gospels and Acts* (3d ed.; Oxford: Clarendon, 1967)
AAS	*Acta apostolicae sedis*
AbhTANT	Abhandlungen zur Theologie des Alten und Neuen Testaments
AER	*American Ecclesiastical Review*
AGSU	Arbeiten zur Geschichte des Spätjudentums und Urchristentums
AJP	*American Journal of Philology*
AJT	*American Journal of Theology*
ALBO	Analecta lovaniensia biblica et orientalia
AnBib	Analecta biblica
ANEP	J. B. Pritchard, *The Ancient Near East in Pictures* (Princeton: Princeton University, 1954)
ANET	J. B. Pritchard, *Ancient Near Eastern Texts* (Princeton: Princeton University, 1950) and *Supplement* (1968)
AnGreg	Analecta gregoriana
ANT	M. R. James, *The Apocryphal New Testament* (Oxford: Clarendon, 1924)
AOS	American Oriental Society
APOT	*Apocrypha and Pseudepigrapha of the Old Testament* (ed. R. H. Charles, 2 vols.; Oxford: Clarendon, 1913)
ASAE	Annales du service des antiquités de l'Egypte
ASNU	Acta seminarii neotestamentici upsaliensis
ASOR	American Schools of Oriental Research
AsSeign	*Assemblées du Seigneur*
ASTI	*Annual of the Swedish Theological Institute*
ATANT	Abhandlungen zur Theologie des Alten und Neuen Testaments
ATR	*Anglican Theological Review*
A.U.C.	AB URBE CONDITA (from the foundation of Rome, in Roman dates)
AzNTT	Arbeiten zur neutestamentlichen Textforschung
BA	*Biblical Archaeologist*
BAG	Bauer-Arndt-Gingrich, *Greek-English Lexicon of the New Testament* (Chicago: University of Chicago, 1957)
BASOR	*Bulletin of the American Schools of Oriental Research*
BBB	Bonner biblische Beiträge
BDF	Blass-Debrunner-Funk, *Greek Grammar of the New Testament* (Chicago: University of Chicago, 1961)

BDR	Blass-Debrunner-Rehkopf, *Grammatik des neutestamentlichen Griechisch* (Göttingen: Vandenhoeck und Ruprecht, 1976)
Beginnings	F. J. Foakes Jackson and K. Lake (eds.), *The Beginnings of Christianity: The Acts of the Apostles* (5 vols.; London: Macmillan, 1920-1933; repr., Grand Rapids: Baker, 1979)
BeO	*Bibbia e oriente*
BETL	Bibliotheca ephemeridum theologicarum lovaniensium
BEvT	Beiträge zur evangelischen Theologie
BFCT	Beiträge zur Förderung christlicher Theologie
BGBE	Beiträge zur Geschichte der biblischen Exegese
BGD	Bauer-Gingrich-Danker, *Greek-English Lexicon of the New Testament* (Chicago: University of Chicago, 1979)
BHT	Beiträge zur historischen Theologie
Bib	*Biblica*
BibLeb	*Bibel und Leben*
BibOr	Biblica et orientalia
BibS(N)	Biblische Studien (Neukirchen: Erziehungsverein, 1951-)
BJ	*La Bible de Jérusalem*
BJRL	*Bulletin of the John Rylands* (University) *Library* (of Manchester)
BK	*Bibel und Kirche*
BLit	*Bibel und Liturgie*
BNTC	Black's New Testament Commentaries
Boh	Bohairic (an ancient Coptic version of the New Testament)
BR	*Biblical Research*
BSac	*Bibliotheca sacra*
BT	*The Bible Translator*
BTB	*Biblical Theology Bulletin*
BTS	*Bible et terre sainte*
BVC	*Bible et vie chrétienne*
BW	*Biblical World*
BWANT	Beiträge zur Wissenschaft vom Alten und Neuen Testaments
BZ	*Biblische Zeitschrift*
BZNW	Beihefte zur *ZNW*
CB	*Cultura bíblica*
CBQ	*Catholic Biblical Quarterly*
CCD	*Confraternity of Christian Doctrine* (version of the Bible)
CCLat	Corpus christianorum, series latina
CHR	*Church History Review*
CIG	*Corpus inscriptionum graecarum*
CII	*Corpus inscriptionum iudaicarum* (2 vols.; ed. J.-B. Frey; Vatican City: Institute of Christian Archaeology, 1936, 1952)
CIS	*Corpus inscriptionum semiticarum*
CJRT	*Canadian Journal of Religious Thought*
ConNT	*Coniectanea neotestamentica*
CQR	*Church Quarterly Review*

CRev	*Classical Review*
CSCO	Corpus scriptorum christianorum orientalium
CSEL	Corpus scriptorum ecclesiasticorum latinorum
CSS	Cursus sacrae Scripturae
CTM	*Concordia Theological Monthly*
CurrTM	*Currents in Theology and Mission*
DBS	*Dictionnaire de la Bible, Supplément*
DJD	Discoveries in the Judaean Desert (of Jordan) (Oxford: Clarendon)
DS	Denzinger-Schönmetzer, *Enchiridion symbolorum*
DunRev	*Dunwoodie Review*
EBib	Études bibliques
ELS	D. Baldi, *Enchiridion locorum sanctorum* (Jerusalem: Franciscan, 1955)
ESBNT	J. A. Fitzmyer, *Essays on the Semitic Background of the New Testament* (London: Chapman, 1971; repr., Missoula, MT: Scholars Press, 1974)
EstBíb	*Estudios bíblicos*
EstEcl	*Estudios eclesiásticos*
ETL	*Ephemerides theologicae lovanienses*
ETR	*Études théologiques et religieuses*
EvQ	*Evangelical Quarterly*
EvT	*Evangelische Theologie*
EWNT	*Exegetisches Wörterbuch zum Neuen Testament* (eds. H. Balz and G. Schneider; Stuttgart: Kohlhammer, 1978-)
Expos	*Expositor*
ExpTim	*Expository Times*
FC	Fathers of the Church
FGT	V. Taylor, *Formation of the Gospel Tradition* (London: Macmillan, 1949)
FRLANT	Forschungen zur Religion und Literatur des Alten und Neuen Testaments
FTG	M. Dibelius, *From Tradition to Gospel* (New York: Scribner, 1935)
GCS	Griechische christliche Schriftsteller
GKC	Gesenius-Kautzsch-Cowley, *Hebrew Grammar*
Greg	*Gregorianum*
HALAT	W. Baumgartner, *Hebräisches und aramäisches Lexikon zum Alten Testament* (Leiden: Brill, 1967, 1974, 198?)
Hennecke-Schneemelcher, *NTApocrypha*	E. Hennecke and W. Schneemelcher, *New Testament Apocrypha* (2 vols.; London: Lutterworth, 1963, 1965)

HeyJ	*Heythrop Journal*
HNT	Handbuch zum Neuen Testament
HSCP	*Harvard Studies in Classical Philology*
HSM	Harvard Semitic Monographs
HST	R. Bultmann, *History of the Synoptic Tradition* (Oxford: Blackwell, 1968)
HTKNT	Herders theologischer Kommentar zum Neuen Testament
HTR	*Harvard Theological Review*
HTS	Harvard Theological Studies
IB	*Interpreter's Bible* (Nashville: Abingdon, 1952)
ICC	International Critical Commentary
IDB	*Interpreter's Dictionary of the Bible* (Nashville: Abingdon, 1962)
IDBSup	*Interpreter's Dictionary of the Bible, Supplementary Volume* (1976)
IEJ	*Israel Exploration Journal*
ILS	H. Dessau (ed.), *Inscriptiones latinae selectae* (Berlin: Weidmann, 1892-1916)
Int	*Interpretation*
ITQ	*Irish Theological Quarterly*
JAAR	*Journal of the American Academy of Religion* (successor to *JBR*)
JAOS	*Journal of the American Oriental Society*
JB	*Jerusalem Bible*
JBC	*The Jerome Biblical Commentary* (eds. R. E. Brown et al.; Englewood Cliffs, NJ: Prentice-Hall, 1968)
JBL	*Journal of Biblical Literature*
JBR	*Journal of Bible and Religion*
JETS	*Journal of the Evangelical Theological Society*
JJS	*Journal of Jewish Studies*
JPOS	*Journal of the Palestine Oriental Society*
JQR	*Jewish Quarterly Review*
JR	*Journal of Religion*
JRS	*Journal of Roman Studies*
JSNT	*Journal for the Study of the New Testament*
JTS	*Journal of Theological Studies*
KD	*Kerygma und Dogma*
"L"	The Lucan private source
LAE	A. Deissmann, *Light from the Ancient East* (2d ed.; London: Hodder & Stoughton, 1927)
LCL	Loeb Classical Library
LD	Lectio divina
LQ	*Lutheran Quarterly*
LSJ	Liddell-Scott-Jones, *Greek-English Lexicon*

LTK	*Lexikon für Theologie und Kirche*
LumVie	*Lumière et vie*
LXX	The Septuagint
m.	Mishna
MeyerK	H. A. W. Meyer, Kritisch-exegetischer Kommentar über das Neue Testament
"Mk"	The Marcan source
MM	J. H. Moulton and G. Milligan, *The Vocabulary of the Greek Testament* (London: Hodder & Stoughton, 1930)
MNT	R. E. Brown et al. (eds.), *Mary in the New Testament* (Philadelphia: Fortress; New York: Paulist, 1978)
MNTC	Moffatt New Testament Commentaries
MPAT	J. A. Fitzmyer and D. J. Harrington, *A Manual of Palestinian Aramaic Texts* (BibOr 34; Rome: Biblical Institute, 1979)
MT	Masoretic Text
MTZ	*Münchener theologische Zeitschrift*
NAB	*New American Bible* (successor to *CCD*)
NCCHS	R. C. Fuller et al. (eds.), *A New Catholic Commentary on Holy Scripture* (London: Nelson, 1969)
NEB	*New English Bible*
NHS	Nag Hammadi Studies
NICNT	New International Commentary on the New Testament
NIDNTT	C. Brown (ed.), *New International Dictionary of New Testament Theology* (3 vols.; Grand Rapids: Zondervan, 1975-1978)
NKZ	*Neue kirchliche Zeitschrift*
NovT	*Novum Testamentum*
NovTSup	Novum Testamentum, Supplements
NRT	*La nouvelle revue théologique*
ns	new series (any language)
NTA	*New Testament Abstracts*
NTAbh	Neutestamentliche Abhandlungen
NTB	C. K. Barrett, *The New Testament Background: Selected Documents* (London: SPCK, 1956)
NTD	Das Neue Testament deutsch
NTS	*New Testament Studies*
OGIS	W. Dittenberger, *Orientis graeci inscriptiones selectae* (Leipzig: Hirzel, 1903-1905)
OL	Old Latin (Vetus latina)
OS	Old Syriac (Vetus syra)
os	old series (any language)
OxyP	Oxyrhynchus Papyri
PG	Patrologia graeca (ed. J. Migne)
PJ	*Palästina-Jahrbuch*
PL	Patrologia latina (ed. J. Migne)

Prot. Jas.	*Protevangelium of James*
PW	*Paulys Real-Encyclopädie der classischen Altertumswissenschaft* (ed. G. Wissowa; Stuttgart: Metzler, 1893-)
"Q"	Quelle (source of the Double Tradition in Luke and Matthew)
QD	Quaestiones disputatae
QDAP	*Quarterly of the Department of Antiquities in Palestine*
RAC	*Reallexikon für Antike und Christentum* (ed. T. Klausner; Stuttgart: Hiersmann, 1950-)
RB	*Revue biblique*
RBén	*Revue bénédictine*
RCB	*Revista de cultura bíblica*
RechBib	Recherches bibliques
RevExp	*Review and Expositor*
RevistB	*Revista bíblica*
RevQ	*Revue de Qumrân*
RevScRel	*Revue des sciences religieuses*
RevThom	*Revue thomiste*
RGG	*Die Religion in Geschichte und Gegenwart* (3d ed.; ed. K. Galling; Tübingen: Mohr [Siebeck], 1957-1965)
RHE	*Revue d'histoire ecclésiastique*
RHPR	*Revue d'histoire et de philosophie religieuses*
RivB	*Rivista biblica*
RNT	Regensburger Neues Testament
RSR	*Recherches de science religieuse*
RSV	*Revised Standard Version*
RTP	*Revue de théologie et de philosophie*
RUO	*Revue de l'université d'Ottawa*
Sah	Sahidic (an ancient Coptic version of the New Testament)
SANT	Studien zum Alten und Neuen Testaments
SBB	Stuttgarter biblische Beiträge
SBFLA	*Studii biblici franciscani liber annuus*
SBL	Society of Biblical Literature
SBLDS	SBL Dissertation Series
SBLMS	SBL Monograph Series
SBS	Stuttgarter Bibelstudien
SBT	Studies in Biblical Theology
SC	Sources chrétiennes
ScCatt	*Scuola cattolica*
ScEccl	*Sciences ecclésiastiques*
ScEsp	*Science et esprit*
Scr	*Scripture*
SE I, II, III, etc.	*Studia evangelica I* (TU 73; ed. F. L. Cross; Berlin: Akademie, 1959); *II* (TU 87, 1964); *III* (TU 88, 1964); *IV* (TU 102, 1968); *V* (TU 103, 1968); *VI* (TU 112; ed. E. A. Livingstone, 1973)

SEÅ	*Svensk exegetisk årsbok*
SJLA	Studies in Judaism in Late Antiquity
SJT	*Scottish Journal of Theology*
SNT	Studien zum Neuen Testament
SNTSMS	Studiorum Novi Testamenti Societas, Monograph Series
SPAW	*Sitzungsberichte der preussischen Akademie der Wissenschaften*
SQE	K. Aland, *Synopsis quattuor Evangeliorum* (Stuttgart: Württembergische Bibelanstalt, 1964)
ST	*Studia theologica*
StudNeot	Studia neotestamentica, Studia
SUNT	Studien zur Umwelt des Neuen Testaments
Str-B	[H. Strack und] P. Billerbeck, *Kommentar zum Neuen Testament* (6 vols.; Munich: Beck, 1922-1961)
SymOs	*Symbolae osloenses*
TBl	*Theologische Blätter*
TBT	*The Bible Today*
TCGNT	B. M. Metzger, *A Textual Commentary on the Greek New Testament* (London/New York: United Bible Societies, 1971)
TD	*Theology Digest*
TDNT	G. Kittel and G. Friedrich (eds.), *Theological Dictionary of the New Testament* (10 vols.; Grand Rapids: Eerdmans, 1964-1976; Engl. version of *TWNT*)
TDOT	G. J. Botterweck and H. Ringgren (eds.), *Theological Dictionary of the Old Testament* (Grand Rapids: Eerdmans, 1974-)
TF	*Theologische Forschung*
THKNT	Theologisches Handkommentar zum Neuen Testament
TLZ	*Theologische Literaturzeitung*
TynNTC	Tyndale New Testament Commentary
TPQ	*Theologisch-praktische Quartalschrift*
TQ	*Theologische Quartalschrift*
TRu	*Theologische Rundschau*
TS	*Theological Studies*
TSK	*Theologische Studien und Kritiken*
TTod	*Theology Today*
TTZ	*Trierer theologische Zeitschrift*
TU	Texte und Untersuchungen
TvT	*Tijdschrift voor Theologie*
TWNT	G. Kittel and G. Friedrich (eds.), *Theologisches Wörterbuch zum Neuen Testament* (10 vols.; Stuttgart: Kohlhammer, 1933-1979)
TZ	*Theologische Zeitschrift*
UBS	United Bible Societies
UBSGNT	*UBS Greek New Testament*
VC	*Vigiliae christianae*
VCaro	*Verbum caro*

VD	*Verbum domini*
VF	*Verkündigung und Forschung*
Vg	Vulgate (Vulgata latina)
VKGNT	K. Aland (ed.), *Vollständige Konkordanz zum griechischen Neuen Testament*
VS	Verbum salutis
VSpir	*Vie spirituelle*
WA	J. A. Fitzmyer, *A Wandering Aramean* (SBLMS 25; Missoula, MT: Scholars Press, 1979)
WJT	*Westminster Journal of Theology*
WMANT	Wissenschaftliche Monographien zum Alten und Neuen Testament
WUNT	Wissenschaftliche Untersuchungen zum Neuen Testament
ZBG	M. Zerwick, *Biblical Greek* (Rome: Biblical Institute, 1963)
ZKT	*Zeitschrift für katholische Theologie*
ZNW	*Zeitschrift für die neutestamentliche Wissenschaft*
ZRGG	*Zeitschrift für Religions- und Geistesgeschichte*
ZST	*Zeitschrift für systematische Theologie*
ZTK	*Zeitschrift für Theologie und Kirche*

GRAMMATICAL ABBREVIATIONS

absol.	absolute		infin.	infinitive
acc.	accusative		interj.	interjection
act.	active		intrans.	intransitive
adj.	adjective		masc.	masculine
adv.	adverb		neut.	neuter
aor.	aorist		nom.	nominative
art.	article		obj.	object
cl.	clause		opt.	optative
dat.	dative		pass.	passive
def.	definite		pers.	person
dem.	demonstrative		pf.	perfect
dir.	direct		pl.	plural
fem.	feminine		prep.	preposition
fut.	future		pres.	present
gen.	genitive		pron.	pronoun
impers.	impersonal		ptc.	participle
impf.	imperfect		rel.	relative
impv.	imperative		sg.	singular
indef.	indefinite		subjunc.	subjunctive
indic.	indicative		voc.	vocative
indir.	indirect			

OTHER ABBREVIATIONS

app. crit.	*apparatus criticus*
(*bis*)	two occurrences
c.	century
Comm. in	Commentary on
E	English version (bracketed, immediately following chapter and verse)
Ep.	*Epistula*, Epistle
Gos.	Gospel
Hom. in	*Homilia in*, Homily on
Oxy	Oxyrhynchus
P	Papyrus
T.	Testament
Josephus *Ag.Ap.*	*Against Apion*
Ant.	*Antiquities*
J.W.	*The Jewish War*

Dead Sea Scrolls and Related Texts

CD	Cairo (Genizah text of the) Damascus (Document)
Mur	Wadi Murabba'at texts
p	Pesher (commentary)
Q	Qumran
1Q, 2Q, etc.	Numbered caves of Qumran, yielding written material; followed by abbreviation of biblical or apocryphal book
1QapGen	*Genesis Apocryphon* of Cave 1
1QH	*Hôdāyôt* (*Thanksgiving Hymns*) from Cave 1
1QpHab	*Pesher on Habakkuk* from Cave 1
1QM	*Milḥāmah* (*War Scroll*)
1QS	*Serek hayyaḥad* (*Rule of the Community, Manual of Discipline*)
1QSa	Appendix A (*Rule of the Congregation*) to 1QS
4QEn	Enoch texts from Cave 4
4QFlor	Florilegium from Cave 4
4QMess ar	Aramaic "Messianic" text from Cave 4
4QPBless	Patriarchal Blessings from Cave 4
11QtgJob	Targum of Job from Cave 11

Targumic Material

Tg. Neb.	*Targum of the Prophets*
Tg. Yer. I	*Targum Yerušalmi 1*

Orders and Tractates in Mishnaic and Related Literature

To distinguish the same-named tractates in the Mishna, Tosepta, Babylonian Talmud, and Jerusalem Talmud, an italicized *m.*, *t.*, *b.*, or *y.* is used before the title of the tractate. Thus *m. Para, t. Para, b. Para, y. Para.*

INTRODUCTION

I. THE CURRENT STATE OF LUCAN STUDIES

No one who undertakes to write a commentary on a NT book can do so in a vacuum. Such a writer must take into account current interpretations of the biblical book and adopt a perspective vis-à-vis at least the major modes of interpretation of it. On the other hand, it is practically impossible for any one writer to cope with all the numerous interpretations that have been proposed for the various problems in the book under discussion. The problem which confronts the commentator of the Lucan Gospel is perhaps aggravated by the prevailing attitudes toward Luke-Acts in the last two or three decades. This sketch of contemporary Lucan studies is intended to accomplish two things: to survey the more important recent approaches to Luke-Acts and to relate the present commentary on the Lucan Gospel to them.

The Dutch scholar, W. C. van Unnik, once called Luke-Acts "one of the great storm-centers of New Testament scholarship" ("Luke-Acts," 16). That was in 1966. Five years earlier, C. K. Barrett had written that "the focus of New Testament studies is now moving to the Lucan writings" (*Luke the Historian,* 50). But van Unnik also noted that "the exegetical basis for many statements in the modern approach to Luke-Acts is often far from convincing" ("Luke-Acts," 28) and was forced to admit that the current state of affairs was scarcely a debate, since so few of the issues in the modern approach had really been tested or criticized, accepted or rejected. The "real debate" had hardly begun. Van Unnik wrote that assessment almost fifteen years ago; in the meantime some of the issues have begun to be treated more adequately.

No little part of the problem in approaching the Lucan writings is precisely their complexity. The writings of no other single author in the NT occupies the amount of space that Luke-Acts does. The relation of the first volume to the second is admitted almost unanimously today. But the problems of the first volume are not those of the second, and what constitutes the continuity in the two is the source of still further problems. On the one hand, there are the obvious Synoptic relationships of the Lucan Gospel to Mark and to Matthew and problems of possible contacts with the Johannine gospel tradition. On the other, there is the unique aspect of the Lucan Gospel, in that it alone is fitted in the NT with a sequel—and with a sequel that has its own literary, didactic, apologetic, geographical, historical, and theological perspectives. Some of the latter can be detected in the Gospel itself and used to account for the Lucan redaction of the traditional material with which Luke works. Only when the whole Lucan story is understood, does one see that in small ways Luke had actually been preparing by literary foreshadowing for details important for the end of his account.

Too much, however, of the attitude that has been adopted toward the Lucan writings in the last two or three decades has been dominated by views of the Acts of the Apostles. Even though one detects traces of Luke's redactional work in the Gospel, which are clear evidence of his purposeful composition, his gospel-account nevertheless clearly depends on much inherited material—material that can be compared with the other gospel writers. The skepticism that is characteristic of the radical critical approach to Luke-Acts is *engendered far more by Acts* than it is by the Lucan Gospel. This, of course, makes it difficult to write a commentary on the Lucan Gospel and try to cope with the prevailing attitudes toward Lucan writings. Yet what is most strange is that, despite the wide-spread admission of the common authorship of Luke-Acts, rare is the modern interpreter who has attempted to compose a commentary on the two volumes, precisely as two volumes dominated by a single conception.

In looking back at the interpretation of Lucan writings in the past quarter of a century, one sees that it has been the writings of four German scholars in particular which have contributed most to the recent radical critical approach to Luke-Acts. The beginnings of this approach must be traced to Martin Dibelius, especially to his essays which have been collected in the volume, *Studies in the Acts of the Apostles,* which deals mainly with the literary criticism of Acts. Though they were all composed before 1950, they have proved to be seminal for this approach. Two books by Hans Conzelmann have been the more recent major catalysts for this approach: his analysis of Lucan theology in *Die Mitte der Zeit* (1953), translated into English under the title, *The Theology of St Luke* (1960), which was largely devoted to the Lucan Gospel, and his commentary on Acts, *Die Apostelgeschichte* (1963). The extensive commentary of Ernst Haenchen, *The Acts of the Apostles* (1965), adopted many of the viewpoints of Conzelmann and has proved to be the main critical commentary on that NT book. Of no little importance to this approach was the early article of Philipp Vielhauer, "On the 'Paulinism' of Acts" (1950), which has been translated into English and used in various publications. To these four writers one could add a good list of others who, either in isolated remarks or in short articles, have contributed to this analysis of Lucan writings: R. Bultmann, E. Dinkler, E. Grässer, E. Käsemann, G. Klein, S. Schulz, et al. This approach to the Lucan writings has resulted not only in skepticism about their historical worth, but in a negative judgment of what is regarded as Luke's "theology" and his tendentious view of early Christianity—and even about the very identity of Luke himself. Van Unnik summed up the situation, when he wrote about

how "the Rev. Mr. Luke—we keep this traditional name for the author of
Luke-Acts without any prejudice—became one of the heroes or, perhaps
in some cases, more or less the villain of the play on the New Testament
stage" ("Luke-Acts," 16). Indeed, he has been billed as "the dim wit
among the evangelists" (a phrase attributed to G. W. H. Lampe by
R. H. Fuller, *The New Testament in Current Study* [New York: Scribner,
1962] 89).

In the last decade and a half the debate over the issues involved in this
radical critical approach to Lucan writings has been taking shape. It has
involved NT scholars in Germany, where that approach developed, and in
the English- and French-speaking scholarly world as well. Point after
point in this approach to Luke-Acts has been taken up and subjected to
minute analysis. In this connection one has to mention in particular the
survey of W. Gasque, *A History of the Criticism of the Acts of the Apostles* (1975), which despite its exaggerated concern for the historical
worth of Acts has pointed out weaknesses in that approach. Gasque's
work has not gone without a telling caveat from N. A. Dahl ("The Purpose of Luke-Acts" 94, n. 16). The work of H. Flender, *St Luke: Theologian of Redemptive History* (1967), despite its overly systematic concerns has correctives to the radical critical approach. Similar estimates
would have to be given for the works of I. H. Marshall, *Luke: Historian
and Theologian* (1970), W. C. Robinson, Jr., *Der Weg des Herrn*
(1964), and E. Franklin, *Christ the Lord: A Study in the Purpose and
Theology of Luke-Acts* (1975). Two important, crucial assessments of
the entire debate have been written by W. G. Kümmel ("Current Theological Accusations against Luke," 1970) and F. Bovon (*Luc le théologien: Vingt-cinq ans de recherches [1950–1975]*, 1978).

The debate that has thus been shaping up concerns mainly the questions of the historicity and the theology of Lucan writings. But another
aspect of them has also begun to receive greater attention, viz. the literary
aspect of Luke-Acts. Recent Lucan studies have emphasized more and
more that Luke was the first consciously Christian literary writer or *littérateur,* and investigations of his redaction-critical methods and his deliberate stylistic techniques and patterns reveal that these aspects of his
writings bear in no small way on the debate itself. The literary aspect of
Luke's writings was never wholly neglected, for H. J. Cadbury in a series
of writings (e.g. *The Style and Literary Method of Luke* [1920]; *The
Making of Luke-Acts* [1927], and in many articles) had analyzed features of it. More recently, the writings of R. Morgenthaler (*Die lukanische Geschichtsschreibung als Zeugnis* [1949]) and of C. H. Talbert (*Literary Patterns, Theological Themes and the Genre of Luke-Acts*
[1974]) have been devoted to it. This aspect of Lucan writings is
clearly important, but what is valid in studies devoted to it is constantly

bedeviled by as much subjectivism as the redaction-critical studies that they have often sought to curb.

A proper analysis and interpretation of the Lucan writings obviously has to cope with all these problems or aspects of them (not to mention some other minor ones). *The* problem is to steer a judicious course between Scylla and Charybdis, between a hypercritical attitude which makes Luke not only the "villain of the play on the New Testament stage" (van Unnik), but even the whipping boy, and an unreflective acceptance of his conscious, deliberate tendencies as expressive of something historical. To understand the Lucan writings today, it is not sufficient to say, "That is merely Lucan," and to imply thereby that it is either unhistorical, or theologically tendentious, or patterned and structured. It may, in a given case, be all of these; it may be none. The important thing is to determine what it is that Luke has written, why he has written it, why his writings have found a place in the canon of Christian Scripture, and what role they play there.

The current study of the Lucan writings is more dominated by theses about Luke-Acts than by a detailed analysis of these writings. These theses have often been developed by a summary consideration of only part of the evidence (e.g. Conzelmann's dismissal of the infancy narratives from a proper consideration of Lucan "theology"); or by an extrinsic comparison of Luke-Acts with Pauline or Johannine writings (as if only what reflected Paul or John were valid early Christian testimony in the Lucan writings); or even by preoccupations born of later systematic theology (e.g. whether Lucan theology is a theology of the cross or a theology of glory; whether Lucan salvation-history has replaced *Apokalyptik,* or, even less appropriately, "spoiled" the kerygma). These preoccupations may raise legitimate questions about the Lucan writings, but they have to be recognized for what they are: *theses* about Lucan theology, often born of preoccupations other than the study of Lucan theology as such.

Later on I shall attempt a brief sketch of Lucan theology, but I feel that it is necessary to make clear here that Lucan "theology" (in the positive sense) has to be distinguished from the theses that are often proposed about it. Students of NT theology have long since grown acquainted with the idea of Pauline or Johannine theology; attempts to synthesize the teachings of Paul or John are numerous. Yet it is precisely the defect of the books of both Conzelmann (especially in its English form with the misleading title, *The Theology of St Luke*) and J. C. O'Neill (*The Theology of Acts*) that they present not a synthesis of Lucan teaching, but theses about Lucan theology, which never finds adequate treatment in them.

An attempt to present a brief sketch of Lucan theology is made difficult by the complexity of Luke and Acts taken as related works. No little part of Lucan theology will be the Lucan portrait of Jesus in the Gospel itself. This has to be distinguished not only from the way Luke makes his principal preachers in Acts proclaim him, but also from the theology involved in the narrative account of the Christian movement and church which he relates not only to the kerygma but traces even to its Palestinian roots in the ministry of Jesus of Nazareth. The Lucan portrait of Jesus in the Gospel has at times clear traces of Luke's redactional hand and gives evidence of its purposeful construction. But it also depends—and in great measure—on inherited material. This dependence makes his account in the Gospel not only different from its sequel in Acts, but makes it subordinate to elements in Lucan theology that only begin to emerge as the latter part of the account unfolds. Though I have already lamented the predominance of attention that is paid to Acts, the relation of Luke to Acts is a problem with which any summary of Lucan theology has to reckon.

The result is that often in commentaries on the Lucan Gospel the sketch of Lucan theology is largely an attempt to synthesize the portrait of Jesus in the Third Gospel. Nevertheless, an attempt will be made here to keep an eye on the follow-up of that portrait in Acts, to recognize the foreshadowing when it is present, and to allow its presence to color the interpretation of the redactional activity that is involved.

Even such a sketch of Lucan theology has to assume a position vis-à-vis the theses about Lucan theology proposed in recent times; the discussion of them is relegated here to the description of the current state of Lucan studies, not because the questions raised are not important, but because they are for the most part extrinsic to the sketch of Lucan theology itself. What I mean by a "thesis" about Lucan theology, then, is a proposal that does not refer to the understanding of Luke and Acts in themselves. It is, in effect, what U. Wilckens has called "a theological viewpoint" or "a theological persuasion" ("Interpreting Luke-Acts," 60). Wilckens insists that "biblical exegesis in fact always presupposes a theological viewpoint" and acknowledges the part that "subjective prejudice" plays in it. Sometimes this element is more closely related to exegesis than on other occasions; sometimes it is quite extrinsic to it and born of other or later preoccupations. In any case, one has to cope with such theses or viewpoints, without allowing them to obscure what should be the major preoccupation: a descriptive synthetic account of Lucan theology. Wilckens has also shown how the dialectical theology of the 1920s has colored the interpretation of Paul so that what Luke attempted has come to be judged negatively in contrast to a peculiarly dialectical view of Pauline theology (ibid. 69-77). In other words, what often passes today as "Lucan theology" is not merely an eccentric view of Luke-Acts, but one that suffers as a result of comparing Luke with an equally eccen-

tric view of Pauline theology. As a result, Wilckens concludes: "Luke
with his concept of redemptive history stands indeed within a broad early
Christian tradition. So the question seems justified, whether a critical
comparison of Luke with Paul should not find this profound theological
agreement between them of greater importance than is generally assumed" (ibid. 75).

My comments here on a number of these theses about Luke-Acts and
its theology will replace discussion of them in the context of the theology
itself. The full discussion of a given point obviously may depend on details that will be presented later in the positive description of Lucan theology; in such cases, I shall refer the reader to the later presentation.

Before taking up some of these controverted theses, however, I should
like to make here two preliminary remarks. They concern minor issues in
the modern debate about Luke-Acts, and it may be well to set forth
where I stand on them. The first remark has to do with the common
authorship of the Third Gospel and Acts. This too might seem like a current thesis; but it is so widely admitted that we can assume it here. Second, I shall present my reasons below (see pp. 35-53) for regarding the
author of Luke-Acts as the traditional Luke, the one spoken of in Phlm
24; Col 4:14; and 2 Tim 4:11. Here I need only note that, since I distance this Luke sufficiently from Paul in the long run, it is possible to live
with the traditional identification of him and regard the Lucan writings as
compositions which emerged toward the close of the second last decade
of the first Christian century. In the long run, as most people realize, the
question of authorship of these writings is relatively unimportant. But it
does not seem necessary to speak of "the Rev. Mr. Luke . . . without
prejudice" to discuss Lucan theology critically or even the theses that are
often proposed about Luke-Acts. In adopting this position, however, I do
not share the view of J. D. Quinn that this Luke is also the author of the
Pastoral Epistles (see the forthcoming AB 35, I & II Timothy, Titus).

1. *The Purpose of Luke-Acts.* A commentary on the Lucan Gospel has
to cope with the purpose that the author had in mind in writing it. That
purpose is also intimately related to a sketch of Lucan theology. But the
modern problem about the purpose of Luke-Acts arises from discussion
of the two-volume work and thus transcends what might be the limited
intent of the Gospel alone. In 1960 W. C. van Unnik noted that, save for
the monograph of B. S. Easton, *The Purpose of Acts* (1936), "the problem of the purpose of Acts" had been practically neglected ("The 'Book
of Acts' the Confirmation of the Gospel"). More recently, as Dahl ("The
Purpose of Luke-Acts") has commented, it has been receiving greater attention, as a glance at the bibliography which follows reveals. But it is

now finally being put into proper perspective, viz. the purpose of the double-work, Luke-Acts.

The starting point in the discussion of the aim of Luke-Acts has to be the stated purpose of Luke 1:4. Despite the reluctance of Haenchen back in 1965 (*Acts,* 136 n. 3) to consider the Lucan prologue (1:1-4) as the introduction to the two volumes, it has to be so understood, as is generally recognized among commentators today. The main reason is the reference in Acts 1:1; otherwise why speak of the "first book," *prōtos logos?* In Luke 1:4 the purpose is stated thus: "So that your Excellency may realize what assurance you have for the instruction you have received" (see p. 289 below for the explanation of this translation). The "assurance" (*asphaleia*) that is involved has often been assumed to be historical assurance (cf. G. Klein, "Lukas 1,1-4 als theologisches Programm"). But it almost certainly involves more than that, for the Lucan historical perspective transcends the mere question of historicity. Luke writes from the period of the church and intends to assure Theophilus and other readers like him that what the church of his day was teaching and practicing was rooted in the Period of Jesus, to strengthen them in fidelity to that teaching and practice. The "assurance" is, then, mainly doctrinal or didactic: to explain how God's salvation, first sent to Israel in the mission and person of Jesus of Nazareth, has spread as the Word of God—without the Law—to the Gentiles and to the end of the earth (Acts 1:8). Relating Luke 1:1-4 to Acts 1:1 and 8, we see that Luke-Acts purports to be basically "a work of edification" (Haenchen, *Acts,* 103).

Luke insists, indeed, that all "this was not done in a corner" (Acts 26:26), and the historical perspective which he has adopted and which runs through the two-volume work in a way that is unique in the NT becomes precisely the vehicle whereby he presents Christianity as the logical and legitimate outgrowth or continuation of Judaism, and specifically of Pharisaic Judaism (see Acts 23:6; cf. 24:21). Dahl has said that Luke wanted to "write a continuation of biblical history" ("The Purpose of Luke-Acts" 88). This seems to be true, but one has to be a little more specific, for Luke-Acts is unique in the NT not only in insisting that "the God of Abraham and of Isaac and Jacob, the God of our fathers" (Acts 3:13) is the one who "glorified his servant Jesus" and "raised him from the dead" (3:15) but also in depicting Peter and Paul as the transmitters to the Gentiles of this salvation brought about in Jesus, which had been promised to the people of Israel and actually made available first of all to them. Thus Luke is concerned to pass on to a postapostolic age a Jesus-tradition that is related to the biblical history of Israel and to insist that it is only within the stream of apostolic tradition, represented by Peter and by Paul, that one finds this divinely destined salvation.

This concern of Luke to stress the connection and the continuation between Judaism and Christianity is seen clearly in his use of the OT to interpret the Christ-event. He cites many passages of the Hebrew Scriptures, which formally lack predictive elements, but which he reads not
only as prophecy, but even as predictions of what came to be in the ministry of Jesus and in its sequel. This has been variously labeled as promise
and fulfillment in Luke-Acts, as the proof-from-prophecy motif, etc. It is
no small factor in the motivation of Luke as he gathered up the tradition about Jesus and the movement that he began. It is intimately connected with the reversal-theme related to his view of salvation-history
(see further Dahl, "The Purpose of Luke-Acts," 95-96). What has happened, happened indeed, and God has made something out of it—something related to what was foreshadowed in the biblical history of Israel.

The goal of presenting Christianity as intimately related to the history
of Judaism has another, subordinate aspect to it. It may be called a subordinate purpose in Luke-Acts, because it appears only here in the NT; it
is also one of those elements in the Lucan writings which are foreshadowed in many ways in the Gospel, but which are clearly seen only toward the end of Acts itself: Luke's concern to show that Christianity,
rooted in Israel by the birth of its founder to Jewish parents and by the
mark of the covenant (circumcision; cf. Gen 17:11), has as much right

to recognition as *religio licita*, a lawful religion, in the Roman empire as
Judaism itself. It is the logical continuation of Judaism. Luke refers to the
Christian movement in Acts as a "party," "sect" (*hairesis*, 24:5,14;
28:22), using of it the very word that characterizes Pharisaism (Acts
15:5; 26:5) and Sadducaism (Acts 5:17) and that Josephus predicates
of the Pharisees, Sadducees, and Essenes (*Life* 2 § 10; cf. 2 § 12; *Ant.*
13.5,9 § 171). This apologetic concern is present in Luke-Acts; it has
sometimes been considered as the major aim of the Lucan writings, but
that is an exaggeration. Details of this will be further discussed below.

As a means of presenting the "assurance" which marks his concern in
both volumes, Luke has indeed historicized the Christ-event beyond any
mode of presentation of it in other NT books, making of it "a life of
Jesus" (Conzelmann), adopting for it contemporary "literary forms"
(Haenchen), and pinpointing salvation as something (objectively) realized in the past (in *die Mitte der Zeit*). In his presentation, Luke not
only distinguished himself clearly from "eyewitnesses" and "ministers of
the word" (Luke 1:2), he even depicts Jesus in the so-called Travel Account (Luke 9:51 - 19:27) preparing and instructing those Galileans "who
were chosen in advance by God as witnesses" (Acts 10:41) and who
were destined to carry "the word which was proclaimed throughout all
Judea, beginning from Galilee" (Acts 10:37). All of this reveals his concern for an assured tradition about Jesus; yet this tradition is not yet

presented as "the deposit" of faith that has to be guarded (cf. 1 Tim 6:20; 2 Tim 1:14).

Several modern writers have related Luke's intention to Gnosticism. Barrett (*Luke the Historian*, 62) contrasted Luke with John; the latter is supposed to have had "a positive approach to Gnosticism, using some of its language in order to destroy its errors," whereas Luke's attitude is "a direct negative." Luke is said to have pilloried Gnostic leaders in the person of Simon Magus (Acts 8:9-24), but he studiously avoided Gnostic thought and language. This sort of analysis of the Lucan writings has emerged in the writings of various interpreters (G. Klein, E. Käsemann ["Neutestamentliche Fragen von heute," *ZTK* 54 (1957) 1-21, esp. p. 20], et al.). Indeed, Talbert has gone so far as to say that "Luke-Acts was written to serve as a defense against Gnosticism" (*Luke and the Gnostics*, 111).

All of this remains problematic. There is not the slightest suggestion that Luke regarded Simon Magus as a Gnostic; Talbert himself has to admit (p. 83) that he is not "described in unambiguously Gnostic terms" and disagrees with Conzelmann (*Apostelgeschichte*, 53) who describes him as "der Vater der Gnosis." That he was so regarded in patristic literature is one thing; that Luke shares that view is quite another. Even Talbert's attempt to interpret the so-called silence of Luke about heresy in the apostolic age as a device of Lucan defense against Gnosticism is strange and contorted (pp. 83-97). Moreover, W. Schmithals, known for his "discovery" of Gnosticism in other NT writings, eventually had to admit that "other than Mark and Matthew, no NT writer shows so little connection with Gnosticism as does Luke. In other words, it appears impossible to interpret the Lucan image of Paul as anti-Gnostic, as I myself at an earlier time had considered possible" [cf. his article, "Die Häretiker in Galatien," *ZNW* 47 (1956) 62] (in *The Office of Apostle*, 271). Merely because some modern writers (e.g. R. Reitzenstein, R. Bultmann) have labeled certain phrases in the Lucan writings as Gnostic or as echoes of Gnosticism does not make them such. Moreover, there have been in recent times so many queries about would-be evidence of Gnosticism in the first century A.D. which have cast considerable doubt on its existence at that time that one cannot take anti-Gnosticism seriously as a feature of the purpose of the writing of Luke-Acts. See further R. McL. Wilson, *Gnosis and the New Testament*, 44-45; cf. *The Gnostic Problem*, 84; E. M. Yamauchi, *Pre-Christian Gnosticism*, 170-186; W. C. van Unnik, "Die Apostelgeschichte und die Häresien," *ZNW* 58 (1967) 240-246.

2. *Luke-Acts and the Kerygma*. Another "thesis" about Luke-Acts in the current study of these writings criticizes the condition of the kerygma in them. The first major part of my sketch of Lucan theology will be

devoted to the kerygma in Luke-Acts (see pp. 145-162 below). It is necessary to say something here about the thesis of the distortion of the original kerygma in the Lucan writings. Whether one understands "kerygma" in the active sense of the faith-eliciting proclamation of God's eschatological salvation in the Christ-event, or in the content sense of the essential elements of such preaching, one has to admit that it is present in Luke-Acts. Years ago R. Bultmann (*Theology* 2. 117) stated that Luke "surrendered the original kerygmatic sense of the Jesus-tradition," and since that time it has been fashionable to repeat this idea in one form or another. Part of Bultmann's reason for so regarding the Jesus-tradition in Luke-Acts was his contention that Christianity had become in it "an entity of world history" (2. 116). The kerygmatic character of the gospel has thus been made subservient to a theology of history. Moreover, it has been subjected to a historicization and a periodization, and the upshot is that Luke has deformed the Christian kerygma.

However, when one looks at what is proclaimed in the Lucan Gospel by Jesus and what is proclaimed about him in Acts, one can scarcely call it anything else but a proclamation to Theophilus (and other readers like him). It is Luke's way of announcing that Jesus is the Christ and God's sole agent of eschatological salvation for all human beings: "There is salvation in no other name under heaven given among men by which we must be saved" (Acts 4:12). That that statement should cease to qualify as kerygma, because it is surrounded by other considerations, is somewhat baffling. Luke certainly emphasizes, perhaps more than other NT writers, the *traditional* character of what he proclaims about Jesus and he certainly historicizes it. But he is not concerned with historicization for its own sake. As O. Betz has noted, Luke has not written the *Antiquities of the Christians,* as a counterpart of Josephus' *Antiquities of the Jews.* Luke-Acts contains a proclamation of the Christ-event and addresses it to the reader, seeking from him/her the reaction of Christian faith and allegiance. Perhaps the Lucan form of the kerygma is no longer cast in terms of "gospel" or of "power" (*dynamis,* Rom 1:16), but the basic proclamation is not for that reason intended to be any less of an accosting process or of a testimony to the risen Jesus. See further Flender, *St. Luke: Theologian of Redemptive History,* 26, 66, 161-162; O. Betz, "The Kerygma of Luke," 132-134; Kümmel, "Current Theological Accusations," 139-140.

In part, the current pejorative thesis about the spoiled or deformed Lucan kerygma is derived, not from the NT itself, as from an understanding of kerygma born of existentialist philosophy and dialectical theology. No one can criticize the attempt to cast the early Christian kerygma in terms of a modern philosophy such as existentialism. To address the scandal of the cross to human beings of today through a radical understanding of existence and to elicit from them a fundamental reaction to it is a valid endeavor. Such a recasting may imply, indeed, a de-historicization of the gospel-message itself. But it is another thing to insist that the NT kerygma is only valid when so recast, or that this recasting is demanded by the NT itself. The existentialist understanding of the kerygma has, consequently, to be labeled a thesis, when it is brought to bear on Lucan theology and the Lucan understanding of kerygma.

It is not that Luke has spoiled the kerygma. He has simply played it in another key. He proclaims the basic Christian message to the church of his day, assuring it that what is being proclaimed differs not from what was proclaimed at the outset. He makes the proclamation, moreover, to Theophilus in a context of providing a guarantee for the Christian way of life. There is more, indeed, to the Lucan writings than a mere repetition of the kerygma as a means of eliciting from human beings a response of faith. *Asphaleia,* "assurance," is introduced as a guarantee of the instruction which Theophilus has received. To read the Lucan writings as if they were offering a guarantee to the kerygma itself or even as "guarantees for the rightness and the necessity of faith" and to maintain that Luke "doubtless intends on his part to hand on such guarantees" (E. Käsemann, "Probleme der neutestamentlichen Arbeit," 220) is not only to confuse the Lucan kerygma with other aims of Luke, but also to misunderstand the basic source of the Lucan *asphaleia.* The assurance comes not from Luke or the human transmission of the kerygma, or even from "the teaching of the apostles" (Acts 2:42), but from the Spirit of God which is depicted as operative in the inauguration of the ministry of Jesus (Luke 4:1,14) and authenticating the proclamation about him in Acts 2:14-21. See further U. Luck, "Kerygma, Tradition," in *Das Lukas-Evangelium,* 112. Yet, even if the Spirit-filled guarantee for the Jesus-tradition is set aside, it is still hard to see in what way Luke's kerygmatic message about the Christ-event differs from Mark's or Matthew's—save that he has added to it a historical perspective and a sequel that heavily marks its historicization. It is not, for that reason, spoiled.

Also implicit in the accusation that Luke has spoiled the kerygma is a comparison with Paul. One looks in vain in Lucan writings for a succinct kerygmatic summary such as Rom 4:24-25, "It [righteousness] will be reckoned to us who believe in him that raised from the dead Jesus our Lord, who was put to death for our trespasses and raised for our justification" (or other such summaries as 1 Cor 15:1-7; Rom 1:3-4; 8:34; 10:8-9, etc.). But is the kerygma deformed because the effects of the Christ-event are not cast in Pauline figures and images but rather in terms of "salvation," "forgiveness of sins," "peace"? Or because the reaction of human beings to it is now expected not only in terms of "faith" but also of "repentance" and "conversion"?

In sum, the current thesis about the spoiled or deformed or surrendered Lucan kerygma has not attended sufficiently to the kerygma that is, indeed, presented in the Lucan writings.

3. *The Historical Value of the Lucan Writings.* One of the current theses about the kerygma in the Lucan writings is that it has been historicized and even been cast in terms of "salvation-history." No one can deny that this has happened. See the evidence to be recounted below (pp. 171-192) and the discussion of salvation-history in the next section. But there is another aspect of the question that needs to be treated separately, since it too is one of the current theses about Lucan theology, in that it concerns Luke "the historian." At the beginning of this century and up to roughly 1950 the emphasis in Lucan studies was centered mainly on Luke as a writer of history. The basis of this mode of study of the Lucan writings was not only the historical perspective just mentioned, but also the numerous details that have been incorporated into his account, especially in the second part (Acts), which seemed to have considerable extrabiblical support. In this regard, the judgments of important scholars were often invoked: E. Meyer (*Ursprung und Anfänge des Christentums,* 1924, 1. 1), W. M. Ramsay (*The Bearing of Recent Discovery on the Trustworthiness of the New Testament,* 1915: Luke was "a historian of the first rank" [p. 222]), F. H. Chase (*The Credibility of the Book of Acts of the Apostles,* 1902). A number of the essays in vol. 5 of *Beginnings of Christianity,* edited by F. Foakes Jackson and K. Lake, also contributed to this view of the Lucan writings.

With the shift in emphasis and interest to the literary and theological aspects of the Lucan writings that has characterized the radical critical approach to them, the historical value of the Lucan writings has at times been seriously called in question. This shift in emphasis and interest was inevitable. But it remains to be seen whether the picture painted about the historical value of Luke-Acts is as black as it is often said to be. No little attention has been given to this character of Acts, especially in the survey of Gasque, *A History of the Criticism of the Acts of the Apostles,* in the commentaries of F. F. Bruce, (indirectly) in a series of articles by A. J. Mattill, and in the monograph of Marshall, *Luke: Historian and Theologian.*

No little part of the problem comes from the Gospel prologue itself. There Luke clearly distinguishes himself from the "eyewitnesses" of the events narrated. Moreover, his entire composition gives evidence of originating in a decade toward the end of the first century A.D. His account of Jesus and of the movement that came to be associated with him, then, can scarcely be regarded as on-the-spot reporting. Its ex post facto stance has to be admitted, whether or not Luke is understood to be claiming that he was around for the events recorded in the so-called We-Sections of Acts. But from another viewpoint the prologue creates further problems, because it announces in staid formality that the account will be thorough (*pasin*), traced from the beginning (*anōthen*), orderly (*kathexēs*), and accurate (*akribōs*). These are four qualities that any historian would be proud of, if they were included in an assessment of his work. Yet, standing in the prologue as they do, they amount to a statement of purpose, to a protestation. And in the modern discussion of the historical value of the Lucan writings, they can scarcely be pressed. The question is, in fact, whether Luke's opus has measured up to the protestation. It is a problem which cannot be avoided.

When one listens to such a protestation, there arise constantly in the mind the problems associated with the Lucan references to the census of Quirinius (Luke 2:1-2; Acts 5:37), the chronological reference to the priesthood of Annas and Caiaphas (Luke 3:2), Theudas and Judas the Galilean (Acts 5:36-37), the presence of the cohort *Italica* in Caesarea Maritima in the time of Herod Agrippa (Acts 10:1), the historical geography of Palestine (e.g. Luke 4:44; 17:11; cf. Conzelmann, *The Theology of St Luke*, 41 n. 1, 68-73), and other notorious *cruces interpretum*. It seems rather apparent that on many of these issues Luke's information was not the best.

No little part of the difficulty in treating the question of the historical value of the Lucan writings is the tendency to judge Luke in terms of categories of modern historical writing. There have been numerous attempts in modern times to insist that Luke's narrative should not be so judged and that one should rather look to the norms of historiography which would have been characteristic of contemporary historians. C. K. Barrett (*Luke the Historian*, 9-12; cf. pp. 51-52) has insisted on this point and sought briefly to compare Luke with Lucian of Samosata. A much more extensive treatment of the problem can be found in the work of E. Plümacher, *Lukas als hellenistischer Schriftsteller: Studien zur Apostelgeschichte*, 1972. And Dahl has summarized the thinking of many interpreters today, in insisting that Luke was not only influenced by Hellenistic historiography, but was "himself a minor Hellenistic historian, albeit one who dealt with a very special subject matter and who imitated biblical rather than Attic style" ("Purpose of Luke-Acts," 88). In other words, as Barrett has put it, "Luke's vocation as a historian did not arise out of idle curiosity, but was (humanly speaking) forced upon him by the theological and ecclesiastical environment in which he lived" (*Luke the Historian*, 51). Since Luke's is a form of historical writing laced with a concern for religious guarantee, proclamation, and didactic, it may well fit into categories of ancient literary writing but fail to live up to the standards of modern historiography. This is widely admitted today among

many interpreters of the Lucan writings. It is often accompanied by protests that exponents of the modern critical approach to Luke-Acts would
not be so naïve as to judge these writings by such an anachronistic standard. But the difficulty is that the norms of modern historical writing do
enter, however covertly, into judgments about the Lucan writings, protests to the contrary notwithstanding. A modern commentator on the
Lucan Gospel or Acts is expected to answer the questions that readers of
these writings may have today, which include the extent to which certain
details are traditional or historical and accurate.

Luke's peers are not von Ranke or Lord Acton, but rather writers like
Polybius and Plutarch, Josephus and Tacitus; and even these persons are
sometimes criticized today in terms of historical accuracy. It must be
recalled, however, that even in antiquity the distinction between fact and
fiction was recognized. The second-century Greek writer Lucian of
Samosata devoted a short treatise to the standards of historical writing,
How to Write History. In it he expresses a norm that may surprise the
modern reader: "the historian's sole task is to tell the tale as it happened" (§ 39, *hōs eprachthē eipein*); "this . . . is the one thing peculiar
to history: only to truth must sacrifice be made" (§ 40, *monē thyteon tē
alētheia;* see K. Kilburn, *Lucian* [LCL; Cambridge, MA: Harvard University] 6 [1949] 54-55). Lucian was not far removed from Luke in either time or space. Yet his standard for historiography sounds much like
the standard attributed to the renowned historian, L. von Ranke, that history should describe the past "wie es eigentlich gewesen," as it actually
was.

If Lucian's words warn us against making too facile a distinction between ancient and modern historians in their concern for details or facts
as they tell their story, they must also caution us against an oversimplified
understanding of the historian's craft in antiquity. Lucian's standard is no
more telling than Luke's protestation, when the end-result has to be
assessed. Even if we prescind from the almost impossible ideal of objectivity that such a standard, ancient or modern, implies and grant that history cannot be anything but an interpretation of past events, nevertheless
it must be recognized that Luke's purpose in recounting the story of Jesus
and its sequel is not simply, or even primarily, that of an ancient
Hellenistic historian. Herein lies the real difference between Luke the
evangelist and both ancient and modern historians. For his historical
concern serves a theological end; he sees the "events" that he is to narrate as a fulfillment (Luke 1:1) and this reveals his historical concern as
subordinate to a theological one.

In discussing the historical value of the Lucan Gospel, we can compare
Luke's version of many of the episodes with their Synoptic counterparts
in Matthew or Mark. It is often not difficult to decide which form of a

given episode represents the more primitive tradition of an incident or saying. But the step back from that more primitive tradition to the event or saying itself is another matter. A verdict about the authenticity of a saying of Jesus presented in the Lucan Gospel would entail an investigation that goes far beyond the concerns of a commentator on this text. Moreover, in composing his Gospel, Luke has clearly made use of earlier traditions and even written sources. His dependence on Mark and "Q" (see pp. 66-80 below) means that for such material the historical value of what he recounts as the words and deeds of Jesus may be as good as that of his sources, though perhaps colored by his own redaction. Modern commentators on the Lucan Gospel recognize that Luke has also had independent sources of information about the Jesus-tradition (perhaps written, perhaps oral). But it is always difficult to draw the line between what is "L" (the Lucan source) and what is of Lucan composition.

As for the Acts of the Apostles, the question of the historical value is even more acute, since the problems are different and the episodes are generally without parallels. J. Jervell has called our attention to a neglected amount of material in the NT that lends support to certain details in the account of Acts ("The Problem of Traditions in Acts," in *Luke and the People of God,* 19-39). And T. H. Campbell has studied in a stimulating article the routes of Paul's vagaries in the Pauline letters, comparing them in a positive way to those of the so-called missionary journeys of Paul in Acts ("Paul's 'Missionary Journeys' as Reflected in His Letters," *JBL* 74 [1955] 80-87). Despite such considerations there still remain the classic problems of the divergences of the three accounts of the conversion of Paul (Acts 9:1-19; 22:1-21; 26:2-18) and the relation of Acts 15 to Galatians. One cannot ignore such problems.

Luke has not called his account *historia* any more than he called it *euangelion;* he uses of it *diēgēsis,* "narrative account," which tends to relate it in a generic way to historiography. But what he has composed still has to be assessed for its historical value in the mind of a twentieth-century reader. If the modern reader remains skeptical, that is simply because, when the modern question about historicity is asked, the only possible answer is a frankly expressed "We do not know."

(For the sake of Roman Catholic readers, I should like to add a further remark, for it is often asked how one can square such a skeptical attitude about the historical value of the Lucan writings with teachings about biblical inspiration. To answer this question in detail is out of place here; but this much at least should be said: None of the ecclesiastical dogmatic documents which treat of biblical inspiration or the discussions of theologians who have sought to explicate this teaching have ever maintained that a necessary formal effect of inspiration is historicity. Biblical inspiration does not make history out of what was not such or intended to be such. The guarantee that is implied in biblical inspiration concerns truth, but the truth that is involved is often not literal but analogous and differs with the literary form being used: poetic truth, rhetorical truth, parabolic truth, epistolary truth, even "gospel truth"—apart from historical truth itself. Nor is every affirmation in the past tense, even in a narrative, necessarily meant to be "historical." The extent to which it is metaphorical or symbolic would still have to be assessed [and excluded] before one comes down on the side of historical truth. If it is historical, there will be ways of assessing it apart from inspiration. For further study, one should consult the 1964 Instruction of the Biblical Commission, "On the Historical Truth of the Gospels," *AAS* 56 [1964] 712-718; *CBQ* 26 [1964] 305-312; see my commentary on it, *TS* 25 [1964] 386-408; *Die Wahrheit der Evangelien* [SBS 1; Stuttgart: Katholisches Bibelwerk, 1965].)

4. *Lucan Salvation-History and Eschatology*. One of the ways in which Luke presents the kerygma is to cast it in terms of salvation-history—he plays it in this key. The historical perspective that he has adopted and its relation to "salvation-history" and eschatology will be discussed more fully below. One of the current theses about Lucan theology involves the effect that this recasting of the kerygma has had on the eschatological character of the early Christian message. An adequate description of Lucan eschatology is not easily drawn; and Conzelmann's view of Lucan eschatology constitutes the part of his thesis that has come under greatest fire. Some comments, therefore, have to be made here about the relationship between these ideas—salvation-history and eschatology—and between them and other Lucan perspectives, which are not properly part of the positive synthesis of Lucan teaching on these topics.

As will be made clear, I consider the description of the threefold division of Lucan salvation-history presented by Conzelmann in his *Theology of St Luke* to be correct. Some modifications of it are necessary, but by and large it is still valid. Hence, in discussing the Lucan historical perspective, one has to reckon with three periods: the Period of Israel (from creation to John the Baptist), the Period of Jesus (from the beginning of his ministry to his ascension), and the Period of the Church under Stress (from the ascension to the parousia). It is likewise correct that Luke has historicized the Christ-event, casting "salvation" as something that happened in the past (in the Period of Jesus), for his concern is to root in that period what is being taught and practiced in the church of his own day. This threefold periodization of salvation-history is not fully explicit in Luke. Luke 16:16 seems to speak of a demarcation of two periods, Israel and Jesus; but its exact sense needs further explanation. In any case, it makes mention of only two periods. However, no one can ignore the further periodization that is implicit in the addition of the sequel of Acts to the Gospel itself. The threefold division of salvation-history in Lucan writings actually antedates Conzelmann, being found earlier in the writings of H. von Baer, *Der heilige Geist in den Lukasschriften*, 45. Conzelmann's treatment has been adopted by others (e.g. Haenchen, 96). However, the threefold division of Lucan salvation-history has also been called in question (see W. G. Kümmel, "Current Theological Accusations," 137; "'Das Gesetz und die Propheten,'" 89-102; U. Luck, "Kerygma, Tradition," 53 n. 5). In any case, that Luke had made use of a view of salvation-history in his account of the Christ-event and its sequel is widely admitted today.

It is, however, precisely the notion of salvation-history in the Lucan writings that has drawn the most fire in the radical critical approach to them. E. Käsemann, in particular, has found fault with it, asserting that in Luke "primitive Christian eschatology is replaced by salvation history" ("The Problem of the Historical Jesus," 28). Again, "You do not write the history of the Church, if you are expecting the end of the world to come any day" (ibid.). Hence, "apocalyptic hope" no longer possesses for Luke "any pivotal interest" (ibid.). Similarly, for H. Conzelmann, the Spirit has become the substitute for the expected imminent parousia of Jesus. Consequently, this Lucan device of salvation-history becomes but a further manifestation of the way in which the primitive Christian kerygma has been spoiled or surrendered. For Haenchen (*Acts,* 96), "the Third Evangelist . . . denied the imminent expectation." Unlike John, "he took the chronological dimension . . . into serious consideration, and asked himself where and how God's work of salvation proceeds in time. He saw the history of salvation as a great unity which ended in the parousia" (ibid.).

Involved at times in such criticism of these writings is the idea that Luke *invented* salvation-history. S. Schulz has said, "The Hellenist Luke is the creator of Salvation History" ("Gottes Vorsehung bei Lukas," 104). Indeed, Schulz even queries whether salvation-history is a valid category in NT theology at all. But writers such as U. Wilckens ("Interpreting Luke-Acts," 66) and Kümmel ("Current Theological Accusations," 137) have strongly reacted against Schulz's position, and rightly so. For Luke is not the only NT writer who makes use of this device to interpret the Christ-event, nor is he the earliest. Aside from the fact that "salvation" is one of the ways in which Paul too describes an effect of the Christ-event, he too has a view of salvation-history. I tried to describe it elsewhere (*Pauline Theology: A Brief Sketch* [Englewood Cliffs, NJ: Prentice-Hall, 1967] 23-31; *JBC,* art. 79, § 35-51). What Paul writes in 1 Cor 7:29-31; 10:11; Rom 4:23; 5:14; 10:4; 13:11-14; 2 Cor 6:2 certainly implies some such view. Moreover, in a reply to Schulz, W. G. Küm-

mel offered a list of interpreters of Pauline theology who have recog-
nized this as a valid element in the Apostle's thinking (among them,
R. Bultmann, K. Deissner, M. Dibelius, P. Feine, H. J. Holtzmann,
T. Hoppe, K. Mittring, W. Wrede); see "Heilsgeschichte im Neuen Testa-
ment?". The phases of Pauline salvation-history are, indeed, different from
Luke's, but the basic idea of a divine plan of salvation as adumbrated in the
OT and realized in the earthly career and death/resurrection of Jesus of
Nazareth is common to both. Moreover, the fulfillment motifs which one
finds in Matthew and John (e.g. the "fulfillment" quotations in the
Matthean Gospel, and passages like John 12:38; 13:18) reveal that an
ordering of the affairs of human history according to a *boulē* or *thelēma*
("will, counsel, plan") of God and its coming to realization in the
career of Jesus were not uncommon early Christian beliefs. Luke's
view of such "history" may be more properly called *salvation*-history because of his more frequent use of *sōtēria, sōtērion,* "salvation" and of his
predilection for the title *sōtēr,* "savior," for Jesus. See further O. Cullmann, *Salvation in History,* 186-291; Marshall, *Luke: Historian and Theologian,* 77-102.

For neither Paul nor Luke was salvation to be achieved in some historically unrooted or existential act. Here I can only echo what others like
Wilckens and E. Dinkler have said, that "it is most assuredly not the
opinion of the historical Paul that 'history means the perpetually new decision of the individual'" ("Interpreting Luke-Acts," 76; cf. E. Dinkler,
"Earliest Christianity," 190). What Christ Jesus did had a once-for-all
character to it; the historicization of it and the Christian response to it
were inevitable.

The specific periodization of salvation-history that one finds in the
Lucan writings has to be regarded as a Lucan creation; but it is not for
that reason any less valid a view than Paul's. Luke obviously distinguishes
the phases to insist on their continuity and logical connection; this insistence is part of his purpose. Moreover, the Spirit is not solely for him the
substitute for the expected imminent parousia, since it is first met in his
story as the creative and prophetic presence of God in the earthly career
of Jesus himself: in the Period of Israel, prior to and at his birth
(1:15,35,41,67; 2:25-26); in the Period of Jesus, guiding his ministry
(3:22; 4:1,18); and in the Period of the Church, poured out on the Jewish Christian community in Jerusalem (Acts 2:4) and later on Gentile
converts (Acts 10:44-48).

No one will deny that Luke has shifted the emphasis from the expectation of an imminent parousia to the concerns of the Christian community
in its day-to-day existence and to the reality of evil that can affect the
lives of Christians. This shift was partly achieved by his decision to add

the sequel of Acts to the story of Jesus. Moreover, passages such as Luke 19:11; Acts 1:7; and the eschatological discourse in Luke 21 (with its distinct separation of what refers to Jerusalem from what refers to the end-time) reveal that he is aware of the delayed parousia. However, Luke has not completely eliminated all reference to the parousia in the inherited sayings of Jesus or John the Baptist. It has assumed for him a position on the periphery and is not so central as it may be in some other NT writers.

No little part of the negative view of Lucan salvation-history and of what it has done to so-called primitive Christian eschatology is the exaggerated emphasis given to eschatology as "the decisive, all-inclusive force permeating the whole tradition" about Jesus (cf. Wilckens, "Interpreting Luke-Acts," 65). I describe it as exaggerated, because most of it is derived from certain Pauline passages (especially 1 Thessalonians 4-5; 1 Cor 7:26,29) which are emphasized to the neglect of others in the same corpus. Elsewhere Paul shows that he too was beginning to reckon with the fact that he might die before that great moment and considers death itself as a chance to be "with Christ" (Phil 1:20-23; 2 Cor 1:8-10; 5:1-5).

Luke's salvation-history is also found to be at fault when it is considered as a replacement for *Apokalyptik*. It has been said that *Apokalyptik* has been rediscovered in our day. This is correct, if it means that we have come to realize better what this *literary form* is and have learned to distinguish it more properly from the eschatological, or soteriological content which it normally invests. All such content can be adequately expressed without apocalyptic stage-props, and, indeed, has been so expressed in the NT itself. If one regards *Apokalyptik* as somehow the mother of all Christian theology, then one can see how Lucan salvation-history has taken the edge off of what had been apocalyptically expressed. By casting the primitive Christian message in terms of salvation-history rather than as apocalyptic, however, Luke has again merely played that message in a different key. It is, moreover, far from sure that apocalyptic is a key "superior" to salvation-history. Perhaps he has reduced the "apocalyptic hope" somewhat, for he has eliminated some of the crisis-oriented vigilance with which the apocalyptic stage-props enhanced the eschatological confrontation of human beings with the parousiac Jesus or Lord. But is that apocalyptic expression of cringing vigilance any less of a bourgeois pietistic attitude than Luke's call to the Christian to take up his/her cross each day and follow Jesus (Luke 9:23)? As I see it, the parousia may not be as imminent for Luke as for some other NT writers, but it is still for him a reality to be expected, which will come suddenly and unpredictably. His counsel to the Christians of his day may well be that it is not their lot to "know the times or the seasons that the Father has set by his own authority" (Acts 1:7), but his challenge to authentic living has not completely lost an eschatological dimension.

5. *Theology of the Cross vs. Theology of Glory.* Years ago, when C. H. Dodd was discussing various manifestations of the early kerygma in the NT, he wrote, "The Jerusalem *kerygma* does not assert that Christ died *for our sins.* The result of the life, death, and resurrection of Christ is the forgiveness of sins, but this forgiveness is not specifically connected with his death" (*The Apostolic Preaching,* 25). This was part of Dodd's comparison of the kerygma as found in the speeches of Acts with that of the Pauline letters. What Dodd had written of the Jerusalem kerygma has come to be related more specifically to Lucan theology itself. Indeed, J. M. Creed about the same time noted "the entire absence of a Pauline interpretation of the Cross" in Lucan writings: "There is indeed no *theologia crucis* beyond the affirmation that the Christ must suffer, since so the prophetic scriptures had foretold" (*The Gospel* [1930] lxxii). Yet Barrett found that Creed's view was "not the whole truth": "The fact is that Luke stands far enough from the historical Jesus to have digested the raw, perplexing traditions which stand in Mark in all their crudity and offensiveness, and to have made them something less scandalous, and more easily assimilable" (*Luke the Historian,* 23). Yet it is precisely this which evokes stern criticism from a commentator like E. Käsemann. In discussing the speeches of Acts, he finds that "fabrication is interwoven with proclamation. A *theologia gloriae* is now in process of replacing the *theologia crucis.*" And because apocalyptic has been replaced by a theology of history, "the Cross of Jesus is no longer a scandal but only a misunderstanding on the part of the Jews which the intervention of God at Easter palpably and manifestly corrects" ("Ministry and Community," 92).

Again, the soteriology of Luke is being compared with Marcan ideas (cf. Mark 10:45, which has no counterpart in Luke) or with Pauline theology. Why must one expect that Luke should have the same emphasis as Mark or as Paul? Even Kümmel, who has noted important aspects of Lucan soteriological teaching that are often bypassed or neglected in various discussions of the death of Jesus in Luke-Acts, quotes G. Voss approvingly, when he says, "In Luke the death of Jesus neither has the character of a sacrifice nor is it understood as an atoning work" ("Current Theological Accusations," 138; cf. G. Voss, *Die Christologie,* 130). But one can still ask whether these are the only ways in which the salvific character of that death could be expressed. Instead of allowing Luke to present the life, death, and resurrection of Jesus as he sees it, Lucan soteriology is being censured for not being Marcan or Pauline. This is, again, an extrinsic consideration.

Another aspect of this thesis about Lucan theology is seen in the tell-tale Latin phrases that are used of it. Perhaps it is for brevity's sake that one speaks of *theologia crucis* or *theologia gloriae;* but how does one safeguard such consecrated expressions from the connotations of later theological controversy when applying them to Lucan theology? They tend to import into Lucan ideas connotations that are not necessarily his.

It is true that in the Acts of the Apostles the minor "summaries" (1:14; 2:41; 4:4; 5:14; 6:7; 9:31; 11:21,24; 12:24; 14:1; 16:5; 19:20; 28:30-31) enhance the continuing growth of the Christian community and record the success of the spreading Word of God. They can, of course, be read with a sense of triumphalism, as an expression of Lucan glory, or perhaps even of pride. But is that really intended?

Is Paul's "scandal" (1 Cor 1:23) so significantly different from Luke's claim that "this child is marked for the fall and rise of many in Israel, to be a symbol that will be rejected" (Luke 2:34)? It may not be "the cross," but it is at least the person of Jesus himself that is such. Again, is Luke's solution to the problem of Israel's place in God's salvific plan (viz. its ignorance) that much more of a watering down of the scandal than Paul's own way of explaining it in Romans 9-11—especially in Rom 11:13-16, "to make my fellow Jews jealous"? Finally, it has always puzzled me how one can refer to Luke's neglect of the salvific character of Jesus' death, in light of one of the peculiarly Lucan episodes of the passion narrative that brings it out expressly. Only in the Lucan Gospel does the already crucified Jesus say to the thief beside him: "Today you shall be with me in Paradise" (23:43). No matter how one may explain the meaning of the phrase "in Paradise," one cannot help but realize that the crucified Jesus is assuring the repentant thief that that very day he would be with him. That scene certainly conveys to the reader of the Lucan Gospel in a highly literary way something about the salvific character of Jesus' death. And it might be recalled that Paul uses the same expression for the destiny of a Christian (1 Thess 4:17b [described with apocalyptic stage-props]; Phil 1:23 [without the apocalyptic stage-props]). Further details about the Lucan understanding of the death of Jesus will be given below (pp. 219-221). What has been said here should suffice to cast at least some doubt on the validity of a rather widespread thesis about Lucan soteriology. See further R. Zehnle, "The Salvific Character"; A. George, "Le sens de la mort de Jésus pour Luc," *RB* 80 (1973) 186-217.

6. *Early Catholicism in Luke-Acts.* Another current thesis about Lucan theology is that it is a manifestation of "early Catholicism." The notion of *Frühkatholizismus* apparently was first used toward the beginning of this century in the writings of E. Troeltsch, *Die Soziallehren der christlichen Kirchen und Gruppen* (Gesammelte Schriften 1; Tübingen: Mohr

[Siebeck], 1922; reprinted: Aalen: Scientia, 1962) 1. 83; *The Social Teaching of the Christian Churches* (New York: Macmillan, 1931) 1. 89. Used as a term first of all in sociological writings, it found its way into theological discussions, apparently for the first time, in A. Ehrhard, *Urkirche und Frühkatholizismus* (Bonn: Buchgemeinde, 1935); cf. K. H. Neufeld, " 'Frühkatholizismus'—Idee und Begriff," *ZKT* 94 (1972) 1-28. It was used to describe those elements of the early Christian community which characterize it as an ordered institution of salvation, a church with sacraments, hierarchical offices, and a tradition involving a deposit of faith. It was used to characterize the picture of the church found in early patristic writers and in the Pastoral Epistles. In the last quarter of a century or so, it has been applied to Luke-Acts, beginning in 1950 in the article of Vielhauer on the Paulinism of Acts; perhaps the application even antedates him. In any case, E. Käsemann eventually wrote: "It was Luke who was the first to propagate the theories of tradition and legitimate succession which mark the advent of early Catholicism" ("Ministry and Community," 91). Similar attribution of it to Luke can be found in the writings of G. Klein, J. C. O'Neill, S. Schulz, C. K. Barrett (with hesitation), et al. Indeed, this development has even been seen as a defense against Gnosticism. But this thesis is a highly contested one, even among those who otherwise espouse the radical critical approach to Luke-Acts.

Just how much Early Catholicism can be found in the Lucan *Gospel* is quite problematic, if one prescinds from stressing (or overinterpreting) certain phrases in the Lucan prologue. Those who regard Luke-Acts as an Early-Catholic document usually concentrate their attention on Acts. And in this regard it is a clear example of the way problems in Acts have tended to dominate and characterize Lucan theology as a whole.

This aspect of Lucan thought will not be treated below, because I consider the topic extrinsic to Lucan theology, and one born of another preoccupation. But I shall make certain comments about it here, because it is part of the current study of the Lucan writings.

First of all, one has to realize that there is no univocal understanding of the term "Early Catholicism." J. H. Elliott, for one, has struggled to sum up what is often meant by it ("A Catholic Gospel: Reflections on 'Early Catholicism' in the New Testament," 213-223, esp. p. 214). See further W. Marxsen, *Der "Frühkatholizismus"*; Haenchen, *Acts* 94; F. Mussner, "Frühkatholizismus," *LTK* 6 (1961) 89-90.

Second, the implication that "catholicism" might have "a foothold in the canon" (to use a phrase of R. H. Fuller, *The New Testament in Current Study* [New York: Scribner, 1962] 89 n. 3, 95) is difficult for many to accept, despite the "far-reaching implications for contemporary ecumenical discussion" that it may have (ibid. 95). This makes it particularly difficult to judge whether this notion is properly predicated of Luke-

Acts. It bears in one way or another on the problem of "the canon within the canon" and embarrasses some radical critical scholars, whose views of the issue are diverse. See further I. H. Marshall, " 'Early Catholicism' in the New Testament," in *New Dimensions in New Testament Study* (eds. R. N. Longenecker and M. C. Tenney; Grand Rapids: Zondervan, 1974) 217-231.

Third, it is significant that so critical a commentator of the Lucan writings as Conzelmann will admit no more than "initial traces" of its presence in Acts. See "Luke's Place in the Development of Early Christianity," esp. p. 304; cf. *The Theology of St Luke,* 159; *An Outline of the Theology of the New Testament,* 149. See also P. Borgen, "From Paul to Luke," 182; O. Betz, "The Kerygma of Luke," 145-146.

Fourth, one cannot deny that Luke depicts in Acts the development of the primitive Jewish Christian community of Jerusalem into the established *ekklēsia* dotting the eastern Mediterranean world as far as Rome. It is, moreover, a Spirit-guided institution, with presbyters set up in all the churches (Acts 14:23), by those who are called "apostles" (Barnabas and Paul—they are given this title in Acts only in 14:4,14) and who are implicitly emissaries of "the church in Jerusalem" (see 11:22,25-26; 13:2-3). The picture of the growing and spreading community that emerges is one through which the Spirit works; indeed, the Spirit is normally received only when a member of the Twelve or one of their representatives (e.g. Paul) is present (cf. Acts 8:16-17; 19:1-7). The community's dedication is to "the teaching of the apostles," breaking of bread, etc. (2:42). There is, moreover, a concern that the presbyters be *episkopoi,* "overseers," caring for God's flock and guarding it against the "fierce wolves" that appear, "speaking perverse things, to draw away the disciples after them" (20:28-30).

There is, however, no *unique* or *uniform* "structured hierarchy" (see Conzelmann, "Luke's Place," 313). The Twelve, initially regarded in Acts as a group necessarily to be reconstituted (1:15-26), is not so considered later on when James, the son of Zebedee, is put to death by Herod Agrippa (12:1-2). The Twelve were involved in the commission of the Seven "to serve tables" (6:1-6), but, having "summoned the body of the disciples" for a decision, the Twelve as such disappear from the story (although "the apostles" who imposed hands on them [6:6] are almost certainly meant to be the same). Moreover, the new structure thus inaugurated by the disciples with the Twelve/apostles, distinguishing those who were "to serve tables" from those who were "to pray" and "minister to the word" (6:2,4), seems to have been lacking in definition, for two of the Seven, Stephen and Philip, are depicted shortly thereafter "preaching the word" or "proclaiming the Christ" (6:8 - 7:53; 8:5-13). "Apostles" and "elders" both play an important role in the decisions made by those assembled in Acts 15 about circumcision and the regulations to be imposed on Gentile Christians living in mixed communities of the local churches of Antioch, Syria, and Cilicia. But the "apostles" are last heard of in Acts 16:4, and when Paul returns to Jerusalem, he goes up to greet James and "all the elders" (21:17), in a scene that makes James look like a residential bishop of later times, though he is never given the title of *episkopos*. In other words, one cannot deny that Luke has at least sketched elements of a structured *ekklēsia*, but that structure is far from uniform. This must be noted, because for him the Spirit works or is poured out through the structure, no matter what it was (see, e.g. 2:4; 7:55; 8:29,39; 10:44; 13:2; 15:28). The one exception to this is the way the Spirit is received through the imposition of Ananias' hands on Saul, just before his baptism (9:17)—possibly a special case, related to the unique election of Saul as "a chosen instrument."

Fifth, Luke thus sets off the primitive period of the church, when the Twelve/apostles functioned in it, from the church of his own day. He is concerned about the origins of that apostolic community, its relation to the commission of the risen Jesus to the "apostles" (1:2) to be his "witnesses" (1:8) and also to the "time that the Lord Jesus went in and out among us" (1:21). This certainly implies a rooting of the "apostles' teaching" (2:42) in what Jesus had "begun to do and teach" (1:1) and probably also explains why Luke normally hesitated to give Paul the title of "apostle."

Sixth, if one sees in this Lucan continuity of teaching and community life a notion of tradition, it should at least be noted that *paradosis*, "tradition," is not a Lucan term (contrast 1 Cor 11:2; 2 Thess 2:15; 3:6). The closest that one comes to it is the cognate verb *paradidonai* used in Luke 1:2 and Acts 16:4. The nuance in these passages stands in remarkable contrast to the numerous other uses of the verb in Lucan writings which lack this nuance (cf. Rom 6:17; 1 Cor 11:2,23; 15:3). But in any case the claim that this implied notion of tradition guarantees the gospel or the kerygma or that it controls the Spirit is certainly an overstatement of the case. For all his concern about *asphaleia*, what Luke assures Theophilus about is not yet the "deposit" (*parathēkē*), as Kümmel correctly notes ("Current Theological Accusations," 139). The gospel traditions that Luke passes on are "primarily testimony to Christ. He listens to them and applies them anew to his own situation" (ibid.). And even admitting this Lucan concern, we still find it difficult to see the Lucan writings as a *demonstration* of the basic unity of the Christian faith. To read Luke-Acts in this way is to introduce another preoccupation of later *Kontroverstheologie* (theological controversy).

Seventh, one can, moreover, query whether the installation of elders in the churches (Acts 14:23; 16:4; 20:28-32), even with their obligation to preserve their flocks from teachers of "perverse things" is to be labeled "apostolic succession." One might see in the sending of Barnabas to Antioch by "the church in Jerusalem" (Acts 11:22), his further seeking out of Saul of Tarsus (11:25-26), the subsequent setting apart of Barnabas and Saul for the work of the first missionary journey—with an imposition of hands, to boot (13:2-3)—and their setting up of elders in every town (14:23) some notion of succession. But it would be a perverse reading of the Lucan text thus to pass over the independent choice of Saul by "the Lord" (9:10-17), his being filled with the holy Spirit (9:17), and the initiative of the Spirit in the start of the missionary journey itself (13:2-3). Once again, *diadochē*, "succession," is not a Lucan term at all —in fact, it does not occur in the NT—and to read Luke-Acts in terms of the classic problem of "apostolic succession," a notion dear to patristic writers, is to fail to respect the primitive character of what these writings pass on to us.

If the Lucan elements of a Spirit-guided structured church as an ordered instrument of salvation with the seeds of a sacramental system were to be labeled "early Catholicism," that would be one thing. But one would still have to ask whether or not that portrayal is a bad thing. The answer to that question depends on something beyond exegesis and biblical theology—which are our concerns here—for it is really a query proper to *Kontroverstheologie*. See further I. H. Marshall, " 'Early Catholicism' in the New Testament," 224. And the same would have to be said about Luke's supposed concern for "the undisputed authority of the one, holy, apostolic church."

7. *Luke and Paul.* Interwoven in a number of the topics discussed above is at least an implicit comparison of Luke with Paul. Paul may be a Christian theologian superior to Luke, and his writings may represent an earlier stage of Christian thinking and teaching. His mode of presenting the Christian message is more engaging and profound than Luke's. But the comparison of Lucan theology with that of Paul invariably involves unfairness. I can admit that the demands of the Pauline story of the cross are more radical, a *skandalon,* but I am not sure that the Lucan call to "repentance and conversion" is any less Christian than Paul's. The comparison is unfair because it implies that Pauline theology is a norm for what Luke writes, a criterion by which Lucan teaching is to be judged. This comparison is not only extrinsic to the study of Lucan theology in itself; it is also born of a later systematic concern with a "canon within the canon." If one, for instance, were to admit with E. Käsemann that "the doctrine of justification is the heart of the Christian message" and that it "establishes the legitimacy and sets the limits on all varieties and even interpretations of NT teaching" ("Some Thoughts on the Theme 'The Doc-

trine of Reconciliation in the New Testament,' " 63), then one can understand how Lucan theology is treated as it is by certain radical critical
interpreters. But that is a big "if."

However, Käsemann is not alone in this view of the matter. Even so
perspicacious a critic as W. G. Kümmel has maintained that the kernel of
the NT is to be "defined by the agreement of Jesus, Paul and John"
("Current Theological Accusations," 141). Note the title of his book,
*Theology of the New Testament According to Its Major Witnesses:
Jesus—Paul—John,* 1973 (cf. his " 'Mitte des Neuen Testaments,' "
1968). Aside from the problem in linguistic analysis created by the
collocation of "Jesus" along with "John and Paul" in such a threesome or
of regarding "Jesus" as a "major witness" of the *theology* of the NT, how
can one seriously write a theology of the NT and not consider as one of
its major witnesses the views of the writer whose books occupy almost a
quarter of the NT itself? At work in all of this is the extrinsic comparison
of Luke with Paul (and other writers of the NT). It tends to obscure the
genuine theological values in Luke-Acts.

Moreover, we must ask whether the differences between Paul and Luke
have not been overdrawn to the extent that their fundamental theological
agreement has been obscured. The Paul of Acts differs from the Paul of the
epistolary corpus, and I admit by and large the thesis of P. Vielhauer on
the Paulinism of Acts. But I hesitate to see the differences as contradic-
tories; they are contraries at most. Moreover, Paul was obviously for Luke
a hero of the early Christian community; he so presents him in the latter
part of Acts. I think that this idealization of Paul comes in part from a
brief association with him. There is, indeed, no evidence that Luke had
ever read any of Paul's letters, *pace* E. E. Ellis, M. S. Enslin, J. Knox,
C. K. Barrett et al. (see below). But one should also recall the studies of
P. Borgen, M. Carrez and others who have sought to offset the differences
between Luke and Paul with considerations of their more fundamental
agreement.

Finally, as was noted above (p. 21), the interpretation of Paul that is
often used in this comparison has a definite philosophical character, related to a dialectical theology of the early part of this century.

In sum, when one considers the modern theses about Luke-Acts and
their theology, one realizes that they have tended to obscure the basic
thrust of Lucan theology and to denigrate it by a questionable comparison with other NT writers. In the light of contemporary studies we have
to realize that Luke was an early Christian author, who was an evangelist
as much as Mark, Matthew, or John (despite his general reluctance to
use *euangelion*—a reluctance shared by the author of the Fourth Gospel), who sought to compose his account of the Jesus-story and its sequel
with the interest of a minor Hellenistic historian, writing in a biblical

mold, and with the concern of a theologian, apologete, and propagandist who consciously strove to enhance his account with literary patterns and themes that would make it palatable to the contemporary Hellenistic world in which he lived and wrote.

BIBLIOGRAPHY

Anderson, W. "Die Autorität der apostolischen Zeugnisse," *EvT* 12 (1953-1954) 467-481.

Baer, H. von. *Der heilige Geist in den Lukasschriften* (BWANT 39; Stuttgart: Kohlhammer, 1926).

Barrett, C. K. *Luke the Historian in Recent Study* (London: Epworth, 1961).

Berchmans, J. "Lukan Studies," *Biblebhashyam* 2 (1976) 81-90.

Betz, H. D. "Das Verständnis der Apokalyptik in der Theologie der Pannenberg-Gruppe," *ZTK* 65 (1968) 257-270.

Betz, O. "The Kerygma of Luke," *Int* 22 (1968) 131-146.

Boice, J. M. "The Reliability of the Writings of Luke and Paul," *Christianity Today* 12 (1967-1968) 176-178.

Borgen, P. "From Paul to Luke: Observations toward Clarification of the Theology of Luke-Acts," *CBQ* 31 (1969) 168-182; German original: *ST* 20 (1966) 140-157.

Boulgarēs, C. S. "Historikē anaskopēsis tēs peri ton Loukan kai tas Praxeis ereunēs," *Deltion* 1 (1972) 212-223, 329-352.

Bovon, F. "Orientations actuelles des études lucaniennes," *RTP* 26 (1976) 161-190.

———— *Luc le théologien: Vingt-cinq ans de recherches (1950-1975)* (Le monde de la Bible; Neuchâtel: Delachaux & Niestlé, 1978).

Braumann, G. "Das Mittel der Zeit: Erwägungen zur Theologie des Lukasevangeliums," *ZNW* 54 (1963) 117-145.

Bultmann, R. *The Theology of the New Testament* (2 vols.; London: SCM, 1952, 1955) 2. 116-118, 125-127. Cited as Bultmann, *Theology*.

Burnier, J. "Art littéraire, témoignage et histoire chez Saint Luc," *RTP* 38 (1950) 219-225.

Cadbury, H. J. *The Making of Luke-Acts* (London: SPCK, 1927; reprinted, 1958).

———— *The Style and Literary Method of Luke* (HTS 6; Cambridge, MA: Harvard University, 1920).

Cairns, E. E. "Luke as a Historian," *BSac* 122 (1965) 220-226.

Carrez, M. "L'herméneutique paulinienne peut-elle aider à apprécier la conception lucanienne de l'histoire?" *RTP* 3/19 (1969) 247-258.

Chase, F. H. *The Crediblity of the Book of Acts of the Apostles* (London/New York: Macmillan, 1902).

Conzelmann, H. *Die Apostelgeschichte* (HNT 7; Tübingen: Mohr [Siebeck], 1963).

——— "Luke's Place in the Development of Early Christianity," in *Studies in Luke-Acts*, 298-316.

——— *The Theology of St Luke* (New York: Harper, 1960); a translation of the 2d ed. of *Die Mitte der Zeit: Studien zur Theologie des Lukas* (BHT 17; Tübingen: Mohr [Siebeck], 1957).

———*An Outline of the Theology of the New Testament* (New York: Harper & Row, 1969).

——— "Zur Lukasanalyse," *ZTK* 49 (1952) 16-33.

Cullmann, O. *Salvation in History* (New York: Harper & Row, 1967).

Dahl, N. A. "The Purpose of Luke-Acts," in *Jesus in the Memory of the Early Church: Essays* (Minneapolis: Augsburg, 1976) 87-98.

Dibelius, M. *Studies in the Acts of the Apostles* (ed. H. Greeven; London: SCM, 1956).

Dinkler, E. "Earliest Christianity," in *The Idea of History in the Ancient Near East* (ed. R. C. Dentan; AOS 38; New Haven: American Oriental Society, 1955) 169-214. Reprinted as "The Idea of History in Earliest Christianity," in *Signum crucis: Aufsätze zum Neuen Testament und zur christlichen Archäologie* (Tübingen: Mohr [Siebeck], 1967) 313-350.

——— "Tradition, V. Im Urchristentum," *RGG* 6. 970-974.

Dodd, C. H. *The Apostolic Preaching and Its Developments* (London: Hodder & Stoughton, 1936).

Easton, B. S. *The Purpose of Acts* (London: SPCK, 1936).

Edwards, W. T. "Preparing to Teach the Gospel of Luke," *RevExp* 64 (1967) 433-440.

Ehrhardt, A. "The Construction and Purpose of the Acts of the Apostles," *ST* 12 (1958) 45-79; reprinted in *The Framework of New Testament Stories* (Manchester: Manchester University, 1965) 64-102.

Elliott, J. H. "A Catholic Gospel: Reflections on 'Early Catholicism' in the New Testament," *CBQ* 31 (1969) 213-223.

Flender, H. *St. Luke: Theologian of Redemptive History* (Philadelphia: Fortress, 1967).

Francis, F. O. "Eschatology and History in Luke-Acts," *JAAR* 37 (1969) 49-63.

Franklin, E. *Christ the Lord: A Study in the Purpose and Theology of Luke-Acts* (Philadelphia: Westminster, 1975).

Funk, R. W. "Conzelmann on Luke," *JBR* 30 (1962) 299-301.

Gärtner, B. "Den historiske Jesus och trons Kristus: Några reflexioner kring Bultmannskolan och Lukas," *SEÅ* 37-38 (1972-1973) 175-184.

Gasque, W. *A History of the Criticism of the Acts of the Apostles* (BGBE 17; Tübingen: Mohr [Siebeck], 1975).

George, A. "Israël dans l'oeuvre de Luc," *RB* 75 (1968) 481-525.

——— "Tradition et rédaction chez Luc: La construction du troisième évangile," *ETL* 43 (1967) 100-129.

——— *Etudes sur l'oeuvre de Luc* (Sources bibliques; Paris: Gabalda, 1978).

Ghiberti, G. "Letteratura e problematica attuale su S. Luca," *Parole di vita* 6 (1971) 405-415.

Goppelt, L. "Paulus und die Heilsgeschichte: Schlussfolgerungen aus Röm. IV and I. Kor. X. 1-13," *NTS* 13 (1966-1967) 31-42.

Grässer, E. "Die Apostelgeschichte in der Forschung der Gegenwart," *TRu* ns 26 (1960-1961) 93-167.

—————— *Das Problem der Parusieverzögerung in den synoptischen Evangelien und in der Apostelgeschichte* (BZNW 22; Berlin: Töpelmann, 1957; 2d ed., 1960).

Haenchen, E. *The Acts of the Apostles: A Commentary* (Philadelphia: Westminster, 1971); a translation of *Die Apostelgeschichte* (MeyerK 3; 15th ed.; Göttingen: Vandenhoeck und Ruprecht, 1965). Cited as Haenchen, *Acts*.

Harrington, D. J. "The 'Early Catholic' Writings of the New Testament: The Church Adjusting to World-History," in *The Word in the World: Essays in Honor of Frederick L. Moriarty, S.J.* (eds. R. J. Clifford and G. W. MacRae; Cambridge, MA: Weston College, 1973).

Jervell, J. *Luke and the People of God: A New Look at Luke-Acts* (Minneapolis: Augsburg, 1972).

Käsemann, E. "Aus der neutestamentlichen Arbeit der letzten Jahre," *VF 1947-1948* (1949-1950) 196-223.

—————— "Ministry and Community in the New Testament," in *Essays on New Testament Themes* (SBT 41; London: SCM, 1964) 63-94.

—————— "Ein neutestamentlicher Überblick," *VF 1949-1950* (1951-1952) 191-218.

—————— "The Problem of the Historical Jesus," in *Essays on New Testament Themes*, 15-47.

—————— "Probleme der neutestamentlichen Arbeit in Deutschland," *Die Freiheit des Evangeliums und die Ordnung der Gesellschaft* (BEvT 15; Munich: Kaiser, 1952) 133-152.

—————— "Some Thoughts on the Theme 'The Doctrine of Reconciliation in the New Testament,'" in *The Future of Our Religious Past: Essays in Honour of Rudolf Bultmann* (ed. J. M. Robinson; New York: Harper & Row, 1971) 49-64.

Klein, G. "Lukas 1,1-4 als theologisches Programm," in *Zeit und Geschichte: Dankesgabe an Rudolf Bultmann zum 80. Geburtstag* (ed. E. Dinkler; Tübingen: Mohr [Siebeck], 1964) 193-216.

Kodell, J. "The Theology of Luke in Recent Study," *BTB* 1 (1971) 115-144.

Kümmel, W. G. "Current Theological Accusations against Luke," *Andover Newton Quarterly* 16 (1975) 131-145; original in *ETL* 46 (1970) 265-281; cf. *ZNW* 63 (1972) 149-165; *Das Lukas-Evangelium* (Wege der Forschung 280; Darmstadt: Wissenschaftliche Buchgesellschaft, 1974) 416-436.

—————— "Futurische und präsentische Eschatologie im ältesten Christentum," *NTS* 5 (1958-1959) 113-126.

—————— "'Das Gesetz und die Propheten gehen bis Johannes,' Lukas 16,16 im Zusammenhang der heilsgeschichtlichen Theologie der Lukasschriften," in *Verborum veritas: Festschrift für Gustav Stählin zum 70. Geburtstag* (eds. O. Böcher und K. Haacker; Wuppertal: R. Brockhaus, 1970) 89-102.

——— "Heilsgeschichte im Neuen Testament?" in *Neues Testament und Kirche: Für Rudolf Schnackenburg* (ed. J. Gnilka; Freiburg: Herder, 1974) 434-457.

——— " 'Mitte des Neuen Testaments,' " *L'Evangile, hier et aujourd'hui: Mélanges offerts au Professeur Franz-J. Leenhardt* (Geneva: Labor et Fides, 1968) 71-85.

——— *Promise and Fulfilment: The Eschatological Message of Jesus* (SBT 23; London: SCM, 1957).

——— *The Theology of the New Testament According to Its Major Witnesses, Jesus—Paul—John* (Nashville: Abingdon, 1973).

Lindsey, F. D. "Lucan Theology in Contemporary Perspective," *BSac* 125 (1968) 346-351.

Lohse, E. "Lukas als Theologe der Heilsgeschichte," *EvT* 14 (1964) 256-275.

Luck, U. "Kerygma, Tradition und Geschichte Jesu bei Lukas," *ZTK* 57 (1960) 51-66; reprinted in *Das Lukas-Evangelium* (ed. G. Braumann), 95-114.

Marshall, I. H. *Luke: Historian and Theologian* (Exeter: Paternoster, 1970).

——— "Recent Study of the Gospel According to St. Luke," *ExpTim* 80 (1968-1969) 4-8.

Marxsen, W. *Der "Frühkatholizismus" im Neuen Testament* (BibS[N] 21; Neukirchen: Neukirchener, 1958).

Mattill, A. J., Jr. "The Jesus-Paul Parallels and the Purpose of Luke-Acts: H. H. Evans Reconsidered," *NovT* 17 (1975) 15-46.

——— "The Good Samaritan and the Purpose of Luke-Acts: Halévy Reconsidered," *Encounter* 33 (1972) 359-376.

——— "*Naherwartung, Fernerwartung,* and the Purpose of Luke-Acts: Weymouth Reconsidered," *CBQ* 34 (1972) 276-293.

——— "The Purpose of Acts: Schneckenburger Reconsidered," in *Apostolic History and the Gospel: Biblical and Historical Essays Presented to F. F. Bruce on His 60th Birthday* (eds. W. W. Gasque and R. P. Martin; Grand Rapids: Eerdmans, 1970), 108-122.

Meyer, E. *Ursprung und Anfänge des Christentums* (3 vols.; Darmstadt: Wissenschaftliche Buchgesellschaft, 1962); originally published, 1921-1923, by J. G. Gotta.

Morgenthaler, R. *Die lukanische Geschichtsschreibung als Zeugnis* (2 vols.; Zürich: Zwingli, 1949).

Morris, L. "Luke and Early Catholicism," *WJT* 35 (1972-1973) 121-136.

——— "Luke the Theologian," *Christianity Today* 15 (1970-1971) 1067.

Moule, C. F. D. "The Intention of the Evangelists," in *New Testament Essays: Studies in Memory of Thomas Walter Manson 1893–1958* (ed. A. J. B. Higgins; Manchester: Manchester University, 1959) 165-179.

Müller, P.-G. "Conzelmann und die Folgen: Zwanzig Jahre redaktionsgeschichtliche Forschung am Lukas-Evangelium," *BK* 28 (1974) 138-142.

O'Neill, J. C. *The Theology of Acts in Its Historical Setting* (London: SPCK, 1961; 2d ed., 1970).

Plümacher, E. *Lukas als hellenistischer Schriftsteller: Studien zur Apostelgeschichte* (SUNT 9; Göttingen: Vandenhoeck und Ruprecht, 1972).

Ramsay, W. M. *The Bearing of Recent Discovery on the Trustworthiness of the New Testament* (2d ed.; London: Hodder & Stoughton, 1915).

Rasco, E. "Hans Conzelmann y la 'historia salutis': A proposito de 'Die Mitte der Zeit' y 'Die Apostelgeschichte,' " *Greg* 46 (1965) 286-319.

Rese, M. *Alttestamentliche Motive in der Christologie des Lukas* (SNT 1; Gütersloh: Mohn, 1969).

Robinson, W. C., Jr. "Luke, Gospel of," *IDBSup*, 558-560.

———— *Der Weg des Herrn: Studien zur Geschichte und Eschatologie im Lukas-Evangelium: Ein Gespräch mit Hans Conzelmann* (TF 36; Hamburg-Bergstedt: H. Reich, 1964).

Rohde, J. *Rediscovering the Teaching of the Evangelists* (Philadelphia: Westminster, 1968).

Schmithals, W. *The Office of Apostle in the Early Church* (Nashville: Abingdon, 1969).

Schneider, G. "Der Zweck des lukanischen Doppelwerks," *BZ* 21 (1977) 45-66.

Schulz, S. "Gottes Vorsehung bei Lukas," *ZNW* 54 (1963) 104-116.

———— *Die Stunde der Botschaft: Einführung in die Theologie der vier Evangelien* (Hamburg: Furche, 1967).

Schweizer, E. *Gemeinde und Gemeindeordnung im Neuen Testament* (ATANT 35; Zürich: Zwingli, 1959; 2d ed., 1962) 54-67.

Talbert, C. H. "An Anti-Gnostic Tendency in Lucan Christology," *NTS* 14 (1967-1968) 259-271.

———— *Literary Patterns, Theological Themes and the Genre of Luke-Acts* (SBLMS 20; Missoula, MT: Scholars Press, 1974).

———— *Luke and the Gnostics: An Examination of the Lucan Purpose* (Nashville: Abingdon, 1966).

———— "Shifting Sands: The Recent Study of the Gospel of Luke," *Int* 30 (1976) 381-395.

Tannehill, R. "A Study in the Theology of Luke-Acts," *ATR* 43 (1961) 195-203.

Unnik, W. C. van. "Die Apostelgeschichte und die Häresien," *ZNW* 58 (1967) 240-246; reprinted in *Sparsa collecta I* (NovTSup 29; Leiden: Brill, 1973) 402-409.

———— "The 'Book of Acts' the Confirmation of the Gospel," *NovT* 4 (1960-1961) 26-59.

———— "Luke-Acts, a Storm Center in Contemporary Scholarship," in *Studies in Luke-Acts*, 15-32.

Vielhauer, P. "On the 'Paulinism' of Acts," in *Studies in Luke-Acts*, 33-50.

Voss, G. *Die Christologie der lukanischen Schriften in Grundzügen* (Studia neotestamentica, Studia 2; Bruges: Desclée de Brouwer, 1965).

Wikenhauser, A. *Die Apostelgeschichte und ihr Geschichtswert* (NTAbh 8/3-5; Münster in W.: Aschendorff, 1921).

Wilckens, U. "Interpreting Luke-Acts in a Period of Existentialist Theology," in *Studies in Luke-Acts*, 60-83.

―――― *Die Missionsreden der Apostelgeschichte: Form- und traditions-geschichtliche Untersuchungen* (WMANT 5; Neukirchen: Neukirchener, 1961).

Williams, C. S. C. "Luke-Acts in Recent Study," *ExpTim* 73 (1961-1962) 133-136.

Wilson, R. McL. *Gnosis and the New Testament* (Oxford: Blackwell, 1968).

―――― *The Gnostic Problem: A Study of the Relations between Hellenistic Judaism and the Gnostic Heresy* (London: Mowbray, 1948).

Winn, A. C. "Elusive Mystery: The Purpose of Acts," *Int* 13 (1959) 144-156.

Yamauchi, E. M. *Pre-Christian Gnosticism: A Survey of the Proposed Evidences* (Grand Rapids: Eerdmans, 1973).

Zehnle, R. "The Salvific Character of Jesus' Death in Lucan Soteriology," *TS* 30 (1969) 420-444.

II. LUKE, HIS DATE AND HIS READERS

1. *The Identity of Luke.* The Third Gospel is anonymous, as are the other three canonical Gospels. Nowhere in it does its author reveal his identity, and it cannot be deduced from the extant text. This Gospel is, then, quite different from the writings of Paul, whose name regularly appears at the beginning of his letters, with or without that of co-senders, in the formulaic *praescriptio,* or "address."

From the Gospel itself it emerges that the author is not an eyewitness of the ministry of Jesus, but that he depends on those who were (1:2). He is rather a second- or third-generation Christian. Further, he is scarcely a native Palestinian; his knowledge of its geography and customs seems inadequate and argues in favor of another origin. Third, he is obviously a rather well-educated person, a writer of no little merit, acquainted with both OT literary traditions (especially as they are known from the Greek Bible) and Hellenistic literary techniques. Fourth, he differs from other evangelists in his desire to relate the story of Jesus not only to the contemporary world and culture, but also to the growth and development of the nascent Christian church.

The Third Gospel is clearly related to the Acts of the Apostles. Not only does the author of Acts speak of the Gospel as his "first book" and succinctly describe its contents ("all that Jesus began to do and teach"), but he dedicates it to the same Theophilus (Luke 1:3; Acts 1:1). Though it is on rare occasions called in question (e.g. by A. C. Clark, A. W. Argyle), the common authorship of these two NT writings is so widely admitted in modern times that it calls for little proof here. Modern studies of the language, style, and theological preoccupations of the two works have normally led to this conclusion (see the writings of A. von Harnack, W. L. Knox, and most recently B. E. Beck). But Acts is equally anonymous; nothing in its text-tradition reveals the identity of the author. There is a paraphrase of Acts 20:13 in an Armenian translation of a commentary on Acts by Ephraem of Syria, which names Luke as one of a group, the subject of a verb in the first plural: "We—I, Luke, and those with me—entered the boat" (see *Beginnings* 3. 442). But the introduction of his name into this paraphrase is certainly late and dependent on the existing church tradition. It is worthless in the debate about the authorship of the Third Gospel and Acts so far as the text-tradition goes.

The ancient title, *euangelion kata Loukan,* "Gospel according to Luke," is found at the end of the Gospel in the oldest extant ms. of it, P[75], a papyrus codex dating from A.D. 175-225 (*Papyrus Bodmer XIV* [eds. V. Martin and R. Kasser; Cologny-Genève: Bibliothèque Bodmer, 1961] pl. 61). In general, such ms. titles date from the end of the second century, when the attribution of the four canonical Gospels to their traditional authors was already a common heritage.

The prep. *kata*, "according to," could express some vague association with the person designated by it (see Gal 1:11); but here it is rather the formula for literary authorship (as in 2 Macc 2:13).

The "Luke" who is meant by this ancient attribution is mentioned three times in the NT. In Phlm 24 he appears as Paul's "fellow worker" and sends his greetings along with other companions. In Col 4:14 he is called "the beloved physician" and sends greetings to the church of Colossae. In 2 Tim 4:11 he is named as Paul's "sole companion." Since the time of Chrysostom (*Hom. in II Cor.,* 18.1; PG 61. 523) it has often been suggested that Paul also refers to him in 2 Cor 8:18 as "the brother whose fame in preaching the gospel is known throughout all the churches." Plausible as this interpretation may be, it is scarcely certain.

Objections, however, have been raised in modern times against this identification of Luke as the author of the Third Gospel and Acts. It has been asked, for instance, how Paul could refer to Luke as a "fellow worker," when he is imprisoned. But the objection is dependent on a too literal interpretation of Paul's words. If one were to admit the Roman origin of the Pauline letters to Philemon and the Colossians—which is still the majority opinion among those who regard the latter as authentically Pauline (see W. G. Kümmel, *Introduction to the New Testament* [Nashville: Abingdon, 1975] 340-348)—the Apostle might well be referring to Luke who had been a fellow worker or still was during at least part of his Roman house-arrest (ca. A.D. 61-63), which was not a totally restricting confinement (Acts 28:30). But the identification of Luke as Paul's "fellow worker" is complicated for many commentators today who regard Colossians as Deutero-Pauline.

The identification of Luke as the author of Luke-Acts has found some support in the so-called We-Sections of Acts (16:10-17; 20:5-15; 21:1-18; 27:1-28:16 [and 11:28 in Codex Bezae—of questionable validity]). In these passages the shift from the third person to the first plural in the narrative suggests the association of the author of Acts with Paul in certain parts of the story. Sometimes it is said that Acts 16:17 and 21:18 actually tell against this association, because Paul seems to be distinguished there from the "we" (see Kümmel, *Introduction,* 176). But even though he may be so distinguished in the formula used, the sentence in each case still suggests the association; the distinction is not really an argument against the evidence of the We-Sections. The nature of these sections in Acts is controverted, but one creditable view of them is that they represent a diary of the author, later used in the composition of

Acts. If Luke is to be identified as that author, then the last We-Section (especially Acts 28:16) would suggest that Luke was present in Rome with Paul. We shall return to the We-Sections below.

A reason for the identification of the author as Luke is the long-standing church tradition. Though it is the vogue today to reject this identification, a fresh look at the data may be called for, since there is a tendency to make it say either too much or too little. Most of the texts on which this tradition depends can be found in K. Aland, *SQE,* 531-548 in the original languages; see also *Beginnings* 2. 209-250. We shall present here the substance of the data.

The first reference to the tradition can be found in the Muratorian Canon (*SQE,* 538). Though A. C. Sundberg, Jr. has questioned the early dating of this Latin canonical list ("Canon Muratori: A Fourth-Century List," *HTR* 66 [1973] 1-41), it has usually been assigned a date ca. A.D. 170-180. Lines 2-8 read: "The third book of the Gospel: According to Luke. This Luke was a physician. After the ascension of Christ, when Paul had taken him along with him as one devoted to letters, he wrote it under his own name from hearsay. For he himself had not seen the Lord in person, but, insofar as he was able to follow (it all), he thus began his account with the birth of John."

(The Latin in the eighth-century copy of this text is quite defective. The text of H. Lietzmann and K. Aland, followed above, is heavily emended. The phrase read as *litteris studiosum,* "one devoted to letters," is emended from the text's *iuris studiosum,* "one devoted to law"; others have interpreted it as *itineris sui socium,* "a companion of his journey." Again, *secum,* "with him," is emended from the text's *secundum,* "a second" [?]. The phrase *nomine suo,* "under his own name," is emended from the text's *numeni suo,* "at his own inspiration" [?], and the phrase "from hearsay" is an attempt to render the obscure *ex opinione.* However, none of these problems in the text affect the basic attribution of the Third Gospel to Luke. See further J. Quasten, *Patrology* [3 vols.; Westminster, MD: Newman, 1953] 1. 207-210.)

From the end of the second century comes further testimony, in the writings of Irenaeus *Adversus haereses* 3.1,1 (*SQE,* 533-537): "Luke, too, the companion (*akolouthos, sectator*) of Paul, set forth in a book the gospel as preached by him (i.e. Paul)."

(The pres. ptc., *kēryssomenon,* is not to be pressed as an indication of contemporaneity, meaning that Luke wrote his Gospel while Paul was actually preaching it.)

In *Adv. haer.* 3.14,1 Irenaeus further says, "That this Luke was inseparable from Paul and was his collaborator in [preaching] the gospel, he himself makes clear, not by boasting (of it), but led on by the truth itself. For after Barnabas and John, who was called Mark, had parted company

with Paul and had sailed for Cyprus [Acts 15:39], he says, 'We came to
Troas' [Acts 16:8]. When Paul saw in a dream a man of Macedonia saying, 'Come over to Macedonia,' Paul, 'and help us' [Acts 16:9], immediately he says, 'we sought to set out for Macedonia, realizing that the Lord
had summoned us to preach the gospel to them. So we set sail from Troas
and steered our course toward Samothrace' [Acts 16:11]. Then he carefully indicates all the rest of their journey as far as Philippi, and how they
delivered their first address. For he says, 'Sitting down, we spoke to the
women who had assembled' [Acts 16:13]. . . . And later he recounts,
'But we sailed from Philippi after the days of Unleavened Bread and arrived at Troas . . . where we stayed seven days' [Acts 20:6]. All the rest
(that happened) with Paul he sets forth in due order. . . . In this way
he [Paul, after 2 Tim 4:10-11 has been quoted] shows that Luke was always associated with him and inseparable from him." (See further *Adv.
haer.* 3.14,2-3.)

(In this piece of apologetic writing, Irenaeus clearly ascribes the Third Gospel to Luke, an "inseparable" companion of Paul, because of his desire to establish its "apostolic" origin. Irenaeus' discussion is clearly dependent on the
data of the NT itself. His main argument for the Lucan authorship is derived
from the We-Sections of Acts, which he even extends to include 16:8. Like
other patristic writers, he ascribes to Luke the gospel preached by Paul, undoubtedly because of an oversimplified or literal understanding of the
Pauline expression, "my gospel" [e.g. Rom 2:16]. Once Luke is recognized
as the companion of Paul, he became to him what Mark was believed to
have been to Peter, a compiler of his preaching.)

Likewise coming from the end of the second century A.D. is an ancient
extratextual Prologue to the Gospel (*SQE,* 533), which runs as follows:
"Luke was a Syrian of Antioch, by profession a physician, the disciple of
the apostles, and later a follower (*parakolouthēsas*) of Paul until his
martyrdom. He served the Lord without distraction, without a wife, and
without children. He died at the age of eighty-four in Boeotia, full of the
holy Spirit." The second paragraph of this Ancient Greek Prologue continues: "Though gospels were already in existence, that according to
Matthew, composed in Judea, and that according to Mark in Italy, he was
prompted by the holy Spirit and composed this gospel entirely in the regions about Achaia. He made very clear in the prologue [i.e. Luke 1:1-4]
that other (gospels) had been written before him, but that it was necessary to set forth for Gentile converts the accurate account of the (new)
dispensation that they might not be distracted by Jewish fables or de-
ceived by heretical and foolish fantasies, and so miss the truth itself.
From the very beginning (of his gospel) we have received as of no little
importance (the story of) the birth of John, who is the beginning of the
Gospel. He was the Lord's precursor, the one who shared in the articu-

lation of the good news, in the ministering of baptism, and in the company of the Spirit. Of this dispensation a prophet among the Twelve makes mention. Later the same Luke wrote the Acts of the Apostles."

(This Ancient Prologue actually exists in two forms, one in Greek and one in Latin; the latter has slight variants that are unimportant here. D. de Bruyne ["Les plus anciens prologues latins des évangiles," *RBén* 40 (1928) 193-214] believed that this prologue along with similar prologues for Mark and for John, which survive in Latin versions, had originally been composed in Greek at Rome, that all three had a common origin, and that they were written with anti-Marcionite intent. Thus they are commonly called the Anti-Marcionite Prologues. His thesis was accepted in the main by H. Lietzmann, A. Jülicher, W. F. Howard, and above all by A. von Harnack, who dated them ca. A.D. 160-180.

However, it is clear today that these prologues did not originally form a unity, were not all composed at the same time, are not uniformly anti-Marcionite, and do not in fact refer to questions of canon. The anti-Marcionite character of the Greek form of the prologue to Luke is not evident. Some would date it even later than the Monarchian Prologue to the Third Gospel [e.g. E. Gutwenger, *TS* 7 (1946) 393-406; J. Regul, *Die anti-marcionitischen Evangelienprologe* (Freiburg: Herder, 1969)]; but this is not certain.

Moreover, it seems that one should distinguish two parts in the Greek prologue, which is almost certainly older than the corresponding Latin form. R. G. Heard ["The Old Gospel Prologues," *JTS* 6 (1955) 1-16] recognized that the two parts of the Greek form are of unequal value. The first paragraph contains details that do not come from the NT and may represent a separate tradition. To it has been joined other material, the second paragraph, which may depend only on Irenaeus' testimony. D. de Bruyne and A. von Harnack argued for the dependence of Irenaeus on the Greek prologue; M.-J. Lagrange contested this [*RB* 38 (1929) 115-121; see further W. F. Howard, *ExpTim* 47 (1935-1936) 534-538]. As far as I can see, the Greek prologue to Luke may echo 1 Cor 7:35, but is not certainly echoing 1 Tim 1:4-6 or dependent on Irenaeus.

The first paragraph of the Greek prologue, which shows no clear relation to the other so-called Anti-Marcionite Prologues, has been too quickly written off as an unusable source of information by W. G. Kümmel [*Introduction,* 147]. The serious difficulties encountered in the interpretation of the extratextual prologue to John should not, however, be predicated of the group. Each must be considered in and for itself. It may be difficult to show the priority of the first paragraph of the Greek prologue to Luke over the testimony of Irenaeus, but its testimony to the authorship of the Third Gospel has not really been shown by the modern criticism to be later than Irenaeus!)

From the beginning of the third century comes further testimony, from Tertullian. Writing ca. A.D. 207-208 against Marcion, he made use of the distinction of Gospels written by "apostles" (*apostoli,* Matthew and John) and by "men of apostolic times" (*apostolici,* Mark and Luke). Of the Third Gospel he wrote: "Luke, however, was not an apostle, but only a man of apostolic times (*apostolicus*); not a master, but a disciple, inferior indeed to a master—and at least as much later (than they) as the Apostle whom he followed, undoubtedly Paul (was later than the others)" (*Adversus Marcionem* 4.2,2). He called Paul Luke's "inspirer" (*inluminator Lucae*) and Luke's Gospel "the gospel of his teacher" (4.2,5 [*SQE,* 540]), or a "digest" of Paul's gospel (4.5,3).

The attribution of the Third Gospel, thus attested in the second century, continues in the later centuries in the testimony of Origen (*Comm. in Matth.,* quoted by Eusebius *Historia ecclesiastica* 6.25,6 [*SQE,* 540], from ca. A.D. 254), Eusebius himself ca. A.D. 303 (*Hist. eccl.* 3.4,6-7 [*SQE,* 543]), and Jerome, who recapitulates the earlier tradition (*De viris illustribus* 7 [*SQE,* 545]) ca. A.D. 398. These seven testimonies are the most important from the early Church; but others of less importance could also be added: Clement of Alexandria (quoted in Eusebius *Hist. eccl.* 6.15,5 [*SQE,* 539]), the Monarchian Prologue (*SQE,* 539), Jerome (*Comm. in Isaiam,* 3.6; *Pref. Comm. in Matth.*), Ephraem Syrus (*Comm. on Tatian's Diatessaron,* App. 1.1 [*SQE,* 544]), Adamantius (*Dialogue on True Faith* [GCS 4.8]), Epiphanius (*Panarion* 6.1 [*SQE,* 544]), and the Prologue of the Latin Vulgate (*SQE,* 547).

From such testimony about the author of the Third Gospel one can sift out two groups of details: (a) *Things which cannot be deduced from the NT:* that the author was Luke—indeed, according to some, the Lucius of Rom 16:21; that he was a Syrian of Antioch, who wrote a Gospel derived from Paul; that he wrote it in Achaia (or, according to some, in Rome or Bithynia) and died in Boeotia or Thebes, unmarried, childless, and at the age of eighty-four. (b) *Things that have been deduced from the NT:* that this Luke was a physician, a companion or collaborator of Paul, a disciple who had not witnessed the ministry of Jesus; that he wrote his Gospel for Gentile converts, after the Gospels of Mark and Matthew, and began his with the birth of John the Baptist; that he also composed Acts and was a good Greek stylist.

Most of the information, whether deduced from the NT ultimately or not, is contained in the earliest testimonies, the Muratorian Canon, Irenaeus, and the Ancient Greek Prologue. H. J. Cadbury (*Beginnings* 2. 259) has rightly pointed out that they show that speculation on the origins of the NT was already abundant in the second century. Even if valid external evidence may not have been available, the inner characteristics of the writings were being exploited to answer questions about their dates, purposes, and authority. But it is quite another matter to attribute all the data in the early testimony to such exploitation and speculation.

That some of the details have to be explained as allegorical or legendary has to be admitted (e.g. Luke's marital status, his age [see Luke 2:37], the place of his death, and probably even the place of composition of his writings). They are of little concern. But to dismiss the substance of the tradition—that Luke wrote the Third Gospel and Acts—seems gratuitous. As in all cases, the tradition has to be scrutinized; what cannot be explained as "inferences from the text" of the NT or as obvious legendary accretions should be accepted, unless one encounters serious, insoluble, or contradictory problems. Cadbury (*Beginnings* 2. 250-264) has maintained that "inferences from the text" of the NT would have made it possible to conclude that Luke was the author of the Third Gospel, because a canonical Gospel had to have an "apostle" or "man of apostolic times" as its author, as Tertullian argued. Given this attitude, which itself has not been inferred from the text of the NT, one could have compared the We-Sections in Acts with the data about Paul and his companions during his house-arrest and concluded that Luke was the author. More recently Haenchen (*Acts,* 1-14) has argued similarly. He discussed anew the evidence from tradition in great detail and showed many of its weaknesses from a critical standpoint. But the argument that the second-century church inferred from the NT itself that Luke was the author, while *in se* possible, is all too pat. That an individual in the second century—or even several individuals—might have so reasoned is certainly possible; but that such inferences from the NT text are the sole basis of an otherwise uncontested or unambiguous tradition (unlike that of the First Gospel) is difficult to accept. Too much has indeed been made of such early church tradition in the past, even as late as the beginning of this century, in the attempt to defend the historicity of the Gospels. But I find myself in agreement with J. M. Creed who thus argued for the presumption that the tradition is true: "Luke . . . is not personally a prominent figure in the apostolic age. . . . If the Gospel and Acts did not already pass under his name there is no obvious reason why tradition should have associated them with him" (*The Gospel,* xiii-xiv).

There are some problems that one has to face in accepting the substance of the tradition that Luke, the companion of Paul, was the author of the Third Gospel and Acts, and to these we now turn.

A. LUKE'S ETHNIC BACKGROUND. Scholarly opinion has been divided on the question of Luke's ethnic background. In general, two views are proposed: (1) *Luke was a Gentile Christian:* This view is based mainly on the internal evidence of the Gospel and Acts: the superior quality of the Greek language, the avoidance of Semitic words (except *Amen*), the omission of gospel traditions about Jesus' controversies with the Pharisaic understanding of the Law and about what is clean or unclean, the transformation of Palestinian local color and details into Hellenistic counterparts. These and similar factors have been cited to identify the author as a Gentile Christian, i.e. one converted to Christianity from paganism.

The argument is sometimes pushed still further to maintain that the author was actually a Gentile Christian of *Greek* origin or an Antiochene *Greek*. This is based on Paul's statement in Col 4:11-14, where three persons are listed as his Jewish-Christian co-workers, but Luke seems to be listed among other, presumably, Gentile-Christian collaborators. For instance, K. Lake years ago claimed that the early tradition identified Luke as "an Antiochene Greek" ("Luke," in *Dictionary of the Apostolic Church* [New York: Scribner, 1922] 1. 719); and more recently, K. H. Rengstorf (*Evangelium nach Lukas,* 11) has called him a Gentile Christian, indeed of Greek origin. Many others have followed this view (e.g. W. K. Hobart, A. von Harnack, P. Vielhauer, G. B. Caird, W. G. Kümmel, A. Plummer, W. Manson, J. Schmid).

(2) *Luke was a Jewish Christian*. The view that the author was a Jewish Christian, i.e. a convert from Judaism, is based mainly on the interest displayed in Luke-Acts in the OT and its phraseology, the author's alleged Palestinian language, and the Epiphanian tradition (*Panarion* 51.11) that he was one of the seventy-two disciples; sometimes the mention of Lucius as among Paul's "kinsmen" (Rom 16:21) is also invoked. Among supporters of this view, one may cite A. Schlatter, B. S. Easton, E. E. Ellis, W. F. Albright, N. Q. King, B. Reicke.

For reasons that I shall try to set forth below, I regard Luke as a Gentile Christian, not, however, as a Greek, but as a non-Jewish Semite, a native of Antioch, where he was well educated in a Hellenistic atmosphere and culture. But various factors, which support this view of the author of the Third Gospel and which are involved in the contrasting views, have to be discussed. They involve the form of Luke's name, the NT passages in which he is mentioned, and the ancient tradition about his Antiochene origin. I shall comment on these in turn.

Luke's name is written in NT Greek as *Loukas,* i.e. in a shortened or hypocoristic Greek form of a Latin name (or names): *Loukanos* (=Latin *Lucanus*), *Loukianos* (=*Lucianus*), *Loukios* or *Leukios* (=*Lucius*), *Loukillios* (=*Lucilius*). See W. M. Calder, *CRev* 38 (1924) 30. It has, moreover, been compared with other shortened Greek names in the NT: Paul's companion is called *Silas* (Acts 15:40), but otherwise *Silouanos* (1 Thess 1:1 = Latin *Silvanus*). Similarly, *Epaphras* (Col 4:12), a shortened form of Greek *Epaphroditos* (Phil 2:25); or *Antipas* (Rev 2:13) for Greek *Antipatros* (Josephus *Ant.* 14.1,3 § 10). See BDF § 125. The shortening of the name has been explained as a Greek phenomenon (see W. Schulze, *Graeca latina* [Göttingen: Dieterich, 1901] 12). That *Loukas* is a shortened name seems certain.

Of the various Latin names for which *Loukas* might stand, the only certainly attested equivalent is *Loukios* (=Latin *Lucius*). This equation is based on two inscriptions referring to a family which set up *ex voto* plaques in honor of the god Men Ascaënus at Pisidian Antioch in the Imperial period. In one the son's name is given as *Loukios,* in the other as *Loukas* (see A. Deissmann, *LAE,* 435-438). This evidence makes many interpreters insist on this explanation of Luke's name, even though the other possibilities cannot be absolutely ruled out.

From the use of such a name one cannot tell whether the person who bore it was a Gentile or a Jew. Greek and Roman names were borne by many Jews in Palestine and Syria of this period. They were often indicative of their status either as *liberti,* "freedmen," descendants of Jews once sold into slavery during the Roman conquest of an area, or as *incolae,* "inhabitants," of the area, who in time had been granted the right of Roman citizenship.

Origen knew of persons who identified Luke as the Lucius of Rom 16:21 (*Comm. in Ep. ad Rom.* 10.39), and that identification has persisted into modern times. This would make Luke a kinsman of Paul, and hence a Jewish Christian, because Paul's phrase, "my kinsmen" (*hoi syngeneis mou*) seems to refer to "Lucius, Jason, and Sosipater" (Rom 16:21). Deissmann (*LAE,* 438) sought to get around this, by arguing that the phrase "might be in apposition only to Jason and Sosipater." Though that is possible, the real problem is to explain why Paul would refer to Luke there as *Loukios,* when he elsewhere uses *Loukas* of him (Col 4:14). The identification is further complicated by the fact that the immediately preceding verse, Rom 16:20b, is a greeting, "The grace of our Lord Jesus be with you" (the end of Paul's own message?) and that the following verse, Rom 16:22, contains a greeting from Paul's scribe, Tertius. Hence it is not clear to whom the pronoun "my" in 16:21 refers. So one cannot facilely conclude from Rom 16:21 that Luke was a Jewish Christian.

Col 4:10-14 has been used to show that Luke was a Gentile Christian, indeed a Greek. There Paul seems to say that Aristarchus, Mark, and Jesus Justus "are the only persons of the circumcision" (i.e. converts from Judaism) who are among his fellow workers. Immediately contrasted to them is Epaphras, identified as "one of yourselves," seemingly converts from paganism. Then, after two verses describing Epaphras' prayer, work, and concern for Christians in Colossae, Laodicea, and Hierapolis, Paul mentions the greeting of Luke and Demas, who are not explicitly identified either as Jewish or Gentile converts. Yet the implied contrast would seem to suggest that Luke was a Gentile Christian. Again, Deissmann (*LAE,* 438) has argued that here too it is not certain that Paul is describing all three men as Jews in 4:10, but only the last two. Aristarchus could have been a pagan convert to Christianity. This is again a possibility, but it is not plausible because of the natural sense of the phrase and because the name Aristarchus could have been borne by a Jew.

Moreover, W. F. Albright has argued that it is quite wrong to infer from Col 4:10-11 and 14 that "Luke was not himself circumcised" (AB 31. 266). He insists that the phrase *hoi ontes ek peritomēs* means "those belonging to the circumcision party," because this Greek phrase without the article designates the party which considered circumcision a necessary prerequisite for salvation. The phrase has this meaning in Gal 2:12; it is a plausible meaning for Acts 11:2 and Titus 1:10 (so interpreted by the *RSV* in these places). But that it always designates the circumcision party is not at all certain. It is impossible in Rom 4:12 and is far from demanded in the context of Acts 10:45. As for Col 4:11, what sense would it make for Paul to say that Aristarchus, Mark, and Jesus Justus were "the only men of the circumcision party" who were his fellow workers? It seems incredible that Paul would admit that such persons "have been a comfort" to him. Moreover, the contrast of the phrase with the other one, *ho ex hymōn,* "one of yourselves," calls for the more general meaning, "converts from Judaism," among whom Epaphras was not. The contrast is limited to vv. 10-12, and the greeting that mentions Luke in v. 14 is extrinsic to that contrast. The least one can say is that v. 11 implies that Luke is not among the converts from Judaism.

But does it immediately mean that Luke was a "Greek"? Such a description of him has depended in part on the common estimate of the Greek in which the Third Gospel and Acts are written. For Jerome's high estimate of his Greek, see p. 107 below (cf. *De vir. ill.* 7). That estimate has been often repeated and even grew in time. A tenth-century writer, Symeon Metaphrastes, spun out its implications: Luke had "received the finest education among the Greeks" (*Hypomnema* 1; PG, 115. 1129).

The description is also related to the tradition that Luke came from the Hellenistic city of Antioch. Josephus spoke of Antioch as the capital of Syria, "ranking third among the cities of the Roman world because of its size and prosperity" (*J.W.* 3.2,4 § 29). Founded by Seleucus I Nicator ca. 300 B.C., it was situated on the Orontes River near the plateau and springs of Daphne, whence was derived the common epithet, "Antioch near Daphne." The town was divided into various quarters in which lived European settlers and native Syrians. Its population was mixed: Macedonians, Cretans, Cypriotes, Argives, Jews (who had served as mercenaries in the Seleucid army), and native Syrians. Josephus makes it clear that a Jew from Antioch could have been called *Antiocheus* ("our Jewish inhabitants of Antioch are called Antiochenes," *Ag. Ap.* 2.1 § 39; cf. *Ant.* 12.3,1 § 119). See C. H. Kraeling, "The Jewish Community at Antioch," *JBL* 51 (1932) 130-160; G. Downey, *A History of Antioch in Syria from Seleucus to the Arab Conquest* (Princeton: Princeton University, 1961) 54-201; *Ancient Antioch* (Princeton: Princeton University, 1963) 27-142.

The understanding of Luke as a Gentile *Greek* is not necessarily called for by the evidence. To begin with, one should distinguish clearly between the internal evidence for the author's ethnic background and that for the destination of the Gospel, i.e. the readers for whom Luke wrote and destined his work. W. G. Kümmel (*Introduction,* 149-150) writes, "The only thing that can be said with certainty about the author, on the basis of Lk, is that he was a Gentile Christian." Although Kümmel does not call the author of Luke-Acts a "Greek," as others have done, his paragraph mingles indiscriminately evidence about Luke's ethnic background and evidence about the Gentile-readers destination of his Gospel. Aside from the question of Luke's knowledge of Palestinian geography, most of the items which Kümmel mentions support the Gentile destination of the Gospel and are irrelevant to the consideration of the author's ethnic background. The most that one can deduce from the Gospel is Luke's concern for Christians of Gentile background; and the Gentile destination of the Gospel would not necessarily exclude a Jewish background for its author. In the long run, then, the question of the author's ethnic background has to be decided on other grounds, which would include the tradition extrinsic to the Gospel and what might be deduced from Col 4: 10-14.

Here we may consider the phrase mentioning Luke's origin in several of the ancient testimonies which relate the Third Gospel to him. The oldest reference is in the Ancient Greek Prologue: *estin ho Loukas Antiocheus Syros* (with a variant reading, *Syros tō genei;* the [later?] Latin form of the prologue has *Lucas Antiochensis Syrus*), "This Luke is an Antiochene, a Syrian" (with the variant, "by nationality" [or possibly, "by descent"]). Eusebius knows of the same tradition (*Hist. eccl.* 3.4,6): *Loukas de to men genos ōn tōn ap' Antiocheias,* "by descent Luke was of those from Antioch." Jerome (*De vir. ill.* 7) repeats it: "Lucas medicus Antiochensis."

Though Luke in this ancient tradition is said to be from Antioch in Syria, he is not said to be a Greek. The statement quoted from Josephus above could be used to explain that Luke was a "Jew from Antioch." There is a third possibility, simpler than the other two, viz. that Luke was a native Syrian inhabitant of Antioch, a non-Jew from a Semitic cultural background, an *incola* of Antioch, a Gentile. W. F. Albright (AB 31,

264) has argued that since there were at least twenty-four different Antiochs, this phrase means no more than that Luke was a native of Antioch in Syria. But if there were, indeed, twenty-four Antiochs in Syria, the adjective *Syros* is scarcely specific for any one of them. For this reason, the ethnic meaning is to be preferred. Certainly, Eusebius' testimony points in that direction. (Here I have to record that my revered teacher Albright wrote what he did about this matter in opposition to what I was proposing about it, as he queried me at the time that he [with his assistant] was composing the appendix to Munck's commentary. But in the light of further study I stick to my guns.) See the NOTE on 7:3.

The mention of Luke's Syrian and Antiochene connections in the Ancient Greek Prologue has *in se* no apologetic or theological value. But in this connection one should recall the striking acquaintance that the author of Luke-Acts manifests with the Christian community in Antioch (see A. Harnack, *Luke the Physician,* 20-24). Some have tried to support the relationship with the variant reading in Codex Bezae at Acts 11:28, which makes it one of the We-Sections. It is in a context concerning the Antiochene church. But how can one assign that reading "to the second century" (*Beginnings* 4. 130) or be certain that it antedates the Ancient Greek Prologue? Why is it "certainly as early as the tradition of Luke's Antiochian provenance" (ibid. 2. 248)? As J. M. Creed notes (*The Gospel,* xxi), it is hardly likely that that reading is original.

A. Strobel (*ZNW* 49 [1958] 131-134) has argued for the plausibility of Luke's Antiochene origin on the basis of internal evidence from Acts. Haenchen, however, has expressed his skepticism about Strobel's arguments. But, though Haenchen has rightly argued that the ancient so-called Anti-Marcionite Prologues do not form a literary unit and are not directed against Marcion (*Acts,* 10-12), he has offered no evidence that the attribution of the Third Gospel and Acts to Luke, a Syrian of Antioch, is untenable.

Luke's acquaintance with Antioch would have to be limited to an early phase of the church there, as it can be deduced from Acts 11:19-20; 13:1-4; 14:26-28; 15:1-3,13-40; and 18:22-23. He knows of it as a city where many converts were made to Christianity from Gentile and Jewish Antiochenes by people from Jerusalem, Cyprus, and Cyrene; where the disciples were first called Christians; and where the Jerusalem prophet Agabus told of a famine coming to a vast area. Much of his story about Barnabas (aside from his work with Paul on Mission I [A.D. 46-49]) is related to Antioch, to which Barnabas was sent by the Jerusalem community and to which he brought Saul. Again, Luke is aware of the Antiochene efforts to alleviate the stricken brethren in Jerusalem. He is acquainted with five prophets and teachers of the Antiochene community, perhaps intimately with Barnabas, Manaen, and Saul. He knows too of the dispatch of Barnabas and Saul by that church on missionary work and of the sending of these men to Jerusalem for an official resolution of the Antiochene problem of the circumcision of Gentile converts. After the "council" of Jerusalem, he tells of the brief Antiochene sojourn of Paul and Barnabas before their separation. At this point Barnabas disappears not only from Antioch but also from the story of Acts. Antioch does too, save for a fleeting mention in 18:22-23, in a way that suggests that Luke was not on hand at all. This would then imply an *early* acquaintance of Luke with the Antiochene church.

It has been further suggested by R. Glover ("'Luke the Antiochene' and Acts," *NTS* 11 [1964-1965] 97-106) that Luke was no longer associated with Antioch after a date in the late 40s when Barnabas went off to Cyprus, and that unless the common interpretation of the We-Sections has erred, Luke soon thereafter turned up in Troas (Acts 16:8-10). From there he sailed with Paul to Europe, where he seems to have made a long stay at Philippi (Acts 16:12; 20:5-6). From there he further returned with Paul to Caesarea Maritima, visited Jerusalem, followed Paul back to Caesarea, and then accompanied him to Rome.

If the author of the Third Gospel and Acts were a native of Antioch in Syria, one could rule out the possibility of his coming from other places that are at times proposed: Pisidian Antioch, Philippi, and Cyrene in Northern Africa. W. T. Whitley ("Luke of Antioch in Pisidia," *ExpTim* 21 [1909-1910] 164-166) proposed Pisidian Antioch as Luke's hometown on the basis of the "we" in Acts 14:22, which is not for him a verbatim quotation, but a neglected We-Section. Others, such as J. H. Moulton (*A Grammar of New Testament Greek,* 1. 19), think that the author was referring to himself as the "man of Macedonia" in Paul's dream at Troas and that hence he would have been a citizen of Philippi. The identification of Luke with "Lucius of Cyrene" (Acts 13:1) was suggested ages ago by Ephraem of Syria (Armenian *Comm. on Acts,* 12:25 - 13:3; *Beginnings* 3. 416); it has been more recently espoused by R. C. Ford and B. Reicke (*Gospel of Luke,* 10-24). The latter thinks that the "men of Cyprus and Cyrene" (Acts 11:20), who carried the Christian message to the Greeks at Antioch, included converted Jews and proselytes such as Barnabas (Acts 4:36) and Luke, who is none other than Lucius of Cyrene. In all these instances, we are dealing with speculation. It would seem preferable to give a little more credit to the ancient tradition, that Luke was a native of Antioch (near Daphne) - and a Syrian

B. LUKE AS A COMPANION OF PAUL. If the substance of the ancient tradition about the author of the Third Gospel and Acts still has something to be said for it, what about that aspect of it that claims that Luke was Paul's companion? It is particularly this aspect that evokes the loudest objections today.

Paul's statements in Phlm 24 and Col 4:14 refer to Luke as a fellow worker or companion. As we have seen, this association finds some support in the We-Sections of Acts (16:10-17; 20:5-15; 21:1-18; 27:1 - 28:16), at least if one is willing to admit the explanation of them as diary material. In this sense, they were understood by Irenaeus in antiquity and by R. Glover in recent times.

Irenaeus (*Adv. haer.* 3.14,1) appealed to those passages in Acts to establish his thesis that Luke had been Paul's "inseparable" companion. In doing so, Irenaeus read into the text of Acts more than is there. The author of Acts relates, indeed, Paul's missionary activity after the "council" of Jerusalem (ca. A.D. 49), and in the We-Sections that only begin after it implies that he has traveled with Paul from Troas to Philippi on Mission II (ca. A.D. 49-52) and stayed there until Paul returned to that town at the end of Mission III (ca. A.D. 54-57). Paul was then en route to Jerusalem, traveling overland from Achaia to Philippi and then by boat to Troas and eventually to Caesarea Maritima. "We sailed from Philippi after the days of Unleavened Bread, and in five days came to those at Troas, where we stayed for seven days" (Acts 20:6). This would have been the spring of A.D. 58 (or thereabouts), about eight years after the brief association of Luke with Paul between Troas and Philippi on Mission II. Even granting, then, that Luke was with Paul for some other intervals in the period described in Acts, he was scarcely Paul's "inseparable" companion. In other words, if one takes the We-Sections at face value—and does not overinterpret them, as Irenaeus did—one could still admit that Luke was a companion or fellow worker of Paul for a time, without having been with him inseparably.

If this understanding, which is basically that of R. Glover, has any validity, then it would reveal that Luke was not with Paul during the major part of his missionary activity, or during the period when Paul's most important letters were being written. It would also mean that Luke was not on the scene when Paul was facing the major crises in his evangelization of the eastern Mediterranean world, e.g. the Judaizing problem, the struggle with the factions in Corinth, or the questions that arose in Thessalonica. Luke would not have been with Paul when he was formulating the essence of his theology or wrestling with the meaning of the gospel. This would explain why there is such a difference between the Paul of Acts and the Paul of Paul's letters. In this connection we must recall T. H. Campbell's analysis of Paul's missionary journeys as they are reflected in his letters and his argument about their agreement with the sequence of Paul's movements in Acts (*JBL* 74 [1955] 80-87).

Moreover, there is no real evidence that Luke ever read any of Paul's letters, not even those that are ascribed to his Roman house-arrest. This point has often been questioned (E. E. Ellis, *Gospel of Luke,* 51; M. S. Enslin, " 'Luke' and Paul," *JAOS* 58 [1938] 81-91; J. Knox, "Acts and the Pauline Letter Corpus," in *Studies in Luke-Acts,* 279-287), but no convincing arguments have been brought forth to show that he did.

If this is so, then one has an explanation for a number of things in Acts that puzzle us with regard to Paul: the number of his visits to Jerusalem after his conversion, the omission of his sojourn in Arabia (Gal 1:17-22), the failure to mention Paul's various floggings and shipwrecks (2 Cor 11:24-25), the almost complete disregard of the collection as the motive for Paul's return to Jerusalem at the end of Mission III, and the silence about his plans to visit Spain.

Because Luke would have spent only a short time with Paul, it is also possible that he misunderstood a number of events in the earlier career of the Apostle, which he presents in a fashion that conflicts somewhat with what Paul himself says in his letters. For instance, Luke has apparently historicized the so-called Famine Visit (Acts 11:27-30; 12:25), by distinguishing it from the "council" visit (15:1-12), whereas the references in diverse sources of his information may really have pertained to one and the same visit. At any rate, this classic problem, for all its complexity, can no more be used to prove that Luke was never Paul's companion than to prove that he was such at some time. One thing is clear: Luke was not Paul's companion at the time of these visits, and the source of his information about them is not apparent. If, as has been suggested, Luke derived his information about the "council" of Jerusalem from an Antiochene source, he could have done this as one who had been a sometime companion of Paul just as easily as one who had never been his companion. In reporting the "council," he has undoubtedly telescoped two classic decisions that were made at Jerusalem: the one at the "council" about the non-circumcision of Gentile Christians (Acts 15:1-12) and the one made by James with apostles and elders of Jerusalem about dietary regulations for local churches of Antioch, Syria, and Cilicia (Acts 15:13-33; for further details, see *JBC,* art. 45, § 72-78; art. 46, § 28-34). Because this *crux interpretum* is almost insoluble, we must be more nuanced in our estimate of Luke's relation to Paul. Certainly, W. G. Kümmel has overstated the case when he says that Luke could scarcely have been a companion of Paul on his missionary journeys, because he is so misinformed on three essential points of Paul's activity, viz. his journey to Jerusalem (Acts 11:30), his failure to mention Paul's compromise with the "pillars" of the Jerusalem church (Gal 2:1-10), and Paul's unacquaintance with the dietary decree of Acts 15:22-29 (*Introduction,* 180).

In recent times it has been especially the thesis of P. Vielhauer ("On the 'Paulinism' of Acts," in *Studies in Luke-Acts,* 33-50) that has provoked the skepticism about the ancient tradition of the author of the Third Gospel and Acts. Building on the work of earlier interpreters such as F. C. Baur, M. Dibelius, R. Bultmann, and F. Overbeck, Vielhauer summarized the major differences between Paul's own theology and the "Paulinism" of Acts (i.e. what Luke attributes to Paul in speeches and theological statements) under four headings: natural theology, the Law, christology, and eschatology. Vielhauer compares the natural theology of Paul's speech on the Areopagus (Acts 17:22-30) with Paul's own words on the inexcusable ignorance of God among pagans (Rom 1:18-21). The speech in Acts 17 is a sample discourse of Paul's proclamation to the Gentiles, a Lucan composition with a Stoic cast that emphasizes not their ignorance of God, but the fundamental knowledge of him that they actually have. Vielhauer further contrasts Paul's attitude toward the Law in Acts with that in the letters: in Acts Paul is utterly loyal to the Law, does not insist on freedom from the Law, does not contrast Christ and the Law, and does not preach justification by faith alone. Again, Vielhauer contends that the christology attributed to Paul in his speeches before Jewish audiences (Acts 13:17-41 and 26:22-23) is adoptionist, neglects the value of the cross, and really is neither specifically Pauline nor Lucan, but rather derived from the primitive community. Finally, Vielhauer maintains that in Acts Paul's eschatology has disappeared, since it becomes peripheral to his speeches, a mere hope in the resurrection or faith in the return of Christ; it has been removed from the center of faith and become one of the last things. Vielhauer summed up his contention thus: In his christology the author of Acts is pre-Pauline; in his natural theology, idea of the law, and eschatology, he is post-Pauline. He has presented no specifically Pauline ideas. He has rather depicted Paul in his zeal for the worldwide evangelization of the Gentiles. He considers the theological distance between Luke and Paul to be such as to raise the question whether there was not also temporal distance between them, i.e. whether one may really consider Luke, the physician and travel companion of Paul, as the author of Acts (p. 48).

With much of the detail of Vielhauer's argument I find myself in agreement. I should not disagree with the four areas of difference that he has pointed out; but I should want to nuance a bit more carefully his remarks about natural theology (especially in the light of 1 Cor 1:20-21) and concerning the Law (especially in the light of Rom 7:12 and Acts 13:39). J. A. T. Robinson (*Redating,* 87) has recently characterized Luke's statement about justification in Acts 13:39 as a "typical 'lay' summary" of a theologian's position, inadequate in precision (since it could be taken to mean that for some things justification by the law was possible), but sufficient in its general intent." As for Vielhauer's contention that the christology attributed to Paul in Acts 13:17-41 and 26:22-23 was derived from the early Christian community, I should hesitate to agree, if he intends to ascribe the formula, "the Messiah must suffer" (Acts 26:23), to such a source. Finally, in maintaining that Paul's eschatology disappears in Acts, Vielhauer accentuates the Lucan emphases, without ever clearly stating what he means by Pauline eschatology. In his treatment of the latter there is something of an oversimplification, for his discussion is limited to Galatians, 1 Corinthians 7 and 15, and Romans, but neglects crucial passages in Philippians and 2 Corinthians.

Differences do exist between Paul's theology and Luke's "Paulinism," but they need not be explained by a complete lack of relationship between Luke and Paul. As others have noted (e.g. E. Troemé, Le livre des Actes et l'histoire [Paris: Presses universitaires, 1957] 143), these differences may come from an insufficient and brief acquaintance. If one takes more seriously the indications furnished by the We-Sections of Acts and admits that Luke did not write his two volumes until a decade or two after Paul's house-arrest (and his death), is there not reason to expect differences between Paul's theology and Lucan "Paulinism"? If Luke were not a collaborator of Paul during the crucial time of the latter's struggle with the Judaizers and if he had never read Paul's letters, would we not expect that his view of Paul, idyllic as it is in many ways, should differ from what we read in Paul's own letters? Most of the arguments brought forth in modern times to substantiate the distance of Luke from Paul do not militate against the traditional identification of the author of the Third Gospel and Acts with Luke, the Syrian from Antioch, who had been a sometime collaborator of the Apostle Paul.

M. A. Siotis has also discussed many of these questions about Luke's relationship to Paul. Though he is right in querying "the results of the [modern] critical analysis of the written sources, and . . . the underestimation of ecclesiastical tradition" ("Luke the Evangelist as St. Paul's Collaborator," 105), much of his own discussion of the relationship between Luke and Paul relies on details that themselves require "critical analysis." *—what about "we" parallels in other ancient lit that make "we-sections" of Acts look like a literary device when narrating sea voyages?*

c. LUKE THE PHYSICIAN. In Col 4:14 Luke is identified as "the beloved physician." This detail is picked up and used in subsequent church tradition about the author of the Third Gospel and Acts. Since this description of Luke comes from the NT itself, there is, in my opinion, no need to disregard it. But it should be understood that it is historically plausible solely because of that reference.

In the early part of this century the author's medical background was taken much more seriously. This was so because of the book of W. K. Hobart, who in 1882 published a detailed comparison of the language and style of Luke with "the language of the Greek Medical Schools," and especially with that of writers such as Hippocrates, Galen, Dioscurides, and Arataeus. Hobart sought to show from internal evidence that Luke-Acts were written by the same person and that the writer was a medical man. He insisted that the author used expressions found in medical writing and contrasted numerous phrases in the Gospel with their counterparts in the Marcan Gospel; he argued that the language of the Third Gospel was more technical. He appealed to such phrases as "suffering from a very high fever" (Luke 4:38, *synechomenē pyretō megalō;* contrast Mark 1:30); "a man covered with leprosy" (Luke 5:12, *plērēs lepras;* contrast Mark 1:40); "paralyzed" (Luke 5:18,24, *paralelymenos;* contrast Mark 2:3-10), or "her hemorrhage stopped" (Luke 8:44, *estē hē rysis tou haimatos autēs;* contrast Mark 5:29). See further Luke 7:15; Acts 5:5,10; 9:40; 12:23; 28:8. Hobart's contention drew varied support from a number of scholars (M. Albertz, J. Behm, N. Geldenhuys, B. Gut, A. von Harnack, R. J. Knowling, M.-J. Lagrange, W. Michaelis, W. M. Ramsay, A. Wikenhauser, T. Zahn).

In 1912 H. J. Cadbury reopened the debate, questioning the presuppositions of Hobart's argument and showing that most of the "alleged medical language" of Luke could also be found in the LXX and in cultivated Hellenistic non-medical writers such as Josephus, Lucian, and Plutarch. Cadbury concludes: "The style of Luke bears no more evidence of medical training and interest than does the language of other writers who were not physicians. This result, it must be confessed, is a purely negative one. . . . The so-called medical language of these books cannot be used as a proof that Luke was their author, nor even as an argument confirming the tradition of his authorship" (*The Style,* 50-51). Later on, in a partly humorous lexical note, entitled, "Luke and the Horse Doctors," Cadbury showed that a good part of the alleged medical vocabulary could also be found in the *Corpus hippiatricorum graecorum* (eds. E. Oder and C. Hoppe; Leipzig: Teubner, 1924, 1927). Consequently, though such expressions as those listed above might seem to be more technical than their Marcan parallels, they are not necessarily more technical than expressions used by educated Greek writers who were not physicians. Ancient medical writers did not use an exclusive technical jargon such as the modern argument once presupposed. Indeed, Galen claimed to be writing in clear everyday language, "which the bulk of the people (*hoi polloi*) are accustomed to use." Hence, neither the alleged medical language of Luke, nor the attitude manifest in the care of the wounded man attended by the Good Samaritan (10:34-35) or in the elimination of the pejorative saying about "many physicians" who were unable to cure a woman (contrast Mark 5:26 and Luke 8:43) necessarily prove that he was a physician.

More recently G. A. Lindeboom has shown that there does not really exist any similarity between the Lucan prologue and the prologues of Galen, Hippocrates, and Dioscurides, despite suggestions by commentators to this effect.

In reality, it is a matter of little consequence for the interpretation of the Third Gospel whether its author was a physician or not. He is said to have been such in Col 4:14, if one accepts the traditional ascription of the Third Gospel to him; but that is the extent of the matter.

In fact, it makes little difference to the interpretation of the Lucan Gospel whether or not one can establish that its author was the traditional Luke, a sometime companion of Paul, even a physician. I think that some of the modern objections to the traditional identification are not all that cogent; hence the foregoing reassessment of them and of the traditional thesis. The important thing is the text of the Lucan Gospel and what it may say to Christians, regardless of the identity of its author.

2. *The Date and Place of the Composition of the Lucan Gospel.* The identification of the author of the Third Gospel and Acts as Luke, a Syrian of Antioch, a physician, and a sometime collaborator of Paul, in no way necessitates an early dating (i.e. pre-70) of the composition of these two NT books. In the prologue to the Gospel Luke speaks of his dependence on the first generation of Christian disciples ("eyewitnesses"), possibly on some of the second generation ("ministers of the word"—if these are to be understood as distinct from the eyewitnesses), and on "many" others who undertook to write accounts of the Christ-event before him. Among the latter must be included Mark, whose Gospel was composed about A.D. 65-70. The Lucan Gospel should be dated, therefore, later than the Marcan, but how much later?

Despite the suggestions of F. H. Chase, R. Koh, P. Parker, H. G. Russell, C. S. C. Williams, and others, that Acts was composed before the Lucan Gospel (or at least the final form of it), there is really no serious reason to question Luke's reference in Acts 1:1 to his "first book," or its implication that the Gospel was written before Acts. Williams and others have argued that Luke sent Theophilus not his Gospel, but an early draft of it, a collection of the sayings and doings of the Lord; later on he wrote Acts, and still later he revised the Gospel-draft, making use of a copy of Mark that he had actually acquired before he wrote Acts. This sort of explanation, however, is highly speculative and depends in part on the questionable theory of Proto-Luke (see below).

The story in Acts comes to a close with the house-arrest of Paul in

Rome, in the early sixties, perhaps A.D. 61-63 (28:30). The abrupt ending of that story has always been problematic, and many commentators have concluded from it that Luke-Acts was composed prior to the death of Paul, of which Luke makes no mention. Among these are Jerome, M. Albertz, F. Blass, J. Cambier, L. Cerfaux, E. E. Ellis, N. Geldenhuys, F. Godet, B. Gut, A. von Harnack, M. Meinertz, W. Michaelis, B. Reicke, H. Sahlin, J. A. T. Robinson, etc. No one knows why the story ends where it does, despite many attempts to explain it. But the straightforward reading of it, and the conclusion that the Lucan writings must have been composed prior to Paul's trial or death, are not warranted. They encounter too many problems.

First, Luke's own allusion to "many" other attempts to recount the Jesus-story (Luke 1:1) before his own would be difficult to understand at such an early date. Second, Luke 13:35a ("your house is abandoned," addressed to Jersualem) is almost certainly a reference to the destruction of Jerusalem. Third, Jesus' judgment about the Temple (Mark 13:2; cf. Luke 21:5) and his announcement about the desecration of it by the "abomination of desolation" (Mark 13:14) become in the Lucan version a saying about "Jerusalem surrounded by camps" (21:20). The Marcan apocalyptic prophecy, making an allusion to Dan 12:11 or 9:27, about the destruction or desolation of the Temple has given way to a description of a siege and capture of the *city* of Jerusalem itself. Many commentators agree that this is in part a *vaticinium ex eventu,* with allusion being made to the details of the taking of the city by Titus. Again, Luke 19:43-44 seems to be an allusion to earthworks of the sort that Josephus described as being used in the siege (*J.W.* 6.2,7 §§ 150, 156). In my opinion, these allusions make it clear that Luke has modified his Marcan source in the light of what little he knew about the destruction of Jerusalem by the Romans.

C. H. Dodd sought to counter this interpretation of the Lucan material by treating the two Lucan oracles (19:42-44 and 21:20-24) as "composed *entirely* from the language of the Old Testament." For him, the picture of the coming disaster which Luke has in mind was a generalized one about the fall of Jerusalem as imaginatively presented in OT prophets; insofar as any historical event has colored the picture, it was not Titus' capture of Jerusalem (A.D. 70) but rather Nebuchadnezzar's (587 B.C.) ("The Fall of Jerusalem," 79). Some of the vocabulary used by Luke may, indeed, have been influenced by the OT prophetic passages about the destruction of cities. But the use of such vocabulary does not rule out an allusion to the destruction of Jerusalem itself in A.D. 70. The shift of emphasis from the Temple (in Mark) to the city of Jerusalem (in Luke) is not to be overlooked. Moreover, even Dodd was convinced that it was "fairly certain" on other grounds that "the Third Gospel was in fact produced after the Fall of Jerusalem" (ibid. 69).

Building in part on Dodd's analysis of these predictions, J. A. T. Robinson has recently sought to date the Lucan Gospel ca. A.D. 57-60 (*Redating*, 57-60). He does well to remind us all how little evidence there really is for dating any of the NT writings and how odd it is that "what on any showing would appear to be the single most datable and climactic event of the period"—the fall of Jerusalem in A.D. 70—is never mentioned as a past fact in those writings (ibid. 13). From this he concludes, using other internal criticism as well, that all of the NT books were composed prior to A.D. 70.

Specifically with reference to Luke, he discusses the alleged "three 'hard' pieces of evidence" (ibid. 88): (1) prophecies about the destruction of Jerusalem; (2) dependence (according to the most widely held solution of the Synoptic problem) of the Lucan Gospel on the Marcan; and (3) the ending of Acts. His discussion of these pieces of evidence can be summarized thus: (1) The prophecies afford no ground for supposing that they were *vaticinia ex eventu;* Jesus could have predicted the destruction of Jerusalem just as another Jesus, the son of Ananias, did in the autumn of A.D. 62 (ibid. 15, referring to Josephus, *J.W.* 6.5,3 §§ 300-309). (2) Robinson writes off the dependence of Luke on Mark, preferring to see the Gospels as parallel, though not isolated, developments of common material from different communities (ibid. 94). (3) Following A. von Harnack, Robinson reiterates the view that Luke-Acts must be dated prior to Paul's trial and death at Rome, because that is where Acts ends. If the outcome of Paul's trial were already known, it surpasses belief that no reference to it or no foreshadowing of it would appear in Acts (ibid. 91). Hence Robinson concludes that the burden of proof is on those who would argue that Acts comes from a later period.

It is difficult to respond to a writer who likes to shift the burden of proof to others and characterizes as "dogmatic" (an adjective very dear to Robinson) any view that he opposes. But perhaps a few comments here might be in order.

a) Modern interpreters have long been puzzled by the failure of NT writers to mention the destruction of Jerusalem by the Romans in A.D. 70. Much was made of the event by the Jewish historian Josephus, on whose writings we depend so heavily for what little is known of that part of the eastern Mediterranean world in which Christianity was born and developed. This emphasis is understandable in the writings of a Jew, and especially of one who was so intimately involved in the event itself. But the real question is, Why should Christian writers not have made more of the destruction of Jerusalem than they do? Even Robinson's carefully honed prose subconsciously raises the problem when he comments on the oddity of "what *on any showing would appear* to be the single most datable . . . event" (my italics). After all, the destruction of Jerusalem took place at least a generation after the crucifixion of Jesus, and Christianity had by that time moved out of its Palestinian matrix. Moreover, how few of the NT writings were actually composed in Palestine, where we would expect Jewish Christians to have been concerned about the destruction of the city of their mother-church! A case has been made for the composition of James and 1 Peter in Palestine (see J. N. Sevenster, *Do You Know Greek? How Much Greek Could the First Jewish Christians Have Known?* [NovTSup 19; Leiden: Brill, 1968]). Those who would argue for the Caesarean imprisonment as the place where the captivity letters of the Pauline corpus were composed would thus relate them too to a Palestinian origin; but that is definitely a minority opinion. The real question, however, is why the Christian authors of NT books should have shown as much interest in the destruction of Jerusalem as they do, when the focus of their attention and the spread of Christianity into the Mediterranean world and among European Gentiles were obviously more important to them than the Palestinian matrix which, in general, showed itself so unreceptive to and uninterested in what was of supreme importance to these writers: the interpretation of the Christ-event. (Paul, with his concern for the collection to be taken to the poor at Jerusalem, is a prime example to the contrary—and that concern manifested itself well before the destruction of the city.)

b) To regard the Synoptic Gospels as parallel, though not isolated, developments of common material and on this basis to deny Lucan dependence on Mark flies in the face of the best NT scholarship and work on the Synoptic problem of the past century—W. R. Farmer and his attempt to resurrect the Griesbach hypothesis notwithstanding. In taking such a position, Robinson is closing his eyes to the obvious Lucan references to the destruction of Jerusalem. It is, indeed, not impossible that Jesus predicted the destruction of the Temple—no more impossible than the prophecy of Jesus, son of Ananias. That could well be a plausible way to interpret Mark 13:2. But when one reflects on the Lucan passages that allude to Jerusalem and its fate (13:35a; 19:43-44; 21:20 [and possibly 23:28-31]) and sees how the emphasis falls not on the Temple, but on the city, it is beyond comprehension how one can say that there is no reference in the Lucan Gospel to the destruction of Jerusalem. Working from a modified form of the Two-Source Theory as the solution of the Synoptic problem, we would say that the "prophetic" passages of the Marcan apocalypse have been deliberately recast in terms of what little Luke, writing outside of Palestine, knew of the Roman siege and final destruction of the city. (To press the text of Luke 21:20 about the impossibility of flight to the mountains from Judea or "the city" at the time of the siege and circumvallation is to miss the point of the apocalyptic style of writing. Possibly the same should be said for 23:30; cf. Hosea 10:8.)

c) Finally, I have already alluded to the problematic character of the

ending of Acts. (For a brief survey of attempts to explain it, see my commentary, "Acts of the Apostles," *JBC* art. 45, § 119.) Robinson's treatment of this matter skirts the literary problem involved. Perhaps Luke deliberately ended the book where he did because he thought that he had by
that time written what he wanted to say in his account of the sequel to
the Christ-event. The analysis of that ending should begin with what is
there instead of speculation about what it should have contained. The
boldness of Paul in his preaching, even in Rome, the capital of the empire
in which Christianity was then feeling its way, was more important for
Luke than any foreshadowing of the martyrdom of his hero. Cf. Acts 28:
14c.

For these reasons the dating of Luke-Acts must be not only post-Mark
but also after the destruction of Jerusalem in A.D. 70. But how much
later? There is no way to be certain about the extent of time required. I
should be reluctant to date it in the second century. This has been
suggested at times by such writers as P. W. Schmidt, M. S. Enslin, F. Overbeck, J. Knox, J. C. O'Neill. The last-named has proposed A.D. 115-130.
It was once argued that Luke shows dependence on Josephus, but that is
a view that is largely abandoned today (see A. Ehrhardt, *ST* 12 [1958]
45-79, esp. pp. 64-65). The relationship between Acts and the writings
of Justin Martyr has been greatly overestimated by O'Neill (*Theology*,
1-53); see the review of his book by H. F. D. Sparks, *JTS* 14 (1963)
454-466, esp. pp. 457-466.

On the other hand, Luke-Acts should be dated prior to the formation
or circulation of the Pauline corpus. As we have already noted, there is
no evidence that Luke was acquainted with Paul's letters, much less with
the corpus as such.

Hence the best solution is to adopt the date for Luke-Acts that is used
by many today, ca. A.D. 80-85. See further W. G. Kümmel, *Introduction*,
151 ("between 70 and 90"); A. Wikenhauser and J. Schmid, *Einleitung*,
272 ("zwischen 80 und 90").

As for the place of composition of the Lucan Gospel, it is really anyone's guess. The only thing that seems certain is that it was not written in
Palestine. Ancient tradition about the place of composition varies
greatly: Achaia, Boeotia, Rome. Modern attempts to localize the composition elsewhere are mere guesses: Caesarea (H. Klein), Decapolis
(R. Koh), Asia Minor (K. Löning). In the long run, it is a matter of little
concern, because the interpretation of the Lucan Gospel and Acts does
not depend on it.

3. *Luke's Intended Readers.* A few words must be added here about
the destination of the Lucan Gospel, a topic on which we have touched
briefly above. It is widely held today that Luke has written his Gospel for
a Gentile Christian audience, or at least one that was predominantly Gen-

tile Christian. This view is based on Luke's obvious concern to relate his account of the Christ-event and its sequel to a Greco-Roman literary tradition (e.g. in the prologue of the Gospel), his dedication of his two volumes to a person bearing a Greek name (though it could have been borne by a Jew), and his manifest desire to relate the salvation promised to Israel in the OT to Gentiles or non-Jews.

His elimination of materials from his sources, "Mk" or "Q," that are predominantly Jewish preoccupations (e.g. in the Sermon on the Plain—where most of the matter in the antitheses of Matt 5:21-48 disappears; or the details about Jewish ritual purity and piety; or the controversy about what is clean or unclean, Mark 7:1-23) are best explained by this Gentile Christian destination of his writings. Certain items in the stories or the sayings of Jesus are best regarded as Lucan redactional modifications, adjusting a Palestinian tradition to a non-Jewish Hellenistic situation (e.g. Luke 5:19; cf. Mark 2:4; Luke 6:48-49; cf. Matt 7:24-27). Similarly, the substitution of Greek names for Hebrew or Aramaic names or titles: *kyrios,* "Lord," or *epistatēs,* "teacher," for *rabbi/rab-bouni* (Luke 18:41; cf. Mark 10:51; Luke 9:33; cf. Mark 9:5); *kranion,* "Skull," for *Golgotha* (Luke 23:33; cf. Mark 15:22); *Zēlōtēs,* "zealot," for *Kananaios* (Luke 6:15; cf. Mark 3:18); his occasional substitution of *nomikos,* "lawyer," for *grammateus,* "scribe" (Luke 10:25; cf. Mark 12:28; Luke 11:52; cf. Matt 23:13). His interest in Gentile Christians is likewise responsible for his tracing of Jesus' genealogy back to Adam and God (and not just to David or Abraham, as in Matthew). Most of Luke's quotations from the OT are derived from the Greek version, the so-called LXX (at times with some redactional modification). Finally, his use of the term, "Judea," at times in the generic sense of Palestine as a whole (1:5; 4:44; 6:17; 7:17; 23:5; Acts 2:9; 10:37), suggests that he wrote with non-Palestinians in mind.

The same destination has to be maintained for Acts as well. J. Jervell has ably shown that "Israel" in the Lucan writings always refers to "the Jewish people" and that it is not used "as a technical term for the Christian gathering of Jews and Gentiles." Jews made up a divided people, of "two groups, the repentant (i.e. Christian) and the obdurate" ("Divided People," 49). It seems to me that he has made a convincing case for the idea that the Gentiles have gained a share in what had been given to Israel, i.e. the salvation of God sent first to reconstituted Israel (Acts 15:16-18; cf. 3:23) is by God's own design sent further to the Gentiles without the law, especially when part of Israel rejects the invitation (Acts 13:46). Thus Luke explains the relationship of the Gentile Christians for whom he is writing to Israel of old. Similarly, Jervell has well explained that the Lucan treatment of Paul in Acts is based on a desire to show that the greatest segment of the Christian church does not stem from a

Jewish apostate, but rather from "the teacher of Israel" ("Paul: The Teacher of Israel," 173-174). But less satisfactory is Jervell's further suggestion that "only in a milieu with a Jewish-Christian stamp would such a lengthy explanation of the justification of the circumcision-free Gentile mission be required" (ibid. 175). That Luke writes for Christian readers who are under fire from their Jewish neighbors because of Paul's controversies (ibid. 177) may be true; but that they are therefore themselves Jewish-Christians is not a necessary conclusion. Jervell thus reverts to an older position once espoused by E. R. Goodenough and M. Schneckenburger (with varying nuances). Rather, Luke's discussion serves to explain, precisely to Gentile Christians, what their status is vis-à-vis Israel. They are not, indeed, the new people of God, but belong to the reconstituted people of God. In other words, much of Jervell's thesis stands, except for the suggestion that the composite work of Luke-Acts was destined for Jewish-Christians.

M. Moscato has rightly seen that Luke does not present Paul predominantly as "a missionary to the Gentiles" ("Current Theories," 359), and that his treatment of Paul actually constitutes an excellent portrayal of the "continuity between Judaism and Christianity" (ibid.); nor is it clear that Luke was, therefore, writing "for a community of Jews and Gentiles" (ibid.), or that the Jewish Christian sect of the Nazoreans were part of that mixed community (ibid. 360). The latter identification is entirely too speculative. The readers envisaged by Luke were not Gentile Christians in a predominantly Jewish setting; they were rather Gentile Christians in a predominantly Gentile setting. There may have been some Jews and Jewish Christians among them—as the quotation of Isaiah at the end of Acts suggests. But the audience envisaged by Luke in his writing of Luke-Acts is one that is predominantly Gentile Christian, and Theophilus is one of them.

BIBLIOGRAPHY

The Identity of Luke

Argyle, A. W. "The Greek of Luke and Acts," *NTS* 20 (1973-1974) 441-445.

Bacon, B. W. "Le témoignage de Luc sur lui-même," *RHPR* 8 (1928) 209-226.

Baker, J. "Luke, the Critical Evangelist," *ExpTim* 68 (1956-1957) 123-125.

Beck, B. E. "The Common Authorship of Luke and Acts," *NTS* 23 (1976-1977) 346-352.

Bleiben, T. E. "The Gospel of Luke and the Gospel of Paul," *JTS* 45 (1944) 134-140.

Cadbury, H. J. "The Diction of Luke and Acts," in *The Style and Literary Method of Luke* (HTS 6/1; Cambridge, MA: Harvard University, 1920).

————— "Lexical Notes on Luke-Acts: II. Recent Arguments for Medical Language," *JBL* 45 (1926) 190-206; "V. Luke and the Horse-Doctors," *JBL* 52 (1933) 55-65.

Clark, A. C. *The Acts of the Apostles* (Oxford: Clarendon, 1933) 393-408.

Clemen, C. "Harnack's 'Lukas der Arzt,' " *TRu* 10 (1907) 97-113.

Deissmann, A. "Lukios-Lukas," in *Festgabe von Fachgenossen und Freunden von A. von Harnack zum siebzigsten Geburtstag dargebracht* (ed. K. Hall; Tübingen: Mohr [Siebeck], 1921) 117-120.

Dornseiff, F. "Lukas der Schriftsteller: Mit einem Anhang: Josephus und Tacitus," *ZNW* 35 (1936) 129-155.

Ellis, E. E. "Luke, Saint," *The New Encyclopaedia Britannica* (Chicago: Encyclopaedia Britannica, Inc., 1974) 11. 177-178.

Eltester, W. "Lukas und Paulus," *Eranion* (Tübingen: Niemeyer, 1961) 1-17.

Enslin, M. S. "Luke, the Literary Physician," in *Studies in New Testament and Early Christian Literature: Essays in Honor of Allen P. Wikgren* (ed. D. E. Aune; NovTSup 33; Leiden: Brill, 1972) 135-143.

————— "Once Again, Luke and Paul," *ZNW* 61 (1970) 253-271.

Ford, R. C. "St. Luke and Lucius of Cyrene," *ExpTim* 32 (1920-1921) 219-220.

Friedrich, J. *Das Lukasevangelium und die Apostelgeschichte Werke desselben Verfassers* (Halle a.d. S.: M. Neimeyer, 1890).

Glover, R. " 'Luke the Antiochene' and Acts," *NTS* 11 (1964-1965) 97-106.

Grant, F. C. "A Critique of *The Style and Literary Method of Luke*," *ATR* 2 (1919-1920) 318-323.

Harnack, A. *Luke the Physician: The Author of the Third Gospel and the Acts of the Apostles* (New York: Putnam, 1907).

Harnack, A. von. "Noch einmal Lukas als Verfasser des 3. Evangeliums und der Apostelgeschichte," *TLZ* 31 (1906) 466-468.

Hobart, W. K. *The Medical Language of St. Luke: A Proof from Internal Evidence that "The Gospel according to St. Luke" and "The Acts of the Apostles" Were Written by the Same Person, and that the Writer Was a Medical Man* (Dublin: Hodges, Figgis, 1882; reprinted Grand Rapids: Baker, 1954).

Knowling, R. J. "The Medical Language of St. Luke," *BW* 20 (1902) 260-270, 370-379.

Knox, W. L. *The Acts of the Apostles* (Cambridge: University Press, 1945) 1-15.

Lindeboom, G. A. "Luke the Evangelist and the Ancient Greek Writers on Medicine," in *Janus: Revue internationale de l'histoire des sciences, de la médecine, de la pharmacie et de la technique* 52 (1965) 143-148.

MacRory, J. "The Authorship of the Third Gospel and the Acts," *ITQ* 2 (1907) 190-202.

Manson, T. W. "The Life of Jesus: A Survey of Available Material. (3) The Work of St. Luke," *BJRL* 28 (1944) 382-403; reprinted in *Studies in the Gospels and Epistles* (ed. M. Black; Philadelphia: Westminster, 1962) 46-67.

Moffatt, J. "St. Luke and Literary Criticism," *Expos* 8/24 (1922) 1-18.

Price, S. H. "The Authorship of Luke-Acts," *ExpTim* 55 (1943-1944) 194.

Ramsay, W. M. *Luke the Physician and Other Studies in the History of Religion* (London: Hodder & Stoughton, 1908; reprinted, Grand Rapids: Baker, 1956).

Scott, J. A. *Luke: Greek Physician and Historian* (Evanston: Northwestern University, 1930).

Siotis M. A. "Luke the Evangelist as St. Paul's Collaborator," in *Neues Testament und Geschichte: Historisches Geschehen und Deutung im Neuen Testament: Oscar Cullmann zum 70. Geburtstag* (eds. H. Baltensweiler und B. Reicke; Zürich: Theologischer Verlag; Tübingen: Mohr [Siebeck], 1972) 105-111.

Strobel, A. "Lukas der Antiochener (Bemerkungen zu Act 11,28D)," *ZNW* 49 (1958) 131-134.

Vielhauer, P. "On the 'Paulinism' of Acts," in *Studies in Luke-Acts*, 33-50.

Whitley, W. T. "Luke of Antioch in Pisidia," *ExpTim* 21 (1909-1910) 164-166.

Wikenhauser, A., and J. Schmid. *Einleitung in das Neue Testament* (6th ed.; Freiburg: Herder, 1973) 247-272, 344-379.

The Date and Place of Composition

Dodd, C. H. "The Fall of Jerusalem and the 'Abomination of Desolation,'" *JRS* 37 (1947) 47-54; reprinted in *More New Testament Essays* (Grand Rapids: Eerdmans, 1968) 69-83.

Harnack, A. von. *The Date of the Acts and of the Synoptic Gospels* (New Testament Studies, IV; London: Williams & Norgate; New York: Putnam, 1911).

Hemer, C. J. "Luke the Historian," *BJRL* 60 (1977) 28-51.

Klein, H. "Zur Frage nach dem Abfassungsort der Lukasschriften," *EvT* 32 (1972) 467-477.

Koh, R. *The Writings of St. Luke* (Hongkong: Diocesan Literature Committee, 1953) 23-35.

O'Neill, J. C. *The Theology of Acts in Its Historical Setting* (London: SPCK, 1961).

Parker, P. "The 'Former Treatise' and the Date of Acts," *JBL* 84 (1965) 52-58.

Reicke, B. "Synoptic Prophecies on the Destruction of Jerusalem," in *Studies in New Testament and Early Christian Literature: Essays in Honor of Allen P. Wikgren* (ed. D. E. Aune; NovTSup 33; Leiden: Brill, 1972) 121-134.

Robinson, J. A. T. *Redating the New Testament* (Philadelphia: Westminster, 1976) 86-117.

Russell, H. G. "Which Was Written First, Luke or Acts?" *HTR* 48 (1955) 167-174.

Sutcliffe, E. F. "A Note on the Date of St. Luke's Gospel," *Scr* 3 (1948) 45-46.

Williams, C. S. C. "The Date of Luke-Acts," *ExpTim* 64 (1952-1953) 283-284.

Wilshire, L. E. "Was Canonical Luke Written in the Second Century?—A Continuing Discussion," *NTS* 20 (1973-1974) 28-51.

Luke's Intended Readers

Goodenough, E. R. "The Perspective of Acts," in *Studies in Luke-Acts,* 51-59.

Jervell, J. *Luke and the People of God: A New Look at Luke-Acts* (Minneapolis: Augsburg, 1972), esp. "The Divided People of God: The Restoration of Israel and Salvation for the Gentiles," 41-74, and "Paul: The Teacher of Israel: The Apologetic Speeches of Paul in Acts," 153-183.

Mattill, A. J., Jr. "The Purpose of Acts: Schneckenburger Reconsidered," in *Apostolic History and the Gospel: Biblical and Historical Essays Presented to F. F. Bruce on His 60th Birthday* (eds. W. W. Gasque and R. P. Martin; Grand Rapids: Eerdmans, 1970) 108-122.

Moscato, M. A. "Current Theories Regarding the Audience of Luke-Acts," *CurrTM* 3 (1976) 355-361.

III. THE COMPOSITION OF THE LUCAN GOSPEL

The Lucan Gospel, in the prologue, makes it clear that it is not the first attempt to write the story of Jesus and that it depends on previous attempts to do so. The prologue thus hints at a complex literary history behind it. Detailed critical analysis of the Third Gospel in recent decades has revealed much about it, though it has scarcely resulted in an indisputable judgment about its complex history; yet certain points about its composition have gained the support of so many scholars, working with varied presuppositions, that a high degree of probability can be accorded them.

We cannot rehearse here all the arguments for the positions to be adopted in this commentary regarding the composition of the Lucan Gospel. That would entail a full-scale exposé of the problem of the relations among Matthew, Mark, and Luke and the various attempts to solve it. Details about this problem can be found in many standard NT introductions (e.g. W. G. Kümmel, *Introduction,* 38-80; A. Wikenhauser and J. Schmid, *Einleitung,* 272-289—see pp. 61, 282) and in specific detailed studies listed in the bibliography. A brief survey, however, of the chief factors involved in the composition of the Lucan Gospel, which form the basis of our position, seems called for, since it may clarify the presuppositions of the interpretation of the Third Gospel to be presented.

The relation of the Lucan Gospel to the Marcan and Matthean Gospels is part of the Synoptic problem—a problem that has thus far failed to find a fully satisfying solution. The main reason for this failure is the absence of adequate data for judgment about it. Extrinsic, historically trustworthy data about the composition of these Gospels are totally lacking, and the complexity of the traditions embedded in them, the evangelists' editorial redaction of them, and their free composition bedevil all attempts to analyze objectively the intrinsic data with critical literary methods.

The solution to the Synoptic problem that is being adopted in this commentary is a modified form of the so-called Two-Document Hypothesis. In its classic form this hypothesis, dating from the time of C. Lachmann, C. H. Weisse, C. G. Wilke, and H. G. A. Ewald in the early nineteenth century, maintains the priority of the Greek text of Mark over both Matthew and Luke (mainly because of the order of the common passages); it also postulates a Greek written source for about 230 verses common to Matthew and Luke, which contain mostly sayings of Jesus and which are not found in Mark. "Mk" and "Q" (the abbreviation of the German word *Quelle,* "source" [see H. K. McArthur, "The Origin of the 'Q' Symbol," *ExpTim* 88 (1976-1977) 119-120], commonly used to label the postulated source) are the "two documents" in this analysis of the Synoptic problem. A corollary of this hypothesis is, then, the independence of Matthew and Luke.

A widely used modification of this hypothesis, dating at least from the time of B. H. Streeter (*The Four Gospels,* 1924), admits the use of a third source ("L") for material peculiar to the Lucan Gospel, lacking parallels in Mark or Matthew. A similar modification has been made to explain material peculiar to the Matthean Gospel ("M"). These modifications have, in effect, radically developed the original Two-Document Hypothesis, and some writers even refer to it as the Four-Document Hypothesis. I prefer to speak of the modified Two-Source Theory, a variation on the title used in English, chosen to manifest at once its dependence on the classic Two-Document Hypothesis, but also to allow for a still further understanding of "L" and "M" as *not necessarily written.*

(A further modification of the original hypothesis is sometimes offered to explain the relation of "Q" to an Aramaic collection of Jesus' sayings [e.g. T. W. Manson, *The Sayings of Jesus* (London: SCM, 1949) 17-18]. This modification has been introduced by those who feel that some credence should still be given to the tradition stemming from Papias of Hierapolis [see Eusebius *Hist. eccl.* 3.39,16], that "Matthew composed the sayings [*logia*] in the 'Hebrew' language." That collection of Aramaic *logia* is lost, if it ever existed, and otherwise unknown; there is no indication that it was substantially the same as "Q," much less that it was substantially the same as canonical Matthew. Since this modification is of little concern to the Third Gospel, we need not pursue it further.)

The main reasons for the adoption of this modified form of the Two-Source Theory will be spelled out below.

In adopting such a position in this commentary, I am laying myself open to the criticism of a number of recent writers who believe that the position is untenable and that the theory is deficient, built on unproved assumptions and badly in need of reexamination. To begin with, my use of this theory is not based on what I had originally been taught in my student days where I was exposed to a form of what has been called the *Traditionshypothese* (see Wikenhauser and Schmid, *Einleitung,* 276-277): that all three Synoptic evangelists had drawn their material from an existing oral tradition about the words and deeds of Jesus, without dependence one on the other, except that Greek Matthew depended on Aramaic Matthew, which represented an earlier composition drawn from the same oral tradition. (*Sous-entendus* were the *responsa* of the Biblical Commission on the chronological order of Synoptics [Matthew, Mark, and Luke], the "substantial agreement" of Aramaic and Greek Matthew, and the inadequacy of the Two-Document Hypothesis; see *Enchiridion biblicum*

[4th ed.; Naples: M. D'Auria; Rome: A. Arnodo, 1961] § 383-400). Cf. *Rome and the Study of Scripture* (St. Meinrad, IN: Grail, 1962) 126-132. More recently, a semiofficial interpretation of the *responsa* allows "full liberty" in such scholarly matters; see E. F. Siegman, *CBQ* 18 (1956) 23-29. Discontented with the *Traditionshypothese,* I examined other attempts at a solution of the Synoptic problem and finally settled on the modified form of the Two-Source Theory. Later on, I set forth my reasons for this view in "The Priority of Mark and the 'Q' Source in Luke" (1970); cf. *To Advance the Gospel* (New York: Crossroad, 1981) 3-40.

The Two-Document Hypothesis and the modified Two-Source Theory have not gone without vigorous opposition on the part of a small group of scholars. The most outspoken critic has been W. R. Farmer, who has sought to resurrect the Griesbach solution: that Mark is in reality only an abridgment of Matthew and Luke. See his book, *The Synoptic Problem,* and article, "A 'Skeleton in the Closet' of Gospel Research." In my article, mentioned above, I set forth the difficulties that I saw in that view of the Synoptic problem—nine difficulties that I still consider valid, despite the attempt of Farmer to answer them (see "Modern Developments"). In not agreeing with Farmer, I have, alas, excluded myself from the group he calls "all careful students of the synoptic problem" (*ATR* 48 [1966] 389) or "the perceptive critic[s]" (ibid. 393). So be it; at least I find myself in good company. One last extrinsic consideration has to be mentioned: Given the practical insolubility of the Synoptic problem, the modified Two-Source Theory has at least led to all sorts of advances in gospel interpretation and has pragmatically established its utility—the *Brauchbarkeit* argument of critics such as G. Strecker and W. Marxsen. For it has been the basis of Form-Criticism, Redaction-Criticism, and Composition-Criticism; and even granting that the connection between the Two-Source Theory and these advances in gospel interpretation is not organic or necessary (because of any essential link), it is a matter of historical fact that they were born of studies conducted along the lines of this theory.

1. *The Sources of the Lucan Gospel.* Practically all commentators on the Lucan Gospel are agreed that its author not only knew but made use of earlier gospel compositions in his writing the story of Jesus. Rare indeed are those who would still try to explain its origin by an exclusive appeal to an earlier oral tradition. Even those who do not use the modified Two-Source Theory or the Two-Document Hypothesis tend to admit that Luke was at least dependent on Matthew. And such dependence seems to be suggested by the Lucan prologue itself. In it Luke speaks of "many" (*polloi*) who have undertaken to compile an account like his own. Writing in a language that uses a singular, a plural, and a dual in its structure,

"many" must mean at least three persons, but we have no way of knowing just what Luke meant by that vague number. In the present commentary I shall posit three main sources and must, therefore, set forth some of the reasons for regarding the Lucan Gospel as dependent on the Marcan source ("Mk"), the source "Q," and a source, not necessarily written, which is called "L."

2. *Luke's Dependence on Mark.* Lucan dependence on the Marcan Gospel can be seen in a number of ways. First, a substantial portion of the Third Gospel is the same as the Marcan. B. H. Streeter (*The Four Gospels,* 160) put the amount of common material at 55 per cent; of Mark's 661 verses (omitting 16:9-20) 350 have substantial similarity in the Lucan Gospel. B. de Solages (*A Greek Synopsis,* 1052) counted the material by words: Luke has 7,036 of Mark's 8,485 words. This is an agreement of common material, which does not speak immediately of dependence in one direction or the other. Even in the larger context of the material common to the Triple Tradition (i.e. including Matthew), the extent of agreement would only argue for an intermediary position of Mark—*if the argument were thus left on an abstract and theoretic level.* But when one considers the material which Mark, if he were dependent on Matthew and Luke, would be omitting, then it is impossible to conclude to Lucan or Matthean priority. For six considerations in support of this, see my article, "The Priority of Mark," 134-135; cf. W. R. Farmer, *NTS* 23 (1976-1977) 283-289.

Second, the sequence of episodes in the Third Gospel closely follows that of Mark, even when Luke otherwise adds or omits something. The relatively same order of pericopes is even more crucially apparent when one considers the sequence of episodes in the Triple Tradition. The episodes which Matthew and Luke have in common with Mark generally agree with the Marcan sequence; when Matthew and Luke depart from this sequence, each differs from the other as well, pursuing an independent course. F. H. Woods has well set this relationship forth:

> (1) The earliest and the latest parallels in all three Gospels coincide with the beginning and end of St. Mark. . . . (2) With but few exceptions we find parallels to the whole of St. Mark in St. Matthew or St. Luke, and to by far the larger part in both. (3) The *order* of the whole of St. Mark, excepting of course what is peculiar to that Gospel, is confirmed either by St. Matthew or St. Luke, and the greater part of it by both. (4) A passage parallel in all three Synoptists is never *immediately* followed in both St. Matthew and St. Luke by a *separate incident or discourse* common to these two evangelists alone ("The Origin," 61-62).

The best illustration of the use of this relative Marcan order is seen in what both Matthew and Luke do with the "Q" material that they insert into it; no portion of "Q" ever appears in the same place (after the temptation scenes). See further W. G. Kümmel, *Introduction*, 57-58.

The Lucan use of Marcan episodes is best seen in the five large blocks of material which Luke takes over and into which his significant additions have been made, and from which he makes two omissions:

(1) Mark 1:1-15 = Luke 3:1 - 4:15 (5 episodes in my outline of Luke: §§ 10-13, 15; see pp. 135-142 below)

(2) Mark 1:21 - 3:19 = Luke 4:31 - 6:19 (11 episodes: §§ 18-21, 23-29) (Luke's Little Interpolation, 6:20 - 8:3, §§ 30-37)

(3) Mark 4:1 - 9:40 = Luke 8:4 - 9:50 (20 episodes: §§ 38-57) (At 9:17, Luke's Big Omission, Mark 6:45 - 8:26) (At 9:50, Luke's Little Omission, Mark 9:41 - 10:12) (Luke's Big Interpolation, 9:51 - 18:14, §§ 58-118)

(4) Mark 10:13 - 13:32 = Luke 18:15 - 21:33 (23 episodes: §§ 119-123, 125-142)

(5) Mark 14:1 - 16:8 = Luke 22:1 - 24:12 (16 episodes: §§ 145-151, 153-156, 159, 160 [in part], 161, 164, 165)

Within these major blocks of Marcan material there are occasional minor insertions of "Q" or "L," which may fill out a Marcan episode. But these do not affect the Marcan order as significantly as the interpolations and omissions mentioned above, since despite them the relative order of the Marcan episodes is still apparent. Such minor insertions are found at:

Luke	3:7-14	(John the Baptist's preaching, §11 in part)
	3:23-38	(Jesus' genealogy, §14)
	4:2b-13	(Jesus' temptation, §15 in part)
	5:1-11	(Role of Simon the Fisherman; the catch of fish, §22)
	19:1-10	(Zacchaeus, §124)
	19:11-27	(Parable of the pounds, §125)
	22:28-33,35-38	(Discourse at the Last Supper, §151 in part, 152)
	23:6-16	(Herod and Pilate, §§ 157-158)
	23:27-31	(The Road to the Cross, §160)
	23:39b-43	(Two Criminals on Crosses, §162 in part)
	23:47b-49	(The Death of Jesus, §163 in part)

All of these insertions reveal themselves as deliberate additions made by Luke to the basic Marcan material. The Marcan sequence of episodes is, moreover, not affected by the peculiarly Lucan Infancy and Resurrection Narratives, since they simply add episodes to the beginning and the end of the Marcan story. Moreover, Marcan order has nothing to do with the Lucan interpolations.

Maintaining that "the statement that both Matthew and Luke generally support Mark's order is a great over-simplification," E. P. Sanders ("Argument from Order," 253) has tried to show that there are many "exceptions to the more particular claims of the argument of order" (p. 254). He cites specifically four main sorts of problems:

A) Places where Matthew and Luke do agree against Mark's order:

1. Matt 7:2b	Luke 6:38c	Mark 4:24b
2. Matt 11:10b	Luke 7:27b	Mark 1:2b
3. Matt 3:1-2	Luke 3:3	Mark 1:4
4. Matt 3:11b	Luke 3:16c	Mark 1:7b-8
5. Matt 21:10-17	Luke 19:45-46	Mark 11:11,15-19 (?)
6. Matt 25:14	Luke 19:12-13	Mark 13:34 (?)
7. Matt 6:33b	Luke 12:31b	Mark 4:24d

B) Passages differently placed by each of the evangelists:

8. Matt 5:13b	Luke 14:34b	Mark 9:50b
9. Matt 10:2-4	Luke 6:13-16	Mark 3:13-19
10. Matt 13:53-58	Luke 4:16-30	Mark 6:1-6a
11. Matt 11:15; 13:43	Luke 14:35	Mark 4:23
12. Matt 22:46	Luke 20:40	Mark 12:34c

C) Either Matthew or Luke differs in order from the Marcan, whereas the other omits:

13. Matt 6:14b	Luke omits	Mark 11:25
14. Matt 3:4-6	Luke omits	Mark 1:4-6
15. Matt 10:42	Luke omits	Mark 9:41
16. Matt 9:36b (14:14a)	Luke omits	Mark 6:34b

D) Matthew and Luke agree in placing the same common (Q) Material at the same place relative to the Marcan order:

17. Matt 3:7-10	Luke 3:7-9	after Mark 1:1-6
18. Matt 13:33	Luke 13:20-21	after Mark 4:30-32
19. Matt 12:38-42,43-45	Luke 11:29-32,24-26	after Mark 3:23-30
20. Matt 18:10-14,15-20,21-22	Luke 17:3,4	after Mark 9:42-48
21. Matt 26:25	Luke 22:23	after Mark 14:21
22. Matt 26:50	Luke 22:48	after Mark 14:45

(To these Sanders adds seven other passages, which even he admits break the Marcan order with "different material"—and that is obviously irrelevant to the matter we are discussing.)

Because of the foregoing problematic passages Sanders feels that "the assurance we have felt in the traditional hypothesis must be correspondingly weakened" (p. 261). But must it? A few comments on the foregoing list are in order.

One. Nos. 13-16 are useless in considering Luke, since they are all omitted by him: therefore, he cannot be said to agree with the Matthean transpositions, which admittedly differ from the order in Mark.

Two. Nos. 1, 2, 4, 7, and 8 are generally considered "Q" material, not Marcan.

Three. No. 17 is invalid, because in the traditional hypothesis the placing of "Q" material has always been judged independently after the temptation scenes.

Four. No. 10 involves a "Lucan transposition," and has to be handled otherwise.

Five. The traditional argument has normally referred to the order of pericopes (Lachmann's *ordo narrationum*); to change the *status quaestionis* or focus by introducing passages which lack "verbatim agreement" (or verbal similarity, Nos. 21, 22), or by arguing about single verses (Nos. 1, 2, 3, 4, etc.) is to raise serious questions about the character of the argument. See further F. Neirynck, "The Argument from Order," 784-790—Bibliography, p. 100.

Finally, many of the cases that Sanders has listed involve minutiae. Any current reformulation of the Two-Source Theory must admit that Matthew and Luke could have freely reworked some of the Marcan source and that this could have involved minor and incidental—but independent—overlapping.

We noted above that Marcan priority over Luke is claimed because of the extent of agreement in general and the relative order of episodes. But a third factor in the case is the actual wording of many passages within the Triple Tradition, which is very often the same. This identity affects at times even the collocation of words and the structure of sentences and clauses. Again, abstractly stated, this identity would not argue to Marcan priority. But that conclusion is unavoidable after concrete comparison of the texts in a *Synopticon* such as that of W. G. Rushbrooke or W. R. Farmer, both of which use various colors to highlight the agreements between the various Gospels. When the Marcan material is examined in either Matthew or Luke, only one conclusion is possible; nothing, furthermore, suggests in such an examination that Mark has borrowed from or abridged Matthew and Luke. All the probabilities lie in the other direction.

Fourth, the priority of Mark over Luke (and Matthew) is seen in the more primitive character of the narrative of the Second Gospel—what has been called its "freshness and circumstantial character." This refers to the greater number of vivid, concrete details in the Marcan story, the use of phrases likely to cause offense, the roughness of style and grammar, and the preservation of Aramaic words. These details have often been used to claim greater historicity for the Marcan story, but they cannot be used to support that sort of judgment; rather they *may* suggest primitiveness, but that is as far as one can conclude.

B. H. Streeter analyzed this Synoptic feature well, regarding the differences in Luke (and Matthew) as improvements and refinements of Mark's manner of writing. He saw the difference as one that existed between spoken and literary language. Even B. C. Butler had to admit that this argument of Streeter tended "to support the theory of Marcan priority to the exclusion of all other solutions . . . , an argument deserving serious attention" (*Originality*, 68). Faced with a mass of details in this matter, Butler sought a solution in Mark's dependence on Matthew, insisting rather that the references in Mark to Peter's remembering (11:21) reveal Peter to have been a preacher who "was using Matthew as his *aide-mémoire*" (ibid. 168). Butler writes:

> Peter made use of Matthew as the source-book for his own "instructions", he selected passages which his own memory could confirm and enlarge upon, he omitted incidents that occurred before he met our Lord, and most of Matthew's discourse-material, as not suitable for his purpose and not such as he could reinforce with a personal and independent recollection. He altered his Palestinian-Jewish source in various ways to make it more palatable to his Gentile audience (ibid. 168-169).

In such an explanation Butler is forced to interpose between Matthew and Mark a *preacher*—in effect, an oral source; thus he explains Streeter's phenomena, but he is obliged to enlarge the framework of the theory rather haphazardly. Butler's views have other difficulties: e.g. the decision to include Aramaic phrases not found in Matthew's Gospel is hardly the way that even Peter would have made his "Palestinian-Jewish source . . . more palatable to his Gentile audience."

Streeter's argument was challenged strongly by W. R. Farmer, who was critical of a supposedly facile distinction between spoken and written languages, of his idea that Mark had resulted from dictation, and of the claim that interesting and picturesque details necessarily point to primitive character. He suggested rather the "well-attested tendency in the church to make the tradition more specific by the addition of just such details," but unfortunately this description is too vague, and Farmer never documented the sort of additions he meant. E. P. Sanders (*The Tendencies of the Synoptic Tradition*) addressed this question in great detail; but the only distinct result from his labor and travail is a word of caution: The criterion of detail cannot be used too quickly to establish the relative antiquity of one document or another (ibid. 188). His work ends with a *non liquet:* "While certain of the useful criteria support Mark's priority, some do not. Both Matthean priorists and Lukan priorists can find some support in this study" (ibid. 276). Sanders' study is important, but it is limited in scope, since these questions do not make up the whole of the argument for Marcan priority. If they did, then the word of caution and the *non liquet* would be in order. But when these matters are considered along with the question of bulk, order, and wording, they incline one to a positive literary judgment about the Lucan dependence on the Marcan Gospel.

3. *Lucan Transpositions of Marcan Material.* There are seven well-known transpositions of Marcan episodes in Luke, which may at first sight seem to militate against the thesis that Luke preserves the Marcan order. These are, however, readily explicable in terms of Lucan composition; in each instance one can detect a clear reason why Luke has made the transposition.

1) The imprisonment of John the Baptist (Mark 6:17-18) is moved up by Luke to 3:19-20 in an effort to finish off the story of John before the ministry—and even the baptism!—of Jesus.

2) Jesus' visit to Nazareth (Mark 6:1-6) is transferred by Luke to the beginning of Jesus' Galilean ministry (4:16-30) to serve a programmatic purpose: it presents in capsule form the theme of fulfillment and symbolizes the rejection that will mark the ministry as a whole.

3) The call of four disciples (Mark 1:16-20) becomes in Luke 5:1-11 a scene about the role of Simon the fisherman, and acquires a more psychologically plausible position, depicting disciples attracted to Jesus after a certain amount of ministry and preaching by him.

4) The choosing of the Twelve (Mark 3:13-19) and the report about the crowds that followed Jesus (3:7-12) are inverted by Luke (6:12-16,17-19); he thus achieves a more logical setting and audience for the Sermon on the Plain (6:20-49).

5) The episode about Jesus' real relatives (Mark 3:31-35), shifted to Luke 8:19-21, after the parable of the sower and its interpretation, provides an illustration of the relationship between the word of God and disciples who hear it.

6) Jesus' foretelling his betrayal at the Last Supper (Mark 14:18-21) becomes part of the discourse after the meal in Luke 22:21-23, being joined to three other sayings (22:24-30,31-34,35-38).

7) The order of Jesus' interrogation before the Sanhedrin is inverted: in Mark 14 Jesus is interrogated (55-64a), mistreated (64b-65), and denied by Peter (66-72); but in Luke 22 Jesus is first of all denied by Peter (54c-62), mistreated (63-65), and finally interrogated (66-71). Here one can see Luke's concern to unite the material about Peter (contrast Mark 14:54 [to which the beginning of the Lucan passage, 22:54c-62, corresponds] and 66-72), and to depict only one appearance of Jesus before the Sanhedrin.

Of less importance is the parable of the Mustard Seed (Luke 13:18-19), which may seem to have been transposed from Mark

4:30-32, but is often judged to be a "Q"-form of the same parable. On Luke 17:1-3, see the COMMENT.

Some of these passages have been explained differently by J. Jeremias, H. Schürmann, and R. Morgenthaler. According to them, Luke 6:17-19 is not to be regarded as "transposition" but rather as a subsequent insertion of Marcan material into a non-Marcan source. Both Jeremias and Schürmann think that the Lucan block of material that begins with 4:31 (=Mark 1:21) ends with Luke 6:11 so that Luke omitted Mark 3:7-30 and that what we have called Luke's "Little Interpolation" begins with Luke 6:12-16 (the Choosing of the Twelve) and runs to 8:3. Into it Luke would have inserted Mark 3:7-12, at 6:17-19. Similarly, Mark 3:31-35 would have been later inserted at 8:19-21 into the block of Marcan material which begins at 8:4 and runs to 9:50 (=Mark 4:1-9:41 [with the omission of 6:45-8:26]). Similarly, the first transpositions listed above are rather regarded as derived from *Urlukas* and not from the Marcan source; and both Jeremias and Schürmann maintain a special Lucan source for the passion narrative. The problems connected with that narrative will be taken up below. I am dubious about a special source for this part of the Gospel, though willing to admit for one scene or other some material from "L." Much of the argumentation about so-called transpositions depends on the existence of Proto-Luke or *Urlukas*, on which see below pp. 89-91. The arguments against the transpositions have been well analyzed by F. Neirynck, and need not be rehearsed here. I am basically in agreement with his approach both to the transpositions and the Lucan passion narrative.

Another discussion of Lucan transpositions by H. F. D. Sparks deals with a larger problem: Lucan words, phrases, and sentences. It misses the point of the transposition of episodes, but does provide a wider background against which the latter might well be studied.

4. *Agreements of Matthew and Luke against Mark in the Triple Tradition.* The biggest chink in the armor of the modified Two-Source Theory has always been the agreements of Matthew and Luke against Mark in the Triple Tradition, the so-called Minor Agreements. For it seems inexplicable that, if Matthew and Luke were both dependent on "Mk," as the theory maintains, there would be a number of—not just a coincidental few—agreements of Matthew and Luke against Mark. This problem was sensed by B. H. Streeter years ago (*The Four Gospels,* 179-181, 293-331), who sought to make the discussion of it the fifth point in his reasons for the priority of Mark. It is the problem on which opponents of the theory have always pounced with unceasing vigor. Part of E. P. Sanders's discussion of the problem of order bears indirectly on this. The whole matter has recently been surveyed by F. Neirynck in a stout volume, *The*

Minor Agreements of Matthew and Luke against Mark, with a Cumulative List. He has surveyed the study of the minor agreements, gives a cumulative list of them with full analysis of the details, and further classifies the stylistic agreements with comparative material from the Triple Tradition. This issue cannot be handled here in a commentary on the Lucan Gospel; its import has been exaggerated. I shall merely list here the main sections of the Marcan Gospel that are omitted in common by Luke and Matthew and refer the reader either to my earlier discussion of the problem or to COMMENTS and NOTES on crucial passages below.

The problem is seen in two main areas: (1) There are certain sections of the Marcan Gospel that both Luke and Matthew omit in common: Mark 1:1; 2:27; 3:20-21; 4:26-29; 7:2-4,32-37; 8:22-26; 9:29,48-49; 13:33-37; 14:51-52. This represents a total of some thirty verses of the Marcan Gospel. (2) There are a number of minor verbal omissions or alterations of Mark's text which appear in both Luke and Matthew and scarcely seem to be fortuitous. Neirynck's cumulative list of them covers pages 55-195 of his book and he numbers 109 of them. See further my article, "The Priority of Mark," 142-146.

5. *Luke's Supposed Dependence on Matthew.* Having discussed the dependence of Luke on the Marcan Gospel, we turn to a discussion of the source of the other material in the Third Gospel. We refer to the so-called Double Tradition material, i.e. the material common to Luke and Matthew: some 230 verses not found in Mark. This common material could be explained theoretically in various ways: either Matthew borrowed it from Luke, or Luke borrowed it from Matthew, or both of them used a common source. Few commentators would consider seriously today the suggestion that Matthew used Luke (see L. Vaganay, *Le problème synoptique* [Tournai: Desclée, 1954] 294-295; for a nuanced position, see H. P. West, Jr.). But a number of commentators have from time to time argued in favor of Luke's dependence on Matthew (e.g. A. W. Argyle, B. C. Butler, W. R. Farmer, J. H. Ropes, E. P. Sanders, R. T. Simpson, A. Schlatter, W. Wilkens). A few comments on this problem are needed to clear the way for the further discussion.

That Luke does not depend on the Matthean Gospel is seen in a number of ways: First, Luke is never seen to reproduce the typically Matthean additions within the Triple Tradition. By "additions" I mean the fuller Matthean formulations of parallels in Mark, such as the exceptive phrases in the prohibition of divorce (Matt 19:9; cf. Mark 10:11 [see my treatment of these phrases in *TS* 37 (1976) 197-226]); Jesus' promise to Peter (Matt 16:16b-19; cf. Mark 8:29); Peter's walking on the waters (Matt 14:28-31; cf. Mark 6:50); and the peculiarly Matthean episodes in the passion narrative (especially the dream of Pilate's wife [Matt

27:19] or Pilate washing his hands [Matt 27:24]). (When Matthew and Mark are considered alone, these Matthean passages are problematic: Are they the result of Matthean addition or should their absence in Mark be regarded as Marcan excision? The *pattern* in these passages is such in the Matthean Gospel that they are best regarded as additions.) But the real issue here is to explain Luke's failure to adopt the extra Matthean materials in his parallels, or at least some of them, if he has written in dependence on Matthew.

The few examples mentioned above have to do with whole verses or pericopes; but the same phenomenon can be illustrated further by smaller Matthean additions to Mark omitted by Luke:

Luke 3:22	Matt 3:17 (the public proclamation)	Cf. Mark 1:11
5:3	4:18 ("who is called Peter")	1:16
5:27	9:9 ("Matthew")	2:14
6:4-5	12:5-7 (plucking grain on the Sabbath)	2:26-27
8:18b	13:12a (being given in excess)	4:25
8:10-11	13:14 (quotation of Isa 6:9-10)	4:12
9:1-5	10:7 (nearness of the kingdom)	6:8-11
9:20b	16:16b (Peter's confession of Jesus as Son of the living God)	8:29b

In these instances it is difficult to discern why Luke would have preferred the simpler Marcan form, when he was supposed to have the Matthean form before him.

Second, this same argument can also be extended to the Double Tradition. If Luke had before him the fuller form of the Beatitudes (Matt 5:3,6) or the fuller form of the Our Father (Matt 6:9-13), what would have motivated him to reformulate them as he has (see Luke 6:20-21; 11:2-4)?

Third, why would Luke have wanted to break up Matthew's sermons, especially the Sermon on the Mount, incorporating only a part of it into his Sermon on the Plain and scattering the rest of it in an unconnected form in the loose context of the travel account? Even though we admit that the latter part of the Third Gospel is compositionally important and constitutes a "mosaic" in its own way, yet the tension between its matter and its form has always been a problem for the commentator. Why would so literary an artist as Luke want to destroy the Matthean masterpiece of the Sermon on the Mount? However one wants to explain the Lucan travel account, it is hardly likely that he quarried the material for it from Matthean sermons.

Fourth, apart from 3:7-9,17 (the preaching of John the Baptist) and 4:2b-13 (the temptations of Jesus) Luke has never inserted the material of the Double Tradition into the same Marcan context as Matthew. If he had before him the Matthean Gospel, from which he were deriving this material, would he not manifest the same respect for this source as he does for the Marcan source? Would not at least some of the remaining Double Tradition material occur sometimes in contexts that parallel the Matthean? The frequent disagreement with the Matthean order in this regard is crucial to any judgment about Luke's dependence on Matthew; indeed, it suggests that he does not depend on him at all.

Fifth, analysis of the Double Tradition material in Luke and in Matthew reveals that it is sometimes Luke and sometimes Matthew who preserves what can only be described as the more original setting of a given episode (see Vaganay, *Le problème synoptique,* 295-299; Streeter, *The Four Gospels,* 183). But if Luke were dependent on Matthew for this material, how can one explain this divergence? It is, however, readily explicable on the hypothesis that both of them have used a common source.

Sixth, if Luke depended on Matthew, why did he constantly omit Matthean material in episodes lacking Marcan parallels, e.g. in the infancy and resurrection narratives?

These are the main reasons why it is unlikely that Luke has depended on Matthew. Many more minute considerations could be entertained, but for these I must refer to others.

6. *Luke's Dependence on "Q."* Luke's dependence on another written source besides Mark is a conclusion that is more difficult to establish. It is a hypothesis which refers to a postulated entity that no one has ever seen, but this does not mean that it is "an unnecessary and vicious hypothesis" (B. C. Butler, *Originality,* 170) or "a nebulosity, a capriciousness, an intractability" (S. Petrie, *NovT* 3 [1959] 28-33).

The main reason for asserting Luke's dependence on a Greek written source other than Mark is the similarity of about 230 verses in the First and Third Gospels. Thus, "Q" represents a considerable amount of gospel tradition not found in Mark and is regarded as the source of the Double Tradition. We have already set forth the reasons why it is unlikely that Luke has derived this material directly from Matthew; it remains to set forth some further reasons for postulating this common source for such material.

As we mentioned above, it is noteworthy that none of the Double Tradition material, save Luke 3:7-9 and 4:2-13, was inserted in the Marcan material at the same spot where it occurs in Matthew.

The reasons for maintaining Lucan dependence on "Q" are diverse. First, there are crucial texts in Matthew and Luke where the wording is so similar, at times word-for-word, that it is difficult to explain such passages otherwise. These passages are not Marcan; and the refractory processes of oral tradition would lead us to expect greater diversity in the wording, if this were the origin of these texts. Consider these examples:

Matt 3:7b-10—Luke 3:7b-9	(Speech of John the Baptist; 60 out of 63 (Matthew)/64 (Luke) words are identical; the differences are Lucan stylistic improvements [*arxēsthe* for *doxēte;* an added adverbial *kai;* use of a plural for a singular in 2 words])
Matt 6:24—Luke 16:13	(Saying about serving two masters; 27 out of 28 words identical; Luke adds *oiketēs*)
Matt 7:3-5—Luke 6:41-42	(On judging; 50 out of 64 words identical)
Matt 7:7-11—Luke 11:9-13	(On the efficacy of prayer; 59 out of 74 words identical; Luke adds a third example of basic prayer)
Matt 11:4-6,7b-11—Luke 7:22-23,24b-28	(Jesus' answer to the Baptist and his testimony about him; 100 out of 121 words identical)
Matt 8:20—Luke 9:58	(On foxes' holes; 25 out of 26 words identical)
Matt 11:21-23—Luke 10:13-15	(Woes against Galilean towns; 43 out of 49 words identical)
Matt 11:25-27—Luke 10:21-22	(Jesus' praise of the Father; 50 out of 69 words identical)
Matt 12:43-45—Luke 11:24-25	(On the return of the evil spirit; 53 out of 61 words identical)
Matt 23:37-38—Luke 13:34-35	(Lament over Jerusalem; 46 out of 55 words identical)
Matt 24:45-51—Luke 12:42b-46	(Sayings about vigilance; 87 out of 104 words identical)

Some of the differences in the above list may seem major, but a number of them are merely stylistic variants (e.g. Luke's elimination of a paratactic *kai* that Matthew has preserved from "Q").

Second, it is scarcely coincidental that the "Q" material used by both Matthew and Luke, inserted into their Gospels in entirely different contexts (after the temptation scene), manifests a general underlying sequence that is common to both of them. This cannot be owing merely to oral tradition. The only logical explanation of this factor is a common written Greek source. Most of the "Q" material is found in Matthew in five sermon blocks (5:1 - 7:27; 10:5-42; 13:3-52; 18:3-35; 23:2 - 25:46); but in Luke it occurs mainly in the big and little interpolations (9:51 - 18: 14; 6:20 - 8:2). Given this situation, one would not expect a common sequence of any sort in the "Q" material. And yet there is a trace of it, for the Lucan and Matthean sequence of sections of major importance at the beginning and end of the list is strikingly similar. The numerous divergences at the center of the list affect mostly short, isolated sayings, which one or the other evangelist has rearranged, apparently for one topical reason or another. The following list of "Q" passages reveals the remnant of a common sequence and thus argues for the existence of the material in a set form prior to its use by either evangelist.

Lucan Order	Number of vv. in Luke	Lucan chap. & vv.	Shortened Title of Episode	Matthean chap. & vv.	Matthean Order
1	3	3:7-9	The Baptist's Preaching, A	3:7b-10	1
2	2	3:16b-17	The Baptist's Preaching, B	3:11-12	2
3	12	4:2b-13	Jesus' Temptations	4:2b-11a	3
4	4	6:20-23	Beatitudes	5:3,6,4,11-12	4
5	7	6:27-33	Love of Enemies, A	5:44,39-42, 46-47	9
6	2	6:35b-36	Love of Enemies, B	5:45,48	10
7	2	6:37a,38b	On Judging, A	7:1-2	16
8	1	6:39bc	On Judging, B	15:14b	46
9	3	6:40-42	On Judging, C	10:24-25; 7:3-5	29, 17
10	3	6:43-45	Test of Goodness	7:16-20 (cf. 12:33-35)	20
11	4	6:46-49	Hearers and Doers of the Word	7:21,24-27	22
12	10	7:1b-10	Cure of the Centurion's Servant	8:5-10,13	23
13	6	7:18-23	The Baptist's Question	11:2-6	35a
14	5	7:24-28	Jesus' Testimony to the Baptist	11:7-11	35b
15	5	7:31-35	Jesus' Judgment of His Generation	11:16-19	37
16	4	9:57-60	Three Would-be Followers	8:19-22	25
17	11	10:2-12	Mission of the Seventy	9:37-38; 10:7-16	26-27
18	3	10:13-15	Woes on Galilean Towns	11:21-23	38
19	1	10:16	Disciples as Representatives	10:40	34

Lucan Order	Number of vv. in Luke	Lucan chap. & vv.	Shortened Title of Episode	Matthean chap. & vv.	Matthean Order
20	2	10:21-22	Praise of the Father	11:25-27	39
21	2	10:23-24	Blessedness of Disciples	13:16-17	43
22	3	11:2-4	"Our Father"	6:9-13	11
23	5	11:9-13	Efficacy of Prayer	7:7-11	18
24	10	11:14-23	Beelzebul Controversy	12:22-30	40
25	3	11:24-26	Return of the Evil Spirit	13:43-45	45
26	4	11:29-32	Sign of Jonah	12:38-42	42
27	3	11:33-35	Sayings about Light	5:15; 6:22-23	6, 13
28	14	11:39-40 42-44, 46-52	Sayings against Pharisees	23:25-26, 23, 6-7, 4, 29-30, 34-35, 13	52
29	8	12:2-9	Exhortation to Fearless Confessing	10:26-33	30
30	1	12:10	The Holy Spirit, A	12:32	41
31	2	12:11-12	The Holy Spirit, B	10:19-20	28
32	10	12:22b-31	Worry about Earthly Things	6:25-33	15
33	2	12:33b-d,34	Treasure in Heaven	6:19-21	12
34	7	12:39-40, 42b-46	Sayings on Vigilance and Faithfulness	24:43-51	58
35	3	12:51,53	Enigma of Jesus' Mission	10:34-36	31
36	2	12:58-59	Agreement with One's Opponent	5:25-26	7b
37	4	13:18-21	Parables of Mustard Seed and Yeast	13:31-33	44
38	5	13:24-29	Reception and Rejection in the Kingdom	7:13-14; 25:10-12; 7:22-23; 8:11-12	19, 59, 21, 24
39	2	13:34-35	Lament over Jerusalem	23:37-39	53
40	6	14:16-21	Parable of the Great Dinner	22:2-10	51

Lucan Order	Number of vv. in Luke	Lucan chap. & vv.	Shortened Title of Episode	Matthean chap. & vv.	Matthean Order
41	2	14:26-27	Conditions of Discipleship	10:37-38	32
42	2	14:34-35	Parable of Salt	5:13	5
43	4	15:4-7	Parable of the Lost Sheep	18:12-14	48
44	1	16:13	Servants and Masters	6:24	14
45	2	16:16-17	Two Sayings about the Law	11:12-13; 5:18	36, 7a
46	1	16:18	On Divorce	5:32	8
47	2	17:3b-4	On Forgiveness	18:21-22	49
48	2	17:5-6	On Faith like a Mustard Seed	17:20	47
49	2	17:23-24	Days of the Son of Man, A	24:26-27	54
50	2	17:26-27	Days of the Son of Man, B	24:37-38	56
51	1	17:33	Days of the Son of Man, C	10:39	33
52	2	17:34-35	Days of the Son of Man, D	24:40-41	57
53	1	17:37b	Days of the Son of Man, E	24:28	55
54	13	19:13, 15b-24,26	Parable of the Pounds	25:14-30	60
55	2	22:28b,30b	Remarks on the Disciples	19:28	50

A third major reason for postulating "Q" is the presence of doublets in the Lucan Gospel; this complicated question is discussed further below.

The overriding problem with the postulated source "Q" is that no one has ever seen it. The attempts to ferret it out of the Gospels of Matthew and Luke have not been perfectly acceptable. The evidence set forth above shows, however, that "Q" is not "only what you make it," despite the protests of S. Petrie (*NovT* 3 [1959] 28-33). The agreement of analysts about it is striking. It may never have been the literary unit that Mark is, and this may account for the difficulty of being sure that certain of the passages listed above actually belonged to it.

Another problem is the amount of redactional work that must be allowed to both Matthew and Luke. It is not possible to discuss this element further in detail here; the issue will be discussed when it arises in the commentary itself. But we may single out at least four passages in the above list where the Lucan redaction (or Matthean redaction) is princi-

pally involved in what must have otherwise been "Q" material: Luke
13:24-29; 14:16-21; 15:4-7; 19:13-26.

Still more problematic are Luke 10:25-28; 12:54-56; and 13:22-23.
These should possibly be regarded either as "L" or as Lucan composition;
they will be discussed at the relevant places in the commentary.

Some commentators have suggested at times that "Q" existed in
different forms, which were used independently by Matthew and Luke
(thus C. K. Barrett, *ExpTim* 54 [1942-1943] 320-323; W. Bussmann,
Synoptische Studien [Halle an d. S.: Waisenhaus, 1925-1931], 2. 110-156)
or that "Q" represents only layers of tradition that existed largely in oral,
catechetical, or liturgical form (J. Jeremias, *ZNW* 29 [1930] 147-149).
Such suggestions, however, are in reality quite speculative and fail to account for the word-for-word identity of phrasing in many of the "Q" passages of Matthew and Luke. As will be seen, I prefer to describe the
source "L" as largely oral, but I cannot convince myself that this is the
underlying situation in the case of "Q."

An objection to "Q" has often been derived from its contents, since it
consists almost entirely of sayings of Jesus, contains few narratives (e.g.
the temptation, the cure of the centurion's servant, and the disciples of
John the Baptist), and lacks a passion narrative. The last defect has been
claimed to be crucial, since it seems inconceivable that the early Christian
community would have composed an evangelical text that lacked the
kerygmatic proclamation of the saving event itself. However, the objection stems from a modern preconception of what a gospel has to be. Regardless of the position one adopts about the origin of the sayings
ascribed to Jesus in the Coptic *Gospel according to Thomas*—whether
they are derived from the canonical Gospels, from Gnostic sources, or
from an independent ancient tradition (possibly oral)—the significant
thing is that it was frankly labeled in antiquity as a Gospel (*peuangelion
pkata Thōmas*, at the end of the text). See below on other aspects of this
Gospel. Save for one or other section which contains a slight bit of narrative (e.g. §§ 12, 60), it is a collection of "sayings" (*šaje*) ascribed to
Jesus and deprived of a setting apart from a question put to Jesus. The
absence of a passion narrative in it is striking. The Coptic text is, moreover, known to be a translation of an earlier Greek form of the Gospel,
partially preserved, which spoke of *logoi* pronounced by Jesus. See further
my article, "The Oxyrhynchus *Logoi* of Jesus and the Coptic Gospel
according to Thomas," *ESBNT*, 355-433, esp. pp. 418-419.

Finally, it has to be recalled that there is evidence in the Synoptic Gospels of an overlapping of "Mk" and "Q." Some episodes or sayings may
well have been present in both sources. In some cases we can see that the
material from the two sources has simply been joined (e.g. in the
preaching of John the Baptist, the temptation of Jesus). But in others it
seems that Luke and Matthew preferred to take a "Q" passage instead of

the Marcan form of the episodes (e.g. the parable of the mustard seed, Luke 13:18-19; the parable of the yeast, Luke 13:20-21). This last issue is related to the question of the agreements of Matthew and Luke in the Triple Tradition against Mark.

7. *Lucan Doublets.* By a "doublet" in the Synoptic tradition is meant a passage occurring twice within the same Gospel, but more specifically twice within the Lucan and Matthean Gospels, where they appear in both the Triple and Double Traditions, or in one of these and in the special source-material as well. In this strict sense passages like Mark 6:35-44 and 8:1-9, the feeding of the five thousand and the four thousand, though sometimes called a doublet, are not meant, since these occur within one tradition. Indeed, the doublets have been used in arguing for Luke's dependence on "Q"; they have been seen as an added argument for the postulate.

However, the question of Lucan doublets is somewhat complicated and calls for a brief exposé here. On the one hand, there are clear instances of doublets, in which Luke has inherited one passage from his Marcan source ("Mk"), and the other from either "Q" or (less frequently) from "L." Yet there are also clear instances of his deliberate effort to avoid doublets; the latter has been called his "fear of doublets" (*Dubletten-furcht,* W. Bussmann).

The doublets which are found in the Lucan Gospel occur in the following passages:

From "Mk"	From "Q"
1. 8:8c (=Mark 4:9 and 4:23)	14:35 (=Matt 11:15; 13:9)
2. 8:16 (=Mark 4:21)	11:33 (=Matt 5:15)
3. 8:17 (=Mark 4:22)	12:2 (=Matt 10:26)
4. 8:18 (=Mark 4:25)	19:26 (=Matt 25:29)
5. 9:3,4,5 (=Mark 6:8,10,11)	10:4,5 + 7,10,11 (=Matt 10:10,11, 12,14)
6. 9:23-24 (=Mark 8:34-35)	14:27; 17:33 (=Matt 10:38-39)
7. 9:26 (=Mark 8:38)	12:8-9 (=Matt 10:32-33)
8. 9:48 (=Mark 9:37)	10:16 (=Matt 10:40?)
9. 20:46 (=Mark 12:38-39)	11:43 (=Matt 23:6-7)
10. 21:14-15 (=Mark 13:11)	12:11-12 (=Matt 10:19-20)
11. 21:18 (probably from "L")	12:7 (=Matt 10:30)
12. 18:14b (probably from "L")	14:11 (=Matt 18:4; 23:12)

What is striking in the vast majority of the foregoing doublets is that they form part of a unit that is derived from the pre-Lucan sources. As H. Schürmann has remarked ("Die Dubletten," 276), "Luke deliberately creates no doublets, but at most permits them in a few instances to occur according to his schematic mode of composition." The only one that is in this regard somewhat problematic is the first in the above list, with the isolated logion, "Let him who has ears to hear with take heed." Schürmann also tries to ascribe the occurrence of doublets in the Lucan Gospel to Luke's forgetfulness (ibid. 277). This could be the case, but it is not always clear. In any event, such an explanation does agree with the studied avoidance of doublets that Luke has found in preexisting source-material.

This is evident when one examines the following passages:

1. Mark 4:23 (ears to hear)   see after Luke 8:17; cf. Luke 8:8b
                                ("Mk")
2. Mark 4:24b (measure)   see after Luke 8:18; cf. Luke 6:38
                                ("Q")
3. Mark 8:1-9 (feeding of   see Luke's Big Omission; cf. Luke
   four thousand)   9:12-17 ("Mk")
4. Mark 10:31 (last will be   see after Luke 18:30; cf. Luke 13:30
   first)   ("L")
5. Mark 12:28-34 (great   see after Luke 20:40; cf. Luke 10:
   commandment)   25-28 ("L")
6. Mark 13:15-16 (person on the see after Luke 21:21-22; cf. Luke
   roof at the end-time)   17:31 ("L," or is it simply "Mk"
                                transposed earlier?)
7. Mark 13:21-23 (culmination of see after Luke 21:24; cf. Luke 17:
   troubles)   23-24 ("Q")
8. Mark 13:33-36 (end of   see after Luke 21:33; cf. Luke
   eschatological discourse)   12:35-40 ("Q")
9. Mark 14:3-9 (anointing in   see after Luke 22:2; cf. Luke 7:36-50
   Bethany)   ("L")

These are all clear instances where Luke has omitted Marcan material because he has used something similar at an earlier occasion in the Gospel. Schürmann has treated these passages extensively ("Die Dublettenvermeidungen," 279-289), with most of which one can easily agree. I hesitate to regard either the gaps after Mark 6:1-6 (visit to Nazareth; cf. Luke 4:16-24) or Mark 6:17-29 (the imprisonment and death of the Baptist; cf. Luke 3:19-20) merely as cases of doublet-avoidance; they are rather transpositions of Marcan material. Finally, it is scarcely correct to think that Luke has omitted Mark 9:9b-13 (sequel to the transfiguration) because he regarded it as a doublet of Luke 9:8-19 (=Mark 6:15-16,30-44; 8:27b-29). But he omits Mark 10:1-12 because of 16:18.

8. *Luke's Dependence on Special Sources.* The material in the Lucan Gospel that is derived from "Mk" and "Q" accounts for almost two-thirds of this Gospel. To explain the provenience of the remaining third is not easy. One can, of course, say that whatever is not "Mk" or "Q" is derived from Luke's private source, designated for convenience "L." But it is not so simple. In the case of "Q" it was easy to show the at-times remarkable correpondences in Matthew and Luke and the generic order of

such material which give rise to the postulate of a Greek written source behind this Double Tradition. But when one considers the material that is peculiar to Luke, there is, first of all, no reason to think in terms of a written source. One cannot rule out free Lucan composition, used not only to formulate factual evidence (such as in Luke 3:1-3), literary sutures and summaries, but even possibly some scenes such as 24:50-53. By "composition" I mean free creative activity on the part of the evangelist, who was not depending on a previous source, oral or written, and not merely redacting or modifying something that he had inherited. Lucan "composition" is often evident from characteristic Lucan style. This is the main problem that has to be faced at this stage in the discussion of the composition of the Lucan Gospel. I shall cite below those passages of the Gospel that I think have been derived from "L" (which is to be understood as a "source" in a broad sense, either oral or written, but which is not to be put on a par with "Mk" or "Q"). The problem is, How can one be sure that such material is really derived from "L" and not freely composed by Luke? The answer is, We shall never know. In those cases in which I am particularly hesitant, I have put a question mark in parentheses after the references. The amount of "L"-material in the infancy narrative is minimal indeed.

"L" Passages

1:5 - 2:52	The infancy narrative—in part at least (see commentary)
3:10-14	John the Baptist's preaching
3:23-38 (?)	The genealogy of Jesus
4:17-21,23,25-30 (?)	Jesus' visit to Nazareth
5:4-9a	The catch of fish
5:39	Old wine and new
7:12-17	Raising of the son of the widow of Nain
8:1-3 (?)	Galilean women followers of Jesus
9:52-55	Departure for Jerusalem and a Samaritan reception
9:61-62	Farewell of a would-be follower
10:17-20	The return of the Seventy(-two)
10:25-28	Commandment for eternal life
10:29-37	Parable of the good Samaritan
10:38-42	Martha and Mary
11:1 (?)	Setting of the "Our Father"
11:5-8	Parable of the persistent friend
11:27-28	Those who are really blessed
12:1	Leaven of the Pharisees
12:13-15	Warning against greed
12:16-21	Parable of the rich fool
12:35-38	Vigilance
12:47-48	The servant's reward
12:49	Jesus' mission

"L" Passages

12:54-56	Signs of the times
13:1-9	Timely reform: Parable of the barren fig tree
13:10-17	Cure of the crippled woman on the Sabbath
13:30	Last will be first
13:31-33	Herod's desire to kill Jesus; his departure from Galilee
14:1-6	Cure of the man with dropsy
14:7-14	Sayings on conduct at dinners
14:28-32	Conditions of discipleship
15:8-10	Parable of the lost coin
15:11-32	Parable of the prodigal son
16:1-8a	Parable of the dishonest manager
16:8b-12	Two applications of the parable
16:14-15	Avaricious Pharisees reproved
16:19-31	Parable of the rich man and Lazarus
17:7-10	Unprofitable servants
17:12-18(?)	Cleansing of the ten lepers
17:20-21	Coming of God's kingdom
17:28-32	Days of the Son of Man
18:2-8a	Parable of the dishonest judge
18:10-14	Parable of the Pharisee and the Toll-Collector
19:1-10	Zaccheus
19:39-40	Answer to Pharisees
19:41-44	Lament over Jerusalem
20:18	Strength of stone
21:18,21b,22,24(?),28	Destruction of Jerusalem
21:34-36	Vigilance
21:37-38 (?)	Ministry of Jesus in Jerusalem
22:3a	Satan entering Judas
22:15-18, 19c-20	Last Supper
22:27	Who is greater, the one who dines or who serves?
22:31-33	Peter's denial foretold
22:35-38	Two Swords
22:63-71 (?)	Mistreatment and interrogation of Jesus
23:6-12	Jesus sent to Herod
23:13-16	Pilate's judgment
23:27-32	On the road to the cross
23:35a,36-37	Witnesses at the crucifixion
23:39b-43	Two criminals on crosses with Jesus
23:46,47b-49	Death of Jesus
23:56	Women preparing spices before the Sabbath
24:13-35	Jesus' appearance on the road to Emmaus
24:36-43	Jesus' appearance to disciples in Jerusalem
24:44-49	Jesus' final commission

It would be an oversimplification to ascribe all of the "L"-material in the Third Gospel to an oral source alone. Luke's dependence on eyewitnesses and ministers of the word (1:1) does not demand this. The existence of a special written source for the passion narrative has been discussed time and again; I am skeptical of it, but I shall reserve my comments on this matter for the introduction to the passion narrative.

It is a further question whether "L"—if it is not necessarily written— depends on one or more persons. It is impossible to be certain about this. I prefer to think about "L" as a designation for source(s) of information about the Jesus-story in the early Christian community Luke would have tapped in various ways. This, it seems to me, is consonant with his reference in the prologue to his effort to "trace everything carefully from the beginning."

There are, of course, some verses in the Third Gospel that were probably freely composed by Luke; these will be pointed out in the commentary proper. These are verses that he wrote to present the story about Jesus and the sequel thereto in the form that he was interested in. But one has to distinguish Lucan "composition" from Lucan "redaction," by which I mean the editorial modification of source-material that Luke has taken over. Both activities in their own way contribute to the Lucan picture of Jesus, and it is hard to say which is more important. But there is a reason to keep the two efforts distinct.

On E. Schweizer's attempts to identify a "hebraizing" source in Luke, see pp. 116, 120-122 below.

9. *Luke and the Gospel according to Thomas.* The question of the sources of the Lucan Gospel has been further raised in recent decades in reference to the apocryphal *Gospel according to Thomas* (see Bibliography). Ever since the discovery of a Coptic version of it at Nag Hammadi in Egypt in December 1945, the question of a relationship between the NT and this apocryphal Gospel has been posed anew. Is it possible that its collection of 114 sayings attributed to Jesus is related to "Q" or to "L"?

Through the writings of Hippolytus and Origen we have known of the apocryphal *Gospel according to Thomas;* and other patristic writers quoted a form of it. The Coptic text that became available in the Nag Hammadi discovery dates roughly from the end of the fourth century A.D. It is a translation of an earlier Greek text, as is manifest not only from the Greek words preserved in the Coptic itself, but also from three fragmentary copies of the Greek form which were found at the beginning of this century at Oxyrhynchus in Egypt. They are Oxyrhynchus Papyri 1, 654 and 655; they preserve (in whole or in part) a Greek form of eighteen of the sayings. The Greek copies are dated roughly to the first half of the third century A.D., but the Gospel itself may well have been composed toward the end of the second century. For a comparison of the

Greek text and the Coptic, see my article, "The Oxyrhynchus Logoi of Jesus and the Coptic Gospel according to Thomas," in *ESBNT*, 355-433.

Of the 114 sayings attributed to Jesus in the Coptic *Gospel according to Thomas,* none of them is identical with sayings in the Synoptic Gospels in either Greek or Coptic—despite what was said in earlier days of pioneer research on the newly found text (Saying 34 comes closest; see Matt 15:14b). There is, however, a number of sayings which are related to sayings of Jesus preserved in the Synoptic tradition; there are others, which are marked by echoes of Gnostic language (and reveal thereby their clearly later origin); and still others that are unrelated to the Synoptic tradition and devoid of Gnostic phraseology. The latter two groups are of little concern to us here. The first category of sayings preserved in this apocryphal Gospel has sparked the controversial discussion of Thomas-Synoptic connections. What is the relation of these sayings to the Synoptic Gospels, and in particular to the Lucan Gospel?

Before we discuss the relationship further, it is wise that we list the Lucan passages which have similarities with the *Gospel according to Thomas.* In the following list I give only those episodes which have a noteworthy similarity, and not with a mere echo of a phrase found in the Lucan Gospel. There are a number of these echoes, and in some cases it is not easy to say from which of the Synoptic Gospels the phrase may have been derived or to which it is most closely parallel (e.g. Luke 2:49—§61; 9:46—§12; 10:22—§61b; 11:9—§92; 12:35,37—§103; 12:39—§§21,103; 13:30—§4). Of the episodes that would require serious consideration, we may list the following:

a) Lucan passages, derived from "Mk," which have parallels in *Gos. Thom.*

Luke	Gos. Thom.	Luke	Gos. Thom.
4:24	31	8:17	5b + 6e
5:33-34	104	8:18	41
5:37,36	47c	8:19-21	99
5:39	47b	20:9b-15,18	65
8:5-8	9	20:17	66
8:8c	8e	20:22-25	100
8:16	33b		

b) Lucan passages, derived from "Q," which have parallels in *Gos. Thom.*

Luke	Gos. Thom.	Luke	Gos. Thom.
6:20b	54	12:2	5b + 6e
6:21a	69b	12:3 (?)	33a
6:22	68(-69a?)	12:10 (?)	44

6:39 (?)	34	12:22	36
6:41-42	26	12:33 (?)	76b
6:44-45	45	12:51-53	16
7:24-25	78	12:56	91b
7:28 (?)	46	13:18-19 (?)	20
9:58 (?)	86	13:20-21 (?)	96
10:2	73	14:16-21	64
10:8-9a	14b	14:26-27	55,101
11:10	94	15:4	107
11:33	33b	16:13	47a
11:39-40 (?)	89	19:26 (?)	41
11:52	39a		

The question mark after the Lucan reference means that it is difficult to say that the similarity is closer to the Lucan form than to the Matthean.

c) Lucan passages, derived from "L," which have parallels in *Gos. Thom.*

Luke	*Gos. Thom.*	*Luke*	*Gos. Thom.*
11:27-28	79	17:20-21	113
12:13-14	72	17:21	3
12:16-20 (?)	63	17:34	61a
12:49	10	23:29	79

This list is shorter than the "L" material that H. Schürmann has considered ("Das Thomasevangelium," reprint, 240-241—Bibliography, p. 103). This is because he considers some Marcan material as "L" and includes some brief phrases, which I have excluded. The passages will have to be dealt with in the course of the commentary. Most of them in the *Gospel according to Thomas* are dependent on the Synoptic Gospels (or perhaps on a form of gospel tradition that was harmonizing the canonical Gospels in the second and third centuries). The extent to which any of these parallels in the *Gospel according to Thomas* depends on a tradition that is independent of the canonical Gospels can only be discussed in specific cases.

I have already mentioned a significant point in the use of *euangelion* as a name for this apocryphal collection of sayings (see p. 80 above). However, I should hesitate to regard this collection of sayings as having anything to do with the postulated "Q" itself.

Similarly, the apocryphal collection and "L" share a number of sayings in common; but that does not immediately argue for a common source on which they both depend.

10. *Luke and John (or Other Sources)*. A special problem about "L" is seen in its possible relation to John or other sources. Some of the "L"-material contains details which are shared with the Fourth Gospel. R. E.

Brown (*The Gospel according to John, I-XII* [AB 29; Garden City, NY:
Doubleday, 1966] xlvi-xlvii) has discussed "the possibility of cross-
influence on John from Luke," especially from "the peculiarly Lucan material." He notes the following points in particular: (1) only one story of
the multiplication of the loaves and fish; (2) the mention of figures like
Lazarus, Martha, and Mary, one of the Twelve named Jude (or Judas,
not Iscariot), and the high priest Annas; (3) no night interrogation before Caiaphas; (4) the double question put to Jesus concerning his messiahship and divine sonship (Luke 22:67,70; John 10:24-25,33); (5) the
three non-guilty statements of Pilate during Jesus' trial; (6) the post-
resurrection appearances of Jesus in the Jerusalem area; and (7) the miraculous catch of fish (Luke 5:4-9; John 21:5-11). To these still further
examples could be added, such as: (8) the discourse of Jesus at the Last
Supper (Luke 22:21-38; John 14-17); (9) the belief among the people
that John the Baptist might be the Messiah (Luke 3:15; John 1:20);
(10) two angels in the tomb (Luke 24:4; John 20:12) in contrast to
Matthew and Mark. See further F. L. Cribbs, "St. Luke and the Johannine Tradition." J. A. Bailey has made a detailed study of the following
Lucan and Johannine passages in which he finds major signs of contact.
His list includes some materials not mentioned above:

Luke	John	Luke	John
7:36-50	12:1-8	22:39-53a	18:1-12
3:15-17	1:19,27	22:53b-71	18:13-27
5:1-11	21:1-14	23:1-25	18:29 - 19:16
19:37-40	12:12-19	23:25-26	19:17-42
22:3	13:2,27a	24	20-21
22:14-38	13-17		

I tend to agree with Brown that nothing suggests (*pace* Bailey) that
the fourth evangelist knew Luke's Gospel. But the independent tradition
behind John had features that were also found in the special source(s) on
which Luke depended, even though the details did not always appear in
the same way in both traditions. In the oral tradition behind both the
Gospels there undoubtedly was cross-influence which affected the more
immediate source(s) of both. Brown sees this as an influence "from the
emerging Gospel tradition" into the Johannine tradition. It does not seem
impossible that the Lucan tradition was equally influenced by the Johannine. Brown seems to admit this when he speaks of the secondary editing
of the parable of Lazarus and the rich man (Luke 16:27-31), which
mentions the possibility of Lazarus coming back from the grave.

Attempts are made at times to determine other special sources that
Luke used. These are sometimes referred to as the "personal sources of
the Evangelist" (E. E. Ellis) or understood as the "eyewitnesses" to
which he refers in 1:2. Among such sources are often cited persons like

Mary, the mother of Jesus ("who cherished all these things within her," 2:51; cf. 2:19; Acts 1:14); she is said to have been Luke's chief informant for the infancy narrative and the Nazareth episode (Luke 4:16-30); disciples of John the Baptist (see Acts 19:1-3), who would have known of John's childhood; Joanna, the "wife of Chuza, Herod's steward" (Luke 8:3) and Manaen, "a member of the court of Herod the tetrarch" (Acts 13:1), who could have told Luke about Jesus' relations with Herod Antipas (Luke 13:31; 23:7-10); Cleopas (24:18), who could have told him about Jesus' meeting with him and his companion on the road to Emmaus; Barnabas, the cousin of John Mark (Col 4:10), who could have supplied him with Jerusalem traditions (Acts 12:12); Philip the evangelist and his daughters (Acts 8:5; 21:8-9), who lived at Caesarea Maritima and had evangelized Samaria and would have been a likely source for Jesus' contacts with the Samaritans (about whom only Luke among the Synoptics informs us [Luke 9:52-56; 17:11-19]); other "brethren" in Jerusalem (Acts 11:17), who would have been able to supply Luke with information about certain episodes in Jerusalem that Luke alone recounts (13:1-9); the "daughters of Jerusalem" (23:28) and the women "from Galilee" (23:49); or, finally, various members of the church of Syrian Antioch (Acts 13:1). See further A. Harnack, *Luke the Physician,* 153-156; E. Osty, *L'Evangile selon saint Luc,* 8-9.

That such informants *could have* been among the eyewitnesses to which Luke refers no one will deny. But the list rests solely on speculation—more pious than critical. It is the result of scouring the NT for likely candidates to document Luke 1:2 in an effort to establish the historical credibility of the Lucan story and support the contention that the evangelist makes in the prologue. However, in the long run there is not a shred of evidence that any of these candidates influenced Luke at all. He knows about them, writes about them, but gives not a clue that any of them could be reckoned among his "sources" (even understood in a wide sense).

11. *The Proto-Luke Hypothesis.* Analyses of the composition of the Third Gospel like the one given thus far have been modified at times to take account of the so-called Proto-Luke hypothesis. Forms of this theory were apparently first proposed by P. Feine, B. Weiss, and others, but its classic form and recent popularity have been largely owing to B. H. Streeter (*The Four Gospels,* 233-270), V. Taylor (especially in *Behind the Third Gospel*), and J. Jeremias (with some variation in details). According to this view, Luke would first have combined "Q" and "L" to produce Proto-Luke, a gospel text that began with what is now 3:1. Later on, when he came across the Marcan Gospel, he would have incorporated blocks of the Marcan material into Proto-Luke and prefixed to it the in-

fancy narrative (1:5 - 2:52), preceded by the prologue (1:1-4). It is, moreover, sometimes maintained that Proto-Luke was written by Paul's collaborator in Caesarea Maritima during the time of the Apostle's imprisonment there (Acts 23:33 - 26:32). After Luke had accompanied Paul to Rome, he would have expanded his text with the material from the Marcan Gospel, which he would have encountered there for the first time.

The main reasons for this hypothesis are the obviously separate character of the infancy and resurrection narratives in the Third Gospel, the grouping of Marcan material in five blocks (listed above, p. 67), the absence of more than 30 per cent of the Marcan material in Luke, the striking differences in the Marcan and Lucan passion narratives, and the verbal deviations of Luke from Mark in certain parallels.

The hypothesis has received the support of a number of British, American and Continental scholars (with varying nuances): C. F. Evans, L. Gaston, F. C. Grant, T. Henshaw, E. Lohse, T. W. Manson, A. M. Perry, F. Rehkopf, C. S. C. Williams, J. de Zwaan. But a group at least as numerous has spoken out against it: F. W. Beare, H. Conzelmann, J. M. Creed, M. Dibelius, S. M. Gilmour, M. Goguel, K. Grobel, A. F. J. Klijn, W. G. Kümmel, A. R. C. Leaney, W. Michaelis, H. Montefiore, J. C. O'Neill, H. Schürmann, A. Wikenhauser and J. Schmid. Some of these, however, would admit the hypothesis at least for the passion narrative.

The difficulties that have been found with the proposal are mainly the following.

1) In this hypothesis the genealogy of Jesus (Luke 3:23-38) is an "L" passage; but Luke would have deliberately decided to flank it with two incidents that are otherwise closely linked in the Marcan account, the baptism of Jesus (Mark 1:9-11) and his temptation (1:12-13). Is this more likely than that he would have inserted the genealogy into the Marcan order, especially in view of his expansion of the latter episode with "Q"-material?

2) The omission of such Marcan material as 3:20-30 right after the section (mostly "Q" and "L") of Luke 6:20 - 8:3 and of other material (=Mark 9:42-50) right before the peculiarly Lucan travel account is strange, if the Marcan material is to be understood as inserted into Proto-Luke. Why should such passages have been omitted? On the other hand, their absence is more intelligible in the supposition that the "L" and "Q" material has been inserted into Mark and that in the case of major insertions some of the Marcan material is deliberately omitted (see the matter of the avoidance of doublets above, p. 81; cf. H. Schürmann, "Dublettenvermeidungen," *ZKT* 76 [1954] 83-93; *Traditionsgeschichtliche Untersuchungen,* 279-289).

3) Among the doublets that do occur, normally the episode that is

derived from "Mk" precedes the doublet from "Q" (see p. 81 above). This argues in general for the precedence of the Marcan text and for the insertion of "Q" or "L" into it.

4) Luke 4:16-30 cannot seriously be taken to have been part of Proto-Luke as a sort of initiation story, since the mention of Capernaum (4:23) is then inexplicable. The mention of ministry already performed there by Jesus clearly shows that the passage has been transposed from a later context in the Jesus-story, as indeed Mark 6:1-6 suggests. There the rejection at Nazareth takes place after a ministry of Jesus in Capernaum. Hence the position of this episode in Luke presupposes that the evangelist has been working with Mark as his base.

5) The attempt of F. Rehkopf and others (Tyson, Taylor) to distinguish pre-Lucan vocabulary in "L" (or "Q") has scarcely been convincing. If there is any validity to such material, it does not certainly establish the unity of Proto-Luke as a connected Gospel narrative.

6) The expansion of the Marcan tradition by "Q" and "L" is best seen in what happens to the announcements of the passion in both Gospels. In Mark they occur with brief intervals (8:31; 9:30-31; 10:32-34); but in Luke the first two correspond to this brief-interval occurrence (9:22; 9:43b-45), but the third is almost lost sight of because of the Big Interpolation, the travel account, that intervenes. It does not occur until Luke 18:31-34, and by that time one has almost forgotten that it had been preceded by two others. Moreover, when one considers the Marcan introduction to the third one, "And they were on the road, going up to Jerusalem," it is hard to understand why, if Luke were inserting this into Proto-Luke, he would not have somehow introduced it earlier into his own story of Jesus' journey to Jerusalem. Rather, the delay produced in Luke is owing to the insertion of "Q" and "L" material into the Marcan order.

7) It is obvious that one could maintain the Proto-Luke hypothesis without insisting on its geographical origin in Caesarea Maritima. But H. Montefiore has raised a question that one would have to consider if one were to insist on the Caesarean origin of Proto-Luke and its development into the Lucan Gospel only after Luke had arrived in Rome. How would the text of Proto-Luke have survived the shipwreck off the island of Malta? The question may seem facetious, but it is as serious as the proposal itself.

See further W. G. Kümmel, *Introduction,* 132-137.

12. *The Literary Composition of the Lucan Gospel.* Luke's use of sources in the writing of his story of Jesus and his followers does not exhaust the problem of the composition of his work. We have already mentioned the problem of distinguishing between "L" and actual Lucan composition and the matter of the Lucan redaction of inherited written source

material. Both of these issues raise, in effect, the further matter of how Luke has made use of his sources. He is not a mere compiler, a scissors-and-paste editor. Indeed, it is above all necessary to stress today what Streeter once wrote years ago, that Luke "though not, as has been rashly alleged, 'a great historian' in the modern sense, is a consummate literary artist" (*The Four Gospels,* 548). For he composed his narrative (*diēgēsis*) not merely as an ancient historian of the Hellenistic mode, nor merely as a theologian of the early church writing in a biblical mold, but also as a conscious littérateur of the Greco-Roman period.

In one respect, Luke's narrative represents, along with Matthew, a reaction to the Gospel of Mark. It hints at this in the prologue, when it speaks of earlier *attempts* to record the story—this factor was at times emphasized in the early church, as can be seen in Eusebius *Hist. eccl.* 3.24,15. What is immediately striking is the over-all general similarity of Luke and Matthew despite the impression that the study of their sources makes. The general similarity involves the infancy narrative that both have prefixed; the use of a genealogy; the insertion of the same sayings-material into "Mk"; the ending of the narrative with accounts of the appearances of the risen Christ commissioning the disciples to proclaim him and his message to all nations. This similarity reflects one attitude among Christians of the last part of the first century which sought to crystallize the account of Jesus' deeds and words in a more set form than the Marcan, an attitude different from that which stimulated the Johannine tradition and which probably also regarded the Marcan tradition as inadequate.

But such similarity between Matthew and Luke remains merely on a general level, for it does not take the reader long to detect how different are the First and Third Gospels and how independent Luke actually is of Matthew. Independent, indeed, are the reworkings of the Marcan and "Q" material in both of these Gospels. In handling his own source-material, Luke has not simply copied it slavishly. One can verify this judgment easily in the material said to be Marcan; in that derived from "Q" the judgment is more difficult, but on occasion the presence of a Lucan characteristic, literary or theological, reveals his redaction of a "Q" passage (e.g. the "Spirit" in Luke 11:13), especially when it is absent in its Matthean counterpart.

Lucan *redaction* of earlier material is seen in many ways in the Gospel. First, Luke has frequently improved the Greek style and language of the Marcan stories or the "Q" sayings. He has often rewritten them in his own characteristic style. See further below, pp. 107-108.

Second, Luke frequently abbreviates the Marcan story by omitting details that are circumstantial or anecdotal or that are not required for his purpose. In this regard, one may compare the following episodes with their Marcan counterparts:

Luke 8:4-8	The parable of the sower	cf. Mark 4:1-9
8:22-25	The calming of the storm	4:35-41
8:26-39	The Gerasene demoniac	5:1-20
8:43-48	The cure of the woman with a hemorrhage	5:24-34
8:40-42, 49-56	The raising of Jairus' daughter	5:21-23, 35-43
9:10-17	The feeding of the five thousand	6:30-44
9:37-43a	The cure of the epileptic demoniac	9:14-29
20:9-19	The parable of the wicked tenant-farmers	12:1-12
21:5-7	The fate of the Jerusalem Temple	13:1-4

In some instances the omission of such details has resulted in less clarity in the Lucan account, and there is then the danger of reading the Marcan details into the Lucan form of the story, a dubious procedure indeed.

Third, certain episodes considered by Luke to be duplicates of those he has already recounted are omitted from his Marcan material. Here a principle of economy may be at work. And yet, it is not fully operative, since such material is not entirely eliminated. We have already discussed this matter in part, in commenting on the problem of the Synoptic "doublets" in the Third Gospel (see pp. 81-82 above). Beyond those passages, we may list the following as probably omitted from "Mk" on this principle of economy:

Mark 4:26-29	The parable of the seed that grows in secret	
10:1-12	The debate about divorce	cf. Luke 16:18
12:28-34	The question about the great commandment	10:25-28
14:3-9	The anointing of Jesus at Bethany	7:36-50
14:55-64	Jesus' appearance at night before the Sanhedrin	22:66-71
15:23	The offering of wine mixed with myrrh	23:36

Other instances come to mind, such as Mark 6:45-52 (Jesus walking on the waters) or 8:1-10 (the second feeding of the crowd [cf. Luke 9:12-17]), but these are part of Luke's Big Omission. Even in the above list, one may query whether Luke has not used other source-material in preference to the Marcan, e.g. in 10:25-28 ("L") or 22:66-71 ("L"). But there are further instances of the omission of Marcan material, where we really have no adequate compositional explanation of it (e.g. Mark 3:20-21; 4:33-34; 9:9-13,42-49; 10:35-45(?); 11:12-14,20-25; 13:21-23,33-37; 14:51-52). Some of these omissions can be explained generically as passages, for instance, dealing with topics that would be of little interest to Gentile Christians for whom Luke was writing (e.g. Mark 9:9-13) or containing Aramaic expressions that Luke has studiously eliminated, for instance, *talitha koum,* "maiden, arise" (Mark 5:41; cf. Luke 8:54).

Fourth, Luke deliberately omits from his source-material what does not contribute to the over-all literary plan that he imposes on the story of Jesus. His depiction of Jesus as preoccupied with Jerusalem as a city of destiny and his concern to move Jesus resolutely toward it result in the omission of geographical designations and certain episodes that are explicitly located in Mark. Here the principle is probably a desire not to distract the reader's attention from Jerusalem. This seems to be the main reason for the Big Omission (=Mark 6:45 - 8:26, where Jesus proceeds in a northern direction, going as far as Tyre and Sidon). "Caesarea Philippi" (Mark 8:27) is undoubtedly omitted for a similar reason in an episode that Luke otherwise considers important (Luke 9:18-20). The rendezvous of the disciples with the risen Christ to take place in Galilee (Mark 14:28) becomes a mere recollection of the time that Jesus spent there with his disciples and of what he said there (Luke 24:6); the risen Christ makes his appearances only in the Jerusalem area in the Lucan resurrection narrative.

Fifth, the pursuit of a literary effect is also responsible for the transposition of some Marcan material, already discussed above (see pp. 71-72).

Sixth, certain redactional modifications of the Marcan source material can be seen to stem from a delicate sensitivity which tends to make Luke eliminate anything that smacks of the violent, the passionate, or the emotional. This, of course, tells us something about Luke—much more, indeed, than about the historical Jesus; but it also contributes to the Lucan portrait of Jesus. This sort of redactional modification is undoubtedly at work, in part at least, in some of the following episodes:

Luke 3:19-20	The imprisonment of John the Baptist (recounted as the summation of Herod's evil; we only learn of John's death subsequently in 9:9)	cf. Mark 6:17-29
———	Jesus' relatives (*hoi par' autou*) want to take hold of him, thinking him to be beside himself	3:21
19:45	The violent details of Jesus' purging of the Temple	11:15b-16

22:70	The striking of Jesus at the interrogation of the Sanhedrin (but cf. 22:63-64)	14:62-65
23:16,22,25	The scourging of Jesus becomes a mere suggestion	15:15
———	The crowning with thorns and mockery of Jesus	15:16-20

Similarly, the description of Jesus moved by human emotions in the Marcan Gospel is normally eliminated in the Lucan story, even if they are expressions of love, compassion, or tenderness. The Marcan episodes depict Jesus in a more human way, perhaps too human for the nobility of character that Luke sought to depict. This may seem somewhat strange to us, even a stroke of what has been labeled his bourgeois piety; but it obviously is an aspect of Luke's concern for *asphaleia*, "assurance," which he offers to the Christians of the period for which he writes. The redactional modifications that he has made in this regard can be seen in the following places:

Luke 5:13	Jesus' compassion is eliminated	cf. Mark 1:41
5:14	Jesus' stern rebuke is eliminated	1:43
6:10	Jesus' gaze of anger and sadness	3:5
9:11	Jesus' pity for the crowd in the desert	6:34
18:16	Jesus' anger	10:14
18:22	Jesus' gaze of love	10:21
9:48; 18:17	Jesus embracing the children	9:36; 10:16
22:40	Jesus' distress and anguish	14:33-34
23:46	Jesus' cry on the cross	15:34

A similar restraint is manifested at times toward the disciples of Jesus, whose wonder and fear at his going up to Jerusalem are recorded by Mark (10:32b), but omitted by Luke (18:31). Again, the embarrassed silence of the disciples (Mark 9:34) is passed over by Luke (9:47).

Luke omits the rebuke of Simon Peter, who is called Satan in Mark 8:33 (cf. Luke 9:22); and the disciples' accusation of Jesus' lack of concern about them (Mark 4:38b; cf. Luke 8:24). Their reaction to his (implicitly uncalled for) query about who touched him (Mark 5:30-32) becomes a Petrine protest (Luke 8:45 [in some mss.]). Luke not only omits the request of the sons of Zebedee (Mark 10:35-40), but also—what is extraordinary—all reference to the apostles' deserting of Jesus and their flight (Mark 14:49). This is heightened by the complete omission of the story of the youth who ran off naked (a Marcan detail symbolizing the utter dereliction of Jesus, 14:51-52). On the other hand, he even goes so far as to include among those standing at Jesus' cross with the women-followers from Galilee "his acquaintances" (masc. *hoi gnōstoi autō,* Luke 23:49). And one wonders whom he meant by that!

To the same sort of redactional modification must be attributed perhaps the simplified description of the results of Jesus' teaching in parables in Luke 8:10 (cf. Mark 4:12), and Jesus' comment about Judas' treachery in Luke 22:22 (cf. Mark 14:21c). Though Luke notes at times that the disciples did not understand (18:34), he tends to offer an explanation of such incomprehension ("this message was hidden from them"; cf. 24:16). Here Luke implicitly sees a reference to the workings of divine providence and, in effect, saves face for the disciples. This is probably also the reason why he eliminates Jesus' remark about their failure to understand a parable (Mark 4:13; cf. Luke 8:11) or the resurrection from the dead (Mark 9:10; cf. Luke 9:37), or even their lack of success in exorcism (Mark 9:28-29; cf. Luke 9:43-45). In the scene of Jesus' agony on the Mount of Olives the disciples fall asleep in the Lucan version, as in Mark, but it is explained that they were "exhausted with grief" (22:45). Indeed, their post-resurrection disbelief is explained as the result of "joy" (24:41).

Against the background of such redactional modification on the part of Luke, one can see the intrinsic difficulty that is met when one considers the verses about the so-called bloody sweat (Luke 22:43-44)—which are questionable also from the text-critical viewpoint (see the commentary).

For further details in this sort of study of Luke's use of his sources, see H. J. Cadbury, *Style and Literary Method,* 73-205.

Has Luke composed his Gospel and Acts with overarching parallels or architectonic patterns? In the past, a number of writers have pointed out interesting parallels in various parts of Luke-Acts, such as the parallelism in the infancy narrative between John the Baptist and Jesus; a two-part development in both the Gospel and Acts (Luke 1:4-9:50, 9:51-24:53 and Acts 1:1-15:35, 15:36-28:31); the similarity in the Peter-stories and the Paul-stories in Acts; the death of Jesus in the Gospel and the death of Stephen in Acts, etc. Some of these parallels seem to be valid, especially those within Acts. However, those in the Gospel itself (save for the infancy narrative) or between the Gospel and Acts are more problematic.

Recently C. H. Talbert (*Literary Patterns, Theological Themes, and the Genre of Luke-Acts*) has sought to set out Lucan patterns or "correspondences both in content and sequence between the events and persons found in Luke and those in Acts" (p. 15) in great detail. Three chapters of his book are devoted to "correspondences" between Acts 1-12 and 13-28; between Luke 9:1-48 and 22:7-23:16; between Acts 1:12-4:23 and 4:24-5:42; between Luke 4:16-7:17 and 7:18-8:56; within Luke 1-2; within Luke 3-4; and chiastic parallels within Luke 10:21-18:30 and the same sort in Acts 15:1-21:26; and finally correspondence between Luke 4 and Acts 1, and between Luke 9 and Acts 1. Such patterns he has sought to relate to theological themes of Luke-Acts.

When one scrutinizes these correspondences, one sees that they are far from cut and dried. They raise the old question, Who is seeing the correspondences, Luke or Talbert? Talbert has tried to forestall this objection by a discussion of controls on "scholarly subjectivity" (ibid. pp. 8-10). The fact that scholars in the field of classics have established that a Virgil or a Herodotus worked with parallels or patterns might raise the question whether Luke has done so too. But their success in establishing the architectonic patterns in classical writers does not mean that Luke has them and that we simply have to ferret them out. The question is rather whether he has them or not. When one looks at the details in Talbert's analysis of many of the alleged patterns, one constantly shakes one's head.

I shall prescind from discussing the parallels in Acts, since they do not really concern us in a commentary on the Gospel. But in Talbert's discussion of the correspondences between Luke 9:1-48 and 22:7-23:16 (pp. 26-29) one notes immediately from the two-column table (p. 26) that the items in the first matching column (from Luke 9) are in order, but those in the second (from Luke 22-23) are not. In other words, the order of Luke 9 has become the Procrustean bed into which the verses from Luke 22-23 had to be fitted. This is not the place for an elaborate criticism of Talbert's book. I shall try to keep in mind the question of architectonic patterns in Luke-Acts in the course of the commentary. However, it does not appear that whatever literary patterns Luke introduced into the gospel tradition are all that certain or important in the composition of the Jesus-story. Luke has, indeed, introduced some of this type of parallel structuring into his story, in a way not found in Mark. Moreover, what he has of such parallelism and architectonic pattern differs considerably from the Matthean. The existence of these patterns affects the way one regards the outline of the Lucan Gospel.

Finally, it should be obvious that the discussion of the composition of the Lucan Gospel cannot be finished without some treatment of Lucan language and style. I have chosen to treat this matter under a separate heading.

BIBLIOGRAPHY

The Griesbach and Related Hypotheses

Badham, F. P. *S. Mark's Indebtedness to S. Matthew* (New York: E. R. Herrick, 1897).

Bleek, F. *Einleitung in das Neue Testament* (2d ed.; Berlin: Reimer, 1866) 245-281.

Buchanan, G. W. "Has the Griesbach Hypothesis Been Falsified?" *JBL* 93 (1974) 550-572.

Butler, B. C. *The Originality of St. Matthew: A Critique of the Two-Document Hypothesis* (Cambridge: University Press, 1951).

Dungan, D. L. "Mark—The Abridgement of Matthew and Luke," in *Jesus and Man's Hope* (ed. D. G. Miller; 2 vols.; Perspective Books; Pittsburgh: Pittsburgh Theological Seminary, 1970) 1. 51-97.

——— "Reactionary Trends in the Gospel Producing Activity of the Early Church: Marcion, Tatian, Mark," in *L'Evangile selon Marc: Tradition et rédaction* (BETL 34; ed. M. Sabbe; Louvain: Leuven University; Gembloux: Duculot, 1974) 179-202.

Farmer, W. R. "Modern Developments of Griesbach's Hypothesis," *NTS* 23 (1976-1977) 275-295.

——— "A Response to Robert Morgenthaler's *Statistische Synopse*," *Bib* 54 (1973) 417-433.

——— "A 'Skeleton in the Closet' of Gospel Research," *BR* 9 (1961) 18-42.

——— *The Synoptic Problem: A Critical Analysis* (New York: Macmillan, 1964; slightly revised ed., Dillsboro, NC: Western North Carolina Press, 1976).

——— "The Synoptic Problem and the Contemporary Theological Chaos," in *Christian Century* 83 (1966) 1204-1206.

——— "The Two-Document Hypothesis as a Methodological Criterion in Synoptic Research," *ATR* 48 (1966) 380-396.

Fitzmyer, J. A. "The Priority of Mark and the 'Q' Source in Luke," in *Jesus and Man's Hope* (ed. D. G. Miller; 2 vols.; Perspective Books; Pittsburgh: Pittsburgh Theological Seminary, 1970) 1. 131-170; repr. in *To Advance the Gospel: New Testament Studies* (New York: Crossroad Publ. Co., 1981) 3-40.

Griesbach, J. J. *Commentatio qua Marci evangelium totum e Matthaei et Lucae commentariis decerptum esse monstratur* (Jena: 1789-1790); reprinted as *Griesbachii opuscula academica* (Jena: 1825) 8. 358-425.

Longstaff, T. R. W. *Evidence of Conflation in Mark? A Study in the Synoptic Problem* (SBLDS 28; Missoula, MT: Scholars Press, 1977).

Orchard, B. *Matthew, Luke and Mark* (2d ed.; Manchester, England: Koinonia, 1977).

Reicke, B. "Griesbach und die synoptische Frage," *TZ* 32 (1976) 341-359.

Talbert, C. H., and E. V. McKnight, "Can the Griesbach Hypothesis Be Falsified?" *JBL* 91 (1972) 338-368.

The Sources of the Lucan Gospel

Bartlett, J. V. "The Sources of St. Luke's Gospel," in *Studies in the Synoptic Problem by Members of the University of Oxford* (ed. W. Sanday; Oxford: Clarendon, 1911) 313-363.

Berg, P. "Die Quellen des Lukasevangeliums," *NKZ* 21 (1910) 330.

Brun, L. "Zur Kompositionstechnick des Lukasevangeliums," *Symbolae Osloenses* 9 (1930) 38-50.

Fuller, R. H. "Die neuere Diskussion über das synoptische Problem," *TZ* 34 (1978) 129-148.

Hawkins, J. C. *Horae synopticae: Contributions to the Study of the Synoptic Problem* (2d ed.; Oxford: Clarendon, 1909).

Lagrange, M.-J. "Les sources du troisième Evangile," *RB* 4 (1895) 5-22; 5 (1896) 5-38.

Salazar, A. M. "Questions about St. Luke's Sources," *NovT* 2 (1958) 316-317.

Tyson, J. B. "Sequential Parallelism in the Synoptic Gospels," *NTS* 22 (1975-1976) 276-308.

Weiss, B. *Die Quellen des Lukasevangeliums* (Stuttgart/Berlin: J. G. Cotta, 1907).

Luke's Dependence on Mark

Abbott, E. A., and W. G. Rushbrooke. *The Common Tradition of the Synoptic Gospels in the Text of the Revised Version* (London: Macmillan, 1884).

Bacon, B. W. "The Treatment of Mk. 6^{14}–8^{26} in Luke," *JBL* 26 (1907) 132-150.

Burkitt, F. C. "The Use of Mark in the Gospel according to Luke," in *Beginnings of Christianity* (5 vols.; eds. F. J. Foakes Jackson and K. Lake; London: Macmillan, 1920-1933) 2. 106-120.

Butler, B. C. *The Originality of St. Matthew: A Critique of the Two-Document Hypothesis* (Cambridge: University Press, 1951).

Farmer, W. R. " 'The Lachmann Fallacy,' " *NTS* 14 (1967-1968) 441-443.

——— *Synopticon: The Verbal Agreement between the Greek Texts of Matthew, Mark and Luke Contextually Exhibited* (Cambridge: Cambridge University, 1969).

Glasson, T. F. "Did Matthew and Luke Use a 'Western' Text of Mark?" *ExpTim* 55 (1943-1944) 180-184; 77 (1965-1966) 120-121.

Hawkins, J. C. "Three Limitations to St. Luke's Use of St. Mark's Gospel," in *Studies in the Synoptic Problem by Members of the University of Oxford* (ed. W. Sanday; Oxford: Clarendon, 1911) 27-94.

Lachmann, C. "De ordine narrationum in evangeliis synopticis," *TSK* 8 (1835) 570-590; reprinted in *Novum Testamentum graece et latine* (2 vols.; Berlin: G. Reimer, 1842, 1850) 2. xiii-xxv.

Longstaff, T. R. W. "The Minor Agreements: An Examination of the Basic Argument," *CBQ* 37 (1975) 184-192.

Neirynck, F. "La matière marcienne dans l'évangile de Luc," in *L'Évangile de Luc: Problèmes littéraires et théologiques: Mémorial Lucien Cerfaux* (BETL 32; ed. F. Neirynck; Gembloux: Duculot, 1973) 157-201.

Palmer, N. H. "Lachmann's Argument," *NTS* 13 (1966-1967) 368-378.

Sanders, E. P. "The Argument from Order and the Relationship between Matthew and Luke," *NTS* 15 (1968-1969) 249-261.

——— *The Tendencies of the Synoptic Tradition* (SNTSMS 9; Cambridge: University Press, 1969).

Schramm, T. *Der Markus-Stoff bei Lukas: Eine literarkritische und redak-tionsgeschichtliche Untersuchung* (SNTSMS 14; Cambridge: University Press, 1971).

Solages, B. de. *A Greek Synopsis of the Gospels: A New Way of Solving the Synoptic Problem* (Leiden: Brill, 1959).

Streeter, B. H. *The Four Gospels: A Study of Origins, Treating of the Manu-script Tradition, Sources, Authorship, & Dates* (London: Macmillan, 1924).

Styler, G. M. "The Priority of Mark," *The Birth of the New Testament* (ed. C. F. D. Moule; New York: Harper & Row, 1962) 223-232.

Throckmorton, B. H., Jr. "Mark and Roger of Hoveden," *CBQ* 39 (1977) 103-106.

Wood, H. G. "The Priority of Mark," *ExpTim* 65 (1953-1954) 17-19.

Woods, F. H. "The Origin and Mutual Relation of the Synoptic Gospels," *Studia biblica et ecclesiastica* (5 vols.; Oxford: Clarendon, 1885, 1890, 1891, 1896, 1903) 2. 59-104.

Lucan Transpositions of Marcan Material

Jeremias, J. "Perikopen-Umstellungen bei Lukas?" *NTS* 4 (1957-1958) 115-119; reprinted in *Abba: Studien zur neutestamentlichen Theologie und Zeitgeschichte* (Göttingen: Vandenhoeck und Ruprecht, 1966) 93-97.

Morgenthaler, R. *Synoptische Synopse,* 232-283.

Neirynck, F. "The Argument from Order and St. Luke's Transpositions," *ETL* 49 (1973) 784-815.

Schürmann, H. "Die Dublettenvermeidungen im Lukasevangelium," *ZKT* 76 (1954) 83-93; reprinted in *Traditionsgeschichtliche Untersuchungen,* 279-289, esp. p. 280.

———— *Das Lukasevangelium,* 318-323, 471-472.

Sparks, H. F. D. "St. Luke's Transpositions," *NTS* 3 (1956-1957) 219-223.

Agreements of Matthew and Luke

Argyle, A. W. "Agreements between Matthew and Luke," *ExpTim* 73 (1961-1962) 19-22.

Burrows, E. W. "The Use of Textual Theories to Explain Agreements of Matthew and Luke against Mark," in *Studies in New Testament Language and Text: Essays in Honour of George D. Kilpatrick on the Occasion of His Sixty-fifth Birthday* (NovTSup 44; ed. J. K. Elliott; Leiden: Brill, 1976) 87-99.

McLoughlin, S. "Les accords mineurs Mt-Lc contre Mc et le problème synoptique: Vers la théorie des deux sources," in *De Jésus aux évangiles: Traduction et rédaction dans les évangiles synoptiques: Donum natalicium Iosepho Coppens . . . II* (ed. I. de la Potterie; Gembloux: Duculot, 1967) 17-40.

Neirynck, F. "Minor Agreements Matthew-Luke in the Transfiguration Story," in *Orientierung an Jesus: Zur Theologie der Synoptiker für Josef Schmid* (eds. P. Hoffmann et al.; Freiburg im B.: Herder, 1973) 253-265.

———— *The Minor Agreements of Matthew and Luke against Mark, with a Cumulative List* (BETL 37; Gembloux: Duculot, 1974) [in collaboration with T. Hansen and F. van Segbroeck].

Simpson, R. T. "The Major Agreements of Matthew and Luke against Mark," *NTS* 12 (1965-1966) 273-284.

Stephenson, T. "The Overlapping of Sources in Matthew and Luke," *JTS* 21 (1920) 127-145.

Turner, N. "The Minor Verbal Agreements of Mt. and Lk. against Mk.," *SE I* (TU 73, 1959) 223-234.

Wilson, R. M. "Farrer and Streeter on the Minor Agreements of Mt and Lk against Mk," *SE I* (TU 73, 1959) 254-257.

Luke's Supposed Dependence on Matthew

Argyle, A. W. "Evidence for the View that St. Luke Used St. Matthew's Gospel," *JBL* 83 (1964) 390-396.

Butler, B. C. "St. Luke's Debt to St. Matthew," *HTR* 32 (1939) 237-308.

Guy, H. A. "Did Luke Use Matthew?" *ExpTim* 83 (1972) 245-247.

Hartl, V. "Zur synoptischen Frage: Schliesst Lukas durch 1,1-3 die Benutzung des Matthäus aus?" *BZ* 13 (1915) 334-337.

Sanders, E. P. "The Argument from Order and the Relationship between Matthew and Luke," *NTS* 15 (1968-1969) 249-261.

Schmid, J. *Matthäus und Lukas: Eine Untersuchung des Verhältnisses ihrer Evangelien* (Biblische Studien 23/2-4; Freiburg im B.: Herder, 1930).

Simons, E. *Hat der dritte Evangelist den kanonischen Matthäus benutzt?* (Bonn: C. Georgi, 1880).

West, H. P., Jr. "A Primitive Version of Luke in the Composition of Matthew," *NTS* 14 (1967-1968) 75-95.

Wilkens, W. "Zur Frage der literarischen Beziehung zwischen Matthäus und Lukas," *NovT* 8 (1966) 48-57.

Luke's Dependence on "Q"

Allen, W. C. "Did St. Matthew and St. Luke Use the Logia?" *ExpTim* 11 (1899-1900) 424-426.

Cerfaux, L. "L'Utilisation de la source Q par Luc," in *L'Evangile de Luc: Problèmes littéraires et théologiques: Mémorial Lucien Cerfaux* (BETL 32; ed. F. Neirynck; Gembloux: Duculot, 1973) 61-69.

Cherry, R. S. "Agreements between Matthew and Luke," *ExpTim* 74 (1962-1963) 63.

Downing, F. G. "Towards the Rehabilitation of Q," *NTS* 11 (1964-1965) 169-181.

Ellis, E. E. *Gospel of Luke*, 21-29.

Farrer, A. "On Dispensing with Q," in *Studies in the Gospels: Essays in Memory of R. H. Lightfoot* (Oxford: Blackwell, 1957) 55-88.

Goulder, M. D. "On Putting Q to the Test," *NTS* 24 (1977-1978) 218-234.

Hawkins, J. C. "Probabilities as to the So-called Double Tradition of St. Matthew and St. Luke," in *Studies in the Synoptic Problem by Members of the University of Oxford* (ed. W. Sanday; Oxford: Clarendon, 1911) 95-138.

————— "Some Internal Evidence for the Use of the Logia in the First and Third Gospels," *ExpTim* 12 (1900-1901) 72-76.

Jeremias, J. "Zur Hypothese einer schriftlichen Logienquelle Q," *ZNW* 29 (1930) 147-149; reprinted in *Abba: Studien zur neutestamentlichen Theologie und Zeitgeschichte* (Göttingen: Vandenhoeck und Ruprecht, 1966) 90-92.

Lührmann, D. *Die Redaktion der Logienquelle* (WMANT 33; Neukirchen: Neukirchener, 1969).

Lummis, E. W. *How Luke was Written: Considerations Affecting the Two-Document Theory with Special Reference to the Phenomena of Order in the Non-Marcan Matter Common to Matthew and Luke* (Cambridge: University Press, 1915).

Petrie, S. " 'Q' Is Only What You Make It," *NovT* 3 (1959) 28-33.

Schulz, S. *Griechisch-deutsche Synopse der Q-Überlieferung* (Zürich: Theologischer, 1972).

————— *Q: Die Spruchquelle der Evangelisten* (Zürich: Theologischer, 1972).

————— *Q-Synopse: Der Text der Spruchquelle bei Matthäus und Lukas* (Zürich: Theologischer, 1972).

Schürmann, H. "Sprachliche Reminiszensen an abgeänderte oder ausgelassene Bestandteile der Spruchsammlung im Lukas- und Matthäus-evangelium," *NTS* 6 (1959-1960) 193-210; reprinted with slightly altered title) in *Traditionsgeschichtliche Untersuchungen zu den synoptischen Evangelien* (Düsseldorf: Patmos, 1968) 111-136.

Snape, H. C. "The Composition of the Lukan Writings: A Re-assessment," *HTR* 53 (1960) 27-46.

Taylor, V. "The Order of Q," *JTS* 4 (1953) 27-31.

————— "The Original Order of Q," *Studies in Memory of Thomas Walter Manson 1893–1958* (ed. A. J. B. Higgins; Manchester: University Press, 1959) 246-269.

————— "Some Outstanding New Testament Problems: I. The Elusive Q," *ExpTim* 46 (1934-1935) 68-74.

Vassiliadis, P. *Hē peri tēs pēgēs tōn logiōn theōria: Kritikē theōrēsis tōn synchronōn philologikōn kai theologikōn problēmatōn tēs pēgēs tōn logiōn* (Athens: Privately published, 1977 [available from author, 16 Dardanellion St., Thessaloniki, Greece]).

Lucan Doublets

Fuchs, A. *Sprachliche Untersuchungen zu Matthäus und Lukas: Ein Beitrag zur Quellenkritik* (AnBib 49; Rome: Biblical Institute, 1971).

Hawkins, J. C. *Horae Synopticae*, 80-106.

Schürmann, H. "Die Dubletten im Lukasevangelium," *ZKT* 75 (1953) 338-345; reprinted in *Traditionsgeschichtliche Untersuchungen zu den synoptischen Evangelien* (Düsseldorf: Patmos, 1968) 272-278.

—————"Die Dublettenvermeidungen im Lukasevangelium," *ZKT* 76 (1954) 83-93; reprinted in *Traditionsgeschichtliche Untersuchungen*, 279-289.

Stephenson, T. "The Classification of Doublets in the Synoptic Gospels," *JTS* 20 (1919) 1-8.

Luke's Dependence on Special Sources

Bornhäuser, K. *Studien zum Sondergut des Lukas* (Gütersloh: C. Bertelsmann, 1934).

Easton, B. S. "Linguistic Evidence for the Lucan Source L.," *JBL* 29 (1910) 139-180.

Farmer, W. R. "Notes on a Literary and Form-Critical Analysis of Some of the Synoptic Material Peculiar to Luke," *NTS* 8 (1961-1962) 301-316.

Montefiore, H. "Does 'L' Hold Water?" *JTS* 12 (1961) 59-60.

Rehkopf, F. *Die lukanische Sonderquelle: Ihr Umfang und Sprachgebrauch* (WUNT 5; Tübingen: Mohr [Siebeck], 1959).

Schürmann, H. "Protolukanische Spracheigentümlichkeiten? Zu Fr. Rehkopf, Die lukanische Sonderquelle. Ihr Umfang und Sprachgebrauch," *BZ* 5 (1961) 266-286; reprinted in *Traditionsgeschichtliche Untersuchungen* 209-227.

——— "Das Thomasevangelium und das lukanische Sondergut," *BZ* 7 (1963) 236-260; reprinted in *Traditionsgeschichtliche Untersuchungen,* 228-247.

Schweizer, E. "Eine hebraisierende Sonderquelle des Lukas?" *TZ* 6 (1950) 161-185.

Taylor, V. "Rehkopf's List of Words and Phrases Illustrative of Pre-Lukan Speech Usage," *JTS* 15 (1964) 59-62.

Luke and the Gospel according to Thomas

Bauer, J. B. "The Synoptic Tradition in the Gospel of Thomas," *SE III* (TU 88, 1964) 314-317.

Dehandschutter, B. "L'Évangile selon Thomas: Témoin d'une tradition prélucanienne?" in *L'Évangile de Luc: Problèmes littéraires et théologiques: Mémorial Lucien Cerfaux* (BETL 32; ed. F. Neirynck; Gembloux: Duculot, 1973) 287-297.

Gaertner, B. *The Theology of the Gospel according to Thomas* (New York: Harper, 1961).

Grant, R. M. et al. *The Secret Sayings of Jesus* (Garden City, NY: Doubleday, 1960).

Guillaumont, A. et al. *The Gospel according to Thomas* (Leiden: Brill; New York: Harper & Bros., 1959).

Higgins, A. J. B. "Non-Gnostic Sayings in the Gospel of Thomas," *NovT* 4 (1960) 292-306.

Kasser, R. *L'Évangile selon Thomas* (Neuchâtel: Delachaux et Niestlé, 1961).

Koester, H., and T. O. Lambdin. "The Gospel of Thomas (II, 2)," *The Nag Hammadi Library in English* (ed. J. M. Robinson; New York: Harper & Row, 1977) 117-130.

Montefiore, H. "A Comparison of the Parables of the Gospel according to Thomas and of the Synoptic Gospels," in *Thomas and the Evangelists* (eds. H. E. W. Turner and H. Montefiore; STB 35; Naperville, IL: Allenson, 1962) 40-78.

Schrage, W. "Evangelienzitate in den Oxyrhynchus-Logien und im koptischen Thomas-Evangelium," in *Apophoreta: Festschrift für Ernst Haenchen zu seinem siebzigsten Geburtstag am 10. Dezember 1964* (BZNW 30; eds. W. Eltester and F. H. Kettler; Berlin: de Gruyter, 1964) 251-268.

———— *Das Verhältnis des Thomas-Evangeliums zur synoptischen Tradition und zu den koptischen Evangelienübersetzungen: Zugleich ein Beitrag zur gnostischen Synoptikerdeutung* (BZNW 29; Berlin: de Gruyter, 1964).

Schürmann, H. "Das Thomasevangelium und das lukanische Sondergut," *BZ* 7 (1963) 236-260; reprinted in *Traditionsgeschichtliche Untersuchungen*, 228-247.

Luke and John

Bailey, J. A. *The Traditions Common to the Gospels of Luke and John* (NovTSup 7; Leiden: Brill, 1963).

Cribbs, F. L. "St. Luke and the Johannine Tradition," *JBL* 90 (1971) 422-450.

Dodd, C. H. "Some Johannine 'Herrenworte' with Parallels in the Synoptic Gospels," *NTS* 2 (1955-1956) 75-86.

Grant, F. C. "Was the Author of John Dependent upon the Gospel of Luke?" *JBL* 56 (1937) 295-307.

Leahy, W. K. *An Historical and Exegetical Study of Luke-John Relationships* (Rome: University of S. Thomas Aquinas, 1964).

Mendner, S. "Zum Problem 'Johannes und die Synoptiker,'" *NTS* 4 (1957-1958) 282-307.

Osty, E. "Les points de contact entre le récit de la passion dans saint Luc et dans saint Jean," in *Mélanges Jules Lebreton* (*RSR* 39 [1951]) 146-154.

Parker, P. "Luke and the Fourth Evangelist," *NTS* 9 (1952-1953) 317-336.

Robinson, B. P. "Gethsemane: The Synoptic and the Johannine Viewpoints," *CQR* 167 (1966) 4-11.

Schniewind, J. *Die Parallelperikopen bei Lukas und Johannes* (2. Aufl.; Hildesheim: G. Olms, 1958).

The Proto-Luke Hypothesis

Broadribb, D. "Proto-Luko," *Biblia revuo* 1 (1968) 7-26.

Cerfaux, L. "A propos des sources du troisième évangile: Proto-Luc ou Proto-Matthieu?" *ETL* 12 (1935) 5-27; reprinted in *Recueil Lucien Cerfaux* (3 vols.; BETL 6, 7, 18; Gembloux: Duculot, 1954, 1954, 1962) 1. 389-414.

Creed, J. M. "'L' and the Structure of the Lucan Gospel: A Study of the Proto-Luke Hypothesis," *ExpTim* 46 (1934-1935) 101-107.

Dibelius, M. "Taylor: *Behind the Third Gospel: A Study of the Proto-Luke Hypothesis*," *TLZ* 52 (1927) 146-148.

Feine, P. "Eine vorkanonische Überlieferung des Lukas," in *Evangelium und Apostelgeschichte* (Gotha: Perthes, 1891).

Gaston, L. *No Stone on Another: Studies in the Significance of the Fall of Jerusalem in the Synoptic Gospels* (NovTSup 23; Leiden: Brill, 1970) 244-256.

Gilmour, S. M. "A Critical Re-examination of Proto-Luke," *JBL* 67 (1948) 143-152.

Goguel, M. "Luke and Mark: With a Discussion of Streeter's Theory," *HTR* 26 (1933) 1-55.

Hanson, R. P. C. "Does *dikaios* in Luke xxiii 47 Explode the Proto-Luke Hypothesis?" *Hermathena* 60 (1942) 74-78.

Hunkin, J. W. "The Composition of the Third Gospel, with Special Reference to Canon Streeter's Theory of Proto-Luke," *JTS* 28 (1926-1927) 250-262.

Jeremias, J. *The Eucharistic Words of Jesus* (Philadelphia: Fortress, 1977) 97-98.

Rehkopf, F. *Die lukanische Sonderquelle: Ihr Umfang und Sprachgebrauch* (WUNT 5; Tübingen: Mohr [Siebeck], 1959).

Robinson, W. C., Jr. *Der Weg des Herrn* (Hamburg-Bergstedt: H. Reich, 1964).

Schürmann, H. "Protolukanische Spracheigentümlichkeiten? Zu Fr. Rehkopf, Die lukanische Sonderquelle. Ihr Umfang und Sprachgebrauch," *BZ* 5 (1961) 266-286; reprinted in *Traditionsgeschichtliche Untersuchungen*, 209-227.

Streeter, B. H. *The Four Gospels*, 233-270.

Taylor, V. *Behind the Third Gospel: A Study of the Proto-Luke Hypothesis* (Oxford: Clarendon, 1926).

———— *The First Draft of St. Luke's Gospel* (London: SPCK, 1927).

———— "Important Hypotheses Reconsidered: The Proto-Luke Hypothesis," *ExpTim* 67 (1955-1956) 12-16.

———— "Is the Proto-Luke Hypothesis Sound?" *JTS* 29 (1927-1928) 147-155.

———— "Luke, Gospel of," *IDB* 3. 180-188.

———— "Professor J. M. Creed and the Proto-Luke Hypothesis," *ExpTim* 46 (1934-1935) 236-238.

———— "Proto-Luke," *ExpTim* 33 (1921-1922) 250-252.

———— "The Proto-Luke Hypothesis: A Rejoinder," *ExpTim* 54 (1942-1943) 219-222.

———— "The Value of the Proto-Luke Hypothesis," *ExpTim* 36 (1924-1925) 476-477.

The Literary Composition of the Lucan Gospel

Drury, J. *Tradition and Design in Luke's Gospel: A Study in Early Christian Historiography* (London: Darton, Longman & Todd, 1976).

Edwards, R. A. "The Redaction of Luke," *JR* 49 (1969) 392-405.

George, A. "Tradition et rédaction chez Luc: La construction du troisième évangile," in *De Jésus aux évangiles: Tradition et rédaction dans les évangiles synoptiques: Donum natalicium Iosepho Coppens . . . II* (BETL 25; ed. I. de la Potterie; Gembloux: Duculot, 1967) 100-129.

Hull, W. E. "A Structural Analysis of the Gospel of Luke," *RevExp* 64 (1967) 421-425.

———— "A Teaching Outline of the Gospel of Luke," *RevExp* 64 (1967) 426-432.

Hultgren, A. J. "Interpreting the Gospel of Luke," *Int* 30 (1976) 353-365.

Leal, J. "La geografía y el plan literario del III Evangelio," in *XV semana bíblica española (20-25 Sept. 1954)* (Madrid: Consejo superior de investigaciones científicas, 1955) 227-246.

—— "El plan literario del III Evangelio y la geografía," *EstEcl* 29 (1955) 197-215.

Mattill, A. J., Jr. "The Jesus-Paul Parallels and the Purpose of Luke-Acts: H. H. Evans Reconsidered," *NovT* 17 (1975) 15-46.

Morgenthaler, R. *Die lukanische Geschichtsschreibung als Zeugnis: Gestalt und Gehalt der Kunst des Lukas* (2 vols.; Zürich: Zwingli-V., 1948).

Morton, A. Q., and G. H. C. Macgregor, *The Structure of Luke and Acts* (London: Hodder & Stoughton, 1964).

Nösgen, C. F. "Der schriftstellerische Plan des dritten Evangeliums," *TSK* 49 (1876) 265-292.

Puech, A. *Histoire de la littérature grecque chrétienne depuis les origines jusqu'à la fin du ive siècle* (3 vols.; Paris: Société d'édition 'Les Belles-Lettres,' 1928) 1. 90-120.

Talbert, C. H. *Literary Patterns, Theological Themes, and the Genre of Luke-Acts* (SBLMS 20; Missoula, MT: Scholars Press, 1974).

—— "The Redaction Critical Quest for Luke the Theologian," in *Jesus and Man's Hope* (2 vols.; ed. D. G. Miller; Perspective Books; Pittsburgh: Pittsburgh Theological Seminary, 1970) 1. 171-222.

Unnik, W. C. van. "Eléments artistiques dans l'évangile de Luc," in *L'Évangile de Luc: Problèmes littéraires et théologiques: Mémorial Lucien Cerfaux* (BETL 32; ed. F. Neirynck; Gembloux: Duculot, 1973) 129-140.

Wilkens, W. "Die theologische Struktur der Komposition des Lukasevangeliums," *TZ* 34 (1978) 1-13.

IV. LUCAN LANGUAGE AND STYLE

The composition of the Lucan Gospel cannot fully be described without some attention to the language and style in which it was written. Centuries ago Jerome recognized that "among all the evangelists" Luke "was the most skilled writer of Greek" (*inter omnes evangelistas graeci sermonis eruditissimus fuit,* Ep. ad Damasum 20.4,4; CSEL, 54.108). His use of good Greek style was in part determined by his Hellenist background. (Even though I prefer to think of him as an *incola* of Antioch, that Seleucid town in Syria had no little Hellenistic influence and culture, which would explain the Hellenist background.) It was also determined in part by his desire to write his account in the mold of contemporary Hellenistic literary composition.

1. *Luke's Treatment of Marcan Material.* One need only consider Luke's wording and reformulation of the Marcan material to become aware of his concern to improve its Greek style. Years ago, J. C. Hawkins said of both Matthew and Luke that "to a large extent they clothed the narratives, and to some extent they clothed the sayings, which they derived from those sources, in their own favourite language" (*Horae synopticae* [2d ed.; Oxford: Clarendon, 1909] 26). Though it is not easy to show it, the same seems to be true of Luke's use of the "Q" material. However, one also notes in the Lucan writing a concern not to change the wording too radically, for he has not simply recast the inherited material into a wholly different idiom. Luke's reformulation is usually the improvement of as much of the Marcan wording as his sense of good Greek demanded.

Some of the ways in which Luke has improved the Greek of his sources may be noted here. Part of the improvement is the result of the use of fewer Semitisms, and part of it the use of more resources of the Greek language. These can be seen in the following ways.

1) Luke regularly changes the Marcan historic present to a past tense. Hawkins (*Horae synopticae,* 144-149) lists the 151 historic present tense examples in the Marcan Gospel together with the parallels in Matthew and Luke, if any. Of these, when Luke has a parallel, only one historic present is retained: Mark 5:35 *erchontai* becomes *erchetai* in Luke 8:49. However, Luke does have a few instances of the historic present in either "L" passages (e.g. 7:40; 13:8; 16:7,23,29; 24:12,36) or "Q" passages (19:22), or in his own redaction (11:37,45; 17:37). He also uses it thirteen times in Acts (see Hawkins, *Horae synopticae,* 149).

2) He frequently eliminates parataxis, substituting for it either the genitive absolute or a subordinate clause. Luke uses the genitive absolute as follows:

a) in the infancy narrative: 2:2,42
b) in redacting Marcan or "Q" passages: 3:21; 4:2,40,42; 6:48; 7:6,(24); 8:4,23,45; 9:34,42,43b; 18:40b; 19:11,33,36,37; 20:1, 45; 21:5,26; 22:10,53,55,59; 23:45; 24:5
c) in phrases derived from Mark: 8:49; 9:37
d) in "L" passages 14:29,32; 15:14,20; 17:12; 21:28; 24:36,41
e) in his own composition: 3:1.

3) He frequently substitutes *de* or *te* for *kai* (see E. Schweizer, "Eine hebraisierende Sonderquelle," 166 n. 18).

4) He introduces the balancing *men . . . de* of literary Greek: e.g. 3:16,18-19; 10:2; 11:48; 13:9; 23:33,41; 23:56b - 24:1a. However, Luke omits it in 20:12 (dropping, in fact, the whole phrase), whereas Mark 12:5 has it; in Luke 22:22, in redacting Mark 14:21, he retains *men* and substitutes *plēn* for *de*. The Marcan use of it in 14:38 falls along with Luke's radical curtailment of the episode; see Luke 22:46.

5) He often eliminates a superfluous personal pronoun, especially when used as the indirect object in many Marcan passages (see N. Turner, *The Style,* 58).

6) He introduces the attraction of the relative pronoun to the case of its antecedent. Mark uses it only once (7:13), but Luke often employs it: e.g. 1:20,72-73; 5:9; 9:36; 12:48; 20:17; Acts 1:22; 10:36; 13:2,38; 24:21.

7) He often introduces the optative mood, which is otherwise only rarely used in the Gospels. Thus:

a) in wishes: 1:38; 20:16; Acts 8:20
b) in indirect discourse: 22:23; Acts 17:11,27; 27:12,39; 25:16,20
c) in indirect questions: 1:29, 3:15; 8:9; 18:36; Acts 5:24; 10:17
d) in conditions: Acts 24:19; 20:16
e) in potential expressions (with *an*): 1:62; 6:11; 9:46; Acts 8:31; 17:18; 24:19; 26:29.

8) He makes use of the acc. neut. def. art. to introduce indirect questions: 1:62; 9:46; 19:48; 22:2,4,23,24; Acts 4:21; 22:30.

9) He frequently uses the gen. of the def. art. with an infinitive (and usually without a preposition) to express purpose, result, or explanation. Thus, e.g. 1:9,57,77,79; 2:6,21,24; 10:19; 22:6,31; 24:16,25; Acts 7:19; 26:18; 27:20. For the Attic and Koine use of this infinitive, see BDF § 398.

2. *Luke's Stylistic Range.* Luke's Gospel is the only one that opens with an excellently composed periodic sentence (1:1-4). This studied, conventional prologue is related to similar passages in contemporary or near-contemporary Greek literature. In the NT only Heb 1:1-4 comes close to it in stylistic excellence. Luke 3:1-2 is similar to the Lucan prologue, but not as well constructed; and the counterpart of the prologue in Acts 1:1-2 is even less successful. Yet all three of these passages reveal a type of writing not found elsewhere in Luke-Acts and stand out by their stylistic formality.

It has, indeed, become commonplace in discussions of Luke's style to distinguish three kinds of Greek in which he wrote: (a) the literary style of the prologue(s); (b) the Semitic-flavored Greek of the infancy narrative; and (c) the normal style in which he wrote the bulk of the Gospel and Acts. (In the latter work Luke seems at times to be composing more freely, but it is not easy to be sure about this because of our uncertainty about the sources that he may have used. The style in Acts is not uniform either, but that is not our concern here.) In any case, as E. Norden (*Antike Kunstprosa* 2. 483) once pointed out, though the prologue shows that Luke could have written the Jesus-story in cultivated, literary Greek, he chose for some reason not to do so. It will undoubtedly remain a mystery why he did not. Norden thought that it would have been "a monstrosity" (*ein Unding*) to have composed a gospel in artistic Greek (*Kunstsprache*), but why he thought so is not clear.

3. *Luke's Characteristic Vocabulary and Its Sources.* According to R. Morgenthaler (*Statistik,* 27), the Lucan vocabulary in the Gospel is numbered at 2,055 words, of which 971 are *hapax legomena* and 352 are *dis legomena.* (In Acts there are 2,038 words, 943 *hapax legomena,* and 335 *dis legomena.*) Of the 2,055 words, 47 of them occur more than fifty times over in the Gospel. The total wordage in the Gospel is 19,404 (ibid. 166). Together with the 18,374 words of Acts, the Lucan writings are the largest single body of material in the NT.

J. C. Hawkins's lists of the words and phrases characteristic of the various Synoptic writers mentions 95 that were distinctive of Matthew, 41 of Mark, but 151 of Luke. By "characteristic of Luke" Hawkins meant words and phrases which occur at least four times in this Gospel and which are either not found at all in Matthew or Mark or are found in Luke at least twice as often as in Matthew and Mark together (*Horae synopticae,* 15). Since such characteristic words, phrases, and constructions are important in studying the Lucan redaction of source material, they are listed here to give the reader some idea of the sort of vocabulary that reveals the Lucan hand. However, the details will be left to

Hawkins's tables (pp. 16-23). The number in parentheses below indicates the number of occurrences in the Lucan Gospel.

agathopoiein (do good, 4)
adikia (wrong, injustice, 4)
adikos (dishonest, 4)
athetein (reject, 5)
an + the optative (4)
anastas (aor. ptc. of anistanai, rising, 16)
anēr (man, 27)
anthrōpe (human being, vocative, 4)
apo tou nyn (from now on, 5)
apolambanein (receive, get, 4)
apostolos (apostle, 6)
archontes (leaders [of Jews], 4)
autos ho (. . . self, 11)
aphairein (take away, 4)
aphistanai (leave, 4)
achri (until, 4)
ballantion (purse, 4)
bios (life, 4)
brephos (child, 5)
ge (indeed, 8)
gegonos (having happened, 4)
ginesthai + epi + acc. (come upon, 6)
goneis (parents, 6)
deisthai (beg, 8)
deka (ten, 10)
de kai (and further, 25)
dialogismos (thought[s], 6)
dianoigein (open, 4)
diatassein (authorize, 4)
dierchesthai (go through, 30)
dikaioun (justify, 5)
doxazein ton theon (praise God, 8)
egeneto + kai (11)
egeneto + finite verb (22)
egeneto + infin. (5)
ei de mēge (if not, 5)
eiē (optative of verb einai, to be, 7)
einai + dat. (have, 15)
einai + prep. + art. (7)

eipen parabolēn (he told a parable, 7)
eipen de (but he said, 59)
eirēnē (peace, 13 [14])
eispherein (bring in, 4)
elachiston (very little thing, 4)
elegen de (but he said, 9)
eleos (mercy, 6)
en mia tōn (in one of . . . , 5)
en tais hemērais tautais (in those days, 4)
en tō + infin. (while X was . . . , 32)
enōpion (before, 22)
exapostellein (send out, 4)
exerchesthai apo (come out of, 13)
epairein (raise, lift up, 6)
epididonai (to hand, 5)
epithymein (desire, 4)
epilambanesthai (take, 5)
epistatēs (teacher, master, 7)
erōtan (ask, 15)
heteros (other, 33)
etos (year, 15)
euangelizesthai (preach, 10)
euphrainein (be merry, 6)
ephistanai (stand by, 7)
echein + infin. (have . . . to . . . , 5)
thaumazein epi (wonder at, 4)
thērapeuein apo (cure of, 4[?])
thyein (sacrifice, 4)
iasthai (heal, 11)
idou gar (look! 5)
Hierousalēm (Jerusalem, 27)
kath' hēmeran (day by day, 5)
kai in the apodosis (4)
kai autos (and he, 41)
kai houtos (and that one, 8)
kaloumenos (named, called, 11)
kataklinein (recline, 5)
katanoein (see clearly, 4)

keisthai (lie down, 6)

klaiein (cry, weep, 11)

klinein (lean, 4)

koilia (womb, 7)

kritēs (judge, 6)

krouein (knock, 4)

Kyrios (Lord, used of Jesus in narratives, 13)

laos (people, 36)

legein parabolēn (tell a parable, 6)

limnē (lake, 5)

limos (famine, 4)

logos tou theou (word of God, 4)

lychnos (lamp, 6)

meta tauta (after this, 5)

mēn (month, 5)

mimnēskesthai (remember, 6)

mna (mina, pound, 7)

nomikos (lawyer, 6)

nyn (now, 14)

oikonomos (manager, 4)

oikos (household, family, 7[?])

homoiōs (likewise, similarly, 11)

onoma ([whose] name [was], 7)

onomati (by name, 7)

hos (relative pronoun, attracted, 11)

ouchi, alla (no, but . . . , 5)

para (=beyond, 4)

para tous podas (at the feet . . . , 4)

paraginesthai (be present, 8)

parachrēma (instantly, immediately, 10)

parechein (offer, present, 4)

(ha)pas ho laos (all the people, 10)

peirasmos (temptation, 6)

pempein (send, 10)

pimplanai (fill, 13)

plēthos (throng, assembly, 8)

plēn (except, but, 15)

plousios (rich, 11)

prassein (do, 6)

pros (to [with verb of speaking], 99)

prosdechesthai (await, expect, 5)

prosdokan (wait for, 6)

prostithenai (add, 7)

prosphōnein (speak to, address, 4)

rēma (word, thing, 19)

strapheis (having turned, 7)

syllambanein (conceive, catch, 7)

syn (with, 23)

synechein (grip, press close, 6)

syngenēs + cognates (relative, kin, 5)

synkalein (call together, 4)

sōtēria (salvation, 4)

te (and, 9)

tís + optative (Who? 7)

tís ex hymōn (Who of you . . . ? 5)

tis + a noun (a certain, 38)

to tís, to tí (what? 5)

to, ta (article before prepositions, 8)

tou + infinitive (20)

touton (him, 7)

hyparchein (be present, exist, 15)

hypostrephein (return, 21)

hypsistos (highest, most high, 7)

hypsoun (lift up, elevate, 6)

phatnē (manger, 4)

philos (friend, 15)

phobeisthai (fear [used in reference to God], 6)

phylassein (guard, 6)

phōnē (with ginesthai, a message arriving, 4)

chairein (rejoice, 11)

charis (favor, 8)

chēra (widow, 9)

hōs (when, 19)

hōsei (as, as if, 9)

To the foregoing list of Lucan characteristic words and phrases three further sorts of material were singled out by Hawkins:

1) Words and phrases that do occur at least four times in Luke but not twice as often as in Matthew and Mark, but are found in Luke-Acts together four times as frequently as in Matthew and Mark:

hagios (holy, 73)   *hikanos* (several, 27)
agein (lead, bring, 39)   *hou* (where [relative], 14)

2) Words and phrases that occur in Luke only two or three times, in Luke-Acts at least six times, but that never occur in Mark or (in six instances) only once in Matthew:

ainein (praise, 6)
anagein (lead, bring up; put out to sea, 20)
anairein (take away, do away with, 21)
apodechesthai (welcome, recognize, 7)
apologeisthai (defend oneself, 9)
atenizein (stare at, 12)
boulē (council, plan, 9)
gnōstos (known, acquaintance, 12)
dioti (because, 8)
ean (allow, permit, 9)
ethos (habit, custom, 10)
eisagein (bring into, 9)
eperchesthai (come upon, 7)
hēmera with *ginesthai* (become day, 9)
katerchesthai (come down, 14)

latreuein (worship, 8)
oikoumenē (inhabited world, 8)
paraklēsis (consolation, 6)
pauesthai (cease, 9)
peritemnein (circumcise, 7)
kata polin, kata poleis (throughout the city, cities, 6)
pynthanesthai (inquire, seek to learn, 9)
sigan (become silent, 6)
statheis (having stationed oneself, 9)
stratēgos (captain, 10)
symballein (ponder, plan, plot, 6)
charizesthai (give freely, grant, 7)
chronoi (times, 6)

3) Other words or phrases "more or less characteristic" of Luke:

akouein with *ton logon* (hear the word)
alēthōs (truly)
hamartōlos (sinner)
anth' hōn (used as a conjunction, because)
dei (it is necessary)
dia to + infin. (because . . .)
engizein (draw near [especially in narratives])
hexēs (next, in the next place)

eulogein (bless)
ēn/ēsan + ptc. (progressive impf.)
kathexēs (in order)
kathōs (as)
kai gar (for)
katechein (hold up, hold back)
legō hymin (I say to you)
metanoia (repentance)
monogenēs (unique, only)

odynasthai (suffer pain)	*speudein* (hasten)
prosechete heautois (look to yourselves)	*synchairein* (rejoice with)
	phobos (fear)

A detailed study of Lucan vocabulary from *alpha* to *epsilon* by H. J. Cadbury (*Style and Literary Method,* 4-39) compared it with that of Attic Greek prose writers, classical poets, and later (Atticist) writers. He gives a concrete, though not complete, demonstration of the studied elegance of Luke's vocabulary. While the Greek of NT writers in general varies considerably from that of writers in the classical period, Luke's writings come closest and are more elegant in diction than most of the others.

It is also true, however, that 90 per cent of his vocabulary is found in the LXX, where it resembles most the vocabulary of Judges, Samuel, Kings, and above all 2 Maccabees.

(On the alleged medical language of the Lucan Gospel, see pp. 51-53 above.)

Yet for all its good Greek, Lucan style has always been noted for a significant amount of Semitisms. This observation refers not only to Luke's retention of the so-called Jewish Greek of his sources or to his use of typically Christian Greek words (explicable only from their OT or Jewish background), but even more to the interference of Septuagintisms or of Hebrew and Aramaic lexical or syntactic expressions in his otherwise good Greek style. The Jewish Greek vocabulary includes such words as *angelos* ("angel," e.g. Luke 1:1), *azyma* ("unleavened bread," Luke 22:1,7, derived from Mark 14:1,12); *amēn* ("amen," 4:24; 12:37; 18:17,29; 21:32; 23:43—six instances, of which the first, second, and sixth are introduced by Luke himself); *aperitmētos* ("uncircumcised," Acts 7:51); *batos* ("jug," lit. "measure" [=Hebrew *bat*], Luke 16:6); *Beelzeboul* ("Beelzebul," 11:15); *geenna* ("Gehenna," 12:5); *grammateus* ("scribe," 5:21); *diabolos* ("devil," 4:2-6); *ethnē* ("Gentiles," 18:32); *eirēnē* ("peace," in OT sense, 24:36); *ephēmeria* ("division," of priests, 1:5); *koros* ("bushel" [=Hebrew *kōr,* "dry measure"], Luke 16:7); possibly *kyrios* ("Lord," for God, 20:37); *mamōnas* ("wealth," 16:13); *pascha* ("passover lamb," 22:7); *sabbata* ("Sabbath," 4:31); *sikera* ("beer" [=Hebrew *šēkār,* Aramaic *šikrā'*]). A number of these words have been ascribed to Luke's "Christian style" by Turner ("The Style of Luke-Acts," 62). However, it seems better to separate the foregoing from another group of words, which are Christian, indeed, but are to be explained in terms of an OT or Jewish cultural background. Such would be *Christos* ("Christ" [=Hebrew *Māšîaḥ,* "Messiah"]); *christianos* ("Christian," Acts 11:26; 26:28); *euangelion* ("gospel," Acts 15:7; 20:24—but see p. 148 below); *apostolos* ("apostle," Luke 6:13;

9:10, etc. from *apostellein,* as are Hebrew *šālûaḥ* or Aramaic *šĕlîaḥ* from *šlḥ,* "send"]); possibly *Kyrios* ("Lord," Luke 20:37).

It is not easy to determine the source of the Semitic lexical and syntactic interference in Lucan Greek. Is it owing to Luke's imitation of Septuagint style and vocabulary or to some direct interference of Hebrew or Aramaic in the Greek language that he used? I shall list and discuss below the Aramaisms and Hebraisms that have been said to occur in his Greek. Having studied these in some detail, I am convinced that Luke's dependence on the Greek OT—specifically the so-called LXX—is such that the Semitisms of Lucan Greek which are found in the LXX should be frankly labeled as "Septuagintisms," and only those that are not should be sorted out as true Aramaisms or Hebraisms.

4. *Septuagintisms in Lucan Greek.* We shall begin with a list of Lucan expressions which are clearly of Septuagintal origin, or at least under Septuagintal influence, because of their frequency. (References to the Psalter make use of the Hebrew numbering of the psalms.)

anastas(*a*), "rising up," used inchoatively (e.g. Luke 1:39; 6:8; 15:20); this use has often been related to Hebrew *qwm wĕ-* or Aramaic *qwm* (joined asyndetically to another verb, 1QapGen 21:13); it is found abundantly in the LXX (e.g. Gen 19:15; 22:3).

apokritheis eipen, lit. "answering, he said" (e.g. Luke 1:19; 5:5; 7:22); often related to Hebrew *wayyaʿan . . . wayyōʾmer;* it is found often in the LXX, sometimes simply for *wayyōʾmer* (e.g. Gen 18:9).

doxazein ton theon, "to glorify God" (e.g. Luke 2:20; 5:25-26; 7:16; 13:13); see the LXX of Exod 15:2; Judg 9:9 (ms. B); Isa 25:1; 42:10; Dan 3:51.

ek koilias mētros, "from (his) mother's womb" (Luke 1:15); see LXX Judg 16:17 (ms. A); Job 1:21; Ps 71:6.

epairein tous ophthalmous, "to lift the eyes" (Luke 6:20; 16:23; 18:13); see LXX Gen 13:10; 2 Sam 18:24; 1 Chr 21:16.

epithymia epethymēsa, "I have intensely desired" (Luke 22:15); often related to the use of the Hebrew infin. absol. as an intensifier or a cognate object of a finite verb; see LXX Gen 31:30 for this phrase; cf. Ezek 26:16; Gen 2:17; also 21:12 (use of an abstract noun in the dative as an intensifier); see *phobeisthai* below.

enōpion, "before, in the sight of" (Luke 1:15; 4:7; 15:18,21); among the Synoptics, it is found only in Luke (twenty-two times, + thirteen instances in Acts); often related to Hebrew *lipnê* or Aramaic *qwdm;* found a few times in extrabiblical Greek papyrus (usually legal) texts, it is abundantly used in the LXX (e.g. Gen 11:28; Exod 3:6; Deut 1:8).

kata prosōpon + gen., "before the face of, in the sight of" (Luke 2:31); see LXX Gen 23:17; 25:18; Exod 26:9; Lev 8:9; Deut 7:24, etc. See *pro prosōpou* below.

legōn, "saying" (e.g. Luke 3:16; 8:8; 12:17), often related to the Hebrew redundant infin., *lē'mōr;* abundantly used in the LXX (e.g. Gen 1:22,28; 4:25 [feminine]; Exod 1:22; Num 1:1).

ho theos, "O God" (nom. with art. = vocative, Luke 18:11); often related to the Aramaic use of emphatic state (definite) and Hebrew use of noun with the definite article for the vocative; but see LXX (e.g. Ps 44:1; 48:10; 51:1; 54:1,3).

poiein eleos meta, "to show mercy to," lit. "to do mercy with" (Luke 1:72; 10:37); see LXX Gen 24:12; cf. Judg 21:22; Jer 9:23; Dan 3:42.

poreuein eis eirēnēn, "to go in peace" (Luke 7:50; 8:48); see LXX Judg 18:6; 1 Sam 1:17; 20:42; 29:7; Jdt 8:35.

poreutheis + finite verb, "he went and . . ." (Luke 7:22; 9:12,52; 13:32; 22:8); abundantly used in the LXX (e.g. Gen 27:13,14; 37:14; 45:28).

pro prosōpou + gen., "before the face of, before" (Luke 1:76 [in some mss.]; 7:27; 9:52; 10:1); see LXX Exod 23:20; 33:2; Lev 18:24; Num 14:42; 27:17; 2 Kgs 6:32.

prosōpon lambanein, "to show partiality" (Luke 20:21); often related to Hebrew *nāśā' pānîm,* "to lift up the face" (of someone); frequently translated in the LXX (e.g. Lev 19:15; Ps 82:2; Lam 4:16; Sir 4:22,27); among the evangelists, only Luke uses the LXX expression.

prostheis + finite verb, lit. "having added, he did something," i.e. "he did again" (Luke 19:11); this asyndetic usage is found in the LXX (e.g. Job 27:1; 29:1; 36:1; Esth 8:3).

prostithenai + infin., lit. "he added to (do something)," i.e. "he did further" (Luke 20:11,12—similar to the foregoing expression); see LXX Gen 4:2,12; 8:12,21, etc.

rēma, "thing, matter" (Luke 1:37,65; 2:15,19,51; Acts 5:32; 13:42); actually the word means "word," but it occurs in the LXX with the sense of Hebrew *dābār,* "word, thing" or Aramaic *pitgām;* see LXX Gen 30:31; 34:19; 1 Sam 4:16; 1 Kgs 1:27.

stomati machairas piptein, "to fall by the edge [lit. mouth] of the sword" (Luke 21:24); see LXX Sir 28:18; parts of the phrase can also be found in LXX Gen 34:26; 2 Sam 15:14; Josh 19:48 (*stoma machairas*); Isa 3:25; 10:34; 13:15 (*machairā piptein*).

tithenai en tē kardia sou, "to place in your heart" (Luke 1:66; 21:14); see LXX 1 Sam 21:13; 29:10; Ps 13:2.

huios (figuratively used), "son of . . ." (Luke 5:34; 10:6; 16:8;

20:34,36); see LXX Deut 32:43; Gen 6:2; 1 Sam 14:52; 26:16; 2 Kgs 14:14; Ps 29:1; Wisd 2:18.

phobeisthai phobon megan, "to fear greatly," lit. "fear (with) a great fear" (Luke 2:9); often related to Hebrew infin. absol. as intensifier of a finite verb (see *epithymia* above). Instead of the more frequent dative, the cognate accusative with a modifier is used; see LXX Ps 53:5; Jonah 1:10; 1 Macc 10:8; cf. Jonah 1:16; Ezek 27:28.

pros + acc. after a verb of speaking, "said to . . ." (Luke 1:13; 4:36; 5:22; 7:24,40; 15:3,22; 22:15,70; 23:4; 24:18,44, and abundantly elsewhere, as well as in Acts). Rare in the other Synoptics, the usage cuts through all levels of Lucan writings. It does occur occasionally in classical and Hellenistic Greek, often for emphasis or in poetry; but these sources cannot explain Luke's frequent use of this construction. It has often been related to Hebrew *lĕ-* or *'el* and Aramaic *lĕ-* or *'al* and called "a Semitism" (see Turner, "Style of Luke-Acts," 54). It is a Septuagintism, however, since it occurs abundantly in that OT translation (e.g. Gen 19:5; Exod 7:1,8; Lev 12:1; Num 1:1; Deut 2:17; Judg 9:1; 1 Sam 11:14; 2 Chr 10:14; Ezek 37:11; Dan 3:36; Bel 34).

Attention will be called in the commentary itself to further examples of Septuagintal expressions that Luke uses only on isolated occasions.

The foregoing list scarcely exhausts the Lucan Septuagintisms, but the most frequent of them are found there; others will appear below in the discussion of Aramaisms or Hebraisms. It should be noted that in some instances these expressions have been found in one or other of the Synoptics (in parallels); Luke retained them in such cases, because of his fondness for Septuagintisms. Further, it should be noted that in many instances these expressions cut across his various blocks of writing (infancy narrative, "Q" material, "L" material, and Lucan redaction and composition). Attempts to treat them as proper to only one or two levels do not succeed.

5. *Supposed Aramaisms, Hebraisms, and Semitisms.* There are Semitisms which have been regarded as direct interference from Aramaic or Hebrew in the Greek that Luke writes; it is not easy to be sure about these. The less controversial group includes the Aramaisms. They are not numerous and can be categorized; in my opinion, the source of such interference could be Luke's origin in Syrian Antioch, where he lived as an *incola,* speaking the Aramaic dialect of the indigenous natives of that country, though he was also educated in the good Hellenistic culture of that town. A Palestinian background of some material cannot be ruled out.

Aramaic interference in the Greek of the Lucan Gospel can be seen in the following items.

1) Parallels between Luke 1:32-35 and the Aramaic text of 4Q246 (the so-called "Son of God" text):

He will be great (Luke 1:32)	(He) will be great upon the earth (1:7)
will be hailed as the Son of the Most High (1:32)	they will call him Son of the Most High (2:1)
he will be king . . . forever (1:33)	his kingdom will be an eternal kingdom (2:5)
will come upon you (1:35)	settled [up]on him (1:1)
will be called the Son of God (1:35)	he will be hailed the Son of God (2:1)

See further *NTS* 20 (1973-1974) 391-394; J. T. Milik, *The Books of Enoch* (Oxford: Clarendon, 1976) 60; *WA*, 90-94.

2) Parallels between Lucan expressions and Qumran Aramaic phrases:

the book of the words of Isaiah (Luke 3:4)	the [book] of the words of Enoch (1QapGen 19:25)
in truth (=I can assure you, 4:25)	in truth (1QapGen 2:5)
Lord of heaven and earth (10:21)	Lord of heaven and earth (1QapGen 22:16)
a spirit of sickness (13:11)	a spirit of purulence, spirit of pestilence (1QapGen 20:26,16)
he began to speak (pleonastic, 4:21); but Turner ("The Style of Luke-Acts" 46) questions this	I . . . began to cultivate the earth (1QapGen 12:13)

3) Lexical items betraying Aramaic influence:

heurōsin (in the sense, "be able," Luke 6:7); root *heuriskein*, "find"	which no one can [*yiškaḥ*] number (1QapGen 21:13); root *škḥ*, "find"
ōphthē (in the sense, "he appeared," 24:34); lit. "he was seen" + dative	God appeared [*'ithăzī*] to Abram (1QapGen 22:27); lit. "was seen" + dative
opheiletai (in the sense, "guilty, sinners," 13:4); lit. "debtors"	will you find me guilty [*tehayyĕbinnánī*] (11QtgJob 34:4); lit. "consider me a debtor"
apo mias ("at once," 14:18) [possibly]	*min hădā'* ("at once," known in Syriac)

4) Alleged Aramaisms:

(*en*) *autē tē hōra*, "at that hour" (the proleptic use of the pronoun, Luke 2:38; 10:21; 12:12; 13:31; 20:19; 24:33; cf. 10:7)	"at that hour," lit. "in it, the hour" (Dan 3:6,15, *bah ša'ătā'*; cf. *hŭ' ṣalmā'*, "that statue," Dan 2:32)

But the exact phrase that Luke uses is found in the LXX itself of Dan 5:5 (cf. 3:6, Theodotion and *app. crit.*). Hence it should rather be regarded as a Septuagintism in the Lucan Gospel. The proleptic use of the pronoun is extended in Luke 10:7 to another expression (cf. M. Black, *AAGA*[3], 98). Similarly,

en autē tē hēmera, "that very day" (Luke 23:12; 24:13)	"that very day," Dan 4:37b (LXX); [missing in MT]
en autō tō kairō, "at that time" (Luke 13:1)	"at that time," *en autō tō kairō*, Tob 3:11, 16 [ms. S]

Here the evidence is a little more problematic; the LXX expressions come from translations of books written in Aramaic. It is probably better, however, to regard these as examples of Septuagintisms, as long as one cannot show the direct influence of the Aramaic. The same should also be said about such examples of proleptic *autos* as Luke 20:42 (*autos gar Dauid*).

A genuinely problematic feature in Luke's Greek, however, is the use of so-called Hebraisms. There is no evidence that Luke knew any Hebrew; hence the source of them is puzzling. We shall list the features which are generally so designated and comment on them.

1) The *kai egeneto/egeneto de* construction, followed by a temporal clause, meaning, "and it happened, while . . . , that . . ." According to F. Neirynck ("La matière marcienne," 187), it was A. Plummer (*Gospel*, 45) who first correctly distinguished three forms of the Lucan use of this construction:

a) *egeneto de* + infin. (with subject acc.): E.g. *egeneto de en tō baptisthēnai hapanta ton laon . . . aneōchthēnai ton ouranon*, lit. "and it happened, when all the people had been baptized . . . , (that) the heavens opened" (Luke 3:21). Similarly, Luke 6:1,6,12; 16:22 (in all, five times); this form is also used in Acts 4:5; 9:3,32,37,43; (10:25); 11:26; 14:1; 16:16; 19:1; 21:1,5; 22:6,17; 27:44; 28:8,17 (in all, seventeen times). In the other Synoptics it is found only at Mark 2:23 (cf. 2:15 [cf. 1 Sam 14:1]); this Marcan passage is scarcely the source of Luke's frequent use of it, especially in Acts. It is rather a Greek extension of the more Hebraic form of the Septuagintisms found in b and c (below); so M. Johannessohn ("Das biblische *kai egeneto*," 211). It is also found on rare occasions in Greek papyri from Egypt; see E. Mayser, *Grammatik* 2/1 (1926) 307 § 50B. It should be regarded as influenced by the more common Greek expression *synebē*, "it happened that" (followed by an accusative and infinitive); Luke even uses this in Acts 21:35: *synebē bastazesthai auton hypo tōn stratiōtōn*, "he happened to be carried along by the soldiers." This use of *synebē* is well known in classical and Hellenistic Greek.

b) *kai egeneto* (*egeneto de*) + a finite verb (indic.) without an intervening conjunction: E.g. *egeneto de en tō hierateuein auton . . . , elache tou thymiasai,* lit. "and it happened, when he was serving as priest . . . , (that) it fell to his lot to burn incense . . ." (Luke 1:8). Similarly, Luke 1:23,41,59; 2:1,6,15,46; 7:11; 9:18,(29 [the verb "to be" is omitted]), 33,37; 11:1,14,27; 17:14; 18:35; 19:29; 20:1; 24:30,51 (in all, twenty-two times). Luke never seems to use this form in Acts (10:25 is problematic because of the initial *hōs*). Though it is found twice in Mark (1:9; 4:4), this is scarcely the source of Luke's use of it, since in those instances he changes what he borrows from the Marcan source (3:21) or omits it (8:5). Rather, it is to be recognized as a Septuagintism, since this asyndetic form is used in that translation of the OT for Hebrew *wayyĕhî . . . wĕ-,* "and it happened . . . that," especially when accompanied by the temporal clause, *en tō* + infinitive (=Hebrew *bĕ-* + infinitive). See the LXX of Gen 14:1-2; 40:1; Exod 12:41; 2 Kgs 5:7; 6:30. Cf. K. Beyer, *Semitische Syntax,* 54, n. 5; M. Johannessohn, "Das biblische *kai egeneto,*" 189-190. (This form is also found in Matthew, significantly in the verses which follow the conclusions of the five big discourses: 7:28; 11:1; 13:53; 19:1; 26:1.)

c) *kai egeneto* (*egeneto de*) + *kai* + finite verb (indic.): E.g. *egeneto de en tō ton ochlon epikeisthai autō . . . , kai autos ēn hestōs . . . kai eiden,* lit. "and it happened, while the crowd was pressing about him . . . and he was standing . . . , that he saw . . ." (Luke 5:1). Similarly, Luke 5:12,17; 8:1,22; 9:28,51; 14:1; 17:11; 19:15; 24:4,15 (in all, twelve times). It is also found in Acts 5:7; 9:19; it is absent from Mark. It is, moreover, the form that represents most closely the Hebrew construction of *wayyĕhî . . . wĕ-.* It is found in the LXX (e.g. 1 Sam 24:17; Gen 4:8; 2 Kgs 19:1; 22:11), and Luke's use of it is again to be understood as a Septuagintism.

The reader should note the frequency of this *kai egeneto*/*egeneto de* construction in Lucan Greek. It occurs so often as to be monotonous. In my translation of the Lucan Gospel I have constantly rendered the various forms of this construction with the English verb "happen." This means that my translation of Lucan Greek acquires some of the monotony of the original. Other translations have changed the phrasing; but I have judged that fidelity to Luke's Greek style demands the retention of some sign of this monotony. That is the way Luke has written his story of Jesus.

2) The dative of the articular infinitive with *en,* especially in a temporal sense: E.g. *en tō hierateuein auton,* "when he was serving as a priest . . ." (Luke 1:8 [see 1b above]). Similarly (with the present infinitive), Luke 1:21; 2:6,43; 5:1,12; 8:5,42; 9:18,29,33,51; 10:35,38; 11:1,27; 12:15; 17:11,14; 18:35; 24:4,15,51; (with the aorist infinitive) 2:27; 3:21; 8:40; 9:34,36; 11:37; 14:1; 19:15; 24:30; (in all, thirty-two

times). The construction is also used in Acts 2:1; 3:26; 4:30; 8:6; 9:3; 11:15; 19:1. This type of temporal clause is often, but not always, used with the three forms of the *kai egeneto* construction. It occurs too in Mark (4:4; 6:48). One may question whether it always occurs in the temporal sense (see Luke 1:21); but it does in the vast majority of the Lucan examples, and since this is not common in extra-Lucan Greek, it has been judged to be a Hebraism (see BDF § 404). The prep. *bě-* + infinitive (often in a construct chain or with a suffix) is well attested in Hebrew (see Gen 2:4; cf. GKC § 114q). Less frequent is its temporal use in Aramaic, but it is not unattested (see 11QtgJob 30:2 [=Hebrew 38:4; LXX, *en tō themelioun me tēn gēn,* "when I laid the foundations of the earth"]; 30:6 [=Hebrew 38:8]). Yet whether the Greek construction is Hebraic or Aramaic in background, it is more important that the equivalent is found abundantly in the LXX (e.g. Gen 4:8; 19:29; 28:6; 1 Sam 2:19; 2 Kgs 2:9; Mal 1:7). See Johannessohn, "Das biblische *kai egeneto,*" 174-175. Hence Luke's use of it is to be judged a Septuagintism (cf. M. Zerwick, *Biblical Greek,* § 387).

3) Unstressed *kai autos:* E.g. *kai autos proeleusetai enōpion autou,* "And he will go before him . . ." (Luke 1:17). Similarly, Luke 1:22; 2:28; 4:15; 5:1,14,17,37; 6:20; 8:1,(22),(41); 9:51; (10:38); 15:14; 16:24; 17:11,16; 19:2*bis*,9; (20:42); 22:41; 24:25,28,31 (in all, twenty-two times [or possibly twenty-six times—see *app. crit.* on the references in parentheses]). From these instances one has to distinguish the intensive use of *kai autos* (Luke 24:15 [see *app. crit.*]; possibly 3:23; but in Acts always, 8:13; 21:24; 24:16; 25:22). W. Michaelis described too broad a range of cases as intensive. Similar to *kai autos* are phrases with other forms of the pronoun:

* unstressed *kai autē:* Luke 2:37 (on this, see BDF § 277[3]); 7:12; 8:42; intensive, 1:36

* unstressed *kai autoi:* Luke 2:50; 9:36; 11:46; 14:1; 17:13; 18:34; 22:23; 24:14,35; intensive, 14:12.

The intensive use of this phrase does not concern us here; it is used normally by Luke as by other writers. It is rather the unstressed *kai autos/ autē/autoi* construction that has been called a Hebraism in Lucan style. It is so regarded because it stands in contrast to Luke's not infrequent use of the more literary Greek *autos de* (4:30; 5:16; 6:8; 8:37,54; 11:17,28; 18:39; 23:9), *autoi de* (6:11). This is also the preferred form in the LXX, although both forms are used to translate the Hebrew phrases, *wěhû', wěhî',* and *wěhēm;* thus *kai autos* (Gen 3:16; 42:38; 49:13,20; ·Num 22:22; 27:3; Deut 29:12, etc.); *kai autē* (Gen 20:5; 40:10; Lev 13:10,21, etc.); and *kai autoi* (Exod 28:5; 36:3; Lev 26:43; Num 1:50; 15:25, etc.). See BDF § 277(3). These examples are sufficient to show that these constructions must be numbered among Luke's Septuagintisms, even though a few examples of *kai autos* are also found in Mark ([4:38]; 6:47; 8:29; 14:15; 15:43), since, wherever Luke has parallels to these Marcan passages, he has changed the phrasing.

It has also to be noted that unstressed *kai autos* functions in a special way in the *kai egeneto* construction in some instances. There Luke uses it to continue a paratactic, epexegetical description which is at times parallel to the temporal clause; in this case it should not be mistaken for the *kai* + finite verb that really is the follow-up of the introductory *kai egeneto*. Thus, *egeneto de en tō ton ochlon epikeisthai autō kai akouein ton logon tou theou kai autos ēn hestōs para tēn limnēn Gennesaret kai eiden dyo ploiaria*, lit. "and it happened, while the crowd was pressing upon him and hearing the word of God and he was standing on the shore of Lake Gennesaret, that he saw two boats . . ." (Luke 5:1). Similarly, Luke 5:17; 8:1,22; 9:51; 14:1; 17:11. See Neirynck, "La matière marcienne," 189-193; M.-J. Lagrange, *Evangile selon Saint Luc,* 156-157. W. Michaelis ("Das unbetonte *kai autos* bei Lukas," 90) has judged these instances differently, but it is clear that he has confused the issue here, even though he has rightly criticized E. Schweizer's counting of the Lucan instances of *kai autos*.

4) Introductory *kai idou*: E.g. *kai idou syllēmpsē . . . kai texē huion*, lit. "and behold, you are going to conceive and bear a son" (Luke 1:31). Similarly, Luke 1:20,36; 2:25; 5:12,18; 7:12,37; 8:41; 9:30,38,(39); 10:25; 11:31,32,41; 13:11,30; 14:2; 19:2; 23:14,15,50; 24:4,13,49 (in all, twenty-six times). The phrase is also found in Acts (5:28; 10:30; 27:24), but there one also finds a fuller phrase, *kai nyn idou*, "and now, behold" (13:11; 20:22,25). Moreover, Luke also employs *idou gar*, lit. "for behold" (1:44,48; 2:10; 6:23; 17:21; Acts 9:11). Neither of the expressions is found in Mark, who uses *idou* alone; *kai idou* seems to have been in "Q," Luke 11:31-32 (=Matt 12:41-42), but in most cases it is part of "L" or Lucan redaction. *Kai idou* has been thought to represent the ubiquitous Hebrew *wěhinnēh* (e.g. as it does in the LXX of Gen 1:31; contrast Gen 6:12), but it could just as readily represent Aramaic *wěhā'* (1QapGen 19:[14]; 20:30; 22:27; 4QEn[e] 1 xxii 1; 4QEn[e] 4 i 16,17; 4QEn[f] 1:4). Since it is found abundantly in the LXX (e.g. Gen 1:31; 15:17; 22:13), where *idou gar* is also found, though with less frequency (e.g. 2 Sam 17:9; Jdt 5:23; 9:7; 12:12; Job 2:9b; 33:2; Ps 51:5; Isa 13:9), its use by Luke is to be regarded as a Septuagintism (see BDF § 4[2]). It should also be noted that in a few instances *kai idou* is substituted for simple *kai* which introduces the finite verb after the *kai egeneto* construction (see Luke 5:12 [verb "to be" is understood], BDF § 128[7]; 14:2; 24:4).

5) The phrase *en mia tōn . . . ,* where the numeral *heis* is used indefi-

nitely with a partitive genitive, "in one (=someone) of the . . .": E.g. *kai egeneto en tō einai auton en mia tōn poleōn kai idou anēr plērēs lepras*, lit. "and it happened, while he was in one of the towns, that, behold (=there was) a man covered with leprosy" (Luke 5:12). Similarly, Luke 5:17; 8:22; 13:10; 20:1 (in all, five times); it is not used in Acts. Schweizer ("Eine hebraisierende Sonderquelle," 163) regards it as a Hebraism because Luke otherwise changes an unstressed *heis* to *tis* or *anēr* (see 9:8 [=Mark 6:15]; 9:19 [=Mark 8:28]; 9:38 [=Mark 9:17]; 18:18 [=Mark 10:17]; 21:2 [=Mark 12:41]). This is a dubious contention. In the first place, the phrase *en mia tōn poleōn* is found word-for-word in the LXX of Deut 13:13; 1 Sam 27:5; cf. 2 Sam 17:9. Furthermore, this indefinite use of *heis* (especially with a partitive genitive) is well attested in classical and Hellenistic Greek. At most it could be regarded as a Septuagintism; yet even that is doubtful. Since the usage singled out by Schweizer is not really different from other instances of *heis* in Luke, one may question the listing of it as a Hebraism. Elsewhere Luke uses this indefinite pronoun in passages when he retains it from sources (see 12:27; 22:47), where it is probably from "L" (15:15,19,26) or from his own redaction (11:46; 17:22).

6) The periphrastic conjugation (the verb "to be" + pres. ptc.): E.g. *kai autos ēn dianeuōn autois, kai diemenen kōphos*, "for he kept beckoning to them and remained speechless" (Luke 1:22). Luke uses many instances of the verb "to be" with the perfect ptc.; this is merely the standard usage in classical and Hellenistic Greek for the pf., plupf., and fut. tenses—one can make nothing of it. One might suspect that he is merely extending this usage to other tenses, especially the impf., but one has to sort out his varied use of the impf. *ēn* with the pres. ptc. Schweizer ("Eine hebraisierende Sonderquelle," 169 n. 20g) gives thirty-four instances of the periphrastic conjugation which he classes as examples of Hebraisms. However, he has not clearly sorted out the pf. ptcs. and adjectival uses in some of the places. According to *VKGNT* (pp. 317-318) there are, indeed, thirty-three instances of pres. ptcs. used with *ēn* in the Lucan Gospel. But four of them are adjectival (2:8; 4:33; 8:32; 13:11a), and eleven of them seem to be the normal Greek usage (1:10,21; 3:23; 4:20,38; 5:29; 8:40; 9:53; 23:53 [taking *keimenos* as = pres. ptc.]; 24:13,32); eighteen others are possible candidates for consideration as influenced by Semitic usage:

* *kai ēn* + ptc.: 2:33,51; 4:31; 5:17b; 6:12; 11:14; 13:11b; 19:47; 24:53
* *kai autos ēn* + ptc.: 1:22; 5:1 (taking *hestōs* as = pres. ptc.); 5:17a; 14:1
* *ēn de/gar* + ptc.: 13:10; 15:1; 21:37; 23:8
* *autos de ēn* + ptc.: 5:16.

In each of these classes the verb either follows the conjunction or is preceded by an unstressed *autos,* with the ptc. following. The usage may be the result of Semitic interference, either of Hebrew *wayyĕhî* + ptc. (e.g. Gen 4:17; Judg 16:21; 2 Kgs 6:26), or Hebrew *wĕhû'* + ptc., or Aramaic *hwh* + ptc. (e.g. *whwyt ktš' lh,* "and it kept afflicting him," 1QapGen 20:17). But some of the constructions are also attested in the LXX. Thus *kai ēn* + ptc. (Gen 4:17; Judg 16:21; 2 Kgs 6:26; Dan 1:16; Sus 1:1; Bel 33; 2 Esdr 4:24 [=Aramaic Ezra 4:24]); *ēn gar* + ptc. (Gen 14:12). Hence the real question about these periphrastic conjugations is whether they are to be explained by Hebraic or Aramaic interference, or more immediately by Luke's imitation of Septuagintal style. The latter seems to be the preferable interpretation of the evidence, since there is nothing that establishes the direct Semitic interference.

Finally, there are several expressions in Lucan Greek that are usually called simply "Semitisms" because one cannot be sure of the interference involved, whether it has been Aramaic or Hebraic, since the feature can be found in both languages. These features are the following:

1) The use of a pleonastic personal pronoun in a relative clause: E.g. *autou* in *erchetai de ho ischyroteros mou, hou ouk eimi hikanos lysai ton himanta tōn hypodēmatōn autou,* lit. "but someone more powerful than I is coming, whose sandal-strap I am not fit to untie" (Luke 3:16). See further 3:17; 13:4; Acts 15:17. First of all, in several of these instances Luke has derived the feature from a source ("Mk," "Q," or the LXX); the question then arises, Why did he retain it? It could be explained, as it often has been, by appealing to Hebrew *'ăšer,* indeclinable, which has to have a following suffixal form of some sort to indicate the oblique case intended, e.g. *'ăšer bô nepeš ḥayyāh,* lit. "which, in it, the breath of life" (=in which [is] the breath of life, Gen 1:30), or Aramaic *dî,* e.g. *'antāh malkā' . . . dî 'ĕlāh šĕmayyā' malkûtā' . . . yĕhab lāk,* lit. "You, O king, . . . whom the God of heaven . . . has given kingship to you" (=to whom the God of heaven has given kingship, Dan 2:37). It has been noted time and again that this pleonastic pronoun is found in relative clauses in classical, Hellenistic, and modern Greek on many occasions (see BDF § 297; BDR § 297; Moulton-Howard-Turner, *A Grammar of New Testament Greek* 3. 325). The reason why Luke has retained this feature and even used it once himself (13:4 [if that were to be regarded, not as "L," but as Lucan composition]) is that the construction is found frequently in the LXX (e.g. Gen 10:14; 20:13; 28:13; 41:19; Exod 4:17; Lev 11:34; 13:52; 15:9,17,20; 16:9,32; 18:5; Deut 11:25; Josh 3:4; 22:19; Judg 18:5,6; 1 Sam 9:10; 1 Kgs 11:34; 13:10,31; 2 Kgs 19:4; Isa 1:21; Joel 3:7; Amos 9:12; Ps 39:5). Cf. *DBS* 3.1356.

2) The so-called Hebraic genitive, i.e. the use of a genitive of a noun to modify another noun, when an adjective would be more in order in

Greek. This is supposed to be influenced by the Hebrew or Aramaic construct chain. The extent to which one should consider this separately from the standard Greek adnominal genitive (see BDF § 162) or the genitive of quality (see BDF § 165) is the first problem that one has to face. The Hebraic genitive has been invoked to explain such Lucan phrases as the following: *kai epēnesen ho kyrios ton oikonomon tēs adikias,* lit. "the master approved of the manager of dishonesty" (=the dishonest manager), Luke 16:8. Similarly, Luke 4:22; 11:20,31; 16:9; [cf. 16:11]; 18:6; Acts 9:15. One could also include here some of the figurative uses of *huios,* discussed above (p. 115). This expression is considered particularly Semitic when it is anarthrous, resembling Hebrew construct chains such as *'al har qodšî Yĕrûsālayīm,* lit "on the mount of my holiness, Jerusalem" (=on my holy mountain, Jerusalem, Isa 66:20) or Aramaic *mrh rbwt',* "the Lord of majesty" (=the majestic Lord, 1QapGen 2:4). In such cases, the LXX sometimes translates the construct chain with a genitive (e.g. Dan 3:6; 1Kgs 21:31), and sometimes with an adjective (e.g. Isa 66:20, cited above, *eis tēn hagian polin;* Gen 17:8). Since it is difficult in this case to insist on the influence of the LXX, perhaps a "Semitic" genitive should be admitted. See further ZBG §§ 40-41; Turner, "The Style of Luke-Acts," 48-49.

3) The use of the positive degree of an adjective instead of a comparative or a superlative: E.g. *Mariam gar tēn agathēn merida exelexato,* "Mary has chosen the best part" (lit. the good part, Luke 10:42). Similarly, Luke 1:42; 13:2; 15:7; 18:14. The positive degree is sometimes used with prepositions (e.g. *en, para*) or the conjunction *ē,* "than" (=an ellipsis for *mallon ē*). This is considered to be "Semitic" because neither Hebrew nor Aramaic have a comparative or superlative degree of adjectives, and these degrees of modification are expressed rather by circumlocutions: the comparative by the preposition *min* (lit. "from") with the adjective (*gābōah mikkol-hā'ām,* "taller than any of the people [lit. "tall from all the people"], 1 Sam 9:2), and the superlative by the definite article (*haqqāṭān,* "the youngest" [lit. "the little (one)"], 1 Sam 17:14) or by the definite article and a prepositional phrase (*w'l kwl nšyn šwpr šprh,* "and beyond all women (was) she exceedingly beautiful," 1QapGen 20:6-7). It would thus be an easy solution to brand all Lucan use of positive adjectives as "Semitic" were it not for the fact that the comparative and superlative degrees in the Hellenistic Greek of the time were on the wane (see BDF §§ 60-61; BDR §§ 60-61).

4) The nominative/accusative absolute (or *casus pendens*): E.g. *kai idou Elisabet hē syngenis sou, kai autē syneilēphen huion,* "and now, (as for) Elizabeth your kinswoman, she has also conceived a son" (Luke 1:36). Similarly, Luke 8:15,18; 12:10; 13:4; 21:6; 23:50-52; Acts 2:22-23; 7:35; 10:36-37. This use is, in reality, anacoluthon, and it is common enough in colloquial forms of any language. Nor is it confined to

the nominative or accusative; see Luke 12:48a (*panti de hō edothē poly, poly zētēthēsetai par' autou,* lit. "to everyone to whom much has been given—much will be required of him"). Similarly, 12:48b. Why this construction has been thought to be particularly Semitic, either Hebrew or Aramaic, is puzzling. It is well attested in all phases of Greek (see ZBG § 31). And even Black (*AAGA*³, 51) had to begin his discussion of this phenomenon with the admission, that *"casus pendens* is not especially a Semitism"!

Whatever one wants to say about the alleged Semitisms in Luke's Greek, one has in the long run to reckon with a great deal of influence from the LXX.

The preceding survey of the main features of Lucan language and style has not exhausted the material. But it has covered the main points and will serve as a guide for the interpretation of Luke's text in the commentary that follows.

BIBLIOGRAPHY

General Studies

Antoniadis, S. *L'Évangile de Luc: Esquisse de grammaire et de style* (Collection de l'institut néo-hellénique de l'Université de Paris 7; Paris: Société d'édition 'Les belles lettres,' 1930).

Cadbury, H. J. "Luke—Translator or Author?" *AJT* 24 (1920) 436-455.

—— *The Style and Literary Method of Luke* (HTS 6; Cambridge, MA: Harvard University, 1920).

Díaz, J. M. "Características literarias de S. Lucas," *Cathedra* 6 (1952) 39-48.

Goodspeed, E. J. "The Vocabulary of Luke and Acts," *JBL* 31 (1912) 92-94.

Grant, F. C. "A Critique of the Style and Literary Method of Luke by Cadbury," *ATR* 2 (1919-1920) 318-323.

Morgenthaler, R. *Statistik des neutestamentlichen Wortschatzes* (Frankfurt am M./Zürich: Gotthelf, 1958).

Norden, E. *Die antike Kunstprosa von vi. Jahrhundert v. Chr. bis in die Zeit der Renaissance* (Leipzig: Teubner, 1923) 2. 480-492; 5th ed., reprinted, Darmstadt: Wissenschaftliche Buchgesellschaft, 1958.

Pernot, H. *Études sur la langue des évangiles* (Collection de l'institut néo-hellénique de l'Université de Paris 6; Paris: Société d'édition 'Les belles lettres,' 1927).

Turner, N. "The Quality of the Greek of Luke-Acts," *Studies in New Testament Language and Text: Essays in Honour of George D. Kilpatrick on the Occasion of His Sixty-fifth Birthday* (ed. J. K. Elliott; NovTSup 44; Leiden: Brill, 1976) 387-400.

—— "The Style of Luke-Acts," in *A Grammar of the Greek New Testament* (by J. H. Moulton; 4th vol. by N. Turner; Edinburgh: Clark, 1976) 45-63.

Vogel, T. *Zur Charakteristik des Lukas nach Sprache und Stil* (2d ed.; Leipzig: Dürr, 1899).

Zerwick, M., *Biblical Greek: Illustrated by Examples* (Rome: Biblical Institute, 1963).

Specific Treatments

Beyer, K. *Semitische Syntax im Neuen Testament: Band I, Satzlehre Teil 1* (SUNT 1; 2d ed.; Göttingen: Vandenhoeck und Ruprecht, 1968).

Cadbury, H. J. "Four Features of Lucan Style," in *Studies in Luke-Acts: Essays Presented in Honor of Paul Schubert* (ed. L. E. Keck and J. L. Martyn; Nashville: Abingdon, 1966) 87-102.

————"Lexical Notes on Luke-Acts, I," *JBL* 44 (1925) 214-227; "II. Recent Arguments for Medical Language," *JBL* 45 (1926) 190-209; "III. Luke's Interest in Lodging," *JBL* 45 (1926) 305-322; "IV. On Direct Quotation, with Some Uses of *hoti* and *ei,*" *JBL* 48 (1929) 412-425; "V. Luke and the Horse Doctors," *JBL* 52 (1933) 55-65; "VI. A Proper Name for Dives," *JBL* 81 (1962) 399-402; "VII. Some Lukan Expressions of Time," *JBL* 82 (1963) 272-278; "IX. Animals and Symbolism in Luke," in *Studies in New Testament and Early Christian Literature: Essays in Honor of Allen P. Wikgren* (ed. D. E. Aune; Leiden: Brill, 1972) 3-15.

————"'We' and 'I' Passages in Luke-Acts," *NTS* 3 (1956-1957) 128-132.

Connolly, R. H. "Syriacisms in St Luke," *JTS* 37 (1936) 374-385.

Davies, David P. "The Position of Adverbs in Luke," in *Studies in New Testament Language and Text* (see above), 106-121.

Graystone, G. "Reflections on Luke's Use of the Deliberative Question," in *Theological Soundings: Notre Dame Seminary Jubilee Studies 1923-1973* (ed. I. Mihalik; New Orleans: Notre Dame Seminary, 1973) 20-29.

Grobel, K. *Formgeschichte und synoptische Quellenanalyse* (FRLANT 53; Göttingen: Vandenhoeck und Ruprecht, 1937).

Hunkin, J. W. "Pleonastic *archomai* in the New Testament," *JTS* 25 (1923-1924) 390-402.

Johannessohn, M. "Das biblische *kai egeneto* und seine Geschichte," *Zeitschrift für vergleichende Sprachforschung* 53 (1925) 161-212.

Kilpatrick, G. D. "The Historic Present in the Gospels and Acts," *ZNW* 68 (1977) 258-262.

Mayser, E. *Grammatik der griechischen Papyri aus der Ptolemäerzeit mit Einschluss der gleichzeitigen Ostraka und der in Ägypten verfassten Inschriften* (2 vols. in 6 parts; Berlin: de Gruyter, 1906-1938).

Michaelis, W. "Das unbetonte *kai autos* bei Lukas," *ST* 4 (1950) 86-93.

Neirynck, F. "La matière marcienne dans l'évangile de Luc," in *L'Evangile de Luc: Problèmes littéraires et théologiques: Mémorial Lucien Cerfaux* (BETL 32; Gembloux: Duculot, 1973) 157-201.

O'Neill, J. C. "The Six Amen Sayings in Luke," *JTS* 10 (1959) 1-9.

O'Rourke, J. J. "The Construction with a Verb of Saying as an Indication of Sources in Luke," *NTS* 21 (1974-1975) 421-423.

Pasqualetti, T. "Note sulle determinazione temporali del vangelo secondo Luca," *RivB* 23 (1975) 399-412.

Ropes, J. H. "An Observation on the Style of S. Luke," *HSCP* 12 (1901) 299-305.

Schramm, T. *Der Markus-Stoff bei Lukas: Eine literarkritische und redaktionsgeschichtliche Untersuchung* (SNTSMS 14; Cambridge: University Press, 1971).

Schweizer, E. "Eine hebraisierende Sonderquelle des Lukas?" *TZ* 6 (1950) 161-185.

Sparks, H. F. D. "The Semitisms of St Luke's Gospel," *JTS* 44 (1943) 129-138.

Wootton, R. W. F. "The Implied Agent in Greek Passive Verbs in Mark, Luke and John," *BT* 19 (1968) 159-164.

V. THE TEXT OF THE LUCAN GOSPEL

As C. K. Barrett once pointed out, there is no other NT writing in which the textual problem is "so vexed" as in Luke-Acts (*Luke the Historian*, 8). He was thinking, of course, mainly of the Acts of the Apostles, where the differences between the mss. of what have been called the Hesychian or Alexandrian tradition and the Western tradition are notorious. Some of this problem affects the Lucan Gospel as well, as we shall see, but only in a minor way in comparison with Acts.

The Greek text of the Lucan Gospel on which this translation and commentary have been based is that of E. Nestle, revised by K. Aland. It is a text that is dominated by the Hesychian or Alexandrian tradition. Nestle's text has been compared continually with that of *The Greek New Testament* of the United Bible Societies, which is also dominated by the Hesychian tradition. Attention has also been paid to the *apparatus criticus* of K. Aland's *Synopsis quattuor evangeliorum*. These editions of the Lucan Gospel-text represent the best of modern NT textual criticism.

It is impossible to go into detail here about the problems that one faces in dealing with the Greek text of the Lucan Gospel, but the bare essentials have to be set forth, because certain decisions have to be made about the inclusion of certain verses in the text of Luke. The reader has a right to know why a decision is made in one direction or another, even though he/she may not understand all the intricacies in this most abstruse aspect of NT scholarship.

The text of the Lucan Gospel, as of the rest of the NT, is by and large well preserved in many ancient papyri and parchment mss. (both uncial and minuscule). In fact, their number is so great that it is almost impossible to catalogue them adequately; but attempts have been made in recent times by K. Aland (*Kurzgefasste Liste*).

Parts of Luke's Gospel-text are preserved in papyrus codices or leaves; none of these is complete. However, they are important, because some of them date from a period earlier than the parchment mss. which preserve the text in its entirety. Portions of the Lucan Gospel are found in seven papyri; four of them date from the third century, and of these two (P^{45} and P^{75}) are the most extensive and most important. A good part of the Lucan text is found in P^{75}, which is the oldest papyrus text of the Gospel. The following are the papyrus texts of Luke.

P^{75} (beginning of 3d c.)	Papyrus Bodmer	3:18-22; 3:33 - 4:2;
	XIV (Cologny	4:34-42; 4:44 - 5:10;
	near Geneva);	5:37 - 6:4; 6:10 - 7:32;

	Alexandrian text-tradition	7:35-43; 7:45 - 17:15; 17:19 - 18:18; 22:4 - 24:53	
P45 (3d c.)	Chester Beatty Papyrus (Dublin); Vienna Papyrus (Vienna, National Library); partly Alexandrian, partly Western	6:31-41; 6:45 - 7:7; 9:26-41; 9:45 - 10:1; 10:6-22; 10:26 - 11:1; 11:6-25; 11:28-46; 11:50 - 12:12; 12:18-37; 12:42 - 13:1; 13:6-24; 13:29 - 14:10; 14:17-33	
P4 (3d c.)	Paris Papyrus (Paris, Bibliothèque Nationale); Alexandrian	1:58-59; 1:62 - 2:1; 2:6-7; 3:8 - 4:2; 4:29- 32; 4:34-35; 5:3-8; 5:30 - 6:16	
P69 (3d c.)	London Papyrus; mixed text	22:41; 22:45-48; 22:58-61	
P7 (4th-6th cc.)	Kiev Papyrus (now lost); ?	4:1-2	
P3 (6th-7th cc.)	Vienna Papyrus (Vienna, Nat. Library); Alexandrian	7:36-45; 10:38-42	
P42 (7th-8th cc.)	Vienna Papyrus (Vienna, Nat. Library); Alexandrian	1:54-55; 2:29-32	

Two of these (P3, P4) are sometimes thought to have been leaves of a lectionary; hence they may never have contained the whole Gospel.

The main copies of the full text written in uncial characters on parchment are the following.

ℵ	(4th c.)	Codex Sinaiticus (London, British Museum)
A	(5th c.)	Codex Alexandrinus (London, British Museum)
B	(4th c.)	Codex Vaticanus (Vatican City, Library)
C	(5th c.)	Codex Ephraemi rescriptus (Paris, Bibliothèque Nationale)
D	(6th c.)	Codex Bezae (Cambridge, University Library)
E	(8th c.)	Name ? (Basel, University Library)
L	(8th c.)	Codex Regius Parisiensis (Paris, Bibliothèque Nationale)
P	(6th c.)	Name ? (Wolfenbüttel, Library)
R	(6th c.)	Codex Nitriensis (London, British Museum)
T	(5th c.)	Codex Borgianus (part in New York, Pierpont Morgan Library; part in Rome, Collegio Propaganda Fide)
W	(5th c.)	Codex Washingtonianus (Washington, Freer Gallery of Art)
Θ	(9th c.)	Codex Koridethi (Tiflis, Library)
Ξ	(6th c.)	Codex Zacynthius rescriptus (London, British and Foreign Bible Society)

For fuller details about other and later mss., uncial and minuscule, see
Aland, *Kurzgefasste Liste,* or the preface of Greek NT texts.

The so-called Western text of the Lucan writings is found mainly in
Codex Bezae (D); and in the Old Latin version(s), and the Curetonian
Syriac version. It is a text-tradition that is known to be old, because certain patristic writers depended on it (e.g. Tatian, Justin, Irenaeus,
Hippolytus, and Tertullian). This text-tradition is characterized by occasional omissions but more frequently by the insertion of whole clauses
and sentences, by changes of words, and by clarificatory alterations which
tend to smooth out problems in the other (Hesychian) tradition. Harmonization with other NT passages, change of introductory formulas, and
the substitution of compound verbs for simple verbs are part of this Western text-tradition. The readings of this Western tradition, being old, have
to be respected, but they are invariably a problem for the modern text-
critic, who does not know what to make of them. From time to time we
shall comment on Lucan passages in which the Western text-tradition appears. Most of its problems are found in the text of Acts.

In the Gospel, however, the most acute facet of the problem concerns
the so-called Western Non-Interpolations. This cumbersome expression
was first used by Westcott and Hort, when they published their critical
edition of the Greek NT text in 1881. They distinguished between "Western omissions" (those due only to capricious oversimplification) and
"Western non-interpolations" (those due to *incorrupt* transmission). The
latter involve material which appears in the so-called Neutral Text (the
agreement of Sinaiticus and Vaticanus), but is missing in the otherwise
full Western text-tradition. This material has been judged to be secondary
to the original text, i.e. the result of interpolations into the Neutral tradition, but which were avoided by the Western. The respect of Westcott
and Hort for Sinaiticus and Vaticanus would not allow them to speak of
interpolations into that Neutral tradition, and so they referred to such
material as Western Non-Interpolations. The material in question was
printed in their edition of 1881 within double brackets and is found in
the following verses or partial verses: Matt 27:49b; Luke 22:19b-20;
24:3b,6a,12,36b,40,51b,52a. (They also enclosed in double brackets
Luke 22:43-44 and 23:34a; but these verses constitute a problem apart.)
A further eighteen NT passages were suspected by Westcott and Hort of
being Western Non-Interpolations and were printed in single brackets.
Those of the Lucan Gospel so treated are found in the following verses:
5:39; 10:41-42a; 12:19c,21,39c; 22:62; and 24:9. Westcott and Hort
started a fad, and many NT text-critics tended to agree with them.

Merk omitted only Matt 27:49b from his edition of the Greek text; in
the eight main Lucan passages he followed the Alexandrian (or Neutral)
text-tradition and admitted the material queried by Westcott and Hort.

Nestle, however, omitted Luke 24:12,36b,40,51b,52a from his text, admitted to it two passages in double brackets (22:19b-20; 24:6a), and only one unconditionally (24:3b). The first edition of the UBS text admitted only Luke 24:9, one of the minor passages, and set only *kyriou* of 24:3b in single brackets; the single brackets were also used for six of the main passages (24:6a,12,36b,40,51b,52a); but 22:19b-20 was admitted only in double brackets. The third edition of the UBS text, however, has admitted all eight Lucan passages to the text without brackets, listing the seven in chap. 24 as D readings (i.e. with a very high degree of doubt about their superiority over what is contained in the *app. crit.*) and 22:19b-20 as a C reading (i.e. with a considerable degree of doubt). The 26th ed. of "Nestle-Aland" (1979) has likewise admitted all eight passages into its text without any brackets. This represents a notable shift away from the fad started by Westcott and Hort almost a hundred years ago.

The reasons for the new trend are the realization of the importance of the papyrus text P[75], a codex that was only published in 1961 and hence was unknown to Westcott and Hort, and an even greater awareness of the rather arbitrary decisions made by those editors. P[75] contains all the eight Lucan passages and joins the witnesses of the Alexandrian text-tradition that were always cited in favor of the inclusion of these passages. In this commentary, even though our translation has been based on the 25th edition of Nestle and Aland, these readings are considered part of the original Lucan text. We shall discuss the evidence in detail at the proper places. Here it is sufficient to mention that the studies of this material undertaken by K. Aland, C. Martini (indirectly), K. Snodgrass, J. Jeremias, and others have been decisive in this matter. What is puzzling is the grade of reading that has been assigned to these texts in the third edition of the UBS text; in my opinion, most of them merit at least a B reading (i.e. texts that have only some degree of doubt).

One last comment on the importance of P[75] in this matter is in order. The work of C. Martini and others on the affiliation of this latest-acquired, yet oldest, text of Luke has shown the value of Codex Vaticanus. In general, P[75] has enhanced the tradition represented by Sinaiticus and Vaticanus; but more importantly, the so-called Neutral text of Westcott and Hort is now seen to be not a product of a fourth-century distillation but to have been in existence ca. A.D. 200. In discussing the text-type represented by P[75]/B, J. Duplacy toys with the idea that this type existed even earlier: "The second century is not excluded" ("P[75] [*Pap. Bodmer XIV-XV*]," 128).

We must mention here another large group of mss. of the Lucan Gospel, which does not enter into the debate about the Alexandrian and Western text-traditions, because reference to its readings will be made from time to time in the course of the commentary. It goes by various names, "Syrian" text, "Byzantine" text, or the "Koine" (common) text. I shall use the last of these names. It is a text-tradition which developed in the fourth century and is largely a conflated text which was widely used in the Byzantine empire. It is found mainly in Codex Alexandrinus (for the Gospels, though not for the rest of the NT), in uncial mss. of later centuries of the first millennium, and in the bulk of minuscule mss. from the ninth century on. It was the merit of Westcott and Hort that they isolated this text-tradition, assessed its value, and showed that it was the basis for the so-called *Textus receptus,* "the received text." This was the form of Greek text used in Erasmus's first printed edition of the NT and which derived its name from the boast contained in the title of the Elzevir Greek NT (2d ed., 1633): *Textum ergo habes, nunc ab omnibus receptum: in quo nihil immutatum aut corruptum damus!* ("[Here] you have the text now received by all, in which we give nothing changed or corrupted"). Though hundreds of Gospel mss. belong to this Koine tradition, the number of readings that are preserved in it which demand attention in a commentary is minimal. Today we recognize that the Koine text-tradition is, by and large, inferior to the Alexandrian (or Neutral), represented by the papyri and the great parchment uncial mss. of the fourth-sixth centuries.

In the translation presented in this commentary textual variants will not be recorded. When variants in the various traditions are of any importance—even minor—they will be discussed in the NOTES. My translation has omitted the following contested verses or partial verses: 22:43-44; 23:17,34a. But NOTES on these verses will clarify the matter.

BIBLIOGRAPHY

Aland, K. "Die Bedeutung des P75 für den Text des Neuen Testaments: Ein Beitrag zur Frage der 'Western non-interpolations,'" in *Studien zur Überlieferung des Neuen Testaments und seines Textes* (AzNTT 2; Berlin: de Gruyter, 1967) 155-172.

———— *Kurzgefasste Liste der griechischen Handschriften des Neuen Testaments: I. Gesamtübersicht* (AzNTT 1; Berlin: de Gruyter, 1963).

———— "Neue neutestamentliche Papyri," *NTS* 3 (1956-1957) 261-286 [on P7]; "Neue neutestamentliche Papyri II," *NTS* 9 (1962-1963) 303-316 [on papyri with Lucan passages]; "Neue neutestamentliche Papyri II," *NTS* 11 (1964-1965) 1-21 [collation of P75 on Luke]; "Neue neutestamentliche Papyri II," *NTS* 12 (1965-1966) 193-210 [on P75 and Western-Non-Interpolations].

———— *Synopsis quattuor evangeliorum locis parallelis evangeliorum apocryphorum et patrum adhibitis* (Stuttgart: Würtembergische Bibelanstalt, 1964).

———— et al. *The Greek New Testament* (New York: American Bible Society, 1966; 3d ed., 1975[=UBS text]).

Birdsall, N. "Rational Eclecticism and the Oldest Manuscripts: A Comparative Study of the Bodmer and Chester Beatty Papyri of the Gospel of Luke," in *Studies in New Testament Text and Language: Essays in Honour of George D. Kilpatrick on the Occasion of His Sixty-fifth Birthday* (NovTSup 44; ed. J. K. Elliott; Leiden: Brill, 1976) 39-51.

Blass, F. W. *Evangelium secundum Lucam, sive Lucae ad Theophilum liber prior secundum formam quae videtur romanam* (Leipzig: Teubner, 1897).

Curtis, K. P. G. "Linguistic Support for Three Western Readings in Luke 24," *ExpTim* 83 (1971-1972) 344-345.

Duplacy, J. "P75 (*Pap. Bodmer XIV-XV*) et les formes les plus anciennes du texte de *Luc*," in *L'Évangile de Luc: Problèmes littéraires et théologiques: Mémorial Lucien Cerfaux* (ed. F. Neirynck; BETL 32; Gembloux: Duculot, 1973) 111-128.

Fitzmyer, J. A. "Papyrus Bodmer XIV: Some Features of Our Oldest Text of Luke," *CBQ* 24 (1962) 170-179.

Hartley, J. E. "Textual Affinities of Papyrus Bodmer XIV (P75)," *EvQ* 40 (1968) 97-102.

Huck, A. *Synopse der drei ersten Evangelien* (10th ed.; rev. H. Lietzmann; Tübingen: Mohr [Siebeck], 1950).

Jeremias, J. *The Eucharistic Words of Jesus* (Philadelphia: Fortress, 1977) 139-159 [on Luke 22:19b-20].

King, M. A. "Notes on the Bodmer Manuscript of Luke," *BSac* 122 (1965) 234-240.

Klijn, A. F. J. *A Survey of the Researches into the Western Text of the Gospels and Acts* (Utrecht: Kemink & Zoon, 1949); *A Survey of the Researches into the Western Text of the Gospels and Acts, Part Two 1949-1969* (NovTSup 21; Leiden: Brill, 1969).

Martini, C. *Il problema della recensionalità del codice B alla luce del papiro Bodmer XIV* (AnBib 26; Rome: Biblical Institute, 1966).

Menoud, P.-H, "Papyrus Bodmer XIV-XV et XVII," *RTP* 12 (1962) 107-116.

Merk, A. *Novum Testamentum graece et latine* (9th ed.; Rome: Biblical Institute, 1964).

Metzger, B. M. *A Textual Commentary on the Greek New Testament* (New York: United Bible Societies, 1971).

Nestle, E. *Novum Testamentum graece cum apparatu critico* (25th ed.; rev. E. Nestle and K. Aland; Stuttgart: Privilegierte Württembergische Bibelanstalt, 1963; 26th ed. ["Nestle-Aland"]; Stuttgart: Deutsche Bibelstiftung, 1979).

Snodgrass, K. " 'Western Non-Interpolations,' " *JBL* 91 (1972) 369-379.

Westcott, B. F., and F. J. A. Hort. *The New Testament in the Original Greek* (2 vols.; 2d ed.; Cambridge/London: Macmillan, 1890, 1896; orig. ed., 1881).

VI. THE OUTLINE OF THE LUCAN GOSPEL

1. *The General Outline.* The Lucan Gospel is easily divided into the following eight parts on which there is general agreement among commentators today.

1:1 - 4   THE PROLOGUE
    Luke's intention in recording the account of what Jesus did and taught: a reliable account addressed to Theophilus.

1:5 - 2:52   THE INFANCY NARRATIVE
    The birth and childhood of John the Baptist and of Jesus set out in parallelism.

3:1 - 4:13   THE PREPARATION FOR THE PUBLIC MINISTRY OF JESUS
    The appearance, career, and imprisonment of John the Baptist set forth as a prelude to the events which initiate the public career of Jesus.

4:14 - 9:50   THE GALILEAN MINISTRY OF JESUS
    The training ground for the disciples who were to give testimony to Jesus later on and the starting point of his great "exodus."

9:51 - 19:27   THE TRAVEL ACCOUNT, JESUS' JOURNEY TO JERUSALEM*
    The "exodus" of Jesus depicted in a specifically Lucan travel account, occupying the central portion of the Gospel (9:51 - 18:14), to which is added the Synoptic travel account (18:15 - 19:27).

19:28 - 21:38   THE MINISTRY OF JESUS IN JERUSALEM
    Jesus' regal entry into the city of destiny initiates a period of ministry in the Temple before the events of the last days of his earthly career.

22:1 - 23:56a   THE PASSION NARRATIVE
    The climax of Jesus' "exodus" in which he begins the "ascent" to the Father.

23:56b - 24:53   THE RESURRECTION NARRATIVE
    The exaltation of Jesus in which he is glorified and officially commissions his disciples as witnesses to him and his role as Savior, as he ascends to the Father.

Differences of style clearly mark off the prologue of the Gospel and the infancy narrative not only from each other, but also from the rest of the Gospel. Once chap. 3 is begun, Luke's account is evidently influenced by the Synoptic tradition to which he is tributary. Though many of the epi-

---

* The present volume, AB 28, covers Luke 1:1 - 9:62. AB 28A will complete the Gospel, 10:1 - 24:53.—Ed.

sodes follow the order of the Marcan Gospel, a notable difference is detected at 9:51 where Luke inserts his own travel account. This makes the division of his Gospel clear, and this section is quite distinctive in the Synoptic tradition; it continues until 18:14, where Luke again takes up episodes in the Marcan order. Finally, the last two parts of the Gospel are clearly demarcated by their subject-matter and correspond to the passion and resurrection narratives with which the other Gospels end. The only question, then, which one might raise about the general outline of the Lucan Gospel would be the reason for separating the preparation for the public ministry of Jesus (3:1 - 4:13) from the Galilean ministry itself (4:14 - 9:50). This division seems to be called for by the way Luke handles Jesus' visit to Nazareth (4:16-30); he has transposed this episode from its position in the Marcan source and put it at the beginning of the narratives which describe the Galilean ministry. It (together with the brief summary which precedes it, 4:14-15) seems intended as a symbolic formulation of the whole set of episodes which follow, up to 9:50. The fuller meaning of the summary and of the visit to Nazareth will be explained in the commentary; it is mentioned here only as a reason for distinguishing these parts of the outline. It would in the long run make little difference if the whole section from 3:1 to 9:50 were to be regarded as one part.

2. *The Detailed Outline.* The following detailed outline of the Gospel is intended to help the reader to see the articulation of the individual episodes of the Lucan account of Jesus' career. At times some of the subdivisions may seem arbitrary, and it is not easy to justify them. This is frankly admitted about the subdivisions of Part Three (A-H) and of Part Four (A, a-c). In the latter case the outline uses as the key to the subdivision the threefold mention of the journey that Jesus is making toward Jerusalem (9:51; 13:22; 17:11). These references call attention to the journey in the midst of episodes which at times seem rather unrelated to it. The only justification for making them serve as the key to the subdivision of the specifically Lucan travel account is that they are the elements in it which alert the reader to the nature of this section (9:51 - 18:14) in Luke. They are, however, scarcely a key to any logical development of the account and should not be regarded as such.

THE PROLOGUE: 1. A Reliable Account Addressed
                         to Theophilus   (1:1-4)

PART ONE: THE INFANCY NARRATIVE (1:5 - 2:52)
A. 1:5-56 Events before the Birth of John the Baptist and of Jesus

C. 6:12-49   The Preaching of Jesus
                    28.   The Choosing of the Twelve   (12-16)
                    29.   Crowds Following Jesus   (17-19)
                    30.   The Sermon on the Plain   (20-49)
D. 7:1 - 8:3   The Reception Accorded to Jesus' Ministry
                    31.   The Cure of the Centurion's
                         Servant   (7:1-10)
                    32.   Nain: Raising of the Widow's
                         Son   (11-17)
                    33.   John the Baptist's Question;
                         Jesus' Answer   (18-23)
                    34.   Jesus' Testimony to John   (24-30)
                    35.   Jesus' Judgment of His Own
                         Generation   (31-35)
                    36.   The Pardon of the Sinful
                       Woman   (36-50)
                    37.   Galilean Women Followers of
                       Jesus   (8:1-3)
E. 8:4-21   The Preached and Accepted Word of God
                    38.   The Parable of the Sowed
                       Seed   (4-8)
                    39.   Why Jesus Spoke in Parables   (9-10)
                    40.   The Explanation of the
                       Parable   (11-15)
                    41.   The Parable of the Lamp   (16-18)
                    42.   Jesus' Mother and Brothers
                       Are the Real Hearers   (19-21)
F. 8:22 - 9:6   The Progressive Revelation of Jesus' Power
                    43.   The Calming of the Storm   (22-25)
                    44.   The Gerasene Demoniac   (26-39)
                    45.   The Cure of the Woman with
                       a Hemorrhage   (40-48)
                    46.   The Raising of Jairus'
                       Daughter   (49-56)
                    47.   The Mission of the Twelve   (9:1-6)
G. 9:7-36   "Who Is This?"
                    48.   Herod's Reaction to Jesus'
                       Reputation   (7-9)
                    49.   The Return of the Apostles;
                       the Feeding of the Five
                       Thousand   (10-17)
                    50.   Peter's Confession   (18-21)
                    51.   The First Announcement of
                       the Passion   (22)

PART SIX: THE PASSION NARRATIVE (22:1 - 23:56a)
A. 22:1-38 The Preliminary Events

VII. A SKETCH OF LUCAN THEOLOGY

It has long been customary to write syntheses of Pauline or Johannine theology. These syntheses exist in the form of separate monographs or as parts of full-scale theologies of the New Testament. In standard handbooks devoted to NT theology that strive to allow for the distinctive teachings of different writers a section on Paul or John invariably appears. This can be found, for instance, in the syntheses of R. Bultmann, W. G. Kümmel, and H. Conzelmann. In such works one finds an initial grappling with the message or proclamation of Jesus, or at least a discussion of the early Christian kerygma, sometimes distinguished according to the forms it took in the primitive (Palestinian) community and in the Hellenistic churches (of the diaspora in the eastern Mediterranean world). Often enough, a nod is made to the Synoptics, to cope with what might be primitive elements in Mark or "Q"; sometimes even a brief summary of the theology of the three Synoptic Gospels is presented. This is followed by a sketch of Pauline theology, and then by another, of Johannine theology. The latter may or may not be regarded as part of the development after Paul or the development toward the ancient church, depending on the writer's view of the Johannine tradition.

What space is given to Lucan theology, however, is usually brief. Luke is lumped together with other representatives of late development and treated in the context of concern for the church's emerging understanding of itself, of ministry and church order, of developing doctrine, of the effects of the delayed parousia, and of problems of Christian living. Whatever Lucan theology appears in such a section is often subsumed under topical headings, resembling the treatment of NT theology in the writings of those who make little effort to distinguish its various thrusts. What has led to this sort of understanding of NT theology can now be traced in the book of G. Strecker, *Das Problem der Theologie des Neuen Testaments* (Wege der Forschung 367; Darmstadt: Wissenschaftliche Buchgesellschaft, 1975).

One reason for the rarity of synthetic presentations of Lucan theology is the negative attitude displayed toward it by many modern interpreters of the NT—an attitude described in the theses dealt with above (pp. 4-6). It is an attitude that ranges from a denial of any real theology in the Lucan writings (M. Goguel, *La naissance du Christianisme* [Paris: Payot, 1946] 367) to the attenuated sense of Lucan theology used by H. Conzelmann.

Attempts have been made, indeed, to redress this imbalance. Syntheses of Lucan theology have been attempted in recent times by, among others, H. Flender (*St. Luke: Theologian of Redemptive History*, 1967), I. H. Marshall (*Luke: Historian and Theologian*, 1970), and E. Franklin (*Christ the Lord: A Study in the Purpose and Theology of Luke-Acts*, 1975). See further the general bibliography at the end of this section (pp. 259-260). However, some of these treatments have been either preoccupied with restoring the reputation of Luke as a historian or have striven to counteract the influence of H. Conzelmann's *The Theology of St Luke*. Though that work has been a significant and widely discussed contribution to the topic, since its first appearance in 1954, it is limited to the Gospel and is scarcely a comprehensive presentation of Lucan theology; it is rather a prime example of a thesis about Lucan theology, or about some part of it.

Lucan theology is, moreover, involved in the problem of the Synoptic relationships. Many parts of the Lucan Gospel, especially its "Q" passages, have been mined for what they might contribute to the message or proclamation of Jesus. What is really needed is a synthetic approach to Lucan theology, not only as it appears in the Lucan redaction of traditional gospel material, but in the thrust of Lucan composition in both the Gospel and Acts. It is the theology of the end product that has to be synthesized. This, in the long run, is more important than what can be ferreted out in the twentieth century as the theology of "Q" or of the teaching of Jesus. (The same could be said, *mutatis mutandis,* of Matthean theology.)

A synthetic presentation of the theology of any NT writer will always remain a step removed from the writings themselves and will never replace them. A synthesis is produced by a modern interpreter who culls from the writings. According to E. Haenchen (*Acts,* 91), "Luke is no systematic theologian." But that could be said equally well of Paul and of John, and yet attempts have been made to synthesize their teachings. The picture Luke has painted of Jesus and of the Christian disciples who spread his message after him and came to be called after him (Acts 11:26) has a relevance for Christians of today unlike that of any other presentation of either Jesus' own teaching or of those NT writers often regarded as his major witnesses. If we have to admit that Lucan theology is not as radical in its demands as Pauline or as sublime in its conception as Johannine theology, it is still a major witness to Jesus and to his significance for the salvation of human beings throughout the centuries since he walked this earth. Hence it deserves close study and an attempt to present a holistic view in a commentary that is otherwise largely analytical.

The evidence for a distinctive Lucan theology can be found in a generic way in a number of features in Luke's literary presentation. They can be summarized briefly at the outset. First, there is the distinctive form which the Lucan kerygma takes, which can be found not only in the proclamation of the Lucan Jesus and of his disciples proclaiming the entire Christ-event in Acts, but also in the proclamatory narrative that Luke himself writes. Whether one understands kerygma in an active sense (the proclaiming of the salvific Christ-event) or in a content sense (the essential elements of that proclamation), a form of it is present in Luke-Acts. Second, Lucan theology can be seen in the very way that Luke has structured his Gospel, for his use of traditional materials is suited to composition with a theological intention. Third, the Lucan geographical perspective anchors the Christ-event in Jerusalem, whence the word of it is to be spread "to the end of the earth." Fourth, the Lucan historical perspective roots the Christ-event in human history, not just for the sake of historicizing it, but to present it as inaugurating a new era in human existence. Thus both the geographical and historical perspectives have a theological aspect and betray a unique form of universalism. Fifth, Lucan christology, in presenting various phases of Jesus' existence and influence, both in recasting inherited titles and in using distinctive titles, and in a particular soteriological emphasis, becomes an important part of Lucan theology. Sixth, the stress that Luke puts on the role of the Spirit in the story of salvation is almost unique in the New Testament, particularly in the way in which he depicts the Spirit's relation to the earthly Jesus, the risen Christ, and his disciples. Seventh, the Lucan treatment of eschatology, which copes more than that of other evangelists with the delayed parousia, clearly manifests a theological concern. Eighth, the picture of Christian disciples in Luke-Acts as those who respond to the word with faith, repentance and conversion, and baptism; as those who conform to the demands of Christian living (in the following of Christ, testimony, prayer, and right use of material possessions); and as those who live in structured communities together across the eastern Mediterranean world, also reveals a Lucan theological concern. Lastly, the overall portrait of Jesus in the Gospel is not without its significance for Lucan theology, beyond the aspects mentioned in relation to other categories.

Each of these elements of Lucan theology calls for more extended discussion, and the treatment of them will constitute the bulk of this sketch.

1. *The Lucan Kerygma.* An attempt will be made here to study those elements in the Lucan narrative that should be recognized as kerygmatic. It makes little difference whether one speaks of the "Lucan kerygma" or the "kerygma in Luke," even though the latter might seem to suggest a discussion of what happened to the kerygma in Luke. The question of what

happened to the primitive kerygma in Luke will be treated eventually; here our attention will rather be brought to bear on the kerygmatic elements in Luke-Acts.

"Kerygma" can be used in a broad sense to describe what Luke is proclaiming in his two volumes. In this sense it has been used in a series of articles in *Interpretation,* which sought to present the kernel of preaching in various OT and NT writings. O. Betz's treatment there of "The Kerygma of Luke" shares at times some of this broader perspective, including some things that I should prefer to discuss under Lucan theology proper. However, I intend to use the term "kerygma" in a narrow sense, recognizing with R. Bultmann (*Theology* 1. 3) that "theological thinking—the theology of the New Testament—begins with the kerygma of the earliest Church and not before." Moreover, I accept the initial definition of the "Christian kerygma" proposed by Bultmann: the proclamation of Jesus Christ, crucified and risen, as God's eschatological act of salvation; or, as the challenging word occurring in the salvific act of Christ—God's proclamation in the crucifixion and resurrection of Jesus the Christ for our salvation. In that early Christian kerygma Jesus was not only a teacher or prophet announcing that act of salvation, but also the one "who formerly had been the *bearer* of the message [but who] was [now] drawn into it and became its essential *content. The proclaimer became the proclaimed*" (ibid. 1. 33 [his italics]). But, as Bultmann himself recognized, the central question is: In what sense did he become it? Bultmann was asking that question in terms of the kerygma of the earliest church; but we shall have to pose it in terms of the Lucan writings. Is there any sense in which such kerygma is found in them?

At the outset, the attempt to isolate kerygmatic elements in Luke-Acts can only be skeleton-like, for the kerygma contained there is embedded in a narrative account which contains much of Lucan theology. At the outset one might wonder, How can one discuss Lucan kerygma without getting into Lucan christology, or Lucan soteriology. This skeleton-like character of the Lucan kerygma is to be recognized, but because of what is often said about the kerygma in Luke it seems necessary to attempt at least to see what one can make of it. Hence, as pointed out above, we are interested at first only in kerygma in a narrow sense.

It has been customary to distinguish in the NT as a whole three senses of kerygma: (a) the *active* sense of proclaiming or preaching (e.g. 1 Cor 2:4; 15:14); (b) the *content*-sense, i.e. what is proclaimed (e.g. Rom 16:25, "the preaching about Jesus Christ," a phrase parallel to "my gospel"; cf. 1 Cor 15:1-3); and (c) the *task*-sense, i.e. the office of preaching given to certain individuals (1 Tim 1:3; 2 Tim 4:17). These are different aspects of the early Christian proclamation (*kērygma*) about God's eschatological act of salvation in Christ Jesus. The third sense hardly concerns us now; but the distinction between kerygma in the active and content senses will be important in the analysis of the kergymatic elements found in Luke-Acts.

Before we probe, however, into various aspects of the kerygma in Luke-Acts, we should make a few preliminary remarks about the use of the Greek word *kērygma* in these writings. The noun occurs only once and is used of the "preaching of Jonah" (Luke 11:32, parallel to Matt 12:41 ["Q"]). These parallel passages are, indeed, the sole instances of it in the Synoptic tradition. The cognate verb, *kēryssein,* however, is often found. Such use echoes the Septuagint, where the verb usually denotes a prophetic or priestly proclamation (see Isa 61:1; Zech 9:9; Joel 1:14; Jonah 3:5; Exod 32:5); it means to "preach, proclaim," and invariably involves the declaration of an event (see G. Friedrich, *TDNT* 3. 703). In the Marcan Gospel (apart from the appendix, 16:15,20) the verb occurs twelve times. It describes the activity of John the Baptist (1:4,7), of the disciples (3:14; 6:12; 13:10; 14:9), of a cured leper (1:45), of an unidentified group of people ("they," 7:36), of the cured demoniac of Gerasa (5:20), and three times of Jesus' own preaching activity (1:14,38,39). The object of such preaching is specified as "the gospel" only in 1:14; 13:10; 14:9.

In the Lucan Gospel the verb occurs nine times, and in Acts eight times. In the Gospel it is used of the preaching of the Twelve (9:2), of the disciples (12:3; also implied in 24:47), of the cured demoniac (8:39), and again four times of Jesus' own preaching (4:18,19,44; 8:1). Although Luke has not taken over all the Marcan uses of the verb—only 4:44 *might* be regarded as influenced by Mark 1:39—he has no fewer instances of it for Jesus' preaching than has Mark. In one instance (4:18-19), where Isa 61:1-2 is quoted, the application of the verb to Jesus is distinctively Lucan. In Acts, the verb is used to describe the activity of Christian disciples: in general (10:42), of Philip (8:5), of Saul/Paul (9:20; 19:13; 20:25; 28:31). *Kēryssein* is further used of the activity of the Baptist (10:37) and of Jewish preachers (15:21). The object of such preaching is either Christ/Jesus (8:5; 9:20; 19:13) or "the kingdom of God" (20:25; 28:31), when Christians proclaim; John the Baptist preaches "baptism" (10:37) and the Jews preach "Moses" (15:21). Thus, though the kerygmatic vocabulary is abundantly used in the Lucan writings—more than in any of the other Synoptics—and though it is used of the preaching activity of Jesus and his disciples, one cannot simply determine the Lucan kerygma in terms of such word-study.

But Luke often substitutes other verbs as stylistic variants of *kēryssein,* and this substitution further complicates the picture; it also reveals how interested he is in the basic notion of proclaiming the Christ-event. As substitutes he uses *euangelizesthai, didaskein, lalein,* and *katangellein* (to mention only those which occur with some frequency). The first of these, *euangelizesthai,* is, in fact, a favorite Lucan word; by contrast, it is never used by Mark and only once in Matthew (11:5). In the Lucan Gospel it occurs ten times, and in Acts fifteen times: of Jesus' preaching it is used seven times (Luke 4:18,43; 7:22; 8:1; 9:6; 16:16; 20:1). Since Luke studiously avoids the use of *euangelion* in his Gospel and uses it only twice in Acts (15:7; 20:24), it seems unlikely that he intends the verb to be understood in the etymological sense of announcing/preaching good news (except perhaps in the quotation from Isaiah in 4:18 and the allusion to it in 7:22). The verb normally means no more than "to preach," often having as its object the "kingdom" (4:43; 8:1), "(Christ) Jesus" (Acts 5:42; 8:35; 11:20; 17:18), or "the word" (Acts 8:4; 15:35). See further Conzelmann, *Theology,* 222; cf. *TDNT* 2. 718.

The verb *didaskein,* "teach," is used in the Lucan Gospel as often as in the Marcan, seventeen times in each. Of Jesus' teaching it is employed fifteen times (Luke 4:15,31; 5:3,17; 6:6; 11:1; 13:10,22,26; 19:47; 20:1,21*bis;* 21:37; 23:5). The connotation that this verb expresses in its relation to kerygma is, of course, debatable; on its relation to proclamation, see Friedrich, *TDNT* 3. 713. It should not in the long run be made to imply an activity of Jesus that is different from his preaching.

The verb *lalein* is used many times in Luke-Acts; sometimes it means nothing more than "to speak, utter." But H. Jaschke ("*'Lalein'* bei Lukas") has shown that Luke uses it, not only in its ordinary sense of an equivalent of *legein* ("to say"), but also with a special connotation for prophetic utterance: It is used of OT prophets (Luke 1:70; 24:25; Acts 3:21); for Spirit-filled utterance in the Period of Jesus (Luke 2:38, etc.), and for Jesus' own preaching (Luke 8:49; 11:37; 22:47—specifically about the kingdom, 9:11), or for that of the apostles (especially in the phrase, "to preach the word [of God]," *logon* [*tou theou*] *lalein,* Acts 4:29,31; 11:19; 13:46; 14:25; 16:32).

Finally, the verb *katangellein,* "to announce, proclaim," is found frequently enough in Acts (4:2; 13:5,38; 15:36; 16:17; 17:3,13,23; 26:23) as a synonym for *kēryssein.*

This survey of the vocabulary related to the process of kerygma in Luke-Acts is not insignificant, because when taken together it manifests a Lucan emphasis on the process to which one might not otherwise attend.

By way of another preliminary remark it should be noted that in the long run other activities of Jesus such as healing, defeating the forces of evil, resolutely proceeding to his death and destiny, are not without kerygmatic impact in the Lucan writings. If we emphasize the kerygmatic aspect of his *message* and that of the early witnesses about him, this is because so much of the modern debate about the kerygma in Luke has centered on this aspect of his activity. The person of Jesus of Nazareth, however, especially given the engaging, challenging portrait of him in the Lucan Gospel, cannot be minimized in the accosting of human beings in view of God's eschatological act of salvation.

As we have already noted above, in discussing the kerygma in Luke-Acts, we have to distinguish between the act of proclamation and what is proclaimed, since both aspects of the kerygma are present and they involve Jesus himself, the disciples, and the author.

A. KERYGMA AS THE ACT OF PROCLAMATION.

1) *The Preaching of Jesus.* In the Lucan Gospel Jesus proclaims the fact of God's eschatological salvation, the event of his decisive intervention in human history, proposing to Israel a new mode of salvation. Even though Jesus is never called a "herald" (*kēryx*), he is in fact depicted in the role of God's herald, God's prophet or mouthpiece, since he is the preacher of the *eschaton*.

Luke has derived his picture of Jesus preaching and teaching from Mark and other sources, but treats this picture in his own way. He draws no line between Jesus' preaching and teaching, as is sometimes done between *kērygma* and *didachē* in later forms of early Christian writings. Whether he preaches or teaches that is part of his proclamation. The various terms used of the proclamation in the Lucan Gospel are no less compelling or demanding in their import than their counterparts in the Marcan Gospel. If anything, they take on an intensification. Moreover, the proclamation is ascribed to no less an historical figure in whom the eschatological word of God confronts mankind than in the Marcan Gospel. In this regard the Lucan kerygma is no less than the Marcan.

It is true, however, that Luke substitutes at the beginning of the account of Jesus' ministry a bland report of Jesus' teaching in the synagogue (Luke 4:14b-15) for the first (and striking) Marcan proclamation: " 'The time is fulfilled, and the kingdom of God is at hand; repent, and believe in the gospel" (Mark 1:15). But in the immediately following Nazareth scene, which is largely of Lucan composition and programmatic for the entire Lucan account of the ministry, Jesus openly applies to himself Isa 61:1-2, "The Spirit of the Lord is upon me for he has anointed me . . . to proclaim the Lord's year of favor," and boldly continues, "Today, this passage of Scripture sees its fulfillment" (4:21). Perhaps this is not as explicit a challenge as the Marcan invitation to repent and to "believe in the gospel," but its implication is unmistakable: A new age is dawning (=the *eschaton* of Mark's fulfilled time); Jesus proclaims God's year of favor (=the Marcan "kingdom"), release, sight, and relief (=the Marcan "gospel"). Thereafter, Jesus travels about "preaching and announcing the kingdom of God" (8:1), so depicted in a Lucan compositional summary. The call to repentance gives way here at the outset to a proclamation of release; but repentance eventually becomes an important part of the Christian message in Luke's treatment of the basic Christian reaction to the message (see below).

The Lucan Jesus makes no more of an attempt to justify his claim that the prophetic words of Isaiah are fulfilled in himself and his preaching than the Marcan Jesus seeks to authenticate his call for repentance. Perhaps one should agree with Conzelmann that there is a difference between the Lucan "today" and the Pauline "now" of 2 Cor 6:2 ("See, now is the favorable time, now is the day of salvation"), in that Paul identifies his own, post-resurrection era as the *eschaton,* whereas Luke looks on salvation as a thing of the past, accomplished in the Period of Jesus. The period of salvation has become a period in time, in human history, which, though it determines the present, is now over and done with (*Theology,* 36). But that is not the entire meaning of the Lucan "today," which is also related to the "anointing" (of Isaiah 61) and clearly insinuates that the new messianic era has begun. The "today" calls attention to the time for decision: one must accept relief, sight, and release or not. The kerygmatic challenge of the Lucan Jesus is linked to "today" because it initiates a proclamation that is eschatological, yet not limited to the Period of Jesus. Whether it be expressed in terms of Isaian release (Luke 4:18-21) or of the kingdom (8:1), the kerygma has its own challenge (or existential demand), since those who enter the kingdom enter it only "with violence" (16:16), i.e. with a pressing demand for decision. And he who announces the word, whether as release or as kingdom, does so as one anointed with the eschatological gift of the Spirit (5:18; cf. 3:22; 4:1,18; Acts 10:38).

The Lucan redaction of Mark 1:38 even sharpens the need that Jesus senses to preach "the kingdom of God" (4:43), "for that is what I was sent for." And the import of his kerygmatic activity, preaching and healing, is stressed in the message that he sends to John in prison, ending with the challenging comment, "Blessed, indeed, is the person who is not shocked at me" (Luke 7:23), i.e. who can accept me for what I am. Certainly, the Lucan form of Jesus' words about reception and rejection in the kingdom (13:22-30) are no less incisive than their "Q" counterparts in Matt 7:13-14,22-23; 25:10b-12.

It is, however, only the Lucan Jesus who during the ministry explicitly begins to train his disciples to carry on his own proclamation, when he says, "Whoever listens to you listens to me" (Luke 10:16). Here Luke has cast the saying, preserved elsewhere in the Synoptic tradition in terms of reception, explicitly in terms of hearing the proclamation. This leads to another form of kerygma in the Lucan writings, viz. the preaching of the disciples.

2) *The Preaching of Disciples.* The activity of proclamation is also

carried on by disciples in the Lucan writings, and this aspect of the Lucan story conveys its own kerygmatic impact. The limited preaching mission of disciples in Mark 6:7-13,30 not only becomes a mission of the Twelve (Luke 9:1-6,10), who are explicitly sent forth "to preach the kingdom of God," but is also paralleled by a separate mission of seventy(-two) others (10:1-16). Aside from the literary aspect of the parallel episodes, the double sending out of disciples in the Lucan Gospel, during the ministry of Jesus itself, drives home the importance of his message. The seriousness of the challenge that they were to convey comes through in the details of the mission charge itself: the sparsity of their *impedimenta*, no need for greetings on the way, etc.

At the end of the Gospel the risen Christ issues his final mission charge in terms that are characteristically Lucan—"in his name repentance for the forgiveness of sins must be preached to all the nations" (24:47; compare Matt 28:18-20). The charge is carried out in scene after scene in Luke's second volume, which narrates the vigorous preaching-activity of disciples like Peter and John, Barnabas and Saul, Paul and Timothy, Stephen and Philip. But the "word" is now preached "with boldness" (*parrēsia,* Acts 4:13,29,31; 28:31), which connotes not only fearless, frank proclamation, but also the earnestness of the challenge being offered to human beings. Two verses, in particular, sum up that character of their proclamation: "Be it known to all of you, and to all the people of Israel, that by the name of Jesus Christ of Nazareth, whom you crucified, but whom God raised from the dead, through him this man stands before you cured. . . . And salvation is found in no one else, for there is no other name under heaven given to human beings by which we are to be saved" (4:10,12). The radical challenge of that preaching cannot be missed. And it comes from the pen of Luke.

Given the nature of Acts as a narrative account, with a somewhat idyllic description of the early Christian community, it is not difficult to trace this sort of kerygmatic activity on the part of the disciples. But one must not, as a result, minimize the part the proclamation of the disciples plays in the Lucan kerygma.

3) *The Preaching of Luke.* It may seem strange to think that Luke in his writing is proclaiming some salvific facts, but he has, in fact, actively contributed to the process of the early Christian kerygma. If we admit with O. Piper that kerygma is "the proclamation of a fact that is announced by God" (*IDB* 2. 444), we must further admit that this is a major Lucan preoccupation. Luke not only states in his prologue that his narrative account is concerned with "the events which have seen fulfillment among us" (1:1), i.e. not with bare historical facts, but he tells us in the prologue to his second volume that he has recounted "what Jesus began to do and teach" (Acts 1:1). Luke has depicted in the Gospel the preaching/

teaching Jesus, and in Acts the preaching about Jesus or the Christ-event. True, his Gospel has become more of "a life of Christ" than that of either Mark or Matthew, but it has not lost its proclamatory character. Though his account is more formal and literary than the other two, it is not for that reason unkerygmatic. After all, the Lucan writings are proclaiming to Theophilus and to others like him God's act of eschatological salvation. The adjective "kerygmatic" may not fully characterize the purpose(s) of Luke-Acts, but it would be wrong to deny that characterization of them, for they proclaim the Christ-event and the kingdom of God and demand from those who are addressed the response of Christian faith as much as the writings of Mark or Paul—albeit in a different way.

Is it then correct to draw so sharp a distinction between Mark and Luke as Conzelmann has done? He sees the Marcan narrative providing a broad unfolding of the kerygma, whereas Luke's narrative sketches the historical foundation that is added as a secondary factor to the kerygma, a knowledge of which he takes for granted (*Theology,* 11). As I read the Lucan prologue, Luke is not taking the kerygma for granted; nor does he limit his foundation solely to what is historical. He is aware that others have attempted to present the kerygma, but insinuates that he can do it better in his own way. Luke's narrative account is no less of a broad unfolding of the kerygma than Mark's; in fact, it may even be a broader one.

The real question that has to be asked in this analysis of the Lucan kerygma is whether it possesses a time-transcending, ever-present, and existential call. When Luke composed his narrative for Theophilus, did he expect his patron to be challenged by what took place in the Period of Jesus and by the proclamation about the Christ-event which he put on the lips of Peter and Paul, echoing the preaching of disciples of an earlier generation? It is difficult to imagine that Luke's purpose did not include an accosting of reader Theophilus and an eliciting from him of an act of Christian faith. And if it is right to say that Luke composed his highly literary narrative account in a contemporary Hellenistic mode, did he not expect that this narrative would be read by others besides Theophilus— whom he as an evangelist would have been accosting? Has not his form of the kerygma taken on as much of the ever-present and existential call as that of Mark, Matthew, Paul, or John? I find it difficult to say that it has not—in its own way. As Betz ("The Kerygma of Luke," 132) has noted, Luke has not imitated Josephus in writing a treatise on the "Antiquities of the Christians." His account of Jesus the Christ and of the witnesses to him reveals Luke's personal commitment, which surpasses that of a secular historian, or even of such an apologete as Josephus. What makes the account different is precisely the kerygmatic character (in the active sense) that it possesses. It is the testimony of a believer who seeks to proclaim the Christ-event and evoke the response of Christian faith from others.

Another way of putting this is to say with C. K. Barrett (*Luke the Historian*, 52) that Lucan literature is more accurately described as preaching than as an historical work for it aims to set out the substratum of Christian kerygma in the life and teaching of Jesus and to illustrate that proclamation itself in a series of classical models. And he quotes Luther to the effect that ". . . by this book St. Luke teaches the whole of Christendom, even to the end of the world . . ." ("Preface to Acts," *Luther's Works* 35 [Philadelphia: Muhlenberg, 1960] 363). Cf. I. H. Marshall, *Luke: Historian and Theologian*, 84.

B. KERYGMA AS WHAT IS PROCLAIMED. In the content-sense of kerygma, Luke-Acts presents the object of the Christian proclamation in ways that are at once similar to other NT writings and specific to its understanding of the message of Jesus himself, of his disciples, and of the author. At the outset of a discussion of the content-sense of kerygma in Luke, we may note what it definitely is not. In his treatment of "The Kerygma in Luke," Betz has rightly noted that the object of that proclamation is neither anthropology nor ecclesiology. The kerygma is not an attempt to formulate a human being's self-understanding or to describe the church as an eschatological community. It is rather Jesus Christ himself who is proclaimed in it.

1) *By Jesus.* The content of Jesus' own proclamation in the Lucan Gospel is presented under various headings. a) Even before "the kingdom of God" appears on his lips for the first time (4:43), Jesus has proclaimed that he and his preaching are the fulfillment of something mentioned in the Scriptures of old associated with God's salvation. In his person and his preaching, he inaugurates the year of God's favor spoken of in Isa 61:1-2. The "year" refers to an era or period which is beginning, and he is the eschatological and prophetic herald of the new mode of release, sight, and liberty spoken of by Isaiah of old. It is, furthermore, noteworthy that his presentation of himself as such not only charms his fellow townspeople at first, but also proves offensive to them; and this comes precisely from the radical character of the kerygma being announced by the Lucan Jesus. That fulfillment of an Isaian prophecy will be reasserted in the message that Jesus sends to the imprisoned Baptist (7:22-23). In a still further, exclusively Lucan episode, the risen Jesus sums up his career by interpreting what pertained to him in the OT Scriptures (24:27,32,45). In Mark 10:29 an identification of Jesus with the gospel is suggested, which insinuates a content-sense of the gospel; the Lucan presentation of Jesus and his preaching in these various places is at least analogous to that of the Marcan passage. It obviously reflects an

early Christian understanding of the kerygma in which the herald is already being presented as the one heralded. Luke, in making use of this in the programmatic Nazareth synagogue scene, may be retrojecting back into the ministry and preaching of Jesus a developed understanding of him; but it is not for that reason less kerygmatic. It is, moreover, significant that this becomes the initial mode of presenting the preaching of Jesus in the Lucan Gospel—prior even to his preaching of the kingdom.

b) In the Lucan Gospel, however, Jesus is the kingdom-preacher par excellence. As Conzelmann has noted (*Theology,* 20), John the Baptist in Luke does not proclaim the kingdom of God, in contrast to Matt 3:2, where the proclamation that Jesus is to make is first heard from the lips of John. The first proclamation of it in the Lucan Gospel is made by Jesus (4:43), even though Luke has omitted any reference to it in his parallel to the first dramatic announcement of it in Mark 1:15. That was omitted to make room for the identification of Jesus as the one in whom Isaiah's words were fulfilled, which is more important than the kingdom in Luke's scheme. When the first proclamation of the kingdom of God is made in Luke (4:43), Jesus is there made to add significantly, "That is what I was sent for!" As Betz has put it, "the kingdom has come with the kerygma" ("The Kerygma of Luke," 133), and Jesus is its herald. His announcement is one of an event, and is not a lecture on the nature of God's kingship or kingdom (see Friedrich, *TDNT* 3. 710). See Luke 8:1; 9:11.

The kingdom-preaching of Jesus is drawn from the tradition to which Luke has been tributary. He derives part of it from Mark (see Luke 8:10; 9:27; 13:19[?]; 18:16,17,24,25; 22:18) and part of it from "Q" (see Luke 6:20; 7:28; 10:9; 11:2,20; 12:31; 13:18[?],20,28,29; 16:16). Basically, therefore, the Lucan Jesus proclaims in this respect what the Marcan and Matthean Jesus does. But there are some specifically Lucan nuances in the manner of Jesus' kingdom-preaching that should be noted here. Whereas Mark 10:29 records Jesus' words about the need of disciples to leave home and family "for my sake and that of the gospel," the reason becomes in Luke 18:29 merely "for the sake of the kingdom of God." This alteration is certainly related to Luke's reluctance to speak of the "gospel."

There is, moreover, a sense in which the Lucan Jesus speaks of the imminence of the kingdom: "Realize that the kingdom of God is near" (21:31; see also 10:11). Yet he does not hesitate to speak of its presence in his own person and acts, "The kingdom of God is among you" (17:21 [see NOTES; cf. 11:20]). Furthermore, he can also speak of certain things being fulfilled in the coming kingdom (22:16,30). We note here that these specifically Lucan passages dealing with the kingdom have a two-pronged reference, to a present and a future aspect of it—a reference that is not without its significance for the eschatology of the Lucan writings (see below). Above all, the Lucan Jesus stresses the radical character of the reaction to kingdom-preaching most notably in the very verse (16:16), of which Conzelmann has made so much in a different respect: "Up until John it was the law and the prophets; from that time on the kingdom of God is being preached, and everyone is pressed to enter it," i.e. everyone who enters it does so only with a radical, demanding invitation to do so. See further below.

Moreover, it is only Luke who depicts the risen Christ speaking to his disciples about the kingdom (Acts 1:3) and reacting against a still-misunderstood sense of it among them (1:6). This is obviously a transitional nuance, which links the disciples' eventual preaching to that of Jesus himself. The same transition is suggested in the specifically Lucan saying recorded in 22:29-30, addressed to the disciples who have followed him in his trials: "I assign you a kingdom such as my Father has assigned me, that you may eat and drink in my kingdom. . . ."

There is no difference in the basic usage of the phrase, "kingdom of God/heaven," in the three Synoptics. Luke employs only the form *hē basileia tou theou,* "the kingdom of God," and he never explains it. It obviously reflects the OT idea of Yahweh as king (1 Sam 12:12; Isa 6:5; 33:22; 43:15; Jer 8:19; Mic 2:13; Zeph 3:15; Zech 14:9,16; Ps 47:3,8) or the kingship and royal authority that are ascribed to him (Obad 21; Pss 103:19; 145:11-13) or his ruling as king (Exod 15:18; Isa 24:23; 52:7; Ezek 20:33; Mic 4:7; Pss 93:1; 97:1; 146:10). In Dan 7:22 God's dominion or kingdom is assigned to the "holy ones" of Israel. The NT phrase finds its closest verbal counterpart in postexilic writings, in 1 Chr 28:5 (*malkût Yhwh, basileia Kyriou*) or 2 Chr 13:8 (*mamleket Yhwh, basileia Kyriou*), "Yahweh's kingship" or "Yahweh's kingdom." In the OT the phrase expresses an eschatological hope for a period when God's salvation would be realized, when his dominion over the minds and lives of human beings would be accomplished, and they would be withdrawn from subjection to danger, evil, and sin. The phrase implies also a divine guidance of human history (Judg 21:25), thwarted no longer by hostile opposition. In this sense the OT idea would assume a specific determination in the NT in view of the Christ-event: The kingdom of God enters history in Jesus' ministry, passion, death, and resurrection. As the Christ and the risen Lord, he is the Father's special anointed agent for the preaching and establishment of this dominion henceforth among human beings.

Hē basileia tou theou is a prime kerygmatic notion in the Synoptic tradition, and it is debated whether one should translate the phrase as

"God's kingship" or as "God's kingdom." The former meaning, "kingship, reign, dominion," is more abstract and essential in its connotation; it may suit most of the OT passages cited above. The latter meaning, "kingdom," is more concrete and spatial in its connotation. The former meaning may suit some Lucan passages (4:43; 8:1; 9:2,11,27[?],60; 11:20; 12:32; 13:18,20,28[?]; 16:16[?]; 17:21; 18:29[?]; 19:11; 21:31; 23:51). But some of these references are ambiguous—even beyond those marked with the question mark. There are other Lucan passages, however, which because of the way in which the kingdom is mentioned imply rather the concrete, spatial sense: those that speak of the *basileia* as belonging to certain persons (6:20; 18:16; cf. 9:62), of certain things being done in it (7:28; 13:29; 14:15), of people entering it (18:17,24,25), of its "coming" (10:9,11; 17:20; 22:16,18), or of its having to be looked for (12:31). S. Aalen ("'Reign' and 'House'") has argued that *basileia* as a "kingdom" in the sense of a house is the only concept that fits the NT data and Jesus' own preaching. There is something to be said for his thesis, even though I should hesitate to go along with his interpretation of all the data he cites. For this reason, I have preferred to retain "kingdom" in my translation of Luke and shall comment on the possibilities that the word has in a given setting in the NOTES.

The data in the Synoptics about the kingdom are such that one must attribute this topic to the preaching of Jesus himself in his ministry. The relationship between him and the kingdom may receive slightly different nuances in the different Synoptic writings, but the basic preaching of the kingdom of God is so diversely attested that it has to be traced to the historical ministry. But, having said this, we have to admit that the topic never appears in the kerygma of either the Pauline letters or the early speeches in Acts alleged to contain kerygmatic elements. And "kingdom of God" occurs in the Johannine Gospel only in 3:3,5. This situation is, of course, puzzling, but if the kingdom-preaching of Jesus is to be regarded as kerygmatic in the Marcan Gospel, then it will have also to be so regarded in Luke.

c) In addition to Jesus' proclamation of himself as fulfilling God's promise of release in Isaiah 61 and of the kingdom of God, we find Jesus also proclaiming "salvation" in the Lucan Gospel. This proclamation is found on his lips only in Luke 19:9, uttered apropos of Zacchaeus, the toll-gatherer: "Salvation has come to this house today." Even if that passage is unique, the topic that it announces is important. Luke plays upon this topic, which is more properly discussed as an effect of the Christ-event in Lucan theology.

2) *By Disciples*. Another aspect of the Lucan kerygma is seen in what is proclaimed by Christian disciples in Luke-Acts. Here we must distin-

guish their proclamation of the kingdom, of the word of God, and of Jesus himself in their testimony to him as witnesses carrying the kerygma to the end of the earth (Acts 1:8).

a) The Kingdom. Even though Jesus is the kingdom-preacher par excellence in the Lucan Gospel, it is significant that he specifies in this Gospel the object of the preaching of the Twelve to be sent out. They are sent explicitly "to proclaim the kingdom of God" (9:2). There is nothing of this in Mark 6:6b-13, where the purpose of the mission of the Twelve is stated solely in terms of repentance. Matt 10:7 mentions kingdom-preaching in the mission of the Twelve, but that verse is parallel to Luke 10:9. Moreover, this object of proclamation is used also in the commission given to other disciples (9:60,62; cf. 10:9,11). Here too one must recall what was said above about Jesus' transitional preaching of the kingdom (in Luke 22:29-30; Acts 1:3). In the Acts of the Apostles the kingdom becomes the topic of the preaching of Philip (8:12), Barnabas and Saul (14:22), and Paul (19:8; 20:25; 28:23,31). This proclamation of the kingdom by disciples in Acts is the logical extension of Jesus' proclamation in the Gospel, and some of the same nuances of the phrase are used in Acts.

b) The Word of God. Even though the kingdom is the first topic of proclamation in Acts (1:3), the topic of the disciples' preaching is most frequently expressed in it as *ho logos tou theou,* "the word of God" (or occasionally as *ho logos tou Kyriou,* "the word of the Lord"), or sometimes simply as *ho logos* or *to rēma,* "the word." It is used by Luke as a brief way of summing up the fundamental Christian message. (Acts 4:4,29,31; 6:2,4; 8:4,14,25; 10:36,37,44; 11:1,19; 13:5,7,44,46,48; 15:35,36; 16:6,32; 17:11,13; 18:5,11; 19:10; 28:25). Bultmann has noted that the notion of the "Word of God" stands for *"the Christian kerygma"* ("The Concept of the Word of God in the New Testament," 298 [his italics]). He further describes it as a word which has power and which acts with power. This may be too Pauline a nuance for the uses in Luke-Acts (cf. Rom 1:16; 1 Cor 1:18), but one may associate with the Lucan use of the phrase the OT connotation of God's effective utterance (see Isa 55:11); even Bultmann referred to Acts 20:32. This use is the extension into Acts of what Jesus himself proclaims in the Gospel (5:1; 8:11-21; 11:28); in the first and last of these references the use is exclusively Lucan, and the second is the explanation of the parable of the sowed seed (on which see the COMMENT).

Implied in the phrase "the word of God" is an address by the revealing and saving God to human beings from whom a response of faith is sought (see Acts 6:7; 13:48). It is described as a word which God has "sent to Israel" (10:36), and is specified at times as "the word of this salvation" (13:26; cf. 11:14) or as "the word of the gospel" (15:7), or as a "word of grace" (14:3; 20:32). Lest the word be taken as too static, one should recall that when it is proclaimed, it cuts to the heart (2:37), and that Luke likes to recount in his summaries how "the word of God grew and prevailed mightily" (19:20; cf. 6:7; 12:24). This growth was due to "the power of the Lord" himself (cf. 2:47). The word of God is made the object of such verbs as *lalein,* "speak, utter," *euangelizesthai,* "preach," *akouein,* "hear," and even on occasion of *didaskein,* "teach."

c) Jesus Christ, the Christ-event. The objects of the disciples' kerygmatic preaching are not solely the kingdom and the word of God, but also Jesus himself, especially as the crucified, risen, and exalted Messiah and Lord, who is present to his followers through his Spirit. The relation of Jesus Christ to the kingdom is succinctly presented by Luke at the very end of Acts: Paul, though in house arrest, preached the kingdom of God and taught openly and unhindered about the Lord Jesus Christ (28:31). This mention of the two objects of preaching activity is based on Jesus' own proclamation about himself and the kingdom. Luke emphasizes these points, spelling out in his own way what Mark 10:29 implies. Thus, in Acts Peter proclaims "this Jesus" whom "God raised up and made Lord and Messiah, this Jesus whom you crucified" (2:32,36). And again, "The God of our fathers raised Jesus whom you killed by hanging him on a tree; God exalted him at his right hand as Leader and Savior, to give to Israel repentance and the forgiveness of sins" (5:30-31). Similar to Peter's preaching is Paul's proclamation of Jesus in his argument with Thessalonian Jews, "explaining from the scriptures and proving that it was necessary for the Messiah to suffer and rise from the dead, saying, 'This Jesus, whom I proclaim to you, is the Messiah'" (17:2-3). See further Acts 3:18-26; 5:42; 8:5,35; 9:20; 10:36-43; 13:26-39; and in particular 11:20, "preaching the Lord Jesus." On one occasion he is presented as "the one ordained by God to be judge of the living and the dead" (10:42).

Related to this proclamation of Jesus as the agent of God's salvation for all mankind is the varied use in Acts of preaching, baptizing, and healing "in the name of Jesus (Christ)": 2:38; 3:6,16; 4:10,12,30; 8:16; 9:14,27,29; 10:43,48; 16:18 (cf. also 4:17,18; 5:28,40,41). Underlying the Lucan use of the phrase "in the name of Jesus" are perhaps the OT use of *šēm,* "name" (e.g. Joel 3:5 [2:32E] cited in Acts 2:21) and the OT connotation of the efficacy of the name, especially of that of the deity. In ancient terminology, especially before the notion of "person" emerged in the history of ideas, the "name" was also often used as a way of referring to what came to be called "person" or "personality" later on. Even Acts hints at this, when it speaks of *ochlos onomatōn,* which literally means "a crowd of names," but which is usually translated as "a company of persons" (1:15, *RSV*). If the Lucan references to "the name of Jesus" were to be so understood as "the person of Jesus," these would be further Lucan nuances about the object of the kerygma in Acts. In any case, what was to be preached by the disciples in connection with his name is clearly stated in the great commission of Luke 24:47: "In his name repentance for the forgiveness of sins must be preached to all the nations—beginning from Jerusalem" (see Acts 10:4). That is a formula replete with Lucan terms; and yet it is scarcely unkerygmatic for all that.

The Lucan formulas of "preaching the Lord Jesus" or "speaking/ teaching in the name of Jesus" are Luke's way of referring to the spreading of the "Christ-event," as it is often called today. The latter is our twentieth-century way of referring to all that was accomplished in and by the person, ministry, death, and resurrection of Jesus of Nazareth for the salvation of mankind. When NT writers looked back on that complex, they often described its effects in terms or images derived from their varied backgrounds. That complex has also been called the "objective redemption" or the "whole work of Christ," terms that often bring with them various *impedimenta* of later theological developments. The term "Christ-event," then, is being used here as a way of summing up the content of the preached word, or Christ proclaimed in all his fullness.

In a few of the quotations from Acts cited above mention was made of the proclamation of the forgiveness of sins (see Luke 24:47; Acts 26:18). It is found on the lips of Peter (Acts 2:38; 5:31; 10:43) and of Paul (13:38). It thus becomes part of the Lucan Easter proclamation, the victory proclaimed about the risen Jesus, "to whom all the prophets bear witness, that everyone who believes in him receives forgiveness of sins through his name" (Acts 10:43). But forgiveness is really an effect of the Christ-event and is better treated as part of Lucan theology (see below).

3) *By Luke.* When discussing the content-sense of the Christian kerygma and the contribution that Luke has made to it, it may be difficult to distinguish between his contribution and that of the disciples (discussed in the previous section). Years ago C. H. Dodd tried to isolate the kerygma in the content-sense found in the speeches of Acts; and he compared it with the kerygmatic passages in Paul's letters. Having appealed to such fragments preserved in 1 Thess 1:9-10; Gal 1:4; 3:1; 1 Cor 15:3-5; 2 Cor 4:4; Rom 1:3-4; 2:16; 8:31-34; 10:8-9; 14:9-10, he summarized the primitive kerygma in Paul as a proclamation of the facts of the death and resurrection of Christ Jesus in an eschatological setting that gave meaning to the facts; they marked the transition from "this evil age" to the "age to come." The latter is the era of fulfillment, for it reveals the importance of the statement that Christ died and rose "according to the scriptures" (*Apostolic Preaching,* 13). Dodd's outline of the Pauline kerygma may be reformulated as follows: OT prophecies have been

fulfilled, and a new age has been inaugurated in the ministry of Jesus. He was born of David's seed; he died in accord with the (OT) Scriptures, in order to deliver human beings from the present evil age. He was buried. He was raised on the third day in accord with the Scriptures. He has been exalted at God's right hand, as God's Son and Lord of the living and the dead. He is to come as Judge and Savior of mankind (ibid. 17).

Dodd made a similar summary of the kerygma in the speeches of Acts (ibid. 21-24), which may be summarized as follows: The age of fulfillment has dawned (2:16; 3:18,24). It has taken place in the ministry, death, and resurrection of Jesus, of which a brief account is given, with proof from Scripture that all this has happened through the "set plan and foreknowledge of God" (2:23): in his Davidic descent (2:30-31), his ministry (2:22; 3:22), his death (2:23; 3:13-14), and his resurrection (2:24-31; 3:15; 4:10). As of the resurrection, Jesus has been exalted at God's right hand, as the messianic leader of the new Israel (2:33-36; 3:13; 4:11; 5:31), and the Spirit in the community is the sign of Christ's present power and glory (2:33; 5:32). The messianic age will shortly reach its consummation in the return of Christ (3:21; cf. 10:42). Repent, therefore, and be converted (2:38-39; 3:16,25-26; 4:12; 5:31; 10:43). Dodd concluded that all this is what Luke meant by the preaching of the kingdom of God (ibid. 24).

Dodd singled out three points in which the kerygma in Acts differed from that of Paul: (a) in the kerygma in Acts Jesus is not called the "Son of God" (contrast Rom 1:3-4); (b) it is not said that he died "for our sins" (cf. 1 Cor 15:3); or (c) that the exalted Christ intercedes for us (cf. Rom 8:34).

Dodd thought that he could regard these kerygmatic fragments in Acts as part of the "Jerusalem *kerygma*" (ibid. 25), i.e. as pre-Lucan and primitive. This is precisely the controversial aspect of his thesis. A number of writers have queried whether the kerygma as outlined reflects the framework of the Marcan Gospel, as Dodd maintained, or whether it only reflects that of Luke's first volume. See, in particular, U. Wilckens, *Die Missionsreden der Apostelgeschichte: Form- und traditionsgeschichtliche Untersuchungen* (WMANT 5; Neukirchen: Neukirchener, 1961) and the review of it by J. Dupont, *RB* 69 (1962) 37-60 (reprinted in *Etudes sur les Actes des Apôtres* [LD 45; Paris: Cerf, 1967] 133-155); C. F. Evans, "The Kerygma," *JTS* 7 (1956) 25-41; D. E. Nineham, "The Order of Events in St. Mark's Gospel—An Examination of Dr. Dodd's Hypothesis," in *Studies in the Gospels: Essays in Memory of R. H. Lightfoot* (ed. D. E. Nineham; Oxford: Blackwell, 1955) 223-239.

We cannot go into a detailed discussion of this matter here. It is clear that there is Lucan formulation involved in some of the material that Dodd has cited from Acts as the pre-Lucan kerygma; but it is far from clear that the basic proclamation of the speeches of Peter and Paul is to be entirely ascribed to Luke. It may seem that, because I have relegated Dodd's suggestions about the kerygma in Acts to this part of my treatment of the Lucan kerygma, I am skeptical about the pre-Lucan character of it. I have done this in order not to seem too naïve. Those who prefer to regard the matter as pre-Lucan can add it easily enough to the preceding section as another form of the kerygma in the content-sense as preached by the disciples. It would then be just another support for my contention that there is kerygma in the Lucan writings—in this case even some pre-Lucan kerygma.

Even if we were to agree that the elements that Dodd has isolated represent rather the Christian preaching of Luke's own day, we still have to attend to the substantial similarity of what is proclaimed there to what is regarded as the Pauline kerygma. Moreover, it is well to recall what Paul wrote in 1 Cor 15:1-2 about the "terms (*tíni logō*) in which I preached to you the gospel, which you received, in which you stand, by which you are saved, if you hold it fast—unless you believed in vain." There, having cited the fragment of pre-Pauline kerygma in vv. 3-5a and the list of (official?) witnesses (vv. 5b-7) and having explained his understanding of his relation to "the apostles," he concluded, "Whether, then, it was I or they, so we preach and so you believed" (15:11). Hence, it is significant that the content of the Lucan kerygma turns out to be similar to the Pauline, with which it is so often pejoratively compared. There are differences, as Dodd pointed out (see above), but the absence of the title, Son of God (cf. Acts 8:37; 9:20), or of the intercession of the exalted Christ are not, in my opinion, so crucial that one could speak of substantial diversity. The absence of the assertion that Christ died for our sins is more significant; we shall comment on that in terms of Lucan soteriology below (see pp. 219-221).

Perhaps this comparison of the Lucan and Pauline kerygma is too material and disregards the formal challenge that the kerygma has in non-Lucan writings. But it should be recalled that we have been speaking of the content-sense of the kerygma. In that sense the similarity outweighs the diversity. Both Paul and Luke speak in their own way of a new age or of an age of fulfillment, i.e. in effect, of the *eschaton*. Moreover, both of them speak of Jesus as the agent of that eschaton's salvation and as the judge of the living and the dead (Rom 2:16; 14:10; cf. Acts 2:19-21; 10:42). Luke has tempered the eschatological aspect with his historical perspective, but has not dulled the capacity of the kerygma in his writings to challenge the Christian believer. What Paul has presented to us as the scandal of the cross (1 Cor 1:23) differs little from the prediction that he was "marked for the fall and rise of many in Israel, a symbol that men will reject" (Luke 2:34).

If we separated the active and content senses of the kerygma in the above discussion, it was simply for the sake of convenience in the discussion of details. Such a distinction cannot always be made with ease, and one may hesitate about some of the details—whether this or that might not have been better discussed elsewhere. As U. Luck ("Kerygma, Tradition, und Geschichte Jesu," 112) has observed, "for Luke kerygma, tradition and the Jesus-story are not really to be separated from each other." Luke presents no abstract kerygma, no mere address, not even a "mass of tradition." All has been worked into his story of the Christ-event. The Gospel is only the first part of Luke's narrative account; it is the inherited gospel tradition and the kerygma shaped into what Luke regards as its proper form—an account of how God's salvific activity in Christ is presently to be comprehended. Even Bultmann, for all his insistence on kerygma as the act/word of God challenging human beings personally in the salvific crucifixion and resurrection of Christ Jesus, could also identify it as "the word of Christ whose contents may also be formulated in a series of abstract propositions" ("Bultmann Replies to His Critics," 209).

Having thus isolated the kerygmatic elements in the Lucan writings, we may now turn to the more distinctively Lucan theological emphases. Even if the kerygma in Luke has its distinctive aspects and at the same time a great deal of similarity with that of other NT writings, we must now make an effort to see what Luke has done with the inherited tradition.

2. *The Structure of the Lucan Gospel.* Having begun the sketch of Lucan theology with a discussion of the kerygma in Luke-Acts, we may now move on to the distinctive cast that Luke has given to traditional material beyond that which may be called kerygmatic. Conzelmann has rightly described the Lucan Gospel as not simply the transmission of the received kerygma, but as a reflection upon it; this he finds present in Luke's "critical attitude to tradition as well as in the positive formation of a new picture of history" (*Theology,* 12). Though it is not clear just what Conzelmann considers Luke's "critical attitude" toward tradition to be, he rightly refers to Luke's positive formation of a new picture of history. Before we come to that aspect of Lucan theology, however, we have to consider the evidence for Lucan theology in the structure of the Gospel itself.

The Third Gospel lacks the pedagogical structure of the Matthean Gospel, with its deliberate alternation of narrative episodes and catechetical discourses, and the symbolical structure of the Johannine Gospel, with its clear division into a Book of Signs and a Book of Glory and its systematic motif of the replacement of Jewish institutions by Jesus himself. Nevertheless the structure of the Lucan Gospel does reveal the author's concern to narrate the story of Jesus from more than an annalist's viewpoint. As is explained elsewhere (see pp. 66-71), Luke has fundamentally followed the order of Mark. But his modification of the order of Mark with additions from "Q" and "L" manifests an emphasis that is not found in Mark, one which is not solely literary.

Luke has, first of all, prefaced the Marcan material with an infancy narrative, which, though dependent on pre-Lucan information, is a stylized composition of parallel episodes. It not only explains the relationship of Jesus to John the Baptist in a way that is lacking in the Marcan Gospel, but incorporates many theological motifs of the Gospel proper. It neither represents Proto-Lucan theology nor is it of questionable authenticity (pace Conzelmann, Theology, 118); it is an integral factor in Lucan theology. Functioning, as it were, as an overture to the Gospel proper, the infancy narrative sounds initially many of the motifs to be orchestrated later on in the Gospel and Acts. Many of the chords of the Lucan composition are first struck in it: for instance, John as the precursor of Jesus, Jesus as Savior, Messiah, and Lord, Jesus as a child marked for the fall and rise of many in Israel, a symbol that people will reject; Jesus as incorporated into Israel, foreshadowing the logical connection between (Pharisaic) Judaism and Christianity that Luke will suggest time and again toward the end of Acts.

Second, the Lucan transposition of Marcan material (e.g. the Nazareth synagogue scene) results not only in a different order of presentation, but has its own symbolic and apologetic intent. The Nazareth scene is programmatic for the ministry, symbolizing the rejection of Jesus by his own townspeople, and preparing for the acceptance of him by Peter and the others.

Third, chapter 9 is of no little importance in the Lucan Gospel, its structure being determined by the so-called Big Omission (see p. 67) and the introduction of the lengthy travel account. Luke's treatment of the retained Marcan material makes his form of Herod's question, "Who is this about whom I hear such talk?" (9:9), pivotal in that part of the Gospel. In the rest of the chapter Luke supplies a whole series of answers to the question, some of which involve christological titles (see further the COMMENT on 9:7-9).

Fourth, the Lucan Gospel is unique in its lengthy travel account (9:51 - 19:27), part of which is distinctively Lucan (9:51 - 18:14). It is a major factor in the Lucan geographical perspective, to be discussed below, which enhances Luke's concern to move Jesus resolutely toward Jerusalem, the city of destiny. No matter what else is to be said about the travel account, it certainly reveals a Lucan theological concern.

Fifth, the Lucan emphasis on Jesus' Jerusalem ministry as one of teaching in the Temple is again a manifestation of a theological concern.

Sixth, chapter 24, with its climactic assertions about a suffering Messiah, bolstered by a proof-from-prophecy argument and a final commission to witnesses who are to await the promise of the Father (the Spirit), provides not only a fitting conclusion to this structured composition of traditional gospel material but also a bridge to the second Lucan volume.

Finally, much of what Luke presents in this structured Gospel finds an unfolding in his second volume, not only in the parallels between Peter and Paul, the two principals of Acts, but also in the parallel patterns between the Gospel and Acts. Here one has to recall the contributions that H. Flender and C. H. Talbert have made in the study of this aspect of Lucan theology. See the general bibliography, pp. 259-260.

3. *The Lucan Geographical Perspective.* It may seem strange to discuss in a sketch of Lucan theology the author's preoccupation with geographical details. But there is reason for doing so, not only because the Third Gospel gives more attention to geography than any of the others or because of what has been called Luke's "geographical ineptitude" (C. C. McCown, "Gospel Geography," 15), but also because this perspective is subservient to a theological concern in the Lucan writings. The perspective not only affects the structure of the Lucan Gospel; it also transcends the structure. The structure of the Third Gospel is basically that of the Marcan Gospel, with only one journey of Jesus to Jerusalem, and differs in this regard from the Johannine Gospel with its three journeys to Jerusalem. But in preserving the one-journey story, Luke has enhanced it with redactional, compositional details that affect the geography of the story and reveal a theological preoccupation.

Building on partial studies of this perspective undertaken by various writers before him, Conzelmann devoted the first part of his five-part *Theology* to a detailed analysis of it (18-94). An extended critique of many points in Conzelmann's study was later undertaken by W. C. Robinson, Jr., *Der Weg des Herrn*. Robinson has been inclined to substitute a spatial or geographical summary, "the Way of the Lord," for Conzelmann's temporal or historical summary of Lucan theology, "the center of time," to which he had in fact subordinated the geographical perspective (see *IDBSup*, 560). But it seems rather that, in explaining Lucan theology, one has to allow for both of these perspectives; both of them are obviously Lucan concerns. Here we must limit ourselves to the essential traits of the geographical perspective; details will be considered at appropriate places in the commentary proper.

The overarching geographical perspective in Luke-Acts can be seen in the author's preoccupation with Jerusalem as the city of destiny for Jesus and the pivot for the salvation of mankind. Luke establishes a special relationship between Jesus' person and ministry and that city of David's throne. He depicts Jesus making his way thither as his goal (13:32). From there too the word of God's salvation must spread to the end of the earth in Acts. It is not merely the place where Jesus suffered, died, and was raised to glory; it is also the place where salvation itself has been accomplished once and for all and from which preordained witnesses carry forth the kerygma about it. Thus the geographical perspective becomes a factor in the divine plan of salvation, to be discussed below.

Unlike the compositions of the other evangelists, the Lucan Gospel begins and ends in Jerusalem: after the prologue, the first scene is that of Zechariah offering incense in the Jerusalem Temple (1:9), where he learns of the birth of a son, and at the end Luke tells how the Eleven and the others returned to Jerusalem from Bethany to spend their time in the Temple (24:53). In its own way the infancy narrative strikes the chord of the journey-to-Jerusalem motif in depicting the child Jesus taken there twice by his parents (2:22,42). The scene of the twelve-year-old Jesus sitting among the Temple teachers, who were astounded at his understanding and his answers, foreshadows in a sense not only his Temple teaching-ministry (19:47), but identifies him as one who has to be in his Father's house (2:49; cf. 19:45-46). Moreover, the angel's words to Mary reveal that the child to be born to her will sit on the throne of David and be king over the house of Jacob (1:32-33)—implying a special relationship to Jerusalem.

The preoccupation with Jerusalem undoubtedly accounts for the order of the temptation scenes in Luke 4:1-13, where what is more likely the original order (desert, pinnacle of the Temple, and high mountain—see Matt 4:1-11) has been altered to give the climactic ending to Jerusalem (desert, high mountain, pinnacle of the Temple—see the COMMENT at 4:5). Thus the climax of Jesus' encounter with Satan comes precisely in his city of destiny in this symbolic scene on the pinnacle of the house of his Father. The locale is, moreover, highlighted as the evangelist adds the remark about Jesus' subsequent withdrawal to Galilee (4:14), the transition between that encounter of opposition and temptation and the real work of his ministry itself, which will depict opposition and temptation in other, concrete forms.

Once the ministry proper begins, the areas of Jesus' activity are defined as Galilee (4:14-9:50), Samaria (9:51-17:11), and Judea/Jerusalem (17:11-21:38). Though some commentators have thought that the Lucan Jesus had a Samaritan mission (E. Lohmeyer, C. C. McCown), it may be questioned whether that is so. The threefold geographic distribution of the ministry would be better put as the Galilean ministry (4:14-9:50), the journey to Jerusalem (through Samaria and Judea, but not through Perea, 9:51-19:27), and the Jerusalem ministry (19:28-21:38). Judea is mentioned in 4:44 as an area of his activity; if it is meant in a specific sense as opposed to Galilee, it creates a notorious problem (see NOTE there), but it may rather be used generically, as in 1:5; 7:17; 23:5. Jesus' reputation spreads to other areas that are mentioned (all Judea and the surrounding countryside, 7:17), and people flock to him from elsewhere (from every village in Galilee and Judea, and even from Jerusalem, 5:17; from Judea, Jerusalem, Tyre, and Sidon, 6:17). Presumably, however, in all of this he is still in Galilee.

One detects in this regard Luke's concern to move Jesus from Galilee to Jerusalem, the city of destiny. In 23:5 Jesus is described as one who has been stirring up people all throughout Judea with his teaching; "he began in Galilee and has come even here." And in Acts 10:37 Luke depicts Peter announcing that word which has been proclaimed throughout Judea, starting from Galilee after the baptism that John preached. Underlying this perspective is the Lucan redaction of 22:22 about the Son of Man going his way (poreuetai, see below), "as it has been determined." This clearly relates the geographic movements of Jesus to a theological preoccupation.

Luke is scarcely unaware of disciples or followers of Jesus in areas to the north of Galilee (e.g. Christians in Phoenicia, Acts 11:19; or people from Tyre and Sidon, Luke 6:17), but he studiously avoids any reference to a ministry of Jesus in such territory. His progress from Galilee to Jerusalem is predetermined, and so Luke omits what corresponds to Mark 6:45 - 8:26 (the so-called Big Omission), thus eliminating Jesus' activity in Bethsaida (Mark 6:45), Tyre and Sidon (Mark 7:24,31), and the Decapolis (Mark 7:31). That this omission was deliberate has been convincingly shown by V. Taylor (Behind the Third Gospel, 91) and accepted by Conzelmann (Theology, 52-55). Even in episodes that Luke has taken over from the Marcan Gospel, he omits mention of the geographical locality: thus Peter's confession of Jesus as the Messiah is not located anywhere (Luke 9:18; cf. Mark 8:27, Caesarea Philippi), and the notice about Jesus' return to Galilee is omitted (Mark 9:30; cf. Luke 9:43). Even when Jesus is depicted going into the region of the Gerasenes, Luke is at pains to identify it as opposite Galilee (8:26).

An important part of the geographical perspective is the so-called travel account (9:51 - 19:27). Luke seems to draw his inspiration for it from Mark 10:1, where Jesus is said to have gone to the region of Judea and beyond the Jordan. But instead of making Jesus go by that route, Luke has his own ideas. He significantly introduces a theological motivation for his starting out from Galilee to go up to Jerusalem: "As the days were drawing near when he was to be taken up, he set his face resolutely toward Jerusalem" (9:51). The problems that the travel account raises at this point in the Gospel will be discussed in the commentary proper. Here it suffices to note that the first part of the account is peculiarly Lucan

(9:51-18:14), being almost wholly independent of Marcan material and composed out of material derived from "Q" and "L". The latter part of it (18:15-19:27) corresponds closely to Mark 10:13-52, being but another form of the Synoptic journey to Jerusalem. Yet three times over in the specifically Lucan form reference is made to the goal of his journey (9:51-53; 13:22; 17:11), lest the details incorporated into this artificially expanded account, which often have little to do with a journey, distract the reader from its main purpose in the Lucan presentation. At the outset Luke notes that Jesus "set his face resolutely toward Jerusalem" (9:51), determined to face his destiny; that notice comes shortly after the transfiguration scene, in which Luke had depicted Moses and Elijah conversing with Jesus about the *exodos,* "departure," that he was to complete in Jerusalem (9:31). Conzelmann (*Theology,* 63) regards the travel account as "a progress toward the Passion." That is certainly true, but it cannot be limited to the passion, since in 9:51 itself Luke is clearly thinking of the ascension of Jesus. Hence, the "departure" has to be understood as the complex of events that forms Jesus' transit to the Father: passion, death, burial, resurrection, and ascension/exaltation.

The peculiarly Lucan material forms only the first part of the travel account; the second part, considerably shorter (18:15-19:27), contains an ending that Luke has significantly altered. One may actually query whether the travel account comes to an end at 19:28 or includes the three following episodes: the regal entry of Jesus into Jerusalem (19:28-40), his lament over the city (19:41-44), and his immediate purging of the Temple (19:45-46). In any case, they are transitional, capable of being regarded as the climax of the travel account or as introductory to the section about Jesus' teaching ministry in the Jerusalem Temple, which begins at 19:47. At any rate, one should note the modification of the scenes that Luke has made.

Arriving at the city of destiny, Jesus enters it as a king in triumph, riding on a colt (19:35-36). As he draws near to the city, he is hailed by crowds, *"Blest be* the king, *the one who comes in the name of the Lord!* Peace in heaven and glory in the highest heaven!" (19:38, with an allusion [italicized] to Ps 118:26). Only in Luke among the Synoptics is Jesus hailed as a "king" at this point. The addition of this title results in a different understanding of the psalm alluded to (see the COMMENT). *Ho erchomenos,* "the one who comes" (i.e. the pilgrim coming to the Temple), now assumes a new meaning, taking on the connotations of "the One Who Is to Come" of the earlier gospel tradition (see Luke 7:19) and now identified explicitly as a "king." Luke's insertion of the title "king" not only makes the entry of Jesus explicitly royal, but alludes to the angel's words to Mary that her son will sit on the throne of David (1:32). Furthermore, it explains why Jesus, having entered the city of

David's throne, goes immediately to the Temple, not just to look around, as in Mark 11:11, but to purge it. "And suddenly to his temple shall come the Lord whom you are seeking" (Mal 3:1, the source of *ho erchomenos* speculation). In an act of authority (*exousia,* Luke 20:2), Jesus the king, the One Who Is to Come, purges his Father's house. This climax of the travel account gathers up any number of Lucan theological strands and again reveals how the geographical perspective subserves the theological concerns of Luke.

The pivotal role of Jerusalem is also clear in Luke 24, which recounts the appearances of the risen Christ only in the vicinity of this city. The Lucan Gospel knows nothing of appearances in Galilee, even though that area is mentioned in 24:6b, to recall what he had told the disciples when he was still in Galilee. But Jerusalem forms rather the geographic link that unites the Gospel to Acts: "In his name repentance for the forgiveness of sins must be preached to all the nations—beginning from Jerusalem" (24:47). The last phrase, *arxamenoi apo Ierousalēm,* echoes 23:5, *arxamenos apo tēs Galilaias heōs hōde,* "beginning from Galilee even to this place." Moreover, the commission expressed in 24:47 is picked up in the programmatic verse of Acts (1:8), which also reveals Jerusalem as the starting-point for the spread of the word of the Lord to "the end of the earth."

This pivotal position of Jerusalem in the two volumes of Luke is important because it is related to "the events that have come to fulfillment among us" (Luke 1:1). Those events included not only what "Jesus began to do and teach" (Acts 1:1), but also the stage-by-stage spread of the word of God from Jerusalem, the mother-church, to outer Judea and Samaria (8:1,5,26), to Caesarea Maritima (8:40) and Galilee (9:31), to Damascus (9:2), to Phoenicia, Cyprus, and Syrian Antioch (11:19), to the Roman provinces of Cilicia, Galatia, Asia, Macedonia, and Achaia, and finally to Rome itself, "the end of the earth" (Acts 1:8; 23:11c; 28:14; cf. *Ps. Sol.* 8:15).

Behind this idea of Jerusalem as the city of destiny and the pivot for the word of God's salvation to the nations may lie certain OT notions. Isa 49:6 may have influenced Luke in this respect: "I will set you as a light to the nations that my salvation may reach to the end of the earth" (cf. Luke 2:32 and Acts 13:47). Or again, "Out of Zion the Law shall go forth, and the word of the Lord from Jerusalem" (Isa 2:3 = Mic 4:2). The word that was proclaimed, "beginning from Galilee" (*arxamenos apo tēs Galilaias,* Acts 10:37), must now go forth from Jerusalem. Though Luke never uses the expression, Jerusalem functions for him as "the navel of the earth" (Ezek 38:12; cf. 5:5; *Jub.* 8:19).

A few other elements of this geographical perspective in Luke-Acts have to be mentioned. First, there is the pregnant use of the verb *poreuesthai,* "go, move along, proceed on one's way." Luke makes frequent use of it, but in certain instances it bears a special connotation when employed of Jesus. For example, this usage is found in 4:30, when at the end of his visit to Nazareth, he slips through the crowd and goes on his way. The context is one of opposition and hostility, and the implication is that his destiny is to be reached despite such opposition. Further noteworthy instances of it are to be found in the travel account in particular (9:51,52,53,56,57; 10:38; 13:33; 17:11; 19:12), though its use is not confined to this section. We have already alluded to the use of it above, concerning the Son of Man who goes his way, "as it has been determined" (22:22).

Second, Luke depicts Jesus' whole career as a course or a way. This view of his career seems to be rooted in the pre-Lucan tradition which used Isa 40:3 to describe John the Baptist's role in the desert, "making ready the way of the Lord" (Mark 1:3; cf. Luke 3:4; 7:27). Regardless of the specific meaning that *hodos,* "way," would have had in John's career, it becomes for Luke a special designation for Jesus' salvific mission. Within the travel account the word occurs in 9:57; 18:35; elsewhere it is found in 19:36; 20:21; 24:32. Possibly a pregnant sense of it can be detected in 1:79; 20:21; 24:32. This "way" is not simply expressive of his physical arrival in Jerusalem or of his progress toward the passion. It describes something greater, which begins with an *eisodos,* "entrance" (a compound of *eis,* "into," and *hodos*), that takes place only once John's "course" (*dromos*) has been run; and it ends with an *exodos,* "departure" (a compound of *ex,* "out of," and *hodos*), about which Jesus conversed with Moses and Elijah in the transfiguration scene. The details of all this are set forth in Paul's speech in Antioch in Pisidia: "According to his promise God brought forth from this man's [i.e. David's] offspring Jesus, a savior for Israel. John heralded his entrance (*eisodos*) in advance, by proclaiming a baptism for all the people of Israel. As John's course (*dromos*) was coming to an end, he used to say, 'What you suspect me to be, that I am not; rather, one is coming after me, the sandals of whose feet I am not worthy to unfasten" (Acts 13:23-25). Thus both John and Jesus are related through details of the Lucan geographical perspective to the Father's salvific plan. (Further aspects of *hodos* will be discussed below in terms of Christian discipleship as Luke understands it.)

Third, it is to be noted that Jesus' way is intimately related to his "being taken up" (Luke 9:51) or his "ascension" (Acts 1:2,11,22). For, as we have noted above, the "departure" is not fully explained unless it includes the ascension/exaltation of Jesus. As Luke sees it, a time has been set for this in the Father's plan of salvation; Luke 9:51 alludes to this ("the days for his being taken up were reaching their full number"). This too explains why the people of Nazareth were not able to do away with him (Luke 4:30). This time-aspect sets the ascension in historical perspective, but it does also have a spatial connotation in Luke's view of it, and as the goal of Jesus' career it has to be considered here, for it is part of the Messiah's transit to glory: "Was not the Messiah bound to suffer all this before entering (*eiselthein*) into his glory?" (Luke 24:26).

A few further aspects of the Lucan geographical perspective can be treated briefly. Conzelmann (*Theology,* 18-27) has sought to use details of the geographical perspective in the Lucan Gospel to dissociate John the Baptist from Jesus' ministry. He has maintained that the locales of the ministry of the two are clearly demarcated in Lucan thinking. The desert first and then all the region about the Jordan would form the scene of John's itinerant preaching, but he has nothing to do with Galilee, Judea, or Jerusalem. John is not a kingdom-preacher, and hence his ministry differs from that of Jesus, even geographically. Moreover, John is imprisoned in the Lucan Gospel even before Jesus is baptized, with the result that we are not told by whom Jesus was baptized (3:19-22). Luke thus avoids bringing the two into contact. The reason would be that, whereas in the pre-Lucan tradition John stands at the dawn of a new age, is the precursor of Jesus, and is Elijah come back, he plays none of these roles in the Lucan Gospel. For Luke would never bring figures of the past into direct connection with future eschatological events. John, then, belongs to the earliest epoch; he is the greatest prophet of the Period of Israel. But with Jesus' arrival on the scene, in a distinct locale, a new stage is begun in the process of salvation. Thus, according to Conzelmann, Luke uses geographic details to separate the locales of John and Jesus in the interest of separating periods of salvation-history.

As will be discussed in the section on the Lucan historical perspective, Conzelmann has not understood the relation of John the Baptist and Jesus correctly. Here comment will be made only on the geographical problems. First of all, Conzelmann has overdrawn the distinction in locales in regarding the region about the Jordan as "the region of the old era" (*Theology,* 20). Here he characterizes a *geographical* area in terms of a *temporal* distinction. His overall thesis about the periods of salvation-history has affected his treatment of geography. Second, Luke depicts Jesus passing through John's locale in the episodes situated at Jericho. As he draws near the town (18:35) he cures a blind man, in an episode derived from "Mk." Again, in an episode peculiar to his Gospel, he encounters Zacchaeus as he passes through the town (19:1-10). If Luke could describe John's locale as "the region all around the Jordan" (3:3), Jericho would have to be included. Conzelmann tries, indeed, to avoid this fact by claiming that Luke would not have known that Jericho was in the region about the Jordan, because he could not have learned this from the LXX (*Theology,* 19). Perhaps. But that seems to presume too much.

(A better reason for tolerating Jesus' passage through the area might have been that John has already been beheaded; see Luke 9:9.) Third, as W. Wink has pointed out, the "desert" is just as much John's area as the region about the Jordan (see Luke 1:80; 3:2,4; 7:24) and Jesus is depicted in it (4:2; 5:16); see *John the Baptist,* 49. Fourth, as Robinson has noted, the generic distinction of locales for John and Jesus is part of the pre-Lucan tradition. Mark 10:1, which mentions Jesus going to the region of Judea and beyond the Jordan, may be omitted by Luke; but it was omitted as part of a block of material (Mark 9:42-10:12) which Luke has left out (*Der Weg des Herrn,* 10-16). Hence it is difficult to see a special geographical concern in the treatment of John beyond the generic separation of their areas, which was already present in the pre-Lucan tradition: John in the desert and near the Jordan, Jesus in Galilee, Samaria, and Judea/Jerusalem. Luke omits Perea and the northern area, which he knew from the pre-Lucan material.

Another aspect of the geographical perspective has, finally, to be pointed out. As will be explained more fully in the commentary proper, the travel account serves a Lucan theological concern in another way. It is the section in the Gospel in which Jesus trains the preordained and chosen witnesses from Galilee. This training, couched largely in the sayings-material used in that section, will serve as the basis for the "assurance" being given to Theophilus that the teaching of Luke's community is rooted in the teaching of Jesus himself (see Luke 8:1-2; 9:51-52; Acts 1:3-8,21-22; 10:41). This aspect of the geographical perspective has been well worked out by W. C. Robinson, Jr. ("The Theological Context," esp. pp. 27-28, 30).

4. *The Lucan Historical Perspective.* A sketch of Lucan theology also has to cope with the author's preoccupation with historical connections in his writing. In fact, this aspect of the Lucan writings is more important for Lucan theology than the geographical perspective just discussed, because it reveals that Luke is, indeed, playing the early Christian kerygma in a new key.

At the outset, it is necessary to insist that one should not confuse the question of the historicity of the Lucan account with its historical perspective. The former has been discussed in relation to a "thesis" about Lucan theology (see pp. 14-18 above). What interests us here is rather the evangelist's concern to anchor the Jesus-story and its sequel in time or in human history. But the question of historicity does raise another, related question: Did the early Christian kerygma ever include the recital of historical facts? Was historical reminiscence ever part of the kerygma? One response lies behind the way some writers speak about the kerygma over against historical concern. The shape of the kerygma in Paul (or even in the form it takes in the speeches of Acts alleged to contain it) is different from the shape of the kerygma in Mark or "Q." In the former the accent is on proclamation, whereas in the latter the kerygmatic message is veiled in narrative that prima facie purports to be historical. N. Perrin (*Rediscovering the Teaching of Jesus* [New York: Harper & Row, 1967] 15) has denied that "historical reminiscence" was one of the purposes of the gospel form in the early church. He is right in the sense that there was no concern to record with exactitude the *ipsissima verba Iesu*. Reminiscence was not the primary purpose of the primitive kerygma, but to divest the kerygma wholly of historical recollection would be to sever it from all relation to the historical Jesus. Historical reminiscence, the recital of historical fact, did become part of the kerygma as found in the gospel-shape of it; and that is why one can still detect some kerygmatic elements in Luke-Acts. But even if we admit this, we still have to insist that the historical perspective in which Luke has cast the kerygma in his writings is far more important for Lucan theology.

A. LUKE'S CONCERN TO SITUATE THE CHRIST-EVENT IN TIME. The best evidence for this concern is found in Paul's statement before King Agrippa toward the end of Acts (26:26). Having briefly rehearsed details of his own conversion and of the Christ-event, Paul announced, "None of these things has escaped the king's notice, for this was not done in a corner." In contrast to this view of the events, what is related in Mark, John, and even Matthew (who does have a fleeting reference to Herod the Great in 2:1) might well have happened in a corner, for all the interest in contemporary history that they manifest. And similar to Paul's statement is that of Cleopas in Luke 24:18: "Are you the only stranger in Jerusalem who has not learned what happened there these last few days?" Only Luke has emphasized the far-reaching connections of the Christ-event and the Christian proclamation of it. He alone relates them to persons, times, institutions, and epochs of world history.

1) *Diēgēsis*, "Narrative Account." The first indication of Luke's perspective is given by the quasi-title that Luke has used for his two-volume composition. Mark had begun his story with "the beginning of the gospel of Jesus Christ" (1:1). Here *euangelion* appears as the quasi-title of Mark's opus, and the word occurs again six times in it (1:14,15; 8:35; 10:29; 13:10; 14:9 [and once in the Marcan appendix, 16:15]). This word is not used by Mark in the sense of a literary genre, "Gospel," to which we have been accustomed ever since the second century (see Justin Martyr *Apologia* 1.66; *Dialogus cum Tryphone Iudaeo* 10.2). For him it rather means the "good news," as its etymology would suggest; it is a summation of the message of the story that he is about to recount. Whether Jesus himself would have used the word *euangelion* or its

Aramaic equivalent is debated (see *TDNT* 2. 727-728). Within the gospel tradition the use of the term seems rather to be a Marcan contribution, for it is absent in John as well as in Luke and is found only four times in Matthew (introduced by him into two summary statements derived from Mark, 4:23; 9:35, and twice derived from Mark, 24:14; 26:13, but used of "this" gospel—the gospel of the kingdom). The Marcan influence on Matthew in this regard is clear. Matthew never uses it independently. (Luke does finally use it late in Acts; see below.)

The Marcan usage of *euangelion* may be related to the usage in the Pauline corpus, where it frequently occurs. This has at least been so argued by W. Marxsen (*Mark the Evangelist: Studies on the Redaction History of the Gospel* [Nashville: Abingdon, 1969]). See further E. Molland, *Die paulinische Euangelion: Das Wort und die Sache* (Avhandlinger utgitt av det norske Videnskaps-Akademie i Oslo, II. Hist.-Filos. Kl., 1934, No. 3; Oslo: Dybwad, 1934); R. J. Dillon, "Mark and the New Meaning of 'Gospel,'" *DunRev* 7 (1967) 131-161. Marxsen even goes so far as to describe the "gospel" in Mark as the means of bringing to human beings the very presence of Jesus himself. He appeals above all to Mark 8:35, where Jesus speaks of losing one's life "for my sake and for the sake of the gospel"; see 10:29; 13:9-10. This identification of the gospel and Jesus himself has been contested by G. Strecker, "Literarkritische Überlegungen zum *euangelion*-Begriff in Markusevangelium," in *Neues Testament und Geschichte: Historisches Geschehen und Deutung im Neuen Testament: Oscar Cullmann zum 70. Geburtstag* (eds. H. Baltensweiler and B. Reicke; Zürich: Theologischer V.; Tübingen: Mohr, 1972) 91-104.

In avoiding *euangelion* in his first volume, Luke seems to be reacting against the Marcan usage of it. He does introduce it, however, in Acts: once on the lips of Peter (15:7), and once on those of Paul (20:24). In using *diēgēsis* as the quasi-title of his opus, he designates it as a "narrative account" and adopts for his work a term current among Hellenistic litterateurs and historians. The frequency with which the word occurs in both classical and Hellenistic Greek writers, especially by those who profess to write history or about history and the way it should be written, makes it impossible to miss the intention with which Luke proposes his account of the Christ-event. M. Hadas in the introduction to his edition of the *Letter of Aristeas*, which also bears the title of *diēgēsis*, quotes the second-century Greek rhetorician Theon, who defined it as *logos ekthetikos pragmatōn gegonotōn ē hōs gegonotōn*, "an expository account of things which happened or might have happened"; Hadas also quotes Cicero's definition of the Latin equivalent: "narratio est rerum gestarum aut ut gestarum expositio," i.e. a narrative is a setting forth of things as done or as might have been done (*De Inv.* 1.19,27). See *Aristeas to*

Philocrates (*Letter of Aristeas*) (ed. M. Hadas; New York: Harper, 1951) 57. For further information on the use of *diēgēsis* in ancient Greek writers, see the NOTE on 1:1.

Why Luke has avoided *euangelion* we shall never be able to say for sure. It may be that he was familiar with the use of *euangelion* in the cult of the Roman emperor in the eastern Mediterranean and preferred to avoid the use of it in his story of Jesus. The word is used in the oft-quoted Priene inscription about Augustus (see p. 394 below; cf. *TDNT* 2 [1964] 724). There the "good news" is the salvation and good fortune that the emperor brings to human beings. But Luke's use of *diēgēsis* as the quasi-title of his work gives it not only a literary dimension, but alerts the reader to the historical implications of the story.

It may seem that we are making too much of the Lucan omission of *euangelion* in the Gospel; after all, Luke does use the verb *euangelizesthai* frequently (see above p. 148). We have already discussed the sense of that verb, which by and large has the meaning "preach, announce, proclaim" in the Lucan writings rather than "announce the good news."

The use of *diēgēsis* as the quasi-title of Luke's writing in the literary prologue relates his work to that of other historians. In this regard one should consult Lucian *Quomodo Historia conscribenda sit* 54-55, who speaks explicitly of the prologues of Herodotus and Thucydides. We have already commented on the four qualities that Luke assigns to his endeavor and the way in which they have to be understood; see pp. 15-16 above. One cannot neglect the historical concern that they give to the Lucan *diēgēsis*.

2) *How Luke Situates the Christ-event in Time.* Years ago Bultmann noted that for Luke Christianity was conceived of as an "entity of world history" (*Theology* 2. 116) and he sought to explain the ways in which the tradition about Jesus was passed on in the three Synoptics. Jesus' words and deeds were passed on, not as those of the church's heavenly Lord, but in the framework of a story. (I have referred to this above as the gospel-shape of the kerygma as contrasted with the Pauline shape.) Yet, Bultmann contends, neither Matthew nor Mark wrote his Gospel out of historical interest, as did Luke. In Mark the Jesus-tradition was still subservient to the kerygma and retained a fundamental challenge, whereas Matthew presented Jesus as the one in whom the history of salvation found its fulfillment. Matthew's account revealed that eschatological salvation had become history; yet Jesus was not presented as a figure of world history, but rather as its conclusion (ibid. 2. 124-126).

 However, one has to ask whether it is evident that, even if in the Lucan Gospel Jesus has become a figure of world history, his eschatological significance has been eliminated or dulled thereby. If the Lucan Jesus, as the risen, exalted Lord, is the one in whose name repentance for the forgiveness of sins is still to be preached to all nations (Luke 24:47), the one whose testimony is to be carried to the end of the earth (Acts 1:8), the one in whose name alone salvation is to be found (Acts 4:12), and the one who will come again in the same way he was seen to go (Acts 1:11), is this account any less challenging or eschatological than the Matthean?

As we shall see, the Lucan historical perspective has colored the eschatological thrust of the early kerygma that it contains, but there is almost as much a sense of the eschatological present in the Lucan writings as in Mark or Matthew. Luke has a clear awareness that a new era of human history has begun in the birth, ministry, death and resurrection of Jesus. He does not express it in the same way as does Matthew (e.g. with formula quotations), but time after time he calls attention to fulfillment. Those allusions imply at least as much concern with the inbreaking of a new age as do the Matthean citations.

In contrasting Luke and Mark, Bultmann also stressed that fulfillment was of minor importance for the latter. In Mark Bultmann found the emphasis falling rather on the miracles and the events of baptism and transfiguration, which express the kerygmatic character of the story being written. Jesus' life has not become an episode of world history but the miraculous manifestation of the divine robed in a cloak of earthly occurrence. But even if Luke has presented Jesus' life as an episode of world history, has he completely eliminated the miraculous manifestation of the divine? There is much of that still left in Luke—some would say too much. These features are not incompatible; the kerygma exists in Luke along with the historical perspective. We turn now to the details of the latter. The story of Jesus is related by Luke to world history in three ways, by connecting it with Roman history, Palestinian history, and church history.

a) *Relation to Roman History*. Luke relates his narrative to the history of the Roman world by several references in the Gospel and Acts. He connects the birth of Jesus with a decree of Caesar Augustus ordering the registration of the whole (Roman) world (2:1). During the reign of Augustus a census was to be carried out in the province of Syria, during the governorship of P. Sulpicius Quirinius (2:2). In the commentary we shall discuss the problem of the dating of this census, and even if we shall have to admit that Luke's information about it leaves something to be desired, his intention is clear: The birth of the person from whom Christianity takes its start is situated in the Roman world and related to Roman history. It was important for Luke, theologically, that Jesus was born in the rule of Caesar Augustus, in the time of the *pax Augusta*, "the Augustan Peace." The peace and security of Augustus' imperial dominion have a counterpart in an effect of the Christ-event to be discussed below.

Again, the word of God which came to John the Baptist in the desert
and which inaugurated his preaching of repentance is dated by Luke to
the fifteenth year of Tiberius Caesar (between August or September
A.D. 28) and to the prefecture of Pontius Pilate (A.D. 26-36) in the
Roman province of Judea (Luke 3:1). This anchoring of the beginning
of John's ministry to Roman history serves to date the beginning of Jesus'
ministry, since he is baptized before John is beheaded.

Further reference is made to Roman history in the mention of the famine in the days of Claudius (Acts 11:28); what was foretold by the Spirit
is thus precisely related to the reign of this Roman emperor (A.D. 41-54).
Luke further refers to him in telling of the arrival of Aquila and Priscilla
in Corinth, because the emperor had ordered all Jews to leave Rome
(Acts 18:2). This is usually dated to A.D. 49, by a combination of information from Suetonius *Claudii vita* 25 and Orosius *Historiae adversum
paganos* 7.6 (CSEL 5.451).

Again, Luke tells of Paul being haled before the governor of the
Roman province of Achaia, "when Gallio was the proconsul" (Acts
18:12). With the aid of an inscription mentioning Gallio in such a post,
found in Greece at Delphi in 1905, it is possible to situate this appearance of Paul before him probably in the summer of A.D. 52 (see *JBC*, art.
46, § 9).

Finally, Luke depicts Paul's encounters with two Roman procurators,
Porcius Festus and Antonius Felix, perhaps about A.D. 60, though the
date of the succession of Festus is not easily established. Related to
Paul's appearance before Festus is his appeal to Caesar (Acts 25:11).
Thereafter Paul is finally sent off to Rome itself in the care of Julius, a
centurion of the cohort Augusta (27:1), and eventually arrives there and
preaches the word of God in the capital of the civilized world of the time.

In this way Luke has presented the Christ-event and its sequel as a
phenomenon rooted in Roman history of the first century of this era.

b) *Relation to Palestinian History.* Matt 2:1 links the birth of Jesus to
the days of King Herod the Great (37-4 B.C.), and we learn from
2:15,19 that his birth took place before the end of that long reign. In the
Lucan Gospel the birth of John the Baptist is announced to his father in
"the days of Herod, king of Judea" (1:5). This date, taken with the announcement of the birth of Jesus six months later (1:36) and his actual
birth at the time of a census in the reign of Augustus (2:1-6), gives an
apparent but problematic synchronism, to which we have already referred. But, no matter how the dating is handled, the concern of Luke to
situate the birth of John and Jesus at a certain point in Palestinian history
is clear.

Similarly, though the other evangelists depict the appearance of Jesus
before the prefect of Judea, Pontius Pilate (e.g. Matt 27:2, where he is

explicitly named as the "governor" [hēgemōn]), only Luke uses him to fix a date, when he ties the call of John in the desert to the period "when Pontius Pilate was governor of Judea" (3:1), sometime between A.D. 26-36. Luke depicts Jesus before Pilate in his passion narrative (23:1-5), and he adds a further link with Palestinian history missing from the other Gospels when he tells how Pilate sent Jesus to Herod Antipas, the tetrarch of Galilee (4 B.C.-A.D. 39). In this case the synchronism is not made explicit, but the link of Jesus' passion to Palestinian history is plain. Cf. Luke 13:1.

Again, the connection of the high priests Annas and Caiaphas with the passion of Jesus is known from other Gospels (e.g. Matt 26:3; John 18:13,24; Luke 22:54, following Mark 14:53, does not name the high priest), but it is only Luke who refers to them in dating, again when telling of John's call to preach, "in the highpriesthood of Annas and Caiaphas" (3:2). The Lucan mode of referring to these two high priests together, implying that they were simultaneously in office, creates an historical problem (see the commentary). Annas was the high priest in A.D. 6-15 and Caiaphas in A.D. 18-36. Indeed, John 11:49 identifies Caiaphas explicitly as "the high priest that year," i.e. the year of Jesus' death. In any case, the intention of Luke is clear, as he pegs the ministry of John and Jesus roughly to a period of Palestinian history when these two high priests were powerful figures in the country. Further reference is made to them in Acts 4:6, when John and Peter are summoned before them and other members "of the high-priestly family." Here again Luke refers to Annas as "the high priest," in an episode that postdates the Christian Pentecost.

The most obvious instance of dating the ministry of Jesus to Palestinian history is found in the passage, to which we have already referred, about the call of John the Baptist, which is linked not only to the prefecture of Pilate and the highpriesthood of Annas and Caiaphas, but also to the reigns of Herod Antipas (tetrarch of Galilee), Philip (tetrarch of Iturea and Trachonitis), and Lysanias (tetrarch of Abilene) in 3:1. Save for Galilee, the first area of Jesus' ministry, these regions do not figure again in the Lucan story geographically; and so their only explanation has to be sought in the synchronism provided. For the details see the commentary.

In any case, Luke seems to be establishing connections between Jesus and such authority-figures in the Palestinian world. Indirectly, these prepare for his confrontation with some of the figures in the course of the narrative.

The explicit synchronisms that Luke uses, however, are limited to the beginning of his story. This fact raises the question why he did not continue the practice that he had introduced. On the other hand, the situation

also the reference to the falling tower in 13.4. + to Pilate in 13.1.

shows that he probably added them at the stage of composition when he was fashioning the infancy narrative and the prologue and that he cannot be accused of having overhistoricized the kerygma, presenting it as a chronicler would. He is still enough of a preacher to let his preaching dominate the story. Toward the end of his volumes the temporal connections are only suggested, no more obviously than in the other Gospels; the loosely dated incidents are the appearance of Jesus before Pontius Pilate or the high priests, and Paul's appearance before Felix, Festus, and King Agrippa in Acts.

c) *Relation to Church History.* Only Luke has written a sequel to the Jesus-story proper. His second volume, the Acts of the Apostles, is no more easily characterized as to its literary form than the Gospels, but the least one can say is that it is intended to give a rapid view of the sequel to the Christ-event itself. In it one sees the spread of the word of God and the emergence of the Christian church in the eastern Mediterranean world in the mid-first century of this era. Thus Luke has related in a peculiar way the Jesus-story to the early history of the Christian church.

The preoccupation with relating the Christ-event to the Christian church has an apologetic concern. It touches on the question of Christianity as a *religio licita,* a legitimate form of worship, in the Roman world, to borrow a term from Tertullian (*Apologeticus* 21:1; CCLat 1.122). We have commented above on the Lucan concentration of temporal references to Roman and Palestinian history mainly in the beginning of his story. Some of the synchronisms occur in the infancy narrative, some immediately after it in the Gospel. One of the purposes of the infancy narrative is to show the incorporation of Jesus into Palestinian Judaism from his very birth. It is only as the story develops, especially in the second volume, that one begins to realize that no little part of Luke's concern for that incorporation at the outset has been to foreshadow an important aspect of his whole work. Though it is not the main purpose of Acts, as has sometimes been argued, one cannot deny that Luke has a concern to depict Christianity as a logical outgrowth and continuation of Judaism, and especially of the Pharisaic form of it. If Judaism had the right to exist in the Roman world, then Christianity has too. This concern is not obvious in the Lucan writings from the outset; but it does emerge clearly in time: first of all, in the triple declaration of Jesus' innocence by Pilate in the passion narrative (Luke 23:4,14,22); and then indirectly in declarations of Paul's innocence toward the end of Acts (23:29; 25:25; 26:30-32; 28:21), declarations put on the lips of both Roman officials and Jews.

Thus the historical perspective in which Luke has played the kerygma in his writings has an obvious theological or apologetic concern. This perspective of the Lucan story is really part of a larger historical concern in the Lucan writings, viz. the sense of salvation-history, of which the foregoing relations are only a part and against which they have to be viewed. The history of the contemporary world, to which Luke has related the Christ-event in these various ways, has to be understood as affected by God himself in the activity of Jesus who appeared in that history. So we must now turn to a discussion of the Lucan view of salvation-history.

B. SALVATION-HISTORY. As we have already explained, an understanding of "salvation-history" is found in several NT writers who have recounted or interpreted the Christ-event. As a generic term, it would suit the view of Matthew or Paul, as well as Luke. The term is used, in a specific sense, of the Lucan writings, because of the numerous elements in them that go to make it up. As F. Bovon has noted ("Le salut," 303), it is not an identification of history as salvation, but rather the entrance of salvation into history. Luke focuses on the inbreaking of divine salvific activity into human history with the appearance of Jesus of Nazareth among mankind. Jesus did not come as the end of history, or of historical development. He is rather seen as the end of one historical period and the beginning of another, and all of this is a manifestation of a plan of God to bring about the salvation of human beings who recognize and accept the plan.

Various elements in the Lucan writings reveal the author's conception of salvation-history. First, Luke alludes at times to a fundamental divine "plan" for the salvation of human beings which is being realized in the activity of Jesus. He refers to it under diverse terms. It is explicitly mentioned in Luke 7:30 as "God's design" (*hē boulē tou theou*); there it is said to be thwarted by Pharisees and Scribes who refused to be baptized by John the Baptist. This is the only place in the Gospel where *boulē* is so used, but it emerges again in Acts 2:23, where Peter refers to God's definite plan and foreknowledge realized in Jesus; in 4:28, which speaks of God's plan and hand arranging for Jesus' passion and death; in 13:36, where David's role in OT history is related to God's design; and in 20:27, where Paul tells the elders of the Ephesian church about the plan. Under the term *thelēma,* (God's) "will," it appears in Jesus' prayer in the agony on the Mount of Olives: "Not my will, but yours be done" (Luke 22:42); see also Acts 21:14; 22:14. Reference is also made to it in Acts 1:7, where Luke speaks of the Father's authority in fixing times.

Second, Luke makes use of several expressions that speak of God's having predetermined things that have taken place: "For the Son of Man goes his way, as it had been determined" (Luke 22:22). Jesus is preached as the one preordained by God to be the judge of the living and the dead (Acts 10:42; cf. 17:26,31). Luke further depicts Paul's conversion as ordered by God in this salvific plan (Acts 22:14; 26:16).

Third, the idea of a plan of salvation underlies the necessity that is often associated in the Lucan story with what Jesus does or says, with what happens as the fulfillment of Scripture, and with the activity of various Christians. This necessity is expressed by the impersonal verb *dei,* "it is necessary (that . . .)." Its frequent use in Luke in contrast to the isolated occurrences of it in Mark (8:31) and Matthew (16:21) reveal the importance of it: Luke 2:49; 4:43; 9:22; 13:33; 17:25; 19:5; 21:9; 22:37; 24:7,26,44; Acts 1:16,21; 3:21; 4:12; 5:29; 9:6,16; 14:22; 15:5; 16:30; 17:3; 19:21; 20:35; 23:11; 24:19; 25:10; 27:24. To this usage one would also have to add Luke's use of *anankaion,* "necessary" in Acts 13:46.

Fourth, the execution or realization of the plan is often spoken of by Luke in terms of "fulfillment." Fulfillment, especially the fulfillment of prophecy, is not, of course, an exclusively Lucan notion, being found in the Matthean and Johannine Gospels as well. But the Lucan use of the notion is related to his idea of salvation-history because he sees many events happening precisely under this aspect. The notion occurs sporadically in the first nine chapters of the Gospel, but then more frequently toward the end of it and in Acts. Both the verb *plēroun* (1:20; 4:21; 9:31; 21:24; 24:44) and *symplēroun* (9:51) are used by Luke in the Gospel to describe fulfillment. Similarly, the verb *telein* takes on this connotation at times (18:31; 22:37). Often enough, Luke interprets OT passages, which were not in themselves prophetic, not only as prophetic, but even as predictive. See Luke 18:31; 22:37; 24:44; Acts 13:29; 10:43. But fulfillment for Luke is not limited to promises made in the OT, for he often sees other things coming about as the fulfillment of God's plan, i.e. the realization or accomplishment of it. Jesus is made to speak of the baptism that faces him and how hard pressed he is until it is accomplished (Luke 12:50). Again, Moses and Elijah are presented in conversation with Jesus at the transfiguration, "speaking of his departure, the one he was to complete (*plēroun*) in Jerusalem" (9:31). See further 21:24.

This notion of fulfillment is hinted at in the otherwise stylized and formal Hellenistic prologue of the Gospel and colors the meaning of the "events" mentioned there. The literary word *plērophorein* may suit the formality of the rest of the prologue, but it has to be understood as carrying the same nuances as the verbs noted above: "the events that have come to fulfillment among us" (1:1). The events are those of the ministry of Jesus and of the early church, set not only in the framework of contemporary Roman and Palestinian history, but related as well to the divine plan of salvation-history. Moreover, even some aspects of the geographical perspective of the Lucan writings have to be understood in this relationship too (e.g. the words that introduce the travel account, "as the days were drawing near [*symplēroun*] when he was to be taken up," 9:51).

Fifth, that this plan of God concerns the "salvation" of human beings receives in the Lucan writings a special emphasis. We shall discuss "salvation" more in detail as an effect of the Christ-event; here it is mentioned only as the major specific way in which Luke presents the goal of the Father's plan that is being realized in human history in the activity of Jesus. Among the Synoptics, only Luke gives Jesus the title, "Savior" (2:11). With his coming this aspect of the Father's plan is achieved: "Salvation has come to this house today" (19:9). The "salvation" of which the prophet Isaiah (25:9; 26:18; 45:17; 61:1) spoke is explicitly depicted as realized in the ministry and person of Jesus (Luke 4:18-21; 7:22). It will also be proclaimed in the ministry of disciples (Acts 4:12; 13:46-47). In view of the striking frequency with which the nouns and verbs referring to salvation have been used in the Lucan writings, it is best to speak in English of Lucan "salvation" history instead of "redemptive" history (as some writers have done on occasion). Luke has not avoided the idea of "redemption" achieved in Jesus' ministry (see 1:68; 2:38; 21:28), but it is neither as frequent a notion with him as "salvation" nor as important.

We have just sketched briefly the idea of a salvific plan which has been realized in the activity of Jesus and his followers. We now turn to the way that plan affects human history.

1) *Phases of Lucan Salvation-History.* It has been debated in recent years whether one should speak of two or three phases in Lucan salvation-history. Conzelmann has been the main advocate of the three-phase view of it (*Theology,* 12-17), having derived it from H. Baer. Others, e.g. W. G. Kümmel ("Current Theological Accusations," 138), prefer to think in terms of two phases of Lucan salvation-history. In the latter view there would be the phase of promise and the phase of fulfillment; included in the second phase would be not only the ministry of Jesus but also the time of the church. Yet promise and fulfillment are not exclusively Lucan ideas, and they do not sufficiently express the distinction that Luke seems to make between the ministry of Jesus and that of his followers, although the two-phase view may better stress the continuity between the two periods of ministry that Luke also has in mind. The demarcation of the phase of Jesus' ministry from that of the church can be seen, as Kümmel himself has noted, in Luke's narrating the ascension of Jesus twice, once as the end of Jesus' own history, and again as the beginning of the church's (see also C. K. Barrett, *Luke the Historian,* 57). The separation is also implied in the question that the apostles pose to the risen Christ, "Lord, will you *at this time* restore the kingdom to Israel?" (Acts 1:6). That seems to hint at a period that is distinct in the disciples' minds from that of the ministry of Jesus, when he had not restored the kingdom, i.e. from the "today" of Jesus' own ministry.

Because Luke did not end his narrative account with the ascension of

Jesus but added a sequel and depicted the kerygma being proclaimed not only by Jesus but by his followers as well in a part of salvation-history dominated by God's Spirit, one has to reckon with a three-phase view of salvation-history. Conzelmann's view of the three phases has come under fire for various reasons, but it is not to be wholly rejected. An attempt will be made to present his view here briefly and then to modify it in the light of various discussions of it.

Conzelmann has seen Lucan salvation-history structured as follows: *Period of Israel*, from creation to the imprisonment of John the Baptist; *Period of Jesus*, from his baptism through his public ministry to his ascension; *Period of the Church under Stress*, from Jesus' ascension to his parousia. (I have slightly simplified Conzelmann's presentation here. He does not always speak consistently of the ascension as the break between the second period and the third; see Robinson, *Der Weg des Herrn*, 23 for the various places where Conzelmann has wavered in indicating the demarcation of these periods.)

This threefold structuring of the salvation-history is based on three main passages in the Lucan writings: (a) In Luke 16:16 one finds a saying of Jesus, isolated in the immediate context, suggesting a demarcation between the first two periods mentioned: "Up until John it was the law and the prophets; from that time on the kingdom of God is being preached." Compared with its "Q" counterpart in Matt 11:12, where the words "from that time on" (*apo tote*) are missing, it seems clear that Lucan redaction has introduced the demarcation. (b) In Luke 22:35-37, Jesus at the Last Supper instructs the Twelve to provide themselves from that time on with purse, knapsack, and sword, whereas in the mission charge at the sending out of disciples during the ministry he forebade these very things (10:4). There was no need of such in the Period of Jesus, but now in the Period of *ecclesia pressa* (the church under stress) the situation will be different. This instruction is to be understood as applicable to the period after his ascension. (c) In Luke 4:21 Jesus in the synagogue of Nazareth interprets Isa 61:1-2: "Today this passage of Scripture sees its fulfillment." The words of Jesus declare the fulfillment of the promises made by God in the Period of Israel through the prophet Isaiah and relate it precisely to the ministry that he is beginning. "Today" thus serves to demarcate the Period of Jesus not only from the Period of Israel, but also from the Period of the Church, because the second period becomes in the Lucan view of things *the* period of salvation. To it the Period of the Church, from which Luke writes, constantly looks back as the period in which salvation *was* achieved once for all.

The first phase of God's salvation-history embraced the time of the law and the prophets, to which, according to Conzelmann, John the Baptist belonged as the last and the greatest of the prophets (Luke 7:26-28).

(One should recall here how Conzelmann sought to distance John from Jesus geographically; see above, pp. 170-171.) The second phase of salvation-history is the time of salvation par excellence, embracing the ministry (not the "life") of Jesus, the time when the kingdom of God was preached and salvation actually achieved—a unique, unrepeatable period. The third phase of the history is the time of *ecclesia pressa,* the church under stress, when the Spirit as the substitute for the no longer imminent parousia, guides the Christian community in its day-to-day existence. Luke writes from the third period, looking back at the Period of Jesus, as the time when salvation was accomplished and the real "beginning" was made. Conzelmann makes much of Luke's use of *archē,* "beginning" (and of a related verb, *archein*), which does not relate to the beginning of Jesus' life, but rather to the beginning of his ministry (see Luke 3:23; 23:5; Acts 1:1,22; 10:37; cf. 13:24-25).

Conzelmann has further subdivided the Period of Jesus into three phases: (a) the period of the gathering of Galilean witnesses, from the baptism of Jesus proclaimed as the Son of God to the end of the Galilean ministry (3:21-9:21); (b) the period of the training of the Galilean witnesses, from Jesus' first announcement of his passion and the transfiguration through the journey to Jerusalem (9:22-19:28); and (c) the period of Jesus' teaching in the Temple and his passion in Jerusalem (19:28-22:53). The basis for this subdivision of the Period of Jesus is the coupling of scenes of heavenly revelation and human rejection at various stages in the Lucan story of the ministry: baptism and Nazareth rejection, transfiguration and the disciples' misunderstanding, and the Mount of Olives scene and the subsequent passion. Once again, Conzelmann has not been consistent in citing the Lucan passages for the demarcation; at one point he even uses the triumphal entry into Jerusalem as the third "epiphany." See Robinson, *Der Weg des Herrn,* 21. This subdivision of the Period of Jesus is, in my opinion, questionable, because it is so subjective. It is not crucial to the three-phase structure of the Lucan salvation-history and can easily be dispensed with.

Certain objections have been raised to Conzelmann's threefold structuring of Lucan salvation-history. P. S. Minear has maintained that Conzelmann's use of Luke 16:16 in dividing the first and second periods is overdrawn ("Rarely has a scholar placed so much weight on so dubious an interpretation of so difficult a logion," "Luke's Use of the Birth Stories," in *Studies in Luke-Acts,* 122). It seems to me that Conzelmann is right in appealing to this verse and to the Lucan redactional modification of it in the phrase, *apo tote,* "from that time on." The problem with Conzelmann's use of it is not that it is an isolated logion, but rather with the interpretation of the prep. *mechri,* "up until," in the verse: Does it mean "up until John (inclusive)" or "up until John (exclusive)"? Conzelmann has taken it in the former sense. But it seems that in the Lucan story the preposition has to be understood in the exclusive sense, for it is with the appearance of John that the new period begins; that is precisely the point of the beginning of chap. 3 and of the view of John in the infancy narrative, where he clearly is seen as the precursor of Jesus.

The basic problem is Conzelmann's neglect of the infancy narrative as part of Lucan theology, as Minear and others have pointed out. For Conzelmann what is contained in Luke 1-2 is really not Lucan (see *Theology*, 118, where Conzelmann even questions the authenticity of these chapters; see further p. 310 below). Even though the view of John that is contained in the infancy narrative has to be understood as composed by Luke in dependence on what he has written in the rest of his Gospel, it can hardly be said not to form a part of Lucan theology. As Minear and others have insisted, the infancy narrative makes a serious contribution to Lucan theology and cannot be disregarded. I do not care for Minear's suggestion that one should rather follow R. Morgenthaler in considering Luke 1:5-4:30 as the prologue of Luke's two volumes. Aside from the fact that the term "prologue" ought to be restricted to Luke 1:1-4 and not used of the infancy narrative, Morgenthaler's suggestion obscures the real function of the infancy narrative. It is a sort of overture to the whole opus. The parallel drawn there between John and Jesus foreshadows the parallel initial ministry of the two agents in God's salvific plan. Moreover, the opening verses of chap. 3, which immediately follow on the infancy narrative, mark by their formal style the "beginning" (*archē*) of the Period of Jesus. They depict John as the forerunner of Jesus; implicit in this treatment of John is Luke's anti-Baptist polemic. John is not the Messiah; he is the one who in God's providence introduces the Messiah. John had to run his course and finish it (Acts 13:25) in the Period of Jesus. Just as Jesus, so he too belongs to both the Period of Israel and the Period of Jesus. John is thus a transitional figure. In Luke 1:80 he appeared in the first period "in the desert"; and the word of God came to him in the desert (3:2). Among the criteria that Peter sets forth for the candidate who is to replace Judas Iscariot among the Twelve in Acts 1:22 is the requirement that he had accompanied them during all the time that the Lord was with them, "beginning from the baptism of John." This verse supports the exclusive reading of the verse of the Gospel of which Conzelmann had tried to make so much (16:16).

Conzelmann is correct in thinking that according to that verse John the Baptist is not a kingdom-preacher in the Third Gospel; he is rather the one who inaugurates the preaching by introducing the preacher himself. The Baptist is a kingdom-preacher only in Matt 3:2; in the Matthean interpretation of John, the evangelist has put on John's lips the very proclamation that Jesus makes (see 4:17). The latter is part of the pre-

followed by Talbert

Matthean (and pre-Lucan) tradition; cf. Mark 1:15. The attribution of the proclamation to John is, therefore, to be regarded as Matthean redaction. Luke does not share that view with him.

Luke does insist that, though no one born of a woman is greater than John, yet one who is less in the kingdom is greater than John (Luke 7:28). Luke also makes of John something more than a prophet (7:26); but, *pace* Conzelmann (*Theology*, 25), he does not become "the greatest prophet," i.e. the greatest of the prophets of the Period of Israel. See Robinson, *Der Weg des Herrn*, 19-20. John the Baptist is rather to be regarded as a transitional figure in the Lucan Gospel. He is not a Christian, but a Jewish reform-preacher, who does not understand Jesus' role (7:18-23).

An adjustment of Conzelmann's structure of the phases of Lucan salvation-history has been proposed by Wink (*John the Baptist in the Gospel Tradition*, 55). Using some of his suggestions, I prefer to think of the threefold structure of this history in the following way:

a) *Period of Israel,* from creation to the appearance of John the Baptist: The period of the law and the prophets (1:5-3:1)

b) *Period of Jesus,* from the baptism of John to the ascension of Jesus: The period of Jesus' ministry, death, and exaltation (3:2-24:51)

c) *Period of the Church,* from Jesus' ascension to his parousia: The period of the spread of the word of God (Luke 24:52-Acts 1:3-28:31)

If one wants to subdivide the Period of Jesus, then the following is suggested:

i) inauguration of the ministry of Jesus by John sent ahead as messenger or precursor (3:1-20; cf. 7:27)

ii) the Galilean ministry and the gathering of witnesses from Galilee (3:21-9:50)

iii) the training of the witnesses from Galilee during the journey to Jerusalem (9:51-19:27)

iv) Jesus' ministry of teaching in the Temple and his death, burial, and ascension in Jerusalem and nearby (19:28-24:51).

It is important to note that, though Luke has toned down the precursor role of John in his Gospel, he has not completely eliminated it. It is not true to say with Wink that Luke "has retained *nothing* of John's role of Elijah" (*John the Baptist,* 42 [italics mine]). Here Wink has been influenced too much by Conzelmann's position. True, Luke omits the post-transfiguration conversation of Jesus with the disciples about Elijah's coming (cf. Mark 9:11-13) and has none of the Matthean parallel's ex-

plicit identification of John as Elijah (17:13). But an implicit identification of John as Elijah is retained in the "Q" passage that Luke has in
7:27 (=Matt 11:10), where Jesus applies to him the words of Mal 3:1.
This identification is foreshadowed in Luke 1:17 about John's coming
"with the spirit and power of Elijah"; that was written with the hindsight
of the gospel tradition and his own use of it in Luke 7. Part of the problem here is the idea of Elijah as the precursor of the Messiah; as I shall
stress in the commentary proper, this should not be read into these texts.
There is no evidence of a pre-Christian Jewish belief in Elijah as the
precursor of the Messiah.

Jesus himself is understood by Luke as a figure in the Period of Israel
(up until his baptism). This view is important in Lucan theology, and the
reason why the infancy narrative cannot be neglected. For Luke is at
pains in this initial part of his Gospel to show that Christianity's founder
was incorporated into Israel itself (see further p. 178 above).

It was important for Luke that the Period of Jesus was the time in
God's plan when salvation was achieved, and Luke, writing from the Period of the Church, sought to anchor the teaching of the church of his
day in that period. Objection has been raised that this anchoring would
seem to imply that the Period of the Church is not a period of salvation
(see W. G. Kümmel, "Current Theological Accusations," 138). This,
however, would be a facile oversimplification. Luke's concern is to stress
the continuity of the two periods: What Jesus proclaimed about himself
and the kingdom is now continued in the apostolic kerygma and in Luke's
own kerygma. But no differently from Paul, Luke can look back on the
Christ-event and maintain that something *was* achieved then, the effects
of which continue to be available to human beings throughout the generations of the *ecclesia pressa,* the church under stress. Paul proclaimed, "He
was put to death for our transgressions and raised for our justification"
(Rom 4:25). Luke puts it this way: "This Jesus whom you crucified God
has made both Lord and Christ" and "there is salvation in no one else"
(Acts 2:36 and 4:12). Both Luke and Paul have a backward glance,
looking at something achieved for human beings at a moment in history
that precedes us and our generation. Luke, with his concern for salvation-
history, preferred to relate the Period of Jesus to the fulfillment of God's
promises in Isa 61:1-2. The "today" of Jesus' ministry (4:21) was a moment in time that could not be repeated—akin to Paul's *ephapax* (Rom
6:10).

One further comment is needed about the threefold structure of Lucan
salvation-history, as presented by Conzelmann. No little reason for his
demarcation of the Period of Jesus was his characterization of it as a Satan-free period. At the end of the temptation scene Luke tells his readers
that the devil, having exhausted every sort of temptation, "departed from

him for a while" (4:13). Then in the passion narrative Satan is said to enter into Judas Iscariot (22:3), marking the return of Satan to dominate "the hour" and represent the "power of darkness" (22:53), i.e. to bring about the betrayal and death of God's herald and prophet. But the Period of Jesus was otherwise free of Satan and thus was the center of salvation-history; it differed from the Period of the Church, when the *ecclesia pressa* would again be threatened by satanic evil. This aspect of the Period of Jesus, as presented by Conzelmann, is not essential to it. It is partly responsible for the fluctuating lines of demarcation between the second and third periods that we mentioned above. The fluctuation has rightly been criticized by S. Brown (*Apostasy and Perseverance in the Theology of Luke*), who has shown, among other things, that most of Jesus' dealings with Satan or the devil are found precisely within this part of the Lucan Gospel (see 8:12; 10:17-18; 11:14-22; 13:11-17). Moreover, the salvation that Jesus is seen bringing in this period, is precisely the defeat of evil in all its forms, physical, psychic, or satanic.

2) *Universalism in Lucan Salvation-History.* Another aspect of the distinctive Lucan view of salvation-history is its universalist dimension. The new inbreaking of divine salvific activity into human history includes the extension of salvation to persons outside of God's chosen people of old. The change involves a distinctive view of Israel and a reordering of attitudes toward levels of human society. Both in the Marcan Gospel and the Matthean, one can find a universalist dimension at times, especially in the journey of Jesus into Gentile territory and his ministry there or in the final commission given to the disciples in Matt 28:19-20. But the abundance of references in the Lucan Gospel (and in Acts) makes obvious the universalist concern of this evangelist.

In a sense Luke's concern resembles that of Paul, who viewed salvation as destined for "the Jew first and also the Greek" (Rom 1:16; 2:10; 3:1-2; 9:3-4), and recognized the prerogatives of Israel. Luke has some of this attitude, when he depicts Paul and Barnabas proclaiming in the synagogue of Antioch in Pisidia that God's word *had to* be addressed "first to you" (Jews) before they were to "turn to the Gentiles" (Acts 13:46). There Luke uses *anankaion,* "it was necessary," suggesting that this priority accorded to Israel was part of God's plan. See further Acts 3:26.

The attempt to explain Lucan universalism, however, must begin with a brief discussion of his attitude toward Israel. The phases of Lucan salvation-history include the Period of Israel, as we have seen; but it is not there merely to be superseded. It is not that God has replaced his chosen people of old with a new one.

Rather, as P. Schubert and N. Dahl have shown, Luke emphasizes in his writings a "proof-from-prophecy" motif. If salvation is now extended to the Gentiles and Samaritans, this is so because the extension is envisaged by Luke as having been part of God's promises to Israel from the beginning. Luke acknowledges clearly the place of Israel in God's salvation-history. More than any of the other Synoptic evangelists Luke refers to Abraham in his writings. He acknowledges his privileged position in that history. Moreover, he does not present him as the prototype of Christian believers as do Paul and the Epistle to the Hebrews; Abraham is not a witness to Christ before his coming, as in John. Rather in the Lucan writings Abraham remains the father of the Jews (1:73; 16:24-31; Acts 7:2). In Luke's treatment of Abraham one sees his underlying concern to show the priority of Israel in the plan of God's salvation-history. This is seen in the infancy narrative of the Gospel, where the various representatives of ancient Jewish piety are depicted; they stand in stark contrast to the picture of the "elders of the people, chief priests, and Scribes" (22:66) which is gradually painted in the rest of the Gospel. The initial portrait shows the real Israel. The same treatment emerges in the Acts of the Apostles, where all the first converts to Christianity are from among Palestinian Jews (2:41; 4:4; 21:20; 6:7). The relation between Abraham's role and salvation is seen best in Jesus' remark to Zacchaeus, "Salvation has come to this house today! For this man too is a son of Abraham" (19:9). See further Dahl, "The Story of Abraham in Luke-Acts," 51.

The peculiar place that Israel occupies in the Lucan view of salvation-history is seen, further, in the story about the need to reconstitute the Twelve after the ascension. It has always been something of an enigma that the early disciples felt the need to put someone in Judas' place at the very beginning of Luke's story in Acts, though once Matthias is chosen by lot, he disappears completely from the scene and is never seen again doing anything (except, presumably, to share in the decision made in 6:2 and the imposition of hands in 6:6). No similar need is felt to replace James, the son of Zebedee, when he is put to death by Herod Agrippa (12:1). Once again, it seems implicit in Luke's story that the priority of Israel is operative; the group of the Twelve, representing the twelve tribes of Israel (Luke 22:30), is reconstituted so that it can confront Israel on the day of Pentecost and show that despite the death of God's anointed one, he still addresses the message of salvation first to the children of Abraham.

This partiality for Israel is seen in the infancy narrative, in the delineation of the role both of John and of Jesus. John is described as one who is to "turn back many of the children of Israel to the Lord, their God" (1:16) and to "make ready a people fit for the Lord" (1:17). The canticle of Zechariah, his father, recognizes the deliverance brought to God's people in the birth of John (1:68), who is to offer them a knowledge of salvation through the forgiveness of sins (1:77). When John appears in his desert ministry, it is because God's word has sent him to preach to children of Abraham (3:3,8). Similarly in the case of Jesus: He is to sit on David's throne and rule as king over the house of Jacob (1:32-33), and Mary's canticle extols God for being "mindful of his mercy" and for "favoring Abraham and his descendants forever" (1:55). Jesus is born as "God's Messiah," "the consolation of Israel" (2:25-26), and the source of "glory for God's people, Israel" (2:32). Though Simeon's words about the child hint at something more ("a symbol that people will reject"), they describe Jesus' relation to the rise of many in Israel (2:34). The words of Anna speak of him in terms of the deliverance of Jerusalem (2:38).

In the Period of Jesus or the ministry Luke depicts Jesus as identifying himself with the role described in Isa 61:1-2, one of proclaiming release, sight, and freedom to his fellow townspeople—who are the symbol of Israel at this point in the Gospel. Once again, though the episode hints at his relation to people outside of Israel, the carrying of the message of salvation first to Israel is obvious. His Galilean ministry is, moreover, not distracted by any activity in the north, as in Mark 6:45; 7:24-31; 8:27. Only in Luke 8:26-39 is it related that he has gone into "the region of the Gerasenes," and the evangelist takes pains to locate it "opposite Galilee." In sending out the Twelve and the Seventy(-two), Jesus never specifies in the Lucan Gospel, as he does in Matt 10:5, that they are not to go to the Samaritans. As he begins his way from Galilee to Jerusalem, he does send disciples ahead of him into Samaritan villages, but he is not welcomed (9:52-53). The rejection here in Samaria recalls his rejection in Nazareth and gradually introduces the note of concern for both Jews and Samaritans, associated by Luke in a way that no other evangelist has done. Though Jesus' concern is extended to Samaritans at times (indirectly in the story of the Good Samaritan, 10:33; directly, in the cure of the ten lepers, 17:16), Luke is really using them as foils for the Jews to whom his message has been mainly addressed.

Luke has tried not only to show the message of salvation being preached by Jesus to the Jews of Galilee and Judea and the Samaritans, but he also depicts his concern at their failure to accept that message. This is seen in the parable of the barren fig tree (13:6-7), in the end of the parable of Lazarus and the rich man (16:27-31), and in Jesus' weeping over Jerusalem (19:41-44), which did not recognize the time of its visitation.

By and large, there is no extension of salvation to Gentiles in the Period of Jesus. The sole exceptions to his activity among non-Jews are the few episodes that deal with Samaritans and the trip to the Gerasenes. But the foreshadowing of the extension of salvation to non-Jews is seen in many ways in the Gospel itself. In the infancy narrative, Simeon praises God for granting him the opportunity to see the salvation made ready for all peoples and the revelation for "the nations" in Jesus himself (2:30-32). The chord of universalism is first struck there. It is heard again when Isa 40:3 is quoted to explain John's presence in the desert; as Luke quotes it (imitating his Marcan source), he continues it to include v. 5 with its note that "all mankind shall see the salvation of God" (3:6). In various minor ways this extension of salvation, promised originally to Israel, is carried on in the ministry of Jesus himself. Thus, his genealogy is traced back, not merely to David or Abraham, as in Matthew, but to Adam and God (3:23-38), envisaging his relation to all mankind as God's son. His programmatic address in the Nazareth synagogue includes the casting of himself in the role of Elijah and Elisha, sent to outcasts beyond the borders of Israel (4:16-30). En route to Jerusalem he cures a Samaritan, one of the ten lepers (17:11-19). His words become dire as he speaks of places at the banquet in the kingdom: the patriarchs and all the prophets will be there, but his contemporaries will see people coming from the north, south, east, and west to sit down with them, whereas they themselves will be put out (13:28-29). Again, the Lucan form of the parable of the great dinner (14:15-24) differs from Matt 22:1-10 in the mention at the end of a double sending-out of servants into "streets and avenues of the town" (to bring in Jews after the invited guests have refused to come) and then into "highways and hedgerows" beyond the town (to bring in non-Jews). The parable of the prodigal son has been interpreted similarly (see J. van Goudoever, "The Place of Israel," 121), though such a reading may be an unintended allegorization of a detail.

It has been questioned whether in such details as these there really is a universalism in the Lucan Gospel. N. Q. King realizes that in the Lucan volumes the word is eventually to be carried to non-Jews, but thinks that there is a motif of partial concealment of this extension of salvation within the Gospel itself. The preaching of salvation is to come to Gentiles only after Jesus himself has been crucified with the involvement of the leaders of his own people. This preaching eventually is depicted in Acts. Because there is in the Third Gospel no full-fledged mission of Jesus into Gentile territory such as one finds in Mark or Matthew, the question is raised. Moreover, it is only the risen Christ who commissions the Eleven and others to be his witnesses and preach in his name repentance for the forgiveness of sins "to all the nations" (24:47-48). Whether one should call this a concealment—King uses the phrase "a partial *krypsis*"—might be debated. The question is whether Luke sought to conceal any ministry of Jesus among non-Jews. We have already mentioned Jesus' limited activity with Samaritans and Gerasenes, the former of whom are conspicuously absent from Mark and Matthew. What is more to be noted is that the question of Lucan universalism is linked to the geographical perspective: there is a gradual spread of the word of God in the Gospel itself, as is also true in Acts. In the second volume the Christian message is preached at first to Jews in Jerusalem, to diaspora-Jews among them (Acts 2:5,6; 6:8), to Samaritans (8:4), to an Ethiopian "worshiper" (8:27, a eunuch [cf. Deut 23:1-2]), to Jews in Lydda, Sharon, and Joppa (9:32-43), and eventually to Gentiles, beginning with the conversion of the Roman centurion Cornelius (Acts 10:1ff). Hence it is much more the geographical perspective that has created this would-be concealment. Indirectly, it affects the Lucan historical perspective for it deprives the Period of Jesus of any ministry among Gentiles.

This matter would be differently put, if one were to try to answer the question whether there actually was a Gentile mission in the ministry of the historical Jesus. To this question S. G. Wilson has addressed himself (see bibliography; also my review in TS 35 [1974] 741-744). Wilson may be right in saying that Luke-Acts lacks any consistent "theology of the Gentiles" (p. 239), but Luke's attitude toward them certainly fits into Lucan theology in a larger sense, as we are trying to show here.

In all of this matter of universalism one sees that salvation is not only extended to others than Jews, but that it demands a reconstituting of Israel itself. As J. Jervell has well shown, Luke does not describe a Jewish people that, as a whole, has rejected Jesus and his message, but among whom there are some exceptions. "Israel" continues to refer to the Jewish people, but they are now a people of repentant (i.e. Christian) Jews and obdurate Jews. It does not refer to a church made up of Jews and Gentiles, but to Jews who have accepted the Christian message and to whom the promises of old have been fulfilled, with whom Gentiles have been associated for a share in those realized promises. It is *not* a *new* Israel, but a reconstituted Israel. But Israel itself has been split over Jesus and his message: those who have accepted the message of repentance and those who have not. See further "The Divided People of God," 41-74.

However, the universalism of the Lucan Gospel has another dimension. It is not limited merely to the question of Jews and non-Jews, since it manifests itself also in the way the Lucan Jesus is depicted dealing with individuals at various levels of society. We have already mentioned the Samaritans, but one would also have to mention his attitude toward or dealings with *toll-collectors* (Levi, 5:27; Zacchaeus, 19:2-10; groups of them, 5:29-30; 7:29,34; 15:1; one unnamed, 18:10-13), *sinners* (the sinful woman, 7:36-50; the prodigal son, 15:11-32; 6:32-34), *women* (the widow of Nain, 7:11-17; the sinful woman, 7:36-50; Galilean women followers, 8:2-3; Martha and Mary, 10:38-42; the cripple, 13:10-17; parable of the lost coin, 15:8-10; parable of the importunate widow, 18:1-8; the widow's mite, 21:1-4; the daughters of Jerusalem, 23:27-31), and *the poor* (in his Nazareth speech, 4:18; first beatitude, 6:20; 7:22; 14:13; the parable of Lazarus, 16:20; 18:22; 21:1-4). Indirectly, this same attitude appears in the preaching of John the Baptist to the crowds, toll-collectors, and soldiers (3:10-14). In a poignant way it is driven home when Jesus promises a share in his kingdom to the penitent criminal hanging next to him (23:39-43). Salvation is now extended to a "daughter of Abraham" (13:16) or "a son of Abraham" (19:9), and Jesus' basic attitude is expressed at the conclusion of the Zacchaeus scene, "The Son of Man has come to seek out and to save what was lost" (19:10). In this regard one may recall the special parables of mercy in the Lucan Gospel.

To appreciate the implications of this range of Jesus' dealings, one would have to investigate further the lack of esteem accorded such persons in the Palestinian society of Jesus' time or at least in Luke's own experience in order to appreciate his reasons for presenting Jesus as he has. In many instances one senses in Luke's Gospel a concern for the disreputable, those beyond the pale of respectable society (see further Moore, *Beginnings* 1. 439-445).

5. *Lucan Christology*. The key figure in Lucan salvation-history is Jesus Christ himself, for he is the one in whom God's activity in human history is now manifested. He is not only the one who proclaims salvation; he becomes himself the object of the proclamation. Moreover, as we have already insisted, for all of Luke's emphasis on the word of God and its spread to the end of the earth, the main thing that his two-volume work proclaims is Jesus of Nazareth: "Salvation comes through no one else, for there is no other name under the heavens given to human beings by which we must be saved" (Acts 4:12). Luke sees Jesus not only as "the climax of God's activity in Israel" (E. Franklin, *Christ the Lord,* 7), but as the very center of salvation-history itself. Hence we must attempt now to synthesize what Luke actually teaches about Jesus. In doing so, we can distinguish two aspects of Luke's teaching: christology, or the Christ-event *in se,* and soteriology, or the salvific effects of the Christ-event.

A. CHRISTOLOGY. Luke presents Jesus as a Palestinian Jew, born in Bethlehem (2:6-7), of Davidic lineage (1:27; 2:4; 3:31), and raised in Nazareth (4:16). He speaks of him as "a man (*andra*) attested to you by God with mighty deeds, wonders, and signs which God did through him in your midst" (Acts 2:22). With many a deft stroke of an artist's brush he has painted a portrait of Jesus as a human being with great concern for others. Despite his tendency to suppress the marks of human emotion, even vehemence, that are found in the Marcan Gospel at times, Luke has depicted him with notably human qualities. The relevant Marcan passages have, however, been retained, especially those which manifest Jesus' own human reaction to his destiny. Though he has curtailed the agony scene and located it on a mountain, Luke has no less dramatically presented Jesus' reaction to that destiny and his ultimate resignation to the Father's will (22:42) than Mark (14:36) and Matthew (26:39) have. Moreover, the end of his earthly existence, his death on the cross, at which he echoes the same resignation, "Father, into your hands I entrust my spirit" (23:46), is a mark of supreme human dedication.

Luke also affirms certain things about Jesus that transcend his human condition. These include: (1) Jesus' virginal conception through the power of the holy Spirit (1:34-35). Luke's treatment of this conception is expressed in figurative language which does not answer all the medieval or modern questions posed about it. It is more implied by the contrast with John's miraculous birth to aged parents than by a direct affirmation about it and stands in contrast to the open affirmation of it in Matt 1:18. (2) Jesus' unique Spirit-guided ministry (3:22; 4:1,14,18; 10:21). Luke found the Spirit mentioned in connection with Jesus' baptism and temptation in the Marcan Gospel, but only he among the Synoptists has emphasized its role in Jesus' ministry. (3) Jesus' special relation to his heavenly Father (2:49; 3:22; 9:35; 10:21-22; 23:46). Aside from the first and the last of these references, Luke shares this teaching with other Synoptic evangelists. (4) Jesus' resurrection from the dead (Luke 24:6a; Acts 2:24,32; 3:15; 4:10; 5:30; 10:40; 13:30,33,37; 26:23). The resurrection is affirmed in Luke-Acts, but it is never depicted outright or described. Despite the formulation that Luke uses in Acts 1:22, where among the criteria for the one who will replace Judas among the Twelve, it is stipulated that he be "a witness to the resurrection," Luke has never depicted anyone witnessing the resurrection. What he means there is "a witness to the risen Christ"; he has simply formulated the criterion abstractly. Cf. Acts 4:33. Luke has not attempted to do what the author of the *Gospel of Peter* (§§ 35-42) has done, i.e. describe Jesus' coming forth from the tomb. Though he puts an interval of forty days between the resurrection and the ascension in Acts 1:3, he never depicts Jesus walking the earth during those days, apart from the accompanying of the two disciples to Emmaus on Easter Sunday itself (24:15). Luke strives to avoid the impression that disciples seeing the risen Christ were seeing a ghost (Luke 24:37). Moreover, he is at pains to insist on the reality of Jesus' resurrection, by portraying him eating broiled fish in front of the disciples in Jerusalem on Easter Sunday night (24:43; cf. Acts 10:41; and possibly 1:4); and by emphasizing that he experienced no decay (Acts 2:27; 13:35,37). Yet Luke never depicts the resurrection of Jesus as if it were a mere resuscitation or return to natural, terrestrial existence (like the resuscitated son of the widow of Nain, 7:15; or Jairus' daughter, 8:54-55). Rather he is aware that Christ has entered "his glory" (24:26). It is from "glory" (the presence of the Father) that Jesus' appearances to his disciples take place. From there he clearly appears to Saul on the road to Damascus (Acts 9:3-6; 22:6-10; 26:13-18); and the only real difference between that appearance and the others (to the disciples on the road to Emmaus, to the Eleven and others in Jerusalem, and the many instances referred to in Acts 1:3) is that it was postpentecostal. Luke, however, is the only NT writer who speaks of "proofs" of the resurrection (Acts 1:3); this reveals that doubts about the resurrection had already emerged in Christian consciousness by the time he was writing, and he has introduced this reference as part of the *asphaleia* that he gives to Theophilus.

5) Jesus' ascension (Luke 24:51c; Acts 1:9) or exaltation to the Father's right hand (Acts 2:33; 5:31). Though Luke has retained some of the primitive mode of referring to the status of the risen Christ as "exalted" (see the pre-Pauline hymn to Christ in Phil 2:8-9 and in the primitive hymn embedded in 1 Tim 3:16), he is the NT writer par excellence who refers to Christ's status as "ascension" (hinted at as early as 9:51). Indeed, he has not only set an interval between the resurrection and the ascension in Acts 1:3, in contrast to the date of both events given in Luke 24, where the temporal adverbs and prepositional phrases in the course of the chapter leave no doubt that they took place on Easter Sunday evening; he has even depicted the ascension as a visibly perceptible event (Acts 1:9-10). This is the sort of description that he avoided for the resurrection itself. The time-references surrounding Luke 24:51 and dating the "carrying of him up into heaven" on Easter Sunday are similar to those in the Marcan appendix (16:19) and John 20:17. They all fix a date (Easter Sunday) and a goal (heaven, Father) for the transit. But only Acts 1:3,9,10 describe the transit, fix it in time (some forty days after the resurrection, 1:3; cf. 13:31), in space (the Mount of Olives, 1:12), in a specific mode ("lifted up," with an apocalyptic cloud taking him out of sight, 1:9), and set its term (heaven, 1:11). Luke has thus done for the ascension of Christ what the *Gospel of Peter* eventually did for the resurrection. In reality, the ascension is but another appearance of the risen Christ to his disciples, described as his final leave-taking from them; they will no longer behold him in such bodily form, but are to await "the Father's promise" (the holy Spirit), which will thereafter be the form of Christ's presence among them in the Period of the Church.

Luke has, in his second book, historicized the ascension of Jesus, by situating it distinctly in time, forty days after the resurrection (Acts 1:3-11). But, in the first, in dating the ascension to Easter Sunday (along with other NT tradition), he reveals that it was intimately connected with the resurrection in his own thought. That is why he can portray the risen Christ, who appeared to the disciples on the way to Emmaus, as saying that the Messiah has entered "his glory" (Luke 24:26). Another Lucan way of expressing his risen status would be to speak of Jesus as having been exalted to God's right hand, where he received the Spirit, which he now pours forth (Acts 2:33). In effect, these are different Lucan ways of describing Jesus' "departure" (*exodos*, Luke 9:31) or his transit to the Father through suffering, death, burial, resurrection, and exaltation to glory (one effect of which will be the outpouring of the holy Spirit). A modern (non-Lucan) phrase for this complex is the "paschal mystery."

Moreover, Luke explicitly links the resurrection of Jesus not only with his own predictions (Luke 24:7; cf. 9:22; 18:32-33) but also with OT scriptures (Acts 17:3; cf. 3:24).

In speaking of the resurrection, Luke uses the transitive verbs *egeirein* and *anastēsai*, "raise," either in the active with God as the subject (*egeirein*, Acts 3:15; 4:10; 5:30; 10:40; 13:30,37; *anastēsai*, Acts 2:24,32; [3:26?]; 13:33,34; 17:31) or in the passive (*egerthē[nai]*, Luke 9:22; 24:34), with God as the implied agent. Though Luke is the only NT writer who uses the transitive *anastēsai*, his use of other transitive forms agrees with the earlier tradition found in Pauline letters (see *JBC*, art. 79, § 72). Luke also formulates references to the resurrection in the intransitive (Luke 18:33; 24:7,46; Acts 10:41; 17:3), using *anastēnai*, "rise," and implying that Jesus rose by his own power.

This difference of vocabulary has been used by H. Braun to support a thesis that Lucan christology in Acts has developed a "subordinationist quality" (*TLZ* 77 [1952] 533), i.e. that Jesus is managed by the Father. This, however, is a too pejorative a term and lays too much emphasis on the Lucan use of *egeirein* (active and passive) and the transitive *anastēsai*, playing down the five intransitive usages. It is also anachronistic. The data given above show that Luke has simply preserved two traditional ways of referring to Jesus' resurrection: one which ascribes the efficient causality of it to the Father (indeed, most probably the older way of expressing it, because "God raises the dead" [Acts 26:8; cf. *Shemoneh Esreh* § 2; Str-B 4. 211]); and the other, which attributes it to Jesus himself, as in Paul's earliest letter, 1 Thess 4:14; Mark 8:31; 9:9,31; 10:34; 16:9; John 20:9. Moreover, it is scarcely true that Luke has "an unmistakable preference" for *egeirein* (*pace* U. Wilckens, *Missionsreden*, 137); cf. I. H. Marshall, "The Resurrection," 101-103.

Related to this question of terminology is whether the passive of *egeirein* should be translated "be raised" or intransitively "rise." That *egerthē* in references to Jesus' resurrection should be translated "was raised" (by the Father) may be seen in the parallel expressions for the ascension. Though Luke can use the abstract noun *anastasis,* "resurrection" (Acts 1:22; 2:31; 4:33; 17:18[?]; 26:23) in referring to Jesus and can speak of his *analēmpsis,* his "being taken up" (Luke 9:51), when the verb for the latter is used it is always in the passive (*analambanein,* Acts 1:2,11,22: "was taken up"; or *anapherein,* Luke 24:51: "was carried up"). The implication is "by God." Only in Acts 2:34 is the intransitive *anabainein* used to deny that David "ascended" to heaven. Cf. Rom 10:6; Eph 4:8-10 (and note the OT passages being used there).

What is at issue here is of more general import for Lucan christology. The five elements just described have to do with the transcendent aspects of Jesus' existence in the Lucan writings. Though not all of equal value, they, taken along with the human aspects, make up what has to be recognized as Luke's view of the "Christ-event." We shall explain this view in more detail below (pp. 221-227); here it suffices to recall that it is a shorthand way of referring to the complex of things or events in Jesus' existence that produced the impact that he made on humanity: his ministry, his passion-death-burial, his resurrection-ascension-exaltation. One may debate the extent to which the events of the infancy narrative are included in the Lucan view of that complex; this is affected by the view one takes of the Lucan *archē,* "beginning," which we have discussed above (p. 183), and of Conzelmann's treatment of the Period of Jesus. In any case, it is the combination of the human and transcendent aspects of Jesus' existence that make up the Lucan view of the Christ-event.

Though he never uses the word *parousia,* Luke's christology reckons with a return as the final phase of Jesus' role. The angel who appears at his ascension tells the Galilean onlookers that "this Jesus, who has been taken up from you into heaven, will come in the same way as you saw him go" (Acts 1:11). And in the Gospel Luke has preserved from the Marcan source a saying about the coming of the Son of Man with power and great glory (21:27; cf. Mark 13:26); see also 21:36. Though Luke says nothing of Jesus' heavenly intercession for humanity in the Father's presence (contrast Rom 8:34; Heb 7:25; 9:24; 1 John 2:1), he regards the exalted Christ as the one who pours out the Spirit (Acts 2:33), who stands on God's right hand (Acts 7:55-56; see H. P. Owen, *NTS* 1 [1954-1955] 224-226), who is appointed as a Messiah still to come (3:20-21), and is to be involved in the judgment of the world on a fixed day (17:31).

In Lucan christology, there are four phases of Christ's existence. The first begins with his virginal conception and continues until his appearance in the desert to be baptized. The second begins with his baptism and continues through the Period of Jesus until his ascension. The third begins with his ascension and continues until the parousia. The fourth is the parousia itself. (In Lucan theology there is no question of Jesus' preexistence or incarnation. Many NT interpreters rightly reckon with the preexistent sonship of Jesus in Pauline theology and with the incarnation of Jesus in Johannine theology; but neither of these aspects of his existence emerge in the Lucan portrait of him.)

It is important to keep these phases of Jesus' existence in mind, because they enter into the discussion of the next aspect of christology, the titles applied to Jesus in the Lucan writings.

B. CHRISTOLOGICAL TITLES. At times some of the titles used for Jesus in the Lucan writings are more expressive of soteriology than of christology. But we shall group the titles together here and reserve for the discussion of Lucan soteriology other aspects of Jesus' significance for humanity.

In a study of christological titles used in the NT one has to discuss three aspects of them: the background or origin of the title (Palestinian Judaism or Hellenistic world?), its meaning, and its application (i.e. to what phase of Jesus' existence has it been applied or to what phase was it originally applied?). Some of the details in the discussion of these aspects will have to be relegated to notes on various passages. We shall concentrate here on the specifically Lucan usage.

1) *Messiah or Christ*. Though not the most frequently used title for Jesus in the Lucan writings, *christos* has to be regarded as the most important. This emerges from the question that the Lucan Jesus poses to the disciples on the road to Emmaus, "Was not the Messiah bound to suffer all this before entering into his glory?" (24:26). Moreover, only Luke in the NT implies its importance by telling us the name, "Christians," by which the disciples came to be known (Acts 11:26; 26:28).

The noun *christos* is used by Luke in a titular sense about twenty-four times (Luke 2:11,26; 3:15; 4:41; 9:20; 20:41; 22:67; 23:2,35,39; 24:26,46; Acts 2:31,36; 3:18,20[?]; 4:26; 5:42; 8:5; 9:22; 17:3; 18:5,28; 26:23). One may debate whether it is better to render it in these passages as "Messiah" or as "the Christ." The latter might seem better for Luke's Gentile Christian readers, but the former conveys the meaning of the title better—especially given the use of Christ as a name for Jesus, a use that tends to obscure its basic meaning. But *christos* has already become a name for Jesus in some Lucan texts, a sort of second name (e.g. Acts 2:38; 3:6; 4:10,33; 8:12,[37]; 9:34; 10:36,48; 11:17; 15:26; 16:18; 17:3[?]; 20:21; 24:24; 28:31). In some of these passages it is actually coupled with the word for "name" (e.g. 4:10; 8:12).

The title is derived from Palestinian Judaism. Its origin is found in the OT use of *māšiaḥ*, "anointed one," which was translated in the LXX as *christos*. Both the Hebrew root *mšḥ* and Greek *chriein* mean "anoint." In the OT the anointing did not have a univocal significance, but the title was generically used of certain historical persons regarded as anointed agents of Yahweh for the service or protection of his people, Israel. It was usually applied to kings of Israel (Saul, David, and successors on the Davidic throne), but at times it was applied to others as well (the high priest, even Cyrus, the Persian king). In the last pre-Christian centuries of Palestinian Judaism there emerged a messianic expectation, i.e. a belief in a future David or in anointed figures to be sent by God; for details on the emergence of this belief, see the NOTES on 3:15 and 9:20.

In the time of Jesus the title "messiah" would have denoted an expected anointed agent sent by God either in the Davidic, kingly or political, tradition for the restoration of Israel and the triumph of God's power and dominion or in the priestly tradition (see *Ps. Sol.* 17:32; 18:title, 5,7; *1 Enoch* 48:10; 52:4; *2 Esdras* 12:32; 1QS 9:11; cf. M. de Jonge, "The Use of the Word 'Anointed'"). Jesus would not have been unaware of this messianic expectation or of a possible relationship of himself to it. But we have no certain way of assessing what form that relationship would have taken in his own consciousness.

Though the pre-Lucan gospel tradition attests the application of the title to Jesus by Peter in his ministry, it also portrays Jesus himself as scarcely tolerating the use of it for him and as correcting it by announcing his destiny of suffering as the Son of Man (Mark 8:30-31). Moreover, whereas the Marcan Gospel later presents Jesus frankly admitting his messiahship before the high priest (14:62), that admission is likewise corrected in the later gospel tradition (cf. Matt 26:64; Luke 22:67). The political overtones of the title were almost certainly the reason for the corrections.

After Jesus' death and in the time before Luke writes, *christos* became the title par excellence for Jesus of Nazareth, even a name for him. *Pace* F. Hahn (*Titles,* 186), Paul has scarcely retained any of its titular sense, save in Rom 9:5 (see W. Kramer, *Christ,* 203-214). But the distinction noted above in Lucan writings between the title and the name is hardly original with Luke. The catalyst for the adoption of the title "messiah" (*christos*) for Jesus has to be recognized in that used for him on the cross, "The king of the Jews" (Mark 15:26). The regal status attributed to him by Pilate led to the clear association of him with the messianic expectation of the time. In other words, he was crucified as such, as N. A. Dahl ("The Crucified Messiah," 23-28) has rightly argued. Crucified as king, he quickly became for his followers "the Messiah," and the title, colored by resurrection-faith, ceased to be a mere appellation for an expected messianic figure and became instead a honorific designation that suited one person alone. Within a few years of the crucifixion "Christ Jesus," "Jesus Christ," or "Jesus the Messiah" emerged. It soon became interesting possibility that the Jesus movement only became a Messianic movement after death of Jesus – this as opposed to other Jewish messianic movements throughout history.

VII. LUCAN THEOLOGY   199

part of the kerygma, as 1 Cor 15:3 reveals: "*Christ* died for our sins in accord with the Scriptures." This passage clearly militates against the thesis of Hahn that in the "earliest times the concept and the title of Messiah were not applied to Jesus" (*Titles*, 161).

Luke has preserved the application of the title to Jesus during his ministry in Peter's confession (9:20, "God's Messiah"), but he has also preserved Jesus' prohibition to use it of him and the correction (9:22), even though he omits the rebuke of Peter. At the interrogation before the high priest he does not answer the question about his messiahship with the frank "I am" of Mark 14:62, but with an evasive, at most half-affirmative reply (Luke 22:67-68). Moreover, Luke further portrays the risen Christ brushing aside the disciples' question whether he was then about to restore the kingdom to Israel (Acts 1:6). Thus the Lucan Jesus does not tolerate the political overtones to the current messianic expectation, even though the close identification of "Messiah" and "king" are predicated of him in 23:2.

If, then, the title is applied to the phase of Jesus' earthly ministry in the Lucan Gospel, Luke does not use it of him solely there. It is expressly linked to his resurrection in Acts. Peter is made to proclaim on Pentecost to the Jews of Jerusalem, "This Jesus God raised up . . . ; this Jesus, whom you crucified, God has made Lord and Messiah" (Acts 2:32,36), and he speaks of him as exalted to God's right hand (2:32-33). Thus the title is applied to him in the third phase of Christ's existence. It is also pressed back into the first, for Luke, writing his infancy narrative with hindsight, makes the angels declare to the shepherds of Bethlehem, "A Savior has been born to you today in the town of David. He is the Messiah, the Lord" (Luke 2:11).

For Luke the title *christos* used of Jesus designates him as God's anointed agent announcing himself as the bearer of a new form of salvation to mankind and its relation to God's kingdom among them in a new form (see Luke 2:26,29-32). Not unrelated to this title is the sense of another one, "king" used of Jesus in a special way in the Lucan writings and expressive of a sense in which *christos* itself has to be understood (see below, pp. 215-216). Furthermore, one should note the distinctively Lucan phrases *ho christos Kyriou,* "the Lord's Messiah" (2:26; Acts 4:26) and *ho christos tou theou,* "God's Messiah" (Luke 9:20; 23:35), where the genitive expresses the author of the anointing, as in the OT (e.g. 1 Sam 24:7).

Two further aspects of Lucan messianism must be recalled here. First, the view of Jesus as a Messiah who is still expected. Peter, in his speech addressed to the people of Jerusalem gathered in the Temple, exhorts them: "So repent and turn, so that your sins may be wiped away, that times of refreshment may come from the presence of the Lord, and that he may send you the Messiah appointed for you, Jesus, whom heaven must welcome until the time for establishing all that God spoke through the mouth of his holy prophets of old" (Acts 3:19-21). One may try to read these verses as if they referred to Jesus, who is already recognized as the Messiah, who has ascended, and who is expected to come again; but that would be to miss the complicated testimony of these verses. For they speak of Jesus as one appointed as a Messiah to come, one whom heaven must preserve until God's good time arrives. J. A. T. Robinson has queried whether we may not have here "the most primitive christology of all" in the NT (see bibliography). That may well be. Since it is a type of messiahship that appears nowhere else in the NT and is not used by Luke himself in any other part of his writings, it may be that we are confronted here with a bit of pre-Lucan para-kerygmatic christology (i.e. a primitive type of christology that emerged in the early church, that was not part of the kerygma itself, but existed alongside it, notably with what became the more common view of Jesus' messiahship). What should be noted about it is that it applied the title *christos* to Jesus as of his parousia, to the fourth phase of his existence. It is the only place in the NT where this title is used of the parousiac Jesus; elsewhere *kyrios* seems to be the preferred title for that phase (see 1 Thess 4:17; 1 Cor 11:26; 16:22).

Second, a peculiarly Lucan theologoumenon is the idea that Jesus was a suffering Messiah. "Was not the Messiah bound to suffer all this before entering his glory?" (Luke 24:26); ". . . the Messiah must suffer and rise from the dead" (24:46). See further Acts 3:18; 17:3; 26:23. The idea of a suffering messiah is found nowhere in the OT or in any Jewish literature prior to or contemporaneous with the NT. This is true despite what Luke says in 24:27,46 about "Moses," "all the prophets," and "all the scriptures." Nor does any other NT writer speak of Jesus as the suffering Messiah. True, Mark 8:29-31 may contain elements that enabled Luke to formulate the matter as he has: Peter is said to acknowledge Jesus to be the Messiah, and immediately thereafter Jesus corrects that confession, speaking of himself as a suffering Son of Man. But Mark himself never spoke of the suffering Messiah. (Needless to say, one should not confuse the idea of a suffering Messiah with that of the suffering Servant of Yahweh in Isa 52:13 - 53:12. In later Jewish tradition, the Servant eventually was given the title, "the Messiah"; cf. *Tg. Neb.,* Isa 52:13 [A. Sperber, *The Bible in Aramaic* (4 vols.; Leiden: Brill, 1959-1973) 3. 107]; see further S. H. Levey, *The Messiah: An Aramaic Interpretation: The Messianic Exegesis of the Targum* [Cincinnati: Hebrew Union College, 1974] 63-67. But that is not known from earlier tradition.)

2) *Lord.* "Lord" or "the Lord" ([*ho*] *kyrios*) is the most frequently

used title for Jesus in Luke-Acts, occurring almost twice as often as *christos;* it remained a real title and did not become a name. Its background or origin is a matter highly contested today.

The title *kyrios* occurs in Luke-Acts for both Yahweh and Jesus. Its use for Yahweh was already found among Christians prior to Luke, as suggested by Mark 11:9; 12:11,29,30,36, the "Q" passages in Luke 4:8 (=Matt 4:10) and 4:12 (=Matt 4:7), and the passage in Luke 10:27, which may be from "L." This early Christian use of *kyrios* for Yahweh has been traced by some scholars to the LXX (e.g. O. Cullmann, *Christology,* 200-201; W. Foerster, *TDNT* 3 [1965] 1086). However, the practice of referring to Yahweh as *kyrios,* "Lord," is said to be found only in Christian copies of the so-called LXX dating from the fourth century A.D. on, whereas in pre-Christian Greek translations of the OT the name *Yhwh* was written in Hebrew characters as a mark of reverence for the sacredness of the name. Origen and Jerome knew of Greek mss. in their day which contained the name in this form (see Jerome *Prologus galeatus,* PL 28. 594-595; *Ep. 25, Ad Marcellam,* CSEL 54. 219). Moreover, in recent times two Greek texts of the OT of early date have been found which reveal the scribal practice: (a) from Palestine: 8ḤevXII gr, a fragmentary Greek text of the Twelve Minor Prophets discovered in the eighth cave of Naḥal Ḥever, dating from 50 B.C.-A.D. 50, with the name *Yhwh* written in paleo-Hebrew characters; (b) from Egypt: Papyrus Fuad 266, a fragmentary Greek text containing parts of Genesis and Deuteronomy, dating from the second/first centuries B.C., with at least thirty-one examples of the name written in Hebrew square characters. Other data could also be adduced. This situation has led a number of NT scholars to ask whether Jews in pre-Christian times ever referred to Yahweh as "(the) Lord." Bultmann (*Theology,* 1. 51) has maintained that it was "unthinkable in Jewish usage" to use "the unmodified expression 'the Lord'" of Yahweh in ancient Palestine. See further P. Vielhauer, "Ein Weg zur neutestamentlichen Christologie? Prüfung der Thesen Ferdinand Hahns," in his *Aufsätze zum Neuen Testament* (Theologische Bücherei 31; Munich: Kaiser, 1965) 141-198; H. Conzelmann, *Outline,* 82-84; Kramer, *Christ, Lord, Son of God,* 70-71.

The corollary to this is that the Christian use of *kyrios* for Jesus in the absolute as "Lord" or "the Lord" cannot be derived from this Septuagintal or Palestinian usage. As a result, many of these same interpreters seek to derive the title for Jesus from a non-Palestinian setting: it would not be part of the primitive kerygma, but would have emerged when the kerygma was carried by missionaries out from Palestine to the eastern Mediterranean world. When their message came into contact with the many other "gods" and many "lords" of that area, then it would have emerged in Christian consciousness that "for us there is one God, the Father, . . . and one Lord, Jesus Christ" (1 Cor 8:5-6). In this regard one may note that Luke uses the absolute *ho kyrios* of the emperor Nero in Acts 25:26.

All this needs further scrutiny. It is impossible to spell out the details here, but suffice it to say that there is now evidence from pre-Christian Palestine that Jews did speak of Yahweh in Hebrew as *'ādōn*, "Lord," in Aramaic as *mārê'* and *māryā'*, and in Greek as *kyrios*, with the result that it is not impossible that early Jewish Christians in Palestine itself trans-ferred the title "Lord" or "the Lord" from Yahweh to Jesus. See further my articles, "The Semitic Background of the New Testament *Kyrios*-Ti-tle," *WA*, 115-142 (originally in German, in *Jesus Christus in Historie und Theologie: Neutestamentliche Festschrift für Hans Conzelmann zum 60. Geburtstag* [ed. G. Strecker; Tübingen: Mohr (Siebeck), 1975] 267-298); "New Testament *Kyrios* and *Maranatha* and Their Aramaic Background," in *To Advance the Gospel: New Testament Studies* (New York: Crossroad, 1981) 218-235. Cf. G. Howard, "The Tetragram and the New Testament," *JBL* 96 (1977) 63-83.

Because pre-Christian Palestinian Jews did on occasion refer to Yah-weh as "Lord," and it was not as "unthinkable" as has been sometimes maintained, the transfer of that title to Jesus undoubtedly took place on Palestinian soil itself. It would thus mean that the primitive confession "Jesus is Lord" (1 Cor 12:3; Rom 10:9) was a response to the early kerygma itself and was not then a product of missionary activity during the evangelization of the eastern Mediterranean. It was probably formu-lated in Greek by the "Hellenists" among the Jewish Christians of Pales-tine and in Aramaic or Hebrew by the "Hebrews" among them.

The use of *kyrios* for Jesus would have meant putting him on the same level as Yahweh, without, however, identifying him, since he is never re-ferred to as *'abbā'*. Moreover, the ancient Aramaic prayer *māranā' thā'*, preserved in Greek in 1 Cor 16:22, "Our Lord, come!" would suggest that the title had been applied to him at first in his parousiac status (cf. 1 Cor 11:26).

Luke never predicates the title *kyrios* of Jesus in his parousia. In Acts 3:19 it is clearly used of Yahweh who is to send the appointed Messiah. Luke does apply the title to Jesus after the resurrection, in Acts 2:36, "God has made him both Lord and Messiah." This is a passage that has been related to the kerygma in Acts and may even represent a pre-Lucan formulation; in any case the passage reveals the use of the NT title par excellence for the risen Christ. Cf. Luke 24:34, "the Lord has been raised."

Luke has time and again retrojected this title into the phase of Jesus' earthly ministry. Whereas the absolute use of *kyrios* is found only once in the Marcan Gospel (11:3), the frequency of its use in Lucan narratives, where the evangelist himself is speaking, is to be noted: Luke 7:13,19; 10:1,39,41; 11:39; 12:42a; 13:15; 17:5,6; 18:6; 19:8a,31,34; (20:44); 22:61bis; 24:3,34. Here Luke is simply using the title that had become current in his own day, as the narrative in Acts also betrays (e.g. 1:21; 4:33; 5:14; 8:16, etc.). During the course of the ministry of Jesus many persons address Jesus with the vocative kyrie (5:8,12; 6:46bis; 7:6; 9:54,59,61; 10:17,40; 11:1; 12:41; 13:23,25; 17:37; 18:41; 22:33,38,49). In these instances it is not easy to decide how one should translate the title, "sir" (in a secular sense) or "Lord" (in a religious sense). This is a more acute problem in the Marcan Gospel; by the time that Luke writes, he may well be intending the religious sense even of the vocative. The same question is raised about the use of the vocative in the accounts of Paul's vision of Jesus on the road to Damascus (9:5,10b,13; 22:8,10,19; 26:15a).

Again, one should note that Luke even retrojects the title kyrios into the first phase of Jesus' earthly existence. In the angels' announcement to the shepherds of Bethlehem he is identified, among other things, as "Lord" (Luke 2:11). And Elizabeth is made to refer to Mary as "the mother of my Lord" in 1:43, whereas Mary in calling herself the "handmaid of the Lord" (1:38) is rather referring to Yahweh with this title.

In using kyrios of both Yahweh and Jesus in his writings Luke continues the sense of the title already being used in the early Christian community, which in some sense regarded Jesus as on a level with Yahweh. This is not yet to be regarded as an expression of divinity, but it speaks at least of his otherness, his transcendent character. The sense of lordship that kyrios, 'ādōn, or mārê' would have carried among Palestinian Jews for Yahweh is now extended to Jesus, especially in his risen status. It is expressive of the dominion that both figures are thought to have over human beings. Luke never uses for Jesus the title reserved twice for Yahweh, despota, "sovereign lord" (Acts 4:24; Luke 2:29). The use of the title kyrios for Jesus in the Lucan writings, then, expresses the influence of the risen Christ on his followers. In retrojecting the title born of the resurrection back into earlier parts of his story, Luke surrounds the character of Jesus with an aura more characteristic of the third phase of his existence. This is again a form of Lucan foreshadowing.

Since I prefer to keep the meaning of the various titles applied to Jesus distinct, I hesitate to go along with I. de la Potterie, who thinks that kyrios in the Lucan Gospel has "an essentially messianic resonance" ("Le titre," 145). This is a careless use of the word "messianic," which M. de Jonge has also criticized ("The Use of the Word 'Anointed,'" 133). Acts 2:36 tells against the tendency to interpret one by the other: "God made

him Lord and Messiah" (see also Luke 2:11). There would be no reason
to use two titles if one were carrying essentially the resonance of the
other. See further J. A. Fitzmyer, *EWNT* 2. 811-20.

3) *Savior.* In discussing salvation-history above (p. 181), we noted a
distinctive Lucan title for Jesus, *sōtēr,* "Savior." John also uses it (4:42),
but among the Synoptics it is found exclusively in the Third Gospel. It
occurs there only once, but it is being discussed third among the titles because of the prominence given to it in the message of the angels to the
shepherds of Bethlehem at the time of Jesus' birth: He is Savior, Messiah,
and Lord (2:11). The title occurs again in Acts 5:31, when Peter and
the apostles answer the charge of the Sanhedrin and declare that God has
exalted "as Savior and Leader" Jesus, "whom you killed by hanging him
on a tree." Here the title is applied to the third phase of Jesus' existence,
whereas in the Gospel Luke has already retrojected it to the first phase.
Again, Paul in his synagogue address in Pisidian Antioch is made to
relate Jesus to David's lineage and declare that God has brought in him
"a Savior to Israel, as he promised" (13:23). Later on in the address,
Paul refers to Jesus whom God has raised from the dead (13:34), and so
Luke is undoubtedly thinking here of *sōtēr* as a title for the risen Christ.

Sōtēr was a title in frequent use in the contemporary Greco-Roman
world; it was often applied to gods, philosophers, physicians, statesmen,
kings, and emperors (see W. Foerster and G. Fohrer, "*Sōzō,* . . . ,"
TDNT 7 [1971] 965-1024). For example, it is found on the Rosetta
Stone, in which Ptolemy V Epiphanes (203-181 B.C.) was hailed as "savior and god," and on an Ephesian inscription of A.D. 48, in which Julius
Caesar was called "god manifest and common savior of human life" (see
MM, 287, 621). It was often linked to Roman *salus* and the awaited return of the Golden Age.

The title *sōtēr* also has an OT background, since *môšiaʿ,* "savior," is
used there of both individuals whom God raises up for the deliverance of
his people (Judg 3:9,15) and of God himself in that capacity (1 Sam
10:19; Isa 45:15,21); and *sōtēr* appears in the corresponding passages in
the LXX. See further LXX Wisd 16:7; 1 Macc 4:30; Sir 51:1; *Ps. Sol.*
3:6; 8:33; 16:4 (all used of God).

The Christian use of the title for Jesus may be influenced by both of
these backgrounds. The title was already current in pre-Lucan Christianity, as Phil 3:20 reveals, where Paul uses it of the Lord Jesus Christ
who is "awaited as a Savior." This parousiac reference to the Savior is
not surprising in Pauline thinking, because most of Paul's references to
"salvation" regard it as a future, eschatological effect of the Christ-event.
Luke uses the title not of the parousiac Lord, but of his risen status
(Acts 5:31; 13:23) or of his earthly appearance (Luke 2:11).
Significantly, it is absent from the Period of Jesus itself, the center of

time, for then salvation was achieved, yet there is no reason to think that the historical Jesus was actually so hailed in that period. As Luke uses the title, it is related to OT promises of salvation, as Acts 13:23 makes clear: From David's lineage God has brought a Savior to Israel, as he promised.

For the meaning of the title, see the discussion of salvation as an effect of the Christ-event (p. 222 below). Luke says nothing of the popular etymology of the name of Jesus, given in Matt 1:21 ("he will save his people from their sins"). Though "Savior" became a common title for Jesus throughout subsequent centuries, probably mainly because of the Lucan usage, it is not a major NT title for him.

4) *Son of God.* The title "Son of God," which became so important for later theology, is likewise used for Jesus in the Lucan writings, and we have to establish its meaning there. We can distinguish three forms in which it has been used by Luke: "Son of God," "Son of the Most High (God)," and simply "the/my Son" (without the dependent genitive). The first identification of Jesus provided in the Gospel reveals to the reader that he will be born as an heir to David's throne and will be "the Son of the Most High" (1:32), the "Son of God" (1:35). Luke has derived from the earlier gospel tradition that use of the full title by Satan or demons during the ministry (4:3,9; 8:28), but he introduces it once in a similar situation (4:41). Otherwise it appears only in the high priest's second question during the interrogation of Jesus (22:70). In Acts, Paul is portrayed preaching in Damascus that Jesus is "the Son of God" (9:20). In the scenes of Jesus' baptism and transfiguration he is proclaimed by a heavenly voice to be "my Son" (Luke 3:22; 9:35), and in 10:22 Jesus refers to himself three times as "the Son." Indirectly, the title is used of him in Acts 13:33, when Paul in the synagogue of Pisidian Antioch applies Ps 2:7 to him: "You are my Son; today I have begotten you." (The reading of "Son" in Acts 20:28 [BJ] is a sheer conjecture, unsupported by any Greek mss.)

The title "Son of God" had a long history in the ancient Near East and could imply many things. Egyptian pharaohs were called "sons of God" because the sun-god Re was regarded as their father (see C. J. Gadd, *Ideas of Divine Rule in the Ancient East* [London: Oxford University, 1948] 45-50; H. Frankfort, *Kingship and the Gods* [Chicago: University of Chicago, 1948] 299-301). In the Hellenistic and Roman worlds it was used of rulers, especially in the phrases *divi filius* or *theou huios* (see A. Deissmann, *Bible Studies* [2d ed.; Edinburgh: Clark, 1909] 166-167; *LAE²*, 346-347; MM, 649). In the same worlds it was often applied to mythical heroes, *thaumaturgoi* (often called *theioi andres,* "divine men"), and famous historical persons (such as Plato, Pythagoras, Apollonius of Tyana, etc.). See further G. P. Wetter, *"Der Sohn Gottes": Eine Unter-*

suchung über den Charakter und die Tendenz des Johannesevangeliums (FRLANT 26; Göttingen: Vandenheock und Ruprecht, 1916); W. Grundmann, *Die Gotteskindschaft in der Geschichte Jesu und ihre religionsgeschichtlichen Voraussetzungen* (Weimar: Deutsche Christen, 1938). In such a context the use of this title implied divine favor, divine adoption, and even divine power, being conferred often at the time of enthronement.

As used of Jesus in the NT, it has been said to reflect this Hellenistic or Roman background. Bultmann (*Theology*, 1. 50) regarded most of the Synoptic passages in which Jesus is given this title either as secondary and of Hellenistic-Christian origin or else as formulated by the respective evangelists, whereas the use of it in the transfiguration scene (Mark 9:7) and by Paul (Rom 1:3) could go back to a tradition of the earliest church because the resurrection made Jesus the Son in a messianic sense. Cf. H.-J. Schoeps, *Paulus* (Tübingen: Mohr [Siebeck], 1959) 163.

One also has to consider the OT and Jewish background of the title. In the OT "son(s) of God" is used with diverse nuances. It is a mythological title given to angels (Gen 6:2; Job 1:6; 2:1; Ps 29:1; Dan 3:25); a title of predilection for Israel in a collective sense (Exod 4:22, "my firstborn son"; Deut 14:1; Hos 11:1; Isa 1:2; Wisd 18:13); a title of adoption for a Davidic king (2 Sam 7:14; Ps 2:7; cf. Ps 89:27), for judges ([or angels?] Ps 82:6), or for the upright individual Jew (Sir 4:10, "son of the Most High"; Wisd 2:18). The singular occurs mostly in postexilic passages. What should be noted here is that the full title is never found in the OT predicated directly of a future, expected Messiah. *Pace* Conzelmann (*Outline*, 76), the title is not "synonymous with 'Messiah,'" even when used of a king. Psalm 2 speaks of Yahweh and "his anointed" and refers to the latter as "my Son," but that is at best a royal psalm, addressed to some historic king at his enthronement and not clearly "messianic" in the future sense. See further G. Dalmann, *The Words of Jesus* (Edinburgh: Clark, 1909) 268-272.

In Palestinian Judaism of the late pre-Christian centuries the title is used at times. 4QFlor 1-2 i 10 (see DJD 5. 53-55) identifies a person called "the Shoot of David" (cf. Jer 23:5) as such, quoting 2 Sam 7:14, the oracle of Nathan. The text does not use *māšîaḥ* of him, even though it includes a midrash on the opening verses of Psalms 1-2. The titles "Son of God" and "Son of the Most High" occur in an Aramaic text with phraseology very similar to Luke 1:32,35 (see my article, *NTS* 20 [1973-1974] 382-407). Here, however, they are not predicated of anyone called "messiah" in the text; they may refer to the son of some Jewish king or ruler. Hence there is nothing in the OT or Palestinian Jewish tradition that we know of to show that "Son of God" had a messianic nuance. Yet, even if that cannot be shown, the data listed above show at least that the title "Son of God" was as much at home in Palestinian Judaism as in the contemporary Hellenistic world of the eastern Mediterranean. The chances are that the use of it in both areas has to be respected in the discussion of the origin of the NT title.

Like *kyrios,* "Son of God" used of Jesus must be regarded as an element of the early kerygma itself, as Conzelmann (*Outline,* 76-82) recognized. This is suggested by its occurrence in pre-Pauline kerygmatic fragments embedded in Paul's letters (1 Thess 1:10; Rom 1:3-4). M. Hengel has recently pleaded for the recognition of it as such in an excellent discussion of the title, *The Son of God.*

When Luke adopts the title and uses it in Acts, he relates it to the resurrection, applying Ps 2:7 to Jesus, whom God raised "from the dead" (13:33-34). In this he seems to have been influenced by the primitive kerygma reflected in Rom 1:3-4, where sonship, resurrection, and the holy Spirit are combined in the affirmation. Two of these elements, sonship and influence of the Spirit, are taken by Luke from the resurrection-context of the kerygma and made part of his christology of the first phase of Jesus' existence: By the power of the Spirit Mary will conceive, and therefore her child will be "the Son of God" (1:35). It is strange that, when the heavenly angels identify the child to the shepherds, they do not identify him as God's Son (2:11). The puzzling two-staged question posed by the high priest at Jesus' interrogation, first about messiahship and then about divine sonship, is a literary echo of the identification of Jesus by Gabriel in the infancy narrative: He will sit on David's throne; he will be the Son of God (cf. 1:32,35 and 22:67,70). Finally, the title is used by Luke during his account of Jesus' ministry (the second phase), being derived either from "Q" (4:3,9; 10:22) or from "Mk" (8:28); only in 4:41 does it stem from Luke's own pen.

In the Lucan writings "Son of God" attributes to Jesus a unique relationship with Yahweh, the God of Israel. Even though Luke uses "sons of the Most High" of disciples (6:35), that scarcely detracts from the unique sense of filiation suggested by Gabriel's declaration to Mary before Jesus' birth (1:35). Used in that context, and related to the overshadowing of the holy Spirit, it carries a connotation that cannot be missed. Luke 10:22 suggests the uniqueness of the filiation, too. This aspect of the sonship in the Lucan writings has to be recognized, even if it does not yet carry the later connotations of physical or metaphysical sonship or identity of substance associated with the later Nicene or Constantinopolitan creeds. Luke does not intend that Jesus should be recognized as God's son merely in the adoptive sense in which a king on David's throne could be called his son (2 Sam 7:14; 1 Chr 17:13); his explicit relation of the title to the conception of Jesus connotes much more. We shall discuss below some ambiguous passages in the Lucan writings, where Luke might even be suggesting that Jesus is God. But not even Luke comes out boldly and says what Ignatius of Antioch eventually arrived at, "For our God, Jesus the Christ, was conceived of Mary" (*Ep. ad Ephesios* 18. 2, *ho gar theos hēmōn Iēsous ho christos*), as R. E. Brown (*Birth*, 316 n. 56) has pointed out.

Just how the "revelation" of Jesus' divine filiation took place in the first stage of the gospel tradition—in the ministry of Jesus itself—we shall never know. What we can trace, however, are various stages or phases of awareness on the part of NT writers as they gradually recognized the implications of that revelation, when or however it took place. I do not care for Brown's term, "christological moments," because it is open to the objection that the revelation of Jesus' unique relationship to the Father may have actually been made at the resurrection.

The NT title of Son of God has been understood by O. Cullmann (*Christology*, 270) in a different way, when he stresses that it "essentially implies his obedience to the Father." That suggestion can certainly be admitted and is found to be applicable, in particular, in the Lucan Gospel. For there Jesus is tempted as Son (4:3,9), and as such he cannot become a *theios anēr* and use his powers for his own interest. His dedication to the plan of his Father, which that scene stresses, is what drives him on.

5) *Son of Man*. Along with the other evangelists Luke preserves the tradition of the early church in putting the title *ho huios tou anthrōpou* on the lips of Jesus himself. In classical Greek that phrase would mean "the man's son," i.e. "the son of the man (human being)." Yet it is usually translated "Son of Man," because it is used in the same way as the anarthrous phrase *huios anthrōpou* (John 5:27; Rev 1:13; 14:14, in an allusion to Dan 7:13). The latter is usually explained as a Semitism.

Given its strange Greek formulation with two definite articles and its synonymous relation to the Semitic anarthrous form, it is hardly to be traced to a Hellenistic or Roman background. But its origin in the Jewish world is not easily explained. The titular use of the phrase in the New Testament is scarcely to be derived from Hebrew vocative *ben 'ādām*, "son of man" (=mortal man), in Ezekiel, God's mode of address to the prophet. (This explanation has been proposed at times, e.g. by A. Richardson, *An Introduction to the Theology of the New Testament* [New York: Harper & Row, 1958] 145-146; P. Parker, *JBL* 60 [1941] 151-157.) The two uses are entirely distinct.

More frequently this title is explained as a Greek translation of Aramaic *bar 'ĕnāš* or *bar 'ĕnōš*, "son of man." This phrase is now attested in several pre-Christian Syrian and Palestinian texts (Sefire III 16; 1QapGen 21:13; 11QtgJob 9:9; 26:3) so that there cannot be any doubt about its existence. In these texts it is used either in a generic sense (=a human being, a mortal) or in an indefinite sense (=someone [or, if in a negation, no one]). In such pre-Christian extrabiblical texts it is never found either as a vocative (like the ben 'ādām of Ezekiel), or as a title for some apocalyptic figure, or as a surrogate for "I" or "he." (The last usage is now attested, indeed, in targumic texts of a later period; cf. Gen 4:14 in Tg. Neofiti I and in the Cairo targum B text. But that is scarcely of relevance to the NT, pace G. Vermes, Jesus the Jew [London: Collins, 1973] 163-168, since both targums stem from such a late date.) Bultmann (Theology 1. 30) sought to use the indefinite sense mentioned above as the explanation of those Son of Man sayings in the Synoptics in which it refers to Jesus "now at work." The problem, then, is to explain how the phrase could have one meaning for certain occurrences and another elsewhere.

The attempt, however, has often been made to relate the Greek phrase to bar 'ěnāš in Dan 7:13, where it is used of a figure "like a son of man." There it seems to be a symbol for the collectivity of the "holy ones of Israel" who have been promised to inherit a kingdom (7:18). The problem has always been to explain how that collective sense of the phrase would have developed into a title for an individual in the NT.

As a step in the process of development between Daniel and the NT, commentators have often referred to the individual use of the phrase in 1 Enoch (46:2-4; 48:2; 62:5-7,13-14; 69:27-29). Here the phrase is applied to a mysterious hidden figure who is to be revealed; he is also called "the Elect One" (49:2-4; 51:5a,2-3; 61:8-9; 62:1), "the Righteous and Elect One" (53:6), "the Lord's Anointed" (48:10; 52:4), and "the Light of the Gentiles" (48:4). Thus, it would seem that this is a transitional use, referring to an apocalyptic figure. The trouble is that all these passages occur in the so-called Book of Parables, the second part of Ethiopic 1 Enoch, chaps. 37-71. This part of Enochic literature, however, is missing from the Greek fragments and from the Aramaic form of the Books of Enoch recently recovered from pre-Christian Palestinian caves of Qumran. J. T. Milik (The Books of Enoch [Oxford: Clarendon, 1976] 91-92) has concluded that the Parables represent a "Christian Greek composition" inspired by the NT Gospels and substituted for the original second part of Enochic literature, the Book of Giants, preserved in Qumran and also in Manichean literature. If his thesis were acceptable, it would mean that one cannot appeal to the use of the title in Enochic literature to trace the development from Daniel to the NT and its emergence as a title for an apocalyptic figure. However, Milik's thesis has not gone without objection. One of the main problems is that the Parables of Enoch do not betray anything that is really Christian; they still read like a Jewish composition and seem to be dependent on Daniel 7. See further my article in TS 38 (1977) 332-345; J. C. Greenfield, "Prolegomenon," in H. Odeberg, 3 Enoch or the Hebrew Book of Enoch (New York: Ktav,

1973) xvii; P. Grelot, "Le messie dans les apocryphes de l'Ancien Testament," *La venue du Messie: Messianisme et eschatologie* (RechBib 6;
Bruges: Desclée de Brouwer, 1962) 19-50, esp. pp. 43-47; M. de Jonge,
"The Use of the Word 'Anointed,'" 142-143; M. A. Knibb, "The Date
of the Parables of Enoch: A Critical Review," *NTS* 25 (1978-1979)
345-359. The upshot of this is that we may still have to reckon with the
Parables of Enoch as a transitional piece of evidence. If so, then there
would be some evidence for the use of the title for an apocalyptic individual figure.

The real problem with the title is the fact that in most instances it is
found in the Gospels—all four of them—on the lips of Jesus himself. In
Acts 7:56, however, it is not; rather, Stephen at his stoning sees Jesus as
the Son of Man standing at God's right hand. This represents Luke's extension of the title to another speaker. In still another passage that has
often been misunderstood it is actually used by the evangelists in a narrative statement about Jesus. Both Luke (5:24) and Matthew (9:6) have
taken over verbatim from Mark 2:10 the declaration, "but to let you
know that the Son of Man has authority on earth to forgive sins." That is
addressed to the reader; but because of the usually admitted thesis that
the phrase is found in the Gospels only on the lips of Jesus, an
anacoluthon is usually invoked to retain this instance on his lips too (see
the *RSV*). Since the phrase usually so occurs, and since it is never used in
the NT outside the Gospels, Acts, and Revelation, it is a peculiar title.
Its really problematic aspect is whether Jesus himself ever used the phrase.
We cannot discuss this in detail here. Briefly, my own view of the matter
is that he probably used *bar 'ĕnāš* in the generic sense (=a human being,
a mortal) and that this was later understood in the early tradition in a
titular sense and applied to him. The title has been secondarily introduced
by Luke himself in passages where the parallels in other Gospels do not
have it. Hence we have to reckon with the putting of the title on Jesus'
lips by the evangelist. Thus in 6:22 (cf. Matt 5:11, "me"); 9:22 (cf.
Matt 16:21, "he"); 12:8 (cf. Matt 10:32, "I"); 12:40 (cf. *Gos. Thomas*
§ 21,103[?]); 19:10 (introduced into an allusion to Ezek 34:16); 22:48
(added to Mark 16:7). These are instances of the surrogate or circum-
locutional use of the phrase, as G. Vermes would regard them. The problem is whether that usage existed in Aramaic of the time of Jesus or is a
coincidental creation of the evangelists.

Luke always employs the arthrous form of the phrase *ho huios tou
anthrōpou*. He uses it of Jesus' earthly ministry, in which it expresses his
mortal condition (Luke 5:24; 6:5; 11:30; 12:10; 19:10; 22:48, with a
connotation of dignity; and in 6:22; 7:34; 9:58, with a connotation of
service or lowliness). Luke also employs it in sayings that refer to Jesus'
passion (Luke 9:22,44; 18:31; 22:22; 24:7—in the announcements of

the suffering that is awaited). And he also uses it in a future sense of Jesus' coming in glory or judgment (Luke 9:26; 12:8,40; 17:22,24,26,30; 18:8; 21:27,36; 22:69). Though the question has been raised by NT interpreters whether Jesus himself possibly used the phrase to refer at times to some other expected apocalyptic figure (e.g. in Luke 9:26; 12:8; 17:22,24,26,30), it is hardly likely that this is the connotation in the Lucan Gospel. Luke 17:25, alluding to Jesus' suffering and rejection, makes it clear that for this evangelist the title is meant to refer to Jesus himself.

This title is unlike the others because it occurs for the most part on the lips of Jesus himself. Does it represent a confession that the evangelist makes? Since the title was already in the gospel tradition, and Luke's use of it is scarcely distinctive, it is not easy to say just what he would have meant by it. As an expression of Jesus' mortal condition, as applied to him in his ministry, it would express the aspect of his humanity, and this would be even truer of the application of it to his passion. But the use of it in contexts referring to his coming in glory or as judge obviously transcends the aspect of humanity. If one is right in relating the title to Dan 7:13, then the title would suggest a heavenly figure. It is not easy to be sure that all this is connoted every time the title appears, especially in the later Gospels of Luke, Matthew, and John. — *definitely a heavenly figure in*

I leave aside all connection of this title with any *Urmensch*-speculation *fn, but* and see no reason to relate it to the Pauline Adam-Christ typology. These *not in* aspects of the modern debate are farfetched; they are born of the desper- *sense of* ation sensed by all commentators in trying to explain the background *Daniel;* question as sketched above. *rather in*

6) *Servant.* Luke has also cast Jesus in the role of God's "Servant." *sense of* Though he uses of him in Acts (3:13,26; 4:27,30) the term *pais,* its *revealer* sense is controverted. The word can mean "child" (as in Luke 2:43); yet *who descends* it was often used in the sense of "slave" or "servant" as a designation of *from heaven* social condition (see Luke 7:7). If one could show that Luke is alluding *and then* to the *pais* of the Isaian Servant Songs (LXX of 42:1; 50:10; 52:13), *re ascends.* then "servant" would be the preferred interpretation of the passages in Acts. But the question is complicated by the use of *pais* in Greek literature and in the Hellenistic world of the time. There it was used in a religious sense, to express a special relationship to a god. *Kronou pais,* "a child of Cronus," is found in *The Iliad* 2. 205. Similarly in Greek OT writings, the righteous Jew is called *paida kyriou,* "a child of the Lord," where this meaning is certain because of the later use of *huios theou* of the same person (Wisd 2:13,18). From this variety of usages arises the hesitation about the sense of the term in Acts.

However, in view of several other allusions to or quotations of the Isaian Servant Songs in the Lucan writings, one should probably prefer this interpretation of *pais* in Acts. Thus in Luke 2:32 Jesus is predicted to be a light to the nations, an allusion to Isa 42:6 or 49:6. In Luke 22:37 Jesus at the Last Supper is portrayed quoting part of Isa 53:12 and saying that it finds fulfillment in him: "He was classed even with outlaws." In Acts 8:32-33 the eunuch of Candace reads Isa 53:7-8, the passage about the sheep being led to its slaughterers, which Philip then applies to Jesus (8:35). These allusions to or quotations of the Servant Songs in the Lucan writings, therefore, make it plausible that Luke, in using *pais* of Jesus in Acts 3-4 understood it in the sense of "Servant."

This at least seems to me to be preferable to the explanation suggested by R. H. Fuller that *pais,* meaning "servant," should rather be understood in the OT sense of *'ebed* as that is applied to Moses or David. The only passage that he cites for evidence of this is 1 Kgs 11:34, where David is called in the LXX, not *pais,* but *doulos* (*Foundations,* 44, 58 n. 67). Fuller has, furthermore, fused his treatment of two titles, servant and "prophet like Moses," which should have been kept distinct.

Luke has omitted from his Gospel for some inscrutable reason the allusion to Isa 53:12 found in Mark 10:45. This deprives his account of the vicarious nature of Jesus' service and suffering that the other Synoptics have.

However, as in Mark, the Lucan Jesus speaks of himself as the suffering Son of Man (9:22; cf. Mark 8:31). Since there is no OT passage which speaks of a suffering Son of Man nor any trace of such a figure in pre-Christian Palestinian Jewish literature, we conclude that the pre-Lucan Christian tradition had already fused aspects of the Suffering Servant with the Son of Man role that was developing in the post-Easter period. The extent to which Jesus would ever have so presented himself in his ministry is highly debatable; but that does not concern us here.

This question of suffering is, however, related to the idea of a suffering Messiah that we mentioned earlier (see p. 200 above). It is undoubtedly Luke's allusions to and quotations of the Isaian Servant passages that enabled him to fuse these two ideas and form his distinctive theologoumenon. For it is highly questionable whether Isaian Servant passages such as 42:1; 43:10; 49:6; 52:13; 53:11 were ever interpreted in a messianic sense in pre-Christian Palestinian Judaism. None of the evidence that J. Jeremias tried to amass (*The Servant of God* [SBT 20; London: SCM, 1957] 57-78) is pertinent, as others have already shown (M. D. Hooker, *Jesus and the Servant* [London: SPCK, 1959] 55-58; E. Lohse, *Märtyrer und Gottesknecht* [FRLANT 64; Göttingen: Vandenhoeck und Ruprecht, 1966] 66-78). For it comes either from questionable sources or periods much later than the NT itself. The most that one might concede is that in the Parables of *1 Enoch* (cf. the problems of that part of

Enochic literature already discussed), where one figure is given the various titles, "Son of Man," "Anointed One," "Righteous One," "Elect One," and "Light of the Gentiles," the last two depend on Isa 42:6 and 49:6. Thus the Isaian Servant function would be suggested for one who is an "Anointed One" (a Messiah); but one looks in vain in that part of Enochic literature for any suggestion that that figure is to suffer.

(Finally, it is to be recalled that Luke does cast Paul also in the role of the Servant; see Acts 13:46-47; 26:16-18, where Isa 49:6 and 42:7 are so used of him.)

7) *Prophet*. Another primitive title that Luke has picked up from the gospel tradition before him is *prophētēs*. Jesus is depicted using the title of himself (by implication at least) in the Nazareth synagogue: "No prophet is accepted in his own country," a saying based on Mark 6:4. Later in the same episode he compares himself to Elijah and Elisha. Still later, he is explicitly recognized by the people as "a great prophet" (7:16, in an episode exclusive to Luke), as "one of the prophets of old" (9:8,19 [the latter is dependent on Mark 6:15]), and as "a prophet mighty in deed and word in the eyes of God and all the people" (so identified by Cleopas on the road to Emmaus, 24:19). Cf. Luke 7:39.

In a passage exclusive to Luke, Jesus refers to himself as a prophet and links his destiny in Jerusalem to this role: "It is impossible that a prophet should perish outside of Jerusalem" (13:33). Indeed, as that destiny begins to work itself out, he is taunted by those who hold him in custody and have blindfolded him, "Now prophesy! Who was it that hit you?" (22:64).

More specifically, Luke casts Jesus in the role of the prophet like Moses promised in Deut 18:15-18. This role is implied in the transfiguration scene, where he converses with Moses (and Elijah) about his "departure" to be accomplished in Jerusalem and where the instruction given to the disciples by the heavenly voice, "Listen to him" (9:35), echoes that of Deut 18:15. The role is even more explicitly given to him in Peter's speech in the Temple, where a form of Deut 18:15,18-19 is quoted (Acts 3:22-23), and again in Stephen's speech, where Deut 18:15 is cited (Acts 7:37).

In dealing with another prophetic role Luke treats Jesus as Elijah returned. There is, in fact, in the Lucan writings a double Elijah theme. On the one hand, Jesus rejects the identification of himself as the "One Who Is to Come," the title for *Elias redivivus* derived from Mal 3:1-23 (3:1-4:6E). This role is attributed to Jesus by John the Baptist, implicitly in Luke 3:16 and explicitly in 7:19. But Jesus reverses the role (7:27) and identifies John as the messenger of Mal 3:1 (eventually recognized in the OT book as Elijah). This rejection of the Elijah role is further seen in

Jesus' rebuke of the disciples, James and John, who expect him to act like
the OT prophet and call down fire from heaven on the inhospitable Samaritan villages (9:54-55 cf. 1 Kgs 18:36-38; 2 Kgs 1:9-14). On the
other hand, Jesus is portrayed as *Elias redivivus.* This is seen, first of all,
in the estimate of him found among the people (9:8,19); but also in the
Nazareth scene, where he compares himself to Elijah (and Elisha) sent to
heal people outside of Israel (4:25-27; cf. 1 Kgs 17:8-16; 2 Kgs 5:1-14).
Further, Jesus plays an Elijah role, when he addresses a would-be follower about putting one's hand to the plow and turning back, since he
there alludes to 1 Kgs 19:19-21. What is to be noted here is the implication of this double use of the Elijah role. Jesus rejects the idea that he has
come as a fiery social reformer (see Sir 48:10); but he tolerates the
identification of himself with Elijah because of his miracles, especially the
recognition of him as "a great prophet" after the raising of the son of
the widow of Nain (7:16; cf. 1 Kgs 17:23).

If R. E. Brown ("Jesus and Elisha") is right about the Elisha role that
Jesus plays in the Gospels, especially in contending that the Elisha cycle of
miracles is the best analogue for the collected miracles of Jesus, then
there would be still another implication of Jesus' prophetic role in this aspect.

There is still another aspect of the Elijah role that needs to be considered. Elijah was said to have been taken up to heaven in a whirlwind
(2 Kgs 2:11); and because he was taken up (without dying as other mortals), he was expected to return. This expectation gave rise to the notion
of *Elias redivivus,* referred to above. Elijah's "being taken up" is also
reflected in Luke's use of *analēmpsis* for Jesus in 9:51 at the beginning of
the travel account; and it also explains the appearance of Elijah with
Moses in the conversation with Jesus about his "departure" to be accomplished in Jerusalem.

These different ways in which Luke casts Jesus in a prophetic mold reveal that he saw him as a mouthpiece of God (cf. Exod 4:15-16), uttering with authority God's word to human beings (see Luke 4:32,43; 5:1;
Acts 10:36). In the context of Palestinian Judaism in the last pre-Christian centuries it was often thought that prophets had ceased to appear
among the people (see 1 Macc 9:27; Ps 74:9; cf. Josephus *Ag. Ap.* 1.8
§ 41). Consequently, there arose the expectation of a "trustworthy
prophet" (1 Macc 14:41; cf. 4:46), who was at times linked to the
prophet like Moses or to the expected *Elias redivivus.* Such an expectation is attested in Qumran literature: " . . . until there come a prophet
and the Messiahs of Aaron and Israel" (1QS 9:11). Cf. *T. Levi* 8:15.
Jesus is thus considered to be an eschatological prophet. It is in this sense
that one has to understand the role of Jesus in the Lucan writings. It is

not that he is just depicted at times as *Elias redivivus,* the prophet like Moses, or even Elisha, but rather through him God now pours forth his Spirit "in the last days" (see Acts 2:17,33).

It does not detract from Jesus' prophetic role in the Lucan writings that John the Baptist is also so portrayed (20:6; cf. 1:76; 3:2). The Lucan Jesus makes it clear that John was actually something "more than a prophet" (7:26). Indeed, one of the lesser purposes of the Lucan writings is to define the role of John the Baptist vis-à-vis Jesus. This is done by presenting John as the precursor of Jesus, at least by implication. Because of the double treatment of Elijah in the Lucan writings, Luke never explicitly identifies John with Elijah, as does Matt 11:14; and he omits the post-transfiguration scene in which Jesus says in Mark 9:9-13 that Elijah must come first. These traditions are undoubtedly omitted because there is a sense in which Jesus is *Elias redivivus.*

If Luke has portrayed Jesus as the eschatological prophet, he uses this title solely of the second phase of Jesus' existence, of his earthly ministry. It has no relevance in the first, third, or fourth phases. It attributes to Jesus an activity that launches the new phase of salvation-history. He is the bringer of "God's word" to mankind, precisely because he is a prophet. In the first phase, John the Baptist is recognized as a "prophet" (1:76), and as one coming in the spirit and power of Elijah (1:17). But there "prophet" is not used of Jesus, for he is something more: he is "great" (1:32), "Son of the Most High" (1:32), and "Savior, Messiah, and Lord" (2:11).

8) *King.* Given the early recognition of Jesus as "the Messiah," it is not surprising that the developing christology of the early community eventually adopted for him an even more explicitly regal title, *basileus,* "King." As we have already seen, Pilate's title on the cross, "the king of the Jews," was the catalyst for the swift attribution of the title "Messiah" to the crucified (and risen) Jesus. That title was used by Pilate because of the charges that were made against Jesus by those who thought of him in terms of messianic conduct. This motivation emerges clearly in the Lucan account (23:2). Though the title on the cross occurs with minor verbal variations in the different accounts—one might have thought that the early Christians would have at least recorded exactly what Pilate wrote— the substance of it is found in all four Gospels (Mark 15:26; Matt 27:37; Luke 23:38; John 19:19), *ho basileus tōn Ioudaiōn,* "the king of the Jews." Variations of this title are found also in different parts of the passion narratives; Luke uses forms of it in 23:2,3,37.

Just as Pilate's formulation brought early Christians to acknowledge Jesus as "the Messiah," it may also have prompted the use of *basileus* for him in other contexts. Luke is the only evangelist who has introduced it into the quotation from Ps 118:26, which was chanted by the people who greeted Jesus as he entered Jerusalem seated on a colt: *"Blest be the king, the one who comes in the name of the Lord!"* (19:38). Whereas the use of Ps 118:26 in the other Gospels hails Jesus as a pilgrim, coming to Jerusalem for the feast of Passover, Luke makes his arrival a regal one.

Reference is further made to Jesus' status as a king in Acts 17:7, where Jason and other disciples are haled before the city authorities in Thessalonica on the charge that they acknowledged Jesus as "another king" contrary to the "decrees of Caesar."

Both the title on the cross, "the king of the Jews" (23:38), its use elsewhere (23:2,3,37), and the use of "king" for Jesus in Acts 17:7 obviously carry a political connotation, as is made clear in Luke 23:2. It is, however, scarcely in a political sense that "king" is used at the entry of Jesus into Jerusalem. Luke, in introducing it there, seems to give it a religious sense. Coming to Jerusalem in the name of the Lord (Yahweh), Jesus arrives on a kingly mission, bringing peace to the city that unfortunately does not recognize the hour of its visitation (19:38,41,44).

Indirectly, Jesus' status as king in the Lucan Gospel colors his role as its kingdom-preacher. If the soldiers can taunt him about his kingship and challenge him to save himself (23:37), the penitent criminal acknowledges his kingship, requesting that he be remembered when Jesus comes into his kingdom (23:42). Here once again one detects the nuances of political and non-political kingship in the two attitudes.

The title "King" emerges in the Lucan account only at the end of the second phase of Jesus' existence, in the passion narrative. It carries no real significance for the other phases, except that in the infancy narrative Gabriel declares to Mary that Jesus will reign over the house of Jacob forever (1:33). This may imply a kingly role that extends beyond the ministry to Israel.

9) *Other, Less Frequently Used Titles in Lucan Christology.* The most important titles employed by Luke for Jesus are listed above; but there are a number of others that occur only once or twice and express other insights into Luke's view of Jesus.

a) *Son of David.* Derived from the pre-Lucan gospel tradition is the title "Son of David." It is not surprising that this title emerged, given the independent attestation of Jesus' Davidic descent in other NT writings (Rom 1:3; 2 Tim 2:8).

The title occurs in Luke only in the episode of the healing of a blind man outside Jericho, "Jesus, Son of David, have mercy on me" (18:38,39), and in the debate of Jesus with the scribes about how the Messiah could be called David's Son (20:41,44). Both passages are derived from Mark (10:47; 12:35). But the title is implied in several other passages: in Gabriel's message to Mary about his receiving the throne of his father David (1:32), in Zechariah's canticle, praising God for raising up a horn of salvation in the house of David, his servant (1:69), in Jesus' birth in the city of David (2:11), and in his genealogy (3:31).

The title is obviously related to Jesus' messiahship. This relationship can be seen in *Ps. Sol.* 17:21 in a pre-Christian writing and is the subject of the debate mentioned above. The title refers to an aspect of Jesus distinct from his status as "anointed," because there were Davidids who were not messiahs and "anointed ones" who were not Davidids (e.g. Cyrus). For the interpretation of the debate in chap. 20, see the commentary proper.

That Jesus should be addressed as "Son of David" in a miracle-story raises an interesting question: Why should such miraculous power be associated with a Davidid? Perhaps a Lucan answer to that question may be found in the words of Zechariah's canticle, praising God for having raised a "horn of salvation" in David's house. Through Jesus, the "Son of David," salvation came to the blind man of Jericho (18:35-43).

b) *Leader.* In the Acts of the Apostles Luke twice uses of Jesus the title *archēgos,* "leader" (5:31), or *archēgos tēs zōēs,* "leader of life" (3:15). In the former instance it is coupled with "Savior." The sense of the title is not absolutely clear; it seems to mean a pioneer, author, or originator, i.e. a person who begins something and is thus regarded as the source of its effects, blessings, etc. It may be related to the Lucan *archē,* "beginning," noted above (p. 183), designating Jesus as the initiator of the period of salvation. Or again, it may be related to the Lucan geographical perspective, designating him as a pioneer leading people along the way of salvation. Cf. Heb 2:10. The title has no clear OT or Jewish background and is best explained as derived by Luke from the Hellenistic world, where it was used of various rulers looked upon as the source of bounty to their peoples (see MM, 81).

c) *Holy One.* The adjective *hagios,* "holy," is used substantively as a title for Jesus in various Lucan contexts. It is employed by a demon (Luke 4:34) and by Peter in two of his speeches in Acts (2:27 [*hosios,* in OT quotation]; 3:14). The simple adjectival sense of the word is also found (Luke 1:35; Acts 4:27,30). The adjective is found both in Hellenistic Greek inscriptions and literature and in the Greek OT. In both bodies of literature it is applied to gods and to objects or persons dedicated to them. Luke has derived it from the pre-Lucan gospel tradition (see Mark 1:24). As a designation for Jesus in the Lucan writings, it has to be understood as expressing a special dedication of him to

Yahweh and his divine plan of salvation. It is applied to him in the first, second, and third phases of his existence.

d) *Righteous One*. Related to the preceding title is another, which sometimes occurs with it, *ho dikaios,* "the Righteous One." It is used as a title for Jesus in Acts 3:14 (with *hagios*); 22:14. As a simple adjective it is applied to Jesus by the Roman centurion at his crucifixion (Luke 23:47); there its meaning is "innocent." As a title for Jesus, it should rather be understood as it is used of upright Jewish individuals of the Period of Israel (see Luke 1:17; 23:50; Acts 10:22).

e) *Judge*. This title for Jesus is significantly absent from the Synoptic tradition itself, but it does emerge in the Acts of the Apostles. In 10:42 Jesus is proclaimed to be "the judge of the living and dead," and a similar function is ascribed to him in 17:31 (God will judge the world in righteousness by a man whom he has appointed). The title thus expresses Jesus' role in the goal of the salvific plan itself; it is applied to the fourth phase of his existence.

f) *Teacher*. If we end this list of titles used of Jesus in the Lucan writings with two for "Teacher," it is with the recognition that they are often used, either in the vocative *didaskale* (Luke 7:40; 9:38; 10:25; 11:45; 12:13; 18:18; 19:39; 20:21,28,39; 21:7) or in the exclusively Lucan word *epistata* (sometimes translated "master," Luke 5:5; 8:24*bis;* 9:33,49; 17:13). See also 8:49; 22:11. On the relation of these titles to *rabbi/rabbouni,* see NOTE on 7:40. The title "Teacher" attributes to Jesus authority in speaking of God and his salvation, but it is doubtful whether it makes any contribution to Lucan christology. The same title is given to John the Baptist in 3:12. The scene of Jesus' finding in the Temple is often thought to be a portrayal of him teaching the teachers of Israel, but in reality that scene depicts him as a disciple or learner (see the COMMENT), even though the emphasis given there to his comprehension and answers foreshadows his teaching role later in the Gospel, especially that of his teaching in the Jerusalem Temple. The two titles imply a relationship to Jesus' disciples. It is a relationship that continues even after his earthly ministry is over, as the absolute use of the expression, "the disciples," makes clear in Acts 6:1-2,7, etc.

g) *God(?)*. It is well known that the title *theos* is eventually given to Jesus in some NT writings. R. E. Brown (*Jesus God and Man,* 1-38) has studied the various NT passages, dubious and clear, where the title occurs. He considers John 1:1; 20:28; and Heb 1:8-9 to be among the certain uses. There are at least three passages in the Lucan writings in which the title might be intended. However, none of them is entirely clear. They are Luke 8:39; 9:43; and Acts 20:28; the last is involved in a major textual problem. They are mentioned here as problematic passages and will be discussed at length in the commentary proper. What should be noted here, however, is that by the time Luke wrote his Gospel and Acts it would not have been impossible for a Christian author to refer to Jesus as God.

C. SOTERIOLOGY. Having sketched Luke's basic christology, we turn to his view of the significance of Jesus' role in the Father's plan of salvation. If he has presented Jesus as a man attested by God with mighty deeds, wonders, and signs and as one to whom he attributes characteristics transcending the normal human condition and suggesting that he is "other," he has not done this in a vacuum. Such affirmations have been made about Jesus to serve the description of the essential role that he plays in the Father's plan. As we have already maintained, Luke has not written the story of Jesus with the intention that it be an anthropology, i.e. an explanation of the human condition, or merely as an ecclesiology, i.e. an explanation of the Christian church. Rather, he has retold the Jesus-story with a definite christological and soteriological intent: what Jesus did, said, and suffered had and has a significance and bearing on human history. Acts 4:12 makes that clear: "There is salvation in no one else, for there is no other name under heaven given among human beings by which we are to be saved."

In a discussion of Lucan soteriology, one has to devote some space to two main areas: (1) the treatment of the death of Jesus in the Lucan writings; and (2) the effects of the Christ-event, as Luke views them.

1) *The Death of Jesus.* This topic was briefly treated in the discussion of the thesis about Lucan theology entitled "Theology of the Cross vs. Theology of Glory" (see pp. 22-23 above). The problem of the Lucan presentation of the death of Jesus was briefly touched upon there, but more has now to be said about it. We cited there the views of C. H. Dodd, J. M. Creed, E. Käsemann, G. Voss; to which one could further add Conzelmann (*Theology,* 201: "there is no trace of any Passion mysticism, nor is any direct soteriological significance drawn from Jesus' suffering or death"), H. J. Cadbury (*Making of Luke-Acts,* 280-282), C. H. Talbert (*Luke and the Gnostics,* 71-82), etc. Has Luke really downplayed "the Cross," or ascribed the death of Jesus to Jewish misunderstanding and ignorance (of the Scriptures) so that the resurrection turns out to be God's corrective of that event? Is there no "saving significance" to the death of Jesus in the Lucan writings? This is the problem much discussed today.

True, Luke has no story of "the Cross." Conzelmann (*Theology,* 201) says, "The idea of the Cross plays no part in the proclamation." This is true only if one is looking for the Pauline way of expressing the significance of Jesus' death in the Lucan writings. (Incidentally, one might recall that a more frequent Lucan mode of expression is "hanging on a tree" [Acts 5:30; 10:39; cf. 13:29].) Nor does Luke regard Jesus' death as a sacrifice (cf. Eph 5:2) or as an expiation for sin (cf. Rom 3:25).

But the real question that has to be asked is whether in the Lucan story God is so depicted as bringing his salvific plan into realization *despite* the suffering and death of Jesus or *through* it (see G. Baumbach, *BLit* 45 [1972] 242). Even if one recognizes that in the Lucan account place is made for the misunderstanding of certain Jewish leaders involved in the death of Jesus (Luke 23:34; Acts 3:14-17; 13:27), that does not deprive his view of the death of all saving significance.

In this regard one has to recall that it is solely Luke who depicts Jesus as a suffering Messiah, as the Messiah who "must suffer" (see pp. 200, 212 above). No less than the other Synoptists he portrays Jesus praying on the Mount of Olives, "Yet not my will but yours be done" (22:42). He further depicts him as the prophet aware that he has to perish in Jerusalem (Luke 13:33), and Acts 13:28-30 clearly explains that what happened to him was divinely related to God's salvific plan. "But first he [the Son of Man] must suffer many things and be repudiated by this generation" (Luke 17:25). In other words, the Lucan "necessity" involved in the plan of salvation-history has a bearing on the death of Jesus (see pp. 179-180 above).

Though Luke has for some inscrutable reason omitted the Marcan saying about the Son of Man who had to give his life as a ransom for many (Mark 10:45), he is the only Synoptist who has preserved the words pronounced over the bread at the Last Supper as, "This is my body which is given for you" (22:19). The sacrificial nuance of this phrase has been stressed by A. George, W. G. Kümmel, and others. It is clearly akin to 1 Cor 11:24, but it has long been neglected in this regard because of the short reading that many interpreters have preferred. That neglect, however, can no longer be sustained [see NOTE on 22:19-20]. Similarly, a sacrificial nuance of the death of Jesus must be recognized in the covenant-blood spoken of in 22:20.

Again, no matter how one resolves the textual difficulties of Acts 20:28 ("the church of God/the Lord, which he acquired through his own blood/through the blood of his Own" [see B. M. Metzger, *TCGNT*, 480-482]), the acquisition of a people—an OT allusion (Isa 43:21; Mal 3:17)—by God through blood/death certainly alludes to the saving significance of Jesus' death.

Hence one has to admit with H. Flender (*St Luke*, 159) that "Luke regards the cross as an eschatological event"—even though "the cross" is a more Pauline turn of phrase. The death of Jesus is one of the events that has come to fulfillment among us (1:1), and in that sense is eschatological. "Its saving significance can only be comprehended in the context of the whole drama of salvation" (ibid.), or better, in the whole drama of the salvific plan being realized. The Lucan way of putting it: "This is what stands written: the Messiah must suffer and rise from the dead on the third day; in his name repentance for the forgiveness of sins must be preached to all the nations" (24:46-47). That certainly implies that forgiveness of sins comes only in the name of him who is the suffering Messiah. Luke may in the long run attach more saving significance to the resurrection of Jesus, but that is not because he regards it as a corrective of the misunderstanding of some Jewish leaders. Rather, through it Jesus became the "leader of life" (*archēgos tēs zōēs,* Acts 3:15; see p. 217 above).

Finally, one should recall what was said above (p. 23) about the episode of Jesus and the penitent thief, which is a Lucan symbolic way of highlighting the effect of the crucified Jesus on human beings. / *no!*

A. George (*RB* 80 [1973] 186-217) has amassed all the references to the death of Jesus in the Lucan writings, and the sum total of them makes a striking impression. It may be that they do not all underline the saving significance of it in a Pauline or Marcan way, but in the whole picture of the suffering Messiah it is difficult not to see Luke's way of presenting that significance. George speaks of the Lucan presentation of Jesus' death as "original," and in a sense he is right, even though one has to recognize that some of the data Luke uses are traditional. But he rightly concludes: "In fact, Luke does not suppress the cross, nor its tragedy, nor its mystery, nor even at times its salvific role, nor the necessity for the disciple of Jesus to deny himself, to take up the cross, and follow the Master" (pp. 216-217).

2) *Effects of the Christ-Event as Seen by Luke.* The NT writer who has best summed up the significance of what Jesus of Nazareth did for human beings is Paul. Under a variety of images or figures drawn from his diverse background, he presents those effects. For a list of them, see my article, "Reconciliation in Pauline Theology," *No Famine in the Land: Studies in Honor of John L. McKenzie* (eds. J. W. Flanagan and A. W. Robinson; Missoula, MT: Scholars Press, 1975) 155-177, esp. pp. 156-157. Actually, the various effects represent different aspects of the one reality, viewed in different ways. The one reality is that which was achieved by the Christ-event, i.e. the complex of the ministry, suffering, death, burial, resurrection, and ascension or exaltation of Christ; or the sum total of the impact on humanity of what Jesus was, what he said, and what he did. In terms of later theology this complex has been called the "whole work of Christ" or the "objective redemption," terms that can be used, provided one realizes that they are born of another matrix and are used to state what Jesus achieved *ephapax,* "once for all" (Rom 6:10).

Luke, however, also has his way of looking at the effects of the Christ-event. The three-phase view of salvation-history, espoused by Conzelmann, provides a background for this explanation. Luke writes from the Period of the Church, looking back at the Period of Jesus precisely as the time of salvation. When he looks back at it he sums up the effects of the Christ-event or that period under various images or figures. These are mainly the following: (a) Salvation; (b) Forgiveness of sins; (c) Peace; and (d) Life. Some minor ones will be mentioned later.

a) *Salvation.* In discussing the Lucan view of history and its various elements (see p. 181 above), we mentioned "salvation" among them, reserving for this point the description or definition of what is to be understood by that term. "Salvation" denotes the deliverance of human beings from evil, physical, moral, political, or cataclysmic. It connotes a victory, a rescue of them from a state of negation and a restoration to wholeness or integrity. As applied to the Christ-event, the wholeness to which human beings are restored is a sound relation to God himself. That would imply a rescue from sin, the state of alienation from God and, in terms of a post-NT theology, a deliverance from eternal damnation.

The use of the image to describe an effect of the Christ-event is, of course, pre-Lucan. It is based on sayings of Jesus preserved in the Marcan tradition (e.g. Mark 5:34; 15:31), but absent from the "Q" tradition. The Pauline use of the image shows that it had already assumed the abstract formulation in pre-Lucan times (e.g 2 Cor 7:10; Rom 1:16; 10:10; 13:11). In most instances, where Paul uses the image, it expresses an element of his futurist eschatology, denoting an effect still to be fully achieved in the future (in contrast to that of justification). Thus he speaks of the Christian's need to work out one's "salvation with fear and trembling" (Phil 2:12) and of the Christian awaiting a "Savior" from the heavenly commonwealth (Phil 3:20). By contrast, when Luke refers to salvation, it is something already achieved, though Luke 21:28 admits a future aspect of it.

As we have already indicated in the discussion of the christological title "Savior," it is not really possible to say for sure whence this image has been derived—whether from the OT idea of salvation (*yĕšû'āh*) or from the contemporary Greco-Roman use of it (e.g. Latin *salus*, Greek *sōtēria*). The OT background is often favored (e.g. Exod 14:13; 15:2), because a NT writer at times cites OT passages in connection with it (thus Luke quotes Isa 49:6 in Acts 13:47). On the other hand, Luke's insistence that "salvation" comes to human beings through no other name under heaven (Acts 4:12) may well reflect his awareness of the contemporary custom of ascribing it to the Roman emperor and other "benefactors" of humanity, and his denial of such deliverance through anyone else but Jesus whom he proclaims.

In any case, "salvation" is clearly an important effect of the Christ-event for Luke. He alone among the Synoptists calls Jesus "Savior"

(2:11; cf. Acts 5:31; 13:23) and uses the abstract noun, either fem. *sōtēria* (1:69,71,77; 19:9; cf. Acts 4:12; 7:25; 13:26,47; 16:17; 27:34) or neut. *sōtērion* (Luke 2:30; 3:6; cf. Acts 28:28). He also uses the verb *sōzein* more frequently than the others (Mark has it thirteen times, Matthew fifteen times, but Luke seventeen times [and thirteen times in Acts]).

In the Gospel "salvation" often denotes deliverance from such evils as sickness, infirmity, or sin; and its relation to "faith" (*pistis*) is often noted (e.g. 7:50; 8:48,50; 17:19). In contrast, both the noun and the verb in Acts express the more comprehensive salvation brought by him who is now the object of the proclamation. Luke recognizes that Jesus has brought salvation to Israel (Acts 13:23) and depicts him bringing it to all sorts of underprivileged human beings (on its universality, see pp. 187-192 above). "Salvation" is best summed up in one of Jesus' sayings preserved in 19:10: "The Son of Man has come to seek out and save what was lost." Further comments on its meaning in individual passages will be made in the NOTES on them. Even though the verb *sōzein* often depicts Jesus' effect on individuals during his ministry, the title *sōtēr* is never given to him during that ministry. It is a title born of the totality of his work, especially as that was understood after the resurrection. As O. Cullmann has put it (*Christology*, 241): "Like *Kyrios,* the title *Soter* presupposes the completion of Jesus' earthly work and its confirmation in his exaltation."

b) *Forgiveness of Sins.* When Luke looks back at the Christ-event, another way in which he sums up its effect is "the forgiveness of sins" (*aphesis hamartiōn*).

The image being used in *aphesis* is derived from an economic and social background in antiquity, either from the remission of debts or punishment or from the release from captivity or imprisonment. The noun *aphesis* is often found in the Greek OT as the translation of Hebrew *yôbēl*, "jubilee" (e.g. Lev 25:30), or *děrôr*, "release" (e.g. Jer 41:8 [=MT 34:8]) or *šěmiṭṭāh*, "release" (from debt, Deut 15:1). Only in Lev 16:26 does it occur in the LXX in a context involving "sin." However, the verbal form *aphienai* is often used in the OT with *hamartia* as its object (Exod 32:32; Lev 4:20; 5:6, etc.). In the contemporary Greek world too *aphesis* was often used in the sense of the pardon of debts or punishment and release from captivity (see MM, 96).

The association of *aphesis* with "sin" came from the Jewish religious use of the word "debt" in the sense of sin. This is not easily shown in the OT, in relation to the vocabulary of forgiveness. But the terms "sin" and "debt/guilt" (*ḥṭ'h whwbt*) are now found in juxtaposition in a fragmentary Qumran text, 4QMess ar (see *MPAT* § 28:2.17; cf. *ESBNT*, 142-143; M. Black, *AAGA*[3], 140). Moreover, God's "remission" of the sins of Job's friends is explicitly mentioned in 11QtgJob 38:2-3 (see *MPAT* § 5:38.2-3).

"To forgive sins"—the verbal form of the expression—is, of course, found abundantly, not only in the Lucan Gospel, but in the other Synoptics as well. But what is of interest to us here is the abstract form of the expression, *aphesis hamartiōn,* which never turns up in the LXX as such, and is found in the Synoptics only in Mark 1:4 and Matt 26:28. Its anarthrous form in these instances and in the Lucan passages to be cited below, reflecting undoubtedly a Semitic construct chain, stands in contrast to the two occurrences of the expression in the Pauline corpus (Col 1:14; Eph 1:7 [with "transgressions" instead of "sins"]). (Moreover, unless one admits that *paresis* in Rom 3:25c means nothing more than *aphesis,* there is no instance of "forgiveness of sins" in the undisputed authentic letters of Paul.) Hence the significance of the Lucan formula as an expression of an effect of the Christ-event.

It is true that Luke derives the expression from Mark 1:4 (see Luke 3:3). There and in 1:77 it is used in connection with John the Baptist. But the next time that it occurs in the Lucan Gospel is in the great commission given by the risen Christ to the Eleven and others on Easter Sunday night: "In his name repentance for the forgiveness of sins must be preached to all the nations" (24:47); and it is used frequently in Acts (see 2:38; 5:31; 10:43; 13:38; 26:18). Related to it earlier in the Lucan Gospel is the scene of Jesus' preaching in the Nazareth synagogue, which speaks of "release" for prisoners and the downtrodden (4:18, quoting Isa 61:1 and 58:6, but using *aphesis* in the general OT sense, without the modifier "of sins").

In other words, though Luke often depicts Jesus "forgiving sins" in the ministry of the Gospel, when he comes to sum up the corresponding effect of Jesus' total work that must be proclaimed, it is stated in terms of his releasing human beings from their debts (=sins) in the sight of God. He has, by all that he was and did, cancelled the debt of guilt incurred by their evil conduct.

c) *Peace.* Another effect brought about by the Christ-event, as viewed by Luke, is "peace" (*eirēnē*). Once again it is not easy to say whether the proper background of this image is the pervasive *pax Augusta* in the contemporary Roman world (see COMMENT on 2:2) or the OT understanding of *šālôm.* It may be that both are at work. Certainly Luke's dating of the birth of Jesus to a census taken during the reign of the emperor Augustus implies an association, if not a contrast, with the peace of that long reign. On the other hand, the connotations of the Hebrew root *šlm,* "be whole, complete," seem to be implied in the Lucan use of the term "peace." In the OT, *šālôm* expresses not merely an absence of war or hostilities, but much more the state of bounty or well-being that comes from God and includes concord, harmony, order, security, and prosperity. See Isa 48:18; 54:10; Ezek 34:25-29; Pss 29:11; 85:8-10; Jer 16:5; Num 6:24-26. In time "peace" became the mark of the awaited messianic kingdom, derived from Isa 52:7 (the heralds of peace). In Acts 10:36 Luke reflects this notion: "the word which he sent to the children of Israel, preaching peace through Jesus Christ (he is the Lord of all!)."

In a few of the sayings of Jesus the term "peace" has the meaning of the absence of war (Luke 11:21; 14:32). More often it is a figure for the bounty that he and his ministry bring to human beings. Peace is proclaimed by the angels to the shepherds at the announcement of his birth: "Peace on earth for the people whom he favors" (2:14). For he now brings God's peace in a new way. It is a quality characteristic of heaven itself: "Peace in heaven" (19:38). But it is also that which Jerusalem has unfortunately failed to comprehend: "If you yourself only knew what would make for your peace" (19:42).

On the lips of Jesus it is sometimes associated with salvation (7:50; 8:48). When Jesus sends out disciples during his ministry to precede him to the various towns to which he is to come, he instructs them that their announcement is to be "Peace be to this house" (10:5). Even though this echoes a common enough OT greeting, šālôm lĕkā, "Peace be to you!" (Judg 6:23; 19:20; cf. Gen 43:23), the fact that they are to say this "first" betokens the effect that he and his message are to have on the "peaceful people" who dwell there (10:6). Finally, that greeting appears again on his own lips, as he appears in his risen state to the Eleven and others on Easter Sunday evening in 24:36.

Paradoxically, Jesus denies that he has come to bring peace in a passage preserved from "Q." There the Lucan Jesus is presented asking, "Do you think that I have come to put peace on earth? No, I tell you, rather discord" (12:51). This note of discord or division, however, belongs to another theme in the Lucan Gospel, foreshadowed already in the infancy narrative, when Simeon says of the child that he holds that he is set for the fall and the rise of many in Israel (2:34). Jesus denies that his coming brings peace because he realizes that human beings will have to make a decision about him, either for or against him. But, in the long run, those who accept him as an influence in their lives will experience that comprehensive peace which is the effect of the Christ-event itself.

Finally, at one point in Acts an idyllic description of the early community shows the church at peace in a political sense (9:31).

This figure is not as important for Luke as either of the two preceding ones; but it does convey an aspect of the Christ-event that he presents.

d) *Life*. In a few instances Luke speaks of an effect of the Christ-event as "life," i.e. as a share in "eternal life." Though he never speaks of "newness of life" or of a "new creation," as does Paul (Rom 6:4; Gal 6:15; 2 Cor 5:17), it is clear that he is speaking of a form of life that transcends the ordinary existence of mortal human beings. As does Matt 4:4, Luke depicts Jesus, being tempted by Satan, quoting Deut 8:3 in reply, "Not on bread alone is man to live." Jesus thus suggests that there is a mode of life fed by other things. Again, Jesus' words to the inquiring lawyer, "Do this and you shall live," answer an explicit question about how one is to "inherit eternal life" (10:25-28). See further 18:18,30.

Jesus is not only depicted in the Lucan Gospel as speaking about this "eternal life"; he also shares in it through his own resurrection. The men who greet the women at the tomb ask them, "Why look for the living among the dead?" (24:5c). And in Acts Luke not only recounts how the risen Christ presented himself "alive" to the apostles (1:3), but regards him as "the author of life" (see p. 217 above). The apostles are instructed by the angel who frees them from prison to go and "speak to the people all the words of this life" (Acts 5:20), i.e. to rehearse for them the message of the life-giving Christ-event. It is a "life" in which even the Gentiles have been granted a share (Acts 11:18; cf. 13:46-48).

This image of "life" or "eternal life" as an effect of the Christ-event is almost certainly derived from pre-Christian Judaism; see Dan 12:2; 2 Macc 7:9; 4 Macc 15:3; 1QS 4:7; CD 3:20; 4Q181 1:4,6; Ps. Sol. 3:12; 13:11.

e) *Other Modes of Expressing the Effects.* The four foregoing modes of expressing the effects of the Christ-event in the Lucan writings are the most important and the most frequently used. There remain one or two other modes that ought to be mentioned here at the end. The first of these is "justification," which Luke, surprisingly enough, uses in a speech of Paul in the synagogue in Pisidian Antioch: "Be it known to you, therefore, brothers, that through him the forgiveness of sins is proclaimed to you, and (that) in all those things in which you could not be justified in Mosaic Law everyone who has faith is (now) justified through him" (Acts 13:38-39—contrast the *RSV*). This is the only time that Luke speaks of justification as an effect of the Christ-event, and he links it explicitly to his own more common notion of "the forgiveness of sins" (see above p. 223). He seems to be making known to his readers that he knows of Pauline justification, but prefers to cast it into the—for him—more genial note of forgiveness.

Still another mode of expressing an effect of the Christ-event may be found in the words of the crucified Jesus who replies to the penitent thief, "Today you shall be with me in Paradise" (23:43). Here the effect is seen as an intimate association "with Jesus", i.e. a share in the destiny of the Christian, "to be with the Lord," of which Paul speaks in 1 Thess 4:17c; Phil 1:23c. See p. 23 above.

6. *The Spirit.* No adequate description of Lucan christology or soteriology is possible without a discussion of the role of the Spirit in Luke-Acts. More than either of the other Synoptic evangelists Luke has made the Spirit an important feature of his Gospel and its sequel. Whether one should speak of "the centrality of the Spirit in the thought of St Luke," as does W. B. Tatum ("The Epoch of Israel," *NTS* 13 [1966-1967] 185), or of "the operation of the Spirit of God" as "the connecting thread which runs through both parts" (i.e. Gospel and Acts), as does G. W. H. Lampe ("Holy Spirit," 159), may be debated. But that the Spirit plays an important part in certain stages of the Lucan story no one will deny. What is necessary in a sketch of Lucan theology is to set forth the relationship of the Spirit to the Father and his salvific plan, to Jesus himself, and to the emergent Christian community, as this is depicted by Luke.

Sometimes Luke speaks merely of "the Spirit," sometimes of "the holy Spirit," and sometimes of "the Spirit of Jesus" or "the Spirit of the Lord." These may be in part merely rhetorical variants, or in part variants determined by the character of a given passage. But it is more important to realize the frequency with which the Spirit appears in his writings. Whereas Mark has only six places in which the Spirit is mentioned (1:8,10,12; 3:29; 12:36; 13:11) and Matthew twelve (1:18,20; 3:11,16; 4:1; 10:20; 12:18,28,31,32; 22:43; 28:19), Luke has seventeen, or possibly eighteen, in his Gospel alone (1:15,35,41,67,80[?]; 2:25,26,27; 3:16,22; 4:1[*bis*],14,18; 10:21; 11:13; 12:10,12); and in Acts the Spirit appears fifty-seven times (1:2,5,8,16; 2:4,4,17,18,33,38; 4:8,25,31; 5:3,9, 32; 6:3,5,10; 7:51,55; 8:15,17,18,19,29,39; 9:17,31; 10:19,38,44,45, 47; 11:12,15,16,24,28; 13:2,4,9,52; 15:8,28; 16:6,7; 19:2[*bis*],6,21[?]; 20:22,23,28; 21:4,11; 28:25). (In the Johannine Gospel the Spirit occurs about fifteen times.)

What should be noted at the outset about the list of passages given above is that Luke introduces the Spirit mainly at the beginning of certain stages of his account. He mentions the Spirit seven times at least in the infancy narrative, six times in the chapters that inaugurate Jesus' public ministry (chaps. 3-4), and four times in chaps. 10-12 (passages near the beginning of the travel account, derived from "Q," into three of the four of which he has introduced the Spirit by way of redactional correction). It is hard to explain why the Spirit never appears in the final part of the travel account (chaps. 13-19), in the story of Jesus' Jerusalem ministry (19:28-21:38), in the passion narrative, or in the resurrection narrative (though allusion is made to it in the phrase "the promise of my Father" in 24:49, which really looks to the beginning of Acts [1:4]). Similarly, it is noteworthy that the Spirit figures often in the early part of Acts (chaps. 1-16) and then only occasionally, about twelve times, from chap. 17 on. But what is remarkable is that, whereas Luke retains the mention of the Spirit from Mark 1:8,10,12 (=Luke 3:16,22; 4:1), he suppresses Mark's mention of it in 3:29; 12:36; 13:11—in half of the passages in his Marcan source (cf. Luke 11:23; 20:42; 21:14). Likewise in two "Q" passages (see Matt 12:28,31-32 [but see the COMMENT on Luke 11:20]). What seems, then, to be important for Luke is that various stages of his narrative be initiated under the influence of the Spirit. This is obvious in the parallel passages that inaugurate the Period of Jesus (baptism, temptation, and Nazareth scenes) and the Period of the Church (ascension, pentecost), but it is true also of his Period of Israel.

In most instances Luke depicts the Spirit as it appears in the OT: God's presence in nature or human beings as a breath or wind of force which actively creates (Ps 33:6; Jdt 16:14), raises up leaders (Judg 6:34; 11:29; Isa 11:1-5), inspires prophecy (Num 24:2; Hos 9:7; 1 Sam 11:6), and judges (Isa 4:4). In other words, it is mainly an impersonal active force; occasionally Luke has attributed to it personal actions (e.g. Luke 2:26; 4:1[?]; Acts 16:7). In particular, certain specific OT passages have influenced him most, Isa 61:1-2 and Joel 3:1-2 (2:28-29E). Thus in most instances the Lucan Spirit denotes God's active, creative, or prophetic presence to his world or his people.

Conzelmann may be partly right in thinking that the Spirit in Luke-Acts is no longer regarded as God's gift in the eschaton, as Joel 3:1-2 (2:28-29E) originally suggested, but has become instead a solution to the problem of the delayed parousia (*Theology*, 136) or "the substitute in the meantime for the possession of ultimate salvation" (ibid. 95). In other words, "the Father's promise" (Luke 24:49) has indeed become in the Period of the Church the source of power for Christian missionary endeavor and endurance in the face of problems and persecution. But one can scarcely reduce the Lucan notion of the Spirit to that. Tatum has done well to insist on the role of the Spirit even in the Period of Israel, the "period of preparation." This he has done in order to correct Conzelmann's neglect of the infancy narrative in the study of Lucan theology. But one must emphasize that in the Lucan writings it is the same Spirit that is promised for the eschaton, now inaugurated in the Period of the Church (Acts 1:4; 2:4,17), which is active in the infancy narrative, the Period of Israel, and at the inception of the ministry, the Period of Jesus.

By referring to the Spirit twice as "the Father's promise" (Luke 24:49; Acts 1:4), and relating the outpouring of it on Pentecost to the prophecy of Joel 3:1-2 (2:28-29E), Luke implies a relation of the Spirit to the

OT, to Yahweh, precisely as Jesus' Father, and to Jesus himself. The relation of the Spirit to the Father is not further explained, except that in Acts 2:33 Luke makes Peter proclaim that Jesus, "having been exalted to the right hand of God, received from the Father the promised holy Spirit and poured it out."

This implies that the Spirit is poured out anew. Though Luke never appeals to a passage like Ezek 36:26, which promises a "new spirit" to be put within Israel, he seems to be thinking along these lines. Hence his use of Joel, and his depiction of the Spirit operative in the Period of Israel. From the beginning of his narrative Luke portrays the Spirit active as God's prophetic presence in this period of preparation. The Spirit fills John the Baptist from his mother's womb (1:15), which explains why he will be regarded as "the prophet of the Most High" (1:76; cf. 1:80a). And a similar influence affects Elizabeth (1:41), Zechariah (1:67), and Simeon (2:25,27), as these faithful representatives of Israel of old are moved to comment on the significance of the two children born or to be born and incorporated into Israel. But as God's creative presence the Spirit is most active in Mary, overshadowing her and coming upon her, to bring about the virginal conception of Jesus. The miracle involved in the conception of John is not, however, ascribed to the Spirit. However, the way in which the Spirit affects the two children born is involved in the step-parallelism that runs through the infancy narrative: filled with the Spirit of prophecy, John becomes a prophet of the Most High; overshadowed by the creative presence of God, Jesus is born as God's Son.

Another way in which Luke depicts the Spirit active in the Period of Israel is to have Peter or Paul declare that the Spirit actually spoke through David (Acts 1:16; 4:25) or through Isaiah (28:26).

The Period of Jesus is inaugurated by the preaching of John the Baptist. As one coming from the Period of Israel, he announces the imminent arrival of the One-Who-Is-to-Come, who will baptize with the holy Spirit (Luke 3:16). Such a Spirit-baptism will transcend his own water-baptism. Luke retains from his Marcan source the descent of the Spirit on Jesus at his own baptism as a way of explaining the relationship of Jesus to the Spirit. In a sense, this is superfluous, since Luke has already set forth the relation of Jesus to the Spirit in the infancy narrative, by the story of the virginal conception. Mark, lacking an infancy narrative, uses the baptism scene to establish Jesus' relation to heaven. This was the function of the baptism scene in the first draft of the Lucan Gospel too; but the infancy narrative was written with hindsight and thus foreshadows a detail of the start of the ministry. See p. 311 below. The baptism is retained because Luke wants to show the ministry of Jesus under the Spirit's influence. Moreover, as the COMMENT on 3:21-22 will explain, nothing in that passage determines that relationship as messianic, but in

Acts 10:38 Luke interprets it as an anointing of Jesus with the holy Spirit, thus going beyond the details in the scene itself.

Jesus is further led by the Spirit into the desert to be tempted by the devil (4:1), a detail which Luke derives from Mark 1:12 but softens. Jesus later returns from the desert "with the power of the Spirit" (4:14) to begin his Galilean ministry. Among the various ways in which the Nazareth synagogue scene is programmatic in the Lucan Gospel, one is the role of the Spirit that is set forth there as the ministry is begun: "The Spirit of the Lord is upon me for he has anointed me," quoting Isa 61:1 (4:18). What Isaiah spoke of centuries before now sees fulfillment in a new sense "today" (4:21). Thus the entire beginning of Jesus' ministry is put under the aegis of the Spirit, and the role of the Spirit as a starter is clearly not limited to the beginning of the Period of the Church.

After these initial references to the Spirit, Luke makes mention of it only in 10:21; 11:13; 12:10,12. In the last three instances the Spirit is mentioned in sayings of Jesus, whereas it is introduced into Luke's narrative in 10:21, as Jesus delights in the Spirit.

At the end of the Lucan Gospel a special relation between the Spirit and the risen Christ is noted, as he tells the Eleven and others to await "the Father's promise" (24:49), an enigmatic phrase that only becomes clear in Acts 1:4-5. A new role for the Spirit is now envisaged in that its influence is no longer limited to an effect on John or Jesus; all Israel is to be reconstituted anew. The Spirit is seen in Acts as the creative and prophetic presence of God (Acts 5:9; 8:39), and even of Jesus himself (16:7). Here the Spirit is not merely "a solution to the problem of the delayed parousia" but a substitute for the risen Christ himself, when he is no longer physically present to his followers. Having taken his last leave from them in the ascension, Christ will henceforth be "recognized" as present among them in "the breaking of the bread" (Luke 24:35) and in "the Father's promise," poured out among them.

The Spirit poured out on Pentecost inaugurates a new age—that is the whole point of the Pentecost-experience narrated in Acts 2. That is also the reason why one must reckon with a three-phase view of salvation-history in Lucan theology. The role of the Spirit as initiator was important for the inception both of Jesus' life and his ministry; but now it has become the initiator of a new era of salvation-history, when the Spirit becomes God's presence to his people anew. This may explain in part why the Spirit is not involved in the Lucan passion narrative at all or in the major part of the resurrection narrative. Only at the end of the latter does it appear with reference to a future role.

In Acts the Spirit becomes the guiding force of Christian disciples and witnesses. It is explicitly so depicted, either directing their activity (see

Acts 2:4c; 4:31; 8:29,39; 10:19,44; 11:28; 13:2,4; 15:28; 19:21[?]; 20:22,28) or hindering it (16:6,7; 21:4).

Moreover, it becomes plain in Acts that the Spirit is given only when the Twelve are present or a member or delegate of the Twelve is on the scene. Thus Luke depicts the Spirit-guided Christian community. The reconstitution of the Twelve (1:15-26) is the necessary preparation for the outpouring of the Spirit (2:1-4). This also explains why, though Philip (not one of the Twelve, but one of the Seven appointed to serve tables [6:2-6]) evangelizes Samaria and baptizes there (8:5-13), Peter and John have to be sent before the people in Samaria receive the Spirit (8:17). Similarly, it is only when Paul, indirectly a delegate of the Twelve (see 11:22,25-26; 13:2-4), arrives in Ephesus that "some disciples" (i.e. neophyte Christians) are baptized in the name of the Lord Jesus and receive the Spirit through the laying on of Paul's hands (19:1-6). The only exception to this bestowal of the Spirit is the case of Saul himself, who is baptized by Ananias and receives the Spirit through the laying on of his hands (9:17-18). This obvious exception is made at this point in Luke's narrative to manifest the extraordinary grace shown to Paul, who thus becomes the "chosen instrument" (or vessel of election) to carry Jesus' name to Gentiles, kings, and the children of Israel (9:15)—the hero of the second part of Acts.

As E. Schweizer has rightly pointed out ("Pneuma . . . ," TDNT 6 [1968] 412), Luke has taken "an important step beyond Mark and Matthew," in not considering it sufficient to present Jesus as a bearer of the Spirit in individual pneumatic features or in birth and baptism stories. In the Period of the Church, the promises of old are fulfilled and the Spirit is given to the people of God as a whole. For, if in the Gospel the Spirit is that in or with which Jesus moves and has "the power of the Lord to heal" (5:17), in Acts it is clear that the Spirit's guidance is behind the growth of the church and guarantees the disciples' kerygma. This concern to depict the work of the Spirit in the Christian church is obviously introduced because of Luke's own view of the parousia of Christ. But to discuss that further is to broach the next topic, Lucan eschatology.

7. *Eschatology.* This is the most difficult and most controverted aspect of Lucan theology today, and it cannot be adequately discussed without recalling some of the ideas that we have already treated in relation to Luke's view of salvation-history, the kingdom of God, the parousia, and the Spirit. The biggest problem derives from the fact that Luke wrote Acts as a sequel to his Jesus-story, for to take up the story of the early Christian community as immediately as he did implies that he had a dis-

tinctive view of the imminence of what the other Synoptic evangelists spoke of as the coming of the kingdom, or the coming of the Son of Man with power and glory, or of the wrath that is coming. There has been a Lucan reinterpretation of some of these sayings, as we shall see, but it should be recalled that it is not Luke who has dismissed the parousia. He alone among the Synoptists openly affirms that Jesus is to return in the same way as he was seen going to heaven—and this in Acts (1:11). Recall further his other references to the parousia (p. 196 above) and his unique mention of the "times of refreshing" and the "restoration (*apokatastasis*) of all things" (Acts 3:19-21). That Luke reckons with an end-time is clear; the problem is how near or distant it is for him. For Conzelmann and those who follow or agree with him, the question is whether "Luke has definitely abandoned belief in the early expectation" of the end-time (*Theology*, 135). To try to answer that question one has to consider several aspects of the Lucan writings.

First, Luke has at times either omitted sayings from his sources that manifestly express an imminent eschaton or modified them so as to dull, at least, their eschatological edge. Thus, the proclamation of Mark 1:15, "The time has come; the kingdom of God has drawn near (*ēngiken*); repent and believe in the gospel," becomes in the Lucan parallel a bland narrative statement about Jesus' teaching in synagogues and being praised by all the people (4:15). In his subsequent inaugural sermon in the synagogue of Nazareth the Lucan Jesus shifts the emphasis to himself and to the fulfillment of Isa 61:1 as they sit listening to him "today" (4:18-21). What he says to them is kerygmatic, but without any reference to an imminent coming of the kingdom. Again, the saying of Jesus in Mark 9:1 about those standing by who will not taste death until they see the kingdom come with power becomes a statement which eliminates all reference to its coming (Luke 9:27). Conzelmann writes of this saying, "The idea of the coming of the Kingdom is replaced by a timeless conception of it" (*Theology*, 104). In a redacted statement about the coming of the kingdom, inherited most likely from "L," Luke makes Jesus deny that the kingdom comes with observation and affirm rather that "the kingdom of God is among you" (17:20-21). Again, in the parable of the pounds, which Luke has inherited from "Q," he adds his own introduction, which is unmistakable: Jesus tells the parable because "people thought that the kingdom of God was to appear immediately" (19:11; contrast Matt 25:13).

Second, there are a number of statements in the Lucan Gospel that imply a delay or postponement of the end-time. These are the sayings that have to do with vigilance or preparation for it; thus those about the servant who knows not when his master will return (12:38,45) or the parable of the barren fig tree (13:8). They warn against counting on the delay.

Third, some of the apocalyptic stage props in the eschatological discourse of Mark 13 have been either eliminated or reduced in the Lucan parallel (chap. 21). The terrible sign of the end, the "desolating abomination standing where it ought not" (Mark 13:14) is eliminated; instead, "Jerusalem surrounded by camps" serves as a sign that "her desolation has drawn near" (21:20). Here what is almost certainly a reference to the historical destruction of the city by the Romans has been used instead of apocalyptic stage props drawn from Dan 9:27; 12:11. In this case, one may query whether the substitution has been made because of Luke's concern to de-eschatologize the sermon or his concern that his predominantly Gentile Christian readers would not understand the allusion. Though he has separated the references to the historical destruction from those alluding to the end-time, he has not completely de-eschatologized the sermon or eliminated all of its apocalyptic stage props. It still contains mention of "the Son of Man coming on a cloud with power and great glory" (21:27), associating with it the news that "your deliverance is near." Rather, Luke has anchored his form of the eschatological sermon in the historic destruction of Jerusalem, implying that, as that happened, so one should be certain that God's deliverance will come about too.

Fourth, there are, on the other hand, a number of sayings of either John the Baptist or Jesus that Luke has retained from the primitive gospel tradition about an imminent judgment or an imminent coming of the kingdom or the Son of Man. These are neither few in number nor negligible, as if they did not matter in view of the emphasis found in the sayings cited above. Thus, John the Baptist is portrayed challenging the crowds about "the wrath that is coming" (3:7) and preaching how "the ax already lies at the root of the trees" (3:9; cf. Matt 3:7-10) and how the winnowing fan of judgment has already been taken up (3:17; cf. Matt 3:12). These are inherited "Q" passages that Luke has not de-eschatologized. Similarly, when Jesus sends out the Seventy(-two) disciples, he instructs them to announce that God's kingdom "has drawn near" (10:9, cf. Matt 10:7; though a "Q" verse, it echoes Mark 1:15!). Again, in addition to 21:27, quoted above and almost verbatim identical with Mark 13:26, Jesus says in the same eschatological discourse, "Believe me, it will all happen before this generation passes away" (21:32, close to Mark 13:30).

Fifth, Luke himself did not shrink from adding to his traditions further sayings about an imminent coming of the kingdom or of judgment. Thus he has redacted the mission charge to the Seventy(-two) disciples with an added note about the kingdom that has drawn near (10:11, echoing 10:9; contrast Matt 10:14). Again, he has added to the parable of the dishonest judge (or possibly so received and preserved its conclusion), "Will he delay long over them? I tell you, he will make haste to vindicate them" (18:7-8). Similarly, only the Lucan form of the parable of the fig tree ends with the conclusion, "Realize that the kingdom of God is near" (21:31; contrast Mark 13:29). Moreover, the peculiarly Lucan ending of the eschatological discourse leaves no doubt about the sermon's purpose in its admonition to pray for strength to stand before the Son of Man (21:36).

When one reflects on these sayings, one realizes that Luke has not completely abandoned belief in an early expectation of the end-time. He has obviously coped with the delay of the parousia, which puzzled early Christians. But the two-pronged set of statements that one finds in the Lucan Gospel is not necessarily all of Luke's own making. There is reason to think that this double attitude was part of a pre-Lucan tradition. In discussing Luke 21, even Conzelmann finally admitted that Mark was himself using traditional material in the eschatological discourse and that in his version one could trace "a certain postponement of the Parousia" (*Theology,* 126 [his footnote refers to Mark 13:10]). Moreover, in the Pauline corpus one can detect a shift in the Apostle's attitude toward this event. In 1 Thess 4:13-17 he clearly reckons with its imminence, but in Phil 1:22-24 and 2 Cor 5:1-10 one sees Paul toying with the idea that he might die before it takes place. A comparable ambivalence in the pre-Lucan tradition has to be recognized, even though it does not explain entirely the Lucan emphasis on the length of the interval between the Period of Jesus and the parousia.

The Lucan emphasis is not to be ascribed to a crisis in the early Church over the delay, nor is it to be understood as a warning against a Gnostic identification of the parousia with Jesus' resurrection/ascension. The emphasis is rather owing to Luke's desire to shift the emphasis in many of Jesus' sayings from the *eschaton* to the *sēmeron* to show that they are still valid guides for conduct in his generation. This is particularly evident in the Lucan use of *sēmeron,* "today" (4:21; 5:26; 19:5,9; 23:43) or of the related prep. phrase *kath' hēmeran,* "daily" (9:23; 11:3; 16:19; 19:47): "If anyone wishes to come with me, let him disregard himself, take up his cross *each day,* and follow me" (9:23; cf. Mark 8:34). This subtle shift directs Christian attention from the following of Christ in view of an imminent reckoning to an understanding of Jesus' conduct as an inspiration and guide for Christian life in the Period of *ecclesia pressa,* the church under stress. Admittedly, Luke has thus dulled the eschatological edge of some of the sayings of Jesus to make of them a hortatory device for everyday Christian living.

When one reflects further on the varied factors in Lucan eschatological thinking, one realizes that he has not simply de-eschatologized the kerygma. He does retain some of the traditional references to the imminent coming of the kingdom/Son of Man/judgment. These cannot be ignored in looking for the more widespread pattern of the Lucan shift, because Luke could have omitted all the traditional material about an imminent coming. He was aware of the importance of it in the tradition, and that is why he has retained some of it. But he also has sought to shift Christian attention from an exclusive focus on imminence to a realization that the present Period of the Church also has place in God's salvation-history.

Just as we qualified the idea that the Spirit has become in Lucan thinking a substitute for a solution to a delayed parousia, so too we qualify the idea that salvation-history itself is a substitute for it. Rather, Luke has shown, in view of the delay, what can be made of Jesus' words and deeds in an era of Christian existence which is not that of the Period of Jesus itself. For Christians who live in the twentieth century and who realize that the interval between the original proclamation of the Christian message and their own time has grown longer than what even Luke coped with, his shifted eschatology and his form of the kerygma may be even more suitable than others in the NT.

8. *Discipleship.* Luke's shift of emphasis from the *eschaton* to the *sēmeron* eliminated the need to focus on the imminent coming of the kingdom and enabled him to present in his own way the important role of Christian discipleship. What we have been discussing up to this point is the shape that the Christ-event has objectively taken in the Lucan writings. Now we turn to that part of Lucan teaching which sets forth what ought to be the subjective reaction of human beings to it. This includes what Luke considers as the fundamental response of human beings to the Christian kerygma, and how he regards Christian discipleship.

A. THE RESPONSE TO THE CHRISTIAN KERYGMA. There are three main ways in which Luke speaks of the reaction of human beings to the proclamation of Christ and his disciples; they are common to other NT writers as well. These are faith, repentance and conversion, and baptism.

1) *Faith.* In his speech at the conversion of Cornelius, Peter sums up succinctly the basic Lucan outlook: "Everyone who believes in him [Jesus] receives forgiveness of sins through his name" (Acts 10:43). Similarly, Paul announces to the jailer at Philippi, "Believe in the Lord Jesus and you and your household will be saved" (Acts 16:31). What is meant by "faith" in the Lucan writings is perhaps best gleaned from Luke's redaction of the explanation of the parable of the sower. There he

describes the disciples characterized by the seed fallen into good soil thus: "Those who listen to the word and hold on to it with a noble and generous mind: these yield a crop through their persistence" (Luke 8:15). Here we note that faith begins as a listening, just as in Pauline theology, but it does not end there. If faith for Paul begins with a "listening" (*akoē*) to the preaching of Christ (Rom 10:17), it ends as a "submission" (*hypakoē pisteōs*, Rom 1:5; 16:26), or better as a personal commitment to God in Christ. Though this way of expressing the response is not foreign to Luke, since he notes in Acts 6:7 that many of the (Jewish) priests "submitted to the faith" (*hypēkouon tē pistei*), he has his own way of describing what follows on the listening: an allegiance of openness ("a noble and generous mind") and persistence (subject to neither uprooting, nor apostasy, nor worldly distraction; see Luke 8:11-14).

At times Luke uses the absolute form, "the faith," as a synonym for Christianity (see Acts 6:7 [quoted above]; 13:8; 14:22[?]), and at times speaks of "the believers" or "those who came to believe" (=Christians; see, e.g. Acts 2:44; 4:4,32; 5:14; 11:21; 14:1; 15:5,7; 17:12,34; 18:8,27; 19:2,18; 21:20,25; 22:19). Confronted with such diverse descriptions, one tends to think of the distinction between *fides qua* and *fides quae*, i.e. the faith by which one believes and the faith that one believes (in a content-sense). But one has to remember that this is a distinction born of a later theological problem, one that is not formulated by NT writers, either Paul or Luke. This has to be kept in mind especially in Luke 22:32, where Jesus prays that Peter's "faith" will not give out.

On one occasion Luke joins "faith" and "justification," and its juxtaposition is significant: "through him the forgiveness of sins is proclaimed to you, and in all those things in which you could not be justified in Mosaic Law everyone who has faith (*pas ho pisteuōn*) is (now) justified through him" (Acts 13:38-39). What is noteworthy here is that Luke does not link the human response of faith as closely to justification as does Paul. He speaks far more frequently of the role of faith in the forgiveness of sins and salvation.

The relation of "faith" and "salvation" is often referred to in the Gospel itself. Here there is a problem. In what sense are we to understand the faith involved in such statements as "Your faith has brought you salvation" (7:50; 8:48; 17:19; cf. Acts 14:9)? Obviously, in the Gospel passages one has to reckon with stages of the gospel tradition (see Preface, p. viii), and in stage I *pistis* would hardly have had the full sense of post-resurrection faith in Jesus. But in stage III, on the level of Lucan composition, it may well carry that connotation. The statement belongs to the pre-Lucan gospel tradition, as Mark 5:34; 10:52 show. If it is to be regarded as an authentic statement of Jesus, it must express some recognition of him at least as God's envoy; it is difficult to say how much more it would connote.

It is possible that Luke is aware of a relationship between "faith" and "grace." He says of Apollos that, when he arrived in Corinth, "he helped considerably those who had come to believe through grace" (Acts 18:27). The problem is that the prepositional phrase *dia tēs charitos*, "through grace," may refer not to "those who had come to believe," as we have rendered it above, but may modify the verb "helped": "he considerably helped through grace those . . ." (see Haenchen, *Acts*, 551; H. Conzelmann, *"Charis . . . ," TDNT* 9 [1974] 393).

In any case, the Lucan redaction of the "Q" passage in 17:5-6 suggests that a person's faith could be increased; the apostles beg of Jesus, "Grant us more faith!" And Jesus' reply implies that their faith was actually smaller than a mustard seed.

In contrast to the Marcan Gospel, in which Mary seems to be among Jesus' family (*hoi par' autou*, 3:21; cf. 3:31-35), who think that he is beside himself, Luke depicts her rather as the first person in his Gospel "who has believed" (1:45) and portrays her praying with the Eleven and others awaiting the gift of the Spirit on Pentecost, i.e. she is among the first believers in the post-resurrection era.

2) *Repentance and Conversion.* Another Lucan way of presenting the ideal Christian reaction to the proclamation of Jesus and the disciples is "repentance and conversion." The Greek word for "repentance" is *metanoia*, which literally denotes a change of mind. But in the NT it is almost always used in the religious sense of a turning from sin, repentance for sin. It connotes a new beginning in moral conduct. In the Marcan Gospel the noun is used only once (1:4), and the verb *metanoein* only twice (1:15; 6:12); in the Matthean Gospel the noun is found twice (3:8,11 in the preaching of John the Baptist) and the verb five times (3:2; 4:17; 11:20,21; 12:41). In the Lucan writings the noun appears five times in the Gospel (3:3,8; 5:32; 15:7; 24:47) and six times in Acts (5:31; 11:18; 13:24; 19:4; 20:21; 26:20), whereas the verb is used nine times in the Gospel (10:13; 11:32; 13:3,5; 15:7,10; 16:30; 17:3,4) and five times in Acts (2:38; 3:19; 8:22; 17:30; 26:20). This frequency in the Lucan writings is significant and is closely linked with Luke's view of the effect of the Christ-event as the forgiveness of sins.

Closely related to "repentance" is "conversion," which means a turning. The noun *epistrophē* is found only once, in Acts 15:3, where there is mention of "the conversion of the Gentiles." But the verb *epistrephein* is frequently used in the religious sense of "turning, being converted." Again, both Mark and Matthew use it only once in the sense of religious conversion, and then in a quotation of Isa 6:10 (Mark 4:12; Matt

13:15). It denotes the turning of a human being to God or to the Lord (from sin or paganism). It is so used by Luke in 1:16,17; 17:4; 22:32; Acts 9:35; 11:21; 14:15; 15:19; 26:18 (under the figure of turning from darkness to light); 28:27; as well as in the cases cited below.

In three places Luke links *epistrephein* and *metanoein:* "Repent, then, and turn, that your sins may be blotted out" (Acts 3:19); "that they [the Gentiles] should repent and turn to God and do deeds worthy of repentance" (Acts 26:20); and "If (your brother) sins against you seven times a day and seven times turns back to you to say, 'I am sorry,' you must forgive him" (17:4). Although the two words are used in the last passage of human intercourse and conduct, even there the linking of the two reveals their close connection in Lucan thought. Actually, they are seen to be two sides of the same coin; one expresses a negative aspect, a changing from sinful conduct; the other a positive aspect, a turning to God or to the Lord. In a similar way, the two are found together in the LXX, in Joel 2:14.

Both processes are complementary to "faith," in the Lucan view of things, because they could not exist without it. As Conzelmann has put it (*Theology*, 226), both faith and conversion are thought of as God's work. Yet Luke does not think of the Christian as one possessed by the Spirit, but rather describes his/her existence in ethical categories. That is why repentance and conversion, though just as much God-given as faith itself, have to be understood as its complement.

In two places Luke speaks of "repentance and the forgiveness of sins" (Luke 24:47; Acts 5:31), taken together, as having been given to Israel and as being destined to be preached to all nations. Conzelmann (*Theology,* 228) is certainly correct in saying that the two are "inseparably connected," but his view of their relationship is puzzling. He thinks that *metanoia* in Mark 1:4,15 stands for a way of summing up the whole process of salvation, whereas in the Lucan view it becomes merely one definite point and is not an adequate description of salvation. What Conzelmann has done is to confuse the effects of the Christ-event, viz. forgiveness of sins, salvation, or life, with the reaction expected of humans to those effects. In the sense of reaction, one can speak of repentance as a condition for the forgiveness of sins. What was brought about by Christ in his passion, death, and resurrection and made possible by the gift of the Spirit is appropriated by human beings—in the Lucan view—through faith, repentance and conversion (and baptism).

As J. Dupont (*ScEccl* 12 [1960] 137-173) has noted, a call to repentance and conversion usually forms the practical conclusion of the missionary sermons in Acts, the practical conclusion to the Easter proclamation. Thus these reactions are elicited from those who have put their faith in the risen Christ, who have turned to the Lord in the full Christian sense of that title. If John the Baptist's role was seen to be one of turning many of the children of Israel to the Lord their God (1:16), so Luke notes how, when the disciples spread from Jerusalem to proclaim the Lord in Antioch, a great number of Jews and Greeks believed and turned to the Lord (Acts 11:20).

3) *Baptism.* As did Paul before him, Luke inherited from the early Christian community the requirement that a person not only had to believe in Jesus Christ and his role in the Father's plan of salvation, but also had to be baptized in his name. In fact, though the ritual washing is nowhere described, it is taken for granted in the Lucan story that everyone would know of it as a fundamental part of the expected human reaction to the proclamation of the Christ-event.

Unlike John 3:26, which depicts Jesus himself baptizing people—a detail that is corrected in 4:2—the Synoptic evangelists have never so presented Jesus. It is, consequently, difficult to say whether Christian baptism is rooted in any *action* of Jesus himself. The need to be baptized is, of course, based on the great commission at the end of the Matthean Gospel (28:19), with which that in the Marcan appendix (16:16) agrees. However, there is no mention of baptism in the commission which the Lucan Jesus gives to the Eleven and others in 24:47-49, as he charges them to preach repentance and forgiveness of sins in his name.

Luke is at pains to stress the difference between the "baptism of John" and Christian baptism, even though he is aware of the heavenly origin of the former (7:30; 20:4). He inherits the distinction between John's baptism and that of Jesus from Mark 1:8 (or possibly some other source) and is concerned to stress this difference; see Luke 3:16; Acts 1:5; 11:16; 18:25; 19:3-4. John's baptism is related to the "beginning" of the Period of Jesus; it inaugurates it. But it is different because it does not confer the Spirit, even though it was administered by John as a baptism of repentance for the forgiveness of sins (3:3)—two ideas otherwise related to the Christ-event itself. This contrast between the two baptisms does not surprise the reader of the Lucan writings, since Luke has been preparing for it by the step-parallelism in the infancy narrative itself.

Once the sequel to the Jesus-story begins in Acts, the need to be baptized is constantly stressed. Peter's speech on Pentecost terminates: "Repent, and let each of you be baptized in the name of Jesus Christ for the forgiveness of your sins; and you shall receive the gift of the holy Spirit" (2:38). Here baptism is linked to one of the classic Lucan forms of kerygmatic preaching. Cf. Acts 10:48. One looks in vain, however, in the Lucan writings for any direct affirmation of the necessity of baptism (contrast John 3:5), but its necessity is implied in such passages as Acts 2:38 (quoted above); 8:12,37; 9:18; 10:48. Nor does one find any explanation of the nature of Christian baptism, as one finds in Rom 6:3-11;

Gal 3:27-28. However, Acts 22:16 implies that baptism washes away sins.

We are never told of the baptism of the original apostles or disciples; the Pentecost scene suggests that their experience of the Spirit on that occasion, when they received "the Father's promise," was what enabled them to go forth and preach boldly the Christian message and call others to baptism, through which these others received the "gift of the holy Spirit" (Acts 2:38). By contrast, we are told in Acts 9:18 that Saul was baptized.

Though the relation of the Spirit to baptism is made clear in Acts (1:5; 11:16), this ritual washing is never said to have taken place *in the name* of the Spirit—much less in the name of the Father, and of the Son, and of the holy Spirit (as in Matt 28:19). That so-called trinitarian form most likely represents a liturgical formula derived from some other, possibly later, Christian tradition. For in Acts it is often said that baptism was administered "in the name of Jesus Christ" (2:38; 10:48) or "in the name of the Lord Jesus" (8:16; 19:5; cf. 22:16). The ritual washing undergone with the invocation of the name of Jesus Christ, the Lord, is thus seen as the means whereby the Christian shares in the effects of the Christ-event and partakes of the Spirit.

In this regard three texts have always created a problem: in Acts 8:16 it seems to say that Samaritans, though baptized by the evangelist Philip in the name of the Lord, have not yet received the holy Spirit; for this Peter and John have to be sent down to them by the apostles in Jerusalem. In Acts 10:44-48, the Spirit falls on the Gentile household of Cornelius, while Peter was still speaking to it; then Peter orders its members to be baptized in the name of Jesus Christ. Still later, in Acts 19:1-6, Paul arrives in Ephesus and finds some "disciples" (apparently Christian neophytes), who have received only John's baptism and do not so much as know of the Spirit. Then they are baptized in the name of the Lord Jesus, and receive the Spirit when Paul lays hands on them. In other words, there seems to be in these passages some distinction between baptism in the name of Jesus and the reception of the Spirit. Various solutions have been attempted for this notorious problem: Some theologians of later date have sought to root in this distinction the difference of the sacraments of baptism and confirmation; other interpreters have tried to distinguish two forms of baptism in the early church, in which the baptism of the holy Spirit really differed from the baptism in the name of Jesus. Neither of these solutions, however, seems to account for what is really going on in the Lucan story. As the story of Paul's conversion seems to suggest (9:17-18), the reception of the Spirit is more important in Luke's eyes and so he mentions it prior to the baptism; it is singled out to show that the incorporation of Paul into the Christian church was a gift of God himself. Hence Luke gives priority to the reception of the Spirit. Similarly, in the other episodes: the distinction is made between baptism and the reception of the Spirit as a literary device to insist that the Spirit is given through the church, especially through the Twelve or members of the Twelve (e.g. Peter and John in chap. 8) or their delegate (e.g. Paul in chap. 19). See further p. 231 above. Another way of putting it might be to say with E. Käsemann that Luke is concerned about the process by which the immature forms of early Christianity were to be assimilated into its mainstream (see *Essays on New Testament Themes* [SBT 41; Naperville: Allenson, 1964] 136-148). That would be true of chaps. 8 and 19 in particular. Finally, it may be that we are faced in these passages with but further instances of Lucan inconsistency.

B. THE DEMANDS OF CHRISTIAN LIFE. In addition to the three main reactions to the Christian message described above, one finds in the Lucan writings a number of other ways in which the evangelist describes what Christian life should be or sets forth its requirements. Though these are not as important as the basic response, they do make their own contribution to distinctive Lucan theology. Among these we may list several.

1) *The Following of Jesus.* This aspect of Christian discipleship was hinted at above, when the geographical perspective in the Lucan writings was discussed. To be a disciple of Christ one has to follow him along the road that he walks to his destiny in Jerusalem, his *exodos,* his transit to the Father. There are scenes in the ministry of Jesus in which this idea comes to the fore; and the Lucan redaction of some of Jesus' sayings on the subject sharpen the demand, applying it in a figurative way to the daily existence of the Christian reader of his Gospel.

The following of Jesus is not exclusive to Luke, since the impv. *akolouthei moi,* "follow me," is already found in Mark 2:14; 10:21 (cf. Mark 8:34). But the stress that this idea receives in the Lucan Gospel is noteworthy. In particular, its relation to the travel account is to be noted, since immediately after the introduction to it (9:51-56) come sayings of Jesus to three would-be followers, "as they moved along the road" (9:57-62). The first two of them are derived from "Q" (see Matt 8:19-22), and the third may be from "L" or composed by Luke himself (probably the latter).

Thus for Luke Christian discipleship is portrayed not only as the acceptance of a master's teaching, but as the identification of oneself with the master's way of life and destiny in an intimate, personal following of him. Because of the geographical perspective in the Gospel, the "following" has a pronounced spatial nuance: the disciple must walk in the footsteps of Jesus.

Underlying this notion is the Lucan view of God's revelation of salvation in Jesus as the revelation of a way. For salvation is not made manifest in merely isolated, saving events in Jesus' ministry—in cures, exorcisms, or resuscitations—or even in Jesus' suffering or death on the cross understood in an isolated way. All of these elements must be seen as parts of a pattern described as a way (*hodos*), on which Jesus has entered (*eisodos*), moves along (*poreuesthai*), and heads for its outcome (*exodos*, the transit to the Father). Christian discipleship, then, suits this pattern by being a close following of Jesus en route.

The notion first appears with the call of Peter as a fisher of men (5:11). It appears again in the call of Levi (5:27-28) and is encountered in the first mention of Jesus' disciples (5:30; 6:1). In time a distinction is made between them and the crowds (6:17). Yet at times we read of crowd(s) that follow Jesus too (7:9; 9:11). But Luke actually uses the verb *akolouthein* in two senses: (a) as a generic term for people following Jesus physically (e.g. out of curiosity or to see a miracle: 7:9; 9:11; 18:43; 22:10,39,54; 23:27; Acts 12:8,9; 13:43; 21:36); and (b) as a figurative expression for discipleship (e.g. Acts 9:23,49,57,59,61; 18:22,28).

A special corporate sense of following is found in the Acts of the Apostles, where the primitive Palestinian Christian community is designated "the Way" (*hē hodos*). The absolute use of this term is exclusively Lucan in the NT, being found in Acts 9:2; 19:9,23; 22:4; 24:14,22. Elsewhere Luke speaks of "a way of salvation" (16:17), "the way of the Lord" (Acts 18:25), or "the way of God" (Acts 18:26), and one might be tempted to think that "the Way" is simply an abbreviation of such fuller phrases, which have at times been said to be, in part at least, allusions to Isa 40:3, "make straight the way of the Lord." Indeed, it may be that Luke has heard of this expression as one used by Palestinian Christians of themselves, as may be suggested by Acts 24:14 (being opposed to a sect [*hairesis*]). This verse and 24:5 seem to imply that the community was called by others "the sect of the Nazoreans" (*hairesis* is again used, the term employed to designate the Sadducees in Acts 5:17 and the Pharisees in Acts 15:5).

In his commentary on Acts, Haenchen maintains that we do not know for certain the origin of the Lucan absolute expression, "the Way" (*Acts*, 320). Theoretically, it could be a Lucan creation. But it is more likely a pre-Lucan name for the community. I have suggested elsewhere that the absolute use of Hebrew *derek/had-derek*, "Way, the Way," as a designation of the Essene community in Qumran literature, may be at the root of this Lucan usage. Various Qumran passages suggest this: "Those who have chosen the Way" (*lbwḥry drk*, 1QS 9:17-18); "these are they who turn away from the Way" (*hm sry drk*, CD 1:13; cf. 2:6; 1QS 10:21); "these are the regulations of the Way for the Master" (*'lh tkwny hdrk lmśkyl,* 1QS 9:21). (See further 1QS 4:22; 8:10,18,21; 9:5,9; 11:11; 1QM 14:7; 1QH 1:36; 1QSa 1:28. Cf. *ESBNT*, 281-284; E. Repo, *Der 'Weg';* S. V. McCasland, "'The Way,'" *JBL* 77 [1958] 222-230.) Given the existence of such a Palestinian designation for a community, considered as a "sect" within Judaism of the time (see Josephus *Ant.* 13.5,9 § 171), it is not impossible that early Christians would have borrowed it as a designation of their way of life too. Just what its meaning would have been in the pre-Lucan tradition might be queried; but, as it is used in Acts, it suits well the Lucan geographical perspective and serves to recall the motif of discipleship as a following of Jesus along his way. This notion has a bearing too on Lucan ecclesiology.

2) *Testimony.* Another aspect of Christian life in the Lucan view of things involves the disciple's duty to give witness to the risen Christ. Testimony (*martyria*) is an important idea in the Johannine Gospel, but little is made of it in the Synoptic Gospels, apart from the last chapter of the Lucan Gospel, where it emerges. It then becomes a motif in Acts. As we have already noted, whereas the great commission in the Matthean (and Marcan) Gospel(s) involves preaching, teaching, and making disciples by baptism (Matt 28:19-20 [Mark 16:15-16]), it, rather, is formulated in Luke 24:48 in terms of testimony: "You are the witnesses to all this." The importance of *martyria* is further clarified in Peter's speech at the conversion of Cornelius: "We are witnesses of all that he did both in the country of the Jews and in Jerusalem. . . . God raised him on the third day and made him visible, not to all the people, but to us who were preordained by God as witnesses and who ate and drank with him after he rose from the dead" (Acts 10:39-41).

Such a statement of Peter makes one appreciate the earlier Lucan emphasis on Galilean disciples being gathered by Jesus during his ministry, on the training given to them in the travel account as witnesses from Galilee, and on the form of the great commission. Indeed, that commission is picked up in the programmatic verse in Acts 1:8: "You will be my witnesses in Jerusalem and in all Judea and Samaria and to the end of the earth." The disciples' realization of this role is further seen in Acts 2:32; 3:15; 5:32; 13:31.

This aspect of Christian discipleship is not unrelated to the following of Jesus discussed above. It also explains why the person to be chosen to take Judas' place among the Twelve has to be one who had gone along with the Eleven throughout the time that the Lord Jesus went in and out among them from the baptism of John until the Ascension (Acts 1:21-22): Joseph Barsabbas and Matthias had to have been among the preordained witnesses. Even though not one of the Twelve, Paul too is cast in the role of a witness (Acts 22:15; 26:16), at least in the sense of a witness to the risen Christ.

3) *Prayer*. Another important aspect of Christian life in Lucan thinking is the disciple's ongoing communing with God. The emphasis that Luke gives to it begins in the Gospel itself, in which he depicts Jesus at prayer more often than any of the other evangelists, and then continues reference to it in the lives of the early Christians about whom he writes in Acts. He depicts Jesus often at prayer, because this is to become one of the ways in which the disciple is to follow him.

Because of this emphasis on prayer, it is not surprising that the first episode in the Gospel, the announcement of the birth of John the Baptist, takes place when all the people assisting at the incense-offering were standing outside the sanctuary praying (1:10). Thus Luke's entire account begins in the context of Jewish communal prayer, and during it Zechariah is told that his prayer has been heard (1:13). The Temple piety that surrounds the infancy narrative includes the notice about Anna, the prophetess, spending her days in the courts, joining in its common worship, fasting, and praying (2:36-38); and her declaration about the role of Jesus in the deliverance of Jerusalem implicitly flows from her communing with God. Thus the chord of prayer is struck in the infancy narrative.

Moreover, it is only Luke who tells us that John the Baptist used to teach his disciples how to pray (11:1; cf. 5:33), without, however, giving any details about how they went about it. That note, at the introduction of the "Our Father," when the disciples ask Jesus to teach them, proves to be the basis of the Lucan view of prayer in the lives of Christian disciples.

Such details associate prayer with the Period of Israel. So it is not surprising that Luke depicts Jesus too at prayer. Many of the major episodes in Jesus' ministry are explicitly linked with his prayer, occurring either before or during them. Thus, at his baptism (3:21), before the choosing of the Twelve (6:12), before Peter's confession and the first announcement of the passion (9:18), at his transfiguration (9:28), before he teaches the "Our Father" (11:2), at the Last Supper (to strengthen Peter's faith, 22:32), during his agony on the Mount of Olives (22:41), and on the cross itself (23:46). In some of these episodes Luke has preserved the details from the tradition before him that at times Jesus withdrew from his disciples or from the crowds to a secluded place to pray. On occasion he goes up the Mount of Olives or on some unnamed mountain to do so—a mountain being regarded as a special place for communing with the Father. Indeed, on one occasion Luke adds to his notice of Jesus' retiring to the Mount of Olives the phrase, "as usual" (22:39).

Luke not only portrays Jesus often withdrawing to pray (e.g. 5:16; 6:12), but on occasion tells us about how he prayed or about the substance of his prayer. This is done even above and beyond the implications of the context in which his prayer is mentioned (as above). Thus, in a passage derived from "Q," he records Jesus' thanksgiving to the Father, uttered in a moment of exultation in the holy Spirit, for what has been revealed to mere children about himself and his filial relation to the Father, something kept hidden from the wise and the learned, from prophets and kings (10:21-23). Again, after the Last Supper and on the Mount of Olives he prays, "Please, Father, take this cup away from me; yet not my will but yours be done" (22:42 [vv. 43-44 add details which are omitted in the best Greek mss.; see the NOTE]). The prayer of supplication that he utters, not to have to face the ordeal that awaits him, ends in filial submission to the salvific plan that is to come to realization. Again, his filial confidence is recorded as he prays on the cross, "Father, into your hands I entrust my spirit," echoing the words of Ps 31:6 (23:46). In these various prayers Jesus communes with his heavenly Father in praise or thanksgiving, supplication, resignation, and filial confidence.

Alone among the evangelists, Luke portrays the disciples asking Jesus during his ministry to teach them to pray, making reference to the practice of John mentioned above (11:1). And in this context he derived from "Q" a form of the "Our Father." Here too the content of Christian prayer is displayed: God is acknowledged as Father, is praised, recognized as the source of material sustenance, forgiveness, and freedom from temptation (see further the COMMENT at 11:2-4).

Against the background of this plea for instruction in prayer, one reads a number of other injunctions of the Lucan Jesus that bear on it. Thus he tells the parable of the dishonest judge because of "the need to pray always and never give up" (18:1), citing the example of the importunate widow and commenting on the value of supplicating God: "Will not God then vindicate his chosen ones who cry out to him day and night?" (18:6). As Jesus sends out the Seventy(-two), he instructs them not only about what they are to do (preach, heal, etc.), but also about prayer: "Beg the owner of the harvest to send out laborers enough for his harvest" (10:2). Again, his instruction about prayer given in the "Our Father" is followed by the parable of the persistent friend (11:5-8) and further sayings on the efficacy of prayer (11:9-13).

This characteristic of Christian discipleship is inculcated in the Lucan account not merely by the instruction and example of Jesus himself during his ministry, but is depicted as part of the life of the early Christians. From the very beginning of Acts the community is engaged in the activity of communing with God. The Eleven, Mary and his "brothers" (now clearly depicted among the believers), and other women devote themselves to common prayer with one accord (Acts 1:14). This is noted even prior to Pentecost and the reception of the gift of the Spirit. Reference is further made to community prayer in the summary statement of Acts 2:42; cf. 4:31; 12:12.

It is interesting that Peter and John, even after Pentecost, go up to the Temple at the ninth hour, the hour of mid-afternoon prayer (3:1), thus still associating themselves with the prayer life of Israel (compare Luke 24:53 and the actions of Peter and Cornelius, the God-fearer, in Acts 10:9,30; 11:5, where the liberating vision is accorded to Peter in the context of prayer).

When the Seven are appointed to serve tables, this is done to allow the Twelve to engage in "prayer and ministry of the word" (Acts 6:4). Note the order of terms here: Luke clearly suggests that prayer is as important for the life of the Christian apostle as "the ministry of the word," i.e. the preaching of the Christian message. For he boldly takes over and makes part of Christian life two features of Jewish piety, prayer and almsgiving, suggesting that they rise before God as a memorial (Acts 10:2-4).

Luke does not hesitate to supply an example of Christian prayer, addressed to God as the Sovereign Lord (despota), in which he is recognized to be the creator, the inspirer of David in the composition of the psalms, and fashioner of the plan of salvation that saw its realization in the death of Jesus. It begs of God that disciples may be emboldened to preach the Christian message about him and his Anointed One fearlessly in the face of threats from kings and rulers and to heal in the name of his servant Jesus (Acts 4:24-30). Here one sees the sort of prayer that Luke has formulated on behalf of Peter and John, a petition for courage and boldness, that the disciples may carry out the roles expected of them. But the prayer becomes the context of their being filled with the holy Spirit.

Just as important episodes in the life of Jesus took place in the context of prayer, so too important events in the life of the early community occur in the same context. The early Christians beg God to manifest his choice of a successor for Judas in the casting of lots (1:24); they pray earnestly for the deliverance of Peter from the hands of Herod Agrippa (12:5). Prayer accompanies the imposition of hands, as the Seven are appointed by the apostles (6:6) and as Barnabas and Saul are set apart for their mission (13:3); it also accompanies the appointment of elders in every church by these two (14:23).

Nor does Luke pass over the place of prayer in the life of Paul, the hero of the latter part of Acts. Having been struck blind on the road to Damascus, his initiation into Christian life is begun as he is at prayer and accorded a vision of Ananias coming to help him (9:11; cf. 22:17), i.e. that he might regain his sight and be filled with the holy Spirit. Though he carries the Christian message to the Gentiles, he is presented insisting on his worship of the God of "our fathers" (24:14; cf. 27:23). His departure from the Ephesian elders summoned to Miletus takes place only after he has fallen to his knees to pray with them (20:36; cf. 21:5).

Thus Luke does not hesitate to insist in diverse ways on the need of prayer in Christian life and on its varied forms and occasions. What begins in his account as a manifestation of Temple piety is made into a characteristic of Christian life—dependence on God and his Anointed, manifested now on both a common and an individual basis as a mode of communing with them. The reason for this exhortation to prayer in the Lucan writings is best expressed in the Gospel (22:46), when Jesus finds his disciples asleep while he himself prayed, "Get up and pray so that you may not be subjected to temptation" (*peirasmos*). Ceaseless prayer is demanded of them lest apostasy be their lot. For this communing with God is the mark of their faith, as Luke 18:1-8 makes clear: God will vindicate those who cry out to him, but will the Son of Man find faith on the earth when he comes?

4) *The Disciple's Right Use of Material Possessions.* No other NT writer—save perhaps the author of the Epistle of James, and then only in an analogous way—speaks out as emphatically as does Luke about the Christian disciple's use of material possessions, wealth, and money. More than any of the other evangelists Luke either preserves sayings of Jesus about the rich and the poor or puts on his lips statements that reflect Luke's own attitude in this matter, extending such sayings. In Acts he further presents an idyllic picture of the first Jewish Christians of Jerusalem in the matter of common ownership and sharing of wealth as a model for the community of his own day. Obviously, he is not satisfied with what he has seen of the Christian use of wealth in his ecclesial community and makes use of sayings of Jesus to correct attitudes within it.

Elements of an attitude toward material wealth or possessions can be found in the pre-Lucan gospel tradition, for a number of sayings of Jesus found in his Gospel are likewise recorded in his Marcan source. Thus Luke has preserved (18:25) the saying about the greater ease a camel will have to pass through the eye of a needle than for a rich man to enter the kingdom of God (see Mark 10:25), or about the significance of the widow's mite (21:1-4, where, however, he has suppressed the Marcan note that many rich people contributed large sums to the Temple treasury, Mark 12:41c); and Jesus' advice to pay tribute in coins to Caesar (20:20-26; cf. Mark 12:13-17). Like Mark before him (14:11), Luke has implied his horror at the willingness of Judas to betray Jesus for "a sum of money" (22:5). The Marcan source depicted Jesus telling a rich young man to sell what he possessed, give the proceeds to the poor, and come, follow him (10:21). But in characteristic fashion Luke has sharpened the instruction, making Jesus tell "the ruler," "Sell *all* that you have" (18:22). Again, whereas in the Marcan source Simon and Andrew, James and John leave their nets to follow Jesus immediately (1:18,20), Luke depicts Simon, James, and John leaving "everything" to follow him (5:11). (Yet Luke is not always consistent; compare Mark 10:28 and Luke 18:28.) Similarly, Luke has preserved from the "Q" source the saying about Jesus as the Son of Man not having a place to lay his head (9:58; cf. Matt 8:20); the advice about avoiding anxiety over food and clothing (12:22-32; cf. Matt 6:25-33); the lines about giving one's tunic as well as one's cloak (6:29; cf. Matt 5:40); and about giving something to every beggar (6:30; cf. Matt 5:42). The point here is that this attitude toward material wealth in the Lucan Gospel did not originate with Luke himself. There is no need to think that it is not rooted in the preaching of the historical Jesus. But for his own reasons Luke has chosen to accentuate it, and he sees it as an imperative need in the Christian community for which he writes.

Luke's own emphasis and keen awareness of the difference between "the poor" and "the rich" can be noted initially in various ways. In the infancy narrative the chords of this motif are struck for the first time in Mary's Magnificat, when she extols God for filling the hungry with good things and sending the rich away empty (1:53). This chord thus struck announces a certain reversal of human values associated with the birth of a new heir to the heritage of David and Abraham. It introduces a motif that will be more fully commented on below.

The distinctively Lucan forms of the preaching of John the Baptist include, furthermore, the instruction to the people that they should share tunics and food with those who need them (3:11) and to soldiers that they avoid extortion and blackmail and be content with their wages (3:14). Later on, Luke sharpens the contrast between John in the desert and those who wear elegant robes (cf. Matt 11:8, "Q"), by adding to the latter, "and who live in luxury" (Luke 7:24-25).

The programmatic Nazareth scene with its quotation of Isa 61:1 sets the tone in the Lucan writings for Jesus' preaching to "the poor" (4:18). That theme is again picked up in the beatitudes, the first of which is pronounced over "you who are poor" and in its counterpart, the first woe, uttered against "you who are rich" (6:20,24). The beatitude was derived from the "Q" source (see Matt 5:3, where Matthean redaction has spiritualized it); but the parallel woe makes it clear that in the Lucan writings "the poor" are the economically and socially poor. The programmatic announcement of 4:18 is further picked up and commented on in Luke 7:21-22.

This basic Lucan motif is further played upon in the exclusively Lucan passages in the Gospel that contrast the rich and the poor, and deal with material possessions. These are found in first woe (just mentioned, 6:24), the parable of the rich fool (12:16-21), the story of the rich man and Lazarus (16:19-26), the story of the good Samaritan (which was actually told for another purpose, but which exemplifies a right use of material possession to aid an unfortunate human being, 10:35-37), the advice to "invite the poor" to dinner instead of rich neighbors (14:13). A unique place in the Lucan Gospel is occupied by Zacchaeus, who is obviously a model for the Christian disciple; but he is "a chief toll-collector and quite wealthy" (19:2). He comes off well, however, because he gives away "half of what I own to the poor" (19:8). In an analogous way, in a parable told for another purpose, the rich owner, who has had a dishonest manager swindling him (16:1), commends the manager for the prudent use of his commission (16:8a).

In the foregoing passages, whether derived from the pre-Lucan written tradition of Mark or "Q," or from his own special tradition, one detects an attitude toward material possessions which Luke would instill in his readers, but it is not uncomplicated. It is best described as a twofold attitude: (a) a moderate attitude, which advocates a prudent use of material possessions to give assistance to human beings less fortunate or to manifest a basic openness to the message that Jesus is preaching; and (b) a radical attitude, which recommends the renunciation of all wealth or possessions. This twofold Lucan attitude is not so explicitly formulated in the Gospel and Acts as it is here; but it can be found in various ways in the two volumes.

The moderate attitude, advocating a prudent use of material possessions, is detected in the advice to share them (3:11), to use them prudently (16:8a), to give alms (12:33). In this regard one should note the Lucan description of the Galilean women who provided for Jesus and the Twelve "with their own means" (8:3), the addition about almsgiving to the sayings about Pharisees and lawyers otherwise derived from "Q" (11:41; cf. Matt 23:26), the commendation of the dishonest manager and the application that is made of it: "Use the mammon of dishonesty to make friends, so that, when it gives out, you will be welcomed into dwellings that are everlasting" (16:9). In Acts Tabitha is spoken of highly because of her many "good works and alms" (9:36); similarly Cornelius (10:2,4,31, where the custom of almsgiving is commended as a prayer rising to God). By contrast, Simon of Samaria is cursed by Peter for trying to buy "the gift of God" (the Spirit) with money (8:18-20). Moreover, Paul reminds the elders of Ephesus to toil to help the weak, recalling the words of the Lord Jesus, "It is better to give than to receive" (Acts 20:35).

But along with such a moderate attitude toward material possessions, one detects a more radical Lucan attitude. Under this heading one can list the advice about lending and "looking for nothing in return" (6:35), about taking no provisions for the missionary journey (no walking-stick, bread, money, purse, knapsack, or sandals, 9:3; 10:4), about selling what one owns and giving it away as alms (12:33). "Everyone of you who does not say goodbye to all he has cannot be a disciple of mine" (14:33)— that sums up the radical Lucan attitude in one saying. "No servant can serve two masters; either he will hate the one and love the other, or he will be devoted to the one and despise the other. You cannot serve both God and mammon" (16:13). If we insisted above that for Luke "the poor" are the economically and socially poor, we begin to see in these sayings of Jesus that more is involved. It is what wealth tends to do to a human being, and to this we shall return below.

This radical attitude toward material possessions underlies the picture of the early Jewish Christian community in Acts. Peter, who cures the lame beggar at the Beautiful Gate in the Jerusalem Temple precincts, tells him: "Gold and silver I do not have, but what I have, I give you: In the name of Jesus of Nazareth, start walking" (3:6). Luke depicts the Jerusalem Christian community as having no needy persons among its members because all those who owned lands or houses sold them and pooled their resources so that they could be distributed to each as one needed things (4:35; cf. 2:44-45; 4:37). Just how widespread this community of holdings was, is not clear. But the details that Luke has singled out contribute in a general way to the idyllic picture of unanimity of the primitive community, a unanimity that was eventually sullied by the deception of Ananias and Sapphira (5:2-11) and the squabble between the Hellenists and the Hebrews over the dole to their widows (6:1-7).

Luke, however, does not stop with the description of the rich and the poor as the haves and have-nots of humanity. If he sees it as an obligation of Christian disciples of the former category to assist those of the latter, he sees the contrast in yet other ways. There is, for instance, an eschatological dimension to the contrast, in that God in his providence will eventually bring about the reversal of the human condition. This aspect of the contrast is found at the very beginning of the Lucan Gospel, in Mary's Magnificat (1:53), in the first beatitude and first woe (6:20,24), and in the parable of the rich man and Lazarus (16:19-26). But there is still another dimension, because Luke uses the contrast between the poor and the rich as a divider of human attitudes toward God, Jesus the prophet, and his message to human beings. For "the poor" in the Lucan Gospel are not only to be understood as the economically and socially poor (in contrast to the Matthean "poor in spirit"), but are associated with prisoners, blind persons, the downtrodden (4:18), or with those who hunger, weep, are hated, persecuted, and rejected (6:20b-22), or with blind people, cripples, lepers, and deaf people—even the dead (7:22). In other words, "the poor" represent generically the neglected mass of humanity. They are not the servants of mammon (16:13); they are not piling up treasures for themselves, but are rather "rich for God" (12:21). The characteristic of the rich fool was that he felt no need of God, whereas the poor are those that do and those to whom Jesus the prophet preaches.

This aspect of the portrayal of the poor in the Lucan writings has been emphasized in one way or another in recent times by such writers as J. Dupont, I. H. Marshall, and L. T. Johnson. The last has rightly insisted on the Lucan use of the language of possessions "not only literally, but also metaphorically, or symbolically." For it has been used by Luke to express the inner response of human hearts to God's visitation of his people in the ministry of Jesus and to his authority. The rich and the poor in the Lucan writings symbolize, in effect, the rejection and acceptance of Jesus the prophet announcing the new message of God's salvation and peace. *but how do we reconcile the "moderate" and the "radical" attitudes towards ∄? when is one appropriate? is one appropriate more appropriate than the other?*

C. CHRISTIAN LIFE TOGETHER. Luke's views on discipleship are not exhausted by the consideration of what he regards as demands made on individual Christians; he also envisages a certain organized and communal way of life for Christians—in effect, life in the Christian church. In discussing the Lucan idea of the following of Christ, we have already hinted at a designation used by him for the early Christian community, "the Way" (see B 1 above). Indeed, it is possibly a pre-Lucan designation for the early community, even though it is found only in Lucan writings. It does not say much, however, about the organized or communal aspects of Christian life.

From the first Easter-Sunday Luke depicts the followers of Jesus as the Eleven and other disciples banded together (24:33) and spending their time together in the Jerusalem Temple (24:52). Similarly, at the beginning of Acts they are portrayed praying together with one accord, "along with the women, Mary the mother of Jesus, and his brothers" (1:14). This nucleus is numbered as 120 persons (Acts 1:15), and the earliest designation that Luke uses of the group is "community" (koinōnia)—a sort of fellowship to which they devoted themselves, along with apostolic teaching, breaking of bread, and prayers (Acts 2:42). Just as yaḥad, "community," serves in Qumran literature to designate the specific Essene mode of communal life (1QS 1:1,16; 5:1,2,16; 6:21; 7:20, etc.; 1QSa 1:26,27 etc.), so koinōnia expresses for Luke the corporate spirit of the early Christian group, even if one cannot regard this term as a name for it.

However, ekklēsia, "church," soon emerges in the Lucan account in Acts as the name of the early community in Jerusalem and elsewhere. Absent from the first four chapters of Acts, it appears in 5:11, at the end of the story about Ananias and Sapphira: "Great fear came upon the whole church." This is, however, Luke's own comment in which he uses the term current in his day for the Christian community as he reflects upon that early scandal. It is not until the story of Paul begins in Acts that *ekklēsia* really appears (8:1,3) in the sense of "church"; and thereafter it is used continually. Since *ekklēsia* rarely occurs in the canonical Gospels—appearing only in Matt 16:18; 18:17—its abundant use in the Pauline letters and in Acts is striking. Was the Pauline use of this term a major factor in the designation of the community as "church"? Does the gradual introduction of it into the Lucan story in Acts betray the amount of time that it took early Christians to realize that their communal model of life (*koinōnia*) was best described as "church"? These are tantalizing questions which affect Lucan ecclesiology.

Not even the Lucan accounts of Paul's conversion relate it specifically to "the church." The heavenly voice on the road to Damascus calls out, "Saul, Saul, why do you persecute me" (9:4; 22:7; 26:14). But what is being identified as "me"? In the immediate contexts Saul is never depicted as persecuting "the church." In Acts 9:1-2 he has been persecuting "the disciples of the Lord" or "the Way"; in 22:4, "this Way"; and in 26:9-10, "the name of Jesus of Nazareth" and "many of the saints." Luke may, indeed, be preserving in these contexts primitive designations of the Christian community. But in any case, it is clear that the church as the body of Christ, a good Pauline theologoumenon, has no place in Lucan theology. Paul's insight into the meaning of Jesus Christ for humanity on the road to Damascus did not immediately include *that* theologoumenon; nor does he include it in his own reference to that experience (Gal 1:16).

Paul and Luke in Acts are the two main NT writers that use *ekklēsia* as the name for the "called assembly," the organized Christian community, either local or universal; beside the two above-mentioned Matthean passages and its frequent occurrence in Revelation 1-3 (in the letters to the seven local churches), it is used but rarely elsewhere (Jas 5:14; 3 John 6,9,10; Rev 22:16).

Luke refers to the members of the church in different ways, sometimes with terms that reveal some sort of structure, sometimes with terms that do not. He knows, for instance, that the followers of Jesus, the Christ, have come to be known generically as "Christians" (*Christianoi*, Acts 11:26). Sometimes he refers to them simply as *mathētai/mathētria*, "disciple(s)," using a term that suggests their following of Christ rather than any ministry or function that they may have within the community (Acts 6:1,2,7; 9:1,36, etc.). Again, sometimes he refers to them as *adelphoi*, "brothers, brethren," using a term that implies community rather than a function or ministry within it (1:15; 9:30; 10:23; 11:1,29, etc.). Both of these terms have roots in the ministry of Jesus itself (see Luke 6:1,13; 22:32).

Luke is also aware that some members of the church served in special functions or ministries: "elders," "the Twelve," and "apostles." These reveal that the Christian community was organized or structured, and that some members played roles in it that others did not. However, it is not always clear just what these roles were.

If there is no evidence in the Pauline letters that the churches with which Paul dealt were presbyterally structured (but cf. Phil 1:1), Luke depicts Paul (and Barnabas) on Mission I (A.D. 46-49; cf. JBC, art. 46, § 25-27) setting up "elders" (presbyteroi) "in every church" (Acts 14:23). When Paul is returning to Jerusalem from Mission III (A.D. 58), he summons the elders of Ephesus to Miletus and addresses them, telling them to be responsible "overseers" (episkopoi) of the church of God (20:17,28—the only place in Acts where this term appears for church officials; cf. 1:20). The "elders" appear elsewhere as functionaries or leaders in local churches (11:30; 15:2,4,6,22,23; 16:4; 20:17; 21:18). It seems, then, that Luke has attributed to Paul the structure of the community with which he was familiar in his own day. That elders were understood by him to be persons of authority can be seen from the way that they are coupled with "the apostles" in Acts 15-16.

Luke too is aware of a group in the early church called "the Twelve." Like the other Synoptic evangelists he traces the origin of this group to the ministry of Jesus himself (Luke 6:13; cf. Mark 3:14; Matt 10:1-5). That there is much to be said for this origin can be seen in the way the early church remembered with horror that Jesus was betrayed by Judas, who was "one of the Twelve" (Mark 14:10,43; echoed by Luke 22:3,47; Matt 26:14; cf. John 6:71). Luke follows Mark in making further use of them in his Gospel (see 8:1; 9:1,12 [their mission]; 18:31; 22:3,47; cf. 24:9,33 [the Eleven, minus Judas]). That they serve as an important link between Jesus and the early church is seen in the beginning of Acts, where the initial nucleus of disciples feels that it is necessary to reconstitute the Twelve and Matthias is chosen by lot to be with "the Eleven" in the place vacated by Judas' death (1:26). Luke sought to explain this necessity by the relation of the new community to be fashioned on Pentecost to that of Israel (represented by its twelve tribes). Yet, as the story in Acts progresses and James, the son of Zebedee, one of the Twelve, is put to death by Herod Agrippa (12:2), no need is then felt to reconstitute the Twelve anew. Indeed, once it was reconstituted in chap. 1, the Twelve appear in the Lucan account only on Pentecost (2:14) and in the selection of the seven table-servers (6:2—in 6:6 they are referred to as "the apostles"). This ephemeral existence and the function of the Twelve in the Lucan story raise problems in the understanding of the structure of the community that is recounted as stemming from Jesus himself. How does one account for the ephemeral existence of this group? Why does its influence disappear in Acts? Why is its only function, after the testimony to Israel on Pentecost, to change the community-structure by overseeing the democratic appointment of the seven table-servers? If this Lucan awareness of special ministries in the early church reveals something of its structure, it does not answer all possible questions about it.

But the problem of the special ministry of the Twelve in the early Jerusalem church is compounded by the fact that Luke seems to identify the Twelve with "the apostles." The "twelve apostles" occurs as a label put at the head of the list of the Twelve in Matt 10:2; it occurs again in Rev 21:14. But aside from these two late occurrences of what is by now a stereotyped phrase, only Luke brings the Twelve into close relationship with the apostles. In reality, these seem to have been originally distinct groups; that seems to be how 1 Cor 15:5 and 7 understood them, and v. 7 implies that they may have numbered more than twelve. In Mark 3:14 Jesus is said to have simply called those who were following him and appointed twelve of them to be with him; Matt 10:1,5 specifies that Jesus called the Twelve from among "the disciples." Luke does the same (6:13), adding, however, "whom he named apostles." When one considers the frequency with which "the apostles" appear in the Lucan account (Luke 9:10; 11:49; 17:5; 22:14; 24:10; Acts 1:2,26 ["eleven apostles"]; 2:37,42,43; 4:33,35,36,37; 5:2,12,18,29,40; 6:6; 8:1,14,18; 9:27; 11:1; 14:4,14; 15:2,4,6,22,23; 16:4), over against the very rare use of *apostolos* in the other Gospels (Mark 6:30; the *varia lectio* in 3:14 is a scribal harmonization in some Marcan mss. with Luke 6:13; Matt 10:2; John 13:16 [only in a generic sense!]), one realizes the problem that this group presents in the understanding of members in the Lucan view of the early church.

It seems obvious that Luke has identified the Twelve with the apostles, or at least represents a mode of thinking in the Christian community, in which they have already been so identified. As their name indicates, they would be the missionaries par excellence, those "sent" to carry the Word to the end of the earth. Though Paul is Luke's hero in the second half of Acts, he begrudgingly bestows the title "apostle" on him only in Acts 14:4,14. This may reflect the reluctance that Christians in the early church experienced in regarding Paul as such; and his own letters manifest the struggle that he put up to be so recognized: "Am I not an apostle? Have I not seen Jesus our Lord?" (1 Cor 9:1-2; cf. Gal 1:1,17,19; 2 Cor 12:11-12). It may also reflect the criteria that Luke set up for membership in the Twelve in Acts 1:21-22, which would, in effect, be criteria for membership among the apostles, if we are to take Luke 6:13 at face value. Among the criteria one finds that one had to be one of those who accompanied the other members of the Twelve during all the time that the Lord Jesus went in and out among them (Acts 1:21). It seems that the group of the apostles was actually in Luke's mind an important link between the church of his day and the historical Jesus; that is why he depicts the small nucleus at the beginning of Acts devoted to "the teaching of the Apostles" (2:42). In restricting the apostles to the Twelve, he combines their roles and increases their authority. In all of this one wonders, then, why he gives the title "apostle" to Barnabas, who was not one of the Twelve (Acts 14:4,14).

Even apart from this problem of the identification of the Twelve with the apostles in Lucan thinking, another crucial problem is why, after the "Council" of Jerusalem, the "apostles" also disappear from the structure of the Jerusalem church. They last appear in Acts 16:4, where it is said that Paul, Silas, and Timothy announced to the churches in the cities in Asia Minor through which they passed the decisions reached by "the apostles and elders in Jerusalem." When Paul returns to Jerusalem at the end of Mission III he goes up to greet James and "all the elders" (21:18), no mention being made any longer of apostles—unless we are to suppose that James was regarded by Luke as an "apostle" (which is never said!). (He is almost certainly the same as the James of Gal 1:19, whom Paul identifies as "the brother of the Lord" and possibly as an "apostle"—depending on how one translates the crucial *ei mē* in that verse: "except" or "but" [see *JBC,* art. 49, § 15].)

Lastly, in this matter of Lucan thinking about the organized or structured Christian community, one has to mention the seven table-servers, appointed by the "whole assembly" under the supervision of the Twelve or "the apostles" (Acts 6:1-6). They represent a structure that the community itself introduces; they are to "serve tables" (*diakonein trapezais*) in order that the Twelve might devote themselves to preaching, prayer, and the ministry of the word (6:2,4). The irony of it is that two of those so appointed, on whom the apostles prayed and imposed hands, are subsequently depicted by Luke as preaching and disputing with the Jews: Stephen (6:8-7:53), and Philip (8:4-13). Again, it is not clear just what we are to make of this structure thus introduced into the Jerusalem church.

If Luke shows an awareness of the organized Christian community or structured church, he does not conceal its changeable and ephemeral character. E. Schweizer (*Church Order in the New Testament* [SBT 32; London: SCM, 1961] 72) has called the Lucan mention of special office-bearers in the early church "casual"; he thinks that the forms of church service mentioned are "not fundamental to the Lucan church." This may be so. In any case, what we have set forth above shows the difficulty in trying to be definite about the structures of the Lucan church.

In reality, Luke is much more concerned about tracing the growth of the church in various parts of the eastern Mediterranean world and with the spread of the Word of God through it to "the end of the earth" (Acts 1:8) than in the details of church-structure. This accounts for his use of the numerical summaries in Acts, i.e. those isolated summary statements that insinuate the growth of the church, its peace, and its upbuilding (see 2:41; 4:4; 5:14; 6:1,7; 9:31; 11:21,24b; 12:24; 14:1; 19:20). In three of these summaries (6:7; 12:24; 19:20) he even stresses the growth of the Word itself. Another aspect of church-life may be seen in the esprit de corps manifested when Christians of one local church (Antioch) send a collection to relieve the desperate situation of their "brethren who lived in Judea" at the time of the famine under Emperor Claudius (Acts 11:29).

Still another aspect of the church for Luke was its character as the Spirit-guided organized community. As E. Käsemann has put it, "the Spirit bestowed upon the . . . disciples is precisely *not* the mark of a community without cultus or ministry but the seal of incorporation into the organized Church" ("The Disciples of John the Baptist in Ephesus," in his *Essays on New Testament Themes* [SBT 41; London: SCM, 1964] 141). That is why, normally speaking, the Spirit is given only when the Twelve are present or a member or delegate of the Twelve is on hand (see p. 231 above). Luke is concerned in Acts to draw fringe-Christians, like those evangelized by Philip (8:4-13), Apollos (18:25), and the "disciples" at Ephesus (19:1) into the Spirit-guided organized church. He sees the church as the locus in which the Word of God is rightly preached and in which salvation in the name of Jesus is offered to human beings. But does that make of the church in Lucan thinking an institution of salvation, tolerating no rival, the *Una sancta* ("the one holy [church]")—or even the beginning of it? So Käsemann would like to have us believe. But is Luke any more unique in this regard than any other NT writer? To be incorporated into the church in Lucan thinking means baptism and the laying on of hands, conditions for the reception of the Spirit. This is a certain sacramentalism (to use an anachronistic term, which is not Lucan); but is Luke alone in this in the NT? And even if one admits that Luke is concerned about tracing what the church of his day teaches back to Jesus himself (through the "teaching of the apostles"), is one not guilty of further anachronism in ascribing to Luke the beginning of "the *Una sancta*, the integrity of which is guaranteed by the teaching office of the Church resting upon the apostolic succession" (Käsemann, ibid., 145)? Luke may have the seeds of something like this —and that is why Käsemann can take refuge in the phrase, "the beginning of"—but it is not fair to ascribe to Luke all the implications of *Una sancta*, "teaching office," or "apostolic succession." This stems from *Kon-*

troverstheologie, not from exegesis. The point is that the Lucan treatment of these matters could have developed in terms of such a notion of "early Catholicism," but it could also have developed otherwise. That only Lucan theology developed exclusively in the former direction is a question that might be hotly debated.

If in the Lucan view of things salvation comes to human beings through the church, through the organized Christian community, that is because in it the Word of God is rightly preached and baptism is conferred "in the name of the Lord Jesus." But it would be a truncation of the Lucan view to consider the church in this manner alone. It is also the community that breaks bread together (Acts 2:42,46; 20:7,11)—without insinuating that salvation depends on it—that prays together (1:14; 2:42; 4:24, etc.), and that is guided by the Spirit of God.

If Luke has an ecclesiology, it grows from an awareness of Christians sharing life together, structured indeed (even though we may have difficulty today in sorting out all the details of that structure). If his vagueness about church-structure or even if his implication that church-structure has a somewhat ephemeral character has to be recognized, that does not mean that structure is of no importance. He gives enough detail to show that church-structure, even though it might have changed or displayed an ephemeral character, was indispensable. He even revealed that the change introduced by the appointment of the seven table-servers by the assembly was supervised or initiated by "the Twelve" (Acts 6:2).

9. *The Lucan Portrait of Jesus.* In section 5 above we tried to analyze the distinctive elements of Lucan christology and soteriology. That analysis concentrated on the essential theological aspects of the Lucan Jesus and his significance for human beings of all ages. But we cannot terminate this sketch of Lucan theology without referring to other features of the way Jesus is presented in the Third Gospel, features of the portrait of the Lucan Jesus that have often been noticed and do not adequately fit into the categories discussed in section 5.

The Lucan portrait has not only incorporated the essential christological teaching but has also made use of deft strokes to depict a person who is at once very human, dramatic, and at times even romantic. It is the sort of details or qualities that one would expect from the writer who sought to compose the first life of Christ. They are, moreover, qualities that Luke thinks should dominate the lives of Christians themselves and the Christian church.

Furthermore, they are probably qualities which reflect the sensibilities of Luke himself. Centuries ago Dante described Luke as *scriba mansuetudinis Christi* (*De monarchia* 1.18), "the scribe of the gentleness of Christ." For the qualities of mercy, love, charm, joy, and delicacy that are part of the Lucan portrait of Jesus in the Third Gospel tend to soften the starker reality that is at times portrayed in the other Gospels. This aspect of the Lucan Gospel perhaps deprives it of some of the radical and critical character associated with Jesus in the other Gospels, but it is part of the picture Luke wanted to paint.

Ernest Renan, in his own inimitable way, once wrote of the Lucan Gospel, "C'est le plus beau livre qu'il y ait" (*Les évangiles et la seconde génération chrétienne* [3d ed.; Paris: Calmann Lévy, 1877] 283). A writer in the early part of this century, D. A. Hayes, entitled a book about Luke in imitation of Renan's estimate, *The Most Beautiful Book Ever Written: The Gospel According to Luke* (New York: Eaton and Mains, 1913). Yet one cannot quote that estimate of Renan without appending the sage remark of Barrett, ". . . the Third Gospel has survived this damning faint praise, pronounced by the learned but sentimental French rationalist" (*Luke the Historian,* 7). Say what one may, there is something in the Lucan portrait of Jesus that such writers sense and perceive that transcends even Gallic sentimentality. For when the synthesis of Lucan thought is done, there remains something about the story of Jesus in the Gospel that almost defies proper analysis.

Years ago, M.-J. Lagrange tried to sum it up thus:

> In reading this Gospel of mercy, but also of repentance, of stark renunciation, but with a view to charity, these miracles inspired by goodness, this forgiveness for sin which is not complacency but rather a divine gift for sanctification—in learning to appreciate how a virgin and tender mother gave birth to the Son of God and how He suffered to bring human beings to His Father, the noble Theophilus would have comprehended the reasons for the moral transformation at work before his eyes and undoubtedly already begun in his heart. And he would have recognized them as good and secure: the world has possessed a Savior indeed (*Luc,* xlvii).

There are aspects of the Lucan portrait of Jesus that we have not included in our synthetic sketch which tend to build up the impression that such writers have got of the Third Gospel. Let a few of them be mentioned here; they include the Lucan parables of mercy (the two debtors, 7:41-43; the good Samaritan, 10:29-37; the barren fig tree, 13:6-9; the lost sheep, 15:3-7; the lost silver coin, 15:8-10; the prodigal son, 15:11-32; the Pharisee and the Toll-collector, 18:9-14), the episodes about Zacchaeus and Emmaus; the prominence of women in various episodes of Jesus' ministry; the pairing off of parables of men and women. Such things may not really be part of the theology of the Lucan writings, but they deserve to be mentioned here at least, if only to fill out the impression that the rest may have made.

BIBLIOGRAPHY

General Studies

Bovon, F. "L'Importance des médiations dans le projet théologique de Luc," *NTS* 21 (1974-1975) 23-39.

────── *Luc le théologien: Vingt-cinq ans de recherches (1950-1975)* (Le monde de la Bible; Neuchâtel/Paris: Delachaux et Niestlé, 1978).

Brown, S. *Apostasy and Perseverance in the Theology of Luke* (AnBib 36; Rome: Biblical Institute, 1969).

Bultmann, R. *The Theology of the New Testament* (2 vols.; London: SCM, 1952, 1955) 2. 95-236. Cited as Bultmann, *Theology*.

Conzelmann, H. *An Outline of the Theology of the New Testament* (New York: Harper & Row, 1969).

────── *The Theology of St Luke* (New York: Harper, 1960).

Dömer, H. *Das Heil Gottes: Studien zur Theologie des lukanischen Doppelwerks* (BBB 51; Bonn: P. Hanstein, 1978).

Flender, H. *St. Luke: Theologian of Redemptive History* (Philadelphia: Fortress, 1967).

Franklin, E. *Christ the Lord: A Study in the Purpose and Theology of Luke-Acts* (Philadelphia: Westminster, 1975).

George, A. *Études sur l'oeuvre de St. Luc* (Sources bibliques; Paris: Gabalda, 1978).

Gewiess, J. *Die urapostolische Heilsverkündigung nach der Apostelgeschichte* (Breslauer Studien z. historischen Theologie, ns 5; Breslau: Mueller und Seiffert, 1939).

Goguel, M. "Quelques observations sur l'oeuvre de Luc," *RHPR* 33 (1953) 37-51.

Haenchen, E. *The Acts of the Apostles: A Commentary* (Philadelphia: Westminster, 1971).

Hastings, A. *Prophet and Witness in Jerusalem: A Study of the Teaching of Saint Luke* (Baltimore: Helicon, 1958).

Hegermann, H. "Zur Theologie des Lukas," in . . . *und fragten nach Jesus: Beiträge aus Theologie, Kirche und Geschichte: Festschrift für Ernst Barnikol* (Berlin: Evangelische Verlagsanstalt, 1964) 27-34.

Hultgren, A. J. "Interpreting the Gospel of Luke," *Int* 30 (1976) 353-365.

Jervell, J. *Luke and the People of God: A New Look at Luke-Acts* (Minneapolis: Augsburg, 1972).

Koh, R. *The Writings of St. Luke* (Hongkong: Diocesan Literature Committee, 1953).

Kümmel, W. G. *The Theology of the New Testament According to Its Major Witnesses, Jesus—Paul—John* (Nashville: Abingdon, 1973).

Marshall, I. H. *Luke: Historian and Theologian* (Exeter: Paternoster; Grand Rapids, MI: Zondervan, 1971).

Navone, J. *Themes of St. Luke* (Rome: Gregorian University, [1970]).

O'Neill, J. C. *The Theology of Acts in Its Historical Setting* (2d ed.; London: SPCK, 1970).

Rasco, E. "Hans Conzelmann y la 'Historia Salutis': A propósito de 'Die Mitte der Zeit' y 'Die Apostelgeschichte,'" *Greg* 46 (1965) 286-319.

―――― *La teologia de Lucas: Origen, desarrollo, orientaciones* (AnGreg 201; Rome: Gregorian University, 1976).

Rohde, J. "Luke's Two Books," in *Rediscovering the Teaching of the Evangelists* (Philadelphia: Westminster, 1968) 153-239.

Schulz, S. "Lukas," in *Die Stunde der Botschaft: Einführung in die Theologie der vier Evangelisten* (Hamburg: Furche, 1967) 235-296.

Stöger, A. "Die Theologie des Lukasevangeliums," *BLit* 46 (1973) 227-236.

Talbert, C. H. *Literary Patterns, Theological Themes and the Genre of Luke-Acts* (SBLMS 20; Missoula, MT: Scholars Press, 1974).

―――― "The Redaction Critical Quest for Luke the Theologian," *Perspective* 11/1-2 (1970) 171-222.

Tolbert, M. "Leading Ideas of the Gospel of Luke," *RevExp* 64 (1967) 441-451.

The Lucan Kerygma

Aalen, S. "'Reign' and 'House' in the Kingdom of God in the Gospels," *NTS* 8 (1961-1962) 215-240.

Asting, R. K. *Die Verkündigung des Wortes Gottes im Urchristentum, dargestellt an den Begriffen "Wort Gottes," "Evangelium" und "Zeugnis"* (Stuttgart: Kohlhammer, 1939).

Baird, W. "What is the Kerygma? A Study of I Cor 15:3-8 and Gal 1:15-17," *JBL* 76 (1957) 181-191.

Betz, O. "The Kerygma of Luke," *Int* 22 (1968) 131-146.

Bultmann, R. "Bultmann Replies to His Critics," in *Kerygma and Myth: A Theological Debate* (ed. H. W. Bartsch; 2 vols.; London: SPCK) 1 (1953) 191-211.

―――― "The Concept of the Word of God in the New Testament," in *Faith and Understanding* (tr. L. P. Smith; ed. R. W. Funk; New York: Harper & Row, 1969) 286-312.

Dinkler, E. "Existentialist Interpretation of the New Testament," *JR* 32 (1952) 87-96.

Dodd, C. H. *The Apostolic Preaching and Its Developments* (London: Hodder & Stoughton, 1936).

Evans, C. F. "The Kerygma," *JTS* 7 (1956) 25-41.

Friedrich, G. "*Kēryx . . . ,*" *TDNT* 3 (1965) 683-718.

Higgins, A. J. B. "The Preface to Luke and the Kerygma in Acts," in *Apostolic History and the Gospel: Biblical and Historical Essays Presented to F. F. Bruce on His 60th Birthday* (eds. W. W. Gasque and R. P. Martin; Grand Rapids: Eerdmans, 1970) 78-91.

Hillmann, W. "Grundzüge der urkirchlichen Glaubensverkündigung," *Wissenschaft und Weisheit* 20 (1957) 163-180.

Jaschke, H. "'*Lalein*' bei Lukas: Ein Beitrag zur lukanischen Theologie," *BZ* 15 (1971) 109-114.

Leijs, R. "Prédication des Apôtres," *NRT* 69 (1947) 605-618.

Luck, U. "Kerygma, Tradition und Geschichte Jesu bei Lukas," *ZTK* 57 (1960) 51-66; reprinted in *Das Lukas-Evangelium: Die redaktions- und kompositionsgeschichtliche Forschung* (Wege der Forschung 280; ed. G. Braumann; Darmstadt: Wissenschaftliche Buchgesellschaft, 1974) 95-114.

März, C.-P. *Das Wort Gottes bei Lukas: Die lukanische Worttheologie als Frage an die neuere Lukasforschung* (Erfurter theologische Schriften 11; Leipzig: St. Benno, 1974).

Merk, O. "Das Reich Gottes in den lukanischen Schriften," in *Jesus und Paulus: Festschrift für Werner Georg Kümmel* (eds. E. E. Ellis and E. Grässer; Göttingen: Vandenhoeck und Ruprecht, 1975) 201-220.

Perrin, N. *Jesus and the Language of the Kingdom: Symbol and Metaphor in New Testament Interpretation* (Philadelphia: Fortress, 1976).

Staudinger, F. " 'Verkündigen' im lukanischen Geschichtswerk," *TPQ* 120 (1972) 211-218.

The Lucan Geographical Perspective

Baltzer, K. "The Meaning of the Temple in the Lukan Writings," *HTR* 58 (1965) 263-277.

Lohmeyer, E. "Galiläa und Jerusalem bei Lukas," in *Das Lukas-Evangelium* (Wege der Forschung, 280; ed. G. Braumann; Darmstadt: Wissenschaftliche Buchgesellschaft, 1974) 7-12.

Mánek, J. "The New Exodus in the Books of Luke," *NovT* 2 (1957) 8-23.

McCown, C. C. "The Geography of Luke's Central Section," *JBL* 57 (1938) 51-66.

——— "Gospel Geography: Fiction, Fact, and Truth," *JBL* 60 (1941) 1-25, esp. pp. 14-18.

Navone, J. "The Journey Theme in Luke-Acts," *TBT* 58 (1972) 616-619.

——— "The Way of the Lord," *Scr* 20 (1968) 24-30.

Robinson, W. C., Jr. "The Theological Context for Interpreting Luke's Travel Narrative (9,51ff.)," *JBL* 79 (1960) 20-31.

——— *"The Way of the Lord: A Study of History and Eschatology in the Gospel of Luke* (Basel: Dissertation, 1962).

——— *Der Weg des Herrn: Studien zur Geschichte und Eschatologie im Lukas-Evangelium: Ein Gespräch mit Hans Conzelmann* (Theologische Forschung, 36; Hamburg-Bergstedt: H. Reich, 1964).

Simson, P. "The Drama of the City of God: Jerusalem in St. Luke's Gospel," *Scr* 15 (1963) 65-80.

Wink, W. *John the Baptist in the Gospel Tradition* (SNTSMS 7; Cambridge: University Press, 1968) 49-51.

The Lucan Historical Perspective

Barrett, C. K. *Luke the Historian in Recent Study* (London: Epworth, 1961).

Dibelius, M. "The First Christian Historian," *Religion in Life* 25 (1955-1956) 223-236; reprinted in *Studies in the Acts of the Apostles* (London: SCM, 1956) 123-137.

Morgenthaler, R. *Die lukanische Geschichtsschreibung als Zeugnis: Gestalt und Gehalt der Kunst des Lukas* (AbhTANT 14/15; Zürich: Zwingli, 1949).

Navone, J. "Three Aspects of the Lucan Theology of History," *BTB* 3 (1973) 115-132.

Salvation-History

Bovon, F. "Le salut dans les écrits de Luc," *RPT* 3/23 (1973) 296-307.

Cullmann, O. *Salvation in History* (New York: Harper & Row, 1967).

Flender, H. *St Luke: Theologian of Redemptive History* (Philadelphia: Fortress, 1967).

Kümmel, W. G. " 'Das Gesetz und die Propheten gehen bis Johannes,' Lukas 16,16 im Zusammenhang der heilsgeschichtlichen Theologie der Lukasschriften," in *Verborum veritas: Festschrift für Gustav Stählin zum 70. Geburtstag* (eds. O. Böcher and K. Haacker; Wuppertal: R. Brockhaus, 1970) 89-102; reprinted in *Das Lukas-Evangelium* (Wege der Forschung 280; ed. G. Braumann; Darmstadt: Wissenschaftliche Buchgesellschaft, 1974) 398-415.

———— "Heilsgeschichte im Neuen Testament?" in *Neues Testament und Kirche: Für Rudolf Schnackenburg* (ed. J. Gnilka; Freiburg im B.: Herder, 1974) 434-457.

Lohse, E., "Lukas als Theologe der Heilsgeschichte," *EvT* 14 (1954) 256-275; reprinted in *Das Lukas-Evangelium* (Wege der Forschung 280), 64-90.

Lönning, K. "Lukas—Theologe der von Gott geführten Heilsgeschichte," in *Gestalt und Anspruch des Neuen Testaments* (ed. J. Schreiner; Würzburg: Echter, 1969) 200-228.

Reumann, J. "Heilsgeschichte in Luke: Some Remarks on Its Background and Comparison with Paul," *SE IV* (TU 102, 1968) 86-115.

Schulz, S. "Gottes Vorsehung bei Lukas," *ZNW* 54 (1963) 104-116.

Universalism in Lucan Salvation-History

Dahl, N. A. "The Story of Abraham in Luke-Acts," in *Studies in Luke-Acts,* 139-158.

Dupont J. "Le salut des gentiles et la signification théologique du livre des Actes," *NTS* 6 (1959-1960) 132-155.

Gamba, J. "Praeoccupatio universalistica in evangelio S. Lucae," *VD* 40 (1962) 131-135.

George, A. "Israël dans l'oeuvre de Luc," *RB* 75 (1968) 481-525.

Goudoever, J. van "The Place of Israel in Luke's Gospel," in *Placita Pleiadia: Opstellen aangeboden aan Prof. Dr. G. Sevenster* (=*NovT* 8 [1966] 85-307; eds. J. Smit Sibinga and W. C. van Unnik; Leiden: Brill, 1966) 111-123.

Haenchen, E. "Judentum und Christentum in der Apostelgeschichte," *ZNW* 54 (1963) 155-187; reprinted in *Die Bibel und Wir: Gesammelte Aufsätze* (2 vols.; Tübingen: Mohr [Siebeck], 1968) 2. 338-374.

Hanford, W. R. "Deutero-Isaiah and Luke-Acts: Straightforward Universalism?" *CQR* 168 (1967) 141-152.

Jervell, J. "The Divided People of God: The Restoration of Israel and Salvation for the Gentiles," in *Luke and the People of God: A New Look at Luke-Acts* (Minneapolis: Augsburg, 1972) 41-74.

Kiddle, M. "The Admission of the Gentiles in St Luke's Gospel and Acts," *JTS* 36 (1935) 160-173.

King, N. Q. "The 'Universalism' of the Third Gospel," *SE I* (TU 73, 1959) 199-205.

Wilson, S. G. *The Gentiles and the Gentile Mission in Luke-Acts* (SNTSMS 23; New York/London: Cambridge University, 1973).

Zingg, P. "Die Stellung des Lukas zur Heidenmission," *Neue Zeitschrift für Missionswissenschaft/Nouvelle revue de science missionaire* 29 (1973) 200-209.

Lucan Christology

Berchmans, J. "Some Aspects of Lukan Christology," *Biblebhashyam* 2 (1976) 5-22.

Bouwman, G. "Die Erhöhung Jesu in der lukanischen Theologie," *BZ* 14 (1970) 257-263.

Lampe, G. W. H. "The Lucan Portrait of Christ," *NTS* 2 (1955-1956) 160-175.

Lohfink, G. *Die Himmelfahrt Jesu: Untersuchungen zu den Himmelfahrts- und Erhöhungstexten bei Lukas* (SANT 26; Munich: Kösel, 1971).

Lohse, E. *Die Auferstehung Jesu Christi im Zeugnis des Lukasevangeliums* (BibS[N] 31; Neukirchen: Neukirchener, 1961).

Marshall, I. H. "The Resurrection in the Acts of the Apostles," in *Apostolic History and the Gospel: Biblical and Historical Essays Presented to F. F. Bruce on His 60th Birthday* (eds. W. W. Gasque and R. P. Martin; Grand Rapids: Eerdmans, 1970) 92-107.

Martin, H. *Luke's Portrait of Jesus* (London: SCM, 1949).

Martini, C. "Riflessioni sulla cristologia degli Atti," *Sacra doctrina* 16 (1971) 525-534.

Moule, C. F. D. "The Christology of Acts," in *Studies in Luke-Acts*, 159-185.

Owen, H. P. "Stephen's Vision in Acts vii. 55-56," *NTS* 1 (1954-1955) 224-226.

Rese, M. *Alttestamentliche Motive in der Christologie des Lukas* (SNT 1; Gütersloh: Mohn, 1969).

Resseguie, J. L. "The Lukan Portrait of Christ," *Studia biblica et theologica* 4 (1974) 5-20.

Stempvoort, P. A. van. "The Interpretation of the Ascension in Luke and Acts," *NTS* 5 (1958-1959) 30-42.

Voss, G. *Die Christologie der lukanischen Schriften in Grundzügen* (Studia neotestamentica, studia 2; Paris/Bruges: Desclée de Brouwer, 1965).

Wilckens, U. *Die Missionsreden der Apostelgeschichte: Form- und traditionsgeschichtliche Untersuchungen* (WMANT 5; Neukirchen: Neukirchener, 1961).

Christological Titles

Brown, R. E. "Jesus and Elisha," *Perspective* 12 (1971) 84-104.

—— *Jesus God and Man: Modern Biblical Reflections* (Milwaukee: Bruce, 1967) 1-38.

Burger, C. *Jesus als Davidssohn: Eine traditionsgeschichtliche Untersuchung* (FRLANT 98; Göttingen: Vandenhoeck und Ruprecht, 1970).

Busse, U. *Die Wunder des Propheten Jesus: Die Rezeption, Komposition und Interpretation der Wundertradition im Evangelium des Lukas* (Forschung zur Bibel 24; Stuttgart: Katholisches Bibelwerk, 1977).

Cullmann, O. *The Christology of the New Testament* (Philadelphia: Westminster, 1959).

Dahl, N. A., *The Crucified Messiah and Other Essays* (Minneapolis: Augsburg, 1974).

Dubois, J.-D. "La figure d'Elie dans la perspective lucanienne," *RHPR* 53 (1973) 155-176.

Dupont, J. "Jésus, Messie et Seigneur dans la foi des premiers chrétiens," *VSpir* 83 (1950) 385-416.

Franklin, E. "Jesus of Nazareth," in *Christ the Lord*, 1-8, 48-69.

Fuller, R. H. *The Foundations of New Testament Christology* (New York: Scribner, 1965).

George, A. "Jésus fils de Dieu dans l'évangile selon Saint Luc," *RB* 72 (1965) 185-209 (digested in *TD* 15 [1967] 128-133).

—— "La royauté de Jésus selon l'évangile de Luc," *ScEccl* 14 (1962) 57-69.

Gils, F. *Jésus prophète d'après les évangiles synoptiques* (Orientalia et biblica lovaniensia 2; Louvain: Publications universitaires, 1957).

Hahn, F. *The Titles of Jesus in Christology: Their History in Early Christianity* (London: Lutterworth, 1969).

Hengel, M. *The Son of God: The Origin of Christology and the History of Jewish-Hellenistic Religion* (Philadelphia: Fortress, 1976).

Higgins, A. J. B. "Jesus as Prophet," *ExpTim* 57 (1945-1946) 292-294.

Hinnebusch, P. "Jesus, the New Elijah, in Saint Luke," *TBT* 31 (1967) 2175-2182; 32 (1967) 2237-2244.

Iersel, B. M. F. van. *'Der Sohn' in den synoptischen Jesusworten* (NovTSup 3; 2d ed.; Leiden: Brill, 1964).

Jones, D. L. "The Title *Christos* in Luke-Acts," *CBQ* 32 (1970) 69-76.

—— "The Title *Kyrios* in Luke-Acts," in *SBL 1974 Seminar Papers* (ed. G. W. MacRae; 2 vols.; Cambridge, MA: Society of Biblical Literature, 1974) 2.85-101.

Jonge, M. de "The Use of the Word 'Anointed' in the Time of Jesus," *NovT* 8 (1966) 132-148.

Kilpatrick, G. D. " 'Kurios' in the Gospels," *L'Évangile hier et aujourd'hui: Mélanges offerts au Professeur Franz-J. Leenhardt* (eds. les professeurs de la faculté autonome de théologie de Genève; Geneva: Labor et Fides, 1968) 65-70.

Kramer, W. *Christ, Lord, Son of God* (SBT 50; Naperville: Allenson, 1966).

Kränkl, E. *Jesus der Knecht Gottes: Die heilsgeschichtliche Stellung Jesu in den Reden der Apostelgeschichte* (Biblische Untersuchungen 8; Regensburg: Pustet, 1972).

Müller, P. G. *Christos Archêgos: Der religionsgeschichtliche und theologische Hintergrund einer neutestamentlichen Christusprädikation* (Europäische Hochschulschriften, 23/28; Bern: H. Lang; Frankfurt: P. Lang, 1973).

Nevius, R. C. "*Kyrios* and *Iēsous* in St. Luke," *ATR* 48 (1966) 75-77.

Normann, F. *Christos Didaskalos: Die Vorstellung von Christus als Lehrer des ersten und zweiten Jahrhunderts* (Münsterische Beiträge zur Theologie 32; Münster in W.: Aschendorff, 1967).

Potterie, I. de la. "Le titre *kyrios* appliqué à Jésus dans l'évangile de Luc," *Mélanges bibliques en hommage au R. P. Béda Rigaux* (eds. A. Descamps et A. de Halleux; Gembloux: Duculot, 1970) 117-146.

Robinson, J. A. T. "The Most Primitive Christology of All?" *JTS* 7 (1956) 177-189; reprinted in *Twelve New Testament Studies* (SBT 34; Naperville: Allenson, 1962) 139-153.

Young, F. W. "Jesus as Prophet: A Re-examination," *JBL* 68 (1949) 285-299.

Zimmerli, W., and J. Jeremias. *The Servant of God* (SBT 20; London: SCM, 1957).

Soteriology

Baumbach, G. "Gott und Welt in der Theologie des Lukas," *BLit* 45 (1972) 241-255.

Frizzi, G. "La soteriologia nell'opera lucana," *RivB* 23 (1975) 113-145.

George, A. "Le sens de la mort de Jésus pour Luc," *RB* 80 (1973) 186-217.

Kümmel, W. G. "Current Theological Accusations against Luke," *Andover Newton Quarterly* 16 (1975) 131-145, esp. p. 138.

Larkin, W. J., Jr. "Luke's Use of the Old Testament as a Key to His Soteriology," *JETS* 20 (1977) 325-335.

Schütz, F. *Der leidende Christus: Die angefochtene Gemeinde und das Christuskerygma der lukanischen Schriften* (BWANT 5/8; Stuttgart: Kohlhammer, 1969).

Tannehill, R. "A Study in the Theology of Luke-Acts," *ATR* 43 (1961) 195-203.

Voss, G. *Die Christologie der lukanischen Schriften in Grundzügen* (Studia neotestamentica, Studia 2; Paris/Bruges: Desclée de Brouwer, 1965), 99-130.

Zehnle, R. "The Salvific Character of Jesus' Death in Lucan Soteriology," *TS* 30 (1969) 420-444.

Effects of the Christ-Event as Seen by Luke

Bovon, F. "Le salut dans les écrits de Luc," *RTP* 3 (1973) 296-307.

Colon, J.-B. "La conception du salut d'après les évangiles synoptiques," *RevScRel* 3 (1923) 62-92, 472-507; 10 (1930) 1-39, 189-217, 370-415; 11 (1931) 27-70, 193-223, 382-412.

Comblin, J. "La paix dans la théologie de saint Luc," *ETL* 32 (1956) 439-460.

Descamps, A. "Le pardon divin dans les paraboles de miséricorde," *Revue diocésaine de Tournai* 6 (1951) 310-314.

George, A. "L'Emploi chez Luc du vocabulaire de salut," *NTS* 23 (1976-1977) 308-320.

Glöckner, R. *Die Verkündigung des Heils beim Evangelisten Lukas* (Walberger Studien 9: Mainz: Matthias-Grünewald, [1976]).

Martin, R. P. "Salvation and Discipleship in Luke's Gospel," *Int* 30 (1976) 366-380.

Rad, G. von, and W. Foerster. "*Eirēnē*, . . . ," *TDNT* 2 (1964) 400-420.

Taylor, V. *Forgiveness and Reconciliation: A Study in New Testament Theology* (London: Macmillan, 1941).

Throckmorton, B. H. "*Sōzein, sōtēria* in Luke-Acts," *SE* VI (TU 112, 1973) 515-526.

Thyen, H. *Studien zur Sündenvergebung im Neuen Testament und seinen alttestamentlichen und jüdischen Voraussetzungen* (FRLANT 96; Göttingen: Vandenhoeck und Ruprecht, 1970).

Unnik, W. C. van. "L'Usage de *sōzein* 'sauver' et les dérivés dans les évangiles synoptiques," *La formation des évangiles* (RechBib 2; Bruges: Desclée de Brouwer, 1957) 178-194.

Vriezen, T. C. and K. Stendahl, "Sündenvergebung," *RGG*³ 6 (1962) 507-513.

Wagner, W. "Über *sōzein* und sein Derivate im Neuen Testament," *ZNW* 6 (1905) 205-235.

Whiteley, D. E. H. "The Doctrine of Salvation in the Synoptic Gospels," *SE* IV (TU 102, 1968) 116-130.

The Spirit

Baer, H. von. *Der heilige Geist in den Lukasschriften* (BWANT 39; Stuttgart: Kohlhammer, 1926).

———— "Der heilige Geist in den Lukasschriften," in *Das Lukas-Evangelium: Die redaktions- und kompositionsgeschichtliche Forschung* (Wege der Forschung 280; ed. G. Braumann; Darmstadt: Wissenschaftliche Buchgesellschaft, 1974) 1-6.

Beasley-Murray, G. R. "Jesus and the Spirit," in *Mélanges bibliques en hommage au R. P. Béda Rigaux* (eds. A. Descamps and A. de Halleux; Gembloux: Duculot, 1970) 463-478.

Dana, H. E. *The Holy Spirit in Acts* (2d ed.; Kansas City, KS: Central Seminary Press, 1943).

Hull, J. H. E. *The Holy Spirit in the Acts of the Apostles* (London: Lutterworth, 1967).

Lampe, G. W. H. "The Holy Spirit in the Writings of St. Luke," in *Studies in the Gospels: Essays in Memory of R. H. Lightfoot* (ed. D. E. Nineham; Oxford: Blackwell, 1957) 159-200.

Samain, P. "L'Esprit et le royaume de Dieu d'après saint Luc," *Revue diocésaine de Tournai* 2 (1947) 481-492.

Schweizer, E. "*Pneuma*, . . . ," *TDNT* 6 (1968) 332-445, esp. pp. 404-415.

Smalley, S. S. "Spirit, Kingdom and Prayer in Luke-Acts," *NovT* 15 (1973) 59-71.

Stalder, K. "Der heilige Geist in der lukanischen Ekklesiologie," *Una sancta* 30 (1975) 287-293.

Tatum, W. B. "The Epoch of Israel: Luke i-ii and the Theological Plan of Luke-Acts," *NTS* 13 (1966-1967) 184-195.

Eschatology

Dupont, J. "Die individuelle Eschatologie im Lukasevangelium und in der Apostelgeschichte," *Orientierung an Jesus: Zur Theologie der Synoptiker: Für Josef Schmid* (eds. P. Hoffman et al.; Freiburg: Herder, 1973) 37-47.

Ellis, E. E. *Eschatology in Luke* (Facet Books, Biblical Series, 30; Philadelphia: Fortress, 1972).

———— "Present and Future Eschatology in Luke," *NTS* 12 (1965-1966) 27-41.

Ernst, J. *Herr der Geschichte: Perspektiven der lukanischen Eschatologie* (SBS 88; Stuttgart: Katholisches Bibelwerk, 1978).

Francis, F. O. "Eschatology and History in Luke-Acts," *JAAR* 37 (1969) 49-63.

Franklin, E. "The Ascension and the Eschatology of Luke-Acts," *SJT* 23 (1970) 191-200.

———— "Luke's Eschatology," *Christ the Lord* (London: SPCK, 1975) 9-47.

Geiger, R. *Die lukanischen Endzeitsreden: Studien zur Eschatologie des Lukas-Evangeliums* (Europäische Hochschulschriften, 23/16; Bern: H. Lang; Frankfurt: P. Lang, 1976).

Grässer, E. *Das Problem der Parusieverzögerung in den synoptischen Evangelien und in der Apostelgeschichte* (BZNW 22; Berlin: Töpelmann, 1957; 2d ed., 1960).

Hiers, R. H. "The Problem of the Delay of the Parousia in Luke-Acts," *NTS* 20 (1973-1974) 145-155.

Kaestli, J.-D. *L'Eschatologie dans l'oeuvre de Luc: Ses caractéristiques et sa place dans le développement du christianisme primitif* (Geneva: Labor et Fides, 1969).

Kümmel, W. G. "Futurische und präsentische Eschatologie im ältesten Christentum," *NTS* 5 (1958-1959) 113-126.

Mattill, A. J. *"Naherwartung, Fernerwartung,* and the Purpose of Luke-Acts: Weymouth Reconsidered," *CBQ* 34 (1972) 276-293.

Schneider, G. *Parusiegleichnisse im Lukas-Evangelium* (SBS 74; Stuttgart: Katholisches Bibelwerk, 1975).

Smith, R. H. "History and Eschatology in Luke-Acts," *CTM* 29 (1958) 881-890.

Wilson, S. G. "Lukan Eschatology," *NTS* 16 (1969-1970) 330-347.

Discipleship

Benoit, P. "La foi dans les évangiles synoptiques," *Lumière et vie* 22 (1955) 45-64.

Brown, S. "Apostasy and Perseverance in the Theology of Luke," *TBT* 63 (1972) 985-993.

Dupont, J. "Repentir et conversion d'après les Actes des Apôtres," *ScEccl* 12 (1960) 137-173.

Meunier, A. "La foi dans les Actes des Apôtres," *Revue ecclésiastique de Liège* 43 (1956) 50-53.

Michiels, R. "La conception lucanienne de la conversion," *ETL* 41 (1965) 42-78.

Rétif, A. "La foi missionnaire ou kérygmatique et ses signes," *RUO* 21 (1951) 151*-172*.

Schnackenburg, R. "Typen der Metanoia-Predigt im Neuen Testament," *MTZ* 1 (1950) 1-13.

Sheridan, M. "Disciples and Discipleship in Matthew and Luke," *TBT* 3 (1973) 235-255.

The Demands of Christian Life

Repo, E. *Der 'Weg' als Selbstbezeichnung des Urchristentums: Eine traditionsgeschichtliche und semasiologische Untersuchung* (Annales academiae scientiarum fennicae B132/2; Helsinki: Suomalainen Tiedeakatemia, 1964) 55-138, 150-158, 167-180.

Sheridan, M. "Disciples and Discipleship in Matthew and Luke," *BTB* 3 (1973) 235-255.

Thysman, R. "L'Ethique de l'imitation du Christ dans le Nouveau Testament: Situation, notations et variations du thème," *ETL* 42 (1966) 138-175

Testimony

Andersen, W. "Die Autorität der apostolischen Zeugniss!" *EvT* 12 (1952-1953) 467-481.

Cerfaux, L. "Témoins du Christ (d'après le Livre des Actes)," *Angelicum* 20 (1943) 166-183; reprinted in *Recueil Lucien Cerfaux* (Gembloux: Duculot, 1954) 2. 157-174.

Jauregui, J. A. *Testimonio, apostolado-misión: Justificación teológica del concepto lucano apóstol-testigo de Act 1, 15-26* (Teología-Deusto 3; Bilbao: Universidad de Deusto, 1973).

Menoud, P.-H. "Jésus et ses témoins: Remarques sur l'unité de l'oeuvre de Luc," *Église et theologie* (Paris: Presses universitaires de France, 1960) 1-14.

Nellessen, E. *Zeugnis für Jesus und das Wort: Exegetische Untersuchungen zum lukanischen Zeugnisbegriff* (BBB 43; Bonn: Hanstein, 1976).

Rétif, A. "Témoignage et prédication missionaire dans les Actes des Apôtres," *NRT* 73 (1951) 152-165.

Prayer

Conn, H. M. "Luke's Theology of Prayer," *Christianity Today* 17 (1972) 290-292.

Harris, L. O. "Prayer in the Gospel of Luke," *Southwest Journal of Theology* 10 (1967) 59-69.

Monloubou, L. *La prière selon saint Luc* (LD 89; Paris: Cerf, 1976).

Ott, W. *Gebet und Heil: Die Bedeutung der Gebetsparänese in der lukanischen Theologie* (SANT 12; Munich: Kösel, 1965).

Samain, P. "Luc, évangéliste de la prière," *Revue diocésaine de Tournai* 2 (1947) 422-426.

Material Possessions

Degenhardt, H.-J. *Lukas Evangelist der Armen: Besitz und Besitzverzicht in den lukanischen Schriften: Eine traditions- und redaktionsgeschichtliche Untersuchung* (Stuttgart: Katholisches Bibelwerk, 1965).

Dupont, J. "Les pauvres et la pauvreté dans les évangiles et les Actes," *La pauvreté évangélique* (Lire la Bible 27; Paris: Cerf, 1971) 37-63.

Hauerwas, S. "The Politics of Charity," *Int* 31 (1977) 251-262.

Henry, A.-M. " 'Rompre ton pain avec celui qui a faim,' " *VSpir* 96 (1957) 227-265.

Koch, R. "Die Wertung des Besitzes im Lukasevangelium," *Bib* 38 (1957) 151-169.

Johnson, L. T. *The Literary Function of Possessions in Luke-Acts* (SBLDS 39; Missoula, MT: Scholars Press, 1977).

Mueller, H. "St. Luke on Poverty," *Cross and Crown* 18 (1966) 429-435.

Stöger, A. "Armut und Ehelosigkeit—Besitz und Ehe der Jünger nach dem Lukasevangelium," *Geist und Leben* 40 (1967) 43-59.

Wansbrough, H., "St. Luke and Christian Ideals in an Affluent Society," *New Blackfriars* 49 (1967-1968) 582-587.

Christian Life Together

Bernadicou, P. J. "Christian Community according to Luke," *Worship* 44 (1970) 205-219.

Bori, P. C. KOINŌNIA: *L'idea della comunione nell'ecclesiologia recente e nel Nuovo Testamento* (Testi e ricerche di scienze religiose 7; Brescia: Paideia, 1972).

Bruni, G. "La comunità in Luca," *Servitium* 7 (1973) 726-739.

Campenhausen, H. von. "Der urchristliche Apostelbegriff," *ST* 1 (1947) 96-130.

Flender, H. "Die Kirche in den Lukas-Schriften als Frage an ihre heutige Gestalt," in *Das Lukas-Evangelium* . . . (Wege der Forschung 280; ed. G. Braumann; Darmstadt: Wissenschaftliche Buchgesellschaft, 1974) 261-286.

LaVerdiere, E. A., and W. G. Thompson. "New Testament Communities in Transition: A Study in Matthew and Luke," *TS* 37 (1976) 567-597.

Lohfink, G. *Die Sammlung Israels: Eine Untersuchung zur lukanischen Ekklesiologie* (SANT 39; Munich: Kösel, 1975).

Menoud, P.-H. *La vie de l'église naissante* (Cahiers théologiques 31; Neuchâtel: Delachaux et Niestlé, 1952).

Roloff, J. *Apostolat—Verkündigung—Kirche: Ursprung, Inhalt und Funktion des kirchlichen Apostelamts nach Paulus, Lukas und den Pastoralbriefen* (Gütersloh: Mohn, 1965).

Schlier, H. "Die Kirche in den lukanischen Schriften," *Mysterium salutis* (eds. J. Feiner and M. Löhrer; Einsiedeln: Benziger, 1972) 4/1. 116-135.

Schnackenburg, R. *The Church in the New Testament* (New York: Herder & Herder, 1965) 55-68.

———— "Lukas als Zeuge verschiedener Gemeindestrukturen," *BibLeb* 12 (1972) 232-247.

Schneider, G. "Die zwölf Apostel als 'Zeugen': Wesen, Ursprung und Funktion einer lukanischen Konzeption," in *Christuszeugnis der Kirche* (eds. P.-W. Scheele und G. Schneider; Essen: Fredebeul und Koenen, 1970) 41-65.

Zingg, P. *Das Wachsen der Kirche: Beiträge zur Frage der lukanischen Redaktion und Theologie* (Orbis biblicus et orientalis 3; Fribourg: Universitätsverlag; Göttingen: Vandenhoeck und Ruprecht, 1974).

The Lucan Portrait of Jesus

Bernadicou, P. J. "Joy in the Gospel of Luke" (Dissertation extract; Rome: Gregorian University, 1970).

———— "The Lucan Theology of Joy," *ScEsp* 25 (1973) 75-98.

Samain, P. "Luc évangéliste de la bonté," *Revue diocésaine de Tournai* 2 (1947) 31-37.

———— "Luc évangéliste de la joie," *Revue diocésaine de Tournai* 2 (1947) 144-149.

VIII. SELECT BIBLIOGRAPHY

1. COMMENTARIES: MODERN

Anon. *Luc: Evangile; Actes des apôtres: Edition oecuménique* (Tournai: Casterman, 1966).

Abbott, L. *The Gospel according to Luke: With Notes, Comments, Maps and Illustrations* (New York: A. S. Barnes, 1878).

Arndt, W. *Bible Commentary: The Gospel according to St. Luke* (St. Louis: Concordia Publishing House, 1956).

Baird, W. "The Gospel according to Luke," in *The Interpreter's One-Volume Commentary on the Bible* (ed. C. M. Laymon; Nashville: Abingdon, 1971) 672-706.

Balmforth, H. *The Gospel according to St. Luke in the Revised Version with Introduction and Commentary* (Oxford: Clarendon, 1930; reprinted, 1958).

Barclay, W. *The Gospel of Luke* (2d ed.; Daily Study Bible series; Philadelphia: Westminster, 1956).

Bartelt, W. *Das Evangelium des hl. Lukas übersetzt und erklärt* (Die heilige Schrift für das Leben erklärt 12; Freiburg im B.: Herder, 1937).

Berkelbach van der Sprenkel, S. F. H. J. *Het evangelie van Lukas* ('s-Gravenhage: Boekencentrum, 1964).

Bisping, A. *Erklärung der Evangelien nach Markus und Lukas* (2d ed.; Exegetisches Handbuch zum Neuen Testament 2; Münster: Aschendorff, 1868) 137-498.

Blass, F. W. *Evangelium secundum Lucam, sive, Lucae ad Theophilum liber prior: Secundum formam quae videtur romanam* (Leipzig: Teubner, 1897).

Bliss, G. R. *Commentary on the Gospel of Luke* (Philadelphia: American Baptist Publication Society, 1884).

Browning, W. R. F. *The Gospel According to Saint Luke: Introduction and Commentary* (Torch Bible Paperbacks; 3d ed.; London: SCM, 1972; New York: Macmillan, 1960).

Bundy, W. E. *Jesus and the First Three Gospels: An Introduction to the Synoptic Tradition* (Cambridge, MA: Harvard University, 1955).

Burnside, W. F. *The Gospel according to St. Luke* (Cambridge: University Press, 1913).

Burton, H. *The Gospel according to St. Luke* (Expositor's Bible; London: Hodder & Stoughton, 1890).

Caird, G. B. *The Gospel of St Luke* (Pelican Gospel Commentary; Baltimore: Penguin, 1963).

Callan, C. J. *The Four Gospels: With a Practical Critical Commentary for Priests and Students* (3d ed.; New York: J. F. Wagner, 1918).

Cecilia, Madame. *The Gospel according to St Luke: With Introduction and Annotations* (Catholic Scripture Manuals; 2d ed.; London: Burns, Oates & Washbourne, 1930).

Ceulemans, F. C. *Commentarius in evangelium secundum Marcum et in evangelium secundum Lucam* (3d ed.; Mechlin: H. Dessain, 1931).

Clark, K. S. L. *The Gospel According to Saint Luke: With Commentary* (The Students' J.B.; London: Darton, Longman & Todd, [1972]).

Cleverley Ford, D. W. *A Reading of Saint Luke's Gospel* (London: Hodder & Stoughton, 1967).

Cook, F. C. *The Holy Bible . . . Commentary: New Testament, 1. St. Matthew—St. Mark—St. Luke* (New York: Scribner, 1889) 309-472.

Creed, J. M. *The Gospel according to St. Luke: The Greek Text, with Introduction, Notes, and Indices* (London: Macmillan, 1930).

Danker, F. W. *Jesus and the New Age According to St. Luke: A Commentary on the Third Gospel* (St. Louis: Clayton Publishing House, 1972).

———— *Luke* (Proclamation Commentaries; Philadelphia: Fortress, 1976).

De Wette, W. M. L. *Kurze Erklärung der Evangelien des Lukas und Markus* (3d ed.; Kurzgefasstes exegetisches Handbuch zum Neuen Testament 1/2; Leipzig: Weidmann, 1846).

Díaz, J. M. *El santo evangelio según San Lucas: Traducción y comentario* (Bogota: Editorial el Catolicismo, 1961).

Dillersberger, J. *The Gospel of Saint Luke* (Westminster, MD: Newman, 1958).

———— *Lukas: Das Evangelium des heiligen Lukas in theologischer und heilsgeschichtlicher Schau* (6 vols.; Salzburg: O. Müller, 1947-1949).

Drury, J. *Luke* (J. B. Phillips' Commentaries; New York: Macmillan, 1973).

Easton, B. S. *The Gospel according to St. Luke: A Critical and Exegetical Commentary* (New York: Scribner, 1926).

Eaton, R. O. *The Gospel according to Saint Luke: With Introduction, Text and Notes* (London: Catholic Truth Society, 1916).

Ellis, E. E. *The Gospel of Luke* (Century Bible; London: Nelson, 1966; 2d ed.; London: Oliphants, 1974).

Erdman, C. R. *The Gospel of Luke* (Philadelphia: Westminster, 1942).

Ernst, J. *Das Evangelium nach Lukas übersetzt und erklärt* (RNT; Pustet: Regensburg, 1977).

Farrar, F. W. *The Gospel According to St. Luke* (Cambridge Bible for Schools and Colleges; Cambridge: University Press, 1888).

Fendt, L. *Der Christus der Gemeinde: Eine Einführung in das Evangelium nach Lukas* (Die urchristliche Botschaft 3; 2d ed.; Berlin: Furche-V., 1937).

Fillion, L.-C. *La Sainte Bible . . . avec commentaires: 33. Evangile selon S. Luc* (Paris: Lethielleux, 1882).

———— *La Sainte Bible* (*texte latin et traduction française*) *commentée d'après la Vulgate et les textes originaux* (Paris: Letouzey et Ané, 1912) 285-460.

Foote, J. *Lectures on the Gospel According to Luke* (3d ed.; Edinburgh: Ogle and Murray, Oliver & Boyd, 1858).

Geldenhuys, N. *Commentary on the Gospel of Luke: The English Text with Introduction, Exposition, and Notes* (NICNT; Grand Rapids: Eerdmans, 1951; repr. 1972; London: Marshall, Morgan & Scott, 1950).

George, A. *L'annonce du salut de Dieu: Lecture de l'évangile de Luc* (Paris: Équipes enseignantes, 1963).

Gilmour, S. M. "The Gospel according to St. Luke," *IB* (Nashville: Abingdon, 1952) 8. 1-434.

Ginns, R. "The Gospel of Jesus Christ according to St. Luke," in *A Catholic Commentary on Holy Scripture* (eds. B. Orchard et al.; New York: Nelson, 1953) 935-970.

Godet, F. *Commentaire sur l'évangile de saint Luc* (2 vols.; 3d ed.; Paris: Librairie Fischbacher, 1888-1889).

————— *A Commentary on the Gospel of St. Luke* (trs. E. W. Shalders and M. D. Cusin; 2 vols.; 4th ed.; Edinburgh: Clark, 1887, 1889).

Gollwitzer, H. *La joie de Dieu* (Neuchâtel: Delachaux et Niestlé, 1958).

Gore, C. "The Gospel according to St. Luke," in his *A New Commentary on Holy Scripture Including the Apocrypha* (London: SPCK, 1928) part III, 207-239.

Gourbillon, R. P., and R. P. Rose. *L'évangile selon Saint Luc et les Actes des Apôtres* (Paris: Editions S. O. S., 1960).

Grant, F. C. "The Gospel according to Luke" *Nelson's Bible Commentary: Based on the Revised Standard Version* (New York: Nelson, 1962) 6. 209-323.

Gressmann, H. *Das Lukasevangelium* (rev. E. Klostermann; HNT II/1; Tübingen: Mohr, 1919).

Grundmann, W. *Das Evangelium nach Lukas* (2d ed.; THKNT 3; East Berlin: Evangelische Verlagsanstalt, 1961) [rev. ed. of F. Hauck, 1934].

Gutzwiller, Richard. *Meditationen über Lukas* (2 vols.; Zürich: Benziger, 1954).

Hahn, G. L. *Das Evangelium des Lucas erklärt* (2 vols.; Breslau: Morgenstern, 1892, 1894).

Harrington, W. *The Gospel according to St. Luke: A Commentary* (Westminster, MD: Newman, 1967).

————— "St. Luke," in *NCCHS* (eds. R. C. Fuller et al.; London: Nelson, 1969) 986-1021.

Hauck, F. *Das Evangelium nach Lukas* (THKNT 3; Leipzig: Deichert, 1934).

Herbst, W. *Das Lukasevangelium übersetzt und ausgelegt* (Bibelhilfe für die Gemeinde, Neues Testament 3; Kassel: Oncken, 1957).

Hillard, A. E. *The Gospel according to St. Luke with Introduction, Notes, and Maps* (London: Rivingtons, 1916).

Holtzmann, H. J. "Die Synoptiker," in *Handcommentar zum Neuen Testament* (2d ed.; Freiburg im B.: Mohr, 1892) 1. 1-304.

Iglesias, E. *El Salvador de los hombres: Comentarios al evangelio de S. Lucas* (2d ed.; Mexico: Buena Prensa, 1950).

Innitzer, T. *Kommentar zum Evangelium des heiligen Lukas mit Ausschluss der Leidensgeschichte* (3d ed.; Graz/Wien: Styria, 1922).

Javet, J. S. *L'évangile de la grâce. Commentaire sur l'évangile selon S. Luc* (Génève: Editions Labor et Fides, 1957).

Karris, R. J. *Invitation to Luke: A Commentary on the Gospel of Luke with the Complete Text from the Jerusalem Bible* (Image Books; Garden City, NY: Doubleday, 1977).

Klostermann, E. *Das Lukasevangelium* (HNT 5; 3d ed.; Tübingen: Mohr [Siebeck], 1975).

Knabenbauer, J. *Commentarius in quatuor s. evangelia, III: Evangelium secundum Lucam* (CSS 3/3; 2d ed.; Paris: Lethielleux, 1926).

Lagrange, M.-J. *Evangile selon Saint Luc* (Études bibliques; Paris: Gabalda, 1921; 3d ed., 1927; 4th ed., 1927; 8th ed., 1948).

Lampe, G. W. H. "Luke," in *Peake's Commentary on the Bible* (rev. ed.; eds. M. Black and H. H. Rowley; London: Nelson, 1962) 820-843.

Larère, C. *L'évangile selon saint Luc* (Le témoignage chrétien; Le Puy: X. Mappus, 1942).

Leal, J. "Evangelio según san Lucas," in *La sagrada escritura, Nuevo Testamento I* (Biblioteca de autores cristianos 207; Madrid: Editorial católica, 1961) 509-777.

Leaney, A. R. C. *A Commentary on the Gospel according to St. Luke* (BNTC; London: A. & C. Black, 1958).

Lenski, R. C. H. *The Interpretation of St. Mark's and St. Luke's Gospels* (Columbus, OH: Lutheran Book Concern, 1934).

Lindsay, T. M. *The Gospel according to St. Luke, with Introduction, Notes and Maps* (Edinburgh: T. & T. Clark, 1887).

Loisy, A. *Les évangiles synoptiques I et II* (Ceffonds: Chez l'auteur, 1907-1908).

——— *L'Evangile selon Luc* (Paris: E. Nourry, 1924; reprinted, Frankfurt am M.: Minerva, 1971).

Luce, H. K. *The Gospel according to St. Luke: With Introduction and Notes* (Cambridge: University Press, 1936).

MacEvilly, J. *An Exposition of the Gospel of St. Luke: Consisting of an Analysis of Each Chapter and of a Commentary Critical, Exegetical, Doctrinal, and Moral* (2d ed.; Dublin: Gill and Son, 1887).

Mandolfo, S. *Commento al Vangelo di Luca* (Turin: Marietti, 1970).

Manson, W. *The Gospel of Luke* (MNTC; London: Hodder & Stoughton, 1930; repr. New York: R. R. Smith, 1963).

Marchal, L. "Evangile selon Saint Luc," *La sainte Bible* (eds. L. Pirot and A. Clamer; new ed.; Paris: Letouzey et Ané, 1950) 10. 7-292.

Martindale, C. C. *The Gospel according to Saint Luke: With an Introduction and Commentary* (Westminster: Newman, 1957).

Melinsky, H. *Luke* (The Modern Reader's Guide to the Gospels; Libra book; London: Darton, Longman & Todd, 1966).

Meyer, H. A. W. *Critical and Exegetical Handbook to the Gospels of Mark and Luke* (tr. from 5th Germ. ed. by R. E. Wallis; rev. and ed., W. Stewart; Edinburgh: Clark, 1880) vol. 2.

Migne, J.-P. "In Evangelium secundum Lucam commentaria," *Scripturae sacrae cursus completus* (Paris: Montrouge, 1842) 22. 229-1448.

Moorman, J. R. H. *The Path to Glory: Studies in the Gospel according to Saint Luke* (London: SPCK; Greenwich, CT: Seabury, 1960).

Morgan, G. C. *The Gospel according to St. Luke* (New York: F. H. Revell, 1931).

Morris, L. *The Gospel according to St. Luke: An Introduction and Commentary* (TNTC; Grand Rapids, MI: Eerdmans; London: Inter-Varsity, 1974).

Mueller-Jurgens, W. *Das Evangelium des Lukas: Neu bearbeitet nach der Vulgata und mit Erläuterungen versehen* (Nürnberg: Glock und Lutz, 1958).

Norwood, F. W., and F. R. Barry. *St. Luke: A Little Library of Exposition, with New Studies* (London: Cassell, 1926).

Oosterzee, J. J. van. "The Gospel according to Luke," in *A Commentary on the Holy Scriptures: Critical, Doctrinal, and Homiletical* (ed. P. Schaff; New York: Scribner, 1866) 2, part 2.

Osty, E. *L'Evangile selon Saint Luc* (BJ; Paris: Cerf, 1948; 3d ed., 1961).

Owen, J. J. *A Commentary, Critical, Expository and Practical on the Gospel of Luke* (New York: Leavitt & Allen, 1857).

Phillips, J. B. *St. Luke's Life of Christ: Translated into Modern English* (London: Collins, 1956).

Plummer, A. *A Critical and Exegetical Commentary on the Gospel according to S. Luke* (ICC; 5th ed.; New York: Scribner, 1922; 8th impr., 1964). Cited as Plummer, *Gospel*.

Prete, B. *Vangelo secondo Luca: I. Vangelo dell'infanzia; II. Vangelo della vita publica* (Biblioteca universale Rizzoli; Milan: Rizzoli, 1961).

Ragg, L. *St. Luke with Introduction and Notes* (Westminster Commentaries; rev. ed.; London: Methuen, 1922).

Rengstorf, K. H. *Das Evangelium nach Lukas* (NTD 3; 9th ed.; Göttingen: Vandenhoeck und Ruprecht, 1962; 14th ed., 1969).

Rienecker, F. *Das Evangelium des Lukas* (Wuppertaler Studienbibel; Wuppertal: Brockhaus, 1959; 4th ed., 1972).

Rigaux, B. *Témoignage de l'Évangile de Luc* (Pour une histoire de Jésus 4; Bruges: Desclée de Brouwer, 1970).

Robertson, A. T. *A Translation of Luke's Gospel with Grammatical Notes* (New York: Doran, 1923).

Rose, V. *Évangile selon saint Luc: Traduction et commentaire* (Paris: Bloud, 1909).

Schanz, P. *Commentar über das Evangelium des heiligen Lucas* (Tübingen: F. Fues, 1883).

Schegg, P. *Evangelium nach Lukas übersetzt und erklärt* (2 vols.; Munich: J. T. Lentner, 1863).

Schlatter, A. *Das Evangelium des Lukas: aus seinen Quellen erklärt* (2d ed.; Stuttgart: Calwer, 1960).

——— "Das Evangelium nach Lukas," in *Erläuterungen zum Neuen Testament* (3 vols.; 5th ed.; Stuttgart: Calwer, 1936) 1. 153-406.

Schmid, J. *Das Evangelium nach Lukas* (RNT 3; 3d ed.; Regensburg: Pustet, 1955; 4th ed., 1960).

Schneider, G. *Das Evangelium nach Lukas* (2 vols.; Ökumenischer Taschenbuchkommentar zum Neuen Testament, 3/1-2; Gütersloh: G. Mohn; Würzburg: Echter, 1977).

Schürmann, H. *Das Lukasevangelium: Erster Teil: Kommentar zu Kap. 1, 1-9, 50* (HTKNT 3/1; Freiburg: Herder, 1969).

Soubigou, L. *Sous le charme de l'évangile selon Saint Luc* (Paris: Desclée de Brouwer, 1933).

Staab, K. *Das Evangelium nach Markus und Lukas* (Echterbibel 5/1; Würzburg: Echter, 1956).

Stöger, A. *Das Evangelium nach Lukas* (Geistliche Schriftlesung 3/1-2; Düsseldorf: Patmos, 1964).

———— *The Gospel according to St. Luke* (New Testament for Spir. Reading, 5-6; 2 vols.; New York: Herder, 1969).

Stoll, R. F. *The Gospel according to St. Luke: A Study of the Third Gospel with a Translation and Commentary* (New York: Pustet, 1931).

Stuhlmueller, C. "The Gospel according to Luke," in *JBC* 2. 115-164 (※44).

———— "Evangelio según san Lucas," in *Comentario biblico "San Jeronimo"* (Madrid: Ediciones Cristiandad, 1972) 3. 295-420.

Summers, R. *Commentary on Luke: Jesus, the Universal Savior* (Waco, TX: Word Books, 1972).

Tenney, M. C. "The Gospel according to Luke," *The Wycliffe Bible Commentary* (eds. C. F. Pfeiffer and E. F. Harrison; Chicago: Moody, 1962) 1027-1070.

Thompson, G. H. P. *The Gospel according to Luke in the Revised Standard Version* (New Clarendon Bible; New York: Oxford University, Oxford: Clarendon, 1972).

Tinsley, E. J. *The Gospel according to Luke* (Cambridge Bible Commentary: *NEB;* Cambridge: University Press, 1965).

Tolbert, M. O. *Luke* (The Broadman Bible Commentary 9; Nashville: Broadman, 1970) 1-187.

Tuya, M. de. "Evangelio de San Lucas," *Biblia comentada: Texto de la Nácar-Colunga* (ed. profesores de Salamanca; BAC 239; Madrid: Editorial católica, 1964) 5. 731-935.

Valensin, A., and J. Huby. *Evangile selon Saint Luc* (VS 3; 41st ed.; Paris: Beauchesne, 1952).

Ward, B. *The Holy Gospel according to Saint Luke with Introduction and Notes* (London: Catholic Truth Society, 1915).

Weiss, B. *Die Evangelien des Markus und Lukas* (Meyerkommentar 1/2; 7th ed.; Göttingen: Vandenhoeck und Ruprecht, 1883).

———— "The Gospel according to Luke," *A Commentary on the New Testament* (4 vols.; trs. G. H. Schodde and E. Wilson; New York: Funk & Wagnalls, 1906) 2. 1-212.

Weiss, J. *Die Evangelien des Markus und Lukas* (MeyerK 1/2; 9th ed.; Göttingen: Vandenhoeck und Ruprecht, 1901).

Wellhausen, J. *Das Evangelium Lucae übersetzt und erklärt* (Berlin: G. Reimer, 1904).

Zahn, T. *Das Evangelium des Lucas ausgelegt* (4th ed.; Leipzig: Deichert, 1930).

2. COMMENTARIES: PATRISTIC, MEDIEVAL, RENAISSANCE, REFORMATION

Origen (A.D. 185-254), *Homilies on Luke.*

Rauer, M. *Origenes Werke: Die Homilien zu Lukas in der Übersetzung des Hieronymus und die griechischen Reste der Homilien und des Lukas-Kommentars* (GCS 35; Leipzig: Hinrichs, 1930; 2d rev. ed. [GCS 49], 1959).

"Homiliae in Lucam," PG 13. 1801-1902.

"Scholia in evangelium secundum Lucam," PG 17. 311-370.

"Fragmenta (ex Makarii Chrysocephali orationibus) in Lucam," PG 13. 1901-1910.

Crouzel, H., F. Fournier, and P. Périchon. *Origène: Homélies sur S. Luc* (SC 87; Paris: Cerf, 1962).

Lomiento, G. *L'esegesi origeniana del vangelo di Luca (Studio filologico)* (Quaderni di "Vetera christianorum" 1; Bari: Istituto di letteratura cristiana antica, 1966).

Eusebius of Caesarea (260-340), *Eis to kata Loukan euangelion*, PG 24. 529-606.

Ephraem of Syria (306-373), *Commentary on the Diatessaron.*

Leloir, L. *Saint Ephrem: Commentaire de l'évangile concordant: Version arménienne* (CSCO 145; Louvain: Durbecq, 1954; CSCO 137, 1953).

Ambrose of Milan (339-397), *Expositio evangelii secundum Lucam libris X comprehensa*, PL 15. 1607-1944; CSEL 32/4 (ed. C. Schenkel, 1902); CCLat 14 (ed. M. Adriaen, 1957).

Rollero, P. *La "Expositio evangelii secundum Lucam" di Ambrogio come fonte della esegesi agostiniana* (Pubblicazioni della facoltà di lettere e filosofia 10/4; Turin: Università di Torino, 1958).

Titus of Bostra (d. ca. 378), *Homilies on Luke.*

Sickenberger, J. *Titus von Bostra: Studien zu dessen Lukashomilien* (TU 21/1; Leipzig: Hinrichs, 1901).

John Chrysostom (347-407), *Commentarii, qui extant in sacrosanctum Iesu Christi evangelium secundum Marcum et Lucam* (Antwerp: I. Steels, 1547).

Cyril of Alexandria (d. 444), *Homilies on Luke*, PG 72. 475-950.

Sickenberger, J. "Fragmente der Homilien des Cyrill von Alexandrien zum Lukasevangelium," *TU* 34/1 (1909) 63-108.

Chabot, I.-B. *S. Cyrilli Alexandrini commentarii in Lucam* (CSCO 70 [=Syriac 27]; Louvain: L. Durbecq, 1954; tr. R.-M. Tonneau, CSCO 140 [=Syriac 70], 1-227).

Rücker, A. *Die Lukas-Homilien des hl. Cyrill von Alexandrien: Ein Beitrag zur Geschichte der Exegese* (Leipzig: Drugulin, 1911).

Eucherius of Lyons (d. ca. 449), "Liber instructionum ad Salonium libri duo (in Lucae evangelium)," PL 50. 799-800; CSEL 31 (ed. C. Wotke, 1894) 121-123.

Arnobius (junior, d. ca. 451), *Adnotationes ad quaedam evangeliorum loca*, PL 53. 569-580, esp. pp. 578-580.

Anon. *Synopsis latina evangeliorum ibericorum antiquissimorum secundum Matthaeum, Marcum, Lucam* (ed. J. Molitor; CSCO 256, subsidia, 24; Louvain: Secrétariat du CSCO, 1965).

Anon. *Catenae graecorum patrum in Novum Testamentum: Tomus II. In evangelia S. Lucae et S. Joannis* (ed. J. A. Cramer; Oxford: University Press, 1844) 1-174.

Paterius of Brescia (d. 604), "Expositio veteris et novi testamenti, lib. III," PL 79. 1057-1074.

Bede the Venerable (673-735), "In Lucae evangelium expositio, libri VI," PL 92. 307-634; CCLat 120 (ed. D. Hurst, 1960) 1-425.

Sedulius Scotus (d. 830), "Expositiuncula in argumentum secundum Lucam," PL 103. 285-290.

Walafrid Strabo (808-849), "Expositio in evangelium Lucae," PL 114. 893-904; "Glossa ordinaria" [rightly ascribed?], PL 114. 243-356.

Christian Druthmarus (d. 850), "Expositio brevis in Lucam evangelistam," PL 106. 1503-1514.

Alulf (11th century), "Expositio evangelii secundum Lucam," PL 79. 1199-1240.

Nicetas of Heracleia (11th century), *Catena on Luke.*

Sickenberger, J. *Die Lukaskatene des Niketas von Herakleia untersucht* (TU 22/4; Leipzig: Hinrichs, 1902).

Theophylact of Euboea (11th century), "Hermeneia eis to kata Loukan euangelion," PG 123. 683-1126.

Euthymius Zigabenus (d. 1118), "To kata Loukan euangelion," PG 129. 853-1102.

Bruno Astensis (d. 1125), "Commentaria in Lucam," PL 165. 333-452.

Dionysius bar Salibi (d. 1171), *Commentarii in evangelia, f. 196r—f. 256r: Explicatio evangelii s. Lucae* (CSCO 95 [=Syriac 47, 1953]; 113 [=Syriac 60, 1939] 225-412; Latin tr., CSCO 114 [=Syriac 61, 1940] 117-337).

Peter Comestor (d. 1179), "Historia scholastica: Historia evangelica," PL 198. 1537-1644.

Petrus Comestor, *Historia scholastica* (Lyon: N. Petit and H. Penet, 1534) 184-226.

Thomas Aquinas (d. 1274), "Catena super Lucae evangelium," *Opera omnia* (25 vols.; New York: Musurgia, 1949) 12. 1-255.

Albert the Great (d. 1280), "In Lucam," *Opera omnia* (38 vols.; ed. A. Borgnet; Paris: Vivès, 1890), vols. 22-23.

Cajetan, Thomas de Vio (1469-1534). *In quattuor evangelia et acta apostolorum commentarii* (5 vols.; Lyon: Jacobus et Petrus, 1639) 4. 171-276.

Erasmus, D. (1469-1536), "In evangelium Lucae paraphrasis," *Opera* (Basel: Froben, 1540) 7. 213-369.

Luther, Martin (1483-1546), "Evangelion Sanct Lucas," *Die deutsche Bibel* (WA DB 6; Weimar: H. Böhlaus, 1929) 208-325.

Hoffmeister, J. (1509-1547), *Commentaria in Marcum et Lucam evangelistas* (Louvain: A. Byrckmann, 1562) 133-592.

Calvin, John (1509-1564), *Harmonia ex evangelistis tribus composita, Mat-*

thaeo, Marco & Luca commentariis . . . exposita . . . (Geneva: E. Vignon, 1595) 1-376.

Pringle, W. (tr.) *Commentary on a Harmony of the Evangelists, Matthew, Mark and Luke* (Calvin's Commentaries 31-33; Grand Rapids: Eerdmans, 1957).

Estella, Diego de (d. 1575), *In sacrosanctum Iesu Christi evangelium secundum Lucam enarrationum tomus I [-II]* (2 vols. in one; Lyon: S. Beraud, 1581).

Maldonado, J. (1533-1583), "Commentarii in evangelium D. Lucae," *Commentarii in quatuor evangelistas* (Paris: J. Billaine, 1651; 3d ed., rev. C. Martin; 2 vols.; Mainz: F. Kirchhem, 1863) 2. 1-370.

Cornelius à Lapide (Cornelis Cornelissen van den Steen, 1567-1637), "Commentarius in evangelium S. Lucae," in *Commentaria in Scripturam Sacram* (ed. nova, A. Crampon; Paris: L. Vivès, 1877) 16. 1-284.

Cordier, B. (1592-1650), *Catena sexaginta quinque graecorum patrum in S. Lucam, quae quatuor simul evangelistarum introducit explicationem, luce et latinitate donata . . .* (Antwerp: Plantin, 1628).

Hugo Grotius (1583-1645), "Annotationes in evangelium Lucae," *Annotationes in Novum Testamentum* (ed. nova; Halle: Orphanotrophei bibliopolium, 1769) 1. 669-942.

Chemnitz, M., P. Leyser, and J. Gerhard (16-17th cc.), *Harmonia quatuor evangelistarum* (2 vols.; Frankfurt/Hamburg: Z. Hertelij, 1652).

Calovius, A. (1612-1686), *Biblia novi Testamenti illustrata: Tomus 1. exhibens harmoniam evangelistarum* (Dresden/Leipzig: J. C. Zimmermann, 1719).

Bengel, J. A. (1687-1752), *Gnomon of the New Testament . . .* (2 vols.; trs. C. T. Lewis and M. R. Vincent; Philadelphia: Perkinpine & Higgins, 1888).

3. MONOGRAPHS OF A GENERAL NATURE

Barrett, C. K. *Luke the Historian in Recent Study* (London: Epworth, 1961).

Bartsch, H. W. *Wachet aber zu jeder Zeit: Entwurf einer Auslegung des Lukasevangeliums* (Hamburg-Bergstedt: H. Reich, 1963).

Bouwman, G. *Das dritte Evangelium: Einübung in die formgeschichtliche Methode* (Düsseldorf: Patmos, 1968).

Bovon, F. *Luc le théologien: Vingt-cinq ans de recherches (1950-1975)* (Le monde de la Bible; Neuchâtel/Paris: Delachaux et Niestlé, 1978).

Braumann, G., ed. *Das Lukas-Evangelium: Die redaktions- und kompositionsgeschichtliche Forschung* (Wege der Forschung 280; Darmstadt: Wissenschaftliche Buchgesellschaft, 1974).

Brown, S. *Apostasy and Perseverance in the Theology of Luke* (AnBib 36; Rome: Biblical Institute, 1969).

Busse, U. *Die Wunder des Propheten Jesus: Die Rezeption, Komposition und Interpretation der Wundertradition im Evangelium des Lukas* (Forschung zur Bibel 24; Stuttgart: Katholisches Bibelwerk, 1977).

Cadbury, H. J. *The Making of Luke-Acts* (New York: Macmillan, 1927).

Cassidy, R. J. *Jesus, Politics, and Society: A Study of Luke's Gospel* (Maryknoll, NY: Orbis, 1978).

Conzelmann, H. *The Theology of St Luke* (New York: Harper & Brothers, 1960).

Flender, H. *St Luke: Theologian of Redemptive History* (Philadelphia: Fortress, 1967).

Foakes Jackson, F. J., and K. Lake. *The Beginnings of Christianity, Part I, The Acts of the Apostles* (5 vols.; London: Macmillan, 1939, 1922, 1926, 1933, 1933).

Franklin, E. *Christ the Lord: A Study in the Purpose and Theology of Luke-Acts* (London: SPCK, 1975).

George, A. *Études sur l'oeuvre de Luc* (Sources bibliques; Paris: Gabalda, 1978).

Green-Armytage, A. H. N. *A Portrait of St Luke* (London: Burns and Oates, 1955).

Hannam, W. L. *Luke the Evangelist: A Study of His Purpose* (New York/Cincinnati: Abingdon, 1935); British title, *In the Things of My Father: A Study of the Purpose of Luke the Evangelist* (London: Epworth, 1954).

Harnack, A. *New Testament Studies, I: Luke the Physician: The Author of the Third Gospel and the Acts of the Apostles* (London: Williams and Norgate, 1908).

Hayes, D. A. *The Most Beautiful Book Ever Written: The Gospel according to Luke* (New York: Eaton and Mains, 1913).

Hobart, W. K. *The Medical Language of St. Luke: A Proof from Internal Evidence that "the Gospel according to St. Luke" and "the Acts of the Apostles" Were Written by the Same Person, and That the Writer Was a Medical Man* (Dublin: Hodges, Figgis; London: Longmans, Green, 1882).

Holtz, T. *Untersuchungen über die alttestamentlichen Zitate bei Lukas* (TU 104; Berlin: Akademie, 1968).

Immer, K. *Erzähltes Evangelium: Aus dem Sondergut des Lukas, 1. Teil* (BibS[N] 11; Neukirchen: Erziehungsverein, 1956).

Jervell, J. *Luke and the People of God: A New Look at Luke-Acts* (Minneapolis: Augsburg, 1972).

Keck, L. E., and J. L. Martyn, eds. *Studies in Luke-Acts: Essays Presented in Honor of Paul Schubert* (Nashville: Abingdon, 1966). Cited as *Studies in Luke-Acts*.

McLachlan, H. *St. Luke, the Man and His Work* (Manchester: University Press; New York: Longmans, Green, 1920) [Publications of the University of Manchester, Theology Series, no. 3].

Marshall, I. H. *Luke: Historian and Theologian* (Grand Rapids, MI: Zondervan, 1970).

Maurice, F. D. *The Gospel of the Kingdom of Heaven: A Course of Lectures on the Gospel of St. Luke* (London/New York: Macmillan, 1888).

Meinertz, M. *Das Lukasevangelium* (Biblische Zeitfragen 3/2; 3. Aufl.; Münster i.W.: Aschendorff, 1912).

Minear, P. S. *To Heal and to Reveal: The Prophetic Vocation according to Luke* (New York: Seabury, 1976).

Morgenthaler, R. *Die lukanische Geschichtsschreibung als Zeugnis: Gestalt und Gehalt der Kunst des Lukas* (2 vols.; Zürich: Zwingli, 1949).

Moorman, J. R. H. *The Path to Glory: Studies in the Gospel according to Saint Luke* (London: SPCK, 1960).

Morton, A. Q., and G. H. C. Macgregor. *The Structure of Luke and Acts* (London: Hodder & Stoughton, 1964).

Neirynck, F., ed. *L'Evangile de Luc: Problèmes littéraries et théologiques: Mémorial Lucien Cerfaux* (Bibliotheca ephemeridum theologicarum lovaniensium 32; Gembloux: Duculot, 1973).

Pallis, A. *Notes on St Luke and the Acts* (London: Oxford University, 1928).

Radl, W. *Paulus und Jesus im lukanischen Doppelwerk: Untersuchungen zu Parallelmotiven im Lukasevangelium und in der Apostelgeschichte* (Europäische Hochschulschriften 23/49; Frankfurt: P. Lang, 1975).

Ramsay, W. M. *Was Christ Born at Bethlehem? A Study on the Credibility of St. Luke* (3d ed.; London: Hodder & Stoughton, 1905).

Reicke, B. I. *The Gospel of Luke* (tr. R. Mackenzie; Richmond: John Knox, 1964).

Reiling, J., and J. L. Swellengrebel, *A Translator's Handbook on the Gospel of Luke* (Helps for Translators 10; Leiden: Brill, 1971).

Rese, M. *Alttestamentliche Motive in der Christologie des Lukas* (SNT 1; Gütersloh: Gerd Mohn, 1969).

Sahlin, H. *Der Messias und das Gottesvolk: Studien zur protolukanischen Theologie* (ASNU 12; Uppsala: Almqvist & Wiksell, 1945).

Schleiermacher, F. E. D. *A Critical Essay on the Gospel of St. Luke* (London: J. Taylor, 1825).

Schneider, G. *Parusiegleichnisse im Lukas-Evangelium* (SBS 74; Stuttgart: Katholisches Bibelwerk, 1975).

Schütz, F. *Der leidende Christus: Die angefochtene Gemeinde und das Christuskerygma der lukanischen Schriften* (BWANT 89; Stuttgart: Kohlhammer, 1969).

Stonehouse, N. B. *The Witness of Luke to Christ* (London: Tyndale, 1951).

Talbert, C. H. *Literary Patterns, Theological Themes, and the Genre of Luke-Acts* (SBLMS 20; Missoula, MT: Scholars Press, 1974).

———— *Luke and the Gnostics: An Examination of the Lucan Purpose* (Nashville: Abingdon, 1966).

———— ed. *Perspectives on Luke-Acts* (Special Studies Series 5; Danville, VA: Association of Baptist Professors of Religion; Edinburgh: Clark, 1978).

Wilson, S. G. *The Gentiles and the Gentile Mission in Luke-Acts* (SNTSMS 23; Cambridge: University Press, 1973).

Zingg, P. *Das Wachsen der Kirche: Beiträge zur Frage der lukanischen Redaktion und Theologie* (Orbis biblicus et orientalis 3; Fribourg: Universitätsverlag; Göttingen: Vandenhoeck und Ruprecht, 1974).

4. GENERAL WORKS FREQUENTLY QUOTED

Banks, R., ed. *Reconciliation and Hope: New Testament Essays on Atonement and Eschatology Presented to L. L. Morris on His 60th Birthday* (Grand Rapids, MI: Eerdmans, 1974).

Blinzler, J. *The Trial of Jesus* (Westminster, MD: Newman, 1959).

Brown, R. E. *Jesus God and Man: Modern Biblical Reflections* (Milwaukee: Bruce, 1967).

Bultmann, R. *Exegetica: Aufsätze zur Erforschung des Neuen Testaments* (ed. E. Dinkler; Tübingen: Mohr [Siebeck], 1967).

Bundy, W. E. *Jesus and the First Three Gospels* (Cambridge, MA: Harvard University, 1955).

Cerfaux, L., *Recueil Lucien Cerfaux: Etudes d'exégèse et d'histoire religieuse* (3 vols.; Gembloux: Duculot, 1954, 1954, 1962).

Dodd, C. H. *The Parables of the Kingdom* (New York: Scribner, 1961).

Finegan, J. *The Archeology of the New Testament* (Princeton: Princeton University, 1969).

Fitzmyer, J. A. *The Genesis Apocryphon of Qumran Cave 1: A Commentary* (BibOr 18A; Rome: Biblical Institute, 1971).

Hahn, F. *The Titles of Jesus in Christology: Their History in Early Christianity* (London: Lutterworth, 1969).

Jeremias, J. *The Eucharistic Words of Jesus* (Philadelphia: Fortress, 1977).

———— *Jerusalem in the Time of Jesus* (Philadelphia: Fortress, 1969).

———— *New Testament Theology: The Proclamation of Jesus* (New York: Scribner, 1971).

———— *The Parables of Jesus* (rev. ed.; New York: Scribner, 1963).

Kertelge, K. *Die Wunder Jesu im Markusevangelium: Eine redaktionsgeschichtliche Untersuchung* (SANT 23; Munich: Kösel, 1970).

Kümmel, W. G. *Introduction to the New Testament* (Nashville: Abingdon, 1975).

———— *Promise and Fulfilment: The Eschatological Message of Jesus* (SBT 23; Naperville, IL: Allenson, 1957).

Lindars, B., and S. S. Smalley, eds. *Christ and the Spirit in the New Testament in Honour of Charles Francis Digby Moule* (Cambridge: University Press, 1973).

Milik, J. T. *Ten Years of Discovery in the Wilderness of Judaea* (Naperville, IL: Allenson, 1959).

Moule, C. F. D. *An Idiom-Book of New Testament Greek* (Cambridge: University Press, 1953).

Moulton, J. H., and W. F. Howard, *A Grammar of New Testament Greek* (4 vols.; vols. 3 and 4 by N. Turner; Edinburgh: Clark, 1906, 1929, 1963, 1976).

Perrin, N. *Rediscovering the Teaching of Jesus* (New York: Harper & Row, 1967).

Schrage, W. *Das Verhältnis des Thomasevangeliums zur synoptischen Tradition und zu den koptischen Evangelienübersetzungen: Zugleich ein Beitrag zur gnostischen Synoptikerdeutung* (BZNW 29; Berlin: de Gruyter, 1964).

Schramm, T. *Der Markus-Stoff bei Lukas: Eine literarkritische und redaktionsgeschichtliche Untersuchung* (SNTSMS 14; Cambridge: University Press, 1971).

Streeter, B. H. *The Four Gospels: A Study of Origins, Treating of the Manu-*

script Tradition, Sources, Authorship, & Dates (London: Macmillan, 1924).

Turner, N. *Grammatical Insights into the New Testament* (Edinburgh: Clark, 1965).

5. BIBLIOGRAPHIES ON THE LUCAN GOSPEL

Anon. "Bibliographie des études récentes sur l'évangile de Luc," BVC 98 (1971) 90-94.

Navone, J. *Bibliografia lucana* (Rome: Gregorian University, 1969).

Williams, C. S. C. "Commentaries and Books on St Luke's Gospel," *Theology* 62 (1959) 408-414.

TRANSLATION
AND COMMENTARY

THE PROLOGUE

Luke's intention in recording the account of what Jesus did and taught: a reliable account addressed to Theophilus

---

1. THE PROLOGUE
(1:1-4)

1 [1] Since many writers have undertaken to compile an orderly account of the events that have come to fulfillment among us, [2] just as the original eyewitnesses and ministers of the word passed them on to us, [3] I too have decided, after tracing everything carefully from the beginning, to put them systematically in writing for you, Theophilus, [4] so that Your Excellency may realize what assurance you have for the instruction you have received.

COMMENT

None of the other canonical Gospels begins, as does the Lucan Gospel, with a distinctive literary prologue. The earliest Gospel, Mark, begins almost *in medias res*, with at most one line of introduction. Matthew begins his "book" with a genealogy in imitation of OT models, which relates it to earlier Palestinian Jewish literary types; this opening lacks the formality of the Lucan prologue. The Johannine Gospel begins with an adapted hymnic composition which shares with the Lucan prologue a certain detachment from the rest of the work. The Third Gospel from its very outset betrays the author's intention of relating his work consciously to contemporary literature of the Greco-Roman world.

Luke's prologue is constructed as a formal literary period. Some modern English translations, in breaking up the long sentence for the benefit of present-day readers, thereby obscure its obvious literary character. By its very style the prologue stands out not only from other Gospels, but also from the rest of the Lucan writings themselves. It is a formal beginning of the composition and has to be compared with two other passages in the Lucan writings, which resemble it somewhat in style but do not match it in perfection. They are Luke 3:1-2, the formal beginning of the traditional gospel material at the start of Jesus' ministry, and Acts 1:1-2, the prologue to the second volume. All three instances are examples of free Lucan composition, independent of any source-material, in which Luke displays his ability to write in a literary mode that was contemporary.

In studying the prologue, the reader should not fail to note its balanced form, in which both the protasis (vv. 1-2) and the apodosis (vv. 3-4) contain three parallel phrases. This is best seen in the Greek text itself because it cannot be preserved easily in translation. There is also a formal contrast between the "many" and "I too," between "compile an orderly account" and "put them systematically in writing," and lastly between the secondary subordinate clauses in both the protasis and the apodosis ("just as . . . ," "so that . . ."). See BDF § 464.

Commentators have often compared Luke's prologue with the classical historical prefaces of Herodotus, Thucydides, and Polybius and with the prefaces of Hellenistic treatises on various subjects, such as Dioscorides Pedanius (*De materia medica* 1.1; a pharmacological treatise), Hippocrates (*De prisca medicina*), Aristeas (*Ep. ad Philocraten* § 1), and Josephus (*Ag. Ap.* 1.1 §§ 1-3; 2.1 § 1). *Against Apion* is particularly pertinent to illustrate the Lucan composition, for this two-volume treatise of Josephus offers close parallels in its prologues to those of Luke.

> In the history of the *Antiquities,* most excellent Epaphroditus, I believe that I have made sufficiently clear to any who would come upon that work the antiquity of our Jewish race, the purity of its original stock, and the manner in which it established itself in the land that we occupy today. That history embraces a period of five thousand years and was written by me in Greek on the basis of our sacred books. But since I see that a number of persons, influenced by malicious slander from certain people, discredit statements in my history concerning our antiquity and offer as proof of the comparative modernity of our race the fact that it has not been considered worthy of mention by the best-known Greek historians, I consider it my duty to write briefly about all these points, to convict our detractors of opprobrium and deliberate falsehood, to correct the ignorance of others, and to instruct whoever desires to know the truth about the antiquity of our race (1.1 §§ 1-3).

> In the first volume of this work, most esteemed Epaphroditus, I proved the antiquity of our race, substantiating my statements with the writings of Phoenicians, Chaldeans, and Egyptians, in addition to citing as witnesses many Greek historians . . . (2.1 § 1).

Luke's prologue is not only characterized by its periodic structure, in imitation of Hellenistic literary prologues, but also by the use of formal, literary language. The NOTES call attention to this quality of such words as "since," "many," "have undertaken," "compile an orderly account," "events," "passed on," and "Excellency." Such vocabulary is paralleled at times in Hellenistic writers. Luke's imitation of them, however, is not slavish. It may relate the work that he is composing to contemporary literary fashion, but the nuances of the language have also to be understood in terms of his account of the Christ-event.

Luke writes as a third-generation Christian, carefully marking his distance from the "events," and the eyewitnesses and ministers of the word (see the NOTE on 1:2 about whether one or two groups are involved in this phrase) on whom he depends. He clearly sets out his own proper contribution: He "has done his homework," in investigating the story of Jesus and its sequel, with a claim that rivals the boast of any historian. Three qualities are claimed for his investigation, completeness, accuracy, and thoroughness ("from the beginning"); and another for his composition, order ("systematically"). (The role these four qualities play in a modern assessment of Luke's historical value is another question; see p. 15 above.)

The prologue also makes it clear that Luke was not interested solely in recounting the "facts" of the Christian movement like a secular historian, or in merely giving an interpretation of them from some aloof or uninvolved position. Moreover, the prologue has also to be understood in relation to that of Acts, which explicitly names Jesus, unlike the prologue of the first volume. Furthermore, it has to be related to the two volumes as a whole, for the "events" in the two of them are the subject-matter of his "narrative." Yet in the prologue Luke refers to them as having the note of "fulfillment"—they belong to a past and a present which are not unrelated to what God has promised in the OT. They are the stuff of salvation-history, even though Luke does not so put it in the prologue itself.

Moreover, the end of the prologue announces to Theophilus and readers like him Luke's goal; his stated purpose is set forth in v. 4, "so that Your Excellency may realize what assurance you have for the instruction you have received." Asphaleia, "assurance," is put in the emphatic position at the end of the periodic sentence. But what is the nature of that assurance? It has been said that Luke's purpose was apologetic, "to defend Christians against unfavorable reports which had come to the ears of Theophilus" (H. J. Cadbury, Expositor 8/21 [1921] 432); and others have proposed similar apologetic views, even making Theophilus an influential Roman official. This view of the matter, however, is based on a minimal interpretation of v. 4 and fails to reckon with the relation of the prologue to the Lucan work as a whole.

The NOTES will make clear the reasons for our view that Luke has in mind a broader perspective. According to it the "assurance" would rather be an aspect of the teaching of the church in Luke's own day. In seeking to trace matters to their beginning, Luke discloses the solidity of the early church's catechetical instruction (see further M. Devoldère, *NRT* 56 [1929] 714-719).

This does not mean that Luke has sought to guarantee the kerygma. His aim is quite different from that. What guarantees the kerygma for Luke is the Spirit, guiding the ministry and preaching of Jesus itself, and thereafter, when he becomes the one proclaimed, that of the disciples as well.

Thus Luke makes his literary ambition serve his theological intention. He acknowledges that he has made use of earlier presentations of the Jesus-story and of other sources of apostolic tradition. He is aware of the fact that he is dependent on tradents before him and associates himself with them ("I too have decided . . ."). Whether one will want to characterize all that Luke does in his two volumes as "theological reflection," as G. Klein ("Lukas 1,1-4," 200) seems to, one can agree with him that Luke has written his prologue as a "theological program." (This is not to admit all the interpretations of details in Klein's article.) There is more to the prologue than the bland interpretation of Cadbury would tolerate.

Luke insists that he has a larger goal than the mere recounting of what he was able to get from his predecessors. He wants to recount the Jesus-story and its sequel as a historian writing in a certain mold. But that mold is not that of the secular Hellenistic historian, for once the prologue is complete one realizes that Luke writes far more in the mode of OT biblical history.

The "everything" that he has investigated and recounted includes the infancy narrative and the sequel to the Jesus-story. These enable him to recount the events "systematically," i.e. in a given literary order, periodized, and guided by promise and fulfillment.

Though the prologue is the first part of the Lucan Gospel that the reader encounters, it was probably the last part composed, being added at the time the infancy narrative was written, as will be seen below.

NOTES

1 1. *Since.* The first word of Luke's prologue is the formal literary causal conjunction *epeidēper*, "since, inasmuch as," which expresses a reason for some fact or condition already known. Normally, it introduces a causal clause which follows the main clause (e.g. Josephus *J.W.* 1.1,6 § 17; Philo *Legatio ad Gaium* § 164). It occurs only here in the entire Greek Bible (the LXX and the NT). Luke's use of it, then, even though it is not in the usual postpositive position, indicates his concern to relate his entire composition to a well-known lit-

erary introductory form; and other literary expressions in the prologue confirm
this impression. The sentence of Luke should be compared with Acts 15:24-26
which is another formal statement, opening with *epeidē* and recording the results of deliberation.

many writers. It is not easy to say how many Luke would have had in mind
in using *polloi.* One suggestion has been made in the Introduction (see p. 65
above). The use of *polys,* alone and in compounds, in prologues and epilogues
is a known rhetorical device, and its meaning is perhaps not to be pressed for
this reason. Cf. Sir Prologue:1; Heb 1:1; Acts 24:2,10; John 20:30; see further examples in H. J. Cadbury, *Beginnings* 2. 492; J. Bauer, *NovT* 4 (1960)
263-266. In mentioning predecessors, Luke is implying his dependence on earlier written records of what "Jesus began to do and teach" (Acts 1:1) and his
right to attempt something similar. From the rest of the prologue, with its assertions about accuracy, acquaintance, completeness, and order, it would not
be amiss to think that Luke also implies that in some sense he is going beyond
the attempts of his predecessors.

Is it possible to mention some of the writers whom Luke might have had in
mind, in referring to *polloi?* Luke's dependence on "Mk," "Q," and "L" is a
widely admitted conclusion of modern Synoptic studies (see pp. 63-65 above).
These would at least be implied, but we must remember that "L" does not designate a source that was solely written. Moreover, despite V. Hartl (*BZ* 13
[1915] 334-337) and the proponents of the Griesbach hypothesis, it is quite
unlikely that Matthew in any form is to be considered among the "many"
about whom Luke writes here. Moreover, there is no reason to think that these
"many writers" were necessarily or in all cases distinct from the "eyewitnesses"
and "ministers of the word" in v. 2, though the general tenor of the statement
would suggest that they were, like Luke, recipients of a church tradition. In
mentioning them, even in a stereotyped and conventional way, Luke is
implicitly taking a position with reference to them; and that position becomes
clearer in the following words.

have undertaken. Or "have attempted." Etymologically, the verb *epecheir-
ēsan* means "have set their hand to. . . ." It too is a word found in the prologues of literary treatises of Hellenistic writers (e.g. Hippocrates *De prisca
medicina*) to describe the effort of literary composition. It is sometimes used in
a neutral sense (Josephus *Ag. Ap.* 1.2 § 13; Polybius *Histories* 2.37,4; 3.1,4;
12.28,3) and may be so understood here. It is, however, sometimes used with a
pejorative nuance, "they attempted (but did not really succeed)." It thus may
connote a presumptuous undertaking (see Acts 9:29; 19:13); it is used in this
way by Josephus, of others who tried to write Jewish history (*Life* 9 § 40; 65 §
338). See also Hermas *Similitude* 9.2,6. Commentators, then, from Origen on
(*Hom. in Lucam* 1; ed. C. Lommatzsch, 5.87), have often suggested that Luke
too intends this nuance here. It is hard to be certain. On the one hand, Luke
writes *kamoi,* "I too," in v. 3, which might suggest that he looks to his many
predecessors as examples. On the other, the contrast of himself with them and
his pretensions to accuracy, acquaintance, completeness, and order as well as
his claim to offer "assurance" (*asphaleia*) suggest that he envisages his task as

one needed in the church of his day. Their works seemed perhaps mere attempts to record the tradition about the momentous events that had taken place. They were faced with the problem of handing on a tradition; Luke is conscious of this task too and proposes to do it again, in his own better way (which is still to be specified).

to compile an orderly account. Lit. "to arrange in proper order an account." The meaning of the rare literary verb *anatassesthai* is "to arrange, repeat in order" (Plutarch *Moralia* 968C). It also occurs in a wider sense of "drawing up, compiling" (Aristeas *Ep. ad Philocraten* § 144). Luke seems to imply that this is his aim too. His composition is also to be an "account" (*diēgēsis*), different from the tradition referred to in v. 2.

The term *diēgēsis*, "a narrative account," was often used in classical and Hellenistic Greek literature of historical writing, even though it was not so confined. Plato (*Republic* 3.392D) used it of an account of things past, present, or future; Aristotle (*Rhetorica* 3.16, 1) of the past. The orator Isocrates used the related verb *diēgeisthai* in the sense of narrating past achievements (*Panathenaicus* 152; *Trapeziticus* 3). The *Letter of Aristeas* used it three times, of the narrative of the author's visit to Eleazar the high priest of the Jews (§ 1, 8, 322). Josephus likewise uses it in the sense of an account about the Jews who returned from the Babylonian Captivity to Jerusalem (*Ant.* 11.13,10 § 68); and he often describes his own writing precisely with this term (*J.W.* 7.3,2 § 42; 8.8,1 § 274; *Ant.* 1.2,3 § 67; 4.8,4 § 196; 9.10,2 § 214; 12.3,3 §§ 136, 137; 19.9,1 § 357; 20.8,3 § 157). In his *Life* (65 § 336) he relates the word specifically to the writing of history. The same relationship is known to Plutarch (*Non posse suaviter* 10, 1093B [*historia kai diēgēsis*]) and to Lucian (*Quomodo Historia conscribenda sit* 55). Compare the use of it in 2 Macc 2:32, at the end of the epitomist's prologue; also 6:17. Etymologically, it would denote a composition that "leads through to an end," a comprehensive story which aims at being something more than a mere collection of notes or a compilation of anecdotes. One should contrast with *diēgēsis*, used here of the two volumes, the quasi-title that Luke uses for the Gospel at the start of Acts, *prōtos logos*, "first account" (lit. "first word"). See further pp. 172-174 above.

events. The *pragmata* about which Luke writes can be compared to the "facts" or "happenings" that any historian would be interested in. But as the Lucan account unfolds, the reader learns that the "events" are not being recounted merely as facts, nor even with the concern of a secular historian (ancient or modern). They are for Luke events of salvation-history, and the significance of them depends on the way one interprets the fulfillment mentioned. In the concrete, the "events" refer not only to the deeds of the ministry of Jesus, his passion, death, burial, and resurrection, but also to the sequel to all this, the spread of the "word of the Lord" from Jerusalem to the end of the earth in the activity of the chosen witnesses.

that have come to fulfillment. The pf. ptc. *peplērophorēmenōn* expresses a condition of the events which have come to pass in Luke's recent past and continue in their effect into his present. Etymologically, *plērophorein* means "bear to full measure, bring to fullness." It was not much used by pre-Christian Greek writers. In the LXX it occurs only at Eccl 8:11 ("is filled up," rendering Hebrew *mālē'*). It is found often enough, however, in Greek papyrus texts from Egypt in the sense of "paying in full" (debts), or "satisfying" (legal obligations); see MM, 519; A. Deissmann, *LAE*[2], 86-87. In Rom 4:21; 14:5 it has the meaning of "being fully convinced." Cf. Col 4:12.

For the Lucan use of the verb here three different interpretations have been proposed. First, the simplest meaning, exploiting the sense that is found in the papyri, is "have been completed, accomplished." This is used in the *RSV* and *NEB*, undoubtedly under the influence of H. J. Cadbury (*Beginnings* 2. 495-496); see also M.-J. Lagrange, *Luc*, 3. It was also used in many ancient versions (OL, OS, Vg, Sah, Boh). It is supported by the use of the verb in 2 Tim 4:5,17. This meaning would involve a bland admission that some events have come to pass in Luke's time. Second, making use of the sense in Romans, K. H. Rengstorf (*Lukas*, 14) proposes the meaning "have been fully assured." Rengstorf uses the first meaning in his translation, but then comments that the word actually has a double meaning: not only "have been accomplished," but also "have been fully assured." This he finds suggested by the end of the prologue itself, where Luke is concerned to give "assurance" to Theophilus. Origen too seems to have understood the word in this way. But Cadbury (ibid.) sensed the difficulty in this interpretation: Can one apply to events the passive of a verb meaning "convince," in the sense of things of which one is convinced? Third, a number of modern commentators prefer the meaning, "have been fulfilled," or "have come to fulfillment" (thus G. H. Whitaker, *Expos* 8/20 [1920] 264; O. A. Piper; E. Lohse, *EvT* 14 [1954] 261; G. Delling, *TDNT* 6. 310; E. Trocmé, *"Le 'livre des Actes'* . . ." 46; A. M. Pope).

The third meaning is the one that should be preferred. The first is too non-committal and does not do justice to the sense of the Lucan prologue. Cadbury says the suggestion that the fulfillment of Scripture is being intended needs hardly to be taken seriously. But one wonders why. The verb *plērophorein* should be regarded as a more literary or formal expression, suited to the prologue, for the verbs *plēroun* or *pimplanai* that Luke uses frequently enough in his Gospel to bring out the idea of fulfillment (see 1:20,57; 2:6,21,22; 4:21; 9:31; 21:22,24; 24:44). Luke intends something more here, in using *plērophorein*, than such neutral verbs as *ginesthai* (Josephus *Ag. Ap.* 1.9 § 47) *tynchanein*, or the passive of *poiein*, which he could well have used to express mere occurrence or accomplishment. There is no other known instance of *pragmata* being used with *plērophorein*, and this remains a difficulty. But the emphasis in the Lucan writings on the fulfillment of what was spoken of in the OT seems to call for the third meaning of the verb here. W. Grundmann (*Lukas*, 44) has tried to combine the second and the third meanings, but this is scarcely correct.

among us. The first pl. pronoun is not simply editorial; nor is it to be identified with the "us" in v. 2. It denotes the people who are now affected by salvation-history. In v. 1 it includes the "many writers" as well as "the original eyewitnesses and ministers of the word" from whom Luke distinguishes himself in v. 2. It undoubtedly includes also Luke and other third-generation Christians, which is the sense of "us" in v. 2. But it is scarcely to be restricted to that sense. Furthermore, Luke's use of "us" here has to be related to the use of the first pl. pron. in the We-Sections of Acts (see p. 36 above). Luke implies that he has been a contemporary of and a witness to *at least some* of the events which he is going to recount; it does not mean that he witnessed any of the ministry of Jesus or that he was present for the majority of the events of the early church recounted in Acts. (This relation between the "us" of v. 1 and the We-Sections can be maintained, even with the sense of the participle *parēkolouthēkoti* adopted in v. 3 below.)

2. *just as.* In the best Greek mss. the form of this conjunction is *kathōs,* "just as, even as," a form that is frowned on by strict ancient Atticist grammarians like Phrynichus (see BDF § 453). The Codex Bezae has *katha,* a more correct post-classical form, which expresses the same comparison. This conjunction introduces a statement of the reliability of the earlier accounts, which is important for Luke, even though he is inclined to present the matter in a better way (see H. Schürmann, *Lukasevangelium* 1.8).

the original eyewitnesses and ministers of the word. The Greek of this phrase is not easily translated. Another, more literal, translation of *hoi ap' archēs autoptai kai hypēretai genomenoi tou logou* might be: "the original eyewitnesses who became ministers of the word." The problem lies in whether Luke is referring here to one or to two groups of persons who shaped the early tradition. K. Stendahl (*The School of St. Matthew* [ASNU 20; Lund: Gleerup, 1954] 32-34) and R. Balducelli (*CBQ* 22 [1960] 419) think that two groups in the early church are meant. The order of the nouns and the use of the conj. *kai,* "and," would seem to favor this interpretation. But the single art. *hoi,* which governs the whole construction, the position of the ptc. *genomenoi,* "becoming," which separates not the two nouns but the noun *hypēretai,* "ministers," from the prep. phrase "of the word," and the position of the other prep. phrase *ap' archēs,* "from the beginning," would seem to favor the view that the two phrases are a double description of one group. If the latter interpretation were correct, the double description would refer to the disciples of Jesus, who were the "eyewitnesses" of his ministry, and who eventually became the "ministers of the word." When this phrase so understood is related to Acts 1:21-22, where the criteria for the Twelve are set forth—a "man" (*andra*), a witness of the resurrection, and one who "shared our company all the time that the Lord Jesus moved among us, from the baptism of John until the day he was taken up"—it would seem to refer to the Apostles, understood as the Twelve. The same idea would be confirmed by Acts 10:37-39. The choice is difficult; I prefer the latter interpretation. See R. J. Dillon, *From Eyewitnesses to Ministers of the Word* (AnBib 82; Rome: Biblical Institute, 1978) 269-272.

In any case, Luke is distancing himself from the ministry of Jesus by two layers of tradition; between him and it there is the testimony of eyewitnesses who have become ministers of the word.

In itself, *hypēretēs* means "a servant, helper, assistant," and it designated assistants to physicians, kings, courts, the Sanhedrin, and in a synagogue (Luke 4:20). In Acts 13:5 John Mark is called an "assistant" of Barnabas and Saul, precisely in a context in which they announced "the word of God" in a Jewish synagogue at Salamis in Cyprus. See R. O. P. Taylor, *ExpTim* 54 (1942-1943) 136-138.

Even though "the word" may be intended here merely as a "general term applicable to the story of Christian origins" (Cadbury, *Beginnings* 2. 500), the use which the absolute form *ho logos* acquires in Acts (e.g. 8:4; 10:36; 11:19; 14:25; cf. Luke 8:12-15) gives it the significant overtone of "the word of God." In Acts 6:4 we read of the "ministry (*diakonia*) of the word," and that should be considered here. See further A. Feuillet, " 'Témoins oculaires. . . .' "

Not too much should be made of the tense or the position of the Greek ptc. *genomenoi,* because *autoptēs genomenos* is an ordinary Greek phrase (see Josephus *Ag. Ap.* 1.10 § 55) for "being an eyewitness." Luke has expanded it by the addition of "and ministers of the word."

No matter how one resolves the first question about Luke's reference to one or two groups in this phrase, there is a further question about the specific meaning of "the ministers (of the word)." Does the phrase refer to an "exactly defined group with the community," instructors in the early church who exercised a function analogous to the Pharisaic-rabbinic institution which controlled the transmission of its "traditions of the fathers" (Gal 1:14)? According to H. Riesenfeld (*The Gospel Tradition and Its Beginnings* [London: Mowbray, 1957]), "the beginning of the Gospel tradition lies with Jesus himself," and this phrase designates a group of "authorized transmitters" of the tradition about Jesus which already possessed a special character as "holy word."

B. Gerhardsson (*Memory and Manuscript* [ASNU 22; Lund: Gleerup, 1961] 243-245) specifically relates this group to "the ministry of the word" (Acts 6:4), which the apostles were to perform. That they might not be distracted from it, aides were chosen in the early Jerusalem church to "serve tables." Moreover, this may be the "apostolic ministry" (hendiadys, *diakonia kai apostolē*) used of the Twelve in Acts 1:25. This activity may suggest that there was a controlled transmission of the words and deeds of Jesus in the early church that shaped the tradition to which Luke refers in these verses. This attempt to define the meaning of "ministers of the word" more specifically has some attraction, but it is not without its difficulties. It would seem to cast Jesus in the role of a rabbi vis-à-vis his disciples. Yet for all of Luke's concern to depict Jesus training his Galilean witnesses, especially during the travel account, he is rarely so portrayed in the Gospel itself (and even less so earlier in the gospel tradition, e.g. in Mark). Moreover, the developed methods of rabbinic transmission of traditions in Judaism after A.D. 70 cannot without further ado be predicated of the pre-70 situation, especially of the form of Pharisaism then current in Palestine. But even granting that the Riesenfeld-Gerhardsson thesis is somewhat overdrawn, there is something in it. Not only is Luke aware of a tradition prior to him, but Paul also alludes to something similar in 1 Cor 15:1-2 (especially *tíni logō,* "in what form"), 11; cf. 11:23. See further M. Smith, "A Comparison of Early Christian and Early Rabbinic Tradition," *JBL* 82 (1963) 169-176; B. Gerhardsson, *Tradition and Transmission in Early Christianity* (ConNT 20; Lund: Gleerup, 1964); J. Neusner, "The Rabbinic Traditions about the Pharisees before A.D. 70: The Problem of Oral Transmission," *JJS* 22 (1971) 1-18; B. Gerhardsson, *Die Anfänge der Evangelientradition* (Wuppertal: Brockhaus, 1977); J. A. Fitzmyer, "Judaic Studies and the Gospels: The Seminar," in *The Relationships among the Gospels: An Interdisciplinary Dialogue* (ed. W. O. Walker, Jr.; San Antonio: Trinity University, 1978) 237-258, esp. pp. 254-256.

original. Lit. "from the beginning." On this phrase, see the NOTE on v. 3 below.

passed them on. The verb *paredosan* occurs here in a literary, classical form, not elsewhere attested in the NT. The more usual NT aor. indic. of *didonai* (with *-k-*) is found in Luke 24:20,42; Acts 1:26; 3:13; 15:30 (cf. BDF § 95.1). This is another indication of the literary form of the prologue.

The verb *paradidonai* is the technical NT word for handing on a tradition in the early church; see 1 Cor 11:2,23; 15:3; Mark 7:13; Jude 3; cf. B. Gerhardsson, *Memory and Manuscript,* 288-306. Though the tradition to which Luke refers here could include written forms, it is more likely an oral tradition, because of the contrast with the "accounts" attempted already by other writers.

to us. Here Luke distinguishes his own generation of Christians from the eyewitnesses and ministers of the word.

3. *I too have decided.* Lit. "it seemed good to me too," to which some OL mss. add, "and to the holy Spirit." The latter phrase, however, is a scribal gloss introduced from Acts 15:28. For grammatical parallels to *edoxe kamoi,* see Acts 15:22,25,28,[34]. Luke states here that he writes because others have attempted an account in no more advantageous a situation than his; indeed, he seems to imply that he is really in a better position.

after tracing everything carefully. The meaning of the pf. act. ptc. *parēkolouthēkoti* is quite disputed—in fact, it is the crucial word in the modern interpretation of the Lucan prologue. Several senses are attested for the compound verb *par-akolouthein:*

1) "follow" (physically), "accompany" (at one's side), Demosthenes *Orationes* 42.21;
2) "follow with the mind" (as a speech, a teaching, a rule), 1 Tim 4:6; 2 Tim 3:10; cf. Cadbury, *Beginnings* 2. 501;
3) "follow, result from" (logically; intransitive use), Mark 16:17;
4) "follow closely, keep in touch with" (as some event or movement), Demosthenes *De corona* 53; cf. MM, 485-486;
5) "follow up, trace, investigate, inform oneself about" (past events), Demosthenes *Orationes* 18.172; 19.257; Josephus *Ag. Ap.* 1.10 § 53; cf. BAG, 624.

In which sense does Luke intend the word to be understood?

Patristic writers, who sought to stress the apostolicity of NT writings, called Luke *sectator apostolorum,* "a follower of the apostles," understanding *parēkolouthēkoti* in the first sense (see Irenaeus *Adv. haer.* 3.10; Justin *Dialogus cum Tryphone Judaeo* 103). This scarcely fits the context; the modern debate centers on the fourth and fifth senses. In recent times Cadbury (especially in *Beginnings* 2. 501-503; but also *Expos* 8/24 [1922] 401-420) has sought to show that *parakolouthein,* used figuratively in contexts dealing with events, means either "having kept in close touch" with them or "having been intimately associated" with them (=sense 4 above). Indeed, Cadbury insisted that there is no Hellenistic example of the verb meaning "to investigate" (*NTS* 3 [1956-1957] 131). He would, therefore, "leave the possibility open that the author is claiming for himself actual presence and participation in the events described and that this participle is a paraphrase of *autoptai kai hypēretai genomenoi*" (*Beginnings* 2. 502). Such presence or contact would contradict Luke's distinguishing himself from the eyewitnesses and ministers, precisely as a recipient of their tradition. For this reason, J. Dupont, who otherwise follows Cadbury closely, sums up the sense of the prologue, using the same interpretation of this crucial word as Cadbury, thus: "The writer is presenting himself as a contemporary and eyewitness of *a part of the facts* he recounts and this statement indicates the importance that should be attributed to the passages he writes in the first person" (*Sources of Acts*, 102 [my italics]). Cadbury's interpretation has been used by many interpreters (e.g. E. Trocmé, B. W. Bacon).

It has not, however, gone without objection. In particular, E. Haenchen (*ZTK* 58 [1961] 363-365; *TLZ* 87 [1962] 43) has insisted that the verb can mean "investigate, follow up, trace" and that it is so used by Josephus. Moreover, one cannot be "intimately associated" with an event *akribōs*, "accurately, carefully," and the adverb *anōthen* has to be given the unusual meaning, "for a long time." Haenchen thus returns to what has been the traditional interpretation of *parēkolouthēkoti*, "having traced, investigated." See further M. Goguel, W. Grundmann, M.-J. Lagrange, K. Rengstorf, J. Schmid, N. Stonehouse, M. Zerwick, etc. It seems to be the preferable sense, although this choice does not rule out Luke's being contemporary with some of the events (see the comment on "among us" in v. 1). The ptc. should not be made the basis of any discussion of the historical value of the Lucan account.

everything. I.e. all the "events" and the accounts of the "many" who preceded him. This is the first of the three characteristics of Luke's investigation, completeness, accuracy, and thoroughness. It is a rhetorical protestation about completeness.

In my translation of the word *pasin* I have taken the pronoun to be neuter, referring to the *pragmata*, "events," mentioned above. It could be taken as masculine, referring to the many writers, eyewitnesses, and ministers. This seems to have been the way in which Justin Martyr understood the phrase (*Dial.* 103; cf. Eusebius *Hist. eccl.* 3.4,6; Epiphanius *Panarion* 51.7). But the intervening adv. *anōthen* and the lack of a def. art. with *pasin* favor the vaguer neuter meaning.

The use of *pasin* has been called a "pardonable exaggeration" (J. H. Ropes, *JTS* 25 [1923-1924] 71). It is such in the interpretation of the ptc. *parēkolouthēkoti* as meaning close contact or intimate association with the events; but if the ptc. be understood of investigation, "everything" could apply to those events that Luke actually records.

carefully. Or "accurately." This is the second characteristic of Luke's investigation. The adv. *akribōs* is also used by Josephus in a context in which he uses *parakolouthein* (*Ag. Ap.* 1.10 § 53). It suggests a quality of the investigation Luke had engaged in.

However, some commentators (e.g. Rinaldi, " 'Risalendo,' " 252; F. Mussner,

"Kathexēs," 253) have preferred to take this adv. *akribōs* with the following infin. *grapsai,* i.e., "to put accurately in writing." This is not impossible, but it is not the most convincing way to understand the adv. See Schürmann, *Lukasevangelium,* 10 n. 61.

from the beginning. This is the third characteristic of his investigation. The adv. *anōthen* means "from above." When used in a temporal sense, it can be the equivalent of *ap' archēs* (1:2), as Acts 26:4-5 suggests. There Luke uses the same expressions in parallelism about Paul's life, without any difference in meaning (see E. Haenchen, *ZTK* 58 [1961] 363-364; *TLZ* 87 [1962] 43; *Acts,* 682). See further Philo *De Vita Mosis* 2.48; cf. BAG, 76.

Another meaning of *anōthen,* "for a long time," has been favored by Cadbury (*Beginnings* 2. 502-503), and J. Dupont (*Sources of Acts,* 106-107). But this disregards the parallelism of *ap' archēs.* It is favored because of the meaning given to the ptc. *parēkolouthēkoti* by them.

But if *anōthen* and *ap' archēs* are to be understood as parallel, what is the *archē* to which they refer? They have been understood as referring to the births of John the Baptist and Jesus, with which the Lucan Gospel begins. Thus E. Osty, A. Plummer (*Gospel,* 4), G. Schneider (*Evangelium nach Lukas,* 39). But given that Luke associates *archē* and cognate forms with the beginning of the period of Jesus (see 3:23; 23:5; Acts 1:1,22; 10:37; cf. Luke 5:10), it may be asked whether he does not mean this here too. (Much of the decision about this will depend on how much historical detail one will admit is contained in the Lucan infancy narrative.) Here the beginning seems to be that of the apostolic tradition.

to put them systematically in writing for you. Lit. "to write for you in order." As in the case of the adv. *akribōs,* so too here with *kathexēs,* one may ask whether it is used with the ptc. *parēkolouthēkoti* or with the infin. *grapsai.* It could refer to the former, denoting an "orderly" investigation, but, as Cadbury (*Beginnings* 2. 505) has noted, that would make the new colon (after the participial clause) begin with the enclitic *soi,* which is most unnatural. Hence it denotes a mode of composition.

The meaning of the adv. *kathexēs* is quite contested. In the NT it is peculiar to Luke (see 8:1; Acts 3:24; 11:4; 18:23). The word is a compound of *kata* and *hexēs,* an adverb that Luke also uses (7:11; 9:37; Acts 21:1; 25:17; 27:18). Years ago, Cadbury (*Beginnings* 2. 504-505) regarded them as synonyms, and although M. Völkel (*NTS* 20 [1973-1974] 295) has contested this, I fail to see any difference between *kathexēs* in Luke 8:1 and *hexēs* in 7:11. This is, however, a minor issue. The meaning of *kathexēs* was said by Cadbury to be "successively" or "continuously" (*Beginnings* 2. 505), and it has usually been understood to denote either a well-ordered presentation of the Jesus-story (K. H. Rengstorf, *Evangelium nach Lukas,* 15) or one which agrees with the actual succession of events (E. Lohse, "Lukas als Theologe," 260). G. Klein has more recently tried to depart from the idea of order or succession in the adverb, to stress its reference to content (*Umfang des Stoffes*). Though he admits that it occurs at times with a chronological aspect, the real emphasis is on the "complete presentation of material" ("Lukas 1,1-4," 194-195). But M. Völkel (*NTS* 20 [1973-1974] 289-299) has investigated all the Lucan passages anew and a number of extrabiblical occurrences of the adverb and shown that the best meaning to be given to the word is "in a continuous series." About the same time J. Kürzinger ("Lk 1, 3," 249-255) suggested, using material that Cadbury (*Beginnings* 2. 505) had discussed, that *kathexēs* should really be understood as "hereinafter," i.e. in the account that follows on the prologue. A little later F. Mussner ("*Kathexēs* im Lukasprolog," 253-255) tried to establish that it meant that Luke would write "without a gap" (*lückenlos*), i.e. without leaving anything out. He based this opinion on the material Völkel had amassed from extrabiblical texts where *kathexēs* stood together with some expression for completion or wholeness (as it does in the Lucan prologue, where it is used with *pasin*, "everything"). The trouble with this interpretation is that, compared with Mark, Luke has left out a considerable amount of material. Kürzinger's interpretation is not impossible, but the material presented by Völkel seems to indicate that the adverb does express a succession or order.

But what kind of order? Cadbury (*Beginnings* 2. 505), having admitted that the best meaning is "successively" or "continuously," then made the strange remark that this need not "imply accordance with some fixed order, either chronological, geographical, or literary." This is baffling. I readily agree that attempts to insist on Luke's historical sense have overstated the chance of chronological agreement with the actual succession of events. But why rule out literary order? To me that is the most evident sense of the adverb, and it is suggested by the use of *kathexēs* by Luke himself in Acts 11:4, where Peter explains his Joppa visit to the apostles and brethren in Judea, "speaking to them in order," i.e. in a systematic presentation.

More recently, G. Schneider, taking up this same notion, has contended that the systematic presentation involves the phases of salvation-history in the Lucan account and the motif of promise and fulfillment. This makes sense, as long as one realizes that the involvement is not explicit here. Luke merely says that he is going to write for Theophilus in a systematic presentation; that is a veiled reference to the Period of Israel, the Period of Jesus, and the Period of the Church.

Theophilus. Though my translation separates "Your Excellency" from Theophilus, the Greek text actually has the voc. *kratiste Theophile,* "most excellent Theophilus." Theophilus is a proper name commonly used from the third century B.C. on, found in both Greek papyri from Egypt and inscriptions (see MM, 288). It was used by both Gentiles and Jews (for the latter see Aristeas *Ep. ad Philocraten* § 49). The Theophilus mentioned here is met again in the introduction to the second volume (Acts 1:1); he is otherwise unknown.

There is no reason to doubt his existence as a real person to whom Luke dedicates his two-volume composition. Though the dedication does not mean that he was the *patronus* of Luke, who was to see to the copying or publication of the Lucan work, dedication did at times mean that in the Greco-Roman world of the time (compare Maecenas and Horace *Odes* 1:1; Atticus and Cicero). The Ps.-Clementine *Recognitions* (10.71) subsequently identified Theophilus as a great personage of Antioch, who made his house into a basilica and eventually became the bishop of Antioch. This is undoubtedly a worthless legend of later date. There is no reason to interpret the name symbolically, as if it were a designation for the Christian reader of Luke's writings, someone "beloved of God" or "loving God." This symbolic interpretation is said to date from the time of Origen. It would understand *theophile* as a substantivized adjective. But *theophilos* as an adjective is hardly attested before the Byzantine period; its earlier form, which would then be expected here, would be *theophilēs* (cf. Aristeas *Ep. ad Philocraten* § 287; *Martyrium Polycarpi* 3).

It is not possible to say for certain whether Theophilus was an official of some sort. The adj. *kratiste,* which also occurs in Acts 23:26; 24:3; 26:25 (of the procurator of Judea), is the common Greek equivalent for the Latin *egregius* in the Roman world of the time. The latter was often used as a title for a member of the *ordo equester,* the "knights" of Roman society. But was it so used this early? From the time of the emperor Septimius Severus on, it became the title of an equestrian *procurator. Kratistos* is also attested from the first century A.D. as the equivalent of Latin *optimus,* a honorific appellation for any official. At most it would imply that Theophilus was socially respected and probably well off, or highly placed in the society to which Luke had access.

Was Theophilus a Christian, an influential non-Christian, or a God-fearer? It is almost impossible to answer this question with certainty. Part of the reason is the evidence already presented about the name and title; part of it is the interpretation that is given to the last clause of v. 4. As the latter is interpreted below, Theophilus is best regarded not as an interested non-Christian, but as a catechumen or a neophyte. Because Luke dedicates the two volumes to Theophilus, it means that his opus is not a private writing; Theophilus stands for the Christian readers of Luke's own day and thereafter.

4. *may realize.* Or "may come to know." The verb *epiginōskein* in Lucan usage means either "to recognize" an object or fact, or "to learn" or "acquire knowledge" (see Acts 19:34; 22:24; 23:28; 24:8,11). Being a compound verb in *epi-,* it may imply the acquiring of profound knowledge. If so, it would stand in contrast to the rest of the verse.

what assurance you have for the instruction you have received. The interpretation of this last clause is not easy, and it has been diversely translated. H. J. Cadbury (*The Making of Luke-Acts,* 347) rendered it: "that you may gather the correctness as regards the accounts that you have been given to understand." Or, it could be translated with similar implications, "in order that you may know the reliability of the stories which have been reported to you" (H. W. Beyer, *TDNT* 3. 639, who also gives an alternate: "in order that you may have certainty concerning the doctrines in which you have been instructed").

Crucial in the understanding of the clause are three words: (a) *asphaleia,* (b) *logōn,* and (c) the verb *katēchein.* Luke has put *asphaleia* in the emphatic position at the end of the periodic sentence. Fundamentally, *asphaleia* means "safety" (either physical or societal [="security"]). In Greek papyri it can also denote a document that serves as a "written security," sometimes even in a commercial sense (see MM, 88). In Lucan writings it would seem to be the same as the expression *to asphales* used as the object of verbs of knowing or writing (Acts 21:34; 22:30; 25:26). This limits the meaning of it to something like "reliability, assurance, guarantee," in a cognitive or communicative context.

As for the meaning of *logos* in this context, opinions again vary. Cadbury (*Beginnings* 2. 509) took it as the equivalent of *pragmata* in v. 1, i.e. "events reported," and noted the use of *logos* in Luke 7:17 as a paraphrase of *ēchos*, "talk, report." That *logos* could have this meaning is shown by the fact that Luke uses it at times in the sense of "thing, matter" (Acts 8:21; 15:6), as the LXX uses *logos* to translate Hebrew *dābār* in the same sense (e.g. Gen 29:13). But the sense of *logos* here must depend in part on what one understands of the next word to be discussed, for Luke also uses *logos* at times in the sense of "instruction, teaching" (Luke 4:32; 10:39) or of a "message" to be accepted (Luke 1:20; 6:47). The verb *katēchein* can mean simply "report, tell, inform" (as Acts 21:21,24 make clear). But it is also used by Luke in the sense "to instruct, teach," as can be seen from Acts 18:25. Cf. Gal 6:6; Rom 2:18.

When the Lucan writings, and especially Acts, were treated as an *apologia* for Paul, a bland interpretation of this last clause, such as was proposed by Cadbury, would have been regarded as preferable. But the other interpretation fits the Lucan writings better, viz. that Luke writes for Theophilus, a catechumen or neophyte, in order to give him assurance about the initial instruction that he has received. The last clause would then be literally translated, "so that you may realize the assurance of the matters (*or* the teachings) about which you have been instructed." In the Greek text the rel. pron. obj. of *katēchēthēs* should be *hous* (acc. masc. pl.), but has been attracted to the gen. case of *logōn*. This is a common Lucan feature (see BDF § 294).

BIBLIOGRAPHY (1:1-4)

Bacon, B. W. "Le témoignage de Luc sur lui-même," *RHPR* 8 (1928) 209-226.

Bauer, J. "Polloi Luk 1,1," *NovT* 4 (1960) 263-266.

Cadbury, H. J. "Commentary on the Preface of Luke," in *Beginnings* 2. 489-510.

———— "The Knowledge Claimed in Luke's Preface," *Expos* 8/24 (1922) 401-420.

———— *The Making of Luke-Acts* (New York: Macmillan, 1927) 344-348, 358-359.

———— "The Purpose Expressed in Luke's Preface," *Expos* 8/21 (1921) 431-441.

———— "'We' and 'I' in Luke-Acts," *NTS* 3 (1956-1957) 128-132.

Devoldère, M. "Le prologue du troisième évangile," *NRT* 56 (1929) 714-719.

Du Plessis, I. I. "Once More: The Purpose of Luke's Prologue (Lk i 1-4)," *NovT* 16 (1974) 259-271.

Dupont, J. *The Sources of Acts: The Present Position* (London: Darton, Longman & Todd, 1964) 101-112.

Feuillet, A. "'Témoins oculaires et serviteurs de la parole' (Lc i 2ᵇ)," *NovT* 15 (1973) 241-259.

Goodspeed, E. J. "Some Greek Notes: I. Was Theophilus Luke's Publisher?" *JBL* 73 (1954) 84.

Haenchen, E. "Das 'Wir' in der Apostelgeschichte und das Itinerar," *ZTK* 58 (1961) 329-366.

———— Review of J. Dupont, *Les sources du livre des Actes* (Bruges: Desclée de Brouwer, 1960), *TLZ* 87 (1962) 42-43.

Hartl, V., "Zur synoptischen Frage: Schliesst Lukas 1,1-3 die Benutzung des Matthäus aus?" *BZ* 13 (1915) 334-337.

Klein, G. "Lukas 1,1-4 als theologisches Programm," in *Zeit und Geschichte: Dankesgabe an R. Bultmann* (ed. E. Dinkler; Tübingen: Mohr [Siebeck], 1964) 193-216; reprinted in *Das Lukas-Evangelium* (ed. G. Braumann; Wege der Forschung, 280; Darmstadt: Wissenschaftliche Buchgesellschaft, 1974) 170-203.

Kürzinger, J. "Lk 1, 3: . . . *akribōs kathexēs soi grapsai,*" *BZ* 18 (1974) 249-255.

Lohse, E. "Lukas als Theologe der Heilsgeschichte," *EvT* 14 (1954) 256-275; reprinted in *Das Lukas-Evangelium* (ed. G. Braumann) 65-94.

Mulder, H. "Theophilus, de 'godvrezende,' " in *Arcana revelata: Een bundel Nieuw-Testamentische Studiën aangeboden aan F. W. Grosheide* (eds. N. J. Hommes et al.; Kampen: Kok, 1951) 77-88.

Mussner, F. *"Kathexēs* im Lukasprolog," in *Jesus und Paulus: Festschrift für Werner Georg Kümmel* (eds. E. E. Ellis and E. Grässer; Göttingen: Vandenhoeck und Ruprecht, 1975) 253-255.

Pope, A. M. "The Key Word of the Lucan Narratives," *CJRT* 3 (1926) 44-52.

Rinaldi, G. " 'Risalendo alle più lontane origini della tradizione' (*Luca* 1,3)," *BeO* 7 (1965) 252-258.

Robertson, A. T. "The Implications in Luke's Preface," *ExpTim* 35 (1923-1924) 319-321.

Ropes, J. H. "St Luke's Preface; *asphaleia* and *parakolouthein,*" *JTS* 25 (1923-1924) 67-71.

Schneider, G. "Zur Bedeutung von *kathexēs* im lukanischen Doppelwerk," *ZNW* 68 (1977) 128-131.

Schürmann, H. "Evangelienschrift und kirchliche Unterweisung: Die repräsentative Funktion der Schrift nach Lk 1,1-4," in *Miscellanea erfordiana* (=Erfurter theologische Studien 12; eds. E. Kleineidam and H. Schürmann; Leipzig: St. Benno, 1962) 48-73; reprinted in *Das Lukas-Evangelium* (ed. G. Braumann) 135-169.

Trocmé, E. *Le 'livre des Actes' et l'histoire* (Études d'histoire et de philosophie religieuses, 45; Paris: Presses universitaires, 1957) 39-49, 78, 122-128.

Vögtle, A. "Was hatte die Widmung des lukanischen Doppelwerks an Theophilus zu bedeuten?" in *Das Evangelium und die Evangelien: Beiträge zur Evangelienforschung* (Düsseldorf: Patmos, 1971) 31-42.

Völkel, M. "Exegetische Erwägungen zum Verständnis des Begriffs *kathexēs* im lukanischen Prolog," *NTS* 20 (1973-1974) 289-299.

Wijngaards, J. "Saint Luke's Prologue in the Light of Modern Research," *Clergy Monthly* 31 (1967) 172-179, 251-258.

I. THE INFANCY NARRATIVE

The Lucan Overture to the Account of Jesus

"A Savior has been born to you today in the town of David.
He is the Messiah, the Lord!"

A. EVENTS BEFORE THE BIRTH OF JOHN THE BAPTIST AND OF JESUS

2. THE BIRTH OF JOHN IS ANNOUNCED
(1:5-25)

1 ⁵There was in the days of Herod, king of Judea, a priest named Zechariah, who belonged to the priestly course of Abijah. His wife was a descendant of Aaron, and her name was Elizabeth. ⁶Both of them were upright in God's sight and lived blamelessly according to all the commandments and requirements of the Lord. ⁷But they had no children, because Elizabeth was barren, and both were well along in years.

⁸Once when Zechariah was serving before God during the turn of his priestly course, ⁹it fell to his lot according to the custom of the priests to enter the sanctuary of the Lord and burn incense. ¹⁰Meanwhile, all the people were assembled outside, praying at the time of the incense-offering. ¹¹There appeared to Zechariah the angel of the Lord, standing to the right of the altar of incense. ¹²At the sight of him Zechariah became alarmed and fear came over him. ¹³Then the angel said to him, "Do not be afraid, Zechariah; your prayer has been heard. Your wife Elizabeth is to bear you a son, and you are to name him John. ¹⁴Joy and delight will be yours, and many will rejoice at his birth, ¹⁵for he is to be great in the sight of the Lord. *He shall drink*

no wine or beer,[a] but even from his birth he will be filled with a holy Spirit. [16] He will turn many of the children of Israel to the Lord, their God. [17] He will go before him with the spirit and power of Elijah, *to turn the hearts of parents to children,*[b] to turn the disobedient to the understanding of the upright, and to make ready a people fit for the Lord." [18] But Zechariah said to the angel, *"How shall I know*[c] that this is so? I am an old man, and my wife is well on in years!" [19] The angel replied, "I am Gabriel and I stand in the presence of God. I have been sent to speak to you and to announce this to you. [20] Now, you shall become mute, and be unable to speak, until the day these things take place, because you have not believed my words, which will find fulfillment in their own time."

[21] Meanwhile, the people who were waiting for Zechariah began to wonder at his lingering in the sanctuary. [22] And when he did come out and could not speak to them, they realized that he had seen a vision in the sanctuary, for he kept beckoning to them and remained speechless. [23] Now when the period of his Temple service was over, he went back to his home.

[24] Sometime later his wife Elizabeth became pregnant, and she remained in seclusion for five months, thinking, [25] "This is how the Lord has dealt with me, at the time he saw fit to take away the disgrace I have endured among people."

a Num 6:3; Judg 13:4   b Mal 3:24   c Gen 15:8

COMMENT

The Lucan Gospel shares with the Matthean an introductory section, a complex of stories about the birth and childhood of Jesus, which neither the Marcan nor the Johannine Gospel has. Mark begins his Gospel with a flat statement, "The beginning of the good news of Jesus Christ, the Son of God" (1:1), and immediately starts his account with the ministry of John the Baptist. John's Gospel prefixes a hymnic prologue to the story of the Baptist's ministry. The first two chapters of Matthew and Luke, however, begin with stories purporting to tell of Jesus' origins, usually called "infancy narratives" in English discussions of them, although they contain information about more than his infancy only. Here we must devote a few paragraphs to the general character of the infancy narrative in the gospel tradition and to the Lucan infancy narrative in particular, before we can comment on the first episode in it.

I. *An Infancy Narrative.* Like the passion narrative or the resurrection narrative, the infancy narrative is a subform in the literary genre of gospel in Christian literature. *Per se* it fits into none of the usual categories of form criticism, since those categories were mainly worked out in the analysis of the public ministry accounts. However, the episodes in the infancy narratives have at times been classed with the "Stories about Jesus" or the "Legends"; this has also been contested (see G. Schneider, *Evangelium nach Lukas,* 77).

The reader, in picking up the Lucan or Matthean Gospels, is first confronted with the infancy narrative and might not be aware that this actually represents the latest part of the gospel tradition to take shape (see V. Taylor, *FGT,* 168-189; R. Bultmann *HST,* 354; O. Cullmann, "Infancy Gospels," Hennecke-Schneemelcher, *NTApocrypha* 1. 363-369). The Gospels are recognized as the outgrowth of the early Christian *kērygma,* fragments of which are preserved in 1 Cor 15:3-4; Rom 1:3-4; 1 Thess 1:9-10 (and possibly also in Acts 2:23-24,32,36; 3:14-15; 4:10; 10:39b-40). The first stage in development would have been a passion narrative, to which an account of Jesus' ministry (built up out of the early Christian *didachē,* based on recollections of what Jesus did and taught), was eventually prefixed. Then, at a still later stage, the resurrection narratives and infancy narratives were added. If one prescinds from its appendix (16:9-20, not found in the best of Greek mss.), Mark, the earliest Gospel to attain shape, lacked both an infancy narrative and resurrection appearances; it is similar, in fact, in structure to the summary of Jesus' career in Acts 10:36-41.

Though biographical concern was scarcely responsible for the formation of the rest of the gospel tradition, it eventually emerged in that tradition and is responsible (in part, at least) for the accretion to it of stories about the origins of Jesus and his identity. Mark used the baptism scene to identify Jesus to his readers, but he had no interest in Jesus' origins and does not even mention Joseph's name. The biographical concern yielded in its turn to curiosity, as is seen in the tradition that eventually developed into the apocryphal infancy Gospels (e.g. the *Protevangelium of James* in the second century A.D.; and the *Infancy Gospel of Thomas* see Hennecke-Schneemelcher, *NTApocrypha* 1. 363-401).

Yet that biographical concern must not be understood in terms of modern historical biography. Early tradition tended to take to itself legendary details, literary embellishment, folklore, astrology, and the interpretation of the OT. These are known features in much ancient tracing of origins, where the sophisticated modern use of genealogical and historical records was unknown.

Moreover, the infancy narrative materials were never part of the early *kērygma* or *didachē* itself. The only exception might involve the indirect relation to the *kērygma* of such details as that Jesus was the Son of God, descended from David, and related to the holy Spirit. These are found in Rom 1:3-4. That identification of him in Romans is made apropos of the resurrection, and the extent to which it is to be associated with the tradition of his virginal conception will be discussed more fully below (see p. 340). I am trying to stress here that the infancy narrative materials were not really part of the "gospel" in the theological sense, such as Paul would have meant, when he spoke of "my gospel" (Rom 2:16) or "the gospel of God" (Rom 1:1; 15:16).

A process of theologizing was certainly at work in the fashioning of the infancy narratives (e.g. in the parallels implied in the Matthean Gospel between Joseph and Joseph the patriarch, or between Jesus and Moses; or the apologetics involved in the Jesus-John parallelism in the Lucan Gospel). Theological motives were also operative in the retrojection of the identity of Jesus as the Son of God, Lord, and Messiah from the time of his resurrection to his very birth and conception (1:32-35; 2:11). This resulted in the multi-phase christology of the later Gospels in contrast to the two-phase form in Mark.

Again, it should be noted that in both Matthew and Luke the infancy narratives function as a sort of overture to the Gospels proper, striking the chords that will be heard again and again in the coming narratives. This is, indeed, more evident in the Lucan Gospel than in the Matthean, since, as we shall see, the Lucan infancy narrative was composed with the hindsight not only of the gospel tradition prior to Luke but also of the Lucan Gospel proper.

Given the character of the infancy narrative just described, the historical value of this part of the gospel tradition has been questioned extensively. That Jesus exercised a ministry in Galilee, was baptized by John, taught authoritatively, traveled to Jerusalem, ate there a final supper with disciples before he was betrayed by Judas, was crucified in Jerusalem, died, and was buried nearby—such details of his life can be substantiated because of their multiple attestation in the NT itself (e.g. besides the Synoptic and Johannine traditions about them, see 1 Cor 11:23-25; Phil 3:10; Gal 3:13; Col 2:14; 1 Thess 2:14-15; 1 Tim 6:13; Heb 6:6; cf. J. A. Fitzmyer, *Chicago Studies* 17 [1978] 77-80). The details in the infancy narratives themselves often present problems we cannot run away from.

On the one hand, Matthew and Luke both depend on a certain body of information in the tradition that existed prior to their writing. Since there is no evidence that Luke depends on Matthew or vice versa (see pp. 73-75 above), the details that they share must be regarded as derived from an earlier tradition. Opinions will vary as to the historical value of such traditional details, but I tend to regard them as the historical nucleus of what the evangelists worked with. The following are the details that the two evangelists share in their infancy narratives:

1) Jesus' birth is related to the reign of Herod (Luke 1:5; Matt 2:1)
2) Mary, his mother to be, is a virgin engaged to Joseph, but they have not yet come to live together (Luke 1:27,34; 2:5; Matt 1:18)
3) Joseph is of the house of David (Luke 1:27; 2:4; Matt 1:16, 20).
4) An angel from heaven announces the coming birth of Jesus (Luke 1:28-30; Matt 1:20-21)
5) Jesus is recognized himself to be a son of David (Luke 1:32; Matt 1:1)
6) His conception is to take place through the holy Spirit (Luke 1:35; Matt 1:18,20)
7) Joseph is not involved in the conception (Luke 1:34; Matt 1:18-25)
8) The name "Jesus" is imposed by heaven prior to his birth (Luke 1:31; Matt 1:21)
9) The angel identifies Jesus as "Savior" (Luke 2:11; Matt 1:21)
10) Jesus is born after Mary and Joseph come to live together (Luke 2:4-7; Matt 1:24-25)
11) Jesus is born at Bethlehem (Luke 2:4-7; Matt 2:1)
12) Jesus settles, with Mary and Joseph, in Nazareth in Galilee (Luke 2:39,51; Matt 2:22-23)

(Cf. J. Schmid, *Evangelium nach Lukas,* 90; X. Léon Dufour, *Les évangiles et l'histoire de Jésus* [Paris: Ed. du Seuil, 1963] 90; Schneider, *Evangelium nach Lukas,* 78; R. E. Brown, *Birth,* 34-35.)

Such agreement of the two evangelists on these details is important, and the Lucan attestation can be used as a control for the Matthean, and vice versa. One instance, however, that of Jesus' residence at Nazareth, might have been deduced from the tradition of his ministry in his own country (Luke 4:16,23; cf. Matt 13:54).

There are problems that the infancy narratives themselves create in the matter of historicity. First, the striking structural difference of the two accounts; they cannot be put in parallel columns in a Synopsis. Second, the angelic announcement about Jesus' birth comes to Mary in the Lucan Gospel and to Joseph in the Matthean; its discrepancy raises the question: Who was actually informed of this important birth to come? The discrepancy is hardly to be explained by the claim that Matthew has recorded Joseph's recollections, whereas Luke has preserved Mary's. (See e.g. P. Sträter, *VD* 25 [1947] 321-327; H. Schürmann, *Lukasevan-*

gelium, 61.) This solution has so many problems that it can scarcely be correct: Why would not Mary and Joseph have exchanged their stories? And why would not the tradition have a composite form of them? This touches on the larger question, whether there were at the basis of the episodes in the infancy narratives traditions handed down in family seclusion which only later seeped into the church traditions. The Lucan infancy narrative has been more subject to this sort of explanation, because many have thought that at the root of it lie Mary's memoirs. But all such claims have only speculation for their basis, sheer conjecture. Not even Luke 2:19,33-35,51b can be read in support of such claims. Third, Matthew's narrative has a genealogy, Luke's does not—and how different the Lucan one in 3:23-38 is! Fourth, Luke knows nothing of the Magi, the flight to Egypt, the massacre of the innocents, and the return from Egypt, just as Matthew knows nothing of the presentation of Jesus in the Temple, Simeon, Anna, the Magnificat, the Benedictus, or the finding of Jesus in the Temple. Fifth, more crucial still, Matthew knows nothing of the census of Quirinius, the reason Luke gives for Jesus' being born in Bethlehem. (See further A. Vögtle, "Offene Fragen," 43-54.)

It has, of course, been popular to harmonize these accounts: Luke 1, Matthew 1, Luke 2:1-38, a postulated return to Bethlehem, Matthew 2. But with what right, apart from pious speculation? The harmonization tends to obscure the individual thrusts of the two narratives, and it does not summon up great credence for them.

In recent times it has often been asked whether the infancy narratives may be characterized as midrashic. The word *midrāš* is found in the OT (2 Chr 13:22 [*RSV,* "story"]; 24:27 [*RSV,* "commentary"], in Qumran literature (1QS 6:24; 8:15,26; 4QFlor 1:14; CD 20:6 [where it denotes the "study" or "interpretation" of Scripture]), and often in rabbinic literature, where it is used of a certain literary genre (extended "commentary" on OT books, either of the haggadic [anecdotal] type, or of the halakhic [legalistic, ethical] type). The word *midrāš* itself is derived from *drš,* "seek, resort to" or "consult, inquire of." To "seek Yahweh" (Deut 4:29, etc.) came to mean the seeking of the will of Yahweh as expressed in Scripture, as Isa 34:16 makes clear. The midrashic use of the OT came to mean not only extended commentaries on OT books (as in the Tannaitic midrashim, or the *Midraš Rabbah*), but even in the latter books of the OT it involved the homiletic retelling of older stories (cf. Psalm 105; Sirach 44-50; Wisdom 16-19, etc.). Because the Lucan infancy narrative is heavily Semitized in its language and the Matthean is structured about five OT quotations, the question has been raised whether the NT infancy narratives could be midrashic, especially in the story-telling sense. The term would be more accurately used of the Matthean text than the Lucan, because Matthew at least quotes the OT, and a starting-point in an OT text is an essential of midrash. Even then it would have to be used only in the broadest of senses. The term is better avoided and is, in any case, quite unsuitable for the Lucan form. See further J. Riedl, *Die Vorge-schichte Jesu*, 8-10; A. G. Wright, "The Literary Genre Midrash," *CBQ* 28 (1966) 105-138, 417-457, esp. pp. 454-456.

Some years ago E. Burrows (*The Gospel of the Infancy and Other Bib-lical Essays* [London: Burns, Oates, 1940] 1-58) coined the term "imita-tive historiography," which I borrow from him and use in a slightly different way. Calling the infancy narratives "imitative historiography" means that whatever historical matter has been preserved by the two evangelists has been assimilated by them to other literary accounts, either biblical or extrabiblical. Matthew has modeled his infancy narrative in part at least on a contemporary Palestinian haggada about the birth of Moses (see M. M. Bourke, "The Literary Genus of Matthew 1-2," *CBQ* 22 [1960] 160-175). Luke's story of Jesus not only parallels his story of John in part, but has unmistakable resonances of the story of the child-hood of Samuel in the OT (1 Samuel 1-3). See S. Muñoz Iglesias, "El evangelio de la infancia en San Lucas y las infancias de los héroes bíblicos," *EstBíb* 16 (1957) 329-382. Further details of the Lucan tech-nique will be given below.

II. *The Lucan Infancy Narrative.* In contrast to the Matthean infancy narrative, which after the introductory genealogy (1:1-17) has five epi-sodes (1:18-25; 2:1-12,13-15,16-18,19-23) that either end or come to a climax in an OT quotation with a fulfillment formula, the Lucan narrative is less obviously structured, though it manifests parallelism of scenes about John the Baptist and Jesus in places. Its obvious purpose is to introduce and identify these two children, especially Jesus, as agents of God's sal-vation-history; both come from God.

The infancy narrative was in large part freely composed by Luke on the basis of information obtained from earlier models and in imitation of some OT motifs. In addition to the twelve details that this narrative shares with the Matthean (see p. 307 above), which Luke inherited from earlier Christian tradition, one has to reckon with his use of other source material too, in a preexistent form, either written or oral. Thus (a) from a Jewish-Christian source: the canticles, Magnificat (1:46-55) and Bene-dictus (1:67-79), possibly the Nunc Dimittis (2:29-32), and probably also the last scene of chap. 2 (vv. 41-50); (b) from an earlier Baptist source: the story of the announcement of John's birth (1:5-25) and the story of his birth, circumcision, and manifestation (1:57-66b). The rest is most likely to be ascribed to Lucan composition, based at times on some information that may have been available. To admit such sources, however, does not mean that Luke has not reworked them in his own style.

The infancy narrative, even though dependent on prior source-material, has become an integral part of the Lucan Gospel. This has to be stressed over against H. Conzelmann's contention that "the authenticity of these first two chapters is questionable" (*Theology*, 118), a contention which belies his claim that his study of Lucan theology "is concerned with the whole of Luke's writings as they stand" (ibid. 9; for more of his comments on the infancy narrative, see 18 n. 1; 22 n. 2; 24-25; 75 n. 4; 172; 174 n. 1; 193 n. 5). I tend to agree (at least substantially) with writers like H. H. Oliver and W. B. Tatum that the data of the infancy narrative can be worked into the basic insight of Conzelmann about the three stages of Lucan salvation-history (see pp. 181-186 above). John is presented, indeed, in the infancy narrative as the precursor of Jesus, because that is also the way that he is presented in the Gospel proper. John's appearance is an aspect of the time of fulfillment, and he plays a transitional role, being part of the Period of Israel, but also the inaugurator of the Period of Jesus. Much of the analysis of P. S. Minear has shown the close relationship of the infancy narrative to the rest of the Gospel, but he has overreacted against Conzelmann's basic insight.

This relationship, however, does not mean that Luke composed the infancy narrative as the very first part of his Gospel. Rather, it seems obvious that 3:1-2 was at one time a formal introduction to the work—this we maintain, without subscribing to the Proto-Luke hypothesis (see pp. 88-91 above). Luke 3:1-2 resembles the prologue (1:1-4), even though it is not as perfectly composed a periodic sentence. Introducing, as it does, the ministry of John the Baptist, it shows that the Lucan Gospel once began at the point at which the Marcan Gospel now begins and at which the Johannine Gospel follows on its own prologue. Moreover, the position of John the Baptist in Luke 3 explains the peculiar Lucan emphasis on a "beginning" (*archē*) associated with the baptism-preaching of John (see the NOTE on 1:3; cf. Acts 10:37; 1:22). Further, H. J. Cadbury (*The Making of Luke-Acts*, 204-209) has drawn attention to the parallels to this sort of opening in Greek papyri from Egypt, Dionysius Halicarnassus (*Roman antiquities* 9.61), Thucydides (*History* 2.2,1) and Josephus (*Ant.* 20.11,1 § 257; *J.W.* 2.14,4 § 284). John's ministry is dated by a synchronism of contemporary rulers in an introductory formula. Recognizing this feature of the beginning of chap. 3 makes it imperative to acknowledge the independent character of the infancy narrative and its telltale quality of a later addition. This recognition makes impossible the suggestion that one should regard 1:5-4:13 as the introductory part (*Vorgeschichte*) of the Lucan Gospel (so W. G. Kümmel, *Introduction*, 125; Schmid, *Evangelium nach Lukas*, 33), or even 1:5-4:30 (so R. Morgenthaler, *Die lukanische Geschichtsschreibung*, 155,

165). That would be to neglect the formal introductory character of 3:1-2. Nor does Acts 1:1 refer to Luke 1-2 as part of the first book.

All of this suggests that Luke composed his Gospel, beginning with 3:1-2, and having written it (and Acts too, if R. E. Brown's evidence for the dependence of the infancy narrative on Acts is accepted [*Birth,* 242-243]), he then composed the infancy narrative. There are foreshadowings in the infancy narrative of things to come in the rest of Luke-Acts, but they are there because the infancy narrative has been composed with hindsight.

This observation about the secondary character of the Lucan infancy narrative is not merely the conjecture of modern scholars. Years ago F. C. Conybeare pointed out that a note in the commentary of Ephraem of Syria on Tatian's *Diatessaron,* which regards Luke 1:5 - 2:52 as a later insert into the Lucan Gospel, confirms this suggestion. (See "Ein Zeugnis Ephräms über das Fehlen von c. 1 and 2 im Texte des Lucas," *ZNW* 3 [1902] 192-197.) This makes one immediately think of Marcion's version of the Gospel and its relation to the Lucan, because it too lacked the infancy narrative. Conybeare commented: "But when he [Marcion] allowed 3:1 to follow on 1:4, he simply preserved the original form of the Gospel." See further J. Knox, *Marcion and the New Testament: An Essay in the Early History of the Canon* (Chicago: University of Chicago, 1942) 77-113.

Whether Luke composed the infancy narrative all in one draft or wrote a first form of it and later made some additions may remain moot. Brown (*Birth,* 250-253) opts for the latter. The absence of a tight connection between the Magnificat and its context, and the Benedictus and its context might suggest that at least these passages were added at a later date than the rest. Whether other verses should be put in that category must remain questionable.

Chapter 1 of the infancy narrative is a unit in itself and chap. 2 scarcely presupposes any of it. In fact, not only does John the Baptist not appear in the latter, but Mary is again introduced as Joseph's betrothed (2:5), even though she was already so described in 1:27. Moreover, Luke speaks of Mary and Joseph as "his parents" (2:41) and portrays Mary speaking to Jesus about Joseph as "your father" (2:48), as if nothing had been said in 1:35 about the virginal conception. Furthermore, the distant relation of 2:41-52, which reads like a pronouncement story and goes beyond anything connected with Jesus' infancy, to the rest of chap. 2—and a fortiori to chap. 1—reveals some of the nature of these two introductory chapters. These are some of the reasons why the "sources" that were mentioned above have often been isolated.

This view of chaps. 1 and 2 of the Lucan Gospel as an introductory unit has at times been questioned. J. H. Davies would prefer to regard chaps. 1-3 as "the Lucan prologue," because he considers that they have a coherence and distinctness from what follows. While there is some Lucan redaction (and composition) in the third chapter (e.g. the introduction in vv. 1-2, the genealogy at the end), the rest of it is so closely related to the beginning of the gospel tradition, as known from Mark and seen in the Matthean Gospel right after its infancy narrative, that one has to resist any attempt to associate chap. 3 closely with the two foregoing chapters, which constitute the infancy narrative. (See Davies, "The Lucan Prologue [1-3]: An attempt at Objective Redaction Criticism," *SE VI* [TU 112, 1973] 78-85).

Did Luke use sources written or formulated in languages other than Greek? This question has often been raised in modern times, since, especially after the formal literary Greek of the prologue, one notes a heavy Semitic flavor to the Greek of the infancy narrative. This characteristic of the first two chapters likewise stands in contrast to that of the rest of the Gospel and Acts, although there is some Semitizing Greek in Acts too. Scholars have at times sought to show that Luke has translated some of the material from a Hebrew source (so G. Dalman, G. H. Box, P. de Lagarde, H. Gunkel, B. H. Streeter, V. Taylor, R. Laurentin) or from an Aramaic source (B. Weiss, A. Plummer, M. Dibelius, W. Michaelis) or that he used an existing Greek translation of a Semitic source (K.-H. Schelkle). Some of the arguments for such positions have been linked to the problem of the canticles, Magnificat and Benedictus; these cento-like compositions, abounding in OT phrases, should not be allowed to obscure the problem of the rest of the infancy narrative. In my own discussion of the language and style of the Lucan Gospel I have allowed for a few possible Aramaisms (see p. 117 above), but I account for the vast majority of Hebraisms as Septuagintisms, i.e. Lucan imitation of Septuagintal Greek style. If there is any plausibility to the thesis of the Baptist-source for certain passages in the infancy narrative, it does not stand on the question of a difference of language in which that source would have been written. The sooner one reckons with the rather uniform Lucan Greek style in the infancy narrative the better. In this I line myself up with H. J. Cadbury, A. von Harnack, P. Benoit, and others.

Is one to reckon with the Johannine tradition as a source of information for the Lucan infancy narrative? This has been suggested at times (e.g. C. Stuhlmueller, *JBC*, art. 44, § 13; J. McHugh, *The Mother of Jesus in the New Testament* [New York: Doubleday, 1975] 8-10, 147-149). Parallels between the story of John in Luke 1 and the Johannine prologue, where all references to him are in prose inserts in an otherwise hymnic composition, have at times been pointed out. Or one maintains the affinity between the Lucan and Johannine Gospels is "nowhere more marked than in the Infancy Narrative," and because "the Johannine Gospel cannot be wholly detached from John the son of Zebedee" (McHugh, *Mother of Jesus,* 147), Luke must include him among "the eyewitnesses from the beginning." Or again, "it is *a priori* likely that Mary gave some account of the infancy of Jesus to the first disciples" (ibid. 148). This is sheer speculation. None of the standard discussions about contacts between the Johannine and Lucan Gospels includes details in Luke 1-2; see, e.g. J. A. Bailey, *The Traditions Common to the Gospels of Luke and John* [NovTSup 7; Leiden: Brill, 1963]; R. E. Brown, *John, I-XII,* xlvi-xlvii; R. Schnackenburg, *Gospel according to John* (New York: Herder & Herder, 1968) 30-32; Kümmel, *Introduction,* 203. Moreover, as Brown points out (*Birth,* 238), the Johannine Gospel shows no awareness of the birth and childhood stories of Jesus (save possibly that he was from Bethlehem, *if* John 7:41-42 be interpreted ironically).

We may now turn to the structure of the Lucan infancy narrative. Modern commentators have generally noted the parallelism of certain scenes in it. There is, however, little unanimity on the best way to view the structure. Brown (*Birth,* 248-249, Table IX) displays six attempts (by Galbiati, Burrows, Dibelius, Gaechter, Lyonnet, and Laurentin) and discusses the various problems met in them. In what I shall propose below, I am mainly influenced by M. Dibelius, but also in part by S. Lyonnet and R. Laurentin. Perhaps my table presents more parallelism than others have been willing to admit; none of the analyses of the structure has been able to avoid a certain amount of subjectivism.

THE STRUCTURE OF THE LUCAN INFANCY NARRATIVE
I. The Angelic Announcements of the Births (1:5-56)

1. *About John* (1:5-25)	2. *About Jesus* (1:26-38)
The parents introduced, expecting no child (because barren) (5-10)	The parents introduced, expecting no child (because unmarried) (26-27)
Appearance of the angel (11)	Entrance of the angel (28)
Zechariah is troubled (*etarachthē*) (12)	Mary is troubled (*dietarachthē*) (29)
"Do not fear . . ." (*mē phobou*) (13)	"Do not fear . . ." (*mē phobou*) (30)
Your wife will bear a son (13)	You will bear a son (31)
You shall call him John (13)	You shall call him Jesus (31)
He shall be great before the Lord (15)	He shall be Great (32)
Zechariah's question: "How shall I know?" (18)	Mary's question: "How shall this be?" (34)
Angel's answer: I have been sent to announce this to you (19)	Angel's answer: The holy Spirit will come upon you (35)

Sign given: You shall become mute (20)	Sign given: Your aged cousin Elizabeth has conceived (36)
Zechariah's forced silence (22)	Mary's spontaneous answer (38)
Refrain A: Zechariah "went back" (apēlthen) (23)	Refrain A: The angel "went away" (apēlthen) (38)

3. *Complementary Episode:* The Visitation (1:39-45)
    Canticle: Magnificat (46-55)
    Refrain A: Mary "returned" to her home (56)

II. *The Birth, Circumcision, and Manifestation of the Children* (1:57-2:52)

4. *The Birth of John* (1:57-58)

The birth of John (57)

Joy over the birth (58)

5. *The Birth of Jesus* (2:1-20)

The birth of Jesus (1-12)
Canticle of the Angels (13-14)
Joy over the birth (15-18)
Refrain B: Mary treasured all this (19)
Refrain A: The shepherds returned (20)

6. *The Circumcision and Manifestation of John* (1:59-80)

John circumcised and named (59-64)
Reaction of the neighbors (65-66)
Canticle: Benedictus (68-79)

Refrain C: "The child grew . . ." (80)

7. *The Circumcision and Manifestation of Jesus* (2:21-40)

Jesus circumcised and named (21)
Reaction of Simeon and Anna (25-38)
Canticle: Nunc dimittis (29-32)
Refrain A: They returned (39)
Refrain C: "The child grew . . ." (40)

8. *Complementary Episode:* The Finding in the Temple (2:41-52)
    Refrain A: "went" to Nazareth (51)
    Refrain B: His mother kept all this in her heart (51)
    Refrain C: Jesus grew in wisdom, age, and grace (52)

The outline given above brings out the parallels in the two stories of John and Jesus in the infancy narrative. The greatest parallels exist between the announcement episodes. The parallels between the births are less pronounced, since only two verses are devoted to John's, whereas Jesus' birth gets twelve verses. Again, more space is devoted to the manifestation of Jesus, which takes place not among neighbors, but before two Period of Israel figures in the Temple itself. There is no parallelism in the complementary episodes; the first of them links by its details the first two episodes that precede it. The second complementary episode is unrelated to what precedes. Its only connection is that Jesus is in the Temple once again, following the Lucan motif of moving Jesus toward Jerusalem and its Temple. The canticles are only loosely joined to the outline. The Magnificat occurs in the first complementary episode, but the Benedictus and Nunc Dimittis have some parallel function. That of the angels (2:13-14) is in a parallel episode, but without any parallel of its own.

Luke has not used parallelism just for the sake of parallelism. There is more. The parallelism does not merely suggest that John and Jesus are twin agents of God's salvation on the same level. Rather, there is a step-parallelism at work, i.e. a parallelism with one-upmanship. The Jesus-side always comes off better. For instance, John's parents are "upright in God's sight" (1:6), but Mary is the favored one (1:28). John's mother, though aged and barren, eventually bears him naturally, but Jesus' mother bears him wondrously. John will be great before the Lord (1:15), but Jesus will be Great (1:32—for the connotation of this, see the NOTE). John will walk before the *Kyrios* (1:16-17), but Jesus will be called *Kyrios* (2:11 [in a different sense, of course]), as well as Savior and Messiah. John's father queries the angel and is struck dumb (1:19-22), but Jesus' mother queries the angel and is reassured, declaring herself the handmaid of the Lord (1:34-38). Though the question, "What is this child to become" (1:66), is asked only about John, the reader senses that this is to be asked as well about the child with whom he is implicitly compared.

One senses here in the infancy narrative an attempt to put John in the proper perspective vis-à-vis Jesus. Yes, John is an agent of God's salvation; what is written here about him is formulated in view of Luke 20:4, where Luke makes it clear that John's baptism did come from heaven. Brown (*Birth*, 250) notes that there is further parallelism between Jesus and John in the Gospel proper, but he fails to reckon with the purpose of it adequately. Even though John is something greater than a prophet, he is not part of the kingdom (7:26-28), and his baptism is not that of Jesus (3:16). Cf. Acts 13:23-25; 18:25; 19:3. Only Luke, among the Synoptists, asserts that John was not the Messiah (3:15). In the infancy narrative Luke is making it clear that John is the precursor of the Messiah.

As a whole, the Lucan infancy narrative is stressing that the origin of these two agents of salvation is in God himself: John is the prophet of the Most High, Jesus is his Son—and the latter relationship is affirmed again in its own way in the last scene of the narrative (2:49). Jesus is not just someone filled with the Spirit (1:15), but, though his earthly existence is begun under the Spirit's influence, he is God's Son. So, if the early christology incorporated in Peter's speech in Acts 2:36 ("God made him Lord and Messiah") sounds adoptionist, Luke 1:32-35 aims at giving another impression. Written with the hindsight of the rest of the Gospel (and probably Acts), it makes Jesus Son of God as of his conception.

The Lucan infancy narrative makes use of some OT themes in the development of its story of John and Jesus, which we should note here. One complex of them includes the dawning of messianic times, the coming of the great and awesome Day of the Lord, and the coming of the Lord to his Temple. This group is presented by allusions to Dan 9:20-26; 10:7,

12,16-17 and to Mal 2:6; 3:1,23-24(4:5-6E). Thus "the angel of the Lord" (1:11) is identified as "Gabriel" (1:19), who in Daniel announces the prophecy of Seventy Weeks and the coming of an Anointed One, a prince (Dan 9:25). This messianic era is associated with "the great and awesome Day of Yahweh" (Mal 3:23[4:5E]) as the term for John's preparation of the people in the spirit and power of Elijah (1:17). Moreover, Jesus is identified as "Lord" (2:11) and made to come to the Temple (2:22,42) in the spirit of Mal 3:1. The following Lucan verses should be noted more in detail:

Luke 1:12-13	Dan 10:7,12
1:16	Mal 2:6
1:17	Mal 3:1,23-24 (cf. Sir 48:1,3,10)
1:19	Dan 9:20-21
1:26-29	Dan 9:21-24
1:64-65	Dan 10:16-17
1:76	Mal 3:1,23

Two other motifs in the infancy narrative should be noted: the Temple-piety of some of the figures of the Period of Israel and the beginnings of Christian faith. The former is manifested in the parents of John and Jesus, and in Simeon and Anna. They embody a piety that foreshadows that of the early Jerusalem Christians in Acts 2:46; 3:1; 5:12. The beginnings of faith can be seen when God's *charis,* "favor," is manifested to Mary (1:28,30), who becomes the first believer in the Lucan Gospel (1:38,45; 2:19,51). (Contrast her attitude in Mark 3:21,31-35.)

III. *Comment on 1:5-25.* The announcement to Zechariah about John's birth may be subdivided into four sections (a) the setting and dramatis personae (vv. 5-7); (b) the announcement proper (vv. 8-20); (c) the manifestation to the people that something extraordinary has occurred (vv. 21-23); (d) the fulfillment of the promise (vv. 24-25).

As already suggested above, Luke is most likely making use here of a source (from "L"), or more specifically a Baptist source, as it has often been called. The same is probably true for the story of John's birth, circumcision, and manifestation. To the source-material he has joined the stories of Jesus in parallelism, in order to achieve the step-parallelism already pointed out. This earlier Baptist source was not the same as the Jewish Christian source from which he derived the canticles and 2:41-50. That does not mean that it came from a group of anti-Christian disciples of John. More than likely it comes from his disciples who eventually became Christian (see Acts 19:3-4). In espousing this source, I am lining myself up in part with commentators such as R. Bultmann, M. Dibelius, H. Gunkel, R. C. Leaney, G. Schneider and others who have postulated this source in one form or another. But, as it will become clear below, I do not necessarily admit all the claims that are made about this source. A Baptist source has been resisted by Brown (*Birth*, 244-245, 265-279), and many of his objections against it have to be reckoned with. The dependence of the Lucan announcement stories on the OT is clear, but it is likely that the Baptist source itself depended on the stereotyped five-element OT story before the Lucan incorporation of it into the Infancy narrative. Brown (*Birth*, 279) finally admits that there "is no real way to disprove the theory that Luke drew" the angelic message in vv. 13-17 from a Baptist source. As far as content is concerned, the theory of the source is certainly possible; as far as Lucan theology is concerned, that depends on what one thinks Luke made of the source.

The setting for the angelic announcement, the first section of this episode, is provided in vv. 5-7; it is specified in terms of time and space: in the days of Herod, in Judea. The chronological setting is from a pre-Lucan tradition, as the parallel dating in Matt 2:1 shows. The names of Zechariah and Elizabeth and their relation to priestly families come from the same tradition. The information is undoubtedly to be ascribed to disciples of John, about whom Luke certainly knew (see Luke 7:18; Acts 19:1-4; he tells too of "priests" who had been converted to Christianity, Acts 6:7). There is no serious reason to think that Luke has fabricated these items on the basis of their occurrence in the OT (see NOTES). The barrenness of Elizabeth recalls especially the condition of Hannah in 1 Sam 1:2 (see NOTES for examples of other barren women in the OT whose condition was relieved by divine intervention), since the Lucan phraseology in these verses even echoes this OT passage. Moreover, in mentioning the old age of Zechariah and Elizabeth as well, the author is alluding to the condition of Abraham and Sarah in Gen 16:1; 18:11. Luke could conceivably have composed this himself, but there is nothing in the verses that would make us ascribe them exclusively to his hand. The setting for the announcement of the birth of John, however, does set the stage for seeing John's birth in relation to that of two famous figures in Israel's history, Isaac and Samuel. John is not only to be born of priestly stock and dedicated to the service of Yahweh's house, but is associated by implication to a patriarchal and prophetic figure of Israel's past.

Verses 8-20 contain the announcement proper, the second section of this episode. Its introduction (vv. 8-10) stresses the cultic context for the angelic appearance and message. God's providence has been at work in the choice of Zechariah to be the one to offer incense; he was not elected, but chosen by lot (just as Matthias is chosen in the later reconstitution of the Twelve in Acts 1:26). Time and place are again indicated: during the week of Temple service performed by the course of

Abijah and at the hour of the (afternoon) incense offering; in the holy place of the Jerusalem Temple.

The announcement proper is presented in vv. 13b-20, which are hardly to be understood as poetry, since there is no clear indication of this in the Greek text. The announcement itself follows the five-element pattern of OT birth announcements: (a) the appearance of an angel (or the Lord) to someone (mother or father); (b) fear on the part of the person confronted by the heavenly figure; (c) the heavenly message (often with stereotyped details); (d) an objection expressed by the person confronted or a request for a sign; and (e) the giving of some sign or reassurance. This pattern can be found in the announcements of the births of Ishmael (Gen 16:7-13), Isaac (Gen 17:1-21; 18:1-15), and Samson (Judg 13:3-20). It will be used by Luke again in the announcement of the birth of Jesus (1:26-37). Only the first and third elements are found in Matt 1:20-21. The pattern is pre-Lucan, and there is no reason to think that it could not have been in a Baptist source. As taken up by Luke, the five elements appear in the following verses:

   a) the appearance of an angel (1:11)
   b) Zechariah's fear (1:12)
   c) the heavenly message (1:13b-17, with Zechariah addressed by
      name, told not to be afraid [1:13b], told that his wife will bear a
      son [1:13d], told what he is to name him [1:13e], and told what
      the son's role will be [1:15-17])
   d) Zechariah's objection (1:18)
   e) the sign of dumbness (1:20).

In phraseology echoing Gen 17:19, where the father, Abraham, is told that his wife, Sarah, will bear him a son in his old age, Zechariah, the father, is now told (1:13d), "Your wife Elizabeth is to bear you a son." God's "favor" toward Zechariah is manifested in the name that he is to give the child (see NOTE). This is precisely the point in the heavenly imposition of the name "John." See OT counterparts in Gen 16:11; 17:19; Isa 7:14. Whether Gentile converts would have grasped the nuance may be missing the point; the implication is that God's grace or favor is now to come to humanity in a new form; otherwise why should Yĕhôḥānān be born of barren and aged parents precisely at this point in human history?

The birth of the child is to be attended with joy and delight, not yet the messianic joy of Jesus' birth, but a preparatory joy, heralding an age to come.

Verses 15-17 define the role of the Baptist: he is to be great in the Lord's sight, a Nazirite, one filled with the holy Spirit, and one sent for the conversion of Israel like the reformer Elijah. Nothing in the verses is said about John being an anointed figure, so that attempts to think that the Baptist source described him as a Messiah are baseless. Moreover, in 3:15-16, alone among the Synoptists Luke shows that he was aware people were thinking of John as a royal Messiah, and that is denied of him. Even if the Pseudo-Clementine literature (*Recognitions* 1.54,60) reveals that Luke may not have been the only one to show this awareness, there is no evidence that it was in the Baptist source.

John's greatness is certainly pre-Lucan, since it is found in "Q" (Luke 7:28; Matt 11:11). His Nazirite role is described in terms taken from the OT (see NOTE for details); it sets him in the ascetic tradition of Israel. His going "before the Lord" is set forth in terms of Mal 3:1,23, and possibly also of Hannah in 1 Sam 1:19 and of her son thereafter. From the same Malachi passages comes the description of Elijah's role as a reformer; see also Sir 48:10. So far, none of these descriptions of John must necessarily come from Luke alone; they could have been part of the Baptist source.

That John is to be "filled with the holy Spirit" certainly sounds like a peculiarly Lucan phrase, for he often uses it elsewhere (1:41,67; 4:1; Acts 2:4; 4:31; 7:55; 9:17,[31]; 11:24; 13:9). I agree with Brown (*Birth,* 274) that the contention that in the Lucan writings the Spirit is associated with Jesus and that the association of it here with John reveals the passage's non-Christian origin is really groundless and overworked. There are two ways of understanding what is operative here, if Luke is really using a Baptist source. On the one hand, this detail could be a Lucan redactional modification of the source, made by Luke to stress the Spirit-guided activity of John's prophetic role. On the other hand, the relation of "Spirit" and "filling" is not unknown in the OT (see Exod 35:31; Wisd 1:7; the spirit of Elijah fills Elisha in ms. A of Sir 48:12 LXX). So some form of this expression may well have been used in the Baptist source, suggesting a relationship of John to the prophets of old, who were often said to be under the Spirit's influence in the OT (e.g. 1 Sam 10:10; Isa 61:1). In the Lucan story other figures of the Period of Israel are said to be filled with the holy Spirit (e.g. Zechariah, 1:67; Elizabeth, 1:41). Luke does not separate that period from the Spirit.

Verses 15-16, then, describe John as one who will be a Nazirite prophet who is to summon Israel to turn again to the Lord (an echo of Mal 3:24 [or Sir 48:10]).

In v. 17a John is explicitly related to Elijah, as one endowed with his "spirit" (see 2 Kgs 2:9-16), as was Elisha, and with his "power." The first part of this verse specifies, in effect, how John is to be "great" in the Lord's sight (v. 15). In the Gospel proper we shall see John carrying out his role of the reform prophet, thus acting in the "spirit" of Elijah; but he is never depicted exercising the "power" of Elijah, by which is usually meant his power to work miracles (see NOTE). Luke retains this reference to power from the Baptist source, even though it does not agree with his own account of John. In retaining the entire description of John as one endowed with the spirit and power of Elijah, Luke identifies John with him, more explicitly than he does in 7:27, where what he writes amounts to an implicit identification (using Mal 3:1) and where he does not do what Matthew does in his parallel, i.e. name him explicitly as "Elijah who is to come" (11:14). Here, however, the equivalent is being said. On the double Elijah-theme in Lucan writings, see p. 213 above. The identification of John and Elijah is pre-Lucan, as its presence in "Q" shows. There is no reason to think that it was not already in the Baptist source. The "messenger" of Mal 3:1 had already become "Elijah" sent before the great and awesome Day of the Lord in the appendix of Malachi (3:23-24) and in Sir 48:10. The identification continued in the pre-Lucan tradition about John, and Luke picks it up and uses it here.

In v. 17b-d, which resumes v. 16, the mode in which the turning to the Lord is to happen is made specific. The first specification alludes to only one form of conversion mentioned in Mal 3:34, omitting the reciprocal turning of children to their fathers (or of a people to their neighbors, in the LXX-form). The conversion is to remedy a paternal neglect of the young in Israel; Luke is hinting, in adopting this phrase, at the neglect shown by Israel of old toward those who are to become Abraham's children (3:8). The second specification is a turning of the disobedient to the understanding (or wisdom) of those who stand upright in the sight of God. The third specification of the turning emphasizes John's role in preparing Israel for the coming of the Lord.

In vv. 18-20 the fourth and fifth elements of the OT birth-announcement pattern are presented. Zechariah echoes Abraham's objection (Gen 15:8), when God promised the patriarch a progeny as numerous as heaven's stars. In reply, Gabriel identifies himself and promises Zechariah that he will be struck dumb. Part of Zechariah's objection (v. 18b), about his and Elizabeth's old age, echoes v. 7. In identifying himself as Gabriel, the angel alludes to Dan 9:21. Still another allusion to Daniel (10:15) is found in the muteness of Zechariah. The sign given to Zechariah, then, differs considerably from that given to Abraham (Gen 15:7-21) and to Mary (1:35-37).

The third section of this episode (vv. 21-23) makes it clear to the people that something extraordinary has happened to Zechariah. The sign promised to Zechariah is immediately manifested: As he emerges from the holy place of the Temple, he is speechless, unable to pronounce the customary priestly blessing (see NOTE).

The final section of this episode is found in vv. 24-25. Only the first half of v. 24 was derived from the Baptist source by Luke. What begins in v. 57 is the logical sequel to it. Lucan redaction has introduced the five-month seclusion of Elizabeth. This seclusion is not to be explained psychologically as the result of some modesty or as part of a device embracing the various time-indications in the infancy narrative (e.g. five months here, six months in 1:26, three months in 1:56, and eight days in 2:21) to equal [supposedly] 490 days, a hidden allusion to the Danielic Seventy Weeks prophecy—see Burrows, *Gospel of the Infancy,* 41-42; R. Laurentin, *Structure,* 49. Rather, as Schneider (*Evangelium nach Lukas,* 46) and Brown (*Birth,* 282) maintain, the five-month seclusion is a preparation for the sign to be given to Mary (1:36). If Elizabeth had not been in seclusion, her pregnancy would have become known (certainly within her family) and could not have been used as a sign to be given to Mary's question (1:36). This modification of the Baptist source is made in preparation for the sign to Mary.

Just as no announcement was made to Sarah by an angel, after Abraham had been informed by the Lord (Gen 17:16), so no announcement is made to Elizabeth. The economy of storytelling is at work here. The promise made to Zechariah about the birth of a son is straightway fulfilled, just as in 1 Sam 1:19-20 Elkanah returns home to Ramah and Hannah conceives shortly thereafter.

This first episode of the Lucan infancy narrative has, then, as its purpose to introduce him who will be the precursor of Jesus in the new age of salvation-history that is soon to begin. John will be transitional, bridging the Period of Israel and the Period of Jesus. His work as one great before the Lord, an ascetic Nazirite prophet, sent to turn back Israel to the Lord in the spirit and power of Elijah, is thus laid before the reader of the Lucan Gospel.

NOTES

1 5. *in the days of Herod, king of Judea.* So Luke pinpoints the story that he is about to tell to his extra-Palestinian readers. But, despite his protestation about completeness, thoroughness, and accuracy (1:3), his dating of the birth of John (and of Jesus) in Palestinian history remains vague at this point. The "days of Herod" covered a long period. Matthew has a similar dating in 2:1, "in the days of Herod, the king," but he at least tells his readers that Jesus was born shortly before the death of Herod (2:15,19-20).

Luke refers to Herod the Great, the son of the Idumean Antipater. When driven out of Palestine by the alliance of the Hasmoneans and the Parthians, Herod was given support by Mark Antony and granted the title, "king of Judea," by the Roman Senate in 40 B.C. However, he had to return to Palestine and win his kingdom (see Josephus *Ant.* 14.14,5 § 386; 14.15,1 § 398). He began to rule in 37 B.C. "In the days of Herod" could refer to any time between 37 and 4 B.C., when the king died (*Ant.* 15.8,1 § 191). The date, however, will be narrowed down by the reference to the census under Quirinius the governor in Luke 2:1-2.

The vague dating used here is probably derived by Luke from a characteristic OT expression; see Tob 1:16; Jdt 1:1; cf. 2 Chr 14:1.

"Judea" must be understood here generically, as the land of the Jews (=Palestine); see Luke 4:44; 6:17; 7:17; 23:5; Acts 2:9; 10:37. Herod's dominion also included Galilee, Samaria, and much of Perea and Coele-Syria. Hence, it is not to be restricted to the specific sense of "Judea," as it is used in 1:65 or 2:4; 21:21.

a priest named Zechariah. Lit. "a certain priest by (the) name of Zechariah." He is a member of a priestly family that served in the Jerusalem Temple. John is being introduced to the readers through his priestly father, and thus related already to the Period of Israel. Other priests of earlier days named Zechariah are mentioned in the OT (1 Chr 15:24; 2 Chr 35:8; Neh 11:12). His name is typically Hebraic; Zĕkaryāh means "Yahweh has remembered (again)," in giving the parents this child.

the priestly course of Abijah. Zechariah is further identified as a member of the eighth "course" or "division" of the priests who served in the Jerusalem Temple. The word ephēmeria denotes the "daily" duties to be performed by the priests (Neh 13:30), but it came to be the Greek word for the classes or divisions into which David with the aid of Zadok and Ahimelech organized the sons of Aaron (see 1 Chr 23:6; 24:7-18, where the twenty-four courses are named). After the Babylonian Captivity priests of only four courses returned to Jerusalem: Jedaiah, Immer, Pashhur, and Harim (Ezra 2:36-39; cf. 10:18-22). These seem to have been redivided into twenty-four courses with the old names (Neh 12:1-7). Josephus speaks of both seven courses (Life 1 § 2; Ant. 7.14,7 § 365-366 [here called phylai, "families"]) and four courses (Ag. Ap. 2.8 § 108 [here called tribus, "clans"]). Each course served twice a year in the Jerusalem Temple, for a week at a time (see Str-B, 2. 55-68 for details). Luke's description of Zechariah reveals that he was a simple priest of the course of Abijah, not a high priest (as the Protevangelium of James 8:1-3 eventually depicted him).

His wife was a descendant of Aaron. Lit. "(was) of the daughters of Aaron." John's parents are thus both described as being of priestly stock; this should mean that John would one day appear serving in the Temple too. But he is never so portrayed. The Lucan expression used here is paralleled in 2 Chr 2:14, apo thygaterōn Dan, "of the daughters of Dan." Though Lev 21:7,14 forbids a Jewish priest to marry a harlot, a defiled woman, a widow, or a divorcee (for he "is holy to his God"), he was not obliged to marry a virgin of priestly descent.

her name was Elizabeth. Cf. Luke 1:27 and the LXX of Gen 17:5,15 for similar expressions. Elizabeth was the name of Aaron's wife in Exod 6:23. Hebrew 'Elíšeba' may mean "My God is the one by whom to swear," but the sense is contested; sometimes it is explained as "my God is satiety, fortune" (see W. Baumgartner, HALAT, 55; cf. L. Koehler, ZAW 55 [1937] 165-166).

6. upright in God's sight. Here the adj. dikaios expresses the conformity of John's parents to the will of God, expressed especially in his law, as the rest of the verse makes clear (cf. Deut 6:25 for an OT expression of the same idea).

See further A. Descamps, *Les justes et la justice dans les évangiles et le christi-anisme primitif hormis la doctrine proprement paulinienne* (Louvain: Publica-tions universitaires, 1950) 32-34. This description is added by Luke to make sure that the couple's childlessness is not understood by the reader as resulting from any wickedness or unworthiness in the sight of God.

lived blamelessly. Lit. "walking blamelessly." Luke uses the verb *poreuesthai* in the sense of ethical conduct, as does the LXX of Ps 119:1. Cf. 1 Kgs 8:61.

the commandments and requirements of the Lord. As often in the rest of the infancy narrative, *kyrios* is here used of Yahweh. See p. 201 above. The rest of the phrase is formulated in imitation of OT expressions; see Gen 26:5; Num 36:13; Deut 4:40.

7. *no children.* The situation has its OT precedent; see Gen 18:11. For a couple to be childless in Judaism was a misfortune, even a disgrace or a pun-ishment for sin (see Gen 16:4,11; 29:32; 30:1; Lev 20:20-21; 1 Sam 1:5-6; 2 Sam 6:23). But Elizabeth's barrenness is intended by Luke in a class with that of Sarah (Gen 16:1), Rebecca (Gen 25:21), Rachel (Gen 30:1), the mother of Samson (Judg 13:2), and Hannah (1 Sam 1-2), i.e. the mothers of famous OT patriarchs or leaders. To such antecedents John himself is now understood to belong. Their barrenness was remedied by God's intervention, and so will Elizabeth's be. A special similarity between Elizabeth and Sarah is evident in that both were not only barren but beyond the normal age of childbearing.

because. This is the first occurrence of *kathoti*, which is used solely by Luke in the NT (Luke 19:9; Acts 2:24,45; 4:35; 17:31).

both were well along in years. Lit. "advanced in their days," an expression frequently used in the LXX (Gen 18:11; 24:1; Josh 13:1, etc.). Elizabeth's barrenness has been mentioned, and this phrase reveals that she was also be-yond the age of childbearing. The detail heightens the miraculous aspect of the birth to come. The same description will be used of Anna in 2:36.

8. *Once when Zechariah was serving before God.* Lit. "and it happened, when Zechariah . . . , (that) it fell to his lot. . . ." This is the first instance of the *egeneto de* construction in the Lucan writings (see p. 119 above). Here it occurs with a finite verb (*elache*), but without an intervening *kai*. The temporal clause is expressed by *en* + the dat. of the articular infin., *tō hiera-teuein*, "in his serving (as priest)." Thus Luke sets the stage for the angelic an-nouncement that is to come to this lowly priest.

during the turn of his priestly course. I.e. during one of the two turns when his course was performing the priestly duties during the year.

9. *it fell to his lot.* The member of the course who would be privileged to enter the sanctuary to offer the incense was chosen by casting lots; the regula-tions for the lot are given in *m. Tamid* 5:2 - 6:3. Cf. *TDNT* 4.1.

to enter the sanctuary of the Lord. Luke uses the word *naos* (as in 1:21-22), which may designate both the "holy place," the front part, in which stood the altar of incense, the golden seven-branched lampstand, and the table of show-bread (see 1 Macc 1:21-22), and "the holy of holies," the rear, separated by a curtain from the front part (Luke 23:45). Into the latter, however, only the high priest entered, and then only once a year, on the Day of Atonement (Heb 9:6-7). Zechariah's duty was to enter the holy place to clean the altar of incense and offer fresh incense. The *naos* was distinct from the *hieron*, the term used by Luke to designate either the Temple in general or the Temple precincts (Luke 2:27,37,46; 4:9; 18:10; 19:45,47; 20:1; 21:5,37,38; 22:52,53; 24:53).

10. *all the people were assembled outside.* Lit. "all the assemblage of people was praying outside." This is a typically Lucan rhetorical exaggeration; it probably should be understood to mean, "the people who were assembled outside were all praying." Normally, the OT does not mention the praying of people at the time of sacrifices, unless Solomon's prayer in 2 Chr 6:12-42 is to be so understood. "Outside" would refer to the people gathered in the courts of the men and the women.

at the time of the incense offering. Exod 30:7-8 prescribes that Aaron should burn incense "every morning when he dresses the lamps" and again when "he sets up the lamps in the evening." The parallels with Dan 9:21 otherwise found in the infancy narrative would suggest that it is the time of the evening offering that is to be understood here, since at that hour Gabriel appeared in Daniel 9. Acts 3:1 speaks of the ninth hour as the hour of prayer, i.e. about 3 P.M. Cf. Josephus *Ant.* 13.10,3 § 282.

11. *There appeared to Zechariah the angel of the Lord.* Lit. "there was seen to him." Luke here uses the aor. pass. indic. of *horan,* "see," the form *ōphthē,* which he uses again in 24:34; Acts 2:3; 7:2,26,30,35; 9:17; 13:31; 16:9; 26:16 to denote various epiphanies or appearances. It is also used frequently in the LXX in the same sense (e.g. Gen 12:7; 17:1; 18:1). Its Aramaic counterpart (*'ithăzî*) can be found in the *Genesis Apocryphon* (1QapGen 22:27).

"The angel of the Lord" also appears to the barren wife of Manoah, the father of Samson in Judg 13:3. Though Luke is combining two OT figures in this passage, the name of the angel is not given until 1:19. The Greek phrase *angelos kyriou* is a Semitism, reflecting the Hebrew construct chain, *mal'ak Yhwh,* "messenger of Yahweh," as the lack of Greek def. arts. reveals. This is the exalted OT figure who appears at times to be indistinguishable from Yahweh himself (Gen 16:7-13; 21:17; 22:10-18; 31:11-13; Exod 3:2-6; 14:19-24; Judg 2:1-5). Originally, it was a personification of a theophanic element, a way of describing God's presence to human beings. But in the course of time it becomes a definite heavenly being (Zech 1:11-14), even though it is never given a proper name in the OT. Especially in the postexilic period Jewish angelology developed, mostly owing to the contact of exiled Jews with other cultures in which lesser gods and divine heroes were a commonplace. To preserve the transcendence of Yahweh, angels of various types were introduced, and there developed names for specific angelic beings, especially in apocalyptic and related literature. In identifying "the angel of the Lord" as Gabriel (1:19), Luke not only goes beyond the contemporary Jewish custom, but depicts him as a personal being. In introducing such a being, he would be adopting an element from Pharisaic belief, not admitted by the Sadducees (see Acts 23:8). "The angel of the Lord" further appears in Luke 2:9; Acts 5:19; 8:26; 12:7,23.

to the right of the altar of incense. For a description of the altar of incense, see Exod 30:1-10; 37:25-29. The "right side," being usually considered the favored side, would convey to Zechariah that the angel's visit to him was not ominous.

12. *fear came over him.* Lit. "fear fell upon him," possibly an allusion to Dan 10:7. In the OT alarm and fear are the standard reactions to heavenly epiphanies. See, e.g. Exod 15:16.

13. *the angel said to him.* This is the first occurrence of a verb of saying with the prep. *pros* + accus. instead of the dative—a construction common in the Lucan writings; see further p. 116 above.

Do not be afraid. This is again a standard OT reassurance given by heavenly visitors (e.g. Gen 15:1; Dan 10:12,19). See further Luke 1:30; 2:10; 8:50.

your prayer has been heard. The object of Zechariah's prayer is not specified, but the immediate context and the following words of the angel would imply that he had been praying not only for the good of Israel but also for a child (vv. 6-7). The angel's words imply too that the child to be born to him will also help Israel. See v. 16. It is not impossible to think that Zechariah's generic prayer (for "the redemption of Israel," 2:38) is answered in a specific way by the announcement of the birth of a son to him. Indeed, the specific aspect of the announcement or answer to his generic prayer may be the reason for his hesitation and doubt.

you are to name him John. Lit. "you will call his name John"; the same formula will appear again in 1:31; cf. 1:59; 2:21. It is also used in Matt 1:21,25; cf. 1:23. It is an OT expression; see Gen 3:20; Isa 9:5; Jer 11:16; Tob 1:9. The name given by the angel for the child expresses the situation, for *Yôḥānān* means "Yahweh has shown favor." The child will be graced, and his special character is thus made known to his father, who will name him (cf. Gen 4:26; 5:3). Like other heaven-imposed names (Gen 16:11; Isa 7:14; 1 Kgs 13:2), it implies that the child will have a role in the drama of God's salvation, one in accord with the meaning of the name.

14. *Joy and delight.* This is the first indication of the atmosphere that pervades the Lucan infancy narrative (see further 1:28,46,58; 2:10). Verse 15 gives the reason for the joy, which is not limited solely to his parents, but will also come to "many."

15. *great in the sight of the Lord.* The Greek phrase *estai megas enōpion kyriou* could mean no more than *estai megas* in *T. Levi* 17.2, "he will grow up before God." Cf. 1 Sam 2:21 (*emegalynthē*). So H. Sahlin, *Der Messias und das Gottesvolk: Studien zur protolukanischen Theologie* (ASNU 12; Lund: Gleerup, 1945) 77. However, a contrast seems to be implied with 1:32, where it is said of Jesus that *houtos estai megas.* Laurentin (*Structure,* 36) calls attention to the absolute use of *megas,* "great," there and to the fact that in the LXX the absolute *megas* is an attribute of Yahweh himself (see Pss 48:2 =145:3; 86:10; 135:5) whereas the adjective is qualified when it is used of human beings (see 2 Sam 19:33 LXX; Sir 48:22). So it is here in the case of John. John's greatness (see Luke 7:28) is here measured in terms of the *Kyrios,* who in this context is to be understood as Yahweh. This is not an allusion to Mal 3:1.

He shall drink no wine or beer. This is an allusion to Num 6:3, "he shall abstain from wine and beer," or perhaps to Judg 13:4, where the mother of Samson is cautioned to drink "no wine or beer" because she is to bear a child who will be a Nazirite, i.e. one consecrated by vow (Hebrew *nēzer*) and set apart for the Lord. Luke is implying that John is to come as a Nazirite, assimilating him to Samson and also to Samuel (see 1 Sam 1:11, "he drinks no wine or intoxicating beverage," according to the LXX and 4QSamᵃ). A Qumran Hebrew text, 4QSamᵃ 1:3 reads 1 Sam 1:22 thus: *nzyr 'd 'wlm kwl ymy* [*ḥyyw*], "a Nazirite forever all the days of [his life]," making Samuel's status as *nāzîr* explicit, which is not said in the LXX. See F. M. Cross, *BASOR* 132 (1953) 18. The allusion to the Samuel story is but a part of the larger Lucan dependence on that story in the infancy narrative. In depicting John thus, Luke is hinting at his prophetic role; cf. 1:76; 7:26-27.

The Greek word *sikera* is often translated simply as "strong drink" (BAG, 758); but that English expression may imply a beverage stronger than what is intended. The word is the Greek transcription of Aramaic *šikrā'* (=Hebrew *šēkār;* Akkadian *šikaru*), the word for an alcoholic drink distinct from wine and commonly used of "barley beer," though it was made at times of other substances.

even from his birth. Lit. "still from the womb of his mother." Ms. W reads rather *en koilia,* "while still in the womb." The substitution of prep. *en* for *ek* is an obvious correction smoothing out the relation between the prep. phrase and the adv. *eti,* "still." In the OT the phrase *ek/apo koilias mētros* can mean either "from birth on" (Isa 48:8; Ps 22:11) or "while still in the womb" (Judg 13:3-5; 16:17; Isa 44:2). That the latter is meant here is evident from 1:41. But the phrase is also used in a broad sense, meaning that John's whole existence will be graced. Later theological speculation will interpret it as the sanctification of John in his mother's womb (see 1:41; cf. DS 790).

filled with a holy Spirit. John's satiety will not be found in that of ordinary mortals, but in the gift of the Spirit. As a Nazirite, he will be consecrated to the Lord; Yahweh's Spirit will fill him instead of the drink from which he is to abstain. A typically Lucan expression, "filled with a/the holy Spirit" (e.g. 1:41,67; Acts 2:4; 4:8,31; 9:17; 13:9), denotes the gift of God's creative or prophetic presence. Since in Lucan theology John plays a transitional role (see p. 184 above), he shares the new manifestation of the Spirit that is to guide the Period of Jesus and the Period of the Church. On the role of the Spirit in Lucan theology, see pp. 227-231 above.

16. *He will turn many . . . to the Lord.* Fitted out with prophetic spirit and power, John will become Yahweh's instrument to convert Israel from its estrangement. The words *pollous epistrepsei* seem to be an allusion to Mal 2:6 (*pollous epestrepsen,* "he turned many" from iniquity). Cf. Sir 48:10. They imply again John's role as Elijah, introduced into the infancy narrative by Luke with hindsight from the developed gospel tradition.

the children of Israel. An OT phrase (Hos 3:4-5; Mic 5:2; Sir 46:10; 47:2) often used by Luke (Acts 5:21; 7:23,37; 9:15; 10:36).

to the Lord, their God. Here *Kyrios* clearly refers to Yahweh.

17. *go before him.* I.e. before Yahweh, as the messenger of Mal 3:1.

with the spirit and power of Elijah. In the OT the prophet Elijah the Tishbite, promised that Elisha would receive a double share of his "spirit" if Elisha saw him as he was being taken away from him (2 Kgs 2:9-10; cf. Sir 48:12). The vision that followed revealed Elisha as the successor of Elijah in Israel. Elijah's power is known in the OT in his miracles (1 Kgs 17-18). Having called down fire from heaven in the contest with the prophets of Baal and rid Israel of their influence, Elijah was cast in the role of a reformer. In Mal 3:23 4:5-6E) he is identified as the messenger to be sent before "the great and awesome day of Yahweh" (cf. Mal 3:2). Cf. Sir 48:1-10. It is in this sense that the angel now tells Zechariah that his son John is to go before the Lord (=Yahweh). See Luke 1:76.

The parallelism of the stories of John and Jesus suggests that John "goes before" Jesus, who is also called "the Lord" (1:43; 2:11). But that cannot be meant here, since Zechariah is told nothing of the birth of yet another child in God's plan. Moreover, neither in the OT nor in any other pre-Christian Jewish literature is Elijah ever depicted as the precursor of the Messiah. That notion developed only in Christian times (see J. A. T. Robinson, "Elijah, John and Jesus"). Cf. Justin *Dial.* 9.8; 49.1 One has to insist on this absence in pre-Christian times, *pace* J. Jeremias, *TDNT* 2. 931; the figure in *1 Enoch* 89:52 and 90:31 may be Elijah, but he is not presented as the precursor of the Messiah. J. Starcky (*RB* 70 [1963] 497-498) has revealed that a fragment from Qumran Cave 4 reads in part, *lkn 'šlḥ l'lyh qd[m . . .],* "to you I shall send Elijah bef[ore . . .]," and the text breaks off! Starcky rightly sees that one can refer it to Mal 3:23, but there is no certainty that the lacuna would have to be restored with [*mšyḥ*], "[the Messiah]." (For another understanding of Elijah's precedence, see Mark 9:10-12.) Cf. M. M. Faierstein, *JBL* 100 (1981) 75-86.

to turn the hearts of parents to children. This is an allusion to Mal 3:24 (4:6E) or Sir 48:10; the plural is closer to the MT of Mal 3:24. John's role will be a continuation of the reform effort of the famous prophet of old. Cf. P. Winter, *ZNW* 49 (1958) 65-66.

turn the disobedient to the understanding of the upright. A wisdom role is also assigned to John, for in the Wisdom literature of the OT *phronēsis*, "understanding," is often associated with *sophia*, "wisdom." "Understanding," "wisdom," and "righteousness" are associated in 4 Macc 1:18.

to make ready a people fit for the Lord. The first part of the clause is an OT expression, "to make ready a people" (2 Sam 7:24); cf. Exod 19:10-11. The added ptc. *kateskeuasmenon* is redundant, unless the emphasis is put on a people equipped, i.e. fitted out for the Day of the Lord (Mal 3:24). Cf. Luke 1:76.

18. *How shall I know?* Like the incredulous Abraham of old (Gen 15:8), Zechariah queries the angel, knowing that God in the past had given signs in such contexts (Judg 6:37-40, Gideon's trial of God with the fleece; 2 Kgs 20:8-11, Hezekiah's request; Isa 7:11).

19. *I am Gabriel.* Luke identifies "the angel of the Lord" as the angel of the prophecy of seventy weeks in Daniel 9, Gabriel, who came to Daniel "at the time of the evening sacrifice" (9:21; cf. 8:16). Along with Michael (Dan 10:13; 12:1) and Raphael (Tob 3:17), Gabriel is one of the three angels specifically named in the OT; elsewhere in pre-Christian Jewish literature four

others are named, Sariel, Uriel, Penuel, and Baraqiel (at times with some variants attested). They were the seven angels of the presence (see Tob 12:15; *1 Enoch* 20; Rev 8:2; cf. J. T. Milik, *The Books of Enoch*, 152-156 [but beware of the meanings given there]). The developing angelology of postexilic Judaism made use of archaism in giving such heavenly beings names ending in *-ēl*, "God," i.e. the ancient theophoric type of name compounded with the name of the old Canaanite god (*'El*), which eventually became a name of Yahweh himself. The name *Gabrî-'ēl* means, not "Man of God" or "God has shown himself strong" (so Brown, *Birth*, 262), but "God is my hero/warrior." See J. A. Fitzmyer, *CBQ* 39 (1977) 438.

I have been sent. I.e. by God; the so-called theological passive is common in Lucan writings. See ZBG § 236.

to announce this to you. Luke uses here the verb *euangelizesthai* for the first time. For K. H. Rengstorf (*Evangelium nach Lukas*, 22) it means "to preach the gospel," and Zechariah would be the first to whom it is preached. However, given Luke's attitude toward *euangelion* (see p. 173 above), it is highly questionable whether we should so interpret it.

20. *Now.* Lit. "and behold," the words being *kai idou*, on which see p. 121 above.

you shall become mute, and be unable to speak. This is the sign by which Zechariah is to know. This sort of miracle differs significantly from those which Jesus performs in the gospel tradition. It is a punitive miracle, related to the stories in Acts 5:1-10; 13:16-11. The further implication in the action is that God himself closes the lips of Zechariah to conceal from human beings what he is about—for a time at least. Deafness must also have been part of Zechariah's condition, because the people have to make signs to him in 1:62.

which will find fulfillment. Luke uses the verb *plēroun* here, referring to the words (*logoi*) of the angel. The same verb will be used in 4:21 about the fulfillment of the words of Isaiah and in 24:44 about what was written in the law of Moses, the prophets, and the psalms. The angel had hinted at God's plan of salvation-history, but Zechariah had not comprehended it.

in their own time. Here the noun *kairos* has its nuance of a point in God's determination. See further 12:56; 18:30; 19:44; 21:8,24; Acts 1:7; 3:20; 17:26.

21. *who were waiting.* In Luke's account Zechariah is portrayed alone in the holy place, expected to return from it without undue delay to prevent anxiety on the part of the people. Luke is unaware of the prescription in the Mishnah (*Tamid* 5:4-6; 6:1-3; 7:1-2) that several priests entered the holy place together. The Mishnah (*Yoma* 5:1) forbids the high priest in the Day of Atonement to prolong his prayer before the curtain of the holy of holies lest "he put Israel in terror." Whether this was applied also to the *tamid*-offering, we do not know.

22. *he . . . could not speak to them.* According to *m. Tamid* 7:2, the priests, on coming out of the holy place, were expected to pronounce together the priestly blessing (Num 6:24-26) over the assembled people. For the sake of his story about Zechariah's vision in the holy place Luke has limited the

priestly role to one person and now portrays Zechariah as unable to utter the blessing.

they realized that he had seen a vision. Luke does not tell us how the crowd could have been so perceptive; but to ask how is to miss the point of his story. Cf. Josephus *Ant.* 13.10,3 §§ 282-283.

remained speechless. The Greek adj. *kōphos* means "blunt, dull," and in a figurative sense both "deaf" and "dumb." From the immediate context it would seem to mean "mute" (and so it is understood in BAG, 463); but 1:62 implies that Zechariah could not hear either; so perhaps one should translate it "deaf and dumb."

23. *when the period of his Temple service was over.* Lit. "and it happened, when the days of his service were completed, he went back. . . ." Luke uses here *kai egeneto* + a finite verb (without a conj.), with the temporal clause introduced by *hōs.* See p. 119 above. The period of service lasted for a week. Luke here uses the verb *pimplanai,* "fill, complete," and it probably does not have any connotation of fulfillment; contrast *plēroun* in v. 20.

he went back. This is the beginning of what will be a refrain of departure in several episodes in the infancy narrative; see 1:38,56; 2:15,20,39,51. See the COMMENT. No indication is given here about the location of Zechariah's home; but 1:39 makes it clear that he and Elizabeth did not live in Jerusalem. Their home was in the "hill country" (1:39).

24. *Some time later.* Lit. "after these days."

Elizabeth became pregnant. The promise that was made to Zechariah in 1:13 finds fulfillment in this notice that Elizabeth has conceived. Luke is more reserved than the author of 1 Sam 1:19-20, but his story contains the same motif. The notice foreshadows what will be said to Mary by the angel in 1:36.

remained in seclusion for five months. Lit. "she hid herself (for) five months." This refers to the first five months of her nine-month pregnancy (cf. 2 Macc 7:27; 2 Esdr 4:40). It might seem puzzling that Luke should note that she hid herself during the first part of her pregnancy; no Palestinian custom is known that would call for it. The seclusion prepares for 1:36, where Mary, her cousin, learns of her condition first from an angel. Moreover, the following verse explains the motivation. Her seclusion, like Zechariah's muteness, preserved the secret until the plan of salvation-history reaches the point at which it is to be made known.

25. *This is how the Lord has dealt with me.* So Elizabeth expresses her joy over the divine removal of her embarrassment. In this she is not only like Sarah (Gen 21:6) and Rachel (Gen 30:23), who rejoice after the birth of their children, but also like Mary. She does not utter a Magnificat, but she understands the implications of what God has done for her.

The *hoti* at the beginning of this verse in the Greek text creates something of a problem. It is best taken as *hoti recitativum,* despite the Latin Vg, which translates it as *quia,* "because," and makes the rest sound like a reason why Elizabeth has secluded herself. But cf. P. Winter, *HTR* 48 (1955) 213-216.

he saw fit. The Greek verb *epeiden* means "fixed his gaze on, looked at." It expresses God's concern for human beings. Since it has no pronominal object and is followed by an infin., it should be understood absolutely, with the infin. expressing purpose.

the disgrace. I.e. of childlessness. See the NOTE on v. 7 above. Elizabeth's comment echoes the words of Rebecca in Gen 30:23.

LUCAN INFANCY NARRATIVE: GENERAL BIBLIOGRAPHY

Audet, J.-M. "Autour de la théologie de Luc I-II," *ScEccl* 11 (1959) 409-418.

Bornhäuser, K. *Die Geburts- und Kindheitsgeschichte Jesu: Versuch einer zeitgenössischen Auslegung von Matthäus 1 und 2 und Lukas 1-3* (BFCT 2/23; Gütersloh: Bertelsmann, 1930).

Box, G. H. "The Gospel Narratives of the Nativity and the Alleged Influence of Heathen Ideas," *ZNW* 6 (1905) 80-101.

Brown, R. E. *The Birth of the Messiah: A Commentary on the Infancy Narratives in Matthew and Luke* (New York: Doubleday, 1977) 233-499.

Brunner-Traut, E. "Die Geburtsgeschichte der Evangelien im Lichte ägyptologischer Forschungen," *ZRGG* 12 (1960) 97-111.

Burrows, E. *The Gospel of the Infancy and Other Biblical Essays* (Bellarmine Series 6; London: Burns, Oates and Washbourne, 1940) 1-58.

Daniélou, J. *The Infancy Narratives* (New York: Herder & Herder, 1968).

Derrett, J. D. M. "Further Light on the Narratives of the Nativity," *NovT* 17 (1975) 81-108.

Dibelius, M. "Jungfrauensohn und Krippenkind: Untersuchungen zur Geburtsgeschichte Jesu im Lukas-Evangelium," in *Sitzungsberichte der Heidelberger Akademie der Wissenschaften*, Philos.-histor. Kl., 4 (1932); reprinted in *Botschaft und Geschichte* (Tübingen: Mohr [Siebeck]) 1 (1953) 1-78.

Dignath, W. *Die lukanische Vorgeschichte* (Gütersloh: Mohn, 1971).

Erdmann, G. *Die Vorgeschichten des Lukas- und Matthäus-Evangeliums und Vergils vierte Ekloge* (FRLANT 47; Göttingen: Vandenhoeck und Ruprecht, 1932).

Feuillet, A. *Jésus et sa mère, d'après les récits lucaniens de l'enfance et d'après Saint Jean* (Paris: Gabalda, 1974).

——— "Quelques observations sur les récits de l'enfance chez S. Luc," *Esprit et vie* 82 (1972) 721-724.

Ford, J. M. "Zealotism and the Lukan Infancy Narratives," *NovT* 18 (1976) 280-292.

Gaechter, P. *Maria im Erdenleben: Neutestamentliche Marienstudien* (3d ed.; Innsbruck: Tyrolia, 1955).

George, A. "Le parallèle entre Jean-Baptiste et Jésus en Lc 1-2," in *Mélanges bibliques en hommage au R. P. Béda Rigaux* (eds. A. Descamps and A. de Halleux; Gembloux: Duculot, 1970) 147-171.

Glöckner, R. *Die Verkündigung des Heils beim Evangelisten Lukas* (Mainz: Grünewald, n.d. [1976]) 68-124.

Goulder, M. D., and M. L. Sanderson. "St. Luke's Genesis," *JTS* 8 (1957) 12-30.

Gressmann, H. *Das Weihnachtsevangelium auf Ursprung und Geschichte untersucht* (Göttingen: Vandenhoeck und Ruprecht, 1914).

Isaacs, M. E. "Mary in the Lucan Infancy Narrative," *Way*, Suppl. 25 (1975) 80-95.

Kraaft, E. "Die Vorgeschichte des Lukas: Eine Frage nach ihrer sachgemässen Interpretation," in *Zeit und Geschichte: Dankesgabe an Rudolf Bultmann zum 80. Geburtstag* (ed. E. Dinkler; Tübingen: Mohr [Siebeck], 1964) 217-223.

Lagrange, M.-J. "Le récit de l'enfance de Jésus dans S. Luc," *RB* os 4 (1895) 160-185.

Laurentin, R. *Structure et théologie de Luc I-II* (EBib; Paris: Gabalda, 1957).

———— "Traces d'allusions étymologiques en Luc 1-2," *Bib* 37 (1956) 435-456; 38 (1957) 1-23.

Leaney, R. "The Birth Narratives in St Luke and St Matthew," *NTS* 8 (1961-1962) 158-166.

Machen, J. G. "The Origin of the First Two Chapters of Luke," *Princeton Theological Review* 10 (1912) 212-277.

MacNeill, H. L. "The *Sitz im Leben* of Luke 1:5-2:20," *JBL* 65 (1946) 123-130.

Mann, C. S. "The Historicity of the Birth Narratives," in *Historicity and Chronology in the New Testament* (Theological Collections 6; eds. D. E. Nineham et al.; London: SPCK, 1965) 46-58.

Meagher, G. "The Prophetic Call Narrative," *ITQ* 39 (1972) 164-177.

Minear, P. S. "The Interpreter and the Nativity Stories," *TTod* 7 (1950-1951) 358-375.

———— "Luke's Use of the Birth Stories," in *Studies in Luke-Acts*, 111-130.

Muñoz Iglesias, S. "Estructura y teología de Lucas I-II," *EstBíb* 17 (1958) 101-107.

———— "El evangelio de la infancia en S. Lucas y las infancias de los héroes bíblicos," *EstBíb* 16 (1957) 329-382.

———— "Midrás y evangelios de la infancia," *EstEcl* 47 (1972) 331-359.

Neirynck, F. "L'évangile de Noël selon S. Luc," *Études religieuses* 749 (Paris/Bruxelles: Pensée catholique, 1960).

———— "Visitatio B. M. V.: Bijdrage tot de Quellenkritik van Lc. 1-2," *Collationes brugenses et gandavenses* 6 (1960) 387-404.

Nellessen, E. "Zu den Kindheitsgeschichten bei Matthäus und Lukas: Bericht über neuere deutschsprachige Literatur," *TTZ* 78 (1969) 305-309.

Norden, E. *Die Geburt des Kindes: Geschichte einer religiösen Idee* (Stuttgart: Teubner, 1924; reprinted, Darmstadt: Wissenschaftliche Buchgesellschaft, 1958).

Oliver, H. H. "The Lucan Birth Stories and the Purpose of Luke-Acts," *NTS* 10 (1963-1964) 202-226.

Räisänen, H. *Die Mutter Jesu im Neuen Testament* (Annales academiae scientiarum fennicae B/158; Helsinki: Suomalainen Tiedeakatemia, 1969).

Riedl, J. *Die Vorgeschichte Jesu: Die Heilsbotschaft von Mt 1-2 und Lk 1-2* (Biblisches Forum 3; Stuttgart: Katholisches Bibelwerk, n.d. [1968]).

Ruddick, C. T., Jr. "Birth Narratives in Genesis and Luke," *NovT* 12 (1970) 343-348.

Sahlin, H. *Der Messias und das Gottesvolk: Studien zur protolukanischen Theologie* (ASNU 12; Uppsala: Almsqvist, 1945) 63-342.

Salazar, A. M. "Questions about St. Luke's Sources," *NovT* 2 (1957-1958) 316-317.

Schelkle, K. H. "Die Kindheitsgeschichte Jesu," in *Wort und Schrift: Beiträge zur Auslegung und Auslegungsgeschichte des Neuen Testaments* (Düsseldorf: Patmos, 1966) 59-75.

Schierse, F. J. "Weihnachtliche Christusverkündigung: Zum Verständnis der Kindheitsgechichten," *BibLeb* 1 (1960) 217-222.

Schürmann, H. "Aufbau, Eigenart und Geschichtswert der Vorgeschichte, LK 1-2," *Bibel und Kirche* 21 (1966) 106-111; reprinted in *Traditionsgeschichtliche Untersuchungen zu den synoptischen Evangelien* (Düsseldorf: Patmos, 1968) 198-208.

Songer, H. S. "Luke's Portrayal of the Origins of Jesus," *RevExp* 64 (1967) 453-463.

Staudinger, J. "Testis 'primarius' evangelii secundum Lucam," *VD* 33 (1955) 65-77, 129-142.

Sträter, P. "De probabili origine historiae infantiae Christi," *VD* 25 (1947) 321-327.

Tatum, W. B. "The Epoch of Israel: Luke i-ii and the Theological Plan of Luke-Acts," *NTS* 13 (1966-1967) 184-195.

Thompson, P. J. "The Infancy Gospels of St. Matthew and St. Luke Compared," *SE I* (TU 73; 1959) 217-222.

Turner, N. "The Relation of Luke i and ii to Hebraic Sources and to the Rest of Luke-Acts," *NTS* 2 (1955-1956) 100-109.

Usener, H. "Geburt und Kindheit Christi," *ZNW* 4 (1903) 1-21.

Vögtle, A. "Offene Fragen zur lukanischen Geburts- und Kindheitsgeschichte," *BibLeb* 11 (1970) 51-67; reprinted in *Das Evangelium und die Evangelien: Beiträge zur Evangelienforschung* (Düsseldorf: Patmos, 1971) 43-56.

Wickings, H. F. "The Nativity Stories and Docetism," *NTS* 23 (1976-1977) 457-460.

Wilson, R. M. "Some Recent Studies in the Lucan Infancy Narratives," *SE I* (TU 73; 1959) 235-253.

Winter, P. "The Cultural Background of the Narrative in Luke I and II," *JQR* 45 (1954-1955) 159-167, 230-242, 287.

———— "Lukanische Miszellen," *ZNW* 49 (1958) 65-77.

———— "The Main Literary Problem of the Lucan Infancy Story," *ATR* 40 (1958) 257-264.

———— "'Nazareth' and 'Jerusalem' in Luke chs. i and ii," *NTS* 3 (1956-1957) 136-142.

———— "On Luke and Lucan Sources: A Reply to the Reverend N. Turner," *ZNW* 47 (1956) 217-242.

—————— "On the Margin of Luke I, II," *ST* 12 (1958) 103-107.

—————— "The Proto-source of Luke I," *NovT* 1 (1956) 184-199.

—————— "Some Observations on the Language in the Birth and Infancy Stories of the Third Gospel," *NTS* 1 (1954-1955) 111-121.

—————— "Two Notes on Luke I, II with Regard to the Theory of 'Imitation Hebraisms,'" *ST* 7 (1953) 158-165.

BIBLIOGRAPHY (1:5-25)

Badham, F. P. "The Integrity of Luke i. 5-11," *ExpTim* 8 (1896-1897) 116-119.

Baltzer, K. "The Meaning of the Temple in the Lukan Writings," *HTR* 58 (1965) 263-277.

Benoit, P. "L'Enfance de Jean-Baptiste selon Luc i," *NTS* 3 (1956-1957) 169-194.

Dubois, J.-D. "La figure d'Elie dans la perspective lucanienne," *RHPR* 53 (1973) 155-176.

Milik, J. T. (with the collaboration of M. Black), *The Books of Enoch: Aramaic Fragments of Qumrân Cave 4* (Oxford: Clarendon, 1976).

Scott, R. B. Y. "The Expectation of Elijah," *CJRT* 3 (1926) 1-13.

Winter, P. *"Hoti* 'recitativum' in Lc 1, 25.61; 2,23," *ZNW* 46 (1955) 261-263; cf. *HTR* 48 (1955) 213-216.

3. THE BIRTH OF JESUS IS ANNOUNCED
(1:26-38)

1 ²⁶ In the sixth month the angel Gabriel was sent by God to a town in Galilee called Nazareth, ²⁷ to a virgin engaged to a man named Joseph, a descendant of the house of David. The virgin's name was Mary. ²⁸ The angel entered and said to her, "Hail, favored woman! The Lord is with you!" ²⁹ But Mary was quite perplexed at his words and pondered what sort of a greeting this might be. ³⁰ The angel said to her, "Do not be afraid, Mary; you have been favored by God. ³¹ You are going to conceive in your womb and bear a son, and you will name him Jesus. ³² He will be great and will be hailed as Son of the Most High, and the Lord God will bestow on him the throne of his father David. ³³ He will be king over the house of Jacob forever, and of his kingship there will be no end." ³⁴ But Mary said to the angel, "How can this be, since I have no relations with a man?" ³⁵ The angel said to her in reply, "The holy Spirit will come upon you, and the power of the Most High will cast a shadow over you. Therefore the child to be born will be holy; he will be called Son of God. ³⁶ And now, your relative Elizabeth, even in her old age, has also conceived a son; in fact, it is already the sixth month for her who has been called barren, ³⁷ since *nothing is impossible for God*."ᵃ ³⁸ Then Mary said, "The Lord's handmaid am I! Let it be with me as you say!" At that the angel left her.

ᵃ Gen 18:14 LXX

COMMENT

The second episode of the Lucan infancy narrative is parallel to the first: As the wondrous birth of John was announced to his father, Zechariah, so Jesus' wondrous birth will be made known to his mother, Mary. Some of the details of the parallelism can be seen in the discussion of the structure of the infancy narrative given above (p. 313). For a more elaborate comparison, see R. E. Brown, *Birth*, 294-297.

As in the announcement of John's birth, so too here the five-element pattern of the OT birth-announcement is present:

a) the entrance of the angel (1:28)
b) Mary's perplexity (1:29)
c) the heavenly message (1:30-33, with Mary addressed by name, told not to be afraid [1:30b], told that she would conceive and bear a son [1:31a], told what he would be named [1:31b], and told what his role was to be [1:32-33])
d) Mary's objection (1:34bc)
e) the reassurance and sign: Mary's virginal conception and Elizabeth's pregnancy in her old age (1:35b-37).

Thus Luke has taken some of the details of the pre-Lucan and pre-Matthean tradition about the birth of Jesus (see p. 307 above) and modeled an announcement of Jesus' birth on the stereotyped OT pattern, in imitation of the announcement of John's birth in the Baptist-source. He has inserted it into his reworking of the source, which ended with 1:24a, and will be picked up again in 1:57.

If this sort of imitative historiography is at work in assimilating the account of the announcement of Jesus' birth to that of Ishmael, Isaac, Samson, and Samuel, it may raise a question about the historical value of the account itself. This is not an easy question to answer. It should be recalled that Matthew—independently of Luke—knows of a tradition about a heavenly announcement of the birth of Jesus, prior to the living together of Mary and Joseph, and about a virginal conception involving the holy Spirit. There are significant differences between the stories, however, that have to be considered: in Matthew the announcement comes to Joseph, presumably in Bethlehem (in that infancy narrative we learn about Nazareth only in 2:23); in Luke it comes to Mary, in Nazareth. Matthew has little of the stereotyped OT pattern of birth-announcement; Luke has made use of it. That means that both evangelists, having picked up elements of the tradition, have freely cast them in their own molds—one in terms of dreams, the other in an OT birth-announcement pattern. What really happened? We shall never know. Writers like J.-P. Audet (*RB* 63 [1956] 355) and J. McHugh (*Mother of Jesus,* 128) have toyed with the idea that the announcement to Mary may be Luke's way of presenting an account of an interior, spiritual experience, to which no bystander could have been witness. That is possible. In this matter the important thing is to attend to the message about the child that is made known, whether one can establish the historicity of the details of the account or not. Just as the angelic message of a wondrous birth made known the character and special role of John to his father Zechariah, so too does the announcement of the even more wondrous birth of Jesus to Mary reveal his identity and role. This is the purpose of the episodes and the reason for the Lucan parallelism.

The announcement about the birth of Jesus may be subdivided into three sections: (a) the setting and the dramatis personae (vv. 26-27); (b) the announcement proper (vv. 28-37); and (c) Mary's acceptance (v. 38).

In vv. 26-27, the setting of the episode, Luke makes use of the same angel, Gabriel, to announce the birth of Jesus. The temporal setting of "the sixth month" clearly reflects Lucan composition, linking this episode to the conclusion of the reworked Baptist-source (1:24b-25).

The new element in this announcement-story is the virginity of Mary. This is not to be understood as derived from Isa 7:14, *pace* G. Schneider (*Evangelium nach Lukas,* 49); G. Voss (*Die Christologie,* 65-81), and many others. The possible Lucan parallels to the phrases of Isa 7:10-17 are the following seven: "house of David" (1:27; cf. Isa 7:13); "the Lord" (1:28; cf. Isa 7:10); "virgin" (1:27; cf. LXX Isa 7:14) "are going to conceive" (1:31; cf. Isa 7:14 LXX); "will bear a son" (1:31; cf. Isa 7:14); "you will name him" (1:31; cf. Isa 7:14); and "over the house" (1:33; cf. Isa 7:17). But each one of these phrases occurs elsewhere in the OT, as the NOTES make clear, and sometimes with great frequency. Indeed, the description of Mary in 1:27 is far closer to Deut 22:23 than to Isa 7:14. The tradition of Mary's virginity prior to the birth of Jesus is known to Matthew as well (1:18-25). It is Matthew who has related her condition to a Greek form of Isa 7:14, and that Matthean theologoumenon should not be imported into the interpretation of the Lucan account. Moreover, Matthew has made the connection in using a fulfillment quotation which he has added to an account that already asserted the virginal conception.

The announcement proper (vv. 28-37) begins with the angel's greeting. It has at times been proposed that vv. 28-33 originally formed a unit composed by Luke himself and that vv. 34-35 (Mary's question and the angel's reassurance) were a later addition to an earlier draft of the episode. So, e.g. A. von Harnack ("Zu Lk 1,34-35," *ZNW* 2 [1901] 53-57); R. Bultmann (*HST,* 295), who regarded vv. 34-37 as a "secondary addition"; F. C. Grant (*JBL* 59 [1940] 18-21), who thought that v. 34c was a "gloss introduced under the influence of the doctrine of the Virgin Birth"—a "gloss, undoubtedly very early, but by a hand that lacked the skill of the author of Luke." Without vv. 34-35 the announcement of the birth of Jesus would have implied normal marital relations.

But these verses are found in all the Greek mss. of the Lucan Gospel (see B. Brinkmann, *Bib* 34 [1953] 327-332). The style of these verses is certainly Lucan (see V. Taylor, *The Historical Evidence for the Virgin Birth* [Oxford: Clarendon, 1920] 40-87). These items raise a further question: Did Luke himself add them to a form of the announcement story that did not originally contain them? Reasons have often been sought in support of this. For instance, it is said that vv. 36-37 follow smoothly on vv. 30-33; that Mary's question is not really parallel to Zechariah's (1:18) in that she is reassured, whereas he was punished; that the title "Son of the Most High" (1:32) is needlessly repeated in "Son of God" (1:35); or that the former reflects a Palestinian christology, the latter a Hellenistic christology. But in considering these items, it must be recalled that the pattern of OT birth-announcements calls for a question or objection; that would make the presence of vv. 34-35 crucial in this episode in its most basic form. Again, other motifs were at work in the Gabriel/Zechariah confrontation (viz. the dumbness of the seer in Dan 10:15), which would have no place here—to say nothing of the step-parallelism that is obviously being exploited here. Finally, the two christological titles are found in parallelism—strikingly similar to the Lucan usage—in a Palestinian Aramaic text from Qumran (see NOTE on 1:32) so that one cannot regard the title "Son of God" as Hellenistic. The upshot is that there is no real reason to query the unit-character of vv. 28-37. Bultmann (*HST*, 295) maintains that "Mary's question in v. 34 is absurd for a bride"; it is not absurd for one who was only engaged and had not yet come to live with her husband.

The announcement story in vv. 28-37 is a dramatic, two-stage declaration made to Mary about the extraordinary character of the child that is to be born to her and about divine involvement in his origin. The passage is primarily christological, and only secondarily mariological: it shows that he comes from humanity, just as he comes from God. Just as Elizabeth's disgrace was removed by divine intervention resulting in a son who would be an agent of Yahweh, a prophet before His coming, so Mary's virginal status will be exploited by divine influence so that she too will bear a son, who will be David's heir and the Son of God. He will be "Great" (bearing a title given to Yahweh in the LXX—see NOTE on 1:15), will be hailed as Son of the Most High, and will sit on the Davidic throne in an eternal kingship. So runs the first stage of the identification of the child. In the second stage he is further identified as the holy one, the Son of God. If the conception of John required a miracle, the step-parallelism requires an even greater one in Jesus' conception. Hence the conception by a virgin.

Jesus' conception is to occur by the coming of the holy Spirit on Mary and the power of the Most High overshadowing her (1:35); as a result Jesus will be the Son of God. The language used here is highly figurative; neither verb, *eperchesthai,* "come upon," or *episkiazein,* "overshadow, cast a shadow over," has an immediate connotation of conception, let alone a sexual implication. They are otherwise unattested in a context that would suggest these nuances. They are figurative expressions of the mysterious intervention of God's Spirit and power which will bring about Jesus' Davidic role and his divine filiation. Paul interjects the work of Spirit in his allusion to the birth of Isaac, who was born "according to the Spirit" (Gal 4:29), a detail that is not present in the Genesis story. Such intervention does not imply virginal conception.

In an earlier discussion of the virginal conception (*TS* 34 [1973] 567-570) in the Lucan Gospel, I queried whether Luke's words, read in and for themselves—and without the overtones of the Matthean announcement to Joseph, where the virginal conception is clearly formulated—could not be understood of a child to be born of Mary in an ordinary human way. The Spirit's role would be one of endowing the child with a special character suiting him to bear the title Son of God. I still think that the words themselves in v. 35 could tolerate that meaning; but I now agree with Brown that the step-parallelism in the two announcements demands that the miraculous divine intervention, precisely invoking the creative power of the Spirit, has to result in a more extraordinary conception, hence, virginal. See Brown, *Birth,* 299-301; *TS* 35 (1974) 360-362.

In the two-stage declaration made to Mary, Jesus and his future role are set forth. In the first stage (vv. 32-33) his extraordinary character is set forth in terms of his Davidic and messianic role with clear allusions to the dynastic oracle of Nathan in 2 Samuel 7. Compare the following:

2 Sam 7:9 "a great name"	Luke 1:32 "he will be great"
13 "the throne of his kingdom"	32 "throne of his father David"
14 "he will be my son"	32 "Son of the Most High"
16 "your house and your kingdom"	33 "king over the house of Jacob forever"

But it should be noted that the Lucan use of this oracle reflects more the postexilic understanding of it such as one reads in 1 Chr 17:11-14, where the oracle that in 2 Samuel spoke of a "son" in a collective sense (referring to the dynasty as a whole) becomes specific and speaks of David's offspring, "who shall be *one* of your own sons."

Luke's identification of Jesus as the Davidic Messiah ties in, of course, with the development of Palestinian pre-Christian messianic expectations (see p. 198 above). But it should be noted that nowhere in pre-Christian Jewish literature is the expected Messiah given the explicit title "Son of God." The text closest to this is 4QFlor 10-13 (DJD 5. 53), where the Qumran author, having cited parts of 2 Sam 7:11-14, identifies the "my son" of v. 14 as the "shoot of David," who will arise in the last days, sit upon David's throne, and save Israel. Though *māšîaḥ,* "messiah," is not used of this Davidic heir, he is identified as the one about whom Nathan's oracle spoke. Because the title "Son of God" is now attested in a Qumran text (see NOTE on 1:32), but not clearly used there of anyone said to be a Messiah, it is not to be concluded from this 4QFlor text that "son of God" could be understood in some messianic sense. This is important for the understanding of the Lucan two-stage identification of Jesus. If he is the Davidic Messiah (as vv. 32-33 seem to suggest), he is not simply "Son of God" in a messianic sense. That is the point of the second stage of the angel's announcement: he is not only the Davidic Messiah, he is also God's Son.

There is, however, one other Qumran text that should be considered here. In 1QS, the *Manual of Discipline* of the Qumran community, a fragmentary part of the appendix, sometimes called the "Rule of the Congregation for the Last Days," may speak of God's begetting the Messiah. It reads: "[This is the ses]sion of the men of renown, [summoned] to assembly for the Council of the community when (*or* if) [God] begets the Messiah among them" (1QSa 2.11-12; DJD 1. 110). But the reading and interpretation of the text are highly debated. First of all, *'l,* "God," has been restored. Second, the original editor (D. Barthélemy) at first read the last word of line 11 (*ywlyd*) as *ywlyk,* translating it "would lead," instead of "begets." But many others, who have inspected the text (Allegro, Cross, et al.), insist that *ywlyd,* "begets," must be read. The subject of the verb almost certainly has to be *'l,* "God." A further problem is that this would be the sole pre-Christian Palestinian text in which the title, "the Messiah," in the singular and with the def. art. is found. Though the text is debatable, one should keep it in mind at least as a possible attestation of the idea of God's begetting the Messiah. (See further O. Michel and O. Betz, "Von Gott gezeugt," *Judentum, Urchristentum, Kirche: Festschrift für Joachim Jeremias* [ed. W. Eltester; Berlin: Töpelmann, 1960] 11-12; "Nocheinmal: 'Von Gott gezeugt,'" *NTS* 9 [1962-1963] 129-130; E. F. Sutcliffe, "The Rule of the Congregation (1QSa) II, 11-12: Text and Meaning," *RevQ* 2 [1959-1960] 541-547; M. Smith, "'God's Begetting the Messiah' in 1QSa," *NTS* 5 [1958-1959] 218-224.)

Even if this text speaks of God's begetting the Messiah, it still would not be the same as the Lucan v. 35, which speaks of the virginal conception of Jesus through the holy Spirit and the power of the Most High. God's "begetting" of the Messiah is also a figurative expression and may be an echo of 2 Sam 7:14 (or Ps 2:6-7?), although there is nothing in the context of 1QSa to suggest that.

In the second stage of the angel's declaration to Mary about Jesus' identity and his role, a parallel construction of the sort common in He-

brew poetry is used to tell her that she will conceive through God's intervention, and *therefore* her child will be the Son of God. The "holy Spirit"
coming upon her and the "power of the Most High" overshadowing her
are parallel expressions for God's intervention. The result of it will be
that the child will not be merely a Davidic Messiah but God's own Son.

In v. 35, then, Luke picks up and makes use of an existing tradition in
the Christian community about the virginal conception of Jesus announced by a heavenly being. This is pre-Lucan tradition, because
Matthew also has it (1:18-25). But there is more involved. Luke is working here with elements from a pre-Lucan christology, such as one sees
attested in Rom 1:3-4, where Paul, himself making use of a pre-Pauline
kerygmatic fragment, acknowledges that Jesus was born of the seed of
David according to the flesh, but constituted Son of God in power according to a Spirit of holiness as of the resurrection from the dead. Here
four elements are involved: Son of God, power, Spirit of holiness (=a
non-Pauline way of referring to the Holy Spirit), and Davidic descent.
Luke, undoubtedly aware of such a christological formulation, makes use
of the elements to fashion a statement about the origins of the child to be
born. Whereas in the Pauline and probably pre-Pauline use of the formulation, the resurrection of Jesus was the moment when the title Son of
God became attached to him, Luke pushes the christological affirmation
back to the conception of Jesus. What is involved here is the growing understanding of the early church about the identity of Jesus. Though at
first such titles as Son of God were attached to him primarily as of the
resurrection (besides Rom 1:4, see Acts 13:33), the time came when
early Christians began to realize that he had to have been such even
earlier in his career, even though it had not been recognized. It is not so
much that the "christological moment" (Brown, *Birth,* passim) was
pushed back as that there was a growth in awareness as time passed
among early Christians that what Jesus was recognized to be after the resurrection he must have been still earlier. Luke, in affirming that Jesus was
Son of God, not only at his conception, but through his conception, is
representative of early Christians among whom such an awareness was
achieved. Still later, in the Johannine community, the awareness will grow
into the idea of incarnation—a notion foreign to Luke (as to Matthew).

This, then, is the primary import of this passage, its christological
affirmation: the announcement to Mary identifies Jesus to the reader of
the Lucan Gospel as the Davidic Messiah and the Son of God. However,
I did admit above that the passage also had a secondary, mariological import. This is not to be seen in the affirmation of Mary's virginity
(1:27,34), which is never presented in any biological sense, as the figurative character of the verbs "coming upon" and "casting a shadow over"
clearly imply. Indeed, the virginal conception of Jesus is affirmed, but it is

set forth in order to explain something about him, not primarily about Mary: "therefore he shall be called God's Son."

Much more important, however, in the mariological sense is the depiction of Mary as "the favored one," chosen to be the mother of him who will be hailed the Savior, Messiah, and Lord (2:11). This element of Mary's motherhood will appear again in the Lucan account (8:19-21; 11:27-28) and in Acts 1:14; her motherhood will serve the Lucan picture of Christian discipleship.

And still more important is Luke's portrayal of Mary as "the handmaid of the Lord" (1:38). Here Luke writes with hindsight, and foreshadows the way in which he will depict Mary in the Gospel proper, especially in 8:19-21, where she will be, along with his "brothers," among those "who hear the word of God and act on it." Here, Mary's enthusiastic response to the angel depicts her from the very beginning of the account as one who cooperates with God's plan of salvation. As we shall see in the discussion of 8:19-21, this differs considerably from the way that she is presented in the earlier gospel tradition, especially in Mark 3:21,33-35. For Luke, Mary is the model believer (see 1:45), pronounced blessed; and because she has been favored, she will be declared blessed by all generations (1:48). In Acts 1:14 she sits among the believers awaiting the promised holy Spirit.

This entire episode of the angelic announcement to Mary of Jesus' identity has to be rightly understood. It has been composed by Luke in a highly dramatic way to get across to the reader of his Gospel who Jesus is. Because it is largely the result of literary composition, refashioning elements of a tradition, it should not be used to answer such questions as whether Mary during the lifetime of Jesus knew him to be the Son of God (see, e.g. R. Laurentin, *Jésus au Temple* [Paris: Gabalda, 1966]). To try to answer that question on the basis of the Lucan account is to confuse the stages of gospel tradition. What Luke recounts here belongs to the third stage of that tradition. The question posed, however, concerns the Mary of history, or the first stage of the tradition. We have no way of answering that sort of question. Moreover, the negative attitude toward her in Mark 3:33-35, and her reaction to Jesus in 3:21, would suggest a different view of her in the earlier tradition from what one finds here in the Lucan story.

The Virginal Conception of Jesus. Since both Luke and Matthew have this notion in their infancy narratives, it is generally concluded that both evangelists have been tributary to an earlier gospel tradition about it (from Stage II). But how would such a tradition have developed? Various answers have been given to this question.

a) It was based on family secrets (the memoirs of Joseph or Mary) that were eventually passed on to the church community—i.e. it was rooted in Stage I. We have already seen that the whole question of the infancy narratives being dependent on a family tradition is the result solely of speculation. If they were so dependent, then why have no other NT writers picked the matter up, and why have the Lucan and Matthean accounts of it turned out so differently?

b) It was a deduction made by early Christians from the title "Son of God" which they were already using of him. But why would anyone be inclined so to conclude? The title was widespread in use in the ancient world in a figurative sense (see pp. 205-208 above); the same Christians must have known that the OT used the title (by implication at least—see 2 Sam 7:14; 1 Chr 17:13; Ps 2:7) of the king, when the king's human father was well known.

c) It has been described as a borrowing from the pagan world, which knew of heroes born of gods and human women. But no one has ever been able to show that any of the alleged parallels in literature were really virginal conceptions such as the Lucan or Matthean accounts imply. They were all instances of a god taking the place of a male human parent and having intercourse with a woman (see T. Boslooper, *The Virgin Birth* [Philadelphia: Westminster, 1962]; *Religion in Life* 26 [1956-1957] 87-97).

d) It has been pointed out that Philo knew of a tradition that the patriarchs were begotten of God (*De Cherubim* 12-15, esp. 13.45), in particular that Isaac was born of the holy Spirit and Sarah without the intervention of Abraham. Thus there was a tradition in diaspora Judaism of the virginal conception of patriarchs. To associate this with the conception of Jesus, however, would be to read in a literal fashion what Philo has written allegorically about the generation of virtues in the human soul (see P. Grelot, "La naissance d'Isaac et celle de Jésus: Sur une interprétation 'mythologique' de la conception virginale," *NRT* 94 [1972] 462-487; cf. *MNT*, 46-49).

None of these proposals has explained adequately how there came to be some sort of a tradition in the early Christian community prior to both Luke and Matthew about the virginal conception of Jesus. In a commentary of this sort there is no need to go into this matter in great detail; the reader who wants to pursue it at greater length can find a recent discussion of it in Brown, *Birth*, Appendix IV, 517-534.

As was clear in the Preface, this commentary is concerned with Stage III of the gospel tradition; there is, as far as I am concerned, no real proof for or against the fact of the virginal birth in Stage I. Christian belief in it is governed by factors other than what one can ascertain by careful exegesis (see *MNT*, 96; *TS* 34 [1973] 541-575).

NOTES

1 26. *In the sixth month.* I.e. of Elizabeth's pregnancy. This dating not only opens a new episode but also links it with the preceding (see 1:24), preparing for the announcement to be made in 1:36.

the angel Gabriel. See the NOTES on 1:11,19.

was sent by God. Or possibly "from God." The Greek phrase *apo tou theou* should prima facie have the latter spatial sense; but with passive verbs the prep. *apo* sometimes replaces the more proper *hypo* and expresses the agent of an action. This use of *apo* is found elsewhere in Lucan writings (6:18; 7:35; 8:43; 16:18[?]; 17:25; Acts 2:22; 4:36; 15:4). But the mss. also vary considerably (e.g. ms. D on Luke 10:22; cf. Acts 10:33). Though this substitution of *apo* for *hypo* is attested in extrabiblical Greek (see BAG, 87; BDF § 210.2), in NT Greek it may be influenced by the Semitic use of *min*, "from," which is also used commonly not only for separation, but also for agency.

called Nazareth. Lit. "the name of which was Nazareth." Though this phrase is lacking in ms. D and the OL, it is otherwise attested by the best Greek mss. Nazareth is not mentioned in the OT, Josephus, or rabbinical writings (either talmudic or midrashic). The existence of this insignificant Galilean hamlet is known, however, from a Hebrew inscription found in 1962 at Caesarea Maritima which, though now fragmentary, listed the twenty-four priestly courses (see NOTE on 1:5) and the villages or towns where they were resident. It locates the eighteenth course, Happizzez (1 Chr 24:15), at *Nṣrt*, "Nazareth." The inscription dates from the end of the third or the beginning of the fourth century A.D. See M. Avi-Yonah, "A List of Priestly Courses from Caesarea," *IEJ* 12 (1962) 137-139; "The Caesarea Inscription of the Twenty-Four Priestly Courses," in *The Teacher's Yoke: Studies in Memory of Henry Trantham* (eds. E. J. Vardaman and J. L. Garrett, Jr.; Waco, TX: Baylor University, 1964) 46-57. The later prominence of the town is the result of the Christian gospel tradition; for ancient descriptions of it, see D. Baldi, *ELS* § 1-42. Here the Greek name is spelled *Nazareth*, but in Luke 4:16 it is *Nazara*, as in Matt 4:13. See further J. Finegan, *Archeology*, 27-33. On Galilee, see NOTE on 17:11.

27. *to a virgin.* Luke does not call Mary *pais*, "girl" (cf. 8:51), *paidiskē*, "little girl, maid" (cf. 12:45), or *korasion*, "maiden" (cf. ms. D of 8:51), but rather *parthenos*, the normal understanding of which is "virgin" (BAG, 632). This term and the following phrase prepare for 1:34.

engaged to a man. Luke uses the pf. pass. ptc. of *mnēsteuein* and his whole phrase seems to be derived from the LXX of Deut 22:23 (*parthenos memnēsteumenē andri*); cf. Matt 1:18. In Palestine of the time the marriage of a young girl took place in two acts: (a) the engagement (Hebrew *'ērûsîn* = Latin *sponsalia*) or formal exchange of agreement to marry in the presence of witnesses (cf. Mal 2:14) and the paying of the *mōhar*, "bride price"; (b) the marriage proper (Hebrew *niśśû'în*) or the "taking" of the girl to the man's home (see Matt 1:18; 25:1-13). The engagement gave the groom legal rights over the girl, who could already be called his "wife" (*gynē*, see Matt 1:20,24). It could only be broken by his divorcing her, and any violation of his marital rights by her was regarded as adultery. After the engagement the girl usually continued to live in her family home for about a year before being taken to her husband's home. See further Str-B, 1. 45-47; 2. 293; *m. Ketubot* 4:4-5.

named Joseph. Lit. "whose name was Joseph." Mary's fiancé bears an ancient biblical name, widely used among Jews in the postexilic period (see Ezra 10:42; Neh 12:14; 1 Chr 25:2,9). It was probably a shortened form of a theophoric name such as *Yôsîp-yāh,* "May Yahweh add" (other children to the one just born); cf. Ezra 8:10, English Josiphiah; Gen 30:24 (for the meaning). Luke's narrative makes less of Joseph's OT background than does Matthew, which exploits details of the Genesis story of the patriarch Joseph (dreams, Egypt, flight). But both Josephs are similar in their attempt to fathom divine intention in humanly difficult situations.

of the house of David. In the Greek text this stereotyped OT phrase (e.g. 1 Kgs 12:19; 2 Chr 23:3) follows immediately on the name of Joseph and expresses his Davidic lineage (also mentioned in 2:4 and 3:23). Origen, however, understood the phrase to modify *parthenon,* and his understanding (along with the *Prot. Jas.* 10:1; Ignatius *Eph.* 18.2) gave rise to the view that Mary too was of Davidic descent—which is nowhere asserted in the NT. In fact, from Luke 1:5,36 one could conclude that she was of Aaronic lineage. The phrase is preparing for 1:32-33, where Jesus will be related to the Davidic dynasty. For the early Christian tradition of Jesus' Davidic descent, see Rom 1:3; Matt 1:1,20; 2 Tim 2:8. Joseph's genealogy will be given in Luke 3:23-38. My translation has supplied "a descendant."

The virgin's name was Mary. Cf. 1:5. Jesus' mother bears the name of the famous sister of Moses, Miriam (Hebrew *Miryām,* Exod 15:20). In the LXX this was normally written as *Mariam,* the form that Luke uses here. In 2:19 the better reading is *Maria,* a form that is attested extrabiblically (see BAG, 492). On the phenomenon behind the alternation of *Maryam/Maryāh,* which underlies the two Greek forms, see my commentary on 1QapGen 21:24 (*Genesis Apocryphon,* 162). *Miryām,* from which *Maria(m)* developed, is a Semitic name, of Canaanite origin, and most likely was related to the noun *mrym,* found in both Ugaritic and Hebrew (cf. Prov 3:35), meaning "height, summit." As the name of a woman, it probably connoted something like "Excellence," and is to be related to other abstract fem. names, such as *Ḥannāh,* "Grace," or *'Ednāh,* "Pleasure." See further E. Vogt, *VD* 26 (1948) 163-168; J. B. Bauer, *Marianum* 19 (1957) 231-234.

28. *Hail!* The angel uses the sg. impv. of *chairein,* lit. "rejoice." It is a common salutation or greeting, well known in Greek literature and used even by Semites in the NT (Matt 26:49; cf. 28:9). This seems to be the sense demanded by Mary's subsequent pondering about the "greeting."

However, a number of commentators (H. Gressmann, H. Sahlin, S. Lyonnet, R. Laurentin) insist rather that the impv. be understood literally, "rejoice." S. Lyonnet (*Bib* 20 [1939] 131-141) has argued that the more usual greeting in the NT for a Semite is *eirēnē,* "peace" (Luke 10:5; 24:36; John 20:19,21,

26), a translation of Hebrew *šālôm* or Aramaic *šĕlām*, as in the LXX, which never uses *chaire* in this sense. The impv. *chaire*, "rejoice," is not unknown, however, in the LXX, occurring four times (Zeph 3:14; Joel 2:21; Zech 9:9; Lam 4:21). In the first three instances it introduces a prophecy addressed to Israel or Jerusalem about the restoration of God's people. Luke's phrase has in common with these OT passages, according to these commentators, the positive exhortation to joy and the negative counsel, "Do not be afraid" (*mē phobou*). Hence, it is argued that the OT daughter of Zion is being alluded to here. Luke would be referring to Zeph 3:14-17:

chaire (Luke 1:28), "Rejoice"	*chaire, . . . thygater Siōn* (Zeph 3:14), "Rejoice, daughter of Zion"
"the Lord is with you!" (1:28)	"the king of Israel, Yahweh, is in your midst" (3:15b)
"do not be afraid, Mary" (1:30)	"do not be afraid, Zion" (3:16 in the MT; the LXX reads *tharsei*, "take courage")
"you are going to conceive" (1:31)	"Yahweh, your God, is in your midst" (3:17 in the MT; for *bĕqirbēk* the LXX has *en soi*, "in you")
"Jesus" (1:31)	"a warrior (who) saves (3:17 in the MT; the LXX reads, "will save you")

This would be an impressive array of allusions, if it could be shown that Luke is really the one who is seeing the connection. The list, however, uses the MT or the LXX freely, to exploit the maximum connection with Zephaniah, depending on which text happens to be closer to Luke's. This lack of consistency makes the suggestion somewhat unconvincing. In particular, the appeal to *qereb* (Zeph 3:17), meaning not only "midst" but even a part of the body, while barely intelligible in Hebrew, is scarcely transparent in Greek, and is lacking in the LXX. Similarly, the popular etymology of the name of Jesus (=Savior) is a Matthean explanation; see the NOTE on 1:31 for the proper meaning of the name. Despite the Lucan emphasis on "salvation," Luke does not make use of such a meaning of Jesus' name in the infancy narrative. Cf. Acts 4:12. Since the main argument for the interpretation of *chaire* as "rejoice" begins with an appeal to the LXX, the rest of the allusions would have to be shown from that text of Zephaniah, and that is not possible. Hence the interpretation of *chaire* as an ordinary greeting should be retained.

It seems rather likely, however, that there is a play on the Greek words *chaire* and *kecharitōmenē*, to be explained in the next NOTE.

favored woman. This phrase functions here almost as a proper name; cf. Judg 6:12 for a similar use of an epithet. Though the pf. pass. ptc. *kecharitōmenos* is found in the LXX of Sir 18:17 in the sense of a "gracious man," here it rather designates Mary as the recipient of divine favor; it means "favored by God," another instance of the so-called theological passive (see ZGB § 236). She is favored by God to be the mother of the descendant of David and the Son of the Most High. Even though the pf. ptc. might express a state or condition of divine favor, that favor is to be understood of the unique role that she is to perform in conceiving God's Messiah. In later scholastic theological tradition that favor would be classed as a charism, a *gratia gratis data*, "a grace freely given." Beginning in patristic times, theological tradition understood *kecharitōmenē* in a fuller sense, which does not contradict the Lucan pf. ptc., but which certainly goes beyond it. The translation of the ptc. in the Latin Vg. as *gratia plena* heavily influenced the Western theological tradition about the fullness of Mary's grace and was mainly responsible for the understanding of the word in terms of *gratia gratum faciens,* or sanctifying grace. See further M. Cambe, "La *charis* chez Saint Luc," 193-207; C. Mohrmann, "Ave gratificata," 1-6.

The Koine text-tradition and mss. C*, D, and ⊕ add to the phrase, "blessed are you among women." This is, however, a scribal gloss introduced from Luke 1:42.

The Lord is with you! This is a frequently used OT phrase, but it occurs as a greeting only in two places in the OT, Ruth 2:4 and Judg 6:12. In both cases it lacks a verb, as here in Luke. The phrase in Ruth 2:4 has been understood as a wish, "May the Lord be with you!" (so *RSV, NAB, NEB*), whereas in Judg 6:12 it is rather a declaration (so *RSV, NAB, NEB*). The appearance of the angel of the Lord to Gideon in the latter passage and the similarity of greeting there to what one finds in Luke suggests that the phrase be understood here too as a declaration. Moreover, it supplies a better explanation for Mary's perplexity in the following verse. In the OT the phrase often expresses Yahweh's help and assistance and carries a military connotation. Obviously, *kyrios* here is to be understood of Yahweh.

29. *was quite perplexed.* Lit. "was greatly troubled." The Greek verb is a compound of the verb used to express Zechariah's alarm in 1:12. Some mss. (C, ⊕, and the Koine text-tradition) explain the perplexity by adding *idousa,* "seeing (him)." But the text itself explains the perplexity by referring to the angel's "words" (*epi tō logō*). Perhaps underlying the reaction was the realization that she, a woman, was being greeted by someone not a woman, since later rabbinical tradition has recorded an opinion, attributed to R. Shemuel, that males extend "to a woman no greeting at all" (*b. Qiddušin* 70a).

might be. Luke uses the opt. mood here; see p. 108 above.

30. *Do not be afraid, Mary.* See NOTE on 1:13. Cf. BDF § 336.3.

you have been favored by God. Lit. "you have found favor (*charis*) with God," an OT expression (see Gen 6:8; 18:3; cf. 1 Sam 1:18). It explains the real sense of the ptc. in v. 28. *Charis* is a favorite Lucan word, not used by either Mark or Matthew.

31. *You are going to conceive in your womb and bear a son.* The angel's words to Mary actually begin with the Lucan *kai idou,* "and behold"; see p. 121 above. I have omitted them in the translation. The message to Mary is couched in rather stereotyped OT phraseology for announcing the conception and birth of an extraordinary child. Compare Gen 16:11 ("Behold you are pregnant and will bear a son; you will call him Ishmael" [the Hebrew text has *hinnāk hārāh,* and the LXX uses the present, *en gastri echeis*]); Judg 13:3,5 ("you will conceive and bear a son" [the Hebrew has again *hinnāk hārāh,* "you are pregnant"; the ms. A of the LXX makes a future of it, *sy en gastri*

hexeis, "you will conceive"]), but ms. B reads as in Gen 16:11; Isa 7:14 ("Lo, a young woman is pregnant and bearing a son" [the Hebrew has *hāʻalmāh hārāh wĕyôledet bēn,* but the LXX again makes a future of it, *hē parthenos en gastri hexei kai texetai huion,* "the virgin will conceive and bear a son"]).

In the OT the expression is addressed sometimes to a woman who is already pregnant, and sometimes to one who will conceive in the immediate future. Luke has followed the Septuagintal future, and that tense will appear in v. 35 again.

and you will name him Jesus. Lit. "you will call his name Jesus"; see NOTE on 1:13. The future tense here is almost the equivalent of an impv. (see ZBG § 280). Luke makes no issue of the meaning of the name, despite his concern for salvation; contrast Matt 1:21. The name *Iēsous* is a Greek form of the late development of the Hebrew name for Joshua. In Hebrew the latter is *Yĕhôšûaʻ* (Josh 1:1), a theophoric name, the first element of which is a form of *Yāhû* (=Yahweh) and the last the impv. of *šwʻ,* "help." The name would mean, "Yahweh, help!", expressing the cry of the mother in childbirth. In time *Yĕhôšûaʻ* was contracted to *Yôšûaʻ* and then to *Yēšûaʻ* (e.g. Ezra 2:6), transcribed in the LXX as *Iēsous.* But because the name *Yēšûaʻ* sounds like *yĕšûʻāh,* which is from a different root, *yšʻ,* and means "salvation," Jesus' name came to be popularly understood as a form of *yšʻ,* "save." It is this popular etymology to which Matt 1:21 alludes. But the real root of the name of Jesus/Joshua is *šwʻ,* "help." See *HALAT,* 379-380; also M. Noth, *Die israelitischen Personennamen* (Stuttgart: Kohlhammer, 1928; reprinted, Hildesheim: Olms, 1966) 101-110, 154.

32. *He will be great.* This verse begins the description of the role that the child to be born to Mary is to play. The phrase itself is similar to that used of Ishmael in Gen 16:12, "he will be a wild ass of a man." For the connotation of the absolute use of *megas,* "great," see NOTE on 1:15. An interesting parallel to this affirmation is found in a Palestinian Aramaic text from Qumran Cave 4, not yet fully published (see my article, *NTS* 20 [1973-1974] 393-394). In it some person, possibly the son of a king, is spoken of: "(he) shall be great upon the earth, [O King!]." Unfortunately, the text that contains this startling parallel to Luke's Greek is fragmentary, and it is not at all clear to whom the statement refers.

will be hailed as Son of the Most High. This phrase too finds an exact counterpart in the Qumran fragment mentioned in the previous note. The Aramaic text runs: [*whwʼ br ʼl r]bʼ ytqr wbšmh ytknh / brh dy ʼl ytʼmr wbr ʻlywn yqrwnh,* "he shall be called [son of] the [g]reat [God], and by his name shall he be named. He shall be hailed (as) the Son of God, and they shall call him Son of the Most High" (*NTS* 20 [1973-1974] 393; *WA,* 92). Not only is the title "Son of the Most High" found here, but also a form of the title "Son of God"; the significance of this text for the background of these NT titles has already been discussed in the sketch of Lucan theology (see p. 206 above). Though *hypsistos,* "highest" is found as a titular adjective for Zeus as early as Pindar (*Nemean Ode* 1.60; 11.2) and the phrase *theos hypsistos* is not uncommon in inscriptions from the Greco-Roman world (see BAG, 858), the absolute use of it for Yahweh is undoubtedly to be related to the Hebrew title *ʻElyôn* or the

Aramaic title *'Illāy,* "High, Exalted One," which is usually translated as "Most High." In pre-Christian Jewish literature this title appears frequently for Yahweh (e.g. *Jub.* 16:18; *1 Enoch* 9:3; 10:1; 46:7; 60:1,22 [unfortunately, none of these passages is preserved in Aramaic Enoch]; 1QapGen 12:17; 20:12,16). In the LXX the Hebrew and Aramaic titles were translated by *hypsistos* (e.g. Gen 14:18; Dan 4:14). Luke uses this title for God more frequently than any other NT writer (1:35,76; 6:35; 8:28; Acts 7:48; 16:17; elsewhere it occurs only in Mark 5:7 and Heb 7:1).

the throne of his father David. An allusion to 2 Sam 7:12-13.

33. *He will be king.* The chord of Jesus' kingship is thus struck here in the infancy narrative; see further 19:14,27,38; 23:2,3,37-38. See p. 215 above.

the house of Jacob. A traditional OT term for Israel; see Exod 19:3; Isa 2:5-6; 8:17; 48:1.

of his kingship there will be no end. Possibly Luke alludes here to Isa 9:6 (LXX) or to Dan 7:14, where promise of an everlasting kingdom is made. The endless character of this kingship is thus one of the qualities of the messianic kingdom. At this point in the Lucan Gospel the kingship should be understood in terms of the OT theme of kingdom (e.g. as in Ps 45:7). Jesus in some sense is to be anointed descendant of David and restorer of ancient kingship (Amos 9:11).

34. *How can this be?* Mary's perplexity is only increased by the substance of the angel's message in vv. 32-33. Compare Zechariah's objection (1:18).

since I have no relations with a man. Lit. "since I do not know a man (*or* a husband [Greek *andra,* not *anthrōpon*])." The verb *ginōskein* is used euphemistically of marital relations, a usage well attested in Hellenistic Greek and in the LXX (e.g. Judg 11:39; 21:12; Gen 19:8); cf. Matt 1:25. Mary's words explain the description of her in 1:27. But they should not be translated, "since I have no husband" (*RSV,* which obscures the fact that Mary has indeed a fiancé), or "I am a virgin" (*JB,* which is a "loaded" version), or "I am still a virgin" (*NEB,* which carries the same oversimplification), or even "I do not know man" (*NAB,* which sounds as though Mary might be saying that she did not know how children were conceived—a mode of interpretation that has been used at times!).

The recognition that Mary's question is part of the literary device of dramatization that Luke employs excludes all attempts to interpret her words as an expression of her inner psyche. Such psychological interpretations have often been used; e.g.:

a) Mary's words are said to refer to a vow of perpetual virginity that she had made. This mode of interpretation goes back to patristic writers (e.g. Gregory of Nyssa *In diem natalem Christi;* PG 46.1140D; Augustine *De sancta virginitate* 4.4; CSEL 41. 237-238). It has been called "the usual interpretation of Roman Catholic exegetes" (J. M. Creed, *The Gospel,* 19). Though some modern interpreters have still espoused it (e.g. O. Graber, "Wollte Maria . . ."; R. Laurentin, *Structure,* 176-179; McHugh, *The Mother of Jesus,* 446) or cast it in terms of a resolve instead of a vow (G. Graystone, *Virgin of All Virgins*), it is more and more abandoned by Roman Catholic exegetes today (see P. Benoit, review of Laurentin, *Structure, RB* 65 [1958] 431); it is not an interpretation that must be held. Support, however, for the interpretation has been sought in Luke's use of the pres. tense to express the future, i.e. "since I shall not know a man" (cf. Luke 12:40,54-55; 14:19; 22:10 for examples of such present tenses; cf. ZBG § 278; BDF § 323), and the existence of celibacy among the Essene Jews of Palestine (see Josephus *J.W.* 2.8,2 §§ 120-121) or among the related Therapeutae of Egypt (Philo *Hypothetica*, 11.14-17 §§ 380-381). The words in themselves merely express a simple denial of sexual intercourse and have nothing to do with an antecedent vow or resolve of perpetual virginity; the context in which they occur scarcely implies anything of the sort. We have no information that Mary shared those specific Essene or Therapeutic views of marriage. If she did, why is she depicted as engaged? Given that status and the normal OT esteem for a family and children (see Sir 7:24-25; Ps 128:3), Mary's expectation would have been that of any young Jewish girl who was engaged, i.e. firmly committed to marriage in the full sense. Lastly, a vow of virginity is unknown in the OT; not even Jeremiah's celibate life (16:1-2) can be invoked to explain Mary's situation or words.

b) Mary's words are understood as a protest because, realizing that she is already engaged, she wonders how this can be reconciled with the virginity that Israel's history expected of the mother of the Messiah: "How can this be, since (in that case) I am not to know a man?" This interpretation has been proposed by J.-P. Audet ("L'Annonce à Marie"). It depicts Mary as a pious Israelite, like Simeon and Anna, "looking for the consolation of Israel" (2:25). Acquainted with the OT stories about famous leaders, with the message given to Gideon, Judg 6:11-18, and with the prophecy of Isa 7:14, Mary would have shared the desire of many young Jewish girls to become the virgin-mother of the Messiah and carry such a son. Aware of the import of the Isaian prophecy, that a virgin would be the mother of the Messiah, Mary immediately caught the implication of the angel's words to her. Hence her perplexity. Audet supports the elliptical sense of the conj. *epei* ("puisque alors"), by appealing to 1 Cor 5:10; 7:14; 15:29; Heb 9:26; 10:2. But the elliptical use of *epei*, though found in NT Greek (BDF § 360.2 § 456.3), has rather the nuance of a contrary-to-fact or unreal condition, "for otherwise," as the very passages cited by Audet show. Then Mary's words would mean, "For, if it were not so, then I should know no man." And they would be meaningless in the context (see J. Gewiess, "Die Marienfrage, Lk 1,34," *BZ* 5 [1961] 238-239). But much more fundamental is the presupposition of Audet that Mary would have understood Isa 7:14 as a prophecy of the virgin-birth of the Messiah. Such an interpretation is unknown in pre-Christian Jewish literature. Finally, as explained in the COMMENT, there is no proof that Isa 7:14 influenced the composition of the *Lucan* announcement story.

c) Mary's words have been understood as an expression of surprise, that she, as Joseph's fiancée but not yet cohabiting with him, would conceive then and there, or else would do so in the immediate future (rather than in the still distant time when she would go to live with Joseph). So P. Gächter, *Maria im Erdenleben* (3d ed.; Innsbruck: Tyrolia, 1955) 92-98; J. B. Bauer, *MTZ* 9 (1958) 124-135; A. Plummer, *Gospel*, 24—with varying nuances among them. But, though this interpretation is the best of the four psychological interpretations, it tends to obscure the future tense that the angel used in v. 32 and will use in v. 35.

d) Mary's words have been cast in the past tense, "since I have not known a man." This interpretation is found in a number of ancient versions: *"Quoniam virum non cognovi"* (in the OL and some patristic writers who exploit the ambiguous meaning that the pf. *cognovi* has). The same translation can be found in Syriac and Sahidic versions of Luke and in the Arabic and Persian translations of Tatian's Diatessaron (see H. Quecke, *Bib* 44 [1963] 499-520; 47 [1966] 113-114). This interpretation would mean that Mary understood the angel to mean that she was already pregnant.

All of these interpretations have in common the naïve obscuring of the third stage of the gospel tradition (what is written in the Lucan Gospel) with its first stage (what was in the mind of the historical Mary: a vow, surprise, or misunderstanding). They presume that Luke has written a biographical account here, whereas the literary device of the OT birth-announcements makes it obvious that the words are to be understood rather in the light of that pattern. The question is asked to advance the dialogue, to give the angel the opening to explain how the conception is to come about. See further the COMMENT on this verse (34). The literary interpretation of the words has been used by Creed (*The Gospel,* 19); S. Muñoz Iglesias, *EstBib* 16 (1957) 329-382; Brown, *Birth,* 307-309; *MNT,* 114-115.

In my translation I have left the words of Mary as vague as they are in the Greek; "since I have no relations with a man" (*andra ou ginōskō*). Brown (*Birth,* 286, 289) removes the vagueness by translating, "since I have had no relations with a man," and explaining that the Greek tense, though present, describes a state resultant from a past pattern of behavior. That may be, but then one expects the Greek pf. tense, and that is why some of the ancient versions rendered it that way. See J. Carmignac, *BT* 28 (1977) 327-330.

Luke uses here *epei* for "since," the only time that it occurs in his writings. This is the one word that cannot be documented as Lucan (he uses *epeidē* in a casual sense in Luke 11:6; Acts 13:46; 14:12; 15:24; and *epeidēper* in Luke 1:1). But it is scarcely enough to make v. 34 non-Lucan.

35. *The holy Spirit.* See NOTE on 1:15. The Greek text has no def. art. The parallelism of "holy Spirit" and "power of the Most High" is intended to let the phrases explain each other. The latter phrase indicates that the Spirit is understood in the OT sense of God's creative and active power present to human beings. The *parallelismus membrorum* here is reminiscent of Hebrew poetry. See further 4:14; Acts 1:8; 6:8; 10:38, where Luke further uses the two ideas of "power" and "Spirit/grace" in conjunction.

Later church tradition made something quite other out of this verse. Justin Martyr wrote, "It is not right, therefore, to understand the Spirit and the power of God as anything else than the Word, who is also the First-begotten of God" (*Apologia* 1.33; FC, 6. 71). In this interpretation the two expressions are being understood of the Second Person of the Trinity. It was, however, scarcely before the fourth century that the "holy Spirit" was understood as the Third Person; see O. Bardenhewer, *Mariä Verkündigung: Ein Kommentar zu Lukas 1,26-38* (Freiburg: Herder, 1910). On the other hand, the collocation in this verse of "the Most High," "the Son of God," and "the holy Spirit" prepared in its own way for the Trinitarian doctrine of a later date. Only the elements of that doctrine are to be found here, not the doctrine itself. It is, moreover, to be noted that there is no evidence here in the Lucan infancy narrative of Jesus' preexistence or incarnation. Luke's sole concern is to assert that the origin of God's Messiah is the effect of his creative Spirit on Mary.

will come upon you. The verb *eperchesthai* is used by Luke alone among the evangelists; it occurs in 11:22; 21:26; Acts 1:8; 8:24; 13:40; 14:19 (also in Eph 2:7; Jas 5:1). Only in the programmatic verse of Acts 1:8 is it again used by Luke of the "coming" of the Spirit on the disciples. The use of it here in connection with the conception of Jesus is unique and is not to be understood of any sexual union. It is thought to be a Septuagintism, derived in particular from Isa 32:15, "until the Spirit comes upon you from on high." There it is used of the fertility of the land (of Carmel). But it also occurs with *pneuma*, "spirit," in other LXX passages, such as Num 5:14,30; Job 1:19; 4:15. But the sense of "spirit" differs. Here the phrase is intended to convey that the child to be born will be a "gift" of God in a full sense.

the power of the Most High. See NOTE on 1:32. A similar phrase will be found again in 5:17. Here the phrase is a Semitic parallel for the holy Spirit.

will cast a shadow over you. The verb *episkiazein* occurs again in the transfiguration scene (9:34), and again in Acts 5:15. In both cases it may have a literal sense, especially in Acts. Here the verb has to be understood in a figurative sense, denoting God's presence to Mary. Since the verb is used in Exod 40:35 of the cloud of God's glory filling the desert tabernacle, commentators have suggested that this connotation may be present here too (cf. Ps 91:4). This is possible, but not certain (see Voss, *Christologie,* 73-76). At any rate, there is no hint that Luke intends this to be understood as a *hieros gamos.*

Therefore. Luke uses the conj. *dio,* as in 7:7; Acts 10:29; 15:19; 20:31; 24:26; 25:26; 26:3; 27:25,34. As in the other places, it expresses a causal connection between the virginal conception and Jesus' divine sonship; it is another indication that Luke does not have a notion of Jesus' preexistence. See S. Lyonnet, "L'annonciation," 45 n. 3.

the child to be born. Luke uses to *gennōmenon,* pres. ptc. pass. neut. of *gennan,* "beget" (used of the father) or "bear" (used of the mother). It could theoretically mean "the one begotten," but since the words are being addressed to the mother to be, it means rather "the one being born." Probably the neut. noun to *brephos,* "baby" (see Luke 1:41,44; 2:12,16) is to be understood here, but it could mean simply "what is to be born." For the future sense of the pres. ptc., see BDF § 339.2b; cf. 4 Macc 13:19. Some mss. (C*, ⊙) add "of you."

holy. The function of the adj. *hagion* is not easily determined. I have taken it as the predicate of a verbless clause preceding the naming clause, "will be holy; he will be called Son of God." But it could also be rendered, "will be called holy, Son of God" (as predicate of the verb *klēthēsetai*), or even substantivally, "the Holy One to be born will be called Son of God" (as the subj. of the verb *klēthēsetai*). But, as C. F. D. Moule (*An Idiom-book of New Testament Greek* [Cambridge University Press, 1953], 107) notes, this last is a distinctly irregular usage. In the first possibility, one could understand the fut. verb *estai*, "the child to be born will be holy," i.e. set apart, consecrated to the service of Yahweh. The sense of the expression can be seen in Luke 2:23; cf. Isa 4:3.

Son of God. This first occurrence of this title in the Lucan writings is related to the other, "Son of the Most High" (1:32; see NOTE there; also p. 206 above).

36. *And now*. Lit. "and behold," see NOTE on 1:20 above. As it introduced the sign given to Zechariah there, so too here.

your relative Elizabeth. The degree of kinship is not stated. And Luke does not use a form of *anepsios*, "cousin," otherwise known in the NT (Col 4:10), and thus renders questionable a popular interpretation of this kinship. The phrase implies the kinship of John and Jesus as well, which must be considered in the light of John 1:33, where John the Baptist says that he did not know Jesus. The traditions here are obviously mixed.

it is already the sixth month. The secret that has been kept for five months (1:24) is now made known.

37. *nothing is impossible for God*. Lit. "not impossible will be word (*or* thing) with God." The angelic message ends with an OT allusion, probably to Gen 18:14 (LXX), i.e. to the words Yahweh addressed to Sarah, the barren wife of Abraham, when she was informed she would bear Isaac in her old age. Similar phrases are found elsewhere (see Job 42:2; Zech 8:6). Greek *rēma* properly means "word, speech," but here it carries the Septuagintal nuance of Hebrew *dābār*, "word, matter, thing."

38. *The Lord's handmaid am I!* Luke uses here *doulē*, the fem. of *doulos*, "slave, servant." See Luke 1:48; Acts 2:18. Mary is made to identify herself with the OT term used by Hannah in 1 Sam 1:11, expressive of her lowly condition before Yahweh, who is here the *Kyrios*.

Let it be with me as you say! Lit. "may it be done to me according to your word" (*rēma*, see NOTE on v. 37). Luke uses the opt. *genoito*, expressing a wish that is attainable. See BDF § 384.

At that the angel left her. The refrain A (of departure—see p. 314) closes the scene.

BIBLIOGRAPHY (1:26-38)

Aldama, J. A. de. "Una opinión mariológica reciente, censurada por teólogos antiguos," *Divinitas* 4 (1960) 123-140.

Allard, M. "L'Annonce à Marie et les annonces de naissance miraculeuses de l'Ancien Testament," *NRT* 78 (1956) 730-733.

Allgeier, A. "*Episkiazein* Lk 1,35," *BZ* 14 (1917) 338-343.

Audet, J.-P. "L'Annonce à Marie," *RB* 63 (1956) 346-374.

Auer, J. "Maria und das christliche Jungfräulichkeitsideal: Eine biblischdogmatische Studie," *Geist und Leben* 23 (1950) 411-425.

Avi-Yonah, M. "L'Inscription 'Nazareth' à Césarée," *BTS* 61 (1964) 2-5.

Baarda, T. "Dionysios bar Ṣalībī and the Text of Luke i, 35," *VC* 17 (1963) 225-229.

Bauer, J. B. "De nominis 'Mariae' vero etymo," *Marianum* 19 (1957) 231-234.

——— "Philologische Bemerkungen zu Lk 1,34," *Bib* 45 (1964) 535-540.

Beckermann, C. " 'Et nomen virginis Maria' (Luc. 1, 27b)," *VD* 1 (1921) 130-136.

Benko, S. "The Perpetual Virginity of the Mother of Jesus," *LQ* 16 (1964) 147-163.

Boslooper, T. "Jesus' Virgin Birth and Non-Christian 'Parallels,' " *Religion in Life* 26 (1956-1957) 87-97.

Brinkmann, B. "Die Jungfrauengeburt und das Lukasevangelium," *Bib* 34 (1953) 327-332.

Brodmann, B. "Mariens Jungfräulichkeit nach Lk 1, 34 in der Auseinandersetzung von heute," *BK* (1955) 98-110; *Antonianum* 30 (1955) 27-44.

Brown, R. E. "Luke's Description of the Virginal Conception," *TS* 35 (1974) 360-362.

——— "Luke's Method in the Annunciation Narrative of Chapter One," in *No Famine in the Land: Studies in Honor of John L. McKenzie* (eds. J. W. Flannagan and A. W. Robinson; Missoula, MT: Scholars Press, 1975) 179-194; reprinted in *Perspectives on Luke-Acts* (ed. C. H. Talbert; Danville, VA: Association of Baptist Professors of Religion, 1978) 126-138.

——— "The Problem of the Virginal Conception of Jesus," *TS* 33 (1972) 3-34; reprinted, with some revisions, in *The Virginal Conception and Bodily Resurrection of Jesus* (New York: Paulist, 1973) 21-68.

——— "Virgin Birth," *IDBSup* (1976) 940-941.

Brown, R. E. et al. (eds.) *Mary in the New Testament* (Philadelphia: Fortress; New York: Paulist, 1978) 105-134. Cited as *MNT*.

Cambe, M. "La *charis* chez saint Luc: Remarques sur quelques textes, notamment le *kecharitōmenē*," *RB* 70 (1963) 193-207.

Campenhausen, H. von. *The Virgin Birth in the Theology of the Ancient Church* (Studies in Historical Theology 2; Naperville: Allenson, 1964).

Cantalamessa, R. "La primitiva esegesi cristologica di Romani I, 3-4 e Luca I, 35," *Rivista di storia e letteratura religiosa* 2 (1966) 69-80.

Carmignac, J. "The Meaning of *parthenos* in Luke 1.27—A Reply to C. H. Dodd," *BT* 28 (1977) 327-330.

Cole, E. R. "What Did St. Luke Mean by *kecharitōmenē?*" *AER* 139 (1958) 228-239.

Collins, J. J. "Our Lady's Vow of Virginity (Lk. 1:34)," *CBQ* 5 (1943) 369-380.

Craghan, J. F. "Mary's 'Ante Partum' Virginity: The Biblical View," *AER* 162 (1970) 361-372.

Delling, G. "*Parthenos*," *TDNT* 5 (1967) 826-837.

Escudero Freire, C. "Alcance cristológico de Lc. 1,35 y 2,49," *Communio* 8 (1975) 5-77.

——— *Alcance cristológico y traducción de Lc. 1,35: Aportación al estudio de los titulos* Santo *e* Hijo de Dios *en la obra lucana* (Seville: Centro de estudios teológicos, 1975).

Fitzmyer, J. A. "The Contribution of Qumran Aramaic to the Study of the New Testament," *NTS* 20 (1973-1974) 382-407, esp. pp. 391-394; reprinted in *WA*, 85-113, esp. pp. 90-94, 102-107.

———— "The Virginal Conception of Jesus in the New Testament," *TS* 34 (1973) 541-575.

Flanagan, N. M. "Our Lady's Vow of Virginity," *Marian Studies* 7 (1956) 103-121.

Fuller, R. H. "The Virgin Birth: Historical Fact or Kerygmatic Truth?" *BR* 1 (1956) 1-8.

Gächter, P. "Der Verkündigungsbericht Lk 1, 26-38," *ZKT* 91 (1969) 322-363, 567-586.

Gewiess, J. "Die Marienfrage, Lk 1,34," *BZ* 5 (1961) 221-254; digested in *TD* 11 (1963) 39-42.

Graber, O. "Wollte Maria eine normale Ehe eingehen?" *Marianum* 20 (1958) 1-9.

Grant, F. C. "Where Form Criticism and Textual Criticism Overlap," *JBL* 59 (1940) 11-21.

Graystone, G. *Virgin of All Virgins: The Interpretation of Lk 1:34* (Rome: Tipografia S. Pio X, 1968).

Harnack, A. von. "Zu Lk 1,34-35," *ZNW* 2 (1901) 53-57.

Haugg, D. *Das erste biblische Marienwort: Eine exegetische Studie zu Lukas 1,34* (Bibelwissenschaftliche Reihe, 1; Stuttgart: Katholisches Bibelwerk, 1938).

Hebert, A. G. "The Virgin Mary as the Daughter of Zion," *Theology* 53 (1950) 403-410.

Hehn, J. *"Episkiazein* Lk, 1,35," *BZ* 14 (1917) 147-152.

Hoyos, F. "Darás a luz un hijo y le pondrás por nombre Jesús," *RevistB* 28 (1966) 239-246.

Jellouschek, C. J. "Mariä Verkündigung in neuer Sicht," *MTZ* 10 (1959) 102-113.

Kasteren, J. van. "Analecta exegetica," *RB* os 3 (1894) 52-61.

Lagrange, M.-J. "La conception surnaturelle du Christ d'après saint Luc," *RB* 11 (1914) 60-71, 188-208.

Lattke, G. "Lukas 1 und die Jungfrauengeburt," in *Zum Thema Jungfrauengeburt* (Stuttgart: Katholisches Bibelwerk, 1970) 61-89.

Legrand, L. "Fécondité virginale selon l'Esprit dans le Nouveau Testament," *NRT* 84 (1962) 785-805.

Lyonnet, S. *"Chaire, kecharitōmenē,"* *Bib* 20 (1939) 131-141.

———— "Le récit de l'annonciation et la maternité divine de la sainte Vierge," *Ami du clergé* 66 (1956) 33-46; reprinted, Rome: Biblical Institute, 1956; translated, in part, as "St. Luke's Infancy Narrative," in *Word and Mystery: Biblical Essays on the Person and Mission of Christ* (ed. L. J. O'Donovan; Glen Rock, NJ: Newman, 1968) 143-154.

McHugh, J. *The Mother of Jesus in the New Testament* (Garden City, NY: Doubleday, 1975).

Mohrmann, C. "Ave gratificata," *Rivista di storia della chiesa in Italia* 5 (1951) 1-6.

Muñoz Iglesias, S. "Lucas 1,35b," *La idea de Dios en la Biblia: XXVIII semana bíblica española* (*Madrid 23-27 Sept. 1968*) (Madrid: Consejo superior de investigaciones científicas, 1971) 303-324 (=*EstBíb* 27 [1968] 275-299).

Páramo, S. del. "La anunciación de la Virgen: Reparos exegéticos y doctrinales a una reciente interpretación," *EstBíb* 16 (1957) 161-185.

Piper, O. A. "The Virgin Birth: The Meaning of the Gospel Accounts," *Int* 18 (1964) 131-148.

Prete, B. "A proposito di Luca 1,34," *RivB* 18 (1970) 379-393.

Quecke, H. "Lk 1,34 in den alten Übersetzungen und im Protevangelium des Jakobus," *Bib* 44 (1963) 499-520.

———— "Lk 1,34 im Diatessaron," *Bib* 45 (1964) 85-88.

———— "Lukas 1,31 in den alten Übersetzungen," *Bib* 46 (1965) 333-348.

———— "Zur Auslegungsgeschichte von Lk 1,34," *Bib* 47 (1966) 113-114.

Schneider, G. "Jesu geistgewirkte Empfängnis (Lk 1,34f): Zur Interpretation einer christologischen Aussage," *TPQ* 119 (1971) 105-116.

———— "Lk 1, 34.35 als redaktionelle Einheit," *BZ* 15 (1971) 255-259.

Schürmann, H. "Die geistgewirkte Lebensentstehung Jesu: Eine kritische Besinnung auf den Beitrag der Exegese zur Frage," *Einheit in Vielfalt: Festgabe für Hugo Aufderbeck zum 65. Geburtstag* (Erfurter theologische Studien, 32; eds. W. Ernst and K. Feiereis; Leipzig: St.-Benno, 1974) 156-169.

Smith, D. M. "Luke 1:26-38," *Int* 29 (1975) 411-417.

Strobel, A. "Der Gruss an Maria (Lc 1,28): Eine philologische Betrachtung zu seinem Sinngehalt," *ZNW* 53 (1962) 86-110.

Turner, H. E. W. "The Virgin Birth," *ExpTim* 68 (1956-1957) 12-17.

Vicent, A. "La presunta sustantivación *to gennōmenon* en Lc 11,35b [*sic!* read 1,35b]," *EstBíb* 33 (1974) 265-273.

Vogels, H. "Zur Textgeschichte von Lc 1,34ff.," *ZNW* 43 (1950-1951) 256-260.

Vogt, E. "De nominis Mariae etymologia," *VD* 26 (1948) 163-168.

Völkel, M. "Der Anfang Jesu in Galiläa: Bemerkungen zum Gebrauch und zur Funktion Galiläas in den lukanischen Schriften," *ZNW* 64 (1973) 222-232.

Zerwick, M. "'. . . quoniam virum non cognosco' (Lc 1,34) (Conspectus criticus de opinionibus recentioribus)," *VD* 37 (1959) 212-224, 276-288.

4. MARY VISITS ELIZABETH
(1:39-56)

1 39 About the same time Mary set out and went in haste to a Judean town in the hill country. 40 She entered Zechariah's house and greeted Elizabeth. 41 When Elizabeth heard Mary's greeting, the child in her womb leaped. Elizabeth was filled with the holy Spirit 42 and uttered in a loud voice,

> "Blest, indeed, are you among women,
> and blest is the fruit of your womb!"

43 "But why should this happen to me that the mother of my Lord comes to me? 44 For as the sound of your greeting reached my ears, the child in my womb leaped with delight."

> 45 "Blessed, indeed, is the woman who has believed,
> because what the Lord has promised her will see fulfillment."

46 And Mary said,

My soul declares the greatness of the Lord,	1 Sam 2:1-10
47 and my spirit finds delight in *God my Savior*,	Ps 25:5 (LXX)
48 because he has *had regard for the lowliness of his handmaid.* From now on all generations will count me blessed,	1 Sam 1:11; Ps 113:5-6
49 for he who is mighty *has done great things* for me, he *whose name is holy.*	Deut 10:21 Ps 111:9
50 His *mercy* is for *those who fear him from generation to generation.*	Ps 103:17
51 He has displayed the might of his arm; he *has put to rout* the arrogant in the conceit of their hearts.	Ps 89:11
52 He has put down mighty rulers from their thrones and exalted the lowly.	1 Sam 2:4,7

53 *He has filled the hungry with good things* and   Ps 107:9;
                                                         1 Sam 2:5
    sent the rich *away empty.*   Job 22:9
54 *He has come to the aid of his servant Israel,*   Isa 41:8-9
    mindful of his mercy,   Ps 98:3
55 as he promised *our fathers,* Abraham and his   Mic 7:20
descendants forever."

56 Then Mary stayed with her about three months, before she returned home.

COMMENT

The third episode in the Lucan infancy narrative is complementary to the two preceding announcement stories and presupposes them. It brings together elements from each of them and acts as a link for the two, especially to vv. 24-25 and 36-37. Having composed the announcement of Jesus' birth in imitation of the Baptist-source's story of the announcement of John's birth, Luke makes use of the visit of Mary to Elizabeth to join the two announcement stories more closely. The story in 1:5-24a from the source is continued in vv. 57-66.

This episode has two main parts and a conclusion: (a) Mary's visit to Elizabeth and the latter's recognition of Mary as "the mother of my Lord" (1:39-45); and (b) Mary's reaction to Elizabeth's praise of her and to God's favor bestowed on her—the canticle, the Magnificat (1:46-55). The concluding verse (1:56) echoes the refrain A of vv. 23 and 38. In the episode both women utter praise, Elizabeth of Mary, and Mary of God.

As we have already mentioned (p. 309 above), the canticle is to be ascribed to a pre-Lucan Jewish Christian source; further discussion will be devoted to this judgment below. The rest of the episode is to be attributed to Luke's free composition. This would not mean, however, that he had not derived from the tradition before him that John the Baptist came from a town in Judea in the hill country of Palestine; that geographical detail may well reflect an earlier tradition.

In vv. 39-45 Mary is portrayed as making her way in haste to her relative's house in a town of Judea in the hill country. Mary knows about Elizabeth's condition because of the angel's declaration to her (v. 36); this is why she goes to Elizabeth, whose seclusion thus comes to an end (1:24). As Mary greets her, the child in Elizabeth's womb leaps prophetically, and from that Elizabeth, filled with the holy Spirit, concludes that

Mary is to give birth to "the Lord." Thus each mother learns from heaven about the child of the other. And John goes before the Lord (1:17) to become—even in the womb—his precursor. Note that in the episode there is no mention of Jesus as Messiah. Elizabeth greets Mary as "the mother of my Lord" (1:43). Then she utters a blessing and a beatitude over Mary: She is blest (*eulogēmenē*) among women because of the fruit of her womb; she is blessed (*makaria*) because of her faith. Two aspects of Mary are thus praised, her motherhood of him who is *kyrios,* but above all her faith.

Elizabeth's praise of Mary is found in vv. 42-45. A. Plummer (*Gospel,* 27) calls it "the Song of Elisabeth" and refers to its structure as two strophes of four lines each. This is hardly correct, since Elizabeth's praise does not have the structured parallelism of either the Magnificat or the Benedictus. The parallelism is clear in v. 42b,c, and possibly in v. 45. What occurs in between (vv. 43-44) is scarcely to be understood as poetic. Elizabeth, filled with God's prophetic Spirit, utters first a blessing over Mary that echoes that of the prophet Deborah over Jael, "Blest be Jael among women" (Judg 5:24), or that of Uzziah over Judith, "Blest of God Most High are you, daughter, above all the women of the earth" (Jdt 13:18). The reason for the blessing is expressed in parataxis: "and blest is the fruit of your womb," because she bears within her the *Kyrios.* The beatitude in v. 45 serves to foreshadow the beatitude that will be expressed over Mary by the woman in the crowd in 11:27-28: here Mary's faith is explicitly mentioned; in 11:28 the second beatitude, Jesus' reply to the woman, implies Mary's hearing the word of God and keeping it (cf. 8:21).

The leaping of the child in Elizabeth's womb also has an OT precedent in the leaping of the twins in Rebecca's womb (Gen 25:22), which symbolized the roles Jacob and Esau were to play as adversary peoples.

In the visitation scene proper Mary's child is thus recognized as the *Kyrios,* and Mary as the "mother of the Lord," a believer, a model of faith. Luke is picking up the lowly handmaid motif of 1:38 and making her a disciple from the beginning of his account (cf. 8:19-21; Acts 1:14).

In answer to Elizabeth's praise of Mary, Mary utters her canticle of praise (vv. 46-55). As the NOTE on 1:46 explains, the canticle is ascribed to Mary in the best textual tradition, and it has to be regarded as an expression of her praise of God for what has happened to her. It is similar to three other passages in the Lucan infancy narrative that have hymnic properties and structure: the Benedictus (1:67-79), the Angels' Song (2:13-14), and the Nunc Dimittis (2:28-32). As I shall explain, I consider the Angels' Song to be a Lucan composition. But one has to reckon with the preexistence of the Magnificat, the Benedictus, and possibly the Nunc Dimittis from an earlier tradition that Luke has taken over.

Since they are all so loosely connected with the contexts into which they have been fitted, R. E. Brown (*Birth,* 251-253) may well be right in maintaining that Luke himself added these secondarily—at a stage in his writing when the infancy narrative had otherwise taken shape.

Since there is no evidence that the Magnificat ever existed in a Semitic (Hebrew or Aramaic) form, there is no reason to think of Mary as the one who has composed it. It has not been preserved by a family tradition. The heavy dependence on the Greek OT makes it evident that it is a *cento*-like composition, a mosaic of OT expressions drawn from the LXX. In the translation of the canticle I have italicized the phrases that show clear dependence. But there are many other allusions, to which the NOTES on various verses call attention. The best way to ascertain the extent of dependence of the Magnificat on the OT is to compare its Greek text with the Greek form of the OT verses involved, especially with the Song of Hannah (1 Sam 2:1-10), its principal model. One can do this easily by consulting A. Plummer, *Gospel,* 30-31; or J. M. Creed, *The Gospel,* 303-304; some of the allusions disappear in translation. Moreover, it is hardly likely that Luke composed the Magnificat himself, since it fits so loosely into the present context. It has often been compared to the speeches in Acts, in which largely Lucan compositions give utterance to ideal sentiments of the speakers involved. This is true of the Magnificat, but it could be omitted without anything essential being lost to the narrative of the visitation itself. The song praises God's salvific activity in generic terms without anything specifically referring to Mary's visit to Elizabeth.

Part of the reason for regarding the canticle as non-Lucan is that, aside from v. 48, which Luke may well have composed himself—in whole or in part—and inserted into the hymn he inherited from an earlier Jewish Christian tradition, much of the Magnificat does not suit Mary specifically. Indeed, this has been part of the reason for attempts to attribute it to Elizabeth, and is even more apparent when the structure of the canticle is considered.

The Magnificat is not unlike some psalms of praise in the canonical Psalter. However, it is not as perfectly structured or built with the same amount of parallelism as they usually are. In this regard it resembles rather some of the hymnic compositions of late pre-Christian Jewish literature found in 1 Maccabees, the Qumran Thanksgiving Psalms (*Hôdāyôt*), or Qumran War Scroll (*Milḥāmāh*).

Basically, the canticle resembles what have been called "hymns of praise" among the canonical psalms and may be compared with such psalms as 33, 47, 48, 113, 117, 135, and especially 136. Such a psalm usually contains an introductory invitation to praise God or a statement of praise of him, then the body of the psalm, giving the reason(s) for the praise (usually introduced by Hebrew *kî*, "because, for" [cf. Hannah's canticle, 1 Sam 2:3b]), and a concluding part, which is often repetitious of elements of the body.

In the Magnificat the introduction is found in vv. 46b–47; and the rest of the verses may either be regarded as the body of the hymn with three strophes (vv. 48–50, 51–53, 54–55) or as a two-strophe body (vv. 48–50, 51–53) with a conclusion (vv. 54–55). The latter seems to be preferable, because vv. 54–55 repeat, in effect, what vv. 51–53 set forth as Yahweh's great deeds, making them specific in relating them to Israel, "our fathers," and Abraham. It should be noted that the Greek conj. *hoti* (=Hebrew *kî*) occurs at the beginning of both v. 48 and v. 49. Verses 49–50 are closely related in that they sing of three attributes of Yahweh: his might, his holiness, his mercy. This is the reason for regarding these as part of a single strophe. Verses 51–53 sing rather of Yahweh's great deeds, and they belong together. Verse 48, in reality, stands out alone, and it has often been thought to be a Lucan composition, inserted to bring the otherwise generic praise of Yahweh in the hymn into reference to Mary herself. It makes mention of Mary's status as "handmaid" (echoing 1:38) and her "blessedness" (echoing the beatitude of 1:45). This, then, would explain the double *hoti,* the generic character of vv. 49–50, and the parallelism in vv. 51a–51b, 52a–52b, 53a–53b.

In the parallel introductory verses (vv. 46b–47) Mary, like Hannah of 1 Sam 2:1–10, extols Yahweh's greatness and recognizes in him her Savior. He is so hailed, because she acknowledges the new form of salvation that is to come through the birth of her child. She speaks as the "favored" one of 1:28, and her "delight" sets the tone and atmosphere for the new era that is dawning.

In the Lucan insert of v. 48 she is made to contrast her humble station with Yahweh's greatness, might, holiness, and mercy. "All generations" will count her blessed, not because of any intrinsic, personal holiness or merit, but because of him whom she is bearing. Verses 49–50 extol three attributes of Yahweh. Two of them echo elements in the story of Mary in the infancy narratives, but the third does not. Yahweh is the mighty one (*dynatos*), and it was announced to Mary by the angel that the power (*dynamis*) of the Most High would cast its shadow over her (1:35). Similarly, from him whose name is "holy" would come the child to be born to her, who would be called "holy" (1:35). Only Yahweh's "mercy" has not figured earlier in the story about Mary; it is present because of the pre-Lucan composition of the hymn. It suits her situation in a generic sense, without any specific application.

The second strophe (vv. 51–53) stands out from the preceding in that the verses contain six verbs all in the aorist tense. The aorists are scarcely to be interpreted as rendering Hebrew prophetic perfects, since we have already excluded the composition of this hymn in a Semitic language. That they could be gnomic aorists (see BDF § 333), descriptive of Yahweh's tendency to reverse the conditions that human beings create for themselves, is possible. But it seems more likely that they reflect the situation for which the hymn was originally composed in its pre-Lucan setting. The battle-like tone of these verses was taken by P. Winter to suggest that the Magnificat was originally composed to celebrate a victory of the Maccabees. This might seem plausible for these three verses, but it hardly explains the full hymn, which echoes much more a Jewish Christian setting. On the lips of Mary, the great deeds of Yahweh, manifested for his people of old, are now seen to be manifested in a new form in the conception of the child to be born to her. Luke can put such sentiments on Mary's lips at this stage in his narrative because he is writing with hindsight and knows that each of the details can be interpreted figuratively of the career of Jesus himself.

In the conclusion to the Magnificat (vv. 54-55) Mary recognizes that the salvation that is to come through the birth, life, and career of Jesus is related to the covenant made by God with Abraham of old. The nation of Israel, God's Servant, is recalled, as are the patriarchs. The remnant of Israel is to have a new meaning, for it is to be reconstituted in a way that will extend the promises of old to others not under the Law.

Whence did Luke derive the Magnificat, i.e. vv. 46b-47, 49-55? Though some commentators (e.g. A. von Harnack, H. D. F. Sparks, N. Turner) think that Luke composed the hymn in imitation of contemporary Jewish hymns, it is noteworthy that the hymn is more heavily Semitized than the rest of the surrounding, otherwise Semitized Greek of the infancy narrative. Other commentators (e.g. H. Gunkel, S. Mowinckel, P. Winter) have argued that the hymn was originally a Jewish composition that was taken over by Luke and adapted to his Christian purpose and usage. While this is not absolutely impossible, it is more likely that the emphasis on salvation now coming to Israel in a new way is indicative of the Jewish Christian early community. Attempts have been made to specify this background even more. In dependence on others before him, Brown has argued forcefully that the source of both the Magnificat and the Benedictus was the Jewish Christian circle of the Poor Ones or Anawim (see *Birth*, 350-355). The Hebrew term *'ănāwîm* was used originally to denote the physically poor, but in time it came to be applied to people in Israel who were unfortunate, lowly, sick, downtrodden. Their opposites were not simply the rich, but included the proud, the arrogant, those who felt no need of God. See Ps 149:4; Isa 49:13; 66:2 for descriptions of these "poor ones." They were often identified as the remnant of Israel, and developed in time a piety of dependence on God and even a "Temple piety." Converts to Christianity undoubtedly carried over their piety into a form of Jewish Christianity. Certain elements of the early community described in the early chapters of Acts (the summaries in 2:43-47; 4:32-37) may be derived from them. Brown's conclusion is worth quoting: "Thus, it is not impossible that, in the last third of the century when he was composing Luke/Acts, Luke came upon these canticles in a Greek-speaking Jewish Christian community in an area influenced by Jerusalem Christianity" (ibid., 355).

The concluding verse of the episode (1:56) belongs to the visitation proper. It has been given various psychologizing interpretations (e.g. that Mary's pregnancy was now becoming obvious, or was now discovered [Matt 1:18]), but the real reason has to be understood in terms of Luke's literary composition. He wants to clear the stage before he returns to the narrative of the birth of John in his Baptist-source; the parallelism of the scenes involving the birth, circumcision, and manifestation of John and Jesus take over. Mary will return to the stage when her time comes.

NOTES

1 39. *About the same time.* Lit. "in those days," a vague time reference to 1:36, linking the new episode to the angel's message about Elizabeth's advanced pregnancy. This phrase, or another with a different demonstrative (having the same meaning), can be found frequently in Lucan writings (see 2:1; 4:2; 5:35; 6:12; 9:36; 23:7; Acts 1:15; 11:27, etc.).

Mary set out and went in haste. Lit. "having arisen, Mary went with haste." Luke uses here the pleonastic or redundant ptc. *anastas(a)* with another verb (see 4:29; 5:28; 6:8; 11:7,8; 15:18,20; 17:19; 22:46; 23:1; 24:12,33; Acts 5:6; 8:27; 9:18,39; 10:13,20,23; 11:7,28; 14:20; 15:7; 22:10,16; 23:9); cf. BDF § 419.2. The usage is a Septuagintism (see p. 114 above), being a translation of *qwm*, "rise," and another verb in either Hebrew (see Gen 13:17; 19:14) or Aramaic (1QapGen 21:13). The combination connotes inception.

The other verb, *poreuesthai*, "make one's way, go," is a Lucan favorite, especially for depicting Jesus en route (see NOTE on 4:30).

The prep. phrase *meta spoudēs*, "in haste," is found with this meaning in Mark 6:25; Exod 12:11; Wisd 19:2. However, it is possible that it means "with eagerness," a meaning that it has in 3 Macc 5:24,27; Josephus *Ag. Ap.* 2.4 § 42. See B. Hospodar, *CBQ* 18 (1956) 14-18. However, it should not, in either case, be used to analyze Mary's psychology; it suggests merely the proper reaction to the heavenly sign that has just been given.

to a Judean town. From 1:23 we learned that Zechariah returned to his home after his Temple service, but it was not stated where that was, in Jerusalem or elsewhere. Here it is made clear that he and Elizabeth dwelled in a town in the hill country of Judea (ancient Judah). The town is unspecified, and Luke's description of it may depend merely on 2 Sam 2:1, where David is said to have inquired of the Lord whether he should go up "into one of the towns of Judah" (LXX). A Christian tradition, well antedating the Crusades, eventually localized the dwelling of Zechariah at 'Ain Karim, eight kms. W of Jerusalem (see C. Kopp, *Holy Places*, 87-96; D. Baldi, *ELS*, § 44-81). Neh 11:3 reveals that priests who served in the Jerusalem Temple could live outside of the city.

Luke actually refers to "Judah" (*Iouda*) in the indeclinable Greek form that reflects the Hebrew *Yĕhûdāh*. Since there is no def. art. before it, "Judah" looks like a Semitism and resembles the Greek of LXX 2 Sam 2:1. Years ago C. C. Torrey (*HTR* 17 [1924] 83-91) argued that Luke's Greek phrase was really a mistaken rendering of Hebrew/Aramaic *'l mdynt yhwdh*, which would really mean "to the province of Judea." Challenged by J. F. Springer (*ATR* 5 [1922] 324-332), he insisted that *mĕdînāh* in Hebrew and Aramaic from its earliest attestation among Palestinian Jews meant "province" and that only in Gentile usage did it mean "city, town" (=Greek *polis*). This was called a brilliant suggestion by M. Black (*AAGA*[3], 12). However, this suggestion raises more problems than it solves. Was there a "province of Judea/Judah" in the time of Herod the Great (see 1:5)? His realm included not only Judea, but also Galilee, Samaria, Perea, and Idumea. Even in Luke's day it might be asked whether there was a "province" of Judea. Again, if Luke meant to speak of the "province" of Judea, he would undoubtedly have used the technical Greek word for it, *eparcheia,* which he uses in Acts 23:34; 25:1(?). Cf. F. L. Horten, "Reflections on the Semitisms of Luke-Acts," in *Perspectives on Luke-Acts* (ed. C. H. Talbert; Danville, VA: Association of Baptist Professors of Religion, 1978) 1-23, esp. pp. 21-22.

in the hill country. Lit. "into the hilly" (region [understood]). Josephus (*Ant.* 12.1,1 § 7) used the same adj. as a substantive of Judea. Cf. *J.W.* 4.8,2 § 451. See Luke 1:65.

40. *Zechariah's house.* Both Zechariah and Elizabeth, who are mentioned here, are known from 1:5.

greeted Elizabeth. Luke does not tell us what the greeting was or how it was phrased.

41. *when Elizabeth heard.* Lit. "and it happened that, when . . . , the child in her womb leaped." Luke uses *kai egeneto* + finite verb without the conj. *kai* (see p. 119 above).

leaped. The movement of the unborn child in Elizabeth's womb is intended as a recognition by him of his relation to Jesus. The verb *eskirtēsen* is the same as that used in LXX Gen 25:22 (*eskirtōn*), where Rebecca's twins similarly leaped, foreshadowing their future relations. In v. 44 we are told that Elizabeth's child leaped "with delight." As Luke presents the scene, the mere utterance of Mary's greeting (which must be understood as not disclosing any information about the angelic revelation to her of Elizabeth's condition) causes the movement of the child. Elizabeth is filled with the Spirit and inspired to interpret the sign thus given to her. The unborn child is thus made to acknowledge not only the "Lord" but also the presence of the "mother of my Lord."

filled with the holy Spirit. What was promised to Zechariah (1:15) is now fulfilled. This "filling" of Elizabeth is the source of her inspiration. Because of it she understands Mary's condition.

42. *uttered in a loud voice*. Lit. "with a great cry." Luke makes use of an exaggerated expression to stress the importance of the event. The ms. D and the Koine text-tradition read *phonē*, "voice," instead of *kraugē*, "cry." Contrast 1 Sam 1:12-13, Hannah's muttering.

Blest, indeed, are you among women. The reason for her being blest is set forth in the following parallel clause. Elizabeth thus recognizes the "favor" (1:28) with which Mary has been graced by God. Luke uses here the Greek perf. pass. ptc. *eulogēmenē*, which, like the adj. *eulogētos* (1:68), either pronounces praise of the person so characterized or recognizes the condition of God's blessing or favor bestowed upon him/her. Used in the positive degree along with a prep. phrase *en gynaixin*, "among women," it is a Semitic way of expressing the superlative, "most blest" (see BDF § 245.3). Cf. Judg 5:24, where a similar blessing is uttered over Jael "among women" (where the Hebrew *min*, lit. "from," usually used to express comparison, is translated in the LXX by *en* [the prep. used here]). Also Cant 1:8; Jdt 13:18; 1QapGen 20:6-7. Since according to contemporary Jewish ideas a woman's greatness was measured by the children that she bore, the mother of the *Kyrios* would naturally be said to surpass all others. Luke here is foreshadowing 11:27, where a woman from the crowd utters a similar recognition of her.

blest is the fruit of your womb! An OT phrase is used here (see Gen 30:2; Lam 2:20; cf. Deut 7:13; 28:4) to convey to the reader that Mary's conception has already taken place. Luke has not mentioned this, whereas he did in the case of Elizabeth (1:24). Cf. 1QapGen 2:15. For another double "blessing," cf. Gen 14:19-20.

43. *why should this happen to me that the mother of my Lord comes to me?* Lit. "whence (is) this to me that the mother of my Lord should come to me?" A clause, introduced by *hina* with the subjunc., replaces the epexegetical infin. usual in this construction (see BDF § 394; ZBG § 410). Thus Mary is recognized by Elizabeth: as the "mother of my Lord," where *kyrios* is used of Jesus himself.

Some commentators have noted the similarity of this question to either 2 Sam 6:9 ("How can the ark of the Lord come to me?") or 2 Sam 24:21 ("Why has my lord, the king, come to his servant?"). For E. Burrows (*Gospel of the Infancy*, 47) and R. Laurentin (*Structure*, 79-81), Elizabeth's question compares Mary with the ark of the covenant. This link is supposed to be confirmed in 1:56, where Mary is said to remain three months with Elizabeth, just as the ark stayed "three months" with Obededom. But this is subtle. If, indeed, the story may be compared with 2 Sam 24:21, then what connection does it have with the ark? Again, the question has to be asked: Who is seeing the connections here? Luke, or Burrows and others? See further P. Benoit, *RB* 65 (1958) 429; Brown, *Birth*, 327-328.

On the basis of 2 Sam 24:21, where "my lord" has as an appositive "the king" (*ho basileus*), D. M. Stanley (*Worship* 34 [1959-1960] 330-332) has argued that Luke's phrase, "the mother of my Lord," casts Mary in the role of a queen mother. He compares the mention of Bathsheba, "the king's mother" (2 Kgs 2:19), and the mother of Belshazzar (Dan 5:10-12). He thinks that the Lucan phrase reflects an early Christian attitude toward Mary in a queenly role. This too is, indeed, subtle. The title *kyrios* is given to Jesus here, and its meaning in Lucan theology as a whole must be considered (see p. 200 above). That it eventually suggests putting Jesus on a level with Yahweh would have to be admitted; that it has regal connotations is also possible. However, when Luke wants to get across the role of Jesus as king, he calls him precisely that (see p. 215 above). Thus it seems better to limit the meaning of the phrase as used here.

The expression "my Lord" will turn up again in the Lucan Gospel (20:41-44) and in Acts (2:34), where a line from Ps 110:1 is used of Jesus, "The Lord said to my lord, 'Sit at my right hand.'" (See NOTE on 20:42 for the sense in which it is applied to him.)

44. *For.* Lit. "for behold (*idou gar,* used also in 1:48; 2:10; 6:23; 17:21; Acts 9:11).

with delight. This phrase interprets the movement of the child within Elizabeth and supplies the reason for Elizabeth's recognition of Mary's condition and acknowledgment of her as "the mother of my Lord." The delight (*agalliasis*) echoes that conveyed by the angel's words in 1:14 and the cognate verb is used in Mary's canticle (1:47). It is a mood-word in the Lucan infancy narrative, creating a suitable atmosphere for the messianic period that is dawning (see R. Bultmann, *TDNT* 1. 18-20).

45. *Blessed, indeed, is the woman who has believed.* In contrast to v. 42 above, where a double "blessing" was uttered (using *eulogēmenē*), Luke here introduces the first beatitude into his Gospel. The adj. is *makaria* (see NOTE on 6:20). It is uttered over Mary, whose faith stands in contrast to Zechariah's incredulity (1:20). Elizabeth's extolling of Mary is to be understood from the standpoint of the reader of the Gospel, because Luke's story is abbreviated; he has not yet said anything about Mary's "faith" (except to imply it in 1:38).

Sometimes the attempt is made to understand the ptc. *pisteusasa* with the def. art. as a vocative, "blessed (are you), O believing woman" (see *ZBG* § 34); cf. Vg. *beata quae credidisti.* However, the translation in the lemma is preferred because of the third sg. fem. pron. in the following subordinate clause.

because what the Lord has promised her will see fulfillment. Lit. "because there will be fulfillment for those things spoken to her by the Lord." Or possibly, "that there will be. . . ." It is not easy here to say whether the conj. *hoti* introduces the object of Mary's faith ("that") or expresses the cause of the blessing ("because"). In either case Elizabeth seems to know fully what the promise is. The "fulfillment" (*teleiōsis,* used only here in the Lucan writings; cf. Jdt 10:9) is part of the Lucan theme of the fulfillment of salvation-history.

46. *And Mary said.* This is, in the long run, the best reading of the introduction to the following canticle. "Mary" is attested as the speaker in all Greek mss. (*Mariam,* but *Maria* in mss. C*, D), almost all the ancient versions, and patristic quotations.

But three copies of the OL version (mss. a, b, 1*) read *Elisabet, Elisabel,* and *Elisabeth* (respectively), and Elizabeth is taken as the speaker by Irenaeus, *Adv. haer.* 4.7,1 (Armenian and Latin translations; but cf. 3.10,1-2); Jerome's translation of Origen *Hom. in Luc. 7;* and Nicetas of Remesiana (in modern Yugoslavia) *De psalmodiae bono* 9.11. This variant comes mainly from the Latin tradition.

Ever since A. Loisy's discussion of the problem (1897) and A. von Harnack's study of the Magnificat (1900) it has been maintained by a number of commentators (e.g. J. M. Creed, B. S. Easton, M. Goguel, E. Klostermann, J. R. Harris) that the Magnificat was actually composed by Luke for Elizabeth, as the Benedictus was for Zechariah. The canticle on Elizabeth's lips would suit the "filling" of her with the holy Spirit (1:41), would remove the awkward reintroduction of Mary's name in v. 56, and would associate Elizabeth's condition with the barrenness and disgrace mentioned in vv. 48-49. Indeed, von Harnack suggested that the text originally read simply *kai eipen,* "and she said," thus making the introduction of Mary's name in v. 56 proper. It is far more likely, however, that the reading *Elisabet* is not the *lectio difficilior,* but the result of a change introduced by some copyists who sought to relate the canticle to 1:41 and the "her" (*autē*) of v. 56, which presently has a very remote antecedent, to Elizabeth. See further R. Laurentin, *Bib* 38 (1957) 15-23; Brown, *Birth,* 334-336.

My soul declares the greatness of the Lord. Lit. "extols the Lord." This first phrase may be echoing an OT phrase, such as Ps 69:31, "I extol him" (*megalynō auton*); cf. Ps 34:3; Sir 43:31. It expresses praise and thanksgiving for Yahweh's greatness and majesty which are recognized as the source of the blessings that have come to Mary. It also stands in contrast to her lowly condition to be mentioned in v. 48.

"My soul" is a Hebrew surrogate for "I" (see Gen 27:4,25; Ps 34:3); in literary parallelism with "my spirit" (v. 47) it can be found in the LXX (Ps 77:3-4; cf. Job 12:10; Wisd 15:11). It would be a way of expressing what we call in English the "self." In 1 Sam 2:1 Hannah uses another parallelism with similar meaning, "my heart" and "my horn."

The contention that the Greek verb *megalynei* represents a Hebrew ptc. *mĕrîmāh,* "raises on high, exalts," playing on Mary's name in Hebrew *miryām* (so R. Laurentin, "Traces d'allusions étymologiques en Lc 1-2 (II)," *Bib* 38 [1957] 1-23) is farfetched. There is no evidence that this canticle ever existed in a Semitic language.

47. *my spirit finds delight.* Lit. "has delighted." The verb is aor. but, being in parallelism with the pres. *megalynei,* it must be understood as a timeless aor., such as is found in lyric passages of the LXX (see BDF § 333.2). It is also taken at times as an ingressive aor., "has begun to delight" (see BDF § 331). A more subtle explanation of the aor. has been offered (see ZBG § 260), that it reflects a Hebrew pf. with *waw*-conversive, which would tolerate, then, a pres. meaning. That explanation presupposes that the canticle existed at some point in Hebrew, which is hardly likely.

"My spirit" is again a Hebrew surrogate for "I" (see Gen 6:3; Ps 143:4). If one were to substitute "my soul" for it, one would find a very close parallel to the first part of this verse in Ps 35:9, where the LXX has *hē de psychē mou agalliasetai epi* (or *en*) *tō kyriō,* "my soul shall delight in the Lord."

God my Savior. This phrase is parallel to "Lord" in v. 46, showing that *kyrios* there is to be understood of Yahweh, the source of blessing to Mary.

The two following verses, both introduced by *hoti*, explain the reasons for Mary's extolling of the Lord. This phrase is derived from the LXX of Ps 25:5; one can also compare with it Isa 12:2 and Mic 7:7. It is the first occurrence of the title "Savior" in the Lucan writings and introduces the theme of salvation (see p. 222 above). The title is here applied to Yahweh, but in 2:11 it will be given to Jesus. Mary's "delight" in God echoes vv. 14 and 44; it conveys the atmosphere of conscious and spontaneous rejoicing, characteristic of those who are aware of the new period about to begin, to be inaugurated by God's saving act in Jesus Christ. It is the delight of the eschaton (see further R. Bultmann, *TDNT* 1. 19-21).

48. *he has had regard for the lowliness of his handmaid.* This is the first reason for Mary's praise. This part of the verse is a direct allusion to the vow of Hannah (1 Sam 1:11), "If you have regard for the affliction (Hebrew *'ŏnî*, Greek *tapeinōsis*, as in Gen 16:11; 29:32) of your handmaid. . . ." Luke too uses *tapeinōsis* of Mary. Basically, it means "humiliation," and in the OT passages cited it is applied to a woman's barrenness. This use, indeed, is one of the reasons why some commentators have thought that the canticle was originally ascribed to Elizabeth (see NOTE on v. 46), since she—like Hannah—would have been a better candidate for the condition described in this verse. However, on this verse as a whole, see the COMMENT. Mary has already referred to herself as "handmaid" in v. 38, in her reply to the angel; so the noun should be understood here of her "humble station" (so BAG, 812). It expresses her unworthiness to be the mother of the Davidic Messiah and the Son of God. Because of it she can declare that Yahweh is great. Cf. Jdt 6:19.

From now on. The temporal phrase, *apo tou nyn*, lit. "from the now," refers to the coming inauguration of a new age of salvation, as often in Luke (see 5:10; 12:52; 22:18,69; Acts 18:6).

all generations will count me blessed. I.e. will pronounce a beatitude over me. The verb *makariousin* (fut. tense) reflects the adj. *makaria* of Elizabeth's pronouncement in v. 45. The connection of these two words can be illustrated from Gen 30:13, *makaria egō, hoti makarizousin me pasai hai gynaikes,* "Blessed am I that all women count me blessed." If the *tapeinōsis* of the first part of the verse might have seemed to suit Elizabeth better than Mary, the beatitude here mentioned certainly suits Mary better than Elizabeth, despite the parallel with the once-barren Leah in Genesis 30. Luke has also changed "all women" to "all generations" and implies a respect for her who is the mother of the Lord and the first representative of faith in his account vis-à-vis all those who will accept her Son in faith. The verse expresses a fundamental attitude of all Christians toward the believing Mother of the Lord.

49. *for he who is mighty.* This is the second reason for Mary's praise. Literally, it runs, "for the Mighty One" (*ho dynatos*), a title used of Yahweh in the LXX of Zeph 3:17; Ps 89:9. The name of God is no longer used; instead there is a title recalling his exalted power, by which he has done great things for Mary—given her both a child who will be the Savior, Lord, and Messiah and a chance to express her faith in him.

has done great things for me. This phrase reflects Deut 10:21, "He is your God who has done these great and awesome things for you." What Yahweh has done for Mary, by making her the mother of the Lord, is related to the OT tradition about his great saving acts toward Israel of old (see Deut 11:7; Judg 2:7).

whose name is holy. Or "whose name is the Holy One." Ps 111:9 is reflected here. The holiness of God is explained in Isa 57:15 in terms of his exaltation; he "inhabits eternity" and is "exalted" (*mārôm*), though he dwells with the lowly. As such, he is the source of the bounty manifested to Mary.

50. *His mercy is for those who fear him.* The phraseology of this verse is derived from Ps 103:17, "The Lord's mercy is from generation to generation on those who fear him." It does not mean that Yahweh's merciful bounty is manifested solely to those who stand in servile fear before him; rather it is shown to those who recognize and reverence his sovereignty. The canticle has moved from the personal level to the praise of Yahweh for what he does for Israel as a whole.

51. *has displayed the might of his arm.* Lit. "he has produced the might of his arm." This strange expression seems to be an allusion to Ps 89:11, "with your mighty arm you scattered your enemies." The anthropomorphism of God's arm is meant to symbolize his strength or power (see Exod 6:6; Deut 4:34; Isa 40:10; 51:5,9; 53:1), by which he reverses the condition in which human beings find themselves or which they have fashioned for themselves.

the arrogant. Or "the proud," i.e. the enemies of God. See Isa 2:12; 13:11.

in the conceit of their hearts. The prep. phrase explains in what the arrogance consisted. *Dianoia,* which I have translated as "conceit," denotes at times "plotting" or "scheming" (see LXX Bar 1:22). For *kardia,* "heart," used in the sense of "mind," see LXX 1 Kgs 10:2; Job 12:3; 17:4; Luke 12:45.

52. *has put down mighty rulers from their thrones.* The canticle plays on the title given to God in v. 49 (*ho dynatos*); he is the one who brings low *dynastas,* i.e. "princes, potentates." There is possibly an allusion here to Job 12:19, "overthrows the mighty." See also 1 Sam 2:7.

exalted the lowly. Possibly an allusion to Job 5:11.

53. *has filled the hungry with good things.* The phraseology is derived from Ps 107:9, "the hungry person he has filled with good things." See also 1 Sam 2:5.

and sent the rich away empty. The divine reversal of the human condition continues with a phrase similar to Job 22:9; 15:29. Cf. 1 Sam 2:7.

54. *has come to the aid of his servant Israel.* These words reflect those of Isa 41:8-9 (LXX), "You, Israel, my servant, Jacob, whom I have chosen . . . , You are my servant, I have chosen you and not cast you off." In the Lucan context they are to be understood of Yahweh's intervention in Jesus' conception on behalf of his people Israel. The Davidic heir to be born is yet another instance of Yahweh coming to the aid of his people.

servant Israel. Luke uses here a form of *pais,* "boy, servant," as in the Servant passage of Isa 42:1; 52:13. Cf. Isa 44:1; 45:4.

mindful of his mercy. Lit. "to recall (his) mercy," the phrase actually being an infin. of purpose. It is an allusion to Ps 98:3, "He has recalled his mercy and fidelity to the house of Israel."

55. *as he promised our fathers.* This is most likely an allusion to Mic

7:20, "You will show fidelity to Jacob, mercy to Abraham, as you swore to our fathers from days of old." The canticle thus ends with a recollection of promises made by Yahweh to the patriarchs (Gen 17:7; 18:18; 22:17) and to David (2 Sam 7:11-16). Here the canticle uses a form of *lalein*, "speak" (as Hebrew *dbr* also means "promise" at times) with *pros* + acc. (see p. 116 above), but the following phrase that seems to be parallel to it is introduced by the simple dative.

Abraham and his descendants. Lit. "and his seed." The phrase echoes Gen 17:9, with the name of Abraham substituted for "you." Some commentators would take the dative as one of interest (see *ZBG* § 55).

Finally, at the end of our comments on the Magnificat it is good to recall again the similarity of this canticle with that of Hannah in 1 Sam 2:1-10 in general. Both Mary and Hannah are women who praise God for the action that he has taken in choosing them to be mothers of instruments of his salvific intervention in Israel's history. The general pattern and purpose of the canticles are the same, and many of the details in the Magnificat echo those of the canticle of Hannah (see the references to parallels given in the translation).

56. *Mary.* Though this name is given as the subj. of the verb *eipen* before the canticle (see NOTE on 1:46), it is repeated here. Its repetition is seen as problematic, since it might seem to imply that a different person uttered the canticle. This is prima facie a difficulty, but it would not be out of place after a long quotation such as the canticle is. Moreover, one should compare Num 24:25; Deut 32:44,45,48; 34:1; 2 Sam 2:1; Tob 14:1.

stayed with her about three months. Luke has deliberately used *hōs*, "about." Coming after the mention of the "sixth month" (1:36), this might seem to mean that Mary stayed until Elizabeth had given birth to John. The following verse (1:57) corrects this impression. It might seem strange that Mary would not be expected to stay with her relative precisely at the time when she would need her most, i.e. at the delivery of the child John. But Luke has his own literary purposes. Nonetheless, there is no reason to think that Luke is reckoning with a pregnancy of ten lunar months (*pace* Brown, *Birth*, 338). That would mean a pregnancy of 295 days, since the lunar month was reckoned at 29.5 days (see J. Finegan, *Handbook of Biblical Chronology*, § 29). All of Luke's time references are vague; cf. "for five months" (1:24); "the six month" (1:36); "about three months" (1:56). They should not be pressed.

returned home. Lit. "returned to her house." It is impossible to say whether this means her family's house or that of her husband Joseph. The scene ends again with refrain A (see 1:23,38). Cf. 1 Sam 1:19.

BIBLIOGRAPHY (1:39-56)

Arce, P. A. "El topónimo natal del Precursor," *Miscelanea bíblica Andres Fernandez* (=*EstEcl* 34 [1960]) 825-836.

Craviotti, J. C. "La visitación de la Sma. Virgen," *RevistB* 17 (1955) 84-88, 123-125; 18 (1956) 25-29.

Dahl, N. A. "The Story of Abraham in Luke-Acts," in *Studies in Luke-Acts*, 139-158.

Dattler, F. "A casa de Zacarías (Lc 1,40)," *RCB* 5/10-11 (1968) 112-114.
———— "La casa de Zacarías (Lc 1,40)," *RevistB* 31 (1969) 202-203.
Galbiati, E. "La visitazione (Luca 1,41-50)," *BeO* 4 (1962) 139-144.
Hospodar, B. *"Meta spoudēs* in Lk 1,39," *CBQ* 18 (1956) 14-18.
Kopp, C. *The Holy Places of the Gospels* (New York: Herder and Herder, 1963) 87-96.
Mussner, F. "Lukas 1,48 f.; 11, 27 f. und die Anfänge der Marienverehrung in der Urkirche," in *De primordiis cultus mariani: Acta congressus mariologici-mariani in Lusitania anno 1967 celebrati* (2 vols.; Rome: Academia mariana, 1970) 2. 25-34.
Nevius, R. C. *"Kyrios* and *Iēsous* in St. Luke," *ATR* 48 (1966) 75-77.
Rábanos, R. "¿De dónde a mí esto, que la madre di mi señor venga a mí? (Luc. 1, 43)," *Estudios marianos* 8 (1949) 9-27.
Schoonheim, P. L. "Der alttestamentliche Boden der Vokabel *hyperēphanos* in Lukas i 51," *NovT* 8 (1966) 235-246.
Springer, J. F. "M'dinah and *polis,*" *ATR* 5 (1922) 324-332.
———— "No Mistranslation in Luke 1:39," *ATR* 10 (1927-1928) 37-46.
———— "St. Luke 1:64 and 39," *ATR* 4 (1921-1922) 332-337.
Stanley, D. M. "The Mother of My Lord," *Worship* 34 (1959-1960) 330-332.
Torrey, C. C. "Medina and *Polis,* and Luke i.39," *HTR* 17 (1924) 83-91.
———— "The Translations Made from the Original Aramaic Gospels," in *Studies in the History of Religions Presented to Crawford Howell Toy* (eds. D. G. Lyon and G. F. Moore; New York: Macmillan, 1912) 269-317.

Bibliography on the Lucan Canticles

Aytoun, R. A. "The Ten Lucan Hymns of the Nativity in Their Original Language," *JTS* 18 (1916-1917) 274-288.
Flood, E. "The Bible and the People: The Magnificat and the Benedictus," *Clergy Review* 51 (1966) 205-210.
Gryglewicz, F. "Die Herkunft der Hymnen des Kindheitsevangeliums des Lucas," *NTS* 21 (1974-1975) 265-273.
Gunkel, H. "Die Lieder in der Kindheitsgeschichte Jesu bei Lukas," in *Festgabe von Fachgenossen und Freunden A. von Harnack zum siebzigsten Geburtstag dargebracht* (Tübingen: Mohr, 1921) 43-60.
Haupt, P. "Magnificat and Benedictus," *AJP* 40 (1919) 64-75.
Jones, D. "The Background and Character of the Lukan Psalms," *JTS* 19 (1968) 19-50.
Marty, J. "Études des textes cultuels de prière contenus dans le Nouveau Testament," *RHPR* 9 (1929) 234-268, 368-376, esp. pp. 371-375.
Spitta, F. "Die chronologischen Notizen und die Hymnen in Lc 1 u. 2," *ZNW* 7 (1906) 281-317, esp. pp. 313-317.
Winter, P. "Magnificat and Benedictus—Maccabean Psalms?" *BJRL* 37 (1954) 328-347.

Bibliography on the Magnificat

Balagué M. "La geografía del Magnificat," *CB* 12 (1955) 31-34.

―――― "El Magnificat," *CB* 14 (1957) 158-164.

Barns, T. "The *Magnificat* in Niceta of Remesiana and Cyril of Jerusalem," *JTS* 7 (1905-1906) 449-453.

Benko, S. "The Magnificat: A History of the Controversy," *JBL* 86 (1967) 263-275.

Bover, J. M. "El 'Magnificat': Su estructura y su significación mariológica," *EstEcl* 19 (1945) 31-43.

Castellino, G. "Osservazioni sulla struttura letteraria del 'Magnificat,'" in *Studi dedicati alla memoria di Paolo Ubaldi* (Pubblicazione della università cattolica del Sacro Cuore, ser. 5, sc. storiche, 16; Milano: "Vita e pensiero," 1937) 413-429.

Cepeda, J. G. "La Virgen, poetisa sagrada (Lc 1,39-56)," *CB* 11 (1954) 391-394.

Davies, J. G. "The Ascription of the Magnificat to Mary," *JTS* 15 (1964) 307-308.

Durand, A. "L'Origine du Magnificat," *RB* 7 (1898) 74-77.

Forestell, J. T. "Old Testament Background of the Magnificat," *Marian Studies* 12 (1961) 205-244.

Guillet, J. "Le Magnificat," *Maison Dieu* 38 (1954) 56-69.

Harnack, A. von. "Das Magnificat der Elisabet (Luc. 1, 46-55) nebst einigen Bemerkungen zu Luc. 1 und 2," *SPAW* 27 (1900) 538-556.

Jacobé, F. (=A. Loisy). "L'Origine du *Magnificat*," *Revue d'histoire et de littérature religieuses* 2 (1897) 424-432.

Joüon, P. "Notes de philologie évangélique: Luc, 1, 54-55: Une difficulté grammaticale du *Magnificat*," *RSR* 15 (1925) 438-441, esp. pp. 440-441.

Koontz, J. V. G. "Mary's Magnificat," *BSac* 116 (1959) 336-349.

Köstlin, H. A. "Das Magnificat Lc 1,46-55, Lobgesang der Maria oder der Elisabeth?" *ZNW* 3 (1902) 142-145.

Ladeuze, P. "De l'origine du Magnificat et son attribution dans le troisième évangile à Marie ou à Elisabeth," *RHE* 4 (1903) 623-644.

Ramaroson, L. "Ad structuram cantici 'Magnificat,'" *VD* 46 (1968) 30-46.

Roschini, G. "Il 'Magnificat' cantico della Vergine," *Marianum* 31 (1969) 260-323.

Sabbe, M. "Het Magnificat," *Collationes brugenses* 50 (1954) 313-321.

Schnackenburg, R. "Das Magnificat, seine Spiritualität und Theologie," *Geist und Leben* 38 (1965) 342-357.

Spitta, F. "Das Magnificat, ein Psalm der Maria und nicht der Elisabeth," in *Theologische Abhandlungen: Eine Festgabe zum 17. Mai 1902 für Heinrich Julius Holtzmann dargebracht* (eds. W. Nowack et al.; Tübingen: Mohr, 1902) 63-94.

Tannehill, R. C. "The Magnificat as Poem," *JBL* 93 (1974) 263-275.

Ter-Minassiantz, E. "Hat Irenäus Lc 1,46 *Mariam* oder *Elisabet* gelesen?" *ZNW* 7 (1906) 191-192.

Zorell, F. "Das Magnificat ein Kunstwerk hebräischer oder aramäischer Poesie?" *ZKT* 29 (1905) 754-758.

B. THE BIRTH AND THE INFANCY OF
JOHN AND JESUS

5. THE BIRTH OF JOHN
(1:57-58)

1 ⁵⁷ The time came for Elizabeth to deliver and she bore a son.
⁵⁸ When her neighbors and relatives heard that the Lord had shown her
his great mercy, they shared her joy.

COMMENT

In this episode Luke resumes the use of the Baptist-source; it will run
from 1:57 to 1:66b, telling the story of the birth, circumcision (and naming) of John, and his manifestation to Israel.

This short episode recounts the birth of John the Baptist and the joy
that attended it. As in the first series of parallel stories in the infancy narrative, announcements of the birth of John and Jesus, so now John is the
subject of the story that opens the second series. This birth story is considerably shorter than that of Jesus (2:1-20). In this second series the
parallelism is not as explicit as in the first. Indeed, one might question
why we separate the birth of John (1:57-58) from the following episode
of the circumcision and manifestation (1:59-80). This is done so that the
parallelism that is here may not be completely overlooked.

The birth of John the Baptist is recounted by Luke with two nuances.
The event manifests the favor or mercy that Yahweh shows to his people
in removing from Elizabeth the stigma of barrenness, a special burden for
her as the wife of a Jerusalem priest. It also emphasizes the manifestation
of God's mercy in playing on the name of John, *Yěhôḥānān,* "Yahweh
has shown favor." The grace that he thus manifests to his people Israel
favors not only Elizabeth but will be given to the people as a whole. With
the birth of John the promise made to Zechariah is fulfilled. This child,
born to barren parents, becomes the source of joy to neighbors and relatives, as the angel had predicted.

Whereas the announcement of John's birth had exploited certain details of the story of Abraham and Sarah, so now the birth story exploits details from the birth of Esau and Jacob to Rebecca (Gen 25:24). But the OT atmosphere is unmistakable in the recounting of the birth and attendant joy.

NOTES

1 57. *The time came for Elizabeth.* Lit. "for Elizabeth, the time of her giving birth was filled up (*or* fulfilled)." The text here makes use of an OT expression, found in Gen 25:24; it is not an exact quotation in that "days" is there used to describe Rebecca's giving birth to Jacob and Esau. Cf. Luke 2:6 apropos of Mary. The verb used here is *eplēsthē,* which could simply denote the completion of the time of pregnancy; but in the Lucan narrative, which makes so much of fulfillment, the overtone is unmistakable. The OT echo brings this out, though there is a parallel to the phrase in classical Greek literature (see Herodotus 6.63).

bore a son. The verb used here is *gennan,* the same as in the promise made to Zechariah by the angel (1:13).

58. *heard.* Elizabeth had remained in seclusion (see 1:24) even after her condition had been made known to her relative, Mary (1:36), so that her neighbors and other kin were kept in ignorance of her pregnancy until the child was born. Lucan dramatic heightening abandons all verisimilitude.

had shown her his great mercy. Lit. "had made great his mercy." The verb *megalynein* is used here; it is that used by Mary in 1:46 ("declares the greatness of the Lord"). The different nuance is undoubtedly to be ascribed to the difference of sources involved. Here the words refer directly to the divine favor shown to Elizabeth in the birth of a child that removed the stigma of her barrenness. There is more, however, involved in the words that play on the meaning of the name of the child, John (see fourth NOTE on 1:13).

they shared her joy. Or possibly, "they congratulated her." As I prefer it, the verb *synechairon* (governing the dat. *autē*) would have its full etymological force, "and they rejoiced with her." The phrase expresses the joy that was predicted in the time of the promise made to Zechariah (1:14), that "many will rejoice at his birth."

BIBLIOGRAPHY (1:57-58)

(See the items listed under the next section.)

6. THE CIRCUMCISION AND MANIFESTATION OF JOHN
(1:59-80)

1 59 On the eighth day they came to circumcise the child and would have named him Zechariah after his father. 60 But his mother spoke up: "No," she said, "he is rather to be called John." 61 But they said to her, "There is no one in your family who has this name." 62 Then they made signs to his father to see what he wanted the child called. 63 He asked for a writing tablet and to the surprise of all he wrote, "His name is to be John." 64 Instantly, he opened his mouth, and his tongue was loosed; he began to speak in praise of God. 65 Fear came over all their neighbors, and all these things became the talk of the entire hill country of Judea. 66 All who heard of them pondered them and asked, "Now what is this child to become?" For the hand of the Lord, indeed, was with him.

67 Then his father Zechariah was filled with the holy Spirit and spoke in prophecy:

68 *Blest be the Lord, the God of Israel:*	Pss 41:14; 72:18; 106:48
For he has taken note of *his people* and brought them *redemption,*	Ps 111:9
69 and has raised up for us a *horn of salvation* in	Ps 18:3; 1 Sam 2:10
the house of his servant David, 70 as he promised through the mouth of his holy prophets of old:	
71 to save us *from* our *enemies*	Ps 18:18=2 Sam 22:18;
and *from the hands of all who hate us,*	Ps 106:10
72 to *show mercy to* our fathers,	Gen 24:12
mindful of his holy *covenant*	Pss 105:8; 106:45
73 and of *the oath he swore to* our *father Abraham;*	Gen 26:3

⁷⁴ to grant us to be rescued from the hands of
our enemies

⁷⁵ that we might *worship* in his presence with-
out fear, *in* holiness and *uprightness as long as
we live.*

Josh 24:14

Isa 38:20

⁷⁶ Now you, my child, will be hailed as the
prophet of the Most High,

for you will *go before the Lord to prepare his
way,*

Mal 3:1;

Isa 40:3

⁷⁷ to offer his people a knowledge of salvation
through the forgiveness of their sins.

⁷⁸ In the merciful compassion of our God, the
Dawn from on High will take note of us

⁷⁹ and shine on *those who sit in darkness, in the
shadow of death,*

to guide our feet into *the path of peace.*"

Ps 107:10

Isa 59:8

⁸⁰ As the child grew up, he became strong in spirit. He lived out in
the desert until the day he was manifested to Israel.

COMMENT

The episode which follows on the notice of the birth of John tells of his
circumcision, naming, and manifestation to relatives and neighbors, and
eventually hints at his manifestation to all of Israel. The question that the
relatives and neighbors pose at the end of the episode (before Zechariah's
canticle) is important in the infancy narrative as a whole, "Now what is
this child to become?" (1:66). It is asked explicitly of John, and the
reader implicitly asks the same question—though it is never posed by the
evangelist—of Jesus. This is the effect of the step-parallelism in this series
of the parallel episodes.

The relatives and neighbors learn of the divine intervention in the birth
of John to barren Elizabeth from the attendant sign given to Zechariah,
his condition of being deaf and dumb up until the birth and naming of
the child (see 1:20). The crucial question is asked by the relatives and
neighbors not only because they realize that God has removed Elizabeth's
barrenness in her old age, but because they see that Zechariah's deafness
and dumbness have been cured. Thus God has intervened twice.

Zechariah's canticle follows on the manifestation of John to the relatives and neighbors, and it serves two functions: (a) it expresses his

"praise of God" (1:64); and (b) it acts as an answer to the question posed (1:66b).

The episode falls, then, into two parts: (1) the account of the circumcision, naming, and manifestation of John to the relatives and neighbors (1:59-66b); and (2) Zechariah's canticle—the Benedictus (1:68-79). The intervening verses (66c,67) and the concluding verse (80) are clearly Lucan composition. The Baptist-source has been used in vv. 59-66b, and the Jewish Christian source in the canticle (with Lucan inserts in vv. 70,76-77).

The episode proper stresses three things about John: his circumcision, his naming, and his manifestation. The circumcision marks him with "the sign of the covenant" (Gen 17:11) and incorporates him into Israel (Josh 5:2-9). As he would share in the blessings promised to Yahweh's chosen people (Josh 5:6-7), he could celebrate the passover with them (Exod 12:44-49) and could look forward to an association with his fathers in the world to come (Str-B, 4/1. 37). Circumcision also meant the eventual obligation of observing the Mosaic Law (Rom 2:25-28; Gal 5:3). The incorporation of the forerunner of Jesus the Messiah into Israel is important in the Lucan story because of the eventual incorporation of Jesus himself, for Luke will be at pains at the end of his two-volume work to show that Christianity is a logical outgrowth of Judaism. Those who inaugurate it and found it must be shown to be part of Judaism. And so John from the very beginning is so marked and incorporated. The naming of the child of Zechariah and Elizabeth as "John," against all their family traditions, is a further sign of God's favor and mercy that is being manifested, not only to them in their old age, blameless lives (1:6), but also to Israel at large. That general dispensation of mercy is the point to which the manifestation of the child eventually leads. For *news* of the birth of the child caused joy (1:58), but the child is first manifested to his parents' neighbors and relatives; and eventually the talk is spread to the entire hill country of Judea (1:65). This rumor thus prepares for John's retirement in the desert until the time comes for his manifestation to Israel as a whole. It is recognized that the hand of the Lord was with him in birth and determination of his destiny.

Zechariah's canticle, the Benedictus, is an expression of his praise of God (*eulogōn ton theon*, 1:64), introduced as a Spirit-filled prophetic utterance (1:67). Verses 76-77 give an answer to the question posed by the neighbors and relatives in v. 66b. Like the Magnificat, the canticle is separable from its present context, and v. 80 could follow smoothly on v. 66b (or 66c). Like the Magnificat and the speeches in Acts, it expresses the ideal sentiments of Zechariah, now that the day has come when "all these things" were "to take place" (1:20). As in the case of the Magnificat, the Benedictus is a *cento*-like composition, built up like a mosaic from numerous phrases drawn from the Greek OT. For a comparison of the Greek text of the canticle with its OT parallels, see A. Plummer, *Gospel*, 39; J. M. Creed, *The Gospel*, 305-306. My translation of the Benedictus has italicized phrases that show clear dependence on such OT parallels; the NOTES will call attention to less clear allusions.

As in the case of the Magnificat, the Benedictus cannot be thought of as derived from an old family tradition by Luke. Such traditions would scarcely have been preserved in Greek.

Years ago A. von Harnack tried to defend the literary unity of the Benedictus and its Lucan composition; more recently a form of that thesis has been espoused by J. Ernst (*Evangelium nach Lukas*, 93-94). However, P. Benoit (*NTS* 3 [1956-1957] 182-183) has discredited the arguments proposed for such an assessment. And yet a number of students have tried to insist on its unity (J. G. Machen, F. Hauck, H. Sahlin, A. Plummer, etc.).

Several specific problems in the canticle have to be recognized, all related to its loose Greek composition. Verses 68-75 make up only one long sentence, with a subordinate clause (v. 70) and several epexegetical or purpose infinitives, loosely strung together (vv. 71-75). Verse 76, which starts anew with an address to the child John, begins a series of four further infinitives, two of which have the definite article (the second and fourth), and two do not (the first and the third). Are the four infinitives in vv. 76-79 so closely joined that they can refer only to John— making him, for instance, the "Dawn from on High" (v. 78)? Most readers at first sight would think that Jesus was meant thereby. Since it seems unlikely that John is being so designated, what is the relation between vv. 76-77 and vv. 78-79? The former have to be understood of John; the future tense in v. 76 refers clearly to him; the allusions to Mal 3:1 and Isa 40:3 in the rest of the verse echo traditional gospel phraseology used of him elsewhere (cf. Mark 1:2-3); v. 77 contains Lucan terminology ("salvation"), and the Lucan description of the purpose of John's baptism (cf. 3:3) is reflected here. This is clear. But what of vv. 78-79? The future in v. 78b ("will take note of" or "will visit") would seem to continue that of v. 76; but there is a textual problem (see NOTE). Moreover, the use of the first plural pronouns ("us, our") seems to relate these concluding verses of the canticle to the first part (vv. 69,71-75).

Faced with these and some other minor problems, commentators have proposed various divisions of the canticle. (1) Some commentators (e.g. H. Gunkel, R. Bultmann, E. Klostermann, M. Goguel, P. Vielhauer, P. Winter—with varying nuances) would regard vv. 68-75 as an adopted Jewish hymn (of varying character—Maccabean, martial, messianic, eschatological, etc.). (2) Some others (J. Weiss, A. Loisy, J. Marty) would derive the same verses from a Jewish Christian source. (These two points will be dealt with below.) (3) Verses 76-79 have been regularly ascribed either to a Johannite (or Baptist) source (so M. Goguel, P. Winter, P. Vielhauer) or to a Christian source (H. Gunkel). (4) H. Schürmann (*Lukasevangelium,* 84-94) regards vv. 76-79 as the Lucan canticle, which originally answered the question of v. 66b, and which was attached to v. 67; vv. 68-75 were secondarily inserted. (5) M. Dibelius, P. Benoit, and R. E. Brown look upon vv. 76-77 as the main insertion (a Lucan composition) into an otherwise adopted hymn, taken over from a Jewish-Christian source. In the long run, the last opinion has the best chance of being the right one. Although Brown suggests the possibility only to dismiss it, I would look on v. 70 as Lucan in its composition.

Nothing in vv. 68-75 links them specifically to the episode of the circumcision, naming, and manifestation of John. The same has to be said of vv. 78-79. The break at v. 75 is clear; and the phrase, "as long as we live" (lit. "all the days of our lives"), with which it ends, is similar to expressions of eternity or "forever" often found at the end of hymns (e.g. Isa 38:20; Pss 23:6; 30:13). This has been used as an argument to define the first part of the canticle as a hymn of praise, to which a birthday hymn or a hymn of good fortune for the newborn child has been added. Yet, as R. E. Brown (*Birth,* 381) rightly points out, such expressions are also found in the midst of hymns (e.g. Pss 90:14; 128:5; cf. Ps 27:4).

There is no real evidence that this canticle ever existed in either Hebrew or Aramaic. One can retrovert most of it easily, but its dependence on the phraseology of the LXX has to be reckoned with. Speculation is the only way to characterize the attempt to ascribe this canticle to the Baptist (or Johannite) source. The traces of Temple piety in v. 75 suggest a plausible background in the Jewish Christian Anawim of the early community. This seems the best solution, even though the traces of Anawim piety in this canticle are less manifest than those in the Magnificat.

Given this situation I prefer to regard the structure of the Benedictus as follows: v. 68a, the introductory utterance of praise; vv. 68b-77b, the body of the hymn of praise, divided into three parts (68b-71b [with v. 70 as a Lucan insert], 72a-75b, 76a-77b); and the conclusion of the hymn in vv. 78-79.

In treating the Magnificat, we saw that some minor textual variants attribute the canticle to Elizabeth. That fact has sparked speculation about the Benedictus too. Though there is no variant for the speaker in v. 67, the Benedictus has at times been ascribed to Anna (of Luke 2:36), without a shred of evidence for such a suggestion.

Given the context in which the Benedictus now appears in the Lucan infancy narrative and its close relation to the episodes of the birth, circumcision, naming, and manifestation of John, which convey the idea of the incorporation of John into Israel, the canticle serves to enhance that connection of John with God's chosen people of old. This child, who is now born and named, has a special role in Israel's destiny, and it is this that the canticle seeks to explain.

However, the main thrust of the canticle is an affirmation of the messianic role of Jesus, and only in the Lucan insert of vv. 76-77 is the connection of John to Jesus explained. The major part of the canticle, which Luke inherited from his Jewish Christian source and fitted out with a note of promise and fulfillment by adding v. 70, sings of a christological theme. What the Jewish Christian community praised God for in generic terms is now in the Lucan context seen to have specific relevance to the messianic role of Jesus.

The canticle begins with an introductory utterance of Zechariah, which according to v. 67 was supposed to be prophetic, but which manifests itself as a formula of praise.

The first part of the body of the hymn (vv. 68b-71b) introduced by *hoti* (=Hebrew *kî*), sets forth the first reason for uttering such praise: Yahweh has taken note of or visited his people, bringing them redemption and salvation by raising up in their midst "a horn of salvation" in the house of David. The "horn of salvation" is to be understood of Jesus, who is the Christ. The salvation is from enemies and those that hate his people.

The second part of the hymn (vv. 72a-75b) then relates that redemption and salvation to the covenant of old and the oath sworn to Abraham —and the theme of promise and fulfillment is introduced. What God has so wrought was done to enable his people to worship him in holiness and uprightness all the days of their lives.

The third part, the insert about John (vv. 76-77), relates John's role to God's visiting his people and the recalling of his covenant made with them. John is now to be Yahweh's prophet, making known a new knowledge of salvation and preparing the people for the coming of the Lord (=Jesus), before whom he is now to walk (*proporeusē*). John is the precursor of Jesus.

In the concluding verses of the canticle (vv. 78-79) elements of the earlier parts of the canticle are recapitulated. The visitation of God's people will proceed from his merciful compassion, and "the horn of salvation" in David's house is now presented as the messianic "Dawn from on High," with the canticle ending on the notes of peace and of light shining on those who now sit in darkness.

After the Benedictus is ended, Luke concludes the scene with a statement about the growth of the child (refrain B on outline, p. 314 above), and a note that foreshadows the presence of John in the desert (3:2), where the word of the Lord will come to him, commissioning him for his ministry.

NOTES

1 59. *On the eighth day*. According to the injunction given to Abraham (Gen 17:12; cf. 21:4), taken up and formalized in the Mosaic Law (Lev 12:3), the newborn boy was to be circumcised on the eighth day. Even the sanctity of the Sabbath yielded to the regulation of circumcision on the eighth day according to John 7:22-23 and the rabbis of a later date: "They may perform on the Sabbath all things that are needful for circumcision" (*m. Šabbat* 18:3; 19:1-4). See Str-B, 4/1. 23-40 for details.

they came. Lit. "and it happened . . . (that) they came." Luke uses *kai egeneto* + finite verb, without the conj. *kai;* see p. 119 above. "They" refers presumably to the relatives and neighbors of v. 58, those who would witness the circumcision (cf. v. 65).

to circumcise. According to Gen 17:11, this would mean to mark the boy with "the sign of the covenant." The OT associates the origin of the Jewish practice of circumcision with Israel's patriarch Abraham, whose male descendants were so marked as members of the continuing covenant of Israel with Yahweh.

the child. Whereas in the foregoing visitation scene Luke had used *brephos* of the child in the womb (1:41,44), here the word for "child" is *paidion*, as in 1:66,76,80. *Brephos* is used in 2:12,16, of Jesus. *Paidion* may be derived from Luke's sources (Baptist and Jewish Christian) and then further used by him in v. 80 and 2:17,27,40.

would have named . . . after his father. Lit. "they were calling (or possibly, "were trying to call," if a conative impf. be understood here) him by the name of his father." The Greek expression is a Septuagintism (2 Esdr 7:63).

According to this passage (and 2:21) the child was named at his circumcision. Such a custom of naming children at circumcision is not otherwise attested among Palestinian Jews until several centuries later. Some commentators have consequently thought that the references to such a practice might be imported here from Greek practice, since in ancient Greece it was common to name the child on the seventh or tenth day after birth. Among Palestinian Jews it had been the practice to name the child at birth (see Gen 4:1; 21:3; 25:25-26). Moreover, it was usually the concern of the parents, either the father or the mother. Luke's words here must be understood, not so much as a proposal made by the neighbors and relatives, as a supposition; people were referring to the child already as "little Zechariah." Yet even such a supposition is strange, for though the naming of a child after his Jewish father is attested (Tob 1:1,9[?]; Josephus *Ant.* 14.1,3 § 10; 20.9,1 § 197; *J.W.* 5.13,2 § 534; Mur 29:10 [*Yĕhûdāh bar Yĕhûdāh*]; 42:12 [*Yĕhôsēp bar Yĕhôsēp*]), it was apparently not common. The more usual practice seems to have been papponymy, or the naming of a child after his grandfather (1 Macc 2:1-2; *Jub.* 11:15; Josephus *Life*, 1.1 § 5—cf. E. L. Sukenik, *JPOS* 8 [1928] 119). That would at least explain in part the subsequent comment of the neighbors and relatives (1:61).

The extent to which these customs have a bearing on Luke's story is another matter. In the long run the association of the name with the circumcision of John serves only as a background for the account of the loosing of Zechariah's tongue and for the sign that is thereby given about the character and role of the child so circumcised and named.

60. *his mother spoke up.* Lit. "having answered, his mother said." Luke uses the aor. pass. ptc. *apokritheisa.* Cf. 1:19,35. See p. 114 above.

For the sake of the story we must suppose that the name John was communicated to Elizabeth somehow, so that she reacts to the attempt of the neighbors and relatives. Then Zechariah confirms what she says on the authority of the angelic announcement to him (1:13). Even though he had become deaf and dumb after learning the name, would he not have communicated it to his wife in the interval before the child's birth? Yet, to ask that question is to fail to understand Luke's narrative, which was not meant to bear such scrutiny. Its simple account should be allowed to tell its own story.

John. For the meaning of the name, see NOTE on 1:13. The repetition of the name contributes to the emphasis on divine favor and graciousness which marks the period of salvation-history now coming to be with the birth of this child.

61. *they said to her.* Luke again uses the verb *eipan* with *pros* + acc. See p. 116 above.

no one in your family. However, John/ *Yĕhôḥānān* was a name in use among priestly-family members in the postexilic period as Neh 12:13,42; 1 Macc 2:1-2 make clear. The statement is introduced in Greek by *hoti* recitativum; see NOTE on 1:25.

62. *made signs.* Lit. "nodded." Zechariah is here understood to be both deaf and dumb; see NOTES on 1:20,22. The indirect question is here introduced by the neut. def. art., as in 9:46; 19:48; 22:4,23,24; Acts 4:21; 22:30 (see BDF § 267.2).

63. *to the surprise of all.* This is introduced because Zechariah is not supposed to have heard what Elizabeth called the child, but also because of the name.

he wrote. Lit. "he wrote, saying." The pres. ptc. *legōn* is the stereotyped LXX equivalent of Hebrew infin. *lē'mōr,* which introduces direct discourse (see 2 Kgs 10:6, for its use with a form of the verb *graphein*).

64. *Instantly.* This is the first occurrence of the adv. *parachrēma,* which, apart from two occurrences in Matt 21:19,20, is used exclusively by Luke in the NT. See further 4:39; 5:25; 8:44,47,55; 13:13; 18:43; 19:11; 22:60 (and six times in Acts). As here, it is often used by Luke in connection with miracles.

he opened his mouth, and his tongue was loosed. Lit. "his mouth was opened, and his tongue." No verb is expressed with the mention of "his tongue," and that of the first phrase is to be extended (by zeugma) to it. In English we have had to supply a verb. Ms. D, however, solves the problem by reading *kai parachrēma elythē hē glōssa autou kai ethaumasan pantes. aneōchthē de to stoma autou,* "and instantly his tongue was loosed and all were surprised; and his mouth was opened. . . ." That solves the problem, but it cannot be accepted as the original reading; it is a copyist's correction.

The loosing of Zechariah's tongue is a new wonder, a further sign of the character and role of the child now born and named. The first utterance that Zechariah makes is not his son's name, but a blessing of his God, who has so wondrously intervened in human history.

65. *Fear.* This is a typically Lucan reaction to the miraculous intervention of God (see NOTE on 7:16).

all these things became the talk of the entire hill country of Judea. This might seem as though Luke is giving a basis for the tradition that he is incorporating here; the widespread publicity serves rather to enhance the role of John. On the hill country, see NOTE on 1:39.

66. *pondered them.* Lit. "all who heard (them) laid (them) up in their hearts." Cf. Luke 2:19,51; 3:15; 5:22. It is a Septuagintism (see 1 Sam 21:13; Mal 2:2). It is a comment of the evangelist, just as the last clause in the verse is.

the hand of the Lord. An OT anthropomorphism (see 1 Chr 28:19; 4:10) expresses the powerful divine protection and direction which are guaranteed to John. Yet it will not spare him imprisonment and death at the hand of Herod Antipas (3:20; 9:8). In the NT this expression is exclusively Lucan (see Acts 11:21), but it may also have the nuance of divine punishment (see Acts 13:11; cf. 1 Sam 5:9; 12:15). There is little doubt that *kyrios* here refers to Yahweh.

67. *filled with the holy Spirit.* See NOTE on 1:15. As Elizabeth was filled (1:41), so is Zechariah. It refers here to the prophetic presence of God to Zechariah, manifest in the canticle that is to be uttered. This verse is undoubtedly Lucan in composition; it is transitional between the matter derived from the Baptist source and that which Luke now uses from the early Jewish Christian source. The designation of Zechariah as "his father" is obviously superfluous after 1:5-24a and 59.

spoke in prophecy. I.e. as a result of being filled with the holy Spirit. As Elizabeth was so filled (1:41–42), Zechariah is cast in the role of a mouthpiece of God. The emphasis on prophecy will reappear in the hymn to be uttered, as Zechariah declares his son John to be a prophet of the Most High (1:76); this reference was introduced by Luke with hindsight, for in the Gospel proper he will be said to be even greater than a prophet (7:27).

68. *Blest be the Lord, the God of Israel.* Zechariah's prophetic utterance takes the form of a canticle or hymn of praise, beginning with a well-known praise-formula from the psalter (see Pss 41:14; 72:18; 106:48). A slight variant of it is also found in 1 Chr 16:36, at the end of a conflate composition resembling what we have here. It is also found in 1 Kgs 1:48, where it is used by David at the enthronement of his son Solomon. As an opening formula, it resembles the beginning of the Hymn of Return in the Qumran War Scroll (which omits the tetragrammaton that would correspond to *Kyrios* here): "Blessed be the God of Israel, who preserves mercy for his covenant and periods of salvation for the people he redeems" (1QM 14:4; cf. 13:2). On the verbal adj. *eulogētos,* "blest," see NOTE on 6:20.

he has taken note of his people. Or "he has visited his people." The Greek verb *episkeptesthai* can mean "look at, examine," and also "go to see, visit." In the Greek OT it often denotes God's gracious visitation of his people, bringing them deliverance of various sorts (see Exod 4:31; Ruth 1:6; Pss 80:14; 106:4). This religious sense of the verb, apparently unattested in extrabiblical Greek, renders the Hebrew *pāqad*. Yahweh's visitation is associated with "salvation" in Ps 106:4, whereas here it is specifically related to his raising of "the horn of salvation." The same verb will be met again in 1:78; 7:16 to refer to the coming of some personal instrument of salvation. This use of *episkeptesthai* should be compared with the use of Hebrew *pqd* in the Qumran Damascus Document (CD 1:7-11, where God is said to have raised up a Teacher of Righteousness in a similar "visitation").

brought them redemption. Lit. "made (*or* brought about) redemption" for his people. Though the phrase probably echoes Ps 111:9, "He sent redemption (*lytrōsin*) to his people," the combination of the noun *lytrōsis* with the verb *poiein* is strange. But the sense of the combination is clear, for it describes Yahweh's activity on behalf of his people in terms of ransom or release (see Luke 2:38; 21:28; 24:21). Both of the verbs in this verse are aor., as are the rest in the first part of the canticle. The sense of the aor. is debated. Zechariah's words could refer to the past, but the christological thrust of the first part of the canticle makes one realize that Zechariah is praising God for what he has done in the conception and coming birth of Jesus.

69. *a horn of salvation.* This phrase alludes to Ps 18:3 (=2 Sam 22:3), where God is hailed by the psalmist as "the horn of my salvation." There may also be an allusion to 1 Sam 2:10, where Hannah sings of Yahweh raising on high "the horn of his Anointed One" (an allusion to some Davidic or Israelite monarch). See further Ps 132:17 ("I shall cause a horn to sprout for David"); Ezek 29:21. The figure is derived from an animal's horns, especially that of wild buffalo or oxen, which symbolize strength and power (see Deut 33:17). The lifting up of the horn in the OT refers to the animal's tossing of its horns in a display of might (see Ps 148:14). But in the Greek OT neither "horn" nor the "horn of salvation" occurs with the verb *egeirein*, "raise up," which may thus seem to be a mere synonym for other expressions used, such as *hypsoun, epairein*, "lift on high." But *egeirein* is used of God's providential summoning into existence favored or anointed instruments of salvation for his people (see Judg 2:16,18; 3:9,15; cf. Acts 13:22). In any case, "horn of salvation" must be understood here as a title for an agent of God's salvation in David's house, i.e. in a loose sense a messianic title.

"Salvation" occurs here for the first time in the Lucan Gospel; see the sketch of Lucan theology above (p. 222).

in the house of his servant David. The canticle alludes to the dynastic oracle of Nathan (2 Sam 7:12-13). Just how the birth, naming, and circumcision of John is related to this raising of a horn of salvation in David's house is not immediately explained. That will emerge with the insert of Luke in vv. 76-77. The reader of the Lucan Gospel, however, knowing of the announcement made to Mary (1:32-35), understands what is meant.

For David as "servant" (*pais*) of Yahweh, see Ps 18:1; Isa 37:35. The term occurs again in Acts 4:25. Cf. J. Jeremias, *TDNT* 5. 681.

70. *through the mouth of his holy prophets of old.* Lit. "through the mouth of the holy ones of old [*ap' aiōnos*], his prophets." Because v. 70 is the only

subordinate clause in this part of the canticle and because the word-order is close to that of Acts 3:21, this verse should be regarded as a Lucan insertion into the inherited hymn of praise. It would thus be stressing the Lucan theme of promise and fulfillment. It might seem to be an OT expression, but it is not found as such in the OT; the closest one comes to it is found in Qumran literature: *k'šr ṣwh byd mwšh wbyd kwl 'bdyw hnby'ym,* "as he commanded through (lit. 'by the hand of') Moses and through all his servants, the prophets" (1QS 1:3). Cf. 4QpHos^a 2:5 (DJD 5. 31). Another reason for regarding it as a Lucanism is that it is unlikely that a messianic expectation would have been so formulated in pre-Christian times. This is an especially acute problem for those who, like P. Winter, want to see the nucleus of the Benedictus as a pre-Christian Jewish hymn. The text reflects the Lucan understanding of the OT (see 24:27,44-46). Cf. Acts 1:16; 3:18. For "holy prophets," see *2 Apoc. Bar.* 85:1.

"Of old" must be understood, not as "from the beginning of time," but rather "from a long time back." As a phrase used in the Lucan insert, it could mean, of course, from the beginning of the Period of Israel, but that may be pressing its meaning too much.

71. *to save us from our enemies.* Lit. "salvation from our enemies," an abstract appositive to the "horn of salvation" (1:69). The phrase echoes Ps 18:18 (=2 Sam 22:18), "He delivered me from my strong enemies, and from those hating me." Cf. 2 Sam 22:18; Ps 106:10. On the lips of Zechariah, it scarcely refers to the Roman occupiers of Palestine, but rather to all the forms that hostility to the chosen people took over the ages. In the Lucan setting of the canticle the "enemies" would include all those who resist or refuse to accept the new form of God's salvation-history.

72. *to show mercy.* Lit. "to do mercy with." This is a frequent OT expression (see LXX of Gen 24:12; Judg 1:24; 8:35; Ruth 1:8). The use of "covenant" in the latter part of the verse reveals "mercy" here as Yahweh's covenantal attribute, *ḥesed,* which is often translated as *eleos* in the LXX. The infin. *poiēsai,* used with *eleos,* is to be understood as an appositive to the noun "salvation" (1:71) and through it to the "horn of salvation" (1:69).

our fathers. This phrase is probably an allusion to Mic 7:20, which is perhaps reflected in the next verse too, "You will show fidelity to Jacob, mercy to Abraham, as you have sworn to our fathers from days of old."

mindful of his holy covenant. The phrase is an echo of Ps 105:8 or 106:45. Cf. Exod 2:24; Lev 26:42. The salvation that is now coming from Yahweh, in raising his horn in David's house, is seen as an extension of his covenant promises to Israel's ancestors of long ago. Cf. 1 Macc 4:10; Acts 3:25.

73. *the oath.* My English translation makes the acc. *horkon* parallel (an appositive) to "covenant" (1:72). The latter word is in the gen. case, *diathēkēs.* However, it is a question of the antecedent being attracted to the case of the following rel. pron. (see BDF § 295; ZGB § 19).

he swore to our father Abraham. This phrase is an allusion to such OT formulas as those in Mic 7:20; Gen 26:3; Jer 11:5. The oath itself to which it refers is found in Gen 22:16-17. What was promised there is interpreted in a broad sense. It is not the gift of the promised land, but the gift of deliverance from enemies for the continual service and worship of Yahweh. The canticle deserts the OT precedent, and echoes the Temple piety of the Anawim, making it likely that this is the origin of adopted canticle.

74. *to grant us to be rescued.* This infinitival construction explains the content of the oath (1:73), as now understood by the author. Cf. Ps 97:10.

75. *we might worship in his presence without fear.* The Greek word-order of vv. 74-75 is complicated; the adv. *aphobōs,* "without fear," occupies an emphatic position, following immediately on the infin. phrase, *tou dounai hēmin,* "to grant us," in v. 74. The infin. *latreuein,* "to worship" expresses the consequence of the deliverance brought about by Yahweh for his people, expected to result in a way of life that is really a cultic service of him. Though it denotes acts of worship, it is used analogously of the entire way in which the chosen people was to conduct itself. Since "worship" was not restricted to priestly service, it is not true that the canticle is here alluding to the "priestly service of the whole people" or to Exod 19:6, *pace* W. Grundmann.

76. *Now you, my child.* The end of v. 75 was the end also of the long sentence that began in v. 68a. Whether one thinks that Luke has merely inserted two verses here about John or appended a birthday hymn of four verses, it is generally agreed that a new part of the canticle begins here. Zechariah sings of his newborn son and the prophetic mission that he will have.

will be hailed as the prophet of the Most High. The title "prophet of the Most High" is found in *T. Levi* 8:15, used of a new king to arise from Levi. Does this mean that the title has a messianic connotation? A. R. C. Leaney (*NTS* 8 [1961-1962] 161) seems to think so. This connotation would mean that John was here being regarded as a messianic figure. This is hardly likely, because the title, even though found outside of the NT and only in an alleged messianic sense, has to be understood in the Lucan infancy narrative over against the title used for Jesus in 1:32, "the Son of the Most High." John, however, is to be Yahweh's prophet, or mouthpiece. On "Most High," see NOTE on 1:32. Note the shift of the tense of the verb here; from the aorists that preceded, one now moves to the future.

you will go before the Lord to prepare his way. Though these phrases echo Mal 3:1 and Isa 40:3, they reflect much more the use made of them in the Lucan Gospel proper. These OT phrases were already associated with John in the pre-Lucan tradition (see Mark 1:2-3). Cf. Luke 3:4.

Who is the *kyrios* in this verse, Yahweh or Jesus? When we posed this question at 1:17, we identified "the Lord" as Yahweh, since there was not yet any reason in the infancy narrative up to that point to think that Jesus was meant by it. However, even though this verse echoes Mal 3:1 (and 3:23 indirectly), where *kyrios* in the LXX is used of Yahweh, the title has been given to Jesus in 1:43, "the mother of my Lord." If we are to understand *kyrios* here as a title for Jesus, then John's role as a precursor of Jesus is clear. If we are to think that Luke is simply preserving traditional language about John, then the precursor role is less obvious, though that role will be presented in v. 77. But it is far from certain that *kyrios* is "obviously" (selbstverständlich) Yahweh, *pace* G. Schneider, *Evangelium nach Lukas,* 62. The hindsight with which the infancy narrative has been composed by Luke makes it likely that *kyrios* here would be understood by him as Jesus. That identification makes the canticle itself hang together better as a unit: Jesus is not only the horn of salvation in the house of David (1:69), the Dawn from on High (1:78), but also the *Kyrios* before whom John prepares the way (1:76).

Here one need not inquire whether Zechariah was aware of Jesus' impending birth. The reader of Luke's Gospel knows of the coming birth, and that answers the question about the *kyrios* to be born.

77. *a knowledge of salvation.* John's task will be to make known to his compatriots the coming salvation in the Davidic lineage. John's role was described to Zechariah by Gabriel as one of preparing a people fit for the Lord (1:17). "Salvation" is, of course, a favorite word of Luke (see NOTE on 1:71 above). In the first part of the canticle it has more overtones of political deliverance from Israel's enemies; but now it is given a more spiritual meaning by the following prep. phrase. The phrase, "knowledge of salvation," is not found in the OT or in Qumran literature. In the Gospel proper John is not depicted transmitting anything so named; however, it is possible that it is a summary way of referring to the kinds of preaching in which he engages, in 3:7-18.

through the forgiveness of their sins. This is the first time that this Lucan phrase (used often of an effect of the Christ-event) turns up in this Gospel. It is based on such OT passages as Ps 25:18; Isa 55:7, even though the phrase itself is not found there. Luke picks it up from Mark 1:4 and makes more frequent use of it than the other evangelists (see p. 223 above). The introduction of it here undoubtedly depends directly on Luke 3:3; that notice was derived from the Marcan passage just mentioned. John's role here is cast in terms of the effect of the Christ-event itself, and John is thus portrayed as spreading salvation in a form that will be characteristic of Jesus' role. In this sense he is taken as the precursor of Jesus, the horn of salvation in David's house. Thus salvation moves a step beyond that associated with contemporary Palestinian messianism (see W. Foerster, *TDNT* 7. 991).

78. *in the merciful compassion of our God.* This phrase introduces the conclusion of the original canticle inherited by Luke; lit. it reads, "through the compassion of our God's mercy." In the last two verses of the canticle there is no main verb; the clauses are simply appended to vv. 76-77; but they imitate the loose connection that one found in vv. 68a-75. Thus vv. 78-79 could have followed on v. 75 originally.

The Greek word *splanchna* basically means "entrails, bowels," that part of the body that in antiquity was often regarded as the seat of compassion. Its figurative use is well known. The combination of *splanchna* and *eleos* found here does not occur in the LXX as a translation of *raḥămîm* and *ḥesed,* for which it rather uses *eleos* and *oiktirmoi* (see Hos 2:21). The Greek combination does appear in *T. Zebulun* 7:3; 8:2,6. It could be the translation of the double abstract Hebrew synonyms found in Qumran literature: *raḥămê ḥesed* (1QS 2:1; 4QSl 39 1 i 23) or *ḥasdê raḥămîm* (1QS 1:22). A significant parallel to this verse is found in *T. Levi* 4:4, where, however, *splanchna* occurs alone: ". . . till the Lord takes note of all the nations through the compassion of his son forever." See further H. Koester, *TDNT* 7. 552-555; he stresses the eschatological character of the revelation attributed to this merciful compassion of God.

the Dawn from on High. Lit. "(the) rising from (the) height." This unique, enigmatic phrase has long been a *crux interpretum.* Its difficulty lies not in the last part, *ex hypsous,* found again in Luke 24:49, meaning, "from the height (of heaven)," i.e. from God's abode (see Eph 3:18; 4:8), but in the meaning of *anatolē.* This can denote the "rising" of luminaries (e.g. stars [cf. Matt 2:2,9; *T. Levi* 18:3] or the sun), as can its cognate verb, *anatellein.* The word might be used here in this sense in dependence on Mal 3:20 (4:2E): "for you who fear my name the sun of righteousness shall rise (*anatelei*) with healing in its wings." The phrase then alludes to the ancient Near Eastern winged sun-disc, a symbol for a manifestation of divine mercy, shining from heaven and illumining human beings. Cf. J. B. Pritchard, *ANEP* § 281, 320-321, 447, etc. It might be another way of expressing the "knowledge of salvation" that John is to bring, and thus might refer to John.

Remaining within this same OT background, the phrase, however, could refer to Yahweh: in which "he (Yahweh) will visit us as the Dawn from on High." But this encounters the difficulty that *anatolē,* as a title of a person, seems to refer to someone other than "our God" in 1:78a.

However, there is still another OT usage that must be considered, for the word *anatolē* occurs three times in the LXX as the translation of Hebrew *ṣemaḥ,* "sprout, shoot, scion," a word that designates a Davidic heir. Thus, "I will raise up for David a legitimate scion" (Hebrew *ṣemaḥ ṣaddîq;* LXX *ana-tolēn dikaian,* Jer 23:5); "my servant, the scion" (Hebrew *'abdî ṣemaḥ;* LXX *ton doulon mou Anatolēn,* Zech 3:8); "the man whose name is Scion" (Hebrew *'îš ṣemaḥ šĕmô;* LXX *Anatolē onoma autō,* Zech 6:12). As a title for the Messiah, "the shoot" seems to be derived from Isa 11:1 (*ḥoṭer//nēṣer = rhabdos//anthos*), and it persists in later Jewish literature, in which *ṣemaḥ* is the preferred term. In the patriarchal-blessings text of Qumran Cave 4 we read: "Until there comes (the) righteous Messiah, the Scion of David" (*'d bw' mšyḥ hṣdq ṣmḥ Dwyd,* 4QPBless 3; *JBL* 75 [1956] 175). Again, in 4QFlor 1:11 (=4Q*174* 1-2 i 11; DJD 5. 53-54): "He is the Scion of David who will arise with the Interpreter of the Law" (*hw'h ṣmḥ Dwyd h'wmd 'm dwrš htwrh*). Cf. 4QpIsa[a] 8-10:17 (with partial restoration). Though one cannot exclude the possibility of the dawning sense (whether of John or of Yahweh), this messianic meaning of *anatolē* makes better sense in the concluding verses of the Benedictus. Zechariah would be referring to Jesus as the Messiah, as the "Dawn from on High"—the Davidic Scion sent by God. As in v. 69, the text would refer to David's house. Zechariah would be implying a preparatory role for his son, John. He will give human beings a "knowledge of salvation," but the Davidic Scion will visit them and illumine them still more, as they sit in darkness. See further the use of *anatellein* in *T. Naphtali* 8:2; *T. Gad* 8:1. — Though I prefer the messianic sense of the phrase, I have retained the ambiguity of the Greek phrase in my translation.

The phrase, "the Dawn from on high," is preceded in Greek by a prep. rel. phrase, *en hois,* which has *splanchna* as its antecedent: "through the merciful compassion of our God, in which the Dawn from on High will take note of us and shine. . . ." This is part of the problem mentioned above resulting from the lack of a main verb in these two verses. I have omitted *en hois* in my translation, making the verb in the rel. clause into a main verb and thereby splitting the single loose sentence of vv. 76-79 into two sentences.

will take note of us. Or "will visit us"; the same verb is used here as in v. 68. The fut. tense *episkepsetai* is read by P⁴, B, ℵ*, W, ⊙, etc. and is thus better attested than the aor. read by mss. A, C, D, and the Koine text-tradition. The fut. is preferred by Nestle, Merk, UBSGNT, and Aland. It suits the preceding verb *proporeusē* in v. 76. However, P. Benoit (*NTS* 3 [1956-1957] 185) and Brown (*Birth*, 373) have argued in favor of the aor. *epeskepsato*, maintaining that the latter was changed to the fut. precisely because of the fut. verb in v. 76; it is therefore suspect. That treatment fits more easily into the view that both Benoit and Brown espouse about vv. 78-79 being the conclusion to the original canticle. Though I agree with their analysis of the canticle—with their interpretation, in other words—I am reluctant to let that interpretation answer a textual question. The original canticle must be thought of as having past verbs in the first part of the structure, and a shift to an eschatological future in the conclusion.

79. *and shine on.* Or "and appear to," since the verb is a form of *epiphainein*, "appear." The illumination will be the work of the Dawn from on High. Those to be so illumined, "those who sit in darkness, in the shadow of death" (an allusion to Ps 107:10), are the sinners referred to in v. 77. See further Isa 9:1; 42:7.

our feet. Zechariah regards himself as one of those sitting in darkness; he belongs to the Period of Israel, which even in the Lucan infancy narrative is edging toward its end.

into the path of peace. Possibly an allusion to Isa 59:8, "they know not the way of peace." This is the first Lucan mention of *eirēnē*, "peace," which expresses in the Lucan writings another effect of the Christ-event (see Sketch of Lucan Theology, p. 224 above).

80. *grew up.* This is another Lucan refrain (B) in the infancy narrative; see 2:40,52. The verse itself, which brings to a close the story of John's birth and childhood, is modeled on Judg 13:24-25 and 1 Sam 2:26.

strong in spirit. Or possibly, "in the Spirit," since the holy Spirit has been mentioned in his regard in vv. 15,41,67.

out in the desert. Lit. "in the deserts, or desert places." R. W. Funk (*JBL* 78 [1959] 205-214) has maintained that the phrase *en tais erēmois* here must mean a particular "wilderness place," because the plural is never used in the LXX to render Hebrew *midbār*, "the desert." Both in the LXX and in the NT generally *hē erēmos* (sg.) means "desert," referring either to the wilderness of Sinai (which is out of question here) or to the wilderness of Judea, a definitely localized area on the eastern slopes of Judea and possibly the Jordan valley. He concludes that "if John's youth is to be connected with the wilderness [of Judea], it must be done on some other basis than grammatical and lexical evidence" (p. 214). But can one discuss this phrase in isolation from Luke 3:2 and only against its LXX background usage? Luke 3:2 locates John "in the desert," using the very phrase that otherwise consistently denoted the localized wilderness of Judea. Hence this must be the intention of this phrase here too.

This phrase has served as the basis, along with other considerations, for the plausible hypothesis—which cannot be proved or disproved—that John the Baptist spent some of his youth among the Essenes of Qumran. Born of elderly parents, he is located as a child by the Lucan infancy narrative "in the desert." For all the parallelism in the stories of John and Jesus in the infancy narrative, there is no further indication of any contact between the families. In 3:2 we are simply told that a "message came from God to John, the son of Zechariah, in the desert." This could be understood as a turning point, when he broke off from the Essenes with whom he had lived for some time, and went forth to preach a baptism for the forgiveness of sins. Part of the reason for this hypothesis is the fact that John, born into a priestly family, is never depicted in the gospel tradition as serving in or associated with the Jerusalem Temple, as was his father Zechariah (1:5). It is not implausible that John, perhaps after the death of his parents, was adopted by the Essenes, who were known to take "other men's children, while yet pliable and docile . . . and mould them according to their own ways" (Josephus *J.W.* 2.8,2 § 120). When we consider the question of John's baptism in chap. 3, we shall add further reasons which tend to make the hypothesis plausible. See J. A. T. Robinson, "The Baptism of John and the Qumran Community," *HTR* 50 [1957] 175-191; reprinted in *Twelve New Testament Studies* (SBT 34; Naperville, IL: Allenson, 1962) 11-27; W. H. Brownlee, "John the Baptist in the New Light of Ancient Scrolls," *The Scrolls and the New Testament* (ed. K. Stendahl; New York: Harper, 1957) 33-53; A. S. Geyser, "The Youth of John the Baptist," *NovT* 1 (1956) 70-75.

A difficulty found with the hypothesis is the esteem in which the Essene community held the Jerusalem priesthood; they considered them lax in levitical purity, grasping, and politically inclined (see 1QpHab 9:4-7; 4QpNah 3-4 i 12). But having at one time been associated with the Zadokite priesthood, they might still have been inclined to take into their midst even those who came from the Jerusalem Temple priests.

until the day he was manifested to Israel. Lit. "until the day of his manifestation to Israel." This is a foreshadowing of the Gospel proper, viz. 3:2-6. Luke depicts John as part of God's formal disclosure of a new way of salvation now becoming available to mankind. However, the Greek word *anadeixis* used here can also have a technical meaning, found in the papyri, of "commissioning" or "installation." This would then be a solemn expression for the public ministry of John. See H. Schlier, *TDNT* 2. 31. Is v. 80b supposed to be a parallel to the last episode of the infancy narrative, the manifestation of Jesus? If so, it is very short, even cryptic.

BIBLIOGRAPHY (1:59-80)

Fridrichsen, A. "*Sophia, hēlikia, charis* (Luc 1:80; 2:40, 52)," *Symbolae osloenses* 6 (1928) 36-38.

Funk, R. W. "The Wilderness," *JBL* 78 (1959) 205-214.

Geyser, A. S. "The Youth of John the Baptist: A Deduction from the Break in the Parallel Account of the Lucan Infancy Story," *NovT* 1 (1956) 70-75.

McCown, C. C. "The Scene of John's Ministry and Its Relation to the Purpose and Outcome of His Mission," *JBL* 59 (1940) 113-131.

Bibliography on the Benedictus

Auffret, P. "Note sur la structure littéraire de Lc i. 68-79," *NTS* 24 (1977-1978) 248-258.

Bover, J. M. " 'Mariae' nomen in cantico Zechariae," *VD* 4 (1924) 133-134.

Gnilka, J. "Der Hymnus des Zacharias," *BZ* 6 (1962) 215-238.

Jacoby, A. *"Anatolē ex hypsous,"* *ZNW* 20 (1921) 205-214.

Kasteren, J. van. "Analecta exegetica—Luc. 1, 76s.," *RB* os 3 (1894) 54-56.

Vanhoye, A. "Structure du 'Benedictus,' " *NTS* 12 (1965-1966) 382-389.

Vielhauer, P. "Das Benedictus des Zacharias," *ZTK* 49 (1952) 255-272; reprinted in his *Aufsätze zum Neuen Testament* (Theologische Bücherei 31; Munich: Kaiser, 1965) 28-46.

(See further the bibliography on the Lucan Canticles, p. 370 above.)

7. THE BIRTH OF JESUS
(2:1-20)

2 1 Now in those days an edict happened to be issued by Caesar Augustus, ordering the whole world to be registered. 2 This registration was the first, and it took place when Quirinius was governor of Syria. 3 All had to go to be registered, each in one's own town. 4 So Joseph too went up from the Galilean town of Nazareth to Judea to be registered in the town of David called Bethlehem, because he was descended from the house and family of David. 5 He went up with Mary, his fiancée, who was pregnant.

6 While they were there, the time came for Mary to deliver her child, 7 and she bore her firstborn son, wrapped him in cloth bands, and laid him in a manger, because there was no room for them in the lodge.

8 Now there were shepherds in the same district who lived out-of-doors and kept night-watch over their flocks. 9 When the angel of the Lord stood by them and God's glory shone about them, they were struck with great fear. 10 But the angel said to them, "Do not be afraid, for I announce to you a cause for great joy among all the people: 11 A Savior has been born to you today in the town of David; he is the Messiah, the Lord! 12 This will be a sign for you: You will find a child wrapped in cloth bands and lying in a manger!"

13 Then suddenly a throng of the heavenly host appeared with the angel, praising God and singing,

> 14 "Glory to God in highest heaven;
> peace on earth for people whom he favors."

15 When the angels had left them and had gone back to heaven, the shepherds said to one another, "Quick! Let's go over to Bethlehem and see this thing that has taken place, which the Lord has made known to us." 16 So they came in haste and found Mary and Joseph, and the baby lying in the manger. 17 Having seen the sight, they made known the message which had been given to them about the child. 18 All who heard of it wondered at what the shepherds told them.

¹⁹ But Mary treasured all these things and pondered over them.
²⁰ The shepherds returned to their flocks, glorifying God and praising him because they had seen and heard everything just as it had been told to them.

COMMENT

The episodes of chap. 2 of Luke's Gospel strikingly have nothing in them about the John-Jesus relationship. The first and most important episode, narrating the birth of Jesus (2:1-20), does parallel the notice of John's birth (1:57-58). There is further parallelism in the subsequent episode of the circumcision, naming, and manifestation of Jesus (2:21-40). But the parallels make no mention of John, and Jesus is introduced anew as Messiah and Lord in 2:11, as if the reader had not already learned of these titles in 1:32-35 (implicitly as Messiah) and 1:43 (explicitly as Lord).

The first episode (2:1-20) clearly falls into three main parts: (1) the setting for the birth of Jesus in Bethlehem (2:1-5); (2) the birth itself (2:6-7); and (3) the manifestation of the newborn child to the shepherds and the reaction of all who heard of it to the birth and manifestation (2:8-20). In fact, the third part can be subdivided: (a) 2:8-14, the manifestation of the child; (b) 2:15-20, the reaction to the manifestation.

To what extent is Luke dependent here on source-material? The question has often been posed and discussed. For instance, K. L. Schmidt (*Der Rahmen der Geschichte Jesu* [Berlin: Trowitzsch, 1919] 312) recognized the literary qualities of vv. 1-5 over against an older folk-narrative in vv. 6-20. F. Hahn (*Titles,* 259) likewise attributes vv. 1-5 to "the redactional work of Luke," believing that the original beginning of the older narrative has been lost. He ascribes to Luke "the comprehensive cosmo-historical horizon" of the introductory verses, but thinks that the census was the occasion for the journey in the older narrative (against M. Dibelius, "Jungfrauensohn," 55-60). Similarly, vv. 6-7 would have been designed by Luke to introduce the shepherd scene. The older narrative would, then, have been preserved in vv. 8-14,15-18,20 (v. 19 is clearly Lucan composition, being echoed in 2:51). In a similar way, A. Vögtle ("Öffene Fragen," 56) speaks of an older narrative, but regards vv. 6-7 as a derived form of vv. 11-12 of that narrative. This scarcely exhausts the analyses that have been attempted. They are all the product of literary analysis, with all its plusses and minuses.

I find such analyses of the episode highly speculative. I share R. E. Brown's hesitation about this approach (*Birth,* 411). I regard vv. 1-5 as Lucan composition. The reason: Luke's failure to understand the date of the census of Quirinius, just as he fails to understand it in Acts 5:37, where he dates it after the uprising of Theudas (Acts 5:36; cf. Josephus *Ant.* 20.5,1 § 97, in which the Theudas revolt is dated to the procuratorship of Fadus [A.D. 44-46]).

The elements of a pre-Lucan tradition in this episode are the following: the principal dramatis personae (Jesus and his parents, Mary and Joseph), Jesus' birth in Bethlehem, the connection of the dramatis personae with Nazareth, and the relation of a Galilean with "the days of the census" (Acts 5:37). Talk of the last of those elements probably floated around the early community in a vague form which Luke picked and then fashioned more explicitly into what we now have in vv. 1-5. There is, however, no trace of this dating in Matthew, who merely relates the birth of Jesus to the days of Herod, as does Luke too (by cross-reference, 2:1 referring to 1:5).

The setting for the birth of Jesus (2:1-5) describes the edict for a worldwide census issued by Augustus and carried out in Syria by Quirinius and the effects of it in bringing the Galilean Joseph and his fiancée, Mary, from Nazareth to Bethlehem, his ancestral town. As the NOTES seek to make clear, there are many difficulties with the details of this setting: There is no extra-Lucan evidence for such a worldwide census under Augustus, for the requirement of people to register in their ancestral towns; or for a census under Quirinius, the legate of Syria (A.D. 6-7), which would have occurred in the days of Herod the Great and which would have affected people in territory outside the former tetrarchy of Archelaus (either Judea, Samaria and Idumea [Josephus *Ant.* 17.11,4 § 319; 17.13,5 § 355] or only Judea [ibid., 18.1,1 § 2]). Moreover, since Luke's reference to "the days of the census" (Acts 5:37) is also confused—dated after the uprising of Theudas (see above)—it is clear that the census is a purely literary device used by him to associate Mary and Joseph, residents of Nazareth, with Bethlehem, the town of David, because he knows of a tradition, also attested in Matthew 2, that Jesus was born in Bethlehem. He is also aware of a tradition about the birth of Jesus in the days of Herod, as is Matthew; Luke's form of the tradition, unlike Matthew's, tied the birth in a vague way to a time of political disturbance associated with a census.

In introducing Caesar Augustus, the supreme ruler of the Roman world, Luke depicts him as an agent of God, who by his edict of registration brings it about that Jesus is born in the town of David. Jesus' Davidic connection is thus dramatically emphasized. But, unlike Second Isaiah, Luke does not hail the secular ruler as "my [i.e. Yahweh's] shepherd" (Isa 44:28), said of the Persian king Cyrus, or as "his anointed" (Isa 45:1). Luke does associate the birth of Jesus with the reign of Augustus (27 B.C.-A.D. 14), a lengthy period widely regarded as the era of peace. Augustus managed to put an end to the civil strife in the

Roman world of his day (see his boast in *Res gestae divi Augusti,* lines
12-45; cf. C. K. Barrett, *NTB,* § 1). In his principate the Roman senate
decreed three times that the doors of the Shrine of Janus, which usually
stood open in the time of war, be closed. It ordered the erection and consecration of an altar to *Pax Augusta* in the Campus Martius, the so-called
Ara pacis augustae, which still stands in Rome today (in restored condition). In the eastern Mediterranean world Augustus was further hailed as
"savior" and "god" in many Greek inscriptions: *sōtera tou sympantos
kosmou,* "savior of the whole world" (Myra inscription [see V. Ehrenberg and A. H. M. Jones, *Documents Illustrating the Reigns of Augustus
and Tiberius* (Oxford: Clarendon, 1949) § 72]). His birthday (23 September) was celebrated: "[the birthday] of the god has marked the beginning of the good news through him for the world" (Priene inscription,
40-42 [see W. Dittenberger, *OGIS,* 2. § 458]).

Thus Luke, writing from a later period in the Roman age, associates
the birth of Jesus with a famous Roman emperor and suggests that the
real bearer of peace and salvation to the whole world is the one whose
birth occurred in the town of David and was made known by angels of
heaven. By relating Jesus' birth to a worldwide census, Luke hints at the
worldwide significance of that birth. Jesus' birth is recounted in terms of
lowly circumstances to contrast with the majesty and renown of him
whom the rest of the Roman world regarded as its savior. The birth in the
city of David gives the story a Jewish atmosphere, but that is transformed
by the larger reference to Roman history. The child thus born under *Pax
Augusta* will eventually be hailed as "the king, the One Who is to come
in the name of the Lord"—and the result will be, "Peace in heaven and
glory in the highest heaven" (Luke 19:38).

In vv. 6-7 Luke recounts the birth itself. The two verses parallel the
two-verse account of the birth of John (1:57-58). Jesus is simply described as Mary's firstborn, a description that prepares for 2:23 (see
NOTE on 2:7 for its meaning and significance). The rest of the details are
here more important, not only because they will become part of the sign
given to the shepherds, but because of their symbolic character. They are
like allusions in a tone poem to OT motifs. Jesus is swaddled or wrapped
in cloth bands, as the wise King Solomon once described his birth:
"Cared for with cloth bands and concern, no king ever had another beginning of existence" (Wisd 7:4-5). Jesus is laid by Mary in a manger,
evoking the memory of the LXX of Isa 1:3, "An ox knows its owner and
an ass the manger of its lord; but Israel knows not me, and my people
does not comprehend." Palestinian shepherds will be directed by heaven
itself to find him in the Lord's manger, the sign of God's sustenance of his
people. And the reference to the "lodge" may allude to Jer 14:8, which
speaks of Yahweh as the hope of Israel, its savior in time of evils, "Why

are you like an alien in the land, like a wayfarer who goes to a lodge (*katalyma*) for the night?" The symbolism in all of this is that Jesus is born in the town of David, not in a lodge like a stranger, but in the manger of the Lord, who is the sustainer of his people. Like Solomon, David's most famous son in the past, Jesus is swaddled in token of his regal condition, but also of his human condition. See further C. H. Giblin, "Reflections on the Sign of the Manger," *CBQ* 29 (1967) 87-101.

In any case, this description of the birth of Jesus would stand in contrast to an expectation of a Davidic Messiah—one who was "to restore the kingdom to Israel" (Acts 1:6) in a political or military sense.

The manifestation of the child in 2:8-14 contains the account of the angelic message (vv. 8-12) and the Song of the Angels (vv. 13-14). Why should the first announcement of Jesus' birth to outsiders be made to shepherds? Both in ancient Near Eastern literature, including the OT (e.g. 2 Sam 5:2), and in classical Greek and Latin literature "shepherd" was often used for a political and sometimes for a military leader. However, no such connotation is meant here, for the Lucan story clearly envisages shepherds in the literal sense. R. Bultmann (*HST*, 298-299) thinks that they have been introduced here because they often appear in Hellenistic bucolic poetry as representatives of an ideal humanity. Furthermore, in the stories of the birth of many famous persons there is often mention of shepherds (e.g. Cyrus, Romulus and Remus, Mithras; see J. M. Creed, *The Gospel,* 31). But it is really difficult to see any connection between these poems and stories and the Lucan account, save for a generic reference to shepherds.

For J. Jeremias (*TDNT* 6 [1968] 491) the shepherds appear in the Lucan story because they "are obviously owners of the stall; this is why they can be told without further elaboration that the manger is the site of the sign from God, 2:12." That, of course, is possible; but it goes beyond what Luke says.

The shepherds are almost certainly introduced by Luke into the story because of the association of Jesus' birth with Bethlehem, the town of David. We first learn of David as a shepherd tending the flocks of Jesse, his father, in 1 Sam 16:11; see further references to this activity of his in 1 Sam 17:14-15,20,28,34—especially his boast of having killed lions and bears in defense of the flock (and hence his ability to slay the Philistine Goliath). Moreover, Mic 5:1 speaks of Bethlehem as a place from which shall come forth a "ruler in Israel" (like David), even though it was among the insignificant clans of Judah. This OT verse is actually quoted (in a slightly expanded form which makes the ruler into a "shepherd") in Matt 2:6. But Luke makes no allusion to this OT passage, even though he undoubtedly knew it; and it may well have figured in his thinking in depicting Jesus as a ruler born in shepherd-country. This is as far as I am willing to go with the OT background of the shepherd motif in the Lucan birth-story.

Some commentators (e.g. Creed, *The Gospel*, 31-32; Brown, *Birth*, 421-424) think that Luke also has in mind Migdal Eder ("the Tower of the Flock"), mentioned in Gen 35:21 and Mic 4:8, and may even have known of the tradition, preserved in *Tg. Ps.-Jonathan* of Gen 35:21, that "the King Messiah will be revealed at the end of days" from the Tower of the Flock. This is, however, rather unlikely, because (1) Gen 35:21 makes it clear that Migdal Eder is at some distance from Bethlehem; (2) Mic 4:8 uses it as a parallel name for Zion/Jerusalem; (3) the *Tg. Ps.-Jon.* dates in its final form from about the seventh century A.D., since it mentions the wife of Muhammed (*'Adîša'*) and his daughter (*Faṭîma'*) in Gen 21:21, mentions "Constantinople" in Num 24:19 and Rome and Constantinople in Num 24:24; and it knows about the six orders of the Mishnah in Exod 26:9. To maintain, as does J. Bowker (*The Targums and Rabbinic Literature* [Cambridge: University Press, 1969] 26), that "it [the targum] rests on a tradition going back to pre-Christian times" is unbridled speculation. That can only be admitted for those literary traditions which can be shown to exist in pre-Christian sources or contemporary writers (like Philo or Josephus). In this case, there is simply no such evidence. (4) That Luke may have shifted Migdal Eder (Mic 4:8) from Jerusalem to Bethlehem is, of course, not impossible; but it is highly speculative and scarcely warranted by his shift of the name "town of David" from Jerusalem to Bethlehem.

There is enough in the OT tradition about Bethlehem and David to explain the relation of the shepherds to the birth of Jesus. One final aspect of the shepherds has to be added. They are not to be taken as examples of sinners (even though in later rabbinic tradition they were often regarded as thieves, see Str-B, 2. 113-114), to whom the word of salvation is now brought by heavenly messengers; or even as examples of the poor, since the implication of "their flock" (2:8) may mean that they owned them. Rather their presence is another example in the infancy narrative of Luke's predilection for the lowly of human society; recall 1:38,52.

In vv. 9-12 we have the announcement proper. As in the announcements of the birth of John and Jesus, one can find the stereotyped elements of an announcement story. However, in this case one of the five elements is missing, viz. the objection. Otherwise, one has (a) the appearance of the angel of the Lord (v. 9a); (b) the fear on the part of the shepherds (v. 9b); (c) the heavenly message (vv. 10-11, including the injunction, "Do not be afraid!"); and (d) the giving of a sign or reassurance (v. 12).

The angel's message to the shepherds stands in this whole episode in contrast to the edict of Caesar Augustus to the whole world. The essential message is that in God's providence a child is born who is to become for human history Savior, Messiah, and Lord. Born in the time of the *Pax Augusta* and in the town of David, the Palestinian shepherds are invited to recognize in him cause of great joy for them and all the people.

The three christological titles applied to Jesus in this scene are titles born of resurrection-faith, which are being pressed back to the very beginning of his earthly existence. But Phil 3:20 shows that they were already being applied to Jesus in pre-Lucan tradition. Certainly "Messiah" and "Lord" would have to be regarded as kerygmatic titles, stemming from the Jewish Christian community of Palestine. Whether "Savior" is likewise solely to be derived from that tradition may be debated.

After the angel of the Lord has announced his message to the shepherds, he is joined by a throng of the heavenly host that praises God at this announcement of the birth of a Savior. The praise is given in a hymn that is inserted at this point. As in the case of the Magnificat and the Benedictus, this canticle may well have been inserted secondarily, after the original infancy narrative was written, as Brown (*Birth*, 426) suggests. Brown holds (p. 427) that this canticle too was originally composed by a community of Jewish Christian Anawim. That is certainly possible, but given the acclamation that is found in Luke 19:38, with a certain similarity to the hymn here, I prefer to think of this as a Lucan composition. The angelic chorus invites the Christian reader to sing God's glory too, because the birth of this child means a manifestation of God's peace to the people of his predilection. This is the source of the joy that will be among all the people.

In vv. 15-20 Luke records the reaction to the angelic manifestation of the birth of the Savior, Messiah, and Lord. It is actually a series of three reactions: (a) the reaction of the shepherds; (b) the reaction of those to whom the shepherds told the story of the angelic declaration; and (c) the reaction of Mary. The first reaction is that of the shepherds, who go in haste to verify what they had been told. They come and see. They find the child lying in the manger, and Mary and Joseph with him. The scene ends with their departure and further reaction of praise and glory to God for all that they had seen and heard. They are not to be regarded as eyewitnesses whom Luke decades later contacted in order to get the story. Their function is that of showing spontaneous trust in the heavenly message, which results in their hastening to the child. It is an example of the kind of spontaneous faith of which the Lucan Gospel is full.

The second reaction comes from those to whom the shepherds recounted their story, and it is one of wonder or astonishment. Compare the reaction in 1:66.

The third reaction is that of Mary herself: She treasured all these things and pondered over them. As the NOTE on 2:19 seeks to explain, this means that Luke depicts Mary trying to hit upon the meaning of all that she has witnessed herself and heard about from the shepherds. Since this notice of Mary's preserving all this is echoed again in 2:51 (as a refrain), it should be clear that she has not perceived the deep implications of everything. As we have already explained, Luke presents Mary as the first Christian believer (1:45), and this theme will appear later in his account (8:21; Acts 1:14). He has already portrayed her with some knowledge of her child as the Davidic Messiah, Son of God, and Lord (1:32-35,43). Now from the shepherds she has learned of him as "Savior." But Luke's picture of Mary here should not be overplayed, since in 2:50 he will still speak of her misunderstanding.

The Lucan infancy narrative should not be read as if it were an account of Stage I of the gospel tradition, as if the text reflected what actually went on in the historical Mary's mind. For it obviously has to be understood in contrast to what one finds in Mark 3:21, where "his family" (*RSV*, Greek *hoi par' autou*), thinks that he is out of his mind, and Mark 3:31 speaks of "his mother and his brothers" as part of that family. No, one has to recognize that Mary's pondering and treasuring of all these things did not result in an immediate insight into Jesus' status as divine. Luke never puts it that way, and the Christian reader should not too facilely so conclude.

Verse 19 should not be read as a reflection of memories preserved within Mary's family, which later became known to the Christian community, and on which Luke has based his account. There is no evidence for such memoirs, despite the attempts of serious commentators at times to suggest or hint at such. For instance, E. Osty (*Luc* [BJ], 39) asks in his comment on v. 19: "Is this a delicate way of letting it be known that Luke has garnished the confidence of Mary?" Or A. Plummer (*Gospel*, 60), in his comment on the ptc. *symballousa*, "pondering," asks, "From whom could Lk. learn this?" Such reflections miss the point.

Mary's reaction to what has happened is something that she keeps to herself, and is contrasted to the reaction of the shepherds who go forth to spread the news, and to the reaction of wonder and astonishment of those who heard the news. Her treasuring and pondering is part of the picture of the "believing woman," "the handmaid of the Lord."

The episode finally ends with the departure of the shepherds who return to the flocks, echoing the Song of the Angels in their praise and glorifying of God.

NOTES

2 1. *in those days.* See NOTE on 1:39.

Reference is made to "the days of Herod, king of Judea" (1:5), and to the time sequences mentioned in 1:24 (Elizabeth's seclusion for "five months"), 1:36 (her sixth month), and 1:56 (Mary's stay with her "about three months"). Luke's story of Jesus' birth, which is now to be recounted, does not mention the last six months of Mary's pregnancy. Hence his birth is to be reckoned about fifteen months from the time of the announcement of John's birth to which the dating in the days of Herod (1:5) refers. For all its vagueness the present phrase dates the birth of Jesus in "the days of Herod." The problem that this dating raises will be posed in the NOTE on v. 2. See also 3:1,23.

an edict happened to be issued. Lit. "and it happened in those days (that) an edict went forth." Luke uses *egeneto de* + a finite verb, without the intervening conj. *kai;* see p. 119 above. The word *dogma* was used in classical Greek to denote an "opinion" (what *seems,* from *dokein*), and by extension even a philosophical "notion." By Roman times it had developed an official meaning, "public decree, ordinance," being used especially of a Roman *senatusconsultum,* a decree of the Roman senate. Here, as in Acts 17:7, it is used of an imperial edict; this usage is found also in Josephus (*J.W.* 1.20,3 § 393) and Greek papyri (e.g. FayumP 20:22). A later ecclesiastical sense of the word developed from the use made of it by Luke in Acts 16:4, where it denotes the "decision" passed by the apostles and elders at the "Council" of Jerusalem.

by Caesar Augustus. The ruler of the Roman world of the time. Born Gaius Octavius on 23 September 63 B.C., he was in Spain at the time of the assassination of Julius Caesar on the Ides of March 44. Through his granduncle's will he became his chief heir, and in 43 was named his adopted son, under the name Gaius Julius Caesar Octavianus. The triumvirate set up to rule the Roman world included Octavian along with Mark Antony and M. Lepidus. It began to rule on 27 November 43 B.C. On 1 January 42 Caesar was recognized as a god, and Octavian became *divi filius.* The downfall of the triumvir Lepidus took place in 36, and Octavian defeated Cleopatra and Mark Antony at Actium in 31, in the same year in which he assumed the consulship. In the following year (30) he was recognized as the master of Egypt. This year is often regarded as the effective beginning of his sole, imperial reign. His title of *imperator,* though won earlier, was ratified in 29. It was only on 16 January 27 that the Roman senate bestowed on him the title of *Augustus,* thus acknowledging his supreme position in the restored "republic." From that time one usually dates the beginning of the reign of the emperor Caesar Augustus.

Augustus was a title and was intended to be borne by all subsequent emperors; only Vitellius (A.D. 69) did not receive it. Luke transcribes the Latin title in Greek as *Augoustos,* treating the title as the emperor's proper name, which it actually became in time. Normally, the title *Augustus* was translated into Greek as *Sebastos* (see Acts 25:21,25).

Augustus died in A.D. 14 and was succeeded by his stepson, Tiberius, who ruled from 14-37. He will be mentioned in 3:1.

the whole world to be registered. Or "to register itself." Luke employs here *apographesthai,* and in v. 2 *apographē,* "registration," the technical Greek equivalents for Latin *census* (see BDF § 5.3).

Though *oikoumenē* means "inhabited earth" (originally a ptc., with the noun *gē,* "earth," understood), the substantived adj. was often used with hyperbole in the official rhetoric of decrees and inscriptions for the Roman empire itself. See Acts 11:28; O. Michel, *TDNT* 5. 157. Nero, for instance, was hailed the "savior and benefactor of the inhabited world" (W. Dittenberger, *OGIS,* § 668.5; cf. § 666.3; § 669.10; OxyP 7.1021:5). It was meant to include Italy and the provinces. There is no evidence that it designated only the latter, as distinct from Italy, much less Palestine alone (for which Luke uses *pasa hē gē* in 4:25).

Aside from this statement here in Luke (and of later Christian and pagan writers who depend on him), there is no ancient evidence of a universal, worldwide registration or census ordered by Caesar Augustus. No ancient historian tells of a Roman census conducted on this scale in the time of Herod the Great (37-4 B.C.).

Augustus, however, did conduct enrollments of the population in the empire during his long reign. These were of two sorts: (a) a census of Roman citizens, both in Italy and in the provinces; and (b) a census of provincial inhabitants (*incolae,* or people who were not *cives romani*). The census of Roman citizens was called *census populi* (or in Greek *apotimēsis tou dēmou*); it was conducted mainly for the purpose of taxation and military service. It usually included a "declaration" (*apographē*) and an "assessment of property" (*timēsis*). It is known that such censuses were taken up in 28 B.C., 8 B.C., and A.D. 14 (see *Res gestae divi Aug.* § 8; cf. Suetonius *Aug.* 27.5). The census of provincial inhabitants came to be known simply as *apographē,* the word Luke uses in v. 2, but it was scarcely carried out on a worldwide scale. It was administered in individual provinces and suited to the conditions of individual areas. It is know that in Roman Egypt a province census was taken every fourteen years from A.D. 33/34 to 257/58 (see OxyP 2.254,255,256); a province census is also known in Gaul for 27 B.C., 12 B.C., and A.D. 14-16. And references are found to similar census-taking in Lusitania, Spain, and Judea (see below). In imperial provinces (i.e. in provinces under the supervision of the emperor, and not the senate, where the emperor appointed the legate [or governor]) legates, prefects, and procurators were delegated by imperial authority to carry out the provincial census. Syria was such a province.

Hence it seems that Luke, living in the Roman world of his day—and if I am right, an *incola* of his native Syria—was aware of censuses under Augustus (perhaps of both sorts) and indulged in some rhetoric in his desire to locate the birth of Jesus in Bethlehem under the two famous reigns, of Herod the Great and Caesar Augustus, using a vague recollection of an Augustan census to do so.

2. *This registration was the first.* Or, "this was the first registration." Here we read *autē apographē prōtē egeneto,* which is awkward Greek, and creates a

problem with the following gen. clause. Some mss. (C and the Koine text-tradition—not the best) insert the def. art. *hē* between the first two words, making it clearly mean, "this registration was the first." The better reading, omitting the def. art., can be translated either way. The clause means that this was the first time that a census took place in Judea.

After Herod the Great died in 4 B.C., the territory over which he ruled was divided according to a codicil in his will among three of his sons: Archelaus (4 B.C.-A.D. 6) became the ethnarch over Judea, Samaria, and Idumea; Herod Antipas (4 B.C.-A.D. 39), the tetrarch over Galilee and Perea; and Philip (4 B.C.-A.D. 34), the tetrarch over Auranitis, Batanea, Gaulanitis, Paneas, and Trachonitis (regions in the northeast, mainly east of the Jordan). In A.D. 6 Archelaus was exiled to Vienne in southern Gaul, and his tetrarchy became a Roman territory subject to the legate of the province of Syria (see Josephus *Ant.* 17.11,4 § 319; 17.13,5 § 355). At that time a census of Judea was ordered, including an assessment of property and the liquidation of Archelaus' estate (see Josephus *Ant.* 18.1,1 §§ 1-10). Luke knew of this census, since he refers to it in Acts 5:37 (cf. Josephus *Ant.* 18.1,6 § 23).

The trouble is that Luke speaks of the census here as the "first" and links it to the legateship of Quirinius, using this as a way of dating the birth of Jesus. If he is referring to the census under Quirinius, then, as we shall see, it could not have occurred in "the days of Herod."

Various attempts have been made to get around the difficulty, and they will be discussed apropos of the various phrases that Luke uses. One of the attempts affects the first four words in this verse.

Prōtē, "first," is sometimes used in Hellenistic and NT Greek in the sense of *protera*, the comparative, "former, prior" (see Acts 1:1; John 1:15,30; 15:18), since the use of the comparative degree was on the wane, and other means were taken to express it (BDF §§ 244-245). Understood thus, *prōtē* might govern the following gen. and be translated, "This registration took place before Quirinius was governor of Syria," or (with an ellipsis of the term of comparison, as in John 5:36; 1 Cor 1:25), "This registration was before (that of) Quirinius, governor of Syria." This interpretation, apparently first proposed in the seventeenth century, was adopted by M.-J. Lagrange (*Luc*, 67; *RB* 8 [1911] 60-84) and supported by no less a grammarian than N. Turner (*Grammatical Insights*, 23-24). Either of these interpretations would mean that Luke was referring to a registration conducted prior to Quirinius's well-known census in A.D. 6-7. The comparative sense of *prōtē* is attested. But the following gen. is a gen. absolute, since the first word is a ptc. If Luke had written *hēgemonos tēs Syrias Kyrēniou*, then it would be possible. But the use of the ptc. and the word-order are fatal to such interpretations. Moreover, it is obviously a last-ditch solution to save the historicity involved. It is trying to make Luke more accurate than he really is.

when Quirinius was governor of Syria. Lit. "Quirinius being in charge of Syria." The gen. absolute contains the ptc. *hēgemoneuontos*. When the noun *hēgemōn* (or its derivatives) is used as a technical term by writers of this period, it refers to the "prefect" of certain Roman provinces. However, a generic sense of the word (=“ruler, governor”) is also found, and Luke’s use of it in that sense in 3:1 illustrates what can also be found in Greek papyri from Egypt (see NOTE on 3:1; cf. MM, 276–277). Here it is probably used generically of Quirinius, who was a *legatus* in an imperial province, i.e. a legate of the emperor Augustus, and not dependent on the Roman senate. This use of a form of *hēgemōn* for a governor of Syria is paralleled in Josephus (*Ant.* 18.4,2 § 88).

Publius Sulpicius Quirinius’ career is fairly well known and defies all attempts either to attribute to him two censuses in Judea or to date the start of his legateship of Syria to any other period than A.D. 6-7; the only thing in this regard that is uncertain is how long his legateship continued.

He was a native of the municipality of Lanuvium in the Alban Hills of southern Latium and became consul in Rome under Augustus in 12 B.C. (=A.U.C. 742), along with C. Valgius Rufus (see H. Dessau, *ILS* § 3004, § 6095, § 8150). Tacitus (*Annales* 3.48) describes him as an intrepid soldier and assiduous official who successfully campaigned against the Homonadensian bandits in Cilicia, south of the Roman province of Galatia, and was therefore granted a public triumph for it. Strabo (*Geography* 12.6,5) tells how he starved them out, captured and deported four thousand of them alive, settled them in neighboring regions, but left the country destitute of men in the prime of life. This campaign against the Homonadensians took place after his consulship; but neither the exact dates of it nor the rank that he held during it is known. It may have been sometime between 11 and 6 B.C. (so T. Mommsen maintained), but it more likely took place later, ca. 5-3 B.C. It is presumed that he was in Galatia in some official capacity about this time. Some time after 4 B.C. he was appointed by Augustus to be the advisor (*rector*) of Gaius Caesar, the emperor’s adopted son. The son was eventually given proconsular powers and made the vice-regent of eastern provinces, including Syria, between 1 B.C. and A.D. 4. Quirinius was his advisor especially during his command of Armenia.

When Augustus annexed the territory (Josephus *J.W.* 2.8,1 § 117; 2.9,1 §§ 167-168) ruled over by Archelaus (i.e. Judea, Samaria, and Idumea) to the Roman province of Syria, Quirinius was sent as *legatus*, “legate, deputy,” by the emperor to take a census of property in Syria and to sell the estate of Archelaus in Palestine (Josephus *Ant.* 17.18,5 § 355; cf. *Ant.* 18.1,1 §§ 1-2; 18.2,1 § 26). Josephus also tells us that Coponius was sent along to Judea to rule over the Jews (as prefect) and that the census was taken in the thirty-seventh year after Augustus’ defeat of M. Antony at Actium (2 September 31 B.C.). Hence the census of Quirinius took place about A.D. 6-7, following the incorporation of Judea into the province of Syria and the banishment of Archelaus to Vienne in southern Gaul in A.D. 6. Josephus never hints at an earlier Roman census in Judea; nor does he say anything about Quirinius having been governor in Roman Syria at an earlier date. The census of A.D. 6-7 has to be that to which Luke refers in Acts 5:37, which led to a revolt of Palestinian Jews under the leadership of Judas the Galilean. See further Josephus *J.W.* 7.8,1 § 253. Quirinius died in Rome in A.D. 21 (Tacitus *Ann.* 3.48).

Two Latin inscriptions mention Quirinius. One confirms his legateship in Syria (*legato Caesaris Syriae*) and his census in Syria (*idem iussu Quirini censum egi Apamenae . . .*); the other mentions him as a high commissioner or *duovir* in Pisidian Antioch, an honor given him either during his Homonadensian campaign or during his advisory career with Gaius Caesar (see Dessau, *ILS* § 2683; §§ 9502-9503).

A broken inscription from Tivoli (*lapis* or *titulus tiburtinus,* now in the Vatican Museum) mentions a governorship of Syria (Dessau, *ILS* § 918). It has often been attributed to Quirinius, but the beginning of the text and thus the name of the person honored are lost. There is no evidence that it refers to Quirinius, and it has been ascribed to others as well, e.g. to M. Plautius Silvanus, a proconsul of Asia (so E. Groag) or to L. Calpurnius Piso, a legate of Caesar in Galatia (so R. Syme, *Roman Revolution* [Oxford: Clarendon, 1939] 298 n. 8).

The Tivoli inscription is still cited by some to support the view that a second legateship of Syria would have been possible for Quirinius, even if the inscription was not set up in honor of him, because its last line and a half (partly, but certainly restored) read: [*legatus pro praetore*] *divi Augusti iterum Syriam et Pho*[*enicen optinuit*]. This has been translated, "(as) pro-praetorial legate of Divus Augustus, he received again (the province of) Syria and Phoenicia." That would suggest that someone was Augustus' legate in Syria twice. Hence, even if Quirinius is not the person to whom the Tivoli inscription refers, it would at least reveal the possibility of an earlier legateship of Quirinius in Syria. However, it has long since been pointed out that *iterum* does not modify [*optinuit*] but the preceding phrase; the whole clause means rather "(as) pro-praetorial legate of Divus Augustus for a second time, he received Syria and Phoenicia." Moreover, it was unheard of that a proconsul would become a legate of the emperor twice in the same province (see J. G. C. Anderson, *Cambridge Ancient History* 10 [1934] 878; R. Syme, "Titulus Tiburtinus," 590).

The known legates of the province of Syria for the time about the birth of Jesus can easily be listed:

M. Agrippa	23-13 B.C.	C. Caesar	1 B.C.-A.D. 4(?)
M. Titius	ca. 10 B.C.	L. Volusius Saturninus	A.D. 4-5
S. Sentius Saturninus	9-6 B.C.	P. Sulpicius Quirinius	A.D. 6-7 (or later)
P. Quintilius Varus	6-4 B.C.	Q. Caecilius Creticus Silanus	A.D. 12-17

That Quirinius was legate in Syria in A.D. 6-7 must be regarded as certain; Josephus mentions the fact at least three times, and attempts to discredit his testimony (e.g. W. Lodder, T. Corbishley) have been recognized as misguided. An earlier governorship of Syria for Quirinius—if it were possible!—would have had to be prior to 10 B.C.; but then this would push the birth of Jesus back so far that it would be out of harmony with the dates in Luke 3:1,23 about the beginning of his ministry. To put Quirinius' legateship in between 4 and 1 B.C. would solve nothing, since Herod died early in 4 B.C.

Another attempt to solve the problem has been to invoke a possible *imperium maius*, "greater command, jurisdiction," that Quirinius would have had at the time of his Homonadensian campaign. This would have meant that a superior imperial commission had been given to him to take up a census in Syria, when someone else was actually legate there. This has been maintained for the legateship of S. Sentius Saturninus (9-6 B.C.), because of a notice found in Tertullian (*Adv. Marc.* 4.19,10; CSEL, 47. 483). It relates the birth of Jesus to a census taken up under this legate: *census constat actos sub Augusto tunc in Iudaea per Sentium Saturninum,* "It is known that censuses were taken in Augustus' reign at that time in Judea by Sentius Saturninus." How Tertullian got such information has always been a mystery. But it may be queried whether this information is rightly interpreted in reference to Luke 2; see C. F. Evans, "Tertullian's References." The situation is complicated by the fact that Tertullian elsewhere gives a different year for Jesus' birth in *Adversus Iudaeos* 8 (CSEL, 70. 281), viz. in the forty-first year of Augustus' reign! From what is he reckoning?

When all is said and done, there is no reason to doubt that Jesus' birth took place in the days of Herod; this is independently attested in Matt 2:1, where it is also made known that it occurred shortly before the death of Herod (2:15-19), i.e. before 4 B.C. In Acts 5:37 Luke speaks vaguely of Judas the Galilean "in the days of the census," and it is not unlikely that the vagueness of his recollection of that event has given rise to the faulty synchronism of the Quirinius census and "the days of Herod."

In recent years two experts in Roman history and law have turned their attention to the Quirinius problem. One is A. N. Sherwin-White in his Sarum lectures, *Roman Society and Roman Law in the New Testament;* the other is Syme in his article, "The Titulus Tiburtinus." How different are their solutions!

According to Sherwin-White, Luke has dated the birth of Jesus by linking it to the census of Quirinius (A.D. 6), whereas Matthew has dated it in the last years of Herod the Great (ca. 4 B.C.). Sherwin-White regards as "rearguard action" the attempt to reconcile Matthew and Luke, by invoking an earlier legateship of Quirinius in Syria in the years 4-2 B.C. Rather, he maintains that Luke, who alone of the evangelists had a notion of chronology, deliberately dated the birth of Jesus to the census of Quirinius just as he linked the beginning of the ministry to the fifteenth year of Tiberius (3:1). Luke's dating of Jesus' birth under Quirinius "was a deliberate rejection of the tradition of Matthew, which connects the nativity with Herod and Archelaus" (p. 167). Being a classical scholar and having no restraints about the Synoptic problem, Sherwin-White thus assumes that Luke knew Matthew's Gospel, and passes over in silence the problem within the Lucan account itself, the cross-reference in 2:1 and 1:5.

According to Syme, the solution is rather to be sought in the vagueness of recollection of two important events in the history of Palestinian Jews:

Two striking events in Palestinian history would leave their mark in the minds of men. First, the end of Herod in 4 B.C., second the annexation of Judaea in A.D. 6. Either might serve for approximate dating in a society not given to exact documentation. Each event, so it happened, led to disturbances. More serious were those in 4 B. C., according to Josephus. Varus the legate of Syria had to intervene with the whole of his army. But the crisis of A. D. 6 was the more sharply remembered because Roman rule and taxation were imposed. Thus, in Acts 5,37, the speech of the Pharisee Gamaliel: 'In the days of the census' ("Titulus Tiburtinus," 600).

And Syme even recalls the error made about the death of Herod in the writings of a famous historian of ancient Greece: "On his death in A.D. 6 Judaea became a Roman province" (W. W. Tarn, *Hellenistic Civilization* [1st and 2d eds.; London: E. Arnold, 1927, 1930] 208; cf. 3d ed. [1952] 238). It seems rather obvious that Syme's solution is to be preferred. For if a Tarn could do it, then why not Luke?

3. *All.* This is Lucan hyperbole again, like the reference in v. 1 to the "whole world." There is no reason to restrict it solely to the province of Syria.

to be registered, each in one's own town. Ms. D reads, instead of *polin*, "town," the word *patrida*, "native land"; ms. C* has *chōran*, "region." The prep. phrase, *eis tēn heautou polin*, creates a problem alongside 2:39, where Nazareth is called Joseph's and Mary's "own town." Moreover, one wonders why they would be going from Galilee, where they were resident in the territory of Herod Antipas, to Judea to take part in a census in an area in which they did not live. There is no evidence that in a Roman census people were expected to return to their native lands (as the reading in ms. D suggests) or to their ancestral cities. In a Roman census the people were registered for taxation or military service where they happened to be (or possibly in a large town nearby).

It is true, however, that *apographē kat' oikian* or *kat' idian* is known from Greek papyri from Egypt, i.e. a registration according to (one's) house, or according to one's (property). The edict of G. Vibius Maximus, recorded in London Papyrus 904 (from A.D. 104), sets down: "Since registration by household is imminent, it is necessary to notify all who for any reason are absent from their districts to return to their own homes that they may carry out the ordinary business of registration and continue faithfully the farming expected of them" (lines 20-27; see A. Deissmann, *LAE,* 271). Just what pertinence such a regulation in the province of Egypt would have to customs in the province of Syria is hard to say. In any case, it does not say anything about the need to go to one's *ancestral town* in order to register in a census. There is, moreover, not a hint that Joseph owned property in Bethlehem; nor can this be deduced even from Matt 2:11, if that were even remotely pertinent to the Lucan story.

4. *Joseph too went up.* The mention of Joseph links this episode with 1:27. The same verb *anabainein* will be used in 2:42 to describe the journey of Mary and Joseph to Jerusalem. Since Bethlehem was about 2,564 feet above sea level, the reference to an ascent from Galilee in the north is understandable, Nazareth being about 1,830 feet above sea level. See further 18:31; 19:28; Acts 11:2. The expression is also found in the OT; see Ezra 1:3. Customarily, one went "up" to Jerusalem and its vicinity.

from the Galilean town of Nazareth. Lit. "from Galilee, from the town (of)

Nazareth." See NOTE on 1:26. In 2:39 Nazareth will be described as Mary and Joseph's "own town." The Matthean infancy narrative knows nothing of this and implies rather that their "house" was in Bethlehem (2:11). One should not read that into the Lucan account.

Luke implies here that inhabitants of Galilee were affected by a Roman census that applied only to Judea, Samaria, and Idumea, the former territory of Archelaus. Galilee was still at this time under Herod Antipas, who continued to rule it until A.D. 39; there is no reason to suspect that the census would have applied to his territory as well. On Galilee, see NOTE on 17:11.

It seems clear that Luke is not thinking in terms of such historical detail. His purpose is to get Mary (who is with child) to Bethlehem in time for the birth of Jesus there. From Nazareth to Bethlehem was about eighty-five miles by the most direct route, through Samaria.

the town of David called Bethlehem. Usually in the OT the phrase, "the town of David" is used of the citadel of Zion or the former Jebusite fortress that David took over and made into Jerusalem (see 2 Sam 5:7,9 = 1 Chr 11:5,7; 2 Sam 6:10,12,16; 2 Kgs 9:28; 12:22). Yet David himself is known in the OT as the son of "an Ephrathite of Bethlehem in Judah" (1 Sam 17:12) or as the son of "Jesse the Bethlehemite" (1 Sam 17:58; cf. 20:6). Hence the Lucan conflation that is found here, possibly added for extra-Palestinian readers. The prep. phrase is anarthrous, but also a Semitism, with the determination coming from the proper name in the *nomen rectum* of the construct chain.

"Bethlehem in/of Judah" (so named in Judg 17:7-9; 19:1-2; Ruth 1:1-2; 1 Sam 17:12) was a small town ca. five miles S/SW of Jerusalem. In John 7:42 it is called a *kōmē,* "village." It was a town with a long history, being originally a Canaanite town mentioned in the Amarna letters (*ANET*, 489) as *Bit-Laḥmi* ("house of [the god] Laḥmu," and not, *pace* Plummer [*Gospel*, 52], "house of bread"). It was the home of David and the place of his anointing. The specification of it as Bethlehem of Judah served to distinguish it from Bethlehem in Zebulon (Josh 19:15). Luke does not link Jesus' birth in Bethlehem with any OT prophecy, as Matthew does in 2:5-6.

because he was. Some minuscule mss. (348, 1216) read *autous,* "they," and the Sinatic OS reads "both." These are attempts to make Mary a Davidid and are characteristic of a later tradition. Luke knows of no Davidic connection for Mary. Jesus' Davidic descent is clearly traced by Luke through Joseph (see 3:23-38).

from the house and family of David. The prep. phrase is anarthrous, revealing its intention to stress Joseph's Davidic descent. See NOTE on 1:27. The anarthrous forms also prevent one from interpreting the words too literally, as if they meant that Joseph owned a house or some property in Bethlehem that might have become taxable.

5. *He went up with Mary.* As the Greek text is presently divided into verses, one should read, "to be registered (*or* to register himself) with Mary." But Plummer (*Gospel,* 52) is certainly right in linking the prep. phrase with the verb "went up." We have supplied this verb in the lemma from v. 4 to simplify

the understanding of "with Mary." We know nothing about the obligation of women to register in a province census in Judea. There is no reason to think that Luke is suggesting that Mary had property there. In his story she accompanies Joseph so that her child will be born in the city of David.

his fiancée, who was pregnant. Luke used *emnēsteumenē,* the perf. ptc., "engaged, betrothed," of Mary in 1:27, and he simply repeats that description of her marital status here; he has never called her the *gynē,* "wife," of Joseph. Theoretically, he could have used that term of her, even before the *niśśûʾîn* (see NOTE on 1:27)—if he were actually aware of Palestinian Jewish marriage customs. The reader of the Lucan Gospel knows already that Mary is pregnant and should avoid overliteral readings of this description. Such a reading leads to all sorts of questions that the account itself does not intend to answer (such as, "What was she doing on a journey with Joseph, if she were merely his fiancée or betrothed? And, worse still, pregnant as well?"). To ask them is to miss the point of *Luke's* story.

They have been asked, as the text-tradition of this part of the verse reveals. The best mss. (B*, ℵ, C, D, W) and some ancient versions (Syrᵖ, Sah, Boh) read *(m)emnēsteumenē autō,* "engaged to him," or the equivalent. Some ancient versions (OL, Syrˢ) read rather "his wife," or the equivalent. And some mss. (A, Θ, the Koine text-tradition and the Freer family of minuscules) and other versions (Eth, Vg) read *(m)emnēsteumenē autō gynaiki,* "his engaged wife." These, however, are both attempts to tamper with what the best Lucan text has and to eliminate what might seem scandalous. Significantly, the *UBSGNT* does not even mention these variants in its *apparatus criticus;* nor has B. M. Metzger (*TCGNT,* 132) any comment on the problem. See further Brown, *Birth,* 397.

The phrase, "who was pregnant," does not give a reason for Mary's accompanying Joseph; it simply states her condition and prepares for the coming birth of Jesus in Bethlehem.

6. *While they were there.* This implies that Mary and Joseph have arrived in Bethlehem. Luke here uses *egeneto de* + finite verb, without the conj. *kai.* (see p. 119 above), lit. "it happened, in their being there, (that) the days of her giving birth were (ful)filled." In the *Prot. Jas.* 17.3, Mary begins to feel the birth pangs when they have come only "half the way," and in 18:1 the birth takes place in a cave which Joseph finds "in the region of Bethlehem."

the time came for Mary to deliver her child. Compare 1:57 and Gen 25:24 (Rebecca's giving birth to Jacob and Esau).

7. *she bore her firstborn son.* The adj. *prōtotokos* does not necessarily mean "firstborn" of many. Sometimes *monogenēs* is added to it to make this clear (*Ps. Sol.* 18:4; *2 Esdr* 6:58). What it says is merely that no child of Mary preceded Jesus and that he was entitled to have all the privileges and status of the firstborn in the Mosaic Law (see Exod 13:2; Num 3:12-13; 18:15-16; Deut 21:15-17). Luke is preparing for 2:23. Cf. Matt 1:25.

That the adj. *prōtotokos* does not necessarily imply that there were other children after this one can be seen from its extrabiblical usage. An ancient funerary inscription recalling the death of a Jewish woman, Arsinoe, dated to 5 B.C., was found in Leontopolis in Egypt. It runs: "In the pangs of giving birth

to a firstborn child, Fate brought me to the end of my life." Her death in giving birth to her firstborn shows that the adj. does not necessarily imply that
more children were born to her. See further C. C. Edgar, "More Tomb-Stones
from Tell el Yahoudieh," *ASAE* 22 (1922) 7-16; H. Lietzmann, "Jüdisch-
griechische Inschriften aus Tell el Yehudieh," *ZNW* 22 (1923) 280-286 (§21);
J.-B. Frey, "La signification du terme *prōtotokos* d'après une inscription
juive," *Bib* 11 (1930) 373-390; W. Michaelis, "*Prōtotokos, prōtotokeia*,"
TDNT 6 (1968) 871-881, esp. pp. 876-877. For a recent attempt to date Jesus'
birth, see R. T. Beckwith, *RevQ* 9 (1977-1979) 73-94.

wrapped him in cloth bands. Lit. "swaddled him," since the Greek verb
sparganoun is derived from the noun *sparganon*, "cloth band." The statement
declares Mary's maternal care; she did for Jesus what any ancient Palestinian
mother would have done for a newborn babe (see Wisd 7:4; cf. Ezek 16:4). It
is not to be understood as a sign of poverty or of the Messiah's lowly birth.
Much less is it to be used as an argument for a special mode of his birth, as
has at times been done in the debate about virginity *in partu*.

laid him in a manger. I.e. in a feeding trough for domesticated animals (see
MM, 665). It could have been in a barn or in some feeding-place under the
open sky, as the contrast with "lodge" in the rest of the verse would suggest.
However, the word *phatnē* can also mean a "stall, feeding-place" (see H. J.
Cadbury, *JBL* 45 [1926] 317-319; 53 [1933] 61-62), i.e. an enclosure where
animals might be penned, either indoors or outdoors (see Luke 13:15). The
verb *aneklinen* seems to the call for the meaning, "manger." No mention is
made of animals in this text. Their presence in the Christmas cribs of later date
is derived from Isa 1:3. The tradition of Jesus' birth in a "cave" is derived
from the *Prot. Jas.* 18.1; it is also found in Justin *Dial.* 78, and Origen *Contra
Celsum* 1.51.

no room. I.e. no space (*topos*). The implication is that Mary and Joseph
were not the only ones who have come to the town of David for the registration so that there was simply not space enough for all.

in the lodge. In Luke 22:11 *katalyma* occurs again, to denote the "guest-
room" where Jesus and his disciples eat the Last Supper. From the use there
and here it is rather obvious that it does not mean an "inn"; furthermore, Luke
uses the word *pandocheion* for that in 10:34. Actually, *katalyma*, a compound
of *kata* + *lyein*, "loose," denotes a place where one "lets down" one's harness
(or baggage) for the night. Cf. Luke 9:12; 19:7. In 1 Sam 1:18 Elkanah and
Hannah on their visit to the sanctuary of Shiloh stay in a *katalyma* (LXX),
which may have influenced Luke's expression here. It should be understood as
a public caravansary or khan, where groups of travelers would spend the night
under one roof.

8. *shepherds in the same district.* News of the birth of the Messiah is first
made known, not to religious or secular rulers of the land, but to lowly inhabitants of the area, busy with other matters. The chord of "the lowly" has already
been struck in Mary's Magnificat (1:52) and foreshadows the use of it in the
Gospel proper (see the "Q" passage in 7:22); it is part of the universalism in
the Lucan Gospel. In the background of the story is the association of David

as a boy with his father's sheep in a district near Bethlehem (1 Sam 17:15); see further the COMMENT.

who lived out-of-doors. The ptc. *agraulountes* means that the shepherds made the open fields (*agroi*) their house (*aulē,* see Luke 11:21). Attempts to date the birth of Jesus by this detail to certain months of the year have been legion, but they are more speculative than convincing.

kept night-watch. Lit. "watching the watches of the night." The cognate acc. suggests a distributive nuance: the shepherds guarded the flock in shifts. Cf. Num 3:7,8,28; 8:26 for similar expressions. The nocturnal watch of the shepherds is singled out in preparation for the shining glory of v. 9.

9. *the angel of the Lord.* See NOTE on 1:11. In this instance, he is not identified; contrast 1:19. As at times in the OT, what is here announced by "the angel of the Lord" is subsequently attributed to "the Lord" himself (see v. 15).

stood by them. The verb *ephistanai* is almost an exclusively Lucan word in the NT (see 2:38; 4:39; 10:40; 20:1; 21:34; 24:4—and often in Acts), almost always in the second aor. forms. In classical Greek it was often used of gods and heavenly beings who appear in dreams and visions (*Iliad* 10.496; 23.106; Herodotus 1.34,2; 7.14,1).

God's glory. In the LXX *doxa* translates Hebrew *kābôd,* the "splendor, brilliance," associated with Yahweh's perceptible presence to his people (Exod 16:7,10; 24:17; 40:34; Ps 63:3; cf. Num 12:8).

struck with great fear. Lit. "feared (with) a great fear," another cognate acc. (see v. 8), this time with an aor. pass. verb used intransitively (BDF § 153.1, § 313). Cf. Mark 4:41.

10. *Do not be afraid.* See 1:13,30.

I announce to you a cause for great joy. Lit. "I announce to you great joy." Luke uses here the verb *euangelizesthai;* see NOTE on 1:19. The statement begins, *idou gar,* "for behold," on which see NOTE on 1:44. The note of joy is struck again (see 1:14); such is the atmosphere that surrounds the dawn of the messianic age "for all the people" (i.e. of Israel).

11. *Savior.* The Lucan title for Jesus is put first; it had been used of Yahweh in 1:47. Now it is explicitly used of Jesus, having been implied in "the horn of salvation" (1:69). Cf. 2:30. For its meaning, see p. 204 above.

has been born to you. I.e. to the shepherds and to all the people of Israel.

today. This is the first occurrence of the adv. *sēmeron,* which will figure prominently in the rest of the Lucan Gospel (4:21; 5:26; 12:28; 13:32,33; 19:5,9; 22:34,61; 23:43). It often has the nuance of the inaugurated eschaton (see further p. 234 above), and is to be so understood proleptically here.

in the town of David. I.e. Bethlehem, as in 2:4; see NOTE there.

the Messiah, the Lord. Two further titles are added to "Savior" in the angelic announcement, traditional titles inherited by Luke from the early Palestinian Christian community before him, but now predicated by him of Jesus at his very birth. See pp. 197-204 above for a discussion of the meaning of them. They are not to be regarded as additions made by a Hellenist.

Luke actually writes here *christos kyrios,* two anarthrous nominatives. This is the reading in the best Greek mss. But some ancient versions read *christos kyriou,* "the Lord's Messiah." The latter is influenced undoubtedly by Luke 2:26 or the LXX of Lam 4:20; *Ps. Sol.* 17:32. The anarthrous form is open to another interpretation, "(the) anointed Lord," in which the first word is treated as an adj., not as a title. Since this is the only place in the NT where this phrase occurs, it has given rise to some speculation about which may have been the more original form. I prefer to remain with the reading in the best mss. and take the words as titles, because they are almost certainly a reflection of what Luke has written in Acts 2:36, where God is said to have made Jesus "Messiah and Lord" at the resurrection. The titles are now retrojected to his birth by Luke. Cf. P. Winter, *ZNW* 49 (1958) 67-75.

12. *a sign for you.* Many mss. of the Hesychian and Koine text-traditions (as well as mss. D and ⊗) add the def. art., "the sign for you." This is done under the influence of OT parallels (see the LXX of Exod 3:12; 2 Kgs 19:29; Isa 37:30; etc.; cf. 1Q27 1:5, "This is for you the sign that this will take place"). Like Zechariah (1:18-20) and Mary (1:36), the shepherds receive a sign to confirm the announcement of the angel; it is an unusual one, corresponding in no way to the signs that one might have expected of a coming Messiah.

a child. Luke uses *brephos* of the newborn child, as he did of the babe in the womb in his freely composed episode of Mary's visit to Elizabeth; contrast the use of *paidion* in the story of John's birth and circumcision, inherited from the Baptist-source. See the NOTE on *paidion* (1:59).

and lying. These words are omitted in mss. ℵ* and D.

13. *a throng of the heavenly host.* This is a variant of a LXX expression, *he stratia tou ouranou,* "the host of heaven" (1 Kgs 22:19; Jer 19:13; Hos 13:4; 2 Chr 33:3,5; cf. the pl. in Neh 9:6).

praising God. The ptc. *ainountōn* is in the gen. pl., agreeing in sense with the collective sg. *stratias,* "host" (see BDF § 134.1b). "Praising God" is also a LXX expression (see Judg 16:24 ms. A; Jdt 13:14; Ps 147:12); for angels praising God, see Ps 148:2.

14. *"Glory to God in highest heaven."* Lit. "glory in (the) highest to God." This hymnic formula is not found as such in the OT, but it is based on phrases about "giving glory" (*doxan didonai*) to God, i.e. honoring him, in such passages as Bar 2:17-18; I Esdr 9:8; 4 Macc 1:12. Cf. Rom 11:36; Heb 13:21. The glory referred to here differs from the *doxa kyriou,* "the glory of the Lord" (2:9), which expresses the perceptible manifestation of God's presence. The formula used here is, rather, close to that in *Ps. Sol.* 18:10, "Great is our God and glorious (*endoxos*), dwelling in the highest" (abodes, i.e. the heights of heaven). The prep. phrase *en hypsistois* refers, not to degree, but to God's abode (cf. Job 16:19; Ps 148:1; Sir 26:16; 43:9). It is in contrast to "earth" in the next line. The utterance is a jussive or volitive, not a mere declaration, *pace* G. Schneider (*Evangelium nach Lukas,* 67).

peace on earth. Lit. "on earth peace," making a chiastic parallelism with the first two words of the preceding line of the hymn. On the meaning of "peace," one of Luke's ways of summing up the effects of the Christ-event, see p. 224 above. Contrast 19:38.

for people whom he favors. Lit. "for human beings of (God's) good pleasure." The reading in the best mss. here is the gen. *eudokias*, "of good pleasure" (B*, ℵ*, A, D, W, and many ancient versions [including the Vg, whence the Roman Catholic tradition] and patristic citations). It is regarded by Metzger (*TCGNT*, 133) as the *lectio difficilior*. In the Koine text-tradition, ms. Θ, and some ancient versions, one finds the nom. *eudokia*.

This difference of reading led historically to two traditional renderings of the angels' song, one three-membered, the other two-membered:

> Glory to God in the highest,
> and on earth peace,
> good will toward men.
> (*KJV*, using the nom. *eudokia*)

> Glory to God in the highest.
> and on earth peace among men of good will.
> (*CCD*, using the gen. *eudokias*)

In the first form the three nouns in the nom., *doxa, eirēnē,* and *eudokia*, were used to support the structuring of the song. In the second, two-membered form, the chiastic parallelism noted above was used, even though it was not perfect; the second member is longer than the first.

In more recent times both of these renderings have been abandoned in favor of one that is almost certainly correct:

> Glory in highest heaven to God;
> and on earth peace for people whom he favors.

Thus "glory" and "peace" are parallel; "in highest heaven" and "on earth" are so too; and "God" parallels "people whom he favors." Not only is this a better parallelism, but it reckons with the better reading, gen. *eudokias*, "people *of* (*his*) *good pleasure*," i.e. toward whom he manifests his good pleasure, his predilection.

Some reasons for translating *eudokia* as referring to God's "good pleasure" can be mentioned: (a) The term has been subject to recent restudy because it has always been apparent that the difference between the "good will" of the traditional two-membered and three-membered forms of the song were being heard with the overtones of the Reformation/Counter-Reformation debate. (b) J. Jeremias ("*Anthrōpoi eudokias* (Lc 2.14)," *ZNW* 28 [1929] 13-20), on the basis of the LXX translation of Hebrew *rāṣôn* and its cognates by *eudokia* and its cognates (e.g. Ps 51:18), argued that *eudokia* must also refer here to God's "good pleasure." (c) Luke himself uses the word *eudokia* in this sense in 10:21, "Indeed, Father, this was your good pleasure." (d) C.-H. Hunzinger ("Neues Licht auf Lc 2.14 *anthrōpoi eudokias*," *ZNW* 44 [1952-1953] 85-90; see also *ZNW* 49 [1958] 129-130) called attention to Hebrew parallels to the Lucan expression in some Qumran texts: 1QH 4:32-33, *bĕnê rĕṣônô*, "sons of his good will"; 1QH 11:9, *lĕkôl bĕnê rĕṣônĕkā*, "for all the sons of your good pleasure"; possibly also in 4QpPs^a 1-2 ii 24-25, if Allegro's restoration is accepted [*pišrô 'al 'anšê*] *rēṣôn*[*ô*], "[the interpretation of it concerns the people of his] good pleasure." (e) I discovered the same phrase in both an Aramaic

Qumran text, 4Qḥ'Aᶜ 18, *be'ĕnōš rē'ût[ēh]*, "among men of [his] good pleasure," and in the Sahidic translation of Luke 2:14, *hᵉn ᵉnrōme ᵉmpefwōš*, "among men of his pleasure" (see " 'Peace upon Earth among Men of His Good Will' (Lk 2:14)," *ESBNT*, 101-104.

This evidence makes it clear that the angels' song dealt neither with the "good will" to be manifested on earth by human beings toward one another (so the *KJV*), nor with the "good will" as the disposition required of human beings to be recipients of the peace (so the *CCD*), nor even with the "good will" or esteem that some people might enjoy among others (Tatian and the Peshitta [see R. Köbert, *Bib* 42 (1961) 90-91]). Rather, *eudokia* was to be understood of God's "good pleasure," and the complete phrase, *anthrōpoi eudokias*, as "people whom God has favored," i.e. with his grace or predilection.

A remote parallel has been found in an ancient Ugaritic text, *'Anat* 3.10*ff*, "Pour out peace over the earth, loving consideration over the fields" (see A. Goetze, *BASOR* 93 [1944] 17-20). Cf. *ANET*, 136.

15. *When the angels had left them . . . said.* Lit. "and it happened, when the angels left them for heaven, (that) the shepherds said. . . ." Luke uses *kai egeneto* + finite verb, without the conj. *kai* (see p. 119 above). The Koine text-tradition and ms. D read, *kai hoi anthrōpoi*, "that the men," instead of "the shepherds," thus restoring the conj. *kai* before the finite verb. In any case, the sense remains the same.

see this thing that has taken place. The term *rēma*, "word, thing" occurs here again; see NOTES on 1:37 and 38. Cf. 1:65. The Vg. translates: *Videamus hoc verbum quod factum est*, preserving the Semitism, which is impossible in English.

which the Lord has made known to us. I.e. Yahweh (see NOTE on 2:9). The verb *gnōrizein*, "make known," has here both a dir. and indir. obj., as in Acts 2:28 (=Ps 16:11); cf. Acts 7:13.

16. *they came in haste.* Lit. "hurrying," expressed by a circumstantial (modal) ptc., in the aor. tense of *speudein* (BDF § 418.5).

found Mary and Joseph, and the baby lying in the manger. Nothing is said here about how the baby (*brephos*) was conceived. In fact, if we had this story only, there would be no hint of Mary's virginal conception. This is part of the independence of chap. 2 from chap. 1 in the infancy narrative. See further the COMMENT.

lying in the manger. In contrast to v. 12, the Greek text does have a def. art. here.

17. *they made known.* I.e. to Mary and Joseph, and undoubtedly to inhabitants of Bethlehem too. According to the Lucan story thus far, Mary knows that her child is to be the Davidic Messiah (1:32-35) and that he has been recognized as "Lord" (1:43). To these identifications the shepherds add that he is to be "the Savior" (2:11). Here the "child" is referred to as *paidion*.

18. *all who heard of it.* I.e. among the inhabitants of Bethlehem. So it should be understood in the immediate context. Cf. 1:66, where something similar is said of John, and the crucial question is asked, "Now what is this child to be-

come?" Explicitly formulated about John, it is implied by Luke that it will be asked of Jesus. Hence the wonder.

wondered. Or "were surprised." Compare 1:21,63; 2:33.

19. *but Mary treasured all these things.* Lit. "preserved all these words (or things, *rēmata*)," i.e. the arrival of the shepherds on the scene and the things that they told her. Contrast the content of what she is said to preserve in 2:51; here at least there is something extraordinary. In these two verses one meets with refrain C (see the outline of the infancy narrative, p. 314 above). The verb *syntērein* is complemented by a slightly different compound form in v. 51, *diatērein*, "keep, cherish." The latter is used in the LXX of Gen 37:11, where, after Joseph, having told about his dream of the wheat sheaves, incurred the wrath of his brothers, his father is said to have "cherished the saying" (or thing, *rēma*). In Dan 4:28 the LXX has a slightly different text from the Aramaic of 4:25; not only is the verse-number off, but the Greek is fuller: "At the end of the words Nebuchadnezzar, as he heard the judgment of the vision, treasured these words in his heart" (*tous logous en tē kardia synetērēse*). Both the Genesis and Daniel passages show a person puzzled by what he has heard, keeping the words in mind in an effort to fathom their meaning. This too would be the picture of Mary here, as the next phrase makes clear.

pondered over them. Lit. "tossing them together in her heart." The verb *symballein* is used solely by Luke in the NT, but in every other instance it has a meaning that does not suit this passage. In Acts 4:15 it means "to converse, confer," and possibly also in Acts 17:18, where another meaning has also been suggested, viz. "to meet." In Luke 14:31 it means "to meet" in a hostile sense (and again in a variant of 11:53, "quarrel"). In Acts 18:27 the middle voice of the verb occurs in the sense of "coming to the aid" of someone. Yet none of these meanings suits the context of Luke 2:19. Josephus uses it of a dream (*Ant.* 2.5,3 § 72), whose import Joseph sought to learn. W. C. van Unnik studied the occurrences of the verb in many Hellenistic Greek texts and maintains that the sense there is "to hit upon the right meaning." If this were the meaning, the Lucan text would ascribe to Mary comprehension of the significance of the words of the shepherds. Not everyone has accepted van Unnik's data, because it seems to make the verse say more than is really intended (see Brown, *Birth*, 406; *MNT*, 150). The ptc. *symballousa* is circumstantial to the main verb *synetērei*, an impf. (see BDF §§ 417-418), the conative force of which it may share, "trying to hit upon their right meaning." See BDF § 326. Cf. W. C. van Unnik, "Die rechte Bedeutung des Wortes treffen, Lukas II 19," in his *Sparsa collecta: The Collected Essays of W. C. van Unnik* (NovTSup 29; Leiden: Brill, 1973) 1. 72-91.

20. *The shepherds returned.* Refrain A recurs (see 1:23,38,56; 2:40,51).

glorifying God and praising him. The reaction of the shepherds is an echo of the song of the angels (vv. 13-14). Forms of the two verbs are found together in the LXX of Dan 3:26,55.

because they had seen and heard. Lit. "for all which they had heard and seen." The same two verbs occur again in Acts 4:20. This is not to be used as the basis of an attempt to isolate a shepherds' account of this incident.

BIBLIOGRAPHY (2:1-20)

Baily, M. "The Crib and the Exegesis of Luke 2,1-20," *Irish Ecclesiastical Record* 100 (1963) 358-376.

———— "The Shepherds and the Sign of a Child in a Manger: Lk 2:1-20 and I Sam. c. 16," *ITQ* 31 (1964) 1-23.

Beckwith, R. T. "St. Luke, the Date of Christmas and the Priestly Courses at Qumran," *RevQ* 9 (1977-1979) 73-94.

Benoit, P. "'Non erat eis locus in diversorio' (Lc 2,7)," *Mélanges bibliques en hommage du R. P. Béda Rigaux* (eds. A. Descamps and A. de Halleux; Gembloux: Duculot, 1970) 173-186.

Brown, R. E. "The Meaning of the Manger: The Significance of the Shepherds," *Worship* 50 (1976) 528-538.

de Jonge, M. "The Use of the Word 'Anointed' in the Time of Jesus," *NovT* 8 (1966) 132-148.

Derrett, J. D. M. "The Manger at Bethlehem: Light on St. Luke's Technique from Contemporary Jewish Religious Law," *SE VI* (TU 112; Berlin: Akademie, 1973) 86-94.

———— "The Manger: Ritual Law and Soteriology," *Theology* 74 (1971) 566-571.

Dulière, W. L. "Inventaire de quarante-et-un porteurs du nom de Jésus dans l'histoire juive écrite en grec: Un Jésus d'Ananos prédisant la ruine du Temple—Jésus, nom de lieu," *NovT* 3 (1959) 180-217.

Ehrenberg, V., "*Imperium maius* in the Roman Republic," *AJP* 74 (1953) 113-136.

Förster, M. "Nochmals Jesu Geburt in einer Höhle," *ZNW* 4 (1903) 186-187.

Frey, J.-B. "La signification du terme *prōtotokos* d'après une inscription juive," *Bib* 11 (1930) 373-390.

Giblin, C. H. "Reflections on the Sign of the Manger," *CBQ* 29 (1967) 87-101.

Goetz, K. G. "Zum Herdenturm von Bethlehem," *ZNW* 8 (1907) 70-71.

Guillet, J. "'Marie gardait toutes ces paroles dans son coeur,'" *Christus* 3 (1954) 50-59.

Hengel, M. "*Phatnē*," *TDNT* 9 (1974) 49-55.

Jeremias, J. "*Poimēn . . . ,*" *TDNT* 6 (1968) 485-502.

Jones, D. L. "The Title *Christos* in Luke-Acts," *CBQ* 32 (1970) 69-76.

Kasteren, J. van. "Analecta exegetica," *RB* os 3 (1894) 56-57 (on 2:7), 58-61 (on 2:14).

Legrand, L. "L'Evangile aux bergers: Essai sur le genre littéraire de Luc, II, 8-20," *RB* 75 (1968) 161-187.

McNamara, E. A. "'Because There Was No Room for Them in the Inn,'" *AER* 105 (1941) 433-443.

Meyer, B. F. "'But Mary Kept All These Things . . . ,' (Lk 2, 19.51)," *CBQ* 26 (1964) 31-49.

Miguens, M. "'In una mangiatoia, perchè non c'era posto . . . ,'" *BeO* 2 (1960) 193-198.

Nestle, E. "Die Hirten von Bethlehem," *ZNW* 7 (1906) 257-259.

Pax, E. "'Denn sie fanden keinen Platz in der Herberge': Jüdisches und frühchristliches Herbergswesen," *BibLeb* 6 (1965) 285-298.

Preuschen, E. "Jesu Geburt in einer Höhle," *ZNW* 3 (1902) 359-360.

Ramsay, W. M. "Luke's Narrative of the Birth of Christ," *Expos* 8/4 (1912) 385-407, 481-507.

Schmithals, W. "Die Weihnachtsgeschichte Lukas 2,1-20," *Festschrift für Ernst Fuchs* (eds. G. Ebeling et al.; Tübingen: Mohr [Siebeck], 1973) 281-297.

Schürmann, H. "'Sie gebar ihren erstgeborenen Sohn . . .': Lk 2, 1-20 als Beispiel homologetischer Geschichtsschreibung," in *Ursprung und Gestalt* (Düsseldorf: Patmos, 1970) 217-221.

Unnik, W. C. van. "Die rechte Bedeutung des Wortes treffen Lukas 2,19," in *Verbum—Essays on Some Aspects of the Religious Function of Words: Dedicated to Dr. H. W. Obbink* (eds. T. B. van Baaren et al.; Utrecht: Kemink, 1964) 129-147; reprinted in his *Sparsa Collecta: The Collected Essays of W. C. van Unnik* (NovTSup 29; Leiden: Brill, 1973) 1. 72-91.

Vaccari, A. "De vi circumcisionis in Veteri Foedere," *VD* 2 (1922) 14-18.

Westermann, C. "Alttestamentliche Elemente in Lukas 2,1-20," in *Tradition und Glaube: Das Frühe Christentum in seiner Umwelt: Festgabe für Karl Georg Kuhn zum 65. Geburtstag* (eds. G. Jeremias et al.; Göttingen: Vandenhoeck und Ruprecht, 1971) 317-327.

Bibliography on the Census of Quirinius

Accame, S. "Il primo censimento della Giudea," *Rivista di filologia e di istruzione classica* 72-73 (1944-1945) 138-170.

Barnett, P. W. "*Apographē* and *apographesthai* in Luke 2:1-5," *ExpTim* 85 (1973-1974) 377-380.

Benoit, P. "Quirinius (Recensement de)," *DBS* 9 (1978) 693-720.

Bleckmann, F. "Die erste syrische Statthalterschaft des P. Sulpicius Quirinius," *Klio* 17 (1921) 104-112.

Braunert, H. "Der römische Provinzialzensus und der Schätzungsbericht des Lukas-Evangeliums," *Historia* 6 (1957) 192-214.

Corbishley, T. "A Note on the Date of the Syrian Governorship of M. Titius," *JRS* 24 (1934) 43-49.

——— "Quirinius and the Census: A Re-study of the Evidence," *Klio* 29 (1936) 81-93.

Dessau, H. "Zu den neuen Inschriften des Sulpicius Quirinius," *Klio* 17 (1921) 252-258.

Evans, C. F. "Tertullian's References to Sentius Saturninus and the Lukan Census," *JTS* 24 (1973) 24-39.

Grenfell, B. P., and A. S. Hunt. eds. *The Oxyrhynchus Papyri* (London: Egypt Exploration Fund) 2 (1899) 207-214 (=POxy 254, "Census Return"— *apographai kat' oikian*).

Groag, E. "P. Sulpicius Quirinius," PW 2d ser., 4/A1. 822-843.

Instinsky, H. U. *Das Jahr der Geburt Christi: Eine geschichtswissenschaftliche Studie* (Munich: Kösel, 1957).

Lagrange, M.-J. "Où en est la question du recensement de Quirinius?" *RB* 8 (1911) 60-84.

Lazzarato, D. *Chronologia Christi seu discordantium fontium concordantia ad iuris normam* (Naples: M. d'Auria, 1952) 44 n. 7 (older bibliography).

Lodder, W. *Die Schätzung des Quirinius bei Flavius Josephus: Eine Untersuchung* (Leipzig: Dörffling und Franke, 1930).

Marquardt, J. *Römische Staatsverwaltung* (3d ed.; 3 vols.; Darmstadt: Wissenschaftliche Buchgesellschaft, 1957) 2. 180-246.

Moehring, H. R. "The Census in Luke as an Apologetic Device," in *Studies in New Testament and Early Christian Literature: Essays in Honor of Allen P. Wikgren* (ed. D. E. Aune; NovTSup 33; Leiden: Brill, 1972) 144-160.

Mommsen, T. "De Sulpicii Quirinii Titulo Tiburtino," in *Res gestae divi Augusti ex monumentis ancyrano et apolloniensi* (2d ed.; Berlin: Weidmann, 1883) 161-178; reprinted: Aalen: Scientia, 1970.

———— *Römisches Staatsrecht* (3d ed.; Graz: Akademische Druck- und Verlagsanstalt, 1952), 2/1. 415-417. 2/2. 1087-1095.

Murphy, F. X. "The Date of Christ's Birth: Present State of the Question," *CHR* 29 (1943) 307-325.

Nestle, E. "Die Schatzung in Lukas 2 und Psalm 87(86),6," *ZNW* 11 (1910) 87.

Ogg, G. "The Quirinius Question To-day," *ExpTim* 79 (1967-1968) 231-236.

Ramsay, W. M. *The Bearing of Recent Discovery on the Trustworthiness of the New Testament* (4th ed.; London: Hodder & Stoughton, 1920) 238-300.

Schalit, A. *König Herodes: Der Mann und sein Werk* (Studia judaica 4; Berlin; de Gruyter, 1969) 265-282.

Schürer, E. *The History of the Jewish People in the Age of Jesus Christ (175 B.C.-A.D. 135)* (rev. ed.; eds. G. Vermes et al.; Edinburgh: Clark), 1 (1973) 399-427 (older bibliography, 399-400).

Sherwin-White, A. N. "Quirinius: A Note," in *Roman Society and Roman Law in the New Testament* (The Sarum Lectures 1960-1961; Oxford: Clarendon, 1963; reprinted, 1965) 162-171.

Smallwood, E. M. *The Jews under Roman Rule: From Pompey to Diocletian* (SJLA 20; Leiden: Brill, 1976) 568-571.

Stauffer, E. "Die Dauer des Census Augusti: Neue Beiträge zum lukanischen Schatzungsbericht," in *Studien zum Neuen Testament und zur Patristik: E. Klostermann . . . dargebracht* (TU 77; ed. G. Delling; Berlin: Akademie, 1961) 9-34.

———— *Jesus and His Story* (New York: A. A. Knopf, 1960) 21-32.

Steinmetzer, F. X. "Census," *RAC* 2 (1954) 969-972.

Syme, R. "Galatia and Pamphylia under Augustus: The Governorships of Piso, Quirinius and Silvanus," *Klio* 27 (1934) 122-148.

———— "The Titulus Tiburtinus," in *Akten des vi. internationalen Kongresses für griechische und lateinische Epigraphik, München 1972* (Vestigia, Beiträge zur alten Geschichte 17; Munich: Beck, 1973) 585-601.

Taylor, L. R. "Quirinius and the Census of Judaea," *AJP* 54 (1933) 120-133.

Weber, W. "Der Census des Quirinius nach Josephus," *ZNW* 10 (1909) 307-319.

Wilcken, U. *"Apographai," Hermes* 28 (1893) 230-251.

Bibliography on the Gloria

Bishop, E. F. F. "Men of God's Good Pleasure," *ATR* 48 (1966) 63-69.

Bover, J. M. " 'Pax hominibus *bonae voluntatis'* (Lc. 2,14)," *EstBíb* 7 (1948) 441-449.

Deichgräber, R. "Lc 2,14: *anthrōpoi eudokias," ZNW* 51 (1960) 132.

Feuillet, A. "Les hommes de bonne volonté ou les hommes que Dieu aime: Note sur la traduction de Luc 2,14b," *Bulletin de l'association Guillaume Budé* 4 (1974) 91-92.

Fitzmyer, J. A. " 'Peace upon Earth among Men of His Good Will' (Luke 2:14)," *TS* 19 (1958) 225-227; reprinted in *ESBNT,* 101-104.

Flusser, D. "Sanktus und Gloria," in *Abraham unser Vater: Festschrift Otto Michel* (ed. O. Betz et al.; Leiden: Brill, 1963) 129-152.

Goetze, A. "Peace on Earth," *BASOR* 93 (1944) 17-20 (ancient Ugaritic parallel).

Hansack, E. "Luk 2,14: 'Friede den Menschen auf Erden, die guten Willens sind'? Ein Beitrag zur Übersetzungstechnik der Vulgata," *BZ* 21 (1977) 117-118.

Hunzinger, C.-H. "Ein weiterer Beleg zu Lc 2,14 *anthrōpoi eudokias," ZNW* 49 (1958) 129-130.

———— "Neues Licht auf Lc 2,14 *anthrōpoi eudokias," ZNW* 44 (1952-1953) 85-90.

Jeremias, J. *"Anthrōpoi eudokias* (Lc 2,14)," *ZNW* 28 (1929) 13-20.

Rad, G. von. "Noch einmal Lc 2,14 *anthrōpoi eudokias," ZNW* 29 (1930) 111-115.

Ropes, J. H. " 'Good Will toward Men' (Luke 2,14)," *HTR* 10 (1917) 52-56.

Rusche, H. " 'Et in terra pax hominibus bonae voluntatis': Erklärung, Deutung und Betrachtung zum Engelchor in Lk 2,14," *BibLeb* 2 (1961) 229-234.

Schwarz, G. "Der Lobgesang der Engel (Lukas 2,14): Emendation und Rückübersetzung," *BZ* 15 (1971) 260-264.

Vogt, E. " 'Peace among Men of God's Good Pleasure' Lk. 2,14," in *The Scrolls and the New Testament* (ed. K. Stendahl; New York: Harper, 1957) 114-117.

Walker, N. "The Renderings of *Rāṣôn," JBL* 81 (1962) 182-184.

Wobbe. J. "Das Gloria (Lk 2,14)," *BZ* 22 (1934) 118-152, 224-245; 23 (1935-1936) 358-364.

8. THE CIRCUMCISION AND MANIFESTATION OF JESUS
(2:21-40)

2 ²¹ When eight days had passed, it was time to circumcise the child, and he was called Jesus. This was the name given to him by the angel before he was conceived in the womb.

²² When the days of their purification according to the Mosaic Law had passed, they brought him up to Jerusalem to present him to the Lord—²³ as it is written in the Law of the Lord, *"Every male that opens the womb* is to be considered *sacred*[a] to the Lord"*—²⁴ and to offer a sacrifice as is prescribed in the Law of the Lord: *"a pair of turtledoves or two young pigeons."*[b]

²⁵ Now there was at that time in Jerusalem a man named Simeon who was upright and devout, living in expectation of the consolation of Israel, and the holy Spirit was with him. ²⁶ He had been informed by the holy Spirit that he would not see death until he had seen the Lord's Messiah. ²⁷ He now came, guided by the Spirit, into the Temple area. As the parents brought in their child Jesus, to perform for him what was customary under the Law, ²⁸ Simeon took him in his arms and blessed God, saying,

> ²⁹ Now you may dismiss your servant, Lord, in
> peace, according to your promise,
> ³⁰ for my eyes *have seen your salvation,* Isa 40:5
> ³¹ made ready by you in the sight of all peoples,
> ³² *a light* to give revelation *to the Gentiles* and Isa 49:6
> glory to your people Israel.

³³ The child's father and mother were surprised at what was being said about him. ³⁴ Then Simeon blessed them and said to his mother Mary, "Look, this child is marked for the fall and the rise of many in Israel, to be a symbol that will be rejected—³⁵ indeed, a sword shall pierce you too—so that the thoughts of many minds will be laid bare."

³⁶ There was also a prophetess there, Anna, daughter of Phanuel, of the tribe of Asher. She was well along in years, having lived with her

[a] Exod 13:2 [b] Lev 12:8

husband after her marriage for seven years, 37 and had been a widow for eighty-four years. She never left the Temple area, but worshiped day and night with fasting and prayer. 38 At that very time she too came up and publicly praised God; she spoke about the child to all who were waiting for the deliverance of Jerusalem.

39 When they had finished all that was required by the Law of the Lord, they returned to Galilee and their own town of Nazareth. 40 And as the child grew up, he became strong; he was filled with wisdom, and God's favor was upon him.

COMMENT

The infancy narrative continues in the spirit of traditional Jewish piety. This episode tells of the circumcision, naming, and manifestation of Jesus and is the parallel to the circumcision, naming, and manifestation of John (1:59-80). There are two main parts to the episode and a conclusion. The first consists of a double prelude to the manifestation. The first prelude is found in v. 21, which mentions the circumcision and naming of the child. The second prelude is found in vv. 22-24, which describe the purification of Mary and the presentation of Jesus. Both of these lead into the second main part, the double manifestation of Jesus to Simeon (vv. 25-35) and to Anna (vv. 36-38). The concluding vv. 39-40 pick up refrains of the infancy narrative.

Some commentators would separate v. 21 from this whole episode and attach it to the story of the birth of Jesus in Bethlehem (so H. Schürmann, *Lukasevangelium,* 97-98; R. E. Brown, *Birth,* 394, 407), making vv. 22-40 simply the presentation of Jesus. This separation, however, tones down the parallelism of the John/Jesus stories in the infancy narrative.

Verse 21 is redactional, most clearly in its reference to the scene of the announcement of Jesus' birth by the angel to Mary (1:31), and in its parallelism to 1:59-63. Above we raised the question of separating 1:57-58 from 1:59-80 (p. 372). If one were to keep them closely related, then there would be all the more reason to link 2:21 to 2:22-40. As in 1:59 the circumcision and naming of John occasion the manifestation of the child and the prophetic utterance of Zechariah, his father, so too here. The naming of Jesus is given more stress in v. 21 than the circumcision, and his naming does not cause all the discussion that John's did. The step-parallelism is in evidence here when it is said that he is given a heaven-imposed name, which is not said in John's case, even though that was the origin of his name too. The step-parallelism is further in evidence in that there is the double rather than the single prelude for the eventual manifestation of Jesus. This will take place in the context of his presentation in the Jerusalem Temple—an event separate from the circumcision and naming.

The manifestation itself is made on two levels: (a) to Simeon, from whom a double pronouncement is evoked, a canticle and an oracle; and (b) to Anna, the "prophetess," who goes about spreading word of this child. The whole scene does not presuppose the birth episode that precedes (2:1-20) so much as it does the story of the circumcision, naming, and manifestation of John. If the circumcision and naming of John caused a reaction among people, how much more do the circumcision and naming of Jesus? That is the thrust of the parallel. Moreover, it should be noted that Brown does not list v. 21 under his "reactions" to the birth of Jesus, which he has restricted to vv. 15-20, despite the attachment of v. 21 to the preceding (*Birth,* 410). For these reasons I prefer to regard vv. 21-40 as a unit in the infancy narrative, along with J. M. Creed, *The Gospel,* 37; A. Plummer, *Gospel,* 61; J. Ernst, *Evangelium nach Lukas,* 112; G. Schneider, *Evangelium nach Lukas,* 69.

Some scholars have thought that vv. 21-40 may have existed in a different form at one time. The references to Jesus' "parents" (v. 27b) and his "father and mother" (v. 33), along with the notice about their "surprise" at what was being said, coming as it does on the heels of an announcement to Mary in chap. 1 and of the shepherds' revelation to them (2:17), make some commentators think that possibly the story existed in an earlier form. There is no solid reason to think that the presentation story was really part of the Baptist-source at one time and that it has been shifted to Jesus by Luke. The details in it resemble features of the story of Samuel from 1 Samuel 1-2 and lead one to realize that Luke is writing his story in imitation of the Samuel story. The canticle of Simeon, however, is another matter. That may well have been added by Luke at the secondary stage of his composition of the infancy narrative, as Brown (*Birth,* 454) has argued. It is, however, unclear whether this canticle is derived from the same early Jewish-Christian circle as the Magnificat and Benedictus. Brown argues plausibly that the transition from v. 27 to v. 34 is smooth. On the other hand, Schneider (*Evangelium nach Lukas,* 70) toys with the idea that 2:6-7 was originally followed by 2:22-38. This, however, is unlikely, since v. 21 would almost have to be included, and again the canticle in vv. 28-33 would have to be omitted. In any case, one does detect signs that the story could have been composed in a more coherent fashion.

In v. 21 the circumcision and naming of Jesus are recounted. Jesus is marked, as was John, with the sign of the covenant (Gen 17:11) and incorporated into Israel (cf. Josh 5:2-9). He is given a heaven-imposed name, Jesus; the stress falls on the naming rather than on the circumcision.

In vv. 22-24 two events are recounted that occasion the eventual manifestation of Jesus: (a) the purification of Mary, forty days after Jesus' birth (v. 22a,24); and (b) the redeeming of Jesus, the firstborn, a month after his birth (vv. 22b,23). The redeeming is treated by (the Syrian) Luke as the presentation of Jesus in the Temple, with no mention being made of the payment of the five shekels. For, as the NOTES on 2:22b make clear, there is no evidence of a regulation requiring the presentation of the firstborn in either the OT or the Mishnah. This scene has become a presentation in imitation of the presentation of Samuel in 1 Sam 1:22-24. It may also be partly motivated by Luke's desire to explain something about birth practices in Palestinian Judaism to his predominantly Gentile readership. It should further be noted that Luke depicts Mary offering a pair of turtledoves and two young pigeons; one of the pair of birds was, according to Lev 16:6, a sin-offering. Despite some later mariological speculation, Luke thinks that Mary had to be purified after the birth of Jesus.

What is operative in vv. 22-24 is a stress on the fidelity of Mary and Joseph, as devout and pious Jews, to all the requirements of the Mosaic Law. They carry out on behalf of Jesus all the things that Luke thought were required by that Law for the birth of a child. In these verses the Law is mentioned three times (vv. 22a,23a,24a), and it will be referred to later in the manifestation to Simeon (v. 27) and in the conclusion of the episode (v. 39). The NOTES on these verses call attention to certain problems in them (to whom does "their" in v. 22 refer? what was the presentation? do the datings since birth that are involved [forty days, one month] fit together?). These problems make it highly unlikely that Luke has been dependent here on accurate information, let alone on Mary's recollections. His aim is to stress fidelity to the Mosaic Law. The new form of God's salvation comes with obedience to this Law.

In vv. 25-35 we meet the first manifestation of Jesus, to Simeon, a devout, upright, and aged Jew, apparently of a non-priestly family, who reminds one not only of the aged priest Eli in the Samuel story of 1 Samuel 1-2, but also of Zechariah in the John the Baptist story. Just as the greatness of John was predicted by Zechariah in the Benedictus, so now the greatness of Jesus will be hymned by Simeon. Because of the step-parallelism, however, Simeon utters a double pronouncement, a canticle in vv. 29-32 and an oracle in vv. 34-35.

Simeon is described not only as upright and devout, but as one living in expectation of the consolation of Israel. Though the expression as such, "the consolation of Israel," does not occur in the OT, it is an allusion to the Book of Consolation in Deutero-Isaiah (see NOTE on 2:25). Both the consolation of Israel and the redemption/deliverance of Jerusalem (v. 38) are the message of the herald of good news in Isa 52:9. Recall too the heralds of Deutero-Isaiah, masculine in 41:27 and 52:7 (for Simeon) and feminine in 40:9 (for Anna).

Moreover, Simeon is described as particularly endowed with God's holy Spirit, which has made known to him that he would not die until he had seen the Lord's Messiah. Guided by that same Spirit to come to the Temple area at the right time, he takes the child from Mary and pronounces his canticle. He is made to recognize the new form of salvation that has come in the birth of this child.

The canticle of Simeon, the Nunc Dimittis, is composed of three distichs (vv. 29,30-31,32). In uttering his canticle, Simeon casts himself in the role of a servant-watchman, posted to wait for the arrival of someone. He praises God as "Lord," using of him the title *despotēs* (voc. *despota*), which is sometimes the translation of *Yhwh* in the LXX and is often used by Jewish writers composing in Greek to refer to Yahweh. He sings of his release from duty, using the expression found in the OT, "to release someone in peace." But more importantly, he recognizes in Jesus the promised bearer of messianic peace, salvation, and light. These are to be revealed through him to the Gentiles and unto the glory of Israel, but they are said to have been made ready for "all peoples," Israel and the Gentiles alike. Here Luke associates with the presentation of Mary's firstborn the effects of the Christ-event; contrast the linking of peace with the death of Jesus in Eph 2:14-16. This tie is part of Luke's tendency to manifest the growing early Christian awareness that these effects were to be retrojected to the beginning of Jesus' earthly existence. We do not have, however, an "Incarnation-soteriology," *pace* Schneider (*Evangelium nach Lukas,* 72), since Luke nowhere manifests the Johannine idea of Jesus' incarnation.

The Nunc Dimittis makes an advance over the Song of Angels at the birth of Jesus (2:14) in that the birth is now related not only to the welfare of Israel (2:32b), but salvation is now announced in the sight of all peoples, the Gentiles as well as Israel (2:32a).

The second pronouncement that Simeon makes is the oracle addressed to Mary (vv. 34bc-35ab). Mary is singled out here in imitation of Hannah in 1 Samuel, who plays a more important role in the presentation of Samuel. In its tone the oracle is ominous and looks to the future. It describes the child as a source of division in Israel, and foreshadows the saying of Jesus himself in 12:51-53, about his setting father against son and son against father, mother against daughter and daughter against mother, etc.: "This child is marked for the fall and the rise of many in Israel." The ominous note is found in that "the fall" precedes "the rise." This is, in fact, Luke's way of expressing the scandal of the cross, the stumbling block. Luke has been castigated for not having expressed the Pauline theology of the cross (see 1 Cor 1:18,23). The critical character of the child's mission is just as sharply expressed here and the force of the language should not be overlooked. The rejection of Jesus by his own people is already announced in the infancy narrative; and the chord now struck will be orchestrated in many ways in the Gospel proper (see e.g. 4:29; 13:33-35; 19:44,47-48; 20:14,17). He is the symbol to be rejected, like Isaiah and his children of old (8:18).

Mary too will be caught in this critical aspect of his mission. For the discriminating sword (see NOTE on 2:35a) will pierce her soul too. She will learn what division can come into a family by the role that her son is to play, for her relation to him will be not merely maternal but one transcending such familial ties, viz. that of the faithful disciple. Simeon's words to Mary about the sword foreshadow, in effect, Jesus' answer to the woman who uttered a beatitude over Mary for having given birth to such a son; he replied, "Blessed rather are those who hear the word of God and observe it" (11:28; cf. 8:21).

Verse 35b is to be understood as the continuation of v. 34bc, with the saying about the discriminatory sword in v. 35a being directed solely to Mary (in the second sing.). The "thoughts" that will be laid bare are those hostile or antagonistic thoughts that will cause human beings to resist the ministry of Jesus itself.

As elsewhere in the Gospel, Luke here pairs off his dramatis personae in terms of man and woman (compare Zechariah and Mary in the announcement scenes, Simon the Pharisee and the sinful woman in chap. 7, the widow of Zarephath and Naaman in chap. 4); so too here. The pronouncement about the future greatness of John came from Zechariah, his father, in his canticle, the Benedictus. Now the pronouncement of the greatness of Jesus comes not only from the aged, venerable Simeon, but also from an aged widow, the prophetess Anna. The step-parallelism is at work, and it involves a man and a woman. However, Anna is not made to utter any pronouncement; her herald's role is rather to spread the word about this child acknowledged by Simeon.

She is to do this to those who await the deliverance or redemption of Jerusalem. Recall the description of Simeon above, and the references to the heralds of Second Isaiah.

The concluding verses (39-40) echo refrains already found in the infancy narrative (see details in the NOTES).

NOTES

2 21. *When eight days had passed.* Lit. "and when (the) eight days of circumcising him were (ful)filled." For the eighth day, see NOTE on 1:59. Luke has referred to filling up days/time in 1:23,57; 2:6,22; the phrase simply means that the time set for a certain activity had come.

The best mss. here read the masc. pronoun, *auton,* "him," but ms. D has rather *to paidion,* "the child," which is perhaps demanded by the sense of the context, but is for that reason suspect as a copyist's improvement. My translation, "the child," is not a preference for ms. D, but a concession to clarity in English.

Through the circumcision Jesus, the Messiah, is made subject to the Law; but Luke does not exploit this aspect of it. Cf. Gal 4:4.

he was called Jesus. Lit. "his name was called Jesus"; see Notes on 1:31,59. This verse provides a link with the second episode in the infancy narrative, the announcement of the birth of Jesus to Mary. Stress is put here more on the naming of Jesus than on his circumcision; contrast the elaborate story of the naming of John in 1:59-80, where no emphasis was given to the heaven-imposed name. We are not told which parent named Jesus.

22. *When the days of their purification . . . had passed.* Lit. "and when the days of their purification were (ful)filled." See Note on 2:21; the time had come for the rite of purification.

The reading *autōn,* "their," is attested in the best Greek mss. (ℵ, B, etc.). To whom would it refer? Mary and Joseph? Mary and Jesus? Since there was no requirement for a purification of the husband, copyists have altered the text: *autou,* "his" (i.e. Jesus' purification) is found in ms. D and some ancient versions; the OS and Vg read a form that could be understood as either "his" or "her" (*eius*). Understood as "his," the correction, like the *autou* reading, makes no sense, since there was no requirement that the newborn child be purified. Understood as "her," it is an obvious correction based on Lev 12:4 (see next Note), which cannot be preferred to the *lectio difficilior,* "their." See further W. H. P. Hatch, *HTR* 14 (1921) 377-381.

The pron., "their," must be understood to refer to Joseph and Mary because of the main verb *anēgagon,* "they (i.e. his parents) brought him up." But since the time of Origen, commentators have tried to make "their" refer to Mary and Jesus (so, e.g. Creed, *The Gospel,* 39), despite the difficulty mentioned above. What has to be recognized is that Luke, not being a Palestinian Jewish Christian, is not accurately informed about this custom of the purification of a woman after childbirth. It is also an indication that his information is not derived from Mary's recollections or memoirs—which might be presumed to have got the matter correct.

according to the Mosaic Law. This is the first of several references to the Mosaic Law that run through the episode; see vv. 23,24,27,39. According to Lev 12:2-8 a woman who bore a male child was considered unclean for forty days; after seven days the child had to be circumcised (on the eighth), and the mother had to wait at home for thirty-three days, "until the days of her purifying were completed" (*heōs an plērōthōsin hai hēmerai katharseōs autēs,* 12:4), before she could touch anything sacred or enter the Temple courts. The time was doubled for a female child, fourteen + sixty-six days. After the fortieth (or eightieth) day she was to bring to a priest serving that week in the tent/Temple a one-year old lamb for a whole burnt offering (or holocaust) and a young pigeon or turtledove for a sin-offering to make expiation. If she could not afford the lamb, then she was to offer two turtledoves or two young pigeons.

they brought him up. I.e. Mary and Joseph, or his "parents," as they are called in v. 27, bringing him from Bethlehem presumably, unless we are to think that Joseph and Mary had returned to Nazareth in the meantime. Nazareth is first mentioned again only at the end of this episode. The verb *anagein,* "bring up," is used again in Luke 4:5; Acts 7:41; 9:39; 12:4; 16:34—and frequently in Acts in the sense of "embarking" (e.g. 13:13; 16:11). Compare the presentation of Samuel in the sanctuary of Shiloh in 1 Sam 1:22-24.

to Jerusalem. Luke uses here *eis Hierosolyma,* the Greek spelling of the name of Jerusalem, which occurs again in 13:22; 19:28; 23:7, and twenty-five times in Acts. Beginning with 2:25 he will use the more frequent form *Ierousalēm,* which is almost a transcription of Hebrew *Yĕrûšālēm,* twenty-six times in the Gospel and thirty-nine times in Acts. See J. Jeremias, *ZNW* 65 (1974) 273-276. These forms alternate in some mss. Josephus (*Ant.* 7.3,2 § 67) records that David, having driven out the Jebusites, first "named the city after himself" (see 2 Sam 5:9; 1 Kgs 3:1—see NOTE on 2:4 above); and that in the time of Abraham it had been called *Solyma,* but was later named *Hierosolyma* because of the Temple (*hieron*). Though Josephus makes use of a popular etymology, explaining *Solyma* as meaning "security" in Hebrew, he alludes to Gen 14:18, where Melchizedek, "king of Salem," comes out to meet Abram on his return from the defeat of the kings. In 1QapGen 22:13 Salem is explicitly identified as Jerusalem (cf. Ps 76:3). See further Josephus *Ag. Ap.* 1.22 §§ 173-174; *J.W.* 6.10,1 § 438. In *Ant.* 7.4,12 § 312 Josephus locates Jerusalem as twenty stadia distant from Bethlehem; that would be only two and a half miles, whereas the ancient sites are actually about five and a half miles distant. See further the NOTE on 10:30.

to present him to the Lord. This detail imitates the presentation of Samuel by his mother, Hannah, in 1 Sam 1:22-24. Yet Luke in the next verse relates Jesus' presentation to the law about the firstborn. Jesus was so designated in 2:7, and the obligation of redeeming him lay upon the parents. In Exod 13:1-2 we read: "Yahweh said to Moses, 'Consecrate to me every firstborn—whatever is the first to open every womb among the people of Israel, both human and animal, is mine.'" The implication of the consecration was a blessing on further offspring and well-being. See further Exod 13:11-16; 22:29b-30; Lev 27:26-27; Num 3:13; 8:17-18. The firstborn son was to be redeemed by a payment of five sanctuary shekels to a member of a priestly family (Num 3:47-48; 18:15-16), when the child was a month old. Luke makes no mention of the payment of the shekels to redeem the child. Instead he turns the act into a presentation of the child in the Jerusalem Temple, a custom about which nothing is said either in the OT or in the Mishnah. Such a custom for a firstborn son is simply unknown in Jewish tradition. Moreover, there is nothing either about the need of a purification of the firstborn son.

23. *as it is written.* Luke here uses the introductory formula *kathōs gegraptai,* as in Acts 7:42; 15:15. This formula is found in the LXX of 2 Kgs 14:6, used also of Scripture. It is the Greek equivalent of a formula introducing OT quotations in Qumran literature, *k'šr ktwb* (e.g. 1QS 8:14; 5:17; see J. A. Fitzmyer, *ESBNT,* 8-9). The quotation is introduced by *hoti* recitativum; see NOTE on 1:25.

the Law of the Lord. This is Luke's way (see vv. 24,39) of referring to the Mosaic Law (see v. 22).

Every male that opens the womb. Luke paraphrases here Exod 13:2. The Hebrew text speaks of *kol bĕkôr, peṭer kol reḥem,* "every firstborn, the opener of every womb." This becomes in the LXX *pan prōtotokon, prōtogenes dianoigon pasan mētran,* "every firstborn, the first-being opening every womb." *Bĕkôr* was commonly used to designate the eldest *son* (see Gen 10:15; 22:21; Exod 6:14), and Luke knows of the understanding of Exod 13:2 in terms of the firstborn son; hence his addition of *arsen,* "male." In reality, the whole phrase is simply Luke's way of referring to Jesus as the "firstborn" (see 2:7). His retention of the graphic imagery of Exod 13:2 shows that he knows nothing of either Mary's virginity *in partu,* an idea that surfaced only later (see *Prot. Jas.* 19.1-20.2), or of a miraculous birth (without the rupture of the hymen).

considered sacred. Lit. "will be called holy," i.e. dedicated to Yahweh (see NOTE on 1:35). Luke plays on the title he gave to Jesus in the announcement to Mary.

24. *to offer a sacrifice.* The sacrifice is not for the redemption of the firstborn, but for the purification of the mother (see NOTE on 2:22).

a pair of turtledoves or two young pigeons. Luke derives most of the wording of this prescription from the LXX of Lev 12:8, which speaks of "two turtledoves or two young pigeons." The turtledove, of which three varieties are known in Palestine, is a small type of pigeon. The two species of birds are often linked in OT stipulations about animal sacrifices. Here the implication is that Mary offered these animals because she (or Joseph) could not afford the one-year old lamb for the whole burnt offering.

25. *Now.* Lit. "and behold," see NOTE on *kai idou* (1:20).

Jerusalem. See NOTE on 2:22.

Simeon. This name was commonly used among Jews of first-century Palestine, and the man meant here is otherwise unknown. He is hardly Simeon, son of Hillel and father of Rabban Gamaliel the Elder, *pace* A. Cutler, *JBR* 34 (1966) 29-35. In later legends Simeon becomes a priest (which is nowhere indicated in the Lucan story), indeed a high priest and successor to Zechariah (*Prot. Jas.* 24.3-4), and even a Christian, the Simeon of James' speech at the "Council" of Jerusalem (Acts 15:14; according to "some" known to John Chrysostom *In Actus Apostolorum hom.* 33.1; PG 60. 239). His name is a diminutive of *Šĕma'-'ēl,* "God has heard," or of *šĕma'-yāh,* "Yahweh has heard," shortened to *Šime'ôn,* for which the more common Greek equivalent was *Simōn,* "Simon." In the OT "Simeon" was the name of one of the sons of Jacob (Gen 49:5) and of one of the tribes of Israel (Num 1:23). See further *ESBNT,* 105-112.

upright and devout. The description of Simeon places him, along with Zechariah and Elizabeth, Joseph and Mary, and Anna, among the representatives of faithful Jews of Palestine in the period immediately preceding the birth of Jesus. See NOTE on 1:6 for "upright." "Devout" (*eulabēs*) is used by Luke again in Acts 2:5; 8:2; 22:12 and is expressive of reverence and awe in God's presence (BAG, 322).

in expectation of the consolation of Israel. This description of Simeon will be paralleled in the infancy narrative by the description of those to whom Anna will speak about the child just born, those "waiting for the deliverance of Jerusalem" (2:38) and in the Gospel proper by the description of Joseph of Arimathea (23:50-51). Luke does not further explain the "consolation of Israel," but it is to be understood as the postexilic hope for God's eschatological restoration of the theocracy to Israel. The term plays on the impvs. of Isa 40:1; cf. Isa 61:2. See O. Schmitz, *TDNT* 5 (1967) 798; Str-B, 2. 124-126. In later rabbinic tradition the Messiah was sometimes given the title of *Měnaḥēm,* "Consoler" (Str-B, 1. 66). See further the NOTE on 2:38.

the holy Spirit was with him. Because God's prophetic Spirit was present to him, he will make the coming utterance about the child. The anarthrous use of *pneuma hagion* occurs here again, as in 1:15,35,41,67. Cf. the LXX of Dan 5:12; 6:4; or Theodotion of Dan 4:8,18. That it is to be understood of God's holy Spirit is clear from v. 26. For the verb *einai* with *epi* + acc., compare 3:2 (see NOTE there).

26. *had been informed.* Lit. "it had been disclosed to him" (cf. Acts 10:22).

not see death. I.e. experience it. "Seeing death" is an OT expression (Ps 89:49). From this expression Simeon's old age is usually deduced.

until. Luke uses here the classical Greek construction of *prin an* + subjunc., the only occurrence of it in the NT (see BDF § 383.3; § 395).

the Lord's Messiah. The OT expression, "the Anointed of Yahweh" (see e.g. 1 Sam 24:7,11; 26:9,11,16,23), is used here in the strictly messianic sense, of a future, expected Davidid.

27. *guided by the Spirit.* Lit. "in the Spirit he came." This is the Lucan motivation for his coming to the Temple at the right moment.

Temple area. Luke uses here *eis to hieron,* lit. "into the holy (place)," to designate the Temple in general or its outer courts (court of the women, court of the Gentiles). Contrast his use of *naos* for the "holy place" or "sanctuary," into which only priests entered, in 1:9,21,22. The reason for the specification is that Simeon can meet Mary only in one of the courts just mentioned.

the parents. As in vv. 41,43, Luke speaks of *tous goneis,* "the parents." Later he will speak of Jesus' "father and mother" (v. 33) or of "your father and I" (v. 48). These expressions reveal the independent character of the Simeon episode in chap. 2, and some commentators have argued on the basis of this usage that the account may have existed previously in an independent form, i.e. independent of chap. 1 and its mention of the virginal conception.

their child. See NOTE on *paidion* (1:59).

what was customary under the Law. This expression occurs only here in the NT and is not found in the LXX.

28. *Simeon took him.* Lit. "and he received him." The phrase begins with the unstressed *kai autos* (see p. 120 above).

blessed God. I.e. praised God, as Zechariah did in 1:64. Cf. 24:53. Actually Luke depicts Simeon uttering two blessings over Jesus, one in the Nunc dimittis of vv. 29-32, the other in his oracle-like statement in vv. 34b-35.

29. *Now.* This adv. is placed first in the sentence in both Greek and English for emphasis.

you may dismiss. Lit. "you are dismissing (*or* releasing)," the verb being in the pres. indic. Simeon speaks of himself as a servant (or slave) who has been performing the lengthy task of a watchman. The release from the task will come in death; the verb *apolyein* is used in the OT with that connotation (of Abram in Gen 15:2; of Aaron in Num 20:29; of Tobit in Tob 3:6; and of Antiochus IV Epiphanes in 2 Macc 9:9).

your servant. Simeon describes himself with the masc. form of what Mary applied to herself in 1:38, *doulos*. This word stands in contrast to *despotēs*, "lord, master," used in the voc. of God in the same verse. The latter Greek word was commonly used for gods in classical and Hellenistic Greek literature, and Josephus commonly used it as the Greek translation of *Yhwh* (see J. B. Fischer, "The Term *despotēs* in Josephus," *JQR* 49 [1958-1959] 132-138; cf. J. A. Fitzmyer, *WA*, 121-122). It also occurs occasionally in the LXX for *Yhwh* (e.g. Prov 29:25; cf. Isa 1:24; Jonah 4:3). Luke will use it again in Acts 4:24.

in peace. See the LXX of Gen 15:15.

30. *seen your salvation*. This is an allusion to the LXX of Isa 40:5, "all flesh shall see God's salvation," which Luke will use again in 3:6; cf. Acts 28:28. What Simeon was said above to be expecting is now cast in terms of the distinctively Lucan view of the Christ-event, viz. "salvation." See p. 222 above.

31. *made ready*. See NOTE on 1:17.

in the sight of all peoples. This phrase is inspired by an Isaian expression; see Isa 52:10, "before all the nations" (*enōpion pantōn tōn ethnōn*). Luke uses here *laōn*, "peoples"; in Acts 4:25-27 *ethnē* refers to the tribes of Israel, which are contrasted with *laoi*, "the nations." See G. D. Kilpatrick, *JTS* 16 (1965) 127. *Laōn* here, however, seems to express the two groups that will be mentioned in v. 32.

32. *a light to give revelation to the Gentiles*. This is an allusion to the Servant Song in Isa 49:6, "that you may be a light to the nations, salvation to the end of the earth." Cf. Isa 49:9.

Creed (*The Gospel*, 41) raises the question about the syntax of *phōs*, "light," here. It is coordinated with *doxan*, "glory," in the second part, with both of them in apposition to "your salvation" (v. 30); or is *doxan*, which is in the acc. case, governed by the prep. *eis* that precedes *apokalypsin*, "revelation"? If the former, then the salvation would be both a "light" to the Gentiles and "glory" to Israel. Creed prefers this as being "perhaps in closer agreement with the thought of the Gospel." The two words are also found in coordination in Isa 60:1. Probably the latter is meant, "a light (to give) revelation . . . and (to give) glory . . . ," hinting at the priority accorded to Israel over the Gentiles in God's salvation—a notion that Luke shares with Paul (see Acts 13:46; cf. Rom 1:16; 2:10; 3:1). See further Brown, *Birth*, 440.

and glory to your people Israel. This should preferably be understood as coordinate to "revelation," as explained in the preceding NOTE. We have here an allusion to the LXX of Isa 46:13, "I shall set salvation in Zion, for glory unto Israel."

33. *The child's father and mother*. Lit. "and his father and mother was (sg.!) wondering (pl.)." The text-tradition is somewhat disturbed in this verse.

The sg. verb *ēn*, "was," is read by all mss.; the best Greek mss. (‎‫א‬, B, D, L, and many minuscules) have as subject following it, *ho patēr autou*, "his father" (which would agree with the sg. verb), but also "and mother," which should demand a pl. verb. However, some mss. (A, ⊕ and the Koine text-tradition) read *Iōsēph* instead of *ho patēr autou*. "Joseph," however, is clearly a copyist's correction, which eliminates the designation of Joseph as "his father," in view of the virginal conception of chap. 1. This is probably also the reason for the addition of *autou*, "his," after *hē mētēr*, "mother" in many mss. (including ms. ‎‫א‬). The real problem is the pl. ptc. *thaumazontes*, "wondering," referring to both Joseph and Mary, despite the sg. verb, with which the verse begins. There is no reason to appeal to Hebrew usage to explain away a Greek inconcinnity here.

34. *Simeon blessed them.* Luke uses here the verb *eulogein* in the sense of uttering a blessing over someone or something (see also 6:28; 9:16; 24:50,51; Acts 3:26). Contrast the NOTE on 2:28 above. The blessing does not mean that Simeon was a priest, though such activity was ascribed to priests in the OT (see Gen 14:18b-19; Num 6:23); recall that Eli, the aged priest, blessed Elkanah and Hannah (1 Sam 2:20).

Look, this child is marked for the fall and the rise of many in Israel. Lit. "behold, this one is set for . . . ," *or* "lies (in store) for. . . ." See Luke 12:19. Though *anastasis*, which usually means "resurrection," is employed here, its meaning is rather more generic and contrasted with *ptōsis*, "fall, failure." This utterance is oracular, but is scarcely poetic.

a symbol that will be rejected. Lit. "a rejected (*or* opposed) symbol." The pres. ptc. *antilegomenon* has in this case future force (see BDF § 339.2b). *Sēmeion* is predicated of Jesus here, as it was of Isaiah and his children who were said to be a sign for Israel (8:18).

35. *indeed, a sword shall pierce you too.* Lit. "and a sword shall go through your own soul." For *psychē* in the sense of "self," see NOTE on 1:46. The Greek text here is difficult to translate exactly, since the sentence begins with the emphatic adv. *kai*, preceding the gen. sg. of pers. pron. (*sou*), which is followed by another intensifier, and the pron. *autēs*. Stress is thus put on Mary's individual lot; she is addressed in the second sg. in contrast to the rest of Simeon's oracle. Hence v. 35a should be understood as parenthetical, and v. 35b taken as the continuation of vv. 34b-c.

The sword that is to pass through Mary's *psychē* is related in Simeon's oracle to the fall and the rise of many in Israel. But in what sense? The most common interpretation of these words is that of the sword of anguish that she will experience as she sees Jesus crucified and his side pierced with a lance—her role as *mater dolorosa*. This does not suit the Lucan Gospel, since Mary appears at the foot of the cross only in John's Gospel (19:25-27) and only in John's Gospel is Jesus' side pierced with a lance (19:34). Mary is never said in the Lucan Gospel to be among the women who followed him from Galilee (23:49,55; 24:10). It is necessary to seek the meaning of this part of Simeon's oracle in a Lucan view of Mary.

The OT background for the saying is the idea of the sword of discrimination. The combination of *romphaia*, "sword," and the verb *dierchesthai*, "go through," is found in the LXX of Ezek 14:17, "Let a sword go through the land that I may cut off from it man and beast." The same expression is picked up in *Sibylline Oracle* 3.316, referring to the invasion of Egypt by Antiochus IV Epiphanes, "A sword shall go through the midst of you." In this image, the sword singles out some for destruction and others for mercy (see further Ezek 5:1-2; 6:8-9). In the Lucan context the figure grows out of the idea of Jesus' role causing the fall and the rise of many in Israel. Mary, as part of Israel, will be affected too. In the Gospel proper Jesus will be depicted as one who brings dissension even within families (12:51-53). Thus, with the imagery of the sword piercing Mary, Simeon hints at the difficulty she will have in learning that obedience to the word of God will transcend even family ties. Recall how Mary will be depicted in Luke 8:21 and 11:27-28.

This attempt to explain v. 35a according to data in the Lucan Gospel likewise rules out many other attempts to explain the sword, e.g. as the sword of doubt piercing Mary during the passion of Jesus (Origen *Hom. in Lucae evangelium*, 17; GCS 49.105); or as the sword of her own violent death (Epiphanius *Panarion* 78.11; GCS 37.462); or as the sword of rejection that she too experienced in the public rejection of her son; or as the sword of illegitimacy with which Jesus was reproached because of the virginal conception; or as the sword of tragedy that she experienced at the fall of Jerusalem; or as the sword of enmity set between her seed and the seed of the serpent of Gen 3:15. All such attempts explain the sword on the basis of material extraneous to the Lucan Gospel and could scarcely have been envisaged by Luke. (See further Brown, *Birth*, 462-463; *MNT*, 156-157.)

so that. I.e. in order that. This purpose clause continues the first part of the oracle in v. 34b-c. It does not mean that the sword piercing Mary will lay bare such thoughts. In manifesting the Messiah, God's purpose is revealed; it forces human beings to react, for or against him. The cl. introduced here with *hopōs an* could also be understood as consecutive, "with the result that" (see ZBG §§ 351-353 for the blending of these clause-types, especially in Hellenistic Greek).

thoughts. The *dialogismoi* are to be understood here of evil, critical, or antagonistic thoughts, which lead to the rejection of the symbol. The noun otherwise occurs in a pejorative or hostile sense in Luke 5:22; 6:8; 9:46,47; 24:38. Here it foreshadows the end of Acts (28:27-28). In the OT cf. Pss 56:6; 94:11; 146:4. See G. Schrenk, *TDNT* 2 (1964) 97.

of many minds. Lit. "of many hearts." See NOTE on 1:51.

will be laid bare. Lit. "will be revealed." Luke uses here the verb *apokalyptein,* the cognate of the noun "revelation" which appeared in the last line of the Nunc Dimittis (v. 32).

36. *Anna.* Jesus' manifestation is made not only to an upright and devout Jewish man, but also to a woman. She is identified by Luke with the name of the mother of Samuel (1 Samuel 1-2). *Anna* is the Greek form of the Hebrew name, *Ḥannāh,* "Grace, Favor" (see NOTE on 1:27), derived from the same root (*ḥnn*) as "John" (see NOTE on 1:13). Though called a "prophetess" by Luke, she utters no canticle. Luke knows of other women in the Christian com-

munity who "prophesied" (Acts 21:9), but he never tells us in what sense the term is to be understood. Cf. Acts 2:17.

Phanuel. This is the Greek form of the Hebrew name *Pĕnû'ēl*, used of a man in 1 Chr 4:4 and of a place in Judg 8:8 and Gen 32:32. It is translated in the LXX of the Genesis citation as *eidos tou theou*, "face/appearance of God."

of the tribe of Asher. This identifies Anna as a member of an outlying northern tribe. Asher is the last of the tribes mentioned in the Blessing of Moses (Deut 33:24-25). It was named after Asher, the son of Jacob. In Gen 30:13 Leah plays on the meaning of the name, "Good Fortune," and exclaims, "Fortunate am I! For women (shall) count me fortunate!" Cf. Luke 1:42b,48b. In Gen 49:20 it appears as the ninth tribe in the Blessing of Jacob. What a prophetess from a tribe like Asher would be doing in the Jerusalem Temple is a bit puzzling; Luke is probably little interested in the geographical location of Asher, as his attempt to describe Anna in the following phrases would suggest.

well along in years. See NOTE on 1:7, where the same phrase occurs.

after her marriage. Lit. "from her virginity."

seven years. The Sinaitic OS version shortens it to "seven days."

37. *a widow for eighty-four years.* The prep. *heōs* before the gen. *etōn*, "years," should mean "until, up to" eighty-four years. Though it is omitted by ms. D and some ancient versions (OL, Sinaitic OS), it has to be retained. E. J. Goodspeed (*Problems of New Testament Translation* [Chicago: University of Chicago, 1945] 79-81) understood it as "until the age of eighty-four," i.e. she was now eighty-four years of age (so too Schneider, *Evangelium nach Lukas*, 72). It may also express the length of her widowhood alone.

never left the Temple area. I.e. the *hieron*; see NOTE on 2:27. For some commentators (e.g. Creed, *The Gospel*, 43) this would mean that she lived within the Temple precincts. That may be reading into the text more than Luke intends. The *Prot. Jas.* 7:1 - 8:2 depicts Mary as presented in the Temple by her parents, where she stayed when they left, "nurtured like a dove and receiving food from the hand of an angel." This, of course, is part of the later legends about Mary; and one should hesitate to understand anything similar here in the case of Anna the prophetess.

worshiped day and night. The same phrase occurs in Acts 26:7. It would denote here Anna's participation in the prayers of the people attending the daily sacrifices (see Luke 1:10). The double expressions, "day and night" and "fasting and prayer," are Lucanisms; see R. Morgenthaler, *Die lukanische Geschichtsschreibung* 1. 28.

38. *At that very time.* A Lucanism; see p. 117 above.

came up. Luke again uses the verb *ephistanai*; see NOTE on 2:9. Unlike Simeon, she is not brought there by the Spirit.

publicly praised God. Or, "thanked God." The verb *anthomologeisthai* is used only here in the NT.

she spoke. Lit. "she kept speaking," since the verb is in the impf. Her words are not quoted, but she confirms the interpretation of Simeon. It does not mean on that occasion alone, but rather that she spread abroad the word about the child.

to all who were waiting for the deliverance of Jerusalem. Recall the analo-
gous description of Simeon in 2:25c, and cf. Isa 52:9, "he has redeemed
Jerusalem." Though some mss. (D, ⊕, and the Koine text-tradition) read *en
Ierousalēm,* "deliverance in Jerusalem," the reading "deliverance/redemption
of Jerusalem" is to be preferred. It is synonymous with "the consolation of Israel." The noun *lytrōsis,* "deliverance, redemption," sometimes translates in the
LXX the Hebrew noun *gĕ'ullāh* (e.g. Lev 25:29,29,48). At the time of the
Second Revolt of Palestinian Jews against Rome (A.D. 132-135) documents
were sometimes dated to the years of "the Redemption of Israel" (*lg'lt Yśr'l—*
Mur 24 B 2; Mur 24 D 2; Mur 24 E 2 [DJD 2. 124-132]) or of "the Freedom
of Jerusalem" (*lḥrwt Yrwšlm—*Mur 25 i 1 [DJD 2. 135]). These phrases are
not identical with the Lucan phrases, but they show that the latter reflect actual
aspirations of Palestinian Jews of the time.

A minor ms. (348) and some ancient versions (OL, Vg) read *Israēl* here instead of *Ierousalēm;* though scarcely to be preferred, it would reflect even
more closely the Palestinian expression found in some of the Murabba'at texts.

39. *they.* I.e. Mary and Joseph.

by the Law of the Lord. See NOTE on 2:23.

they returned. Refrain A occurs here again (see the outline of the infancy
narrative, p. 314).

their own town of Nazareth. See NOTES on 1:26 and 2:3. This ms. D
adds, "as was said by the prophet, 'He will be called a Nazorean,' " a copyist's
addition from the Matthean Gospel.

40. *as the child grew up, he became strong.* This description repeats verbatim the description of John in 1:80. It constitutes refrain B (see NOTE on
1:80 and 2:52). Some mss. (⊕, the Koine text-tradition) add *pneumati,* "in
spirit," but that is the result of harmonization of this verse with 1:80.

filled with wisdom. This is not said of John, but it prepares for the next episode, Jesus sitting among the teachers in the Temple (see 2:47; cf. 2:52).

God's favor was upon him. Such favor was claimed for Mary in 1:30.
Whereas the parallel story of John depicted him in the desert until the time of
his manifestation to Israel, Jesus grows up in the circle of his Galilean family.
This entire v. 40 echoes the Samuel story, especially 1 Sam 2:21c, "And the
boy Samuel grew up in the presence of the Lord," and 2:26, "And the boy
Samuel continued to grow and was favored (lit. was good) both by (lit. with)
Yahweh and by human beings."

BIBLIOGRAPHY (2:21-40)

Benoit, P. " 'Et toi-même, un glaive te transpercera l'âme!' (Luc 2,35)," *CBQ*
25 (1963) 251-261.

Brown, R. E. "The Presentation of Jesus (Luke 2:22-40)," *Worship* 51
(1977) 2-11.

Cutler, A. "Does the Simeon of Luke 2 Refer to Simeon the Son of Hillel?"
JBR 34 (1966) 29-35.

Feuillet, A. "L'Épreuve prédite à Marie par le vieillard Siméon (Luc. II, 35a)" in *À la rencontre de Dieu: Mémorial Albert Gelin* (Bibliothèque de la faculté catholique de théologie de Lyon 8; Le Puy: Mappus, 1961) 243-263.

——— "Le jugement messianique et la Vierge Marie dans la prophétie de Siméon (Lc. 2,35)," in *Studia mediaevalia et mariologica P. Carolo Balić OFM . . . dicata* (Rome: Antonianum, 1971) 423-447.

Figueras, P. "Syméon et Anne, ou le témoignage de la loi et des prophètes," *NovT* 20 (1978) 84-99.

Galbiati, E. "La circoncisione di Gesù (Luca 2,21)," *BeO* 8 (1966) 37-45.

——— "La presentazione al Tempio (Luca 2,22-40)," *BeO* 6 (1964) 28-37.

Hatch, W. H. P. "The Text of Luke II, 22," *HTR* 14 (1921) 377-381.

Herranz, A. A. "Presentación de Jesús en el Templo (Lc 2,22-39)," *CB* 6 (1949) 35-42.

Jeremias, J. "Miszelle: *Ierousalēm/Ierosolyma*," *ZNW* 65 (1974) 273-276.

Lagrange, M.-J. "La présentation de Jésus au Temple," *VSpir* 26 (1931) 129-135.

Michel, R. "La purification de la Vierge, la chandeleur et les relevailles," *Revue diocésaine de Tournai* 2 (1947) 385-395.

Schürmann, H. " 'Es wurde ihm der Name Jesus gegeben . . .' (Lk 2,21)," in *Am Tisch des Wortes* 14 (1966) 34-40; reprinted in *Ursprung und Gestalt* (Düsseldorf: Patmos, 1970) 222-226.

Varela, A. T. "Luke 2:36-37: Is Anna's Age What Is Really in Focus," *BT* 27 (1976) 446.

Vogels, H. J. "Die 'Eltern' Jesu (Textkritisches zu Lk 2,33ff.)," *BZ* 11 (1913) 33-43.

——— "Lk 2,36 im Diatessaron," *BZ* 11 (1913) 168-171.

Winandy, J. "La prophétie de Syméon (Lc, ii, 34-35)," *RB* 72 (1965) 321-351.

Bibliography on the Nunc Dimittis

Charue, A. "La prophétie de Siméon. Luc., II, 22-39," *Collationes namurcenses* 26 (1932) 65-72.

Joüon, P. "Notes philologiques sur les évangiles: Luc 2,31," *RSR* 18 (1928) 345-359, esp. p. 352.

Kilpatrick, G. D. *"Laoi* at Luke ii. 31 and Acts iv. 25-27," *JTS* 16 (1965) 127.

Vincent, L.-H. "Luc ii, 32," *RB* os 9 (1900) 601-602.

Zolli, E. "Il Cantico di Simeone," *Marianum* 8 (1946) 273-276.

(See further the bibliography on the Lucan Canticles, p. 370 above.)

9. THE FINDING IN THE TEMPLE
(2:41-52)

2 41 Every year Jesus' parents used to go to Jerusalem for the feast of Passover. 42 Once, when Jesus was twelve years old, they went up as usual for the festival. 43 After completing the days of its observance, the boy Jesus remained behind in Jerusalem, when his parents started for home, but they did not know about it. 44 Thinking rather that he was in the traveling-party, they journeyed along for a whole day. Then they began to look for him among their relatives and acquaintances. 45 When they did not find him, they returned to Jerusalem in search of him. 46 On the third day it happened that they found him in the Temple area, sitting in the middle of the teachers to whom he listened and posed questions. 47 All who heard him were struck by his comprehension and the answers that he gave. 48 When his parents saw him there, they were startled; and his mother said to him, "Child, why have you treated us like this? Look, your father and I have been terribly worried and have been searching for you." 49 He said to them, "Why are you searching for me? Did you not know that I had to be in my Father's house?" 50 But they did not understand what he was saying to them.

51 Then he went back down with them to Nazareth and was obedient to them. His mother cherished all these things within her. 52 And Jesus *advanced* in wisdom, age, and favor *before God and human beings*.[a]

[a] 1 Sam 2:26

COMMENT

The Lucan infancy narrative concludes with a story of Jesus' childhood which has nothing to do with his "infancy." In a sense, it is ill-suited to the rest of the two chapters at the beginning of this Gospel. A greater difficulty is putting an adequate title on the subform of the tradition with which this Gospel begins. It is precisely this episode that raises the question whether the first two chapters are rightly called an "infancy narrative." We have, however, retained that designation for 1:5 - 2:52 because of its common use in English commentaries and because it is practically impossible to get a better term.

It is clear that Luke intended this episode to be part of what we call today the infancy narrative, even though it is concerned with an incident in the adolescent life of Jesus. The last two verses (2:51-52) contain refrains that link it to other episodes in the infancy narrative. The episode, however, is on the whole transitional between those that have told of Jesus' conception, birth, circumcision, naming, and manifestation as an infant and the beginning of his public ministry.

In the general structure of the Lucan infancy narrative the scene of the finding of the boy Jesus in the Temple is complementary to the preceding parallel episodes of the birth, circumcision, and manifestation of both John and Jesus (see outline, p. 314 above). It is somewhat like the story of Mary's visit to Elizabeth (1:39-56). But in reality it differs more from that episode than it resembles it. The visitation scene was integrally linked to the preceding announcement-of-birth stories (1:5-25; 1:26-38), making use of details from both of them and pulling them together to advance the narrative. In this case, however, the story of the finding of Jesus in the Temple is only loosely connected with what precedes. The two concluding verses, which are clearly of Lucan composition, are secondarily added to join what otherwise has little connection. In the present Lucan context v. 50, the evangelist's comment on the lack of understanding on the part of Joseph and Mary, may be an illustration of the sword of discrimination that would pierce Mary's soul (according to Simeon's oracle, 2:35), but that verse could have stood by itself without losing any significance.

As the episode stands now, one may distinguish in it six elements: (1) the setting (2:41-42); (2) the loss of Jesus (2:43-45); (3) the finding of Jesus (2:46-48); (4) Jesus' pronouncement (2:49); (5) the primary conclusion (2:50); and (6) the secondary Lucan conclusion (2:51-52).

The story of the finding in the Temple is in reality an independent unit, which does not depend on anything that precedes in the infancy narrative and which could be dropped without any great loss to the narrative. It is not unlikely that Luke inherited this story from a pre-Lucan source. There are fewer Semitisms in it than in the rest of the infancy narrative. The story shows no awareness of the virginal conception of Jesus, as presented in chap. 1 (it speaks of "his parents" in vv. 41, 43; and makes Mary speak about Joseph as "your father" in v. 48—this problem is not exclusive to this episode, see 2:27). There is no reason to relate this scene to the Baptist source in any form. It may, however, be part of a tradition that grew up about the childhood of Jesus and that continued to manifest itself in the apocryphal gospels, such as the *Infancy Story of Thomas,* which tells what Jesus did or said at the ages of five (2:1), six

(11:1), eight (12:2), and twelve (19:1-5, actually an expanded para-phrase of this Lucan episode). See Hennecke-Schneemelcher, *NTApocry-pha* 1. 392-401; M. R. James, *ANT,* 49-55. This tradition may also be related to stories of what Jesus did *en famille* in his pre-ministry days (among which the Johannine Cana story may also have belonged at one point; cf. *MNT,* 182-187). This is speculative; there is nothing that serves as the basis for a certain analysis.

It has been suggested by B. van Iersel ("The Finding," 161-173) that the story existed at one time in a shorter form, viz. vv. 41-43, 45-46, 48-50. In other words Luke added two verses: v. 44, about the day's journey without Jesus, and v. 47 about his comprehension and answers. In this he has been followed by R. E. Brown (*Birth,* 480) and the task force of *MNT,* 158-159. This is a plausible explanation of the genesis of the episode, but it does face one difficulty, viz. the clearly Lucan *kai egeneto* construction in v. 46 (see NOTE). In any case, it seems likely that Luke added this episode to an earlier stage of the infancy narrative, perhaps at the time that he added the various canticles. Verses 51-52 then became his secondary conclusion, uniting the episode to what preceded.

This scene is the only episode in the Lucan infancy narrative which may fall into a standard form-critical category. R. Bultmann (*HST,* 300-304) has treated the story as an example of a "legend" in the narra-tive material (see pp. 254-255 for his definition of legend); and V. Taylor (*FGT,* 159-163) similarly regarded it—along with the other episodes in the infancy narrative—as a "story about Jesus." But neither of these analyses does justice to the crucial verse in the episode, Jesus' double question addressed to his parents (2:49). Following up a suggestion of R. Laurentin (*Jésus au Temple,* 158-161) and making use of Bultmann's own terminology, Brown (*Birth,* 483) has more plausibly designated it a "biographical apophthegm." This is certainly better, even though the apophthegm is couched in the form of two questions. I prefer to use Taylor's terminology and call it a pronouncement story. It not only pre-sents Jesus' first words in the Lucan Gospel, but it is the Gospel's first pronouncement story. In this instance, the pronouncement is integrally related to the narrative setting. It puts on the lips of Jesus an implied statement about who he is, making manifest to his parents the way in which he is related to Yahweh—as an obedient Son of his heavenly Fa-ther. This manifestation stands in contrast—in the overall Lucan setting —to the revelations that have been made about him by others (by Gabriel, by the shepherds, by Simeon, by Anna).

Bultmann (*HST,* 300) thinks that the episode has a double point to make: (1) the outstanding wisdom of the child Jesus (v. 47); and (2) his staying behind in the Temple, which reveals his religious destiny.

This, however, makes too much of the wisdom motif, which is only mentioned in the Lucan secondary conclusion (v. 52); the overemphasis stems from Bultmann's regarding the episode as a legend, or story about Jesus. Moreover, if van Iersel is correct about the secondary character of v. 47, the remark about Jesus' outstanding comprehension and answers would only come from Lucan redaction.

Bultmann is influenced, as are many other commentators, by the similarity of this story with many other stories of the precocious childhood and outstanding wisdom of famous figures of history or mythology. Bultmann lists the "similar material" that can be found in Josephus and Philo about Moses, in Herodotus about Cyrus, in Plutarch about Alexander, in Philostratus about Apollonius of Tyana (*HST,* 301; see also J. M. Creed, *The Gospel,* 44 and Josephus, *Life* 2 § 8-9 about his own talents). No one will deny that these at times afford striking parallels to 2:47. It may even be that Luke added that verse under the influence of stories current in the Hellenistic world of his time. But that is scarcely the main point of the episode.

Pressing beyond Bultmann's singling out of the wisdom of Jesus, some commentators have tried to find further significance in the mention of Jesus' comprehension (2:47) and wisdom (2:52) in this scene. These are supposed to be reflections of divine Wisdom revealing itself, as it is described in Sir 24:1-12. See Laurentin, *Jésus au temple,* 135-141. But in Sirach Wisdom is depicted as a woman (because the Hebrew noun *ḥokmāh* is fem., as are its Aramaic and Greek counterparts, *ḥokmĕtāh* and *sophia*). Moreover, Wisdom is identified in Sirach with the Torah. It is farfetched to extend this to the person of the adolescent Jesus. See further Brown, *Birth,* 490; G. Schneider, *Evangelium nach Lukas,* 74.

The main point is rather a christological affirmation that is implicit in the second question asked by Jesus of his parents, "Did you not know that I had to be in my Father's house?" If one accepts the suggestion that this independent story once circulated in the pre-Lucan Christian community, it would represent another retrojection of christological faith, born of post-resurrection days, being pushed back to an earlier phase of Jesus' existence—in this case not yet to his birth or conception, but to his adolescence.

In any case, the first words attributed to Jesus in the Lucan Gospel form a statement about his relationship to his heavenly Father. What is significant is that it is uttered by him somewhere in the Jerusalem Temple. This is true, no matter what interpretation is given to *en tois tou patros mou*—for the sense of the relationship comes through no matter which interpretation of these words is used (see NOTE on 2:49c). The link is based not only on the translation "in my Father's house," although that enhances Jesus' manifestation of himself.

The scene is set in the Jerusalem Temple, and Luke thus ends his infancy narrative as he began it, with a Temple scene (1:5-25). This is important as another chord struck in the infancy narrative, because the Gospel proper will end there too (24:53), with the notice about the Eleven and the others being constantly in the Temple praising God. Moreover, the scene depicts the adolescent Jesus making his way to Jerusalem—to the city which will play such an important part in the Lucan travel account and at the end of the Gospel. He was carried there as an infant (presumably from Bethlehem) in 2:22; but in this scene he makes his way there *from Galilee*. As in the case of his being publicly manifested in the Temple as an infant (2:22-38), so here the scene is dominated by Jewish piety, fidelity, and respect for custom, and it goes further in emphasizing the training of the young Jewish male, and the celebration of the most important pilgrim feast in the Jewish calendar. Not only has Jesus been incorporated into Judaism and marked with the sign of the covenant (circumcision, 2:21), but he is now shown to be one trained in the Torah and its requirements and fulfilling his obligations, even in advance. (See further K. Baltzer, *HTR* 58 [1965] 263-277.)

All of this is a setting for his independent conduct. Though the episode ends with the Lucan notice of his obedience to his earthly parents (2:51), his obedience as son toward his heavenly Father transcends even that filial piety and obedience to Mary and Joseph. His independent conduct here strikes a chord that will be heard again in the Gospel proper. When the woman in the crowd praises Mary (11:27-28), he will offer a corrective that reveals that Mary has progressed beyond the stage of misunderstanding attributed to her here (2:50) to one of those who hear the word of God and keep it (see also 8:19-21). In other words, for Luke Mary may be "the mother of the Lord" (1:43), but it is much more important that her maternal ties yield to those of Jesus' heavenly Father. This is foreshadowed here.

As far as Mary is concerned, the Lucan setting for this episode at the end of the infancy narrative reveals a sense in which the sword of discrimination, mentioned in Simeon's oracle (2:35), pierces her. The incomprehension that she manifests in 2:48,50 reveals that she had much to learn.

In trying to understand the fundamental message of this episode, one must avoid psychologizing explanations of the words of Jesus or Mary and of their actions. One must remember that we are confronted here with Stage III of the gospel tradition, what Luke composed or redacted, and not with Stage I, what actually happened in the adolescence of the earthly career of Jesus. If one attempts to analyze the scene from the standpoint of Mary's awareness or Jesus' consciousness, one encounters all sorts of difficulties. For instance, how could Joseph and Mary have started off on the long journey to Galilee from Jerusalem without making sure that their twelve-year old was in tow? Or how could they have gone a whole day's journey without realizing that he was not with them? Or would they have been traveling separately, in groups of men and women? (Luke tries to answer that in v. 44a; but his attempt scarcely satisfies the modern reader.) Or how did Jesus spend the nights in between, until he was found? Where did he spend them? How could he have acted so irresponsibly toward his parents, if he were gifted with such striking comprehension, as v. 47 suggests? To ask such questions is to miss the whole point of the episode. It was not meant to bear such weight. A fortiori, all questions about Mary's awareness of Jesus' divinity, despite Gabriel's pronouncement to her (1:32,35), have to be understood in the light of what Luke writes in 2:50, Joseph and Mary "did not understand what he was saying to them." This is Luke's way of getting across to his readers the difficulty of understanding who Jesus is or was.

NOTES

2 41. *Every year.* Lit. "according to (the) year." Only here does Luke use this expression, but it is similar to other distributive uses of *kata* in his writings (see *kath' hēmeran*, "every day," in 16:19; 22:52; Acts 2:46-47).

Jesus' parents. Lit. "his parents." Cf. 2:27,43. In v. 33 they were called "his father and mother." In a few mss. and ancient versions (ms. 1012, OL, Diatessaron) one finds rather *ho te Iōsēph kai hē Mariam*, "Joseph and Mary," an obvious scribal correction aimed at reconciling this account with the virginal conception of Jesus in chap. 1.

used to go. The impf. of *poreuesthai* here has iterative force; cf. BDF § 325. See NOTE on 1:39 for the use of this verb, and pp. 168-169 above.

to Jerusalem. See NOTE on 2:22. The Hebraizing spelling of 2:25 is also preserved here.

for the feast of Passover. Or, "at the feast of Passover." The expression, "the feast of Passover," is not found in the LXX; in the NT it occurs only here and in John 13:1. In this instance Luke does not identify Passover with the feast of Unleavened Bread, as he does in 22:1,7.

Passover was celebrated at the sundown which marked the beginning of 15 Nisan, the first month in the Babylonian/Jewish calendar (roughly =March/April—the older name of the month, Abib, is sometimes used instead in the OT [e.g. Deut 16:1]). It was the feast when the passover lamb, slain in the late hours of 14 Nisan (i.e. in the afternoon), was roasted and eaten in a family circle at sundown (Lev 23:6). Everything leavened (i.e. prepared with yeast) had to be removed from the house or dwelling before the slaying of the passover lamb (Deut 16:4; for further details see the later regulations in *m. Pesaḥim* 1:1-4). The meal was not only eaten with unleavened bread (Exod 12:8), but unleavened bread continued to be eaten for seven days thereafter (Exod 12:17-20; 23:15; 34:18). This seven-day period was technically "the feast of Unleavened Bread." In time, however, "Passover" became the name for all seven or eight days (Deut 16:1-4; Ezek 45:21-25; Josephus, *Ant.* 6.9,3 § 423; 20.5,3 § 106). The two feasts are mentioned together in 2 Chr 35:17. Though Josephus (*Ant.* 3.10,5 § 249) still distinguished the two feasts, he sometimes referred to the whole period as the feast of Unleavened Bread (*J.W.* 2.14,3 § 280; *Ant.* 17.9,3 § 213), as Luke does (22:1,7).

Passover was most likely a (pre-Israelite) feast proper to transhumance or seminomadic shepherds (Exod 5:1; 10:9), whereas that of Unleavened Bread was most likely derived from a sedentary (pre-Israelite) agricultural origin (Exod 23:15-16—where it is listed with two other agricultural feasts; cf. Exod 34:18-20).

The Greek word in the NT for "Passover" is *to pascha,* which can designate either the feast or the lamb. The Greek form *phaska* is sometimes found in Josephus (*Ant.* 5.1,4 § 20; 17.9,3 § 213). Both represent attempts to transliterate Aramaic *pashā'* (or *pishā'*). The Hebrew form is *pesaḥ,* which is sometimes transliterated in the LXX as *phasek* (e.g. 2 Chr 30:1,2,5) or *phasech* (e.g. 2 Chr 35:1,6,7). The etymology of Hebrew *pesaḥ* is uncertain; it is popularly explained as the "passing over" (i.e. the sparing) of the Hebrew firstborn during the deliverance of the Hebrews from Egyptian bondage (Exod 12:13).

In NT times Passover was one of the pilgrim feasts, when male Jews from other parts of Palestine (e.g. Galilee) or the diaspora were expected to make their way to Jerusalem for its observance. This custom was in part based on Deut 16:16; Exod 23:15d; 34:23, obliging all males to appear in Yahweh's presence and not empty-handed (i.e. without an offering). The celebration of Passover included the ritual slaying of the lamb in the Temple area, a festal meal at sundown in a family circle of at least ten people, and the consumption of the entire animal. According to the later regulation of *m. Pesaḥ.* 8:3 any number could be admitted to the circle, but each one had to be guaranteed at least "an olive's bulk" of the meat of the lamb.

There was no obligation for women or children to participate in this pilgrim feast (see *m. Ḥagiga* 1:1). The fact that Luke depicts both Mary and Jesus accompanying Joseph to Jerusalem is part of the Temple piety that pervades the infancy narrative in general.

42. *when Jesus was twelve years old.* Luke thus relates the story to the adolescence of Jesus. From regulations set down in the later tractate *m. Niddah* 5:6 it was deduced that a Jewish boy became obligated to observe the Torah at the age of thirteen. (Of much later origin is the modern expression, *bar miṣwāh,* "son of [the] commandment," as well as the ceremony related to it.) There is reason to think that some of the later Mishnaic regulations were somewhat applicable to the time of Jesus—at least in this case. From the age of thirteen on, he would have been obliged to take part in the pilgrimage to Jerusalem. That Jesus is here depicted as being taken up to Jerusalem at the age of twelve may reflect the custom said to exist among pious Jews of getting a young boy accustomed to the obligation, by taking him up at a younger age (see *m. Ḥagiga* 1:1; cf. Str-B, 2. 144-147). Josephus (*Ant.* 5.10,4 § 348) dates

the beginning of Samuel's acting as a prophet (i.e. his call narrated in 1 Sam 3:3) to his twelfth year.

they went up as usual for the festival. Lit. "as they were going up (pres. ptc. *anabainontōn*) according to the custom of the feast." See NOTE on *anabainein* (2:4). The detail echoes the Samuel story, Elkanah and Hannah going up yearly to the sanctuary (Shiloh) in 1 Sam 1:3,21; 2:19.

43. *After completing the days of its observance.* I.e. Joseph and Mary would have stayed in Jerusalem for the seven/eight days of Passover and Unleavened Bread (Lev 23:5-6). Luke here uses the aor. ptc. *teleiōsantōn* in contrast to the foregoing pres. ptc.; see ZBG § 276.

the boy Jesus remained behind in Jerusalem. Here Luke describes Jesus as *pais;* contrast 2:17,40 (see NOTE on 1:59). Luke supplies no information on how he was separated from his parents or any motivation for his remaining; the latter emerges in v. 49. In the Temple precincts he would have been separated from his mother, but would have been with Joseph.

when his parents started for home. Lit. "in their returning." Luke uses here the prep. *en* with the articular infin.

but they did not know about it. Lit. "and his parents did not know about it." For the sake of the English, I have transferred the subject, "his parents," to the preceding clause. As in v. 41, a number of Greek mss. (A, C, X, etc.) substitute for the preferred reading, "his parents," another phrase, here "Joseph and his mother," again in order to reconcile this account with the virginal conception of Jesus in chap. 1. But that is a copyist's correction.

44. *Thinking rather that he was in the traveling-party.* Or, "in the caravan." The noun *synodia* is found only here in the NT; it is used by Epictetus (*Dissertationes* 4.1,91), Josephus (*J.W.* 2.21,1 § 587; *Ant.* 6.12,1 § 243), and Strabo (*Geography* 4.6,6) of a group of people traveling together. The reason for a traveling-party of pilgrims going from Galilee to Jerusalem (or vice versa) was the need to pass through inhospitable Samaritan territory (see Luke 9:53; cf. Josephus *Life*, 52 § 269) or to avoid attacks by highway robbers (see Luke 10:30).

they journeyed along for a whole day. Lit. "they came a day's journey." The expression echoes 1 Kgs 19:4 (with a different verb and word order); cf. Num 11:31.

among their relatives and acquaintances. For the Lucan double expression, see NOTE on 2:37.

45. *in search of him.* Lit. "searching for him."

46. *on the third day it happened that they found him.* Lit. "and it happened after three days (that) they found him in the Temple area." Luke uses here *kai egeneto* + finite verb (*heuron*) without the conj. *kai* (see p. 119 above). The temporal phrase *meta hēmeras treis,* "after three days," is found again in Lucan writings in Acts 25:1; 28:17 as an ordinary designation of time. *Pace* Laurentin (*Jésus au temple,* 101-102), this is scarcely a foreshadowing of the resurrection. Whenever Luke refers to that event he uses the expression *tē tritē hēmera,* "on the third day" (see Luke 9:22; 18:33; 24:7,21,46; Acts 10:40). The temporal phrase is ambiguous; it could mean that they spent three days searching for him in Jerusalem, but it probably means that the first day was

spent in traveling from Jerusalem, the second in returning to Jerusalem, and the third in searching for him in Jerusalem.

in the Temple area. See NOTE on 2:27. Here it must mean that he was found in a hall or portico of the outer courts, since Mary and Joseph together come upon him.

sitting in the middle of the teachers. Though Luke later on, in the Gospel proper, portrays Jesus seated as a teacher (5:3), it is scarcely likely that this is meant here. Jesus is rather depicted as a pupil, "a genuine learner" (J. M. Creed, *The Gospel,* 45). That this detail foreshadows his own teaching in the Temple in the latter part of the Gospel, in his Jerusalem ministry, is possible. But he is not yet so depicted here, *pace* G. Schneider (*Evangelium nach Lukas,* 75) and others.

The Jewish *didaskaloi* in the Temple must be understood as the scribes or lawyers of Jesus' day; aside from this passage they are never again called teachers. Elsewhere in the Lucan Gospel *didaskalos* is used only of John the Baptist (3:12) or of Jesus (*passim,* see p. 218 above). For Christians teaching in the Temple area, see Acts 4:2; 5:25.

The apocryphal *Infancy Story of Thomas* (19:2) goes further than Luke in depicting Jesus putting the elders and teachers in the Temple to silence. See Hennecke-Schneemelcher, *NTApocrypha* 1. 398-399.

to whom he listened and posed questions. I.e. as a pupil would. The instruction and questioning concerned the Torah and its place in Jewish life.

47. *All . . . were struck.* Luke will use the verb *existanai* again either intransitively or in the middle voice in 8:56; 24:22, and often in Acts (2:7,12; 8:13; 9:21; 10:45; 12:16) to express a reaction of wonder or surprise at something in the life of Jesus or the sequel to it.

by his comprehension and the answers that he gave. Lit. "by his comprehension and his answers," i.e. his penetrating answers (a hendiadys). Another Lucan double expression; see NOTE on 2:37. This detail has been prepared for by the mention of his growth in *sophia,* "wisdom" (2:40). *Sophia* and *synesis* are often found together in the LXX (see Deut 4:6; Isa 11:2; 1 Chr 22:12; 2 Chr 1:10,11).

48. *When his parents saw him.* Lit. "seeing him (they were startled)." The verb is in the third pl., without a subject expressed. The subject of it, however, is scarcely the "all who heard him" of v. 47. The sense of the verse demands that "his parents" be introduced from vv. 41,43-46; moreover, as is discussed in the COMMENT, it is quite likely that v. 47 is a secondary addition, which would account for the lack of good sequence. This is a typical verse with a generic statement about Jesus' precocious wisdom.

they were startled. Luke uses here the strong verb *ekplēssesthai,* "be struck out of oneself"; see 4:32; 9:43; Acts 13:12. The joy of finding him is overcome by the realization that he would have done something so agonizing to his parents.

Child. The voc. case of *teknon* occurs again in Luke 15:31 and 16:25, with differing nuances; in the latter instance, it has the nuance of reproach.

why have you treated us like this? Lit. "what have you done thus to us?" *or* "why have you done so to us?" Despite all that Mary has been told about her child in the earlier episodes of the infancy narrative, she is here portrayed as uncomprehending and gently rebuking.

your father and I. The expression "his parents" (*hoi goneis autou,* vv. 41,43) now becomes more explicit, "your father and I." One should not immediately think that Mary means "your foster-father," since as we explain in the COMMENT, this episode may have come to Luke from a source that knew nothing of the virginal conception of Jesus. What is strange is that Luke takes no pains to "baptize" the story and bring it into conformity with the details of chap. 1, as he will do in 3:23.

The Curetonian OS and OL versions solved the problem by changing the text, "Behold, we have. . . ."

have been terribly worried and have been searching for you. Lit. "suffering pain, we are searching for you." The ms. D and some ancient versions (OL, Curetonian OS) add another ptc., "and grieving." Still other mss. (C, D, ⊕, the Koine text-tradition) read the impf. *ezētoumen,* "we were searching," instead of the preferred reading, the pres. indic. (translated here as a pf.). The verb *odynasthai* is used exclusively by Luke in the NT (see 16:24,25; Acts 20:38); it expresses mental torment or anguish. Mary's reproach implies that an obedient or responsible son would have acted otherwise.

49. *Why are you searching for me?* Lit. "Why (is it) that you (pl.) search for me?" Answering Mary and Joseph in the plural tones down the reply to Mary's reproach. Indeed, Jesus' own question has something of a reproach in it too.

Did you not know? Again, the verb form is in the second pl. addressed to both parents. The boy Jesus' query prepares for the Lucan statement in v. 50.

that I had to be. Lit. "that . . . it was necessary (for) me to be." This is the first use of the impersonal *dei,* "it is necessary," in the Lucan Gospel. It expresses not only a necessity in general, but the peculiar Lucan connotation of what had to be as part of the Father's salvific plan involving Jesus. See Lucan Theology, p. 180 above. In the Greek text the pers. pron. *me* is put in the final, emphatic position.

in my Father's house. The Greek phrase *en tois tou patros mou* could also mean "(involved) in my Father's affairs" or even "among those people belonging to my Father," if *tois* were understood as masc. pl., i.e. among the teachers of the Torah. It is not easy to say which is the best sense in the Lucan context.

In support of the version that I have preferred, "in my Father's house" (=chez mon Père), a number of instances have been found in biblical and extrabiblical Greek texts of the neut. pl. of the def. art. followed by a gen. (sg. or pl.) in the sense of "the house/household of X." Thus Gen 41:51; Esth 7:9 (*en tois Aman,* "in Haman's house"); Job 18:19; Josephus *Ag. Ap.* 1.18 § 118 (*en tois tou Dios,* "in the temple of Zeus"); *Ant.* 16.10,1 § 302 (*en tois Antipatrou,* "(lodged) in Antipater's home"); OxyP 3. 523:3; see further MM, 436; BAG, 554b; BDF § 162.8. On the lips of a child this concrete meaning of the expression seems better than the other (more abstract) sense; moreover, the Jerusalem Temple is referred to indirectly as

God's house in Luke 19:46. The household meaning of the words is traceable to patristic interpreters and ancient versions. Used in the question put to Mary and Joseph, it would imply that they should have known *where* to find him.

In support of the second meaning, "(involved) in my Father's affairs," it is customary to cite the use of the neut. pl. of the def. art. followed by a gen. in such phrases as *ta tou theou*, "the (things) of God" (Luke 20:25; Mark 8:33; Matt 16:23); cf. 1 Cor 2:11,14; 7:32,34; Phil 2:21; John 9:4. A difficulty is sensed in this interpretation in that such phrases are never found as the obj. of the prep. *en*, as are phrases of the type required in the first interpretation. Some commentators, however, refer to 1 Tim 4:15, *en toutois isthi*, "be (involved) in these things." This phrase not only uses a dem. pron. instead of the neut. pl. art., but also lacks a dependent gen. Such a construction is, moreover, abstract and hence less suited to the speech of a young boy. However, it cannot really be ruled out. It has been used in ancient versions (e.g. Vg) and many translations in vernacular Bibles.

In support of the third meaning, "among those belonging to my Father," support has been found for the masc. pl. of the def. art. in Rom 16:10,11, where Paul greets *tous ek tōn Aristoboulou* and *tous ek tōn Narkissou*, which the *RSV* translates as "who belong to the family of Aristobulus," "who belong to the family of Narcissus." Here the difficulty is that the gen. is an object of the prep. *ek* and does not depend directly on the masc. gen. pl. Moreover, it seems to be an expression for kin, or "the household," which ill suits the heavenly Father about whom Jesus speaks. But, again, one cannot be apodictic in rejecting this interpretation as a possibility. This interpretation was espoused by Theodoret *De incarnatione Domini*, 24; PG 75.1461CD, who understood it to include the "domestics" of the Father.

In any case, it is clear that Jesus is referring to God as his heavenly Father. He expresses disappointment that his earthly parents have not understood that his relation to his heavenly Father transcends all natural family ties (see further the COMMENT on this passage).

Cf. Laurentin, *Jésus au temple*, 38-72; P. J. Temple, "What Is to Be Understood by *en tois*, Lk. 2,49?" *ITQ* 17 (1922) 248-263; " 'House' or 'Business' in Lk. 2:49?" *CBQ* 1 (1939) 342-352.

50. *they did not understand.* Lit. "they did not understand the word/thing (*rēma*) that he said to them." Luke uses again the noun *rēma* (on which see the NOTE on 1:37), but here it almost certainly has to be understood as "word," because of the following rel. cl., as Creed (*The Gospel*, 46) rightly points out. In using the negative of *synienai*, "understand, comprehend," Luke is suggesting a contrast between Jesus' own *synesis*, "comprehension," in v. 47 and the lack of comprehension of what he has just said. Attempts to tone down the evangelist's statement about the misunderstanding of these words must be resisted. It is true that Luke says merely *kai autoi ou synēkan*, "and they did not understand." In the immediate context, however, this can be understood only of Mary and Joseph. Attempts to attribute this misunderstanding to others are far-fetched. See Brown, *Birth*, 477. —On the unstressed *kai autoi*, see p. 120 above.

In the present context of the Lucan infancy narrative the evangelist's remark is really a commentary on the words of Simeon to Mary, about the sword of discrimination that would pierce her. Despite the revelations that have been made to her by others about the nature of the child born to her, she (and Joseph) still fail to comprehend what Jesus himself says to them. His parents did not understand because their coming to understanding was a gradual process, even in the Lucan writings; their lack of comprehension is like that of the disciples in 18:34. However, after the resurrection Mary will be depicted among the first believers in Acts 1:14.

Another interpretation of this verse has been proposed by R. Thibaut (*Le sens des paroles*, 17-18, 245-246), and picked up by others (e.g. J. M. Bover, *EstBíB* 10 [1951] 205-215; J. Cortés and F. M. Gatti, *Marianum* 32 [1970] 404-418). They translate the verse thus: "But they had not understood what he had told them," i.e. his parents had not understood what Jesus had said to them previously, the morning of the departure from Jerusalem, rather than the reply that he made to them in v. 49. The aor. indic. verbs *synēkan* and *elalēsen* are then translated as pluperfect. Though no one will deny that such usage occurs at times in NT, even in the relatively good Greek of Luke (e.g. 5:9; 7:21; 19:37), it is another matter to import that sense here. In most cases where the aor. form bears a pluperf. meaning it is in a subordinate cl.; one could thus admit the pluperf. sense of *elalēsen* here, "what he had said to them," instead of "what he was saying to them." To impose that sense on the main verb as well is difficult. This understanding, moreover, introduces a detail, viz. that Jesus had told his parents where he would be on the morning of the traveling-party's departure from Jerusalem, a detail that Luke himself never mentions! One has the suspicion that Luke's Greek text is being manipulated in the interest of preventing Luke from admitting that Mary—and Joseph—did not understand Jesus' fundamental relation to his heavenly Father. It smacks of eisegesis; and I prefer to avoid it. Luke says that *they*, who can only be "his parents" in the context, did not understand what he said to them. That is the most evident reading of the words, as the history of the exegesis of this verse has shown for centuries, even though many attempts have been made to explain the misunderstanding away.

For all the revelation that has been made to Mary and Joseph about the child born to her, Luke can still record that they did not understand, for he is aware that the comprehension of who Jesus was/is is a complex problem. But recall that he has already told us that the child will be a sword of discernment even for Mary.

51. *he went back down with them to Nazareth.* Lit. "he went with them and came to Nazareth." The theme of departure, refrain A, appears again; see 1:23,38,56; 2:20. On Nazareth, see NOTES on 1:26; 2:4.

was obedient to them. Lit. "was obeying them," the impf. indic. *ēn* is followed by a pres. ptc., *hypotassomenos*, expressing continuous obedience. This is stressed by Luke because of the implication in the story of Jesus' irresponsibility to his earthly parents, and also because, though Jesus recognizes his relation to his heavenly Father as that of an obedient son, he is not prevented thereby from filial respect for his earthly parents.

His mother cherished all these things within her. Lit. "his mother kept all these words/things (*rēmata*) in her heart." See NOTE on 2:19. This line forms refrain C in the infancy narrative. Coming shortly after the evangelist's statement about her misunderstanding, it suggests the gradual awareness of Mary about her son that is the Lucan picture of her. The dem. adj. "these" (*tauta*) is added in some mss. (C, ⊙, W, the Koine text-tradition). Though it is demanded by the context, it is omitted in the better mss. (B, ℵ*, etc.); I have used "these" in my translation, but I recognize the better text-tradition which lacks *tauta*.

52. *Jesus advanced . . . before God and human beings.* This is refrain B in the infancy narrative; see 1:80; 2:40. It is also a clear echo of 1 Sam 2:21,26, even though the Greek wording differs somewhat. No one can miss the Lucan imitative historiography here. One should compare with the description of Jesus in this verse the longer description of Moses' childhood and growth in years, stature, beauty, and understanding in Josephus *Ant.* 2.9,6 §§ 228-231. Cf. Prov 3:4 (especially LXX).

in wisdom, age, and favor. Or, "in wisdom, stature, and grace." Two of these three aspects of Jesus' progress in human life were mentioned in 2:40, wisdom and divine favor. The word *hēlikia* occurs again in Luke 19:3, where it clearly means "stature." But the word is well-attested in both biblical and extrabiblical Greek texts in the sense of "age, time of life" (see BAG, 345-346). Indeed, MM, 279 maintain that they were unable to quote any Greek papyrus text in which the word occurs in the sense of "stature," whereas for "age" they could present "a long list." See the debate on the use of the word in 12:25. Apropos of this verse, Creed (*The Gospel*, 46) writes that "stature" must be intended here, "for it goes without saying that Jesus grew older." But one can turn that around too: it goes without saying that he advanced in stature.

No matter how *charis* is to be understood here, "favor" or "grace," it is clear that the latter is not to be weighed down with the late medieval and Renaissance debate about the kind of grace he enjoyed.

Concluding Note on the Infancy Narrative

When one considers the Lucan infancy narrative as a whole, one sees that its main purpose is not merely to establish a relationship between John the Baptist and Jesus or to identify the latter as a Palestinian Jew born in Bethlehem and raised in Nazareth, but much more to make christological affirmations about him from the beginning of his earthly existence. As R. E. Brown and others have argued, Luke pushes back the affirmations of who Jesus was from the period when he was clearly acknowledged as Messiah, Lord, Savior, Son of God, etc.—i.e. with titles born of the post-resurrection experience of early Christians —to the period of Jesus' childhood, birth, and conception itself. The resurrection and conception have, like other major points in Jesus' existence presented in the developing gospel tradition, been called "christological moments" (Brown). Such terminology, however, is a bit ambiguous; and it might be better to reckon with varied phases of the growing Christian awareness within the community of the first century A.D. about who Jesus was and is. He did not become Messiah, Lord, etc. at such and such a moment in his earthly existence (in Stage I of the gospel tradition). Rather, the moments at which the christological affirmations were made were gradually pushed further and further back in Jesus' existence, as reflection on him and his relation to Yahweh continued to develop.

Furthermore, in certain circles of systematic theology today, people are seeking to substitute for a "christology from above" a so-called christology from below. Say what one will about the legitimacy of this distinction and of the later understanding of Jesus, one has to realize that the Lucan infancy narrative, like that of Matthew, knows only a "christology from above." That is the whole point of the "revelation" that is made to Mary, to the shepherds, and to Jesus' parents (indirectly) by the child in the Temple himself.

BIBLIOGRAPHY (2:41-52)

Argyle, A. W. "A Parallel between Luke ii. 51 and Genesis xxxvii. 17," *ExpTim* 65 (1953-1954) 29.

Bover, J. M. "Una nueva interpretación de Lc 2,50," *EstBíb* 10 (1951) 205-215.

Brown, R. E. "The Finding of the Boy Jesus in the Temple: A Third Christmas Story," *Worship* 51 (1977) 474-485.

Cortés, J. B., and F. M. Gatti. "Jesus' First Recorded Words (Lk. 2:49-50)," *Marianum* 32 (1970) 404-418.

De Jonge, H. J. "Sonship, Wisdom, Infancy: Luke ii. 41-51a," *NTS* 24 (1977-1978) 317-354.

Dupont, J. "L'Evangile (Lc 2,41-52): Jésus à douze ans," *AsSeign* 14 (1961) 25-43.

Elliott, J. K. "Does Luke 2:41-52 Anticipate the Resurrection?" *ExpTim* 83 (1971-1972) 87-89.

Glombitza, O. "Der zwölfjährige Jesus: Lk ii 40-52. Ein Beitrag zur Exegese der lukanischen Vorgeschichte," *NovT* 5 (1962) 1-4.

Goodman, P. "The Mother of Jesus: Thoughts on Her Role," *TBT* 87 (1976) 1006-1009.

Iersel, B. M. F. van, "The Finding of Jesus in the Temple: Some Observations on the Original Form of Luke ii 41-51a," *NovT* 4 (1960) 161-173.

Laurentin, R. *Jésus au temple: Mystère de Pâques et foi de Marie en Luc 2, 48-50* (EBib; Paris: Gabalda, 1966).

Michel, A. "La divinité de Jésus fut-elle connue par Marie?" *Ami du Clergé* 74 (1964) 654-656.

Montefiore, H. W. "God as Father in the Synoptic Gospels," *NTS* 3 (1956-1957) 31-46.

Pax, E. "Jüdische Familienliturgie in biblisch-christlicher Sicht," *BibLeb* 13 (1972) 248-261.

Pesch, R. " 'Kind, warum hast du so an uns getan?' (Lk 2,48)," *BZ* 12 (1968) 245-248.

Renié, J. E. " 'Et Iesus proficiebat sapientia et aetate et gratia apud Deum et homines' (Lc II, 52)," in *Miscellanea biblica et orientalia R. P. Athanasio Miller . . . oblata* (ed. A. Metzinger; Studia anselmiana 27-28; Rome: Herder, 1951) 340-350.

Schmahl, G. "Lk 2,41-52 und die Kindheitserzählung des Thomas 19,1-5: Ein Vergleich," *BibLeb* 15 (1974) 249-258.

Spadafora, F. " 'Et ipsi non intellexerunt' (Lc. 2,50)," *Divinitas* 11 (1967) 55-70.

Steinmetz, F.-J. "Jesu erste Wallfahrt nach Jerusalem: Auslegungen zu Lukas 2, 41-52," *Geist und Leben* 46 (1973) 60-64.

Temple, P. J. *The Boyhood Consciousness of Christ: A Critical Examination of Luke ii. 49* (New York: Macmillan, 1922).

———— "Christ's Holy Youth according to Lk. 2:52," *CBQ* 3 (1941) 243-250.

———— " 'House' or 'Business' in Lk. 2:49?" *CBQ* 1 (1939) 342-352.

———— "What Is to Be Understood by *en tois*, Luke 2,49?" *ITQ* 17 (1922) 248-263.

Thibaut, R. *Le sens des paroles du Christ* (Paris/Brussels: Desclée, 1940).

Watkin, R. " 'Why Hast Thou Done So to Us?' " *Clergy Review* 27 (1947) 304-306.

Winter, P. "Luke 2,49 and Targum Yerushalmi," *ZNW* 45 (1954) 145-179.

———— "Lk 2,49 and Targum Yerushalmi Again," *ZNW* 46 (1955) 140-141.

II. THE PREPARATION FOR THE PUBLIC MINISTRY OF JESUS

John's Career; Jesus' Baptism, Genealogy, and Temptation

"Someone more powerful than I is coming;
and I am not fit to unfasten even the strap of his sandals.
He will baptize you with a holy Spirit and with fire."

---

10. JOHN THE BAPTIST
(3:1-6)

3 ¹ In the fifteenth year of the reign of Tiberius Caesar, when Pontius Pilate was prefect of Judea, and Herod tetrarch of Galilee, and his brother Philip tetrarch of the region of Ituraea and Trachonitis, and Lysanias tetrarch of Abilene, ² in the high-priesthood of Annas and Caiaphas, a message came from God to John, the son of Zechariah, in the desert. ³ And he moved into the region all around the Jordan to preach a baptism of repentance for the forgiveness of sins, ⁴ as it is written in the book of the sayings of Isaiah the prophet:

A voice of someone crying out in the desert,   Isa 40:3-5
"Make ready the way of the Lord,
make straight the paths for him.
⁵ Every ravine must be filled,
every mountain and hill made low.
What is crooked must become straight,
and rough ways made smooth.
⁶ Then shall all human beings see the salvation of
God."

COMMENT

This is the beginning of the Lucan Gospel proper, not only because the account now begins to correspond to Mark 1 (and Matthew 3), but also because Luke explicitly so regards it in Acts 10:37: "starting from Galilee after the baptism that John preached." See also Acts 1:22. It is the *archē*, "beginning," of the Period of Jesus.

Luke begins this part of the Gospel with a long periodic sentence, resembling that of the prologue (1:1-4). These are the only two lengthy sentences in his writings that are so constructed. Though this instance is not so carefully constructed as the prologue, it clearly marks a fresh start in the story, which the reader of the Greek text cannot fail to note. It again suggests what has already been concluded on other grounds, that the Lucan infancy narrative was added to the Gospel at a stage later than the rest.

This sentence introduces the preparation for the public ministry of Jesus. Actually the episode contains a double preparation: the first part describes the call and ministry of John the Baptist (3:1-20), and the second is devoted to the scenes in the life of Jesus which launch his ministry (3:21 - 4:13).

In the first section (3:1-6) of this preparation for the public ministry of Jesus there is redundancy. John now appears on the scene, introduced anew (3:2), almost as if we had not learned in the infancy narrative that he is the precursor of Jesus. Part of the redundancy is owing to Luke's dependence on Mark 1:1-5, a source that lacks an infancy narrative. In that Gospel John's appearance on the scene is a simple preparation for the public ministry of Jesus; but Luke's story is more complicated because of its dependence on Mark and of the prefixing to it of the infancy narrative itself. It is also complicated by the view of the Baptist that Luke has, which is colored in part by the view of salvation-history that he has worked into his two-volumed composition.

All of the Gospels reflect the early tradition that related the beginning of Jesus' ministry to the preaching and baptism of John. This first scene is closely tied in the Lucan Gospel to the following ones (3:7-21). Taken together, they represent Luke's way of telling what is found in Mark 1:1-11; Matt 3:1-17; John 1:19-28. Echoes of this beginning will be found in Luke 16:16; Acts 1:22; 10:37; 13:24. But in interpreting this part of the Lucan Gospel, one has to recall the broad outline of Lucan salvation-history (see pp. 181-187), for we are precisely at the boundary of the Periods of Israel and of Jesus. The Period of Israel lasted from creation until John, "the Law and the Prophets" (Luke 16:16). John is not only a precursor of Jesus, but the transitional figure who inaugurates the Period of Jesus as well.

We have been introduced to John in the infancy narrative. In time Luke will call him by the name by which he has been known in tradition, "John the Baptist" (7:20). Here he is simply "John son of Zechariah." As Luke picks up the thread of the common gospel tradition about him, it is well to recall that Josephus has also devoted a paragraph to him in his *Antiquities* (18.5,2 § § 116-119):

> Some of the Jews thought that Herod's army had been destroyed by God and that he had been justly punished because of the execution of John, called the Baptist (*tou epikaloumenou Baptistou*). For Herod put to death this good man who was exhorting the Jews to live upright lives, in dealing justly with one another and submitting devoutly to God, and to join in baptism (*baptismō synienai*). Indeed, it seemed to John that even this washing would not be acceptable as a pardon for sins, but only as a purification for the body, unless the soul had previously been cleansed through upright conduct. When still others joined the crowds around him, because they were quite enthusiastic in listening to his words, Herod became frightened that such persuasiveness with the people might lead to some uprising; for it seemed that they might go to any length on his advice. So before any new incident might stem from him, Herod considered it far better to seize John in advance and do away with him, rather than wait for an upheaval, become involved in a difficult situation, and regret it. As a result of this suspicion of Herod, John was sent as a prisoner to Machaerus . . . and there was put to death. This made the Jews believe that the destruction of Herod's army was a vindication of this man by God who saw fit to punish Herod.

(On some problems in this text of Josephus, see *Beginnings* 1. 102-103; J. M. Creed, *JTS* 23 [1922] 59-60.)

This lone extrabiblical testimony to the career of John the Baptist is pertinent to other episodes in the Lucan Gospel beyond this introductory paragraph. The testimony has been written, however, from a political viewpoint, giving the reasons for Herod's decision to imprison John and put him to death. As L. H. Feldman has remarked (*Josephus* [LCL 9] 83 n. e), there is no necessary contradiction between Josephus' account and the Gospel accounts, since the evangelists have chosen to emphasize the moral charges brought against Herod, whereas Josephus stressed the political fears John aroused in him. What is of more immediate interest is the way in which Josephus describes John's preaching and baptism. It sheds light on the way Luke depicts John.

Though Luke follows Mark 1:3-4—in beginning his Gospel proper with the notice of John in the desert and with the explanation of that presence by Isa 40:3, the episode is otherwise an independent Lucan composition. Verses 1-3a, with the reference to the desert (now alluding to 1:80) and its sixfold synchronism, are clearly of Lucan composition. Verses 3b-4 are dependent on Mark, as the end of v. 4 with *autou,* "his," instead of *tou theou hēmon,* "of our God" (LXX) plainly shows. Verses 5-6, the extension of the quotation from Isaiah, are again clearly from the Lucan pen. Five features in the passage stand out as Lucan: (1) the sixfold synchronism, relating John's call and ministry to contemporary Roman and Palestinian history (vv. 1-2); (2) the call of John in the form of an OT prophetic vocation (3:2b); (3) the extended quotation of Isaiah 40 to include v. 5, which ends with the vision of God's salvation by all human beings; (4) the omission of the description of the area from which people came to John and of John's garb; and (5) the relation of the desert to the Jordan (3:2-3).

The question has been raised whether Luke is dependent on "Q" in part at least (see T. Schramm, *Der Markus-Stoff,* 34-35; G. Schneider, *Evangelium nach Lukas,* 84; et al.). This question is raised because both Luke and Matthew mention the presence of John in the desert before the quotation of Isaiah 40, whereas Mark 1:2 begins with the quotation and then notes that John was in the desert, preaching. Again neither Matthew nor Luke have the verse from Mal 3:1 preceding the quotation from Isaiah. These two items might seem to suggest that Luke and Matthew both followed a form of an account from "Q," which differed in these regards from "Mk." The suggestion, of course, is not impossible. But clarity in this instance is not quickly arrived at. The minor agreements in this instance of Matthew and Luke against "Mk" can be explained otherwise. For Mark's introduction of his OT quotation(s) as something found in "Isaiah" when the first part of it actually comes from Malachi is something that both later evangelists might have wanted to correct quite incidentally and independently of each other. For another suggestion about its presence in Mark 1:2, see NOTE on Luke 3:4. Again, the phrase *en tē erēmō,* "in the desert," is found in Mark 1:4 and could have been moved up to v. 2 by Luke as part of his introductory formula; note that Matthew differs from Luke in relating it to John's preaching, as it is found in Mark 1:4. Hence, though the suggestion that Luke may be using "Q" material in part here is not impossible, the issue is not easily decided.

The main purpose of this first passage in the Gospel proper is to present John as one called by God to prepare for the inauguration of the period of salvation and to present him as an itinerant preacher who makes "ready the way of the Lord." The quotation of Isaiah 40 serves to enhance his appearance with the note of fulfillment: the consolation of Israel which that prophetic passage once announced is now to be understood in a new way. John is in the desert, preparing the way of the Lord, not merely by a study and strict observance of the Law—as was the understanding of this Isaian passage among the Essenes of Qumran—but by a preaching of reform, of a salvation to come, and a baptism of repentance.

The sixfold synchronism serves the historical perspective of Lucan theology (see p. 175 above). It cannot be understood as an exact dating of the appearance of John on the Palestinian scene—nor, consequently, of the beginning of Jesus' ministry. It is, rather, intended to provide a Roman and Palestinian ambience, a description of the Palestinian situation in which John's appearance and inauguration took place. For the difficulties relating to the exact dating, see the NOTES on 3:1. But the synchronism provides a solemn and significant literary background for the bringing of John on the scene at the opening of the Period of Jesus, in which salvation will be achieved, and in which "all human beings shall see the salvation of God" (3:6).

As the Gospel now stands, John has already been presented in the infancy narrative as one filled from birth with the holy Spirit (1:15,44). Now his role of prophet (1:76) is being inaugurated after the manner of the prophets of old. The beginning of his prophetic career is portrayed as one with repercussions on human history; hence the relating of his call to the great personalities of Roman and Palestinian history.

It is not unlikely that John, the son of Zechariah, as he is again introduced here (3:2; cf. 1:13), spent some time among the Essenes in the desert of Judah until God's call came to him (see NOTE on 1:80). The call would have meant a break with that closed community and an invitation to go forth and preach a baptism of repentance for the forgiveness of sins to all Jews. Since Josephus (*Life* 2 §§ 10-11) tells us that he himself spent some time among the Essenes, it is not improbable to think that the same sort of temporary connection was had by John, the son of Zechariah.

Some further factors (beyond those mentioned in the NOTE on 1:80) point in the direction of that hypothesis. The use of Isa 40:3 by all the evangelists explains the reason why John is in the desert (Mark 1:3; Matt 3:3; Luke 3:3-6; John 1:23); this association of Isa 40:3 with John's presence in the desert is thus multiply attested. But it is the text used in the Essene Rule-Book to explain why they too are there (1QS 8:12-16; see NOTE on 3:4). This may be sheer coincidence. But the Essene use of that text and their own presence in the desert provide a plausible and intelligent matrix for John's existence there. Again, the baptism that John preaches finds a likely explanation as a development of the ritual washings of the Essenes. There is, to be sure, no evidence that the ritual washings in the Essene community were either unique, initiatory, or not-to-be-repeated; and there is none that John's was such (*pace* Schneider, *Evangelium nach Lukas,* 84). Neither of these washings should be understood with such nuances, really derived from Christian baptism. Nor is there any plain evidence that the Essene ritual washings were a "baptism of repentance for the remission of sins." This description of John's baptism, which is not exclusive to Luke (see Mark 1:4), may be a historical description of what he proclaimed or at least a Christian reformulation of his main topic of proclamation. But, in any case, that topic finds a plausible background in the way in which the Essene Rule-Book refers to its ritual washings, the importance of which cannot be minimized. For "to enter the Covenant" was to "enter into water" (1QS 5:8,13). Finally, the relation of "water, spirit, and fire" to John's preaching of baptism (3:16) is plausibly explained against the views expressed in the same Rule-Book (see NOTE on 3:16). This makes it plausible that John did spend some time in his youth with the Essenes and that his ideas on baptism as a means of preparing for the coming salvation in Jesus were influenced in part by this experience. John would have broken off from them at the time of his "call" from God. This accounts for an important distinction, however, that must be kept in mind. For the Essenes of the Qumran community, contact with outsiders, even Palestinian Jews not of their own community, was a source of defilement (Josephus *J.W.* 2,8,10 § 150). We do not know whether this was true of all Essenes, e.g. those who were said by Josephus to live in the towns and villages (*J.W.* 2.8,4 § 124; cf. J. T. Milik, *Ten Years,* 90). In any case, John was apparently prepared to administer his baptism and to preach to all Jews who were willing to accept it, provided that their dispositions were suitable.

If this hypothesis has any validity, then it would alter the view of R. Bultmann (*HST,* 246), who regarded it as a specifically Christian accretion to the tradition about John that he was a wilderness preacher—this resting in all probability on the Christian view of him as the forerunner of Jesus in fulfillment of Isa 40:3. The use of the OT passage naturally makes one think of a Christian interpretation of the event; but when it is now seen that that very Isaian passage was actually used in pre-Christian Jewish circles with an eschatological connotation, one must hesitate in writing off the use of it about John as a merely Christian interpretation.

This episode, of course, is only introductory to the coming episodes about John's preaching and baptizing. Other forms of his preaching will be exemplified, and his entire ministry will be related to that of Jesus, of whom he is here the precursor.

NOTES

3 1. *In the fifteenth year of the reign of Tiberius Caesar.* Or possibly, "of the reign of Tiberius as Caesar." We have no idea where Luke might have come upon this dating. As the beginning of the synchronism used here, it can be understood with the other items. If we must admit with A. N. Sherwin-White (*Roman Society and Roman Law in the New Testament*, 166) that the "internal coherence of the lengthy formula . . . cannot be challenged for accuracy," one also has to note that this dating with which Luke begins, though prima facie pinpointing, is far from clear. The problem is that we do not know the frame of reference which he was using or his mode of calculating the years of the reign of Tiberius.

Five problematic factors complicate the reckoning and have to be admitted: (a) Did Luke begin his reckoning of Tiberius' regnal years from the coregency of Tiberius (with Augustus) over certain Roman provinces, dated to A.D. 11 (=A.U.C. 764) by Velleius Paterculus (2.121) or to A.D. 12 (=A.U.C. 765) by Suetonius (*Tib. vita*, 21)? This seems to be unlikely, but cannot be wholly excluded. (b) Did Luke reckon from the death of Augustus (19 August A.D. 14) or from the vote of the Roman Senate acknowledging Tiberius as Augustus' successor (17 September A.D. 14)? (c) Did Luke distinguish the accession year from the regnal years, i.e. did he count the period from 19 August or 17 September to a following New Year's Day as the accession year so that the first "regnal year" began only on New Year's Day? (d) Or did he count the partial accession year as the first regnal year, with the second beginning on the next New Year's Day? (e) Which calendar would Luke have been using in either of the latter two ways of reckoning Tiberius' regnal years? New Year's Day would be according to various contemporary calendars as follows:

Julian calendar	1 January
Jewish Calendar	1 Nisan
Syrian-Macedonian Calendar	1 October (or 1 Tishri)
Egyptian calendar	29 August

(For a full discussion of these problems with charts giving the various possibilities, see J. Finegan, *Handbook of Biblical Chronology*, 259-280; cf. H. W. Hoehner, *Chronological Aspects of the Life of Christ* [Grand Rapids: Zondervan, 1977] 29-44).

The option preferred by most commentators is to reckon Tiberius' regnal years either from the death of Augustus or the vote of the Roman senate and to make use of the Julian calendar. This would make the fifteenth year of Tiberius August/September A.D. 28-29. But even if this absolute dating is not ascertained with certitude, Luke obviously intended it to be a pinpointing to a period in the reign of the Roman emperor Tiberius. In contrast to it (and the reference to Pontius Pilate), the other references to subordinate local rulers, civil or religious, are vague and permit a considerable expanse of time.

The word *hēgemonia,* here translated as "reign," is a generic term for "leadership, high command, governorship," used of various officials in the Roman empire (*legati, praesides provinciae, praefectus, procuratores, propraetores*), including the principate of the emperor himself, as here (see Josephus *Life* 1 § 5; cf. Aristeas *Ep. ad Philocraten* 219; Josephus *Ant.* 2.16,5 § 348; H. J. Mason, *Greek Terms for Roman Institutions: A Lexicon and Analysis* [American Studies in Papyrology 13; Toronto: Hakkert, 1974] 51,137). Note the related verb-form used of Pilate in the following phrase.

when Pontius Pilate was prefect of Judea. Or simply, "was governor of Judea." Thus Luke introduces a historical personality who is to play a decisive role in the story of salvation about to unfold.

When Herod's son Archelaus was deposed (A.D. 6), Judea (and Samaria) came under the direct control of Roman officials. Pilate was appointed the sixth prefect of Judea by Sejanus, Tiberius' anti-Jewish adviser, and he held the prefecture from A.D. 26-36. A stern, high-handed ruler, he scarcely ingratiated himself with the local Jewish population (see Josephus, *J.W.* 2.9,2-3 § § 169-174; 2.9,4 §§ 175-177; *Ant.* 18.3,1 §§ 53-59; Philo *Legatio ad Gaium* 38 § 299; cf. *JBC,* art. 75, § 143). He appears again in Luke's story in 13:1; 23:1-6,11-13,20-24,52; Acts 3:13; 4:27; 13:28.

Luke uses of Pilate the ptc. *hēgemoneuontos;* in 20:20 he refers to him as *hēgemōn.* As we saw above, this was a generic title for someone holding a high command in a given area; it is also used of Pilate by Josephus (*Ant.* 18.3,1 § 55). It was often employed for the governor of Egypt. Ms. D, however, reads *epitropeuontos,* "when Pilate was procurator of Judea." This reading agrees with the Latin title usually given to Pilate, *procurator* (see Tacitus *Annales* 15.44,2; Tertullian *Apologeticus* 21.18). See Mason, *Greek Terms,* 49,142-143 (Greek *epitropos* = "governing [praesidial] procurators"). This commonly used title, however, is an anachronism for Pilate. It had long been so regarded by Roman historians (e.g. O. Hirschfeld, *Die kaiserlichen Verwaltungsbeamten bis auf Diocletian* [2d ed.; Berlin: Wiedmann, 1905] 382-383; H. G. Pflaum, *Les procurateurs équestres sous le haut-empire romain* [Paris: Maisonneuve, 1950] 23-25; A. H. M. Jones, "Procurators and prefects in the Early Principate," *Studies in Roman Government and Law* [Oxford: Blackwell, 1960] 115-125; A. N. Sherwin-White, "Procurator Augusti," *Papers of the British School at Rome* 15 [1939] 11-26; *Society and Roman Law in the New Testament* [Sarum Lectures, 1960-1961; Oxford: Clarendon, 1963] 6,12). They maintained that Pilate's title was "prefect" of Judea (like the *praefectus Aegypti,* or in Greek, *eparchos Aigyptou*). Their view has been confirmed by the discovery in 1961 of a fragmentary inscription at Caesarea Maritima, recording the dedication of a building, the *Tiberieum,* apparently erected by Pilate in honor of the emperor Tiberius. It not only represents the first epigraphic testimony to Pilate's presence in Judea, but gives him specifically the Latin title, [*praef*]-*ectus Iuda*[*ea*]*e.* See A. Frova, "L'iscrizione di Ponzio Pilato a Cesarea," in *Rendiconti dell'Istituto lombardo, Accademia di scienze e lettere,* cl. di lettere 95 (1961) 419-434; for further bibliography on this inscription, see *WA,* 31,48-49. Since *hēgemōn* is widely used in Greek papyri from Egypt as an equivalent title for the *praefectus Aegypti,* Luke is possibly using it here similarly of another prefect (hence my first translation). But it is difficult to be certain, because he later employs it for the *procurator* Felix (Acts 23:24,26,33). In any case the ptc. *hēgemoneuontos,* found in the best Greek mss., is preferred to *epitropeuontos* of ms. D. As far as can be ascertained today, the title *praefectus* was used for the governor of Judea until the time of the reorganization that took place under the emperor Claudius, ca. A.D. 46, when *procurator* was introduced. Hence *pace* H. Conzelmann (*Theology,* 18), Luke's terminology may not be so inexact.

and Herod tetrarch of Galilee. This is Herod Antipas, the younger son of Malthace and Herod the Great, who received part of his father's realm at his death (see NOTE on 2:2) and ruled from 4 B.C. He "received the revenue of Perea and Galilee, which annually yielded a tribute of two hundred talents" (Josephus *Ant.* 17.11,4 § 318; cf. *J.W.* 1.33,8 §§ 668-669). This is the "Herod" of the rest of the Lucan Gospel (3:19; 8:3; 9:7,9; 13:31; 23:7-15). He ruled as tetrarch until A.D. 39, when the emperor Caligula deposed and exiled him for seeking to make the courtesy title of "king" (cf. Mark 6:14, *basileus,* used of him) into a real title. See H. W. Hoehner, *Herod Antipas* (SNTSMS 17; Cambridge: University Press, 1972).

The title "tetrarch" originally designated one who ruled over a fourth part of an area; by the time of the gospel tradition it had become a sterotyped title for a petty prince. On Galilee, see NOTE on 17:11.

Philip tetrarch of the region of Ituraea and Trachonitis. Philip was the son of Herod the Great and Cleopatra of Jerusalem. His tetrarchy is variously described. Luke here mentions only two of the small areas over which he ruled. Not even Josephus is consistent in naming the areas; in *Ant.* 17.11,4 § 319 he lists them as Batanaea, Trachonitis, Auranitis, and part of the domain of Zenodorus; but in *Ant.* 17.8,1 § 189, as Gaulonitis, Trachonitis, Batanaea, and Paneas. This may be the reason why Luke uses *chōras,* "the region of . . . ," mentioning only two of the areas. At any rate, they were east of the Jordan, to the north, bordering on Syria, roughly north of the Decapolis and south of Damascus. Philip ruled from 4 B.C. until A.D. 34, when he died without an heir; his territory become part of the Roman province of Syria.

Lysanias tetrarch of Abilene. I.e. of a territory northwest of Damascus, surrounding the town of Abila at the southern end of the Anti-Lebanon range. But who was Lysanias? He is scarcely the Lysanias, son of Ptolemaeus, "king" of Chalcis in Coele-Syria; this Lysanias was put to death by M. Antony at the instigation of the Egyptian Cleopatra in 36 B.C. (see Josephus *Ant.* 15.4,1 § 92). Such a "gross chronological blunder" has at times been ascribed to Luke, but gratuitously. However, vague references in Josephus, referring to an "Abila, which belonged to Lysanias" (*Ant.* 19.5,1 § 275) or to "Abila, which had been the Lysanian tetrarchy" (*Ant.* 20.7,1 § 138), or to "the kingdom of Lysanias" (*J.W.* 2.11,5 § 215; 2.12,8 § 247) in contexts mentioning Chalcis or the territory given over to Herod Agrippa, seem to refer to a Lysanias different from the one put to death by M. Antony. This is also suggested by two fragmentary Greek inscriptions which mention a "Lysanias the tetrarch" (*CIG* 4521,4523), one of which names still another Lysanias. Possibly a descendant of the son of Ptolemaeus is involved. But we have no way of identifying the Lucan Lysanias with either of these persons. See further H. S. Cronin, *JTS* 18 (1917) 147-151; Creed, *The Gospel*, 307-309; S. Sandmel, "Lysanias," *IDB* 3. 193; R. Savignac, *RB* 9 (1912) 533-540.

If the identity of this petty prince is problematic, still more so is the reason why Luke has mentioned him at all. The reference to Pilate and the two sons of Herod the Great is comprehensible enough; they are the contemporary Roman and ethnic civil rulers of the land to which John's preaching will first be made known. Herod and Pilate will both reappear in the story. But why Luke singles out the tiny tetrarchy in Syrian territory as a further synchronic factor in his story of the call of John is a mystery. Is it because Luke was a Syrian? Did he come from Abilene? Alas, we shall never know. The suggestion that he has carelessly made use of information from Josephus in this matter raises more problems than it solves; it is more likely that Luke's reference to Lysanias relies on information that is wholly independent.

2. *in the high-priesthood of Annas and Caiaphas.* To the civil rulers Luke now adds mention of religious leaders of Palestinian Judaism. Annas, or Ananus, son of Seth, was appointed high priest by the Roman governor, P. Sulpicius Quirinius (see NOTE on 2:2), in A.D. 6 and held this position until he was deposed in A.D. 15. He was then succeeded by Ishmael, son of Phiabi (A.D. 15), Eleazar, his own son (16-17), Simon, son of Camith (17-18), and eventually by his son-in-law, Joseph, called Caiaphas. The latter held the post of high priest from A.D. 18-36. The Fourth Gospel refers to Caiaphas twice as "the high priest that year" (11:49; 18:13b), viz. the year of Jesus' death, even though it too gives Annas the title "high priest" (John 18:13a,19). In Acts 4:6 Luke again gives the title "high-priest" to Annas, while mentioning Caiaphas simply as a member of "the high-priestly family" (*ex genous archieratikou*). Just what Luke intends by "the high-priesthood of Annas and Caiaphas" is not easy to say. Since there was never more than one high priest at a time, the phrase raises a question again about either the accuracy of Luke's information or of his interpretation. On the other hand, it may have been customary to speak of an ex-high priest as such even when he was already out of office, and Luke may simply be referring to a period when Palestinian Jewry was dominated by two powerful figures; to it he relates the call of John.

a message came from God to John. Lit. "a word of God was (directed) to John." Whereas Mark 1:4 noted simply that John the Baptist was preaching in the desert, Luke depicts his activity as the result of a "call" from God. Here the Lucan use of *ginesthai epi* + acc. resembles that of *einai epi* in 2:25. In this case, however, the phraseology is borrowed from the LXX of Jer 1:1, *to rēma tou theou ho egeneto epi Ieremian ton tou Chelkious . . .*, "the word of God, which was (directed) to Jeremiah, son of Hilkiah. . . ." Cf. Isa 38:4; Jer 13:3. The allusion thus relates the call of John to that of the prophetic figures, Isaiah or Jeremiah, of the OT, specifying the prophetic character of his role (recall 1:76; cf. 7:26). In this sense, then, John belongs to the Period of Israel. But it is precisely the call of God that makes him play a transitional role at the beginning of the period of fulfillment in Lucan salvation-history. If John had been an Essene and a member of the Qumran community up to this point, the prophetic call would mark his break with that community. His call is to a more universal mission, and this aspect of his preaching is given significant stress in the Lucan account with the extended quotation of Isaiah 40.

the son of Zechariah. This identification of John is now redundant, coming as it does after the infancy narrative in the Lucan Gospel, as we now have it (see 1:13,63). But if this episode were at one time the beginning of an earlier form of the Gospel it would make perfect sense so to identify John. Such an identification is found only in Luke.

in the desert. As the Lucan Gospel now stands, this is an allusion to 1:80 (see NOTE there). Again, if this were the beginning of an earlier form of the Gospel, it would take on a slightly different nuance.

The exact area of John's desert sojourn is not given, neither here nor in 3:4 or 7:24; it is immaterial to Luke's concern. He does not call it "the desert of Judea," as does Matt 3:1; but the relation here between "the desert" and "the region all around the Jordan" makes it likely that the wilderness of Judea is meant. Conzelmann (*Theology,* 18) regards this "relation between the desert and the Jordan as the scene of John's ministry" as part of the Lucan geographical separation of John's ministry from Jesus'; on this problem, see p. 170 above.

3. *he moved into the region all around the Jordan.* Luke depicts John as an itinerant desert preacher, addressing his message to all who would come to listen to him in the Jordan valley. Luke does not specify the regions from which the people came; contrast Mark 1:5, "from all Judea," and "all the Jerusalemites." The "region" is not clearly distinct from "the desert" (see 4:1). None of the other Synoptics localizes John's area of ministry differently, but the Fourth Gospel may do so (John 3:23), if Aenon near Salim is not to be located in the Jordan valley (see R. E. Brown, *John, I-XII,* 151).

to preach a baptism of repentance for the forgiveness of sins. Luke calls John explicitly "the Baptist" (*baptistēs*) in 7:20,33; 9:19; here he depicts him preaching a baptism. *Baptisma* must be understood of a ritual washing having a religious connotation, and the following phrases specify the connotation. It is associated with *metanoia,* "repentance" (lit. "a change of mind," but when used in a religious sense, it connotes "conversion, reform of life"; see p. 237 above). For the OT background of the relation of *metanoia* to human sin, see Wisd 11:23; 12:19—and more generically the prophetic emphasis on human beings "turning" to God from sin (Isa 6:10; Ezek 3:19). The phrase *aphesis hamartiōn,* though not found as such in the LXX, is related to the verb *aphienai* which is used with *hamartia* (e.g. Num 14:19; Ps 25:18). The anarthrous, Semitic-sounding phrase expresses the purpose of the "baptism of repentance" that John preaches. Actually, *metanoia* and *aphesis hamartiōn* are two of Luke's favorite ways of summing up the effects of the Christ-event (see pp. 223, 237 above). Here Luke describes John's ministry in the same terms, but he will make clear the distinction between John's baptism and later Christian baptism in 3:16 (cf. Acts 18:25). John's baptism is now being so described because what John preaches inaugurates the Period of Jesus.

John's baptism finds a plausible matrix in the general baptist movement known to have existed in Palestine roughly between 150 B.C. and A.D. 250. A number of Jewish and Christian groups emerged in this period that practiced some form of ritual washing. Though the forms differed and the connotations attached to them varied, the washings of the Essenes, of John and his disciples (Acts 18:25; 19:1[?]; John 3:23-25), of Jesus and his disciples (John 3:22; cf. 4:2), of the Ebionites and a host of later Gnostic groups are examples of this general movement. See J. Thomas, *Le mouvement baptiste en Palestine* (Gembloux: Duculot, 1935). Whereas Lev 5:14 - 6:7 prescribed various sacrifices for sin, John's message urged a ritual washing instead. We are never told what the efficacy of his baptism was considered to be, and one must resist the tendency to regard it in any anachronistic way (associating to it a sacramental effect characteristic of later Christian baptism). John's baptism, however, does find a plausible explanation, if one considers the contemporary view of ritual washings among the Qumran Essenes. It was useless to "enter the water" (i.e. partake in Essene ritual washing as a member of the community) unless one were willing to turn from evildoing: "They shall not enter the water to share in the pure meal of the saints, for they shall not be cleansed unless they turn from their evildoing; for all who transgress his word are unclean" (1QS 5:13-14). Similarly, the OT idea of God's forgiveness of human sin is related by John to a ritual washing and an attitude of repentance.

This also makes it plausible to explain John's baptism as a development of a purificatory rite such as that of the Essenes, rather than as a derivation from Jewish proselyte baptism (J. Jeremias), which cannot certainly be traced back to the first century A.D., let alone to an earlier period. So J. A. T. Robinson, T. M. Taylor.

4. *as it is written in the book of the sayings of Isaiah the prophet.* To explain the nature of John's preaching and baptism, Luke follows the detail in Mark 1:2-3 and quotes Isa 40:3, extending it to include v. 5. This explicit quotation of Isaiah is introduced by the formula *hōs gegraptai* (as in Acts 13:33); it is a variant of *kathōs gegraptai* (see NOTE on 2:23). The formula is found in extrabiblical legal texts and in the LXX as a translation of Hebrew *kktwb* (e.g. 2 Chr 35:12). See *ESBNT*, 8-9. Not only is the simple form (*k'šr ktwb*) frequently found in Qumran literature (e.g. 1QS 5:17; 8:14; CD 7:19; 4QFlor 1:12), but a fuller form also occurs which is very close to the Lucan formulation here: *'šr ktwb bspr yš'yh hnby'*, "as it is written in the Book of Isaiah the prophet" (4QFlor 1:15; cf. 4QCatena^a 7:3; 4QCatena^b 1:4). Since the Marcan introductory formula is simply, "As it is written in Isaiah the prophet," the Lucan addition is noteworthy. In both the NT and Qumran literature the explicit quotation of the OT is intended to interpret events of recent history, clothing them with an aspect of salvation-history. The introductory conj. *hōs*, "as," shows that Luke regards John's baptism and preaching as a fulfillment of Isaiah's prophetic message.

A voice of someone. . . . Luke follows Mark in citing Isa 40:3 to explain why John is found in the desert near the Jordan; in fact, all four evangelists so explain it. The author of the Qumran *Manual of Discipline* also uses this Isaian passage to explain why the Qumran community is in the desert: "When these become (members of) the community in Israel according to these rules, they shall separate from the habitation of unrighteous people to go into the desert to prepare there the way of HIM; as it is written, 'Make ready in the desert the way of. . . . ; make straight in the wilderness a path for our God.' This means the study of the Law which he enacted through Moses, that they may act according to all that has been revealed from age to age and according to what the prophets have made known by his holy Spirit" (8:12-15). The path to be readied in the desert is different: for the Essenes it is the study and observance of the Law and the Prophets; for John it is the acceptance of the baptism of repentance.

Applied to John, the Isaian passage reveals him to be a prophetic voice proclaiming the accessibility of God's "salvation" to *all* people. The Isaiah quotation climactically ends with 40:5, as Luke has extended it, to present in capsule form not only John's preaching, but even the universality of salvation to be made available in Jesus' preaching, of which John's is the anticipation. It also echoes the canticle of Simeon (2:30-31). The following pericope will specify how John proclaims this salvation; he appears as a prophetic preacher of the eschaton, of salvation, and of reform, but not of the kingdom (contrast Matt 3:2; see p. 154 above).

Luke quotes Isaiah according to the LXX, but with a slight omission (40:5a) and a few insignificant word-changes (singulars becoming plurals; the phrase "in the desert" modifies in the original not "crying out" but the verb "make ready"). If Luke has followed Mark here in using Isa 40:3 to explain why John is in the desert, he has not followed him in prefixing Mal 3:1 to the Isaian quotation. Matt 3:3 also omits Mal 3:1 (see COMMENT). Some commentators have regarded the use of Mal 3:1 in Mark 1:3 as a gloss, introduced into the Marcan Gospel by a later hand and reflecting the same sort of hindsight that is evident in the identification of John and Elijah in the Lucan infancy narrative (so M.-J. Lagrange, V. Taylor). This may be, but it would then mean that Luke was dependent on a form of Mark slightly different from what we have today. However, it is more likely that both Luke and Matthew realized independently that the quotation of the OT as given in Mark was not adequately covered by the introductory formula.

Make ready the way of the Lord. If there were any way of being sure that the historical John described his mission in these words of Isaiah, we would have to realize that "the Lord" in his preaching would have meant Yahweh. His historical preaching of a baptism of repentance would have been a preparation for the "day of the Lord" in the OT sense. But, as this phrase is now used by the Christian evangelists, "the Lord" shares the same sort of ambiguity as *kyrios* in 1:76 (see NOTE). Hence, in the Lucan context John's making ready of the way of the Lord takes on another connotation.

The Isaian phrase, "the way of the Lord," now echoes, in the present form of the Gospel, the description of John's role in 1:76,79. See further 20:21; Acts 28:26,28. It underlies the designation of Christianity as "the Way" in Acts (see p. 242 above).

BIBLIOGRAPHY (3:1-6)

Betz, O. "Die Proselytentaufe der Qumransekte und die Taufe im Neuen Testament," *RevQ* 1 (1958-1959) 213-234.

Creed, J. M. "Josephus on John the Baptist," *JTS* 23 (1922) 59-60.

Dahl, N. A. "The Origin of Baptism," in *Interpretationes ad Vetus Testamentum pertinentes Sigmundo Mowinckel septuagenario missae* (Oslo: Forlaget Land og Kirke, 1955) 36-52.

Geyser, A. S. "The Youth of John the Baptist," *NovT* 1 (1956) 70-75.

Gnilka, J. "Die essenischen Tauchbäder und die Johannestaufe," *RevQ* 3 (1961-1962) 185-207.

Jeremias, J. "Proselytentaufe und Neues Testament," *TZ* 5 (1949) 418-428.

——— "Der Ursprung der Johannestaufe," *ZNW* 28 (1929) 312-320.

Michaelis, W. "Zum jüdischen Hintergrund der Johannestaufe," *Judaica* 7 (1951) 81-120.

Robinson, J. A. T. "The Baptism of John and the Qumran Community," *HTR* 50 (1957) 175-191; reprinted in *Twelve New Testament Studies* (SBT 34; Naperville: Allenson, 1962) 11-27.

Rowley, H. H. "The Baptism of John and the Qumran Sect," in *New Testament Essays in Memory of T. W. Manson* (ed. A. J. B. Higgins; Manchester: University Press, 1959) 218-229.

——— "Jewish Proselyte Baptism and the Baptism of John," *HUCA* 15 (1940) 313-334.

Sahlin, H. *Studien zum dritten Kapitel des Lukasevangeliums* (Uppsala Universitets Årsskrift, 1949/2; Uppsala: Lundeqvistska Bokhandeln; Leipzig: Harrassowitz, 1949).

Sutcliffe, E. F. "Baptism and Baptismal Rites at Qumran?" *HeyJ* 1 (1960) 179-188.

Taylor, T. M. "The Beginnings of Jewish Proselyte Baptism," *NTS* 3 (1955-1956) 193-198.

Thyen, H. *"Baptisma metanoias eis aphesin hamartiōn,"* in *The Future of Our Religious Past: Essays in Honour of Rudolf Bultmann* (ed. J. M. Robinson; New York: Harper & Row, 1971) 131-168.

Torrance, T. F. "Proselyte Baptism," *NTS* 1 (1954-1955) 150-154.

11. JOHN'S PREACHING
(3:7-18)

3 7 Accordingly John addressed the crowds that came out to be baptized by him: "Brood of vipers, who has warned you to flee from the wrath that is coming? 8 Come now, produce the fruit of worthy repentance! Do not start saying to yourselves, 'We have Abraham for our father.' For I tell you, God can raise up children for Abraham from these very stones. 9 The ax is indeed already laid to the root of the trees; any tree then that fails to produce good fruit is to be cut down and thrown into a fire."

10 When the crowds asked him, "What then should we do?" 11 his reply to them was, "Whoever has two tunics must share with him who has none; whoever has food to eat must do likewise." 12 Toll-collectors also came to be baptized, and they asked him, "Teacher, what should we do?" 13 And to them he would say, "Collect nothing for yourselves —nothing beyond what is authorized." 14 When enlisted soldiers asked him, "And what are we to do?" he would say to them, "Avoid extortion and blackmail; be content with your pay."

15 Now the people were piqued with curiosity and all were pondering in their minds whether John might not be the Messiah. 16 But John replied to them all, "I am baptizing you with water, but someone more powerful than I is coming; and I am not fit to unfasten even the strap of his sandals. He will baptize you with a holy Spirit and with fire. 17 His winnowing-fan is in his hand, ready to clean up his threshing-floor and to store the wheat in his barn; but the chaff he will burn in a fire that will never go out."

18 With these and many other exhortations John preached to the people.

COMMENT

In 3:3 Luke presented John the Baptist as a prophetic preacher (*kērys-sōn*), calling for repentance and inviting human beings to baptism. He now paints a more specific picture of his prophetic preaching activity. Three samples of it are given, devoted to different aspects of that preaching: eschatological, ethical, and messianic.

From a form-critical viewpoint this passage belongs in the main to the narrative gospel tradition. It is a story about John, a "legend" in R. Bultmann's sense (*HST*, 245-247). But it is actually conflated, for Luke has introduced into his form of it certain "sayings" of John. Verses 7-9, 10-14 belong to the latter category.

In comparing this passage with the other Synoptic accounts, we see that the basic inspiration for it is drawn from "Mk." Even though Luke has inserted into the narrative derived from "Mk" material from the Double Tradition and a private source, the episode itself still forms part of a major block of material common in sequence in Mark and Luke (see p. 67 above). Verse 7a is a Lucan transitional half-verse introducing the preaching samples. That it stems from Lucan composition is seen by comparison with Matt 3:7a. Sayings-material from "Q" are found in vv. 7b-9 and also in vv. 16b-17; in the latter they have been preferred by Luke to the Marcan form (1:7-8) and find their parallel in Matt 3:11-12. In the "Q" form of the latter sayings, that about the "more powerful one" becomes the basis of the baptism with the holy Spirit and fire. Verses 15-16a,18 are to be ascribed to Lucan composition; they are comments of the evangelist. Verses 10-14 are problematic. Though some commentators (e.g. A. Plummer, *Gospel,* 90; H. Schürmann, *Lukasevangelium,* 169) think that these verses come from "Q" too, being omitted by Matthew, they are more likely to be attributed to Luke's private source ("L"). A certain similarity between them and another "L" passage (the Zacchaeus-episode) has been noted by T. W. Manson (*BJRL* 36 [1953-1954] 411-412). But, as often, can one completely exclude the possibility of Lucan composition? If the analysis of vv. 16b-17 that we have preferred, as coming from "Q" rather than from "Mk," be correct, then we would have in these two independent testimonies a double attestation of the basic comparison of John with Jesus in the matter of baptism.

In analyzing the passage, we shall distinguish in it three subsections, according to the kind of preaching present in each: vv. 7-9, 10-14, 15-18.

The first subsection (vv. 7-9) offers a sample of John's eschatological preaching. He does not invite the crowds who come to him to adopt his desert way of life, but calls them rather to reform and to a mode of conduct demanded by the "coming wrath." Addressed not to Pharisees and Sadducees, as in Matt 3:7, but to "crowds," the Baptist's words are intended as an explanation of the "repentance" (*metanoia*) of v. 3 and an eschatological motivation for it. John's "making ready the way of the Lord" (v. 4) is now seen related to what OT prophets called "the Day of the Lord." Significantly, this sample of eschatological preaching is devoid of any reference to a messiah; all is therefore to be understood against the OT background of prophetic teaching.

This first subsection is one of the clearest instances of identical wording in the Double Tradition: sixty out of sixty-three (Matthew) / sixty-four (Luke) words in the Greek text of these verses are identical (see Matt 3:7-10). The differences, Lucan *arxēsthe,* "start," for Matthean *doxēte,* "think," the addition of adverbial *kai* (v. 9), and a plural for a singular in two words, are almost certainly Lucan stylistic improvements.

Addressed to Palestinian Jews, this eschatological sermon has a certain irony in it. For it is not only a call to repentance and to a form of conduct consonant with the faith that they are supposed to be professing, but, in chiding these "children of Abraham," it counters a widespread boast of John's coreligionists (see also John 8:33-39). Lucan concern for the universality of salvation surfaces, as it is made clear that physical descent from Abraham is not the only way that one can become his "children" (cf. Luke 19:10). The "Q" passage echoes the sentiment in John and in Paul (Rom 4:16-25; Gal 3:29).

The second subsection (vv. 10-14) offers a sample of the Baptist's ethical preaching, especially as it was concerned with social conduct. Again, John does not invite the crowds to adopt his mode of life, but by way of contrast with the former mode of preaching, his words here lack any eschatological motivation. Nor are they related to the coming of a messiah. Instead, John advocates a selfless concern for others—good advice for Jews, Christians, or pagans. His counsel is wholly intelligible in terms of Palestinian or OT backgrounds. However, in its present Lucan context, John's ethical preaching follows on the heels of eschatological preaching, and it is obviously colored by the latter. The radical character of John's eschatological preaching here yields to a different emphasis: assistance, honesty, and equity. In a sense, John's counsel is of a mixed sort: on the one hand, he manifests a real concern for the neighbor (in a variety of ways), and yet, on the other, he does not seek to upset the existing social structure—even in view of the "coming wrath." He advocates the sharing of the fundamentals of life (v. 11), the avoidance of extortion, blackmail, and intimidation (vv. 13-14). But he does not tell toll-collectors to sever their relations with the occupying power, nor does he counsel enlisted soldiers to give up their jobs (even as mercenaries—see NOTE on v. 14). Indeed, the last piece of advice he addresses to them, "be content with your pay" (v. 14), does not even envisage the possibility of its being an unjust wage.

The specific things that John recommends to his fellow Jews are intended by Luke to be recommendations for his Christian readers as well. They are examples of the "good fruit" (v. 8) expected of his community. The collocation here of the Baptist's eschatological kerygma and demand for ethical conduct says much about the Lucan view of the relation of kerygma to ordinary daily life.

The third subsection (vv. 15-18) is the most important part of this episode, offering a sample of the Baptist's messianic (or christological) preaching. Its importance is seen in the way that John defines his role vis-à-vis the Messiah, the One Who Is to Come, the more powerful one. An eschatological note is associated with his messianic preaching, especially in v. 17.

Though John does not explicitly deny that he is "the Messiah," as he does in John 1:20, implicitly he does just that—and that implicit denial is found only here in the Synoptic tradition. It forms part of the evangelist's comment in v. 15 and is not on John's lips. The implicit denial is found rather in John's referring to Jesus as the One Who Is to Come and the more powerful one. In effect, this passage conflates three titles, applying to Jesus: "the Messiah," "the One Who Is to Come"—both of distinct OT backgrounds (see the NOTES)—and "the more powerful one." A christological concern thus dominates this part of John's preaching. In contrast to the Marcan form of John's statement ("I baptized you with water, but he will baptize you with a holy Spirit," 1:8), the "Q" form of John's statement makes the baptism with fire and the holy Spirit depend directly on John's identification of Jesus as the more powerful one. Because he is such, he will baptize in a more powerful way. This superiority of Jesus over John is shown in four ways: (1) Though Jesus "comes" (v. 16c) after John in a chronological sense (see Acts 13:24-25), he does not come "after" him as a disciple following a master (see NOTE). (2) John is not even "fit" to perform the lowliest task for Jesus (v. 16d); (3) Jesus' baptism will be one of the holy Spirit and fire in contrast to John's water-baptism (v. 16b, e); (4) Jesus himself will come as the winnower (=judge) to sort out the wheat and the chaff (v. 17). Thus John is not himself an eschatological figure, but as a prophetic preacher he announces the "more powerful one," the messianic figure of the *eschaton* who is about to appear. As such, he is "more than a prophet" (7:26), the inaugurator of the eschaton.

The NOTES will explain in what sense the various titles given to Jesus are to be understood and how we are to understand the baptism of the holy Spirit and of fire. What should be noted here is that the preaching illustrated in the last subsection of this episode is in reality a further specification of the eschatological preaching of the first. The images used in v. 17 recall those of the first subsection.

What should also be noted is the absence in the entire passage of any reference to the kingdom of God. "John does not proclaim the Kingdom of God" (H. Conzelmann, *Theology*, 20). For in the Lucan writings Jesus is the kingdom-preacher (see p. 184 above). Even if we agree with W. Wink that John's ministry forms the preparatory part of the Period of Jesus, his preaching is still not the same as that of Jesus.

NOTES

3 7. *the crowds.* Whereas John's eschatological preaching is addressed in Matt 3:7 to Pharisees and Sadducees, it is here addressed to "the crowds" who came to John for baptism. It is almost impossible to say whether "the Pharisees and Sadducees" belonged originally to "Q," or whether Matthew has introduced this specification. Given the form of address, "Brood of vipers," it is easier to see the Matthean audience as the more original.

This is, however, the first of many instances of the Lucan use of *ochlos,* "crowd," or the pl. *ochloi.* The other Synoptic evangelists use this word frequently, but the Lucan use is baffling; at times he avoids it where they have it, at times he introduces it where they do not have it. In common with Mark, Luke uses the sg. in 5:1; 8:4,19,40; 9:37,38; 22:47; and the pl. in 8:42,45 (in some instances the Marcan parallel may have the sg.). In common with Matthew, Luke uses the sg. in 9:12,16; 6:17; and the pl. in 7:24; 9:11; 11:14. But these passages are few in comparison with those in which Luke introduces the word on his own, either sg. or pl. Quite frequently the word merely designates the crowd that is present (5:19; 6:19; 7:9,11; 8:19,40,42,45; 9:12,16; 11:27; 12:13; 13:14,17 [only here is there a contrast between the crowd and a leader]; 18:36; 19:3,39; 22:47). Sometimes this crowd is specified by a gen. ("a crowd of disciples," "a city crowd": 5:29; 6:17; 7:12). But in many cases, whether it be used in the sg. or pl., it designates simply the anonymous audience that witnesses the ministry of John or Jesus (3:7,10; 4:42; 5:3,15; 7:24; 9:11,18; 11:14,29; 12:54; 14:25; 23:4,48 [pl.]; 5:1; 8:4; 9:37; 12:1; 22:6 [sg.]). In this last sense the Lucan use of the word suits his general stress on the popular, universal reaction to the ministry of both John and Jesus. In the immediate context, the *ochloi* give way to *laos,* "people," in vv. 15,18.

that came out to be baptized by him. Ms. D reads rather, "to be baptized before him." This would suggest that John did not do all the baptizing himself. In any case, Luke's formulation, in contrast to Matt 3:7, depicts many people accepting John's baptism; cf. 7:29, "all the people." Moreover, Luke depicts John's preaching as postbaptismal, if the statement here is taken at face value. But this may be simply the result of the literary mode of presentation. The overall drift of the passage is that the people accept baptism as a result of his exhortation.

Brood of vipers. Lit. "broods of vipers." This phrase occurs only here in Luke, but besides the parallel in Matt 3:7, it occurs again in Matt 12:34 and 23:33; in the latter context it is associated with "serpents" (*opheis*). The image is otherwise unknown in the OT, Josephus, or rabbinical writings. The *echidna* was regarded in antiquity as a poisonous snake (Lucian *Alexander sive Pseudomantis* 10), and the expression is intended to convey the repulsive, even destructive, character of those so described. So characterized, they are being warned against a smugness of certain salvation—which will be their own undoing.

to flee from the wrath that is coming. Luke speaks of "wrath" (*orgē*) only here and in 21:23; in both instances it refers to a future manifestation of God's wrath. He makes use of an OT expression for God's judgment by which evil is to be wiped out; it is associated with the Day of the Lord in Isa 13:9; Zeph 1:14-16; 2:2; Ezek 7:19. Just as OT prophets often depicted it as the manifestation of an eschatological event, from which Israel itself would not escape, though individuals could find shelter in timely conversion, so John carries on the prophetic message. Jewish apocalyptic literature made much of this idea, even depicting God doing battle with his angels on the side of "the sons of light" on that great day (see 1QM 1:1-17; *1 Enoch* 90:18; 91:7). Since "God's wrath" is of little interest to Luke, we never learn in his writings what evokes it; elsewhere in the NT it is called forth by idolatry, disobedience, or disbelief (a smugness that can do without God)—see 1 Thess 1:10; Rom 1:18; Col 3:6; Eph 5:6.

8. *produce the fruit of worthy repentance!* Lit. "produce fruits worthy of repentance," i.e. in keeping with your repentance; show by your actions and conduct that an inner revitalization has taken place. Whereas Matt 3:8 has the sg. *karpon,* "fruit," Luke uses the pl., possibly because of the details to be set forth in vv. 10-14.

Do not start saying. Luke has here substituted *arxēsthe* for the more original *doxēte,* retained in Matt 3:9. This is the first appearance of the verb *archein* in the Lucan writing, and it has to be understood as an instance of a Lucan favorite expression—the new beginning that is being made in the history of salvation. Cf. Luke 3:23; Acts 1:22; 10:37.

We have Abraham for our father. The blessing of Abraham (Gen 12:1-3) became in time Israel's pride and boast. This finds expression in Isa 51:2-3, where the blessing of Abraham and Sarah is regarded as the basis for the consolation of Zion. In various ways rabbinical literature later played on Israel's physical descent from Abraham as protection against God's wrath; much of it was explained in terms of Abraham's merit (see Str-B, 1. 116-121). Salvation tied to "Father Abraham" as a Jewish belief is echoed elsewhere in the NT (see Luke 16:24; John 8:33-39; Acts 7:2; Rom 4:1; cf. Gal 3:29). Cf. *T. Levi* 15:4 (*APOT* 2. 313). This reliance on an ethnic privilege, however, is precisely what the Baptist repudiates. That repudiation is not based, though, on a call to a faith in a messiah, but on conduct expected to be consonant with an inner reform of life.

God can raise up children for Abraham from these very stones. To have "children of Abraham" God does not depend on Jews physically descended from the patriarch. In thus addressing his fellow Jews, John implies that God can even create Israel anew. Implicit in his thinking is the idea that God thereby would not be unfaithful to the promises made to Abraham, but only that he has other ways of extending them to human beings. As it will develop, Lucan theology will not depict God creating a *new* Israel, a substitute for that of old, but rather will reconstitute Israel of old, relating Gentiles to the promises made to the forefathers. Cf. Exod 32:25-34, for an OT precedent of the reconstitution of Israel.

Some commentators think that there might be a pun in these words of John, if the speech were originally delivered in Aramaic: *běnayyā'*, "sons," would be raised up from *'abnayyā'*, "stones" (see J. M. Creed, *The Gospel*, 52; M. Black, *AAGA*³, 145). Perhaps. The text of "Q" uses *tekna*, not *huious;* but *tekna* is found in the LXX of Dan 6:25 as a translation of Aramaic *běnêhôn*.

9. *The ax is indeed already laid to the root of the trees.* Or "already lies at the root," i.e. waiting to be used. The image is not entirely clear, but it probably is meant as an eschatological warning. Perhaps there is an allusion to Isa 10:33-34, where Yahweh is depicted as a forester lopping off the boughs of mighty Assyria. The image, then, would be that of Yahweh's historic deliverance of Israel, now transferred to an eschatological reckoning. However, the allusion is not certain because the Greek word for "ax" in "Q" is *axinē*, whereas the MT of Isaiah has used *barzel*, "iron," and the LXX *machaira*, "sword"—which have been translated into English as "ax" (e.g. *RSV*). In any case, the "ax" seems to be meant as a figure for discrimination between productive and unproductive trees; cf. the figure of the winnowing-fan in v. 17.

any tree then that fails to produce good fruit. Recall the parable of the fig tree (Luke 13:6-9).

thrown into a fire. John's preaching in this passage will again refer to a fire (vv. 16-17). These references serve to depict him as a fiery reformer and fill out details of his role as one sent in the "spirit and power of Elijah" (1:17). The "fire" has here no special connotation, being merely part of the general description of what is done with dead wood; a different connotation is conveyed in v. 17.

10. *the crowds.* See NOTE on v. 7.

What then should we do? This becomes a refrain in this subsection (see vv. 12,14). It is a characteristic Lucan rhetorical question; see further 10:25 (contrast Mark 12:28; Matt 22:36); 18:18; Acts 2:37; 16:30; 22:10). It is expressive of a popular eagerness for salvation.

11. *Whoever has two tunics.* The first piece of practical advice that John gives exemplifies the kind of reform of life that his *metanoia* calls for. It is not tied up with sacrificial offerings for sins or ascetic practices, such as the use of sackcloth and ashes, or even a flight into the solitude of the desert, such as his own withdrawal has been. Luke omits the description of the Baptist's ascetic mode of life (see Mark 1:6), probably because of the emphasis put here on ethical reform and concern for one's neighbor. Even the essentials of life, a tunic to wear and food to eat, are to be shared with one's less fortunate neighbors. Such a mode of preaching fits in with Luke's counsels in general on the use of material goods (see p. 248 above).

12. *Toll-collectors.* In this context, it refers to Jews who were responsible for collecting tolls from various areas in Palestine for the Romans. The *telōnai* will appear again in Luke 5:27,29-30; 7:29,34; 15:1; 18:10-13; cf. 19:2. Neither "publican" nor "tax-collector" is an accurate translation of the Greek term, which technically designates "toll-collectors," i.e. those engaged in the collection of indirect taxes (tolls, tariffs, imposts, and customs).

The collection of taxes in the Roman provinces had at one time been handled by a *societas publicanorum*, wealthy Romans of the equestrian class who usually exploited the provinces and often ruined them. However, J. Caesar broke their power (see Appian *Bella civilia* 5.4,19; J. Caesar *Bellum civile* 3.3,31 § 103). The publican system seems to have been used in Palestine from the time of Pompey's conquest (63 B.C.), but in 47 B.C. Caesar modified the taxation of the Jews, reducing their taxes considerably and making the sabbath years tax-free, and in 44 B.C. abrogated the system entirely so that publicans ceased to function in Palestine. Subsequently, in areas subject to Roman prefects and procurators (Judea, Samaria, Idumea) the direct taxes (poll tax, land tax) were taken up by "tax-collectors" (Greek *dēmosiōnes* [a word never used in the NT]; Hebrew *gabbā'îm*), directly employed by the Roman occupiers. The collection of other taxes (tolls, tariffs, imposts, and customs) was auctioned off to the highest bidder, who became the "chief toll-collector" (*architelōnēs*, Luke 19:2) and had agents (Greek *telōnai;* Hebrew *môkĕsîn*), usually employed in local tollhouses (*telōnia,* cf. 5:27), e.g. at Capernaum. In Galilee, however, both the "tax-collectors" and the "toll-collectors" were less under Roman control than elsewhere because of Herod Antipas' lengthy financial administration of his tetrarchy. Jews were often engaged in the collection of both direct and indirect taxes; they were in the direct employ of Roman occupiers and were used as tax-farmers in the indirect taxation system. Since the *architelōnēs* usually had to pay the expected revenue to the Romans in advance and then seek to recoup the amount, plus expenses and profits, by assessing and collecting the tolls, the system of toll-collection was obviously open to abuse and dishonesty. Various ancient tariff inscriptions in Greek and Aramaic testify to the attempts of governments to regulate the situation. See J. R. Donahue, "Tax Collectors and Sinners: An Attempt at Identification," *CBQ* 33 (1971) 39-61; O. Michel, *TDNT* 8. 88-105. Also the NOTE on 5:30 below.

Teacher. John is here given the honorific title that is used frequently later on for Jesus (7:40; 9:38; 10:25; 11:45; 12:13; 18:18; 19:39; 20:21,28,39; 21:7). Only in the Fourth Gospel is this title (*didaskalos*) equated with *rabbi* (1:38) or *rabbounei* (20:16); for the problems that this equation creates, see R. E. Brown, *John, I-XII,* 74. Cf. *WA,* 117.

13. *nothing beyond what is authorized.* The Palestinian Jews in the service of the occupying power are thus counseled to take only their legitimate tolls and commissions and to resist the temptation to greed or extortion. John's words seem to imply the common understanding of the career of the toll-collector as one of dishonesty; compare 19:8.

14. *enlisted soldiers.* These were not Roman soldiers, since there were no legions stationed in Palestine in this time, nor auxiliaries from other provinces. They should be understood as Jewish men enlisted in the service of Herod Antipas, of whose troops Josephus gives testimony (*Ant.* 18.5,1 § 113). Palestinian Jews were exempt from service in Roman armies since the time of Julius Caesar (Josephus *Ant.* 14.10,6 § 204); some of them, however, did serve as mercenaries. Some of these could have been among the *strateuomenoi,* lit. "men on military duty."

Avoid extortion and blackmail. Lit. "shake no one down or threaten to delate." The position that a soldier held in ancient Palestine apparently enabled him to intimidate people and secure money thereby. John counsels the soldiers not to play the sycophant (in its ancient Greek sense), i.e. to be a "fig-shower" (or one who reveals the figs by shaking the tree), a term used in classical Greece for those who denounced the attempt to export figs from Athens or the theft of fruit from sacred fig trees. It came to be a figure of intimidation and extortion. See E. Nestle, *ZNW* 4 (1903) 271-272. Compare Josephus' advice to his armed followers: not to make war on anyone or soil their hands with rapine, but to encamp in the plain and be content with their rations (*Life* 47 § 244; cf. *J.W.* 2.20,7 § 581).

be content with your pay. Or "with your rations/provisions." The Greek word *opsōnion* originally referred to the cooked rations of the soldiers, but it came in time to denote the money given for the purchase of such rations. See C. C. Caragounis, *NovT* 16 (1974) 35-57.

15. *were piqued with curiosity.* Lit. "were expecting or expectant of (something)." Luke refers at first to the popular reaction to John's mode of preaching, but the rest of the verse introduces the topic of the third subsection, his messianic preaching. The people's interest in this topic is scarcely occasioned by the immediately preceding ethical teaching; it is more likely occasioned by John's eschatological preaching, as in the first subsection.

the Messiah. Luke's comment implies that there were Palestinian Jews who awaited the coming of a messiah, i.e. an "anointed" agent of Yahweh sent for the restoration of Israel and the triumph of God's power and dominion (see p. 197 above). From at least the beginning of the second century B.C. there had crystallized in Palestinian Judaism such an expectation. It developed out of the David-tradition in Israel, especially as this was presented in the Deuteronomist: David as the zealous worshiper of Yahweh, "chosen" by him to rule over Israel in place of Saul (2 Sam 6:21) and favored not for himself alone, but insofar as his kingly role would affect all Israel. The oracle of Nathan (2 Sam 7:14-17) and the "last words of David" (2 Sam 23:1-17) reveal Yahweh's promise of a dynasty and explicitly refer to the historical David as "the anointed" (*māšîaḥ*) of the God of Jacob. That title of David is repeated in the Psalms (18:51; 89:39,52; 132:10,17). Jeremiah, who confronted the last of the Davidic kings before Nebuchadnezzar's invasion, announced that Jehoiakim would "have none (i.e. no heir) to sit upon the throne of David" (36:30); but he was also the prophet who uttered the promise of a "new covenant" (31:31) and proclaimed the divine assurance that the people of Israel would "serve Yahweh their God and David their king, whom I will raise up for them" (30:9). This "David" was no longer the historical David, but a future occupant of the throne to be raised up by Yahweh. This ideal king will be a "David" (Jer 33:15; Ezek 37:23-24). But in all these promises of a future, ideal "David," the title *māšîaḥ* is strikingly absent. The title occurs but twice in all the prophetic books: once applied to Cyrus, the Persian monarch (Isa 45:1); once to the reigning king of Israel, or perhaps to Israel itself (Hab 3:13). Though reference be made to the oracle of Nathan, "the coming of a messiah" is never the phraseology used to announce the hope of a restored kingdom of David. The same absence is noted in the postexilic rewriting of the David story (compare 2 Sam 7:12,16 and 1 Chr 17:11,14). The first clear mention of *māšîaḥ* in the sense of a *future* anointed agent of Yahweh in the Davidic line is found in Dan 9:25, "from the going forth of the Word to restore and build Jerusalem to (the coming of) an anointed one, a prince, there shall be seven weeks." (We prescind here from the problems of interpretation —to whom this would refer; we note only the implied future context in which the title appears.) This Danielic usage, along with various references to "anointed figures" in Qumran literature (1QS 9:11; 1QSa 2:14,20; CD 20:1; 4QPBless 2:4; 4QFlor 1:11-13; 4QpIsaᵃ 8-10:11-17), which attest the Essene expectation of Messiahs of Israel and Aaron, and the (probably Pharisaic) *Psalms of Solomon* (17:23,36; 18:6,8) reveal a clear Jewish expectation of the coming of a messiah (or messiahs) in the period prior to the emergence of Christianity. See further J. A. Fitzmyer, *Concilium* 20 (1967) 75-87; *ESBNT*, 115-121. This evidence indicates how the OT theme of a coming David as an anointed agent of Yahweh developed into an explicit expectation of a Messiah (with a capital M), or of several of them.

Though Luke's phrase, *ho christos*, "the Messiah," is undoubtedly influenced by the early Christian use of the title in reference to Jesus of Nazareth, it would be an oversimplification to maintain that Palestinians of the time of John the Baptist could never have posed the question as framed by Luke. If we are right in thinking that John had at one time been a member of the Qumran community, then the curiosity of "all" the people takes on a still further nuance in Luke's presentation.

16. *John replied*. The variant in ms. D explains why John "replies": "Discerning their thoughts, he said." This is characteristic of the ms. D, which has the tendency to fill out what might seem like a lacuna in the story.

them all. The use of *pasin*, "all," is a Lucan trait, being absent from Mark 1:7 and Matt 3:11; cf. 7:29. It is part of the Lucan stress on the universality involved in the new form of salvation being made available.

I am baptizing you with water. The ms. D adds, "for repentance." This is obviously a harmonization with Matt 3:11.

someone more powerful than I is coming. Lit. "there is coming one who is more powerful than I." The stress is on the initial verb, *erchetai*. Luke's phrase is here derived from Mark 1:7, but with the omission of *opisō mou*, "after me." Matt 3:11 has adapted the Marcan formula more explicitly to the theme of *ho erchomenos*, "the One Who Is to Come," of the gospel tradition. Luke will use the latter in 7:19 and reveal that he too is aware of the theme. But even without the Matthean adaptation the Marcan and Lucan *erchetai*, given its prominent position, is an allusion to Mal 3:1,23 [4:5E], *erchetai*. In other words, John denies that he is the Messiah and insists rather that his role even as a baptizer is subordinate to that of Jesus. Thus Luke takes over from the Marcan tradition not only the idea of Jesus as *ho erchomenos* (coming before the great Day of the Lord, Mal 3:23), but as *ho ischyroteros*, "the more powerful," i.e. as a fiery reformer like *Elias redivivus*. See J. A. T. Robinson, *NTS* 4 (1957-1958) 263-281.

Conzelmann (*Theology*, 24) thinks that Luke has omitted the Marcan *opisō mou* because it would imply that John was the precursor of Jesus, that he belonged to the same period of salvation-history. But W. Wink (*John the Baptist*, 55) has more plausibly explained the omission as a reflection of Luke's embarrassment that Jesus would seem to be a disciple of John, since the phrase often appears as a sort of technical term for discipleship (9:23; 14:27; 21:8). In Acts 10:37; 13:25; 19:4 Luke depicts Jesus coming "after" John in a chronological sense.

I am not fit to unfasten even the strap of his sandals. This statement is likewise derived from Mark 1:7; it finds a very close parallel in John 1:27, especially in P[66] and P[75] (probably a harmonization). Matt 3:11, by contrast, has, "I am not fit to carry his sandals." To unfasten the sandal-strap was the task of a slave, forbidden by the rabbis in later rabbinical tradition as a service to be done by a disciple for his master (see Str-B, 1. 121). The image that John uses thus emphasizes his lowly rank in relation to Jesus, the more powerful one.

He will baptize you with a holy Spirit and with fire. The omission of *hagiō*, "holy," in a few minuscle mss. and patristic writers (Clement of Alexandria, Tertullian, Augustine) is scarcely evidence of the more original Lucan text, *pace* Creed, *The Gospel*, 53.

The problem in this clause is the twofold nature of the baptism that Jesus is being said to confer. As in Matt 3:11, Luke has "and with fire," which differs from the Marcan form, "with a holy Spirit," only. The addition of "and with fire" stands in contrast to the Lucan formulation in Acts 1:5; 11:16. Yet there is no evidence that Luke has added it here as "a Christian *pesher*-ing" of the Marcan text in the light of pentecostal fulfillment (Acts 2:3,19), *pace* E. E. Ellis, *Gospel of Luke*, 90. This would not explain its presence in Matt 3:11, which apparently knows nothing of the Pentecost tradition. Both Matthew and Luke here share an earlier tradition (from "Q," see the COMMENT), which they have preferred to the Marcan form. — *how about an earlier Mark?*

Bultmann (*HST*, 246) toys with the idea that "Q" preserved the original saying in John's prophecy of the baptism of fire and that the holy Spirit was later added, because he finds it difficult to think that the coming Messiah would be proclaimed as the bearer of the Spirit. Yet this would not be an impossible thing for the Baptist to have meant, given the relation between anointing and the Spirit in Isa 11:1-3. The likelihood is that both Spirit and fire were in the original "Q" form of the saying. The problem, then, is to say what they would have meant in contrast to the water-baptism of John.

The pair has been diversely interpreted over the centuries; it has been taken to mean that (1) Jesus' baptism will confer the fire of the holy Spirit, an inflaming, grace-laden outpouring of God's Spirit—an interpretation obviously influenced by the Pentecost scene of Acts 2. So John Chrysostom (*Hom. in Matt.* 11.4; PG, 7. 154); M.-J. Lagrange, *Evangile selon Matthieu* (4th ed.; EBib; Paris: Gabalda, 1927) 53. This is usually considered an anachronistic Christian interpretation, out of place on the lips of John the Baptist. (2) Jesus' baptism will confer the Spirit on the repentant, but bring the fire of judgment on the unrepentant—an interpretation based on v. 17. So Origen (*Hom. in Luc.* 24; GCS, 35. 158); F. Lang, *TDNT* 6 (1968) 943; R. E. Brown, *New Testament Essays*, 136. This interpretation seems to connote two different baptisms, administered to different groups; it seems to neglect the common object, "you" (*hymas*). (3) Jesus' baptism of Spirit and fire will be a baptism of judgment, since "holy Spirit" is to be understood as a mighty wind symbolizing judgment, aided by the fire that consumes what is swept away (see v. 17). So R. Eisler, *The Messiah Jesus and John the Baptist* (New York: Dial, 1931) 274-279; C. K. Barrett, *The Holy Spirit and the Gospel Tradition* (London: SPCK, 1954) 125-126. This interpretation, though it joins properly the functions of the Spirit and fire, tends to understand the baptism too much in terms of judgment or wrath. If John's own water-baptism were intended to produce "repentance," it might at least be thought that a baptism involving God's Spirit and fire would be expected to accomplish something positive too. (4) Jesus' baptism will have a dual character, accomplishing for those persons who would accept it at once a purification and a refinement. Here one could appeal to a number of OT passages in which both God's Spirit and fire play such a role: Isa 4:4-5; 32:15; 44:3; Ezek 36:25-26; Mal 3:2b-3. There is, moreover, in the *Manual of Discipline* from Qumran Cave 1 a text with a remarkable juxtaposition of "holy Spirit," "water," and "refining" (by fire), which forms a plausible matrix for John's own utterance:

> Then [at the season of visitation, when the truth of the world will appear forever] God will purge by his truth all the deeds of man, refining [i.e. by fire] for himself some of mankind in order to remove every evil spirit from the midst of their flesh, to cleanse them with a holy Spirit from all wicked practices and sprinkle them with a spirit of truth like purifying water (1QS 4:20-21).

Here one finds "water," "holy Spirit," and "refining" all used together in an act of God's purging his community. John has separated elements of such an activity, ascribing to himself a refinement by water and to Jesus, the more powerful one, a refinement by the Spirit and fire.

Another Qumran text should also be brought into consideration here, which speaks of God making known through his messiah(s) his holy Spirit: "And he made known to them his holy Spirit through his Messiah (*or* his Messiahs)" (CD 2:12). Against the background of such a notion it is not impossible to understand John speaking of Jesus, the Messiah, as the bearer of the Spirit.

In all of this, however, one has to keep in mind that what John's words might have meant in Stage I of the gospel tradition is one thing—which we have been trying to sort out above—and that his words as used by the Christian evangelist, Luke, at Stage III of that tradition, may convey a further connotation. In the latter, it is difficult to say that Luke would not have had in mind his own understanding of the Spirit poured out by the Risen Christ (Acts 2:33b-c) and of fire related to that Spirit. Obviously, in this way the Spirit of Pentecost would be understood to accomplish the refinement and purification in its own fuller way.

17. *His winnowing-fan.* A fork-like shovel, used to "fan" or toss threshed grain to the wind to separate the light chaff from the heavy kernels, which would fall to the ground in a heap. Cf. Isa 30:24. It is used here as an eschatological image of the sorting out of human beings according to their worth, to be accomplished by him who is the more powerful one. Here the figure has a twofold effect, in contrast to the ax of v. 9 above.

store the wheat. The heaped up heavy kernels of grain symbolize the persons who will be saved by the judge who is to come. His discrimination is expressed by two infinitives, "to clean up" and "to store."

a fire that will never go out. Or possibly, "that cannot be put out." The phrase may echo Isa 66:24. But it is hard to determine its precise nuance. The image may be derived from the ever-burning dumps and kilns in the Valley of Hinnom, south of Jerusalem (*gê Hinnōm,* whence Greek *geenna,* "Gehenna"); see Jer 7:30-34; or it may be derived simply from the intensity of fire raging and inextinguishable (with no connotation of its endless burning). In any case, it adds a detail to that mentioned in v. 9; but one may wonder to what extent it affects the "fire" of v. 16 (see above).

18. *John preached to the people.* Luke here uses the verb *euangelizesthai* (see NOTE on 1:19). Some commentators (e.g. Wink, *John the Baptist,* 52) think that "the Christian message of salvation is indicated"; by applying this word of John's preaching, "Luke makes him the first preacher of the Gospel" (ibid., 53). Would that not apply better to Gabriel in 1:19? But given Luke's attitude toward *euangelion* (see p. 174 above), I find it hard to understand the cognate verb here as meaning "announced the good news." The verse represents a comment of the evangelist, depicting John as an exhorter (as many others will be in the Lucan story).

BIBLIOGRAPHY (3:7-18)
(in addition to that given on 3:1-6 above)

Benoit, P. "Qumran and the New Testament," in *Paul and Qumran: Studies in New Testament Exegesis* (ed J. Murphy-O'Connor; London: Chapman, 1968) 1-30.

Best, E. "Spirit-Baptism," *NovT* 4 (1960) 236-243.

Brown, R. E. "Three Quotations from John the Baptist in the Gospel of John," *CBQ* 22 (1960) 292-298.

Brown, S. "'Water-Baptism' and 'Spirit-Baptism' in Luke-Acts," *ATR* 59 (1977) 135-151.

Dunn, J. D. G. "Spirit-and-Fire Baptism," *NovT* 14 (1972) 81-92.

Glasson, T. F. "Water, Wind and Fire (Luke iii 16) and Orphic Initiation," *NTS* 3 (1956-1957) 69-71.

Grobel, K. "'He That Cometh After Me,'" *JBL* 60 (1941) 397-401.

Manson, T. W. "John the Baptist," *BJRL* 36 (1953-1954) 395-412.

Robinson, J. A. T. "Elijah, John and Jesus: An Essay in Detection," *NTS* 4 (1957-1958) 263-281; reprinted in *Twelve New Testament Studies* (SBT 34; London: SCM, 1962) 28-52.

Sahlin, H. "Die Früchte der Umkehr: Die ethische Verkündigung Johannes des Täufers nach Lk 3:10-14," *ST* 1 (1948) 54-68.

Trilling, W. "Le message de Jean-Baptiste, Lc 3, 10-18," *AsSeign* 2/7 (1969) 65-74.

12. THE IMPRISONMENT OF JOHN
(3:19-20)

3 ¹⁹ Now the tetrarch Herod, who was criticized by John because of Herodias, his brother's wife, and all his other misdeeds, ²⁰ crowned them all by this—by shutting up John in prison.

COMMENT

The Lucan Gospel is unique in its reporting of the imprisonment of John the Baptist, recounting it even before Jesus is baptized. The baptism takes place in the next episode, in which John is not even mentioned. This episode of the imprisonment of John thus finishes off the ministry of the Baptist and serves to remove him from the scene before Jesus appears. This distinction is reflected later on in 16:16 and Acts 13:25. But Luke makes no mention here of John's death, because of the tradition that he will make use of in the episodes of 7:18-30.

This story of the imprisonment of John is influenced by Mark 1:14 (which records John's imprisonment before Jesus' *ministry* begins) and 6:17-18 (which explains the reasons for the imprisonment). These verses (3:19-20) constitute the first of the Lucan transpositions (see p. 71 above). They are, form-critically speaking, a story about John, which preserves only the essential details about the imprisonment in contrast to the lengthy account in Mark 6:17-29. Indeed, if we had only this Lucan account of John's imprisonment, it would be hard to understand what is really behind these verses. They are intelligible only because we know the longer form of the story from Mark or Matthew. We shall probably never discern the reason why Luke chose to omit the details.

H. Conzelmann (*Theology*, 21) is undoubtedly right in seeing these verses as a divider between the ministry of John and that of Jesus. They constitute a literary device, but whether they are as important to the geographical distinction of the locales of John and Jesus as Conzelmann would have it is another matter. W. Wink (*John the Baptist*, 50-51) sees the geographical removal of John from the scene as a means of emphasizing "the discontinuity between the preparatory work of John and the ministry of Jesus, both of which apparently take place within the period of fulfilment." Here one may query whether there is really a "discontinuity." The verses preserve the independence of John's ministry from that of Jesus, but they also explain how John's ministry, now finished, has been the inauguration of the Period of Jesus. They also hint at the reason why Jesus does not continue to appear in the Gospel as the kind of "more powerful one" that John had expected him to be—a fiery reformer.

NOTES

3 19. *the tetrarch Herod.* Herod Antipas (see NOTE on 3:1).

was criticized by John. Or "was accused." This criticism or accusation of Herod on moral grounds stands in contrast to the political motivation for John's imprisonment supplied by Josephus (*Ant.* 18.5,2 §§ 116-119); see p. 451 above.

because of Herodias, his brother's wife. Luke does not identify the brother concerned. In some mss. (C, A, K, W, etc.) and some ancient versions (syr^p, sah, boh) the name, Philip, has been added. This is result of harmonization by copyists who were aware of the name in Mark 6:17 or Matt 14:3. The best Greek mss. of Mark read it there, but the ms. D and some Latin versions also omit it in Matt 14:3; this again is probably due to scribal harmonization.

The omission of the name of the brother in the Lucan form of the story eliminates a difficulty in the account. According to Josephus (*Ant.* 18.5,1 §§ 109-110), Herodias was married to a *Herod,* the half-brother of Herod Antipas. The latter put away his first wife, the daughter of King Aretas IV of Nabatea, in order to marry Herodias, whose affections he had alienated from his half-brother Herod. Philip the tetrarch (see 3:1) was married to Salome, the daughter of Herodias. Schematically:

From the marriage of Herod the Great (who actually had ten wives) with

Cleopatra of Jerusalem came	Mariamme II came	Mariamme I came	Malthake came
Philip the tetrarch (who married Salome)	Herod (who married Herodias)	Aristobulus IV	Herod Antipas (who married the daughter of Aretas and repudiated her for Herodias)
		Herodias	
		Salome	

Some commentators have tried to solve the problem by maintaining that the Herod who married Herodias was really called "Herod Philip," but this appellation is otherwise unattested.

In any case, Luke's refusal to follow Mark in this identification is noteworthy. He is perhaps consciously correcting the erroneous Marcan identification, and it may be another indication of his more intimate knowledge of the Herodian family (see 8:3; Acts 13:1).

John's criticism of Herod would have been based on Lev 18:16, "You must have no intercourse with your brother's wife, since she belongs to your brother." See Lev 20:21.

all his other misdeeds. Lit. "and because of all the evils that Herod had done." The rel. pron., obj. of *epoiēsen,* is attracted to the gen. case of the antecedent *pantōn ponērōn;* the latter is incorporated into the rel. cl. See BDF § 294.5.

20. *crowned them all by this.* Lit. "added even this to all (of them)." The following cl. explains the "this." It is added asyndetically in most mss.; but some add the conj. *kai* before the following cl.

by shutting up John in prison. Lit. "he locked up John in prison." Josephus (*Ant.* 18.5,2 § 119) recounts that John was taken to the fortress Machaerus in chains. Originally built by Alexander Janneus on a precipitous, solitary peak on the east side of the Dead Sea between the Wadi Zerqa Ma'in and the Wadi el-Mojib, it was magnificently restored by Herod the Great. Its ruins can still be seen today. See further C. Kopp, *The Holy Places of the Gospels,* 141-142; J. Finegan, *The Archeology of the New Testament,* § 14. But Luke never tells us where the prison was. Cf. 7:18; 9:7-9.

13. THE BAPTISM OF JESUS
(3:21-22)

3 ²¹ Then when all the people had been baptized and Jesus too was baptized and was praying, the heavens happened to open, ²² and the holy Spirit descended in bodily form like a dove upon him. A voice was heard from heaven, "You are my beloved son; in you *I have taken delight.*"

Isa 42:1

COMMENT

After the two transposed verses about John's imprisonment (3:19-20), Luke continues with a parallel to the next episode in the Marcan sequence, the baptism of Jesus (3:21-22). In the Greek text of Luke these two verses form one long sentence. They are inspired by Mark 1:9-11, but have been reformulated in Lucan language and stripped of some details, though two characteristically Lucan features have been added. It is highly unlikely that Luke is here substituting for Marcan material a "Q" form of this episode, since the minor agreements with Matthew over against Mark in this case are not so clear that one should postulate a source independent of Mark, *pace* H. Schürmann, *Lukasevangelium,* 197, 218-219.

The Lucan redactional modifications of the Marcan source are mainly five. (1) Luke omits the notice that Jesus came from Nazareth in Galilee and was baptized in the Jordan (Mark 1:9). Given the reduced formulation of the imprisonment of John and its transposition to its present Lucan position, it would have made little sense to tell of Jesus' move from Galilean Nazareth to the Jordan after that imprisonment. Luke is content simply to insinuate that Jesus was among "the crowds that came out to be baptized" by John (3:7). H. Conzelmann (*Theology,* 20) considers the omission of the Marcan geographical details to be another conscious Lucan modification intended to separate Jesus from John's locale. But this is overdrawn, since, though Jesus may nowhere in Luke be related to the Jordan, both John and Jesus are connected with the desert (3:2-2; 4:1; cf. W. Wink, *John the Baptist,* 49). Luke is obviously aware from the gospel tradition before him of a story about Jesus' baptism which he feels obliged to retain, but which he also adapts to his own purpose. (2) Luke omits that Jesus was baptized "by John" (Mark 1:9); this modification is the result of the imprisonment of John in the immediately preceding pericope. (3) Luke depicts Jesus at prayer—one of the characteristically Lucan features added to the episode. (4) Luke describes the heavens as "opening" instead of being "rent" (*schizomenous,* Mark 1:10). In this he resembles Matt 3:16; but the verb forms are not identical (Luke has *aneōchthēnai,* aor. pass. infin.; but Matthew has *ēneōchthēsan,* aor. pass. indic.). The resemblance, however, is coincidental, since both have merely substituted an OT verb for the Marcan expression (see Isa 64:1 [LXX 63:19]; Ezek 1:1; cf. Gen 7:11; Mal 3:10; Isa 24:18; 3 Macc 6:18). (5) Luke adds "in bodily form" to the descent of the Spirit like a dove—another characteristically Lucan feature.

Form-critically viewed, this Lucan episode is a Story about Jesus. R. Bultmann (*HST,* 247-248), while not questioning the historicity of the event, regards the Marcan form of the story as "a faith legend," because of its essentially miraculous element and edifying purpose. He rightly rejects the attempt to use the scene to psychoanalyze Jesus and even to regard the episode like an OT "call" story (such as Isa 6:1-13; Jer 1:5-19; Ezek 1-2), noting that there is in the account not even a word about Jesus' inner experience, about a commission given to him, or about a reply from him. (The Lucan form of the story slightly modifies this; see below.) Bultmann thus rightly recognizes that the main purpose of the episode is to tell of "Jesus' consecration"—or, to put it another way, to tell of heaven's identification and approval of him.

Bultmann is not right, however, in labeling the baptism-scene as "Jesus' consecration as messiah" (*HST,* 248). Neither the descent of the Spirit upon Jesus, nor the recognition of him as "Son," nor the implication of his being Yahweh's Servant connote a messianic function. There is simply no evidence that the titles "Son (of God)" or "Servant of Yahweh" were regarded as *messianic* (i.e. belonging to an expected, future anointed agent of Yahweh) in pre-Christian Judaism. Hence Jesus' consecration must be understood more strictly as the Synoptic evangelists have themselves proposed it.

The episode of Jesus' baptism does not play the same role in the Third Gospel that its original counterpart did in Mark. In that Gospel, which lacks an infancy narrative, the scene of Jesus' baptism is intended to tell the reader who Jesus is. The heavenly declaration and the descent of the Spirit reveal him as someone related to heaven and favored by heaven in a special way. The creative and prophetic presence of God's Spirit is to be with him and mark his ministry; he is God's Son and (by implication) is to act as Yahweh's Servant. Thus his heaven-blessed ministry is inaugurated in the Marcan baptismal scene. But in the present form of the

Lucan Gospel the reader has already learned from the infancy narrative that Jesus is "Savior, Lord, and Messiah" (2:11); he has been hailed as "Son" (1:32,35) and the activity of the Spirit in his regard has already been made clear (1:35). Even though the infancy narrative has been written with the hindsight of the Gospel proper and represents the last stage of its composition, what it conveys at the outset tones down the effect of the baptism scene in the Gospel proper. The only distinctive Lucan element in it is the notice that the heavenly identification of Jesus took place while he was at prayer—the added Lucan item touches on Jesus' inner experience, but only in a vague way.

Luke's handling of the baptism scene makes it the least coherent of the three Synoptic forms. In the Marcan account Jesus "saw the heavens rent" and the Spirit descending on him like a dove; the heavenly voice addresses him directly (in the second sg.), "You are my son . . ." It is thus a vision accorded to Jesus alone. Luke follows Mark in that the voice is addressed to Jesus alone; but the "opening" of the heavens is recounted as an observable event, and the reality of the descending Spirit is stressed by the added phrase, "in bodily form." In Matthew, however, the vision has become an epiphany or public manifestation: the opening of heaven is recounted as an observable event, and the heavenly voice proclaims to all present, "This is my son. . . ." The Lucan form of the account is thus peculiar, being no longer a vision accorded solely to Jesus (as in Mark) nor yet the public manifestation (as in Matthew). F.-L. Lentzen-Deis (*Die Taufe Jesu,* 284-286) thinks that Luke has altered the form from a *Deute-Vision* (in Mark) to an *Epiphanie* because of his non-Jewish Hellenistic readers, who would not have understood the former. This is, however, far from clear.

The main purpose, then, of the baptism scene in the Lucan Gospel is to announce the heavenly identification of Jesus as "Son" and (indirectly) as Yahweh's Servant. The descent of the Spirit upon him is a preparation for the ministry, the "beginning" of which is noted in the immediately following context (v. 23). His being fitted out with the Spirit will be noted again in 4:1,14, as the ministry gets under way.

There are, however, two other aspects of this episode that have to be commented on. The first is the implication of Jesus' baptism. In the Lucan context Jesus is associated with "all the people" who thronged to John for baptism (3:21; cf. 3:7), i.e. to submit themselves to the ritual washing for "the forgiveness of sins" (3:3). Why is Jesus depicted submitting to this rite? (This question is often posed in terms of Stage I of the gospel tradition, i.e. about the historical Jesus; but once again, the answer can only be given in terms of the way in which the evangelists have presented this scene, in terms of Stage III of that tradition.)

Answers have been given to the question in various ways: (a) The evangelists wanted to portray Jesus as a person conscious of sin, yet recognizing in John's call for repentance an opportunity for personal conversion. Even if such a view of the man Jesus finds a sympathetic resonance in modern readers, it runs counter to all that the early Christian tradition has recorded about Jesus' consciousness of sin (e.g. John 8:46; 2 Cor 5:21; Heb 4:15; 7:26; 9:14). (b) The evangelists wanted to portray Jesus as approving of John's ministry and recognizing it as a manifestation of God's will for the salvation of people. Though this answer may contain an element of truth in it (see Luke 20:4-7), it is more suited to the Matthean form of the story (with its compositional addition of 3:14-15) than to either the more primitive form of Mark or the Lucan form. (c) The evangelists portray Jesus as a sort of disciple of John, accepting his baptism as a mark of initial association with him and recognizing it as a preparatory stage of his own ministry. This view would not fit into Conzelmann's sharply drawn division of ministries of John and Jesus in the Lucan Gospel; but it is not excluded by any of the Synoptic accounts (even Luke 3:21 could be so understood), and it finds support in the Johannine tradition (see John 1:29-50; 3:26). (d) The evangelists depict Jesus submitting to John's baptism as a symbolic anticipation of his passion and the expiatory significance that it would have—associating with the "outlaws" of Isa 53:12 for whom his life would be poured out. This might seem to be supported by the allusion to a "baptism" (see Luke 12:50) that Jesus still has to undergo (in his passion and death). But it is reading far more into the scene than the text itself will support. If there is an allusion to the Servant of Yahweh in 3:22, it does not immediately take on all the possible nuances of that figure's role. Of these various answers the third is the one that is most suited to the Lucan context. _Jesus as disciple of Jn._

The second aspect of this episode that calls for comment is the relation of the baptism scene to Lucan theology as a whole. Above we rejected Bultmann's interpretation of it as "Jesus' consecration as messiah." The main reason for the rejection is that neither the descent of the Spirit upon him nor the titles used or implied are necessarily messianic (in the strict sense). There is, however, another angle of the matter that has to be considered. In Acts 10:37-38, in the résumé of Jesus' ministry set forth there, Luke reflects on the baptism scene and notes "how God anointed him with the holy Spirit and with power." The wording there alludes to Isa 61:1 (cf. Luke 4:18), and the Lucan reflection in Acts interprets the baptism of Jesus as a messianic anointing. This has to be understood in terms of Lucan theology as a whole, even though the idea of a messianic anointing is not clear in the baptism scene itself.

Finally, it should be recalled that a similar heavenly identification of Jesus will be given again in the Lucan Gospel, in the transfiguration scene

(9:28-36), "This is my Son, my Chosen One! Listen to him." There the declaration will take on the character of a public manifestation. But, as in this case, it will precede an important period in the ministry of Jesus, as this is presented in the Lucan Gospel. The declaration at the baptism precedes the Galilean ministry itself, whereas the declaration in chap. 9 precedes the travel account or the journey of Jesus to the city of destiny, Jerusalem. In both scenes the heavenly identification stresses the relation of Jesus to his Father, as an important phase of his earthly career begins.

NOTES

3 21. *all the people had been baptized.* Lit. "and it happened, when . . . praying, (that) the heaven opened, and the Spirit . . . descended, and a voice was from heaven. . . ." Luke here makes use of the Graecizing form of the *egeneto de* construction with an infin.—actually three of them (*aneōchthēnai, katabēnai,* and *genesthai*)—with subj. acc.; see p. 118 above. The intervening temporal expression is of two forms: *en* + the articular infin. (*baptisthēnai*) and a compound gen. absol. (*Iēsou baptisthentos kai proseuchomenou*).

The phrase "all the people" is a summary reference to "the crowds" that had been mentioned in 3:7. Luke stresses again the universal reaction of the people (*laos*); cf. 7:29. The distinction between the people and their leaders has not yet been introduced; but the stress given to "all" here will heighten the distinction when it is made.

Jesus too was baptized. Jesus is thus associated with the universal reaction to the call that John was making. This association of Jesus with others relates his ministry to that of John; both occur in the period of fulfillment. Luke omits the Marcan detail, "by John." But Jesus at least shares in John's baptism. Recall that in its own way the Fourth Gospel likewise omits any mention of Jesus being baptized by John (1:31-33).

and was praying. The first occurrence of what will become a familiar Lucan motif, Jesus at prayer (see p. 244 above). Luke omits the mention of the coming out of the water.

the heavens happened to open. Lit. "the heaven (sg.) opened." Mark 1:10 is more expressive, "the heavens (pl.) were rent." See the COMMENT.

22. *the holy Spirit descended.* Whereas Mark 1:10 mentions simply "the Spirit," Luke has added the adj. *to hagion,* "holy." By contrast, Matt 3:16 has "God's Spirit." The Lucan wording is otherwise clearly dependent on Mark (save for the obvious addition, "in bodily form").

like a dove. The comparison of the descending Spirit with a dove is also found in Mark 1:10; Matt 3:16; John 1:32; and *Gospel of the Ebionites* 4 (Epiphanius *Panarion* 30.13,7; GCS, 25.350). The precise significance of the dove has been the subject of much discussion. Elaborate surveys of the attempts to identify the origin of the symbol can be found in Lentzen-Deis, *Die Taufe Jesu,* 170-183; L. E. Keck, *NTS* 17 (1970-1971) 41-67. Keck argues strongly and convincingly for a Palestinian, Aramaic-speaking Christian community as the matrix of the baptism story (against a Hellenistic matrix as proposed by R. Bultmann). If he is right, then attempts to explain the symbol of the dove against a Hellenistic background are excluded. The chief explanations, which appeal to OT or Jewish backgrounds, are the following: (a) The Spirit is compared to a dove because the "Spirit of God" was likened to a bird soaring over the waters of the deep in the first creation account (Gen 1:2); it would then be a symbol of a new creation. (b) It is compared to the dove released by Noah (Gen 8:8) after the flood; it would then be a symbol of a new beginning or of deliverance. (c) It has been compared to Yahweh stirring up his people to a new exodus as an eagle stirs its nestlings (Deut 32:11). Yet each of these allusions encounters difficulties: Gen 1:2 does not speak of a "dove," and no rabbinical literature has ever interpreted it so; Gen 8:8 knows, indeed, of a dove, but has nothing to do with the Spirit; in Deut 32:11 the bird is an eagle, not a dove! In later rabbinical literature the Spirit has been identified at times with a turtledove (so *Tg. Canticles* 2:12; this targum, however, does not certainly antedate A.D. 500); further references can be found in Str-B, 1. 124-125, but none of the texts cited there antedate the Christian era, and Str-B concludes: "At any rate there is no passage in the older literature in which the dove would be a clear and distinct symbol for the holy Spirit" (p. 125). Keck concludes similarly (p. 57).

Even if one cannot explain the origin of the symbol, the evangelists have clearly understood it as a sign of the presence of the Spirit to Jesus. Since in the OT the "Spirit" of God is usually a manifestation of his creative or prophetic presence to human beings, it should be so understood here. In Joel 3:1-5 [2:28-32E] an outpouring of the Spirit is associated with the Day of the Lord. Here the Spirit descends upon Jesus as his ministry is being inaugurated, and the outpouring of it is concretized in the symbolic dove. Another outpouring of the same Spirit will be accomplished in the Lucan story, with other symbols, a mighty wind and tongues as of fire (Acts 2:2-4).

in bodily form. This descriptive addition is found only in the Lucan account of the baptism. It has nothing to do with an anti-Docetic concern, but is intended rather to convey the reality of the presence of the Spirit to Jesus. It fits in with the greater attention shown to the Spirit in the Lucan writings than in either of the other Synoptic evangelists. In light of the prominence that the Spirit has in Lucan theology, this detail is not surprising. It also conforms to other devices that Luke uses to stress the reality of non-ordinary experiences (e.g. the risen Jesus asking for something to eat in 24:41; cf. Acts 10:41c). The question to be asked is, Why does Luke add this detail, when it is hard to imagine how else a dove would come down than in bodily form?

upon him. Luke avoids the Marcan *eis auton,* lit. "into him," using instead *ep' auton,* "upon him," as does Matt 3:16. This minor agreement of Matthew and Luke against Mark is an obvious, independent correction.

A voice was heard from heaven. Lit. "and there was a voice from heaven." The idea of the God of heaven speaking to his people is found in the OT (see e.g. Deut 4:10-12). The "voice" of the Lord was often associated with the thunder-clap (Isa 30:30-31; Ps 18:14), thus stressing its heavenly origin. This

OT notion has been carried over into the NT; it occurs again in the Lucan writings (9:35; Acts 10:13,15; 11:7,9). In later rabbinical literature there developed the idea of the *bat qôl*, "daughter of a voice," to convey the echo of God speaking to mankind (see Str-B, 1. 125-134).

You are my beloved son. Or possibly, "You are my son, the beloved one; in you. . . ." This is the reading in the best Greek mss. (P⁴, B, ℵ, A, W, Θ, the Freer and Lake families of minuscules, and the Koine text-tradition); but ms. D, some OL texts, and some patristic writers read rather, "You are my son; today I have begotten you." The latter reading is a quotation of Ps 2:7 and is preferred by a number of commentators (e.g. Grundmann, Harnack, Klostermann, Leaney, W. Manson, Moffatt, Streeter, Zahn). They retain it on the principle of *lectio difficilior*, thinking that it was eliminated by copyists who harmonized the Lucan text with that of Mark 1:11 or Matt 3:17 or eliminated it for other (doctrinal) reasons. However, despite the importance of Codex Bezae, that is not the best-attested reading; moreover, the similarity of wording between the more common reading (*sy ei ho huios mou*) and the Greek of Ps 2:7 (*huios mou ei sy*) was more likely the reason why scribes familiar with the Greek Psalter would have substituted this quotation, derived from a psalm often interpreted in the early Christian centuries as "messianic." If the quotation of Ps 2:7 were authentic, the heavenly voice would be declaring Jesus to be God's Son, relating him specifically to the royal, Davidic tradition of Israel. This would, indeed, suit Lucan theology in one sense. But it would be the only place in the NT in which Ps 2:7 would be applied to some event in the career of Jesus other than the resurrection. For it is otherwise used only of the risen Christ (see Acts 13:33; Heb 1:5; 5:5; cf. Rom 1:4). See further J. Dupont, "'Filius meus es tu,'" *RSR* 35 (1948) 552-543; E. Lövestam, *Son and Saviour* (ConNT 18; Lund: Gleerup, 1951).

The meaning of the heavenly identification is variously understood. Some commentators, who prefer the more commonly attested reading, still interpret the first part of the declaration in the sense of Ps 2:7 (e.g. Aland, Nestle, Schmid). This is not impossible, but it labors under the suspicion that the first words are being so understood because of the preference for the inferior reading in the second part. If the words are really an allusion to the psalm, then it must be added that it is not a clear identification of Jesus as "the Messiah," because there is no evidence that Ps 2:7 was ever understood in a messianic sense in pre-Christian Judaism. The psalm is normally understood as an enthronement psalm for some heir on the Davidic throne. It expresses a special filiation for him, voiced by God. E. E. Ellis (*The Gospel of Luke*, 92) points out that in later Judaism the term "my son" was applied to the Messiah, appealing to 2 Esdr. 7:28 (composed ca. A.D. 100). He thinks that "this is the connotation here." Again, this would not be impossible, if that appellation of the Messiah were really existent earlier. But both of these interpretations encounter the difficulty that we may have to understand the heavenly voice as saying, "You are my beloved son" (i.e. with the addition of *agapētos*). In this case is there really an allusion to Ps 2:7 or a use of that messianic title? The addition of the adj. "beloved" adds a specification about the sonship that is not present in Ps 2:7, expressive of a special love-relationship between the heavenly Father and the Son, Jesus. If it is not clear that the words are meant in a messianic sense, it is at least clear that they do not refer to "His Eternal Sonship" (N. Geldenhuys, *Commentary,* 147), since that would introduce anachronistically into the Lucan story a connotation born of later (trinitarian) theology. The words in the Lucan Gospel reveal that Jesus enjoys a special relationship to God in terms of sonship; the infancy narrative, in the present form of the Gospel, has already expressed this (1:32,35), and Luke will come back to it again (9:35). It is better to leave it thus, in its Lucan vagueness—without excluding the possibility that it could develop a fuller understanding.

The adj. *agapētos,* found in all the Synoptic accounts, means "beloved," and adds a specification to the sonship expressed in the phrase. But because this adj. is used in the LXX to translate Hebrew *yāḥîd,* "only" (e.g. Gen 22:2,12), and is used by Philo in close juxtaposition with *monos,* "only, single" (*De ebrietate* 8 § 30), a number of commentators have asked whether this might not be the nuance intended in these Synoptic passages (see, e.g. G. Schrenk, *TDNT* 2 [1964] 740 n. 7; C. H. Turner, *JTS* 27 [1926] 113-129). Cf. Mark 9:7; 12:5-6. But this is highly unlikely; see B. Marzullo, *Philologus* 101 (1957) 205.

in you I have taken delight. These words are probably to be understood as an allusion to Isa 42:1, the beginning of the first Servant Song. But there are difficulties in so regarding it, which cannot be glossed over. The LXX of Isa 42:1a-b differs considerably from the MT. The latter reads: "Look, my Servant! I uphold him; my chosen one (in whom) my soul delights." But the LXX translates rather thus: "Jacob, my servant, I shall assist him; Israel, my chosen one, my soul has accepted him." Yet another Greek translation of this Isaian passage was known in antiquity; it is found in Matt 12:18: "Look my Servant! Whom I have chosen; my beloved, (in) whom my soul has delighted." For full discussion of this text, see K. Stendahl, *The School of St. Matthew* (Philadelphia: Fortress, 1968) 107-115. It is hardly likely that Luke has derived his wording from Matthew's text (see p. 73 above). But the similarity may show a dependence on a Greek translation of Isaiah other than that of the LXX.

If the allusion is admitted, then the heavenly identification of Jesus would cast him in the role of the Servant of Yahweh. This would add a connotation to that of his sonship expressed in the first part of the declaration, a connotation of obedience and suffering, in that Jesus would be understood as the embodiment of the figure in Isaiah.

The attempt of P. G. Bretscher (*JBL* 87 [1968] 301-311) to see Exod 4:22-23 behind the heavenly identification here is farfetched.

BIBLIOGRAPHY (3:21-22)

Braun, H. "Entscheidende Motive in den Berichten über die Taufe Jesu von Markus bis Iustin," *ZTK* 50 (1953) 39-43.

Bretscher, P. G. "Exodus 4:22-23 and the Voice from Heaven," *JBL* 87 (1968) 301-311.

Collins, R. F. "Luke 3:21-22, Baptism or Anointing," *TBT* 84 (1976) 821-831.

Feuillet, A. "Le baptême de Jésus," *RB* 71 (1964) 321-352.

——— "Le symbolisme de la colombe dans les récits évangéliques du baptême," *RSR* 46 (1958) 524-544.

Keck, L. E. "The Spirit and the Dove," *NTS* 17 (1970-1971) 41-67.

Légault, A. "Le baptême de Jésus et la doctrine du Serviteur souffrant," *ScEccl* 13 (1961) 147-166.

Lentzen-Deis, F.-L. *Die Taufe Jesu nach den Synoptikern: Literarkritische und gattungsgeschichtliche Untersuchungen* (Frankfurter theologische Studien 4; Frankfurt am M.: J. Knecht, 1970).

Potterie, I. de la. "L'Onction du Christ: Etude de théologie biblique," *NRT* 80 (1958) 225-252.

Sabbe, M. "Le baptême de Jésus," *De Jésus aux évangiles* (BETL 25; ed. I. de la Potterie; Gembloux: Duculot, 1967) 184-211.

Schlier, H. "Die Verkündigung der Taufe Jesu nach den Evangelien," *Geist und Leben* 28 (1955) 414-419; reprinted in *Besinnung auf das Neue Testament* (2d ed.; Freiburg im B.: Herder, 1964) 212-218.

Seethaler, P. "Die Taube des Heiligen Geistes," *BibLeb* 4 (1963) 115-130.

Williams, G. O. "The Baptism in Luke's Gospel," *JTS* 45 (1944) 31-38.

14. THE GENEALOGY OF JESUS
(3:23-38)

3 23 As he began his ministry, Jesus was about thirty years of age; and he was, in the minds of the people, the son of Joseph, son of Heli, 24 son of Matthat, son of Levi, son of Melchi, son of Jannai, son of Joseph, 25 son of Mattathias, son of Amos, son of Nahum, son of Esli, son of Naggai, 26 son of Maath, son of Mattathias, son of Semein, son of Josech, son of Joda, 27 son of Joanan, son of Rhesa, son of Zerubbabel, son of Shealtiel, son of Neri, 28 son of Melchi, son of Addi, son of Cosam, son of Elmadam, son of Er, 29 son of Joshua, son of Eliezer, son of Jorim, son of Matthat, son of Levi, 30 son of Simeon, son of Judah, son of Joseph, son of Jonam, son of Eliakim, 31 son of Melea, son of Menna, son of Mattatha, son of Nathan, son of David, 32 son of Jesse, son of Obed, son of Boaz, son of Sala, son of Nahshon, 33 son of Amminadab, son of Admin, son of Arni, son of Hezron, son of Perez, son of Judah, 34 son of Jacob, son of Isaac, son of Abraham, son of Terah, son of Nahor, 35 son of Serug, son of Reu, son of Peleg, son of Eber, son of Shelah, 36 son of Cainan, son of Arphaxad, son of Shem, son of Noah, son of Lamech, 37 son of Methuselah, son of Enoch, son of Jared, son of Mahalaleel, son of Cainan, 38 son of Enos, son of Seth, son of Adam, son of God.

COMMENT

Luke now introduces as a sequel to the baptism of Jesus a list of his ancestors (3:23-38). It has no parallel at this point in the other Synoptics, and it is clear that Luke is inserting a genealogy of Jesus into the otherwise Marcan framework—between the Marcan episodes of Jesus' baptism and temptation in the desert.

It is impossible to say at what point in the composition of the Lucan Gospel this genealogy would have been inserted. If we are right in thinking that the Gospel existed at one time without the infancy narrative and that 3:1 was its real beginning, the genealogy could have been part of that earlier form of the Gospel. In such a case, it is not unlikely that Luke added *hōs enomizeto,* "in the minds of the people" (3:23), to bring the genealogy into line with the affirmation of the virginal conception of Jesus in the newly added infancy narrative. On the other hand, it is not impossible that the genealogy was also added at the stage of the composition of the Gospel that is represented by the infancy narrative. This might seem more probable, if one were persuaded that a genealogy had some connection with infancy narrative material. But this connection would depend on the Matthean use of genealogical material and on nothing really intrinsic to the material as such. The story of Abraham in Genesis 12 is preceded by his genealogy in 11:10-29. But the story of Moses is well under way in Exodus, before his genealogy is introduced (6:14-20). Elsewhere in the OT a genealogy is introduced at a place, where it is needed to explain a relationship: thus Esau's descendants are listed in Gen 36:9-43 to explain the origin of the Edomites. See also Ruth 4:18-22. In the long run, one would have to ask, then, why Luke did not make the genealogy part of the infancy narrative, as did Matthew. Hence, it seems more likely that Luke had already made the genealogy part of the Gospel proper at a stage earlier than that of the addition of the infancy narrative.

When one considers vv. 23-38 from a form-critical viewpoint, they obviously fit into none of the usual categories. Though this passage and its Matthean counterpart (1:1-17) are commonly called "genealogies" of Jesus, neither Matthew nor Luke has used the Greek *genealogia* in them. That word is found in the NT: Tit 3:9 and 1 Tim 1:4—and, significantly enough, in the latter passage in conjunction with *mythoi,* "myths." The collocation of "myths and genealogies" is also known from extrabiblical Greek writers (see BGD, 154). It reveals an aspect of the ancient literary form with which we are dealing and an ancient attitude toward it. It also warns us at the outset against insisting too much on the factual or historical aspect of such ancient pedigree lists. That they evoked idle speculation in antiquity (see 1 Tim 1:4) suggests that artificial schematizing or perhaps periodization was more operative in them than the modern mind might be inclined to suspect.

The OT counterpart of "genealogy" is either *sēpher tôlĕdôt,* "book of generations" (Gen 5:1)—rendered in the LXX as *hē biblos geneseōs* and imitated by Matthew, "book of genealogy" (1:1, *RSV*)—or *sēpher hay-yaḥaś,* "the book of the genealogy" (Neh 7:5). Recent studies of OT genealogies (by M. D. Johnson and R. R. Wilson) have stressed the functions or purposes to which they were put, which often dominated the mode in which they were constructed, since the genealogic form in the OT differs. Interest in one's ancestry was important at times to preserve tribal homogeneity, cohesion, or integrity, to interrelate previously isolated traditions, to establish continuity over periods not covered by such traditions (e.g. the span between the traditions about the primitive age of creation and the patriarchal narratives), or to tie down speculation about world cycles. The establishment of one's identity, status, or legitimacy in a post or office (as priest or king) often demanded the recording of ancestry. The most frequent use of genealogical lists in the OT is found in writings stemming from priestly circles (e.g. the P-document of the Pentateuch). In the postexilic period the question of the ethnic unity of the Jews was raised because of marriage with non-Jews, and genealogical lists were made use of; the identity of priests returning from the Babylonian Captivity became urgent in the time of Ezra (see Ezra 2:59-63; Neh 7:64-65; cf. R. de Vaux, *Ancient Israel* [New York: McGraw-Hill, 1961] 4-13, 371-375, 394-397). Later on, Josephus bore witness to the precautions taken to ensure the purity of priestly lineage (*Ag. Ap.* 1.7 § 30). This was continued long into the rabbinical period, when haggadic exegesis was often employed to support genealogical speculation about biblical families (e.g. Gen 49:10; 2 Sam 3:4). In rabbinical circles speculation also developed about the ancestry of the Messiah: Would he be *ben Dāwîd* or *ben 'Ahăron* (see M. D. Johnson, *Purpose,* 85-138; Str-B, 1. 4-5). In a generic way, the Lucan and Matthean genealogies of Jesus would be related to this sort of genealogic study. But we have no real evidence for a first-century A.D. dating of the rabbinical literature that bears on this messianic speculation.

The ancient genealogies were not only schematized into historical periods and shaped by anecdotal speculation, they were also marked by a concern for numbered groupings. Blocks of seven or ten names were often used. The preoccupation with "seven" is of particular interest because of its occurrence, as we shall see, in both the Lucan and Matthean genealogies. It is not confined to them, since it is reflected in Josephus' reference to Moses as "the seventh from Abraham" (i.e. as son of 'Amram, Caath, Levi, Jacob, Isaac, and Abraham, *Ant.* 2.9,6 § 229). He also tells us that King David bequeathed his dominion to his posterity for twenty-one generations (*Ant.* 5.9,4 § 336). Probably not by sheer coincidence, Josephus gives his own "not ignoble" pedigree, as he found it "recorded in the public registers," by listing seven generations: Simon Psellus, Matthias, Matthias Curtus, Joseph, Matthias, Josephus, and his three sons (*Life* 1 § 3). Jude 14 names Enoch as "the seventh from Adam," and, again, it is scarcely a coincidence that in the Lucan genealogy of Jesus the names of David, Abraham, and Enoch begin the seventh, ninth, and eleventh groups of seven names. The use of the number seven in genealogical lists, like that of ten, is probably due to nothing more sophisticated than a mnemonic device, because oral tradition undoubtedly played a great role in the composition of such lists. But the use of the number(s) contributed to the stylized and artificial character of the lists.

The Lucan genealogy, coming on the heels of the baptism scene, purports to give Jesus' ancestry at the outset of his ministry of preaching and healing. Terminating, as it does, in the recognition of his descent eventually from "Adam, son of God," it is obviously occasioned by the declaration of the heavenly voice at the baptism itself. All told it contains seventy-eight names, counting both Jesus and God and implying seventy-seven generations. The names are given in a single, direct paternity, traced in ascending order backward from Jesus to Adam and God. No comment is made on any of the individuals mentioned and nothing is made of the seventy-seven generations as a multiple of seven. When one compares the names in the list with the OT, it is evident that some of them coincide with figures in the known history of Israel, e.g. the names from Zerubbabel to Abraham can be found in 1 Chronicles 1-3, and those from Abraham to Adam in Gen 5:1-32; 11:10-26 (or in 1 Chron 1:1,24). But thirty-six others are completely unknown.

Where did Luke get this genealogical list? First of all, it is almost certain that it is Luke himself who has added the last item, "son of God." As Johnson (*Purpose,* 237) has noted, "there is no known parallel in the OT or in Rabbinic texts for a genealogy to begin with or culminate with the naming of God." On the other hand, the termination of the list in that name is hardly to be explained by appeal to Greek and Roman attempts to establish the divinity of a ruler by tracing his pedigree to a god, as R. E. Brown notes (*Birth,* 90 n. 68), since there are too many Jewish elements in the genealogy to call in question its Jewish provenience. But what about the rest? It is obvious that Luke could have consulted his Greek OT in the passages cited above and constructed the list accordingly, either digging out the others from literature unknown to us or filling them in himself. Yet many modern commentators (e.g. W. Grundmann, *Evangelium nach Lukas,* 111; H. Schürmann, *Lukasevangelium,* 203; G. Schneider, *Evangelium nach Lukas,* 94) prefer to think that Luke has made use of a previously existing genealogy. This is, in my opinion, more likely. But, obviously, such a genealogy might well have depended on the same OT passages as have been mentioned above.

The genealogy, as we have translated it from the Nestle Greek text, contains seventy-eight names, as we have already mentioned. But it should be noted that this number is not absolute in all Greek mss. For instance, there are only seventy-six in ms. B, seventy-four in ms. A., seventy-two in mss. N, U, and seventy-five in the Sinaitic Syriac version. The Lucan list has been more open to scribal tampering than the Matthean because of the many unknown persons mentioned in it and because nothing is said explicitly about the number of names or structure of the genealogy, such as is found in Matt 1:17. The number of seventy-eight names or seventy-seven generations is found in the rest of the important mss. of Luke, and none of the names is set in brackets in any modern critical edition of the NT. Moreover, it is more likely that names would be lost from a list than added; here "shorter" is not necessarily "better." So the chances are that the seventy-seven-generation list is the original. It should be noted, however, that ms. D (Codex Bezae) has its own peculiar genealogy: It lists in ascending order the names from Jacob (the father of Joseph) to David, using the *Matthean* ancestors.

In the following list an asterisk affixed to a name in the Lucan genealogy means that the reader should consult the *apparatus criticus* or the NOTE on the respective line. The list will seek to highlight the main features and differences of each genealogy, as well as the OT form of the names; but to appreciate the full differences, one should study the Greek texts and the name-forms in the LXX (see K. Aland, *SQE*, 28-30).

Names in Luke (ascending)	Names in the OT	Names in Matthew (descending)
1. Jesus (3:23)		14. Jesus (1:16)
2. Joseph		13. Joseph
3. Heli		12. Jacob (1:15)
4. Matthat* (3:24)		11. Matthan
5. Levi*		
6. Melchi		10. Eleazar
7. Jannai		
		9. Eliud (1:14)
8. Joseph		
9. Mattathias (3:25)		8. Achim
10. Amos		
11. Nahum		7. Zadok
12. Esli		
13. Naggai		6. Azor (1:13)
14. Maath (3:26)		
		5. Eliakim
15. Mattathias		
16. Semein		4. Abiud
17. Josech		
18. Joda		
19. Joanan (3:27)		
20. Rhesa		
21. Zerubbabel	1 Chr 1-3 Zerubbabel (3:19)	3. Zerubbabel (1:12)
22. Shealtiel	Shealtiel (3:17)	2. Shealtiel
23. Neri		
24. Melchi (3:28)		
25. Addi		

Names in Luke (ascending)	Names in the OT	Names in Matthew (descending)
26. Cosam		
27. Elmadam*		
28. Er	Jeconiah-Asir (LXX 3:17)	1. Jechoniah (1:12)
29. Joshua (3:29)	Jeconiah (LXX 3:16)	14. Jechoniah (1:11)
30. Eliezer	Josiah (3:14)	13. Joseph (1:10)
31. Jorim	Amon (3:14)	12. Amos
32. Matthat	Manasseh (3:13)	11. Manasseh
33. Levi	Hezekiah (3:13)	10. Hezekiah (1:9)
34. Simeon (3:30)	Ahaz (3:13)	9. Ahaz
35. Judah	Jotham (3:12)	8. Jotham
36. Joseph	Azariah (= Uzziah, 3:12)	7. Uzziah (1:8)
37. Jonam	Joram (3:11)	6. Joram
38. Eliakim	Jehoshaphat (3:10)	5. Jehoshaphat
39. Melea (3:31)	Asa (3:10)	4. Asa(ph) (1:7)
40. Menna	Abijah (3:10)	3. Abijah
41. Mattatha	Rehoboam (3:10)	2. Rehoboam
42. Nathan	Solomon (3:5)	1. Solomon (1:6)
43. David	David (2:15)	14. David the king
44. Jesse (3:32)	Jesse (2:12)	13. Jesse (1:5)
45. Obed*	Obed (2:12)	12. Obed
46. Boaz	Boaz (2:11)	11. Boaz
47. Sala*	Salmon (MT: Salma, 2:11)	10. Salmon (1:4)
48. Nahshon	Nahshon (2:10)	9. Nahshon
49. Amminadab* (3:33)	Amminadab (2:10)	8. Amminadab
50. Admin*		
51. Arni*	Ram (= Aram, 2:9)	7. Ram (Aram) (1:3)
52. Hezron	Hezron (2:9)	6. Hezron
53. Perez	Perez (2:4)	5. Perez
54. Judah	Judah (2:1)	4. Judah (1:2)

Names in Luke (ascending)		Names in the OT	Names in Matthew (descending)
55. Jacob (3:34)		Jacob (MT: Israel, 1:34)	3. Jacob
56. Isaac		Isaac (1:34)	2. Isaac
57. Abraham		Abraham (1:34)	1. Abraham
58. Terah	Gen 11	Terah (11:24; cf. 1 Chr 1:24)	
59. Nahor		Nahor (11:22)	
60. Serug (3:35)		Serug (11:20)	
61. Reu		Reu (11:18)	
62. Peleg		Peleg (11:16)	
63. Eber		Eber (11:14)	
64. Shelah		Shelah (MT: 11:12; LXX 11:13b, Sala)	
65. Cainan (3:36)		Cainan (11:13a LXX)	
66. Arphaxad		Arpachshad (11:10)	
67. Shem	Gen 5	Shem (5:32; 11:10; cf. 1 Chr 1:1)	
68. Noah		Noah (5:29)	
69. Lamech		Lamech (5:25)	
70. Methuselah (3:37)		Methuselah (5:12)	
71. Enoch		Enoch (5:18)	
72. Jared		Jared (5:15)	
73. Mahalaleel		Mahalalel (5:12)	
74. Cainan		Kenan (5:9)	
75. Enos (3:38)		Enosh (5:6)	
76. Seth		Seth (5:3)	
77. Adam		Adam (5:1)	
GOD			

The main problem in the interpretation of the Lucan genealogy arises from the comparison of it with the Matthean (1:1-17), which differs notably. The two lists agree in tracing Jesus' pedigree through Joseph, in mentioning Zerubbabel and Shealtiel in the postexilic period (Luke 3:27; Matt 1:12), and in tracing part of the pedigree in the monarchic period and earlier from Abraham to Hezron (Luke 3:33-35; Matt 1:2-3) and from Amminadab to David (Luke 3:31-33; Matt 1:3-6). But apart from that they go their own ways, and the main differences are the following:

a) Matthew uses the verbal form, "Abraham was/became the father of Isaac" (*Abraam egennēsen ton Isaak*), whereas Luke uses the simple genitive of the article, "Joseph, son of Heli" (*Iōsēph tou Hēli*).

b) Matthew uses the descending order of generations, beginning with Abraham and ending with Jesus (cf. Gen 5:6-26; 11:10-27), whereas Luke uses the ascending order, beginning with Jesus and ending with "Adam, son of God" (cf. 1 Sam 9:1; Zeph 1:1; Tob 1:1 [none of these is so lengthy as the Lucan]).

c) Matthew traces Jesus' ancestry back only to Abraham, whereas Luke goes back to "Adam, son of God," thus adding pre-patriarchal ancestors from human history prior to the call of Abraham and the fashioning of a Chosen People. Here the names depend on the Sethite genealogy in Genesis 5 and also on Genesis 11. This difference may also be stated in another way: Matthew's genealogy is openly "messianic" (*ho legomenos Christos,* 1:17), highlighting Jesus' relation to Israel and its famous forebears, David and Abraham, whereas Luke's genealogy is that of Jesus, the Son of God, with David and Abraham mentioned only as ordinary ancestors in a line going back to the first of human beings, Adam.

d) Matthew's list introduces explicative words (e.g. David, "the king" [1:6]), phrases (e.g. "to the deportation to Babylonia" [1:11; cf. 1:12]), four women (Tamar, Rahab, Ruth, and the wife of Uriah [see Brown, *Birth,* 71-74]), whereas Luke's is straightforward in its direct paternal lineage—which makes it impossible to understand Rhesa (3:27) as anything but a proper name (see NOTE). Again whereas Matthew's genealogy is formally structured into three groups of fourteen names (to attain which names are dropped or repeated and to which attention is explicitly called in 1:17), Luke's has none of this.

e) From Abraham to Jesus Matthew counts three $\times$ fourteen generations (1:17), which should mean forty-two names (on the problems of counting the names and generations, see Brown, ibid., 81-84), whereas Luke has fifty-seven names. From Zerubbabel to Jesus, Matthew lists twelve names, whereas Luke has twenty-one. If a generation be reckoned roughly as twenty-five-thirty years, it is clear that the Lucan genealogy is the more plausible (reckon Abraham ca. 1750 B.C., Zerubbabel ca. 580 B.C., and Jesus ca. 5-4 B.C.).

f) Still more significantly, for the monarchic period Matthew lists Jesus' Davidic ancestors as Solomon to Jechoniah (1:6-12), whereas Luke lists them as Nathan to Neri (3:27-31), before the two lists coincide again in Shealtiel and Zerubbabel. Matthew uses fourteen names (one mentioned twice, Jechoniah) in this interval, whereas Luke has twenty. Here the names that Matthew has listed for his monarchic "fourteen" can be seen from the table given above to be known in the OT; their stories are recounted in 1-2 Kings. But, save for Nathan, David's third son born in Jerusalem (2 Sam 5:14; 1 Chr 14:4), the rest of the names used by Luke (from Melea to Neri, 3:27-31) are unknown.

Moreover, Luke compounds the problem in this part of the genealogy by listing four ancestors of Jesus who bear patriarchal names: Levi, Simeon, Judah, and Joseph (3:29-30). As far as can be ascertained, such names were not used by Jews in pre-exilic times and represent an anachronism that reveals why this part of the ancestry cannot be otherwise controlled. See J. Jeremias, *Jerusalem in the Time of Jesus* (Philadelphia: Fortress, 1969) 296.

g) In the postexilic part of the genealogy, if Jesus' nine ancestors in the Matthean list (from Abiud to Jacob, 1:13-15) are otherwise unknown, so too are the eighteen in the corresponding part of the Lucan list (3:23-27, Rhesa to Heli), where not one of them agrees with any of the nine in the Matthean genealogy.

From these considerations it is obvious that the NT has preserved for us two strikingly different genealogies of Jesus, which resist all harmonization. Which one of them stands the chance of being more historical or factual? This is hard to say, even if one thinks that both Matthew and Luke have depended on sources for the material so incorporated. It might seem at first sight that the Lucan would have the greater claim, seeing that it lacks the obviously artificial structure of the three × fourteen generations, which almost certainly stems from Matthew himself (see Brown, *Birth,* 70). But if we are correct in speaking of seventy-seven generations in the Lucan genealogy, with David (✻43), Abraham (✻57), and Enoch (✻71) beginning the seventh, ninth, and eleventh group of sevens, then Luke's genealogy is not wholly devoid of structure and use of seven either. In this regard the real problem is to explain the difference in the Davidic descent of Jesus: via Solomon in Matthew and via Nathan in Luke. One has to recall that the Davidic descent of Jesus is insisted on in various other places in the NT. It is affirmed in Rom 1:3; 2 Tim 2:8, assumed in Mark 10:48 and parallels and implied in Acts 2:30; Heb 7:14. Both Matthew and Luke have picked up this tradition from the early community before them, and have incorporated it—each in his own way —into the genealogies. The Matthean line traced through Solomon finds support in the OT stories of Davidic heirs, whereas the Lucan line has none. It seems obvious that Luke is either dependent on a tradition that traced the Davidic heirs differently or deliberately altered the list of them for some reason. It has often been suggested that Luke did not want to list Solomon and some of the other Davidic kings among the ancestors of

Jesus because of the evil deeds that have been reported of them in the OT and the scandals associated with their names (see M. D. Johnson, *The Purpose*, 135-136). But Zech 12:12-13 may hint at a way of understanding a subdividing of the house of David, when it pits "the house of David" over against "the house of Nathan" just as it compares "the house of Levi" to "the family of the Shimeites," which was but a division of the Levites themselves. Some pre-Lucan tradition about the Davidic heirs descended through Nathan may thus have been current. This is highly speculative, but it is to be preferred to the alternative sometimes proposed that Luke is dependent on a tradition which identified the son of David, Nathan, with Nathan the prophet (found in *Tg. Neb.* of Zech 13:12 in the Codex Reuchlinianus, Julius Africanus' *Letter to Aristides,* and Eusebius' *Quaestiones evangelicae*) and that Luke has preferred this tradition in order to present Jesus as a prophet (see Johnson, *The Purpose,* 240-252). This intriguing interpretation would fit in with the Lucan portrait of Jesus as a prophet; but there is no evidence that such an identification existed in pre-Christian Judaism or in the pre-Lucan Christian community.

Even more crucial is the listing of Jesus' grandfather as Jacob in Matt 1:16 and as Heli in Luke 3:23. Various solutions have been suggested to solve this part of the problem. Julius Africanus (cited in Eusebius *Historia ecclesiastica* 1.7,2-15) explained the Lucan text by invoking levirate marriage, as in Deut 25:5-10, whereby on the death of a husband who was childless the next of kin would have intercourse with the widow to beget children in his brother's name and continue his lineage. Thus Luke 3:23 would be understood: "Being the son, as it was supposed of Joseph, (but really) of Heli," so that Joseph could still be the son of Jacob (according to Matthew). But the solution has many problems (on which see Brown, *The Birth,* App. I, 503-504), and in reality solves nothing.

Another solution was to maintain that the Matthean genealogy was Joseph's and the Lucan Mary's; this has been suggested because of the prominence of Joseph in the Matthean infancy narrative and of Mary in the Lucan. This view was made popular by Annius of Viterbo (ca. A.D. 1490) and used in modern times by J. M. Heer. Though tradition has at times thought of Mary's Davidic descent, there is no basis for this in the NT; and Luke has traced the genealogy of Jesus specifically through Joseph (see NOTE on 3:23).

Because of these many difficulties that arise from the comparison of the Matthean and Lucan genealogies, most commentators realize today that we have in them neither official public records nor treasured family lists. Both of the genealogies have in the long run been fashioned by the evangelists, who most likely did depend on different existing Davidic ancestry lists. Since we have already explained that genealogies were often used for special purposes or functions, it is to this that we should rather turn our attention.

We have already alluded briefly to the function of the Lucan genealogy in this part of the Gospel: It serves to explain in still another way the relation of Jesus, about to begin his Galilean ministry of preaching and healing, to God and to the human beings he has come to serve. A. Plummer (*Commentary,* 101) tried to explain the incorporation of the genealogy into the Gospel at this point because it is its real beginning; the "first three chapters are only introductory." This explanation, however, gives to the Lucan genealogy too much of a Matthean connotation. Granted that Luke uses *archomenos,* "beginning," in the verse that introduces the pedigree, it scarcely implies that the "Evangelist is now making a fresh start." We will explain the nuances of the ptc. *archomenos* in Lucan composition (see NOTE on 3:23); it is better not to attach such an interpretation to it. Plummer does not reckon sufficiently with the distinction between the introductory chaps. 1-2 and what is being begun in chaps. 3-4.

Because Luke has inserted the genealogy between two otherwise Marcan scenes, the baptism and the temptation, one may wonder about its relation to the latter. J. Jeremias (*TDNT,* 1. 141-143) sees a connection in the Adam-motif: Jesus, like Adam, is tempted by Satan. This interpretation, however, depends on the view that Luke has traced the genealogy of Jesus back to Adam because he, like Paul, thinks in terms of a "second Adam" or "last Adam" motif (cf. 1 Cor 15:22,45-49; Rom 5:14). However, it is far from certain that Luke is working with such a motif; Johnson (*The Purpose,* 234-235) has effectively disposed of most of Jeremias' arguments. Luke has his own message of the universality of the salvation brought by Jesus; he does not have to be supported by Pauline motifs. The genealogy ends in v. 38 with "son of God," and the typology is therefore not to be sought between Jesus and Adam, the next to last name in the list. In the long run, then, the connection between the genealogy and what follows is minimal; the connection has rather to be sought with what precedes, since it is the genealogy of Jesus, the Son of God, whose relation to heaven was set forth in the preceding episode.

Implicit in the genealogy, however, is the divine origin of the course of history that is sketched by the line of generations. It gives an aspect to the salvation-history operative in the Lucan writings. Now, as the Period of Jesus is about to be begun, it is seen as related to the course of history stemming not only from Israel but from humanity and ultimately from God himself. God's purpose in creating humanity in the beginning is seen to reach a new stage in the *archē* of the Period of Jesus itself.

NOTES

3 23. *As he began his ministry.* Lit. "(in) beginning, Jesus was. . . ." Luke's use of the ptc. *archomenos,* "beginning, starting," is somewhat cryptic, but it is understood once one recalls that Luke elsewhere uses the verb *archein* (or its cognates) to refer to the beginning of Jesus' public ministry (23:5; Acts 1:1, and especially 1:22; 10:37, where it is closely linked to the baptism of Jesus). For Luke this is the start of the Period of Jesus. Recall the NOTE on 1:3. Compare the use of the noun *archē,* "beginning" (Acts 11:15) to designate the beginning of the Period of the Church; cf. Luke 24:47. There is no need to compare Mark 4:1 or to supply an infin. *didaskein,* "to teach." The word is being used absolutely. The cryptic nature of the ptc. *archomenos* is undoubtedly responsible for its omission in some OL and OS versions, and for the variant *erchomenos,* "(he was) coming (for baptism)," in some inferior mss.

Jesus was. The Greek text reads *kai autos ēn Iēsous,* in which *kai autos* is used as unstressed (see p. 120 above).

about thirty years of age. The use of the adv. *hōsei* indicates that the figure is to be taken as a round number; in the context of chap. 3 it means that Jesus' thirtieth birthday was not far removed from Tiberius' fifteenth regnal year. But despite Luke's desire to anchor "events" by reference to Roman and Palestinian history, this indication of Jesus' age should not be pressed too much in conjunction with 1:5; 2:2; or 3:1, since it is clearly an approximation. Dionysius Exiguus pressed it and miscalculated the beginning of the Christian era, and we have had to live with it ever since (see *JBC,* art. 75, § 134). For a discussion of the relation of this dating to the others mentioned, see H. W. Hoehner, *Chronological Aspects of the Life of Christ* (Grand Rapids: Zondervan, 1977) 37-38; J. Finegan, *Handbook of Biblical Chronology,* 273-275.

There is even less reason to see in the mention of "about thirty years" any reference to 2 Sam 5:4 (David's age), or Gen 41:46 (Joseph's age), or Num 4:3 (a generic adult age), *pace* H. Schürmann, *Lukasevangelium,* 199.

in the minds of the people, the son of Joseph. Lit. "being the son, as it was thought, of Joseph . . ." (*ōn huios, hōs enomizeto, Iōsēph tou Hēli*). As in the Matthean genealogy, Jesus' ancestry is traced through Joseph, not through Mary (despite later attempts to label the Lucan genealogy as that of Mary). To Joseph a legal or commonly estimated paternity is thus ascribed; Jesus is regarded as his heir. This is also the reason why Mary and Joseph are described as "his parents" in 2:41, and Mary is made to refer to Joseph, in speaking to Jesus, as "your father" (2:48). Cf. 4:22; John 1:45; 6:42. The cl., "as it was thought," added by Luke (see COMMENT), modifies solely "the son of Joseph," and is not to be understood with the further list of genitives. On a mode of punctuating these words, to permit an interpretation of them in terms of levirate marriage, see the COMMENT.

Joseph, son of Heli. Joseph has been identified in the infancy narrative as "of the house of David" (1:27; cf. 2:4). Now the genealogy explains this Davidic ancestry in detail. His father Heli is otherwise unknown. The name in Greek *Hēli* (=Hebrew *'Ēlî*) is found in the LXX of 1 Sam 1:3, etc.

According to Matt 1:16 Joseph was the son of Jacob. Ms. D at this point in the Lucan text also reads "Joseph, son of Jacob," but it continues the genealogy (in ascending order) with the names of the Matthean list from Jacob to David. It thus harmonizes the genealogies and gets rid of the problem.

In the following NOTES only the crucial text-critical problems will be discussed; there is a host of minor spelling-variants of the names that are inconsequential and do not call for comment (e.g. interchange of final *n* and *m*). Anyone interested can consult the *apparatus criticus* of any modern critical New Testament.

24-27. *son of Matthat . . . Rhesa*. These seventeen ancestors of Jesus are otherwise unknown; they are not to be identified with any OT persons bearing the same or similar names (e.g. the prophets Amos, Nahum).

27. *Rhesa*. The suggestion has been made that this name is actually a Greek transliteration of the Aramaic title *rēšā'*, "prince," and that it should be taken with the former name, "Prince Joanan, son of Zerubbabel," referring to Hananiah, the son of Zerubbabel in 1 Chr 3:19. According to Plummer (*Commentary*, 104), "some Jewish copyist" of the pre-Lucan list would have mistaken it for a proper name. See further Jeremias, *Jerusalem*, 296. This is, however, highly speculative, and the formation of the list, as it now stands in the Lucan text, is against it. See COMMENT.

Zerubbabel. Luke actually uses the Greek form *Zorobabel*, found in the LXX of 1 Chr 3:19; his name means "Offspring of Babylon" (=Akkadian *zēr-Bābili*), referring to his birth in Babylon (Ezra 2:2) before his return with the Jewish exiles from the Captivity. He became the governor of Judah under the Persian domination after Cyrus' decree permitting the Jews to return. He ruled in Jerusalem ca. 520 B.C., a successor of Sheshbazzar, and had a part in the rebuilding of the Temple ca. 520-515 B.C. The MT of 1 Chr 3:19 implies his Davidic descent, making him the son of Pedaiah, the brother of Shealtiel and third son of Jechoniah. Luke, however, is following another (probably more correct) tradition, which makes him the son of Shealtiel (see Hag 1:1,12,14; 2:2,23; Ezra 3:2,8; 5:2; Neh 12:1), as does the LXX of 1 Chr 3:19. Matt 1:12 follows the same tradition too. A. Plummer (*The Gospel*, 104) thinks that Zerubbabel was really the son of Pedaiah and nephew of Shealtiel, whose heir he became because the latter had no sons. But this is scarcely correct; see Jeremias, *Jerusalem*, 295. In this person the Lucan and Matthean genealogies touch (along with Shealtiel) amid a long list of differing names. The appearance of them in the Matthean list does not surprise us. That they should suddenly turn up at this point in the Lucan is surprising. Does Zerubbabel's name appear here because he has been considered as Yahweh's "signet ring" in Hag 2:20-23, a sign of his elect status?

Shealtiel. Luke actually uses the Greek form *Salathiel*, found in the LXX of 1 Chr 3:17. The Hebrew *šĕ'altî-'ēl* means "I have asked God" (for this child). Whereas in Matt 1:17 he is the son of Jechoniah (as in the LXX of 1 Chr 3:17, actually of *Iechonia-asir*, "Jechoniah-prisoner"), in Luke he becomes the son of an unknown Neri.

28-31. *Melchi . . . Mattatha.* These 18 ancestors of Jesus are likewise unknown, though presented as heirs of David according to "the house of Nathan" (see Zech 12:12). On the use of names of some of the patriarchs in this group, see the COMMENT.

31. *Nathan.* The third son of David, born to him in Jerusalem, is known from 2 Sam 5:14; 1 Chr 3:5; 14:4. Corresponding to his name in Matt 1:6b is Solomon. Luke has thus avoided the royal line from Solomon to Jeconiah either because of the OT strictures on the reigns of some of these kings or, more likely, because of the oracles in Jer 22:28-30 and 36:30-31 about the coming extinction of the Davidic dynasty.

David. The name of Israel's famous king appears here in the Lucan genealogy just as one in the long line of seventy-seven ancestors; nothing special is made of him, in contrast to Matt 1:6,17.

From David to Abraham the names in the Lucan list agree with those in the Matthean genealogy, save for Admin and Arni (see below). It is a moot question whether these names in the Lucan list are derived from 1 Chr 1:34-2:15 or not. Jeremias (*Jerusalem,* 295) thinks that the author of the Lucan genealogy did not know the Books of Chronicles, "which even in Palestine were included in the canon only in the course of the first century A.D." However, the canonical status of the books is one thing, their composition and use at an earlier date another. A fragment of Chronicles has been reported among the texts discovered in Qumran Cave 4, but as yet it has not been published (see F. M. Cross, *The Ancient Library of Qumran and Modern Biblical Studies* [rev. ed.; Anchor Books; Garden City, NY: Doubleday, 1961] 41). Hence the dependence of the Lucan list on such passages in Chronicles cannot be excluded.

32. *Jesse.* The father of David, of the tribe of Judah, resided in Bethlehem (1 Sam 16:1e). Luke uses the Greek form *Iessai,* which is found in 1 Chr 2:13 (LXX); the Hebrew form of the name is *'îšay < Yišay* (1 Chr 2:12). Jesse is otherwise known from 1 Sam 17:12; 20:27; Ruth 4:22; cf. Acts 13:22; Rom 15:12.

Obed. This is David's grandfather (Ruth 4:17,21-22), who had been nursed as a child by Naomi. The Greek form preferred by Nestle, Aland, and Merk is *Iōbēd* in this verse, but mss. B, ℵ* read *Iōbēl* because of a confusion of the similar-looking majuscules Δ and Λ. The Koine text-tradition and ms. Θ read *Ōbēd,* along with the LXX of 1 Chr 2:12 and Ruth 4:21-22—whence the English spelling commonly used. The Hebrew form of the name is *'Ōbēd,* "worshiper."

Boaz. He was a rich and upright resident of Bethlehem, who married Ruth of Moab (Ruth 2-4). Luke uses the Greek form *Boos,* found in the LXX of 1 Chr 2:12; the Hebrew form is *Bō'az* (meaning unknown).

Sala. The name of Boaz's father is given in mss. P⁴, B, ℵ* and various Syriac versions as *Sala.* The counterpart in Matt 1:4 is *Salmōn,* which is the name of his father in the LXX of 1 Chr 2:11, whereas that of Ruth 4:20-21 has *Salman.* The MT of 1 Chr 2:11 has *Salmā',* of Ruth 4:20 *Salmāh,* and of Ruth 4:21 *Salmôn.* Because of the latter and its close LXX transcription, some mss. of Luke also read *Salmōn* (the Koine text-tradition, D, Θ).

Nahshon. He was one of the chiefs of the twelve tribes who helped Moses take the census of Israel in the wilderness. The Greek form of the name is *Naassōn,* which is also found in the LXX of 1 Chr 2:10; Exod 6:23; Num 1:7; Ruth 4:20. Its Hebrew form is *Naḥšôn.* His sister Elisheba (Elizabeth) married Aaron; she was the daughter of the following ancestor.

33. *Amminadab.* The father of Nahshon was a leader of the tribe of Judah (Num 1:7). Cf. Exod 6:23; 1 Chr 2:10; Ruth 4:19-20. In both Matt 1:4 and 1 Chr 2:10 he is known as the son of Ram (=Aram); but Luke makes him the son of Admin and grandson of Arni, which names are unknown in the OT.

Admin, son of Arni. Together with the foregoing name, these present the greatest difficulty in the text-critical state of the Lucan genealogy. The number of variants at this point is great, and modern critical editions of the Greek NT have preferred to read these three names (even without brackets), because it is the *lectio difficilior.* Part of the reason for the variety is precisely the inability of copyists to identify them with any persons known in the OT.

Hezron. With this name the Lucan genealogy again parallels the Matthean (1:3). He was an eponymous leader of the tribe of Judah (Gen 46:12; Num 26:21). The Greek form of the name is *Esrom,* found in the LXX of 1 Chr 2:9 (in some mss. *Eserōm*); the Hebrew form is *Ḥeṣrôn,* "the Lean One" (?).

Perez. He was one of the twins (along with Zerah) born to Judah and Tamar (Gen 38:29). The Greek form of the name is *Phares,* as in 1 Chr 2:4 (LXX). The Hebrew form is *Pereṣ.* Cf. Ruth 4:18.

Judah. He was the fourth son of Jacob, born to Leah (Gen 29:35), who became the eponymous hero of the tribe of Judah. See 1 Chr 2:1; cf. Heb 7:14.

34. *Jacob.* He was the son of Isaac and Rebecca, the younger twin of Esau. Both Luke and Matthew use this name of the patriarch, who is rather called "Israel" in the MT of 1 Chr 1:34; in this they are following the LXX tradition, even to the extent of the un-Grecized form of the name. He has appeared in the Lucan infancy narrative in 1:33; with the following two patriarchs he will appear again in 13:28 and 20:37.

Isaac. He was the son of Abraham and Sarah in their older age, the husband of Rebekah (Gen 24:64). His name is derived from 1 Chr 1:34.

Abraham. Israel's first patriarch appears here, as in the case of King David, in no special role. With the mention of him ends the agreement of the Lucan list with 1 Chronicles 1-3. From Abraham to Arphaxad the list seems to be dependent rather on the genealogy in Gen 11:10-26. Yet some of the names that follow appear in 1 Chr 1:24-27. See the NOTE on 1:55 for a hint of Abraham's role in Lucan theology.

Terah. He was a Semite, named after the region from which he came, and the father of Abraham, Nahor, and Haran according to Gen 11:26-27. The Greek form of the name used in the list is *Thara,* as in the LXX of Gen 11:26. Cf. Josh 24:2; 1 Chr 1:26. The Hebrew form is *Teraḥ.*

Nahor. Abraham's grandfather was probably named after the region from which he came (*Naḥuru*), in Mesopotamia. The Greek form is *Nachōr,* as in the LXX of Gen 11:22; cf. 1 Chr 1:26. The Hebrew form is *Nāḥôr.*

35. *Serug.* The name is probably derived from the region of Sarugi, west of

Haran. Its Greek form is *Serouch,* as in the LXX of Gen 11:20; cf. 1 Chr 1:26; the Hebrew form is *Šĕrûg.*

Reu. A Semite, whose name is probably shortened from Reuel or Reuyah, "Friend of God" or "Friend of Yahu." The Greek form of it is *Ragau,* as in the LXX of Gen 11:18; cf. 1 Chr 1:25. The Hebrew form is *Rĕ'û.*

Peleg. A Semite, whose name meant "Division," and probably reflects the story of the Tower of Babel. The Greek form is *Phalek,* as in the LXX of Gen 11:16; cf. 1 Chr 1:25. The Hebrew form is *Peleg,* or (in the pausal form) *Paleg.*

Eber. He was the eponymous ancestor of the "Hebrews." See Gen 11:14; 10:24; cf. 1 Chr 1:25. The Hebrew form is *'Ēber,* "region beyond" (the Euphrates).

Shelah. The Greek form in the genealogy is actually *Sala,* as in v. 32. It is derived from the LXX of Gen 11:13; 10:24; 1 Chr 1:24, whereas the MT has *Šelaḥ*—whence comes the form commonly used in English.

36. *Cainan.* The name *Kaïnam* (or *Kaïnan*) is found in the LXX of Gen 11:12; 10:24; 1 Chr 1:18 (ms. A). In all these OT passages the MT lacks the name and makes Shelah directly the son of Arphaxad.

Arphaxad. He was the third son of Shem, the grandfather (or great-grand-father) of Eber, the eponymous ancestor of the Hebrews. The Greek form of his name, *Arphaxad,* is derived from the LXX of Gen 11:10; 1 Chr 1:23. The Hebrew form is *'Arpakšad* and was probably of Hurrian origin.

Shem. He was the eponymous ancestor of the Semites. The Greek form is *Sēm,* as in the LXX of Gen 11:10. From Shem to Adam the Lucan list probably depends on the Sethite genealogy of Gen 5:1-32, "the book of the generations of Adam." But see Gen 9:26-27; Sir 49:16.

Noah. The Lucan genealogy includes even the pre-patriarchal righteous fig-ure, the exemplary Noah, son of Lamech, survivor of the Flood, who was saved by God himself from destruction. The Greek form of the name is *Nōe,* as in the LXX of Gen 5:29; 6:9; 1 Chr 1:4; Wisd 10:4; Sir 49:17. In the Sethite genealogy of Gen 5:28-29 Noah was born to Lamech, but in the Cainite genealogy (of the Yahwist source) Noah is not mentioned among the children of Lamech (Gen 4:18-22). He figured in the early columns of the *Genesis Apocryphon* from Qumran Cave 1.

Lamech. He was the husband of Bit-Enosh, who bore him the astounding child Noah (see 1QapGen 2:3,19; 5:4,10,25,26); she is not mentioned in the OT. Lamech's name appears in the list as in the LXX of Gen 5:25 (cf. 4:18-22); 1 Chr 1:3.

37. *Methuselah.* He was the Sethite patriarch; see Gen 5:21. The Greek form of his name is *Mathousala,* as in the LXX of 5:21; 1 Chr 1:3. The He-brew form is *Mĕtûšalaḥ.* But the MT of Gen 4:18 gives Lamech's father's name as *Mĕtûšā'ēl* (i.e. in the Cainite genealogy). The latter is a hebraized form of Akkadian *Mutu-ša-ili,* "man of God." The former may represent a de-liberate deformation of this name, since it is otherwise inexplicable. The LXX of Gen 4:18 has deliberately harmonized the name.

Enoch. He is identified in Jude 14 as "the seventh from Adam." In late pre-Christian Jewish tradition he became the one favored by God, "whose lot was apportioned [with the Holy Ones]" (1QapGen 2:20), because "he walked with God" (Gen 5:24), and was taken up by him. He was also known in the same tradition as "the distinguished scribe" (4QEnGiants^a 8:4). See further Gen 5:18; Sir 49:16; 1 Chr 1:3.

Jard. An antediluvian patriarch (see Gen 5:15; 1 Chr 1:1). The Greek form *Iaret* is found in the best mss. of Luke, but the LXX has *Iared;* the Hebrew form is *Yered.*

Mahalaleel. The Greek form is *Maleleēl,* as in the LXX of Gen 5:12; 1 Chr 1:1. The Hebrew form is *Mahălal'el,* "the praise of God."

Cainan. The same name as in v. 36. See Gen 5:9; 1 Chr 1:1.

38. *Enos.* Or *Enosh* (see Gen 5:6; 1 Chr 1:1). The Hebrew form is *'Ēnôš,* "man." Gen 4:26 records that the worship of Yahweh began in his day.

Seth. According to Gen 4:25-26 he was the third son of Adam and Eve; but in 5:3 he is the first son. Cf. 1 Chr 1:1; Sir 49:16.

Adam. See Gen 5:1; 1 Chr 1:1; Sir 49:16. He is here understood as an individual, historic person, as in Rom 5:12—the first human being. In Genesis 1–2 the word *'ādām* is normally intended as a figure symbolic of humanity. Here, as in much of intertestamental literature, Adam's "sin" is forgotten and his "glory" as the first-formed is extolled. Luke even enhances his status by calling him "son of God." Cf. 1 Tim 2:13.

son of God. The Lucan addition of *tou theou* to the genealogy might seem to make of God a "father" in the same sense as it has been meant for the other persons in the list. Yet Luke is obviously implying more than that. It is not just that Adam whom God created is "his child." The addition rather evokes a recollection of the heavenly declaration of Jesus' sonship (3:22). He is the one who is really "the son of God." However, this is not to be so understood as if everything from *hōs enomizeto* (3:23) is to be taken as a gigantic parenthesis between *ōn huios* and *tou theou;* this would be forced and unnatural, as Plummer points out (*The Gospel,* 105). But Luke has not just added *tou theou* for the sake of Gentiles; tracing Jesus' ancestry back to Adam might convey as much, but the last, further step aims at more. In a sense, Jesus is the Son of God.

BIBLIOGRAPHY (3:23-38)

Abel, E. L. "The Genealogies of Jesus *ho Christos,*" *NTS* 20 (1973-1974) 203-210.

Brown, R. E. "Genealogy (Christ)," *IDBSup* (1976) 354.

Burger, C. *Jesus als Davidssohn: Eine traditionsgeschichtliche Untersuchung* (Göttingen: Vandenhoeck und Ruprecht, 1970) 116-123.

Byskov, M. "Verus Deus—verus homo, Luc 3.23-38," *ST* 26 (1972) 25-32.

Farrer, A. M. "Note: The Genealogies of Christ," in *Studies in the Gospels: Essays in Memory of R. H. Lightfoot* (ed. D. E. Nineham; Oxford: Blackwell, 1955) 87-88.

Gordon, C. H. "Paternity at Two Levels," *JBL* 96 (1977) 101.

Hartl, V. "Zum Stammbaum Jesu nach Lukas," *BZ* 7 (1909) 156-173, 290-302.

Heer, J. M. *Die Stammbäume Jesu nach Matthäus und Lukas* (BibS[F] 15/1-2; Freiburg im B.: Herder, 1910).

Holzmeister, U. "Ein Erklärungsversuch der Lk-Genealogie (3,23-38)," *ZKT* 47 (1923) 184-218.

———— "Genealogia S. Lucae (Lc 3,23-38)," *VD* 23 (1943) 9-18.

Hood, R. T. "The Genealogies of Jesus," in *Early Christian Origins: Studies in Honor of H. R. Willoughby* (ed. A. Wikgren; Chicago: Quadrangle Books, 1961) 1-15.

Johnson, M. D. *The Purpose of the Biblical Genealogies with Special Reference to the Setting of the Genealogies of Jesus* (SNTSMS 8; Cambridge: University Press, 1969).

Kaplan, C. "Some New Testament Problems in the Light of the Rabbinics and the Pseudepigrapha: The Generation Schemes in Matthew I:1-17, Luke III:24ff.," *BSac* 87 (1930) 465-471.

Kuhn, G. "Die Geschlechtsregister Jesu bei Lukas und Matthäus nach ihrer Herkunft untersucht," *ZNW* 22 (1923) 206-228.

Lambertz, M. "Die Toledoth im Mt 1,1-17 und Lc 3,23bff.," in *Festschrift Franz Dornseiff* (ed. H. Kusch; Leipzig: VEB Bibliographisches Institut, 1953) 201-225.

Lee, G. M. "Luke iii, 23," *ExpTim* 79 (1967-1968) 310.

Liver, J. "The Problem of the Davidic Family after the Biblical Period," *Tarbiẓ* 26 (1957) 229-254.

Nestle, E. "Salomo und Nathan in Mt I und Lc 3," *ZNW* 8 (1907) 72.

———— "Zur Genealogie in Lukas 3," *ZNW* 4 (1903) 188-189.

Nolle, L. "Old Testament Laws of Inheritance and St. Luke's Genealogy of Christ," *Scr* 2 (1947) 38-42.

Ogg, G. "The Age of Jesus When He Taught," *NTS* 5 (1958-1959) 291-298.

Pous, P. "Genealogia Christi altera," *VD* 7 (1927) 267-271.

Ramlot, M.-L. "Les généalogies bibliques: Un genre littéraire oriental," *BVC* 60 (1964) 53-70.

Saldarini, G. "La genealogia di Gesù," *I vangeli* (eds. L. Moraldi and S. Lyonnet; Turin: Marietti, 1960) 4. 411-425.

Sanders, H. A. "The Genealogies of Jesus," *JBL* 32 (1913) 184-193.

Seethaler, P. "Eine kleine Bemerkung zu den Stammbäumen Jesu nach Matthäus und Lukas," *BZ* 16 (1972) 256-257.

Thompson, P. J. "The Infancy Gospels of St. Matthew and St. Luke Compared," *SE I* (TU 73; 1959) 217-222.

Throckmorton, B. H. "Genealogy (Christ)," *IDB* 2. 365-366.

Wilson, R. R. "Genealogy and History in the Old Testament" (New Haven: Yale University Dissertation, 1972).

———— "The Old Testament Genealogies in Recent Research," *JBL* 94 (1975) 168-189.

15. THE TEMPTATION IN THE DESERT
(4:1-13)

4 ¹ Jesus, filled with the holy Spirit, departed from the Jordan and was led about by the Spirit ² for forty days in the desert where he was tempted by the devil. During those days he ate nothing, and at the end of them he was famished. ³ The devil said to him, "If you are the Son of God, tell this stone to become bread." ⁴ But Jesus answered him, "It is written in Scripture, *'Not on bread alone is man to live.'* "ᵃ ⁵ Then he took Jesus up and showed him in an instant all the kingdoms of the world. ⁶ The devil said to him, "To you I shall give authority over all this, and the glory that goes with it, because it has been made over to me; to anyone I please I can give it. ⁷ So if you bow down before me, it will all be yours." ⁸ But Jesus replied, "It is written in Scripture, *"You shall worship the Lord your God and him* only *shall you adore.'* "ᵇ ⁹ Then the devil took him to Jerusalem and set him on the pinnacle of the Temple, saying to him, "If you are the Son of God, throw yourself down from here; ¹⁰ for it is written in Scripture, *'He shall give his angels orders about you, to protect you,*ᶜ ¹¹ and again, *'Their hands shall bear you up lest you strike your foot against a stone.'* "ᵈ ¹² But Jesus answered him, "In Scripture it is said, *'You shall not put the Lord your God to the test.'* "ᵉ ¹³ So the devil, having exhausted every sort of temptation, departed from him for a while.

ᵃ Deut 8:3 ᵇ Deut 6:13 ᶜ Ps 91:11 ᵈ Ps 91:12 ᵉ Deut 6:16

COMMENT

The temptation or testing of Jesus in the desert forms the last of the preparatory episodes introducing the public ministry in this Gospel (4:1-13). It is closely linked to the baptism scene and the genealogy in that he is now tested precisely as Son of God. It will be seen to have a relation to the Nazareth scene as well. Both of these set a tone for the whole of Jesus' public ministry.

The Lucan sequence is here dependent on Marcan order: baptism followed by temptation. Luke interrupted that order to insert the genealogy, but now he continues with it. Only a few words are retained from the Marcan source in 1:12-13, "for forty days in the desert" and "being tempted by. . . ." In contrast to Matt 4:11, Luke uses none of the Marcan details at the end of the episode. The mode of temptation is left unspecified in Mark, but Luke uses "Q" material to tell of the nature of the temptation, as does Matt 4:2b-10. See R. Schnackenburg, *TQ* 132 (1952) 300-305.

The more important Lucan redactional modifications are the following: "filled with the holy Spirit," "during those days," "authority," "in an instant," the consistent use of *diabolos*, "devil" throughout, the explanation of the devil in v. 6b, and the concluding v. 13. Minor modifications in the story reveal a Lucan concern to present the temptations in a plausible form (e.g. the shift from the pl. "stones" and "loaves" to the sg. in the first scene; the elimination of a "very high mountain" in the second). These modifications have been studied in great detail by J. Dupont, *Les tentations,* 43-72.

More significant, however, is the order of the temptation scenes. In Matthew the order is: desert—pinnacle—high mountain; in Luke: desert —view of world-kingdoms—Jerusalem pinnacle. What was the original order in "Q" and who changed it? Commentators differ. A. Plummer (*Commentary,* 110) speaks of the Lucan order as the "chronological order," but nothing in them really suggests a temporal sequence. The sequence has to be explained in terms of something either theological or literary. K. H. Rengstorf (*Evangelium,* 63) suggests that either Luke or his source rearranged the sequence so that it would be the reverse of the first three petitions in the Lucan form of the Our Father (11:2): "may your name be sanctified; may your kingdom come; give us each day our bread for subsistence." If this is so, then it is subtle indeed. The same has to be said for the suggestion of H. Swanston, who sees a connection between the Lucan order and Psalm 106 (*JTS* 17 [1966] 71). The more plausible explanations have sought to explain the difference of order in terms of the climactic scene. Matthew is said to have put the temptation on the high mountain last either because of the mountain motif in his Gospel (Sermon on the Mount; Matt 28:16-20—implied New-Moses motif) or because of the rejection of Satan-worship for the service of God alone (see A. Feuillet, J. Dupont). On the other hand, Luke is said to have reversed the order of the last two scenes because of his geographical perspective— the climactic scene takes place in Jerusalem (see p. 165 above). The latter explanation is to be preferred.

Other considerations reveal that the Matthean order is the more original. There is not only the progression from desert-floor, to pinnacle, to high mountain, but the quotations of Deuteronomy used by Jesus to rebuff Satan appear in Matthew in a simple reverse of their OT occurrence: Deut 8:3 in Matt 4:4; Deut 6:16 in Matt 4:7; and Deut 6:13 in Matt 4:10. Again, in Matthew the first two temptations challenge Jesus precisely as "Son of God" (which may point to the use of an original pair, to which a third was eventually added). Coupled with the geographical consideration, these seem to argue in favor of the Lucan reordering of the sequence of "Q."

From a form-critical viewpoint, the episode is another Story about Jesus, part of the narrative tradition. R. Bultmann (*HST*, 254) regarded the temptation scenes in "Q" as "a secondary formulation," a "scribal Haggada," with the dialogue between Jesus and the devil reflecting rabbinic disputations; it would have been "the work of Christian scribes," who gave it the form of a controversy dialogue (ibid., 256). On the basis of its form it would belong to Palestinian tradition, but in that it contains the notion of a "son of God" for whom miracle-working would be characteristic one would really have to look to a Hellenistic milieu to explain its matrix, since Judaism had no figure of a messiah as miracle-worker (ibid., 257). Consequently, the story is for him the creation of an early Christian community, seeking to explain apologetically why Jesus never performed miracles on his own behalf and did not conform to contemporary messianic ideas. With varying nuances, this apologetic explanation of the episode has also been used by other commentators, e.g. W. Bousset, M. Dibelius, G. Bornkamm.

The explanation which points to a Palestinian context of sign-seeking as a way of understanding an aspect of the episode may be partly correct. It explains, indeed, the scenes in their isolated existence (e.g. as in "Q"), but it is inadequate for the understanding of them in either Matthew or Luke. It offers no real explanation of the articulation of the temptations about three quotations from the same OT book. The Jewish model of haggadic disputation may be an interesting parallel, but it misses an essential point in the Gospel contexts.

E. Lohmeyer ("Die Versuchung") thought that different, separately transmitted temptation accounts circulated in the early Church, the Marcan verses and the temptation on a high mountain being the more original, to which the other two were subsequently added—all having a different christological preoccupation. A belief that in the messianic era God would again feed his people as he did at the Exodus led to the request for such a sign from Jesus; or a belief that the Messiah would manifest God's solicitude and concern for him led to the request of a sign of this sort from Jesus. The Gospel scenes, then, reply that such demands were of diabolic origin and make known the church's clarification of its understanding of Jesus as Messiah. Again, there may be an element of truth in such an explanation, but it fails to clarify why there are three quotations from Deuteronomy and the unity that such quotation implies.

No little part of the difficulty in explaining this episode of the temptation of Jesus is the determination of its origin. The scenes are recounted as having taken place between Jesus and the devil alone. How did the early community or the evangelists come to learn about them? The Marcan tradition, though it knows of temptation by Satan for forty days in the desert, knows nothing of the details. Again, aside from "Begone, Satan" in Matt 4:10, the only words attributed to Jesus are Scripture quotations; the rest is the narrative of the evangelists. Since the quotation of the OT in so much of the gospel tradition is the work of the early community seeking to relate the Christ-event to God's plan or seeking for a fuller understanding of details of it, the use of Scripture here naturally suggests "Christian scribes."

It is impossible to establish the historicity of these temptation scenes, since there is no basis for a historical judgment or control of them. The fact that they begin and end in the desert, despite the physical transfers recounted, as well as the fantasy involved in some of the details, is sufficient to suggest that these stories have primarily a symbolic value. It is, however, difficult to ascribe the fantastic details to a communal popular imagination. Would early Christians, who had come to venerate Jesus as the Son of God, concoct such fantasies about him, fabricating them out of whole cloth? This is hard to accept. These scenes have a unified literary composition dominated by a theological reflection. They are, moreover, scarcely born of temptations suffered by Christians themselves and retrojected into the ministry of Jesus himself (see further Dupont, *Les tentations,* 97-108).

The three scenes have a common subject in that they correct a false understanding of Jesus' mission as Son. In Luke 22:31-32 Jesus tells his disciples about a confrontation with Satan, who would have sifted them like wheat. Could it not be that Jesus recounted some form of these stories as figurative, parabolic résumés of the seduction latent in the diabolic opposition to him and his ministry? (See further J. Jeremias, *Parables,* 123.)

Dupont and others are correct in looking for a logical setting for these temptation scenes in the request for a sign made of Jesus during his ministry. His only sign was his fidelity to the Father, and that is not simply born of Easter-faith. Dupont himself has sought to steer a middle course between a literalist interpretation of these scenes and a parabolic interpretation, which latter he regards as "entièrement fictive." "Speaking to his disciples about an experience which he had, Jesus could hardly express himself in this way, if he had no experience of this sort. . . ." The parabolic interpretation would deny to these scenes "a real basis in the life of Jesus." He concludes, "Jesus speaks of an experience which he lived through, but translates it into figurative language, suited to strike the minds of his listeners" (*Les tentations,* 113-115). But what is really the difference between this and the parabolic interpretation?

The "real basis in the life of Jesus" is the fact of temptation or testing that confronted him. All three evangelists insist on this in one way or another (Mark 1:13; Matt 4:1; Luke 4:2). Certain verses in John's Gospel reflect this tradition too (6:15,26-34; 7:1-4; cf. R. E. Brown, *CBQ* 23 [1961] 155). The author of the Epistle to the Hebrews makes much of this fact (4:15; 5:2; 2:17). Indeed, Brown goes so far as to admit: "Mt and Lk (or their common source) would be doing no injustice to historic fact if they dramatized such temptations within one scene, and unmasked the real tempter by placing these enticements directly in his mouth" (ibid.). Whether one admits Dupont's "figurative language" or Brown's dramatization or the parabolic interpretation, one is undoubtedly closer to the correct way of understanding these scenes than a naïve literalism. For, in the long run, their theological import is of greater importance than any salvaging of their historicity.

The scenes depict temptations of Jesus coming from external sources; they do not suggest that they proceed from an inner conflict. They symbolize the seduction in the hostility, opposition, and rejection which confronted him constantly throughout his ministry. These are the elements that should be regarded as the "real basis in the life of Jesus." The opposition was such that he was constantly tempted to use his power as Son to overcome it. Without regarding these stories as *ipsissima verba Iesu,* they could well sum up in parabolic fashion the way that Jesus may have spoken to his disciples about this opposition and its diabolic seduction.

To understand the temptations or the testings of Jesus in this way means that they did not take place as a real, external happening in which the devil in some visible form encountered Jesus, and that physical changes of place actually ensued between the acts (so J. Schmid, *Das Evangelium nach Matthäus* [RNT 1; 5th ed.; Regensburg: Pustet, 1965] 67). Yet it does ascribe the origin of these stories to Jesus himself—in some form. Compare again Luke 22:31-32, which also makes use of a confrontation with the devil to express the problem that incredulity and hostility evoked in his life.

The three scenes then depict Jesus as the Son of God obedient to his Father's will and refusing to be seduced into using his power or authority as Son for any reason other than that for which he has been sent. Each of the scenes has to be explained a little more in detail. The unifying link in the three is the series of quotations from Deuteronomy, derived from passages that recall three events of the Exodus in which the Israelites in the desert were put to the test and failed. Jesus is being implicitly compared with them: Where Israel of old failed, there Jesus succeeds. This comparison is found in both Matthew and Luke, but the emphasis is different. In

Matthew it is part of a theme worked out in detail in the Gospel as a whole, whereas in Luke it receives little attention outside of this episode. Here in particular it emphasizes by contrast the fidelity of Jesus as Son (see further A. B. Taylor, *Int* 14 [1960] 300-309).

The first scene ends with the quotation of Deut 8:3, "Not on bread alone is man to live." Jesus is challenged to use his power as Son in his own interest and apart from his heaven-commissioned goal—to seek food for himself apart from his Father's design. Deut 8:1-6 alludes to the Exodus experience of Israel, sighing after the fleshpots and the bread of Egypt and murmuring against Moses and Aaron (Exodus 16; Num 11:7-8). Despite its desire to seek its food apart from Yahweh, Israel was fed with dew, manna, and quail by him. Israel was thus humbled, having been found wanting. By contrast, Jesus rejects the diabolic challenge and alludes to the Deuteronomic hortatory recapitulation of the Exodus event. Jesus' answer is cryptic, but it implies that Yahweh will supply him with "manna" once he lifts his eyes beyond desert stones.

The second scene ends with the quotation of Deut 6:13, "You shall worship the Lord your God and him only shall you adore." Jesus has been challenged to accept dominion over world-kingdoms from someone other than God. This testing is not directed to him explicitly as Son, but it is challenging him to acknowledge someone other than the Father as his master and lord. His answer quotes a directive given by Moses to the Israelites of old, again drawn from a hortatory recapitulation of an event in the Exodus. Deut 6:10-15 alludes to the experience of Israel wandering in the desert and attracted by Canaanite cults (Deut 12:30-31) and constantly warned by Moses not to run after alien gods or to court alien power (Exod 23:23-33). By contrast, Jesus rejects the challenge to worship anything other than Yahweh, his Father, and makes it clear that his mission is solely to see that God's kingship is established over all. Yahweh is the sole king of the world; he alone is to be served. Israel's failure to heed the directives of Moses was often recalled in the OT (e.g. 2 Kgs 16:3-4; 21:5-6; Jer 7:31; Psalm 106).

The third scene ends with the quotation of Deut 6:16, "You shall not put the Lord your God to the test." Jesus is challenged again as Son to use his power to reveal himself with éclat to his contemporaries and to conform to popular ideas of what a heaven-sent leader of the people would be. Whether this challenge reflects the belief about the appearance of the Messiah on the roof of the Jerusalem Temple or not is hard to say (see NOTE on 4:9). In any case, claims of extraordinary power, uttered by persons who called themselves prophets, were current (recall Josephus' account of Theudas, *Ant.* 20.5,1 §§ 97-98; cf. Acts 6:35-37). It is against such a Palestinian background that the devil's challenge to Jesus is to be understood. His answer: another Mosaic directive; Deut 6:16

alludes to the Exodus experience of Israel putting Yahweh to the test at Massah and Meribah (Exod 17:1-7), when it demanded, "Give us water to drink." Yahweh's answer was water from the rock struck by Moses, a miracle accorded to an incredulous people. But Moses sought to curb Israel from seeking to put Yahweh to the test; his directive sums up in hortatory fashion that Exodus experience, when Israel did put Yahweh to the test. By contrast, Jesus rejects the challenge to demand miraculous protection of himself and his heaven-commissioned role. Implicit in his answer is the rebuke to remember that no one can demand such intervention from God merely to suit his fancy or whim.

The three temptations are presented to Jesus in his capacity as Heaven's emissary and Son (3:22). They are said to have a "messianic character." By this is usually meant that they are not recorded in Matthew or Luke for a hortatory purpose (i.e. to give Christians a model for the temptations of their own lives). See H. Riesenfeld, "Le caractère messianique." This label, however, should be used more carefully, since there is no mention in the episode of the title *Christos* or Messiah, and not even "Son of God" is to be understood solely in a messianic sense. Jesus is tempted as Son.

Some commentators (C. Charlier, E. E. Ellis, A. Feuillet, W. Grundmann, J. Jeremias, et al.) think that a New-Adam motif is present in these scenes. Feuillet would see a reference to Adam's sin in 4:6 and the transfer of dominion over all world-kingdoms to Satan as a result of it; he would see an allusion to the temptation of Eve in Genesis 3 in the challenge to Jesus to turn the stone into bread. Part of this is based on the New-Adam interpretation of the genealogy (see p. 498 above). But this is highly eisegetical. The three episodes allude to the temptations of Israel in the desert at the time of the Exodus and not to that of Adam and Eve. Moreover, the New-Adam interpretation lends to these scenes a hortatory or parenetic character that they do not have. Luke does not present Jesus triumphing over the devil as a model for baptized Christians who have to resist his evil suggestions; any attempt to see a connection between the Lucan scenes and 1 John 2:16, the "lust of the flesh, the lust of the eyes, and the pride of life," is misguided. Similarly inadequate is the interpretation of the scenes which sees Jesus overcoming the devil in his capacity as messianic high priest. W. Grundmann (*Evangelium nach Lukas*, 114) appeals to Dan 5:10-11 and *T. Levi* 18:12 to support this along with the New-Adam interpretation. But this is to read more into the text than is there.

In each of the scenes the devil is vanquished by Jesus, the Son of God, quoting Scripture. No other words of Jesus are recorded (save in Matt 4:10). He is thus portrayed as the conqueror because he is armed with "the sword of the Spirit, the word of God," to put it in non-Lucan, but nevertheless apt (Eph 6:17) terminology. The devil may quote Scripture to his purpose (using Ps 91:11-12 in Luke 4:10-11), but he does not prove to be the "more powerful one" (3:16; 11:22). Thus, at the very outset of his ministry, Jesus is portrayed as the "more powerful one" standing guard over his Father's plan and obedient to Scripture itself.

The peculiar ending of the Lucan scenes (v. 13) gives to the episode its forward-looking orientation. Luke omits Mark 1:13b-c, which is imitated by Matt 4:11. Luke makes the devil depart from Jesus "for a while," i.e. until the passion, when he will make another attack on the Father's plan of salvation-history. This does not mean that the coming ministry will be "Satan-free" (see p. 186 above), even though we do not yet know whether the diabolic hostility during the ministry will succeed or not.

NOTES

4 1. *filled with the holy Spirit.* Lit. "full of a holy Spirit." Though the def. art. is omitted here, the phrase obviously refers to the descent of the Spirit on Jesus at the baptism (3:22). Thus endowed, Jesus now undergoes an experience that sums up an aspect of his whole ministry. He conquers the devil, because he is filled with the Spirit. This Lucan detail also prepares for 4:14,18. Being filled with the Spirit is a Lucan theologoumenon; see NOTE on 1:15.

departed from the Jordan. I.e. from the spot where he had been baptized (see 3:3,21-22). The Jordan appears in neither Mark 1:12 nor Matt 4:1; Luke thus redactionally modifies his Marcan source to establish a connection between the temptation and the baptism. The verb *hypestrepsen* can mean either "returned" (i.e. to Nazareth or Galilee) or "withdrew, turned aside" (see BAG, 955). But since Luke has not mentioned earlier that Jesus came from Nazareth (contrast Mark 1:9) or from Galilee (contrast Matt 3:13), there is little reason to read the first sense into Luke's use of the verb here. See further 4:14, where the term of the withdrawal will be specified. The verb is a Lucan favorite (see p. 111 above).

was led about by the Spirit. Lit. "he was being led about in the Spirit." Luke not only notes Jesus' endowment, but makes it clear that his experience in the desert was under the aegis of God's Spirit. Luke uses the prep. *en,* which may differ from the agency expressed in Matt 4:1, *hypo,* "by." It can express agency, however, as in 11:15; Acts 17:31 (see BDF § 219), although some commentators prefer to understand it of the Spirit's interior influence; so Dupont, *Les tentations,* 50, appealing to Luke 1:17; 2:27.

H. Conzelmann (*Theology,* 28) thinks that according to Luke Jesus is not "led" by the Spirit, but rather acts "in the Spirit" (adding in a note that "*ēgeto en tō pneumati* appears to be a correction of the source, signifying that Jesus is not subject to the Spirit." That is, however, a contradiction of the text itself; the verb is passive, and whether *en* be understood of agency or of influence, Luke is certainly suggesting the subjection of Jesus to the Spirit. The latter is not, however, the origin of the temptation or testing.

2. *for forty days in the desert.* These phrases are derived from Mark 1:13; they supply the time and place for the drama. "Forty days" is to be taken as a round number. But they may recall Deut 8:2, "the Lord your God has led you these forty years in the wilderness" (MT; the LXX lacks "these forty years"; but cf. 8:4; Exod 16:35). Contrast Matt 4:1, where we read of "forty days and forty nights" (cf. Deut 9:9); this phrase may also echo the time spent by Moses on the mountain (Exod 24:18; 34:28) or that spent by Elijah (1 Kgs 19:8). The time is predicated there of Jesus' fast, not of the temptations or the Spirit's leading, as in Luke.

Some Lucan mss. (A, Θ, the Koine text-tradition) read "into the desert" (*eis tēn erēmon*); this is the result of harmonization with Mark 1:12, a phrase that Luke does not take up (cf. Matt 4:1).

By the "desert" the wilderness of Judea is meant, perhaps as place of contact with God (see Hos 2:14-15), but more so as an abode of wild beasts and demons (Lev 16:10; Isa 13:21; 34:14; Tob 8:3). This double aspect of the desert thus confronts Jesus. For a different view, see U. W. Mauser, *Christ in the Wilderness* (SBT 39; Naperville: Allenson, 1963) 146-149.

was tempted by the devil. Lit. "being tempted by the devil," with the pres. ptc. indicating the simultaneity of the temptations and the Spirit's escort. The phrase is derived again from Mark 1:13, except for Luke's substitution of *diabolos*, "devil," for *satanas*, "Satan." Luke does not avoid the latter name (10:18; 11:18; 13:16; 22:3,31), but in this episode he consistently refers to Jesus' opponent as the "devil." *Śāṭān* is the Hebrew name for "adversary, accuser, prosecutor"; in the OT he is in the heavenly court (Job 2:1; Zech 3:1-2). In these passages the LXX renders that name with *diabolos*, which basically means in Greek, "calumniator" (< *diaballein*). By this time in Palestinian Judaism, Satan has become the name for the arch-demon in contemporary angelology. See H. A. Kelly, "The Devil in the Desert," *CBQ* 26 (1964) 190-220; "Demonology and Diabolical Temptation," *Thought* 40 (1965) 165-194; *The Devil, Demonology and Witchcraft* (Garden City, NY: Doubleday, 1968).

The verb *peirazein* can mean (a) "try, attempt" (Acts 9:26; 16:7; 24:6); (b) "try, test" with a good intention (John 6:6); (c) "try, put to the test" with a sinister intention (Acts 5:9; 15:10). It is used here in the last sense, but the nuance is not that of testing Jesus' faith as much as an attempt to frustrate the divine plan of salvation. Luke does not call the devil "the tempter" (*ho peirazōn*), as does Matt 4:3. He is much more the opponent, challenging Jesus (see S. Brown, *Apostasy and Perseverance*, 8, 18-19).

During those days. An expression frequently used by Luke; see 2:1; 5:35; 9:36; 21:23; Acts 2:18 [which reveals its LXX origin, Joel 3:2]; 7:41; 9:37.

he ate nothing. Jesus' fast is not mentioned in Mark; it comes from "Q." Matt 4:2 speaks plainly of Jesus "fasting," whereas Luke says simply that he "ate nothing." In Matthew the temptations come at the end of the fast. Luke's version is influenced by the duration of the temptations in Mark. Perhaps he rephrases the notice from "Q" about the fast to suit the duration. G. Schneider (*Evangelium nach Lukas*, 100) thinks rather that Matthew, with interest in fasting (see 6:16-18), has rephrased "Q." It is hard to say. The "forty days" of the fast—clearly a round number, used symbolically—may be influenced by OT stories of the fast of Moses and Elijah (Exod 34:28; Deut 9:9; 1 Kgs 19:8).

3. *If you are the Son of God.* This is a reference to the baptism scene (3:22). The devil is not doubting Jesus' messiahship. The title used here is already found in the infancy narrative (1:32,35); but it is rather dependent on the heavenly declaration in the Gospel proper. The devil challenges his filial status, exploits his hungry situation, and seeks ultimately to thwart his role in salvation-history. For the conditional taunt, compare Luke 23:35-39.

tell this stone to become bread. Whereas Matt 4:3 has the plural ("stones" and "loaves"), Luke uses the singular. Most likely Luke has changed the original version of "Q" in the interest of plausibility (see Dupont, *Les tentations*, 53). Since Jesus is alone, the changing of one stone to a loaf would suit his need and reduce the grotesque image of a desert full of loaves.

4. *It is written in Scripture.* The Greek text has simply *gegraptai*, "it has been written," a stereotyped formula, used again in 4:8,10 to introduce an OT quotation; see NOTE on 3:4; cf. *NTS* (1960-1961) 300-301; *ESBNT*, 8-10.

Not on bread alone is man to live. The devil is rebuffed with the use of Deut 8:3, quoted in a form resembling the LXX, which follows the MT closely. Some mss. of Luke (A, D, ⊕, the Koine text-tradition) add, "but on every word of God." This addition comes from a scribal harmonization of the Lucan text with Matt 4:4, the best mss. of which read, "but on every word coming from the mouth of God," as in Deut 8:3 (LXX). The addition in some Lucan mss. has been made less anthropomorphic. But the longer quotation is undoubtedly not original to "Q"; it has been added because of a Wisdom motif prominent in the Matthean Gospel, in which Jesus is more clearly portrayed as the wise teacher in Israel who feeds his disciples with his wisdom (see Prov 9:1-5; Sir 24:19-27; Wisd 16:26).

5. *Then he took Jesus up.* Save in a few mss. of Luke (⊕, the Koine text-tradition, where harmonization with Matthew is at work), the term of this transfer is left unspecified. Cf. Matt 4:8: "on a very high mountain." Luke's phrase is cryptic and seems to suggest that he omitted the term from the original version in "Q," rather than that Matthew would have inserted it (for the sake of the New-Moses motif mentioned in the COMMENT). How explain the Lucan omission? For Plummer (*Commentary*, 111) the devil transferred Jesus "in thought to a mountain-top." For Conzelmann (*Theology*, 29) Luke has omitted the mention of the mountain because such a locality in his Gospel means a place of prayer and of heavenly communication or revelation; neither temptation nor public preaching would take place on it. For Dupont (*Les tentations*, 55) Luke prefers to use a temporal designation: Jesus was shown all the kingdoms of the world in an instant, since Luke—in the interest of plausibility—knows that there is no mountain from the top of which one can

see the whole earth. Similarly, H. Schürmann, *Lukasevangelium*, 210; J. M. Creed, *The Gospel*, 63. This last view is the most likely.

in an instant. Lit. "in a point of time" (*en stigmē chronou*). The Lucan addition tends to convey a visionary character of the experience.

all the kingdoms of the world. Luke replaces *kosmos* (Matt 4:8) with *oikoumenē*, "inhabited world," the place of settled and civilized occupation. This is a favorite Lucanism (see 2:1; 21:26; Acts 11:28; 17:6,31; 19:27; 24:5). Possibly there is an allusion to the Roman empire, but it is not clear.

6. *To you.* The pron. *soi* is placed emphatically at the head of the sentence, as is *emoi*, "to me," in v. 6b. Contrast is intended.

authority over all this, and the glory that goes with it. Lit. "all this authority, and the glory of them." This phrase is not well turned, for the pron. (*autôn*), modifying "glory," has no immediate antecedent. It has to be understood as referring to the "kingdoms." The awkwardness is the result of a minor Lucan transposition: he has moved the last phrase from the sentence that precedes (see Matt 4:8). The reason for the transposition is seen in the addition of "authority" (*exousia*), a word used by Luke in a political sense (see 12:11; 20:20; 23:7). Contrast Matt 4:9, "These I shall give all to you." Luke has here expanded the "Q" source, *pace* Schürmann, *Lukasevangelium*, 211.

it has been made over to me. Luke does not say by whom. Perhaps a notion like that in Job 1:2, where the Lord says to Satan about Job, "all that he has is in your power," is thought to be operative here too. The verb would then be another instance of the theological passive, i.e. with God as the implied agent (see ZBG § 236).

to anyone I please I can give it. An old legal formula expressing complete dominion is added; it is found in Aramaic legal documents (e.g. *BMAP* 3:12,14-16).

7. *if you bow down before me.* The devil poses as the "prince" or "god" of this world (see John 12:31; 2 Cor 4:4), claiming authority over it and seeking worship because of it. He challenges the Son to accept worldwide dominion from himself and to switch allegiance from the Father to himself, an underling. He seeks to have the Father's Son bow down before him. The prep. *enōpion* is a Lucan favorite (see p. 110 above).

8. *You shall worship the Lord your God and him only shall you adore.* Deut 6:13 is quoted in a form resembling ms. A of the LXX; ms. B reads, "you shall fear," which is closer to the MT. The adj. *monō* is added in both Matthew and Luke; it is also found in some mss. of the LXX of Deut 6:13 (in dependence on these NT passages?). Cf. Deut 32:43 (LXX).

9. *to Jerusalem.* The climax of the temptations in the Lucan Gospel is reached in the city of destiny itself for Jesus (see p. 165 above). Matt 4:5 has "to the holy city," without naming it. Luke has changed the original form of "Q."

the pinnacle of the Temple. The Greek word *pterygion* means "winglet," and was used as a figure for the extremity or tip of something. As a name for an architectural feature of the Jerusalem Temple, it occurs only here (and in Matt 4:6); Eusebius (*Historia Ecclesiastica* 2.23,11) has probably derived it from these Gospel passages. It designates some visibly prominent part of the Temple, but it cannot be more specifically defined, since *to hieron* is used to denote the Jerusalem Temple with its precincts, porticos, courts, and buildings. Josephus (*Ant.* 15.11,5 § 412) speaks of the dizzying height of the Royal Portico over the ravine (probably the Kidron Valley) below. A tradition from Byzantine times, possibly dependent on Josephus' description, has identified the SE corner of the Temple area, when viewed from the Kidron Valley below it, as the "pinnacle of the Temple" (see D. Baldi, *ELS,* 228-237; B. Mazar, *The Mountain of the Lord* [Garden City, NY: Doubleday, 1975] 149). We really do not know what part of the Temple is meant; see M.-J. Lagrange, *RB* 39 (1930) 190; J. Jeremias, *ZDPV* 59 (1936) 195-208; G. Schrenk, *TDNT* 3 (1965) 236.

throw yourself down from here. The devil's second challenge to Jesus' sonship is a temptation to use his power to manifest himself with éclat before his contemporaries and to conform to their ideas about God's emissaries. If the rabbinical saying preserved in *Pesiqta rabbati* § 36 could be shown to be a belief current among first-century Palestinian Jews, then possibly a messianic overtone would be found in the devil's challenge. The saying reads: "Our teachers have taught, 'When the King, the Messiah, reveals himself, he will come and stand on the roof of the Temple.' "

10. *for it is written in Scripture.* See NOTE on 4:4.

He shall give his angels orders about you. The devil is made here to quote Ps 91:11 according to the LXX, but with the omission of the last phrase of it, "on all your paths." In v. 11 he continues with v. 12 of the same psalm, again according to the LXX. The two verses are separated by *kai hoti,* "and that" (the *hoti* is recitative and can be omitted in the translation of the direct quotation). Psalm 91 is often regarded as a Wisdom psalm, incorporating a reflection on Yahweh as the protector of those faithful to him; they are spared peril because he has provided angelic protection of them. Vanquished by Scripture or the Word of God in the first two temptations, the devil now quotes it to his own purpose: Surely, if Jesus is God's Son, then he stands under his benign protection.

12. *In Scripture it is said.* The introductory formula is *eiretai,* "it has been said," a form not found elsewhere in the NT. It can, however, be compared with the participial or periphrastic form used in Luke 2:24; Acts 2:16; 13:40 (cf. Rom 4:18). This formula has no counterpart in the Qumran introductory formulae.

You shall not put the Lord your God to the test. This time the devil is rebuffed by the quotation of Deut 6:16, cited according to the LXX (=MT). Jesus refuses to exploit his power as Son in the interest of a foolish challenge to his personal safety; tempted by the devil, Jesus warns against tempting God. It is an implied rebuke, that the devil should not have tempted Jesus to begin with, for in effect he was trying to put God to the test.

13. *having exhausted every sort of temptation.* Lit. "having finished every temptation." Thus Luke sums up the three scenes; the threesome represents all the temptations that confronted Jesus. The summary is significant because the threesome symbolizes the seduction of the diabolic opposition to Jesus' career

and mission. They set the tone for what is to come. S. Brown (*Apostasy and Perseverance*, 6-19) rightly insists on the exclusive meaning of *peirasmos*, "temptation," used here (and in the episode in general): "Jesus' *peirasmos* is not the typical temptation of the pious faithful but the unique experience of the son of God (Lk 4,3)" (p. 17). This is the only place in the Lucan writings where the word describes an experience with a good outcome. When Luke uses the noun elsewhere of Christians, the outcome is always negative and connotes apostasy (8:13; 11:4; 22:28,40,46).

The adj. *pas* here has the meaning of "every kind of," as often in the NT (see BAG, 636b).

departed from him for a while. Lit. "distanced himself from him until (another) time." The temporal phrase (*achri kairou*) is used again in Acts 13:11, thus marking the Lucan character of this verse. The noun *kairos* has in the NT both the generic meaning of "point of time" or "period of time" and the specific meaning of "fixed time," even "critical time" (e.g. of the eschaton). Some commentators have sought to understand the word in the Lucan phrase here in the last sense. But this abuses the normal sense of the anarthrous phrase (see BDF § 255,3) and reads more into the text than it can bear. Cf. 8:13 below (*pros kairon*).

In any case, the phrase is an instance of Lucan foreshadowing (cp. 9:9b). It clearly refers to the second diabolic onslaught to be made against the Father's plan of salvation-history in the passion and death of Jesus. The devil departs from Jesus "for a while," to return in 23:3 and 53 in the new attack. This does not mean, however, that the Period of Jesus now beginning is "free from Satan" (Conzelmann, *Theology*, 28), for the opposition that the temptations symbolize will continue all through the ministry. Nor is the passion of Jesus to be regarded as a new form of temptation (see S. Brown, *Apostasy and Perseverance*, 9-10).

BIBLIOGRAPHY (4:1-13)

Doble, P. "The Temptations," *ExpTim* 72 (1960-1961) 91-93.

Dupont, J. *Les tentations de Jésus au désert* (StudNeot 4; Bruges: Desclée de Brouwer, 1968).

Duquoc, C. "La tentation de Christ," *LumVie* 53 (1961) 21-41.

Edgar, S. L. "Respect for Context in Quotations from the Old Testament," *NTS* 9 (1962-1963) 55-62, esp. pp. 59-60.

Feuillet, A. "Le récit lucanien de la tentation (Lc 4,1-13)," *Bib* 40 (1959) 613-631.

Fridrichsen, A. *The Problem of Miracle in Primitive Christianity* (Minneapolis: Augsburg, 1972) 121-128.

Gerhardsson, B. *The Testing of God's Son* (*Matt 4:1-11 & Par.*): *Chapters 1-4* (Coniectanea biblica, NT 2/1; Lund: Gleerup, 1966).

Graham, E. "The Temptation in the Wilderness," *CQR* 162 (1961) 17-32.

Hoffmann, P. "Die Versuchungsgeschichte in der Logienquelle: Zur Auseinandersetzung der Judenchristen mit dem politischen Messianismus," *BZ* 13 (1969) 207-223.

Hyldahl, N. "Die Versuchung auf der Zinne des Tempels (Matth 4,5-7≠Luk 4,9-12), *ST* 15 (1961) 113-127.

Iersel, B. M. F. van. *"Der Sohn" in den synoptischen Jesusworten: Christusbezeichnung der Gemeinde oder Selbstbezeichnung Jesu?* (NovTSup 3; 2d ed.; Leiden: Brill, 1964) 165-171.

Ketter, P. *Die Versuchung Jesu nach dem Berichte der Synoptiker* (NTAbh 6/3; Münster: Aschendorff, 1918).

Kirk, J. A. "The Messianic Role of Jesus and the Temptation Narrative: A Contemporary Perspective," *EvQ* 44 (1972) 11-29, 91-102.

Kruse, H. "Das Reich Satans," *Bib* 58 (1977) 29-61, esp. pp. 44-50.

Lohmeyer, E. "Die Versuchung Jesu," *ZST* 14 (1937) 619-650.

Pokorný, P. "The Temptation Stories and Their Intention," *NTS* 20 (1973-1974) 115-127.

Riesenfeld, H. "Le caractère messianique de la tentation au désert," *La venue du Messie* (RechBib 6; Bruges: Desclée de Brouwer, 1962) 51-63.

Sabbe, M. "De tentatione Jesu in deserto," *Collationes brugenses* 50 (1954) 459-466.

Schnackenburg, R. "Der Sinn der Versuchung Jesu bei den Synoptikern," *TQ* 132 (1952) 297-326.

Smyth-Florentin, F. "Jésus, le Fils du Père, vainqueur de Satan: Mt 4,1-11; Mc 1,12-15; Lc 4,1-13," *AsSeign* 14 (1973) 56-75.

Swanston, H. "The Lukan Temptation Narrative," *JTS* 17 (1966) 71.

Taylor, A. B. "Decision in the Desert: The Temptation of Jesus in the Light of Deuteronomy," *Int* 14 (1960) 300-309.

Thompson, G. H. P. "Called—Proved—Obedient: A Study in the Baptism and Temptation Narratives of Matthew and Luke," *JTS* 11 (1960) 1-12.

Wilkens, W. "Die Versuchungsgeschichte Luk. 4,1-13 und die Komposition des Evangeliums," *TZ* 30 (1974) 262-272.

III. THE GALILEAN MINISTRY OF JESUS

Armed with the Power of the Spirit, Jesus Taught in their Synagogues and Released Human Beings from Evil

A. The Beginning of the Ministry in Nazareth and Capernaum; the Role of Simon the Fisherman; the Cleansing of a Leper

16. SUMMARY: BEGINNING OF THE MINISTRY (4:14-15)

4 ¹⁴ Then Jesus withdrew to Galilee, armed with the power of the Spirit; and reports of him circulated throughout the neighboring countryside. ¹⁵ He taught in their synagogues and was praised by all the people.

COMMENT

Whereas the other two Synoptic evangelists associate the beginning of Jesus' public ministry with the imprisonment of John the Baptist (Mark 1:14; Matt 4:12), Luke begins his account of it with a summary statement (4:14-15). Luke's omission of the mention of John's imprisonment is occasioned by his own transposition of it to 3:19-20. Summary statements often indicate structural divisions.

This summary statement is most likely inspired by Mark 1:14-15. H. Schürmann ("Der 'Bericht vom Anfang'") has tried to argue that Luke is here dependent on a variant non-Marcan source. Similarly, B. H. Streeter (*The Four Gospels*, 206-207): "from Q, not Mark." But this is highly questionable and has been examined at length by J. Delobel ("La rédaction"), who rightly argues rather for Lucan redaction.

These verses are to be regarded as an editorial statement, composed by

Luke, who differs with his Marcan source, by which he is otherwise inspired. From the form-critical point of view, they are a "summary" of the sort that Luke uses in Acts (see *JBC,* art. 45, § 4). Whereas the summaries in Acts describe (idyllically) the life of early Christians or the growth of the church in its springtime, this one gives an overview of the Galilean ministry of Jesus. Cf. 4:31-32,40-41; 6:17-19; 8:1-3; 19:47-48; 21:37-38.

In contrast to Mark 1:14-15, these verses omit a significant element. There is no mention at the outset of Jesus' kerygmatic proclamation of the kingdom and the gospel or of his call for repentance. H. Conzelmann (*Theology,* 114) has rightly called attention to this "shift in emphasis." A bland summary statement has replaced the proclamation (see p. 149 above). It serves as a heading for the episodes in part III of this Gospel.

Three distinctive Lucan features mark the summary: (a) A leitmotiv is sounded in the phrase "armed with the power of the Spirit." The Period of Jesus is thus inaugurated. Because the Spirit will later be depicted as a formative factor in the early community, Luke is now at pains to present Jesus' ministry as guided by the same Spirit's "power." There is continuity between the Period of Jesus and the Period of the Church. (b) Though v. 15 does not read like a logical sequel to v. 14, Jesus' activity is first of all described as "teaching." The implication is that this too is being done under the power of the Spirit. This is important for the entire purpose of Luke-Acts: Jesus must be seen "teaching" those things about which Theophilus is being given assurance. (c) The note of Lucan universality appears in the summary in that Jesus is a revered teacher, "praised by *all* the people."

NOTES

4   14. *withdrew.* See NOTE on *hypestrepsen* in 4:1.

to Galilee. The phrase *eis tēn Galilaian* depends on Mark 1:14a, whence Matt 4:12 has also derived it.

The limits of Upper and Lower Galilee are described at length by Josephus *J.W.* 3.3,1-2 §§ 35-43. He notes its fertility, its thickly crowded distribution of towns and villages, and claims that the smallest of them contains "above fifteen thousand inhabitants." He numbered them as "204 cities and villages in Galilee" (*Life* 45 § 235). See further NOTE on 17:11.

Luke shares with the other Synoptic evangelists the notice of Jesus' ministry beginning in Galilee. It has already been mentioned in the infancy narrative (1:26; 2:4,39) and as the territory of Herod Antipas at the beginning of the Gospel proper (3:1). It is only now that the area takes on an important significance in the Lucan Gospel. Though Luke shares with Mark and Matthew the story of a single journey of Jesus to Jerusalem, he alone makes it an important literary feature in his travel account (9:51). Though Luke does depict

Jesus teaching elsewhere, for instance, in "Judea" (=the land of the Jews, Luke 4:44; Acts 10:37,39) and in "Jerusalem" (Luke 23:5; Acts 13:31), the locale par excellence for his activity prior to the beginning of the travel account is Galilee. He notes explicitly that Jesus' ministry began there (23:5; Acts 10:37; 13:31). It is the area from which he derives his disciples and followers (Acts 13:31; Luke 8:1-3; 23:49,55), and where he begins to prepare those who are to be witnesses to him later. When he goes to the "region of the Gerasenes" (8:26), Luke will take pains to note that it is "opposite Galilee," lest the reader's attention be distracted from any non-Jewish territory. His reputation spreads beyond Galilee, and people flock to him from it and other areas (5:17). But from Galilee he ultimately makes his way to the city of destiny.

armed with the power of the Spirit. Lit. "in the power of the Spirit," i.e. which descended on him at the baptism (3:22) and with which he has been filled (4:1). It now leads him to his "own country." See NOTE on 4:1, *en tō pneumati;* here a similar use of the prep. *en* occurs with an intransitive verb.

As in 4:1, a change of locale is effected under the guiding influence of the Spirit. In Lucan theology the *dynamis* that Jesus possesses is not limited to a miraculous power (for healing or exorcising, as chiefly in Mark); it is closely associated with the Spirit under whose guidance he teaches and interprets Scripture (see W. Grundmann, *Evangelium nach Lukas,* 118).

reports of him circulated throughout the neighboring countryside. Lit. "a report about him went forth through the entire neighborhood." This summary explains how the person about whom Luke writes is so widely known, when so far in the story Jesus has been seen as only one of a crowd (at his baptism), identified by a learned genealogical list, and confronted by the devil alone. This impressive person must be announced; Luke's way of doing it prepares for 4:23; cf. 4:37. This verse seems to have a parallel in Matt 9:26; but that is coincidental, being clearly of Matthean redaction at that point.

15. *He taught.* Luke uses the verb *didaskein* absolutely (i.e. with no object) and does not specify what Jesus taught. This is in marked contrast to the Matthean and Marcan parallels. It may be derived from the Marcan parallel (6:2) to the following episode, which it is obviously foreshadowing. But it also introduces a Lucan motif, of Jesus as teacher (see 4:31; 5:3,17; 6:6; 11:1; 13:10,22,26; 19:47; 20:1,21; 21:37; 23:5; cf. p. 218 above). Luke 23:5 sees the beginning of it precisely here in Galilee.

in their synagogues. The Greek word *synagōgē* can denote either a "meeting, gathering" (e.g. LXX Num 16:3; 20:4; 27:17; Acts 13:43; Jas 2:2) or a "place of meeting, a gathering place" (LXX Gen 1:9; Josephus *Ant.* 15.10,1 § 346).

The origin of the Jewish synagogue is usually traced to the Babylonian Captivity, when Jews separated from their homeland and the Temple and, anxious to preserve their religious traditions, congregated on the Sabbath for prayer, reading of the Torah, and instruction. On their return to Palestine, and even after the rebuilding of the Temple, the custom of meetings continued in local communities and even in Jerusalem itself. "Synagogue" came to denote not only the congregation, but even the place of Jewish religious assembly (see

Philo *Quod omnis probus liber sit* 12 § 81; Josephus *J.W.* 2.14,3 § 285). The Theodotus inscription from Jerusalem expresses the purpose of the synagogue: "for the reading of the Law and the teaching of the commandments" (C. K. Barrett, *NTB*, § 50). Luke himself records: "For generations Moses has been preached in every town and has been read aloud on every Sabbath" (Acts 15:21), referring to synagogue services. Possibly ordinary houses were used for such assemblies at first, for though they are mentioned as early as the second century B.C. in Palestinian inscriptions, archeological remains of them all date from later, Christian times (see E. L. Sukenik, *Ancient Synagogues in Palestine and Greece* [Schweich Lectures, 1930; London: British Academy, 1934]; B. Lifshitz, *Donateurs et fondateurs dans les synagogues juives* [Cahiers de la RB 7; Paris: Gabalda, 1967]; S. J. Saller, *A Revised Catalogue of the Ancient Synagogues of the Holy Land* [Publications of the Studium biblicum franciscanum, coll. min. 6; Jerusalem: Franciscan Press, 1969]; F. Hüttenmeister and G. Reeg, *Die antiken Synagogen in Israel* [2 vols.; Beihefte zum Tübinger Atlas des vorderen Orients, B12/1; Wiesbaden: L. Reichert, 1977]).

The detail of Jesus' teaching in the synagogues is added by Luke because this will become the place par excellence in his story where Israel will hear the news about the new phase of salvation-history. The word of God had to spread first to the Jews, then to the Gentiles (cf. Acts 13:46, Paul's words spoken in the synagogue of Antioch in Pisidia, 13:15). This priority is why Jesus is so depicted here, preaching in a synagogue in his hometown, and elsewhere (4:16,44; 6:6; 13:10).

by all the people. Lit. "by all." In the context this should mean by all who heard his teaching; but Luke often emphasizes the universal reaction of people to Jesus' activity (5:26; 7:16; 9:43; 18:43; 19:37). But it also reflects Luke's generic predilection for the adj. *pas, hapas,* "all."

BIBLIOGRAPHY (4:14-15)

Delobel, J. "La rédaction de Lc. IV, 14-16a et le 'Bericht vom Anfang,'" in *L'Evangile de Luc* (BETL 32; ed. F. Neirynck; Gembloux: Duculot, 1973) 203-223.

Escudero Freire, C. "Jésus profeta, libertador del hombre: Visión lucana de su ministerio terrestre," *EstEcl* 51 (1976) 463-495.

Samain, E. "L'Evangile de Luc: Un témoignage ecclésial et missionaire: Lc 1,1-4; 4,14-15," *AsSeign* 34 (1973) 60-73.

Schürmann, H. "Der 'Bericht vom Anfang': Ein Rekonstruktionsversuch auf Grund von Lk 4,14-16," *SE II/1* (TU 87; 1964) 242-258; reprinted in his *Traditionsgeschichtliche Untersuchungen zu den synoptischen Evangelien* (Düsseldorf: Patmos, 1968) 67-80.

Völkel, M. "Der Anfang Jesu in Galiläa: Bemerkungen zum Gebrauch und zur Funktion Galiläas in den lukanischen Schriften," *ZNW* 64 (1973) 222-232.

17. JESUS' VISIT TO NAZARETH
(4:16-30)

4 ¹⁶ When he came to Nazareth, where he had been brought up, he went into the synagogue on the Sabbath, as was his custom. He stood up to read the Scripture ¹⁷ and was handed a scroll of the prophet Isaiah. Unrolling the scroll, he found the passage where it was written,

> ¹⁸ *The Spirit of the Lord is upon me, for he has*   Isa 61:1-2
> *anointed me; he has sent me to preach good news*
> *to the poor, to proclaim release for prisoners and*
> *sight for the blind, to send the downtrodden away*   Isa 58:6
> *relieved,*
> ¹⁹ *and to proclaim the Lord's year of favor.*

²⁰ Jesus rolled up the scroll, returned it to the attendant, and sat down. The eyes of all in the synagogue were fixed intently on him, ²¹ as he began to speak to them: "Today this passage of Scripture sees its fulfillment, as you sit listening." ²² And they all acknowledged it, but were surprised that such gracious words came from his lips. "Is not this Joseph's son?" they asked. ²³ And he said to them, "You will probably quote me the proverb, 'Physician, heal yourself! Do here in your own country what we have heard you have been doing in Capernaum.'" ²⁴ But he said, "Believe me, no prophet is accepted in his own country. ²⁵ I can assure you, there were many widows in Israel in the time of Elijah, when the heavens were stopped up for three and a half years and a great famine befell all the land; ²⁶ yet Elijah was not sent to any of them, but rather *to a widow in Zarephath near Sidon.*ª ²⁷ Again, there were many lepers in Israel, when Elisha was the prophet; yet none of them was cured, but only Naaman of Syria." ²⁸ When the people in the synagogue heard this, they all became furious, ²⁹ got up, and cast him out of the town. They took him to the edge of the cliff on which the town was built, to throw him over it. ³⁰ But he slipped through the crowd and went on his way.

ª 1 Kgs 17:9

COMMENT

The first concrete instance of Jesus' Galilean teaching is presented by Luke in an account of his visit to Nazareth. After the generic summary of the public ministry (4:14-15), it records an incident in the town, "where he had been brought up" (vv. 16-30). It is an important episode in the Lucan Gospel, foreshadowed in a sense in Simeon's oracle in the infancy narrative (2:34) and foreshadowing in a way the account of the entire ministry that is to follow.

From v. 23 it is clear that Luke was aware of a period of Jesus' ministry in Capernaum prior to this visit to Nazareth. He is, then, consciously making this episode the first of the ministry, knowing that it was not really such. At this point in the Marcan Gospel the story is rather told of the call of the disciples (1:16-20); that will find its Lucan counterpart in 5:1-11. Here Luke has transposed the account of Jesus' visit to his home-town from later on in the gospel tradition (see Mark 6:1-6a; Matt 13:53-58), where it is recounted shortly before the end of the Galilean ministry. Luke has no parallel for it at that point, regarding this one as its equivalent. On Lucan transpositions, see p. 71 above.

Though there is little similarity in the details or in the wording of the Lucan and Marcan form of the account of this visit, the substance of the two stories is the same: a visit to a synagogue in Jesus' hometown; a popular reaction to his teaching (positive, and then negative); the recognition of his parentage; the proverb about a prophet without honor or welcome in his own town; and the absence of any "sign" given in Nazareth. However, the Lucan form of the story is over twice as long as that of Mark, and this raises several questions about the source and function of the former. Efforts in the past to save the historicity of the two accounts often postulated two visits of Jesus to Nazareth; but this sort of interpretation fails to cope with the substantial similarity of the two existing accounts of the same incident.

The Lucan form of the story of the Nazareth visit owes its inspiration to Mark 6:1-6a; in vv. 16,22,24 the wording probably comes from "Mk." As for the rest, vv. 17-21,23,25-30, one may debate whether they are derived from Luke's private source ("L") or are to be ascribed to Lucan composition. R. Bultmann (HST, 32) has plausibly maintained that vv. 25-27 have come to Luke from a tradition, probably Aramaic; to make use of it, he thinks that Luke constructed the scene based on Mark 6:1-6a and also incorporated v. 23 (with its mention of Capernaum and the proverb) from another source. The other long passage, vv. 17-21, suits a distinctive

Lucan concern, and it is probably better ascribed to Luke's own pen. Similarly, for vv. 28-30.

However, a number of commentators think that the entire Lucan epi- sode has come to the evangelist from a non-Marcan source and that it simply has coincidental parallels with Mark 6:1-6a (see, e.g. J. Schmid, *Evangelium nach Lukas*, 110). H. Schürmann ("Zur Traditions- geschichte," 191-205) argues for a thesis held at times by others (e.g. B. H. Streeter, A. H. M'Neile, J. V. Bartlet, B. Violet—with varying nuances) that in vv. 16-30 Luke has made use of a Sayings-source vari- ant. The primitive form of the story would have contained the matter now in vv. 16,22,23b,24,28-30, but it was not Luke who first intro- duced vv. 17-21 and 25-27. This suggestion is intriguing; but many of the arguments put forth in support of it are so tenuous that it is impossible to go along with it. It is better to regard the Lucan story as a reworking of the Marcan source (so J. M. Creed, *The Gospel*, 65; E. Klostermann, *Lukasevangelium*, 62; R. C. Tannehill, "The Mission," 52; G. Schneider, *Evangelium nach Lukas*, 106-107)—a reworking with the sources suggested above by Bultmann.

These various suggestions have been made because the story in its pres- ent form is obviously conflated. The sequence of sentences is not smooth. The Marcan form of the story was classified form-critically by Bultmann as a biographical apophthegm (*HST*, 31), with the proverb in 6:4 serving as the pronouncement. In the expanded Lucan form, the episode might still seem to belong to that category, having, however, multiple pro- nouncements (vv. 23 and 25-27, in addition to the proverb in v. 24). Actually, Bultmann considers the pronouncement in vv. 25-27 as a minatory saying (*HST*, 116). However, V. Taylor (*FGT*, 153) considers the expanded Lucan episode to be rather a Story about Jesus, part of the narrative gospel tradition. The difficulty here is that the narrative has been expanded as well as the pronouncement.

The proverb in v. 24, "No prophet is accepted in his own country," has as its Marcan parallel, "No prophet is without honor except in his own country, among his own relatives, and in his own house" (6:4). This say- ing of Jesus is also attested extra-canonically, being found in a variant form in OxyP1: "Jesus says, 'A prophet is not acceptable in his own homeland; and a physician does not work cures on those who know him'" (1:29-35). The Coptic form of it is found in *Gos. Thom.* § 31: "Jesus said, 'No prophet (*prophētēs*) is accepted in his own town; a phy- sician does not heal (*therapeue*) those who know him" (87:5-7). See *ESBNT*, 401-402. Bultmann (*HST*, 31) once thought that the Marcan story was "a typical example of how an imaginary situation is built up out of an independent saying," which he identified with the Greek Oxyrhynchus form of the saying. But the Oxyrhynchus saying is scarcely the more primitive form of the saying (see H. Anderson, *Int* 18 [1964] 264-265). Bultmann has not explained how the double form of the proverb (about a prophet and a physician) would have resulted in a rejection story in Mark that involves only the prophet. Moreover, the Marcan form uses *atimos,* "without honor" (6:4), and is followed by Matt 13:57, whereas Luke has *dektos,* "accepted" (v. 24). Luke has almost certainly changed *atimos* to *dektos* in view of the Isaian quotation in v. 19. Since the Oxyrhynchus saying uses *dektos* and contains the double proverb, which is found in the canonical tradition only in Luke, it is certain that the Oxyrhynchus form of the saying is dependent on Luke. Moreover, the Oxyrhynchus saying has none of the negative saying about the prophet's relatives or household, again revealing its dependence on Luke, who has laundered the Marcan form of the saying, because he depicts Jesus' mother and relatives among the believers (see 1:45; 8:21; Acts 1:14). See further W. Schrage, *Das Verhältnis,* 75-77.

Because Luke's narrative is a conflation, there is, on the one hand, the fulfillment-story ending on the note of Jesus' success; on the other, there is the rejection-story. As the episode now stands, there is a climactic buildup of popular reaction, but it takes place with conflicting reactions. Verses 20-22 record the first reaction, one of pleasant surprise at Jesus' gracious and learned words; it notes the success of a hometown boy. But immediately thereafter v. 23 puts on Jesus' lips the first proverb and his comment about the people's expectation, which together imply their cynicism. The proverb and comment are introduced without apparent motivation and undoubtedly stem from an independent context or source. They seem to reflect a context of sign-seeking that is really foreign to the foregoing verses. Verse 24 contains the second proverb, corresponding to Mark 6:4a, and formulates a still more hostile reaction of non-acceptance or incredulity. This is the non-acceptance of the *patris,* here understood as the "hometown." But vv. 25-27 move the story into a still further dimension; they are derived from a different tradition and lack a strong connection with vv. 23-24. But a connection does exist. Though the word *patris* is not used in these verses, the idea is present—at least in a broad sense. In v. 24 it meant "hometown," in the contrast between Nazareth and Capernaum. But now there is a contrast between Jesus' "homeland" and Syria or Phoenicia, examples of non-Israelite territory. And the ultimate reaction to him takes the form of hostile, even diabolic, rejection, as he is led out of the town.

The climactic buildup of reactions to Jesus reveals a certain artistry in the Lucan story. But the differing reactions and the lack of smooth sutures between different parts of the story are noteworthy. They reveal the conflation that has gone on. In this regard one should note the double introductory asseverative phrases in vv. 24-25, "Believe me," and "I can assure you." They also point to the joining of two traditions.

The Lucan story, transposed to this point in the Gospel, has a definite programmatic character. Jesus' teaching is a fulfillment of OT Scripture—this is his kerygmatic announcement (the Lucan substitute for the omitted proclamation of Mark 1:14b-15). But that same teaching will meet with success and—even more so—with rejection. Luke has deliberately put this story at the beginning of the public ministry to encapsulate the entire ministry of Jesus and the reaction to it. The fulfillment-story stresses the success of his teaching under the guidance of the Spirit, but the rejection story symbolizes the opposition that his ministry will evoke among his own. The rejection of him by the people of his hometown is a miniature of the rejection of him by the people of his own *patris* in the larger sense.

In quoting Second Isaiah, Jesus is presented as consciously aware of the influence of the Spirit on him. What this Isaiah announced to the people of his day is now being announced to the poor, the prisoners, the blind, and the downtrodden of Jesus' day. What was announced in a prophetic way to the exiles returning to Jerusalem by the prophet of old has now been turned by Luke into a prediction, the fulfillment of which is found in the person, words, and deeds of Jesus of Nazareth. But his own people fail to realize it and reject him. When he finally slips away, it is not accomplished by the "power" of the Spirit or any miracle—and he does not go "to the diaspora of the Greeks" (John 7:35)—rather he turns from his townspeople (relatives and friends) to go to strangers, strangers among the Jews of Galilee. This is the first step in the Lucan motif of "to the Jews first," which reaches a climax in Acts 13:46 (cf. Acts 18:6; 26:20; 28:28).

Because of the Deutero-Isaian quotation used in this episode some commentators (e.g. E. E. Ellis, *The Gospel*, 98; Schmid, *Evangelium nach Lukas*, 112) think that Luke is presenting Jesus here as the Servant of Yahweh. But the Isaian passage quoted (61:1-2; 58:6) is not part of a Servant Song. This nuance should not be read into this passage. — based on a servant song —

Similarly, because of the "anointing" (Isa 61:1) Jesus is sometimes thought to be presented here as Messiah (so A. R. C. Leaney, *A Commentary*, 118). We have already noted the interpretation of Jesus' baptism as an "anointing" (Acts 10:38), and it is likely that the use of Isa 61:1 alludes to Jesus' baptism and the descent of the Spirit upon him at that time. But in what sense is the anointing to be understood? This passage certainly contains no reference to a Davidic dynasty or a royal function of Jesus. In the OT *māšîaḥ*, "anointed one," is perhaps used of prophets in Ps 105:15 and 1 Chr 16:22—but see the commentators on these passages. However, the idea of prophets as anointed servants of Yahweh does emerge in later pre-Christian Palestinian Judaism, e.g. in Qumran literature (see CD 2:12; 6:1; 6QD 3:4). Moreover, the "herald" (*měbaśśēr*) of good news in Isa 52:7 appears in 11QMelch 18 precisely as one "anointed with the Spirit" (*mšwḥ hrwḥ*). See further Y. Yadin, *IEJ* 15 (1965) 152-154; M. de Jonge and A. S. van der Woude, *NTS* 12 (1965-66) 301-302; *ESBNT,* 250, 265-266. Unfortunately, the Melchizedek text from Qumran Cave 11 is fragmentary; but its use of Isa 61:1; 52:7 and Lev 25:9-13 provides an interesting Palestinian background to this distinctively Lucan story. Whether the "anointing" of Jesus is to be understood of the "prophetic" sort or the "heraldic" sort, it gives a nuance to his anointing which is not that of the political, kingly sort. This, too, makes it intelligible why Jesus is compared to Elijah and Elisha in the verses toward the end of the episode. Elisha in particular is introduced as "the prophet"; implicitly, Jesus is suggested to be such, too.

Lastly, an effect achieved by the Lucan transposition of this scene is the postponement of the call of the disciples. That episode is found in Mark 1:16-20, following on the heels of Jesus' proclamation of the gospel and the kingdom (1:14-15). Luke will make something other out of it in due time (5:1-11).

NOTES

4 16. *he came to Nazareth.* See NOTE on 1:26. The best Greek mss. read *Nazareth* in the infancy narrative (1:26; 2:4,39,51); but here the preferred reading is *Nazara,* a form also found in Matt 4:13. This may reflect a more ancient Semitic form of the name (see J. K. Zenner, *ZKT* 18 [1894] 744-747). But in the Marcan and Matthean parallels to this verse the name of the village is not given; Mark 6:1 has simply "to his own country," as does Matt 13:54. Schürmann ("Zur Traditionsgeschichte," 196, 201-202) has tried to argue that the form *Nazara* points to a source distinct from Mark (most likely "Q"), but he then has to include the preceding Matthean episode (at least what = Luke 4:13-15,17)—which is highly unlikely.

where he had been brought up. This is now an allusion to 2:51-52 and a foreshadowing of 4:24. The Greek mss. vary between *tethrammenos* (Hesychian text-tradition, ⊛) and *anatethrammenos* (B, Koine text-tradition), but both have the same meaning.

as was his custom. Luke alone among the Synoptic evangelists stresses Jesus' habitual frequenting of the synagogue; he thus presents him conforming to the general Jewish custom described by Josephus (*Ant.* 16.2,4 § 43) of giving "every seventh day over to the study of our customs and law." See 4:15. In Acts Luke will depict the apostles and early Jerusalem Christians as habitually frequenting the Temple (2:46; 3:1; 4:1; 5:12,42; 21:26). This brings out for Luke the initial relation of Jesus and the nascent church to Israel; indeed, the relation of the church to Israel is depicted as based on the practice of Jesus himself (see H. Conzelmann, *Theology,* 190).

He stood up to read. Instead of the Marcan phrase, "he began to teach in the synagogue" (6:2), which resembles Luke 4:15, the evangelist presents a concrete instance of Jesus' teaching based on Scripture.

Luke may be implying that Jesus was invited by the president of the synagogue assembly (*archisynagōgos*) to read and expound a Scripture text, as happened to Paul and Barnabas at Antioch in Pisidia (Acts 13:15). In first-century Palestine the Sabbath synagogue service apparently consisted of the singing of a psalm, the recitation of the *Šĕma'* (Deut 6:4-9; 11:13-21; Num 15:37-41) and the *Tĕpillāh* (or *Šĕmōnê 'Eśrēh*, the "Eighteen [Blessings]"— for its text, see W. Förster, *Palestinian Judaism in New Testament Times* [Edinburgh: Oliver & Boyd, 1964] 228-229)—and the reading of a *sēder* or *pārāšāh* from the Torah (Law) and a section from the Prophets (*haptārāh*— see Acts 13:15). This was followed by a sermon expounding the Scriptures read, and the service was concluded by a blessing uttered by the president and the priestly blessing of Num 6:24-26. See Str-B, 4. 153-276; P. Billerbeck, *ZNW* 55 (1964) 143-161.

Luke's account here makes no mention of the reading from the Torah, but it must be presupposed. He is more interested in the fulfillment of Second Isaiah's prophetic words and a christological use of the OT. It is not unlikely that there was a fixed or assigned reading of the Pentateuch in the Palestinian synagogue services of this time—perhaps even a triennial cycle, which is certainly attested later. For the first century, some sources suggest a regular reading of the Torah on Sabbaths (see Philo *De somniis* 2.18 § 127; Josephus *Ag. Ap.* 2.17 § 175; Acts 13:14-15).

17. *was handed a scroll of the prophet Isaiah.* Jesus was asked to read a passage from the Hebrew text of "the Prophets." No mention is made here of a *targum,* "Aramaic translation," of such a passage. It is usually claimed that such translation would have been necessary in Palestine at this time, since, save for small pockets or areas where Hebrew was still cultivated, Palestinian Jews used Aramaic as the common Semitic language and did not readily comprehend Hebrew (see *WA*, 38-46). Fragmentary written copies of pre-Christian targums have been discovered in Qumran caves (4QtgJob, 4QtgLev, 11Q-tgJob), but so far none of Isaiah. However, the Isaiah Scroll A from Qumran Cave 1, which is complete and dated paleographically ca. 100 B.C., would be a good example of the sort of scroll that might have been used in a synagogue.

The fact that Jesus "was handed" the scroll of Isaiah has been taken to mean that a passage from Isaiah was assigned for reading, i.e. that there was a cycle of readings for the Prophets as well as for the Torah. But the evidence for a cycle of prophetic readings in first-century Palestine is debatable, despite the claims that have been made for it; see further A. Guilding, *The Fourth Gospel and Jewish Worship* (Oxford: Clarendon, 1960) 125-126, 230-231; C. H. Cave, *SE II/2* (TU 88, 1964) 231-235; L. C. Crockett, *JJS* 17 (1966) 13-46 (esp. p. 27); J. Heinemann, *JJS* 19 (1968) 41-48; C. Perrot, *RevScRel* 47 (1973) 324-340. Acts 13:27 points to no more than a custom of reading prophetic passages after the lessons from the Torah.

Unrolling. The ptc. *anoixas,* "having opened," is the reading preferred by

Nestle and Merk, but *anaptyxas,* "having unrolled," has the strong support of mss. ℵ, D, Θ, and the Koine text-tradition; it is preferred by K. Aland et al., *UBSGNT.* Though it is the more proper word, the sense is not really affected.

he found the passage where it was written. If there is no reason to think of an assigned passage of Second Isaiah (*pace* Ellis, *The Gospel of Luke,* 97), there is no reason either to take this phrase to mean a chance happening upon chap. 61. It sounds as if Jesus deliberately sought out the passage.

18. *The Spirit of the Lord is upon me.* . . . The quotation from Second Isaiah is actually a conflation of 61:1a,b,d; 58:6d; 61:2a. Two phrases are omitted: 61:1c, "to heal the broken-hearted" (at the end of v. 18); and 61:2b, "the day of vengeance of our God" (at the end of v. 19). The omission of the former is of little consequence; but the latter is a deliberate suppression of a negative aspect of the Deutero-Isaian message. The "today" of v. 21 is not to be identified with a day of divine vengeance. The Greek text of Luke's quotation conforms to that of the LXX, save for the infin. *kēryxai,* "to proclaim," instead of *kalesai,* "to call for" (LXX) in 61:2a, and the shift of the impv. *apostelle* (LXX) to an infin. in v. 18. The LXX follows the MT for the most part, but the meaning of the Hebrew text of 61:1d is disputed (lit. "for those bound an opening"—but in what sense? The LXX understood it as an opening of eyes). The Deutero-Isaian verses are part of a hymn (61:1-11), which explains the prophet's mission in the Consolation of Zion. See further J. A. Sanders, "From Isaiah 61 to Luke 4," in *Christianity, Judaism and Other Greco-Roman Cults* (SJLA 12; ed. J. Neusner; Leiden: Brill, 1975) 1. 75-106.

he has anointed me. In the baptism (3:22; cf. Acts 10:38; see the COMMENT on 3:21-22). Here it is to be understood as a prophetic anointing (see COMMENT).

to preach good news. The prophetic function of Jesus' mission is thus set forth in Deutero-Isaian terms. On the verb *euangelizesthai,* see NOTE on 1:19. Its etymological sense is retained here because it is so used in the Deutero-Isaian quotation; cf. 7:22. In the OT it scarcely means the preaching of Jesus or Christian preaching; when put on his lips here, it is not to be assumed that it immediately takes on the full Christian connotation. The point is that what "Isaiah" announced, Jesus is now seen doing himself.

In the Greek text it is not clear whether "to preach the good news" is to be taken with the preceding verb, "he anointed me," or with the following, "he sent me." My translation has followed the sense of the original Hebrew, "to announce good news to the poor he sent me." So too the LXX.

to the poor. Second Isaiah was announcing the Consolation of Zion to various groups in the postexilic Jerusalem community. Luke includes four of them in his quotation. The first is the "poor" (*ptōchoi*), a foreshadowing of a Lucan emphasis on this social class (see 6:20; 7:22; 14:13,21; 16:20,22; 18:22; 19:8; 21:3; cf. p. 248 above).

release for prisoners. In the ministry of Jesus this might refer to imprisoned debtors, the second group. In the Melchizedek text from Qumran Cave 11, Isa 61:1 is used in connection with Lev 25:10-13 and Deut 15:2 of the "release" of the jubilee-year (intended for debtors); see *ESBNT,* 249, 256-257.

sight for the blind. The third group of unfortunates in the Deutero-Isaian quotation, as it appears in the LXX; allusion will be made to them again in 7:22.

to send the downtrodden away relieved. Lit. "with relief, *or* in release." The Greek text uses *en aphesei.* The fourth group is described by a text derived from Isa 58:6d according to the LXX. The conflation of Isa 58:6d with 61:1d is the result of catchword bond: *aphesin,* "release," in the latter, and *en aphesei,* "in release," in the former. Although the word *aphesis* is used in these two verses in the sense of "release," it should be recalled that Luke also uses it in the sense of "forgiveness" (especially of sins); see 1:77; 3:3; 24:47; Acts 2:38; cf. p. 223 above. See further M. Rese, *Alttestamentliche Motive,* 153.

19. *to proclaim the Lord's year of favor.* Lit. "the Lord's acceptable year" (*kēryxai eniauton kyriou dekton*), Isa 61:2a according to the LXX, save for the infin. (see NOTE on v. 18). The Isaian description of a period of favor and deliverance for Zion is now used to proclaim the Period of Jesus, and the new mode of salvation that is to come in him. This is the form that his kerygma takes in the Lucan Gospel in contrast to Mark 1:14b-15 (see p. 153 above). The last part of 61:2 is omitted, "the day of vengeance of our God," since it is scarcely suited to the salvific period now being inaugurated. A similar reworking of this Isaian text to suit the role of Melchizedek and "the holy ones of God" can be found in 11QMelch 9 (*ESBNT,* 249).

20. *returned it to the attendant.* In addition to the "president" of the synagogue (*archisynagōgos*), its officers included "elders" (*presbyteroi,* Luke 7:3), and "attendants" (e.g. the *ḥazzān* or *hypēretēs,* Acts 13:5, who was a sort of sacristan or sexton).

sat down. The reading of Scripture was done standing (v. 16), but the exposition (*logos paraklēseōs,* "word of exhortation," Acts 13:15) was given seated.

fixed intently on him. The verb *atenizein* is a Lucan favorite (see 22:56; Acts 1:10; 3:4,12; 6:15; 7:55; 10:4; 11:6; 13:9; 14:9; 23:1). In most instances it expresses a steadfast gaze of esteem and trust—the nuance intended here. It is part of the assembly's initial reaction of admiration or pleasant surprise, and enhances the interpretation of Isaiah to be given.

21. *as he began to speak.* Lit. "he began to say to them," another instance of the Lucan use of *archesthai.* See NOTE on 3:23.

Today. This adv. *sēmeron* is scarcely to be understood in the generic sense of "nowadays" (*pace* E. P. Rice, *ExpTim* 29 [1917-1918] 45-46). Given its emphatic position at the head of the clause, it marks an important point in Lucan historical perspective. The adverb is used elsewhere in Luke's writings (2:11; 22:34,61; 23:43) and has at times a special connotation in Lucan theology (see p. 234 above); but its use here is significant. According to Conzelmann (*Theology,* 36), it stands in contrast to the Pauline declaration, "*Now* is the acceptable time" (2 Cor 6:2), by which the Apostle identifies his own period as the eschaton. But Luke "sees salvation as a thing of the past," as something brought about in the Period of Jesus, the Center of Time. There is an element of truth in this way of interpreting Lucan theology; but it may be overplaying the significance, because it refers immediately to "fulfillment" (here of the Deutero-Isaian proclamation); but that is not restricted to the Period of Jesus alone. Luke sees fulfillment taking place also in the Period of the Church (Acts 1:16; 3:18). That, however, does not deny the start of it now.

this passage of Scripture sees its fulfillment, as you sit listening. Lit. "this scripture has been fulfilled in your ears." The last phrase is an OT expression, *bě'oznêkem* (Deut 5:1; 2 Sam 3:19), "in your hearing." In Mark 1:15, as Jesus proclaims the kingdom, he announces that "the time is fulfilled" (i.e. has come), whereas in Luke it is Scripture that sees its fulfillment. This is part of the way he reads the OT, making out of much of it—sometimes even passages that are not even prophetic (in the OT sense)—predictions, which are now being realized. What was promised by Second Isaiah as consolation for Zion is now being granted in a new sense and a new way. The Consolation of Zion takes place anew (see 2:25; cf. 7:22).

Note the subtle joining of "eyes" (v. 20b) and "ears" (v. 21b) with the activity of the synagogue congregation mentioned in the following verse, "testifying" (as witnesses).

22. *acknowledged it.* Lit. "were testifying to it (*or possibly*, to him)." The sense of *martyrein* with the dat. is contested here. Most commentators understand the pron. *autō* as masculine and interpret the phrase, "bore witness to him," i.e. praised him (e.g. Creed, *The Gospel,* 67) or "spoke well of him" (*RSV*). B. Violet (*ZNW* 37 [1938] 251-271) and J. Jeremias (*Jesus' Promise to the Nations* [SBT 24; Naperville: Allenson, 1958] 44-46) contest this interpretation. Noting that *autō* could be a dative of disadvantage (BDF § 188.1) as well as a dative of advantage (as in the common interpretation), and comparing Hebrew and Aramaic phrases such as *'ashădûn 'ălôhî,* "they witnessed for *or* against him," Jeremias argues that the verb here should be understood in the hostile sense: "they all bore witness against him and were astonished at the words about (God's) mercy that came from his lips." Jeremias is concerned to eliminate the conflict of reactions in the common interpretation existing between the beginning and end of this passage. He explains the initial reaction as hostile because the people would be amazed that Jesus stopped the quotation of Isa 61:2 in the middle of the verse and left out all mention of "the day of God's vengeance" (61:2b). But this interpretation, intriguing though it be, is too forced to be convincing; it strains the sense of the following phrases (see below; cf. Anderson, "Broadening Horizons," 266-270).

My interpretation agrees in general with the common interpretation, save that *autō* is regarded as neuter (admitted as possible by BAG, 494a).

were surprised. The verb *thaumazein* can express astonishment (coupled with criticism, doubt, or censure) or else admiration (coupled with unexpected pleasure); see G. Bertram, *TDNT* 3. 28. The nuance intended can only be gained from the context; the common interpretation rightly understands it as admiration.

gracious words. Lit. "words of grace (*or possibly,* of charm)." The phrase could express the captivating eloquence of Jesus or (in a content-sense) words conveying God's favor (see Acts 14:3; 20:32). Cf. Eccl 10:12; Sir 21:16; Col 4:6. Violet (*ZNW* 37 [1938] 264-269) sought to explain *charis,* "grace" as a reference to *šěnat rāṣôn laYhwh,* "the Lord's year of favor" (Isa 61:2). This, however, does not succeed because the Lucan quotation of Isaiah depends on the LXX, which does not use *charis,* but *dekton* (see NOTE on v. 19 above), a word that is crucial to the development of the Lucan story (see v. 24).

came from his lips. Lit. "(words) proceeding from his mouth." This phrase seems to tip the sense of the foregoing phrase in terms of eloquence. It is, indeed, hard to understand why the "words of grace" would be coming from his lips, if they were to mean "words about (God's) mercy," as Jeremias suggests, omitted by Jesus. Jeremias blithely passes over this phrase.

Is not this Joseph's son? This query of the townspeople in the Lucan form of the story reflects only their common understanding of who Jesus is. It does not reckon with the precision of the (later added) infancy narrative (1:32-35; but cf. 2:33,48) or even with 3:23. In Mark 6:3, "Is not this the carpenter, Mary's son?" is occasioned by his teaching and his miracles; here the query is occasioned by his interpretation of Scripture and proclamation of God's period of salvation. The query could in itself be one of cynical indignation or one of pleasant surprise or admiration; in my opinion, it records the latter.

23. *he said to them.* The verb *eipen* is used with the prep. *pros* + accus. See p. 116 above.

You will probably quote me the proverb. The word *parabolē* has the meaning "proverb," as in 6:39 and at times in the LXX (1 Sam 10:12). See NOTE on 5:36.

Physician, heal yourself! Though put on Jesus' lips, the proverb reflects the second stage of reaction to Jesus in the Lucan account. Its cynicism is further explained by the comparison between Nazareth and Capernaum in the following remark. The reaction implied here has nothing to do with Jesus' interpretation of Second Isaiah.

The proverb is found in different ancient literatures with varying nuances. In Greek literature, one finds, "A physician for others, but himself teeming with sores" (Euripides *Frag.* 1086); in later rabbinical literature, "Physician, heal your own lameness" (*Genesis Rabbah* 23 [15c]). See further M.-J. Lagrange, *Luc,* 142.

what we have heard you have been doing in Capernaum. This is not simply to be implied in the reference to Jesus' ministry in 4:15. It probably stems from a tradition about his ministry in Capernaum, which Luke has not yet utilized. The reference comes from a source that has been used here in the conflation, and Luke has retained it without eliminating the inconsistency. See the COMMENT.

Capernaum, to be mentioned again in 4:31; 7:1; 10:15, is not mentioned in the OT. It was a town in Galilee (4:31), on the western shore of Lake Gennesaret. Its location is perhaps not yet known with certainty. It is usually identified with Tell Ḥum. But Josephus (*J.W.* 3.10,8 § 519) speaks of its "highly fertilizing spring," which has suggested to some that it might rather have been at Khan Minyeh (see F.-M. Abel, *JPOS* 8 [1928] 24-34; E. F. F. Bishop, *CBQ* 15 [1953] 427-437; J. Finegan, *The Archeology of the New Testament,* 48-56). The name of the town probably means "village of Nahum" (*kĕpar Nāḥûm*).

The Greek text of Luke has *eis tēn Kapharnaoum,* lit. "into Capernaum," an instance of the encroachment of the prep. *eis* on *en* in Hellenistic Greek (see BDF § 205). Cf. Luke 9:61; 21:37. Some Lucan mss. have corrected the phrase to *en tē K.* (⊕, the Koine text-tradition).

24. *Believe me.* Lit. "Amen, I tell you." This is the first occurrence of this asseverative phrase, containing the only Semitic word that has been retained in the Lucan Gospel from the earlier tradition (see further 12:37; 18:17,29; 21:32; 23:43; cf. J. C. O'Neill, *JTS* 10 [1959] 1-9). There is no uniform reason underlying the use of this formula in this Gospel. There is no parallel to it in Mark 6:4. And it is not evident that it is derived from a non-Marcan source, since the rest of the verse is Marcan-inspired. See Schürmann, "Zur Traditionsgeschichte," 190.

The asseveration, "Amen, I tell you," occurs also in the other Gospels: thirteen times in Mark, thirty-one times in Matthew, and twenty-five times (always doubled) in John. Hebrew *'āmēn* is used in the OT as a corroborating statement, often *after* prayer as a response (e.g. Deut 27:15; Ps 106:48), sometimes even doubled (e.g. Num 5:22; Neh 8:6; Pss 41:14; 72:19; 89:53). The doubled form as a response is the only use found in Qumran literature so far (1QS 1:20; 2:10,18; 4QDibHam 1:7; 7:[2]). So far the exact Hebrew equivalent of the NT Greek formula has not yet turned up (*'āmēn* [*'āmēn*], *'ănî 'ômēr lākem*), and this makes some NT commentators think that the prepositive use of Greek *amēn*, whether single or double, in such a phrase is "an authentic reminiscence" of Jesus (so R. E. Brown, *John, I-XII,* 84). It helps little to point merely to the prepositive use of Hebrew *'āmēn* in other formulations; this has been known for a long time (e.g. Jer 28:6 [*'āmēn kēn ya'ăśeh Yhwh*]; the Greek reflex of it in the LXX of Jer 15:11 [*genoito*]).

It has been claimed that prepositive Amen exists in a seventh-century B.C. Hebrew letter written on an ostracon found at Meṣad Ḥashavyahu (Yabneh-Yam); see J. Naveh, "A Hebrew Letter from the Seventh Century B.C.," *IEJ* 10 (1960) 129-139: *'ḥy y'nw ly 'mn nqty m'[šm]* (line 11). Three interpretations of these words are possible: (a) With *'mn* as responsorial: "My brothers will testify for me. Amen! I am innocent of any gu[ilt]." (b) With *'mn* as prepositive: "My comrades will testify for me. Truly, I am innocent of any gu[ilt]." So F. M. Cross (*BASOR* 165 [1962] 45); S. Talmon (*BASOR* 176 [1964] 34-35 [comparing *'mn* with Hebrew *'omnāh* or *'omnām*, Josh 7:20; Gen 20:12; Ruth 3:12]; *Textus* 7 [1969] 124-129); H. Bietenhard (*NIDNTT*, 1. 98); J. Strugnell (*HTR* 67 [1974] 177-182). (c) With *'mn* taken with what precedes, but regarded as a shorthand or direct-address quotation of the "brothers": "My comrades can bear me witness that it was as I say—I am not guilty of any (crime)" (J. C. L. Gibson, *Textbook of Syrian Semitic Inscriptions* [2 vols.; Oxford: Clarendon, 1971, 1975] 1. 29); similarly, K. Berger, (*Die Amen-Worte Jesu* [BZNW 39; Berlin: de Gruyter, 1970] 1-3); J. Jeremias (*ZNW* 64 [1973] 122-123); D. Pardee (*Maarav* 1 [1978-1979] 37). The upshot is that this instance of *'mn* is far from clear; it is not certainly prepositive. Moreover, it scarcely sheds any light on the NT use before a verb of saying.

However, the prepositive use of Greek *amēn* with a verb of saying is not found in the NT on the lips of anyone other than Jesus, nor is this specific use of it "followed by any apostle or prophet of the early Church" (J. Hempel, *IDB* 1. 105).

Berger's attempt to explain the prepositive Amen as an imitation of the oath-particles in Greek (*nai, nai mēn, ē mēn*) is almost certainly misguided. Cf. V. Hasler, *Amen* (Zürich: Gotthelf, 1969).

no prophet is accepted in his own country. Substantially, this is the same proverb as that found in Mark 6:4 and Matt 13:57; but the wording differs. Mark has, "A prophet is not without honor (*atimos*) except in his own country, among his own relatives, and in his own house." Matthew follows Mark, but omits "among his own relatives." See John 4:44, "A prophet has no honor in his own country." For the form of the proverb in the Oxyrhynchus Papyri and Gospel of Thomas; see the COMMENT. Note that Luke omits here all reference to the lack of acceptance of Jesus "among his own relatives, and in his own house." This omission suits the Lucan treatment of Mary and Jesus' relatives elsewhere (see 8:21; cf. *MNT*, 164-167).

By using the proverb, Jesus identifies himself as a prophet; see further 11:49-50; 13:33 (in the latter case a connection is stated between this role and death in Jerusalem). But as a prophet, Jesus is not welcome in his hometown because he does not work the desired miracles there.

The Lucan form of the proverb, in using *dektos*, "accepted," is playing on the use of that adj. in v. 19 above.

25. *I can assure you.* Lit. "in truth I tell you," an asseverative saying which resembles the sense of "Amen, I tell you" (v. 24). The phrase *ep' alētheias* is further found in Mark 12:14,32; Luke 20:21; 22:59; Acts 4:27; 10:34. It is also found in classical and Hellenistic Greek (e.g. Philo *Legatio ad Gaium* 60, 248); but its peculiarly adverbial usage is influenced by the LXX (Job 36:4; Dan 2:8,9,47) and possibly by the Palestinian Aramaic *bĕqûšṭ(ā')*, 1QapGen 2:5,[6],7,10,18,22; 4QEn^e 5 ii 22,30. In using it, Jesus insists on the truth of the comparison to follow.

in the time of Elijah. That Jesus' experience in the town of Nazareth has for Luke a symbolic and programmatic character is seen in the appeal now made to the careers of Elijah and Elisha. What Jesus says about himself as prophet is now compared to the experience of two great prophets of Israel. Jesus is another Elijah and another Elisha. These vv. 25-27 provide a justification from the OT for the Christian mission to the Gentiles (see R. C. Tannehill, "The Mission," 60).

Elijah appeared briefly in the description of the Baptist's role in the infancy narrative (1:17). But this is the real beginning of another treatment of him in the Gospel proper (see p. 213 above).

for three and a half years. According to 1 Kgs 18:1 the rain finally came "in the third year" of the drought. Luke has inherited another tradition about the duration of the drought and the famine, which is also found in Jas 5:17. According to this tradition the duration was equated with the stereotyped length of the period of distress in apocalyptic literature (apparently derived from the length of persecution under Antiochus IV Epiphanes; see Dan 7:25; 12:7; Rev

11:2; 12:6,14). This apocalyptic detail is meaningless in the Lucan account; the evangelist has simply inherited it.

26. *was not sent.* I.e. by God, another instance of the so-called theological passive (see ZBG § 236). The same can be said for "were stopped up" (v. 25) and "was cured" (v. 27). Cf. 4:6.

to a widow in Zarephath near Sidon. Lit. "Zarephath of the Sidonian" (region). This is an allusion to 1 Kgs 17:9 (LXX). The widow was a Gentile, not an Israelite, living in a Phoenician town on the Mediterranean coast between Tyre and Sidon. Josephus (*Ant.* 8.13,2 § 320) thus locates the town and spells its name *Sarephtha,* an aspirated form of the Lucan *Sarepta,* which is derived from the LXX. Both of these forms are closer to the real name of the town (cf. Akkadian *Ṣariptu*) than that of the MT, which has *Ṣārĕpat* (Obad 20; cf. 1 Kgs 17:9,10), whence the English form.

27. *lepers in Israel.* Another example from the OT prophets confirms Jesus' point. See 2 Kgs 7:3-10; 2 Chr 26:19-21. The prophet Elijah and his disciple Elisha are coupled here in a context in which Jesus appears as prophet and teacher.

On leprosy, see NOTE on 5:12 below.

when Elisha was the prophet. This is an allusion to 2 Kgs 5:1-19, esp. vv. 9-10. Naaman was the commander of the army of Syria and was sent by the Syrian king to the king of Israel to be cured of his leprosy. The Israelite king interpreted this as a pretext for starting a war against him. But Elisha in Samaria insisted that Naaman be sent to him; he ordered the commander to bathe seven times in the Jordan. Despite his complaints that the Syrian rivers Abana and Pharphar were "better than all the waters of Israel," the commander bathed in the Jordan and was cured, even though he was not an Israelite, i.e. a person from the *patris.* So Jesus drives home his point about an accepted prophet.

28. *they all became furious.* Lit. "all were filled with fury." The assembly reacts to Jesus' implication that his activity would have better results among those who are not his townspeople and that they are like the persecutors of prophets of old. The maximum of annoyance is expressed in the phrases, "not . . . to any of them," and "none of them."

See Mark 6:5 for a different reason for leaving Nazareth.

29. *cast him out of the town.* This crucial statement in Luke's account foreshadows the locale of the crucifixion itself (23:26).

to the edge of the cliff on which the town was built. Modern Nazareth is a small village built on a slope and ringed about by hills, but it is impossible to point to any such spot as that envisaged in this sentence. Since the ninth century a tradition has associated the Lucan verse with a place about three kms. SE of Nazareth (Jebel el-Kafze), but this is also contested. See D. Baldi, *ELS,* 6 for ancient testimonies. Creed (*The Gospel,* 69) regards it as a "mistake to attempt topographical verification." It is probably only another instance of Luke's vague awareness of Palestinian geography.

30. *slipped through the crowd.* Lit. "having gone through the midst of them." This detail is often considered miraculous, but there is no need to inter-

pret it so. For it would then give to the Nazarenes precisely the sign that they were seeking. The evangelist's intention, however, is clear: the opposition to Jesus is diabolic, but it is not yet time for the opposition to succeed. See 4:13. Moreover, Luke's story demands Jesus' escape, since the spread of the word of God must continue (see Acts 13:46; 18:6; 19:9 for the spelling out of what is implied here).

went on his way. Lit. "proceeded." This is the first occurrence of the significant verb *poreuesthai* in the Gospel proper. It has been used in the infancy narrative (1:6,39; 2:3,41) in a more general sense. But now it is predicated of Jesus with the nuance of his "proceeding" on his way—a way that will eventually lead him to Jerusalem, the city of destiny. See 4:42; 7:6,11; 9:51,52,53,56,57; 13:33; 17:11; 22:22,39; 24:28; also p. 169 above.

BIBLIOGRAPHY (4:16-30)

Anderson, H. "Broadening Horizons: The Rejection of Nazareth Pericope of Lk 4,16-30 in Light of Recent Critical Trends," *Int* 18 (1964) 259-275.

Bornhäuser, K. *Studien zum Sondergut des Lukas* (Gütersloh: Bertelsmann, 1934) 20-33.

Busse, U. *Das Nazareth-Manifest: Eine Einführung in das lukanische Jesusbild nach Lk 4,16-30* (SBS 91; Stuttgart: Katholisches Bibelwerk, 1978).

Crockett, L. C. "Luke 4:25-27 and Jewish-Gentile Relations in Luke-Acts," *JBL* 88 (1969) 177-183.

Eltester, W. "Israel im lukanischen Werk und die Nazarethperikope," in *Jesus in Nazareth* (BZNW 40; ed. W. Eltester; Berlin: de Gruyer, 1972) 76-147.

Finkel, A. "Jesus' Sermon at Nazareth (Luk. 4,16-30)," in *Abraham unser Vater: Juden und Christen im Gespräch über die Bibel: Festschrift für Otto Michel* (eds. O. Betz et al.; Leiden: Brill, 1963) 106-115.

Goguel, M. "Le rejet de Jésus à Nazareth," *ZNW* 12 (1911) 321-324.

George, A. "La prédication inaugurale de Jésus dans la synagogue de Nazareth: Luc 4, 16-30," *BVC* 59 (1964) 17-29.

Haenchen, E. "Historie und Verkündigung bei Markus und Lukas," *Das Lukas-Evangelium* (Wege der Forschung 280; ed. G. Braumann; Darmstadt: Wissenschaftliche Buchgesellschaft, 1974) 287-316.

Hill, D. "The Rejection of Jesus at Nazareth (Luke iv 16-30)," *NovT* 13 (1971) 161-180.

Kirk, A. "La conciencia mesiánica de Jesús en el sermón de Nazaret, Lc 4,16ss," *RevistB* 33 (1971) 127-137.

Reicke, B. "Jesus in Nazareth—Lk 4:14-30," in *Das Wort und die Wörter: Festschrift G. Friedrich zum 65. Geburtstag* (eds. H. Balz and S. Schulz; Stuttgart: Kohlhammer, 1973) 47-55.

Rese, M. *Alttestamentliche Motive in der Christologie des Lukas* (Gütersloh: G. Mohn, 1969).

Samain, E. "Aucun prophète n'est bien reçu dans sa patrie: Lc 4, 21-30," *As-Seign* 35 (1973) 63-72.

Schrage, W., *Das Verhältnis des Thomasevangeliums zur synoptischen Tradition* (BZNW 29; Berlin: de Gruyter, 1964).

Schürmann, H. "Zur Traditionsgeschichte der Nazareth-Perikope Lk 4, 16-30," in *Mélanges bibliques en hommage au R. P. Béda Rigaux* (eds. A. Descamps et A. de Halleux; Gembloux: Duculot, 1970) 187-205.

Strobel, A. "Das apokalyptische Terminproblem in der sogen. Antrittspredigt Jesu (Lk 4,16-30)," *TLZ* 92 (1967) 251-254.

———— "Die Ausrufung des Jobeljahres in der Nazarethpredigt Jesu: Zur apokalyptischen Tradition Lc 4:16-30," in *Jesus in Nazareth* (see above) 38-50.

Sturch, R. L. "The 'Patris' of Jesus," *JTS* 28 (1977) 94-96.

Tannehill, R. C. "The Mission of Jesus according to Luke iv 16-30," in *Jesus in Nazareth* (see above) 51-75.

Violet, B. "Zum rechten Verständnis der Nazarethperikope Lc 4:16-30," in *In memoriam Carl Schmidt* (=*ZNW* 37 [1938]) 251-271.

18. TEACHING AND CURE IN THE CAPERNAUM SYNAGOGUE
(4:31-37)

4 31 He went down to Capernaum, a town in Galilee, where he used to teach the people on the Sabbath. 32 They were struck by his teaching, because it was proposed with authority.

33 There was a man in the synagogue under the influence of an unclean spirit; once he screamed at the top of his voice, 34 "Ha! What do you want with us, Jesus of Nazareth? Have you come to put an end to us? I know who you are, the Holy One of God!" 35 But Jesus charged him, "Silence! Come out of him!" Then the demon threw the man down before them and came out without doing him any harm. 36 Amazement took hold of all of them, as they said to one another, "What is there in this man's words? For with authority and power he gives commands even to unclean spirits, and they come out!" 37 And talk about him began to spread through every part of the countryside.

COMMENT

After the programmatic scene of Jesus' teaching in the Nazareth synagogue, Luke introduces the reader to the first characteristic incidents of his Galilean ministry outside of his hometown. The four following episodes illustrate concretely what had been reported about him in Nazareth concerning his Capernaum activity (4:23). In these scenes Jesus is at work alone in Capernaum; he is not yet surrounded by followers or disciples.

Some commentators make a division of the Lucan Gospel at this point, regarding 4:31 - 9:50 as the Galilean ministry (so E. E. Ellis, W. Grundmann, C. H. Talbert). This, however, isolates the foregoing Nazareth incident and is too dependent on the Marcan order of episodes. The Galilean ministry in the Lucan Gospel clearly begins with 4:14.

The next four episodes in Capernaum are derived from the Marcan source by Luke; in these he follows its order and sequence. He has omitted 1:16-20, to make use of it later. But the first of these four episodes (4:31-37) is parallel to Mark 1:21-28. The episode itself, which tells of the exorcism of a demoniac in the Capernaum synagogue, is preceded by two verses which contain a generic statement about Jesus' Sabbath teaching and of the reaction of the people of Capernaum to it. It is not easy to decide how vv. 31-32 should be regarded. Though they resemble the summary of 4:14-15, they are best taken with the rest as a simple introduction to the specifically Capernaum ministry. Part of the problem in judging them comes from Matt 7:28-29, which seems to parallel Mark 1:21-22, but may not be its real parallel at all.

Luke's version of the first episode is clearly dependent on Mark 1:21-28, especially in vv. 33-37. Aside from some minor verbal changes (e.g. the elimination of *kai euthys,* "and immediately"), the major Lucan redactional modifications are the following: (1) the use of the sg. verb, "he went down" (v. 31), instead of the Marcan "they entered"; (2) the addition of "a town in Galilee" (v. 31); (3) the omission of the comparison of Jesus' authority with that of the Scribes (v. 32; cf. Mark 1:22); (4) the description of the demoniac, "a man . . . under the influence of an unclean spirit" (v. 33; cf. Mark 1:23); (5) the addition of the interjection, "Ha!" (v. 34); (6) the addition of the detail that the demon threw him down in their midst and left "without doing him any harm" (v. 35); and (7) the substitution of "words" for the Marcan "new teaching" (v. 36; cf. Mark 1:27). These details have been studied thoroughly by T. Schramm, *Der Markus-Stoff,* 85-91.

This is the first of twenty-one miracle-stories in the Lucan Gospel. As Bultmann notes (*HST,* 210), it has all the characteristics of the typical exorcism story: (a) The demon recognizes the exorcist and puts up a struggle; (b) the exorcist utters a threat or command; (c) the demon departs, making a scene; and (d) the spectators' reaction is recorded. These characteristics will be verified in the three other exorcism stories (8:26-39; 9:37-43a; 11:14-15).

Hellenistic literature has been scoured for examples of exorcisms or the casting out of demons by magic spells to provide a background for such Gospel episodes. When it is a question of an exorcism as distinct from a healing, the examples are not numerous (e.g. Josephus *Ant.* 8.2,5 §§ 46-49; Lucian *Philopseudes* 16, §§ 30-31; Philostratus *Vita Apollonii* 3.38; 4.20). Qumran literature also knows of exorcism in a Palestinian Jewish context: Abraham prays and imposes his hands on Pharaoh to exorcise him of the evil spirit that has afflicted him and his household (1QapGen 20:16-29).

The exorcism stories are but one of the four kinds of miracle stories in this Gospel; there are, in addition, healing stories (sometimes not easily distinguished from exorcisms), resuscitations, and nature miracles.

Though it is customary to label such Gospel episodes as "miracle" stories, one has to beware of the connotation that this Latin-derived title brings with it, a connotation that is not necessarily conveyed by the Gospel accounts. Latin *miraculum* means "a thing causing wonder"; its Greek equivalent would be *thaumasion,* which is found only in Matt 21:15 in the NT. In Luke one finds on occasion *paradoxa,* "remarkable things" (lit. "unexpected things") or *ta endoxa,* "glorious things" (see 5:26; 13:17). But this element of wonder or surprise (especially at what might seem out of the ordinary) is not per se the reaction that these accounts usually evoke. Behind the NT miracles is the OT idea of *mōpēt,* "portent, prodigious sign," usually translated in the LXX as *teras.* Yet it is often a symbolic action authenticating a prophet's mission and is not necessarily preternatural (see Ezek 12:1-6). The Greek *teras* is never used alone of Jesus' miracles in the NT; but in Acts 2:22,43 Luke uses of them the OT expression *terata kai sēmeia,* "wonders and signs" (cf. Deut 28:46; 13:2; 29:2), along with the normal Greek word used in the Synoptics for them, *dynameis,* "powers, powerful deeds." Contrast the Johannine use of "signs" (*semeia*) and "works" (*erga*). The Lucan use of *dynameis* will be met in 10:13; 19:37. This Synoptic designation for Jesus' miracles better reveals the character of these deeds; and in this very episode there will be mention of his power (4:36). They are not meant in the Gospels as apologetic proofs of Jesus' mission (though Luke does refer to them in this way in Acts 2:22) or of his divinity. They are rather the powerful manifestations and means whereby the dominion of God is established over human beings in place of the "dominion of Belial," freeing them from the evil to which they have been subjected. They also reveal that a new phase of salvation-history is at work. Jesus' *exousia,* "authority," makes his teaching carry weight, as his *dynamis,* "power," reveals that God's dominion is being established in him.

This, then, is the real implication of the present scene. It concretely illustrates Jesus' teaching and power over evils that beset unfortunate human beings. In the Lucan context that authority and power are rooted in Jesus' anointing with the Spirit (3:22; 4:18). Because of that he is now recognized to be not only "Jesus of Nazareth," but even "the Holy One of God" (4:34).

NOTES

4 31. *He went down to Capernaum, a town in Galilee.* See NOTE on 4:23. Ms. D adds a geographic detail, "the seaside (town) in the territory of Zebulun and Naphthali," a scribal harmonization introduced from Matt 4:13. The best mss. of Luke omit it. Luke specifies that Capernaum was a "town in Galilee" for the benefit of his Gentile Christian readers. Capernaum, which appears in Mark as the center of Jesus' Galilean ministry, would have been about six hun-

dred meters lower than Nazareth; hence the distinctive Lucan verb *kathēlthen,* "he went down," which is substituted for the Marcan historical present, *eisporeuontai,* "they entered," referring to Jesus and his disciples (just called in Mark 1:16-20). Because Luke has transposed that Marcan scene to 5:1-11, he must depict Jesus going alone to Capernaum. H. Conzelmann (*Theology,* 38) sought to weaken the implied "accurate geographical knowledge" by saying that *kata* may well "be deduced from the incorrect idea that Nazareth stands on a hill." Perhaps; but even Conzelmann would have to admit that in this instance Luke's knowledge of Palestinian terrain *is* more accurate than usual.

he used to teach. To stress the habitual character of Jesus' activity, Luke uses the impf. of the verb "to be" and the ptc., *ēn didaskōn;* contrast 4:15.

on the Sabbath. Or possibly "on the Sabbaths." Luke uses the pl. *ta sabbata* both for the single Sabbath (cf. 13:10; 6:2 in ms. D) and for more than one (Acts 17:2). Its use for a single Sabbath is sometimes said to be an Aramaism; but the pl. form, accompanied by the Greek pl. def. art. *ta,* is too well attested in Hellenistic Greek to be the result solely of such influence (see BDF § 141.3; BAG, 746b).

32. *struck by his teaching.* Lit. "were amazed, astounded," a strong expression used again in 9:43.

it was proposed with authority. Lit. "his word was with (*or* in) authority," i.e. was authoritative. The *exousia* with which Jesus is said to speak in these introductory verses refers to his ability to elicit conviction from his hearers, an authority that is rooted in the "power of the Spirit" (4:14), with which he has been "anointed" (4:18). The word *exousia* will occur in v. 36 below and then will be associated with his exorcising commands. But nothing in the text suggests that it should be understood in a quasi-magical sense, connoting a knowledge of recondite powers.

Luke omits the Marcan comparison, "and not as the Scribes" (1:22), i.e. the learned interpreters of the Torah. The Christians for whom he writes are not those preoccupied with opposition from the rabbis and their interpretation of the OT. This is why Jesus' authority is rooted in something more than mere learning.

33. *in the synagogue.* See NOTE on 4:15. This is perhaps the synagogue referred to in 7:5 as built by a Roman centurion. Ruins of a synagogue still exist today at Tell Ḥum, but they are scarcely from the first century (see J. Finegan, *Archeology of the New Testament,* 51-55). For details about the debate over its dating, see *MPAT* § A15 (p. 286).

under the influence of an unclean spirit. Lit. "having the spirit of an unclean demon." Mark 1:23 described the man simply as "with an unclean spirit" (*anthrōpos en pneumati akathartō*), but Luke has changed the description, using a cumbersome phrase. The normal Palestinian Jewish expressions would have been either "evil spirit" (*pneuma ponēron,* Luke 7:21; 8:2) or "unclean spirit" (*pneuma akatharton,* Luke 4:36; 6:18), or an expression involving "spirit" with some adjective. Aramaic counterparts of these are known; thus *rûaḥ bĕ'îšā',* "evil spirit" (1QapGen 20:16-17); *rûaḥ mikdaš,* "spirit of affliction" (1QapGen 20:16); *rûaḥ šaḥlānāyā',* "spirit of purulence" (1QapGen 20:26). In the Lucan expression the genitive in *pneuma daimoniou akathartou* may be appositional (the spirit = the unclean demon); Luke would then have made use of a more Greek term *daimonion* for the more Semitic *pneuma*. But *pneuma* may rather denote the man's spirit afflicted by the unclean demon. My translation is something of a paraphrase, which conveys the minimum of the cumbersome Greek text.

The "demons," "unclean spirits," or "evil spirits" of the Synoptic Gospels are rarely associated with Satan, and their control of a person is normally not an indication of moral turpitude. Usually demonic possession is associated with physical or psychic illness. No indication is given in this episode of the illness involved. At times afflictions of some sort are indicated, such as dumbness (Luke 11:14), lameness (Luke 13:11), epilepsy (Luke 9:39), delirium (Luke 8:29). Though the evangelists seem to distinguish at times between possession and illness (e.g. Luke 7:21; 13:32) and do not explain all illness in terms of demonic influence, there is little doubt that they have closely related the two. It might be best to speak of "demon-sickness." It is a form of protological thinking which cannot ascribe physical or psychic disorders to proper secondary causes that makes ancient writers attribute them to beings of an intermediate spirit-world. The same is implied at times in descriptions of violent disturbances of physical nature. This is why Jesus is said to "charge" (*epitiman*) a fever (4:39) or the winds (8:24)—in reality, he charges the spirit controlling the fever or the raging winds. See further J. B. Cortés and F. M. Gatti, *The Case against Possessions and Exorcisms* (New York: Vantage, 1975).

screamed at the top of his voice. Lit. "cried out with a great voice." See 1 Sam 4:5, whence the phrase may be derived. The cry reveals that the demon knows who is confronting him (Jesus of Nazareth) and who he really is (the Holy One of God). How the demon knows this we are not told, but it is assumed that demons have a special knowledge and can assess the value of their superiors.

34. *Ha!* The Greek particle *ea* has nothing to do with the Semitic interjection *wāy* (*pace* Str-B, 2. 157). It is a particle known in Attic Greek poetry, Hellenistic literature, and the LXX (Job 15:16; 25:6); it expresses displeasure or surprise.

What do you want with us? The Greek formula, *tí hēmin kai soi,* lit. "what to us and to you?" expresses here not only a denial of common interest (as in 2 Kgs 3:13; Hos 14:9), but real hostility (as in LXX Judg 11:12; 1 Kgs 17:18; 2 Chr 35:21). The demoniac's cry is very similar to that of the widow of Zarephath in 1 Kgs 17:18. Because it is used there in a situation not involving a demon, it reveals that it does not necessarily belong to apotropaic incantations (*pace* K. Kertelge, *Wunder Jesu,* 53). The hostility expressed reveals that the demon-world would have nothing to do with Jesus' authority and power.

Have you come to put an end to us? Lit. "to destroy us." The pl. "us" does not refer to the man and the demon, but to demons as such. It reflects the belief that the demonic control of human beings would come to an end before the eschaton or the Day of the Lord, when God's control would be established over all on behalf of those faithful to him (see 1QM 1:10-14; 14:10-11). This explains why the demons go off to the abyss (Luke 8:31; cf. Rev 20:2,9-10). The expected subjection of evil spirits (Luke 10:19) is used to convey the idea that a new phase of God's dominion replaces the "dominion of Belial" (1QM 4:9). This now comes in the advent of "Jesus of Nazareth."

the Holy One of God! The title, *ho hagios tou theou,* is derived from Mark 1:24, where alone it otherwise occurs in the Synoptics (see John 6:69). It is unknown outside the NT. It may be inspired by Ps 106:16, where Aaron is called *ho hagios Kyriou,* "the holy one of the Lord." It is farfetched to think that the demon is referring to Jesus as the messianic high priest (*pace* Kertelge, *Wunder Jesu,* 53). Rather, it expresses the demon's recognition of Jesus as one closely associated with Yahweh. In the Lucan context Jesus' "holiness" would have to be explained by his "sonship" (3:22) and "anointing" with the Spirit (4:18). In any case, the title is hardly intended as flattery on the part of the demon.

35. *charged him.* Or "commanded him." Though the Greek verb *epitiman* often means merely "rebuke, reproach" (e.g. 9:55; 17:3; 18:15), its use with reference to demons or unclean spirits is more technical. It occurs regularly in the LXX as a translation of Hebrew *gā'ar,* "shout at, exorcise" (e.g. Zech 3:2 [of Satan]; Pss 68:31 [of beasts], 106:9 [of the Red Sea]). The Aramaic verb *gĕ'ar* is also used in the sense of exorcising the evil spirit that afflicts Pharaoh and his household in 1QapGen 20:28-29. H. C. Kee (*NTS* 14 [1967-1968] 232-246) has shown that this technical usage denotes the pronouncement of a commanding word whereby God or his spokesman brings evil powers into submission. It is part of the vocabulary belonging to the description of the final defeat of Belial and his minions. The fact that this technical sense of *epitiman* is never found in any of the exorcism-stories about Alexander and Peregrinus (in Lucian of Samosata) or about Apollonius of Tyana (in Philostratus), or in any of the Greek papyri—magical or otherwise—indicates that this verb is hardly evidence for the alleged Hellenistic picture of Jesus as a *theios anēr* in the Synoptic Gospels (see MM, 248). The verb, then, should not be simply translated as "rebuked" when used in this technical sense.

To use this verb of the demon reveals the lordship of Jesus; that is what is connoted by the authority and power invested in the command that he utters. See E. Stauffer, *TDNT* 2. 625.

Silence! Lit. "be muzzled," the word being derived from Mark 1:25. The Greek verb *phimoun* is attested extrabiblically as a slang word for stifling evil spirits with a magic spell (MM, 672). Here the gospel tradition has taken over a term from Hellenistic spells. It is used to enshrine Jesus' mighty word on behalf of an unfortunate human being.

Come out of him! In both places Luke uses the same verb *exelthe/exēlthen* as does Mark, but changes the prep. from *ex* to *ap'*. See 4:41; 5:8; 8:29,33,38,46; 9:5; 11:24; 17:29; Acts 16:18,40.

before them. Lit. "into the midst (of them)." A Lucan addition to the description of the departure of the demon which enables all present to see what has happened. This is Luke's way of insisting on the reality of the miracle.

36. *What is there in this man's words?* Lit. "what is this word?" The phrase may be derived from 2 Sam 1:4 (LXX); in that case, one should perhaps

rather translate, "What is this thing?" *Logos* would be used in the sense of Hebrew *dābār,* "word, thing, matter." For this sense of *logos* in Lucan writings, see Acts 8:21; 15:6. However, in the context of the command that Jesus has just given to the demon, the sense is rather, "What kind of a word/command is this?"

This reaction of the people differs considerably in the Lucan story from the Marcan form, where they speak of a "new teaching with power" (1:27).

with authority and power he gives commands even to unclean spirits. The words *exousia* and *dynamis* joined here echo those of 4:32 and 4:14. Cf. 9:1. The *dynamis* with which he has worked the miracle is that of the Spirit. The pair recalls that Jesus is the Spirit-guided agent vested with the power of God who now dominates the world of evil opposition.

37. *through every part of the countryside.* I.e. of Galilee (see 4:31). The phrase is an echo of 4:14 and implies that Jesus' reputation goes even beyond the regions which he himself visits.

BIBLIOGRAPHY (4:31-37)

Busse, U. *Die Wunder des Propheten Jesus: Die Rezeption, Komposition und Interpretation der Wundertradition im Evangelium des Lukas* (Forschung zur Bibel 24; Stuttgart: Katholisches Bibelwerk, 1977).

Buzy, D. "Le premier séjour de Jésus à Capharnaüm," in *Mélanges bibliques rédigés en l'honneur de André Robert* (Travaux de l'Institut Catholique de Paris 4; Paris: Bloud et Gay, 1957) 411-419.

Kertelge, K. *Die Wunder Jesu im Markusevangelium* (SANT 23; Munich: Kösel, 1970) 50-60.

McGinley, L. J. *Form-Criticism of the Synoptic Healing Narratives* (Woodstock, MD: Woodstock College, 1944).

Pesch, R. "'Eine neue Lehre aus Macht': Eine Studie zu Mk 1,21-28," in *Evangelienforschung: Ausgewählte Aufsätze deutscher Exegeten* (ed. J.-B. Bauer; Graz: Styria, 1968) 241-276.

Schramm, T. *Der Markus-Stoff,* 85-91.

Talbert, C. H. "The Lukan Presentation of Jesus' Ministry in Galilee: Luke 4:31-9:50," *RevExp* 64 (1967) 485-497.

19. SIMON'S MOTHER-IN-LAW
(4:38-39)

4 ^{38} On leaving the synagogue, Jesus entered the house of Simon. Simon's mother-in-law was suffering from a very high fever, and they asked him about her. ^{39} He stood over her and commanded the fever; and it left her. Immediately she got up and began to serve them.

COMMENT

Another example of Jesus' Capernaum ministry is given by Luke in the healing of Simon's mother-in-law (4:38-39). It is a scene that he has taken over from Mark 1:29-31 (cf. Matt 8:14-15); his dependence on the Marcan source is clear (see T. Schramm, *Der Markus-Stoff*, 85-91).

Luke has, however, trimmed the Marcan story to his own account at this point. Besides the usual avoidance of *kai euthys* (Mark 1:29), he has introduced the following main redactional modifications: (1) He omits the mention of Andrew, Simon's brother, and the accompaniment of James and John (v. 38a; cf. Mark 1:29). Logically, he has to do so, since he has not yet narrated the calling of disciples by Jesus. Hence he comes alone to Simon's house, who is thus otherwise an unidentified inhabitant of Capernaum. (2) Luke heightens the description of the fever that afflicts Simon's mother-in-law (v. 38b; cf. Mark 1:30). (3) He introduces a request made by an unidentified "them" in place of the report about her in Mark (v. 38c; cf. Mark 1:30b). (4) He depicts Jesus healing the woman by a "command" alone, omitting the Marcan detail of touching her hand (v. 39; cf. Mark 1:31). (5) He introduces the adv. "immediately," to stress the instantaneous nature of the cure (v. 39b; cf. Mark 1:31b).

From a form-critical viewpoint, the scene is another miracle-story, but this time one belonging to the category of healings (see further 5:12-15,17-26; 6:6-11; 7:1-10; 8:43-48; 13:10-17; 14:1-6; 17:11-18; 18:35-43; 22:49-51). Sometimes it is not easy to decide whether the healing is strictly such or borders on an exorcism (see NOTE on v. 39).

Jesus goes alone to the house of a Galilean Jew whose mother-in-law is ill and he cures her. The scene is thus another manifestation of his "authority" and "power" (v. 35), even over an evil in which a demon is not explicitly involved, as in the foregoing episode. In the Lucan form of the story he cures her by a command of his all-powerful word. The first miracle that Jesus performed in this Gospel benefits a man, whereas the second helps a woman. Though it is not yet apparent in the flow of the story, it will emerge in time that Jesus uses his power here on behalf of a relative of one who will become the leader of his disciples. This miracle on her behalf provides in the Lucan account part of the psychological background for the call of Simon the fisherman. The woman's immediate reaction of getting up and serving them is undoubtedly recounted to stress the instantaneous and complete character of her restoration. But it was also undoubtedly recounted in the early Christian community to emphasize her service and implicit gratitude. She is a paradigm of other women from Galilee who will serve Jesus in the Lucan account (8:1-3; 23:49,55).

NOTES

4 38. *On leaving the synagogue.* Lit. "having got up from the synagogue." Luke uses his favorite ptc. *anastas* with the prep. *apo* (see 22:45), but the use is elliptic, for one would expect a finite verb such as *exēlthen*, "he went out," to follow. The following *eisēlthen*, "entered," probably induced Luke to syncopate the formulation.

Simon. He is mentioned here for the first time as one having a house in Capernaum. The phrase, "the house of Simon," naturally suggests that Simon is the owner of it. See NOTE on 5:3. This detail has come to Luke from Mark 1:29, but it seems to conflict with John 1:43, which speaks of Bethsaida as "the town of Andrew and Peter." The two evangelists could, of course, mean different things: John could be speaking of the birthplace of Peter and Andrew, whereas Mark (and Luke) would mean the place where Simon Peter later resided.

The Greek name *Simōn* was used as a common equivalent of Greek *Symeōn* = Hebrew *Šimě'ôn* (see NOTE on 2:25). The latter Greek form is used of Simon Peter in Acts 15:15 (on the problem of this usage, see *JBC*, art. 46, § 33). Luke will allude to the change of name from Simon to Peter in 6:14. On the frequency of the use of this name among Jews of first-century Palestine, see *ESBNT*, 105-112. Note that Matt 8:14 has altered the text to "Peter's house."

Luke further uses the name *Simōn* for the leader of the disciples in 5:3,4,5,10; 22:31; 24:34. The double name *Simōn Petros* occurs only in 5:8; but "Simon" named/called "Peter" is used in 6:14; Acts 10:5,18,32; 11:13. "Peter" alone occurs in 8:45,51; 9:20,28,32,33; 12:41; 18:28; 22:34, 54,55,58,60,61—and often in Acts 1-15 (fifty-six times in all). Luke never uses the Aramaic name *Kēphas*, "Cephas." See further the COMMENT on 5:1-11.

mother-in-law. That Simon Peter was married is clear from 1 Cor 9:5. The

Lucan text seems to suggest that Simon's mother-in-law was actually living in Simon's house, or at least was visiting there. It is scarcely likely that she was the real owner of the house, which was being visited by Simon, in view of the phrase, "the house of Simon," discussed in the previous NOTE.

suffering from a very high fever. Whereas Mark 1:30 describes the mother-in-law as "lying abed feverish" (*katekeito pyressousa*), Luke describes her as (lit.) "seized/tormented by a great fever" (*synechomenē pyretō megalō*). In discussing this phrase, W. K. Hobart, *The Medical Language of St. Luke* (Dublin: Hoges, Figgs & Co., 1882) 3-5, compared Acts 28:8 and various medical writers who used *synechomenos* of seizures and cited in particular Galen *De differentiis febrium* 1:1, "It is a custom for physicians in this sort of difference [of heat] to speak of high and low fever" (*ton megan te kai mikron pyreton*). Hobart wanted to show from such allegedly medical language that the author was the traditional Luke, "the beloved physician" (Col 1:14). H. J. Cadbury disposed of that general thesis (see p. 52 above) and in particular of this argument about fevers in *JBL* 45 (1926) 190-209, esp. pp. 194-195, 203, 207n. He pointed out that Galen actually goes on to object to that customary usage among physicians.

Luke probably uses "a great fever" here because he wants his readers to understand that it will take a powerful deed of Jesus to cure it.

they asked him about her. The plural subject is unexplained; in the Lucan story it would have to be understood of members of Simon's household. But in the Marcan form it could be understood of the four disciples, who "reported" to him about her. Luke avoids the Marcan historical present, *legousin.*

39. *stood over her.* Luke again uses the verb *ephistanai* (see NOTE on 2:9). Mark has, "he came to her and raised her up."

commanded the fever. See NOTES on 4:33,35. The verb *epetimēsen* is not used by Mark; it is introduced as a catchword bond with vv. 35,41. The three episodes, thus linked, depict Jesus making use of the commanding word of salvation and deliverance.

Immediately. See NOTE on *parachrēma*, 1:64. It is introduced here to show that her cure was not gradual, and her service stresses its wondrous character.

began to serve them. Or "kept serving them." Luke uses the impf. tense of *diakonein*, which like the English "serve" is ambiguous; it could mean, when used absolutely, to serve table or serve in a more generic sense.

BIBLIOGRAPHY (4:38-39)

Busse, U. *Die Wunder des Propheten Jesus* (Forschung zur Bibel 24; Stuttgart: Katholisches Bibelwerk, 1977) 66-90.

Dietrich, W. *Das Petrusbild der lukanischen Schriften* (BWANT 94; Stuttgart: Kohlhammer, 1972) 19-23.

Kertelge, K. *Die Wunder Jesu*, 60-62.

Lamarche, P. "La guérison de la belle-mère de Pierre et le genre littéraire des évangiles," *NRT* 87 (1965) 515-526.

Léon-Dufour, X. "La guérison de la belle-mère de Simon-Pierre," *EstBíb* 24 (1965) 193-216; reprinted in *Etudes d'Evangile* (Paris: Seuil, 1965) 123-148.

Pesch, R. "Die Heilung der Schwiegermutter des Simon-Petrus: Ein Beispiel heutiger Synoptikerexegese," *Neuere Exegese—Verlust oder Gewinn?* (Freiburg im B.: Herder, 1968) 143-175.

Sanders, E. P. "Priorités et dépendances dans la tradition synoptique," *RSR* 60 (1972) 519-540.

Schenke, L. *Die Wundererzählungen des Markusevangeliums* (Stuttgart: Katholisches Bibelwerk, 1974) 109-129.

20. EVENING CURES
(4:40-41)

4 ⁴⁰ As the sun was setting, all the people who had (relatives) sick with one disease or another brought them to him. He would lay his hands on each one of them and cure them. ⁴¹ Demons too would come out of many of them, shouting, "You are the Son of God." But he would charge them and forbid them to speak, since they knew that he was the Messiah.

COMMENT

Inspired by the Marcan summary report (Mark 1:32-34) of cures and exorcisms wrought by Jesus at evening, Luke composes his third Capernaum scene in a similar way (4:40-41). It too has the nature of summary, like 4:14-15, 31-32. In this case it is more clearly his own composition.

Bultmann (*HST,* 341) ascribed the Marcan verses to the evangelist's "editorial formulation." The clearly summary tone of them is expressed by the initial main verb, in the imperfect (to stress continuous activity). Luke makes use of this same device, but even multiplies the impf. verbs in his summary (*etherapeuen, exērcheto, ouk eia*), translated with "would" in my rendering of the verses, in an effort to capture the proper nuance.

The reworking of the Marcan summary is such that one hesitates to call it merely redactional modification. The main differences that Luke has introduced are the following: (1) He has simplified the temporal expressions at the outset (v. 40; cf. Mark 1:32). (2) He has separated the reports of cures from those of exorcisms. (3) For the sake of plausibility he has omitted the detail about the gathering of "the whole city" at the gate (cf. Mark 1:33). (4) He has introduced the healing gesture of the laying on of hands and the exorcistic charge. (5) He has supplied the titles by which the demons recognize Jesus. But Luke knows nothing of the quotation from Isa 53:4,11, with which Matthew ends his form of the inherited summary (8:17); that is one of the characteristically Matthean formula quotations.

The meaning of the Lucan summary is simple. It again presents Jesus as healer and exorcist, this time allowing the demons to recognize him as the Son of God and the Messiah. These titles, joined to the one used earlier in Capernaum, "the Holy One of God" (4:34), stress Jesus' nearness to God (Yahweh) in his role in salvation-history.

NOTES

4 40. *As the sun was setting.* Thus Luke simplifies the cumbersome Marcan double expression about the time of day, "as it became evening, when the sun had set" (1:32). Instead, Luke makes use of a simple genitive absolute, *dynontos de tou hēliou,* "and (while) the sun (was) setting." Matthew uses one too (8:16), but retains the initial Marcan gen. absol. Nothing in these phrases suggests that the gathering took place on only one occasion.

all the people who had (relatives) sick with one disease or another. Lit. "all who had (relatives [or friends or neighbors]) ailing with various diseases led them to him." Whereas Mark used the impf. *epheron,* "they were bringing," Luke uses the aor. *ēgagon,* "they led." W. R. Farmer (*The Synoptic Problem* [New York: Macmillan, 1964] 128-130) argues that Mark's use of *pherein* (with personal object) is the result of a Hellenistic encroachment of the late verb *pherein* on an older use of *agein.* He uses this to maintain that the Marcan text is later than Luke: "In epitomizing Matthew or in combining Matthew and Luke, Mark . . . allowed his stylistic preference to influence his text" (p. 129). But this use of *pherein* is as old as Homer, and Luke has simply introduced a more proper Greek verb (*agein*). See my article, "The Use of *Agein* and *Pherein* in the Synoptic Gospels," *Festschrift to Honor F. Wilbur Gingrich* (eds. E. H. Barth and R. E. Cocroft; Leiden: Brill, 1972) 147-160. Cf. BGD, 14.

He would lay his hands. The imposition of hands as a gesture of healing is unknown in the OT and in rabbinical literature, but it has turned up in 1Qap-Gen 20.28-29, where Abram prays, lays his hands on the head of the Pharaoh, and exorcises the plague/"evil spirit" afflicting the Pharaoh (and his household) for having carried off Sarai. See NOTES on 4:35,39 above. In comparison, the only ritual element not mentioned in the Lucan account of Jesus' laying on of hands is the prayer—noteworthy by its absence, given the Lucan emphasis on Jesus' prayer elsewhere (see p. 244 above). See further D. Flusser, "Healing through the Laying-On of Hands in a Dead Sea Scroll," *IEJ* 7 (1957) 107-108; A. Dupont-Sommer, "Exorcismes et guérisons dans les écrits de Qumran," *Congress Volume, Oxford 1959* (VTSup 7; Leiden: Brill, 1960) 246-261; my commentary on *The Genesis Apocryphon of Qumran Cave 1* (BibOr 18A; 2d. ed.; Rome: Biblical Institute, 1971) 140-141.

on each one. Luke extends the number treated, as does Matt 8:16 ("all"); Mark 1:34 speaks only of "many."

41. *You are the Son of God.* This recognition-formula is not in the parallels of Mark 1:34 or of Matt 8:16. It stems from Luke's pen, making his summary

more dramatic and concrete. The inspiration for it is found in Mark 1:34b, where Jesus would not allow the demons to speak, "because they knew him." That was part of the messianic secret in the Marcan Gospel. Luke dispenses with it, in general, though he too has a bit of it in the last part of v. 41. The identification of Jesus as "the Son of God" echoes that given in the baptism scene (3:22)—and by hindsight in the infancy narrative (1:32,35). The context here suggests that Luke equates this title with that of "Messiah," even though they are otherwise used independently, given their distinct and discrete OT origins.

he would charge them. Or "command them." The impf. of *epitiman* is used again; see the NOTES on 4:35,39.

he was the Messiah. Or "the Christ." See NOTE on 2:11. The last part of v. 41 is a comment of the evangelist and differs from the title "the Son of God" put on the lips of the demons. This last part is obviously written from the standpoint of the evangelist composing his account several generations after the ministry of Jesus itself.

21. DEPARTURE FROM CAPERNAUM
(4:42-44)

4 ⁴²Once at daybreak Jesus went out and moved on to a deserted spot. But crowds of people came looking for him, and when they caught up with him, they would not permit him to move on from them. ⁴³But he said to them, "I must proclaim the kingdom of God in other towns as well, for that is what I was sent for." ⁴⁴And he went on preaching in the synagogues of Judea.

COMMENT

Luke's fourth Capernaum episode (4:42-44) recounts Jesus' departure from the town. In a sense, it brings to a close the account of the beginnings of the Galilean ministry (4:14-44). Verse 44 hints at a ministry of Jesus in a wider sense, even though he will be based in Galilee.

Though this episode lacks a counterpart in the Matthean Gospel, it is inspired by Mark 1:35-39. Luke, however, has modified it; the main redactional differences are the following: (1) He makes use of a single reference to the time of day (v. 42; cf. Mark 1:35a). (2) He omits the mention of Jesus' prayer in a place of solitude (cf. Mark 1:35b,c). (3) He substitutes "crowds" for the Marcan phrase, "Simon and those with him" (v. 42c; cf. Mark 1:36); this is done partly because he has not yet recounted the call of Simon and other disciples, and partly because he eliminates the reference to "everyone" searching for him (Mark 1:37). (4) He introduces the attempts of people to hinder him from moving on (v. 42d). (5) He substitutes for Jesus' statement a declaration about his mission to preach the kingdom of God (v. 43; cf. Mark 1:38).

This passage is not easy to judge from a form-critical viewpoint. Bultmann (*HST*, 155) classified the Marcan form of Jesus' statement with other "I-Sayings" in the Synoptic tradition, but denied that it is an old piece of tradition, belonging rather to an "editorial section" (1:35-39). V. Taylor (*FGT*, 148-149; cf. p. 39) treats it as a Story about Jesus, the last of four episodes. But one wonders whether it might not be better to think that Luke has cast his version into the form of a Pronouncement Story. Certainly, the first declaration of Jesus in this Gospel about the kingdom of God would seem to call for some such recognition.

The episode is important because of a number of implicit contrasts that it suggests. First, there is the contrast between the daytime activity of Jesus on one occasion and his evening-cures of vv. 40-41. Second, there is the contrast of the people of Capernaum who seek to restrain him from moving on from them with the conduct of those of his hometown, Nazareth, who wanted to do away with him (4:16-30). Third, there is the contrast between the beginnings of his Galilean ministry and the mission in synagogues of Judea (v. 44).

Still more important is the first appearance of Jesus in this Gospel as the kingdom-preacher. So far he has been presented in the Gospel proper as prophet, teacher, healer, exorcist, the heaven-sent Son, the Messiah, and (probably) the Lord's Servant. Now Luke introduces an important aspect of his role: He has been sent as *the* preacher of the kingdom of God. This stands in contrast to the Matthean theologoumenon, according to which John the Baptist is first presented as the kingdom-preacher (3:2; see further p. 154 above). But as this aspect of his role is being introduced, Jesus is not depicted announcing the kingdom of God as imminent; its time-aspect will be treated later. Here that is omitted, and Jesus is portrayed as one constrained to *proclaim* God's kingship over human beings (see H. Conzelmann, *Theology*, 113-119).

The constraint that is expressed in this passage is related to the Lucan notion of salvation-history (see p. 179 above). No effort, however, is made in it to explain what "the kingdom of God" really means. It is taken for granted that the reader will know what it meant.

In contrast to the Marcan episode, on which it depends, Luke introduces the idea of a wider ministry of Jesus: "other towns" in Galilee (see Mark 1:38), but also in Judea (v. 44). Jesus' preaching is to have effect in the country of the Jews (Acts 10:39).

Notes

4 42. *Once at daybreak.* Lit. "(while) it (was) becoming morning." Luke has again simplified the time reference; Mark has "early, (when it was) still quite dark" (*prōi ennycha lian*), for which Luke substitutes a more elegant genitive absolute. Cf. 4:40.

moved on to. Lit. "proceeded toward." The verb is again the Lucan *poreuesthai*, used twice in this verse; see NOTE on 4:30.

a deserted spot. This is not to be interpreted as a part of the wilderness of Judea. Jesus is depicted seeking solitude from the people.

crowds of people. Lit. "the crowds." This is substituted for the Marcan phrase (1:36), "Simon and those with him." See COMMENT, and NOTE on *ochloi*, 3:7.

they would not permit him to move on from them. Lit. "they tried to prevent him from going on his way (*poreuesthai*) from them."

43. *I must proclaim.* Or "I must preach." Luke here uses *euangelizesthai* with a concrete direct object; see NOTES on 1:19 and 3:18 (also p. 148 above). Note the shift to *kēryssein* in v. 44.

Much more important is the impersonal verb *dei*, "it is necessary"; see NOTE on 2:49. He begins a mission from which he will not be diverted.

the kingdom of God. This is the first reference to the kingdom in the Gospel proper. In most cases Luke refers to it in this way (6:20; 7:28; 8:1,10; 9:2,11,27,60,62; 10:9,11; 11:20; 13:18,20,28,29; 14:15; 16:16; 17:20*bis*,21; 18:16,17,24,25,29; 19:11; 21:31; 22:16,18; 23:51). Sometimes, however, he speaks of it merely as "the kingdom" (11:2; 12:31,32; 22:29,30; 23:42). But he never uses the "kingdom of heaven," which Matthew often employs.

The "kingdom" is the prime kerygmatic announcement in the Synoptic tradition, especially in Matthew, where it appears fifty-five times, whereas it occurs in Luke only thirty-eight times, and in Mark fourteen times. John uses it five times. In earlier Pauline literature it is sometimes found, but it is scarcely the operative or dynamic element that it has become in the Synoptic kerygma. In fact, save for a few places (e.g. 1 Cor 15:24; Col 1:13), it is otherwise mostly used in the Pauline corpus in catalogues of vices or similar statements that reflect early Christian catechesis.

Surprisingly, no attempt is made at this first occurrence of the expression in the Lucan Gospel to define what "the kingdom of God" is. But this is equally true of the other Synoptics. Jesus is presented as taking over an OT idea and giving a new emphasis to it in his kerygmatic preaching. See further p. 154 above.

in other towns as well. Luke substitutes *kai tais heterais polesin*, lit. "even the other towns," for the Marcan *eis tas echomenas kōmopoleis*, "to the neighboring market-towns." The difference between the Marcan *kōmopolis* and Lucan *polis* has been explained by G. Schwarz (*NTS* 23 [1976-1977] 344) as different translations of Aramaic *māḥōzā'*, which he claims could mean "market-town," "city," or "country." Perhaps. It seems more likely that Luke has simply substituted a more usual Greek word for a rare Marcan one. *Kōmopolis* is actually a compound of *kōmē*, "village" and *polis*, "town, city." It is used by Strabo, *Geogr.* 12.2,6 and becomes frequent in Byzantine writers (perhaps influenced by Mark).

what I was sent for. Compare Mark 1:38, "for that is why I came forth." The Lucan formulation shifts the emphasis to the Father's plan of salvation-history and relates his kingdom-preaching to a mission to execute that plan. The second aor. pass. *apestalēn*, "I was sent," is another instance of the theological passive, "sent (by God)"; see ZBG § 236.

44. *went on preaching.* Lit. "was preaching," the impf. of the verb "to be" being used to express continuous or progressive action.

in. The preferred reading here is *eis*, lit. "into"; but see NOTE on *eis tēn K.*, 4:23.

Judea. The best mss. (P75, ℵ, B, and minuscules of the Lake Family) and some Syriac versions, read *Ioudaias*. Another group of mss. (A, D, ⊕, and the Koine text-tradition) reads rather *Galilaias*, "Galilee." The latter is an obvious correction to harmonize the text with the thrust of the Lucan story at this point in the Gospel. But "Judea" is to be retained as the *lectio difficilior*. However, it should most probably not be understood as the specific area of Palestine (in contrast to Galilee), but rather in the comprehensive sense of all the country of the Jews, a sense that it sometimes has elsewhere (1:5; 6:17; 7:17; 23:5; Acts 10:37).

But this phrase creates a problem. When one compares it with Luke 5:17; 6:17; 7:17, one might get the impression prima facie that the geographical sphere is broader than the confines of Galilee; and yet, in those passages, it is more of a question of people coming to Jesus—wherever he was (actually left unspecified)—from "every village of Galilee and Judea, and from Jerusalem" or "from all over Judea, and from Jerusalem" or the reports were made about him "in all Judea." This is again part of Lucan inconsistency. Does he want the reader to conclude that Jesus has left Galilee or not? In 7:1 he will enter Capernaum in Galilee again; in 8:26 he will go to a region "opposite Galilee." It is obvious that Luke is still thinking in general about a Galilean ministry of Jesus, but notes that his influence has reached "the country of the Jews." It is, then, not until 9:51, when Jesus' journey to Jerusalem begins, that we shall see a different specific geographic detail introduced. But at this point in the ministry, before the gathering of disciples and future witnesses will begin, it is immaterial to Luke that his Galilean ministry should be more broadly understood.

22. THE ROLE OF SIMON THE FISHERMAN; THE CATCH OF FISH
(5:1-11)

5 ¹ Once when the crowd was pressing about Jesus, listening to the word of God, and he was standing on the shore of Lake Gennesaret, ² he happened to see two boats moored there, which the fishermen who were washing their nets had just left. ³ He got into one of the boats, which belonged to Simon, and asked him to push off a little from the shore. He sat down in it and taught the crowds of people from the boat. ⁴ When he had finished speaking, he said to Simon, "Put out into deeper water and let down your nets for a haul." ⁵ But Simon answered, "Master, all night long we worked and caught nothing. But if you say so, I shall let down the nets." ⁶ So they did and swept in so great a haul of fish that their nets were beginning to break. ⁷ They waved to their partners in the other boat to come and help them. They too came out and filled both boats till they were almost sinking. ⁸ When Simon Peter saw this, he dropped to his knees before Jesus and said, "Go and leave me, Lord, because I am a sinner." ⁹ Amazement had gripped him and all that were with him over the haul of fish which they had pulled in— ¹⁰ and so it was with James and John too, the sons of Zebedee, Simon's companions. But Jesus said to Simon, "Do not be afraid; from now on you shall be catching human beings." ¹¹ And once they had brought the boats to shore, they left everything and followed him.

COMMENT

The four preceding episodes provided a view of a ministry conducted by Jesus himself. There he appears alone in Galilee, teaching and healing. Yet the last episode (4:42-44) also reveals that his mission as the kingdom-preacher is destined for a wider scope than just Capernaum. In fact, v. 44 suggests that "Judea" in a broad sense is also to be involved. However, Luke now presents Jesus again in Galilee, on the shore of the Lake of Gennesaret (5:1-11), associating to himself Simon, to whom he promises a new career, and being followed by two others as well. This episode and the one following it precede any mention of controversy that Jesus' ministry of teaching and healing eventually evoke; they belong then to the "beginnings" of his (mainly) Galilean ministry. From another viewpoint, this episode telling of the promise made to Simon foreshadows the choosing of the Twelve (6:12-16), of whom Simon will be the leader.

This episode is another Lucan transposition (see p. 71 above), for it is influenced by Mark 1:16-20, even though the Lucan account is largely independent of it. By transposing the scene from its Marcan setting, Luke has eliminated the oft-noted implausibility of the Marcan story about the call of the four disciples—the first thing that Jesus does in that Gospel after his baptism and desert sojourn. In the Lucan context, Jesus has been seen preaching and healing, and Simon (at least) has witnessed one of his mighty deeds (4:38-39). The preceding Lucan scenes thus provide a psychologically plausible setting for the call of Simon the fisherman.

This Lucan episode is scarcely a mere parallel to Mark 1:16-20. Apart from its new setting provided by the transposition, three main things are different: (a) Jesus is not a mere passerby; he preaches from Simon's boat to crowds on the lakeshore (vv. 1-3); (b) Simon lets down his net for a miraculous haul of fish at Jesus' word (vv. 4-9a); (c) Jesus promises *Simon* a new career, which results in his (and two of his companions') abandoning everything to follow Jesus (vv. 9b-11). The whole episode is thus composed by Luke from transposed and redacted Marcan material and other material from Luke's private source ("L").

The episode's setting (vv. 1-3) is inspired by Mark 4:1-2, the introduction to Jesus' sermon in parables in that Gospel: Jesus enters a boat to teach people on the shore. This detail is later omitted by Luke, when he introduces some of the same parables (8:4), a sign that, having borrowed it for the present episode, he does not want to repeat it there. Verse 1, with its characteristic *egeneto de* construction (see NOTE), is clearly of Lucan redaction. On the other hand, the shift from *ploiaria*, "boats" (v. 2, if it is to be read—see NOTE) to *ploiōn/ploiou*, "boat(s)," in v. 3 suggests Marcan influence in the latter (see Mark 4:1). Marcan influence is further seen in vv. 9b-11, where the story rejoins Mark 1:16-20 (especially vv. 17c,19,20). Yet even these parallels have undergone Lucan redactional modification ("Simon's companions," the bringing of the boats to shore). When one separates out such Marcan-inspired material, one has left the story of the miraculous haul of fish (vv. 4-9a).

This story, however, is associated with the call of Simon only in this Gospel. Its similarity to details in John 21:1-11 has often been noted. R. E. Brown (*John, XIII-XXI*, 1090) singles out ten points of similarity between the Lucan and Johannine accounts: (1) disciples who fished all night and caught nothing; (2) Jesus' directive to cast the net(s) for a catch; (3) the directive followed yields an extraordinary haul of fish; (4) its effect on the net(s); (5) Simon Peter reacts to the haul (a clearly Johannine touch makes the Beloved Disciple precede him); (6) Jesus is addressed as "Lord"; (7) other fishermen take part in the haul, but say nothing; (8) the "following" of Jesus occurs at the end (see John 21:19,22); (9) the haul of fish symbolizes a successful missionary endeavor (more explicitly in Luke); (10) the same words used for getting aboard, landing, net, etc. are probably coincidental; but the use of "Simon Peter" (Luke 5:8; John 21:7) is not—it occurs only here in Luke. One might also add: (11) the absence of any mention of Andrew in either account (cf. Mark 1:16).

On the other hand, seven points of dissimilarity have been noted (see A. Plummer, *Gospel,* 147): (1) in John Jesus is not recognized at first; (2) in John Jesus is on shore, not in a boat; (3) in John Simon Peter and the Beloved Disciple are in the same boat; (4) in John Peter leaves the hauling of the fish to others; (5) in John the net is not torn, in Luke it is breaking; (6) in John the fish are caught close to shore and dragged to it; and (7) in John Peter rushes through the water to the Lord, whom he has recently denied; in Luke he begs the Lord to depart from him.

Whereas Plummer concluded to two miracles of a similar sort wrought by Jesus—one to illustrate Simon's call; the other, the recall of the chief apostle—today commentators more rightly regard the Lucan and Johannine scenes as accounts of the same miracle. They represent a piece of the gospel tradition that has come independently to the two evangelists; Luke has made it part of his story of the call of Simon, but John has made it into a story of the appearance of the risen Jesus. G. Klein ("Berufung des Petrus," 34-35) rightly argues that it is scarcely a scene originally derived from Jesus' ministry and secondarily made into a Johannine report of an appearance of the risen Jesus; there are no parallels for this sort of transposition in the gospel tradition, whereas other known cases involve retrojection of post-resurrection scenes into the ministry (e.g. Matt 16:16b-19; cf. R. E. Brown et al. [eds.], *Peter in the New Testament* [New York: Paulist, 1973] 83-101). On the other hand, the Lucan form of the story has little trace of the elements of an appearance-story (see C. H. Dodd, "The Appearances," 22-23). By the time that Luke has inherited the tradition, it is already a simple miracle-story coming to him from "L"; he joins it to the Marcan material and fashions it into a story about the call of Simon. Another reason for thinking that it originally stems from a post-resurrection setting is the reaction of Simon Peter in v. 8, addressing Jesus as "Lord" and regarding himself as a "sinner," a reaction that more plausibly suits one who has denied his Lord. Moreover, v. 8 reveals itself as a suture-verse. Peter's reaction to Jesus after the haul of fish seems strange; one would expect a comment of awe or gratitude toward the wonder-worker rather than a confession of unworthiness. Or, one might expect Peter to defend his ability as a fisherman rather than apologize for his sinfulness. Peter's reaction reflects a guilt-feeling, which is strange in the light of a miracle worked on his behalf, and which would more logically arise from some action or behavior of which he is now ashamed. Nor can it be understood as an expression of shame for having worked all night long and caught nothing. Hence the post-resurrection setting for the original episode again seems plausible. See pp. 87-88 above.

R. Bultmann (*HST*, 28) considered Mark 1:16-20 to be a biographical apophthegm, an ideal scene depicting a sudden summons of disciples from business to a "following." He regarded the scene as one fashioned from an already formulated metaphor, "fishers of men," used of early disciples. Bultmann listed the Lucan story of the catch of fish as a nature miracle (*HST*, 217), an example of how the same metaphor developed into a miracle-story. But, as the story stands now in the Lucan Gospel, this episode has to be regarded form-critically as a pronouncement-story. The "punch line" is v. 10d, "From now on you shall be catching human beings," a Lucan redactional modification of the more original metaphor of Mark 1:17. Verses 4-9a may have been a miracle-story in the pre-Lucan tradition, but he has made it subservient to the pronouncement-story; it is part of the narrative leading up to it. The commission to Simon was not originally part of the miracle-story, as I see it (*pace* Klein et al.). The pronouncement takes the form of a promise addressed to Simon alone (in the second sg.), introduced by the characteristic Lucan phrase, "from now on" (see NOTE). Though "do not be afraid" might seem like a saying more suited to an appearance-story (see Matt 28:5, 10), it is used frequently enough by Luke (see NOTE on 5:10) in different contexts to show that it is derived from Luke's redactional work.

One has to admit that the more original Marcan story of the call of four disciples is somewhat idealistic; but it is going too far to ascribe the call of Simon (and other disciples) solely to a post-resurrectional context. This will be discussed again apropos of 6:12-16. Again, the association of a miracle-story with the call of Simon, such as Luke has here composed, heightens the idealistic character of the scene. But this is not sufficient to question the basic historicity of a call of Simon by the historical Jesus during his ministry. Despite attempts to prove the contrary, the tradition of Peter as the first-called is not simply an extension of the tradition about him as the first witness of the risen Christ (1 Cor 15:5; cf. Luke 24:34). (The Greek tradition about Andrew as *prōtoklētos*, "first-called," is dependent on John 1:40-42.)

However, much more important than the question of the historicity of the call is the meaning of this scene in the Lucan Gospel. As Luke has presented it, Simon is brought personally into the sphere of Jesus' mighty power, and that experience becomes the basis of a promise that is made to him. Though Simon, conscious of his utter sinfulness and unworthiness to associate with such a person as Jesus, drops to his knees in reaction, he is reassured by the latter, who promises him that he will play a role of gathering human beings into the kingdom that Jesus has come to preach.

This he will do much as a fisher gathers in fish in a net. He has been singled out as the first Galilean to witness Jesus' miraculous power (4:38; 5:6); now he is promised a role that will gradually take more definite shape as the story in the Gospel and Acts develops. The miracle-story (vv. 4-9a) which has been associated with the call of Simon enhances the promise made to him; it is a symbol of the success that will attend his fishing for the kingdom. But Simon is not alone. Though he is the first-called, others "leave everything" to follow Jesus too (5:10a-c,11b), but the promise is not made to them, as it is in Mark. Thus the promise made to Simon in the second singular foreshadows the leadership role that he will have in the Lucan story to follow (see 6:14, where his name heads the list of the Twelve). As the first-called, he will be the first to witness to the risen Christ (24:34; cf. Acts 2:14-40).

The Lucan redaction of this scene has also reformulated the saying of Jesus to Simon. In Mark 1:17 Jesus says, "Come along with me, and I shall make you fishers of human beings" (lit. "Come after me, and I shall make you become fishers . . ."). It has often been noted how strange a metaphor is used—indeed, it is "inappropriate if the mission of the disciples is thought of as rescuing men or bringing them to salvation" (C. W. F. Smith, HTR 52 [1959] 187). For what fishermen do to fish is not salutary. That metaphor has often been contrasted with that of the shepherd in Mark 6:34, one that suggests concern, care, and love. Perhaps this is the reason for the Lucan reformulation of the promise, "From now on you shall be catching human beings" (lit. "you shall be taking them alive" [esē zōgrōn]). The implication is that they shall be saved from death and preserved for life, as they are gathered to become followers in the kingdom (see L. Grollenberg, TvT 5 [1965] 330-336). Thus Simon is to become "from now on" a leading missionary in the cause of Jesus.

Does the episode have "an obvious apologetic motive" (R. Leaney, ExpTim 65 [1953-1954] 381), i.e. do Simon's words in v. 8 and Jesus' reply in v. 10 explain to Gentile Christian readers and others on the fringe of the early community the failings of the most famous of the disciples? Perhaps, but if one recognizes the more original setting for Peter's words in v. 8, as suggested above, the apologetic character of this episode may be questioned.

More significant, however, is H. Conzelmann's suggestion (Theology, 42) that this scene serves as a foil to the Nazareth episode (4:16-30). Both are Lucan transpositions and create a literary contrast: the criticism and rejection of Jesus by his own townspeople now yields to the genuine and personal following of Simon and his companions. To respond as a disciple is to follow him on his way—a following which will involve the "catching alive" of other human beings for the kingdom.

Because Jesus is now depicted associating to himself followers who will share in his ministry, some commentators have seen an ecclesiological concern emerging in this episode (e.g. H. Schürmann, *Lukasevangelium,* 264; J. Ernst, *Evangelium nach Lukas,* 185); indeed, G. Schneider thinks that 5:1 - 6:49 must be read in this sense (*Evangelium nach Lukas,* 120). Is this really intended by Luke? It may have some basis, if one tolerates the allegorization of some details of the story. Because Jesus is here portrayed teaching "the word of God" to the crowds from the boat which belonged to Simon, is Luke suggesting that Jesus' real message comes through "the bark of Peter"? This became an image and a mode of interpretation dear to commentators of later centuries; but to read all of that into this episode seems to make more of it than what Luke really intended.

Though Simon Peter has been introduced earlier in the Lucan story (4:38), this episode begins to reveal the esteem that Luke has for him— an esteem inherited, to be sure, from the early community before him. This is the beginning of the special story that Luke will tell about Simon in his own narrative account. Luke has derived from "Mk" the story of Simon's call (5:3,10), his first place among the Twelve (6:14), his role as a spokesman for the disciples (9:20,33; 18:28), his close association with Jesus, along with James and John (8:51; 9:28), and his denial of Jesus (22:33-34,54b-60). But Luke has also omitted some of the less flattering details in "Mk": Jesus' rebuke of him (Mark 8:32-33), Jesus' reproach of the sleeping Peter (Mark 14:37); Peter's running to the tomb (24:12). (Mark 16:7 is omitted because Luke 24 is centered about Jerusalem.) But some of the special material in the Lucan Gospel is derived from the special source "L": his role here in the miraculous haul of fish (5:4-8); Jesus' prayer for Simon (22:31-32); and the notice about an appearance of the risen Christ to him (24:34). There was apparently nothing in the "Q" source about Simon; and Lucan redaction is probably responsible for the appearance of his name in 12:41; 22:8,61. The different names that Luke uses for this disciple have been mentioned in the NOTE on 4:38. They are scarcely determined by the sources that he has used. But Luke is consistent at least in calling him "Simon" prior to 6:14, where he mentions Jesus' naming of him as Peter. For further treatment of Simon Peter in Luke Acts, see Brown et al. (eds.), *Peter in the New Testament,* 39-56, 109-28; W. Dietrich, *Das Petrusbild der lukanischen Schriften* (BWANT 94; Stuttgart: Kohlhammer, 1972).

NOTES

5 1-2. *Once . . . he happened to see.* Lit. "and it happened, as the crowd pressed about him . . . , and he was standing . . . , that he saw. . . ." Luke here uses the *egeneto de* construction with the conj. *kai* + a finite verb, *eiden* (see p. 119 above); there are also two articular infinitives to express time and the unstressed use of *kai autos* (see p. 120 above).

1. *listening*. The infin. *akouein* is actually coordinate with the first one, *epikeisthai*, "was pressing." Some mss. (C, D, ☉, the Koine text-tradition), however, substitute the def. art. *tou* for the conj. *kai*, which makes of *akouein* an infin. of purpose, "in order to listen to the word of God."

the word of God. This is the first occurrence of this phrase, *ho logos tou theou*, in the Lucan Gospel. It is almost peculiarly Lucan in the NT, occurring but once in Mark (7:13) and in John (10:35), and probably only once in Matthew (15:6, but with a variant *nomos*, "law," in some mss.). Luke, however, uses it four times in the Gospel (5:1; 8:11,21; 11:28) and fourteen times in Acts (4:31; 6:2,7; 8:14; 11:1; 12:24(?); 13:5,7,44,46,48; 16:32; 17:13; 18:11). In most of the instances in Acts the phrase denotes the Christian message as preached by the apostles; here Luke uses it of Jesus' own preaching. Thus he roots the Christian community's proclamation in the teaching of Jesus himself. But, as the phrase suggests, the ultimate root of this preaching/teaching is God himself, for the phrase means "God's word" or "the word coming from God" (a subjective genitive or genitive of author) rather than "the word telling about God" (objective genitive). Though these verses are Marcan-inspired, the phrase does not appear in Mark 4:1. See further J. Dupont, " 'Parole de Dieu' et 'parole du Seigneur,' " *RB* 62 (1955) 47-49.

Jesus' preaching of the word of God to the crowds that press about him has little to do with the coming miracle; but it does explain his activity as a kingdom-preacher and prepares for the function to which Simon is to be called.

on the shore of Lake Gennesaret. Lit. "standing alongside the Lake G." According to 4:42 Jesus was preaching in the synagogues of "Judea" (see NOTE there). Luke has derived this geographical notice from Mark 4:1, "began to teach beside the sea" (i.e. of Gennesaret, not far from Capernaum [see Mark 2:1; 3:19b]). That this localization was part of the miracle-story incorporated in vv. 4-9a is not impossible. But that the lake lies, for Luke, somewhere in "Judea" (so Schneider, *Evangelium nach Lukas*, 123-124) is far from clear. To make the text-critical problem of 4:44 dominate all the geographical notices in Luke is to make the tail wag the dog; it is better to reckon with Lucan inconsistencies. Here he is thinking, because of his dependence on Mark, of a Galilean area. Moreover, vv. 42-44 were a Lucan summary, introduced at the end of the Capernaum ministry, but this episode is to be understood as the sequel to that in vv. 40-41.

Gennesaret is the Greek name of a small, fertile, and heavily populated district west of the lake that some writers refer to as the Sea of Galilee; it lay south of Capernaum. From the district the name was extended to the lake. Other evangelists refer to it as a "sea" (*thalassa*—the term used of it also in the LXX of Num 34:11; Josh 12:3). Luke uses the more proper name, "lake" (*limnē*), which is also used by Josephus *Ant*. 18.2,1 § 28). In this instance, Luke's knowledge of Palestinian geography is scarcely deficient. See Conzelmann (*Theology*, 42) for another, less attractive, way of explaining it.

Only here in the Lucan Gospel does Jesus teach from the lakeside; cf. Mark 2:13; 3:7; 4:1-2. Conzelmann (ibid.) thinks that for Luke the lake features as more a "theological" than a geographical designation, the place of manifestations showing Jesus' power. Perhaps.

2. *two boats.* The best mss. of the Gospel use *dyo ploia* (P⁷⁵, ℵ, Cᶜ, D, Θ and the Koine text-tradition); but mss. A, C* read *dyo ploiaria.* The latter has been defended as the *lectio difficilior* and less suspect of harmonization with v. 3, which has *ploiōn* and *ploiou,* dependent on Mark 4:1. Cf. John 21:8. *Ploiarion* would mean "a little boat."

In mentioning "two boats," Luke consciously prepares for the miracle in v. 6 and the summoning of the second boat in v. 7.

the fishermen. The plural is influenced by Mark 1:16, which identifies both Andrew and Simon as such (*haleeis*). Luke never mentions Andrew, but the pl. verbs in vv. 4,6,7,9 imply that someone else is present in the boat with Simon and Jesus—again, a remnant from the Marcan parallel.

washing their nets. So Luke modifies a detail from Mark 1:19, "repairing the nets." For information on the historical background of Palestinian fishing, see E. F. F. Bishop, "Jesus and the Lake," *CBQ* 13 (1951) 398-414; W. H. Wuellner, *The Meaning,* 26-63.

3. *which belonged to Simon.* Lit. "which was of Simon." For the possessive genitive, see 4:38. Both here and in vv. 4,5 he is called simply *Simōn,* but in v. 8 the double name *Simōn Petros* is used, undoubtedly from the "L" source. The choice of Simon's boat gives prominence to him who is to play the leader's role in the group of disciples that Jesus will form.

He sat down. The natural position of a companion in a small boat may be all that is implied. But then the position of a seated teacher may also be suggested (see 4:20).

and taught. The Lucan emphasis on Jesus' activity as a teacher continues; see NOTE on 4:15. The recurrence of the motif here serves to link this episode with the last two verses of the preceding one (4:43-44); it supplies a kingdom-preaching context for the promise to be made to Simon. For attempts to allegorize Jesus' teaching from Peter's boat (=the church), see K. Zillessen, *ZNW* 57 (1966) 137-139; E. Hilgert, *The Ship and Related Symbols in the New Testament* (Assen: Van Gorcum, 1962) 105-110.

the crowds of people. See NOTE on *ochloi* in 3:7.

4. *let down your nets.* The verb *chalasate* is in the second pl., whereas the preceding impv. is sg., *epanagage,* "put out." *Pace* Plummer (*The Gospel,* 144), even though Jesus at first gives the command to Simon alone, someone else is implied to be in the boat with him, as the work on the heavy dragnet would also suggest. However, one cannot immmediately conclude that it is Andrew, since the account in this verse now comes from the non-Marcan "L" source; Andrew is not mentioned in John 21:1-11 either.

5. *Master.* Luke uses here for the first time *epistata,* the voc. of *epistatēs;* see further 8:24,45; 9:33,49; 17:13. Only Luke uses it, whereas the Synoptic parallels have either *didaskale,* "Teacher," or *rabbi,* "Rabbi." As a title used in Greek literature or inscriptions, *epistatēs* often had a wider connotation, "commander, administrator, supervisor" (e.g. in the training of youth). In the Lucan writings it is used of Jesus only by followers or disciples, whereas *didaskalos* is used by non-disciples. As in 8:24; 17:13, *epistata* suits better the context of the miracle to be wrought. See O. Glombitza, "Die Titel *didaskalos* und *epistatēs* für Jesus bei Lukas," *ZNW* 49 (1958) 275-278.

if you say so. Lit. "at your word." Despite the frustration of the night-long toil, Simon's willingness to follow Jesus' suggestion prepares for the miracle. The following sg. verb again singles out Simon's activity.

6. *swept in so great a haul of fish.* Both the ptc. *poiēsantes,* lit. "doing (this)," and the finite verb *synekleisan* are pl., referring to Simon and some unmentioned companion. The huge catch of fish is obviously meant as something extraordinary, manifesting Jesus' power in preparation for the promise to be made to Simon. It is achieved in response to a willing acceptance of a directive from Jesus.

their nets were beginning to break. Lit. "were breaking," the impf. *dierrēseto* is here used like *emellen* + infin., "were about to break" (BDF § 323.4). They did not break actually, because the fishermen were still able to fill two boats with fish. Cf. John 21:11, the net "did not break," despite the Johannine haul of 153 fish.

7. *They waved.* Again the pl. verb is to be noted; it scarcely means Simon and Jesus. See NOTE on v. 4 above.

to their partners. In the miracle-story of vv. 4-9a the technical term for partners (*metochoi*) is used; contrast the more generic "companions" (*koinōnoi*) of v. 10, where the Marcan story is resumed. For the technical use, see Wuellner, *The Meaning,* 23-24.

to come and help them. Luke uses here the articular infin., with a circumstantial ptc., *tou elthontas syllabesthai autois,* to express purpose, after the verb, "they waved." See 4:10; 17:1; Acts 3:12; 15:20; 21:12 (ZBG § 386). The summoning of help underscores the greatness of the miracle and the power of Jesus' word.

till they were almost sinking. Lit. "so that they were sinking"; the pres. infin. with *hōste* is in a result cl. marking tendency, not actual effect (see BDF § 338.1; ZBG § 274). The ms. D adds *para ti,* "almost," to make the tendency clear (see BDF § 236.4).

8. *Simon Peter.* Some mss. (D, W, the Freer family of minuscules) and some ancient versions (OL, OS) omit *Petros;* this is clearly a case of scribal harmonization with vv. 3,5. On the double name, see NOTE on 4:38; it reflects the tradition inherited from "L." The use of *Simōn* alone in v. 5 is constant in the mss. and is probably the result of Lucan redaction. Cf. John 21:7.

dropped to his knees before Jesus. Lit. "fell at the knees of Jesus." Some mss. (D, 579, the Lake family of minuscules) read *posin,* "feet," instead of *gonasin,* "knees," in an attempt to remove the awkwardness of the picture. Leaney (*ExpTim* 65 [1953-1954] 382) suggests that Greek *Iēsou* may be dative, not genitive, and reflect the Hebrew expression, *kāra' 'al birkayim lĕ-* (or *lipnê*), "he fell upon (his) knees to (or before). . . ." That is to read too much into Luke's cryptic expression.

Go and leave me, Lord, for I am a sinner. Lit. "go forth from me," not in the sense of, "Get out of the boat," but rather, "Leave my vicinity." Simon's reaction to the power shown in the miraculous haul of fish relates Jesus to a realm or sphere to which he himself does not belong. He is *anēr hamartōlos,* "a sinful man." His reaction is similar to that of Isaiah (6:5). Simon's self-description is not to be proleptically understood of his coming defection

(22:54-60). See the COMMENT on the suture-problem of the two sources joined here.

Lord. Simon, the sinner, kneels before his "Lord," using the title that is normally reserved for the risen Christ (see p. 200 above). Here it is found in the Greek text in an unemphatic final position, a form of polite address. It reflects again the more original setting of the miracle-story itself (see COMMENT). It is retained here because of the evangelist's hindsight, as he writes from Stage III of the gospel tradition.

9. *Amazement had gripped him.* Lit. "enveloped or enshrouded him," a distinctly Lucan expression (see 4:36; Acts 3:10). But it may have been part of the miracle-story that Luke inherited. We cannot be certain in this part of v. 9.

and all that were with him. Ms. D omits this phrase; see NOTE on v. 4 above. This phrase and the one that follows read awkwardly in the Greek text and may have been added to the inherited miracle-story.

10. *James and John too.* Luke makes the sons of Zebedee (a detail derived from Mark 1:19) share the reaction of Simon. The two will appear again in Luke 6:14; 8:51; 9:28,54; Acts 1:13; 12:2.

Simon's companions. This is a Lucan identification, added to join the miracle-story to the resumed Marcan-derived call of Simon. On "companions," see NOTE on v. 7 above.

Do not be afraid. The negative impv., *mē phobou*, though not exclusively Lucan, is used frequently in his writings (1:13,30; 8:50; 12:32; Acts 18:9; 27:24). It seems to be a strange comment in its present context, in which Simon has just expressed his sinfulness and his reaction of amazement has been noted. The phrase is often at home in an epiphany scene (e.g. 1:13,30; Acts 18:9; 27:24), and is perhaps used here by Luke to mark the revelatory character of the miracle just performed. On the other hand, it may well be a remnant from the more original post-resurrectional miracle-story, which Luke has moved to this part of his story. See COMMENT.

from now on. The phrase *apo tou nyn* is exclusively Lucan; see NOTE on 1:48. F. Rehkopf (*Die lukanische Sonderquelle,* 92) tries to label it as pre-Lucan within the Synoptic tradition; but its occurrence in Acts 18:6 argues rather that it is Lucan.

The phrase changes the sense of the call as it appears in Mark 1:17, introducing a note of immediacy that is not present there. It obviously enhances the role of Simon, who as of now is to be associated with Jesus' own ministry, even if the Lucan promise omits the impv., "come after me." L. Brun (*SymOs* 11 [1932] 48) thinks this anticipation of Simon's role actually contradicts the call of the Twelve in 6:14; but that is to press the meaning of the phrase too much. It is being used here in a proleptic sense, as in 12:52 and 22:69 (see Klein, "Die Berufung des Petrus," 13).

you shall be catching human beings. Lit. "taking human beings alive." The ptc. *zōgrōn* is a combination of *zōos,* "alive" + *agrein,* "catch, hunt." Jesus' words are addressed to Simon alone, in the second sg. In the manner of a fisherman, Simon will gather in human beings for God's kingdom (see further the COMMENT). *Pace* J. Mánek, *NovT* 2 (1957) 138-141, the metaphor used here is not to be explained in terms of old cosmological myths depicting the waters of chaos as an enemy to be subdued; there is not a hint of that in the Lucan text. Nor should one think that Simon as a fisherman will draw human beings out of the dark sea in which they live and into a new world; this not only allegorizes the figure too much, but carries the nuance of misfortune in that fish usually do not survive out of water. The metaphor is rather to be explained on a superficial level of gathering in. It is similar to the OT use of it: "Look, I am sending for many fishers, says Yahweh, and they shall catch them" (Jer 16:16; cf. Amos 4:2; Hab 1:14-15). The nuance of eschatological judgment may be more prominent in the OT passages, but one cannot exclude such a nuance in the NT idea. Cf. 1QH 5:7-9, where the Teacher of Righteousness similarly refers to the gathering of strict observers of the Torah in a context of judgment.

The metaphor of the fisherman catching human beings for the kingdom implies a role of agency, linked to the ministry of Jesus himself. It does not, however, immediately imply discipleship, at least in the Lucan form of the call. As Smith (*HTR* 52 [1959] 197) points out, this role to which Simon is being commissioned by Jesus is not to be interpreted "of all Christians." It is rather used to express a Petrine function.

11. *brought the boats to shore.* The verb *katagein* is exclusively Lucan, appearing only here in the Gospel; but see Acts 9:30; 22:30; 23:15,20,28; 27:3; 28:12. Luke has composed this first part of the verse to join the Marcan material to that of the miracle-story from "L."

left everything. Luke derives from Mark 1:18 the ptc. *aphentes,* where it was used to denote the disciples' "leaving" their nets. Cf. Mark 1:20. In typical fashion, Luke modifies this, making the three of them "leave everything" (*panta*). See NOTES on 3:16; 4:15. Cf. Luke 18:28.

and followed him. Again, a detail is derived from Mark 1:18. This is the first occurrence of *akolouthein* in the Lucan Gospel, where it often will be used of Christian discipleship (5:27-28; 9:23,49,57,59,61; 18:22,28). Josephus (*Ant.* 8.13,8 § 354) uses it of Elisha as a disciple of Elijah (cf. 1 Kgs 19:21 LXX). Cf. CD 4:19; 19:32. In later rabbinical literature "following" (*hālak 'aḥărê,* "walk after") is often used of the relationship of disciples to rabbis (sometimes following on foot a rabbi who rode on an ass). There is, however, a further nuance in the NT use of *akolouthein,* for it occurs in the four Gospels in the sense of "self-commitment . . . which breaks all other ties" (G. Kittel, *TDNT* 1. 213). The disciple may do what the pupil of the rabbi did in an external way, but implied is an internal attachment and commitment to Jesus and the cause that he preaches. In the Lucan writings it takes on a still further nuance because of the geographical perspective into which it fits (see p. 242 above); cf. T. Aerts, "A la suite de Jésus: Le verbe *akolouthein* dans la tradition synoptique," ALBO 4/37 (1967) 1-71.

Bibliography (5:1-11)

Agnew, F. "Vocatio primorum discipulorum in traditione synoptica," *VD* 46 (1968) 129-147.

Betz, O. "Donnersöhne, Menschenfischer und der davidische Messias," *RevQ* 3 (1961-1962) 41-70, esp. pp. 53-56.

Brun, L. "Die Berufung der ersten Jünger Jesu in der evangelischen Tradition," *SymOs* 11 (1932) 35-54.

Delorme, J. "Luc v. 1-11: Analyse structurale et histoire de la rédaction," *NTS* 18 (1971-1972) 331-350.

Dietrich, W. *Das Petrusbild der lukanischen Schriften* (BWANT 94; Stuttgart: Kohlhammer, 1972) 23-81.

Dodd, C. H. "The Appearances of the Risen Christ: An Essay in Form-Criticism of the Gospels," *Studies in the Gospels: Essays in Memory of R. H. Lightfoot* (ed. D. E. Nineham; Oxford: Blackwell, 1957) 9-35; reprinted in his *More New Testament Studies* (Grand Rapids, MI: Eerdmans, 1968) 102-133.

Fuller, R. H. *Interpreting the Miracles* (Philadelphia: Westminster, 1963) 120-123.

Grollenberg, L. "Mensen 'vangen' (Lk. 5,10): Het redden van de dood," *Tijdschrift voor Theologie* 5 (1965) 330-336.

Hengel, M. *Nachfolge und Charisma* (BZNW 34; Berlin: De Gruyter, 1968) 85-87.

Klein, G. "Die Berufung des Petrus," *ZNW* 58 (1967) 1-44.

Leaney, R. "Jesus and Peter: The Call and Post-Resurrection Appearance (Luke v. 1-11 and xxiv. 34)," *ExpTim* 65 (1953-1954) 381-382.

Mánek, J. "Fishers of Men," *NovT* 2 (1957) 138-141.

Matthews, A. J. " 'Depart from Me; for I am a Sinful Man, O Lord' (Luke v. 8)," *ExpTim* 30 (1918-1919) 425.

Pesch, R. "La rédaction lucanienne du logion des pêcheurs d'homme (Lc., V, 10c)," in *L'Evangile de Luc* (ed. F. Neirynck; BETL 32; Gembloux: Duculot, 1973) 225-244.

——— *Der reiche Fischfang: Lk 5,1-11/Jo 21,1-14: Wundergeschichte—Berufungserzählung—Erscheinungsbericht* (Düsseldorf: Patmos, 1969).

Schürmann, H. "La promesse à Simon-Pierre: Lc 5,1-11," *AsSeign* 36 (1974) 63-70.

——— "Die Verheissung an Simon Petrus: Auslegung von Lk 5,1-11," *BibLeb* 5 (1964) 18-24; reprinted in *Ursprung und Gestalt* (Düsseldorf: Patmos, 1970) 268-273.

Smith, C. W. F. "Fishers of Men: Footnotes on a Gospel Figure," *HTR* 52 (1959) 187-203.

Wuellner, W. H. *The Meaning of "Fishers of Men"* (Philadelphia: Westminster, 1967).

23. THE CLEANSING OF A LEPER
(5:12-16)

5 ¹² While Jesus was in one of the towns, a man covered with leprosy happened to be there. Seeing him, he bowed with his face to the ground and begged, "Sir, if you want to, you can make me clean." ¹³ Then Jesus stretched out his hand, touched him, and said, "I want to, indeed; be clean again!" Immediately the leprosy left him. ¹⁴ Jesus instructed him to say nothing to anyone about it. "Go instead and *show* yourself *to the priest*,ᵃ and make an offering for your purification, as Moses prescribed. This will be a proof for them." ¹⁵ Yet so much more did the talk about Jesus spread abroad; many crowds of people gathered to listen to him and to be cured of their illnesses. ¹⁶ But Jesus himself would often retire to deserted places to pray.

ᵃ Lev 13:49

COMMENT

With the story of Jesus' cleansing of a leper (5:12-16) Luke picks up the thread of the Marcan sequence which he had been following in 4:31-44. It was interrupted to accommodate the transposed story about the call of Simon. The cleansing is part of the Synoptic Triple Tradition; the Lucan form of it clearly depends on Mark 1:40-45 and is parallel to Matt 8: 1-4. Because there are some minor agreements of the Matthean and Lucan versions against the Marcan form, some commentators have argued that Luke is dependent here on another form of the story. T. Schramm (*Der Markus-Stoff*, 91-99) argues on the basis of these and other details in Luke that the evangelist knew another form of tradition beyond Mark and was making use of it. But there are other ways of explaining some of these minor agreements; see the NOTES.

In the present Lucan context this episode is only loosely connected with the development of his Gospel. This is evident from the redactional introductory phrase, "in one of the towns" (5:12), added in an attempt to link this scene from Mark to the beginnings of Jesus' Galilean ministry. The episode is a good example of Luke's fidelity to his source; the NOTES will call attention to the many words and phrases in it that are repeated verbatim. But Luke also strives to enliven his account and present it in a more literary fashion than the Marcan source.

The main redactional differences in this episode, in addition to the introductory phrase already mentioned, are the following: (1) in Mark the leper comes to Jesus and falls at his feet (1:40); Luke depicts the leper simply on the scene and falling to the ground at the sight of Jesus (5:12). (2) Luke suppresses the mention of Jesus' emotion in v. 13 (cf. Mark 1:41,43). (3) Luke omits the mention of Jesus sending the leper off (*exebalen*, Mark 1:43). (4) Luke notes the general reaction of the crowds (5:15; cf. Mark 1:45). (5) Luke makes Jesus withdraw to "desert places" in order to pray (5:16; cf. Mark 1:45c).

As the episode stands in the Lucan Gospel, it is a simple miracle-story of healing (so R. Bultmann, *HST,* 212, 240; likewise V. Taylor, *FGT,* 122); but M. Dibelius (*FTG,* 11) strangely lists it as a "tale" (*Novelle*), which is certainly wrong. According to Bultmann, it is a tradition derived from the Palestinian early Christian community. Taylor also calls attention to its perfect form as a miracle-story.

The episode concentrates on the miracle that Jesus performs on behalf of a poor social outcast of a Palestinian Jewish town. On his behalf Jesus uses the power which the Lucan Gospel has already attributed to him (4:14). In contrast to Mark, Luke eliminates the mention of Jesus' emotion ("moved with pity," 1:41; "sternly charged him," 1:43). The result is that all the emphasis in the Lucan form of the story lies on Jesus' will. He does touch the leper, but his all-powerful word gives utterance to an act of his will. The omission of the mention of Jesus' human emotions probably results from a developing christological awareness in the early community, by the time Luke writes. Herein lies the emphasis, but there is more. For Jesus is depicted complying with the Mosaic regulations about ceremonial defilement and the removal of it. This compliance is derived from the Marcan source, but it also fits into Luke's own peculiar emphasis on the continuity of the Christian community with its Mosaic roots. This emerges more clearly in Acts, but there is a trace of it here. The Lucan form of the story stresses too the effect that such a cleansing has on the people, who flock to Jesus. And, in typically Lucan fashion, he unites to the powerful deed wrought by Jesus' willing the notice of Jesus' withdrawal from the notoriety of it all to desert places in order to pray, to commune with his Father.

A variant of this miracle-story is preserved in Papyrus Egerton 2, frag. 1 r, dated ca. A.D. 150. It reads: "[8] And suddenly a leper drew nea[r to him] and said: 'Teacher, Je(su)s, in travelling about [with] le[pers] and eatin[g] with [them], I too became leprous in the inn. If [t]hen [you (really) want to], I am cleansed!' [9] The L(or)d [said to him], '[I] want to (indeed); be cleansed.' [And immediately the lepro[sy l]eft him. ¹⁰ The L(or)d said to him, 'Go your [way, and show yourse]lf to t[he priests . . .]" (see K. Aland, *SQE*, 60; Hennecke-Schneemelcher, *NTApocrypha* 1. 96-97). This variant, however, scarcely represents a tradition independent of the Synoptics; in fact, it is most likely dependent on Luke. See further J. Jeremias, *TBl* 15 (1936) 40-42.

Some commentators have thought that the cleansing depicted in the episode took place by suggestion on Jesus' part (see the comments of V. Taylor, *The Gospel according to St. Mark* [London: Macmillan, 1953] 186). Whether the condition was one of "true leprosy" or a serious inflammatory skin-disease (see NOTE on v. 12), Luke presents Jesus curing the man instantaneously. This, together with the crowds' reaction, achieves the real effect at which the evangelist aims: though Jesus again displays his mighty power on behalf of an unfortunate human being, he yet can retire in solitude to commune with his Father. It thus contributes in its own way to Lucan universalism in salvation (see p. 187 above).

One should read Leviticus 13-14 as background for the understanding of the episode; see further Num 5:2-3; 2 Kgs 7:3-9; 15:5, where one finds the OT reasons for the ostracism of the "leper" from cities, unwalled towns, and general intercourse with other people. This ostracism continued in later rabbinical times (see Str-B, 4/2. 745-763). Needless to say, what is called "leprosy" in the Bible should not be extended to modern "true leprosy" or be used as the basis of any stigma for such as might be afflicted with it—much less the basis of a special missionary activity to such unfortunate persons, simply because "Jesus once touched a leper."

NOTES

5 12. *in one of the towns.* The Marcan parallel takes place in Galilee, even though it contains no designation of a locality. Here Luke adds his redactional introduction, a vague identification, which may mean "in one of the towns" near the Lake of Gennesaret (5:1), as a sequel to the preceding episode. It is farfetched to think that Luke is referring to "Judea" (4:44; so H. Conzelmann, *Theology,* 43). If the latter were meant, it would have to be understood in the broad sense of "the country of the Jews" (see NOTE on 4:44).

a man covered with leprosy. Lit. "a man full of leprosy." In extrabiblical Greek the word *lepra* usually designated something like psoriasis. In the Greek OT it translates Hebrew *ṣāra'at* (e.g. Leviticus 13-14). Some think that the latter may denote there "true leprosy" (Hansen's disease, caused by *mycobacterium leprae*). But it more likely refers to several inflammatory or scaly skin-diseases (e.g. favus, lupus, psoriasis, ringworm, or white spots). The descriptions in Leviticus 13-14 conform much more to the latter than to "true leprosy." Though Hansen's disease was apparently isolated only ca. A.D. 1870, it was known in antiquity, appearing at least in the sixth century B.C. in India (to judge from literary descriptions of it), but known by a different name. But what is known as *ṣāra'at* in the OT was regarded as the cause of ceremonial defilement; persons so afflicted were excluded from normal intercourse with others, having to live often outside of towns (see Exod 4:6; Num 5:2-3; 12:10-12; Deut 24:8; 2 Kgs 5:27; 7:3-9). See further L. Goldman et al., "White Spots in Biblical Times," in *Archives of Dermatology* 93 (1966) 744-753; S. G. Browne, *Leprosy in the Bible* (London: Christian Medical Fellowship, 1970); F. C. Lendrum, "The Name 'Leprosy,'" *American Journal of Tropical Medicine and Hygiene* 1 (1952) 999-1008.

happened to be there. Lit. "and it happened, while he was in one of the towns, that behold a man covered with leprosy (was there)." Luke here uses *kai egeneto* with the conj. *kai* + the interjection *idou;* see p. 119 above. The phrase *kai idou* is used elsewhere (7:37; 11:31; 13:11; 19:2; 23:50; Acts 8:27), often with the sense, "there is, was."

bowed with his face to the ground. Lit. "having fallen upon (his) face." Luke uses a phrase from the LXX, which translates the Hebrew *nāpal 'al pānāyw,* "he fell upon his face" (Gen 17:3,17). The LXX sometimes omits "his," as does Luke here. It is substituted for the Marcan ptc. *gonypetōn,* "kneeling down." It is a gesture of reverence without any necessary religious connotation (see Ruth 2:10; Num 14:5).

Sir. The vocative *kyrie* is absent in Mark, but present in Matt 8:1—a minor agreement of Matthew and Luke against Mark in the Triple Tradition. It is a coincidental addition, that would be called for by the reverential gesture and request of the context. The translation, "Sir," suits the gospel tradition in Stage I; for Luke, writing at Stage III, it may have the connotation of "Lord."

if you want to, you can make me clean. The sentence is borrowed verbatim from Mark 1:40c; cf. Matt 8:2. The words suggest that the afflicted man recognizes something special in Jesus, probably because of his reputation (4:37). He insinuates that Jesus can cure him by an act of his will alone. Recall the OT story of the cure of the leper Naaman by "the prophet of God in Samaria" (2 Kgs 5:3 LXX).

13. *stretched out his hand, touched him, and said.* Lit. "having stretched out the hand, he touched him, saying." The words are identical with Matt 8:3, but both differ from Mark 1:41 in using the pron. *autou,* not as a possessive gen., "his" (hand), but as the obj. of the verb *hēpsato.* Again, a coincidental minor agreement of Matthew and Luke against Mark, because the verb almost demands an object in good Greek.

Both Matthew and Luke also omit the ptc. *splanchnistheis* (Mark 1:41a), "moved with pity" (see COMMENT). Ms. D of Mark reads instead *orgistheis,* "moved with anger," an even stranger emotion for the context. The omission makes the miracle depend on Jesus' power and will, not on his emotions.

Luke does not use here the technical Greek verb for imposing hands; see NOTE on 4:40.

Immediately the leprosy left him. These words are derived from Mark 1:42 with a slight change of word order. They call attention to the instantaneous effect of Jesus' mighty deed. Cf. 4:39. Both Matthew and Luke use the adv. *eutheōs*, instead of the Marcan favorite *euthys*. Luke uses the latter in 6:49 and Acts 10:16 only; otherwise *eutheōs*, in all fifteen times.

14. *to say nothing to anyone about it*. The counsel to keep silent about the cure is derived from Mark 1:44. Luke omits the ptc. *embrimēsamenos*, "sternly charging," and the verb *exebalen*, "sent off." The retention of the counsel is vestigial in the Lucan account, since it has none of the Marcan messianic-secret motif. Later on Luke will omit the mention of the leper's failure to comply. See F. W. Danker, *CTM* 37 (1966) 492-499.

show yourself to the priest. Jesus' words allude to the Mosaic regulation of Lev 13:49 (cf. 14:1-32). A similar instruction will be given to ten lepers in Luke 17:14. The instruction is derived from Mark 1:44 with a slight change of word order. "The priest" (sg.) refers to the one on duty in the Temple at the time.

make an offering. . . . The instruction is again derived from Mark 1:44. For the offering, see Lev 14:4-7 (two living clean birds, cedarwood, scarlet stuff, and hyssop), 10-20 (two male lambs without blemish and one ewe, a cereal offering of three-tenths of an ephah of fine flour mixed with oil, and one measure of oil). Cf. the fragmentary 11QTemple 48:17 - 49:4.

a proof for them. Lit. "for a proof (*or* testimony) to them." This is a difficult phrase, derived from Mark 1:44. Luke has not modified it, probably because he did not understand it either. Part of the difficulty is the pl. *autois*, "to/for them." Does it refer to "the priests" with a transfer of thought from the sg. "priest" mentioned earlier in the verse? Or to "the people" (in general)? A variant reading in ms. D, the Itala, and Marcion has rather *hymein*, "(a proof) for you (pl.)." That just complicates the matter. Part of the difficulty is also the meaning of the noun *martyrion*. Does it mean "proof" (that the leprosy is gone), or "testimony" (that Jesus' power has cured the condition)?

At the end of v. 14 ms. D has a significant addition, quite similar to Mark 1:45: "But he went out and began to talk freely about it, and to spread the news, so that he (Jesus) could no longer openly enter a town, but was out in deserted places; people came to him, and he went back to Capernaum." This is obviously a harmonization of the Lucan account to the Marcan. Conzelmann (*Theology*, 43) sees it as an assimilation of the setting of the story of the paralytic (in the next episode) to the parallel passages and believes that it contradicts Luke's account. This is, however, overdrawn. Even if Luke does not think of Capernaum as Jesus' fixed abode, he does think of Jesus on a tour that does not exclude Galilee.

15. *talk about Jesus spread abroad*. Here Luke omits mention of the leper's disregard of Jesus' instruction (cf. Mark 1:45). He is more concerned to note the publicity of the event and the general reaction to it. This verse echoes the notice of 4:42-43. Cf. 7:17.

crowds. See NOTE on 3:7.

16. *would often retire to deserted places to pray*. Lit. "he was (in the habit of) retiring . . . and praying." Two ptcs. are used with the impf. of the verb "to be" to express iterative action (see BDF § 325, 353). Though Luke

omitted the notice of Jesus' prayer in 4:42 (cf. Mark 1:35), he now introduces it. He depicts Jesus as not interested in the fame that was spreading; he is not fleeing from it, but his detachment relates his activity of teaching and healing to a communing with his heavenly Father.

BIBLIOGRAPHY (5:12-16)

Mussner, F. *Die Wunder Jesu: Eine Hinführung* (Munich: Kösel, 1967) 34-42.

Pesch, R. *Jesu ureigene Taten? Ein Beitrag zur Wunderfrage* (QD 52; Freiburg im B.: Herder, 1970) 98-113.

Schramm, T. *Der Markus-Stoff*, 91-99.

Zimmermann, H. *Neutestamentliche Methodenlehre: Darstellung der historischkritischen Methode* (Stuttgart: Katholisches Bibelwerk, 1967) 237-242.

B. The First Controversies with the Pharisees

Against the background of the enthusiastic reaction of the crowds, the motif of controversy is introduced in the next four episodes

24. THE CURE OF A PARALYZED MAN
(5:17-26)

5 ¹⁷ As he was teaching one day, and Pharisees and teachers of the Law, who had come from every village of Galilee and Judea and from Jerusalem, were sitting around, the power of the Lord happened to be with him that he might heal people. ¹⁸ Then some men came carrying a paralyzed man on a stretcher; they sought to bring him in and lay him before Jesus. ¹⁹ But finding no way to do so on account of the crowd, they went up onto the roof and lowered him on his pallet through the tiles into the midst of the people in front of Jesus. ²⁰ When he saw their faith, he said to the man, "Your sins are forgiven you!" ²¹ Then the Scribes and the Pharisees began to ponder and say, "Who is this who speaks so blasphemously? Who but God alone can forgive sins?" ²² But Jesus perceived their thoughts, spoke up, and said to them, "Why do you ponder over this? ²³ Which is easier to say, 'Your sins are forgiven you,' or 'Get up and walk'?" ²⁴ But to let you know that the Son of Man has authority on earth to forgive sins, he said to the paralyzed man, "I say to you, 'Get up, pick up your pallet, and go home!'" ²⁵ At once the man stood up in front of them, picked up what he was lying on, and went back home, glorifying God. ²⁶ Astonishment gripped all present, and they too glorified God. Filled with deep awe, they commented, "Today we have seen remarkable things."

COMMENT

This passage is the first of a series of controversies that Luke has introduced into his Gospel, deriving them from his Marcan source. Such stories about Jesus' altercations with Scribes and Pharisees have come into the gospel tradition in various groupings. What is presented now is undoubtedly even a pre-Marcan gathering of such material. The series may preserve the early church's recollection of debates that Jesus himself had with leaders of Palestinian Jewry; but even more probably they reflect controversies that early Palestinian Christians had, as their community grew and took shape. It is never easy to say whether the words and replies to Jewish leaders which the evangelists have put on Jesus' lips represent his actual sayings as recalled and used in later controversy or whether later controversies gave rise to sayings attributed to him. The latter is likely and cannot be dismissed; but it may not be the full story. One has to allow for an original tradition and a further shaping of it in the light of later developments.

The first controversy deals with a dispute that arose between Jesus and Pharisees and Scribes about his power to cure and to forgive sins. The setting for the dispute is a miracle that Jesus performs on a paralyzed man who has been brought to him, as he sat teaching (Luke 5:17-26). The story is derived from Mark 2:1-12; a Matthean form of it is found in 9:1-8. Luke's form is dependent solely on the Marcan source; a non-Marcan variant of it need not be postulated as an additional source, *pace* T. Schramm, *Der Markus-Stoff*, 99-103. Luke has, of course, introduced redactional modifications into his form of the story, of which the main ones are the following: (1) he eliminates the geographical reference to Capernaum and Jesus' home there in the introductory verse (5:17; cf. Mark 2:1); (2) he creates a better setting for the miracle in depicting Pharisees and teachers of the Law from all over Galilee, Judea, and even Jerusalem as present from the beginning (5:17b-c; cf. Mark 2:1,6); (3) he calls attention to "the power of the Lord" that was present in Jesus for healing (5:17d); (4) he expands the description of the difficulty that the men had who were carrying in the paralytic (5:18b); (5) he depicts the roof made of tiles (5:19; cf. Mark 2:4); (6) he makes Jesus address the paralytic as "man" (*anthrōpe*, 5:20) instead of "child" (*teknon*, Mark 2:5); (7) he adds "alone" to the Scribes' thoughts about God forgiving sins (5:21c; cf. Mark 2:7); (8) he introduces his favorite adv. *parachrēma*, "at once," to stress the instantaneous character of the cure (5:25a); (9) he intensifies the reaction of the cured man (5:25c) and of "all present" (5:26). Other minor modifications will be mentioned in the NOTES.

In its present Lucan form the episode has to be regarded as a pronouncement-story, with the pronouncement preserved in 5:23, "Which is easier to say, 'Your sins are forgiven you' or 'Get up and walk'?" It also reflects the earlier form in v. 20, "Your sins are forgiven you." But the form-critical analysis of this passage is not easy. On the one hand, this passage is similar to Luke 5:1-11 in that it is conflated, composed of a miracle-story and a pronouncement-story, which has been inserted into the former; so understood, the passage would include a miracle-story (5:17-20a-b,

24c-26 = Mark 2:1-5a,11-12) and the pronouncement-story (5:20c-24ab = Mark 2:5b-10). Cf. R. Bultmann, *HST*, 66. On the other, it is even more complicated because of one verse difficult to interpret, 5:24a-b, preserved almost verbatim from Mark 2:10. (Matthew has also preserved it in 9:6a-b.) Luke changes the word order slightly and avoids the Marcan historical present, *legei*. The verse is problematic because of the shift in the person of the verb, from second pl. ("that you may know") to the third sg. ("he said"). Many commentators, realizing that the first part of v. 24 contains an instance of the title "Son of Man," consider it part of Jesus' comment and introduce an anacoluthon at "he said to the paralytic" (so, e.g. the *RSV, NEB, NAB*). Indeed, this makes the first part of v. 24 the pronouncement of Jesus. The question has been raised whether it is correct to introduce an anacoluthon in v. 24 (Mark 2:10). An alternate way of interpreting the verse is to make of it a comment of the evangelist (or of the pre-Marcan compiler), which is addressed to the readers of the Gospel as "you" (see G. H. Boobyer, *HTR* 47 [1954] 115-120; *NTS* 6 (1959-1960) 225-235; C. P. Ceroke, *CBQ* 22 [1960] 380; C. E. B. Cranfield, *The Gospel according to Saint Mark* [Cambridge: University Press, 1959] 100). This would mean that the Son of Man saying is no longer on the lips of Jesus—a view contrary to a pet thesis of many modern interpreters of the christological titles (cf. Ceroke, ibid., 383-388). It seems to me that this is a better solution to the problematic v. 24; it forms a suture joining the pronouncement-story to the second part of the miracle-story. Such comments to the reader are rare, indeed, in the Synoptic tradition, but not wholly unknown (see Mark 13:14b), and more frequent in the Johannine tradition (e.g. 4:2; 17:3; 19:35; 20:30-31). In such a case, this Lucan passage would then be made up of a miracle-story (5:17-20ab, 24c-26), a pronouncement-story (5:20c-23), and an evangelist's comment (5:24ab). The comment would be explaining the pronouncement of Jesus preserved in v. 23 (or v. 20).

The miracle-story depicts Jesus using the "power of the Lord" (5:17e) to cure a paralyzed man who has been brought to him on a stretcher, lowered by friends through a roof because of the crowd that had gathered to hear his teaching. This expression of their (and his) faith, overcoming physical and material hindrances to bring such an unfortunate into the presence of such power, elicits from Jesus a mighty word of healing, "Get up, pick up your pallet, and go home!" (5:24c). The astonishment at the cure results in the glorification of God for it.

Into this miracle-story a pronouncement-story has been inserted, which relates to it Jesus' power to forgive sins. In fact, it makes of the whole episode a story more concerned with this than with the cure itself. The joining of the two stories gives evidence of a new manifestation of Jesus' power; hitherto he has been depicted curing (4:38-39,40-41; 5:12-16), exorcising (4:31-37), and working a miracle over nature (5:4-9a); now the power of the Lord that attends him is related not only to a cure but also to the forgiveness of sins. Jesus' *dynamis* and *exousia* were linked together in 4:36; here they appear again in the same episode (5:17e,24).

The general sense of the conflated story presents Jesus as the Son of Man, a heaven-sent agent, able to do what people normally ascribe to Yahweh alone (5:21c). The implied equality is heightened in this Lucan form of the episode by the addition of the adj. *monos,* "alone." A new dimension of Jesus' role is thus seen, and a new title is given to him. All of this takes place in the context of his teaching.

The conflation of the miracle-story and the pronouncement-story in this case creates a difficulty, for it links the paralytic condition of the man to sin. It suggests that the former was owing to the latter. We shall meet this sort of thinking again in 13:2; cf. John 5:14; 9:2; Jas 5:15; 1 Cor 11:29-30. In this the NT writers are reflecting a common Palestinian conviction about the relation of sin and suffering inherited from the OT (see Exod 20:5; cf. 1QapGen 20:16-29). There was, however, another OT conviction that sought to correct such impressions (see Jer 31:29-30; Ezek 18:1-4; the Book of Job). Jesus is here depicted reacting to the first of these popular traditions; but it is not the major emphasis in the episode. To concentrate on this relation would be to miss the point of the episode. G. B. Caird (*St Luke*, 94) rightly emphasizes that Jesus' words to the paralytic do not mean that all illness is caused by sin, but he thinks that Jesus has in this case diagnosed the "ailment as psychosomatic (i.e. a physical disease with a mental or emotional cause)," and that "where illness is caused by sin, a cure is proof of forgiveness." Even this may be an anachronistic interpretation of a detail of the story that was not intended to be stressed.

NOTES

5 17. *As he was teaching one day.* Lit. "and it happened on one of the days as he was teaching, and Pharisees and teachers . . . were sitting around, that the power of the Lord was with him." Luke here uses *kai egeneto* with the conj. *kai* + a finite verb *ēn* (in v. 17e); see p. 119 above. Unstressed *kai autos* introduces a circumstantial clause (see p. 120 above). Luke also uses the impf. *ēn* with a pres. ptc. *didaskōn* to depict the continuing progress of his teaching (BDF § 352). It stresses the context of teaching in which the controversy is to take place. Jesus has left the "desert places" (5:11) and is again in the midst of a crowd (v. 19). The phrase, "on one of the days" (*en mia tōn hēmerōn*), resembles that used in 5:12, "in one of the towns" (*en mia tōn poleōn*).

Pharisees. According to Josephus (*Ant.* 18.1,2 § 11), the Pharisees were one of the three "philosophies" among the Palestinian Jews of his day; sometimes he calls them "sects" (*haireseis, Ant.* 13.5,9 § 171; cf. Acts 15:5). Their origin is to be traced to non-priestly interpreters of the Torah in the postexilic period; but they seem to have first emerged as an organized group in the Maccabean period, perhaps shortly before the time of John Hyrcanus (*Ant.* 13.5,9 § 171). The Greek name *Pharisaioi* is probably a transcription of Aramaic *Pěrīšāyē,* "separated ones," undoubtedly used of them by others who differed with them. It may have expressed a certain aloofness and avoidance of dealings with other Jews less observant of the Torah; for Luke's evaluation of them, see Acts 26:5. They advocated a rigorous interpretation of the Mosaic Law, insisting not only on the observance of the written Torah, but also of the oral Torah, i.e. the tradition ascribed to Moses and the elders, which were interpretations of the written Torah propounded since postexilic times. These "Sayings of the Fathers" (cf. Mark 7:3) were intended to be a "fence for the Law," guarding it against violation (*Pirqe 'Abot* 1:1). Influenced by Hellenistic ideas of the value of *paideia,* these interpreters regarded knowledge of the Torah and its prescriptions and prohibitions as the mark and guarantee of piety. To be a holy nation, sacred and dedicated to Yahweh, was a goal of all Jews; but to achieve this by education and knowledge of the Torah was specifically Pharisaic. Meticulous observance of the Sabbath and feast days, of ritual purity regulations, of tithing, of dietary rules was their practice; their tenets numbered belief in human freedom under the control of providence, bodily resurrection, angels, the coming of a Messiah (see *Pss. Sol.* 17:23 - 18:14), and the ingathering of Israel and its tribes at the end of time (Josephus *Ant.* 13.5,9 § 172). Some of these tenets set them off from other "philosophies" among the Jews, such as Sadducees. See further R. Meier and K. F. Weiss, *TDNT* 9. 11-48; J. Neusner, *From Politics to Piety* (Englewood Cliffs, NJ: Prentice-Hall, 1973).

teachers of the Law. The term *nomodidaskaloi* occurs only here in the gospel tradition; in Acts 5:34 it is used of Gamaliel, identified as a Pharisee in the Jerusalem Sanhedrin. They are probably to be understood as a specific group within the Pharisees and probably are the same as the "Scribes" of v. 21, leaders of the Pharisaic group, the "rabbis" of later tradition. The title "Scribes" is undoubtedly part of the inherited pronouncement-story, whereas here in the redactional introductory verse to the miracle-story Luke uses his own word. *Nomodidaskalos* is not used in the LXX or by Philo or Josephus, and may not reflect a Jewish origin at all. It occurs in 1 Tim 1:7 of legalistic false teachers. Here the word may be a Lucan variant for *nomikos,* "lawyer" (see NOTE on 7:30). Cf. K. H. Rengstorf, *TDNT* 2. 159.

Galilee . . . Judea . . . Jerusalem. Luke has already portrayed "crowds" flocking to Jesus (5:15); now he specifies prominent members of certain types of Jews who come from near and far, for Jesus' reputation is spreading abroad, far beyond Galilee. These Pharisees and teachers come *from* these places; they are not mentioned as merely the "area covered by the ministry" of Jesus (*pace* H. Conzelmann, *Theology,* 43). In this instance, "Judea" must be understood in a restricted sense, in contradistinction to Galilee. See NOTE on 4:44.

the power of the Lord happened to be with him. Lit. "the power of the Lord was that he might heal (people)," or "was for his healing" (*eis to iasthai auton*). The mss. אָ, B, L, W read *auton*, "him," the acc. subj. of the infin. But some others (C, D, Θ, and the Koine text-tradition) read *autous*, "was for healing them" (obj. of the infin.). And ms. K reads *pantas*, "was for healing all." The last variant is clearly to be excluded, since it is an obvious embellishment of the second. If the second one is preferred as the *lectio difficilior*, the "them" must refer to unnamed people; it cannot mean the Pharisees and teachers.

This phrase is clearly a Lucan creation, a description of Yahweh's power present in Jesus for the sake of curing people. In effect, it echoes 4:14,36 and prepares for the miracle and the pronouncement that are to come. Here *Kyrios* is clearly distinguished from Jesus and means Yahweh; recall 1:6,9,11, 15,16,17, etc.

18. *Then some men came carrying.* Lit. "and behold (there were) men carrying" (see Note on 5:12). Luke omits the number of the men, "four" (Mark 2:3).

a paralyzed man. Lit. "a human being who was paralyzed." Whereas the other evangelists use *paralytikos*, "a paralytic," Luke prefers the pf. pass. ptc. *paralelymenos*, which better expresses the condition of the man.

they sought to bring him in. Luke has omitted the mention of Jesus being "in a house" (Mark 2:1) and substituted this part of the verse instead. Thus we learn for the first time that Jesus has been teaching indoors.

19. *finding no way.* Lit. "not finding by what (way)"; the noun *hodou* has to be supplied with the interrogative adj. *poias*, a genitive of place.

on his pallet. Lit. "with his pallet." Luke often uses the prep. *syn* in the sense "along with." "Pallet" here translates Greek *klinidion*, the diminutive of *klinē*, "stretcher" (v. 18). It is probably a mere stylistic variant, but it could imply that the man was lowered on only part of what he had been carried on earlier.

through the tiles. The roof of the common Palestinian house was made of wooden beams placed across stone or mudbrick walls; the beams were covered with reeds, matted layers of thorns, and several inches of clay. It was sloped and usually rolled before the rainy season. Such a roof could have been dug through (see Mark 2:4). Luke, however, has changed the description, introducing the tiled roof of Hellenistic houses in the eastern Mediterranean area— making the action more intelligible to Greek-speaking Christian readers outside of the Palestinian context. See further G. Dalman, *Arbeit und Sitte in Palästina* (Gütersloh: Bertelsmann) 10 (1940) 75, 87, 119; C. C. McCown, "Luke's Translation of Semitic into Hellenistic Custom," *JBL* 58 (1939) 213-220, esp. pp. 213-216. H. Jahnow has tried to interpret the letting down of the paralytic through the roof as an act of magical exorcism, citing Indian ritual parallels (*ZNW* 24 [1925] 155-158; but see L. Fonck, *Bib* 6 [1925] 450-454).

20. *When he saw their faith.* This clause, common to the three Synoptics, describes the attitude of the paralytic and his attendants. "Faith" (*pistis*, inherited from Mark) would have meant in Stage I of the gospel tradition a conviction that Jesus would be able to do something for the man's condition, a sense of confidence in the power manifest in Jesus (see R. Bultmann, *TDNT* 6.

206). Such a meaning would suit most of the other passages in Luke where the word occurs (7:9,50; 8:25,48; 17:5,6,19; 18:8,42). Luke has also taken over from Mark (5:34; 10:52) the expression "Your faith has saved you," using it not only in his parallel passages (8:48; 18:42), but even elsewhere (7:50; 17:19), undoubtedly because it was so apt for his theology of salvation. But in Luke 17:5; 18:8 (possibly); 22:32 *pistis* may carry more of the nuance of personal commitment to Jesus, an attitude that can grow or diminish, involving the nuance of Christian discipleship. This would reflect more of the understanding of the word in Stage III of the gospel tradition. It is found in this sense in Acts (e.g. 6:5; 11:24; see further p. 235 above).

he said to the man, "Your sins are forgiven you!" Lit. "he said, 'Man, your sins have been forgiven you!'" My translation has made an indirect object of the voc. *anthrōpe* because of the connotation that "Man!" has in American English. The vocative occurs again in 12:14; 22:58. Luke has added the indirect object *soi* to the Marcan saying of Jesus. He has also substituted for the Marcan verb-form *aphientai* the Doric-Ionic dialectal form of the pf. pass. *apheōntai* (see BDF § 97.3, 340). It is used in the sense of the theological passive (see ZBG § 236), "by God." Jesus' words, however, are understood as a *declaration* by the Pharisees and the teachers.

21. *the Scribes.* Those called "teachers of the Law" (v. 17) now become "Scribes" (*grammateis,* a term derived from Mark 2:6). Mark 2:16 speaks of "the Scribes of the Pharisees," relating them to that "philosophy" among the Jews (see NOTE on 5:17 above). Cf. Acts 23:9. In the LXX *grammateus* translates Hebrew *sōphēr,* "clerk, scribe," a title for court officials (2 Sam 8:17; 1 Kgs 4:3). In postexilic Israel it came to be used of one learned in the Mosaic Law (Ezra 7:6,11; Neh 8:1); it may even be traced back to Jer 8:8. Neither Philo nor Josephus use *grammateus* for the specialists in the Law of their day, though the latter does use *hierogrammateus* once (*J.W.* 6.5,3 § 291). Aside from Acts 19:35, Luke uses the term only for Jewish specialists in the Law, whom he sometimes calls *nomikoi,* "lawyers" (see NOTE on 7:30). Cf. *1 Enoch* 12:4 (Greek).

Who is this who speaks so blasphemously? Lit. "who utters blasphemies." Luke reformulates the Marcan clause, "Why does this man speak thus? He blasphemes" (2:7), which M. Black (*AAGA*[3], 65, 122) regards as an Aramaism. Both Mark and Luke use the deprecatory dem. pron. *houtos,* "this (fellow)" (see *KJV* and *RSV* on Matt 26:61). The Pharisees and Scribes are thus depicted posing the crucial question about Jesus, "Who is he?"

Why blasphemy? The Jewish attitude toward it is derived from Lev 24:10-11,14-16,23, where it refers to an abusive use of the "name of Yahweh." It was to be punished with death. According to later rabbinical tradition, crystallized in the Mishna, "the blasphemer is not culpable unless he pronounces the Name [i.e. *Yhwh*] itself" (*Sanhedrin* 7:5). This tradition may represent the Pharisaic tendency to mitigate penal laws, especially those involving capital punishment. A wider use of the term, reflected in the NT, may belong to another Jewish tradition linking human arrogance to implied attacks on God's salvific power (see 2 Kgs 19:4,6,22) or on his glory through a derision of Israel's mountains (Ezek 35:12) or of his people (2 Macc 15:24). See further H. W. Beyer, *TDNT* 1. 621-625. In most of the NT passages, where the charge is leveled against Jesus, the implication is that he has somehow claimed or implied that he is an equal of Yahweh.

The charge of "blasphemy" obviously echoed in the ears of early Christians time and again. It is associated with the trial of Jesus in Mark 14:64; Matt 26:65 (but omitted by Luke). It turns up in the ministry of Jesus in the Johannine tradition (5:18; 10:30-39). A reference to it is sometimes seen in the "stoning" of Yeshu' in a Baraita of *b. Sanhedrin* 43a. But in none of these passages is it easy to determine precisely the nature of charge being made.

Who but God alone can forgive sins? Underlying the charge of blasphemy here seems to be the notion of sin as an offense against God. If God is offended, only he can pardon the offense. In ascribing to himself a power to forgive sins, Jesus would be judged guilty of an attack on God's majesty. This might imply that he was putting himself on a par with Yahweh.

22. *Jesus perceived their thoughts.* Despite the addition of the ptc. *legontes,* "saying" (v. 21), Luke here follows his Marcan source and understands the criticism of the Scribes and Pharisees to be more in thought than uttered aloud. Cf. 12:17-18. Jesus' perception is an acute awareness of what their reaction to him was (see 4:23; 6:8; 7:40; 9:47). There is no need to invoke his "divine wisdom" (H. Schürmann, *Lukasevangelium,* 1. 283) or his "prophetic knowledge" (G. Schneider, *Evangelium nach Lukas,* 134).

Why do you ponder over this? Lit. "why do you ponder in your hearts (=minds)"? For the connotation of the verb *dialogizesthai* and the noun *dialogismos* in the preceding clause, see NOTE on 2:35.

23. *Which is easier. . . .* The agreement in wording among the three Synoptics in this and the following verse is striking. However, both Matthew and Luke omit the Marcan phrases, "to the paralytic" and "take up your pallet"— another minor agreement between them in the Triple Tradition.

Jesus' comparison implies that the Scribes and Pharisees would consider it easier to declare the forgiveness of sins, because they could not tell whether the effect has been achieved or not, than to heal the paralyzed man, which could be directly verified. Though he himself regards them of equal facility, he will display his power (v. 17e) by doing what they regard as more difficult. In curing the man and forgiving his sins, Jesus fulfills the mission for which he has been sent (4:18).

24. *But to let you know.* The verb *eidēte* is in the second pl. in all three Synoptics. Luke has not removed the inconcinnity it creates with the third sg. *legei* later in the verse, undoubtedly because he respects his source. For the difficulty that this creates, see the COMMENT.

the Son of Man. This is the first appearance of this title for Jesus in the Lucan Gospel; see further 6:5,22; 7:34; 9:22,26,44,58; 11:30; 12:8,10,40; 17:22,24,26,30; 18:8,31; 19:10; 21:27,36; 22:22,48,69; 24:7—in all twenty-four times, always in the arthrous form, *ho huios tou anthrōpou.* For a discussion of the philological problems that this strange Greek expression raises, see *WA,* 143-160; also *JSNT* 4 (1979) 58-68. See p. 208 above.

Luke has clearly inherited the phrase here from Mark 2:10. In the COM-MENT on this passage I have maintained that this verse is addressed by the evangelist to the readers ("you"). In its present form it is certainly Marcan, but it is not unlikely that it belongs even to a pre-Marcan tradition. However, it is almost impossible to decide whether in such a tradition the phrase was in-troduced from other titular uses of it in the gospel tradition or used there in the generic sense of a "human being." In other words, in the pre-Marcan tradi-tion it could have meant simply, "To let you know that a human being has au-thority on earth to forgive sins, he said. . . ." So Bultmann, *HST,* 149; J. Jeremias, *ZNW* 58 (1967) 165; and others. Part of the reason for saying this is that Matt 9:8 records a reaction to the miracle thus, "and they glorified God who gave such authority to human beings" (*tois anthrōpois*). This Matthean verse is clearly a secondary addition to the form of this passsage in the First Gospel and is hardly parallel to the Son of Man saying (cf. 9:6); but it reveals that the generic understanding of the phrase is not an entirely modern concoc-tion. However, by the time that the phrase was used by Mark, especially in its strange Greek form, it was understood as titular. This is the reason why the arthrous Greek phrase is preserved in Stage III of the gospel tradition—even here, where it is not on the lips of Jesus himself.

has authority on earth to forgive sins. Above Luke spoke of "the power of the Lord" being with Jesus (v. 17e), but now it is phrased in terms of his "au-thority" (*exousia*), i.e. an authority rooted in a spokesman for God himself. This is the term inherited from Mark 2:10.

If the phrase, "the Son of Man," originally meant only "a human being" (in Stage I of the gospel tradition), it might find a plausible matrix for its use in a context of forgiving sins in a text from Qumran Cave 4. In 4QPrNab 1-3:4 an exorcist, a Jew from among the deportees in Babylonia, is said to have "remit-ted" the sins of Nabonidus "for Him" (viz. God); see *MPAT,* 2:4 (p. 2). The text is damaged, and Milik's original publication of it changed the prep. *lh,* "for him" (i.e. God) to *ly,* "for me" (i.e. Nabonidus)! See J. T. Milik, *RB* 63 (1956) 407-411. But Milik's change of the text is arbitrary and has obscured an important piece of evidence showing that some Palestinian Jews thought that a human being on earth could remit sins for God.

If, however, there is any connection between the "Son of Man" and the use of *bar 'ĕnāš* in Dan 7:13, as is often suggested, then that use for a corporate figure, which has become the title of an individual in the NT, is now related in a new sense to the forgiveness of sins. The kingdom that is promised to the "saints" in Daniel takes on a special nuance here, involved in the preaching of the forgiveness of sins that Jesus now announces.

25. *At once.* See NOTE on *parachrēma* in 1:64.

the man stood up. The cure is wrought at the word of Jesus, expressive at once of his power and his authority. The physical miracle is the sign of the res-cue of the man from the bonds of moral evil.

glorifying God. This notice of the gratitude of the paralytic is found only in the Lucan version of the story. It is probably Luke's extension of the reaction mentioned in v. 26, which he has derived in part from Mark 2:12c. But this is a characteristic reaction of persons in Luke's Gospel (see 13:13; 17:15; 18:43; 23:47).

26. *they too glorified God.* The reaction of all present is described partly in terms of "glorifying" God in Mark 2:12c. Cf. Luke 7:16.

deep awe. See NOTE on 7:16.

Today we have seen remarkable things. Lit. "things contrary to expectation" (*paradoxa*). This Greek word is used only here in the NT, and it is noteworthy that it is related to a miracle. It is one of the terms that would come closest to the modern term "miracle" for the powerful deeds of Jesus (*dynameis*—as his deeds are usually called in the Synoptic tradition). It suggests the extraordinary character of the new dimension in human life that comes with Jesus' power and authority. Note the use of *sēmeron,* "today." In the Greek text it is given an emphatic position at the end of the sentence; my translation has tried to capture that by putting it first. See NOTE on 4:21 above.

BIBLIOGRAPHY (5:17-26)

Albertz, M. *Die synoptischen Streitgespräche: Ein Beitrag zur Formgeschichte des Urchristentums* (Berlin: Trowitzsch & Sohn, 1921).

Boobyer, G. H. "Mark II, 10a and the Interpretation of the Healing of the Paralytic," *HTR* 47 (1954) 115-120.

Ceroke, C. P. "Is Mk 2,10 a Saying of Jesus?" *CBQ* 22 (1960) 369-390.

Dupont, J. "Le paralytique pardonné (Mt 9,1-8)," *NRT* 82 (1960) 940-958.

Feuillet, A. "L'*Exousia* du fils de l'homme (d'après Mc. II, 10-28 et parr.)," *RSR* 42 (1954) 161-192.

Kertelge, K. "Die Vollmacht des Menschensohnes zur Sündenvergebung (Mk 2,10)," in *Orientierung an Jesus: Festschrift für Josef Schmid* (eds. P. Hoffmann et al.; Freiburg im B.: Herder, 1973) 205-213.

Loos, H. van der. *The Miracles of Jesus* (NovTSup 9; Leiden: Brill, 1965) 440-449.

Maisch, I. *Die Heilung des Gelähmten: Eine exegetisch-traditionsgeschichtliche Untersuchung zu Mk 2,1-12* (SBS 52; Stuttgart: Katholisches Bibelwerk, 1971).

Mead, R. T. "The Healing of the Paralytic—A Unit?" *JBL* 80 (1961) 348-354.

25. THE CALL OF LEVI; THE BANQUET
(5:27-32)

5 ²⁷Later on, when he went out, Jesus saw a toll-collector named Levi sitting in the tollhouse. He said to him, "Follow me!" ²⁸Levi got up, left everything behind, and followed him.

²⁹Then in Jesus' honor Levi gave a sumptuous banquet at his own house, and there was a great crowd of toll-collectors and other people who were there as guests. ³⁰The Pharisees and their Scribes grumbled at this to his disciples, "Why do you eat and drink with toll-collectors and sinners?" ³¹But it was Jesus who spoke up and answered them, "The healthy have no need of a physician, but the sick do. ³²I have come not to invite the upright to reform, but rather sinners."

COMMENT

The second controversy used by Luke recounts the call of Levi and Jesus' altercations with Pharisees and Scribes over his association with toll-collectors and sinners at a banquet given in his honor by Levi, a former toll-collector (5:27-32). Topical arrangement has undoubtedly linked this controversy with Pharisees and Scribes to the former one; likewise the pronouncement about the forgiveness of sins in the former provides the background for Jesus' association with sinners in this scene.

The Lucan story is dependent on Mark 2:13-17; there is no need to postulate the use of another non-Marcan source by Luke. Even T. Schramm (*Der Markus-Stoff*, 104) is inclined to admit this. The agreements of Luke and Matthew against Mark are quite insignificant in this passage (the omission of Levi's father's name [because the toll-collector is called Matthew in Matt 9:9]; "the Pharisees" instead of the "Scribes of the Pharisees" [Mark 2:16] in v. 30, whereas Matt 9:11 omits the Scribes entirely).

Even in the Marcan form of the story, the episode is already conflated: Mark 2:13-14 (=Luke 5:27-28) recounts the call of Levi; Mark 2:15-17 (=Luke 5:29-32) tells of the controversy with the Scribes and Pharisees over Jesus' association with toll-collectors and sinners. In the Marcan form vv. 13-14 served as a mere redactional introduction to vv.

15-17 (see R. Pesch, *ZNW* 59 [1968] 43-45). The gospel tradition had to identify Levi, the toll-collector, as a disciple before the controversy-story would make its proper sense. Hence the two parts were joined in a unit, though the connection is really loose between them.

Luke has again modified the Marcan material, however, mainly by redacting it in the following ways: (1) He omits all reference to Jesus moving "along the sea" and teaching (5:27a; cf. Mark 2:13). (2) He omits the identification of Levi as "son of Alphaeus," probably because it was immaterial. (3) He characteristically adds the detail that Levi "left everything behind" (5:28). (4) He makes it plain that Levi gave the banquet in Jesus' honor in his own house (5:29; cf. the ambiguous formulation in Mark 2:15). (5) The Marcan phrase, "the Scribes of the Pharisees" (2:16) becomes "the Pharisees and their Scribes" (5:30; cf. 5:21). (6) Strangely enough, Luke suppresses the ptc. *idontes,* "seeing," which provided a background for the comment of the Scribes and Pharisees in Mark 2:16. (7) Luke uses the double verbal expression in the second pl., "do you eat and drink" (5:30b), referring to Jesus and his disciples, whereas Mark 2:16c uses simply *esthiei,* "eats" (third sg.) of Jesus alone. (8) Luke adds the goal of Jesus' call or invitation, "to reform" (5:32). Some of these modifications reveal Luke's own theological concerns. For other minor modifications, see the NOTES.

The first part (Mark 2:14) has been classified form-critically by R. Bultmann as a biographical apophthegm (*HST,* 28), but his comments deal much more with Mark 1:16-20, for which such a classification is more accurate. V. Taylor (*FGT,* 75) rejects Bultmann's classification of the first part, preferring to label it a Story about Jesus. Whatever one wants to say about Mark 1:16-20, this passage (2:14) and its Lucan parallel (5:27-28) scarcely belong to the class of pronouncement-stories or apophthegms. As for the second part, Jesus' eating with the toll-collectors and sinners, Bultmann (*HST,* 18) more correctly regarded it as a pronouncement-story. But he noted that the pronouncement in Mark 2:17 (=Luke 5:31) was originally unattached in the gospel tradition, having no close connection with the described situation, i.e. dining with toll-collectors and sinners. It has even less to do with the call of Levi. Mark 2:15-16 (=Luke 5:29-30) provides the setting for a pronouncement in the present form of the episode. Yet the setting is not without its problems, since the Pharisees and Scribes seem to be present at the banquet. Luke, indeed, omits the ptc. *idontes,* "seeing," which both the Marcan and Matthean versions have. They still grumble at Jesus' eating with such people, but presumably *they* are not eating with them, even though somehow present. This problem and the shift in the persons (see NOTE on v. 30) make it likely that the story reflects much more of an early Christian controversy than an explicit confrontation in Jesus' own ministry; the early church is answering an objection about its consorting with such undesirables in Palestinian society, by depicting Jesus so engaged. Its answer was to quote two of his sayings, which really had nothing to do with the call of Levi or his banquet, but which nevertheless characterize the situation. Of the two sayings the second is more related to the situation because of its explicit reference to "sinners."

Since the objection comes from "the Pharisees and their Scribes," its origin is important for the understanding of the episode as a whole. It has already been noted that the Pharisees were the "separatists" in contemporary Jewish groups (see NOTE on 5:17). Their attitude was based on Lev 10:10, "You must distinguish between the holy and the common, between the unclean and the clean." From this resulted "the Pharisaic idea of salvation by segregation" (W. Manson, *Gospel of Luke*, 55). By way of contrast, Jesus is depicted setting up a "new principle of salvation by association." Levi, the toll-collector, an outcast, is called to association as a follower, a disciple. There is an *inclusio* in the conflated episode: Jesus *calls* Levi to follow him, because he has come to *call* not the righteous but sinners to reform. The Lucan reformulation stresses this; for Mark 2:17c reads simply, "I came not to call the upright, but sinners," whereas Luke 5:32 states, "I have come not to invite the upright to reform, but rather sinners." Luke intimates that mere external association with Jesus is not enough; to "follow" him as a Christian disciple includes all that *metanoia,* "repentance, reform," implies (see NOTE on 3:3). This is why Luke depicts Levi "leaving everything behind," and giving "a sumptuous banquet at his own house" in Jesus' honor. He is the toll-collector who has been called to *metanoia.* And so are all the other toll-collectors and other guests, with whom Jesus dines. To ask how Levi could have abandoned everything and then provide a banquet to which Jesus was invited is to miss the whole point of the passage. To ask it is to spoil the story!

NOTES

5 27. *he went out.* I.e. probably from the house implied in 5:19; but it could also mean from "one of the towns" (5:12). The sea is not mentioned (Mark 2:13), but ms. D tries to remedy this: "Going along the sea again, he taught the crowd that was following him; as he passed along, he saw Levi, the son of Alphaeus. . . ." This is clearly a harmonization of the Lucan and Marcan texts.

saw. Instead of the simple verb *eiden* of Mark 2:14, Luke has *etheasato,* a more formal verb, "he observed."

a toll-collector. See NOTE on 3:12.

Levi. In Mark the toll-collector is identified as "Levi, son of Alphaeus"; in Matt 9:9 he is named "Matthew" (*Maththaion*). "Levi" represents the contemporary use of the names of the twelve patriarchs for children in postexilic times (see J. Jeremias, *Jerusalem in the Time of Jesus*, 296). Cf. Luke 3:24,29. "Matthew" rather reflects some form of the Hebrew name *Mattatyāh*, "the gift of Yahweh."

The name "Matthew" is found in the four lists of the Twelve (Mark 3:16-19; Matt 10:2-3; Luke 6:14-16; Acts 1:13), but only in Matt 10:3 is he identified as *ho telōnēs*, "the toll-collector." That addition provides the only link between the traditional list of the Twelve and the call of the toll-collector in the First Gospel (Matt 9:9), a link not made in either Mark or Luke. Were the Levi of this episode in Mark and Luke and the Matthew of the list of the Twelve the same person? We would never know, if we had only the Marcan and Lucan Gospels.

The problem is complicated by the fact that in Mark 2:14 a variant reading in mss. D, ⊕, the Freer family of minuscules, and the Itala identifies the toll-collector as "James, son of Alphaeus" (*Iakōbon*). This is an obvious scribal change, influenced by Mark 3:18, where the second James in the list of Twelve is identified as "son of Alphaeus." But "Levi" is the better reading in the Marcan passage.

First-century Palestinian Jews often had two names, one Semitic (Hebrew or Aramaic) and the other in a Greek or Latin form (cf. Acts 1:23; 12:25; 13:9). Rare instances of two Semitic names are also found: Joseph Barnabas (Acts 4:36), Joseph Caiaphas (Josephus *Ant.* 18.2,2 § 35). Hence it is theoretically possible that the toll-collector was called Levi Matthew. But writers as early as the patristic period have insisted on the distinction of these persons (e.g. Heracleon in Clement of Alexandria *Stromata* 4.9; GCS, 15. 280; Origen *Contra Celsum* 1.62; GCS, 1. 112).

the tollhouse. Levi is depicted as an agent at work for a "chief toll-collector" (19:2), seated at his post, probably in a town like Capernaum, one of the toll-posts in Galilee (see J. R. Donahue, *CBQ* 33 [1971] 54). Luke, however, does not localize the house.

Follow me! I.e. become one of my disciples (see NOTE on 5:11). This provides a transition to the mention of them in 5:30.

28. *got up.* The ptc. *anastas* actually follows another ptc. *katalipōn*, "having left behind," which one would have expected to be in reverse order. Hence, in this case it may not be the mere Greek equivalent of Hebrew/Aramaic *qûm*, which often asyndetically precedes another verb to express the inception of an action (see NOTE on 1:39). Here it is hard to say, because Levi has been depicted seated in v. 27.

left everything behind. This typically Lucan addition has no counterpart in either Mark or Matthew. Cf. 5:11; 14:33. Being part of the introductory verses of the episode, it obviously means left "everything" in the tollhouse behind; Levi leaves one occupation to take up another. Having read that, one is immediately struck by the mention of a "sumptuous banquet" that Levi gives in Jesus' honor in his own house. The suture in the two elements of the episode is thus more apparent in the Lucan version. See further p. 588 above.

followed. The verb is in the impf. tense, lit. "was following him," to stress the continuous nature of the act. Mark 2:14 had the aor. tense.

29. *gave a sumptuous banquet.* Though Luke is fond of the *kai egeneto* or *egeneto de* construction (see p. 119 above), he deliberately avoids following the Marcan construction *kai ginetai katakeisthai,* because he usually changes the Marcan historical present (used in 2:15).

The banquet is intended to give a concrete expression of Levi's "following." Though proffered by an obviously rich Palestinian Jew, the Lucan Jesus does not decline the invitation to attend it.

at his own house. I.e. at Levi's house. Luke preserves the possessive pron. *autou* from Mark 2:15; but it must be understood in a reflexive sense as *heautou* (see BDF § 283-284), since Luke has inserted Levi's name as the subject, and the dative of the pron. *autō* referring to Jesus. Thus he eliminates the ambiguity of Mark 2:15, which might seem to say that Jesus was at dinner with toll-collectors and sinners in his (own) house.

other people who were there as guests. Lit. "and of others who were reclining with them." So Luke changes the description of those who were with the invited toll-collectors; Mark 2:15 has "many toll-collectors and sinners." The "others" are only gradually so labeled in the Lucan version.

30. *The Pharisees and their Scribes.* See NOTES on 5:17,21 above. The pron. *autōn,* "their," seems strange here; thus has Luke modified the Marcan designation, "the Scribes of the Pharisees" (2:16). One group in the Marcan source has become two in Luke's version. Cf. Acts 23:9.

to his disciples. This and the following phrase undoubtedly reflect criticism leveled at early Christians and preserve an indication of the *Sitz im Leben* of this part of the episode. Mark has the criticism leveled at Jesus himself.

Why do you eat and drink. Whereas Mark 2:16 has the third sg. *esthiei* (referring to Jesus), Luke introduces the second pl. He has also made use of an OT double verbal expression (see LXX of Gen 26:30; cf. Luke 7:33-34).

with toll-collectors and sinners. The juxtaposition of these two groups is noteworthy, depicting Jesus' association with segments of Palestinian Jewry often regarded as outcasts. Because of the contextual reference to Pharisees and Scribes, "sinners" might at first sight be thought of in the sense of "this rabble that knows not the law" (John 7:49), those who would not care about Pharisaic interpretations of ritual or dietary regulations (cf. Mark 7:1-12). But "sinners" should most likely be understood in a wider sense, referring to two groups: (a) Jews who fell short of Mosaic obligations (without restricting these to the Pharisaic interpretation), but who could repent and be reconciled to God; and (b) Gentiles, who were *a-nomoi* (Law-less) and *a-theoi* (God-less), often considered hopeless in Jewish apocalyptic literature (see J. Jeremias, *ZNW* 30 [1931] 293-300).

The juxtaposition of "toll-collectors" and "sinners" occurs again in 7:34 (=Matt 11:19); 15:1; and implicitly in 19:7. On "toll-collectors," see NOTE on 3:12; they are associated with other evil people: with "robbers, evildoers, adulterers" (18:11); with "harlots" (Matt 21:32); with "Gentiles" (Matt 18:17). "Toll-collectors" were thus categorized not because they were Jews who had made themselves like Gentiles, i.e. quislings or persons in the service of a foreign occupying power, *pace* N. Perrin, *Rediscovering the Teaching of Jesus*

(New York: Harper & Row, 1967) 93-102. They were not involved in direct taxation, and their ill repute was rather the result of dishonesty and extortion. This is echoed in the Baptist's counsel to them (3:12-13); cf. the Zacchaeus episode (19:1-10). This attitude is also found in later rabbinical writings, especially in those dealing with the môkĕsîn (m. Sanhedrin 3:3, and its Gemara in b. Sanh. 25b; m. Baba Qamma 10:2). Cf. L. Goldschmid, "Les impôts et droits de douane en Judée sous les Romains," REJ 34 (1897) 214-217. "Toll-collectors" were associated with "sinners," then, mainly because of the dishonesty which often characterized their activity.

31. Jesus . . . spoke up and answered them. Though Luke omits the ptc. akousas, "having heard" (Mark 2:17), he follows the Marcan source in having Jesus answer the criticism. Whence the pronouncement in double form.

but the sick do. The first part of Jesus' pronouncement is the quotation of a proverb or wisdom-saying, identical in all three Synoptics, save for the Lucan substitution of hoi hygiainontes, "the healthy," for the Marcan hoi ischyontes, "those who are well." Jesus' saying preserved in OxyP 1224 follows the form of the Lucan pronouncement: "The Scribes a[nd Pharise]es and priests, observ-[ing h]im, were angry [because he reclined] in the mid[st of sin]ners. But Je(sus), having heard (it), [said], 'The he[althy ha]ve [no need of a physi-cian]. . . .'" (see K. Aland, SQE, 63; cf. Hennecke-Schneemelcher, NTApo-crypha, 1. 113-114).

The contrast of the "healthy" and the "sick" prepares for the "upright" and the "sinners" of v. 32. Again, there is the implied association of sin and sickness (see the COMMENT on 5:17-26). More important, however, is the figurative use of the "sick" for outcasts and a despised element of contemporary Palestinian society.

32. I have come. Luke uses the pf. elēlytha to depict Jesus' mission as already in progress; cf. 7:34; 18:8; 19:10. It has effects that perdure into the present (BDF § 340).

not to invite the upright to reform. Jesus' mission is described in terms that echo that of John the Baptist (3:3). Luke's formulation follows that of Mark 2:17c, but adds, significantly, "to reform" (eis metanoian, lit. "for repentance, reform"). See p. 237 above. Cf. 19:10.

sinners. I.e. those whose lives have not been God-oriented and have been missing the mark of essential human existence.

BIBLIOGRAPHY (5:27-32)

Burkitt, F. C. "Levi Son of Alphaeus," JTS 28 (1926-1927) 273-274.

Iersel, B. M. F. van. "La vocation de Lévi (Mc., II, 13-17; Mt., IX, 9-13; Lc., V, 27-32): Traditions et rédactions," De Jésus aux évangiles (BETL 25/2; ed. I. de la Potterie; Gembloux: Duculot, 1967) 212-232.

Jeremias, J. "Zöllner und Sünder," ZNW 30 (1931) 293-300; RGG 6. cols. 1927-1928.

Mouson, J. "'Non veni vocare iustos, sed peccatores' (Mt. ix, 13=Mc. ii, 17=Lc. v, 32)," Collectanea mechliniensia ns 28 (1958) 134-139.

Pesch, R. "Levi-Matthäus (Mc 2,14/Mt 9,9; 10,3)," *ZNW* 59 (1968) 40-56.

———— "Das Zöllnergastmahl (Mk 2,15-17," in *Mélanges bibliques en hommage au R. P. Béda Rigaux* (eds. A. Descamps et A. de Halleux; Gembloux: Duculot, 1970) 63-87.

Schulz, A. *Nachfolgen und Nachahmen: Studien über das Verhältnis der neutestamentlichen Jüngerschaft zur urchristlichen Vorbildethik* (SANT 6; Munich: Kösel, 1962) 97-116.

26. THE DEBATE ABOUT FASTING; PARABLES
(5:33-39)

5 33 Then they said to him, "John's disciples fast frequently and say prayers, as do those of the Pharisees too; but your disciples eat and drink." 34 Jesus replied, "You cannot make the bridegroom's attendants fast, while the bridegroom is with them, can you? 35 Days will come when the bridegroom is taken away from them; then they will fast—when those days come!"

36 He also proposed to them a parable: "No one cuts a patch out of a new garment and sews it on an old one; if one does, one will be cutting up the new, and the patch from it will fail to match the old. 37 Again, no one puts new wine into old wineskins; if one does, the new wine will burst the skins, the wine will spill out, and the skins will be ruined. 38 Rather, new wine is to be put into fresh wineskins. 39 Again, no one who has sipped an old wine prefers a new wine; for he says, 'The old is what is good.'"

COMMENT

The third controversy depicts Jesus answering the criticism of unnamed opponents who find fault with him because he does not teach his disciples to fast, as do John the Baptist and the Pharisees. Jesus' reply to such criticism is followed by two similitudes (or extended metaphors) and a proverb—all three joined by the catchword bond of the "old" and the "new." The whole unit (5:33-39) raises the question of the relation of the old way of Jewish piety to that of Christians.

Luke has derived this episode from Mark 2:18-22; its Matthean parallel is found in 9:14-17. But Luke has again modified the Marcan form, chiefly in the following ways: (1) He omits the Marcan narrative about the fasting done by John's disciples and those of the Pharisees (Mark 2:18a). (2) He adds to the comment of Jesus' opponents the note of the frequency of their fasting and of the prayers of John's disciples—a note characteristic of Luke (see 11:1d), which never really is picked up in the controversy itself, dealing only with fasting. (3) He changes the second part of the opponents' question so that Jesus' disciples are said to "eat and drink" (5:33d; cf. Mark 2:18d). (4) The explanatory statement in Mark 2:19b, following the question that enshrines the pronouncement of Jesus, is omitted by Luke—and also by Matt (9:15). (5) Luke changes the Marcan phrase, "in that day" (2:20c) to the plural, to agree with the first part of the verse. (6) Luke introduces the similitudes expressly (v. 36a). (7) He considerably changes the sense of the first similitude: "a piece of unshrunk cloth" (Mark 2:21) becomes "a patch cut out of a new garment" (5:36b). (8) He adds v. 39 with its proverb, a verse that is exclusive to him. That Luke has reworked the Marcan episode is clear; but that he is influenced by a parallel tradition, save for v. 39 (which comes to him from "L") is not "certainly provable," *pace* T. Schramm (*Der Markus-Stoff*, 111).

There are, however, three minor agreements of Matthew and Luke against Mark in this episode: (1) *epiballei*, "sew on" (Luke 5:36; Matt 9:16) instead of the Marcan *epiraptei*. That, however, is simply the cognate verb of *epiblēma*, "patch," which both of the other evangelists naturally and independently prefer to the Marcan verb. (2) *ei de mē ge*, "otherwise" (Luke 5:37; Matt 9:17) instead of the Marcan *ei de mē*. But Luke has already used the fuller form in v. 36 and makes the later one conform to it. (3) Both Luke (5:34) and Matt (9:15) omit a half-verse from Mark 2:19c—and its repetitive character makes it clear why both evangelists would have independently so reacted to it.

From the form-critical point of view, the episode, as it appears in both Luke and his Marcan source, is again conflated. Luke 5:33-35 (=Mark 2:18-19b, 20) is a pronouncement-story, a controversy dialogue (*HST*, 18-19). And, as Bultmann notes, Mark 2:19b-20 is really a secondary addition to the pronouncement itself. That would correspond to Luke 5:35. Luke 5:36-38 are similitudes (or extended metaphors). They were joined to the pronouncement in the Marcan source, and probably also in a pre-Marcan grouping (see H.-W. Kuhn, *Ältere Sammlungen*, 61-72). To these Luke has added the proverb in v. 39 (a secular mashal, according to Bultmann, *HST*, 103).

Two of the sayings of Jesus recorded in the Coptic *Gos. Thomas* preserve variants of material in this episode. A parallel to the pronouncement in v. 34 is found in *Gos. Thom.* § 104: "They said [to him], 'Come, let us pray today and let us fast (*nēsteuein*).' Jesus said, 'But what then (*gar*) is the sin that I committed, or (*ē*) in what have I been overcome? But (*alla*) when (*hotan*) the bridegroom (*nymphios*) comes out of the marriage-chamber (*nymphōn*), then (*tote*) let them fast (*nēsteuein*) and let them pray.' " This parallel, however, is only "a weak echo of Mark 2:19-20 parr." (W. Schrage, *Das Verhältnis*, 193); and the Lucan addition to v. 33 about prayer is brought to its logical conclusion in Jesus' final words, "Let them fast and let them pray." This saying is clearly dependent on the Lucan form.

Another saying is parallel to the proverb and the similitudes; it is found in *Gos. Thom.* § 47bc:

> "No one drinks old wine and straightway desires (*epithymei*) to drink new wine. They do not put new wine into old wineskins (*askos*) lest they burst; they do not put old wine into a new wineskin lest it ruin it. They do not sew an old patch on a new garment, since (*epei*) a rip might develop."

Even though the last similitude differs from both the Marcan and Lucan form, it is clear that the collection here is basically dependent on the Lucan form; it not only includes the equivalent of v. 39, but reverses the order of the similitude and proverb. See further Schrage, *Das Verhältnis*, 112-116.

In the Lucan Gospel this controversy and the further sayings of Jesus are presented in the context of the banquet of 5:27-32. The narrative setting of Mark 2:18ab has been eliminated, and the contrast between the banquet and the question of fasting is sharper. The unnamed opponents seem, then, to be the Pharisees and their Scribes of v. 30, which creates a bit of a problem in the mention of disciples of the Pharisees in v. 33c.

The controversy-story is intended to give a different perspective to the Jewish custom of fasting. Among Jews fasting was practiced for the expiation of sins (on the Day of Atonement, Lev 16:29-31), for penitence (1 Kgs 21:27; Joel 1:14; 2:15-27; Isa 58:1-9), and for mourning (Esth 4:3). Jesus' reply, however, makes a distinction. He does not reject the practice of fasting, but reveals that it will have its time and place in the new economy of salvation being inaugurated. His disciples are not to fast *now* (v. 34), but they will have to *in time* (v. 35). Jesus' reply also suggests the inconsequential aspect of fasting, when the economy that he is inaugurating is considered as a whole. His presence among his followers, as that inauguration takes place, has to be understood as a joyous occasion, like the time when a married couple are still considered bride and groom. That period is marked by celebration, not by the gloom associated with fasting (see Joel 1:13-16). His disciples are "the bridegroom's attendants" and must share in the joy of the inauguration of this new period.

Because the Lucan Jesus does not rule out fasting completely for his followers, it is clear that the evangelist, following Mark, is telling Theophilus (and others like him) that the fasting practiced in the church of his (their) day is rooted in an attitude of Jesus himself.

To the controversy-story Luke, following Mark and even more deliberately than Mark, now joins two similitudes, which explain another aspect of fasting. Fasting was a practice well-rooted in Judaism; and even though there would come a time for it in Christian life, it has an aspect of the "old" that has to yield to a "new" understanding of God's economy of salvation. The two similitudes make this point. In their Lucan forms they are distinctive (see NOTES for detailed comparison). In the first similitude Jesus' opponents are told that in their demand that Jesus' disciples fast as do those of John and the Pharisees they are equivalently cutting up a new garment (and ruining it) to put a patch on an old garment which it does not match. The incompatibility of the old and the new is thus stressed. The new does not just repair the old; rather, the old must give way. What is interesting here is Luke's emphasis on the difference between (Pharisaic) Judaism and Christianity—whereas he is otherwise at pains to stress the continuity between them (see p. 178 above).

Luke is not content to make the point of incompatibility only once. He picks up the second similitude (vv. 37-38) from Mark as well. Trying to bring the old and the new together just does not work. New wine in old wineskins means the loss of both the new wine and the old skins: "new wine is to be put into fresh wineskins" (v. 38). New forms of piety have to be found; the old observances and practices are not simply to be taken over.

Finally, Luke makes Jesus add a comment on those who have become enamored of the old practices. Using a proverb (v. 39), Jesus wryly comments on the effect of such practices: they result in closing a person off from the new. Verse 39 does not contradict the sayings in vv. 37-38, but it points up the difficulty that those who cling to the old have in accepting the new—the "new wine" that Jesus offers. It is merely another way of commenting on the incompatibility of the "old" and the "new"; it explains the negative attitude of Jesus' opponents. The proverb is also the evangelist's way of explaining why Jesus' claims were so unacceptable to many of his contemporaries: "No one who has sipped an old wine prefers a new wine; for he says, 'The old is what is good.'"

NOTES

5 33. *they said to him*. In the Lucan context the unnamed opponents have to be those mentioned in v. 30, since Luke has omitted the narrative setting of Mark 2:18. In Matt 9:14 the question is put by "John's disciples." Luke uses here a verb of saying (*eipan*) and the prep. *pros* + acc. (see NOTE on 1:13); this construction will appear again in vv. 34,36.

John's disciples. Disciples of the Baptist are known from Luke 7:18-19; 11:1. They seem to be a group of Palestinian Jews (but cf. Acts 18:25-26), who had accepted John's baptism, used some set form of prayer, and fasted regularly. Mark 6:29 suggests that their corporate activity continued even after the Baptist's imprisonment and death. Some commentators have argued that the "disciples" of Acts 19:1 are likewise John's; but this is unlikely (see *JBC*, art. 45, § 90). This passage may suggest that some rivalry existed between the disciples of John and of Jesus; cf. John 3:25-26; 4:1-2.

fast frequently. Luke has added the adverbial acc. (*pykna*). There is no way of telling how often or in what this temporary abstention from food for a religious purpose lasted for John's disciples. Mark 1:6 tells of the Baptist's ordinary ascetic diet ("locusts and wild honey"); spartan though it was, that is not what is usually meant by fasting. That he also fasted is suggested by 7:33. In the OT "fasting" meant abstention from eating bread (food) and drinking water (e.g. Exod 34:28; Deut 9:9); it is often listed along with the ascetic use of sackcloth and ashes (e.g. Dan 9:3). The renunciation of self implied in it apparently contributed to a notion of self-achieved holiness, against which the prophets inveighed at times (see Jer 14:12; Isa 58:3-9).

say prayers. Lit. "make supplications." This Lucan addition seems to suggest that John had taught his disciples certain prayer-forms (see 11:1). Luke uses a classical Greek idiom here: the middle voice of the verb *poiein* with an abstract verbal noun (*deēseis poiountai*). Cf. 3 Macc 2:1; Josephus *J.W.* 7.5,2 § 107; BDF § 310.1.

your disciples eat and drink. So Luke has reformulated his source, Mark 2:18, which reads, "your disciples do not fast." The reformulation provides a link with the preceding episode, where Jesus and his disciples are accused of "eating and drinking" with toll-collectors and sinners (v. 30). The tone of the remark is pejorative; it is meant as a reproof to Jesus. See further 7:33-34, where Jesus himself will be included.

34. *Jesus replied.* Lit. "Jesus said to them" (*eipen pros autous;* see NOTE on v. 33 above).

You cannot make the bridegroom's attendants fast, . . . can you? Lit. "the sons of the bridal-chamber." Jesus takes up the defense of his disciples, implying that fasting is an expression of sorrow and gloom, something out of place in the presence of a bridegroom, whose moment of joy is at hand. The connotation of "fasting" in contemporary Judaism can perhaps be gathered from a classic rabbinical text, the *Mĕgillat Ta'ănît* or "Scroll of Fasting." It is a calendaric list of days in the twelve months of the year when fasting (and mourning) was forbidden because of the joy that was to be associated with historic achievements of Israel commemorated on them. See *MPAT* § 150.

Whereas Luke follows Mark 2:19b in speaking of "fasting," Matt 9:15 changes the saying to "mourning" (*penthein*); see further J. A. Ziesler, *NTS* 19 (1972-1973) 190-194.

The Greek *huioi tou nymphōnos,* "sons of the bridal-chamber," is a Semitism, a translation of Hebrew *bĕnê ha-ḥuppāh* (*t. Berakot* 2:10; cf. J. Jeremias, *TDNT* 4. 1099-1106). The use of "son" expresses the close relationship of the wedding guests so designated to the groom because of the role that they played in attending him on his wedding occasion.

the bridegroom. Jesus' pronouncement, cast here in the form of a question, identifies himself as the bridegroom whose celebration inaugurates a new period. His disciples are the attendants who must share his joy on this occasion of inauguration. For a survey of various ways in which this saying (and the following one) has been interpreted, see R. Dunkerley, *ExpTim* 64 (1952-1953) 303-304.

Neither in the OT nor in early rabbinical writings is "bridegroom" used as a messianic title (see J. Jeremias, *TDNT* 4. 1101-1103). But W. H. Brownlee ("Messianic Motifs of Qumran and the New Testament," *NTS* 3 [1956-1957] 195-210, esp. p. 205) has tried so to understand it. Basing himself on "a sectarian reading" of Isa 61:10, which has *kkwhn,* "like a priest," instead of the verb *yĕkahēn* of the MT, he thinks that the Qumran community understood 1QIsaᵃ 61:10 to refer to the Messiah of Aaron: "he covered me with a garment of righteousness, like a bridegroom, like a priest with a garland" (cf. *RSV*). In this text of Isaiah "bridegroom" would be juxtaposed to "priest." Since in another Qumran text (1QSa 2:19) a "priest" who is said to take precedence over the Messiah of Israel is often interpreted as the Messiah of Aaron, Brownlee thinks that this could be the connotation of "priest" in 1QIsaᵃ as well. However, this is a tenuous argument. If the text of 1QIsaᵃ is to be preferred to that of the MT, then it surely must refer to the splendidly robed high priest, as even the later targum of Isaiah once understood it (see J. F. Stenning, *The Targum of Isaiah* [Oxford: Clarendon, 1949] 205). Moreover, it is far from certain that the "priest" of 1QSa is the Messiah of Aaron. See further J. Gnilka, *TTZ* 69 (1960) 298-301.

35. *Days will come.* I.e. days different from the joyous occasion of the presence of the bridegroom. For the expression, see further 17:22; 19:43; 21:6; 23:29. Here Luke follows his Marcan source. Cf. 22:35-36 for another difference between the Period of Jesus and the Period of the Church.

is taken away from them. The verb *aparthē* is derived from Mark 2:20 and occurs only in this episode in the three Synoptics. It clearly refers to a "departure" or the end of Jesus' presence among his disciples; but it cannot be shown to connote a departure by violent death. Ms. D uses this verb of the ascension of Jesus in Acts 1:9; but it would be reading too much into Jesus' saying here to give it that connotation.

then they will fast. Thus Luke anchors the custom of early Christian fasting in a saying of Jesus. But it is not apparent, even from the general context, that this is meant as a fasting of mourning for the passion and death of Christ.

when those days come. Lit. "in those days." Luke uses the plural here for the singular of the Marcan source (*en ekeinē tē hēmera*) to agree with the phrase at the beginning of the verse.

36. *He also proposed to them a parable.* Lit. "he spoke a parable to them" (*elegen pros autous,* see NOTE on v. 33 above). This is a typically Lucan formula: 12:16,41; 14:7; 15:3; 18:9; 20:9,19; sometimes he substitutes the dat. *autois* for the prep. phrase (6:39; 18:1; 21:29). Here it provides a suture to join the similitudes to the controversy-story; they will illustrate another aspect of the pronouncement, in effect allegorizing it.

a parable. Greek *parabolē* first appeared in 4:23 in the sense of "proverb" (in which sense it would also refer to v. 39). Here, however, it is used in the more normal gospel-sense of "parable" or "similitude." The variety of meanings for *parabolē* is to be attributed to its OT background, since *parabolē* (used only by the Synoptic evangelists) and *paroimia* (its Johannine counterpart; see John 10:6; 16:25,29) both translate Hebrew *māšāl* in the LXX. The Hebrew word has a variety of meanings: "maxim" (Proverbs), "proverb" (1 Sam 10:11-12; 24:14), "obscure prophecy" (Num 23:7), "parable" (2 Sam 12:1-6), "allegory" (Ezek 17:2-24), "taunt" (Isa 14:4). *Parabolē* also translates *ḥîdāh*, "riddle" (Prov 1:6). In the gospel tradition *parabolē* usually denotes a literary form used to achieve a certain esthetic effect, by making an illustrative comparison, usually of a generic nature and not time-conditioned, as many other gospel-stories are. The "parable" proper is a comparison, using storytelling techniques and details drawn from Palestinian daily life, which presents a Christian truth in some clarity and attracts the reader's attention by its vividness or strangeness, but which teases the reader into further reflection, inquiry, judgment, or application. The comparison is often made explicitly (e.g. 6:47-49); then it resembles an extended simile narrated usually in the past tense. But sometimes the comparison is only implied (e.g. 8:5-8); then it resembles an extended metaphor. "Similitude" is sometimes used for the literary comparison that employs descriptive rather than narrative details and is often recounted in the present tense; the comparison can again be either explicit or implicit (as in this instance). But the distinction between "parable" and "similitude" is really of minor significance.

The above description of *parabolē* is concerned with its literary features. The form of this figure is important, but it is in reality subordinate to the content or the message that it is intended to convey. For the figure is not meant merely to compare Christian truths to everyday realities, but rather to confront readers with Christian truths in a dramatic and non-ordinary way. It is, in effect, a revelatory process, used to carry nuances that the abstract formulation of a truth could never express, and designed to capture the adherence of the reader or listener.

Usually the "parable" has only one point of comparison, as has been recognized ever since the studies of A. Jülicher (1899). This has to be kept in mind to prevent the overinterpretation of details in the figure. But it is an aspect of parable study that has often been exaggerated, since some gospel parables have obviously been meant to have more than one point of comparison. Each has to be scrutinized individually. (See further F. Hauck, *TDNT* 5. 744-761; C. H. Dodd, *The Parables of the Kingdom* [New York: Scribner, 1961]; J. Jeremias, *The Parables of Jesus* [rev. ed.; New York: Scribner, 1963]; J. S. Glen, *The Parables of Conflict in Luke* [Philadelphia: Westminster, 1962]; R. E. Brown, *NovT* 5 [1962] 36-45; A. N. Wilder, "The Parable," in *The Language of the Gospel: Early Christian Rhetoric* [New York: Harper & Row, 1964] 79-96.)

No one cuts a patch out of a new garment. This is the Lucan reformulation of the first similitude, which brings the sense of it closer to that of the second. Mark 2:21 reads: "No one sews a piece of unshrunk cloth on an old garment; if one does, the patch tears away from it, the new from the old, and a worse tear is made" (cf. Matt 9:16). The Marcan form has been variously interpreted. According to Jeremias (*Parables,* 118) the point is: "The old world's age has run out; it is compared to the old garment which is no longer worth patching with new cloth; the New Age has arrived." But this does not explain the "worse tear" that is made. According to A. Kee (*NovT* 12 [1970] 13-21), the comparison presupposes that the old worn-out garment is still worth patching; but if the repair is badly done (i.e. with a piece of unshrunk cloth), a "worse tear" is made in the old garment and so there is danger of loss. Perhaps. But the real point seems to be the incompatibility of the old and the new: "the patch tears away from it, the new from the old," and the old is in a worse condition as a result.

In the Lucan form of the similitude the note of incompatibility of the new and the old is also present, but with a different emphasis. The Marcan form (and the Matthean form, following it) concentrates the reader's attention on the old garment, whereas the attention in the Lucan form is on the new garment, which would be sacrificed, and the patch from the new cloth would not match any way. Thus the Lucan form is a better illustration of an aspect of the controversy-story. To ask why anyone would want to tear up a new garment to patch an old one is to miss the point of the illustration.

if one does. Lit. "but if not" (*ei de mē ge*), a phrase that carries the nuance of "otherwise," when it follows a negative, as here.

37. *new wine into old wineskins.* Luke takes over the second similitude from Mark 2:22 with slight redactional modifications.

Dehaired skins of small animals, usually of goats, were sewn up to form containers for liquids: for water (Gen 21:15), for milk (Judg 4:19), or for wine (Josh 9:4,13).

will burst. The strength of the newly fermented wine will be too much for the weakened and aged fibers of the old skins.

the wine will spill out, and the skins will be ruined. As in the first similitude, the effect is double; but the note of incompatibility is not as expressly spelled out as there. In this case, the detriment happens to both the old and the new. The reader's attention, however, is not directed to the superiority of the new over the old, but rather to their incompatibility.

38. *new wine is to be put into fresh wineskins.* This sentence emphasizes the need of compatibility; it says positively what the last clause of v. 36 said negatively. The new economy of salvation must find for itself forms of piety that suit it. Luke has added to the Marcan formulation the verbal adj. *blēteon,* "must be put" (cf. Mark 2:22d).

39. *no one who has sipped an old wine prefers a new wine.* Lit. "no one drinking old (wine) desires new (wine)." Some Greek mss. (A, ⊗, and the Koine text-tradition) add the adv. *eutheōs,* "immediately," to the verb, "desires." This introduces a different nuance into the comparison, one which implies that in time one may so desire; but on the basis of external evidence of the mss., it is to be omitted. It is also found in *Gos. Thom.* § 47 (see COMMENT).

The proverb echoes an ancient conviction, a truism found often, though in different formulations, in many writers. See Sir 9:10b; *b. Berakot* 51a.

It has often been thought that this proverb contradicts the two preceding sayings of Jesus; so, e.g. J. Schmid, *Evangelium nach Lukas*, 126; H. Seesemann, *TDNT* 5. 165. Moreover, because it is lacking in Mark and absent from some forms of Luke (ms. D, OL, and some patristic writers), the text-tradition has been questioned at times. J. M. Creed (*The Gospel*, 83), in dependence on Westcott-Hort, even brackets the entire verse. But the external evidence in support of the proverb is such that one cannot omit it (see mss. P[75], P[4], B, ℵ, etc.). The proverb used by Jesus is a wry comment on the effect that clinging to the old has on those who have closed their minds to his message about the new economy of salvation.

The old is what is good. This is, in fact, a banal explanation of the main proverb in the first part of the verse. It is omitted in the *Gos. Thom.* § 47. But it resembles other explanatory clauses that Luke adds at times to his form of various gospel-stories (see 20:39-40, cf. Mark 12:25; 11:18, cf. Matt 12:26).

The Greek text has the adj. *chrēstos* in the positive degree, "good." The comparative degree *chrēstoteros* is found in mss. C, A, Θ, in the Koine text-tradition, and Latin versions; but it is scarcely to be preferred to *chrēstos*, read by P[4], P[57(?)], B, ℵ, W, etc. Because Luke sometimes uses the positive degree of an adj. in the sense of a comparative (or even a superlative), the clause could be translated, "The old is what is better." See 9:48; 10:42. His Greek, then, would be simply reflecting the breakdown of the degrees of adjectives in Hellenistic Greek in general (see BDF §§ 60-62; ZBG §§ 143-153; cf. P. Joüon, *RSR* 18 [1928] 345). On the textual problem, see p. 130 above.

On the face of it, the saying would support Jewish rejection of Jesus' preaching. But by its irony the saying carries just the opposite meaning.

BIBLIOGRAPHY (5:33-39)

Beilner, W. *Christus und die Pharisäer* (Vienna: Herder [1959]) 19-25.

Braumann, G. "'An jenem Tag' Mk 2,20," *NovT* 6 (1963) 264-267.

Cremer, F. G. "Lukanisches Sondergut zum Fastenstreitgespräch: Lk 5,33-39 im Urteil der patristischen und scholastischen Exegese," *TTZ* 76 (1967) 129-154.

Dillistone, F. W. "St Mark ii. 18-22: A Suggested Reinterpretation," *ExpTim* 48 (1936-1937) 253-254.

Dunkerley, R. "The Bridegroom Passage," *ExpTim* 64 (1952-1953) 303-304.

Dupont, J. "Vin vieux, vin nouveau (Luc 5,39)," *CBQ* 25 (1963) 286-304.

Feuillet, A. "La controverse sur le jeûne (*Mc* 2,18-20; *Mt* 9,14-15; *Lc* 5,33-35)," *NRT* 90 (1968) 113-136, 252-277.

Gnilka, J. "'Bräutigam'—spätjüdisches Messiasprädikat?" *TTZ* 69 (1960) 298-301.

Hahn, F. "Die Bildworte vom neuen Flicken und vom jungen Wein," *EvT* 31 (1971) 357-375.

Kee, A. "The Old Coat and the New Wine: A Parable of Repentance," *NovT* 12 (1970) 13-21.

———— "The Question about Fasting," *NovT* 11 (1969) 161-173.

Kuhn, H.-W. *Ältere Sammlungen im Markusevangelium* (SUNT 8; Göttingen: Vandenhoeck und Ruprecht, 1971) 61-72.

O'Hara, J. "Christian Fasting Mk. 2, 18-22," *Scr* 19 (1967) 82-95.

Reicke, B. "Die Fastenfrage nach Luk 5,33-39," *TZ* (1974) 321-328.

Roloff, J. *Das Kerygma und der irdische Jesus: Historische Motive in den Jesus-Erzählungen der Evangelien* (Göttingen: Vandenhoeck und Ruprecht, 1970) 235-237.

Schäfer, K. T. "'. . . und dann werden sie fasten, an jenem Tage' (Mk 2,20 und Parallelen)," in *Synoptische Studien Alfred Wikenhauser . . . dargebracht* (ed. J. Schmid and A. Vögtle; Munich: K. Zink [1953] 124-147.

Synge, F. C. "Mark ii.21=Matthew ix.16=Luke v.36: The Parable of the Patch," *ExpTim* 56 (1944-1945) 26-27.

Ziesler, J. A. "The Removal of the Bridegroom: A Note on Mark ii. 18-22 and Parallels," *NTS* 19 (1972-1973) 190-194.

27. DEBATES ABOUT THE SABBATH
(6:1-11)

6 1 One Sabbath Jesus happened to be walking through fields of grain, and his disciples plucked some ears and, rubbing them in their hands, began to eat them. 2 Some of the Pharisees remarked, "Why do you do what is prohibited on the Sabbath?" 3 Jesus replied to them, "Have you not even read what David did when he got hungry, he and those with him? 4 How he entered the house of God and took *the presentation-loaves*ᵃ to eat and gave them to those with him, even though no one but the priests alone were allowed to eat them?" 5 And he added, "The Son of Man is lord of the Sabbath."

6 On another Sabbath he happened to go into the synagogue and teach. A man was there whose right hand was stunted. 7 The Scribes and the Pharisees kept watching him to see whether he would cure on the Sabbath, that they might be able to file a charge against him. 8 But Jesus was aware of their thoughts. So he said to the man with the stunted hand, "Get up and stand in front of them." He got up and stood there. 9 Then Jesus said to them, "Let me ask you: Is it allowed on the Sabbath to do good to people or do harm, to save a life or do away with it?" 10 And taking them all in with a glance, he said to the man, "Stretch out your hand!" The man did so, and the use of his hand was restored. 11 Beside themselves with fury, they began to debate what they might do with Jesus.

ᵃ 1 Sam 21:7

COMMENT

The last controversy-story of the present group which Luke has inserted into his Gospel at this point deals with Jesus' attitude toward the observance of the Sabbath (6:1-11). Actually, it is a double controversy, inherited as a pair from Mark 2:23-3:6. They are often treated separately, partly because of the separation of them in the Marcan Gospel by the medieval chapter-division and partly because of the Lucan introduction of the second one by "on another Sabbath" (6:6), whereas in the

Marcan sequence the would-be second controversy takes place in a synagogue on the same Sabbath, "and he entered a synagogue" (3:1).
Topically, however, the two deal with Jesus' attitude to Sabbath-observ-
ance and probably stem from a topical collocation of them in a pre-Marcan collection of episodes (see H.-W. Kuhn, *Ältere Sammlungen*, 72-81;
F. Neirynck, "Jesus and the Sabbath," 229).

The two controversies not only follow the sequence of the Marcan stories (2:23-28; 3:1-6), but are also best regarded as derived by Luke
from the Marcan source, with some redactional modification. For the first
part of the episode (6:1-5), the chief modifications are the following:
(1) Luke omits the unnecessary phrase about the disciples' making their
way (*hodon poiein*, 2:23b) and adds instead that they were rubbing the
grain in their hands and eating it (6:1). (2) He omits the dating of the
David-incident "under Abiathar the high priest" (2:26). (3) He omits
the saying of Jesus in 2:27, "The Sabbath was made for man, not man for
the Sabbath." (4) He changes the word order in 6:5 (see Mark 2:28).
For the second part of the episode (6:6-11), the chief modifications are:
(1) Luke makes the second controversy take place "on another Sabbath"
(6:6). (2) He depicts the man in the synagogue with a stunted "right"
hand (6:6b; cf. Mark 3:1). (3) He introduces "the Scribes and the Pharisees" as those who are watching Jesus (6:7; cf. Mark 3:2. (4) He adds
the notice that Jesus was aware of their thoughts (6:8a). (5) He omits
the mention of the adversaries reduced to silence (see Mark 3:4d). (6)
He drops all reference to the consultation of the Pharisees with the
Herodians (Mark 3:6). See NOTES for other, minor cases.

Though T. Schramm (*Der Markus-Stoff*, 111-112) has minutely cata-
logued the differences in the Lucan and Matthean forms of the story over
against Mark and is inclined to appeal to a variant-source beyond Mark
2:23-28 for the first part (6:1-5), he had to admit that there was "no
certain evidence" for it; and he postulates no variant at all for the second
part (6:6-11). Part of the problem in the first part is the minor
agreements of Matthew and Luke against Mark, but they can be exaggerated. For instance, though *hodon poiein*, "make one's way," is found in
the LXX of Judg 17:8, the better way of expressing it would be with the
middle voice of the infin. *poieisthai* (see F. Neirynck, "Jesus and the Sabbath," 257-258) and is perhaps avoided for this reason, or because it is really unnecessary and repetitious (for an attempt to give it a different
meaning, see B. Murmelstein, "Jesu Gang," 111-120; P. Benoit, "Les
épis," 236-238; on this view, which does not concern us here, see
F. Neirynck, "Jesus and the Sabbath," 254-261). Or, again, both Matthew
and Luke omit the dating of the David-incident under Abiathar because
they both independently recognized it as wrong. Again, the change in
word order in Luke 6:5 and Matt 12:8 merely reveals their independent
preference for a better order. The common omission of Mark 2:27 is the

real problem. The reason for the omission depends in part on how one explains the relation of v. 27 to v. 28 in the Marcan source (on which see Neirynck, ibid., 231-246); the addition of v. 28 to v. 27 undoubtedly was intended as a restriction of the freedom expressed in the former verse. The common omission of v. 27 may well be a reaction of the same sort (see E. Haenchen, *Der Weg Jesu* [2d ed.; Berlin: de Gruyter, 1968] 121).

No matter how one wants to explain the relation of Jesus' sayings in Mark 2:27-28 and 3:4 to the contexts in which they are now found, it is clear that Luke has inherited two of them (2:28 and 3:4) from Mark (=Luke 6:5,9). In fact, they are the pronouncements in the pair of stories used here. E. Lohse ("Jesu Worte") may well be right in regarding the first part of this episode as a community creation, because it deals with a Pharisaic reaction to Jesus' disciples, though preserving an authentic saying of Jesus in Mark 2:27, and in tracing the second part (in its Marcan form) back to the ministry of Jesus itself, with its authentic saying in 3:4. No matter how one wants to view Mark 2:28, it has now become the pronouncement in Luke 6:5, and the reaction of the opponents (to the disciples in the first part, and to Jesus in the second) reveals a certain difference in the two stories. In the Lucan form of these stories one finds the attitude of early Christians toward the Sabbath observance of the Jews not only enshrined, but traced to an attitude of Jesus himself.

The Lucan message in this double episode is easily discerned: even such an institution as the Sabbath-rest, depicted in Genesis 1 as of divine origin, has to yield to other considerations. Verse 1 describes the first consideration: hungry disciples plucking ears of grain from a neighbor's field can do this even on the Sabbath. Their act, which seems at first to be nonchalant plucking, is explained by the story of David and his companions who were hungry. Ahimelech, the priest in Yahweh's sanctuary, knew how to make an exception to the regulations about "holy bread" to ease the hunger and material needs of his fellowmen. Jesus cites this example from Scripture itself to the critical Pharisees, even though it has nothing to do per se with the Sabbath. The joining to this example of David (from 1 Sam 21:2-7 [1-6E]) of the pronouncement in 6:5, "The Son of Man is lord of the Sabbath," not only forestalls a retort from the Pharisees that after all he is not David, but provides a basis for Jesus' defense of his disciples. It is an implicit christological affirmation: he is greater than David, for he is lord of the Sabbath. His "lordship" is now added to his "power" (4:14,36; 5:17) and his "authority" (4:32,36; 5:24); and he is "lord" precisely as "the Son of Man."

Another consideration to which the institution of Sabbath-rest must yield is a charitable deed that Jesus himself would perform, not on behalf of his disciples, but on behalf of an unfortunate individual, a man with a stunted hand, scarcely *in extremis*. The Pharisaic tradition knew of exceptions that could be made to Sabbath-rest, at least if we may judge by the later rabbinical tradition (see Str-B, 1. 622-629): "Whenever there is doubt whether life is in danger, this overrides the Sabbath" (*m. Yoma* 8:6). But the gospel tradition, which depicts Jesus curing a less extreme case, seems to know nothing of that tradition. Jesus' query (6:9), which is the pronouncement in this scene, appeals to common sense. It emphasizes the freedom that his followers will have in the face of such regulations, when there is the opportunity to do good for people or save a life. The second story, which ends with the recounting of a miracle, enshrines his pronouncement and exemplifies his ministry of love. Coming on the heels of the preceding controversy, it elucidates in yet another way how "the Son of Man is lord of the Sabbath."

The end of the story reveals the beginning of an opposition to Jesus that will mount. Luke does not follow Mark in depicting the Pharisees going into consultation with the Herodians about how they might destroy him. Luke prefers to tone down the notice of such specific opposition.

NOTES

6 1. *One Sabbath.* Lit. "on a Sabbath." Luke here uses the sg. *sabbatō* (see NOTE on 4:31) in contrast to the Marcan pl., *tois sabbasin*.

The reading *en sabbatō* is found in a number of important mss. (P⁴, P⁷⁵⁽⁷⁾, ℵ, B, L, W, the Lake family of minuscules, etc.). However, a number of other (important) mss. (A, C, D, K, X, Θ, etc.) have a strange variant, *en sabbatō deuteroprōtō*, which is almost untranslatable (lit. "on [the] second-first Sabbath"). The Freer family of minuscules writes the adj. as two words, *deuterō prōtō*. The adj. occurs nowhere else in Greek writings of any sort; it has been labeled a *vox nihili* (MM, 143). In desperation, BGD (177) has translated it, "first but one," referring to Epiphanius *Panarion* 30.32; GCS, 25. 378. For centuries it has been a *crux interpretum*. Support for it has been sought at times on the principle of the more difficult reading, and more recently it has been thought to reflect a Semitic expression derived from an ancient priestly calendar once in use among Palestinian Jews and preserved among the Essenes of Qumran. This interpretation would take it to refer to the Sabbath of the wave-offering of firstfruits, the Sabbath from which Pentecost was to be reckoned. According to Lev 23:15 it was to be counted as fifty days "from the morrow after the Sabbath" (*mimmohŏrat haššabbāt*), an obscure phrase that evoked much controversy in dating even in antiquity. Those using the old priestly calendar would explain the "second-first Sabbath" as the first Sabbath after the feast of unleavened bread, but the second after passover itself. Cf. 11QTemple 18:10 - 19:9. See further J.-P. Audet, "Jésus et le 'calendrier sacerdotal ancien': Autour d'une variante de Luc 6,1," *ScEccl* 10 (1958) 361-383; J. Baumgarten, "The Counting of the Sabbath in Ancient Sources,"

VT 16 (1966) 277-286; G. W. Buchanan and C. Wolfe, "The 'Second-first Sabbath' (Luke 6:1)," *JBL* 97 (1978) 259-262; E. Vogt, "Sabbatum 'deuteró-prôton' in Lc 6,1 et antiquum kalendarium sacredotale," *Bib* 40 (1959) 102-105; E. Mezger, "Le sabbat 'second-premier' de Luc," *TZ* 32 (1976) 138-143 (he would interpret it to mean "on the second Sabbath of the first [month]"); E. Delebecque, "Sur un certain Sabbat," *Revue de philologie* 48 (1974) 26-29.

The best solution of this problematic word is to regard it as the result of a scribal gloss. Luke has mentioned a Sabbath three times (4:31; 6:1 and 6:6); in the last he has added *heterō*, "another." Some copyist may have put *prōtō*, "first," in 6:1, to which another added *deuterō* in view of 4:31 (as in the Freer family of minuscule mss.); in time the two words became *deuteroprōtō*. Cf. B. M. Metzger, *TCGNT*, 139. We prefer to retain the simple reading in the best Greek mss.

Jesus happened to be walking. Lit. "and it happened (that) he was making his way through standing grain." Luke uses here *egeneto de* + infin. *diaporeuesthai* (see p. 118 above). Here the Marcan parallel (2:23) has the sole instance of a variant of this construction in that Gospel (*kai egeneto auton paraporeuesthai*).

plucked. To pluck ears of grain from a neighbor's field was permitted according to Deut 23:26 [25E], provided that one did not presume to put a sickle to the standing grain. But cf. B. Cohen, *HTR* 23 (1930) 91-92.

rubbing them in their hands. I.e. to separate the kernels from the chaff. This is a Lucan addition to the inherited text.

began to eat them. Lit. "were eating (them)," the impf. tense of *esthiōn* expresses continuous action.

2. *Some of the Pharisees.* Luke has modified the mention of the opponents, using the indef. pron. *tines* and the partitive genitive. Mark 2:24 has simply "the Pharisees."

Why do you do. The Marcan source used the third pl. *poiousin* of the disciples, but Luke has changed it to the second pl. to include Jesus in the Pharisees' criticism.

what is prohibited on the Sabbath. Exod 34:21 enjoins the Sabbath-rest even at harvesttime. To ensure respect for its observance, tradition "built a fence" for it by explaining "plucking" as a form of proscribed "reaping" (see *m. Šabbat* 7:2; cf. *y. Šabb.* 7.9b; Str-B, 1. 617).

3. *Jesus replied to them.* Lit. "in reply, Jesus said to them" (see NOTE on 5:33). Luke adds the ptc. *apokritheis*, thus making Jesus answer directly the criticism addressed to them all in the second pl. One detects here the early Christian community presenting itself in controversy with contemporary Jews and defended by Jesus himself.

Have you not even read. I.e. in the Scriptures. The Lucan counterquestion with *oude*, "not even," instead of the Marcan *oudepote*, "never," heightens the irony of Jesus' words. He implies that the action of the disciples is even justified by Scripture itself.

what David did when he got hungry. Jesus first appeals to Scripture, to the story of the eating of the "holy bread" by David and his hungry young companions at the sanctuary of Nob (1 Sam 21:2-7 [1-6E]).

4. *entered the house of God.* This anachronistic detail is derived from Mark; the Solomonic "house of God" had not yet been built. At the sanctuary of Nob the priest Ahimelech "gave him the holy bread" (1 Sam 21:7). Luke omits Mark's erroneous identification of the priest as Abiathar (as does Matt 12:4).

took. Luke adds the ptc. *labōn* to the Marcan finite verbs *ephagen,* "ate," and *edōken,* "gave." J. A. Grassi (*NovT* 7 [1964-1965] 119-122), in dependence on patristic interpreters, sees in this modification an echo of early Christian eucharistic catechesis, based on a Christian reading of 1 Samuel 21.

the presentation-loaves. Or "the shewbread" (*KJV*), or "the bread of the Presence" (*RSV*). In Hebrew *leḥem happānîm,* lit. "the bread of the face," denotes the loaves set out in Yahweh's presence (see Exod 25:30; 35:13; 39:36; 40:23). The Mosaic instructions for the desert-tabernacle included the setting of it out on a table of acacia wood before Yahweh and the continual renewing of it. In the Solomonic Temple the "continual bread" was placed on a golden table spread with a blue cloth (Num 4:7; 1 Kgs 7:48; 2 Chr 4:19). Because twelve loaves were arranged in two rows with frankincense, they were also called "the bread of the row" (*leḥem hamma'āreket,* 1 Chr 9:32). The NT term, "the loaves of presentation" (*artoi tēs protheseōs*), is derived from the LXX, where it is used rather uniformly to translate the various Hebrew expressions. See Lev 24:5-9 for the prescriptions for making of this bread. It was set out every Sabbath, when the loaves of the preceding week were to be consumed by "Aaron and his sons" (Lev 24:9).

Ahimelech, the priest at Nob, having no other bread to feed David and his companions, gave them the "holy bread," once he had learned that they "had kept themselves from women" (v. 4), a detail on which David insisted, "whenever I go on an expedition." In recounting the story of David at Nob (*Naba*), Josephus says that he received from "Abimelech the high priest" [*sic!*] some "provisions" (*ephodia*), making no mention of the "holy bread" (*Ant.* 6.12,1 §§ 242-243). This treatment of the biblical narrative is also found at times in later rabbinical literature, which sought to defend David's act (e.g. by explaining that it was shewbread already removed from the table, or that it was profane bread; see Str-B, 1. 618-619).

no one but the priests alone. Luke has added *monous;* Matt 12:4 has *monois* (an insignificant minor agreement). The prohibition is implicit in the David story (1 Samuel 21), but set forth explicitly in Lev 24:9, "for Aaron and his sons."

It should be noted that there is no mention of the Sabbath in the David story. The connection is made already in the Marcan source. It has often been thought that the David story was only secondarily added to the tradition of Jesus' defense of his disciples and the saying about the Sabbath (e.g. 2:23,24,27). See commentaries on Mark.

5. *And he added.* Lit. "and he said to them." Here Luke has not used his favorite expression (see NOTE on 5:33), but the Marcan phrase, *elegen* + the dative.

The Son of Man. See NOTE on 5:24. Here the phrase refers to Jesus' earthly ministry and even implies a certain dignity, a superiority over regulations in Scripture.

Mark 2:27-28 reads, "The Sabbath was made for human beings, not human beings for the Sabbath; so the Son of Man is lord even of the Sabbath." Because of this collocation in the earlier tradition, "Son of Man" may have meant no more than "human being" (in the generic sense). In this sense it would suit the context and be an apt answer to the disciples' critics. But here in Luke *ho huios tou anthrōpou* is almost certainly used in the titular sense for Jesus. It is part of the christological buildup of the Gospel as it develops.

lord of the Sabbath. Luke has omitted the adv. *kai* in Mark 2:28 and changed the word order (as does Matt 12:8). In Mark the adverb heightens the contrast, as does the position of the genitive at the end of the sentence. Luke puts "the Son of Man" at the end.

In Luke Jesus is presented as the lord of the Sabbath because of his *exousia* as the Son of Man in preaching the kingdom. If a human being can in certain cases dispense with regulations set down in Scripture, then so can the Son of Man. Without formally abolishing the Sabbath regulations, Jesus subordinates them to his person and mission.

Marcion and ms. D read v. 5 after v. 10, and the latter reads in place of v. 5 the following: "That same day he saw a man working on the Sabbath and said to him, 'Sir, if you know what you are doing, you are fortunate; but if you do not, then you are accursed and a violator of the law." This saying, however, is similar to a number of sayings in the Coptic *Gos. Thomas* (e.g. § 3, 14) and undoubtedly belongs to the same apocryphal gospel tradition. See W. Käser, *ZTK* 65 (1968) 414-430.

6. *On another Sabbath.* This Lucan addition separates the second Sabbath debate from the first more clearly than in Mark 3:1.

he happened to go into the synagogue and teach. Lit. "and it happened on another Sabbath (that) he entered the synagogue and taught." Luke uses here *egeneto de* + two coordinated infins. (see p. 118 above). He has also added the detail of Jesus' teaching (see NOTE on 4:15), precisely as the background for the coming pronouncement.

right hand. This Lucan addition probably stresses what is for most people the hand for work, and it thus heightens the condition of the unfortunate person. Cf. 22:50, where the "right ear" will be cut off. It is a storyteller's detail that makes it clear that the person is not *in extremis.*

stunted. Lit. "dried up," i.e. atrophied in its growth. Luke uses the adj. *xēra*, whereas Mark 3:1 has the ptc. *exērammenēn;* but the adj. follows in 3:3. Luke's description is thus more consistent.

7. *they might be able to file a charge against him.* Lit. "they might find to accuse him." The awkward Greek expression uses the subjunctive of the verb *heuriskein* with an infin. *katēgorein.* It is often translated, "find a charge against him" (BAG, 325), making a noun out of the infin. A supposed parallel is said to be in Paris Papyrus 45:7 (from 153 B.C.): *mē heurē ti kata sou <e>ipein,* "lest he find something to say against you." But it is not exact, since the papyrus contains the direct object *ti,* "something," precisely what is

lacking in Luke's expression. The awkward phrase is not found in Mark 3:2, *hina katēgorēsōsin autou,* "that they might accuse him." Luke's expression, however, may reflect an Aramaism; the verb *škḥ,* which usually means "find," has long been known to mean "be able" in Eastern Aramaic; but it is now attested as well in Western (Palestinian) Aramaic, e.g. in 1QapGen 21:13; 4QEnGiants[b] 1 ii 13 (see *MPAT,* 74, 116). Hence, Greek *heurōsin* is used here with an Aramaic nuance. Cf. BGD § 325b.

8. *was aware of their thoughts.* This is another Lucan addition, which depicts Jesus sizing up his critics' close watch of him. See NOTES on 2:35; 5:22.

and stand in front of them. Lit. "and stand in the middle." The Marcan text has merely "get up in the middle"; Luke's addition smooths out the injunction, as does the further phrase, "he got up and stood (there)." See NOTE on 1:39. The unfortunate man is made to take a position center-stage.

9. *Let me ask you.* This Lucan addition points up the question to be asked; it is a deliberate provocation of the Scribes and Pharisees by Jesus the teacher.

Is it allowed . . . to do good. His question again enshrines the pronouncement of this story. It is a casuistic question, but one that appeals to ordinary common sense. It reflects the kind of debate about works on the Sabbath that is known from later rabbinic discussions (see Str-B, 1. 622-630). Implied in the question is an accusation that to refuse to do good is to do evil. Can one do evil on the Sabbath?

save a life. Greek *psychē* is used here, clearly in the sense of "life." See NOTE on 9:24.

10. *taking them all in with a glance.* Luke omits the mention of the silence of his critics (see Mark 3:4), but retains the Marcan description of Jesus' reaction, adding "all" (*pantas*) and omitting Jesus' emotion, "in anger" (Mark 3:5). See NOTE on "all," 4:15.

did so. Instead of the Marcan form, "he stretched it out," Luke prefers a generic description of the man's compliance.

11. *Beside themselves with fury.* Lit. "they were filled with madness." The Greek noun *a-noia* actually describes a state of unthinking or thoughtlessness and often means no more than "folly." But Plato (*Timaeus* 86B) distinguished two kinds of it: *mania* ("madness, fury") and *amathia* ("ignorance"). The former meaning suits the Lucan context better; it expresses the hardness of the hearts of Jesus' critics.

what they might do with Jesus. Luke mollifies the plans made by the Pharisees with the Herodians, who seek in Mark (3:6) to "destroy him."

BIBLIOGRAPHY (6:1-11)

Beare, F. W. " 'The Sabbath Was Made for Man?' " *JBL* 79 (1960) 130-136.

Benoit, P. "Les épis arrachés (Mt 12,1-8 et par.)," *SBFLA* 13 (1962-1963) 76-92.

Gils, F. "Le sabbat a été fait pour l'homme et non l'homme pour le sabbat,' (Mc, II, 27)," *RB* 69 (1962) 506-523.

Grassi, J. A. "The Five Loaves of the High Priest (Mt xii, 1-8; Mk ii, 23-28; Lk vi, 1-5; 1 Sam xxi, 1-6)," *NovT* 7 (1964-1965) 119-122.

Hinz, C. "Jesus und der Sabbat," *KD* 19 (1973) 91-108.

Hultgren, A. J. "The Formation of the Sabbath Pericope in Mark 2:23-28," *JBL* 91 (1972) 38-43.

Kuhn, H.-W. *Ältere Sammlungen im Markusevangelium* (SUNT 8; Göttingen: Vandenhoeck und Ruprecht, 1971) 72-81.

Lohse, E. "Jesu Worte über den Sabbat," in *Judentum—Urchristentum— Kirche: Festschrift für Joachim Jeremias* (BZNW 26; ed. W. Eltester; Berlin: Töpelmann, 1960) 79-89.

Murmelstein, B. "Jesu Gang durch die Saatfelder," *Angelos* 3 (1930) 111-120.

Neirynck, F. "Jesus and the Sabbath: Some Observations on Mark II, 27," *Jésus aux origines de la christologie* (BETL 40; ed. J. Dupont; Gembloux: Duculot, 1975) 227-270.

Neuhäusler, E. "Jesu Stellung zum Sabbat," *BibLeb* 12 (1971) 1-16.

Pfättisch, J. M. "Der Herr des Sabbats," *BZ* 6 (1908) 172-178.

Troadec, H. "Le fils de l'homme est maître même du sabbat (Marc 2,23-26)," *BVC* 21 (1958) 73-83.

C. THE PREACHING OF JESUS

Jesus chooses twelve special disciples and preaches his first great sermon to the crowds

28. THE CHOOSING OF THE TWELVE
(6:12-16)

6 ¹² Once during those days Jesus happened to go out to the mountain to pray and spent the night in prayer to God. ¹³ When it was day, he called his disciples and chose twelve of them whom he also named apostles: ¹⁴ Simon, whom he named Peter, and his brother Andrew; James and John; Philip and Bartholomew; ¹⁵ Matthew and Thomas; James, son of Alphaeus, and Simon, surnamed the zealot; ¹⁶ Judas, son of James, and Judas Iscariot, who became a traitor.

COMMENT

Luke's account of Jesus' ministry now moves into a new phase. The beginnings in Galilee were described in various traditional scenes of teaching and healing centered about two episodes that Luke had transposed for programmatic effect, the visit to Nazareth and the role of Simon the fisherman. That account of beginnings was followed by a block of controversy-stories in which Jesus was portrayed offsetting Pharisaic and scribal criticism of himself and his disciples; they ended with the mention of talk among them about what to do with Jesus. Now Luke's story moves a step further, as it presents Jesus fashioning for himself a small group of special disciples and giving samples of his preaching to the crowds.

This section is begun with another Lucan transposition. Two scenes that are dependent on the Marcan order are taken up (3:7-12 and 3:13-19) but are now reversed, becoming respectively Luke 6:17-19 and 6:12-16. The reason for this shift is not wholly clear; but it may be that Luke is following the order in another source (some say "Q"), for the transposition creates a parallel with Matt 4:24-25, a summary of cures that precedes the sermon on the mount. The effect of the transposition in Luke is to put a similar summary mentioning multiple cures just before the extended sermon associated with Jesus' early ministry, the so-called sermon on the plain. Some have also seen the order of names in the first episode as closer to that in Matthew than in Mark; but this is more problematic. In any case, as H. Conzelmann has put it (*Theology*, 45), the transposition is made "for literary reasons." It contrasts the discipleship of the Twelve (6:12-16) with the opposition and debate of the Scribes and the Pharisees in the preceding episode (6:1-11). The choosing of the Twelve is a foreshadowing, not only of their mission in 9:1-6, but also of their role in Acts 1:2,8,26; 2:14. See further T. Schramm, *Der Markus-Stoff*, 113-114.

Even though transposed, the first episode, the choosing of the Twelve (6:12-16), is under Marcan influence; but most of it has to be ascribed to Lucan redaction. The introductory verses (6:12-13a) are characteristically Lucan with its *egeneto de* construction, mention of "the mountain," and the prayer of Jesus; likewise Lucan is the distinction between the "disciples" and the "Twelve" (v. 13), a distinction that will be exploited in the separate mission of the Twelve (9:1-6) and of the "seventy(-two)" (10:1-12,17-20). A further Lucan trait is seen in the identification of the Twelve as "apostles." The order of the names in this passage agrees neither with that of Matthew or Mark, nor even with the other Lucan list in Acts 1:13. The four lists given below show three groups of four names, in which Peter, Philip, and James, son of Alphaeus, are always the first in each group, whereas the other names, while remaining constant within the group, vary in order. The grouping is probably a mnemonic device—but not a very successful one at that, as the variation makes plain. That the lists preserve the names of some of the companions of Jesus during his ministry is beyond doubt. But the fluctuation in the names reveals that they were not all precisely remembered as time wore on. D. N. Freedman has called my attention to a similar fluctuation in the order of the names of the twelve tribes in Genesis 49, Deuteronomy 33, and Judges 5. With these one can also compare the order in the *Testaments of the Twelve Patriarchs* and in Rev 7:5-8. Other factors, like the transmission of names over a longer period of time, the migration of tribes, and the absorption or splitting of them, would explain this fluctuation.

The Twelve and the apostolate are hardly the creation of Luke; if they were he would have made more of them (see further pp. 253-255 above). He utilizes a tradition about disciples of Jesus, about the Twelve, and about apostles and uses it in a way that differs from Mark and Matthew.

But even his own account reveals that the role of both the Twelve and the apostles waned in time.

The following chart lists the names of the Twelve as they appear in four places in the NT:

Mark 3:16-19	Luke 6:12-16	Acts 1:13	Matt 10:2-4
Simon, . . . Peter	Simon, . . . Peter	Peter	Simon, . . . Peter
James, son of Zebedee	Andrew, his brother	John	Andrew, his brother
John, brother of James	James	James	James, son of Zebedee
Andrew	John	Andrew	John, his brother
Philip	Philip	Philip	Philip
Bartholomew	Bartholomew	Thomas	Bartholomew
Matthew	Matthew	Bartholomew	Thomas
Thomas	Thomas	Matthew	Matthew, the toll-collector
James, son of Alphaeus	James, (son) of Alphaeus	James, (son) of Alphaeus	James, (son) of Alphaeus
Thaddaeus	Simon, surnamed the zealot	Simon, the zealot	Thaddaeus (or Lebbaeus)
Simon, *ho Kananaios*	Judas, (son) of James	Judas, (son) of James	Simon, *ho Kananaios*
Judas Iscariot, who even betrayed him	Judas Iscariot, who became a traitor	————	Judas Iscariot, who even betrayed him

The special purpose of the Lucan list can be seen in the omission of the Marcan statement of the purpose of the Twelve and the attribution of the title for them, "apostles," to Jesus himself. For Luke these special disciples were not simply to "be with him" (Mark 3:14), but they were to be his "emissaries" (*apostoloi*, i.e. persons sent out), indeed, even witnesses to him. This note is caught up again in Luke 11:49; 24:46-48. This is also one of the reasons why the Twelve has to be reconstituted after the death of Judas Iscariot for the reception of the Pentecostal outpouring of the Spirit and the carrying of Jesus' message first of all to Israel.

The criteria for an "apostle" elsewhere in the NT seem to be mainly two: (a) a witness of the risen Christ (e.g. 1 Cor 9:1, "Am I not an apostle? Have I not seen Jesus our Lord"; cf. 1 Cor 15:8); and (b) a commission by Jesus to proclaim the Christ-event (e.g. Gal 1:15-16). But the criteria that Luke sets forth in Acts for "the Twelve" build on these. First of all, he reformulates the above criteria in an abstract way: the one who will take Judas' place will have to be "a witness to his [i.e.

Jesus'] resurrection" (1:22), i.e. not someone who had physically witnessed the resurrection, but a witness to the risen Christ; he will also take over Judas' "ministry and apostleship" (1:25). Secondly, Luke adds two further criteria: (c) that he must be a man, "one of the men" (*andrōn*, not *anthrōpōn*); and (d) that he must have accompanied the Eleven "during the whole time that Lord Jesus moved in and out among us" (1:22). For the implications of these criteria, see further pp. 253-257 above.

Even though there are indications in the NT that the "apostles" were a larger group, distinct from the "disciples" and from "the Twelve," this episode in the Lucan Gospel makes the Twelve the clear object of a "choice" by Jesus during his ministry and equates with them the apostles, ascribing even this title to Jesus himself.

NOTES

6 12. *Once during those days Jesus happened to go out.* Lit. "and it happened in those days (that) he went out . . . to pray, and he was spending the night. . . ." Luke uses here *egeneto de* + infin. *exelthein* (see p. 118 above) followed by an infin. of purpose, *proseuxasthai,* and then the impf. of the verb "to be" with a pres. ptc. *dianyktereuōn,* "spending the night." The verse is intended to mark a transition from the controversy-stories to a new topic.

the mountain. Even though "the mountain" is mentioned in Mark 3:13, whence the detail probably comes, it takes on the special connotation as a place of prayer, as elsewhere in Luke (9:28). It is the locale of God's presence, of a nearness to the revealing God. Later on in the Gospel a specific mountain will be mentioned near Jerusalem (19:29; 21:37; 22:39), but the connotation will be continued. *Pace* H. Schürmann (*Lukasevangelium,* 313), it is not part of a New Moses motif in this Gospel.

to pray. Ms. D inserts the conj. *kai* before the infin. *proseuxasthai,* which coordinates it with *exelthein,* making them both dependent on *egeneto de:* "Jesus happened to go out . . . and to pray" (cf. 6:6 above). We follow the better attested Greek text, which eliminates the conj.

spent the night in prayer to God. Lit. "in the prayer of God." *Tou theou* has to be understood as an objective genitive; it is omitted in ms. D, probably because of its awkwardness, or perhaps because Jesus' prayer is mentioned in neither Mark nor Matthew. This Lucan addition enhances the setting for the choice of the Twelve, implying that God's blessing has been invoked upon it. Perhaps too it is the Lucan Jesus' way of saying what is said in John 17:6 about those whom the Father had given to him. In Acts 1:2 Luke will say that he chose the apostles "through the holy Spirit." See further p. 231 above.

13. *When it was day.* A Lucan addition to prepare for the choosing, which is also located here on the mountain (see 6:17).

he called his disciples. Presumably those mentioned in 6:1, who are more numerous than the Twelve to be chosen. Mark 3:13-14 does not call them *mathētai*.

chose. The Greek ptc. *eklexamenos* is a Lucan addition, ascribing to Jesus the choice of a small group from among the disciples. Mark 3:13 says merely that he called those whom he wanted "and made (*RSV:* appointed) twelve to be with him." Luke at least follows Mark in rooting a "call" of the Twelve in the ministry of Jesus.

twelve of them. Reference to the Twelve is found in the primitive tradition of 1 Cor 15:5, the only place in the Pauline corpus where they are mentioned. The phrase, *hoi dōdeka,* is part of the early church tradition, being found also in Mark 3:16; 4:10; 6:7; 9:35; 10:32; 11:11; 14:10,17,20,43; in the Johannine tradition, 6:67,70,71; 20:24; in "L" (Luke 8:1); and reflected in the "Q" passage of 22:29-30 (=Matt. 19:28). Whether the association of the Twelve with the twelve tribes of Israel is primitive or not may be debated. See the COMMENT on Luke 22:29-30.

Writers like W. Schmithals (*The Office,* 67-71) question whether the institution of the Twelve is actually to be ascribed to Jesus himself. See p. 253 above for some considerations in favor of such an ascription. Paul in 1 Cor 15:5 cites a pre-Pauline list that associates their existence to the resurrection of Jesus itself—i.e. to the end of his earthly ministry. The problem is to explain why such companions of Jesus on his journeys would have disappeared so completely later on in the history of the young church. They play no special role in Jerusalem once the seven are appointed (Acts 6:1-6). See further K. H. Rengstorf, *TDNT* 2. 326. But such considerations do not completely rule out the roots of the Twelve in the ministry of Jesus itself.

whom he also named apostles. Here Luke ascribes to Jesus a title for the Twelve, *apostolous,* "apostles." Derived from the verb *apostellein,* "send," the word denoted in earlier Greek, when it was only occasionally used, something or someone sent, e.g. a naval expedition, an envoy (Herodotus 1.21), a colonist, a bill of lading (see MM, 70). Josephus (*Ant.* 17.11,1 § 300) uses it in an abstract sense for the "sending" of a delegation of Jews to Rome. It occurs only once in the LXX, translating the pass. ptc. *šālûaḥ* in 1 Kgs 14:6, "sent" (*RSV,* "charged"; *NAB,* "commissioned"), said of Ahijah sent by God with a message for the wife of Jeroboam.

Despite this background, it is clear that in the NT *apostolos* is a technical term for a Christian emissary or missionary commissioned to preach the Christ-event, or in Lucan terms, "the word of God." This specifically Christian use of the term is evident from the failure of later Christians to translate it into Latin; instead of using *missus* or something similar, they simply transcribed the Greek word, *apostolus,* and transcriptions have persisted in modern languages.

The institution of "apostles" in Christianity has been traced to the Palestinian Jewish institution of *šĕlûḥîm/šĕlîḥîn,* "the (ones) sent," i.e. emissaries commissioned by the Sanhedrin or rabbis to represent them and act in their name with authority to settle calendaric, fiscal, or legal matters (see K. H. Rengstorf, *TDNT* 1. 414-420; H. Vogelstein, "The Development"). This background has been contested by G. Klein (*Die zwölf Apostel*); Schmithals (*The Office,* 95-230), et al. They would trace the apostolate either to Paul or to

Gnostic circles in Syria, i.e. to phenomena in the early church later than the ministry of Jesus. But Paul uses an earlier tradition that already speaks of "apostles" (1 Cor. 15:7) and speaks openly of those who were apostles before him (Gal 1:17). The Palestinian institution, rooted perhaps in 1 Kgs 14:6, provides the best analogy and background to the title *apostolos*, when all is said and done. It certainly suits the role that is to be given to such emissaries in Luke 24:47-48; Acts 1:2,8.

But not even Luke says *when* Jesus gave the Twelve the name of apostles; the rare use of it in the other Gospels (see p. 254 above), however, suggests that Luke has retrojected here a post-resurrectional title, restricting it to the Twelve, in the way it came to be understood in the time of his own writing. See further J. Dupont, "Le nom d'apôtres."

14. *Simon, whom he named Peter.* The first named in the list is the one who was first called (5:1-11). He has already been named "Simon Peter" in 5:8 (see NOTES on 4:38; 5:3,8). The relative clause is Luke's modification of Mark 3:16, "he put the name Peter on Simon." It imitates the last clause of 3:13. Simon alone is here given a surname by Jesus. But since Luke has no counterpart of Matt 16:16b-19, we never learn the reason for giving it or what it is supposed to connote. Luke never relates the Greek name *Petros* ("Rock") to the Aramaic name *Kephā'* (on which see now my article, "Aramaic Kepha' and Peter's Name in the New Testament," in *Text and Interpretation: Studies in the New Testament Presented to Matthew Black* (eds. E. Best and R. M. Wilson; Cambridge: University Press, 1979) 121-132.

Andrew. He is mentioned only here and in Acts 1:13 in the Lucan writings; he is identified only as the brother of Simon Peter. From Mark 1:16,29 we learn that he too was a Galilean fisherman; cf. 13:3. From John 1:40-41,44 we learn that he came from Bethsaida and was regarded as the first called among Jesus' disciples; see further John 6:8; 12:22. His name is Greek, *Andreas*, probably meaning "manly," a name otherwise known to have been used by Palestinian Jews.

James and John. These are the Galilean fishermen, the sons of Zebedee, companions of Simon Peter (see NOTE on 5:10). Since Luke has already so identified them, he omits the details which Mark 3:17 or Matt 10:2 have. This James is often called "the Great" (to distinguish him from the one named in Mark 15:40), and his death will be reported in Acts 12:1-2. His name is derived from that of the patriarch *Iakōbos*, "Jacob" (see NOTE on 3:34). On the name of "John," see NOTE on 1:13.

Philip and Bartholomew. They are otherwise mentioned in Lucan writings only in Acts 1:13. *Philippos*, "lover of horses," was a Greek name often used by Jews, ever since the Seleucid period. According to John 1:44, Philip was from Bethsaida, the town of Andrew and Peter. See John 6:5-8; 12:22. *Bartholomaios* is a Grecized form of Aramaic *bar Tolmai* or *Talmai* (see 2 Sam 3:3 MT and LXX). He is otherwise unknown and has nothing to do with Nathanael (John 1:45-46), despite a ninth-century tradition that identifies them.

15. *Matthew.* See NOTE on 5:27.

Thomas. The Greek name, *Thōmas,* resembles Aramaic *tĕʾōmāʾ,* "the twin," and was used as its equivalent. See John 11:16; 20:24, *ho legomenos Didymos,* "who was called Didymus" (Greek word for "twin"). Both *Thōmas* and *Didymos* were probably originally epithets, because John 14:22 refers to a "Judas, not the Iscariot," who in the Curetonian Syriac version is identified as "Judas Thomas," and in the apocryphal *Acta Thomae* as *Ioudas ho kai Thomas,* "Judas, alias Thomas." In the Coptic *Gos. Thom.,* which is ascribed to him, he appears as "Didymus Judas Thomas" (see *ESBNT,* 365-368). He almost certainly has nothing to do with Judas of Mark 6:3.

James, son of Alphaeus. This member of the Twelve is not to be identified with "James the Little" (Mark 15:40) or with "James, the brother of the Lord" (Gal 1:19; 1 Cor 15:6). The latter may have been an "apostle" (depending on how one interprets *ei mē* in Gal 1:19 [see *JBC,* art. 49 § 15]), but he was scarcely one of "the Twelve." This "James, son of Alphaeus," probably has nothing to do with the James of Mark 6:3, who is probably that of Gal 1:19.

Simon, surnamed the zealot. Luke uses the Greek epithet *zēlōtēs,* a label for individual Palestinian Jews who opposed the Roman occupation of their country. Shortly before the First Revolt against Rome (A.D. 66-70) a nationalistic resistance-movement emerged in Palestine, which was called "the Zealots." Attempts have often been made to push back the emergence of this group into earlier decades, but this is questionable. Josephus is often said to have described the group as "the fourth of the philosophies" among Jews of this time (*Ant.* 18.1,6 § 23), but that is far from clear (see L. H. Feldman, *Josephus* [LCL 9; Cambridge: Harvard University, 1965] 21 n. b; M. Smith, *HTR* 64 [1971] 1-19; cf. W. R. Farmer, *Maccabees, Zealots, and Josephus* [New York: Columbia University, 1956]; M. Hengel, *Die Zeloten* [AGSU 1; Leiden: Brill, 1961]). This raises the question of the sense in which Luke has used the epithet both here and in Acts 1:13. In Mark 3:18 and Matt 10:3 the epithet is *ho Kananaios,* most likely a Greek transcription of Aramaic *qanʾānāʾ,* "zealous," for which Luke has substituted a Greek word. But in what sense does he mean it? Since it is not certain that there were Zealots (as a group) in the time of Jesus' ministry, it cannot be so understood as far as Stage I of the gospel tradition. It could mean, however, that this Simon was a "zealot" in the individual sense; but it could also represent a tag that was put on him later because of an association with the Zealots at the time that they emerged. On the name Simon, see NOTE on 4:38.

16. *Judas, son of James.* Often called Jude, to distinguish him from the following Judas; he is otherwise unknown. His name occurs here and in Acts 1:13; he is not certainly to be identified with the "Jude, brother of James," to whom the Epistle of Jude is ascribed (v. 1). *Ioudas* is a Grecized form of the name of the patriarch "Judah," see NOTE on 3:34.

In the corresponding lists (Mark 3:18; Matt 10:3) "Thaddaeus" appears. In later Christian tradition the two names are joined, "Jude Thaddaeus," but this conflation has no basis in the NT itself. Moreover, some mss. of Matt 10:3 read *Lebbaios* (D, W, Θ, the Lake family of minuscules, and the Koine text-tradition) instead of *Thaddaios*. It is unlikely that the same person had all three names. It is rather an indication that the names of the Twelve were no longer accurately preserved in the early church by the time that Luke and Matthew were writing, and that the group of the Twelve, though important at the outset, gradually lost its significance, even to the extent that people no longer could recall who once constituted the Twelve. Luke's account in Acts even shows them changing the structure of the Jerusalem church (6:1-6). See further B. Lindars, "Matthew, Levi, Lebbaeus, and the Value of the Western Text," *NTS* 4 (1957-1958) 220-222.

Judas Iscariot. He is so named in the Synoptic tradition and John 12:4; but John 6:71 and 13:26 call him "Judas, son of Simon Iscariot." Moreover, the Greek form of the latter name varies in the mss.; here the best mss. have *Iskarioth* (P⁴, ℵ*, B, L, 33); many important mss. of Luke have *Iskariōtēs* (ℵᶜ, A, K, W, X, etc.), the form preferred for Matt 10:4 on the basis of Matthean mss. But one also finds *Skariōtēs* (ms. D for Matt 10:4) and *Skarioth* (ms. D for Luke 6:12). The varied textual transmission of the name is partly connected with its meaning, which is unclear, and partly with the person to whom it belongs (see above). The best explanation is still that it represents a Greek transcription of Hebrew *'îš Qĕriyyôt*, "a man from Kerioth," i.e. from Kerioth-Hezron, a village about twelve miles S of Hebron in Judea (see Josh 15:25). This would suit either Judas or his father as an epithet, but then it would make Judas a non-Galilean among the Twelve (clarified perhaps by the variant in John 6:71, *apo Karyōtou*, "from Kerioth," in mss. ℵ*, Θ, etc.). Other less likely interpretations seek to explain the name as related to Latin *sicarius*, "daggerman" (assassin), a name used for some Palestinians who opposed the Romans (see Smith, *HTR* 64 [1971] 1-19; so O. Cullmann, *RHPR* 42 [1962] 133-140). Or as related to Aramaic *šĕqaryā'*, "the false one, liar" (so C. C. Torrey, *HTR* 36 [1943] 51-62); very unlikely. Or, again, as related to Aramaic *sĕqar*, "to dye red"—Judas would have been a "dyer" (so A. Ehrman, *JBL* 97 [1978] 572-573); highly unlikely. See further B. Gärtner, *Die rätselhaften Termini Nazoräer und Iskariot* (Horae soederblomianae 4; Uppsala/Lund: Gleerup, 1957) 37-68; D. Haugg, *Judas Iskarioth in den neutestamentlichen Berichten* (Freiburg im B.: Herder, 1930); H. Ingholt, "The Surname of Judas Iscariot," in *Studia orientalia Ioanni Pedersen . . . dicata* (Copenhagen: Munksgaard, 1953) 159-160. For a highly speculative attempt to explain the suffix *-ōth/ōtēs* on the name, see Y. Arbeitman, "The Suffix of Iscariot," *JBL* 99 (1980) 122-124.

who became a traitor. Judas thus becomes the only one in the list whose future role is mentioned. The added phrase for the last of the Twelve in each of the lists reflects the horror of the early Christian community's recollection which Judas' name conjured up (see p. 253 above).

BIBLIOGRAPHY (6:12-16)

Barrett, C. K. "The Apostles in and after the New Testament," *SEÅ* 21 (1956) 30-49.

———— *The Signs of an Apostle: The Cato Lecture 1969* (Philadelphia: Fortress, 1972).

Campenhausen, H. von. "Der urchristliche Apostelbegriff," *ST* 1 (1947) 96-130.

Cerfaux, L. "Pour l'histoire du titre *apostolos* dans le Nouveau Testament," in *Recueil L. Cerfaux* (BETL 7; Gembloux: Duculot, 1954) 2. 185-200

———— "L'Unité du corps apostolique dans le Nouveau Testament," *L'Église et les églises: Mélanges Dom Lambert Beauduin* (Chevetogne: Abbey, 1954) 99-110; reprinted in *Recueil L. Cerfaux* 2. 227-237.

Dupont, J. "Le nom d'apôtres a-t-il été donné aux Douze par Jésus," *L'Orient syrien* 1 (1956) 267-290, 425-444.

Giblet, J. "Les Douze: Histoire et théologie," *Aux origines de l'église* (RechBib 7; Bruges: Desclée de Brouwer, 1964) 51-64.

Klein, G. *Die zwölf Apostel: Ursprung und Gestalt einer Idee* (FRLANT 77; Göttingen: Vandenhoeck und Ruprecht, 1961).

Kredel, E. M. "Der Apostelbegriff in der neueren Exegese: Historisch-kritische Darstellung," *ZKT* 78 (1956) 169-193, 257-305.

Rigaux, B. "The Twelve Apostles," *Concilium* 34 (1968) 5-15.

———— "Die 'Zwölf' in Geschichte und Kerygma," in *Der historische Jesus und der kerygmatische Christus* (Berlin: Evangelische Verlagsanstalt, 1960) 468-486.

Schmahl, G. "Die Berufung der Zwölf im Markusevangelium," *TTZ* 81 (1972) 203-213.

Schmithals, W. *The Office of Apostle in the Early Church* (Nashville: Abingdon, 1969).

Schnackenburg, R. "Apostles before and during Paul's Time," in *Apostolic History and the Gospel: Biblical and Historical Essays Presented to F. F. Bruce on His 60th Birthday* (eds. W. W. Gasque and R. P. Martin; Grand Rapids: Eerdmans, 1970) 287-303; reprinted in German, *Schriften zum Neuen Testament* (Munich: Kösel, 1971) 338-358.

Trilling, W. "Zur Entstehung des Zwölferkreises: Eine geschichtskritische Überlegung," *Die Kirche des Anfangs: Festschrift für Heinz Schürmann zum 65. Geburtstag* (eds. R. Schnackenburg et al.; Leipzig: St. Benno, 1977) 201-222.

Vogelstein, H. "The Development of the Apostolate in Judaism and Its Transformation in Christianity," *HUCA* 2 (1925) 99-123.

29. CROWDS FOLLOWING JESUS
(6:17-19)

6 17 Going down with them, Jesus stopped at a level spot. There was a great crowd of his disciples, and quite a throng of people from all over Judea, from Jerusalem, and from the seacoast towns of Tyre and Sidon. 18 They came to listen to him and to be healed of their illnesses. Those who were troubled by unclean spirits were cured; 19 and all in the crowd sought to touch him, because power went forth from him, and he healed them all.

COMMENT

This is the transposed parallel to Mark 3:7-12, which Luke has considerably shortened. Even though the transposition may have been made under the influence of a source different from Mark (see p. 613 above; T. Schramm, *Der Markus-Stoff*, 113-114), Luke has clearly modified the Marcan text in the writing of this episode. Above all, the mention of Judea, Jerusalem, Tyre, and Sidon reveal the connection between this passage and the Marcan source. The main Lucan modifications of it are the following: (1) Jesus descends to a plain (6:17) and does not go "to the sea" (Mark 3:7); (2) mention of the boat (Mark 3:9) is consequently omitted; (3) people flock to "listen" to him (6:18), a conscious preparation for the sermon to come; (4) Jesus is not recognized by unclean spirits as "the Son of God" (Mark 3:11), a detail that Luke has already used in an earlier summary (4:41); (5) Luke adds the notice about the power that goes forth from Jesus to heal (6:19b).

From a form-critical point of view, this episode is another summary statement about Jesus' ministry and attraction of people to him; they come to him to listen and to be healed by him. It is similar to earlier summaries (4:14-15,31-32,40-41).

Though Jesus in the Lucan Gospel is made to move in his ministry from Galilee to Jerusalem without leaving Jewish soil (save momentarily in 8:28), Luke is at pains here to depict crowds coming to him to *listen* and to be healed by him from *all* Judea (including Jerusalem) and even from pagan Tyre and Sidon. The emphasis in the Lucan form of the summary is on listening to him; this note has been added to the Marcan source, which rather concentrates on healings and exorcisms. This emphasis has been added in view of the sermon to come. It should also be noted that the people come not as idle curiosity-seekers who have heard about his reputation (*ēchos*, 4:37); they come to listen to him. If Luke mentions the healings and exorcisms, this is because they were in the Marcan source.

NOTES

6 17. *Going down with them.* I.e. from the mountain (6:12) with the Twelve and those disciples from whom he chose them. The Lucan Jesus descends from the mountain for the coming instruction of the disciples and crowds; he does not preach on it (see NOTE on 6:12). H. Schürmann (*Lukasevangelium*, 320) sees a parallel in Jesus' descent to that of Moses in Exod 32:7-15 or 34:29; but this is overdrawn, since it introduces a Matthean motif (the New Moses) into this Gospel, a notion which scarcely interests Luke.

stopped at a level spot. Lit. "came to a stop on a level place," i.e. some plain near the mountain. This Lucan detail differs not only from the Matthean setting for the coming sermon (5:1), but also from the Marcan withdrawal to the sea (i.e. Lake Gennesaret; see NOTE on 5:1). H. Conzelmann (*Theology*, 44) rightly characterizes the plain as "the place of meeting with the people." The verb *estē* means "he stood, came to stand" and is scarcely intended as an indication of the position/posture of Jesus as he begins his sermon (contrast 4:20).

a great crowd of his disciples. This phrase adds significance to the choice of the Twelve recounted in the preceding episode. It and the following phrase are afterthoughts of the evangelist, because they have to be construed with the preceding sg. verb *estē*, despite the plurality that is now introduced. Luke scarcely means that a throng of people were on the mountain with him. He adds "a great crowd of disciples" to the Marcan notice of *poly plēthos*, "a great throng" (3:7), which is retained in the following expression along with the addition of "of people," to distinguish them from the disciples. *Pace* W. Grundmann (*Evangelium nach Lukas*, 138), Jesus, disciples, and crowds are not figures of the structure of the church. Eisegesis!

from all over Judea. Luke again adds *pasēs*, "all (over)," but omits "from Galilee" and "from Idumea and across the Jordan" (Mark 3:7). The omission of the latter is not surprising, since in Luke Jesus does not pass through or preach in Idumea or Perea. A variant in some mss. (ℵ*, W) and some versions adds *kai* (*tēs*) *Peraias*, "and from Perea," but that is clearly a copyist's effort to harmonize Luke with Mark.

Luke makes a distinction between the geographical areas into which Jesus goes to preach and those from which people flock to hear him. But the omission of Galilee here (cf. Mark 3:7) is seen by Conzelmann (*Theology*, 45) as connected with the picture of the spread of Christian communities of a later time; he says that Galilee is absent from Acts. But it is explicitly mentioned in

Acts 9:31. Moreover, one of the motifs in the Lucan writings is the preparation of witnesses from Galilee (see Acts 10:37-42), and Galilee is mentioned in 5:17. On the other hand, it is possible to think that by "all Judea" Luke actually meant "Galilee, Judea, Idumea, and the country across the Jordan" (Mark 3:7-8), given the understanding of "Judea" in 4:44 (so J. M. Creed, *The Gospel,* 89). But it is much more likely that Luke thinks that his readers will understand that Jesus is still in Galilee and that people are pressing to him from elsewhere.

from Jerusalem. As in 5:17, the holy city is singled out from Judea.

from the seacoast towns of Tyre and Sidon. Two ancient, important cities of Phoenicia on the coast of the Mediterranean Sea are mentioned; they lay in Syria in NT times but are in Lebanon today, south of Beirut. See Acts 21:3,7; 27:3. Luke retains the mention of these cities from Mark 3:8 and depicts Gentiles flocking from them to hear Jesus. It adds a motif already sounded in Luke 2:31-32; 3:6; 4:24-27; it will be exploited in the missionary activity in Acts. More immediately, it prepares for Luke 10:13-14.

18. *to be healed.* To the listening to Jesus that Luke has added to his source, the mention of the cures is now appended. Thus Luke prepares a setting for the sermon on the plain, similar to that in Matt 4:24. Luke uses here and in v. 19 the verb *iasthai,* which occurred in 5:17; it will appear again in 7:7; 8:47; 9:2,11,42; 14:4; 17:15; 22:51; Acts 9:34; 10:38; 28:8,27.

troubled by unclean spirits. See NOTE on 4:33. On the prep. "by" (*apo*), see NOTE on 1:26. Luke omits all mention of the silencing of the spirits, since the motif of the messianic secret is of no concern to him (see NOTE on 4:41).

19. *all in the crowd sought.* Lit. "the whole crowd sought," but the verb *ezētoun* is pl., agreeing with the collective sg. subject.

to touch him. Contrast 5:13. Here Luke stresses that the crowd wanted to come into real contact with him.

power went forth from him. Luke's comment refers to "the power of the Lord" (5:17) that attended him; it was a *dynamis* for healing, derived from Yahweh. This is again a way of explaining the source of Jesus' cures. See 8:46, where Jesus will admit that "power has gone forth from me," after he has been touched by the woman with the hemorrhage. See E. May, *CBQ* 14 (1952) 93-103.

healed them all. The comprehensive character of Jesus' ministry is thus stressed by Luke, once again.

BIBLIOGRAPHY (6:17-19)

Egger, E. "Die Verborgenheit Jesu in Mk 3,7-12," *Bib* 50 (1969) 466-490.

Keck, L. E. "Mark 3:7-12 and Mark's Christology," *JBL* 84 (1964) 341-358.

Mánek, J. "On the Mount—on the Plain (Mt v 1—Lk vi 17)," *NovT* 9 (1967) 124-131.

May, E. " '. . . For Power Went forth from Him . . .' (Luke 6,19)," *CBQ* 14 (1952) 93-103.

30. THE SERMON ON THE PLAIN
(6:20-49)

6 **20** Then Jesus fixed his eyes on his disciples and addressed them:
"Blessed are you who are poor, for the kingdom of God is yours.
21 Blessed are you who go hungry now, for you shall have your
fill.

Blessed are you who weep now, for you shall laugh.

22 Blessed are you when people hate you and outlaw you,
denounce you and reject your name as evil, on account of
the Son of Man. **23** That is the time to rejoice and to leap
with joy, for great shall be your reward in heaven; in just
the same way did their fathers treat the prophets.

24 But woe to you who are rich, for you have your consolation
already.

25 Woe to you who are well-fed now, for you shall go hungry.
Woe to you who laugh now, for you shall mourn and weep.

26 Woe to you when all people speak well of you; in just the
same way did their fathers treat the false prophets.

27 But to you who listen I say, 'Love your enemies; do good to
those who hate you; **28** bless those who curse you; pray for
those who mistreat you.' **29** If someone strikes you on one
cheek, offer the other as well. If someone would take your
cloak from you, do not hinder the taking of your tunic as
well. **30** Give to everyone who begs from you; if someone
takes what is yours, do not strive to get it back. **31** And
treat people just as you wish them to treat you.

32 If you love only those who love you, what credit is there in
that? Even sinners love those who love them. **33** If you help
only those who help you, what credit is there in that? Even
sinners act in this way. **34** If you lend only to those from
whom you hope to get something, what credit is there in
that? Even sinners lend to sinners, to get back as much
again. **35** Rather, love your enemies; help people, and lend
to them, looking for nothing in return. Your reward will

then be great, and you will be sons of the Most High, for he too is kind to the ungrateful and the wicked. 36 Be merciful, even as your Father is merciful.

37 Do not judge, and you will not be judged; do not condemn, and you will not be condemned; forgive, and you will be forgiven. 38 Give, and gifts will be given to you—good measure, pressed down, shaken together, and running over, will be poured into the lap of your garment. For the measure you use with others will be the measure by which return is made to you."

39 And he addressed to them a proverb, "Can the blind lead the blind? Will not both of them fall into a ditch? 40 Is a pupil superior to his teacher? Rather, everyone who is fully schooled will someday be like his teacher.

41 Why do you keep staring at the speck in your brother's eye and fail to see the beam in your own? 42 How can you say to your brother, 'Brother, let me take out that speck in your eye,' when you do not see the beam in your own? Hypocrite! First, get the beam out of your own eye; then you will have the sight to take the speck out of your brother's eye.

43 No good tree produces rotten fruit, nor again does a rotten tree produce good fruit; 44 for each tree is known by its own fruit. Figs are not plucked from thornbushes, nor are grapes picked from brambles. 45 The good individual brings forth good from the store of good in his heart; but the wicked brings forth only wickedness from the wickedness that is in him. After all, out of the abundance of the heart his mouth speaks.

46 Why do you address me, 'Lord, Lord,' and fail to do what I tell you? 47 Whoever comes to me listens to my words and acts on them. I shall show you what such a one is like: 48 He is like the person who, in building his house, dug deep and laid its foundations on bedrock; when the flood came, the river burst against that house, but it could not shake it loose because it was well built. 49 But the one who listens and does not act is like a person who built his house on the surface without foundations; when the river burst against it, it collapsed immediately. And great was the wreck of that house."

COMMENT

Luke now introduces into his Gospel a major sermon of Jesus, addressed specifically to the disciples (6:20-49). It epitomizes for him the instruction that Jesus gives to these persons, who are to become the Galilean "witnesses" of his preaching, teaching, and healing. The "sermon on the plain," as it is usually called (because of 6:12,17), is the counterpart of the Matthean "sermon on the mount" (5:1 - 7:27). Whereas the latter is addressed to "the crowds" and to "his disciples" (5:1), Luke's sermon is initially intended for the "disciples" only. It thus becomes a major factor in the Lucan account.

This sermon is the first part of the so-called Little Interpolation, the series of episodes that runs from 6:20 - 8:3, which has been inserted into the Marcan material that he has been using (see p. 67 above). It introduces material from "Q" and "L" as well as modifications from his own editorial pen.

The following verses of the sermon are derived from "Q": 20b-23 (=Matt 5:3,4,6,11-12); 27-33,35b-36 (=Matt 5:39-42,44-48; 7:12); 37a,38b,39bc,40-42 (=Matt 7:1-5 [10:24-25; 15:14]); 43-45 (=Matt 7:16-20 [cf. 12:33-35]); 46-49 (=Matt 7:21,24-27). Verses 24-26 are problematic; some commentators (e.g. H. Frankemölle, "Die Makarismen," 64) think that the woes were part of "Q" and have been left out by Matthew as unsuited to his sermon; others (e.g. J. Dupont, *Béatitudes* 1. 299-342) argue rather that Luke has added them. The latter is the more likely solution, in my opinion, given the heavy incidence of Lucan vocabulary in these verses. Hence they should be ascribed to Lucan composition, and Lucan redaction should be maintained for vv. 27c,28a,34-35a,37bc,38a,39a. (See further the NOTES.)

The Lucan sermon is considerably shorter than the Matthean sermon on the mount (5:3 - 7:27). Whereas Luke's sermon consists of a mere thirty verses, Matthew's has at least 107 verses (some count 109 verses, but there are some text-critical problems that do not concern us here). Despite many differences in the two sermons, there is a basic similarity in them that makes one argue to a nucleus sermon that was inherited by "Q" and that the two evangelists have reworked each in his own way. The similarities are such that they suggest that the tradition has preserved here something from an extended sermon delivered by Jesus toward the beginning of his ministry. Even though the Marcan Gospel has no counterpart of the sermon on the mount/plain, the topically arranged sermon in parables in chap. 4 of that Gospel may also be a recollection of such an early extended sermon of Jesus.

The similarities between the Matthean and Lucan forms of this extended sermon are found in the following points:

> *subject-matter* (teaching about conduct expected of disciples [or following crowds])
>
> *exordium* (the beatitudes)
>
> *content* (almost all of the Lucan sayings are found in the Matthean sermon; also an eschatological dimension of Jesus' words; and above all, the teaching about love of one's neighbor and even of one's enemies)
>
> *conclusion* (the parable of the two houses, challenging listeners to become doers)
>
> *occasion* (early in Jesus' one-year ministry and preceding the cure of a centurion's servant)
>
> *relation to a common place* (in Matt 5:1, on the "mountain"; in Luke, after descent from "the mountain" [6:12,17]).

The differences between the two sermons are largely owing to Matthew's additional use of "Q" material—material that Luke has mostly reserved for his travel account (this can best be seen by a glance at the analytical tables in a synopsis (e.g. K. Aland, *SQE,* 554-555; B. H. Throckmorton, *Gospel Parallels: A Synopsis of the First Three Gospels* [Camden, NJ: Nelson, 1967] xxi-xxii). In many of these episodes Luke has preserved the more original order of "Q" and sometimes even a more natural (perhaps the original) setting for sayings or pronouncements, whereas Matthew has topically arranged otherwise scattered, but related, sayings. For instance, contrast the use of the Our Father in Matt 6:9-13 and Luke 11:2-4.

Luke seems also to have eliminated some material that was in the nucleus sermon (and in "Q"?) because it was more suited to Jewish Christian concerns and less suited to the Gentile Christians for whom he has primarily destined his account. However one wants to assess this material, Luke clearly has no counterparts of the following Matthean verses: 5:17,19-20,21-24,27-28 (29-30?), 33-39a,43; 6:1-8,16-18; 7:6,15.

Finally, as we have already mentioned, Luke has fashioned a few verses on his own (24-26,27c,28a,34-35a,37bc,38a,39a). These, then, account for the major differences in the two sermons.

Another difference can be seen in the structure of the two sermons. In contrast to the relatively well-constructed Matthean sermon on the mount, the Lucan sermon is loose and rambling. The order of the Matthean sermon is simple: (1) *Exordium* (beatitudes and introductory sayings, 5:3-12,13-16); (2) *Proposition* (contrast of the three kinds of righteousness, implied in v. 20, 5:17-20); (3) *the righteousness of the Scribes* (six antitheses, 5:21-48); (4) *the righteousness of the Pharisees* (three practices: almsgiving, prayer, fasting, 6:1-18); (5) *the right-eousness of Christian disciples* (a series of loosely related sayings, 6:19 - 7:27). The order of the Lucan sermon, however, is not universally agreed on. It can be outlined as follows: (1) Exordium (four beatitudes and four woes, 6:20-26); (2) love even your enemies (6:27-36); (3) judge not one another (6:37-42); (4) the role of good deeds (6:43-45); (5) the need to act on these words (with a parable, 6:46-49). Some of the sayings, however, are only loosely related to these generic topics.

From a form-critical point of view, the sermon is made up of dominical sayings (beatitudes and woes, and other isolated unstructured sayings) and parables (the latter in vv. 39,48-49). See R. Bultmann, *HST*, 96, 135-136.

There is probably no other part of the gospel tradition that has under-gone more diverse interpretation over the centuries than the sermon on the mount. The Lucan sermon on the plain has suffered less of that, mostly because of benign neglect. The sayings of Jesus enshrined in the Matthean sermon have been subjected to allegorical, eschatological, fun-damentalist, sociological, and theological interpretations, most of which have since been recognized as blatantly eisegetical. From the patristic view of the sermon on the mount as an epitome of Christian ethics, to the medieval use for its distinction of precepts and counsels of perfection, to the reformation doctrine of the two kingdoms, to the theory of the impos-sible ideal of Lutheran orthodoxy, to the modern theories of interim-ethics and political non-resistance of evil, the gamut has been run—and probably not yet exhausted. Modern interpreters of the sermon, who seek to understand it in terms of its setting in the Gospel in which it is found, realize that "the message of Jesus" is not "contained in the Sermon on the Mount unadulterated and taken as a whole" (a view attributed to Gandhi). It may be a sample of the preaching of the Matthean Jesus, the *magna charta* for the kingdom as proposed in that Gospel, with its ideals, but also with its radical demands.

The sermon on the plain is a sample of the preaching of the Lucan Jesus. Its peculiar emphasis and theological import can only be judged from its place within the Lucan Gospel. Presented as an instruction to "disciples" (6:20), it is intended to shape their conduct. But it has also to be related to the mission of Jesus as presented thus far in the Gospel: he has come to preach to the poor, the prisoners, the blind, and the downtrodden of his day (in the words of Isaiah, quoted in 4:18). In the last episode Luke stressed the flocking of people to him from all over, who wanted to "listen to him" (6:18); now he presents Jesus responding and throwing out challenges even to them. The detail of 6:18 is picked up in the sermon itself: "to you who *listen* I say" (6:27); "whoever comes to me *listens* to my words and acts on them" (6:47).

Jesus' words in the sermon touch on the concerns of daily existence, poverty, hunger, grief, hatred, and ostracism; and the beatitudes and woes seek to raise those concerns to another dimension. That dimension is eschatological, perhaps less radical than the Matthean form, because Luke is less preoccupied with an imminent eschaton, but the dimension is nonetheless there. His introduction of "now" (6:21a,c; 6:25a,c) reveals his concern for Christian life here and now (see p. 234 above). Yet even these beatitudes and woes serve only as a starting-point for the heart of his message, the love which must dominate the life of the Christian disciple. It is a love of one's neighbor, and even of one's enemy—of those who may hate, curse, mistreat, beat, rob, and deprive Christians of what is rightfully theirs. The motivation proposed for such love is the love or mercy of God himself, the father of Christian existence, which is to be imitated. To those who cannot appreciate the radical contrast implied in what happens to a person in precarious earthly life and what is the reality of a God-oriented existence such as Jesus is advocating here, such motivation of conduct may seem paltry and banal. But the failure to appreciate it stems precisely from the mentality that his sermon is challenging. Contrast the motivation for proceeding against one's "enemies" in 11QTemple 61:12-14.

The teaching on love in vv. 27-36 moves in one area, the love of one's enemies, but in vv. 37-45 it takes on a wider scope, i.e. demands regarding Christians among themselves: the prohibition of judging (or criticizing) is but another application of the counsel of love. Judgment and condemnation must yield to forgiveness, bounteous generosity, upright conduct. Finally, in vv. 46-49 Jesus calls for realistic, effective action, based not only on such love, but on the word that he preaches.

It is only in the first beatitude that the "kingdom" is mentioned, and this initial mention of it relates this sermon to the kingdom-preaching of Jesus in 4:43. But it scarcely gives to the sermon as a whole the emphasis that the theme has in the Matthean sermon on the mount (see Matt 5:3,10,19*bis*,20; 6:10,[13],33; 7:21,[21]).

One other aspect of the sermon on the plain has to be noted. In vv. 39-40 the "Q" material touches on a delicate matter that may reflect the situation in the early church in the time of Luke. These verses have no counterpart in the sermon on the mount, but are found elsewhere in the Matthean Gospel (e.g. 10:24-25; 15:14). Their reference to the blind leading the blind and to pupils superior to teachers are probably aimed at some form of false-teaching in the early Christian community. In contrast, the Lucan Jesus insists on disciples being "fully schooled" (6:40). This may be the reason why Luke initially restricts the audience of the sermon to "disciples" (6:20). It is undoubtedly a foreshadowing of the advice to be given to the elders of Ephesus at Miletus (Acts 20:29-30).

It thus relates the sermon on the plain to the emphasis given to *asphaleia* in the prologue (1:4). If this is so, then it is interesting to see that the Lucan Jesus proclaims not simply the kingdom (shares in *kērygma*), but can spell out his message of God's "salvation" also in demands of Christian love. His *didachē* could not be more radical.

Some of the beatitudes and other sayings of Jesus that are preserved in this sermon have their counterparts in the Coptic *Gospel of Thomas*. They will be commented on in the NOTES on appropriate verses.

The beatitudes (6:20b-23) and the woes (6:24-26) form the exordium of the Lucan sermon; they are like two strophes of a poem and correspond to Matt 5:3,6,4, 11-12. The four beatitudes reflect the fourfold number of them in the nucleus sermon and in "Q," *pace* H. Schürmann (*Lukasevangelium,* 336), Frankemölle, et al. See Bultmann, *HST,* 109. Matthew's tendency to add things to the sayings of Jesus (see below) is undoubtedly responsible for the nine beatitudes that he has—or eight, if 5:5 is to be regarded as a later gloss (some commentators even try to reduce them to seven, claiming that vv. 11-12 are not really part of the list, which is marked by an *inclusio* ["kingdom of heaven" in vv. 3 and 10], and comparing Matthew's seven parables in chap. 13 and seven woes in chap. 23). Topical arrangement has resulted in his lengthened list. Of the four Lucan beatitudes the first three originally formed a unit, as their parallelism reveals, and the fourth was added only secondarily to it either in "Q" or in a pre-"Q" collection. These are not the only beatitudes in the Lucan Gospel (see further 1:45; 7:23; 10:23; 11:27-28; 12:37, 38,43; 14:14-15; 23:29).

In form, the beatitudes are related to macarisms found in Egyptian, Hellenistic, and OT literature. The term *makarios* and its background will be explained in the NOTE on 6:20.

The Lucan beatitudes are addressed to the "disciples" as the real poor, hungry, grief-stricken, and outcasts of this world; they are declared "blessed" because their share in the kingdom will guarantee them abundance, joy, and a reward in heaven. Luke has not spiritualized the condition of the disciples as Matthew has done (in adding to Jesus' words distinctions that would suit the members of his mixed community: "poor in spirit," those hungering and thirsting "for righteousness" [note his further additions in 7:24, "sensible"; 9:4, "wicked"; 6:9, "in heaven"; etc.]). Rather, poverty, hunger, weeping, hatred, and ostracism characterize the real condition of the Christian disciples whom the Lucan Jesus declares "blessed." *— but the "woes" are also addressed to the disciples*

It is a matter of debate about who changed the original "Q" form of the beatitudes. Were they originally couched in the second person and changed by Matthew to the third? So K. H. Rengstorf, W. Grundmann, H. Schürmann, G. Schneider, et al. These commentators think that in using the third person Matthew has produced a "catalogue of virtues." This is far from certain, since the third plural form has better OT antecedents (see NOTE). More likely Luke has changed the third person to the second, partly because of the added woes which are addressed to "you" (*ouai hymin*). Moreover, Luke shows a preference for the second plural (see H. J. Cadbury, *Style and Literary Method,* 124-126; Bultmann, *HST,* 109; F. Hauck, *TDNT* 4, 367-368; Dupont, *Béatitudes* 1. 274-289). Further, there is no reason to postulate different forms of "Q" to explain the remaining differences in the details of the beatitudes (*pace* S. Agouridès, G. Strecker, et al.); see Dupont, *Béatitudes* 1. 344; 3. 12-13).

NOTES

6 20. *Then Jesus fixed his eyes.* Lit. "and he, having raised his eyes on his disciples, said." Another instance of the unemphatic *kai autos* occurs here; see p. 120 above. The "disciples" are those mentioned in 6:17b. Mention of them was undoubtedly included in the introduction to the sermon in "Q" (see Matt 5:1); but Luke restricts the sermon initially to them (see COMMENT).

Blessed are you who are poor, for the kingdom of God is yours. Lit. "blessed (are) the poor, for yours is the kingdom of God." Luke's Greek has the same first three words as Matt 5:3, *makarioi hoi ptōchoi,* but the Matthean form continues, "in spirit, for theirs is the kingdom of heaven." Yet another form of this beatitude is found in *Gos. Thom.* § 54: "Blessed (*makarios*) are the poor, for yours is the kingdom of heaven." This form is clearly dependent on the two canonical forms, being closer to Luke save for "heaven" instead of "God." The Matthean form with the third person and "heaven" instead of "God" is undoubtedly the more original (see COMMENT): "Blessed are the poor, for the kingdom of heaven is theirs." By adding "in spirit," Matthew has adapted the original beatitude to the *'ānāwîm* among the early Jewish Christians; see COMMENT on 1:39-56 (p. 361 above). Some mss. of Luke ($\aleph^3$, Θ, the Freer and Lake families of minuscules) have added "in spirit" to the text; but that is clearly a copyist's harmonization of the text with Matthew.

"Blessèd" is the usual translation of Greek *makarios,* the adj. used to express NT "beatitudes" or "macarisms." Together with the following "woes," they belong to a literary subform that has been called "ascription" (see T. Y. Mullins, *NTS* 19 [1972-1973] 194-205). Counterparts of the NT beatitude/macarism have been found in Egyptian literature (see J. Dupont, " 'Béatitudes' égyptiennes," *Bib* 47 (1966) 185-222), classical and Hellenistic Greek literature (see Hauck, *TDNT* 4. 362-364), and in the OT (see G. Bertram, ibid., 364-367; H. Cazelles, *TDOT* 1. 445-448).

In the Greek world the adj. *makarios* denoted a person's inner happiness. When the beatitude-form developed there, it extolled the good fortune of persons or exalted them because of the good fortune that they have had. In form, the adj. *makarios* was usually followed by a rel. pron. *hos(tis)*, "happy (the person) who. . . ." Another form was *olbios hos(tis)*, "fortunate (the one) who . . . ," or *eutychēs*, "blessed with good fortune," or *eudaimōn*, "blessed with a good spirit." In the LXX the same form is sometimes found: *makarios hos* (Ps 137:8); but the adj. *makarios* is also followed by a pers. pron. (e.g. *sy*, "you," Deut 33:29; Qoh 10:17) or, more frequently, by *anēr hos*, "the man who . . . ," or *anthrōpos hos*, "the human being who . . ." (e.g. Pss 34:9; 127:5; Prov 3:13). The latter forms reflect the Hebrew expression, *'ašrê hā'îš/haggeber 'ǎšer . . .* , "the happiness (*or* happy things) of the man/human being who . . ." (Ps 1:1; Sir 14:20). The beatitude-form was especially used in the OT Wisdom literature and took on a religious sense as the expression of God's favor toward persons. The blessing thus ascribed often connoted a full life, a good wife (Sir 26:1), sons as heirs (Ps 127:3-5), prosperity and honor (Job 29:10-11).

In the Greek world the gods were often considered supremely *makares* (e.g. *Odyssey* 5.7). In the Jewish and Christian tradition the beatitude-form is not used of God (but see 1 Tim 1:11; 6:15 for a different use of *makarios* of him). In the LXX God is, indeed, said to be "blessed" (i.e. blest, praised, extolled), but the term is then the adj. *eulogētos* or the ptc. *eulogēmenos*, both of which translate Hebrew *bārûk*, frequently in prayers, "Blest be God/Yahweh" (e.g. Exod 18:10; Gen 9:26; 24:27). The same Greek terms can also be used of human beings, but they express the condition of one's being "blessed (i.e. blest) by God," whereas *makarios*, "blessèd," emphasizes rather the person's resultant happy, prosperous, or fortunate condition. In the religious sense, the beatitude/macarism admits that the happy condition results from God's blessing, but emphasizes the concrete manifestation of the blessing. See further F. Hauck and G. Bertram, *TDNT* 4. 362-370.

In the NT, the beatitude-form only rarely preserves the Hellenistic formula in its simplicity (e.g. Luke 7:23; 14:15). More frequently, it uses *makarios* in the plural, followed by the def. art., and a noun, substantivized adj., or ptc. Sometimes parts of the body are designated: "eyes" (Luke 10:23), "womb" and "breasts" (11:27). Here the beatitudes only rarely express practical wisdom, since they usually stress a reversal of values that people put on earthly things in view of the kingdom now being preached by Jesus. A paradox is often involved in them. The first part describes the condition of the disciples, but the second promises his/her eschatological lot, often formulated in the theological passive (i.e. with the implied agency of God, "you shall be filled" [by God], 6:21).

In the Lucan Gospel the imminent expectation of the eschaton recedes as the evangelist shifts the emphasis in both the beatitudes and woes to the present condition: those who go hungry and weep "now" and those who are well-fed and laugh "now" (6:21,25). He thus contrasts the present earthly condition of individual Christians with that following their death (see J. Dupont, *Béatitudes* 2. 100-109).

21. *Blessed are you who go hungry now, for you shall have your fill.* Lit. "blessed (are) those hungering now, for you shall be sated," i.e. by God (*ZBG*

§ 236). Luke's second beatitude corresponds to Matthew's fourth (5:6): "Blessed are those who hunger and thirst for righteousness, for they shall have their fill." A form of this beatitude is also found in *Gos. Thom.* § 69b: "Blessed (*makarios*) are the hungry, for the belly of him who desires shall be filled." This form is dependent on the Lucan in the first part, but in the second it goes its own way. Whereas Matthew has added "for righteousness," Luke has shifted the beatitude to the second person, added the adv. "now," and eliminated the second verb, "and thirst." The last change seems to be suggested by the fact that the pair "hunger and thirst" is found in the OT (Isa 49:10; 65:13) and hence comes to Matthew from "Q." Probably the original beatitude read: "Blessed are those who hunger and thirst, they shall have their fill." The Lucan form of the beatitude stresses the immediacy or actuality of the disciples' poverty; to them Jesus now promises consolation. It is awaited from God himself and from him alone; but it will be forthcoming. The second part of the beatitude alludes to the OT motif of the eschatological banquet (see Isa 25:6-8; 49:10-13; Ps 107:3-9). On this motif Luke will play elsewhere (see 12:37; 13:29; 14:14-15,16-24).

Blessed are you who weep now, for you shall laugh. Lit. "blessed (are) those weeping now, for you shall laugh." Luke's third beatitude corresponds to Matthew's second (5:4), "Blessed are those who mourn for they shall be consoled." In this instance it is not easy to say which evangelist has touched up the inherited form. Since Matthew's form may echo the consolation of Deutero-Isaiah for those who mourned for Zion (Isa 61:2), that is perhaps closer to the original. Again, the verb *gelan*, "laugh," appears only here and in the corresponding woe in the gospel tradition; this seems to indicate that it is Luke who has modified his source. In any case, "Luke's expressions are more universally human; those of Matthew are more traditional and biblical" (M.-J. Lagrange, *Luc*, 188). In the Lucan context, the "weeping" would seem to refer to oppression of some sort (cf. the following beatitude). Recall Luke 2:25, "the consolation of Israel," for the oppressed. Laughter is here to be understood of the joy that the kingdom of God will bring into the lives of human beings. Cf. Ps 126:1-2.

22. *Blessed are you when people hate you and outlaw you.* The form of the fourth beatitude changes here, being introduced by *makarioi este hotan . . . ,* as in Matthew's ninth (5:11-12): "Blessed are you when they will denounce you and persecute (you) and say all (sorts of) evil against you, lying because of me." In both forms four outrages are mentioned: Luke has hatred, ostracism, denunciation, and denigration of one's name; Matthew has denunciation, persecution, evil talk, and lying (only "denunciation" is common to the two). A form of this beatitude is also found in the *Gos. Thom.* § 68, 69a: "Blessed (*makarios*) are you when (*hotan*) you are hated and persecuted (*diōkein*), and no place (*topos*) shall be found there where you have been persecuted. . . . Blessed are they who have been persecuted in their heart; these are they who have known the Father in truth." These two sayings are scarcely more primitive than the Matthean or Lucan. One should compare, however, the progress of the reaction to the Christian disciple in the Lucan foursome with that in the parable of the wicked tenant farmers (20:9-19).

The fact that Matthew too has the beatitude in the second plural is scarcely an argument in favor of the original beatitudes in "Q" being in that person; recall what was said in the COMMENT about the relation of this beatitude to the three preceding. Cf. D. Daube, *JTS* 45 (1944) 21-24, for parallels in the OT and Jewish liturgical texts to similar brusk changes.

outlaw you. The hatred will culminate in ostracism. This probably refers to exclusion of Jewish Christians from synagogues, and probably reflects the experience of early Christians of Luke's own day. However, though the formulation of the four outrages differs in Matthew and Luke, the point made by them—persecution of disciples because of Jesus—may well be an idea that is to be traced back to Jesus himself.

reject your name as evil. This does not refer to the personal names of the disciples, but undoubtedly to the name of "Christian," which Luke otherwise knows (Acts 11:26; 26:28). Cf. 1 Pet 4:16. Is Luke aware of an attitude reflected in the twelfth "blessing" of *Shemoneh 'Esreh* (see C. K. Barrett, *NTB,* § 169)?

on account of the Son of Man. Matt 5:11 mentions the persecutions "because of me." The title "Son of Man" has been secondarily introduced here by Luke (see J. Jeremias, *ZNW* 58 [1967] 159-172). Since Matthew has secondarily introduced it at times (e.g. 16:13), it is hardly likely that he would have omitted it here, if it were in "Q" (*pace* G. Schneider, *Evangelium nach Lukas,* 153). The use of the title scarcely refers to the coming Son of Man; it is rather used of Jesus in his active earthly ministry, what he has been doing.

23. *That is the time to rejoice.* Lit. "rejoice in that day and leap for joy." Luke has added here "in that day," which corresponds to his introduction of "now" in the first part of the beatitude. The time of persecution will become a time of joy and festive dancing. This is the consolation that Jesus offers to disciples who must follow in his footsteps. Cf. John 15:20.

leap. The verb *skirtan* is used by Luke alone (see 1:41,44); here he has substituted it for *agalliasthe,* "delight," which Matthew has retained from "Q" and used only in this beatitude (5:12). Elsewhere Luke uses *agallian* (1:47; 10:21).

great shall be your reward in heaven. Lit. "much, abundant shall be. . . ." The Greek *misthos* actually denoted payment or salary for work done. It was used figuratively in both the Greek world and the LXX in a religious sense as a "reward" for moral or ethical conduct. Here Jesus' saying promises a reward for being despised as a Christian disciple; neither Luke nor Matthew (5:12) has shrunk from ascribing to Jesus such a motivation that has often been considered debasing or demoralizing.

in heaven. I.e. in the sight of God, unless one is to think of it being "booked" in heaven (see Rev 20:12). What is connoted here is the salvific effect of persecution; even the sufferings of those persecuted for the sake of the Son of Man will have a role in salvation-history.

in just the same way. The Lucan *kata ta auta* occurs again in 6:26; 17:30.

did their fathers treat the prophets. The phrase *hoi pateres autōn* occurs emphatically at the end of the sentence; it is probably a Lucan addition. Cf. Matt 5:12c, and the ending of the fourth Lucan woe (6:26). Both the

Matthean and the Lucan formulation could refer to the persecution of OT prophets (e.g. 1 Kgs 19:10; Jer 26:20-24; 38:6-13). Luke will refer to the slaying of Zechariah in 11:51 (another "Q" passage); see further Acts 7:52. This notion is scarcely exclusive to "Q" or to Luke; see 1 Thess 2:15. The addition of "their fathers" may have another nuance for Luke: The rejection of the Christian name by descendants of prophet-persecutors undoubtedly insinuates in yet another way the continuity of Christianity with Judaism (see p. 178 above).

The saying also implies that the Christian disciples are thought of in a prophetic role.

24. *woe to you who are rich, for you have your consolation already*. The first woe parallels the first beatitude (v. 20b).

The Greek interjection *ouai* is not found in classical Greek writers, but turns up in writings of the Roman period (MM, 464) and in the LXX. Perhaps it is meant to be a transcription of Hebrew *hôy/'ôy*, or else of Latin *vae* (see BDF § 4.2). In form, *ouai* is followed by the dative of a pers. pron. with an appositive; in a few instances it is followed by a noun or a substantivized adj./ptc. in the nominative (see 6:25b). The woe-form is abundant in the LXX, and even though its usage there varies somewhat, this undoubtedly provides the background for the NT use. The form is found in the gospel tradition prior to Luke (see Mark 13:17; 14:21; "Q" in Luke 11:42 = Matt 23:23; 11:44 = Matt 23:27). But Luke makes the most abundant use of it in the Synoptics (see, in addition, 10:13; 11:43,46,47,52; 17:1; 21:23; 22:22). Since the Lucan woes here use the interj. *ouai*, they are not perfectly parallel to the beatitudes with *makarioi* and adjectives/participles. Hence the parallel cannot be made too perfectly in the translation. The woes are minatory in nature and pronounce the opposite of the beatitudes, viz. displeasure, pain, or grief. They are aimed at the privileged "listeners" of Jesus (see COMMENT), the rich, well-fed, carefree, and those well-spoken of; and they emphasize the ephemeral nature of such privilege.

you have your consolation already. The rich need not look to the kingdom (v. 20b) for encouragement about the situation in which their social and economic status classes them. Jesus' words imply that a certain short-sightedness, induced by that status, leads such persons to think that there is nothing more to have. *Paraklēsis*, "consolation, encouragement," is used by Luke alone among the evangelists (see 2:25; Acts 4:36; 9:31; 13:15; 15:31). This is a sign that the woes were not part of "Q."

25. *Woe to you who are well-fed now*. Lit. "those now filled," the perf. ptc. *empeplēsmenoi* expresses the condition of satiety. Ms. D and the Koine text-tradition omit the adv. *nyn*. The second woe corresponds to the second beatitude.

you shall go hungry. The woe expresses the same reversal of status that one finds in the Magnificat (see 1:53). For the *a*-form of the fut. *peinasete*, see BDF § 70.2.

Woe to you who laugh now. The third woe corresponds to the third beatitude. "Laughter" is to be understood here as the carefree expression of contentment with the success of the present. In OT Wisdom literature it is sometimes the mark of the fool (Sir 21:20; 27:13; Qoh 7:6), and the Lucan Jesus may be alluding to such an attitude.

you shall mourn and weep. When success turns to failure, grief will set in and take the place of laughter. The future used in the first three woes unites them together; it obviously has an eschatological note to it, but it is hard to say just what term is envisaged. The pair, "weep and mourn" (*penthein* and *klaiein*), is found in Greek papyri (MM, 502-503) and in the LXX (2 Sam 19:2; 2 Esdr 18:9). See further Mark 16:10; Jas 4:9; Rev 18:11,15,19.

26. *Woe to you when all people speak well of you.* The last woe departs in its form from the preceding three, just as the last beatitude differed from the three that preceded it. Here too the conj. *hotan* occurs. The Lucan Jesus warns that a widespread good reputation can be a deceptive goal in life for a Christian. Since this one is not formulated with a retribution clause, there is no future; instead, Luke composes a parallel to the end of the fourth beatitude.

in just the same way. See Note on 6:23c.

the false prophets. So Luke adapts the saying in v. 23c. The ending of the verse is again the emphatic *hoi pateres autōn.* The fourth woe insinuates the company in which the rich, the well-fed, and those of good repute find themselves. Prophets of old who enjoyed the esteem of their contemporaries turned out to be deceivers of Israel (Isa 30:10-11; see Jer 5:31; 6:14; 23:16-17; Mic 2:11). Cf. 2 Tim 3:1-9.

27. *But to you who listen I say.* This is Luke's introduction to a new part (6:27-36) of the sermon on the plain. In a sense it is the introduction to the whole middle section of the sermon (vv. 27-45), the most important part, for which the exordium has been preparing. The phrase that he uses here echoes that of 6:18; it will be picked up again in 6:47 (see COMMENT). The position of *hymin,* "to you" (before the verb *legō*), and of the ptc. *tois akouousin* (after the verb) makes this introduction emphatic.

Love your enemies. See Matt 5:44a, where the identical four words are found, *agapate tous echthrous hymōn.* This and the next verse contain four commands of Jesus: love, do good, bless, and pray. Only the first and the last have counterparts in Matt 5:44. Luke has obviously added the other two in view of the four outrages expressed in the fourth beatitude (6:22); thus the three that follow specify the kind of love that the Christian follower is expected to show toward an enemy. The "enemy" is thus the one who hates, outlaws, denounces, and rejects the Christian name, i.e. the enemy of Christians as a group. What Luke has preserved here in vv. 27-28 forms part of the sixth antithesis in the Matthean sermon.

Jesus' words on the love of one's enemies in this sermon have to be understood against the background of an ancient view of enmity. One finds forms of it as early as Hesiod in the Greek world (*Opera et dies* 342), Pindar (*Pythian Odes* 2.83-84), and its best formulation in Lysias: "I considered it established that one should do harm to one's enemies and be of service to one's friends" (*Pro milite* 20). Yet even in the Greek world a different view gradually emerged, when Pericles urged overcoming enemies by generosity and virtue (Thucydides 4.19, 1-4). Especially among the Stoics and Pythagoreans was such conduct advocated: "so to behave . . . as not to make friends into ene-

mies, but to turn enemies into friends" (Diogenes Laertius 8.1,23). Jewish
writers, influenced by such Greek philosophy, express similar ideas (see
T. Benjamin 4.3; *T. Joseph* 18.2). The difference in Jesus' words, which are
usually admitted to be authentic, is that they are cast in the form of a command. He tells his followers that they are to manifest the ultimate form of the
human expression of openness and concern toward those who are their
enemies. He recommends not merely a warm affection (*philia*) such as one
might have for one's family, or a passionate devotion (*eros*) such as one
might expect between spouses, but a gracious, outgoing, active interest (*agapē*)
in the welfare of those persons who are precisely antagonistic. See further
C. Spicq, *Agape in the New Testament* (St. Louis: B. Herder, 1963) 1. 78-80.

do good to those who hate you. The added Lucan elaboration of the injunction to love is evoked by 6:22a.

28. *bless those who curse you.* The second added Lucan elaboration of the
love-commandment is probably formulated in imitation of the OT juxtaposition
of solemn and unretractable utterances (see Gen 12:3; 27:29; Deut 27:12-26;
Judg 17:2). The Essenes of Qumran were to bless their own members, the
"sons of light," and curse those who did not join them or defected, "the sons of
darkness" (1QS 2:2-17). In contrast, Jesus' words here inculcate the opposite
attitude and specify the love expected for one's enemies. Passive acceptance of
an antagonist's cursing is to be met with active blessing. The Pauline exhortation echoes this injunction (Rom 12:14b), but it speaks of persecutors: "Bless
those who persecute (you), bless and do not curse." Cf. 1 Cor 4:12; 1 Pet
2:23.

pray for those who mistreat you. Matt 5:44b has, "those who persecute
you." Rom 12:14a is closer to this Matthean form. Prayer for a persecutor
may be found in the Palestinian Jewish writing, 1QapGen 20:28 (see *NTS* 20
[1973-1974] 398-399; *WA,* 97). The ideas expressed in vv. 27-28 parallel
Matt 5:38, though Luke has no exact verbal counterpart of it. In omitting any
comparison with OT ideas, the Lucan form of these sayings gains in its absolute formulation.

29. *strikes you on one cheek.* Lit. "to the one striking you (sg.) on the
cheek, offer the other too." The directives in vv. 29-30 are given in the second
sg., in contrast to the second pl. in vv. 27-28,31-36. This may suggest a
"conflation of sources" (J. M. Creed, *The Gospel,* 93), but it would mean a
conflation in "Q" (or prior to "Q"), since the same phenomenon is found in
Matt 5:39b-45 (contrast 39a,45-48). Creed also thinks that Matthew has
preserved the more original "Q" form, but Luke's fondness for the "right"
hand/ear (see NOTE on 6:6) makes it difficult to think that he would have
suppressed the adjective here, if it were in his source.

The saying probably refers to an insulting blow, from one who assails the
Christian disciple for his/her allegiance to Christ (see J. Jeremias, *The Sermon,* 28). If so insulted, the disciple does not go to court about it but bears the
insult and is ready to take more in the spirit of love expected of a follower
(6:27). This injunction and that in v. 30b thus cut through the old principle of
retaliation (Exod 21:24; Lev 24:20; Deut 19:21), and this is all that Luke retains of what is in the fifth Matthean antithesis. Cf. 11QTemple 61:11-12.

take your cloak from you. I.e. one's outer garment. It could be meant here as the act of a thief, or of a person in need, or of one seizing a garment in pledge because of a legality (see Exod 22:25-26; Deut 24:10-17; Amos 2:8). An instance of the latter is recorded extrabiblically on a seventh-century ostracon from Meṣad Ḥashavyahu (see NOTE on *amēn,* 4:24). The Matthean parallel (5:40) envisages the last-mentioned action. The Greek *himation,* "cloak, garment," used here occurs frequently in the LXX (e.g. Amos 2:8; Deut 24:17) as the translation of Hebrew *beged,* the word used in line 8 of the ostracon-text.

tunic. The garment (*chitōn*) worn next to the skin.

30. *Give to everyone who begs from you.* The absolute form of the command excludes any consideration of the person's background or condition, or the purpose of the begging. Need must not encounter selfish reserve among disciples of the kingdom (see p. 248 above). It is a call to self-denial and is not restricted. Luke has probably added *panti,* "everyone"; compare Matt 5:42 and see NOTE on 4:15.

takes what is yours. The verb *airein* is used here in the sense of theft, by stealth or force (see Cant 5:7).

do not strive to get it back. Lit. "do not demand (it) back."

31. *treat people just as you wish them to treat you.* Lit. "as you (pl.) wish people to treat you, treat them likewise." This is the Lucan form of the so-called Golden Rule. Matt 7:12 reads, "Whatever then you wish people would do for you, do for them yourselves." To it is added, "For this is the Law and the prophets." The addition probably stems from Matthean redaction; but it is not impossible that it was already in "Q" and has been omitted by Luke as something of little concern to his Gentile Christian readers (see COMMENT). Luke has moved his form of the rule up to an earlier position in his sermon. For him it does not sum up the Law and the prophets, but the injunctions on the love of one's enemies (vv. 27-30). However, the reciprocity expressed in the rule is immediately modified in vv. 32-34; thus the Lucan Jesus may quote the rule but counsels a conduct that transcends mere reciprocity. Love of self cannot be the norm alone, and that seems to be implied in the rule.

The "Golden Rule" is an eighteenth-century label for this verse. In antiquity, many formulations, both positive and negative, were known; e.g. (1) Lev 19:18, "You must love your neighbor as yourself." (2) Tob 4:15, "Do not do to anyone what you hate." (3) Aristeas *Ep. ad Philocraten* 207 (*APOT* 2. 113), "As you wish that no evil should befall you, but to be a partaker of all good things, so you should act on the same principle toward your subjects and offenders" (probably before 70 B.C.). (4) Ms. D of Acts 15:29, "Whatever you do not wish to happen to you, do not do to another" (see also 15:20). (5) *Didache* 1:2, "Whatever you would not have done to you, do not do to another." (6) Attributed to R. Hillel, older contemporary of Jesus, in fourth/fifth century rabbinic tradition, *b. Šabbat* 31a, "What is hateful to you, do not do to anyone else; that is the whole Law, all else is commentary. Go and learn" (see also *Tg. Yerušalmi I* of Lev 19:18). Parallels are also found in classical Greek writers (e.g. Isocrates *Nicocles* 61; Herodotus 3.142) and in those of the Sophist movement. It is useless to try to establish that the positive form used by Jesus in Luke or Matthew is actually superior to the negative; it all depends on the context in which the rule is set. See further A. Dihle, *Die goldene Regel: Eine Einführung in die Geschichte der antiken und frühchristlichen Vulgärethik* (Studienheft zur Altertumswissenschaft 7; Göttingen: Vandenhoeck und Ruprecht, 1962) 109-114.

32. *if you love only those who love you.* The command to love one's enemies, even as summed up in the Golden Rule, is now viewed against the morality of sinners, and reciprocal, measured-out love and esteem are now presented as not enough for a Christian disciple.

what credit is there in that? Lit. "what favor (*charis*) do you have?" I.e. in the sight of someone else, especially of God. Here *charis* has the overtone of "reward," as the use of *misthos* in v. 35b shows (see NOTE on 6:23b). On *charis*, see NOTE on 1:30; cf. 2:52; Acts 7:46. The parallel in Matt 5:46 even uses *misthos*.

sinners. Matt 5:46 has "toll-collectors," and 5:47, "Gentiles" (*ethnikoi*). Luke has probably changed *telōnes* to *hamartōloi* (terms often used together, see NOTE on 5:30), given it a broader connotation, and leveled it through the three examples.

love those who love them. I.e. practice the reciprocity counseled in the Golden Rule.

33. *help.* Lit. "do good to" (*agathopoiein*).

34. *If you lend.* This verse and the first half of v. 35 have no counterpart in the Matthean sermon. Lucan redaction has produced a threesome, summed up in v. 35a, the first element of which harks back to v. 27b.

35. *love your enemies.* Because vv. 31-34 had moved beyond such love to a broader scope of love of neighbors, the command is now repeated.

love . . . help . . . lend. Three manifestations of outgoing service sum up redactionally vv. 32-34.

looking for nothing in return. The meaning of *apelpizein* is usually "despair," but that scarcely suits the context here. The meaning used here is otherwise unattested in earlier or contemporary Greek writing (see MM, 56). The words in this phrase express the basic motivation of Christian love.

sons of the Most High. Matt 5:45 has, "sons of your Father in heaven." Since the latter phrase is also found in the Matthean Our Father (6:9; cf. 7:21), it probably reveals that Matthew has changed the original form of "Q." The Lucan phrase echoes the OT *huioi hypsistou* (Ps 82:6). The singular of this title has been applied to Jesus in 1:32 (see NOTE there). On Christian sonship, see Rom 8:14-15; Gal 4:5-6. Here love is set forth as the mark of that sonship.

36. *Be merciful.* This verse reformulates the last clause of v. 35. Its Matthean counterpart reads, "You must be perfect as your heavenly Father is perfect" (5:48). The Lucan form not only sharpens the saying, by putting it in the manner of a command, but expresses it in terms of mercy. It is hard to say which would have been the more original "Q" form, "perfect" or "merciful." Since Matthew uses *teleios* elsewhere (19:21), he may have redacted the "Q" saying; Luke never uses this adjective and has *oiktirmōn*, "merciful," only here.

In either form the saying is a takeoff from Lev 19:2, "You must be holy, for I, the Lord your God, am holy." The Lucan form proposes an imitation of God, and precisely of a quality that the OT predicates of him. God in the OT is never said to be perfect (*teleios*) or blameless (*amōmos*), but he is said to be merciful (*oiktirmōn*, Exod 34:6; Deut 4:31; Joel 2:13; Jonah 4:2). See further J. Dupont, "'Soyez parfaits' (Mt., *V*, 48), 'Soyez miséricordieux' (Lk., *VI*, 36)," in *Sacra pagina* (BETL 12-13; Paris: Gabalda, 1959) 2. 150-162; "L'Appel à imiter Dieu en Matthieu 5,48 et Luc 6,36," *RivB* 14 (1966) 137-158.

Though v. 36 reformulates what precedes, it is also transitional to what follows, since the question of judging is a further example of the imitation of God's mercy.

37. *Do not judge.* The third section (6:37-42) of the Lucan sermon begins here. It corresponds to Matt 7:1-5, but there are several Lucan additions at this point: Vv. 37bc,38a,39a are redactional modifications; v. 39bc comes from another part of "Q" (=Matt 15:14), as does v. 40 (=Matt 10:24-25). These verses (39b-40) were scarcely part of the nucleus sermon, *pace* Schneider (*Evangelium nach Lukas,* 158); cf. J. Schmid, *Lukas,* 138. They have been introduced here because of the Lucan concern about false teaching.

Instead of the simple form of this command which occurs in Matt 7:1-2, Luke has a foursome, two prohibitions (with their consequences) and two commands (with their consequences) in vv. 37-38a. "Judging" does not refer here to the judicial decision of a constituted judge, but to the human tendency to criticize and find fault with one's neighbor. Mercy in judging should lead also to generosity in giving, and so the foursome is united.

you will not be judged. I.e. by God (theological passive, see ZBG § 236). This is true of the other three consequences. The aor. pass. subj. with *ou mē* in the first two is a way of expressing the emphatic neg. fut. (see BDF § 365.3).

38. *good measure.* The image is that of a full measure for grain (see B. Couroyer, *RB* 77 [1970] 366-370). The fullness becomes a norm of conduct since it connotes an unstinted, merciful standard in judging and giving. Human generosity will be rewarded by divine superabundance. See 8:18; 19:25-26. Contrast Isa 65:7; Jer 32:18; Ps 79:12.

will be poured. Lit. "they will pour"; see NOTE on 12:20.

the measure you use. This part of the verse corresponds to Matt 7:2b; it explains v. 38a, not v. 37. If human conduct is not measured merely by the reciprocity of the Golden Rule, it will find its reward in divine superabundance, unstinted giving. Cf. H. P. Rüger, "'Mit welchem Mass ihr messt, wird euch gemessen werden,'" *ZNW* 60 (1969) 174-182.

39. *he addressed to them a proverb.* Lit. "he spoke" (see NOTES on 4:23 and 5:36). This is a Lucan redactional introduction to these two verses.

Can the blind lead the blind? Cf. Matt 15:14. Another form of the saying is found in *Gos. Thom.* § 34: "If a blind person leads a blind person, the two of them fall into a pit." The conditional form here is dependent on the Matthean.

The disciples are to be leaders of people, but they cannot be blinded guides; they must see the way first. In the context of "not judging," the saying about blindness might seem to refer to one's own faults. If a person has not learned self-criticism, he/she cannot lead others. But the collocation of this verse with the following, and the connection between "the blind" and "leaders" with "pupils" and "teachers" seems to suggest that more is involved, i.e. a reference to false teachers. "Leading" (*hodēgein*) is used here as in Acts 8:31. This emerges from the following context.

40. *Is a pupil superior to his teacher?* The parallel to this is found in Matt 10:24-25, in a context dealing with the lot or fate of disciples, where the point of the saying is patient endurance. Luke not only omits the part of the saying about slave and master, but uses it in a different context, in which it reflects on the preceding saying about the "blind" and "leaders." Clear vision is needed in the guide (the teacher); but since the pupil depends on the teacher, the clear vision of the latter is all the more required. Verses 39-40 undoubtedly refer to instruction in the Christian community.

will someday be like his teacher. I.e. by implication, like Jesus himself.

41. *the speck.* The formulation in vv. 41-42 is very close to that of Matt 7:3-5; Luke adds the voc. *adelphe* in v. 42b. The saying in these verses really follows on v. 37a. A form of the saying is found in *Gos. Thom.* § 26: "The speck that is in your brother's eye you see, but the beam in your own eye you do not see. When you cast the beam out of your eye, then you will see clearly to cast the speck out of your brother's." Cf. OxyP 1:1-4; *ESBNT*, 388-390. Though this form is terse and to the point and shorter than either that of Luke or Matthew, it is scarcely a better reflection of the "Q" saying (see W. Schrage, *Verhältnis*, 72-73). A form of the saying is also found in rabbinic literature. A later tradition attributed it to R. Tarphon (ca. A.D. 100), saddened about people of his day who could not accept reproof: "If someone said, 'Cast out the speck from your eye,' the answer would come back, 'Cast out the log from yours.'" See Str-B, 1. 446-447. The figure in all its forms is intentionally grotesque in order to illustrate the human tendency to criticize and the natural reaction to it. The saying illustrates the need of honest self-evaluation and serious self-improvement; only the one who overcomes one's own fault(s) can gain the sight to help one's fellow. Jesus' words do not forbid Christian disciples to form moral judgments about human conduct, but they proscribe attempts to make others better without a similar and prior application of such judgments to oneself. The saying is not to be understood as restricted to community-leaders.

42. *Hypocrite!* The Greek word *hypokritēs* is found in a vocative form in Matt 7:5 too; it belonged to the "Q" form of the saying. It actually denotes "one who answers" and came to mean in classical and Hellenistic Greek not only "interpreter, expounder," but also "orator" and even an "actor" on a stage (Pindar *Frag.* 140b; Aristophanes *Vespae* 1279; Plato *Respublica* 2. 373b; Philodemus *Rhetorica Frag.* 1.197S). From its use for a play-actor it developed a transferred meaning "dissembler, pretender," but this cannot be shown to have a clearly negative ethical tone in pre-Christian secular Greek (cf. MM, 657). In the LXX it occurs in Job 34:30; 36:13 as a translation of Hebrew *ḥānēp*, "godless," and in the literature of Jews of the diaspora *hypokrisis* came to be listed with terms for lying and deceit (*T. Benjamin* 6:4-5; *Ps. Sol.* 4:6;

2 Macc 6:25). The noun *hypokritēs,* "hypocrite," is found only on the lips of Jesus in the Synoptics (never in John); besides this instance, it is found in Luke 12:56 (possibly "L") and 13:15 ("L"); Mark used it only in 7:5, whereas Matthew has it thirteen times. Cf. Luke 12:1. That it is the translation of Aramaic *šaqqār,* "liar" (M. Black, *AAGA*[3], 177) is highly unlikely. That, on the other hand, it constitutes an argument for Jesus' having spoken Greek in this case is far from clear, *pace* A. W. Argyle, *ExpTim* 75 (1963-1964) 113-114. It probably represents a term used by early Greek-speaking Christians of their Jewish opponents, which was in time attributed to Jesus himself.

43. *No good tree.* This verse begins the fourth section (6:43-45) of the Lucan sermon; it corresponds to Matt 7:16-20, but there is no parallel to 6:45. That is found rather in another section in Matt 12:33-35, viz., vv. 35,34. A connection between this section and the preceding is not hard to discern: An evil person cannot bring others to good conduct through criticism alone; one's deeds must precede and reveal that one is really good. The illustrations used in vv. 43-44 express a law of physical nature; and they are easily understood as figures of moral conduct. Fruit as a figure for deeds, good or bad, is used in the OT (Hos 10:13; Isa 3:10; Jer 17:10; 21:14). It is not impossible that these figures are meant here more specifically of false teachers or false prophets in the Christian community, referred to as thorns and brambles.

44. *figs . . . from thornbushes.* Matt 7:16 has the reverse: grapes from thorns and figs from brambles. The Matthean order is followed by *Gos. Thom.* § 45a: "They do not gather grapes from thorns, nor do they harvest figs from brambles, for they give no fruit." But the general relation of the sayings of Jesus in Luke and *Gos. Thom.* has to be noted (see Schrage, *Verhältnis,* 101-102). The pair *akanthai* and *triboloi* are found in the OT (Gen 3:18; Hos 10:8); cf. Heb 6:8.

45. *store of good in his heart.* Lit. "from the good treasure of the heart." Cf. 11:39-41. This verse now applies the tree and fruit figures of vv. 43-44 to human beings, but shifts the figure slightly in making the human heart a "treasure" or "storehouse." For the sense of *kardia,* "heart," see NOTE on 1:51. Again, *Gos. Thom.* § 45b has a form of this saying: "A good person brings forth good out of his treasure, an evil person brings forth evil things out of his evil treasure, which is in his heart, and speaks evil things."

his mouth speaks. The mouth reveals what the heart contains, i.e. the thoughts of the human mind. *Gos. Thom.* § 45c: "For out of the abundance of the heart he brings forth evil things." If the saying is to be understood of false teachers in the Christian community, then it refers to the evil words and speech that their ideas can produce. Verse 45c has no counterpart in the Matthean sermon, but is found in 12:34.

46. *Why do you address me.* This verse begins the final section (6:46-49) of the Lucan sermon and stresses the need to act on Jesus' words. It corresponds to Matt 7:24-27, the concluding section of the Matthean sermon. The minatory saying in this verse acts as a transition and introduces the parable; it immediately preceded the parable in "Q" too. The Lucan form of this verse agrees better with the parable that follows than does the Matthean, "Not everyone who

says to me, 'Lord, Lord,' will enter the kingdom of heaven, but only the one who does the will of my Father in heaven" (Matt 7:21). The Matthean form has been recast to go with vv. 22-23, and the Lucan form is more original, pace F. Hahn, Titles of Jesus, 91.

Lord, Lord. Jesus rejects a discipleship which is content merely with an external acknowledgment of a relation to him. One has to carry out his instructions as an indication of the reality of that relationship. In the Matthean form attachment to him is expressed in terms of entrance into the kingdom.

Even if we insist that the Lucan form of this saying is the more original, it is very difficult to trace it back to the historical Jesus (in Stage I of the gospel tradition). This is so because of the use of the title *Kyrios* in the sense of "Lord" in the ministry, and the association of it with following his instructions. Though the use of the title in this double form is certainly pre-Lucan, it probably stems from the early community, which was seeking to link *didache* with its *kerygma* (see p. 148 above).

what I tell you. The Lucan form of this part of the saying is less eschatological than the Matthean with its reference to entrance into the kingdom.

47. *comes to me listens to my words.* Contrast Matt 7:24, "Everyone who hears these words of mine." Luke has adapted the introductory formula of the parable to 6:18, "they came to listen to him." In the Greek text three ptcs. (*erchomenos, akouōn, poiōn,* "coming, listening, doing,") are in the nom. case and agree (logically, but not grammatically) with *tíni,* dat. "to whom." There is an anacoluthon here that Matthew does not have.

48. *foundations.* Luke heightens the contrast between the two builders by referring specifically to "foundations" and the lack thereof (v. 49). Elaborate foundations for houses were not customary in Palestine. Matthew's "prudent" builder simply built the house "on rock," in contrast to his "foolish" builder who built on sand.

the river. Luke has the sg. *potamos,* which has simplified the picture for the benefit of extra-Palestinian readers. The coming of the rain, the blowing of the wind, and the torrents (*potamoi,* pl.) of the Matthean form probably represent the more original "Q" form of the parable. They are associated with the rainy season in Palestine. Is it possible that Luke, in using the sg., "the river," is referring to floods caused by the overflow of a river like the Orontes near Antioch in Syria?

49. *great was the wreck of that house.* The contrast between the house that withstood the river and that which collapsed under its onset betokens the condition of the disciple in his/her existential relationship to the challenge of the message of Jesus. In Luke his words are scarcely any less challenging than in Matthew. The implication of the parable used, but not so labeled, is eschatological.

BIBLIOGRAPHY (6:20-49)

The Sermon on the Plain

Bartsch, H.-W. "Feldrede und Bergpredigt: Redaktionsarbeit in Luk. 6," *TZ* 16 (1960) 5-18.

Eichholz, G. *Auslegung der Bergpredigt* (BibS[N] 46; Neukirchen-Vluyn: Neukirchener-V., 1965).

Furnish, V. P. *The Love Command in the New Testament* (Nashville: Abingdon, 1972) 54-59, 84-90.

George, A. "Le disciple fraternel et efficace: Lc 6,39-45," *AsSeign* 39 (1972) 68-77.

Grundmann, W. "Die Bergpredigt nach der Lukasfassung," *SE I* (TU 73; 1959) 180-189.

Häring, B. "The Normative Value of the Sermon on the Mount," *CBQ* 29 (1967) 375-385.

Jeremias, J. *The Sermon on the Mount* (Facet Books, Biblical series 2; Philadelphia: Fortress, 1963).

Kahlefeld, H. *Der Jünger: Eine Auslegung der Rede Lk 6,20-49* (Frankfurt: Knecht, 1962).

Kissinger, W. S. *The Sermon on the Mount: A History of Interpretation and Bibliography* (American Theological Library Association, Bibliography series 3; Metuchen, NJ: Scarecrow Press, 1975).

McArthur, H. K. *Understanding the Sermon on the Mount* (New York: Harper, 1960) 22, 84.

Menestrina, G. "Matteo 5-7 e Luca 6,20-49 nell'Evangelo di Tommaso," *BeO* 18 (1976) 65-67.

Schürmann, H. "Die Warnung des Lukas vor der Falschlehre in der 'Predigt am Berge' Lk 6,20-49," *BZ* ns 10 (1966) 57-81; reprinted in *Traditionsgeschichtliche Untersuchungen zu den synoptischen Evangelien* (Düsseldorf: Patmos, 1968) 290-309.

Windisch, H. *The Meaning of the Sermon on the Mount* (Philadelphia: Westminster, 1951).

Wood, J. *The Sermon on the Mount and Its Application* (London: G. Bles, 1963).

Wrege, H.-T. *Die Überlieferungsgeschichte der Bergpredigt* (WUNT 9; Tübingen: Mohr [Siebeck], 1968).

The Beatitudes

Agouridès, S. "La tradition des béatitudes chez Matthieu et Luc," *Mélanges bibliques en hommage au R. P. Béda Rigaux* (eds. A. Descamps et A. de Halleux; Gembloux: Duculot, 1970) 9-27.

Batsdorf, I. W. *Interpreting the Beatitudes* (Philadelphia: Westminster, 1966).

Braumann, G. "Zum traditionsgeschichtlichen Problem der Seligpreisungen Mt V 3-12," *NovT* 4 (1960) 253-260.

Brown, R. E. "The Beatitudes according to St. Luke," *New Testament Essays* (Milwaukee: Bruce, 1965) 265-271.

Dupont, J. *Les béatitudes* (3 vols.; Louvain: Nauwelaerts, 1958, 1969, 1973).

———— "Introduction aux béatitudes," *NRT* 108 (1976) 97-108.

Frankemölle, H. "Die Makarismen (Mt 5,1-12; Lk 6,20-23): Motive und Umfang der redaktionellen Komposition," *BZ* 15 (1971) 52-75.

Neuhäusler, E. *Anspruch und Antwort: Zur Lehre von den Weisungen innerhalb der synoptischen Jesusverkündigung* (Düsseldorf: Patmos, 1962) 141-169.

Schweizer, E. "Formgeschichtliches zu den Seligpreisungen Jesu," *NTS* 19 (1972-1973) 121-126.

Strecker, G. "Die Makarismen der Bergpredigt," *NTS* 17 (1970-1971) 255-275.

Love of One's Enemies

Lührmann, D. "Liebet eure Feinde (Lk 6,27-36/Mt 5,39-48)," *ZTK* 69 (1972) 412-438.

Schneider, G. "Die Neuheit der christlichen Nächstenliebe," *TTZ* 82 (1973) 257-275.

Schottroff, L. "Gewaltverzicht und Feindesliebe in der urchristlichen Jesustradition: Mt 5,38-48; Lk 6,27-36," in *Jesus Christus in Historie und Theologie: Neutestamentliche Festschrift für Hans Conzelmann zum 60. Geburtstag* (ed. G. Strecker; Tübingen: Mohr [Siebeck], 1975) 197-221.

Seitz, O. J. F. "Love Your Enemies: The Historical Setting of Matthew v. 43f.; Luke vi. 27f.," *NTS* 16 (1969-1970) 39-54.

Unnik, W. C. van. "Die Motivierung der Feindesliebe in Lukas vi 32-35," *NovT* 8 (1966) 284-300.

D. The Reception Accorded to Jesus' Ministry

Though leaders of Israel do not flock gladly to him, Jesus begins to attract Gentiles and sinners—those who will become part of the people of God

31. THE CURE OF THE CENTURION'S SERVANT
(7:1-10)

7 ¹After Jesus had finished all his words to the people, he entered Capernaum. ²A centurion there had a servant whom he prized highly, but who was deathly ill. ³Hearing about Jesus, the centurion sent some Jewish elders to him to ask him to come and save his servant. ⁴They approached Jesus and urged him strongly, "He deserves to be granted this by you, ⁵for he is well disposed toward our nation and has built us the synagogue." ⁶So Jesus went with them. When he was still a little way off from the house, the centurion sent some friends to say to him, "Sir, trouble yourself no more, for I do not deserve to have you come in under my roof. ⁷This is why I did not even presume to approach you in person. So just utter a word that my servant may be healed. ⁸I know, for I am under orders myself and have soldiers under me. If I say to one of them, 'Go,' he goes; or to another, 'Come,' he comes. If I say to my servant, 'Do such and such,' he does it." ⁹When Jesus heard this, he marveled at the man. Turning, he said to the crowd that followed him, "I tell you, not even in Israel have I found such faith as this." ¹⁰When the messengers returned to the house, they found the servant in good health.

COMMENT

There now begins in the Lucan Gospel a series of episodes which highlight the reception accorded to Jesus by various persons or groups of persons as his ministry continues. This series begins with the present episode

of the cure of a centurion's servant (7:1-10) and ends with the distinctively Lucan passage about the Galilean women-followers of Jesus
(8:1-3). It will tell of his reception by a Gentile centurion, villagers of
Nain, "all Judea," disciples of John the Baptist, and sinners. The keynote
of the series is sounded in 7:16cd, "A great prophet has been raised in
our midst, and God has taken note of his people."

The cure of the centurion's servant (7:1-10) is still part of Luke's little
interpolation into the Marcan material and order. As in the Matthean
Gospel (8:5-13), it comes on the heels of the extended sermon of Jesus
in the early part of his ministry. The clear "Q" material is found in
7:1b-2,3a,6e,7b,8-9,10b (=Matt 8:5-6,8-10,13b). But which account
has preserved the more original form of "Q"? Years ago, E. Wendling
(*ZNW* 9 [1908] 96-108) tried to argue that Luke had derived his account secondarily from Matthew. E. Haenchen (*ZTK* 56 [1959] 25-27;
SE I, 495-498) has maintained that the Lucan form of the story with the
two delegations and their implausibility (the first delegation should have
made it clear that the centurion considered himself unworthy that Jesus
should enter his house) reveal that Luke inherited his form of the story
from some source. Similarly, G. Schneider (*Evangelium nach Lukas,*
165) thinks that Luke has preserved the "Q" substratum better than
Matthew. But none of these suggestions is really convincing.

Before we proceed with a further analysis of the Lucan form of the
story, we must mention another form of it in the Johannine tradition
(John 4:46-53). Since patristic times it has been recognized that this
Johannine story is related to the cure of the centurion's servant. There
are obvious similarities and dissimilarities in the traditions. In all three
accounts the official (in Luke and Matthew, a "centurion"; in John, a
"royal official" [*basilikos*]) is located at Capernaum; he may be a non-
Jew in each. A boy close to him lies gravely ill and cannot be brought to
Jesus; the official requests of him a cure. Jesus reacts (by going, or by
saying something). A further reply/request is made to Jesus, and he performs the cure at a distance. In the Johannine account Jesus is at Cana
(probably a location secondarily introduced to relate the Capernaum miracle to the first sign wrought at Cana [2:11; 4:54]); the boy is a "son"
whereas in Matthew/Luke he is a "servant-boy" (*pais* in Matthew;
doulos or *pais* in Luke). The sickness is differently described in each account. But the main difference in the Johannine version is the absence of
the official's statement about authority and the substitution for it of a second request in the light of Jesus' remark about signs and wonders.
Though the same incident undoubtedly underlies both the Synoptic and
Johannine accounts, the latter is almost certainly independent of the
Synoptics. See further R. E. Brown, *John, I-XII,* 192-193.

Further scrutiny reveals that the Matthean account (8:5-13) probably contains the form of the story that was originally in "Q." Matthew has, however, inserted secondarily vv. 11-12 into that form from elsewhere in "Q," as Luke 13:28-29 reveals. But the Matthean form agrees with the Johannine tradition in depicting the official/centurion coming to Jesus personally and requesting his help (John 4:47; Matt 8:6). Moreover, the term used for the boy in Matt 8:6,8,13 is *pais* (lit. "child," but which could mean either "boy" or "servant-boy") and it is found in the strictly "Q" part of the Lucan episode (7:7c). It probably represents the more primitive (even pre-"Q") tradition; whereas it has been understood as "son" (*huios*) in John, it is interpreted as "servant, slave" (*doulos*) by Luke in vv. 2,3 and even extended to v. 10. Again, if the double delegation sent to Jesus were part of "Q," its omission by Matthew would be more difficult to explain than to regard it as a Lucan compositional addition to the "Q" form. For these reasons it is better to regard vv. 1a,7a, and 10a as Lucan redaction and the rest vv. 3b-6d as Lucan composition. Lucan redaction would be further responsible for the omission of "Amen" (see Matt 8:10b) and for the use of the negative "not even" (Luke 7:9).

Though the episode mentions the cure of a gravely ill servant of a centurion, it is not really a miracle-story. The miracle is even less directly referred to in Luke than in Matthew (see v. 13). V. Taylor has sought to classify the episode form-critically as a Story about Jesus: "the interest appears to lie in the incidents themselves rather than in the words of Jesus" (*FGT*, 76). But the modification that Luke has introduced into v. 9, "not even in Israel," clearly makes this episode a pronouncement-story (R. Bultmann, *HST*, 38 rightly listed it among the apophthegms).

Bultmann regards the episode as a variant of the story of the Syro-Phoenician woman (Mark 7:24-31; Matt 15:21-28), an episode that Luke does not have. In both, a miracle is performed by Jesus for a Gentile, at a distance, and after the Gentile has managed to overcome his scruples about asking for help for a non-Jewish child. The similarity is striking, indeed, but one should hesitate to write off all the details as variants of the same miracle. Bultmann does this, because he regards both stories as "products of the Church" and questions the "historicity of a telepathic healing" (*HST*, 39). However one is inclined to view this implied aspect of the story, it obviously has not been told to answer modern questions about such matters.

Haenchen, who thinks that Luke has inherited a fuller form of the story with the two delegations sent to Jesus already part of it, ascribes it to a Jewish Christian who considered it impossible that Jesus would assist a Gentile merely because of his faith and sought to reduce the merit of such faith in favor of the need of good works, i.e. alms for the Jewish people (in building them a synagogue); see *SE I*, 496. If this is truly an aspect of the Lucan story, it is certainly a minor one, Acts 10:35 notwith-standing.

The main point in the Lucan story is not so much the worthiness of this particular Gentile, a point stressed by the elders, but rather his "faith" (*pistis*, 7:9). Its importance is seen not only in the Lucan empha-sis (*"not even in Israel* have I found such faith as this") but in this say-ing of Jesus as a reaction to the double delegation sent to him and the very words of the centurion put on the lips of the second. To analyze the double delegation, as Haenchen has done, and reduce it to banality (the clumsy insertion of the Jewish elders who fail to stress that the centurion considered himself unworthy to have Jesus enter his house, necessitating the sending of another delegation) is to miss the point of the whole story. Part of the problem here is what we alluded to above, the different form-critical assessments of the story by Taylor and Bultmann. The Lucan ad-ditions bring it about that it is not a simple pronouncement-story. The elders have been introduced to provide a background for the centurion's own statement about his authority (*exousia*, v. 8) and his recognition of Jesus' authority (v. 7b). Both of them enhance the implied exercise of Jesus' powerful word (his *dynamis*, 5:17d). Again, the contrast between the elders' statement, that the centurion is "deserving" (*axios*, v. 4), and the centurion's own statement transmitted by friends, that he is "not worthy" (*ou gar hikanos*, v. 6), cannot be missed. The double delegation, introduced by Luke, is clearly a literary device to build up the suspense for the pronouncement of Jesus. Neither the elders nor the friends are depicted in any pejorative way; the elders come to Jesus, and he listens to them and goes along with them. For all their willingness (i.e. that of both the elders and the friends) the implied intensity of the faith of the Gentile centurion is enhanced.

The story may exemplify and foreshadow Acts 10:35: "God shows no partiality, but anyone who fears him and does what is right in every na-tion is acceptable to him." It certainly suits the Lucan concern for the mission to the Gentiles. Jesus is again shown to use his power in behalf of an unfortunate human being, this time the servant of a non-Jewish resi-dent in the area of his evangelization.

NOTES

7 1. *After.* The best reading here is *epeidē*, "when, after," in mss. P⁷⁵, B, C*. This is the only place in the NT where it is used in a temporal sense (see BDF § 455.1, for its usual causal meaning). Mss. ℵ, R, the Koine text-tradition, and the Lake and Freer families of minuscules read *epei de*, which is an obvi-ous copyist's correction.

had finished all his words to the people. Lit. "had brought to completion (*eplērōsen*) all his words in the hearing of the people." Ms. D has a variant: "And it happened, when he (had) finished speaking these words, (that) he came. . . ." This variant, however, is a copyist's harmonization, making the conclusion of the sermon on the plain resemble that of the Matthean sermon (7:28).

Capernaum. The Galilean town mentioned in 4:23 (see NOTE). Cf. John 4:46.

2. *A centurion.* Verse 9 shows that the man is a Gentile. He could be regarded as a Roman, since the title *hekatontarchos/hekatontarchēs* designated an officer at the head of a Roman company of one hundred men. He was not certainly in charge of Roman troops stationed at this time in Capernaum; he may have been in the service of Herod Antipas as the leader of mercenary troops (in John 4:46 he is called *basilikos*, "a royal official"), or may have been in police-service or customs-service. The identification of him is of little concern to Luke, for whom he may be rather a foreshadowing of the Roman centurion Cornelius in Acts 10:1.

servant. The same term occurs in vv. 3,10. The best mss. read *doulos* here, but ms. D has *pais*, an obvious copyist's correction, harmonizing the text with v. 8 or possibly with Matt 8:5. In John 4:47,50,52 the boy is called *huios*, "son." Luke's shift from *pais* in "Q" to *doulos* is interpretative, but it is not clear why he shifted. *Pais* was commonly used for "slave, servant" in classical and Hellenistic Greek (BGD, 604; MM, 475) and would have been understood by Luke's readers.

whom he prized highly. Lit. "who was valuable to him." This is probably a Lucan redactional addition, since *entimos* is used by Luke alone among the evangelists. Ms. D has the adj. *timios*, "precious," again a Lucan term.

deathly ill. Lit. "being badly off, about to die." In Matt 8:6 the boy is "paralytic" and "terribly tormented"; in John 4:47 he is "about to die"; as the story develops, it is because of a fever (4:52).

3. *Hearing about Jesus.* This undoubtedly refers to his reputation as a miracle-worker (4:37). This detail is preserved in John 4:47, and may well have been part of pre-Lucan tradition.

some Jewish elders. *Presbyterous* means here not merely "old men" (as in Acts 2:17), but "elders," i.e. a special group of Jewish community leaders in Capernaum (cf. 20:1; 22:52; Acts 4:5,8,23). They are sent to Jesus, a Jew, by a Gentile who respects Jewish customs. The phrase reveals the non-Jewish character of the author who writes.

save his servant. The verb *diasōzein*, "save," denotes deliverance from illness and imminent death. It is part of Lucan soteriological vocabulary (see p. 222 above); but this is hardly intended here (at least at Stage I of the gospel tradition).

4. *He deserves to be granted this by you.* Lit. "he is worthy, to whom you should grant this." A rel. cl. depends on *axios estin;* this is sometimes considered a Latinism, an imitation of *dignus qui* (see BDF § 653b; C. F. D. Moule, *Idiom Book,* 192 [*dignus est cui hoc praestes*]). Contrast the elders' statement,

"he is deserving" (*axios estin*), with the centurion's, "I am not fit" (*ou gar hikanos eimi*, v. 6) or "I did not consider myself worthy" (*oude emauton ēxiōsa*, v. 7).

5. *he is well disposed.* Lit. "he loves our nation." Though these words may suggest that the centurion was a "God-fearer" (Acts 10:2), they need not be so pressed; Josephus records a rather similar estimate of Alexander the Great, "he honored our nation" (*etima gar hēmōn to ethnos, Ag. Ap.* 2.4 § 43).

has built us the synagogue. Probably that mentioned in 4:33; cf. Mark 1: 21; John 6:59 (see NOTES on 4:15,33). An inscription recording the erection by a Gentile of a *proseuchē,* "a (Jewish) place of prayer," is known (see W. Dittenberger, *OGIS* § 96).

6. *went with them.* Compare Peter's reaction in Acts 10:20,23. In the Lucan form of the story, Jesus accedes to the elders' request immediately. This, however, prepares for the sending of the second delegation ("friends"). In Matt 8:7 Jesus merely says, "I will come and heal him"—or, as some commentators have sought to understand the words (e.g. T. Zahn, J. Wellhausen), "Am I to come and heal him?" See Haenchen, *ZTK* 56 [1959] 23.

some friends. They are unspecified: Gentiles or Jews? Probably the latter.

to say to him. Lit. "saying to him," with the ptc. modifying "the centurion." The words are to be understood as repeated verbatim by the friends, even though they are on the lips of the centurion. This inconcinnity reveals the retention of source-material by Luke; he has not smoothed it out by casting it into indirect discourse.

Sir. The voc. *kyrie* is present here and in Matt 8:8 (derived from "Q"). There is no need to give it any nuance other than a secular greeting, *pace* H. Schürmann, *Lukasevangelium,* 389, 393; see F. Hahn, *The Titles of Jesus,* 81 and n. 106.

trouble yourself no more. Lit. "do not bother." This is a Lucan addition to the material from "Q." The protest has been compared to Mark 5:35 (see Luke 8:49).

come in under my roof. Entrance into the house of a Gentile would be a source of defilement for a Jew; see Acts 10:28; 11:12. Cf. *m. Oholot* 18:7, "The dwelling-places of Gentiles are unclean." The centurion is depicted as knowing this. Hence he considers himself undeserving of Jesus' visit.

7. *just utter a word.* Lit. "speak with a word." The centurion is further depicted as recognizing the power of Jesus' word (see COMMENT on 5:24c) and thinking that he can even cure at a distance.

may be healed. The best reading (from mss. P75, B, etc.) is *iathētō,* the aor. pass. impv., "let him be healed." Some mss. (‭א‬, C, D, the Koine text-tradition) read the fut. pass. indic. *iathēsetai,* "he will be healed." There is little difference in meaning.

8. *I know, for I am under orders myself and have soldiers under me.* Lit. "for, in fact, I too am a human being subjected (pres. ptc.) to authority (*exousia*), having soldiers under me." Luke has added to the "Q" material the ptc. *tassomenos,* "subjected," which clearly implies the centurion's subordination to superior officers and then his delegated authority over others. Matt 8:9 reads,

"I am one under authority, having soldiers under me." But variants in the Sinaitic and Curetonian Syriac version of Matt 8:9 mention only the centurion's possession of authority: "for I also am a man having authority and soldiers under my hand"; or "for I too am a man having those who are subject to my authority." J. Jeremias (*Jesus' Promise*, 30 n. 4) argues from this to a more original Aramaic form, in which *en exousia* would be the translation of *běšulṭānā'*, "in authority," but which was misunderstood and rendered as *hyp' exousian*, "under authority." But this is far from certain. The Syriac variants rather reflect an attempt to cope with the implication of the Greek text, made even more pronounced by Luke's addition of *tassomenos*, that Jesus too was somehow under authority and subordinated. See A. H. Hooke, *ExpTim* 69 [1957] 80. Such an interpretation, arguing *a pari* from the centurion's words to the status of Jesus, has given rise to all sorts of manipulation of the Greek text of v. 8 in older commentaries to avoid such connotations (see, e.g. U. Holzmeister, *VD* 17 [1937] 27-32). The words of the centurion are meant to enhance the power of Jesus' command; they argue *a minore ad maius*, express the centurion's modesty, and eventually evoke a comment from Jesus about his faith. See further M. Frost, *ExpTim* 45 (1933-1934) 477-478; A. E. Garvie, *ExpTim* 20 (1908-1909) 377; H. H. Stainsby, *ExpTim* 30 (1918-1919) 328-329.

9. *marveled.* Luke does not suppress Jesus' surprise at the centurion's words and reaction; see R. E. Brown, *Jesus God and Man,* 45.

Turning, he said to the crowd. Not "turning to the crowd that followed him, he said" (cf. *NEB, NAB*), since the dative is the indirect object of the verb of saying (cf. *RSV, BJ;* see P. Joüon, *RSR* 18 [1928] 352). The ptc. *strapheis* is a Lucan favorite (7:44; 9:55; 10:22,23; 14:25; 22:61; 23:28).

I tell you. Lit. "I say to you." Luke has omitted the introductory *amēn* (cf. Matt 8:10); see NOTE on 4:24.

not even in Israel have I found such faith as this. Jesus' acknowledgment of the Gentile centurion's faith contains a criticism of Israel's faith in him. It is the "pronouncement" addressed to the reader, challenging him/her to a similar response of faith. The centurion thus becomes in Luke a symbol of Gentile belief over against the general reaction of Israel. The words do not mean that Jesus has, in fact, found such faith elsewhere outside of Israel, but only that he was not prepared to admit its existence in a Gentile.

10. *they found the servant in good health.* Luke changed the first part of the verse, omitting the impv. of Matt 8:13; the indirect reporting of the miracle's effect is preferred and has its own literary purpose. It does not concentrate on the cure itself, but on the pronouncement of Jesus. Jesus' power, exercised in the act performed at a distance, reveals that he too is a man of authority (*exousia*); cf. 5:17d,24; 4:36.

BIBLIOGRAPHY (7:1-10)

Derrett, J. D. M. "Law in the New Testament: The Syro-Phoenician Woman and the Centurion of Capernaum," *NovT* 15 (1973) 161-186, esp. pp. 174-183.

George, A. "Guérison de l'esclave d'un centurion: Lc 7,1-10," *AsSeign* 40 (1972) 66-77.

Haenchen, E. "Faith and Miracle," *SE I* (TU 73; Berlin: Akademie, 1959) 495-498.

———— "Johanneische Probleme," *ZTK* 56 (1959) 18-54, esp. pp. 23-31.

Jeremias, J. *Jesus' Promise to the Nations* (SBT 24; London: SCM, 1958) 28-35.

Mouson, J. "De sanatione pueri centurionis (Mt. viii, 5-13)," *Collectanea mechliniensia* 29 (1959) 633-636.

Schnackenburg, R. "Zur Traditionsgeschichte von Joh 4, 46-54," *BZ* 8 (1964) 58-88.

Wendling, E. "Synoptische Studien: II. Der Hauptmann von Kapernaum," *ZNW* 9 (1908) 96-109.

32. NAIN: RAISING OF THE WIDOW'S SON
(7:11-17)

7 ¹¹ Soon afterwards Jesus happened to go to a town called Nain, accompanied by his disciples and a great crowd of people. ¹² As he drew near to the gate of the town, a dead man was being carried out; he was the only son of a woman who was a widow. And a considerable throng of people from the town was with her. ¹³ When the Lord saw her, he had pity on her and said, "Do not cry." ¹⁴ Then he went up and touched the coffin. The bearers stopped, and he said, "Young man, get up, I tell you!" ¹⁵ And the dead man sat up and began to speak, *and he gave him back to his mother.*ᵃ ¹⁶ Deep awe came over all of them, and they glorified God, saying, 'A great prophet has been raised in our midst, and God has taken note of his people." ¹⁷ And talk like this about him went abroad in all Judea and in all the countryside.

ᵃ 1 Kgs 17:23

COMMENT

The episode of Jesus' raising the widow's son at Nain (7:11-17) reports still further on the reception given to Jesus in his Galilean ministry. It is yet another part of his little interpolation of non-Marcan material into the Marcan order (see p. 627 above). It has been inserted here to show progress in yet another way, because Jesus' power has been described at work in the preceding episode on behalf of a gravely ill person, but now it is to be exercised on a person who is dead and about to be buried. It thus further reveals the extent of his power and authority in this part of the Lucan Gospel.

Moreover, it is an episode that foreshadows. In 7:22 Jesus will say to the messengers from John the Baptist that "the dead are being raised to life" as a manifestation of the kind of ministry in which he has been engaged. Luke is not content to illustrate that report solely with the story of the raising of Jairus' daughter, to be recounted subsequently in 8:40-42,49-56. He now introduces a story of the resuscitation of a dead person so that when Jesus sends the messengers back to John in prison, his words in 7:22 will already have a concrete exemplification of this phenomenon in the Lucan account itself.

In the main this episode is derived from Luke's private source, "L." He is, however, responsible for the introductory verse (7:11), *pace* G. Schneider (*Evangelium nach Lukas*, 168). The location of the incident, however, is to be regarded as pre-Lucan; there is no reason why he should gratuitously locate it at such a place. M. Dibelius sought to ascribe vv. 13 and 15b to Luke (*FTG,* 75), the first because Luke "depicts feelings" and "readily mentions women," and the second because of its similarity to 1 Kgs 17:23. However, this is not entirely evident, since Luke often omits the emotions of Jesus that are in his sources (see NOTE on 5:13) and the Lucan occurrences of the verb *splanchnizesthai* are all found in "L" passages (here, 10:33; 15:20). Verses 16-17, however, are to be attributed to Lucan composition, since they resemble other summary reactions that he is fond of adding.

From a form-critical viewpoint, the episode is a miracle-story. R. Bultmann (*HST,* 215) has listed it under "miracles of healing"; so does V. Taylor (*FGT,* 120). It would be better to classify it as a resuscitation, a category admitted by Bultmann later on (*HST,* 233-234). This is the first of three resuscitations that Luke has introduced into his account (see also 8:40-42,49-56; Acts 9:36-43—some would add a fourth, Acts 20:7-12).

The passage recalls the raising of the son of the widow of Zarephath by Elijah in 1 Kgs 17:8-24. Jesus comes to a town (Nain), as did Elijah (Zarephath, 1 Kgs 17:10); a widow is met at the gate of the town (17:10); the son of the widow is restored to life (17:22); and an explicit allusion to 1 Kgs 17:23 is made in Luke 7:15. The proximity of Nain to Shunem (see NOTE on 7:11) suggests to some commentators that there is even a reference in this Lucan story to the raising of the son of the Shunamite woman in the Elisha cycle (2 Kgs 4:18-36). This last point is very tenuous and need not detain us here. The identification of Jesus as "a great prophet" (7:16c) and the allusion to the Elijah story (7:15) suffice to show that Luke uses this incident to cast Jesus in the role of *Elias redivivus* (see p. 215 above). There is, however, one significant difference between this story and the Elijah story: Jesus raises the widow's son by a command of his powerful word, whereas Elijah had to stretch himself over the child three times. If the origin of this episode is to be sought in "a popular tale" christianized by traits drawn from the Elijah story, as R. H. Fuller (*Interpreting,* 64) would have it, then it is not Luke who has first so christianized it.

Parallels to resuscitation-stories in ancient literature have at times been drawn. Thus Pliny *Naturalis historia* 26.13; Apuleius *Florida* 19; and especially Philostratus *Vita Apollonii* 4.45. The last-mentioned has often been cited as particularly pertinent to the resuscitations of the gospel tradition. It tells of a miracle (*thauma*) performed by Apollonius of Tyana in raising a newly wed girl from the dead. While all Rome mourned with her groom, who was following her bier, Apollonius ordered the bier to be put down and asked the name of the girl. "Touching her and saying something over her indistinctly (*ti aphanōs epeipōn*), he woke up the maiden from her seeming death (*tou dokountos thanatou*); the girl uttered a sound and returned to her father's house, just as Alcestis did, having been brought back to life by Heracles." However, Philostratus goes on to comment that whether Apollonius detected some spark of life in her unnoticed by others or whether her life was really extinct and was restored by the warmth of his touch was a problem that neither he—writing some hundred years after the event—nor any of those present were able to decide. Apollonius of Tyana (in Cappadocia) was roughly a contemporary of Jesus and survived into the reign of Nerva (A.D. 96-98). Little is known directly about this Neopythagorean ascetic and wandering teacher, who traveled widely to distant lands (India, Rome, etc.). His life was written by Flavius Philostratus, who was born ca. A.D. 170 and lived in Athens and Rome; at the instigation of Julia Domna, the wife of the emperor Septimius Severus, he wrote a life of Apollonius. Debate goes on constantly in modern times about his sources, the value of them, and how they should be interpreted; it is rivaled only by the debate about Jesus and his story. One thing is certain: this story about a resuscitation by Apollonius does not stem from a writer prior to the NT Gospels themselves. Whether this story about Apollonius' resuscitation can be traced to a source earlier than those of the NT evangelists is not clear. Can one exclude the possibility that the tradition about Jesus' resuscitations has influenced that used by Philostratus? In any case, it is noteworthy that Luke (or his source) introduces no hesitation about what Jesus did and that the Lucan account—or for that matter, any of the NT accounts of resuscitation—makes no mention of "seeming death." Modern readers of such a gospel-story may be inclined to think that Philostratus' comment is closest to their own attitude (e.g. W. K. Lowther Clarke, *Theology* 25 [1932] 36: "The young man was in a state of suspended animation. No decay had set in . . ."). His comment shows at least that the problem of the historicity of such a story is perennial, and there is always the human tendency to rationalize the details. But to do so is to put to the text a question that it was not intending to answer and to miss the import of the story itself. Whether one will ever solve the problem of historicity or not, the episode proclaims to human beings the power of God working through Jesus and accosts them with a challenge of faith in that power. That would be the underlying pitch in all resuscitation stories.

In this particular instance, it is important to note that the miracle is not particularly related to faith in Jesus; that is not demanded either of the mother of the boy or of his friends who are carrying him to burial. It is attributed to Jesus' compassion and recounted for a hagiographic purpose (B. Lindars, "Elijah, Elisha," 76-79).

It does elicit from the bystanders a fundamental christological affirmation; Jesus is recognized to be "a great prophet," one with power over life and death. The episode thus contributes in its own way to the Lucan theology of Jesus as prophet (see pp. 213-215 above).

In recognizing that God has taken note of his people in this mighty act, the crowd not only sums up in typically Lucan fashion (glorifying God) the meaning of the episode, but adds to the general picture of the reception of Jesus that is being portrayed in this part of the Gospel.

NOTES

7 11. *Soon afterwards.* Lit. "and it happened in the following (time) (that) he made his way. . . ." Luke uses *kai egeneto* + finite verb (*eporeuthē,* on which see NOTE on 4:30) without the conj. *kai* (see p. 119 above). In the intervening temporal phrase the adv. *hexēs,* "next," is used as an adj. with the masc. art. *tō,* with which some noun like *chronō,* "time," is to be understood. More frequently in Luke, who alone uses *hexēs* in the NT, it is used with the fem. art. *tē* (understand *hēmerā,* "day"); see 9:37; Acts 21:1; 25:17; 27:18. Some Greek mss. (‭א‬*, C, D) read the fem. art. here too.

Nain. A town in southern Galilee (modern Nein), it is mentioned only here in the Bible. It was situated not far from Endor on the NW side of Nebi Dahi, a hill between Gilboa and Mount Tabor, a few miles SW of Nazareth. See Jerome *Epistulae* 108.13, 6 (CSEL, 55. 323); 46.13,3 (CSEL, 54. 344); *De situ et nominibus locorum hebraicorum* 225 (PL, 23. 961). It would be about twenty-five miles distant from Capernaum, the place last mentioned (7:1). Hence it is far from clear that Luke was thinking of Nain as situated in Judea (in the strict sense), *pace* H. Conzelmann, *Theology,* 46. The spelling *Naim* comes from the Latin tradition.

disciples and a great crowd. See 6:17; 7:9.

12. *As he drew near.* For the use of the verb *engizein* in a spatial sense, see 15:25; 19:29,41.

the gate of the town. Cf. 1 Kgs 17:10.

the only son of a woman who was a widow. Lit. "there was being carried out the only son of his mother, having died, and she was a widow." Luke has a predilection for *monogenēs,* "only," using it in two other miracles: 8:42 (cf. Mark 5:23); 9:38 (cf. Mark 9:17). It means "only" in the sense of "one of a kind" (*monos* + *genos*); see my article in *EWNT* 2. 1081-83. It stresses the straits in which the widowed mother has been put by the death of her only child, and incidentally her only means of support. The verb *ekkomizein* is used by Josephus in the same sense of "carrying out" a dead person (*J.W.* 5.13,7 § 567).

13. *When the Lord saw her.* This is the first instance of the absol. use of *ho kyrios* for Jesus in a narrative section of the Gospel; see further p. 202 above.

he had pity on her. Thus the motive of the miracle is presented. It proceeds from Jesus' spontaneous compassion for the woman; as the "author of life" (Acts 3:15), he manifests his power toward her in her dire need. It does not involve "faith," as did the preceding episode. See H. Koester, *TDNT* 7. 553.

"Do not cry." Lit. "do not go on crying," as the pres. impv. would imply. Jesus does not forbid a mother's grief, but counsels the woman in view of his coming action.

14. *touched the coffin.* Or "bier." The Greek *soros* properly means a vessel for holding the remains of a dead person, often made of stone, like a cinerary urn or an ossuary. It also denoted a "coffin," but here it may have rather the meaning of "bier" (for which Greek *klinē* was more properly used [LXX, Gen 50:26; Josephus *Life* 62 § 323]). In Hellenistic texts of a later period *soros* was used for "bier"; this may then be the earliest attestation of it in this sense.

get up. Lit. "to you I say, 'Get up.' " Jesus' words are addressed to the young man in the hearing of the crowd standing by; contrast the story of Apollonius of Tyana, who raises a girl with a formula whispered "indistinctly" (*aphanōs*). See P. J. Achtemeier, *JBL* 94 (1975) 557.

Luke uses the aor. pass. impv. *egerthēti* with the force of the middle voice (=the intransitive). It has the same meaning as the act. impv. *egeire* (5:23,24; 6:8; 8:54). Cf. the aor. pass. indic. in 11:8; 13:25 (of getting out of bed). The passive of *egeirein* is also used of the dead "being raised" (7:22; 9:7,22; 20:37; 24:6,34; cf. Dan 12:2 [Theodotion]; LXX Sir 48:5). Because of this usage, one might be tempted to think that the impv. should mean, "be raised up." That is an added Christian theological connotation for this verb (and others like it, such as *sōzein*, "save"), which might suit Stage III of the gospel tradition, but might also be too much for Stage I.

15. *the dead man sat up.* The verb *anakathizein* is used in the NT only here and in Acts 9:40 (of Tabitha).

began to speak. Luke—or the tradition before him—refrains from putting anything on the lips of the resuscitated son. He was not just "seemingly dead" (Philostratus *Vita Apoll.* 4.45); but is portrayed as visibly and audibly alive again.

gave him back to his mother. This clause agrees word for word with the LXX of 1 Kgs 17:23. The OT allusion is here worked into the narrative itself without trace of any adventitious character, as such allusions sometimes have.

16. *Deep awe came over all of them.* Lit. "fear seized all," referring to those mentioned in vv. 11-12. Luke often uses *phobos*, "fear," to express the reaction of bystanders to a heavenly intervention or a manifestation of Jesus' power (see 1:65; 5:26; 8:25,37; Acts 2:43; 5:5,11; 19:17). A cringing attitude of fear would be too strong an explanation of what is meant; hence the translation "deep awe." Joined to the glorification, it is intended as a sort of Greek-chorus-like reaction to the miracle that has been wrought. On "all," see NOTE on 4:15.

saying. The double use of the conj. *hoti* introduces direct discourse (see BDF § 470.1). The second one does not have to be taken as "because."

A great prophet. I.e. like Elijah of the OT, as the allusion to his story in

v. 15 suggests; Jesus will be so recognized again in 24:19. "Prophet" was used of him implicitly in 4:24,27 (in the comparison with both Elijah and Elisha).

Could "a great prophet" allude to *the* (expected) eschatological prophet (like Moses; cf. Deut 18:15-18)? F. Hahn (*The Titles of Jesus,* 379) thinks that the lack of the def. art. here does not stand in the way of such an explanation, but O. Cullmann (*Christology,* 30) does. The primary reference is surely to a prophet like Elijah (in view of v. 15); but it is difficult to exclude the further connotation.

One should, however, not refer to this title as having anything to do with Jesus' *messianic* role; there is nothing here about his anointed agency (see H. Schürmann, *Lukasevangelium,* 403; against such commentators as E. E. Ellis, *Gospel of Luke,* 118; A. Richardson, *Miracle Stories,* 113; Fuller, *Interpreting,* 64).

Jesus is seen as "a great prophet" in the service of God's people. His ministry extends not only to the poor, the imprisoned, the blind, and the downtrodden, but even to those in the grip of death.

has been raised. I.e. "has been brought on the scene." The verb is again the aor. pass. indic. of *egeirein,* as in 11:31 and possibly 3:8. Cf. Dan 8:18; Judg 2:16,18; 3:9; Isa 45:13 (LXX).

God has taken note of his people. Or "has visited his people," see NOTE on 1:68; cf. 1:78; Acts 15:14. This reaction of the people now echoes a motif sounded in the infancy narrative. God's compassionate and gracious visitation of his people is seen in the manifestation of Jesus' miraculous power. The collocation of visitation and death may echo that of Gen 50:24-25, where the patriarch Joseph relates his own death to a visitation.

17. *talk like this.* Lit. "this word (*logos*)" or "this comment"; see 4:37 (*ēchos*); 5:15 (*logos*).

in all Judea and in all the countryside. See 4:44. News of what took place in southern Galilee is said to have spread to other parts of Palestine. This could be the sense of "Judea" here, because of the phrase that follows.

Some commentators prefer to give it the sense of the land of the Jews (as in 1:5; 4:44; 6:17; 23:5; Acts 2:9; 10:37; see Schürmann, *Lukasevangelium,* 29 n. 112). This would then give a broader meaning to *perichōros,* "countryside," going beyond the bounds of the land of the Jews. Jesus' reputation is in any case widespread. "The area indicated is not where Jesus has appeared in person, but that of his *phēmē* ['reputation']" (Conzelmann, *Theology,* 46).

BIBLIOGRAPHY (7:11-17)

Achtemeier, P. J. "The Lucan Perspective on the Miracles of Jesus: A Preliminary Sketch," *JBL* 94 (1975) 547-562.

Dibelius, M. *From Tradition to Gospel* (New York: Scribner, n.d.) 72-81.

Dubois, J.-D. "La figure d'Elie dans la perspective lucanienne," *RHPR* 53 (1973) 155-176.

Fuller, R. H. *Interpreting the Miracles* (Philadelphia: Westminster, 1963) 64.

George, A. "Le miracle dans l'oeuvre de Luc," in *Les miracles de Jésus selon le Nouveau Testament* (ed. X. Léon-Dufour; Paris: Ed. du Seuil, 1977) 249-268.

Gils, F. *Jésus prophète d'après les évangiles synoptiques* (Orientalia et biblica lovaniensia 2; Louvain: Publications universitaires, 1957) 26-27.

Lindars, B. "Elijah, Elisha and the Gospel Miracles," in *Miracles: Cambridge Studies in Their Philosophy and History* (ed. C. F. D. Moule; London: Mowbray, 1965) 63-79.

Loos, H. van der. *The Miracles of Jesus* (NovTSup 9; Leiden: Brill, 1965) 573-576.

Richardson, A. *The Miracle Stories of the Gospels* (London: SCM, 1959) 113-114.

Ternant, P. "La résurrection du fils de la veuve de Naïn (Lc 7, 11-16)," *As-Seign* 69 (1964) 29-40.

33. JOHN THE BAPTIST'S QUESTION; JESUS' ANSWER
(7:18-23)

7 18 Now John's disciples kept him informed of all these things. So he summoned two of them and 19 sent them to the Lord to ask, "Are you the *'One who is to come,'*[a] or are we to look for someone else?" 20 When the men came to Jesus, they said, "John the Baptist sent us to you to ask, 'Are you the "One who is to come," or are we to look for someone else?'" 21 Jesus had just then cured many people of diseases, plagues, and evil spirits; and restored sight to many blind persons. 22 So he answered them, "Go and inform John of what you have seen and heard: *Blind people recovering their sight,*[b] cripples walking, lepers being cleansed, *deaf hearing again, dead being raised to life,* and *good news being preached to the poor.*[c] 23 Blessed, indeed, is the person who is not shocked at me."

[a] Mal 3:1   [b] Isa 61:1   [c] Isa 35:5; 26:19; 61:1

COMMENT

There now follow in Luke's little interpolation three passages dealing with John the Baptist and his relation to Jesus and his ministry: (1) the question which the imprisoned John sends to Jesus and his answer to it (7:18-23); (2) Jesus' testimony about John's role and identity (7:24-30); and (3) Jesus' judgment on his own generation's estimate of both John and himself (7:31-35). As a group, they spell out the relation of John and Jesus to the execution of God's plan of salvation and recount the reaction of John's disciples and of Jesus' own generation to him.

These Lucan passages have parallels in Matthew 11 and occur there in the same sequence as here, though with the omission of some material that Luke uses either here or elsewhere. Compare Matt 11:2-6,7-11, 16-19. Hence we are dealing with "Q" material again, even though Luke has modified or transposed some of it. Matt 11:12-13 most likely preserves the more original "Q" form and setting of the saying about John's relation to the Law and the prophets; Luke has moved it from here to 16:16 (see COMMENT there). If Matt 11:14 (the identification of the

Baptist with Elijah) were part of "Q," then Luke has omitted it here; but in this instance it is more likely that Matthew has added it, preparing for the implication of 17:12 (=Mark 9:13, which Luke omits entirely at that point in his account). In any case, Matt 11:15 was scarcely part of "Q," for it is one of those isolated sayings ("Let the one who has ears to hear take heed"), which floated around the early communities and has been added to the gospel tradition at various places (see Matt 13:9,43; Mark 4:9,23; [7:16]; Luke 8:8; 14:35).

As for the first episode, the question which the imprisoned John sends to Jesus (7:18-23), the shorter form found in Matt 11:2-4 is generally regarded as representing the more original "Q" form (see V. Taylor, *FGT*, 65-66; W. G. Kümmel, *Jesu Antwort*, 154). The repetitious v. 20 and the summary in v. 21, resembling 4:40-41; 5:15; 6:17, are to be ascribed to Lucan composition (see NOTES for details).

The use of Mal 3:1 to identify John's understanding of Jesus' role is also found in "Mk," independently of "Q." It is used in Mark 1:2, joined to Isa 40:3 in a conflated quotation. That is a secondary Marcan association, perhaps made at the time of the composition of the Gospel (with "his paths" of Mal 3:1 becoming "your paths" to smooth out the conflation; see E. Schweizer, *The Good News according to Mark* [London: SPCK, 1971] 29; E. Haenchen, *Der Weg Jesu* [2d ed.; Berlin: de Gruyter, 1968] 40; M.-J. Lagrange, *Matthieu,* cxx). This double attestation of the use of Mal 3:1 to identify the roles of John and Jesus undoubtedly represents a primitive Christian tradition.

Form-critically, this episode is to be regarded as a pronouncement-story, with the pronouncement enshrined in vv. 22-23. R. Bultmann (*HST,* 23) classed it among his apophthegms, specifically as an example of school debate. He regarded it as a product of the early community, one of "those passages in which the Baptist is called as a witness to the Messiahship of Jesus" (ibid.). That the passage reflects a controversy of a later date between the disciples of John and of Jesus is not impossible; but does such a context adequately explain the genesis of the pronouncement or only provide an occasion for the recollection of a statement about the relationship of the two stemming from Jesus himself? The double attestation of the use of Mal 3:1 in the gospel tradition argues in favor of the latter.

Another aspect of the difficulty of this passage is whether it is rightly related to "the Messiahship of Jesus." Matt 11:2 speaks of "the deeds of the Messiah," but it is far from certain that that was part of "Q." There is not a hint of messianism in the Lucan form. Moreover, as W. G. Kümmel (*Promise and Fulfilment,* 110-111) has noted, "the Baptist appears here in no way as a witness to Christ, but as an uncertain questioner, which contradicts the tendency of the early Church to make him such a witness."

So most probably the story in its essentials represents an old reliable tradition.

In vv. 18-22 Jesus is depicted as rejecting the role of *Elias redivivus,* in which John had originally cast him (see 3:15-18). Rather than understanding his mission as that of a fiery reformer of the eschaton, Jesus sees his role as the embodiment of the divine blessings promised to be shed on the unfortunate of human society by Isaiah. John initially regarded Jesus as one who would further what he had begun, "someone more powerful than I" (3:16), the "One who is to come." Jesus now makes it clear that he carries no ax or winnowing-fan, cleans no eschatological threshing-floor, and burns no chaff. Instead, he cures, frees, resuscitates; he cares for the blind, cripples, lepers, deaf, and even the dead; and he preaches God's good news to the poor. Luke 7:22 is to be understood as an echo of the quotation of Isa 61:1, as presented by Luke in 4:18 (see NOTE).

The end of Jesus' answer to John is a beatitude uttered over the person who fails not to grasp the real sense of his mission (the second part of his pronouncement). Attempts to explain "John's doubts" over the centuries have been numerous. A good summary of them has been given by J. Dupont, *NRT* 83 (1961) 806-813. The following is a brief sketch of such attempts: (1) John's question has been interpreted by commentators from the patristic period on (at least to the Reformation) as a fictive doubt: The imprisoned John used this device to strengthen and improve the understanding of his own disciples about Jesus. So, e.g. John Chrysostom (*Hom. xxxvi in Matt.* 11:2; PG, 57. 413-415); Augustine (*Sermones de scripturis* 66.3-4; PL, 38. 432-433); Hilary (*Comm. in Matt.* 11:2; PL, 9. 978-979). "But the whole context is against it" (A. Plummer, *Gospel,* 202). Especially in the Lucan form such an interpretation is difficult, where v. 19 reads literally, "John sent (the disciples) to the Lord, saying," and the sg. ptc. *legōn* refers clearly to John. The question is his. (2) John's question has also been interpreted as his first inkling of the role that Jesus might be playing. So, e.g. A. Loisy (*Les évangiles synoptiques* [Ceffonds: Privately published, 1907] 1. 660). This interpretation, however, is a reaction against that which considers the question to be an expression of real doubt on John's part about Jesus, whom he once admitted as Messiah. But does it really reckon sufficiently with the identification of him made in chap. 3? (3) The question has been understood as reflecting merely the polemics of the strife of the disciples in the early community; John's disciples are reproached because their master did not bow to the evidence of Jesus' messianic signs. So M. Goguel (*Au seuil de l'évangile: Jean Baptiste* [Paris: Payot, 1928] 64-65). (4) The most common interpretation has been that the question expresses John's real doubt, hesitation, or surprise that Jesus was not turning out to be the kind of messiah that he expected. Such an interpretation of John's failing faith has been used at least since the time of Tertullian (*Adversus Marcionem* 4.18,4-6; CC, 1. 589-590) and is found, in one form or another, in many modern commentaries. (5) The understanding of the question being used here would fall into the fourth category—with, however, the omission of the word "messiah." John's hesitation stems, not from a failing faith in Jesus' messianic role, but from his failure to see Jesus playing the role of the fiery reformer, *Elias redivivus,* the "One who is to come." See further the COMMENT on vv. 24-30.

The end of Jesus' answer is a beatitude uttered over the person who does not cling to preconceived ideas of him. The person who realizes that he has come as the embodiment of the blessings for humanity once announced by Isaiah and not as a fiery reformer will not find him to be a stumbling block in his/her life. No one is to take offense at him.

Implicit in the whole passage is the idea of fulfillment. The OT promises of bounty and blessings on human beings, associated with the eschaton, are now seen to be begun in the activity of Jesus himself. His deeds and preaching, witnessed by the two disciples of John, already concretize what was promised as eschatological blessings. Nowhere in this passage does Jesus relate his activity to the kingdom; and not even the evangelist, in redacting his form of it, has seen fit to relate this activity to that otherwise well-known gospel-theme.

NOTES

7 18. *John's disciples.* See NOTE on 5:33.

kept him informed. Lit. "and his disciples reported to John about all these things." In the Lucan context "all these things" refers to Jesus' preaching (the sermon on the plain), his teaching, and his miracles (from 3:21 on). Contrast the Matthean formula, "the deeds of the Messiah" (11:2), on which see v. 35 below. This is the occasion for the sending of the emissaries.

he summoned two of them. I.e. to the prison where he was being kept; see NOTE on 3:20. Luke does not mention John's imprisonment here; again contrast Matt 11:2. Luke has introduced "two" disciples who are sent; most likely as a reflection of Deut 19:15, "the evidence of two witnesses." This accounts for his addition of v. 21 below to the story (see J. F. Craghan, CBQ 29 [1967] 353-367). The twosome may even be traced back to older (Canaanite?) mythological tradition about messengers, whether gods or humans, traveling in pairs.

19. *to the Lord.* Again, the absolute use of *ho kyrios* in a narrative statement; see NOTE on 7:13. Some mss. (א, Θ, the Koine text-tradition), however, read "Jesus."

to ask. Lit. "saying." The Greek ptc. refers to John. See COMMENT.

the 'One who is to come.' Lit. "the coming one" (*ho erchomenos*), clearly used here as a title. The question refers to John's statement in 3:16, "is coming" (*erchetai,* the same as the verb in the LXX of Mal 3:1).

Since the "coming" of various expected figures in pre-Christian Jewish tradition is known, one has to sort out what the title *ho erchomenos* would have meant for John and for the evangelist. In this context it scarcely refers to the pilgrim coming to Jerusalem for a feast, as in Ps 118:26 (LXX *ho erchomenos*), alluded to in Luke 13:55 and modified in 19:38. Likewise, it is scarcely used of the coming of Yahweh himself, in a sense found in Zech 14:5 (LXX, *hēxei*). It could, of course, refer to a regal figure, whose coming is mentioned in Zech 9:9 (LXX *erchetai*). It could also have been understood of the coming of a prophet (like Moses) and the Messiahs, as in 1QS 9:11 (*'d bw' nby' wmšyḥy 'hrwn wyśr'l,* "until the coming of a prophet and the Messiahs of Aaron and Israel"; see further 4QPBless 3 (*'d bw' mšyḥ ḥṣdq ṣmḥ dwyd,* "until the coming of the messiah of righteousness, the scion of David" (J. M. Allegro, *JBL* 75 [1956] 174-176); 4QTestim (4Q*175*) 1-8, which quotes Deut 18:15-18 of the coming prophet (reflected in the NT in John 6:14). It could also refer to the coming of Yahweh's "messenger" (*mal'ākî,* LXX *ton angelon mou*) of Mal 3:1, who is eventually identified as Elijah, to be sent before "the great and awesome day of the Lord" (Mal 3:23 [4:5E]). Whether it may refer to the coming of an individual, apocalyptic Son of Man is a matter of no little dispute, since it is far from clear that there was a belief in such a figure in pre-Christian Palestinian Jewish tradition. Much of the dispute hangs on how one assesses the so-called parables of *1 Enoch* (see p. 209 above). The "coming" of an individual Son of Man is known, of course, from the NT (see Mark 8:38; Luke 9:26; Matt 16:27; 25:31), being applied to Jesus, who is otherwise spoken of as *ho erchomenos* in Heb 10:37 (an interpretation of Hab 2:3).

It is hardly likely that in this context the Son of Man, the king, or the prophet (like Moses) is meant, when the Baptist speaks of *ho erchomenos.* The majority of modern commentators understand it as a messianic title (e.g. Creed, Dibelius, Dupont, Ellis, Ernst, Lagrange, Plumacher, Schneider). This interpretation might seem to find some support in Luke 3:15, where people ask John whether he is the Messiah, and where commentators often conclude from his answer that he is implicitly applying the title to Jesus. That implication is far from certain. The messianic interpretation might suit the Matthean form of this episode, where the Baptist is said to have heard of "the deeds of the Messiah" (11:2). Yet that is almost certainly a Matthean redaction of "Q" (in view of 11:19). The messianic interpretation of *ho erchomenos,* however, suits neither the traces of Stage I of this part of the gospel tradition nor the Lucan context. Hence, when the eschatological and so-called messianic preaching of John the Baptist (3:7-9,15-17) are considered with what one finds in this episode (7:18-23 and its "Q" form), the title should rather be understood of the coming of "the messenger of Yahweh," *Elias redivivus*—a role that Jesus rejects here. This has to be recognized even though there is a sense in which Jesus is regarded as a Second Elijah in this Gospel. So too J. A. T. Robinson,

NTS 4 (1957-1958) 263-281; and perhaps A. R. C. Leaney (*A Commentary,* 144).

for someone else. The preferred reading (of mss. D, א, and the Koine text-tradition) is *allon,* meaning "another" of the same kind. Some mss. in the Hesychian tradition read rather *heteron,* which, strictly speaking, would mean "another" of a different kind. The latter is suspect, however, because of its possible harmonization by scribes with Matt 11:3. In this period of Greek the two words were often used indiscriminately (see BDF § 306).

20. *When the men came to Jesus.* Lit. "having become present to him." The ptc. is aor. *paragenomenoi,* a verbal form that is a favorite of Luke (see p. 111 above). It occurs frequently in Acts and is a sign of his compositional hand here. This verse merely repeats v. 19.

John the Baptist. In v. 18 he appears merely as "John," as also in v. 22. Here Luke uses his title too, as in 7:33; 9:19.

sent. The preferred reading is the aor. *apesteilen;* some mss. (D, the Koine text-tradition) have the pf. *apestalken,* which would suit the context better. In v. 19 (from "Q") the verb is the aor. of *pempein.*

21. *had just then cured.* Lit. "in that hour he cured." Luke writes here *en ekeinē tē hōrā,* which occurs only here; his more usual phrase is (*en*) *autē tē hōrā* (on which see p. 117 above). This verse further explains "all these things" in 7:18; it is also a summary that Luke provides so that the two disciples may become witnesses of Jesus' ministry for John. Instead of the aor. *etherapeusen,* ms. D. has the impf. *etherapeuen,* a copyist's correction which smooths out the narration.

diseases, plagues, and evil spirits. All three are made the object of the prep. *apo,* "from, of." The linking of "evil spirits" with "diseases, plagues" as the object of the verb "cured," reveals the ancient way of thinking that did not distinguish between disease and demon-possession (see NOTE on 4:33).

restored sight to many blind persons. Lit. "granted to many blind persons to see." Jesus is depicted carrying out the role promised in Isa 61:1, as quoted in 4:18. Luke is the only evangelist to use the verb *charizesthai* (see 7:42,43; Acts 3:14; 25:11,16; 27:24). So far Luke has reported no specific cure of a blind person (cf. 18:35).

22. *he answered them.* On *apokritheis eipen,* see p. 114 above.

what you have seen and heard. Luke has cast this pair in the past tense (aor.); cf. Matt 11:4 (pres.); for he has just recounted miracles that Jesus has been performing "at that hour" (as they arrived). Jesus thus does not answer John's question directly; instead of admitting or denying that he is *ho erchomenos* (in the sense of *Elias redivivus*), he tells the two messengers to report to John what they have witnessed with their own eyes and ears. Their testimony will depend on their own seeing and hearing. His answer will make use of phrases alluding to several Isaian passages, implying that he has come as the embodiment of the blessings promised to human beings by that prophet. In effect, his answer is, "Yes, I have come, but not in the sense that you mean it, not as a fiery reformer." Moreover, note that the idea of "vengeance," which is in the context of the Isaian passages to be quoted (29:20; 35:5; 61:2) is passed over. See J. Jeremias, *Jesus' Promise to the Nations* [SBT 24; Naperville: Allenson, 1958] 46.

Blind people recovering their sight. Interpreters debate whether Jesus' words here allude to Isa 61:1 or 35:5. Luke writes *typhloi anablepousin,* "(the) blind see again." These words are close to the LXX of Isa 61:1, *typhlois anablepsin,* "sight for (the) blind," a phrase that is not found in the MT. Some think that Jesus' words allude rather to Isa 35:5, which agrees with them in sense, but not in exact terminology, *tote anoichthēsontai opthalmoi typhlōn,* "then the eyes of (the) blind will be opened." In either case the Isaian allusion would express the divine favor manifested toward the physically blind in the deeds of Jesus. But since Isa 61:1 has been quoted in a form somewhat like the LXX in 4:18, it should be so understood here. (Note that some OT scholars ascribe Isaiah 35 to Second Isaiah, so that it would be related to Isaiah 61 in another way; see O. Eissfeldt, *The Old Testament: An Introduction* [New York: Harper & Row, 1965] 328.)

deaf hearing again. Jesus' words seem to allude to Isa 35:5, which in the LXX reads, *kai ōta kophōn akousontai,* "and the ears of (the) deaf will hear." Luke has not yet reported the cure of a deaf person.

dead being raised to life. These words allude to Isa 26:19, which in the LXX reads, *anastēsontai hoi nekroi,* "the dead will rise." Luke's form of the saying uses the verb *egeirontai* (on which see NOTE on 7:14). This verse explains in part the introduction of the raising of the son of the widow of Nain (7:11-17).

good news being preached to the poor. Lit. "the poor are evangelized." The words are a clear allusion to Isa 61:1, *euangelisasthai ptōchois* (LXX). The favor of which Isaiah spoke is being realized in the preaching and teaching of Jesus. On the use of *euangelizesthai,* see p. 148 above. The phrase is from "Q," being in Matt 11:5 too.

Two other classes of persons are also mentioned as cured, the cripples and the lepers, but their cures are not related to any promises of the OT. On leprosy, see NOTE on 5:12. The sum total of six classes of unfortunate persons thus described, whether in allusions to Isaiah or not, stresses the kind of persons to whom the message of the Lucan Jesus is being brought.

23. *Blessed, indeed, is.* . . . Lit. "And blessed is. . . ." Of the sixty-five beatitudes in the Greek Bible, only this one and that in 14:14 are introduced by *kai,* "and." Cf. Job 5:17, *makarios de.* Whereas a beatitude normally has a certain independence as an exclamation, the connection provided by "and" in this case makes Jesus' comment about John all the more significant. See Dupont, *NRT* 83 (1961) 952. See NOTE on 6:20.

who is not shocked at me. The beatitude is formulated in the singular, not in the plural, as is more usual; so too in Matt 11:6. It is, however, intended to be generic, as is made clear by the conj. *hos ean, pace* Dupont (ibid., 953-954). Jesus thus utters a beatitude over the person who properly understands his real identity and finds no "stumbling block" (*skandalon*) in him because of preconceived ideas.

BIBLIOGRAPHY (7:18-23)

Becker, J. *Johannes der Täufer und Jesus von Nazareth* (Neukirchen-Vluyn: Neukirchener-V., 1972) 83-85.

Brunec, M. "De legatione Ioannis Baptistae (Mt. 11,2-24)," *VD* 35 (1957) 193-203, 262-270, 321-331.

Dibelius, M. *Die urchristliche Überlieferung von Johannes dem Täufer* (FRLANT 15; Göttingen: Vandenhoeck und Ruprecht, 1911) 33-39.

Dupont, J. "L'Ambassade de Jean-Baptiste (Matthieu 11,2-6; Luc 7,18-23)," *NRT* 83 (1961) 805-821, 943-959.

Hirsch, S. "Studien zu Matthäus 11,2-26: Zugleich ein Beitrag zur Geschichte Jesu und zur Frage seines Zelbstbewusstseins," *TZ* 6 (1950) 241-260.

Kümmel, W. G. *Jesu Antwort an Johannes den Täufer: Ein Beispiel zum Methodenproblem in der Jesusforschung* (Sitzungsberichte der wissenschaftlichen Gesellschaft an der Johann Wolfgang Goethe-Universität Frankfurt/Main; Wiesbaden: Steiner, 1974) 130-159.

——— *Promise and Fulfilment: The Eschatological Message of Jesus* (SBT 23; Naperville: Allenson, 1957) 109-113.

Sabugal, S. "La embajada mesiánica del Bautista (Mt 11,2-6 = Lc 7,18-23): Análisis histórico-tradicional," *Augustinianum* 13 (1973) 215-278; 14 (1974) 5-39; 17 (1977) 395-424.

Strobel, A. *Untersuchungen zum eschatologischen Verzögerungsproblem* (NovTSup 2; Leiden: Brill, 1961) 265-298.

Stuhlmacher, P. *Das paulinische Evangelium I* (FRLANT 95, Göttingen: Vandenhoeck und Ruprecht, 1968) 218-225.

Vögtle, A. "Wunder und Wort in urchristlicher Glaubenswerbung (Mt 11,2-5/Lk 7,18-22)," in *Das Evangelium und die Evangelien: Beiträge zur Evangelienforschung* (Düsseldorf: Patmos, 1971) 219-242.

Völkel, M. "Anmerkungen zur lukanischen Fassung der Täuferanfrage Luk 7,18-23," in *Festgabe für Karl Heinrich Rengstorf zum 70. Geburtstag* (Theokratia 2; eds. W. Dietrich and H. Schreckenberg; Leiden: Brill, 1973) 166-173.

34. JESUS' TESTIMONY TO JOHN
(7:24-30)

7 24 When the messengers from John had gone away, Jesus began to speak about him to the crowds of people. "What did you go out to the desert to look at? A reed swaying in the wind? 25 What did you go out there to see? A man dressed in fine robes? You know, those who wear elegant garments and live in luxury are found in palaces. 26 What, then, did you really go out to see? A prophet? Yes, and I tell you, something greater than a prophet! 27 He is the one about whom it is written:

> *I am sending my messenger ahead of you,*
> *to prepare your way before you.*
Mal 3:1; Exod 23:20

28 I tell you, not one of the children born of women is greater than John. And yet, the one who is less is greater than he in the kingdom of God." (29 All the people, even the toll-collectors, who had listened to John and accepted his baptism, acknowledged thereby God's claims on them; 30 but the Pharisees and the lawyers thwarted God's design on their behalf, by refusing to be baptized by him.)

COMMENT

Jesus' testimony about John (7:24-30) is appended to the pronouncement-story that preceded (7:18-23); it further defines the relationship of the two of them, to one another and to God's salvific plan. This sequence was already in "Q" and its counterpart is Matt 11:7-11; in this instance the wording is extremely similar (see p. 76 above). For some of its synoptic relationships, see the COMMENT on vv. 18-23. The testimony itself is found in vv. 24b-28, to which the Matthean verses correspond.

The relation of vv. 29-30 to the testimony is problematic. A number of commentators regard them as a continuation of Jesus' words (so H. Schürmann, *Lukasevangelium*, 422; R. A. Edwards, *A Concordance to Q*, iii; G. Schneider, *Evangelium nach Lukas*, 172). But these verses are scarcely to be so interpreted; they are rather a comment of the evangelist. If they come to Luke from a non-Q source (e.g. "L"), then Luke has certainly modified them, for traces of his formulation are present. They were not certainly part of "Q" because they have no specific counterpart in Matthew. Following on Jesus' testimony in Matthew 11 are verses from "Q" (11:12-13) that Luke has used elsewhere or Matthean redactional material (see COMMENT on vv. 18-23). In Matt 21:32 there is a remote Matthean counterpart of vv. 29-30, but the formulation is so different that it is difficult to think that we are dealing with a "Q" parallel.

The last statement in Jesus' testimony is also problematic (v. 28b), "And yet, the one who is less is greater than he in the kingdom of God." It seems to qualify the last of the statements made by Jesus preceding it; that it was part of the testimony in "Q" is clear (see Matt 11:11b). Was it originally part of the testimony itself—or added later from a community reaction to John and his disciples? If the latter is the correct explanation, then it was added at a very early period. See W. Wink, *John the Baptist*, 24-25; J. Ernst, *Evangelium nach Lukas*, 251; R. Bultmann, *HST*, 54.

From the viewpoint of form-criticism, the passage belongs to the sayings of Jesus, in this case, to his sayings about the Baptist (see Bultmann, *HST*, 164-166).

Jesus' testimony clearly relates John to God's plan of salvation; this is the burden not only of the testimony-verses proper but also of the appended comment of the evangelist. The rhetorical questions first reveal what John was not, and his role is suggested by contrast to them. Then Jesus' triple utterance about John spells out his role. He was, indeed, a "prophet," i.e. a mouthpiece of God, to which his desert-preaching in chap. 3 bore witness. But he was "something more than a prophet," which is now explained in two ways: (1) by the quotation of a form of Mal 3:1 (see NOTE on 3:16), which casts John not only in the role of a precursor of Jesus, but also (implicitly) as *Elias redivivus;* and (2) by Jesus' admission that no human being—not even the prophets of old—is greater than John.

Verse 27 identifies John as the precursor of Jesus. The "you" in the quotation can in this Lucan context refer only to Jesus himself; he looks on John as the messenger sent ahead of him. H. Conzelmann (*Theology,* 25) and others who follow him have tried to call this identification in question: "John is not the precursor" (ibid.). Though this notion was in the pre-Lucan tradition, Luke's aim would not allow him to accept this tradition; he rejects it. John is not a forerunner "either *before the coming of Jesus* or before the future Parousia" (ibid., 167 n. 1 [my italics]). This is to deny what is implicitly stated in v. 27.

It must be stressed that John is not presented here as the precursor of the "Messiah" Jesus (see further NOTE on 7:19), even if it is implied that John is *Elias redivivus*. This involves the idea that Elijah was thought of as a precursor of the Messiah. J. Schneider (*TDNT* 2. 670)—to cite but one modern writer—has maintained that "many expressions of the popular belief that the coming of the Messiah must be preceded by the return of Elijah" are found in the Synoptics, and he cites 7:19-20 as an example. But there is no evidence for such a belief in pre-Christian Judaism. The messenger spoken of in Mal 3:1 is identified in (the appendix) 3:23 (4:5E) as Elijah, who is to be sent before "the great and awesome day of the Lord." Nothing there alludes to a "messianic" or anointed agent. *Elias redivivus* is dependent, of course, on 2 Kgs 2:11, where Elijah is taken up from Elisha, not by death and burial, but "by a whirlwind into heaven," from which he is expected to come.

J. Starcky has a small papyrus fragment from Qumran Cave 4, dated no later than 50-25 B.C., which contains the beginnings of two lines:

tmyny' lbḥyr wh' '.[	]	"the eighth as elect, and lo, I [?	]
lkn 'šlḥ l'lyh qd[m	]	to you shall I send Elijah befo[re	]"

(see *RB* 70 [1963] 481-505, esp. p. 498).

Unfortunately, the ends of the lines of the fragment are lost. Starcky says that the following line alludes to Mal 3:23. Even so, this tiny text can scarcely be said to attest the belief in Elijah as a precursor of the *Messiah* in pre-Christian times. Moreover, when Mal 3:23 begins to be quoted or alluded to in the Mishna, there is no evidence of Elijah as the forerunner of the Messiah; see *m. Eduyot* 8:7 (which alludes to Mal 3:23-24; *m. Baba Meṣi'a* 1:8; *m. Šeqalim* 2:5). The "coming" of Elijah is, indeed, mentioned, but there is no idea of his coming before the Messiah. In later rabbinic writings the idea turns up; see Str-B, 4. 784-789, 872-874. Cf. R. B. Y. Scott, "The Expectation of Elijah," *CJRT* 3 (1926) 1-13; W. G. Kümmel, *Promise and Fulfilment,* 110 n. 18. The earliest attestation of this notion is found in Justin Martyr *Dialogus cum Tryphone Judaeo* 8.4; 49.1-7. See further A. J. B. Higgins, *NovT* 9 (1967) 298-305, esp. p. 300; J. A. T. Robinson, *NTS* 4 (1957-1958) 276 (=SBT, 34. 46). Cf. M. M. Faierstein, *JBL* 100 (1981) 75-86.

Yet not even such texts reveal any idea of Elijah as the precursor of the Messiah in pre-Christian Judaism. Hence, if Jesus identifies John as the messenger sent ahead of him (7:27), i.e. as his precursor, it does not mean as precursor of Jesus as "Messiah."

However, there is the further implicit identification of John by Jesus as Elijah, even in the Lucan Gospel. This has been denied, of course, not only by Conzelmann, but also by others (e.g. see Wink, *John the Baptist,* 42). Yet this is a denial of what is implied in Luke 7:27: there Jesus explicitly identifies John as his precursor and implicitly as *Elias redivivus* (equating him with the messenger of Mal 3:1, eventually recognized as Elijah in 3:23).

In Stage I of the gospel tradition, John seems to have thought of Jesus as *Elias redivivus,* the "One who is to come" in the role of the fiery reformer. Jesus arrives on the scene and plays out his role as the bringer of the bounties promised by Isaiah. John hesitates and doubts whether he is really the "One who is to come" (7:19). Then Jesus reverses the roles: John is *Elias redivivus* (7:27). Then, because Jesus is eventually recognized in the gospel tradition (Stages II-III) as the "Messiah," and because John has been identified by Jesus himself as his precursor and as Elijah (implicitly, in Luke), Elijah becomes the precursor of the Messiah. Something like this: John : Jesus :: Elijah : Messiah.

Luke knows nothing of the explicit identification of John as Elijah (Matt 11:14); that comes from Matthean redaction (see p. 320 above). Luke also omits the whole passage in which the coming of Elijah is discussed in Mark 9:9-13 (see COMMENT on 9:37). Again, Luke 1:17,76 certainly know of this identification, but those verses are part of the infancy narrative and have been written with hindsight (see p. 310 above). There Luke reads back into the beginnings of Jesus' career what only emerged later in the tradition about John and Jesus.

Verses 29-30, appended to the testimony of Jesus, are not a commentary on Jesus' sayings; rather, they summarize the reaction of "all the people"—and of toll-collectors (why should they be singled out?) to Jesus—in this context to his testimony about John. Their reaction provides the background to judge that of the Pharisees and the lawyers. Thus Luke begins to pit the authorities in Israel over against the masses of the people and those who are not so highly regarded.

NOTES

7 24. *When the messengers from John had gone away.* Matt 11:7 has simply "when these went on their way," which probably represents the more original "Q" form of the transitional clause; Luke's modification is a better introduction to Jesus' testimony.

to speak about him to the crowds. Luke again uses *legein* with *pros* and the acc.; see NOTE on 1:13.

What did you go out to the desert to look at? The reference to the desert recalls 1:80; 3:2,7. Here the first question uses *theasthai*, "look at" (as in Matt 11:7); the verb in the two following questions will simply be *idein*, "see." It is possible to take the first word *ti* in each of the questions in the sense of "why" and to punctuate the question differently: "Why did you go out to the desert? To look at a reed . . . ?" This is, in fact, the way the sayings of Jesus are preserved in *Gos. Thom.* § 78: "Why did you go out into the field? To see a reed shaken by the wind? To see a man clothed in soft garments? [Look, your] kings and your great one (*megistanos*) are the ones clothed in soft [garments], and they [shall] not be able to know the truth." The saying preserved in the Coptic Gospel thus eliminates all reference to John, reduces the questions to two, and adds an obviously later Gnostic ending.

A reed swaying in the wind? I.e. something quite ordinary, not really worth so long a trip; something frail and fickle. That implies that John is in prison precisely because he was not such. This and the following contrast undoubtedly play on John's relation to the tetrarch Herod (3:19).

25. *A man dressed in fine robes?* I.e. something perhaps worth the trip, but not usually found in the desert; something at any rate worth gazing at. Cf. N. Krieger, *NovT* 1 (1956) 228-230.

You know. Lit. "behold" (*idou*).

are found in palaces. Lit. "among royal (things)." The neut. adj. with the art. (*to basileion*, either sg. or pl.) came in time to mean "the royal palace." It is supposed to connote the extreme of luxury, not usually associated with a desert. The phrase has been thought to be a reference to Essenes (see C. Daniel, *RevQ* 6 [1967-1968] 261-277); but that is farfetched.

26. *A prophet?* Jesus' admission that John was a prophet thus relates him to the Period of Israel.

something greater than a prophet! This clearly shows that John's role, even in the Lucan Gospel, is not limited to a prophetic ministry; he is not simply part of the Period of Israel. For Conzelmann (*Theology,* 25) John "now becomes the greatest prophet." The designation of John used here, however, is not exclusive to the Lucan Gospel; it was already in "Q." Those who went out to the desert were not disappointed; John stood in the line of OT prophets and his desert-preaching was prophetic. But he was "more" than that, and the more is explained in vv. 27-28. On Conzelmann's "greatest prophet," see NOTE on 7:28 below.

27. *the one about whom it is written.* This type of introductory formula for OT quotations is also found in Qumran literature; see CD 1:13: "These are the ones about whom it was written in the Book of Ezekiel, the prophet"; cf. 4QCatena[a] 1-4:7; 5-6:11. Cf. *ESBNT*, 9-10.

I am sending my messenger. The quotation is derived mainly from Mal 3:1, which reads in the LXX, *idou egō apostellō ton angelon mou kai epiblepsetai hodon pro prosōpou mou*, "Look, I am sending forth my messenger and he will examine (the) road before me." The LXX of Exod 23:20 may also have affected the quotation here; it reads, *idou egō apostellō ton angelon mou pro prosōpou sou hina phylaxē se en tē hodō*, "Look, I am sending my messenger before you that he may guard you on the road." The shift from "me" to "you" is the result of an adaptation of the OT text to the gospel tradition (already in "Q"). The verb *kataskeuasei*, "prepare," in v. 27c better reflects the Hebrew of Mal 3:1 than does the *epiblepsetai* of the LXX and differs considerably from the last part of Exod 23:20. Moreover, the "messenger" of this passage is understood as an "angel" (probably = Yahweh himself); it is unlikely that it would be the referent in the OT quotation used here of John. Hence the words are to be understood as a quotation of Mal 3:1, slightly influenced by the wording of Exod 23:20. Isa 40:3 has had no influence here.

The purpose of the OT quotation is to identify John as a precursor of Jesus; in this he is "something more than a prophet."

your way. The OT quotation fits in with a good Lucan theme; see p. 169 above.

28. *I tell you.* Whereas in v. 26b the Greek text reads *nai legō hymin*

(=Matt 11:9b), here Luke has simply *legō hymin*, whereas Matt 11:11 begins *amēn legō hymin*. Either Matthew has added *amēn*, or else Luke has omitted it. Probably the former, since Luke does retain *amēn* at times (see NOTE on 4:24).

not one of the children born of women is greater than John. This is the second reason why John is "something more than a prophet." Considered as a human being, John is the greatest. His superiority is affirmed, but is not explained. Born of a Jewish mother (1:57), John belongs to Israel of old and had no peer in it. "Born of a woman" is an OT expression for pertinence to the human race (see Job 14:1; 15:14; 25:4; the expression is also used in Qumran literature, 1QS 11:21; 1QH 13:14; 18:12-13,16,23-24). It is used of Jesus in Gal 4:4. For a reflection of this verse, see *Gos. Thom.* § 46a.

Ms. D has inserted a variant of this verse into v. 26: "No one is a greater prophet among those born of women than John the Baptist." This joins the two reasons. Is it possible that Conzelmann (*Theology*, 25) is following this reading in maintaining that John "becomes the greatest prophet"?

the one who is less is greater than he in the kingdom of God. The meaning and function of this saying has always been a matter of much discussion. Its meaning is controverted because of two Greek comparative adjs. in it, *ho mikroteros*, "the one who is less," and *meizōn*, "greater." That the second is intended as a real comparative is clear from the dependent genitive (of comparison) that follows. Many commentators take the first in the sense of a superlative, "The least in the kingdom of God is greater than he." This is justified because of the waning use of the superlative degree in Koine Greek and the use of the comparative degree in its stead (see BDF § 60, 244). The saying would thus assert the difference between status in the kingdom and one's natural status: the least in the kingdom is greater even than John, the greatest of human beings.

Since the time of Tertullian (*Adversus Marcionem* 4.18,8; CC, 1. 591) and John Chrysostom (*Hom. xxxvii in Matt.* 11; PG, 57. 421) *ho mikroteros* has been taken as a real comparative and understood to mean Jesus himself (see further Franz Dibelius, *ZNW* 11 [1910] 190-192; O. Cullmann, *Christology*, 24, 32). Jesus would be "less" than John either as "younger" (in age) or because he has just asserted that John is the greatest of those born of a woman. In this interpretation "in the kingdom of God" is less closely associated to the comparison, and it would imply that John too is part of it. It is hard to say which is better.

If this second part of the verse is to be traced back to Jesus himself, the comparative sense would probably be the better. But if it is really the product of the early Christian community (in debate with the disciples of John), then the superlative sense would be better.

the kingdom of God. See NOTE on 4:43.

29. *All the people.* For this typically Lucan expression, see NOTE on 1:10.

even the toll-collectors. I.e. those who listened to John's social preaching; see NOTE on 3:12.

The Greek text is a bit awkward at this point. Literally, it reads, "and all the people having listened and the toll-collectors justified God, being baptized (with) the baptism of John." The phrase *kai hoi telōnai,* "and the toll-collec-tors," looks like an after-thought, strangely inserted after the sg. collective ptc., *akousas,* "having listened." In the context, one would think that *akousas* meant listening to Jesus' testimony about John, but as the sentence goes on, it can only mean listening to John's preaching (and accepting his baptism). Though it is hard to think that Luke would have composed such a sentence, it has enough other Lucanisms in it that one has to understand it in this way.

accepted his baptism. Lit. "having been baptized (with) the baptism of John." Cf. 3:21.

acknowledged thereby God's claims on them. Lit. "justified God," i.e. ac-knowledged God as righteous, or acknowledged God's way of righteousness. The sense is that, in listening to John's preaching and in accepting his baptism for the remission of sins, people were acknowledging what God had done to es-tablish righteousness in the world of human beings and to enable them to at-tain it in his sight. Their actions, in effect, rendered a verdict of approval on God's plan of salvation. For the Lucan use of *dikaioun,* see 10:29; 16:15; 18:14.

30. *the Pharisees.* See NOTE on 5:17.

the lawyers. I.e. Jewish experts in Mosaic Law. They appear again in 10:25; 11:45,46,52; 14:3. The term *nomikos* is probably only a synonym for *gramma-teus,* "scribe." Note the variants in 11:53 and compare 10:25 with Mark 12:28; Matt 22:35. G. D. Kilpatrick has shown that all instances of *nomikos* in the Gospels are in non-Marcan passages in Luke. He further sought to show that Luke's sources, in using this word, were written in non-translation-Greek (*JTS* 1 [1950] 56-60). But this has been questioned by R. Leaney (*JTS* 2 [1951] 166-167); *nomikos* may have been introduced by Luke himself. See NOTE on 5:17.

thwarted God's design. I.e. God's plan of salvation (see p. 179 above). Clinging to the Mosaic Law and not recognizing that John's baptism was a way to righteous status before God is seen here as a mode of frustrating God's own providence. Implied, of course, is a further frustration of that to which John's baptism was only leading.

on their behalf. The Greek phrase *eis heautous* is omitted in some mss. (א, D). It is retained by most commentators as *lectio difficilior* because, with it, the text is not clear. It has been understood as a prep. phrase modifying the verb "thwarted"; it would then emphasize the responsibility of the Pharisees and lawyers. It could also be taken with "God's design"; it would then point out the relevance of his plan to them. This seems to be preferable.

G. Gander (*VCaro* 5 [1951] 141-144) tried to explain it as a misunderstood Aramaism; it would = *běnapšěhôn,* which should have an intensifying force: "mais les pharisiens et les docteurs de la Loi, *eux,* en ne voulant pas se laisser baptiser par lui, ont compromis le dessein de Dieu." But is an Aramaic source at the base of these verses?

35. JESUS' JUDGMENT OF HIS OWN GENERATION
(7:31-35)

7 31 "To what, then, shall I compare the people of this generation? What are they like? 32 They are like children sitting in a marketplace and shouting to one another,

'We piped for you, but you would not dance,
we wailed for you, but you would not weep.'

33 For John the Baptist has come, eating no bread and drinking no wine; but you say, 'He is mad.' 34 The Son of Man has come, eating and drinking, and you say, 'Look at him! A glutton and a sot, a friend of toll-collectors and of sinners.' 35 Wisdom, indeed, is vindicated by all her children."

COMMENT

The third episode that concerns John the Baptist is, in reality, a saying of Jesus about his own generation of Palestinian contemporaries who have failed to understand either John or himself (7:31-35). It finds its counterpart in Matt 11:16-19, as the third of three episodes that both Matthew and Luke have in common order from "Q" since the temptation scenes. Like the preceding episode (7:24-30), it records sayings of Jesus, which are appended to the pronouncement-story of 7:18-23. Actually, this episode consists of a parable (or a simile, vv. 31-32), an explanation of the parable (vv. 33-34), and an added wisdom-saying (v. 35). The whole constitutes in the Lucan context an interesting reflection on the two preceding Lucan verses (7:29-30).

For some of the synoptic-relationship aspects of this passage, see the COMMENT on vv. 18-23. The wisdom-saying of v. 35 was already attached to the simile and its explanation in "Q" (see Matt 11:19c). But it scarcely represents an original joining of Stage I of the gospel tradition. J. Jeremias (*Parables*, 160-162) and N. Perrin (*Rediscovering*, 119-120) seem to think that it did; cf. however, M. J. Suggs, *Wisdom*, 34. As it now stands in the Lucan context, it contains an interesting catchword bond with v. 29 (*edikaiōsan*, "justified, vindicated," and *edikaiōthē*, "is vindicated").

There are indications of the Lucan redaction of the sayings. The double introductory question is probably the more original form of the beginning of the parable; Matthew has shortened it. Luke, however, has added the conj. *oun,* "then," which marks the connection of the parable with vv. 29-30. The better Greek style of v. 32 undoubtedly stems from Luke's pen. It also gives John his title in v. 33, "the Baptist" (see v. 20). Again, Luke has added "bread" and "wine" in v. 33 (see Matt 11:18), whereas in v. 34 he retains the original verbs of "Q" without the objects (as in Matt 11:19a). Again, he has most likely changed the verbs to the second pl. ("you say") in vv. 33-34 (cf. Matt 11:18-19). Finally, in v. 35 Luke has added "all," an echo of "all of the people" of v. 29.

The interpretation of the parable has been contested for centuries. The main difficulty in it lies in the connection between the parable (vv. 31-32) and the following verses that would explain it (vv. 33-34). Did the parable ever exist in independent form, without such an explanation applying it to John and Jesus? R. Bultmann (*HST,* 199) thinks so; he cites it as an example of a similitude whose original meaning is irrecoverable. Verses 31-32 could be an image depicting "capricious people," but whether it originally referred to John and Jesus cannot be established. In effect, Bultmann insinuates that the explanation allegorizes the parable. Commentators like A. Plummer (*Luke,* 207) consider the whole (vv. 31-34) to be an allegory. Within these two extremes lie many varying interpretations.

Bultmann and many others have no difficulty in ascribing the parable itself (vv. 31-32) to Jesus in Stage I of the gospel tradition. Perrin (*Rediscovering,* 120) rightly points out that the accusation of Jesus as a glutton and a sot scarcely reflects controversies of the early Christian community and he relates the whole (parable and explanation) to the polemics of Jesus' own ministry.

As for the meaning of the parable, the first problem is to understand the figure of the children sitting in the marketplace and crying out to one another. Are they two groups, one of which wants to play wedding, the other, funeral, but cannot agree? The point would then be that the people of this generation never do what others want them to do. Or is it rather that the children are two groups, one of which proposes to play first at wedding, then at funeral, but cannot get the other group, sulky and capricious, to go along with either proposal. Then the people of this generation would be spoilsports, refusing an invitation to participate in the seriousness of children's play (in either joy or sorrow).

Each of these understandings might have a still further aspect. (1) In the first instance, one group would have been the followers of John, and the other followers of Jesus, who have been exchanging recriminations. (2) In the second instance, it could be further understood in either of two ways: (a) The children who invite the others to play (first at wedding, then at funeral) would represent John and Jesus and their followers. The children who sulk and refuse to join are their Palestinian contemporaries, "the people of this generation," rejecting both the asceticism of John and the unhampered attitude of Jesus (see 5:33-34). (b) The children who refuse to play and find fault are the people of this generation, who wanted John, coming with his rigorous asceticism, to dance as they piped; later, when Jesus came with his message of freedom and joy, they wanted him to weep, as they wailed. In this understanding, the complaints of the sulking children find even a chronological order. The last mode of interpretation may be allegorizing the passage more than is called for. In any case it reveals the "teasing" character of a NT parable (see NOTE on 5:36). The best solution is that mentioned in 2a above.

The added saying of Jesus in v. 35 not only allegorizes the parable further in identifying the "children" as children of Wisdom, but even recalls the "vindication" of God by all the people and the toll-collectors of v. 29 above. Since it is almost certain that Luke has preserved a more original "Q" form of this verse and that Matthew has changed "children" to "works" (11:19), Jesus and John thus were in the "Q" form the children of Wisdom, i.e. the representatives of God's own Wisdom. Wisdom is here personified, and John and Jesus are her children. But whether that is still the identification of Wisdom's children in the Lucan context is another matter. By the addition of "all" in v. 35, Luke has included Jesus' disciples as well.

NOTES

7 31. *To what . . . shall I compare*. This introductory formula is found again in Luke 13:18,20. Here it was already in the "Q" source, as Matt 11:16 makes clear. It is a formula also found in rabbinical parables; see J. Jeremias, *The Parables*, 101; Str-B, 2. 8. Cf. Lam 2:13; Isa 40:18,25; 46:5; Ezek 31:2. In this instance, the introduction consists of two questions.

the people. This is most likely a Lucan addition to "Q"; it enables the saying to be understood in a less comprehensive way than the simple "this generation" of Matt 11:16.

of this generation. Though Luke uses *genea* in a neutral sense (1:48,50; 21:32), the term usually has, as here, a pejorative connotation (9:41; 11:29-32,50-51; 17:25; Acts 2:40), and often elsewhere in the Synoptics. It is used of the Palestinian contemporaries of John and Jesus. *Pace* Plummer (*Luke*, 206), it scarcely is meant to include John and Jesus as well. For a similar connotation of Hebrew *dôr*, "generation," in the OT, see Jer 2:31; 7:29; Deut 32:5; Ps 78:8.

32. *like children*. Jesus' contemporaries are likened to a group of children sit-ting in a marketplace, sulking, and refusing to play at either wedding or fu-neral (see COMMENT). In the explanation, John and Jesus become the "chil-dren" who invite. Hence the real sense of the introductory formula is, "They are like the case of children . . . ," since the children actually have to be divided into two groups (see further Jeremias, *The Parables*, 101).

sitting in a marketplace. The ptc. *kathēmenois*, "having taken seats," is the key to understanding the groups of children; one group sits and refuses to go along with the other.

shouting to one another. A rel. cl., *ha legei*, is added to the ptc. *prosphonou-sin* in some mss. (B, ℵ*) and complicates the syntax; it seems to mean "what (one) says," and may be a sort of introduction to the ditty that follows (=something that everybody knows). Variants are found in other mss.: *kai legousin*, "and saying" (A, Θ, and the Koine text-tradition), or simply *legontes*, "saying" (D, L, the Freer family of minuscules, OL). These are obvious copyists' corrections of the more difficult reading. The clause has, how-ever, been interpreted differently, understanding the neut. rel. pron. *ha* to refer to the neut. antecedent *paidiois*, "children": "who say." See M. Black, *AAGA*[3], 304. The first explanation seems preferable; it scarcely affects the meaning of the verse, and I have simply omitted it in the translation.

one another. Luke uses the reciprocal pronoun *allēlois*, whereas Matt 11:16 has *tois heterois*, "the others." It is hard to say which is the more original.

We piped for you. I.e. we played on our flutes or pipes as at a round dance during a wedding celebration.

we wailed for you. I.e. like the official mourners (usually wailing women) at a funeral or burial. The surface comparison in the two instances is between comedy and tragedy, a portrayal of life's joys and sorrows. On a deeper level the comparison contrasts "this generation," childish in its reaction, with chil-dren, serious in their play. The sulking of the spoilsports characterizes "people of this generation" in their reaction to John and Jesus, the messengers of God's plan of salvation. In their sulking they have missed the decisive hour. Cf. Sir 7:34; Prov 29:9.

For parallels to the ditty itself, see A. A. T. Ehrhard, "Greek Proverbs in the Gospel," in *The Framework of the New Testament Stories* (Manchester: Manchester University, 1964) 44-63, esp. pp. 50-53. See Herodotus 1.141; *Aesop Fables* 27b.

33. *has come*. Luke's text has the pf. *elēlythen* here and in v. 34, whereas Matt 11:18,19 has the aor., *ēlthen*, "came."

eating no bread and drinking no wine. Matt 11:18 has simply, "neither eat-ing nor drinking," the "Q" form (see COMMENT). The noun *artos* sometimes means "food" generically (2 Thess 3:8,12; see J. Behm, *TDNT* 1. 477). It would then make Luke's phrase closer in meaning to Matthew's. O. Böcher (*NTS* 18 [1971-1972] 90-92) prefers to understand it rather of John's qualita-tive abstention; it tells us what he did not eat, whereas Luke avoided telling us earlier what he did eat (see Mark 1:6). That may be, but Luke has depicted John in the infancy narrative as a Nazirite, abstaining from "wine or beer" (1:15—perhaps composed with the hindsight of this passage). "Bread" and "wine" are stock terms for food. In Gen 14:18 Melchizedek brings out to Abram on his return from the defeat of the four kings "bread and wine"; that is translated in the *Genesis Apocryphon* as "food and drink" (1QapGen 22:15; see my *Commentary*, 175). In any case, John's abstention is intended and has to be understood against the background of his penitential and eschatological preaching. Cf. H. Windisch, *ZNW* 32 (1933) 65-87.

He is mad. Lit. "he has a demon," which drives him into non-conformity with Palestinian social mores. John's asceticism is regarded as unreasonable.

34. *The Son of Man has come.* See NOTE on 5:24. Both in "Q" and in this Lucan context the title refers to Jesus in his earthly ministry. In Stage I of the gospel tradition it could have been used by Jesus himself as a surrogate for "I."

eating and drinking. I.e. manifesting no ascetic restraint in taking ordinary sustenance, as a token of the freedom of the kingdom that he was proclaiming. The verse explains Jesus' presence at meals (7:36-50; 11:37; 14:1).

A glutton and a sot. The phrase is said to echo Deut 21:20 (see Jeremias, *Parables*, 160), but the "Q" phrase *phagos kai oinopotēs* scarcely reflects the LXX (*symbolokopōn oinophlygei*).

a friend of toll-collectors and of sinners. See NOTE on 5:30. The accusation points up the impression left by Jesus in his dealings with social groups of his day, especially the impression made on the "establishment" of his generation. Though he preached the wisdom and freedom of God's kingdom, he did not do it in isolation from those elements upon which Palestinian society generally looked down.

35. *Wisdom, indeed, is vindicated.* I.e. has been shown to be right after all. The gnomic aorist *edikaiōthē* (see BDF § 333) echoes the "vindication" or "justification" of God in v. 29. God's wise, salvific plan has become madness or foolishness for some of Jesus' contemporaries; his wisdom is manifested as a mother whose children are not only John and Jesus, but "all" the people who, like toll-collectors and sinners, are willing to listen to John or Jesus.

Wisdom is here personified. She sends out her messengers like prophets, and they are rejected (see Wisd 7:27). Both John and Jesus arrive as such on the Palestinian scene with a critical, eschatological message, and what they announce, heard at first as insane and offensive, turns out to be the mark of Wisdom. The "people of this generation" turn out to be not the children of Wisdom, but sulking spoilsports who fail to recognize her.

by. The Greek prep. is *apo*, lit. "from," sometimes used in the NT instead of *hypo*, the usual prep. for expressing agency with a pass. verb (see NOTE on 1:26). There is no need to regard it as the translation of an underlying Aramaic *min qŏdām*, "before" (*pace* Jeremias, *Parables*, 162).

all her children. Matt 11:19 reads rather "by her deeds" (*ergōn* instead of *teknōn*). "Deeds" is almost certainly a Matthean modification, since it picks up the "deeds of the Messiah" in 11:2. See Suggs, *Wisdom*, 33. Luke has preserved the more original form of the "Q" saying, but has added "all," as he often does (see NOTE on 4:15). The saying has been added because of the mention of "children" in v. 32, even though the Greek words are different (*paidiois* in v. 32, *teknōn* in v. 35); the connection is not by catchword bonding, but by sense. For Wisdom's children in the OT, see Sir 4:11; Prov 8:32.

Bibliography (7:31-35)

Christ, F. *Jesus Sophia: Die Sophia-Christologie bei den Synoptikern* (ATANT 57; Zürich: Zwingli, 1970) 63-80.

Grundmann, W. "Weisheit im Horizont des Reiches Gottes: Eine Studie zur Verkündigung Jesu nach der Spruchüberlieferung Q," in *Die Kirche des Anfangs: Festschrift für Heinz Schürmann zum 65. Geburtstag* (ed. R. Schnackenburg; Leipzig: St. Benno, 1977) 175-199.

Linton, O. "The Parable of the Children's Game: Baptist and Son of Man (Matt xi. 16-19=Luke vii. 31-35): A Synoptic Text-Critical, Structural and Exegetical Investigation," *NTS* 22 (1975-1976) 159-179.

Mussner, F. "Der nicht erkannte Kairos (Matt 11,16-19=Lk 7,31-35)," *Bib* 40 (1959) 599-612.

Smith, M. "Jesus' Attitude Toward the Law," in *Fourth World Congress of Jewish Studies: Papers* (Jerusalem: World Union of Jewish Studies, 1967) 1. 241-244.

Suggs, M. J. *Wisdom, Christology, and Law in Matthew's Gospel* (Cambridge, MA: Harvard University, 1970) 33-61.

Zeller, D. "Die Bildlogik des Gleichnisses MT 11,16f./Lk 7,31f.," *ZNW* 68 (1977) 252-257.

36. THE PARDON OF THE SINFUL WOMAN
(7:36-50)

7 ³⁶ Then one of the Pharisees invited Jesus to dine with him; he went to the Pharisee's house and reclined at table. ³⁷ Now there was a certain woman in the town known to be a sinner. When she learned that Jesus was at table in the Pharisee's house, she got an alabaster flask of perfume, ³⁸ and went and stood crying at his feet. Her tears bathed his feet, and with the hair of her head she wiped them dry; she kissed them and anointed them with the perfume. ³⁹ The Pharisee who had invited him watched all this and thought to himself, "If this man were really a prophet, he would know who this is and what sort of a woman is touching him—seeing that she is a sinner." ⁴⁰ But Jesus spoke up to him, "Simon, I have something to say to you." "Teacher," he said, "say it." ⁴¹ "A certain moneylender had two debtors. One owed him five hundred pieces of silver, the other fifty. ⁴² Since they could not pay it back, he graciously cancelled both debts. Now which of them should love him more?" ⁴³ Simon replied, "I suppose, the one for whom he cancelled the greater debt." Jesus said to him, "You are right." ⁴⁴ And turning to the woman, he said to Simon, "You see this woman? I came into your house, and you offered me no water for my feet; yet she has bathed my feet with her tears and wiped them dry with her hair. ⁴⁵ You gave me no kiss of welcome; yet ever since I arrived, she has not stopped kissing my feet. ⁴⁶ You did not freshen my face with oil, yet she has anointed my feet, and with perfume. ⁴⁷ For this reason, I tell you, her sins, many though they are, have been forgiven, seeing that she has loved greatly. But the one to whom little is forgiven loves little." ⁴⁸ Then Jesus said to her, "Your sins are forgiven." ⁴⁹ And the guests who reclined at table with him began to say to themselves, "Who is this who even forgives sins?" ⁵⁰ Again he said to the woman, "Your faith has brought you salvation; *go in peace.*"

1 Sam 1:17

COMMENT

To the three episodes that have explained the relationship between John the Baptist and Jesus, Luke now adds the story of Jesus' pardon of a sinful woman during a dinner in the house of a Pharisee named Simon, to which he had been invited (7:36-50). This episode is still part of the Lucan little interpolation (6:20 - 8:3). In itself, it is unrelated to the three preceding passages, and it is not easy to discern the reason why it has been added just at this point. Superficial connections of this episode with the preceding have been seen in the mention of Jesus as the Son of Man who has come "eating and drinking" (7:34), but Luke has not yet really depicted Jesus so in the Gospel. Better, perhaps, is the connection with his consorting with "sinners" (7:34); this episode would give evidence of it. Or again, the episode supplies a Pharisaic reaction to Jesus and implicitly illustrates v. 30. The episode itself, however, is far more complicated.

The story of Jesus' pardon of the sinful woman is derived from "L." It is almost certainly a conflated story, since, form-critically judged, it is made up of a pronouncement-story (vv. 36-40,44-47a-b) and a parable of the two debtors (vv. 41-43). There is no reason to think that Luke has conflated these elements; they should be regarded as having come to him so in the tradition. Verse 47c (*hō de* . . .) is an editorial addition, which relates the parable to the pronouncement-story. Verses 48-50 are an appendage which makes the conflated pronouncement-story and the parable into a narrative (see V. Taylor, *FGT*, 153).

Further evidence for the conflation is seen when one considers the passage synoptically, since it is related to the anointing of Jesus in Bethany (Mark 14:3-9; cf. Matt 26:6-13; John 12:1-8). That Luke 7:36-50 is similar to that Marcan passage is seen from the following details: (1) the omission of any parallel to that anointing in Luke 22; this is part of his concern to avoid doublets (see p. 93 above); (2) the anointing by an unnamed woman, who is an uninvited intruder coming from outside; (3) the reclining of Jesus at table; (4) her carrying of an "alabaster flask of perfume" (*alabastron myrou*); (5) the name of the host as Simon; (6) the reaction of onlookers and their objections; (7) Jesus' reaction to the woman, favoring her. There are, of course, significant differences: in Mark, Jesus is in Bethany, not Galilee; it takes place shortly before the Passover; his head is anointed, not his feet; Simon is a leper, not a Pharisee; the objection about the anointing comes from "some" or "disciples," not from the Pharisee; the one who wastes and the poor are mentioned, nothing being said about the woman's sinful past; and the anointing of

Jesus is related to his burial, not to the woman's love or repentance. Moreover, the Lucan form of the story shares some details with the Johannine form, which is otherwise more closely related to the Marcan and Matthean forms; in both Luke and John the woman anoints Jesus' feet and wipes them with her hair. One sees here some contact between the Lucan and Johannine Gospel traditions; see further R. E. Brown, *John, I-XII,* 449-452.

It has seemed to some commentators that Luke has derived a story of the anointing of Jesus from his private tradition and combined this story with details from Mark 14:3-9. The main evidence for this is that the Pharisee at the beginning of the episode is unnamed (vv. 36,37,39) and only later becomes "Simon" (vv. 40,43,44). T. Schramm (*Der Markus-Stoff,* 44-45) finds Marcan vocabulary in the secondary ending (vv. 48-50): "Your sins are forgiven" (see Mark 2:5; Luke 5:20); compare v. 49 with Mark 2:6-7 (=Luke 5:21). However, there is no certainty that the conflated parable and pronouncement-story have not come to Luke from a prior tradition. I prefer to regard vv. 48-50 as Lucan composition, imitating phrases borrowed elsewhere in his Gospel from Mark. I am, moreover, very hesitant about the interpretation of J. Delobel that it is Luke who has given to the scene a dinner-setting that it did not have in Mark.

Whereas the Marcan story has a certain intrinsic coherence and verisimilitude with its anointing of Jesus' head and the protest about the waster of the precious perfume, the Lucan story has details that have always raised questions (and the Johannine form has similar problems; see Brown, *John, I-XII,* 451). In Luke's form, the conduct of the Pharisee is strange, in inviting Jesus to a formal dinner and failing to show him the customary marks of hospitality; Jesus' rebuke of his host is too. Still more problematic are the remarks of Jesus: the woman's sins are forgiven because of her love (v. 47b) or her faith (v. 50), seemingly the condition(s) of forgiveness; but v. 47c seems to regard love as the effect of forgiveness (see further J. M. Creed, *The Gospel,* 109-110). These elements have often been invoked to manifest the conflation spoken of above.

Underlying the question of conflation is another, whether the pronouncement-story and the Marcan/Matthean, and even Johannine, forms of the anointing of Jesus reflect one incident in the ministry of Jesus or more. One interpretation of this problem recognizes two basic incidents: (1) a penitent sinful woman entered the Galilean Pharisee's house, while Jesus was a guest at dinner, wept at his feet and wiped away the tears that dropped on his feet; she loosed her hair in public, suiting her character, to wipe his feet dry, and this evoked the comment about Jesus from the Pharisee. (This would be the backbone of the Lucan narrative.) (2)

A woman entered the house of Simon the leper in Bethany and anointed Jesus' head with her costly perfume, while he reclined there. In the oral tradition, the two incidents became one, so that by the time the story came to Luke it is an anointing of Jesus' feet with perfume, etc.; and the Johannine form of the story gathers other details, as did the Lucan form the parable. This explanation of two incidents behind the stories of the anointing of Jesus in the gospel tradition is not impossible. It is used by Tatian, John Chrysostom, and many modern commentators: V. Taylor, F. W. Beare, T. W. Bevan, E Grubb, H. Drexler, R. E. Brown, R. K. Orchard.

It has, however, not convinced all interpreters. C. H. Dodd (*Historical Tradition,* 162-173) has rather argued for one incident behind the various Gospel-stories of the anointing of Jesus. He maintains that the variations between Mark, Luke, and John "arose in the course of oral tradition," that "each evangelist used independently a separate strand of tradition," but that "the substance of the *pericopé* in each of its three forms is traditional." Similarly, E. Klostermann, R. Holst, J. K. Elliott. Holst (*JBL* 95 [1976] 435-436) would even consider the Lucan and Johannine forms of the story to be more primitive than Mark's, and Luke's description of the act as the most primitive: the anointing of Jesus' feet would have been later changed to the anointing of the head.

For my part, it is hardly likely that the Lucan story is a deliberate reworking of the Marcan by Luke or some tradition before him. Rather, the story of an anointing of Jesus by a woman intruder into a dinner-scene assumed in the stage of oral tradition various forms, recorded in the Marcan, Lucan, and Johannine traditions. The anointing of the feet would have been the more primitive, since it is easier to explain the tradition shifting from the anointing of the feet to the head than vice versa. A theological reason for the shift can be found in the OT references to the anointing of the head (see 2 Kgs 9:3, the kingly anointing of Jehu; 1 Sam 10:1, Samuel's anointing of Saul; Ps 133:2).

The sense of the Lucan passage as a whole is not difficult. Repentance, forgiveness of sins, and salvation have come to one of the despised persons of Israel; she has shown this by an act of kindness manifesting a more basic love and faith, love shown to Jesus and faith in God himself.

It has often been thought that the sinful woman comes to Jesus as a penitent, seeking forgiveness of him; her love then would be the condition of her pardon. The clause in v. 47b, *hoti ēgapēsen poly,* "seeing that she has loved greatly," is in itself ambiguous; and in this interpretation the conj. *hoti* would be given a consecutive nuance, implying that the forgiveness shown to her is the result of her love. This interpretation, known since patristic times and used in a number of modern commentaries (Wellhausen, Loisy, Lagrange, Holtzmann, etc.), has to cope with the almost opposite sense of v. 47c, "but he to whom little is forgiven loves little." However, it has been pointed out time and again that the conj. *hoti* could be understood not as the reason "why the fact *is* so, but whereby it is known to be so" (ZBG § 422). Consequently, it should rather be understood that the sinful woman comes to Jesus as one already forgiven by God and seeking to pour out signs of love and gratitude (tears, kisses, perfume); in this understanding, the love of v. 47b is the consequence of her forgiveness, and v. 47c integrates the parable with the narrative. It extends the pronouncement of Jesus. Verses 48 and 50, which are of Lucan composition, extend the pronouncement still further. This interpretation had been used basically by some patristic writers (Cyprian *Ad Quirinum, testimoniorum libri tres* 3.115-116 [CSEL 3/1. 182]; and [*pace* M.-J. Lagrange] Ambrose *Expositio in Lucam* 6.26 [CC 14. 183]); also by interpreters of later periods (Schmid, Schneider, Schürmann, Wilckens).

Verse 49 poses a question, "Who is this who even forgives sins?" It understands Jesus' declaration in v. 47a (her sins "have been forgiven" *apheōntai,* pf. tense) in the present and foreshadows the crucial question to be put in chap. 9 by Herod.

The parable of the two debtors, inserted into the pronouncement-story, not only carries its own message about the relation between forgiveness and love (that the sinner turns out to be the one who manifests to God greater gratitude than the upright, critical Pharisee), but also allegorizes the narrative: repentance for the sins of the woman's life has made her more open to God's mercy than the stingy willingness of the host who wanted to honor Jesus with a dinner. The love that the woman manifested to Jesus through the tears, kisses, and perfume revealed her more basic orientation to God himself, i.e. her faith, which brings her salvation. For this reason, Jesus tells her to "go in peace." Thus the episode ends with allusions to two of the basic ways in which Luke views the effects of the Christ-event, salvation, peace (see pp. 222, 224 above).

This scene is one of the great episodes in the Lucan Gospel, for it depicts Jesus not merely defending a sinful woman against the criticism of a Pharisee, but drives home in a special way the relationship between the forgiveness of sins (by God) and the place of human love and the giving of oneself in that whole process. No one can read this passage without perceiving the power of the literary picture painted by Luke. When one compares it with the Marcan counterpart, or even the Johannine, there is something here that surpasses them. Significant as they may be for the sense of the anointing of Jesus' body in view of his burial, they do not come through in the same way as the Lucan story. Luke has divested the story of its connection with the passion narrative; it has always been a problem to explain why the anointing of Jesus in the Marcan Gospel should be recounted at the point where it occurs. Luke may not have a more primitive setting for it; but his version of it has a power, perhaps because of the place in which he uses it in the Gospel, that the others do not have. In it Jesus appears not only as the kingdom-preacher but as an agent of the declaration of God's forgiveness for sinful humanity. Luke's appendage even presses further, making the other guests at table pose the question about his own relation to the forgiveness of sins. What is startling is the strong language that Jesus uses of Simon; he may misunderstand the woman's actions, but he is after all Jesus' host. Jesus' words to him are not intended to be rude.

NOTES

7   36. *one of the Pharisees.* See NOTE on 5:21; further 5:30,33; 6:2,7; 7:30. The Pharisee is here unnamed, as in vv. 37 and 39; but in vv. 40,43,44 he is called Simon. The identification of Jesus' host as a Pharisee may well be secondary to the tradition, but it is not to be ascribed to Luke, *pace* R. Holst (*JBL* 95 [1976] 438 n. 20); the evidence he cites does not really affect this passage. The identification of the Pharisee as Simon in v. 40 may well be influenced by Mark 14:3; but at what stage of the tradition?

to dine with him. See Luke 11:37; 14:1 for other instances of Jesus dining with Pharisees. Here he is depicted treating them in the same way he would treat toll-collectors (19:5) and sinners (7:34). No motive for the invitation is assigned. The Pharisee has heard about Jesus, just as has the sinful woman. Verse 39 will reveal that he has suspected Jesus to be a prophet, hence his invitation probably stemmed from a desire to honor an important person. In v. 40 he calls him "Teacher."

reclined at table. The verb *kateklithē* (or *aneklithē* in the Koine text-tradition; or *katekeito* in ms. ℵ*) reveals that the dinner was a festive banquet, since reclining at table was practiced only for such occasions in Palestine of that time (see J. Jeremias, *Eucharistic Words,* 20-21). Jeremias even regards this as a Sabbath-meal, to which Jesus would have been invited after preaching in the synagogue; if so, Luke does not tell us this.

37. *a certain woman.* She too is unnamed, as is also the woman of Bethany in Mark 14:3 and Matt 26:7. Neither in Mark, Matthew, nor John is she called a "sinner," as here in Luke. In John 12:3 she is Mary, the sister of Martha and Lazarus of Bethany. In Western Church traditions, at least since the time of Gregory the Great, Mary of Bethany has been conflated with the sinner of Galilee, and even with Mary Magdalene, "out of whom seven demons had come" (8:2). There is, however, no basis for this conflation in the NT itself, and no evidence whatsoever that the "possession" of Mary Magdalene was the result of personal sinfulness. The Greek church tradition, by and large, kept these Marys distinct. See C. Lattey, "The Sinner."

known to be a sinner. Lit. "who was in the town a sinner." So Luke describes her, so the Pharisee is depicted regarding her (v. 39), and so Jesus is made to acknowledge her (v. 47). No hint is given of the kind of sins that she has committed. Many commentators (e.g. J. Ernst, A. Plummer, J. Schmid, G. Schneider) identify her as the town harlot, guilty of "habitual unchastity" (Plummer, *ExpTim* 27 [1915-1916] 42-43). Possibly this is implied in the Pharisee's thoughts (v. 39b); but it is at most implied, not being said openly in the text. M. Black (*AAGA*³, 181-183) thinks that the Lucan text is playing on the Aramaic word for "sinner," *ḥayyābtā'*, which really means "debtor," and is thus providing a connection between the pronouncement-story and the parable. Possibly.

alabaster flask of perfume. The flasks were generally made of soft stone (yellow or creamy calcareous sinter) and of variegated shapes (see I. Ben-Dor, "Palestinian Alabaster Vases," *QDAP* 11 [1945] 93-112). Cf. Pliny the Elder *Naturalis historia* 13.3,19: *unguenta optime servantur in alabastris,* "ointments are very well preserved in alabaster flasks." See H. Schlier, *TDNT* 2. 472.

38. *went and stood crying at his feet.* Lit. "having stationed herself behind (him), alongside his feet, crying." Three ptcs. (two aor. and one pres.) are used here to describe her position, close to that part of Jesus to which she could get, as he reclined at table with other guests.

Her tears bathed his feet. Lit. "she began to moisten his feet with tears." The cause for her tears is not expressed; it has usually been assumed to be repentance for her sins (so, e.g. J. K. Elliott, "The Anointing of Jesus," 107). It could also have been weeping for joy at the realization of the forgiveness of her sins by God that she has already experienced. See the COMMENT. In any case, the tears are a caution for any interpretation of the scene that the love mentioned in it was intended in an erotic sense.

with the hair of her head she wiped them dry. Having loosened her headdress, she unbound her hair, and wiped away the tears. Doing so in public, she caused surprise and occasioned the Pharisee's comment. Her action does not confirm her sinfulness; it merely gives rise to an interpretation of her.

she kissed them and anointed them. Marks of honor are accorded to one who is recognized as God's agent of salvation. She spares no lavishness.

39. *watched all this and thought to himself.* Lit. "seeing, he said within himself, saying. . . ." On the use of *legōn,* "saying," see p. 115 above.

a prophet. Or possibly, "the prophet," since the Greek text is not certain. The best Greek mss. read simply *prophētēs;* but the def. art. (*ho*) accompanies it in mss. B* and ℵ, which would make of Jesus "the prophet" like Moses (Deut 18:15; see Acts 3:22-23; 7:37; see further p. 213 above). In any case, the Pharisee's thoughts reflect a common belief: a prophet should be able to perceive the character of persons with whom he deals. - *Like in Jn 1*

40. *Jesus spoke up to him.* Luke here uses the Septuagintisms *apokritheis eipen* and *pros auton;* see pp. 114, 120 above. Jesus perceives Simon's thoughts; see 5:22; 6:8.

Simon. See NOTE on v. 36 above. It is strange that this name is only now introduced. Many commentators think that Luke has introduced it here secondarily under the influence of Mark 14:3. That is not impossible, but the conflated form of the passage, inherited from "L," might be just as well responsible for the introduction of it.

I have something to say to you. This is the first occurrence in the Gospel of the verb *echein,* "have," + an infin.; see further 7:42; 12:4,50; 14:14; Acts 4:14; 23:17,18,19; 25:26; 28:19.

Teacher. Simon sees Jesus as one of the revered teachers of Palestine. The title *didaskalos,* used of John the Baptist in 3:12, is given to Jesus here for the first time; see further p. 218 above. It is a pre-Lucan title for Jesus, being found in Mark (e.g. 4:38; 9:17,38), but oddly enough never in "Q." Significantly, Luke does not translate the Marcan *rabbi/rabbouni* by *didaskalos* (Mark 9:5; 10:51; 11:21; 14:45), using instead *epistata* in 9:33 (where, however, mss. P45, X read *didaskale*) or otherwise simply omitting it, as he usually does with Semitic words in his source. *Didaskalos* was a title revered in contemporary Palestine, as can be seen from its use on a Jerusalem ossuary (*CII,* § 1266). John 1:38 translates *rabbi* as *didaskale,* and 20:16 gives it as the translation for *rabbouni* (see Brown, *John, I-XII,* 74). This Johannine usage is undoubtedly the source of the translation in 9:33 in mss. P45, X, mentioned above. See further *WA,* 134. On "he said," see p. 107 above.

41. *A certain moneylender had two debtors.* The parable is introduced without any formula; it is not a kingdom-parable, but one that finds its point in the narrative into which it has been inserted. Its secondary character can be seen in the conclusion drawn in v. 47a-47c and the ambiguity of the comment in v. 47b (see the COMMENT). It belongs to the type of parable that makes use of a question.

five hundred pieces of silver. Lit. "five hundred denarii," i.e. the equivalent of wages for five hundred days of labor (see Matt 20:2).

42. *he graciously cancelled both debts.* Lit. "he forgave them both." The verb *charizesthai* means "to give us a favor, bestow graciously," but it is also used technically of "remitting" debts or sins. Josephus (*Ant.* 6.7,4 § 144) uses it of the latter; cf. Col 2:13. The motive of the gracious cancellation of the debts, large and small, was the inability of the debtors to pay, a procedure rather unheard of, which drives home the point of the parable.

should love him more? J. Jeremias (*Parables,* 127) suggests that *agapan* means not so much "love" as "feel the deepest thankfulness," since neither Hebrew nor Aramaic has a distinct word for thanks, gratitude. H. G. Wood ("The Use of *agapaō,*" 319-320) has pointed out clear examples of the verb *agapan* being so used in Greek. It should be recalled that the Qumran *Hôdāyôt* (Thanksgiving Psalms) constantly employ the Hebrew verb *hôdāh* (lit. "praise," see *HALAT,* 372) in the sense of "I thank you," addressed to God (cf. BDB, 392, "give thanks, laud, praise"). Perhaps the more literal sense of *agapan,* "love," should then be retained.

43. *one for whom he cancelled the greater debt.* Or "to whom he showed the greater favor."

You are right. Lit. "you judged rightly." Jesus approves of the obvious answer that the Pharisee gives to the parable proposed by him.

44. *you offered me no water for my feet.* Jesus applies the parable to Simon

and the woman, not so much to contrast their deeds, as to stress the love manifested in them, and the implication of the amount of forgiveness both of them find in the sight of God. The Pharisee's omissions should not be emphasized as signs of impoliteness.

45. *ever since I arrived.* The preferred reading here is *eisēlthon,* "I entered" (the house); it is the *lectio difficilior,* but some minor mss. and the Vg have corrected it to *eisēlthen,* "she entered," which suits the context better, but is for that reason suspect. J. Jeremias (*ZNW* 51 [1960] 131) suggested that *eisēlthon* is a mistranslation of Aramaic *'tyt,* the consonants of which could be read either as first sg. perf. peal, "I came," or as third sg. fem. perf. peal, "she came." This is, however, problematic, since one would expect the verb *'ll,* "enter," as the Aramaic substratum of *eisēlthon;* moreover, the third sg. fem. perf. peal of *'ty* at this period would be *'tt ('ătat* or *'ătāt).* The variant is rather the result of a copyist's confusion of the Greek majuscules (omicron and circular epsilon); see B. M. Metzger, *The Text of the New Testament* (New York: Oxford, 1964) 187.

In the translation given above, "ever since," I have taken *aph' hēs* in a temporal sense, understanding some word like *hōras,* "from (the hour) that I arrived." See Acts 24:11; 2 Pet 3:4. W. Grundmann (*Evangelium nach Lukas,* 172) thinks, however, that the phrase is dependent on the first words of v. 45, *hautē de:* "but she, from whom (i.e. from whose house) I arrived." "There would have taken place what drives her now to gratitude for release from guilt and disgrace." Jesus would have forgiven her sins there. Theoretically, this is possible; but it strains the Greek style too much. In any case, Jesus' expression involves hyperbole to make his point.

she has not stopped kissing my feet. The marks of the woman's gratitude are not limited to tears or perfume, but even include that sign of respect and love that human beings esteem most. The Lucan Jesus will be repulsed by the use of it by his betrayer (22:47-48).

46. *You did not freshen my face.* Lit. "you did not anoint my head with oil." For the custom among Jews, see Str-B, 1. 427*f.*

anointed my feet. The contrast between "feet" and "head" is intentional. That the feet were part of the pre-Lucan story can be seen from John 12:3, where they are again mentioned. In the Lucan story the "feet" of Jesus are the object of three of his comments (vv. 44,45,46), since that agrees with the position that the woman took on arrival (see v. 38). The anointing of Jesus' feet is perhaps a "strange picture" (Brown, *John, I-XII,* 452), but it is the one that would more likely be changed in the oral tradition to an anointing of the head than the other way round. Attempts to explain the anointing of the feet by reference to Gen 18:4; 19:2; 24:32; 43:24 fail, because these OT passages speak of water for washing the feet of a guest (see A. Legault, "An Application," 138). The point is that her action even went beyond the washing of feet.

47. *For this reason.* The phrase *hou charin* states the reason for what Jesus will declare next. It is a summation of all that has preceded in vv. 44-46. Some commentators (John Dublin, H. G. Meecham) have rather tried to insist on a causal meaning of the phrase, "because." This is hardly right.

unless Lk changed it to make his special point & to sever connection w/ Passion have been forgiven. I.e. by God (the theological passive is being used; see NOTE on 5:20). Moreover, the pf. tense expresses the state of forgiveness, which Jesus recognizes and declares. We are not told in the passage how the woman came to this state of forgiveness, which is the basis of her manifestations of love. To the Pharisee she was still "a sinner" (v. 39). Jesus does not deny that her sins have been "many," but that she is no longer under the burden of them. For contemporary Aramaic expressions about the forgiveness of sins in Qumran literature, see 11QtgJob 38:2-3: *wšbq lhwn ḥṭ'yhwn bdylh,* "and (God) forgave them (i.e. Job's friends) their sins because of him (i.e. Job)." Contrast M. Black, *AAGA*[3], 180. Cf. J. A. Fitzmyer, *JBL* 99 (1980) 15-17.

seeing that she has loved greatly. The conj. *hoti* is not causal, "because," as if it stresses her love as the reason or basis for forgiveness. That would move against the parable in the Lucan story. Rather, *hoti* is to be understood in its logical sense (cf. John 9:19; 1 John 3:14; Matt 8:27; Heb 2:6; see further ZBG § 420-422). Thus the clause states not the reason for the forgiveness but rather why the forgiveness is known to exist. See the COMMENT. Ms. D eliminates *hoti*, thus cutting the Gordian knot for the exegesis.

the one to whom little is forgiven loves little. This generically stated utterance (in the pres. tense) is not only the conclusion to the parable, but extends Jesus' own pronouncement. "Love" describes the consequence of forgiveness, and the "little love" characterizes the host, who turns out to be the little debtor. In God's sight, little forgiveness is shown to Simon, not because of his conduct, but because of his fundamental attitude. See 18:10-14.

48. *Your sins are forgiven.* The verb is *apheōntai,* the same pf. pass. that was used in v. 47a; it could be translated again as a pf. But in vv. 48-50, the Lucan conclusion to the story (see the COMMENT) relates the forgiveness to Jesus' own activity. Verse 49 will record a reaction of the guests at table to Jesus, understanding his words as if he were forgiving the woman's sins. Hence the translation in the present. See NOTE on 5:20.

49. *who even forgives sins?* The pres. tense of the verb *aphiēsin* ascribes to Jesus a power that was not immediately apparent in the earlier part of the story.

50. *Your faith.* At the end Luke supplies the motive that moved the woman to seek God's forgiveness of her many sins in the first place. Her "faith" is to be understood as a confidence in God despite her sinful past, which restores a relationship with him that was previously absent or lacking. It has moved her to manifest also marks of respect and love toward him whom she has understood to be God's agent (the "prophet" in Simon's eyes). See further the NOTE on 5:20.

go in peace. This common dismissal formula (see Luke 8:48; Acts 16:36) is an echo of an OT saying (1 Sam 1:17; 20:42; 29:7). Its use here is probably influenced by Mark 5:34. For the Lucan meaning of "peace," see p. 224 above.

BIBLIOGRAPHY (7:36-50)

Bevan, T. W. "The Four Anointings," *ExpTim* 39 (1927-1928) 137-139.

Bouman, G. "La pécheresse hospitalière (Lc. vii, 36-50)," *ETL* 45 (1969) 172-179.

Braumann, G. "Die Schuldner und die Sünderin Luk. vii. 36-50," *NTS* 10 (1963-1964) 487-493.

Buzy, D. *Les paraboles traduits et commentées* (VS 6; 2d ed.; Paris: Beauchesne, 1932) 238-267.

Dammers, A. H. "Studies in Texts: A note on Luke vii, 36-50," *Theology* 49 (1946) 78-80.

Delobel, J. "L'Onction de Jésus par la pécheresse: La composition littéraire de Lc., VII, 36-50," *ETL* 42 (1966) 415-475 [=ALBO 4/33 (1966)].

Donahue, J. J. "The Penitent Woman and the Pharisee: Luke 7:36-50," *AER* 142 (1960) 414-421.

Drexler, H. "Die grosse Sünderin Lucas 7,36-50," *ZNW* 59 (1968) 159-173.

Dublin, J. *"hou charin,"* *ExpTim* 37 (1925-1926) 525-526.

Dulau, P. " 'Remittuntur ei peccata multa 'quoniam' dilexit multum' (Luc. 7. 47a)," *DivusThomas* 43 (Piacenza, 1940) 156-160.

Eichholz, G. *Einführung in die Gleichnisse* (BibS[N] 37; Neukirchen-Vluyn; Neukirchener, 1963) 44-53.

Elliott, J. K. "The Anointing of Jesus," *ExpTim* 85 (1973-1974) 105-107.

Fuller, R. C. "The Anointing of Christ in Luke vii," *Scr* 4 (1949) 90-91.

Gallo, S. "Peccatrix in civitate (Lc 7, 36-50)," *VD* 27 (1949) 84-93.

Grubb, E. "The Anointing of Jesus," *ExpTim* 26 (1914-1915) 461-463.

Henss, W. *Das Verhältnis zwischen Diatessaron, christlicher Gnosis und "Western Text": Erläutert an einer unkanonischen Version des Gleichnisses vom gnädigen Gläubiger: Materialien zur Geschichte der Perikope von der namenlosen Sünderin Lk 7,36-50* (BZNW 33; Berlin: Töpelmann, 1967).

Holst, R. "The One Anointing of Jesus: Another Application of the Form-critical Method," *JBL* 95 (1976) 435-446.

Holzmeister, U. "Die Magdalenenfrage in der kirchlichen Überlieferung," *ZKT* 46 (1922) 402-422, 556-584.

Jeremias, J. "Lukas 7: 45: *eisēlthon*," *ZNW* 51 (1960) 131.

Joüon, P. "La pécheresse de Galilée et la parabole des deux debiteurs (*Luc*. 7, 36-50)," *RSR* 29 (1939) 615-619.

———— "Reconnaissance et action de graces dans le Nouveau Testament," *RSR* 29 (1939) 112-114.

Lagrange, M.-J. "Jésus a-t-il été oint plusieurs fois et par plusieurs femmes?" *RB* 21 (1912) 504-532.

Lattey, C. "The Sinner of the City," *Expos* 7/8 (1909) 55-63.

Legault, A. "An Application of the Form-Critique Method to the Anointings in Galilee (Lk 7, 36-50) and Bethany (Mt 26, 6-13; Mk 14, 3-9; Jn 12, 1-8)," *CBQ* 16 (1954) 131-145.

Löning, K. "Ein Platz für die Verlorenen: Zur Formkritik zweier neutes-tamentlicher Legenden (Lk 7,36-50; 19,1-10)," *BibLeb* 12 (1971) 198-208.

Meecham, H. G. "Luke vii. 47," *ExpTim* 38 (1926-1927) 286.

Moretta, R. "Chi fu la peccatrice che unse d'unguento Gesù?" *ScCatt* 81 (1953) 350-370.

Orchard, R. K. "On the Composition of Luke vii 36-50," *JTS* 38 (1937) 243-245.

Plummer, A. "The Woman That Was a Sinner," *ExpTim* 27 (1915-1916) 42-43.

Ramaroson, L. "Simon et la pécheresse anonyme (Lc 7,36-50)," *ScEsp* 24 (1972) 379-383.

Sanders, J. N. " 'Those Whom Jesus Loved' (Joh xi. 5)," *NTS* 1 (1954-1955) 29-41.

Saxer, V. "Les saintes Marie Madeleine et Marie de Béthanie dans la tradition liturgique et homilétique orientale," *RevScRel* 32 (1958) 1-37.

Schramm, T. *Der Markus-Stoff*, 43-45.

Suys, A. " 'Simon, habeo tibi aliquid dicere' (Lc. 7,40)," *VD* 12 (1932) 199-202.

Sybel, L. von. "Die Salbungen: Mt 26, 6-13, Mc 14, 3-9, Lc 7, 36-50, Joh 12, 1-8," *ZNW* 23 (1924) 184-193.

Urrutia, J. L. de. "La parábola de los dos deudores, Lc 7, 39-50," *EstEcl* 38 (1963) 459-482.

Weiss, K. "Der westliche Text von Lc 7,46 und sein Wert," *ZNW* 46 (1955) 241-245.

Wilckens, U. "Vergebung für die Sünderin," in *Orientierung an Jesus: Festschrift für Josef Schmid* (Freiburg im B.: Herder, 1973) 394-424.

Winandy, J. "Simon et la pécheresse (Luc 7,36-50)," *BVC* 47 (1962) 38-46.

Winterbotham, R. "Simon and the Sinner: St. Luke vii. 36-50," *Expos* 1/6 (1877) 214-229.

Wood, H. G. "The Use of *agapaō* in Luke viii [sic] 42, 47," *ExpTim* 66 (1954-1955) 319-320.

37. GALILEAN WOMEN FOLLOWERS OF JESUS
(8:1-3)

8 ¹Soon afterwards, as Jesus was traveling about from town to village, preaching and announcing the kingdom of God, there happened to be with him the Twelve, ²and some women who had been cured of evil spirits and diseases: Mary called Magdalene, out of whom seven demons had come; ³and Joanna, the wife of Chuza, Herod's steward; Susanna, and many others who provided for them out of their own means.

COMMENT

The final episode of the little interpolation (8:1-3) is a Lucan summary of Jesus' Galilean ministry, which echoes that of 4:40-44. Verses 1a-b and 2a mention here details that were used of his generic ministry in chap. 4. The chief difference between this summary and the earlier one is the association with Jesus of two groups of followers: the Twelve (already identified by name in 6:13-16) and "some women," three of whom are explicitly named besides "many others."

The passage is best regarded as a Lucan composition as a whole. As J. M. Creed (*The Gospel*, 112-113) has pointed out, it contains many typically Lucan words and phrases: *kai egeneto en tō . . . kai autos . . . ; kathexēs, diodeuein, euangelizesthai, astheneia*. The names of the women followers could well have come to Luke from a pre-Lucan source ("L"); the description of Mary Magdalene as one "out of whom seven demons had come" rings like a stereotyped, inherited phrase. The information in this episode may well be "exact and minute," but this cannot be simply taken as "evidence" of "the excellence of Luke's sources" (*pace* A. Plummer, *Gospel*, 215). H. Schürmann (*Das Lukasevangelium*, 447) has compared these Lucan verses with Matt 9:35 and 11:1, suggesting that perhaps they are derived from "Q." However, the vocabulary is too diverse to tolerate that suggestion. Moreover, Matt 11:1 is usually regarded as the closing verse of the sermon in chap. 10, similar to other closing verses; its mention of "twelve *disciples*" and of "cities" (in the plural) makes one think rather that it is a Matthean composition, just as 8:1-3 come rather from Luke's composing hand. It may be that Luke is even

influenced here by Mark 15:41, "(women) who followed him and minis-
tered to him, when he was in Galilee," but the names of the women differ,
save for that of Mary Magdalene. Recall the use of frequent summaries in
Acts (see *JBC*, art. 45, § 4).

As a summary, this closing episode of the small interpolation makes it
clear that for Luke it is important that Jesus be seen again preaching the
kingdom "from town to village" and that the Twelve and the women are
associated with him in this ministry. It is part of the Lucan concern to
present Galileans as witnessing his teaching and preaching (see Luke
23:2c; Acts 10:37-39).

The episode is preparing for the "big interpolation," to begin at 9:51
and also for the sending out of the Twelve in 9:1. As H. Conzelmann has
put it (*Theology*, 46), it shows Jesus engaged in incessant travels before
9:51, especially in Galilee; he distinguishes Jesus' "tour" in the first part
of the Gospel from the "journey" that is to begin at 9:51. The "tour" is
through unnamed towns and villages in Galilee, whereas the "journey"
will be to Jerusalem, the city of destiny, and will have a pronounced
christological concern.

In particular, it is noteworthy that Luke at this stage introduces into
his story of Jesus' Galilean ministry women followers. Schürmann (*Das
Lukasevangelium*, 448) has raised the question whether the concern for
women in Luke 7:11-17, 7:36-50, and 8:2-3 might not have constituted
at one time a narrative complex, reflecting a *Sitz im Leben* in the early
community's concern about the question of women. This question, however, is too problematic to give anything but a speculative answer. What
the episode of 8:1-3 does indicate, however, is a recollection about Jesus
which differed radically from the usual understanding of women's role in
contemporary Judaism. His cure of women, his association with them, his
tolerating them among his followers (as here) clearly dissociates him
from such ideas as that reflected in John 4:27 or early rabbinical writings
(e.g. *Pirqe 'Abot* 1:5). See Str-B, 2. 438. The women are depicted by
Luke as ministering to Jesus and the Twelve in roles surprising for their
day: providing for them, and from their own means; at least one of them
was a married woman (Joanna); how many among the "many others"
were so too? In introducing these women followers here, Luke is foreshadowing their role at Jesus' cross (23:49) and at the empty tomb
(24:10); but he will also depict them deliberately in association with the
Twelve, with Mary, and his brothers (Acts 1:14). They are "the women"
who with the other first believers prayerfully await the promised Spirit
"with one accord."

This Lucan episode also depicts a distinction between the women and
the Twelve. The reason for the distinction does not emerge here, but
when one recalls the criteria for membership in the Twelve that Luke

uses (see COMMENT on 6:12-16), the reason becomes a little more intelligible. Luke makes the women "provide for" (or "minister to") not only Jesus, but also the Twelve (cf. Mark 15:41).

NOTES

8 1. *Soon afterwards.* Lit. "and it happened in the near (future) (as) he was traveling about . . . that (there were) with him. . . ." Luke uses *kai egeneto* with the conj. *kai* + a finite verb (understood, "there were"); see p. 119 above. There intervenes not only a temporal prepositional phrase (*en tō kathexēs* [i.e. *chronō*, on a similar phrase, see NOTE on 7:11]), but also the unstressed *kai autos* construction (see p. 120 above). The verb *diodeuein*, "travel through, about," occurs only here and in Acts 17:1 in the NT. It depicts Jesus once again en route, moving about the region of Galilee. See 4:44; 5:12.

from town to village. Or, better perhaps, "from town to town and village to village," since the distributive use of the prep. *kata* (with anarthrous objects) is intended here. Cf. 8:4; Acts 15:21.

preaching. See NOTES on 4:18,19.

announcing. See NOTES on 1:19; 4:18.

kingdom of God. See NOTE on 4:43. Coming on the heels of the preceding episodes (7:31-35,36-50), this notice of the theme of Jesus' preaching sums up that to which he would invite the "people of this generation."

the Twelve. See NOTE on 6:13. They follow him in this passage as his chosen ones and foreordained witnesses (see Acts 10:39-41).

2. *some women who had been cured of evil spirits and diseases.* So far only one woman has been cured in the Lucan story of Jesus' ministry, Simon's mother-in-law (4:38-39); presumably she has remained at home. The others must have been included in such notices as 4:40-41; 6:17-19. The "some" become "many others" in v. 3.

Mary called Magdalene. She is the first named, as in Mark 15:40,47; 16:1; Luke 24:10; contrast John 19:25. Introduced here, she foreshadows 23:49; 24:10, where she becomes a witness to the crucifixion and to the empty tomb. She comes from the town of Magdala. Aside from the references to her, the town is otherwise unmentioned in the NT, Josephus, or contemporary sources. The name of the town may be related to Hebrew *migdōl*, "tower," a word often used either by itself as a proper name (e.g. Exod 14:2; Num 33:7) or in combination with other specifying names (see *HALAT*, 516). It is often thought that Josephus refers to the town from which Mary comes, when he speaks of Tarichaeae in Galilee (e.g. *J.W.* 2.13,2 § 252), not far from Tiberias on the west coast of Lake Gennesaret. This Greek name is related to *tarichos*, "dried or smoked fish" (LSJ, 1748), and perhaps its name in later rabbinic writings, *Migdal nûnayya'*, "Fish Tower," reflects the same tradition (*b. Pesaḥim* 46a).

out of whom seven demons had come. I.e. through an exorcism, presumably performed by Jesus. The number of the demons is supposed to imply the severity of the possession. See NOTE on 7:37.

3. *Joanna.* This woman is mentioned again in 24:10; she is otherwise unknown.

the wife of Chuza, Herod's steward. I.e. of Herod Antipas, the tetrarch of Galilee (3:1). The title *epitropos* (used only here in the Lucan writings) cannot be understood as the Greek equivalent of Latin *praefectus* or *procurator* (see NOTE on Pilate as prefect, 3:1). It should rather be understood as "manager" of Herod's estate (see Josephus *Ant.* 18.6,6 § 194). This detail, used to identify Joanna, suggests that Jesus' influence and preaching was reaching even to high places. The mention of Herod foreshadows the question he will utter in 9:7-9. The name *Chuza* has been found in Nabatean and Syrian inscriptions (*CIS*, 2. 227; E. Littmann, *ZA* 27 [1913] 397) as Aramaic *Kûzā'*). It suggests an Aramean connection, having nothing to do, however, with the Idumean deity Qaws, *pace* J. Ernst, *Evangelium nach Lukas,* 261. For Luke's acquaintance with other members of Herod's entourage, see Acts 13:1 (Manaen, a Christian convert of the church in Antioch).

Susanna. She is otherwise unknown.

who provided for them. Lit. "who were serving them," with the verb *diakonein* not being restricted to table service. Some Greek mss. of the Hesychian tradition (A), the Lake family of minuscules, and some OL texts (along with the Vg^cl) read the sg. *autō,* "him." The better attested reading (B, D, W, Θ) is *autois,* "them." The singular is also suspect because it looks like a harmonization with Matt 27:55 or Mark 15:41. The "them" would refer to Jesus and the Twelve.

out of their own means. I.e. they were "persons of substance" (Plummer, *Gospel,* 216), who were expressing their gratitude to Jesus for the cures wrought. Luke uses here *ta hyparchonta,* lit. "those (things) belonging to someone," in the sense of "possessions"; this expression occurs frequently in Hellenistic Greek. See further Luke 11:21; 12:15,33,44; 14:33; 16:1; 19:8; Acts 4:32.

BIBLIOGRAPHY (8:1-3)

Conzelmann, H. *The Theology of St Luke,* 46-48.
Hastings, A. *Prophet and Witness in Jerusalem* (Baltimore: Helicon, 1958) 38-49.

E. THE PREACHED AND ACCEPTED WORD OF GOD

*The Word of God is presented in a parable;
but who are they that accept it?*

38. THE PARABLE OF THE SOWED SEED
(8:4-8)

8 ⁴ As a great crowd of people was now gathering and they were making their way to Jesus from one town after another, he addressed them, using a parable. ⁵ "A farmer went out to sow his seed; as he did, some of it fell along the footpath and was trampled on, and the birds of the sky gobbled it up. ⁶ Some other seed fell on rocky soil, and when it sprouted, it dried up because it had no moisture. ⁷ Some other seed fell amid thornbushes, and when they grew up together, the thorns choked them off. ⁸ Still other seed fell into good ground, and when it sprouted, it yielded fruit a hundredfold." As he said this, he called out, "Let the one who has ears to hear take heed."

COMMENT

A new section of the Lucan Gospel begins here. That material which Luke had inserted, beginning at 6:20, after Mark 3:19 (transposed) has come to an end, and he returns to his use of Marcan material in sequence. Luke has, it is true, omitted Mark 3:20-21, the passage in which "his own" (=his family) came to take Jesus away, considering him to be "beside himself." Given Luke's treatment of Mary and his "brothers" in Acts 1:14, where they are among the first believers, such a passage was obviously too negative for him, and he has simply omitted it. What Mark has in 3:22-30 (the Beelzebul controversy), Luke will present in 11:14-23, under another form. And the passage about Jesus' relatives (Mark 3:31-35) Luke will modify and transpose to the end of what he has retained from the Marcan discourse in parables.

Luke 8:4 picks up Mark 4:1 and presents a form of that Marcan discourse. The name, "Discourse in Parables," is more proper to the Marcan Gospel than to Luke. The parables that Luke retains give examples of the "preaching" mentioned in 8:1, but now the emphasis is much more on the word of God. Even the two last episodes of this section of the Gospel are centered on that theme (viz. the parable of the lamp, vv. 16-18; and Jesus' saying about his real relatives, vv. 19-21). The Marcan discourse falls into various subdivisions, introduced by characteristic clauses (4:10,13,21,24). All of these disappear in the Lucan form, which makes his example of Jesus' use of parables in this chapter much more cohesive and uninterrupted. The concluding episode about Jesus' relatives (vv. 19-21) rounds off the development and makes this whole section one devoted to the preached and accepted word of God. If we treat, however, the first part of it in three subsections (vv. 4-8,9-10,11-15), that is simply because of the problems they have in their Synoptic relationships.

Verses 4-8 present a Lucan form of the parable of the sower, the source of which is Mark 4:1-9 (cf. Matt 13:1-9). Since Luke has already adapted Mark 4:1 for his introduction in 5:1-3, he omits that verse here. Verse 4a represents an independent Lucan composition (with its double genitive absolute), and v. 4b is Lucan redaction. The main change in the parable, however, is that it is more centered on the sowing of the seed than on the farmer. The farmer is no more prominent in Mark 4:1-9 than he is in Luke 8:4-8, but Luke depicts the farmer going out "to sow *his seed*," and his explanation later on passes over the farmer and concentrates on "the seed" as the word of God (8:11; contrast Mark 9:14). Further Lucan redaction is seen in various additions and omissions, when his text is compared with the Marcan form; but none of them is of any major significance (e.g. the omission of Mark 4:5b-6, details about the shallow depth of soil or the scorching sun; or of 4:7c, the failure of the seed sown among thorns to "bear fruit"). Only at the end is there a significant change, when Luke drastically modifies the report of the yield: "thirtyfold, sixtyfold, and a hundredfold," which becomes simply "it yielded fruit a hundredfold." This modification still drives home the main point of the parable. Finally, stress on the message of the parable is found in Jesus' raising his voice and calling out.

In the Lucan passage there are, however, a few minor agreements of Luke and Matthew against Mark: *tou* added before the infin. in v. 5; *auton* added as the subject of the second infin. in v. 5b (see Matt 13:4); the common omission of *kai karpon ouk edōken* in v. 7 (see Matt 13:7); and finally the participial form *ho echōn* in v. 8 (see Matt 13:9). The latter is especially of little significance, since Luke 14:35 and Matt 11:15 and the participial form in Rev 2:7,11,17,29; 3:6,13,22 show that the commonly used Greek form of the saying was participial and that Luke has undoubtedly adjusted his saying to it independently of Matthew. The others are such minor ameliorations of Mark's Greek that one can draw no firm conclusion from them. H. Schürmann (*Lukasevangelium,* 461) would ascribe them to the influence of oral tradition.

The Lucan introductory verse (8:4) makes it clear that this form of the parable is addressed to the people at large, among whom one would have to reckon the Twelve and the women of 8:1-3. But when the "disciples" ask Jesus for an explanation of the parable (8:9), we are not told in Luke, as we are in Mark 4:10, that they were "alone" (*kata monas*); though a contrast is, indeed, made between them and "the others," that has to be understood in its proper context.

So astute a commentator as R. Bultmann once thought that the meaning of this parable was irretrievably lost. "Is it a consolation for every man when his labour does not all bear fruit? Is it in this sense a monologue by Jesus half of resignation, half of thankfulness? Is it an exhortation to the hearers of the divine Word? Is it Jesus' preaching? . . ." (*HST,* 199-200). All but his last query miss the point because they tend to psychologize the parable.

In the Marcan form the parable was one of contrast, as J. Jeremias (*The Parables,* 149-151) has well shown: despite all the obstacles met in the sowing of the seed on various kinds of soil, the farmer's toil succeeds and yields a harvest duly described in triple fashion. It illustrates the ultimate eschatological success that will attend Jesus' preaching, despite all the human obstacles that will be encountered: ". . . God has made a beginning, bringing with it a harvest of reward beyond all asking or conceiving. In spite of every failure and opposition, from hopeless beginnings, God brings forth the triumphant end which he has promised" (ibid., 150).

The Lucan form of the parable presents the same contrast, even with its more succinct formulation of the yield. Moreover, despite the insertion of "his seed" (v. 5), the parable still carries the same basic message. Luke has added that in view of the coming explanation (vv. 11-15); it gives a greater significance to the seed in the passage as a whole. Hence, the title, the parable of the sowed seed.

The parable of the sowed seed has often been regarded as a kingdom-parable; the yield portends the eschatological success of the kingdom that Jesus was preaching. "Kingdom" does occur in Luke 8:1,10, but the comparison is not otherwise explicit. Given the greater emphasis on the preaching of the word of God in this section of the Lucan Gospel, it seems better to understand the parable itself in vv. 4-8 as illustrating the eschatological success of that preaching.

Another form of the parable is found in the Coptic *Gos. Thom.* § 9, which runs as follows:

Jesus said, "Now the sower went out, filled his hand (with seed), and tossed (it). Some fell upon the path; birds came (and) gathered them (up). Others fell upon rock and did not put down roots into the soil and sent no ears up heavenward. Others fell among thorns; they choked the seed(s), and the worm ate them (up). Still others fell upon good soil and yielded good fruit; it bore sixtyfold and a hundred-and-twenty fold."

Though J. Ménard (*L'Evangile selon Thomas* [NHS 5; Leiden: Brill, 1975] 91) sees no dependence of this form on any of the three canonical forms of the parable, W. Schrage (*Das Verhältnis des Thomasevangeliums* [BZNW 29; Berlin: de Gruyter, 1964] 45) more correctly sees the dependence of this parable in the *Gos. Thom.* on the Sahidic text of Mark itself. Yet, even if it were a representative of an independent tradition, its only advantage would be to stress what has long been maintained that the parable circulated for a time separately from the allegorizing interpretation of Mark 4:13-20 and Luke 8:11-15.

The concluding verse of the parable, "Let the one who has ears to hear take heed," is modeled on Mark 4:9. It too is echoed in the Coptic *Gos. Thom.* § 8, 24, but is significantly absent from § 9, where the parable itself is recorded. It reveals again the independent character of the concluding saying.

The Lucan Jesus, in presenting his preaching of God's message, in the form of this parable of the sowed seed depicts vividly the various ways in which his message is being received by people who listen to it. The parable stresses that despite the obstacles that attend the sowing and growth of the seed the message will be heard and abundantly accepted. Success will attend the sowing of seed in such preaching.

NOTES

8 4. *As a great crowd . . . was now gathering.* The pres. ptc. used in this and the following gen. absol. expresses the continuing and progressive increase of persons who were flocking to hear Jesus' message (see M. B. Walker, *ExpTim* 75 [1963-1964] 151). Verses 4 and 8b form a framework for the parable proper.

and they were making their way. The conj. *kai* can be understood either as copulative, "and" (as in the translation), or as epexegetic, "namely" (so A. Plummer, *Gospel*, 217); this would make the second gen. absol. depend on "crowd," i.e. "even of those who were making their way."

from one town after another. Lit. "of those from town to town making their way. . . ." The distributive phrase *kata polin* was met in 8:1 above (see NOTE there). No indication of the towns is given; presumably those in the vicinity vaguely referred to in 8:1.

he addressed them, using a parable. Lit. "he spoke through a parable," an expression used only here. For *parabolē*, see NOTE on 4:23. Codex D and the OL read, "he spoke such a parable as this to them." Contrast Mark 4:2, "many things in parables," which is a more fitting introduction to the multiple parables to follow in that part of the Marcan Gospel.

5. *A farmer went out to sow his seed.* Lit. "the sower went out. . . ." The definite article is used generically of a class of individuals (see BDF § 252). Luke adds to the Marcan source, "his seed" (*ton sporon autou*), a phrase possibly derived from the parable of the seed growing silently (Mark 4:26-29), which Luke omits; see J. Dupont, "La parabole du semeur," 99.

as he did. Lit. "in his sowing (it)."

some of it fell along the footpath. The phrase *ho men*, "some of it," is not resumed by *ho de*, but rather by *kai heteron* (vv. 6,7,8); *ho men* is masc., referring to *sporon*, "seed," but Luke shifts in the following verses to the neut., even making the ptc. *phyen* agree accordingly. It may be owing to the intervening development in the story (BDF § 447[3]), or it may be that Luke is thinking of neut. *sperma*, "seed."

For a correct understanding of this parable, Jeremias (*The Parables,* 11-12) has argued that one has to "remember that in Palestine sowing preceded ploughing." The farmer has to be understood as moving over an unplowed field, casting the seed widely so that some of it falls on a footpath, on rocky soil, amidst thornbushes, as well as on good soil. All will subsequently be plowed and turned in to await rain and growth. Jeremias depended on information from G. Dalman ("Viererlei Acker," *PJ* 22 [1926] 120-132) and some passages in rabbinic literature which seem to suggest that sowing preceded plowing (*m. Šabbat* 7:2; *b. Šabbat* 73b; *t. Berakot* 7:2). His interpretation has been contested by an economic historian, K. D. White ("The Parable of the Sower," *JTS* 15 [1964] 300-307), appealing to Columella *De re rustica* 2.11 passim; 2.4,2; and Pliny *Naturalis historia* 18.179-181, for evidence of multiple plowings and what he calls the "normal Mediterranean practice," which is against Jeremias' suggestion. However, the material which he cites is not that conclusive. While it may be true of some "parts of the Mediterranean region," it is not clearly applicable to Palestine. Moreover, *Jub.* 11:11 makes it clear that sowing did at times precede plowing in Palestine (as W. G. Essame has pointed out, *ExpTim* 72 [1960-1961] 54). White may have rightly criticized Jeremias for using data in rabbinic texts of later centuries as evidence for the Palestine of the first century. But the *Jubilees* text would argue for an earlier attestation of the practice to which Jeremias has called attention. Moreover, Jeremias has answered most of the criticism of White and strengthened his own position (*NTS* 13 [1966-1967] 48-53). See further P. B. Payne, *NTS* 25 (1978-1979) 123-129.

and was trampled on. I.e. by passersby (before the plowing). The phrase is a Lucan addition to the Marcan material; it makes the eating of the seed by birds a bit harder to envisage. It stresses, however, another obstacle to the growth of the seed, viz. the packed earth. No use of this additional detail is made in the interpretation of vv. 11-15.

and the birds of the sky gobbled it up. The phrase "of the sky" (*tou ouranou*) is missing from some Western mss. (D, W) and some OL texts (it[a, b, d, e]); this omission is probably influenced by the parallels of Mark 4:4 and Matt 13:4. However, "the birds of the sky" is a Lucan expression (see 9:58; 13:19; Acts 10:12; 11:6), imitating such LXX expressions as Dan 4:12,21; Ezek 31:6; Ps 104:12, and giving to the parable more of a biblical tone. Cf. *Jub.* 11:11.

6. *Some other seed fell on rocky soil.* Lit. "upon the rock," which may have been lightly covered with soil. Luke has greatly abridged the details here, besides changing *petrōdes* to *tēn petran.*

it dried up because it had no moisture. Luke has introduced a different detail, speaking of the lack of moisture, whereas Mark said that "it had no root."

7. *when they grew up together.* Again, a Lucan modification; Mark does not depict the grain growing up with the thorns.

8. *other seed fell into good ground.* Luke preserves here the double def. art. of Mark 4:8, but changes the adj. from *kalēn* to *agathēn,* writing *eis tēn gēn tēn agathēn.*

it yielded fruit a hundredfold. For the Marcan *edidou karpon* ("produced, gave grain"), Luke has substituted a LXX expression, "it made fruit" (*epoiēsen karpon;* cf. Gen 1:11-12; Luke 3:8). Contrast 20:10. He has also simplified the expression of the huge yield. Varro (*De re rustica* 1.44,2) reports that seed sown "near Gadara, in Syria" yielded a hundredfold—so the yield is not unlikely. Cf. Gen 26:12. White (*JTS* 15 [1964] 301) maintains that the yield should be understood of the "return of seeds reaped for seeds sown," since that is the way a yield was usually measured in antiquity. This is probably the best explanation of it, but it should be noted that in all three Synoptic accounts the yield is expressed in terms of *karpos,* "fruit," not *sporos* or *sperma;* perhaps *karpos* could be understood in the broader sense. In Hellenistic Greek texts it was used of the produce of vines, fruit trees, dates, and olives (see MM, 321).

he called out. Or possibly, "he kept calling out," since the verb is in the impf. tense.

Let the one who has ears to hear take heed. An identically worded conclusion is also found in 14:35. Its Marcan counterpart is found in 4:9 (*hos echei,* a rel. cl.) and 4:23 (*ei tis echei,* a condition). Matthew uses it twice too (4:8; 11:15), in both cases without the infin. *akouein* but with the ptc. *echōn.* In Revelation 2-3 it occurs at the end of each of the letters to the seven churches. The infin. *akouein,* "to hear," is epexegetic; *pace* A. R. C. Leaney, *A Commentary,* 151, it is not to be taken with the verb *akouetō* in imitation of a Hebrew infin. absol. as an intensifier.

BIBLIOGRAPHY (8:4-8)

Carlston, C. E. *The Parables of the Triple Tradition* (Philadelphia: Fortress, 1975) 70-76.

Courthial, P. "Du texte au sermon, 17: La parabole du semeur en Luc 8/5-15," *ETR* 47 (1972) 397-420.

Crossan, J. D. "The Seed Parables of Jesus," *JBL* 92 (1973) 244-266.

Dietzfelbinger, C. "Das Gleichnis vom ausgestreuten Samen," in *Der Ruf Jesu und die Antwort der Gemeinde: Exegetische Untersuchungen Joachim Jeremias zum 70. Geburtstag gewidmet von seinen Schülern* (Göttingen: Vandenhoeck und Ruprecht, 1970) 80-93.

Dodd, C. H. *The Parables of the Kingdom* (New York: Scribner, 1961) 145-147.

Dupont, J. "Le chapître des paraboles," *NRT* 89 (1967) 800-820.

———— "La parabole de la semence qui pousse toute seule (Marc 4, 26-29)," *RSR* 55 (1967) 367-392.

———— "La parabole du semeur dans la version de Luc," in *Apophoreta: Festschrift für Ernst Haenchen zu seinem siebzigsten Geburtstag am 10. December 1964* (BZNW 30; Berlin: Töpelmann, 1964) 97-108.

Gerhardsson, B. "The Parable of the Sower and Its Interpretation," *NTS* 14 (1967-1968) 165-193.

Haugg, D. "Das Ackergleichnis," *TQ* 127 (1947) 60-81, 166-204.

Jeremias, J. "Palästinakundliches zum Gleichnis vom Säemann (Mark. iv. 3-8 Par.)," *NTS* 13 (1966-1967) 48-53.

———— *The Parables of Jesus* (rev. ed.; New York: Scribner, 1963) 149-151.

Jülicher, A. *Die Gleichnisreden Jesu* (2 vols.; 2d ed.; Tübingen: Mohr [Siebeck], 1910) 2. 514-538.

Léon-Dufour, X. "La parabole du semeur," *Études d'évangile* (Paris: Editions du Seuil, 1965) 255-301.

Marshall, I. H. "Tradition and Theology in Luke (Luke 8:5-15)," *Tyndale Bulletin* 20 (1969) 56-75.

März, C.-P. *Das Wort Gottes bei Lukas: Die lukanische Worttheologie als Frage an die neuere Lukasforschung* (Erfurter theologische Schriften 11; Leipzig: St. Benno-V., 1974) 57-59, 67-69.

Miguens, M. "La predicazione di Gesù in parabole (Mc. 4; Lc. 8, 4-18; Mt. 13)," *BeO* 1 (1959) 35-40.

Neil, W. "Expounding the Parables: II. The Sower (Mk 4:3-8)," *ExpTim* 77 (1965-1966) 74-77.

Robinson, W. C., Jr. "On Preaching the Word of God (Luke 8:4-21)," in *Studies in Luke-Acts,* 131-138.

Schramm, T. *Der Markus-Stoff bei Lukas* (SNTSMS 14; Cambridge: University Press, 1971) 114-123.

Schürmann, H. "Lukanische Reflexionen über die Wortverkündigung in Lk 8,4-21," in *Wahrheit und Verkündigung: Michael Schmaus zum 70. Geburtstag* (eds. L. Scheffczyk et al.; 2 vols.; Paderborn: Schöningh, 1967) 1. 213-228; reprinted in *Ursprung und Gestalt: Erörterungen und Besinnungen zum Neuen Testament* (Düsseldorf: Patmos, 1970) 29-41.

White, K. D. "The Parable of the Sower," *JTS* 15 (1964) 300-307.

Wilder, A. N. "The Parable of the Sower: Naiveté and Method in Interpretation," *Semeia* 2 (1974) 134-151.

39. WHY JESUS SPOKE IN PARABLES
(8:9-10)

8 9 Then his disciples asked him, "What is the meaning of this parable?" 10 And he said, "It has been granted to you to know the secrets of the kingdom of God; but the others have only parables, so that *they look and see nothing, they listen and fail to understand.*"ᵃ

ᵃ Isa 6:9-10

COMMENT

As we have already stated, the following vv. 9-10 are not as distinct from the parable itself in the Lucan Gospel as they are in Mark. Luke gives no indication that Jesus and his disciples have retired in private, as does Mark 4:10. In the Lucan context the disciples apparently ask their question in the full hearing of the crowd mentioned in 8:4. The Marcan form has been considerably abridged and softened by Luke; his disciples ask only about one parable. Verse 9 is a Lucan compositional introduction to v. 10 (revealed as such by the indirect question with the optative—see p. 108 above). It is inspired by Mark 4:10. Verse 10 is a redactional abridgment of Mark 4:11-12. A minor agreement of Luke and Matthew against the Marcan tradition is again met in v. 10, *gnōnai ta mystēria*, "to know the secrets" against the Marcan singular *to mystērion*. Luke has also shortened the allusion to Isa 6:9-10 and recast the Greek wording. But he has retained the controversial conj. *hina*, "so that," which Matthew changed.

What is preserved in these Lucan verses is a Saying of Jesus about why he made use of parables. As R. Bultmann noted (*HST*, 199), it has been secondarily introduced at this point into the gospel tradition, undoubtedly by Mark (*HST*, 325 n. 1), whereas it may come from an entirely different context in Jesus' ministry (i.e. in Stage I of the tradition), one distinct from the parable to which it is now attached. V. Taylor (*FGT*, 80) has tried to make a pronouncement-story out of it, one that could "be related to the life-situation of the first Christians." This is, however, unconvincing, since what little narrative is present in Mark 4:10 is scarcely integral to the would-be pronouncement. The form is rather that of a saying of Jesus. Theoretically, it could be the product of early Christian formation, which was seeking to explain the obscurity of some of Jesus' parables; but, as Taylor himself admitted (ibid.), there is no genuine reason why Jesus himself could not have used the words of Isaiah to explain the lack of success that often attended his preaching. Though Isa 6:9-10 is used elsewhere in the NT to explain why Jews did not accept the Christian preaching (John 12:40; Acts 28:26-27), and in contexts having nothing to do with parables, the use of it here in the parable-context is unique.

The passage distinguishes Jesus' disciples from "the others" in that they are favored by God himself with an understanding of Jesus' kingdom-preaching. Whereas the Marcan form of the saying described God's gift as the "secret of the kingdom itself," i.e. a share in it (and not just "knowledge" about when it would come), the Matthean and Lucan forms of the saying speak rather of the gift as a "knowledge" of the secrets of the kingdom. This shift emphasizes rather an awareness of the transcendent, hidden aspects of the kingdom. It suits well the emphasis in Luke on Jesus as the kingdom-preacher. If the passage seems to distinguish only two classes of hearers, the disciples and the others, the interpretation of the parable to come will distinguish further, mentioning four groups of listeners.

Verse 10 alludes to Isa 6:9-10, which is part of the prophet's inaugural vision, as he was called by Yahweh to go and preach to a people that the prophet considered deaf and blind. The implied comparison is itself eloquent. Luke sees a new sense in the Isaian words: what was true of obstinate Israel of old is now seen in a new form; human beings will be charmed by the simplicity of the parable-preaching of Jesus and yet fail to understand what it should mean to them.

NOTES

8 9. *his disciples.* I.e. the Twelve and the women of 8:1-2. The Marcan parallel has *hoi peri auton syn tois dōdeka*, "those who were about him along with the Twelve." They are set over against the "others" (vs. 10).

10. *It has been granted to you.* I.e. by God, again an instance of the theological passive (see NOTE on 5:20). Jesus' words allude to the gracious election of his disciples by the Father. They are privileged to know what will be described here; implicitly the saying reveals a Lucan understanding of discipleship.

to know the secrets of the kingdom of God. In the Marcan source the secret of the kingdom is given outright to the disciples. Along with Matt 13:11, Luke has changed the sg. *mystērion* to the plural and adds the infin. *gnōnai*, "to know." The Lucan form of the saying thus describes God's gift to the disciples as a cognitive experience of the kingdom. They are not just hearers of the parable, but those who see and understand its implication. What is intended is not an esoteric gnosis given to some closed group, but a knowledge that is to be broadcast—about the kingdom and its role in human life. The disciples' comprehension of the "secrets" does not necessarily come full blown to them with Jesus' explanation of the parable, for Luke insists (Acts 1:3b) that the risen Lord further explained to them about the kingdom of God. Their ultimate comprehension of the "secrets" of the kingdom stands in contrast to the lawyers who have the key of knowledge (11:52) but make no use of it. See H. Schürmann, *Lukasevangelium,* 459.

The plural "secrets of the kingdom" may reflect the contemporary Palestinian use of *rāzê 'El,* "secrets of God," known from various Qumran texts (1QpHab 7:8; 1QS 3:23; 1QM 3:9; 16:11; etc.). The use of the plural is no less eschatological than the Marcan singular. Neither the singular nor the plural should be understood in any gnostic sense; nor should one contend that "the eschatological secrecy" of Mark 4:11 is being replaced by a "timeless secrecy," to which the timeless disclosure of mysteries corresponds, thanks to gnosis (*pace* H. Conzelmann, *Theology,* 103). There is simply no evidence of such a shift of emphasis.

the others. Mark 4:11b distinguished the disciples from *ekeinois de tois exō,* "those who are outside," but since Luke has eliminated the notice that Jesus was "alone" with them (*kata monas,* Mark 4:10) he rephrases here too. Literally, his text reads, "the rest."

have only parables. Lit. "but to the rest (it has been granted) in parables," i.e. illustrations, drawn from everyday Palestinian life; see NOTE on 4:23 above. J. Jeremias (*The Parables,* 16) has tried to insist that the word *parabolai* originally had the sense of "riddles" and was understood of Jesus' preaching in general to those who did not accept his message. This is scarcely convincing, but we need not delay on that now. Luke has borrowed the saying of Jesus from his Marcan source, where the word is used clearly of the foregoing parable of the sowed seed and should therefore be understood of such illustrations.

so that. Luke has preserved here the conj. *hina* from Mark 4:12; but Matt 13:13 has changed it to *hoti* in order to soften the saying and express rather the cause of the people's incomprehension. This is clearly a redactional change of Matthew, and there is no need to invoke a "mistranslation" of an underlying Aramaic *dĕ-,* which should have been understood as a relative pron. but is taken in the sense of causal *hoti* by Matthew and final *hina* by Mark and Luke (*pace* M. Black, *AAGA*[3], 215-216).

The greater problem is the sense of the conj. *hina.* It has normally been understood in a final or teleological sense, expressing the reason why Jesus taught in parables, "in order that those others might look and see nothing, listen and fail to understand." So E. Stauffer, *TDNT* 3. 327; BAG, 378; H. Windisch, *ZNW* 26 (1927) 203-209; BDF § 369(2). Accordingly, it would imply that Jesus deliberately preached in a manner similar to God in the OT sending his prophets to harden the hearts of Israel, or of the Pharaoh. Such a purpose, however, has always seemed to be in conflict with the very nature of the parables, which are illustrations and in many cases clarify elements in Jesus' preaching. Hence commentators have at times sought to take *hina* in a consecutive sense, expressing, not the purpose of Jesus' use of parables, but rather the result of them. Cf. Luke 9:45; 11:50. It is further pointed out that in Hellenistic Greek, *hina* with the subjunctive is used at times as a substitute for *hōste* with an infin. (the more regular result construction). See ZBG § 352; cf. BDF § 391(5); BAG, 378b (§ 2). Our translation has used "so that," which can be understood in either way, but the final sense is preferable (see below).

they look and see nothing, they listen and fail to understand. Thus Luke has abridged and softened the stern statement in Mark 4:12, "so that they look indeed but do not see, hear indeed but do not understand, lest perhaps they turn and forgiveness be shown to them." The Marcan form is itself a paraphrase of the LXX of Isa 6:9-10: *akoē akousete kai ou mē synēte kai blepontes blepsete kai ou mē idēte, epachynthē gar hē kardia tou laou toutou . . . , mēpote idōsin tois ophthalmois kai tois ōsin akousōsin kai tē kardia synōsin kai epistrepsōsin kai iasomai autous,* "You will indeed hear but not understand, and you will indeed look but not see, for the heart of this people has been dulled . . . lest they see with their eyes, hear with their ears, and understand with their heart and turn (to me), and I heal them." Luke has certainly not fashioned his form of this saying on anything resembling the LXX (contrast Matt 13:13-15, where the LXX is actually quoted). His starting-point is clearly Mark 4:12. He makes the ptcs. *blepontes* and *akouontes,* which in the LXX and Mark are the equivalent of the intensifying Hebrew infin. absol., into good Greek circumstantial ptcs., with concessive force. Moreover, the last clause about conversion and forgiveness is completely omitted by Luke, who undoubtedly thought that they did not suit Jesus' preaching (and this omission is an argument in favor of the final interpretation of *hina*). J. Dupont ("La parabole du semeur," 102) rightly thinks that Luke has suppressed it lest it seem that Jesus' use of parables was intended deliberately to impede conversion; accordingly, he adds a similar, less offensive, clause to the interpretation of the first group of hearers in the interpretation of the parable (v. 12).

Again, we hesitate to go along with J. Jeremias' contention that *mēpote* of Mark 4:12 represents Aramaic *dilĕmā',* used in the *Tg. Isaiah* 6:10 in the sense of "unless." The reason for the hesitation is a failure to agree that this is a "contemporary interpretation of Isa. 6.10b" (*The Parables,* 17). The Isaiah targum dates from the fourth/fifth century A.D.

BIBLIOGRAPHY (8:9-10)
(in addition to the titles given in 8:4-8)

Cerfaux, L. "La connaissance des secrets du royaume d'après Matt. xiii. 11 et parallèles," *NTS* 2 (1955-1956) 238-249.

Gnilka, J. *Die Verstockung Israels: Isaias 6,1-10 in der Theologie der Synoptiker* (SANT 3; Munich: Kösel, 1961) 119-129.

Siegman, E. F. "Teaching in Parables (Mk 4,10-12; Lk 8,9-10; Mt 13,10-15)," *CBQ* 23 (1961) 161-181.

40. THE EXPLANATION OF THE PARABLE
(8:11-15)

8 11 "This is the meaning of the parable. The seed is the word of God. 12 Those along the footpath are the ones who have listened to it. When the devil comes, he snatches the word from their minds for fear they might believe and find salvation. 13 Those on rocky soil are the ones who listen at first and accept the word with joy; but, having no root, they believe for a while and in time of trial fall away. 14 What fell among the thornbushes represents those who listened, but who in their pursuit of life are choked off by anxieties, riches, and pleasures; they bring nothing to maturity. 15 But the seed in the good soil represents those who listen to the word and hold on to it with a noble and generous mind; they yield a crop through their persistence."

COMMENT

The Lucan interpretation of the parable of the sowed seed (8:11-15) follows closely on Jesus' explanation of why he spoke in parables. In fact, as we noted above, the whole passage (vv. 4-15) is much more of a homogeneous unit in Luke than it is in Mark. The interpretation (vv. 11-15) lacks an introductory formula such as the Marcan *kai legei autois,* "and he said to them." But it forms the answer to the question of the disciples (8:9).

The Lucan form of the interpretation of the parable is clearly dependent on that of Mark. This is the conclusion of D. Wenham, who has discussed it from all the possible aspects of Synoptic interdependence (*NTS* 20 [1973-1974] 299-319). He has tried to isolate a pre-synoptic form of the passage and thinks that Luke may even have known it; but he still concludes in the long run that Luke's form was "under the baneful influence of Mark" (especially in 8:13). Whether that is the word for it, the dependence of Luke on Mark in this section is clear.

Having identified the seed as "the word of God," Luke retains details of the Marcan interpretation (4:13-20), which do not further interpret the seed, but he passes abruptly to an interpretation of the four kinds of soil into which the seed falls. The transition between 8:11b and 8:12 is abrupt, since the "those" of v. 12 does not really pick up the sg. *sporos,* "seed." The reason for the abruptness is found in the Marcan source itself. Luke has omitted Mark 4:13, a verse that is at once difficult to understand and unflattering to the disciples. But Mark 4:15 is no smoother a transition in Mark than one has here in Luke.

Form-critically, the interpretation belongs to sayings of Jesus. Though some commentators (H. B. Swete, M.-J. Lagrange, A. Plummer, and others) have sought to maintain that it is an authentic interpretation of the parable, given by Jesus himself, it is commonly admitted today that it more likely represents an early-church interpretation which has allegorized and further extended the sense of the parable itself. The interpretation clearly moves the parable beyond the idea of the success of the eschatological harvest to an exhortation about Christian perseverance and faith. The hortatory note is not exclusive to Luke, but is found already in the Marcan form. Certain details in that form have been used to argue for its secondary character: (a) the absol. use of *ho logos* (=the Christian message) occurring here only on the lips of Jesus (Mark 4:14-20), whereas elsewhere in the NT it is often found for "the gospel" (see Mark's use of it in narrative verses: 1:45; 2:2; 4:33; 16:20; Luke 1:2; Acts 4:4; 8:4; 11:19; Gal 6:6; Col 4:3); (b) the use of *speirein,* "to sow," in the sense of preaching (4:14) occurs only here; (c) the Greek compound adjectives *proskairos,* "transitory, ephemeral," and *akarpos,* "unfruitful," lack any Semitic counterparts. Such details suggest that the interpretation might well have come from a setting in the early community, in which the parable of Jesus was further allegorized in a sense beyond that which he really intended at first.

R. E. Brown ("Parable and Allegory Reconsidered," *NovT* 5 [1962] 36-45) has argued against much of the oversimplification that is characteristic of parable-interpretation in this century (since A. Jülicher), rightly stressing that the lines between allegory and parable have been too sharply drawn. He is right in maintaining that some parables do contain allegorical elements and that there is no reason why Jesus in his ministry could not have used allegory as well as parable. He recognizes that the interpretation of this parable "has been adapted to the situation of the early Church," but believes that beneath it there "can be found . . . an allegorical explanation by Jesus himself" (ibid., 40). This is possible, but there is no proof for it.

The Lucan interpretation of the parable exploits some of the elements claimed to be indicative of the secondary character of the Marcan form. The absolute "the word" becomes "the word of God." And the interpretation concentrates not so much on the fate of the seed (*pace*

G. Schneider, *Evangelium nach Lukas,* 183) as on the kinds of soil on which it falls. These are identified as various hearers who react to the word of God.

The Lucan interpretation does not allegorize the parable completely. We are not told who the farmer is (Jesus? the disciples?); the hundred-fold yield is not explained (nor is it in Mark). Nor is anything made in the Lucan form of the details of the trampling or of the lack of moisture. But the seed becomes the word of God, the birds of the heavens the devil, the thorns three kinds of worldly distractions, and the four kinds of soil four groups of hearers.

A parallel to this parable and its interpretation in extrabiblical material should be noted. It is found in 2 Esdr 8:41-44:

> Just as a farmer sows many seeds upon the ground and plants a host of seedlings, yet not all that were sown will be saved nor all that were planted will take root, so too not all of those who have been sown in the world will be saved.

This passage, which is part of the Jewish apocalypse sometimes called *IV Ezra* and may date from about A.D. 100, provides an interesting parallel to the parable under discussion, particularly in its Lucan form with the mention of salvation.

In the interpretation of the parable four classes of hearers of God's word are singled out. (a) Those who have no saving faith. Luke has introduced into it his own ideas of faith and salvation. If "the word of God" is a saving word, one has to react to it with faith; but the opportunity to do so in the case of this first group is snatched away, not by Jesus (as the end of Mark 4:12 might imply), but by evil personified, by the influence of what is opposed to the saving word itself. (b) Those who fall away in time of trial. The second group reacts to the word of God, indeed, with faith, but not for long; they are not constant in adversity and apostatize. The defection of the second group implies that they are no better off than the first. (c) Those who listen to the word of God but really attain to no maturity in Christian life. These persons begin by listening to it, but are distracted by varied concerns of worldly life and fail to bring their listening to a fruitful term. (d) Those who listen to the word of God with an openness of mind (or heart) and mature to a full Christian life. The word of God elicits from them the best of human reactions, an attitude of nobility, generosity, and mature fruition. Two things characterize them: they retain the word and persistently bear the fruit of it within them. It is not enough that one listen to the word of God "with joy" (v. 13); more is expected of the mature Christian. The Lucan form of the interpretation puts more emphasis on faith and perseverance than the Marcan. Finally, even though the interpretation makes nothing of the point of the original parable itself, the assured success at the eschatological harvest, it should not be so read as if the seed sown meets with more failure than success (three groups vs. one group), for the hundredfold yield is completely passed over in the interpretation.

It is also significant that, though we are dealing with one of the parables of growth in the Synoptic tradition and one could see ecclesial dimensions in the interpretation of the parable, especially in the Lucan form of it, the extent to which it is intended to have such reference is debatable. Groups of human beings are envisaged, and the fourth group is intended to be the model for the Christian community; but all of this is proposed here by indirection. B. Gerhardsson (in dependence on L. Cerfaux and J. Dupont) has stressed that in the Lucan interpretation the atmosphere is not that of the scribal schools but rather that of the young missionary church in its fight for the faith and about the faith (*NTS* 14 [1967-1968] 183). The emphasis is on "faith," "trial," "persistence," and "constancy." These are, of course, group concerns, but they do not yet say "church." The awareness of that comes only in Luke's second volume, Acts, where the emphasis on hearing the word of God in an organized community comes to the fore.

NOTES

8 11. *This is the meaning of the parable.* Lit. "but this is the parable." The Lucan formula, in effect, identifies the interpretation of the parable with the parable itself.

The seed is the word of God. The Lucan identification is more explicit than the Marcan, "the farmer sows the word." For the almost peculiarly Lucan use of "the word of God," see NOTE on 5:1. *Sporos*, "seed," is used because of the Lucan addition in 8:5 (see above). In the Matthean form (13:19) it becomes "the word of the kingdom," a formulation suiting the theme of that chapter. It is interesting to compare here 2 Esdr 9:31, "Now look, I am sowing my law in you, and it will bear fruit in you, and through it you will be glorified forever." See further C.-P. März, *Das Wort Gottes*.

12. *Those along the footpath.* The interpretation should continue with "that sown along the footpath," but Luke immediately casts the sentence into the plural as *hoi de*, thinking of the coming personal predicate, "the ones who listen to it." He is influenced by Mark 4:15 (*houtoi de*).

the devil. See NOTE on 4:2. Luke substitutes this Greek name for the Semitic *satanas* of Mark. To the devil is ascribed a power over human "hearts."

for fear they might believe and find salvation. Lit. "lest, believing, they might be saved." This is a Lucan redactional addition to the interpretation; Mark simply noted that Satan took away the seed sown. The parallel mention of "faith" and "salvation" fits in with his emphasis on "the word of God." "Faith" will again appear in v. 13. See NOTE on 8:10 about the relation of this addition to the omission of the last clause of Isa 6:10. Cf. Acts 16:31, for a similar correlation of faith and salvation.

13. *accept the word with joy.* The "joy" refers to the first enthusiasm of conversion.

having no root. This phrase is derived by Luke from the Marcan source, omitting the phrase, "in themselves." But Luke is inconsistent, for he has made no mention of "root" in the parable itself and has limited his description to a lack of moisture (8:6).

they believe for a while. Luke adds the idea of faith again (see v. 12), but he changes the Marcan compound adjective *proskairos,* "transitory, ephemeral," used of human beings, to a better expression in a prep. phrase, *pros kairon.* See NOTE on 4:13.

in time of trial. Luke has deliberately substituted for Mark's *thlipsis,* "(eschatological) tribulation" and *diōgmos,* "persecution," a term, *peirasmos,* usually translated "temptation," but which really refers to apostasy from Christian life, when constancy would be called for. See further S. Brown, *Apostasy and Perseverance,* 12-16; L. Cerfaux, "Fructifier," 481-491.

they . . . fall away. Luke has substituted *aphistantai,* "they stand off," for the Marcan *skandalizontai,* "they stumble," which really denotes a less radical break than Luke's reference to defection. He thus shows that he has little tolerance for enthusiasts or fadists who espouse a cause as long as it suits their pleasure.

14. *listened.* For Luke the reaction of "faith" begins with a "listening," but this and the description of the following group of people make it clear that for him faith involves much more. For a Pauline way of phrasing the initial movement of faith, see Rom 10:17.

who in their pursuit of life are choked off by anxieties, riches, and pleasures. Lit. "who, while advancing (in age?), are choked off by cares, wealth, and pleasures of life." Luke has retained the Marcan mention of three distractions to commitment, but he has changed the wording slightly. With these distractions one may compare the "three nets of Belial" in which the author of the *Damascus Document* saw all Israel ensnared (CD 4:15 - 5:10): defilement of the sanctuary, wealth, and taking two women in one's lifetime. See H. Kosmala, "The Three Nets."

they bring nothing to maturity. Lit. "they bear to term no ripe fruit." The vital faith of the start does not continue to the finish, but is found stunted instead.

15. *hold on to it with a noble and generous mind.* Lit. "hold it fast with a good and noble heart." Luke's use of "heart" recalls that in 8:12 above; it is the OT term for the seat of human reaction to God and his promptings. Luke joins to it the classic Greek humanistic expression of noble generosity, what is "beautiful" and "good" (*kardia kalē kai agathē,* see W. Grundmann, *TDNT* 3. 540-543). This combination (*kalos kai agathos*) is found only here in the NT; but it occurs in the LXX (Tob 5:14; 2 Macc 15:12; 4 Macc 4:1); cf. Josephus, *Ant.* 4.4,3 § 67; 10.10,1 § 188. On "the seed in good soil," see p. 124.

they yield a crop through their persistence. Lit. "they bear fruit in constancy" (in face of adversity).

BIBLIOGRAPHY (8:11-15)
(in addition to that given in 8:4-8 and 8:9-10)

Brown, S. *Apostasy and Perseverance*, 119-125.

Cerfaux, L. "Fructifier en supportant (l'épreuve): A propos de Luc, viii, 15," *RB* 64 (1957) 481-491.

Gervais, J. "Les épines étouffantes: Luc 8, 14-15," *Église et théologie* 4 (1973) 5-39.

Kodell, J. " 'The Word of God Grew': The Ecclesial Tendency of *Logos* in Acts 1,7 [*sic* (read 6:7)]; 12,24; 19,20," *Bib* 55 (1974) 505-519.

Kosmala, H. "The Three Nets of Belial: A Study in the Terminology of Qumran and the New Testament," *ASTI* 4 (1965) 91-113.

März, C.-P. *Das Wort Gottes bei Lukas: Die lukanische Worttheologie als Frage an die neuere Lukasforschung* (Erfurter theologische Schriften 11; Leipzig: St. Benno-V., 1974) 57-59.

Wenham, D. "The Interpretation of the Parable of the Sower," *NTS* 20 (1973-1974) 299-319.

Zedda, S. *"Poreuomenoi sympnigontai* (Lc 8,14)," *Euntes docete* 27 (1974) 92-108.

Zingg, P. *Das Wachsen der Kirche: Beiträge zur Frage der lukanischen Redaktion und Theologie* (Orbis biblicus et orientalis 3; Göttingen: Vandenhoeck und Ruprecht; Fribourg: Universitätsverlag, 1974) 76-100.

41. THE PARABLE OF THE LAMP
(8:16-18)

8 16 "No one lights a lamp and then covers it with a pot or puts it under a bed; rather, one puts it on a stand so that those who come in can see the light. 17 For there is nothing secret that will not become public, nothing hidden that will not be made known or brought to light. 18 So take care how you listen. For the one who has will be given more; and the one who has nothing will be deprived even of what he thinks he has."

COMMENT

The Lucan section on Jesus' preaching of the word of God continues with the so-called parable of the lamp (8:16-18). This is really a misnomer, since the verses are a series of three sayings of Jesus, most likely of independent origin, which have been strung together. R. Bultmann (*HST*, 81) calls them "double-stranded meshallim" or proverbs related to those of the OT. He also notes that they really sound like proverbs of secular wisdom (*HST*, 98). To what extent they represent authentic sayings of Jesus is hard to say. They form a unit in the Marcan chapter on parables (4:21-25), where the evangelist has put them because he probably regarded them as parables (see J. Jeremias, *The Parables*, 41). However, Matthew has omitted them in his parable discourse, save for the last one (13:12). V. Taylor (*FGT*, 90-92) stresses the artificial arrangement of the sayings, comparing them to proverbs in Ecclesiastes or Sirach.

Luke is here following Mark and appends these sayings to the interpretation of the parable of the sowed seed, just as Mark did. In view of the fact that Luke has omitted the following parables from his Marcan source, viz. that of the seed growing silently (4:26-29) and of the mustard seed (4:30-32), along with the conclusion of the chapter (4:33-34), we may wonder why he has retained this material. His retention of it makes clear not only his dependence on Mark at this point, but even his concern to relate these sayings closely to this section of his Gospel. For he not only drops the usual Marcan introductory phrase, which tends to highlight the isolated character of these sayings, but he has joined them to 8:15 with a *de* and introduces a *gar,* "for," in 8:18b to tie the material more closely together. In order to secure an even tighter consistency, Luke has omitted two sayings which are found in Mark (4:23, "If anyone has ears to hear, let him hear," probably because he has already used that in 8:8; and 4:24b, a saying about the measure, a form of which has already appeared in 6:38 [=Matt 7:2]).

The three sayings which Luke uses here appear elsewhere in his Gospel in a slightly different form. Verse 16 has a parallel in 11:33 (=Matt 5:15); v. 17 is a form of 12:2 (=Matt 10:26); and v. 18b-c is a form of 19:26 (=Matt 25:29). In other words, we meet here three Lucan "doublets" (see p. 81 above). In these verses the form is derived from Mark (shown by the sequence and relation to the preceding matter), whereas the later verses come from "Q," but the Q-forms have somewhat influenced his use of the Marcan forms. T. Schramm (*Der Markus-Stoff,* 23-24) notes the dependence of Luke on Mark in these sayings, but he prefers to think that the form met here is influenced by some other source that Luke has had. This is unnecessary.

Each of these sayings is further found in the Coptic *Gos. Thom.* § 33, 5-6, 41, and the second is partly preserved in the earlier Greek recension of it (OxyP 654:29-31, 38-40 [see *ESBNT,* 381-387]).

The first saying about not concealing a lamp just lighted (8:16) is not identical with Mark 4:21 or with Luke 11:33, but in the present form it has been clearly influenced by the latter. *Gos. Thom.* § 33b reads: "For no one lights a lamp and puts it under a bushel-measure; nor does one put it in a hidden place. Rather, one sets it on a lampstand so that everyone who comes in and goes out sees its light." This Coptic version (§ 33b) has been joined to another saying about preaching from the housetops by a catchword bond, *maaje,* which in the first saying (§ 33a) means "ear," but in the second means "bushel-measure." Since this is possible only in Coptic, it is obvious that the joining of the two sayings is not original; unfortunately, no counterpart of it is found in the Greek recension. Otherwise the Coptic saying about the lamp is clearly dependent on Luke, and even more on 11:33 than on 8:16. See W. Schrage, *Das Verhältnis,* 82; J. Ménard, *L'Evangile selon Thomas,* 131.

The second saying about secrets becoming public (8:17) is largely dependent on Mark 4:22, but one detail (their being "made known") is undoubtedly influenced by the "Q" form in 12:2. Moreover, Luke omits 4:23, which merely repeats Mark 4:9. *Gos. Thom.* § 5b reads: "For there is nothing hidden that will not become manifest." The Greek recension of OxyP 654:31 adds, "and (nothing) buried that will no[t be raised up]" (see *ESBNT,* 381-384). *Gos. Thom.* § 6d has still another form, "For there is nothing hidden that will not become manifest and nothing covered that will remain without being uncovered." Here the

Coptic and Greek forms of the saying which correspond to what is in the Synoptic tradition are dependent on Luke 8:17a. See Schrage, *Das Verhältnis,* 35.

The third saying about more being given to the one who has (8:18) is dependent on Mark 4:25, save for the Lucan redactional addition ("of what he thinks he has"). It is not influenced by the "Q" form in 19:26. *Gos. Thom.* § 41 reads: "(As for) the one who has (something) in his hand, they will give him (more); and (as for) the one who has not, even the little that he has they will take away from him." In this case, the Coptic saying, save for its own additions ("in his hand," and "the little"), is derived from Mark 4:25. See Schrage, *Das Verhältnis,* 96-97.

At first, it seems that the three sayings of Jesus are rather obvious. But they have to be understood in their present Lucan context, viz. that of Jesus' preaching the word of God, which began with v. 4. In the preceding passage Luke had contrasted hearers who listened to the word "with joy" (v. 13 [=Mark 4:16]) to those who listened to it "with a noble and generous mind" and "with persistence" (v. 15 [his own redactional addition]). Now in v. 18a he says, "Take care *how* you listen," which picks up the modes used above. He has probably omitted the parable of the seed growing silently because it ill accords with the emphasis that he is putting on the mode of listening to the word. It sounds too automatic for him. The sayings, then, serve to heighten the way one should listen to the word. Verse 16 emphasizes that one does not light a lamp in order to hide it; it is put on the stand so that it will shine forth. And v. 17, closely connected to v. 16, explains that what is secret will become public; the very result of secrecy is that it will some day become manifest (recall 8:10c). This manifestation is closely joined to why one lights a lamp and puts it on a stand. On the heels of this comes Jesus' counsel about *how* one listens to the word. Closely joined to it is v. 18b, the saying about the mature disposition with which one listens will be the reason why the hearer matures still more. To the maturity that one has still more will be given. Thus the lighting of the lamp describes the conduct of the Christian disciple: his/her way of listening to the word must bear fruit. The lamp is not lighted in order to have its light hidden away; rather, it is to shine on those who enter. The gift granted to the disciples to know the secrets of the kingdom is destined by God to a wide and public broadcasting. Thus the mature Christian, because of his retention of the word of God and his persistence, becomes a light to "the others." This is an important notion for Luke, who sees the role of the Christian especially as that of a witness (see 24:48; Acts 1:8—and the development of this theme in Acts as a whole).

The question has been raised whether Jesus does not mean that his own preaching is a light to those who enter (see Luke 2:32), a light which must become publicly manifested. This is not a wholly impossible interpretation, but it ill suits v. 18a (with its emphasis on the *mode* of hearing) and v. 18b (with its stress on how the little one thinks one has will be taken away). It is better to understand the whole complex of the three sayings as bearing on the mode of listening to the word of God expected of disciples. This seems to be the Lucan redactional thrust.

NOTES

8 16. *No one lights a lamp.* Luke has suppressed the Marcan introductory phrase, *kai elegen autois,* "and he said to them." He has also changed the inelegant Marcan form of the saying, eliminating the question, "A lamp does not come, does it, in order to be put under a bushel-measure. . . ." Cf. Luke 11:33.

and then covers it with a pot. Luke's redaction changes the cover from the specific "bushel-measure" (*modion*) of Mark 4:21 to a generic term, "vessel" (*skeuos,* which has a wide variety of meanings, "object, gear, equipment, vessel, pot, instrument"). Covering the lamp with a pot was probably a way of extinguishing it safely. The lamp should be understood as the circular, spouted, partly covered oil lamp, made of terracotta, that was common in Palestine in Hellenistic and Roman times (see *IDB* 3. 63-64).

or puts it under a bed. I.e. where its glow would be concealed.

on a stand. I.e. on a portable holder that sometimes held several oil lamps. The lamp must be put on high so that its effect will be had. For an illustration of a Herodian lamp on a lamp-stand, see *BA* 42 (1979) 192.

so that those who come in can see the light. This clause is not found in P[75] or B (two important ms. copies of Luke), but most modern critical editions of the Greek NT include it. Has it been introduced because of Luke 11:33? The Matthean parallel to that verse does not have it either.

In any case, it is clearly a Lucan redactional addition to the Marcan source material. He envisages a house with an entrance or vestibule, not of a style particularly common in Palestine, but otherwise found in the Greco-Roman world of the time. See C. H. Dodd, "Changes," 40-41; J. Jeremias, "Die Lampe," 237-240. This interpretation has been called in question by H. Schürmann ("Lukanische Reflexionen," 225 n. 43); but his objections have been answered by J. Dupont ("La lampe," 48 n. 17).

"Those who come in" are to be understood as among "the others" (8:10), who have not yet been accorded knowledge of the mysteries of the kingdom, but have to be attracted by the power of the light.

17. *there is nothing secret that will not become public.* This verse is closely related to the foregoing pericope by the conj. *gar,* "for." Luke has, however, simplified the clumsy Marcan conditional-final clause (strangely introduced by *ean mē hina*) by using a simple relative, "that."

This saying is loosely joined to the foregoing one by a free association of contrasts: light/darkness, secret/public, hidden/made known. In the present Lucan context the contrast emphasizes that even the secrets of the kingdom have to be divulged.

will not be made known. Another Lucan redactional addition to the Marcan material, but influenced by the saying in Luke 12:2. See NOTE there.

18. *take care how you listen.* Whereas Mark 4:24a reads *blepete tí akouete,* "attend to what you hear," Luke has changed the conj. which introduces the indir. question, emphasizing the *mode* of listening rather than its object. This is an important modification of the Marcan source; it manifests a Lucan concern that the reader understand the modes of hearing presented in 8:12,15.

the one who has will be given more. In itself, this saying reflects practical wisdom about wealth or possessions. In the present Lucan context, however, it has nothing to do with money or material possessions. It is closely related to the foregoing saying about how to listen (through the repetition of the conj. *gar*): whoever "hears the word profitably will profit yet more; he who hears carelessly will lose even what he seems to have" (J. M. Creed, *Gospel,* 117). So Luke epitomizes what he regards as the essential reaction of a disciple to the preached word of God. On the construction here, see p. 124 above.

what he thinks he has. Luke has introduced a modal expression which complicates the understanding of the saying. Mark 4:25b reads simply *ho echei,* "(what) he has." This is also found in Luke 19:26 (=Matt 25:29). Here Luke introduces a modality, *ho dokei echein,* "what he thinks he has" or "what he seems to have." The Lucan redaction in this passage stresses the *apparent* value and character of the possessions, not the apparent possession of them.

BIBLIOGRAPHY (8:16-18)

Bover, J. M. " 'Nada hay encubierto que no se descubra,' " *EstBíb* 13 (1954) 319-323.

Derrett, J. D. M. "Law in the New Testament: The Parable of the Talents and Two Logia," *ZNW* 56 (1965) 184-195.

Dodd, C. H. "Changes of Scenery in Luke," *ExpTim* 33 (1921-1922) 40-41.

Dupont, J. "La lampe sur le lampadaire dans l'évangile de saint Luc (VIII,16; XI,33)," *Au service de la parole de Dieu: Mélanges offerts à Monseigneur André-Marie Charue* (Gembloux: Duculot, 1969) 43-59.

Gnilka, J. *Die Verstockung Israels: Isaias 6,9-10 in der Theologie der Synoptiker* (SANT 3; Munich: Kösel, 1961) 125-126.

Hahn, F. "Die Worte vom Licht Lk 11,33-36," in *Orientierung an Jesus: Zur Theologie der Synoptiker: Für Josef Schmidt* (eds. P. Hoffmann et al.; Freiburg im B.: Herder, 1973) 107-138, esp. pp. 121-124.

Jeremias, J. "Die Lampe unter dem Scheffel," *ZNW* 39 (1940) 237-240; reprinted in *Abba: Studien zur neutestamentlichen Theologie und Zeitgeschichte* (Göttingen: Vandenhoeck und Ruprecht, 1966) 99-102.

Kennedy, H. A. A. "The Composition of Mark iv. 21-25: A Study in the Synoptic Problem," *ExpTim* 25 (1913-1914) 301-305.

Krämer, M. " 'Ihr seid das Salz der Erde . . . Ihr seid das Licht der Welt: Die vielgestaltige Wirkkraft des Gotteswortes der heiligen Schrift für das Leben der Kirche aufgezeigt am Beispiel Mt 5, 13-16," *MTZ* 28 (1977) 133-157, esp. pp. 143-147.

Schneider, G. "Das Bildwort von der Lampe: Zur Traditionsgeschichte eines Jesus-Wortes," *ZNW* 61 (1970) 183-209, esp. pp. 203-206.

Schramm, T. *Der Markus-Stoff*, 23-26.

Schürmann, H. "Lukanische Reflexionen über die Wortverkündigung in Lk 8, 4-21," in *Wahrheit und Verkündigung: Michael Schmaus zum 70. Geburtstag* (2 vols.; eds. L. Scheffczyk et al.; Paderborn: F. Schöningh, 1967) 1. 213-228.

42. JESUS' MOTHER AND BROTHERS ARE THE REAL HEARERS

(8:19-21)

8 ¹⁹ Then there came to him his mother and his brothers, but they
were unable to come close because of the crowd of people. ²⁰ When
it was reported to him, "Your mother and your brothers are standing
outside and want to see you," ²¹ he said to them in reply, "My mother
and my brothers, they are the ones who listen to the word of God and
act on it."

COMMENT

To conclude this section of the Gospel dealing with the word of God,
Luke introduces a scene (8:19-21) that he had omitted earlier from his
Marcan source, as he resumed its sequence at 8:4. H. Conzelmann (*Theology*, 48) has said that it is introduced here because it follows on the
mention of the Galilean women (8:2-3) and on 8:9-10, where what it
means to be a disciple is described for the first time. But this cannot be
so, since if Luke saw any connection between this passage and the
Galilean women (8:1-3), it is unintelligible why he did not introduce it
immediately. The reason why Luke introduces this story here is that he
sees it in a light that is quite different from Mark. He transposed Mark
3:31-35, indeed; but he has also radically changed the meaning of it.

The Lucan redaction of this episode is seen not only in what he makes
of the pronouncement in v. 21, but especially in his omission of a related
Marcan passage (3:20-21). In the latter "his own" (*hoi par' autou*) have
come to get Jesus because they have considered him to be "beside himself" (*exestē*). Many commentators have related these Marcan verses—
and rightly so—to 3:31-35; there "his own" have to be understood as
Jesus' natural family. (Note the shift in translation to this sense in the
second edition of the *RSV* NT [1972].) In Mark 3:20-21 Jesus' relatives
are not depicted as among his disciples, but as reacting negatively to him.
Moreover, when Jesus is told in Mark 3:31-35 that his mother, brothers,
and sisters are standing outside summoning him, he looks around at those
sitting in a circle about him and says, "Here are my mother and my

brothers; whoever does the will of God is brother and sister and mother to me." Thus the Marcan Jesus substitutes for his natural family his disciples—what has been called his "spiritual family." Nowhere else in the Marcan Gospel do we find either his mother or his kin among his disciples; but Mark does not go so far as to say, as is done in John 7:5, "even his brothers did not believe in him."

Luke omits this negative notice of Mark 3:20-21, as does Matthew. He presents Jesus' mother and his brothers (omitting the sisters completely) as model disciples. They are the prime examples of those who listen to the word of God "with a noble and generous mind" (8:15). See further Luke 11:27-28; Acts 1:14. In this mode of presenting them, the Lucan Jesus' reply does not imply a denial of family ties or a criticism of his kin; it does imply that another relationship to himself can transcend even that of family ties. Genuine relation to him consists not so much in descent from common ancestry as a voluntary attachment involving the acceptance of God's word, which he preaches, as the norm of one's life. Here Jesus' mother and brothers are shown to be prime examples of that relation.

Form-critically viewed, the episode is a pronouncement-story (V. Taylor, *FGT*, 71-72) or a biographical apophthegm (R. Bultmann, *HST*, 29-30).

A form of this saying is preserved in the Coptic *Gos. Thom.* § 99: "The disciples said to him, 'Your brothers and your mother are standing outside.' He said to them, 'Those here who do the will of my Father are my brothers and my mother; these are the ones who will enter the kingdom of my Father.' "

NOTES

8 19. *there came to him his mother.* Only in the infancy narrative is Mary named in this Gospel; cf. 11:27-28. The tradition at this part does not name her; nor does John's Gospel. Cf. Mark 6:3; Matt 13:55. To describe her coming to Jesus, Luke makes use of one of his favorite words, *paregeneto* (see p. 111 above). No reason is given for her (or their) arrival on the scene at this time. Here in the Lucan Gospel this is owing to the transposition of Marcan material.

and his brothers. Luke takes over this phrase from Mark 3:31, omitting, however, the "sisters" of 3:32 (cf. Mark 3:35). The mention of mother, brothers, and sisters in the Marcan context suggests at first sight that blood brothers and blood sisters are meant. Indeed, Mark 6:3 mentions four brothers of Jesus by name: James, Joses, Judas, and Simon (a verse that Luke omitted in his story of Jesus' visit to Nazareth; see 4:22). Here again, *adelphos* would seem to mean "blood brother." But the matter is not so simple in the Marcan

Gospel. For the word *adelphos* can express other relationships: "neighbor" (Matt 5:22-24), "coreligionist" (Rom 9:3 [=*syngenēs*, "kin"]), "stepbrother" (Mark 6:17-18, unless the evangelist has erred there about the relationship of Philip to Herod [see *JBC*, art. 75, § 140]), "relative" or "kinsman" (so at times in the LXX: Gen 13:8; 14:14; 24:27; 29:12). The LXX usage may reflect the broader sense of Hebrew *'āh* or Aramaic *'āhā'*, "brother, kinsman." Thus an Aramaic papyrus letter bears the opening formula, "To my son from your brother," as a father writes to his son who is away on a caravan (see *JNES* 21 [1962] 16-17). In 1QapGen 2:9 Bit-enosh addresses her husband Lamech as "O my brother and my lord." The same is found occasionally in Greek texts; see J. J. Collins, *TS* 5 (1944) 484-494; MM, 8-9. In the Marcan texts the sense of *adelphos* is complicated, not because of those passages in themselves which seem simple, but because of 15:40,47; 16:1. There Mark mentions among the women standing apart from the cross a "Mary, the mother of James the Little and Joses." Yet it is hardly likely that Mark would mean thereby the mother of the person hanging on the cross. Why would he have used such a circumlocution? But, then, since it is not unlikely that the James and the Joses of Mark 15:40 are the same as those of 6:3, what is the degree of kinship expressed there by *adelphos* (and also in Mark 3:32)? See further J. Blinzler, *Die Brüder*, 73-82; *MNT*, 65-72.

The sense in which Luke would have understood the *adelphoi* of Jesus in 8:19, as he took over Mark 3:32, cannot really be determined. It could have meant for him "relative" just as easily as "blood brother." It should be recalled that the only virginity of Mary of which he speaks in the Gospel concerns her status prior to the conception of Jesus (1:27,34). As he can tolerate the use of "son of Joseph" for Jesus in 4:22, it is not surprising that he would speak of Jesus' "brothers" here; he may have known of the appellation given to James, which is found even outside of the gospel tradition (Gal 1:19).

Aside from the Marcan problem discussed above, there is no indication in the NT itself about Mary as *aei parthenos*, "ever virgin." This belief in one form or another can only be traced to the second century A.D. (see *MNT*, chap. 9). Jerome thought that *adelphos* could mean "cousin," but this is almost certainly to be ruled out as the NT meaning, since there was a good word for "cousin," *anepsios*, found in Col 4:10.

Finally, *pace* G. B. Caird (*Gospel of St Luke*, 119) the passage loses none of its point if *adelphoi* is understood as "relatives" instead of "blood brothers," since the sense still comes through about Jesus' relatives as hearers of the word of God.

20. *are standing outside*. Since Luke retains the reason (because of the crowd of the people), there is no cause to think that he implies some pejorative sense in this expression, e.g. that they are outsiders. G. Schneider (*Evangelium nach Lukas*, 188) misunderstands this phrase; Luke has not omitted it, and there is really no difference in sense between it and Mark's phrase, which he incorporates into his version.

want to see you. Conzelmann (*Theology*, 48) tries to relate this phrase to Luke 9:9b, where Herod is said to be seeking to see Jesus. He accordingly thinks that Jesus' relatives have come "to see miracles." This is farfetched; there is not a hint in the Lucan text that this is meant. It is even less true that "the relatives are excluded from playing any essential part in the life of Jesus and therefore also in the Church" (ibid.). What is said by Conzelmann suits the Marcan Gospel; but it cannot be sustained for Luke-Acts. E. E. Ellis (*Gospel*, 127) has uncritically accepted this from Conzelmann. See the COMMENT.

21. *My mother and my brothers.* No article is used before these nouns, and A. Plummer (*Gospel*, 224) interprets this phrase as the predicate: " 'Mother to Me and brethren to Me,' i.e. equal to such, equally dear." This completely misses the point. The phrase is actually a nom. absol. (*casus pendens*) resumed by *houtoi*, "(as for) my mother and my brothers, *they* are the ones who listen. . . ." So runs the literal translation of Luke's Greek, other attempts to interpret these words notwithstanding.

who listen to the word of God and act on it. This is the Lucan redaction of Mark 3:35 ("whoever does the will of God, that one is my brother and sister and mother"). It identifies Jesus' real relatives with those "who do the will of God." Luke has adapted the criterion of discipleship to suit this section of his Gospel, especially to 8:11b,15 (hearing the word of God and bearing fruit); his emphasis is thus quite different. J. M. Creed (*Gospel*, 118) is guilty of understatement when he says that the Lucan narrative "at the least lessens the impression of disharmony between Jesus and his relatives." Luke, in fact, identifies them. Ellis (*Gospel*, 127) completely misses the point in ascribing to Luke what is true of the Marcan parallel. Jesus' relatives may have no priority in the kingdom because of their physical descent; but here in Luke Jesus makes those of physical descent models for those who hear the word of God and keep it.

BIBLIOGRAPHY (8:19-21)

Blinzler, J. *Die Brüder und Schwestern Jesu* (SBS 21; Stuttgart: Katholisches Bibelwerk, 1967).

Brown, R. E. et al., eds. *Mary in the New Testament* (New York: Paulist; Philadelphia: Fortress, 1978) 167-170.

März, C.-P. *Das Wort Gottes bei Lukas*, 67-68.

F. THE PROGRESSIVE REVELATION OF JESUS' POWER

Jesus' mighty power continues to manifest itself against the
evils that afflict disciples and other human beings; it is
shared with his followers

43. THE CALMING OF THE STORM
(8:22-25)

8 22 As he and his disciples got into a boat one day, he happened to
say to them, "Let us cross over to the other side of the lake." So they
pushed off, 23 and as they sailed along, he fell asleep. A sudden squall
came down upon the lake, and they were in serious danger, for they
were being swamped. 24 The disciples came and woke him up, saying,
"Master, Master, we are lost!" Jesus awoke and charged the wind and
the surging deep; they subsided, and a calm ensued. 25 Then he said to
them, "Where is your faith?" In deep awe and wonder they said to
one another, "Who can this be, since he gives his commands even to
the winds and the waves, and they obey him?"

COMMENT

A new section of Luke's description of Jesus' Galilean ministry now begins. It concentrates on manifestations of Jesus' power, beginning with
several miracle stories (8:22-25; 8:26-39; 8:40-48; 8:49-56) and ending
with the sending out of the Twelve "to proclaim the kingdom and to
heal" (9:2). The introductory verse in this section (8:22) clearly breaks
with what has immediately preceded.

The sequence of Lucan episodes in this section of the Gospel makes it
clear that Luke is here dependent on "Mk" in the next five passages, with
one transposition. By and large, he is following and redacting Mark
4:35 - 6:13, but he has already transposed Mark 6:1-6 for use in
4:16-30. It has often been suggested that Mark 4:35 - 5:43 reflects a pre-

Marcan complex of miracle-stories (see R. Bultmann, *HST*, 210; V. Taylor, *FGT*, 39), which Mark has inherited and made use of. In any case, Luke has derived his material in this section from "Mk."

The first miracle-story is that of the calming of the storm (8:22-25), derived from Mark 4:35-41. Attempts have been made to regard it as a "crass transformation" of Jesus' walking on the waters and to explain both of them as variants of a post-Easter appearance of the risen Christ (J. Kreyenbühl). Even Bultmann (*HST*, 215, 230-234, 240) saw reason to question the post-Easter origin of this episode, classing it rather as a nature miracle originating in a Palestinian tradition.

In Luke's reworking of Mark 4:35-41, v. 22 is clearly redactional. It not only severs the new episode from the immediately preceding, but introduces the mention of the boat immediately. The reason for this modification is that in the Marcan Gospel this episode presupposes the beginning of the parable discourse, where Jesus was "by the side of the sea" and got into a boat because of the great crowd. Mark 4:35 recalls that boat. Luke, having omitted that introduction in 8:4 (because of 5:1), now has to change the setting of the miracles that follow. So we find Jesus getting into a boat and making for the other side of the lake. In the course of the following verses Luke further omits Marcan details, many of which are not essential to the story (e.g. Jesus' taking leave of the crowd; the "other boats"; Jesus' being asleep in the stern, on a pillow; his words of rebuke, "Peace, be calm," and the disciples' cowardice and great fear). But the story ends in Luke's version, as in Mark's, with a question about his identity. The last question was undoubtedly secondary in the Marcan form (and perhaps even in the pre-Marcan tradition); but Luke retains it because it serves a purpose—it foreshadows a crucial question that Herod will be made to ask in 9:9.

The story preserves the essential form of a miracle account: (a) the setting and description of the squall; (b) the request for aid (after the disciples awaken Jesus); (c) Jesus' word of command (rebuking the winds and the waves); (d) the effect (the subsiding of the winds and the ensuing calm); and (e) the reaction of the disciples.

This Lucan episode manifests Jesus in his majestic power, as a miracle-worker commanding winds and waves. The emphasis is now not so much on his preaching word, but on his word of power. His ministry began "with the power of the Spirit" or "of the Lord" (4:14; cf. 4:36; 5:17). Now it is depicted in action, being used to bring deliverance and safety to his own disciples. It is a word of power that delivers from a natural cataclysm, from evil manifesting itself against his disciples in a physical way. His word in 8:21 implied a command about the doing of the word of God; now his word is a direct command to evil itself.

But the secondary ending of the episode, already present in Mark 4:40, relates the disciples' "faith" to the miracle itself. Jesus' remark to them is not a word of consolation or of calming of fear; it goes rather to the heart of the matter. A disciple of Jesus, faced even with the worst, must realize where his basic relation to God and Jesus really lies. Jesus' comment thus stands in contrast to the reaction that might have been recorded, viz. amazement about his triumph over nature or about the majesty of God (contrast 9:43). However, the Lucan form of Jesus' words to the disciples takes some of the edge off his reply; the sternness of his answer in Mark 4:40 corresponds to the disciples' query in v. 38c whether he cared about them or not.

In picking up this piece of Synoptic tradition from Mark, Luke has preserved an early Christian view of Jesus being depicted in a manner not unlike Yahweh of the OT. Commentators have often thought that lurking behind this early Christian presentation of him was Yahweh's mastery over the seas and waters in such passages as Pss 18:16; 29:3-4; 65:7; 89:9; 104:6-7; 106:9, and especially 107:23-32. If this is true, then this miracle also has a symbolic value for the role of Jesus' power in human lives. As Yahweh established order over chaos and rescued his people from watery disasters, so now Jesus is presented as having a similar role in their destiny.

Parallels to this story of Jesus' calming the storm have been at times pointed out. Thus the arrogance of Antiochus IV Epiphanes, who thought that he "could command the waves of the sea" (2 Macc 9:8); the story of Jonah in the OT; the story of a Jewish boy on a pagan boat, who invoked Yahweh's help against a storm, when the prayers of the pagans to their own gods had failed (*y. Berakot* 9. 13b [Str-B, 1. 452]); or R. Gamaliel's prayer to calm a storm (*b. Baba Meṣi'a* 59b). Luke presents another parallel in the story of Paul (Acts 27:8-44), in which the Apostle is depicted largely as the cause of the deliverance of the 276 persons after the shipwreck. Because of such parallels readers have often thought that the Gospel accounts of Jesus' calming the winds and the waves are merely literary dependents. But in all of them there are elements that differ radically—e.g. a moral that is being inculcated (in the case of Jonah or R. Gamaliel); the answer to prayer (e.g. in the case of the Jewish boy or Paul); etc. If there is literary dependence, one has to recognize the obviously christological thrust of the story in its Synoptic form: Jesus delivers by a word of power, commanding winds and waves.

Faced with such a miracle-story in the gospel tradition, one is further tempted to ask to what extent it is mythological. It is, indeed, seeking to express in human words an aspect of the impact that Jesus of Nazareth made on his contemporaries. The symbolism of the story comes through, no matter what one says about its historicity. Here one touches on the problem: the authenticity of the miracles of Jesus narrated in the Gospels (see p. 542 above). From the historian's point of view, one can only say that there is no way to prove or disprove it.

NOTES

8 22. *As he and his disciples got into a boat one day.* Lit. "it happened, on one of the days, (while) he was getting into a boat, and his disciples (too), that he said to them." Two (or possibly three) Lucan constructions reveal his redaction of this transitional verse: *en mia tōn . . . , egeneto de + kai + finite verb,* and (possibly) unstressed *kai autos* (see pp. 121, 119, 120 above). Some mss. (e.g. P75) omit the *autos* so that the text would then rather read: "it happened, on one of the days, that he got into a boat." This minor variant scarcely changes the sense of the transition. Luke has given the miracle a vague temporal setting and suppressed the mention of the late hour of the day (see Mark 4:35).

and his disciples. In the Lucan form of the story this phrase would mean the Twelve and the women of 8:1-3; cf. 8:9. This should be noted in contrast to the vague Marcan "they" and "them."

the other side of the lake. Luke has added "of the lake," referring more accurately to the Gennesaret body of water as such. See NOTE on 5:1. In Mark 4:1 Jesus was said to be *para tēn thalassan,* "alongside the sea." We are not told why Jesus sought to get to the other side. H. Conzelmann (*Theology,* 49) sees in the added mention of the lake and the further omission of Marcan details a Lucan effort to situate Jesus' miracle on the edge of solitude; the lake is given a mysterious setting for the manifestation of Jesus' power. No other boat accompanies them so that the disciples alone witness the display of it.

they pushed off. Lit. "they were carried up," i.e. upon the water. Luke uses one of his favorite Greek terms, *anagein,* the technical nautical expression for "putting out" to sea or "setting sail." See Acts 13:13; 16:11; 18:21; 20:3,13; 21:1,2; 27:2,4,12,21; 28:10,11. It is occasionally used by him also in other senses (see 2:22; 4:5; Acts 7:41, etc.).

23. *as they sailed along.* Lucan redaction makes use of a gen. absol. (see p. 108, above).

he fell asleep. Luke's better sense of storytelling depicts Jesus falling asleep before the mention of the squall coming up; contrast Mark 4:37-38. His falling asleep stands in contrast to the power that he will manifest; he is subject to human fatigue.

A sudden squall. Lit. "a hurricane of wind." The descriptive gen. is really unnecessary. Lake Gennesaret in northern Galilee is surrounded by hills with gorges that pour into the lake; whereas the atmosphere is normally still, gusts of cold air from the west often sweep down the gorges and create storms on the lake. To this feature of the lake the story makes allusion. See further J. Finegan, *The Archeology of the New Testament,* 47-48.

they were being swamped. Lit. "they (Jesus and the disciples) were being filled completely." Luke speaks of the persons in the boat rather than of the boat itself. Contrast Mark 4:37.

24. *Master, master. Epistata* (see NOTE on 5:5) is substituted for the Marcan *didaskale,* "teacher," and repeated. Moreover, Luke also omits the disciples' plaintive query about Jesus' nonchalance and apparent lack of concern about his and their safety.

charged the wind and the surging deep. I.e. he rebuked or charged the spirit(s) thought to be causing the sudden squall (see NOTES on 4:35,39). Some commentators (A. Plummer, *Gospel,* 226; H. Schürmann *Lukasevangelium,* 476) seek to avoid this interpretation; but it is not evident that the evangelist was depicting the storm itself as a personal agent. One may also query Conzelmann's description of it as descending like a demon into its element (*Theology,* 49). Cf. Zech 3.2.

they subsided. Lit. "they stopped," i.e. calm ensues at the word of Jesus. See Ps 104:6-7; Nah 1:4 for a similar calming of waters by the word of Yahweh.

25. *Where is your faith?* This question in the Lucan redaction is less strong than the Marcan rebuke, "Why are you so cowardly? How (is it that) you have no faith?" The Lucan form does not say outright that the disciples lack all faith; Jesus merely asks where it is. At first sight the query of Jesus could refer to the disciples' lack of faith in God or his providence; but the following comment of the evangelist makes it clear that some form of faith in him is meant (even if that cannot yet be identified with post-Easter Christian faith). In a sense, the question is strange, because the disciples at least knew to whom they should turn in the face of the disaster that threatened them. However, the point of the episode is that their faith would be roused (perhaps in time) by a realization of the power that Jesus actually possessed.

In deep awe and wonder. Lit. "fearing, they expressed surprise." Luke has thus eliminated a Marcan Septuagintism, "they feared (with) a great fear" (Jon 1:10; 1 Macc 10:8; cf. Luke 2:9). This is the only place where Luke combines "fear" (or "awe") and "surprise." They describe the effect produced on the disciples by the miracle.

Who can this be? Lit. "who then can this be," with the illative *ara* retained from the Marcan source.

since. Or possibly "that." The conj. is *hoti.*

he gives his commands even to the winds and the waves. Lit. "he commands even the winds and the water." Luke improves Mark's Greek, which has two subjects (masc. "wind" and fem. "sea") of a sg. verb. Compare this reaction to the miracle with that in 4:36; 9:43. The disciples' question is intended to reveal to the reader the beginning of a sense of awareness in them, which may not yet be "faith," but which is leading in that direction.

BIBLIOGRAPHY (8:22-25)

Kertelge, K. *Die Wunder Jesu,* 91-100.

Kreyenbühl, J. "Der älteste Auferstehungsbericht und seine Varianten," *ZNW* 9 (1908) 257-296.

Léon-Dufour, X. "La tempête apaisée," *NRT* 87 (1965) 897-922; reprinted in *Études d'évangile* (Paris: Éditions du Seuil, 1965) 149-182.

Schenke, L. *Die Wundererzählungen des Markusevangeliums* (SBB; Stuttgart: Katholisches Bibelwerk, [1974]) 1-93.

Schille, G. "Die Seesturmerzählung Markus 4_{35-41} als Beispiel neutestamentlicher Aktualisierung," *ZNW* 56 (1965) 30-40.

Schmithals, W. *Wunder und Glaube: Eine Auslegung von Markus 4,35-6,6a* (BibS[N] 59; Neukirchen: Neukirchener, 1970).

Van der Loos, H. "The Stilling of the Storm," in *The Miracles of Jesus* (NovTSup 9; Leiden: Brill, 1965) 638-649.

44. THE GERASENE DEMONIAC
(8:26-39)

8 26 Then they came to land in the region of the Gerasenes opposite Galilee. 27 As he stepped ashore, he met a man from the town who was possessed by demons. For some time now he had worn no clothes, and not lived in a house; he had been loitering among the tombs. 28 When he saw Jesus, he screamed, lunged at him, and shouted at the top of his voice, *"What do you want with me,* Jesus,ᵃ Son of God Most High? I beg you, do not torment me." (29 Jesus was about to charge the unclean spirit to come out of the man. It had many times convulsed him; and even though he had to be bound with chains and fetters and closely watched, he would break the bonds and be driven by the demon into deserted places.) 30 Jesus asked him, "What is your name?" "Legion," he said, because many demons had entered him. 31 Now they begged Jesus not to order them off to the abyss. 32 There was feeding, nearby on the hillside, a herd of many pigs, and the demons begged him to give them leave to enter those pigs. So he gave them the order. 33 When the demons came out of the man, they entered the pigs; and the herd rushed down the steep slope into the lake and was drowned.

34 The herdsmen who saw what had happened ran off and told all about it in the town and country. 35 People came out to see what had happened. When they came to where Jesus was, they saw the man from whom the demons had departed sitting there at his feet fully clothed and sound of mind. They were naturally afraid, 36 for those who had seen how the possessed man had been delivered told them all about it. 37 The whole populace of the Gerasene countryside begged him to depart from their vicinity, so great was the fear that gripped them. Then Jesus got into a boat and made his way back. 38 The man from whom the demons had departed begged Jesus that he might stay with him; but Jesus sent him off, saying, 39 "Go back home now, and explain to people all that God has done for you." So he went back through the whole town, proclaiming all that Jesus had done for him.

ᵃ 1 Kgs 17:18

COMMENT

Jesus' mighty deed in calming the storm on the Lake of Gennesaret is followed by another miracle-story, the exorcism of the Gerasene demoniac (8:26-39). Evil threatening human beings in the form of natural cataclysms now has a counterpart in evil afflicting the psychic being of a mortal man.

The story is derived from "Mk" (5:1-20), and the differences between the Lucan and Marcan form are specifically Lucan redactions (see T. Schramm, *Der Markus-Stoff,* 126). Luke has shortened the form of the story but still presents it with one demoniac. Matthew (8:28-34) curtails it even more, but recounts it as the story of two demoniacs. Luke has transposed the details about the description of the demoniac's activity (wrenching apart the chains and fetters that people had used to try to subdue him) and omitted still others (e.g. his living day and night among the tombs, his crying aloud, and his bruising himself with stones). The Marcan direct command of exorcism becomes in Luke an indirect command (8:26), as happens with the request in v. 32. Luke has often made a clearer distinction between the demoniac and the demon(s), which is not always true of the Marcan story (cf. 5:8-10). Whereas the unclean spirit in Mark requests not to be sent "out of the country" (5:10), the demons in Luke (8:31) request not to be sent "into the abyss." Luke also omits mention of the number of the pigs involved (two thousand in Mark 5:13). See the NOTES for further minor differences.

We have already called attention to the complex of miracle-stories that Mark took over from a pre-Marcan tradition (4:25 - 5:43; see p. 726 above), to which this episode belongs in the Marcan Gospel. Recent writers have stressed that the Marcan form of this story is singularly devoid of Marcan editorial modifications (see K. Kertelge, *Die Wunder Jesu,* 101-102; P. J. Achtemeier, *JBL* 89 [1970] 275-276). What features there are in it that raise questions about layers of tradition (repetitions, doublets, afterthoughts, different vocabulary) have rather to be attributed to the development of the story in the pre-Marcan tradition; for details on this sort of analysis, which does not concern us here, see R. Pesch, "The Markan Version," 350-374.

Seven parts of the story can be distinguished in the Marcan form: (a) Jesus' arrival in the area and his meeting with the demoniac (5:1-3a); (b) the description of the demoniac's condition and symptoms (5:3b-5); (c) the demoniac's recognition of Jesus the exorcist (5:6-7); (d) the exorcism itself, with *apopompē* and *epipompē,* i.e. the motifs of "sending away" and "consignment" (5:8-13a); (e) the proof of the exit of the demons (5:13bc); (f) the reaction of spectators and others (5:14-17); and (g) the missionary conclusion (5:18-20). Despite the Lucan transition (8:29bc), his form of the story retains the same parts: (a) 8:26-27a; (b) 8:27b,29bc; (c) 8:28; (d) 8:30-32; (e) 8:33; (f) 8:34-37; (g) 8:38-39. R. Bultmann (*HST,* 210) noted that the story has all the features of the typical exorcism: in b-f above. Kertelge (*Die Wunder Jesu,* 107) has also rightly noted that even in the pre-Marcan tradition the miracle-story or exorcism had already become a missionary story (*Missionserzählung*) because of the final verses (Mark 5:18-20 or Luke 8:38-39).

What we are dealing with in this episode is not a simple miracle-story of an exorcism (compare this one with Luke 4:33-37). For the basic miracle-story has in this instance been enshrouded with elements of the fantastic and the grotesque. According to Pesch, "it presents the unsophisticated with preposterous material to feed his credulity and at the same time invites the scorn of the sceptic" ("The Markan Version," 349). It is quite an understatement to say with J. M. Creed (*The Gospel,* 120), "This is a strange story." It has always raised questions and problems that strain the imagination: Is Jesus not presented here as cruel to animals? How could he have caused the owners of the pigs such a financial loss—obviously they were not keeping two thousand pigs for display? What was a herd of two thousand swine doing in an area into which Jews like Jesus would go? How could swine be so energetic to stampede over the miles that separated them from the slope and the lake? Did Jesus really go along with the popular superstitions of his time about demons and possession? Obviously, such questions miss the point of the gospel-story itself, being recounted for a symbolic and religious purpose. The flamboyant and grotesque details of this story reveal the tendency that was beginning to be associated with basic miracle-stories in the gospel tradition, a tendency that comes to full bloom in the apocryphal gospel tradition. There one reads about the child Jesus profaning the Sabbath by making twelve clay sparrows, clapping his hands, and making them fly chirping away; then becoming enraged when one of his companions spoiled the pools of water (*Infancy Story of Thomas,* Hennecke-Schneemelcher, *NTApocrypha,* 1. 393); or how the young Jesus turned his playmates into goats (*Arabic Infancy Gospel,* ibid. 1. 409).

Bultmann is of the opinion that the story has made use of the literary motif of the "duped devil" (*HST,* 201). The demons sought to control Jesus by pronouncing his name; when asked for their own name, the demons reply not with their name, but with their number (or a pseudonym implying number). When commanded by Jesus to come out of the man (the *apopompē*), they request to be sent into the pigs instead (the *epipompē*), rather than go to the abyss. The exorcist consents, sends them, indeed, into the pigs, only to make the latter stampede to their and the demons' destruction. Thus Jesus duped the demons and "saved" the man. See further A. Wünsche, *Der Sagenkreis vom geprellten Teufel* (Leipzig: Akademischer, 1905); H. A. Kelly, "Demonology and Diabolical Temptation," *Thought* 40 (1965) 157, 165-194.

Bultmann has also asked whether the story might represent originally just a popular jest that has been applied to Jesus. It is really impossible to answer this kind of speculation to which the flamboyant and grotesque elements in it give rise. Writers like A. D. Martin have sought to save the historicity of the scene by trying to downplay the esteem the owners would have had for the pigs lost or by trying to judge their market value (*ExpTim* 25 [1913-1914] 380-381). Such attempts do not carry conviction. Nor do such psychologizing explanations as that of A. H. M'Neile (*The Gospel according to St. Matthew* [London: Macmillan, 1915] 114): If Jesus caused the pigs to stampede, he did it to confirm the man's peace of mind, to complete the miracle by giving him an optical demonstration that what had beset him had now departed forever.

At the end of the story the verses that turn it into a missionary story (Jesus' instructing the cured demoniac to proclaim what God had done for him) also show that he complied and they consequently suggest that the tradition circulated in the form of folklore (8:39). That such a folkloric, popular tradition should make its way into the canon might be surprising; but who can say that biblical inspiration, rightly understood, could not accommodate itself even to such a tradition with flamboyant and grotesque details?

The story depicts Jesus using his power to heal an unfortunate demented human being, an outcast of society, thus restoring him to soundness of mind and wholeness of life. This salvific concern is manifested, moreover, even toward one who is presumably a pagan; this the God of Israel has done for even a Gentile. Luke is at pains to relate this excursion into Gerasene territory to the Galilean ministry of Jesus, adding explicitly in 8:26 that it was "opposite Galilee," and omitting all mention of the Decapolis (contrast Mark 5:20). These two modifications thus relate the episode of the cure in pagan territory to the general Lucan geographical perspective. His concern to depict Jesus exercising his power even toward a pagan foreshadows the Lucan missionary stories among the Gentiles (especially in Acts). If Jesus is here recognized as Son of God Most High, it is important that he subdue the demons with his word. When about to order the demons to depart, he was begged by them for another solution, which he granted and thereby brought about their destruction. He appears as the mighty one, conquering the evil that afflicts the very being of an unfortunate member of the human race. The cured demoniac, who desired to stay with him, thus becomes a pagan disciple declaring throughout the whole town all that Jesus had done for him. He who cured by his word thus becomes the one proclaimed.

NOTES

8 26. *they came to land.* Lit. "they sailed down," from the "high seas" or from the high water to the shore of the lake; the verb *kataplein* expresses the opposite of *anagein* in 8:22d.

in the region of the Gerasenes. The site of this episode is not uniformly stated in the three Gospels, and the difference among them is compounded by variant readings in mss. of the three. In mss. of the Lucan Gospel there are three variants: (a) *Gerasēnōn,* "of the Gerasenes" (mss. P75, B, D, 0267, and some ancient versions); (b) *Gadarēnōn,* "of the Gadarenes" (mss. A, R, W, Ψ, 0135, family 13, and the Koine-text tradition generally); and (c) *Gergesēnōn,* "of the Gergesenes" (mss. ℵ, L, Θ, Ξ, 33, 700* 1241 and family 1).

Gerasa (= modern Jerash) is in Transjordan, about thirty-three miles SE of Lake Gennesaret, a city of the Decapolis in the mountains of Gilead near the edge of the desert to the east. The stampede of the pigs from Gerasa to the Lake would have made them the most energetic herd in history! Centuries ago Origen sensed the difficulty of this reading, recognizing Gerasa as "a city of Arabia, having neither a sea nor a lake nearby" (*Comm. in Ioannem* 6.41 [24]; GCS, 10. 150). See C. H. Kraeling, *Gerasa, City of the Decapolis* (New Haven: ASOR, 1938); J. Finegan, *The Archeology of the New Testament,* 61-70.

Gadara (=modern Umm Qeis) was another city of the Decapolis, about six miles SE of Lake Gennesaret. Josephus (*Life* 9 § 42) speaks of it and Hippos as "villages" (*kōmas*) bordering on Tiberias (=Lake Gennesaret) and the territory of Scythopolis. This would imply some proximity of Gadara to the Lake. But Origen (*Comm. in Ioan.* 6.41 [24]), who knew of the reading *Gadarēnōn* in some mss. of the Gospels, speaks of it as a town of Judea, famous for hot springs, but having no steep slope, lake, or sea.

Gergesa is identified by Origen as "an old city in the neighborhood of the Lake now called Tiberias," which he says has nearby a steep place abutting on the Lake, "from which, it is pointed out, the swine were cast down by the demons" (ibid.). However, Origen does not say that he knew of any manuscripts which read *Gergesēnōn;* he is aware of a local tradition, which derived the name *Gergesaioi* from Gergesa, the meaning of which he explains as "the dwelling of expellers" (i.e. inhabitants of the city who requested Jesus to depart from their vicinity [?]). Gergesa is said to be modern Kersa (or Kursi) on the eastern side of the Lake (see G. E. Wright and F. V. Filson [eds.], *Westminster Historical Atlas of the Bible* [Philadelphia: Westminster, 1946] 86; cf. F.-M. Abel, *Géographie de la Palestine* [Paris: Gabalda, 1938] 2. 332).

It is almost certain that the reading *Gergesēnōn* is not owing to the influence of Origen on the so-called Koine text-tradition, since that reading, being attested in numerous mss. that antedate Origen, is really pre-Origenian. In fact, a good case might be made out for it as the original reading in the mss. of Matthew; but it is scarcely to be preferred for the Lucan Gospel. For this reason I stick with the reading *Gerasēnōn,* "of the Gerasenes," the reading found in the best Lucan mss. It is also the *lectio difficilior.*

This fluctuation in the mss. about the locality of the episode, when taken together with other details in the story, cautions one against trying too hard to reconstruct what actually happened. See further B. M. Metzger, *TCGNT,* 23-24. Whether one can do that or not, the religious message of the episode comes through.

opposite Galilee. This Lucan redactional addition keeps the episode, inherited from "Mk," within the broad scope of Jesus' "Galilean" ministry. Jesus is depicted making an excursion into a territory presumably pagan (as the presence of pigs in the area suggests), where his power is displayed. Though it is actually manifested outside of the normal area of his (Galilean) ministry, the notion is important for the Lucan missionary concern for the Gentiles (see H. Conzelmann, *Theology,* 49-50). Hence, rather than omit the episode, Luke takes pains to integrate it into his geographical perspective.

27. *As he stepped ashore.* Lit. "him going out (of the boat) onto the land there met. . . ." With this not-easily-translatable phrase, Luke has improved the questionable Greek of Mark, which used a gen. absol., followed by a resumptive pron. *autō,* which makes the genitive construction no longer absolute.

who was possessed by demons. Lit. "a man (*anēr*) having demons." Luke introduces the pl., "demons," in light of v. 30 ("Legion"). Many demons possessing one person occur again in Luke 11:26. Mark 5:2 reads simply, "a human being with an unclean spirit." The latter expression, more Semitic than *daimōn,* is retained by Luke in v. 29; he sees no difference in the terms. "Unclean spirit" suits the story better in that the demons eventually enter "unclean" animals. But note the ptcs. *daimonizomenos* and *daimonistheis* in Mark 5:15,16,18; cf. Luke 8:36. Though Luke uses the pl., he still thinks at times of one demon (see v. 30).

For some time now. The phrase *kai chronō hikanō,* "and for a considerable time," is read in mss. P75,ℵ*,b, B, L, etc. It has to be taken with what follows (that the man had worn no clothes for some time). However, a number of important majuscule mss. (ℵa, A, K, W, X, etc.) and many minuscules read *ek chronōn hikanōn kai,* "for considerable periods and," which would relate the temporal phrase to what precedes (that the man was possessed for considerable periods and wore no clothes). The former reading is to be preferred; see Metzger, *TCGNT,* 145. For other minor variants, see the *app. crit.* in *UBSGNT,* 239.

among the tombs. Presumably pagan tombs, which would be a source of ritual uncleanness for a Jew, and probably were not whitewashed (cf. Matt 23:27; Str-B, 1. 936-937). For uncleanness from contact with the dead, see Num 19:11,14,16; Ezek 39:11-15; cf. 11QTemple 48:11-13; 49:5-21; 50:3-8. Some commentators have seen an allusion to Isa 65:1-7 in this (and other) dctail(s) in the episode. The loitering of the man among the tombs may be a sign of his alienation, but it may also signify the relation of the demoniac to the realm of death.

28. *screamed, lunged at him, and shouted at the top of his voice.* So Luke has redacted "Mk," which makes it seem rather that the demoniac ran to Jesus from afar, did him homage, and cried out to him in a loud voice. Luke's modification has made the approach of the demoniac more dramatic.

What do you want with me, . . . ? See NOTE on 4:34. To express the demoniac's hostility to Jesus, Luke (following Mark 5:7) uses the exact words of 1 Kgs 17:18 (LXX), *ti emoi kai soi.* As the story develops, it is the demon speaking through the man.

Son of God Most High. Though, as in the preceding phrase, Luke derives these words from "Mk," the demon here echoes a title given to Jesus in the infancy narrative (see NOTE on 1:32); cf. Luke 4:41; Acts 16:17. In the Marcan Gospel, the use of that title has to be understood in the context of the so-called messianic secret; here it takes on a different purpose, since Jesus has already been so identified.

I beg you. Thus Luke tones down the Marcan adjuration, probably considering it inappropriate that a demoniac or demon would "adjure" someone "by God."

do not torment me. The neg. impv. is again borrowed from Mark. In what the torment of a demon would consist, neither Mark nor Luke ever tells us.

29. *Jesus was about to charge the unclean spirit.* Lit. "for he was charging. . . ." The impf. tense used here is peculiar; it would seem to mean that Jesus was in the act of charging, but that comes later. Hence it must be used as an inceptive aor. (see BDF § 328-329, 331; cf. the similar use of *dierrēseto* in 5:6). Part of the problem is that Luke has transposed some of what was in Mark 5:4-5 to after the demoniac's initial greeting in v. 28 (=Mark 5:6-7); and the pl. "demons" now becomes an "unclean spirit," retained from "Mk." It is best to regard v. 29 as parenthetic in the Lucan account.

many times. I.e. on many occasions. But Moulton-Turner (*Grammar* 3. 243 [ii]) think that this could be an instance of the dat. case expressing duration of time, as it often does in Hellenistic Greek. Cf. ZBG § 54; MM, 694a.

30. *"What is your name?"* The demoniac sought to ward off confrontation with Jesus by revealing knowledge of his name and title. Jesus now seeks to learn the demon's name. Behind this dialogue is the popular belief that domination over a spirit is had through the use of the name. Jesus asks to learn the demon's name, but the demon seeks to distract the exorcist with his number. One need not query why Jesus, as Son of the Most High God, did not know the demon's name; to ask about Jesus' "ignorance" here is to miss the point of the story.

Legion. The demon gives, not a name in reality, but a number. A Latin word *legio* (fem.), transcribed into Greek, *legiōn* is used. In the time of Augustus a Roman *legio* numbered six thousand soldiers. A masc. art. precedes the word supposed to be the demon's proper name. The Lucan following clause explains the reason for its being used; it is the evangelist's comment, whereas in Mark 5:9 it was part of the demon's answer. Luke's redactional modification addresses the explanation to the reader, not to Jesus, thus heightening the enigmatic answer.

31. *to the abyss.* The Greek word *abyssos* can denote either the abode of the dead (see Ps 107:26; Rom 10:7) or the final prison of Satan and the demons (Rev 20:3). It is used often in the LXX to translate Hebrew *tĕhōm,* which designated in OT cosmology the "watery deep," or cosmic sea under the earth, the symbol of chaos and disorder conquered by the creator. Aware that this was their final destination, the demons now beg not to be sent there yet. Meanwhile, according to popular demonology of the time, they were to wander the earth, seeking an abode in desert places, tombs, or even in demented persons. Hence they (violently) resist ejection and even seek to return to garnished abodes (Luke 11:24-26). Here they even request to be sent into pigs, unclean animals that will receive them.

"To the abyss" is a Lucan redactional phrase, introduced instead of the Marcan, "out of the region" (*exō tēs chōras,* 5:10). Some have speculated that a mistranslation from Aramaic may be involved (J. Héring, *RHPR* 46 [1956] 25; G. Schwarz, *NTS* 22 [1975-1976] 214-215): Mark's *chōra* would represent the consonants of *tĕḥūmā',* "boundary," but also "territory," and Luke's *abyssos* those of *tĕhōmā',* "watery deep, underworld, abyss." Schwarz even suggests that the latter was more original. Suggestions of this sort are out of order, since they prescind from Synoptic relationships, fail to show that the two Aramaic words were in fact confused elsewhere, and pay no attention to the different preps. used by Mark (*exō*) and Luke (*eis*). The Marcan form is more original, and Luke has substituted for it a more appropriate literary stage prop in his account.

32. *many pigs.* Mark 5:13 numbers them as two thousand, but Luke omits this. In the sight of Palestinian Jews they were worthless animals because they were "unclean," i.e. not to be eaten (see Lev 11:7; Deut 14:8), since, though they have the hoof cloven and completely divided, they "do not chew the cud." Cf. Luke 15:15.

to enter those pigs. I.e. as their temporary substitute abode.

33. *down the steep slope into the lake.* Luke again changes the Marcan *thalassan,* "sea," to *limnēn,* "lake," which better suits Gennesaret. The "lake" is no longer the area of solitude (see NOTE on 8:22). It rather becomes the way to the abyss for the demons (contrast H. Conzelmann, *Theology,* 44-45, 50). The verb *hōrmēsen,* "rushed," preserved from Mark 5:13, "denotes violent movement uncontrolled by human reason" (G. Bertram, *TDNT* 5. 470). The demonic possession of the pigs propelled their mass movement.

and was drowned. The loss of the pigs symbolizes the destruction of the demons too. The unclean animals, worthless though they may be in the sight of many, become the means whereby unclean spirits cease to molest human beings. Demonic force in the world is brought to an end by Jesus' word.

35. *sitting there at his feet.* A Lucan redactional addition makes the cured demoniac assume the position of a disciple at the feet of the master (cf. Luke 10:39; Acts 22:3). Thus Luke prepares for the man's request in v. 38.

fully clothed. We are not told where the clothes came from; recall v. 27b above.

sound of mind. This detail, retained from "Mk," is an interesting comment on the original condition of the man; for want of a proper explanation of his unsettled mental condition, "spooks" were invoked to account for it, i.e. the deranged condition was ascribed to "demons" or "unclean spirit(s)" who had "entered" him (8:30) or "possessed" him.

36. *possessed.* Lit. "demonized." Luke uses the aor. pass. ptc. *daimonistheis,* found in Mark 5:18 (cf. vv. 15,16). Ms. D strangely reads instead the name *ho Legiōn,* "Legion."

delivered. Lit. "saved." Deliverance by Jesus from the evil that afflicted the man is again expressed by Luke's favorite word (see pp. 222-223 above).

37. *The whole populace of the Gerasene countryside begged him.* Lit. "all the multitude of the surrounding region of the Gerasenes." Ms. D, however, reads: "all (the people [i.e. those who had come out]) and the region asked Jesus. . . ." The clause in itself is another Lucan redactional addition, only differing slightly in sense from "Mk." *Gerasēnōn* is again the best attested reading in Lucan Mss. See NOTE on 8:26.

so great was the fear. The fear was caused not only by the possible further losses that might come, if Jesus were to stay among them, but above all by the numinous power implied in the exorcism. This Gentile reaction to the "Savior" is not much different from that of his own townspeople (4:28-29), who even wanted to do away with him. This detail of great fear has been added by Luke (cf. 7:16 [see NOTE]; Acts 2:43; 5:5,11).

38. *that he might stay with him.* Luke preserves this detail from Mark 5:18, changing only the prep. phrase from *met' autou* to *syn autō.* One may hesitate about the motive of the man; was it fear of relapse or discipleship? Probably the latter is intended in view of the Lucan addition of v. 35 (sitting at Jesus' feet). In this case, his reaction to Jesus stands in contrast to that of the "whole populace" (v. 37).

Jesus sent him off. Lit. "dismissed him." He sends him on a missionary errand that is not yet that of Christian discipleship, since the time for Gentile disciples has not yet come in the Lucan story.

39. *all that God has done for you.* I.e. what the God of Israel has done for you, a pagan, through me, Jesus. Mark 5:19 reads rather, "what the Lord (*ho kyrios*) has done." There, as in Luke, the reference is probably to Yahweh as the next contrasting clause seems to suggest, unless one were to toy with the idea that Luke does at times think of Jesus as *ho theos* (see NOTE on 9:43 below). Recall the textual problem of Acts 20:28.

through the whole town. The unnamed town was implied in v. 26 and mentioned in v. 34. This is a Lucan redactional modification by which he eliminates the Marcan mention of the Decapolis (Mark 5:20).

A certain parallelism is detected in the last two sentences. Jesus tells the man to go home and explain to people all that God has done for him (*hosa soi* [lit. for you] *epoiēsen ho theos*); he goes off and proclaims all that Jesus had done for him (*hosa epoiēsen autō ho Iēsous*). The emphatic position of *ho theos* and *ho Iēsous* is not to be missed. Lucan style is here suggestive.

BIBLIOGRAPHY (8:26-39)

Annen, F. *Heil für die Heiden: Zur Bedeutung und Geschichte der Tradition vom besessenen Gerasener (Mk 5,1-20 parr.)* (Frankfurter theologische Studien, 20; Frankfurt am M.: J. Knecht, 1976).

Burkill, T. A. "Concerning Mk. 5,7 and 5,18-20," *ST* 11 (1957) 159-166.

Cave, C. H. "The Obedience of Unclean Spirits," *NTS* 11 (1964-1965) 93-97.

Craghan, J. "The Gerasene Demoniac," *CBQ* 30 (1968) 522-536.

Cratchley, W. J. "Demoniac of Gadara," *ExpTim* 63 (1951-1952) 193-194.

Kertelge, K. *Die Wunder Jesu,* 101-110.

Kleist, J. A. "The Gadarene Demoniacs," *CBQ* 9 (1947) 101-105.

Lamarche, P. "Le possédé de Gérasa (Mt 8,28-34; Mc 5,1-20; Lc 8,26-39)," *NRT* 100 (1968) 581-597.

Martin, A. D. "The Loss of the Gadarene Swine," *ExpTim* 25 (1913-1914) 380-381.

Pax, E. "Das Heidentum Palästinas in römischer Zeit," *BibLeb* 7 (1966) 278-292.

Pesch, R. *Der Besessene von Gerasa: Entstehung und Überlieferung einer Wundergeschichte* (SBS 56; Stuttgart: Katholisches Bibelwerk, 1972).

——— "The Markan Version of the Healing of the Gerasene Demoniac," *Ecumenical Review* 23 (1971) 349-376.

Robinson, J. M. *The Problem of History in Mark* (SBT 21; London: SCM, 1957) 33-42.

Sahlin, H. "Die Perikope vom gerasenischen Besessenen und der Plan des Markusevangeliums," *ST* 18 (1964) 159-172.

Schramm, T. *Der Markus-Stoff,* 126.

Starobinski, J. "An Essay in Literary Analysis—Mark 5:1-20," *Ecumenical Review* 23 (1971) 377-397.

Vencovský, J. "Der gadarenische Exorzismus: Mt 8, 28-34 und Parallelen," *Communio viatorum* 14 (1971) 13-29.

45. THE CURE OF THE WOMAN WITH A
HEMORRHAGE
(8:40-48)

8 40 Now when Jesus returned, a crowd of people welcomed him, for they were all awaiting him. 41 A man named Jairus, a leader of a synagogue, also arrived on the scene. He fell at Jesus' feet and urged him to come to his house, 42 because his only child, a twelve-year-old daughter, was dying. As he went with him, crowds of people pressed closely about him. 43 Among them was a woman who [though she had spent all her livelihood on physicians] had been suffering from hemorrhages for twelve years, and no one was able to cure her. 44 She came up behind Jesus and touched the border of his cloak; immediately her hemorrhage stopped. 45 Then Jesus asked, "Who touched me?" When no one admitted it, Peter said, "Master, crowds of people are pressing close and hemming you in!" 46 But Jesus said, "Yes, but someone touched me; I know, for power has gone forth from me." 47 When the woman realized that she had not gone unnoticed, she came up trembling and fell before him. In the presence of all the people she explained why she had touched him and how she had been instantly healed. 48 Jesus said to her, "Daughter, it is your faith that has brought you salvation. *Go in peace!*"   1 Sam 1:17

COMMENT

The progressive manifestation of Jesus' power continues in this section of the Lucan Gospel with another miracle-story, the cure of a woman with a hemorrhage (8:40-48). In fact, it continues with two closely related miracle-stories, since the raising of Jairus' daughter that follows (8:49-56) is already begun in the course of this one. Our COMMENT, then, will be on the two episodes taken together, whereas the NOTES will be handled separately.

The two stories have been derived by Luke from Mark 5:21-43, being yet further parts of the complex of miracle-stories that Mark inherited from an earlier tradition as a unit (see p. 726 above). Again, little Marcan redaction has been detected in the form of these stories, save possibly the command to silence in 5:43a, which support the so-called messianic secret in that Gospel (see R. Bultmann, *HST*, 214).

Two separate miracles have been, as it were, woven into one. For a commentator such as J. M. Creed (*The Gospel*, 122) the "obvious explanation" is that so it happened. This explanation does not satisfy most commentators today, who would prefer to think that these stories were originally independent and only later came to be joined as they now are. Reasons for the joining have been seen in the use of "little daughter" (Mark 5:23) and "daughter" (5:34), or in the mention of "twelve years" (5:25,42), i.e. by topical arrangement. Likewise, the joining has the literary effect of an interval during which the dying child actually dies and the miracle passes from a healing to a resuscitation. The two stories also betray different compositional styles: the historical present, short sentences, and few participles characterize the Marcan story of the raising of Jairus' daughter, whereas the Marcan form of the other story has the more usual aorist and imperfect tenses, participles, and longer sentences. P. J. Achtemeier (*JBL* 89 [1970] 276-279) thinks that it was Mark who inserted the story of the woman into that of the raising of Jairus' daughter, because of his otherwise known "sandwiching" technique. But not all agree with this, and some prefer to think that the combination was already in the pre-Marcan tradition (thus K. Kertelge, *Die Wunder Jesu*, 110-111; G. Schneider, *Evangelium nach Lukas*, 196). Further discussion of this analysis does not concern us here, for Luke has clearly derived the "sandwiched" accounts from Mark 5:21-43.

The Lucan form of the stories (8:40-48,49-56) is dependent on "Mk," and the specific differences have to be attributed to Lucan redaction. Minor agreements of Luke and Matthew against Mark are noted in *archōn*, "leader," (8:41); *thygatēr*, "daughter" (8:42); *proselthousa*, *opisthen*, *kraspedou*, "coming up," "behind," "border" (8:44); and *elthōn*, "having come" (8:51). Of these only *kraspedou* is of any significance; the rest are coincidences (see T. Schramm, *Der Markus-Stoff*, 126). Luke has shortened the stories, but not as much as has Matthew (9:18-26). Luke has joined the stories to what precedes more closely than Mark (8:40). He introduces the age of the girl early into his form of the story (contrast Mark 5:42), and adds that she was an "only child." In 8:43 he softens the criticism of the physicians, omitting that the woman "had suffered much from many of them." In 8:45 Peter becomes the spokesman for the disciples in expostulating about the crowds; and the disciples' irreverent comment (Mark 5:31) is suppressed. In 8:46 Jesus is made to say that power has gone forth from him, whereas it was the evangelist's comment in Mark 5:30. Luke explains why the crowd laughs at Jesus in ridicule, when he says that the girl was only sleeping

(8:53). Finally, in 8:55 Luke adds that "her breath returned," making clear that the resuscitation involved a return to former life. However, the curtailment of the story in 8:51-54 has also obscured the flow of the story somewhat. In Mark when Jesus arrives at Jairus' house and finds the mourners, Jesus gets rid of them, and takes Peter, James, and John and the girl's parents into where the girl lies, and there he raises her. In Luke Jesus allows no one to enter except Peter, James, John and the parents; but he has not yet mentioned the mother. And he has not made clear that another room was involved. For other minor modifications, see the NOTES.

The two stories present a picture of Jesus as lord over sickness and death. Coming on the heels of the two former miracle-stories, in which his powerful word was used over a cataclysm of nature and over demonic possession, his comprehensive lordship is gradually being displayed. The first of these two miracles, the cure of the woman, is recounted as an exercise of Jesus' *dynamis*, "power" (8:46), which has to be understood as "the power of the Spirit" learned about in 4:14 or "the power of the Lord . . . to heal" spoken of in 5:17. See further 6:19. In the second miracle-story, the raising of Jairus' daughter, no reference is made explicitly to his power. But an OT gesture (taking hold of her hand) and his word of command convey the message of his power to those who were present. He is the lord not only of the ill, but even of life and death. The two miracle-stories, "sandwiched together," enable the reader to understand that the power spoken of in 8:46 is also at work in the raising of Jairus' daughter.

The resuscitation of the girl has to be related to the earlier resuscitation of the son of the widow of Nain (7:11-17). There it concerned a son and his mother; here it is a daughter and her father. Lucan parallelism is again at work, but with contrast. Both of the resuscitations, moreover, are not without foreshadowing elements for the resurrection of Jesus himself. In 7:14 Jesus raised the son, using the aor. pass. impv. *egerthēti;* here in 8:54 the pres. impv. of the same verb is used, *egeire* (in the form derived from Mark 5:41). The same verb will be used of him in the Easter message, *egerthē,* 24:6, "he has been raised." But a nuance of difference has to be noted; in chaps. 7 and 8 the raising is a resuscitation, a return to physical, earthly existence.

Finally, in both of these miracle-stories one has to note the relation of faith to salvation (8:48, 50). The faith that is intended is the confidence of the individuals in the power of Jesus; that the woman is cured and the girl is raised did not happen as modes of deliverance or salvation without faith. In both stories Luke has introduced this relationship; see J. Roloff, *Das Kerygma,* 153-155.

NOTES

8 40. *Now when Jesus returned.* Lit. "at Jesus' returning." Luke uses here *en tō* + infin. independently of any *kai egeneto* construction (see p. 119). It is a clear Lucan attempt to avoid Mark's clumsy gen. absol. with a following resumptive pron. (as in 8:27 above). Jesus is depicted making his way by boat back to the west shore of Lake Gennesaret, whence he set out.

a crowd of people welcomed him. Lit. "the crowd," referring to 8:4,19.

for they were all awaiting him. This redactional addition ties in with Luke's omission of the dismissal of the crowd in 8:22 (contrast Mark 4:36).

41. *A man named Jairus.* A Jew from some town in Galilee, not further specified. *Iairos* is a Grecized form of Hebrew *Yā'îr*, an OT proper name (Num 32:41; Deut 3:14; Josh 13:30). It is a form from which some theophoric element has been lost. It would mean, "May he (i.e. El, Yahweh) enlighten" the man who bears it. The first-century use of this name among Palestinian Jews is known from Josephus' account of the fall of Masada in A.D. 74. The leader of the Jewish resistance against Rome at that site was *El'azar ben Yā'îr* or (in Greek) *Eleazaros huios Iaeirou* (see *J.W.* 2.17,9 § 447). The Hebrew name has been found on a shard discovered on Masada itself, *ben Yā'îr* (see Y. Yadin, *Masada* [New York: Random House, 1966] 201). Bultmann (*HST,* 215) argues that, since Jairus' name is not found in ms. D and is lacking also in the Matthean account, it has been introduced into the usual Marcan text "from Luke"! This is preposterous. See further R. Pesch, "Jaïrus," 252-256. In introducing Jairus' name, Luke uses the introductory *kai idou,* "and behold," a favorite Septuagintism (see p. 121 above); but this has been omitted in the translation.

a leader of a synagogue. See NOTE on 4:15. Mark 5:22 actually uses *heis tōn archisynagōgōn,* "one of the synagogue-leaders." Since Luke employs the word *archisynagōgos* in 8:49, it is puzzling why he has changed it here (Matt 9:18 does the same). Contrast the coming of this leader to Jesus with that not dared by the centurion of 7:6. Here Luke depicts a leader of the Galilean Jews coming to Jesus with a confidence that is matched only by that of the woman in the following story.

to come to his house. Lit. "to enter into his house." The leader appeals to Jesus' mercy indirectly, without stating that his daughter was dying. Luke tells his readers about this and implies that Jesus knew the reason for the invitation. Contrast Mark 5:23.

42. *his only child, a twelve-year-old daughter.* Lit. "an only daughter was to him, of about twelve years." The Greek text does not imply that the man had sons but was concerned about an only daughter. His anguish is rather about a sole descendant. Compare the son of the widow of Nain (7:12 (see NOTE]); cf. 9:38. The child's age may be mentioned here, brought forward by Luke (see Mark 5:42, where it seems out of place), because she was near to the marriageable age (see Str-B, 2. 374). In the Lucan context the twelve years

links the two stories, and what happens to the woman sick for twelve years becomes a sign of what will be done for the twelve-year-old girl.

was dying. Luke has eliminated the purpose of Jesus' coming to the house for a better literary effect; cf. Mark 5:23b.

As he went with him. Lit. "in his going," another instance of the articular infin. (see p. 119 above). The crowds that pressed close may be considered people desirous of seeing a miracle performed.

43. [*had spent all her livelihood on physicians*]. This phrase is omitted in mss. P[75], B, D, and some versions, but it is found in others, A, K, L, P, W, etc. It looks like a succinct condensation of Mark 5:26 such as Luke would write, but its omission in good mss. causes hesitation about it; hence the brackets. See further B. M. Metzger, *TCGNT*, 145. Luke omits the further criticism of the physicians. If Luke, the Beloved Physician, is the author of Luke-Acts, then one could understand his reluctance to incorporate the Marcan criticism. But on this, see p. 51 above. What is recorded here is the woman's desperation and need for help.

suffering from hemorrhages. Lit. "a woman being with a flow of blood." This descriptive phrase is taken over from "Mk." According to Lev 15:25-31 such a woman would be "unclean" and had to be separated from Israel. Cf. 11QTemple 48:16. Her coming to Jesus in such a crowd is indicative of her desperation and need.

for twelve years. Lit. "since twelve years," a Lucan modification of the Marcan acc. of duration of time (*dōdeka etē*).

and no one was able to cure her. Lit. "and she could not be cured by anyone." On the prep. "by" (*apo*), see NOTE on 9:22.

44. *touched the border of his cloak.* The word *kraspedon*, "edge, hem," is found here and in Matt 9:20, but not in Mark 5:27. It could also mean the "tassle" (Hebrew *ṣîṣît*), which the male Jew was supposed to wear on the corners of his outer garment (see Num 15:38-39; Deut 22:12—where the LXX uses the same Greek word). The words *tou kraspedou* are found in mss. P[75], ℵ, A, B, C, L, P, W, X, etc., but other forms of the phrase are attested in other mss. (see the *app. crit.* in *UBSGNT*, 241).

The woman has approached Jesus to touch the extreme edge of his outer garment, confident that some help would come to her even from this. Luke suppresses her inner thoughts (see Mark 5:28).

immediately. See NOTE on *parachrēma*, 1:64.

her hemorrhage stopped. Lit. "stood still," since the Greek word *rysis* implies a "running" or "flow." Luke has simplified the description of the cure given in Mark 5:29.

45. *"Who touched me?"* Jesus' question sounds a bit stupid, as the reaction of Peter shows. Queries about why Jesus should have asked such a question—since he should have known who touched him—are out of place; they are born of later christological conceptions of him. What is startling is that not even Luke has suppressed his question. He passes over the Marcan comment about power going forth from him in order to make that Jesus' answer to Peter's remark.

When no one admitted it. Lit. "as all were denying (it)," a gen. absol.

Peter. Petros is the reading in mss. P⁷⁵, B, ᴨ, etc.; but many other mss. (ℵ, A, C, D, L, P, etc.) read *Petros kai hoi syn autō,* "Peter and those with him," while others have *Petros kai hoi met' autou,* "Peter and those with him" (K, X, Δ, etc.). The inferior readings, however, are either harmonizations with Mark 5:31, which speaks simply of "his disciples," or attempts to make the others share in Peter's expostulation. The best text of Luke makes Peter the spokesman here for the others (see 9:20; 12:41).

Master. See NOTE on *epistata* in 5:5.

and hemming you in. This is the reading of mss. P⁷⁵, ℵ, B, L, etc. But other mss. (e.g. 1071) have instead, "and you say, 'Who touched me?'" Some, indeed, have a combination of these two readings (A, C³, K, P, W, X). Harmonization of the text with Mark 5:31 has been at work here.

46. *for power has gone forth from me.* What was the evangelist's own comment in Mark 5:30 has become Jesus' here in Luke, where it answers Peter's remark. For the sense of "power," see the COMMENT. Cf. 6:19.

47. *she explained.* So Luke modified the Marcan form of the woman's admission ("she told him the whole truth," 5:33). Luke makes it a confession before all the people; expecting a reprimand from Jesus, she hears only words of absolution.

48. *Daughter.* An affectionate term is used to reassure her that she is now to be recognized as part of Israel.

has brought you salvation. Luke again joins "faith" and "salvation"; see 8:12 above and 8:50 below. Jesus attributes her cure to her own "faith," and thereby all suggestion of any magical connotation is removed from the story. See NOTE on 5:20.

Go in peace! The Lucan Jesus uses an OT formula of dismissal (see NOTE on 7:50). It differs slightly from the Marcan parallel.

46. THE RAISING OF JAIRUS' DAUGHTER
(8:49-56)

8 49 Even as he spoke, someone came from the house of the leader of the synagogue and said, "Your daughter has just died. Do not trouble the teacher any more." 50 But Jesus heard this and replied, "Do not be afraid; just have faith, and she will be saved." 51 When he came to the house, he allowed no one to enter with him but Peter, John, and James, and the child's father and mother. 52 All the others were crying and beating their breasts for her. Jesus said, "Do not cry; she has not died; she is only asleep." 53 But they laughed at him, convinced that she was dead. 54 So he took hold of her hand and spoke to her, "Get up, child." 55 Her breath returned, and instantly she stood up. Then he ordered her to be given something to eat. 56 Her parents were struck with astonishment, but he forbade them to tell anyone what had happened.

(For the COMMENT on this passage, see that on 8:40-48.)

NOTES

8 49. *Even as he spoke.* Luke preserves the Marcan gen. absol. and historical present, but introduces "someone" as a single messenger from the leader's house (instead of the vague Marcan "they came"). See p. 108 above.

has just died. Luke has improved the Greek by using the perf. tense instead of Mark's aorist.

Do not trouble . . . any more. The Marcan question becomes a negative impv. The adv. *mēketi,* "not any longer," is the best reading here (in mss. P[75], ℵ, B, D, etc.), but some others have the simple negative *mē* (mss. A, C, K, L, P, etc.).

the teacher. See NOTE on *didaskalon,* 7:40.

50. *Do not be afraid.* See NOTE on 1:13.

just have faith. Luke presumes that the reader will understand the object or mode of this confidence; no explanation is offered. In Mark 5:36 the impv. is present, "continue to have faith," but Luke has made it aorist.

she will be saved. I.e. delivered from death. The verb *sōthēsetai* is a Lucan favorite (see p. 223 above); here he adds it to the inherited story. Jesus' intervention stresses the essential without specifying the mode of deliverance.

51. *but Peter, John, and James.* For the first time in this Gospel this threesome is singled out (see 9:28), being derived from Mark 5:37. They are introduced as privileged witnesses of Jesus' power and become those to whom the "secrets of the kingdom" are made known (8:10) in a special way. Luke has changed the order of the names from Mark 5:37 (cf. Luke 5:10). Peter and John are closely associated in Acts (3:1,11; 4:13); and Luke is aware that James has been put to death (Acts 12:2). See NOTES on 4:38; 5:8,10.

52. *All the others.* I.e. friends, relatives, official mourners, and the accompanying crowd (8:40). Recall the distinction of 8:10.

beating their breasts for her. The Greek phrase used here is impossible to translate exactly; it should be something like, "they were beating themselves her." The verb *koptein*, "strike, beat" can be used in the middle voice in the sense of "mourning" (for her); see Josephus *Ant.* 13.15,5 § 399. Examples of the middle voice with a following dir. obj. are known from classical Greek (Aristophanes *Lysistrata* 396; Plato, *Republic* 10.619C) and the LXX (Gen 23:2; 1 Sam 25:1).

she has not died; she is only asleep. Thus Jesus sums up the situation, only to evoke scorn and laughter. His words do not mean that the girl was only apparently dead, but rather that her death, like sleep, is limited in time. His words hint at a larger issue: that with his coming death is seen to be like sleep, not a permanent state, but transitional. The hint of the resurrection is not remote.

53. *they laughed at him.* The verb *kategelōn* implies ridicule. This reaction comes because they know that she is dead; but they know nothing of Jesus' power (8:46).

54. *took hold of her hand.* Jesus uses an OT gesture (Isa 41:13; 42:6), as Yahweh took hold of Israel's right hand.

"Get up, child." Lit. "child, wake up." Jesus speaks to her as if she were waking from ordinary sleep. The impv. *egeire* is that of the verb that is often used in the NT of Jesus' own resurrection. Luke makes use here of the nom. with the def. art. (*hē pais*) as a voc.; this usage is probably influenced by Mark's similar voc., the translation of Aramaic *ṭĕlīṭā'* or *ṭalyĕtā'* as *to korasion*. But the usage can also be defended independently as good Greek (see BDF § 147.3). Jesus' word of command brings about the resuscitation. (The Aramaic expression, *talitha koum*, Mark 5:41 is avoided by Luke, who writes for Gentile Christians, presupposed not to be acquainted with the language.)

55. *Her breath returned.* I.e. as the sign of the new life bestowed. This clause is added by Luke to stress the idea of return to earthly life lived before; hence too the command to give her food. Is this possibly an allusion to 1 Kgs 17:21-22 (LXX)?

56. *were struck with astonishment.* Lit. "were beside themselves." See Mark 3:21, where the intended nuance is even stronger.

he forbade them to tell anyone. This is a Lucan reformulation of the prohibition in Mark 5:43a, where it makes better sense, fitting in with the pattern of the messianic secret in that part of the Marcan Gospel. Luke retains it, not because he uses any such pattern, but because he too has depicted Jesus admitting that there were secrets of the kingdom not yet fully disclosed (8:10). It does create a problem, however, since one tends to wonder how the parents could possibly have concealed the fact of the resuscitation. In any case, this prohibition stands in sharp contrast to Jesus' words to the cured demoniac in 8:39.

BIBLIOGRAPHY (8:40-48 and 49-56)

Kertelge, K. *Die Wunder Jesu*, 110-120.

Kreyenbühl, J. "Ursprung und Stammbaum eines biblischen Wunders," *ZNW* 10 (1909) 265-276.

Marxsen, W. "Bibelarbeit über Mk 5,21-43/Mt 9,18-26," in *Der Exeget als Theologe* (Gütersloh: G. Mohn, 1968) 171-182.

Pesch, R. "Jaïrus (Mk 5,22/Lk 8,41)," *BZ* 14 (1970) 252-256.

Potin, J. "L'Évangile (Mt 9,18-26): Guérison d'une hémorroïsse et résurrection de la fille de Jaïre," *AsSeign* 78 (1965) 25-36.

Roloff, J. *Das Kerygma und der irdische Jesus: Historische Motive in den Jesus-Erzählungen der Evangelien* (Göttingen: Vandenhoeck und Ruprecht, 1970) 153-155.

Schmithals, W. *Wunder und Glaube: Eine Auslegung von Markus 4,35-6,6a* (BibS[N] 59; Neukirchen: Neukirchener, 1970) 69-91.

Schramm, T. *Der Markus-Stoff*, 126-127.

Van der Loos, H. "The Healing of the Woman with the Issue of Blood" and "Jairus' Daughter," in *The Miracles of Jesus* (NovTSup 9; Leiden: Brill, 1965) 509-519, 567-573.

47. THE MISSION OF THE TWELVE
(9:1-6)

9 ¹ Jesus now called together the Twelve and gave them power and authority over all demons and to cure diseases. ² He sent them out to proclaim the kingdom of God and to heal. ³ He said to them, "Take no provisions with you for the journey, no walking stick or knapsack, no bread or money—and you have no need of two tunics each. ⁴ Wherever you enter a house, lodge there and go forth from it. ⁵ Whenever people do not welcome you, leave their town and knock its dust from your feet as a warning against them." ⁶ So they went forth and passed from village to village, preaching and curing people everywhere.

COMMENT

The miracle stories recounted by Luke in this section of his Gospel have come to an end in 8:56 and are immediately followed by the episode in which Jesus sends out the Twelve on a mission in Galilee (9:1-6). This episode comes from "Mk," but since Luke has used Mark 6:1-6a in his Nazareth story (4:16-30), the collocation of this episode takes on a different significance in the Lucan Gospel, coming, as it does, on the heels of the miracle-stories, and acting as a sort of conclusion to them. The witnesses from Galilee that Jesus has been in the act of training are now being sent to participate in his own mission, even during the ministry in the Period of Jesus.

The Lucan episode, from the standpoint of its Synoptic relationship, is basically derived from Mark 6:6b-13. There is a doublet of this episode in Luke 10:1-12, derived from "Q," which Luke has made into a separate mission (of the Seventy[-Two]). Some of the material in that mission from "Q" may have influenced the redaction of the Marcan material used here.

The Lucan redaction of the Marcan source can be seen in the following elements. Luke omits the Marcan introductory sentence (6:6b) and changes "authority over unclean spirits" to "power and authority over demons and to cure diseases" (9:1). More significantly, Luke makes the

Twelve into preachers of the kingdom (both in v. 2 and implicitly in v. 6). Concerning the rules for what is to be taken on the journey, Luke makes Jesus forbid the carrying of a staff (9:3; cf. Mark 6:8) and omit all mention of sandals (Mark 6:9). He further omits the Marcan introductory phrase of 6:10, adding the instruction about lodging directly to the preceding. Luke 9:6 alters the conclusion, passing over the Twelve's role as conversion-preachers and anointers (Mark 6:13).

Form-critically, the passage has to be classed with the Stories about Jesus, since it is basically narrative material (despite the words of Jesus in Mark 6:10-11, which Luke recasts in 9:3-5). These sayings are, indeed, speech material, but they have been inserted into narratives (see R. Bultmann, *HST,* 331). In the Lucan form one can distinguish five parts of the episode: (a) the conferral of power and authority on the Twelve; (b) the commission to preach and heal; (c) the rules about the journey; (d) the rules about lodging; and (e) the rules about the non-reception of the preaching. The evangelist himself summarizes the mission of the Twelve that ensues.

The meaning of the passage is not difficult to discern. One now sees the purpose behind the choosing of the Twelve in 6:13: they are to be given a share in Jesus' own mission of preaching the kingdom of God. He has already told them that they have been granted the favor of knowing the secrets of the kingdom (8:10) and that what is secret will become known (8:17). Now he bestows on them "power and authority," yet it is not restricted to preaching, but involves the care of the physical and mental health of human beings. In this passage Luke, more carefully than Mark, distinguishes between healing and exorcism, but both are to be in their ability. But Luke has not only prepared for this commission, but it is itself a foreshadowing of a greater commission to be given in 24:46-47. Now, during his own Galilean ministry, his commission gives them a share in his "power" and "authority"; later, they will be commissioned in a different way.

The external conditions of their mission are set forth by Jesus himself in a series of imperatives. The Twelve are to go forth without encumbering provisions (*impedimenta*) so that nothing will distract them from their purpose. Their adhering to them may seem like a manifestation of their "poverty," but it is much more an indication of their reliance and trust in the providence of God himself. They are to accept the hospitality of those who would welcome them and be content with it. But they are also to prepare themselves for rejection, and their reaction is to be one of complete severance from such as do reject them. Some of these external conditions of the journey will be modified later (see 22:35-38).

Further comments on aspects of this passage will be made when the sending out of the Seventy(-two) is discussed in 10:1-12. The historicity of the sending out of disciples during the ministry by Jesus has often been questioned; it is unknown to the Johannine gospel tradition, and so little is really known about it. The double sending in the Lucan Gospel makes the decision about it even more difficult. No proof can be offered for its historicity; but the call of disciples by Jesus during that ministry would logically speak for an association of them with his own work. There is no reason to question it in the long run, even though the evidence from the Synoptics amounts at most to a plausibility.

NOTES

9 1. *called together the Twelve.* I.e. those disciples singled out in 6:13; cf. 8:1. Luke's phrase is derived from Mark 6:7, but a different ptc. is used; *synkalein* is used, as in Luke 15:6,9; 23:13; Acts 5:21; 10:24; 28:17. *Tous dōdeka* is the reading in the best mss. (P⁷⁵, A, B, D, K, W, etc.); some others (ℵ, C*, L, X, etc.) add "apostles," and others (C³, 1010, 1216, etc.), "disciples." In any case, the group is to be distinguished from the Seventy(-Two) of 10:1.

gave them power and authority. The Greek words *dynamis* and *exousia* have already been used by Luke to describe Jesus' own status, his power (4:14,36; 5:17; 6:19; 8:46) and authority (4:32,36; 5:24). Only the latter is used in Mark 6:7. Jesus is thus granting the Twelve a share in the dominion that he enjoyed as God's special emissary. In the Lucan form Jesus confers the power and authority prior to the sending out; contrast Mark.

over all demons. Lit. "over all the demons." Luke has added "all." The def. art. is used generically (BDF § 263[b]). As in 8:26-39, Luke has again introduced "demons" instead of the Marcan "unclean spirits."

and to cure diseases. This is a Lucan redactional addition which does not suit the syntax of the rest of the sentence very well; the purpose infin. has to depend on "power and authority," but it does not parallel the prep. phrase, "over all demons."

2. *He sent them out.* Luke uses the verb *apesteilen,* inspired by Mark 6:7. Here it recalls the name "apostles" that Luke 6:13 says that Jesus gave the Twelve. Luke has omitted the Marcan detail of the sending out "two by two."

to proclaim the kingdom of God. See NOTE on 4:43. This is a Lucan redactional addition. Since in this Gospel Jesus is the kingdom-preacher par excellence, his commission now closely associates the Twelve with his main role.

and to heal. This Lucan addition seems strange, coming so soon after that added in v. 1. Three concerns are laid before the Twelve: they are to preach the kingdom, free human beings from demonic evil, and heal their ills. In some mss. (ℵ, A, D, L, etc.) an object is added to the last infin., *tous astheneis,* "the sick."

3. *Take no provisions with you for the journey.* Lit. "take nothing for the road." This injunction recalls the custom of the Essenes, described by Josephus (*J.W.* 2.8,4 § 125), who carried nothing with them on their journeys except arms against highway robbers and lodged with other Essenes whom they had

never met before. The following details about the journey also have some parallels in Mishnaic regulations for those coming to the Temple, viz. prohibition of carrying various objects into the Temple precincts (one's staff, sandals, wallet—or dust on one's feet, *m. Berakot* 9:5). The prohibitions have also been compared with the equipment usually associated with the itinerant beggar philosophers of the Cynic tradition in the Greek world.

no walking stick or knapsack. Whereas Mark 6:8 permitted the carrying of a stick, the Lucan Jesus forbids it. This suits the Lucan view of detachment from earthly possessions which is otherwise characteristic of his writings (see p. 247 above). For an older view of this problem, see B. Ahern, "Staff or No Staff?" *CBQ* 5 (1943) 332-337. Is Luke here influenced by "Q," since the prohibition is also found in Matt 10:10? In the Lucan parallel to that verse there is no mention of the walking stick (10:4). There is no way to tell for what purpose the *rabdos,* "walking stick," was intended, a real walking stick or a weapon against highway robbers. Cf. *AAGA*[3], 216-217.

no bread or money. Lit. "no bread or silver." Again, Luke modifies Mark 6:8 which forbids "copper (coins) for the belt." He substitutes the more common metal of Greek coins for that of Roman. Tyrian silver shekels (tetradrachms) and half-shekels were used in Palestine of the time; see R. de Vaux, *Archaeology and the Dead Sea Scrolls* (London: Oxford University, 1973) 34-35, 130.

no need of two tunics each. Lit. "nor to have two tunics each." The construction is not elegant Greek, and is almost untranslatable. The infin. may be imperatival (BDF § 389), "do not have . . . ," and parallel to the neg. impv. *mēden airete,* "take nothing," at the beginning of the verse. The words *ana dyo* are problematic too; they seem to express a distributive idea (BDF § 240). But the prep. *ana* is not certainly read in all mss., being omitted by ℵ, B, C*, L, etc., possibly under the influence of Mark 6:9, which has merely *dyo.*

4. *Wherever you enter a house.* I.e. when you are welcomed into someone's house for lodging in a town, stability is recommended; one should not be seeking out better quarters.

go forth from it. I.e. to preach and to heal. See 10:7.

5. *leave their town and knock its dust from your feet.* I.e. get rid of anything belonging to that town that might still cling to you—an act symbolizing the severance of all association with it. See 10:11. Luke depicts Paul and Barnabas doing just this in Antioch of Pisidia (Acts 13:50). Jews returning to Palestine from pagan territory were expected to do the same (see Str-B, 1. 571; cf. H. J. Cadbury, "Dust and Garments," in *Beginnings* 5. 269-277).

as a warning against them. Lit. "for a testimony against them," i.e, as an act that serves as proof of their rejection of the preaching of the Twelve. Cf. Luke 5:14.

6. *So they went forth.* As does Mark 6:12-13, Luke ends the episode with a brief descriptive comment summarizing the mission itself. Whereas Mark made the Twelve into conversion-preachers, exorcists, anointers with olive oil, and healers, Luke depicts them simply as preaching and healing. Significantly, he avoids the Marcan *hina metanoōsin,* "that people may repent," a notion that is otherwise dear to him; instead he uses *euangelizesthai.*

passed from village to village. This is a Lucan addition.

everywhere. The adv. may imply the zeal of the Twelve, or it may imply their success.

BIBLIOGRAPHY (9:1-6)

Beare, F. W. "The Mission of the Disciples and the Mission Charge: Matthew 10 and Parallels," *JBL* 89 (1970) 1-13.

Ford, J. M. "Money 'Bags' in the Temple (Mk 11, 16)," *Bib* 57 (1976) 249-253.

Hahn, F. *Mission in the New Testament* (SBT 47; Naperville, IL: Allenson, 1965) 41-46, 54-59.

Schott, E. "Die Aussendungsrede Mt 10. Mc 6. Lc 9.10," *ZNW* 7 (1906) 140-150.

Schürmann, H. "Mt 10,5b-6 und die Vorgeschichte des synoptischen Aussendungsberichtes," in *Neutestamentliche Aufsätze: Festschrift für Prof. Josef Schmid zum 70. Geburtstag* (eds. J. Blinzler et al.; Regensburg: Pustet, 1963) 270-282; reprinted in *Traditionsgeschichtliche Untersuchungen zu den synoptischen Evangelien* (Düsseldorf: Patmos, 1968) 137-149.

Testa, G. "Studio di Mc 6, 6b-13 secondo il metodo della storia della tradizione," *DivThom* 75 (1972) 177-191.

G. "Who Is This?"

Herod Antipas poses the question that dominates the central chapter in the Lucan Gospel

48. HEROD'S REACTION TO JESUS' REPUTATION
(9:7-9)

9 ⁷ Now the tetrarch Herod began to hear of all that was happening. He was puzzled by the talk of some of the people that John had been raised from the dead, ⁸ of others that Elijah had appeared, and of still others that one of the prophets of old had arisen. ⁹ And Herod's comment was, "John I beheaded; but who is this about whom I hear such talk?" And he was anxious to see him.

COMMENT

There now begins in the Lucan Gospel a special section in which the evangelist concentrates on the identification of Jesus. He has been identifying him, of course, ever since the beginning (see, e.g. 2:11). But the next forty-four verses do it in a significant way. They serve not only as an introduction to the travel account, which begins at 9:51, but by various modifications of the Marcan material that is taken over they create a section that emphasizes his identity. In the episodes that are mainly derived from "Mk" three main things are to be noted: (a) Luke has already transposed to 3:19-20 what he retains of the Marcan story of the imprisonment of John the Baptist (=Mark 6:17-29); (b) Luke omits what corresponds to Mark 6:45-8:26, the so-called Big Omission in Luke, which occurs at 9:17; and (c) the omission of Mark 9:9-13 (Jesus' words about Elijah as the disciples and he descend from the mountain). Whatever reason is to be assigned for the omissions, the shape of the material that remains gives these episodes a distinctive character, when they are considered as a unit.

In these three verses, which are merely a modification of the Marcan material (6:14-16, see T. Schramm, *Der Markus-Stoff*, 128-129), Herod's reaction to Jesus is retained, but it takes on a different shape and serves a different function. It no longer merely introduces this ruler to tell about his treatment of John. Mark had recounted it on the heels of the other reactions, and it sounds there like a guilty conscience speaking. But the Lucan redaction makes it work differently. The Lucan modification of the Marcan episode includes the following: (a) Luke identifies Herod as *ho tetraarchēs*, undoubtedly because he called him so in 3:1; the title becomes one of the minor agreements of Matthew and Luke against Mark in the Triple Tradition at this point. (b) He makes Herod react to *ta ginomena panta*, "all that was happening," a much vaguer expression than Mark's allusion to Jesus' miracles. (c) He makes Herod's reaction one of perplexity (7:7b), which foreshadows the question that Herod will ask in v. 9. (d) Luke rephrases the reports that come to Herod with a threefold *hoti* clause, "that . . . , that . . . , that . . . ," i.e. three parallel clauses that serve as the subject of the infin. *dia to legesthai*, "by the talk." (e) Luke puts on the lips of Herod a distinctive, dramatic question, "Who is this about whom I hear such talk?" (9:9c). This becomes the crucial question which the episodes in the rest of the chapter up to the travel account answer implicitly or explicitly. Finally, (f) Luke adds that Herod was anxious to see Jesus, thus foreshadowing 13:31 and 23:8.

Form-critically, Luke 9:7-9 has to be understood as a story about Jesus (V. Taylor, *FGT*, 147). It is part of the narrative gospel tradition. R. Bultmann (*HST*, 301-302) regarded its Marcan parallel (6:14-29) as a legend devoid of Christian characteristics, probably derived from Hellenistic Jewish tradition, given its heathen parallels (Herodotus 9.108-113; Livy *Ab urbe condita* 39.43, 3-4; Plutarch *Artaxerxes* 17). He was also inclined to deny its historicity (which was defended by H. Windisch, *ZNW* 18 [1917] 73-81). This Marcan episode, however, is largely concerned with the details of the death of John, which do not concern us here, since Luke has omitted them. His transposition of the notice about the imprisonment of John makes no mention of his death, about which we learn only here. The imprisonment and death of John under Herod are reported by Josephus (*Ant.* 18.5,2 § 116-119) so that one cannot call in question Luke's account of these details. See p. 451 above.

This episode in the Lucan Gospel, however, serves a christological purpose. It poses the crucial question and sets the stage for a number of answers to be given to it. Passages that in the Marcan Gospel served other purposes are now seen in the light of Herod's question. Thus the episode becomes a christological climax to what has preceded and prepares for the central section of the Gospel, the travel account. The answers to be given are not all of equal kind or value; some are explicit, some implicit; some use titles derived from the pre-Lucan tradition, some use Luke's own. They amount to what H. Conzelmann (*Theology*, 56) has called "a series of Christological statements which Luke harmonizes one with the other by altering his sources and introducing variations of Markan motifs."

One may wonder why Luke makes Herod, the tetrarch of Galilee, ask the crucial question at this point in the narrative. It seems that he wants a person of authority, a ruler of Galilee, where Jesus' ministry up to this point has mainly taken place, to pose the question. Then the authority of Jesus reflected in the various answers to follow will be properly appreciated. This will undergird the travel account itself, in which Jesus will be seen authoritatively training the witnesses from Galilee, those who make their way with him to the city of destiny.

A minor element in the episode is the implication of Jesus' own prophetic role. The three figures with whom he is compared in the reports of the people that reach Herod's ears are all of prophetic type: John the Baptist has already been declared to be someone greater than a prophet (7:26), Elijah is the well-known OT prophet, and some query whether Jesus himself is "one of the prophets of old." This threefold report is derived from Mark 6:14-15 (with modifications); but it is found again in Luke 9:19, derived from Mark 8:28. The double use of it in the Marcan Gospel is almost certainly of independent origin in the pre-Marcan tradition (so R. Pesch, *BZ* 19 [1973] 190). As a whole, this episode and the following episodes up to 9:50 are a good example of what E. E. Ellis has called "a Lukan combination and reworking of pre-Lukan traditions" ("The Composition of Luke 9," 125).

NOTES

9 7. the tetrarch Herod. On Herod Antipas, see NOTE on 3:1. He is introduced here as the ruler of Galilee, because of his authority in the area being evangelized at present by Jesus. In Mark 6:14 he is called less properly "King Herod"—a title that was proper for his father, Herod the Great. V. Taylor (*Mark*, 308) tries to defend it as a reflection of local custom.

began to hear. Luke uses an inceptive aor., *ēkousen* (see BDF § 331).

all that was happening. I.e. all that Jesus was doing in preaching and curing. Luke makes no explicit mention of the "powerful deeds" of Jesus (Marcan *dynameis*). Some mss. (A, C³, W, ⊕, etc.) add *hyp' autou*, "(all that was being done) by him," i.e. by Jesus; but this phrase is omitted by P⁷⁵, ℵ, B, C*, D, L, etc., important mss., of wide geographic expanse; this reading must prevail.

puzzled by the talk. Lit. "he was at a loss." This psychological note is introduced by Luke in place of the final statement in Mark 6:16, which rather reveals Herod's guilty conscience. The Lucan perplexity depicts Herod affected more by what people were saying about Jesus than by his own treatment of

John. This perplexity prepares for the question in v. 9 and his desire to see Jesus.

John had been raised from the dead. I.e. people were thinking of Jesus as *Ioannes redivivus.* Previously, Luke has reported only that Herod had imprisoned John (3:19-20); now we learn of his execution.

8. *Elijah had appeared.* For the popular expectation of the return of Elijah, see NOTE on 1:17 and the COMMENT on 7:24-30.

one of the prophets of old. Lucan redaction makes Jesus a certain (*tis*) *propheta redivivus,* whereas Mark 6:15 said merely that people thought he was a prophet, "like one of the prophets." Which one he was supposed to be is left undetermined. Since Elijah has just been mentioned, one might think rather in terms of the "prophet like Moses," but this is not certain. See F. Gils, *Jésus prophète.* Jeremiah was also an expected figure at this time; see Matt 16:14; cf. 2 Macc 2:4-7; 15:13-14; 2 Esdr 2:18 (the last passage also mentions Isaiah).

had arisen. I.e. had appeared on the scene. Though Luke uses forms of *anistanai* (especially the intrans. second aor. and the middle forms) in the sense of "rise" from the dead (16:31; 18:33; 24:46), the verb need not have that connotation here (or in 9:19), although one cannot exclude it either—in light of Luke's use of it in that sense and also of his deliberate change of Mark's phrase identifying Jesus merely as "a prophet like one of the prophets." The verb basically means "to stand one on his feet."

9. *John I beheaded.* Luke retains from Mark 6:16 Herod's admission that he had executed John, but he does not put on Herod's lips the belief that he has returned from the dead, as does Mark. Instead he substitutes the crucial question.

who is this about whom I hear such talk? This question has, in fact, been foreshadowed in 8:25, where the disciples pose it apropos of the stilling of the storm. See also 5:21; 7:20,49 for similar questions. In itself, the question would not be that significant, since it fits such a pattern in Luke's Gospel: various persons asking who Jesus is. It is rather the function that the question has in this section of the Lucan Gospel that is important, especially in the light of vv. 18-20 below. The various modifications of the Marcan source that follow presuppose it.

he was anxious to see him. Contrast 8:20. Herod's desire was to see Jesus perform some miracles; it reveals nothing of any belief in him, only curiosity.

BIBLIOGRAPHY (9:7-9)

Ellis, E. E. "The Composition of Luke 9 and the Source of Its Christology," in *Current Issues in Biblical and Patristic Interpretation: Studies in Honor of Merrill C. Tenney* (Grand Rapids: Eerdmans, 1975) 120-127 [originally presented as an answer to the following entry].

Fitzmyer, J. A. "The Composition of Luke, Chapter 9," in *Perspectives on Luke-Acts* (ed. C. H. Talbert; Special Studies Series 5; Danville, VA: Association of Baptist Professors of Religion; Edinburgh: Clark, 1978) 139-152.

Gils, F. *Jésus prophète d'après les évangiles synoptiques* (Orientalia et biblica lovaniensia 2; Louvain: Publications universitaires, 1957) 20-23.

Schnackenburg, R. "Die Erwartung des 'Propheten' nach dem Neuen Testament und den Qumran-Texten," *SE I* (TU 73, 1959) 622-639.

Schramm, T. *Der Markus-Stoff,* 128-129.

Wilkens, W. "Die Auslassung von Mark. 6,45-8,26 bei Lukas im Licht der Komposition Luk. 9,1-50," *TZ* 32 (1976) 193-200.

49. THE RETURN OF THE APOSTLES; THE FEEDING OF THE FIVE THOUSAND

(9:10-17)

9 10 When the apostles came back, they told Jesus what they had done. He took them along with him and withdrew privately to a town called Bethsaida. 11 But when the crowds of people learned of it, they followed him. He welcomed them, spoke to them about the kingdom of God, and healed those who needed to be cured. 12 As the day began to wear on, the Twelve came to him and said, "Send the crowd away so that the people can go to the villages and farms round about to find lodging and food; for we are in a really deserted place here." 13 And Jesus said to them, "You give them something to eat." But they said, "We have nothing more than five loaves of bread and two fish—unless we ourselves are to go and buy food for all these people." 14 (There were about five thousand men there.) So Jesus said to his disciples, "Have them sit down in groups of about fifty each." 15 They did so, making all the people sit down. 16 Then he took the five loaves and two fish, looked up to heaven, blessed them, and broke them in pieces. He gave them to the disciples to pass out among the crowd. 17 All of them ate of it and were filled; and the leftovers were picked up from them, twelve large baskets of fragments.

COMMENT

The Lucan episode of Herod's perplexity is followed immediately by the notice of the return of the apostles (Luke 9:10) from their mission (9:1-6) and the story of the feeding of the five thousand by the multiplication of five loaves and two fish (9:10-17). It is the only miracle of Jesus' Galilean ministry that is recounted in all four Gospels. The analysis of the episode is complicated because one has to compare it not only with the one story of a multiplication of loaves and fish in John 6:1-15, but with the two stories, the feeding of the five thousand and the feeding of the four thousand, in the other two Synoptics. For this Lucan episode corresponds to Mark 6:30-44 and Matt 14:13-21. Luke's Big Omission is partly responsible for his having no counterpart to Mark 8:1-10 and Matt

15:32-39, the feeding of the four thousand. This is one of the prime examples of his avoidance of doublets in his Gospel (see p. 82 above). It also gives Luke a superficial resemblance to the Johannine Gospel, which has only one account of the multiplication of the loaves and fish.

In a detailed analysis of the various accounts, R. E. Brown (*John, I-XII,* 236-244) has convincingly shown that the Johannine account "was not copied from any one Synoptic Gospel nor pieced together from several Gospels." It represents an independent tradition. Moreover, since there are only two minor points at which the Lucan and Johannine accounts are similar, we need not really be concerned about their general relationship here. These points are the crowds following Jesus (9:11; cf. John 6:2) and the mention of the five thousand present prior to the miracle itself (9:14; cf. John 6:10). Nor does the dating of that independent tradition really concern us. See the NOTES for details.

Much more important is the relation of this Lucan episode to those of the Synoptic tradition. Even though we are only concerned in the Lucan Gospel with one account of a multiplication of the loaves and fish, the question arises about its relation not only to Mark 6:30-44, to which it corresponds, but also to Mark 8:1-10 (and their Matthean parallels). This relationship has to be discussed in three ways. First, does the second account, the feeding of the four thousand, represent a distinct miracle or is it simply a variant of the same one? The latter seems to be the case, having been inherited by Mark from two independent traditions. The puzzled query of the disciples in Mark 8:4 ("How can one feed these people here in a desert place?") is strange, if not inexplicable, if they had witnessed the miracle of 6:30-44. Moreover, V. Taylor (*Mark,* 628-632), in dependence on earlier studies, has shown that Mark 6:30 - 7:37 and 8:1-26 not only both begin with a story of a multiplication of loaves and fish but are parallel in other themes. Hence it seems that Mark has preserved two independent complexes of tradition related to the feeding of crowds. See also A. Heising, *Die Botschaft,* 62 n. 75. Matthew has followed Mark in preserving them, whereas Luke has not.

Second, the Lucan account of the feeding of the five thousand does not depend on Mark 8:1-10. What minor resemblances the Lucan account has with that Marcan passage can all be found in Mark 6:30-44. So there is no need to waste time on such a comparison.

Third, the relationship of Luke 9:10-17 to Mark 6:30-44 is complicated. It is clearly inspired by the Marcan account because it continues the Marcan sequence after the omission of the story about the death of John the Baptist (part of which has been transposed to 3:19-20, and part of which is merely alluded to in 9:7-9). Now the notice about the return of "the apostles" (9:10a; see 9:1, where the Twelve, not "apostles," were sent out; cf. vv. 12,14) and their report of "what they had done" are formulated in dependence on Mark 6:30. But Luke 9:10 would be a considerable abridgment of Mark 6:30-32, where nothing is said about Jesus' invitation to come aside and rest awhile; their departure in a boat and their arrival at a lonely place disappear. Instead, Luke makes their destination a town called Bethsaida. Only Luke so identifies the place. Matt 4:13 also drastically curtails Mark 6:30-32 and omits further all allusion to Num 27:17 or 1 Kgs 22:17, to which Mark 6:34 alludes, as does Luke 9:11. Again, both omit the dividing up of the fish (Luke 9:16; Matt 14:19). These significant omissions by Matthew and Luke over against Mark, when considered with a number of minor agreements of the two (e.g. *hoi ochloi,* 9:11; *ēkolouthēsan autō,* 9:11; *kai,* 9:11; *de,* 9:12; *tas,* 9:12; *hoi de,* 9:13; *ouk,* 9:13; *brōmata,* 9:13; *hōsei,* 9:14; *eipen de,* 9:14; *to,* 9:17; and *klasmatōn,* 9:17), have posed the question whether two different sources lie behind the account of the feeding of the five thousand in the Synoptic tradition. Is it possible that Matthew and Luke knew a "Q" form of this episode, details of which they have both preferred to the Marcan form? This is not impossible, but can scarcely be proved. W. R. Stegner, who has analyzed many of these differences, certainly goes too far in ascribing priority to the Lucan account of the feeding ("Lucan Priority," 19-28). Here, a glance at W. R. Farmer's *Synopticon* (Cambridge: University Press, 1969) 172-173 reveals that the blues and greens he uses to denote Triple Tradition and agreement of Mark and Luke predominate, leaving, however, a wide area for Lucan redaction. Given this situation, I prefer to regard this passage as one that is basically Marcan, but influenced by another tradition known to Luke (not that of Mark 8:1-10) and by his own redaction. It is hardly likely that Luke is joining Matthew and Mark, *pace* Heising (*Die Botschaft,* 75).

Form-critically, we recognize the passage as a miracle-story, specifically a nature miracle (see R. Bultmann, *HST,* 217; cf. V. Taylor, *FGT,* 123). It is recounted to show once again the power of Jesus.

Coming immediately after the question that Herod poses in 9:9, it serves in its own way to provide the first answer, an implicit miraculous answer. The traditional material that Luke incorporates here does not include a specific title for Jesus, but in the Lucan form of the story the miracle that is worked is linked explicitly to his preaching of the kingdom of God (9:11, a frequent Lucan motif; see 4:23). The bounty that is displayed in the miracle linked to such preaching clearly identifies Jesus as a person in whom God's message, activity, power, and creative presence are revealed. Even though in the preceding episode Luke had omitted mention of the *dynameis,* "mighty acts," of the Marcan parallel (6:14), it is striking that the first episode after Herod's question makes explicit reference to one of them. Here is depicted concretely what Luke in Acts 2:22 says openly: "a man attested by God with mighty acts and wonders and signs which God did through him in your midst." But it scarcely "marks the climax of Jesus' Galilean mission" in Luke (*pace* E. E. Ellis [*The Gospel*, 138], A. Plummer [*Gospel*, 242]).

One cannot read Luke 9:16 without detecting a formulation parallel to that of the institution of the Eucharist (see 22:19). Luke has suppressed the motive of compassion that one finds in Mark 6:34; so that cannot be operative in his version of the feeding. Because it is a nature miracle it does not immediately depict Jesus confronting the evils that afflict human beings; no mention is made of their hunger in the episode (even though 9:12c might hint at it). It seems, therefore, that it is a symbolic miracle in the Synoptic tradition. It can be understood as a miracle that fulfills OT promises about God feeding his people (Isa 25:6; 65:13-14; Pss 78:19; 81:16). G. Boobyer (*JTS* 3 [1952] 161-171) has tried to argue that the eucharistic liturgical formulations have not colored the accounts of the multiplication of the loaves in the Synoptic tradition. But his argument is not convincing, because the parallels between the various Synoptic accounts of the feeding and the eucharistic institution are too close to be explained otherwise. The use of the eucharistic formulae in the feeding accounts starts a trajectory of Christian interpretation in which the Eucharist is being prefigured. See further L. Cerfaux, "La section des pains," 75-76. Whether this prefigurement was intended by the historical Jesus in Stage I of the gospel tradition is one thing; but it is scarcely without such symbolic nuance in Stage III, especially when one recalls the typically Lucan expression, "the breaking of the bread" (Acts 2:42,46; 20:7,11). See also Luke 22:19; 24:29-30.

Finally, the multiplication of the loaves and the fish in this Lucan context prepares for the admission that Peter is to make about Jesus. The disciples have been taken by him away from the crowd; but the crowd follows. When the feeding is over, no reaction of the crowd is recorded. Whereas what the disciples had, five loaves of bread and two fish, was inadequate to feed the crowd, what Jesus had feeds them abundantly, and with leftovers. On the heels of this largesse comes a reaction from the spokesmen of the disciples.

NOTES

9 10. *the apostles.* The phrase *hoi apostoloi* is taken over by Luke from Mark 6:33 and suits the Lucan designation of "the Twelve," who were sent out (9:1-6), because of Luke's earlier understanding of them in 6:13. See p. 614 above. "The Twelve" reappear in 9:12, where Luke has changed the Marcan *mathētai*, "disciples," to this expression. But in v. 14 he introduces *mathētai*, and in v. 16 he retains it from his Marcan source.

came back. A similar report about the seventy(-two) will be made in 10:17.

told. Lit. "narrated," for the verb is *diēgēsanto*, a form related to the noun *diēgēsis* (on which see the NOTE on 1:1). Cf. 8:39. It is important for Luke that the "apostles" tell Jesus what they had been doing; this makes for *asphaleia*. See p. 289 above.

what they had done. Luke omits the Marcan phrase, "and what they had taught." There was no charge to "teach" in the original commission of 9:1-2.

took them along with him. The report that the apostles have just made is the basis for this gracious action of Jesus. It will find echoes later on; see 9:28; 18:31.

privately. Luke preserves the prep. phrase *kat' idian* from the Marcan source. Cf. 10:23; Acts 23:19. It expresses Jesus' intention to get away from the crowd.

to a town. The best reading here is *polin*, "town, city" (found in mss. P75, B, ℵc). Ms. D, however, reads *kōmēn legomenēn B.*, "a village named B.," whereas some others (Mss. ℵ*, etc.) as well as the Curetonian Syriac version have *topon erēmon*, "a desert place." The text-tradition is here affected by a problem in Luke's account. Whereas Mark 6:31 and Matt 14:13 depict Jesus retiring with the apostles to a desert place, Luke presents him going to "a town." Then the apostles' request in v. 12 made in that town, to send the crowd away so that the people can go to villages and farms round about for lodging and food is peculiar; and "town" conflicts with their reason, "for we are in a really deserted place here." The reading "village" may be owing to some scribe's knowledge that this word has been used of Bethsaida by Josephus (*Ant.* 18.2,1 § 28), who mentions that the tetrarch Philip raised it to the status of a "city." But "town" has to be retained as the *lectio difficilior*. See further D. Baldi, "Il problema."

Bethsaida. The Greek name represents the Aramaic *bêt ṣaidā'*, "house of hunting" (or possibly, "fishing"); the Greek vocalization would not tolerate *bêt ṣayyādā'*, "house of the hunter." Mysterious, indeed, is the explanation of it as "place of satisfaction" (F. W. Danker, *Jesus*, 112). Luke alone mentions a town as the site of the miracle. John 6:1 locates it across the lake of Tiberias, where the Lucan town would have been. But Luke has obviously derived the name from Mark 6:46, the first verse of the first Marcan episode that he drops in his Big Omission, as J. M. Creed (*The Gospel*, 128) has noted. See also Mark 8:22. The use of this name is a good indication that in this episode Luke is basically working with "Mk."

Bethsaida was situated N of Lake Gennesaret and E of the Jordan River, not far from where it empties into the lake. The tetrarch Philip raised it from a village to a city and renamed it *Iulias*, in honor of the daughter of Augustus (Josephus *Ant.* 18.2,1 § 28). It would seem to be the town from which the apostles Philip, Peter, and Andrew came (John 1:44; 12:21), but the evangelist there regards it as "of Galilee" (12:21). This identification of Bethsaida is also found in Ptolemy *Geographia* 5.16,4. Actually it lay in Gaulanitis, in the territory ruled over by Philip. However, there must have existed some popular confusion about it, because Josephus (*Ant.* 18.1,1 § 4) writes about a Gaulanite rebel named Judas, whom he later refers to as a "Galilean" (*Ant.* 18.1,6 § 23). When Luke depicted Jesus crossing the lake to Gerasene territory, he added that it was "opposite Galilee" in order to keep it related to his geographical perspective. Here he undoubtedly wants the reader to think that Bethsaida is still in Galilee; or he may even have had no clear idea where it was (see H. Conzelmann, *Theology*, 51-52). In any case, it is a factor of his geographical perspective.

Jesus is depicted retiring to Bethsaida for seclusion, as v. 10b suggests, not to avoid an "encounter" with Herod (*pace* Ellis, *The Gospel*, 138).

11. *they followed him.* See John 6:2.

He welcomed them. I.e. despite his desire to be in private with the apostles. For some reason Luke omits mention of the compassion of Jesus (cf. Mark 6:34) and the allusion to the OT (Num 27:17; 1 Kgs 22:17). He accords the crowds the response that they had given him (8:40).

spoke to them about the kingdom of God. Or "continued to speak," since the verb is impf. See the NOTE on "kingdom" in 4:43. This is a Lucan redactional addition about the content of Jesus' teaching; Mark 6:34 ends merely with, "he taught them many things." Luke clearly wants to relate the coming miracle to Jesus' kingdom-preaching.

and healed. This is another Lucan redactional addition. In Matt 14:14, where the same idea is present, the wording is entirely different. This suggests that, if Matthew and Luke both knew of another form of this story, they would be using it to modify "Mk."

12. *the day began to wear on.* Lit. "as the day began to decline," the same expression that occurs in 24:29. The time of the evening meal is being suggested.

the Twelve. See the NOTE on 9:10. In John 6:5 Jesus himself takes the initiative, but in the Synoptic account the disciples come as representatives of the people, or at least as observers of their condition. The shift to "the Twelve" here makes H. Schürmann (*Lukasevangelium*, 514) think that Luke is presenting them in a collegial function, as in Acts 6:2. Perhaps.

Send the crowd away. Some mss. (P[75], ℵ[e], 28, 565, etc.) read the pl. *ochlous*, "crowds," but this is suspect, since it looks like a scribal correction to make the noun agree with the following pl. verbs. The suggestion made by the Twelve creates a problem: Where would five thousand men find food and lodging in villages? In reality, it is a literary suggestion, designed to advance the story.

for we are in a really deserted place. See the NOTE on "town" in v. 10 above.

13. *You give them something to eat.* Luke has changed the Marcan word order, putting the pron. *hymeis* emphatically at the end of the sentence. Jesus indirectly challenges the disciples to perform the miracle. Luke does not make this as explicit as it is done in John 6:6. Jesus' command is more unsuitable than the Twelve's suggestion of dismissal; again it is used to advance the story.

The words used by Jesus may well be an allusion to 2 Kgs 4:42-44, where a man from Baal-shalishah brought to Elisha and his servant twenty barley loaves and fresh grain with the command, "Give to the people that they may eat." When Elisha's servant protests, "How can I set this before a hundred men?" the man repeats his command and quotes Yahweh, "They shall eat and have some left." If this allusion is really present in the Synoptic story, then it may hint that Jesus performs the coming miracle in a prophetic role. See further Heising, *Die Botschaft*, 31-38. In any case, this OT allusion is more plausible than a reference to the desert manna (*pace* Ellis, *The Gospel*, 138-139). That allusion fits the Johannine form of the story, but scarcely the Synoptic.

five loaves of bread and two fish. These details are the same as in Mark 6:38; Matt 14:17; and John 6:9. Contrast Mark 8:5; Matt 15:34, where at the feeding of the four thousand mention is made of "seven loaves," to which Matthew adds, "and a few small fish" (which looks like a harmonization of that story with this one). The Synoptic accounts do not tell us of what the bread was made; the "barley loaves" of John 6:9 may be an allusion to 2 Kgs 4:42. Whereas John 6:9 speaks of *opsarion*, "dried fish," the Synoptic accounts consistently use a form of *ichthys*, "fish," a word that soon became a credal symbol of faith in Christ. It built upon the confession of the Ethiopian eunuch of Acts 8:37 (as read in some mss.), by adding *sōtēr*, "Savior," to produce *Iēsous Christos theou huios, Sōtēr* or ΙΧΘΥΣ. Reference to this symbol is found in the *Epitaph of Abercius* and the *Inscription of Pectorius* (see J. Quasten, *Patrology* [Westminster, MD: Newman, 1951] 1. 24, 172, 174; F. J. Dölger, *ΙΧΘΥΣ: Das Fischsymbol in frühchristlicher Zeit* (2d ed.; 5 vols.; Münster: Aschendorff, 1922-1943).

14. *about five thousand men.* Luke's better sense of storytelling brings up from the end of the story in "Mk" the detail about the number of men, thus explaining how numerous "all the people" were. The stage is thus better set for the multiplication of the loaves, for it heightens the miracle. Recall his similar treatment of the age of Jairus' daughter in 8:42 (cf. Mark 5:42). All the Synoptic accounts have *andres*, "men," not *anthrōpoi;* Matt 14:21 adds, "besides women and children."

his disciples. See NOTE on 9:10.

Have them sit down in groups of about fifty each. Lit. "have them recline (as) dining groups, about in fifties." Luke uses the word *klisias* (acc. pl.) in apposition to the dir. obj.; it is a word found in the same meaning in 3 Macc 6:31. For the distributive prep. phrase *ana pentēkonta*, "in fifties," cf. 10:1. Mark 6:39 had used the more Semitic distributive phrase *symposia symposia*, "(in) banqueting parties," by the repetition of a very Greek word. In this miracle Jesus involves his disciples' activity; see further v. 16. The instruction to group the people in fifties is simply a division of five thousand. It has nothing to do with the OT groupings of Israel into thousands, hundreds, fifties, or tens (Exod 18:21,25, etc.) or with that used in the Qumran community (1QS 2:21; 1QSa 1:14-15). In the Qumran literature the groupings allude to those of the OT, but here "fifties" is used alone. There may be some symbolism in the five loaves, five thousand men, and groups of fifty, but it is not evident. Moreover, it would be hard to say how the two fish fit into it.

16. *he took.* Five actions of Jesus are recounted, beginning with this verb: *labōn . . . , anablepsas eis ton ouranon, eulogēsen autous, kateklasen, edidou,* "taking . . . , looking up to heaven, he blessed them, broke, and gave." The ms. D adds a sixth, *proseuxato kai* (before *eulogēsen*), "he prayed and blessed. . . ." That is scarcely an "original" reading, *pace* Creed, *The Gospel*, 129. The five actions are taken over verbatim by Luke from Mark 6:41, with the addition of *autous* (see below). Matt 14:18 has the same five actions, but with two different forms: *klasas*, the aor. ptc. and *edōken*, the aor. indic. Four of these actions occur in the Last Supper scene of Mark 14:22 (*labōn, eulog-*

ēsas, eklasen, edōken); similarly in Matt 26:26. In Luke 22:19 four again appear, but *eucharistēsas*, "giving thanks," replaces *eulogēsas*. The former ptc. is found in the second multiplication scene (Mark 8:6; Matt 15:36). Cf. 1 Cor 11:24, which has *elaben, eucharistēsas, eklasen*, and *eipen*, "he said" (instead of "gave"). The similarity in all these formulas is noteworthy. Those with *eucharistēsas* should be regarded as reflections of a later stage of the tradition about the Eucharist, when a play on the word was seen; it would hardly have been changed to *eulogēsas*. On the other hand, the formulas used in all these passages are undoubtedly reflections of the early eucharistic liturgies.

The five actions predicated of Jesus stand in contrast to the proclamation of the miracle recounted in 2 Kgs 4:43; Jesus does not proclaim the significance of what he is about.

looked up to heaven. This is an OT expression, found often in the LXX (Gen 15:5; Deut 4:19; Job 22:26; 2 Macc 7:28).

blessed them. Luke has added the dir. obj., *autous*, thus making Jesus bless "them," i.e. the bread and the fish. In Mark 6:41 (and Matt 14:18) the verb appears alone and probably is intended to be understood absolutely, meaning, "he uttered a blessing." An ancient Jewish table grace, recorded in the Mishnah, runs, "Blessed be you, O Lord our God, king of the world, who cause bread to come forth from the earth" (*Berakot* 6:1). In it God is blest (i.e. praised), not the food, as in Luke, who misunderstood the Marcan formula.

Ms. D reads *eulogēsen ep' autous*, "uttered a blessing over them," and some commentators (see M. Black, *AAGA*³, 116) have tried to suggest that this is a more primitive Aramaic formula. This is far from certain; cf. the Greek of Ps.-Clement *Hom.* 1.22,4. Cf. S. P. Brock, "A Note on Luke ix 16 (D)," *JTS* 14 (1963) 391-393; cf. *TLZ* 88 (1963) 352.

broke them in pieces. I.e. both the bread and the fish, apparently. But ms. D omits *kai eklasen*, probably because the fish were understood as included. Normally, *klān* is used in the NT with "bread." It is never said in the Synoptics that Jesus "multiplied" the pieces. The miraculous aspect of his actions is deduced from the number who eat of them and from what is left over, given the small amount with which he began. For Luke, who has added *autous*, the blessing and breaking of the bread and the fish cause the multiplication.

He gave. The verb *edidou*, an impf., following the two aor. ptcs. and aor. indics., is strange. Luke preserves what he found in Mark 6:41, whereas Matt 14:19 makes an aor. out of it, *edōken*. Does the impf. mean "he kept on giving it," with progressive force to indicate the miraculous bounty of the food? M. Zerwick (ZBG § 271) takes it in this sense. Whereas in John 6:11 Jesus himself passes out the food, in the Synoptics Jesus makes his disciples dispensers of the bounty that he brings. Apparently he did not partake of the food himself. At least we are not told that he did.

17. *All of them ate of it.* These words are derived from Mark 6:42. They are common to the Synoptic tradition.

and were filled. Luke uses here *echortasthēsan*, the verb that is found in Mark 6:42 (see Matt 14:20). He had used the same verb in the beatitude of 6:21; see further 15:16 (in some mss.); 16:21. In the LXX the word often occurs (e.g. Pss 37:19; 81:17; 132:15), expressing the bounty with which God had promised to sate his people. Contrast John 6:12.

the leftovers were picked up from them. Lit. "what was excessive to them was picked up." The leftovers express the abundance of the food supplied to God's people through Jesus' activity. Recall the saying in 2 Kgs 4:43-44, which proclaimed the abundance directly; here it is just narrated.

twelve large baskets of fragments. The word *klasmata* denotes the "scraps or broken pieces" of food left over. The word is derived from Mark 6:43; cf. Mark 8:8; Matt 14:20; 15:37; John 6:12. In liturgical texts from later Christian eucharistic celebrations the same word occurs for the "bits" of eucharistic bread (see *Didache* 9:3,4, with allusion to the multiplication of the loaves). The "twelve" baskets obviously has a symbolic reference to the "Twelve" in v. 12; they each bring back a basketful and now have enough to feed still others. The word *kophinos* can also mean a "large wallet, sack," such as was carried by a traveler. Juvenal (*Satires* 3.14) associates *cophinus* with a Jew.

What is striking in the Synoptic account of the feeding of the five thousand, as M.-J. Lagrange (*Luc*, 265) has remarked, is the absence of any audience reaction to the miracle. Contrast John 6:14-15. This absence is particularly noteworthy in Luke 9:17, after which comes the omission of Marcan material and the rather abrupt introduction of Peter's confession of Jesus as God's Messiah.

BIBLIOGRAPHY (9:10-17)

Baldi, D. "Il problema del sito di Bethsaida e delle moltiplicazioni dei pani," *SBFLA* 10 (1959-1960) 120-146.

Boobyer, G. H. "The Eucharistic Interpretation of the Miracles of the Loaves in St. Mark's Gospel," *JTS* 3 (1952) 161-171.

Buse, I. "The Gospel Accounts of the Feeding of the Multitudes," *ExpTim* 74 (1962-1963) 167-170.

Cangh, J.-M. van. "Le thème des poissons dans les récits évangéliques de la multiplication des pains," *RB* 78 (1971) 71-83.

Cerfaux, L. "La section des pains (Mc VI,31-VIII,26; Mt XIV,13-XVI,12)," in *Synoptische Studien: Alfred Wikenhauser zum siebzigsten Geburtstag* . . . (eds. J. Schmid and A. Vögtle; Munich: K. Zink, 1953) 64-77.

Friedrich, G. "Die beiden Erzählungen von der Speisung in Mark, 6,31-44; 8,1-9," *TZ* 20 (1964) 10-22.

Heising, A. *Die Botschaft der Brotvermehrung: Zur Geschichte und Bedeutung eines Christusbekenntnisses im Neuen Testament* (SBS 15; Stuttgart: Katholisches Bibelwerk, 1966).

Kertelge, K. *Die Wunder Jesu*, 129-145.

Knackstedt, J. "Die beiden Brotvermehrungen im Evangelium," *NTS* 10 (1963-1964) 309-335.

Lester-Garland, L. V. "The Feeding of the Five Thousand," *Theology* 36 (1938) 87-92.

Stegner, W. R. "Lucan Priority in the Feeding of the Five Thousand," *BR* 21 (1976) 19-28.

Ziener, G. "Die Brotwunder im Markusevangelium," *BZ* 4 (1960) 282-285.

50. PETER'S CONFESSION
(9:18-21)

9 18 Once when Jesus happened to be praying alone, the disciples were with him; so he asked them, "Who do the crowds say that I am?" 19 They replied, "John the Baptist; but others would say Elijah; and still others a prophet of old who has arisen." 20 Then he asked them, "But who do you say that I am?" Peter spoke up in reply, "You are God's Messiah." 21 So Jesus gave them strict orders not to say this to anyone.

COMMENT

Immediately following the episode of the feeding of the five thousand in the Lucan Gospel comes that of Peter's confession of Jesus as God's Messiah (9:18-21). Whereas the multiplication of the loaves is parallel to Mark 6:30-44, Peter's confession parallels Mark 8:27-30. Luke has passed over the material in Mark 6:45 - 8:26 in his so-called Big Omission. The episodes that follow this one show that Luke is again using the Marcan sequence.

Why has Luke omitted the intervening Marcan material? Several answers have been proposed. (a) Luke sensed a need to curtail because of his own inserts (so H. Schürmann, *Lukasevangelium*, 526). This is a possible reason, but not very convincing, since he still retains so much Marcan material. (b) Luke omits a block of episodes that begin and end at Bethsaida, outside of Galilee (Mark 6:45; 8:22); it is a sort of omission by homoeoteleuton (W. E. Bundy, *Jesus*, 266 n. 4). This is, however, a rather tenuous reason, because Luke has substituted Bethsaida for the Marcan phrase, "deserted place," of 6:32 (see NOTE on 9:10); and then suppresses the mention of Caesarea Philippi as the location of Peter's confession. (c) If, as has been pointed out above, there are two series of similar episodes in Mark 6:30 - 7:37 and 8:1-26, both beginning with a multiplication of loaves and fish, then Luke's tendency to avoid doublets may be a factor in the omission of the Marcan material. That does not wholly explain the matter, because he has no parallel at all to some of the "duplicated" material. (d) Luke is at pains to limit Jesus' ministry to

Galilee in this part of the Gospel; hence he omits the Marcan material in which Jesus goes to the areas of Tyre and Sidon in Phoenicia. This is important to his geographical perspective. The omission is therefore to be understood in terms of Luke's composition. That is why Luke 8:1 is important, as is 8:22, since "the other side of the lake" does not mean something distinct from Galilee for Luke. Though he never refers to the lake as the "sea of Galilee," as does John 6:1, the lake is part of Galilee for him.

The reasons for the omission of the Marcan material are not nearly as important as the resultant shape of this part of the Lucan Gospel. It gives to chap. 9, along with the insertion of the travel account at 9:51, a crucial form. Immediately, it brings the confession of Peter into close proximity, not only with the feeding of the five thousand, but also with the question posed by Herod in 9:9. The relation of Peter's confession to the multiplication of the loaves is found in John 6:1-15, 66-69 (see R. E. Brown, *John, I-XII,* 301). But the echoes of the reports to Herod about Jesus (9:7-8) are now found explicitly in the disciples' reports to Jesus himself, and their similarity cannot be missed. The location of Peter's confession at Caesarea Philippi is of no concern to Luke, who sees the answer given to Jesus' question as an answer given to Herod's earlier question. It provides an explicit christological title as the answer.

Moreover, Luke has significantly shortened the episode by omitting not only the geographical location, but even Peter's protest and Jesus' rebuke of him. Again, the confession of Peter turns out to be no longer a climactic point in the gospel-story, as it is in Mark 8, nor is it a church-founding episode, as it is in Matthew 16 (with the addition of vv. 16b-19). Rather the scene functions as one of the important answers given in this chapter to Herod's question.

Jesus had already been identified as "Messiah" in the infancy narrative (2:11); so the title is not new to the Christian reader of this Gospel. But that is introduced there in the light of what is said of Jesus within the Gospel itself. It is in this episode that we are in contact with the tradition that begins to form as Jesus' messiahship. In 4:41 the title occurs, but there it was part of the evangelist's comment. Jesus' reaction to Peter's confession in v. 21 is a prohibition to repeat the title during the ministry, and it prepares for the correctives to come in vv. 22,23-27,28-36,44-45. Such a prohibition was not imposed on the demon in 8:28, where the reader understood that that was supposed to be a conversation between Jesus and it. Here Peter's admission is made in the context of Jesus' question about what people think of him and what his own followers believe. It thus becomes an important christological answer in the Lucan Gospel. It is a messiahship that involves suffering, repudiation, death, even though it may end in resurrection, as the next episode makes clear.

The confession of Peter is a crucial episode in the Marcan Gospel, being related to the so-called messianic secret of Mark. H. Conzelmann (*Theology,* 56) has maintained that Luke turns the Marcan messianic secret into a misunderstanding of the passion, because he has omitted the rebuke of Peter (8:32) and the sayings in vv. 23-27 are addressed to the people who witnessed the glory of Jesus in the miracle, while the command of secrecy (9:21) is based on the inevitability of the passion. "Peter's protest is omitted, and in place of it is another motif, that of the secrecy of the Passion" (ibid.). This is hardly true, since there is here no misunderstanding of the passion. True, later on Luke says that they do not understand his second announcement; but that is not the substitution of one motif for another, which reveals a Lucan misunderstanding of the passion.

Ever since the time of W. Wrede (1901) the historicity of Peter's confession has been called in question. Later on, R. Bultmann argued that Mark 8:27-33 stemmed not from a historic confession at Caesarea Philippi, but from the faith of the primitive church; Peter's messianic faith grew out of his experience of the resurrection (*ZNW* 19 [1919-1920] 165-174; *HST,* 257-259). But E. Dinkler ("Peter's Confession," 176-188) has made a strong case for the historicity of Peter's confession itself (Mark 8:29b) and Jesus' Satan-saying (8:33b), as part of the pre-Easter tradition. F. Hahn (*Titles,* 223-228) also includes v. 27a, making of them a biographical apophthegm (or pronouncement-story). What seems to be clear is that the Marcan episode, as we have it today, is largely the work of the evangelist. Verses 27a, 27b have two introductory phrases; v. 28 is an echo of 6:14-15; v. 29 is a teaching-question that sounds secondary; v. 30 is the Marcan secret; and v. 31 the passion-announcement (on which see below). Verses 32-33a are redactional narrative material of Mark. Since it is scarcely likely that the Satan-saying would have been preserved if it did not stem from Jesus himself and sounds like an appropriate answer of Jesus to Peter's confession, it is thus argued that both should be ascribed to the pre-Easter tradition. Further details of this sort of analysis do not concern us here, especially since Luke has omitted that part of the episode. But this much consideration of them makes us realize all the more what Luke has done with the little that he has retained from Mark.

Finally, a word about the development of the title that Peter uses of Jesus in this episode into the Christian title, "Christ." Obviously, in this episode Peter's confession is not an admission of full Christian faith. That could only come with the resurrection. On the other hand, if Peter did recognize Jesus as God's Messiah (in the Jewish sense, set forth in the NOTE on 9:20), one has the problem of explaining how that title developed into the Christian title, "Christ," and eventually the name for Jesus.

Once again, Dinkler ("Peter's Confession," 194-198) has made a plausible suggestion. Jesus corrected the title that Peter used; how did it come to be accepted by Christians? He finds this in the title used on the cross, "the king of the Jews" (Mark 15:26; Matt 27:37; Luke 23:38; John 19:19—though none of the evangelists gives it in identical wording). Being a Roman formulation, that is contemptuous of the Jews, its basic historicity is scarcely to be contested. If it were invented by Christians, they would have used *Christos,* for early Christians would scarcely have called their Lord "the king of the Jews." He who died on the cross was raised by God and "made Lord and Messiah" (Acts 2:36). In other words, it was undoubtedly the *titulus* of the cross formulated by the Roman prefect that led to the use of this title par excellence for Jesus in the NT. Indeed, in the earliest writings of Paul it often appears as his name.

A considerably transformed version of this episode can be found in the Coptic *Gos. Thom.* § 13. The question put on Jesus' lips there reveals how the question in Luke 9:18d, which many regard (in its Marcan form) to be secondary in the canonical-gospel tradition, can develop still further. The saying reads: "Jesus said to his disciples: 'Make a comparison of me and tell me whom I resemble.' Simon Peter said to him, 'You resemble a righteous angel.' Matthew said to him, 'You resemble a wise philosopher.' Thomas said to him, 'Master, my mouth is quite incapable of saying whom you resemble.' Jesus said, 'I am not your Master; because you have drunk, you have become intoxicated at the bubbling fountain that I have measured off.'" The saying continues with Jesus taking Thomas aside and telling him three things that his companions try to learn from him; but he refuses to tell them. Because it is the *Gospel of Thomas,* he is the one, not Peter, who is rebuked and finally given further instruction.

NOTES

9 18. *when Jesus happened to be praying.* Luke uses again *kai egeneto* + finite verb (without a conj.) and also *en tō* + infin. as a temporal clause; see p. 119 above. Ms. D reads *autous,* "when they happened to be alone," but this is an inferior reading. Not only the Lucan stylistic features just mentioned, but his introduction of Jesus at prayer reveal his redactional hand in the first part of this verse. The mention of Jesus at prayer enhances the occasion not only for Peter's confession, but much more importantly for the declaration that he himself will make in v. 22; for his prayer is usually introduced when there is some significant episode to be recounted (see p. 244 above). There is no mention of it in Mark 8:27, where Jesus' question is posed rather while they were "on the way," and the place Caesarea Philippi (modern Banyas, NE of the

Lake) is given as the location of Peter's confession. That disappears in the Lucan account, and one has the impression that they were still somewhere in Galilee, in the vicinity of Bethsaida. The next time a geographical indication will be given in the Lucan Gospel is at the beginning of the travel account (9:51).

alone. The Greek phrase *kata monas* is not easily translated, since the adj. is in the acc. pl. fem., with some noun to be understood (see BDF § 241.6). The phrase is found already in both classical (Thucydides 1.32,37; Isaeus, 7.38) and Hellenistic Greek (MM, 417), functioning as an adv. to express solitude. However, it creates a problem here in view of the following clause, "the disciples were with him." How could he then be praying alone? Luke tolerates this inconsistency in his redaction, because he seeks to enhance the occasion with the motif of Jesus' prayer—and it is better that he should be at it alone.

were with him. The best reading is *synēsan autō,* read by mss. P75, C, D, W, the Koine text-tradition, etc.; ms. B* reads rather *synēntēsan,* "met him," or "came upon him." Though B. H. Streeter (*Four Gospels,* 177 n. 1) tried to defend this as the "original reading," it is undoubtedly secondary, being devised by some scribe to eliminate the problem just mentioned above.

Who do the crowds say that I am. Luke's redaction substitutes *ochloi,* "crowds," for the Marcan *anthrōpoi,* "people" (8:27). Luke, however, follows Mark in using "I," whereas Matt 16:13 has secondarily introduced "the Son of Man," being influenced most likely by the following declaration of Jesus (Mark 8:31).

19. *John the Baptist.* On the prophetic threesome used in this reply, see NOTES on 9:7-8. The crowds consider Jesus either a resurrected John, or *Elias redivivus,* or a prophet raised up. The popular reaction thus puts Jesus in a prophetic image, not in that of a messianic figure. This serves as a foil to Peter's confession. Recall that in John 6:14-15 it is explicitly said that because of the multiplication of the loaves the people considered Jesus a *prophet* and wanted to come to make him a *king.*

20. *who do you say that I am?* Instead of making a comment on the popular reaction, Jesus poses the question directly to his own disciples. Indirectly, he implies that "prophet" is not the way to put it.

Peter. See NOTES on 5:8; 6:14; 8:45,51. As in Mark 8:29, Peter appears as the spokesman for the "disciples" (v. 18).

God's Messiah. Or, "the Christ of God," if one would insist that Luke would intend this for his Gentile Christian audience, which would not have understood "Messiah." On the meaning of "Messiah" or "Christ," see NOTE on 2:11. The gen. phrase "of God" is a Lucan addition to Mark's simple "the Messiah." It is unrelated to Matthew's "the Christ, the Son of the living God" (16:16), which represents a topical combination of two Petrine confessions, one from Mark (*ho christos*), the other from a pre-Matthean post-resurrection appearance-tradition (*ho huios tou theou tou zōntos*). Along with vv. 17-19 Matthew has conflated the two; see further R. E. Brown et al., *Peter in the NT,* 86-87. The Lucan additional genitive expresses a special relationship of Jesus as Messiah to the Father; it is related to the Lucan use of a genitive in similar expressions in 2:26 (*christon Kyriou,* "the Lord's Messiah"); 23:35;

Acts 3:18. Possibly Luke has been influenced by Mark 14:62 in the use of it; or possibly by the OT background of the phrase in Ps 2:2; 2 Sam 23:1 (LXX). In any case, the relationship expressed by it is such that it does not prevent Jesus from facing suffering, repudiation, and death.

Peter's confession has to be understood as an admission of what he at that time thought Jesus to be. *Christos* would have to be understood in the Jewish sense of an expected anointed agent sent by God in the Davidic, kingly or political tradition. He would be a figure akin to the expected "Messiah of Israel" in the Qumran community (1QS 9:11, "until there comes a prophet and the Messiahs of Aaron and Israel") or "the king of the ages" awaited from Judah (*T. Reuben* 6:12). See further G. R. Beasley-Murray, *JTS* 48 (1947) 1-12; K. G. Kuhn, *NTS* 1 (1954-1955) 168-179. For Luke *christos* is a title clearly related to this tradition, as 2:11 has already shown: "in the city of David" is born one who is "Messiah, Savior, and Lord." In other words, Peter, having witnessed Jesus' kingdom-preaching, healing, and miracles, is depicted as acknowledging him as God's anointed agent sent "to restore the kingdom of Israel" (Acts 1:6). Cf. Luke 2:26; 4:41. See further Dinkler, "Peter's Confession," 179-184; O. Cullmann, *Peter,* 178-180.

Note that in the Johannine Gospel, in contrast to the Synoptics, Peter acknowledges Jesus as "the holy one of God," not the Messiah. Whereas the latter does appear, transcribed indeed as *Messias* in 1:41; 4:25, the former is never again used of Jesus in that Gospel. It cannot be regarded as more authentic or historical than the Synoptic title, despite its tenuous resemblance to Mark 1:24.

21. *Jesus gave them strict orders.* Lit. "but he, reprimanding them, instructed (them)." The verb *parangellein* has been used earlier in 5:14; 8:29 ("charged"). Here Luke joins to it the aor. ptc. of *epitiman* (on which see 4:35,39,41; 8:24). The prohibition refers to the time of Jesus' own ministry. After the resurrection he will enjoin the disciples to become witnesses of him as the crucified Messiah (see 24:46-48; Acts 2:36; 3:18; 4:26; 10:39-43).

not to say this to anyone. Jesus does not deny that he is God's anointed agent, but he forbids the disciples to use such language about him because of its political connotations. A further corrective is given to it in 9:22.

Luke retains the command of silence from the Marcan source, where it is part of his messianic secret. It is retained precisely as the springboard for the first announcement of the passion, as Luke found it in "Mk."

BIBLIOGRAPHY (9:18-21)

Brown, R. E. et al., *Peter in the New Testament* (Minneapolis: Augsburg; New York: Paulist, 1973) 111-112, 64-69.

Bultmann, R. "Die Frage nach dem messianischen Bewusstsein Jesu und das Petrus-Bekenntnis," *ZNW* 19 (1919-1920) 165-174; reprinted in *Exegetica* (ed. E. Dinkler; Tübingen: Mohr [Siebeck], 1967) 1-9.

Corbin, M. "Le Christ de Dieu: Méditation théologique sur *Lc* 9, 18-27," *NRT* 99 (1977) 641-680.

Cullmann, O. "L'Apôtre Pierre instrument du diable et instrument de Dieu: La place de Matt. 16:16-19 dans la tradition primitive," in *New Testament Essays: Studies in Memory of Thomas Walter Manson 1893-1958* (ed. A. J. B. Higgins; Manchester: Manchester University, 1959) 94-105.

———— *Peter: Disciple, Apostle, Martyr: A Historical and Theological Study* (2d ed.; London: SCM, 1962).

Denaux, A. "Petrusbelijdenis en eerst lijdensvoorspelling: Een exegese van Mc. 8, 27-33 par. Lc. 9, 18-22," *Collationes brugenses et gandavenses* 15 (1969) 188-220, esp. pp. 211-216.

Dietrich, W. *Das Petrusbild der lukanischen Schriften* (BWANT 94; Stuttgart: Kohlhammer, 1972) 94-104.

Dinkler, E. "Peter's Confession and the Satan Saying: The Problem of Jesus' Messiahship," in *The Future of Our Religious Past: Essays in Honour of Rudolf Bultmann* (ed. J. M. Robinson; New York: Harper & Row, 1971) 169-202.

Mundle, W. "Die Geschichtlichkeit des messianischen Bewusstseins Jesu," *ZNW* 21 (1922) 299-311.

Pesch, R. "Das Messiasbekenntnis des Petrus (Mk 8,27-30): Neuverhandlung einer alten Frage," *BZ* 17 (1973) 178-195; 18 (1974) 20-31.

Potterie, I. de la. "La confessione messianica di Pietro in Marco 8,27-33," in *San Pietro: Atti della xix settimana biblica* (Brescia: Paideia, 1967) 59-77.

Vögtle, A. "Messiasbekenntnis und Petrusverheissung: Zur Komposition Mt 16,13-23 Par.," *BZ* 1 (1957) 252-272; 2 (1958) 85-103; reprinted in *Das Evangelium und die Evangelien: Beiträge zur Evangelienforschung* (Düsseldorf: Patmos, 1971) 137-170.

Willaert, B. "La connexion littéraire entre la première prédiction de la passion et la confession de Pierre chez les Synoptiques," *ETL* 32 (1956) 24-45.

51. THE FIRST ANNOUNCEMENT OF THE PASSION
(9:22)

9 22 Then he said, "The Son of Man must suffer many things, be repudiated by the elders, chief priests, and Scribes, and be put to death; and he must be raised on the third day."

COMMENT

Luke follows Mark in making Jesus' first announcement of the passion follow directly on Peter's confession of him as God's Messiah (9:22). In Luke's text it is actually part of the same sentence, being a ptc. added to modify the preceding verb, "instructed." He has eliminated the introductory Marcan phrase, "and he began to teach them that. . . ." He has thus joined the announcement more closely to the preceding than it was in his source. (We have separated it here from the foregoing, not only because of the problems that the interpretation of the announcement creates, but also because of the Lucan curtailment of the Peter-scene. It also deserves separate treatment because of its relation to further announcements in the Lucan Gospel.)

Luke has further omitted Peter's protest that comes on the heels of the announcement and Jesus' subsequent rebuke of him (i.e. Mark 8:32-33). This he has done because he undoubtedly considered the rebuke unflattering to Peter; he deliberately omits as much as he can in his Gospel that may sound blameworthy in Peter's conduct (and often of the apostles as well). For further minor modifications of the Marcan text, see the NOTES.

In the preceding episode Luke presented one explicit answer to Herod's question; now in omitting Peter's protest and the rebuke of him, Luke concentrates on Jesus' own declaration. It too becomes an answer to that crucial question—in fact, it is Jesus' own answer. No reaction of any of the disciples is made to Jesus' declaration, and the subsequent verses (23-27) will in their own way give yet another answer. A reaction of the disciples will eventually be recorded (9:43b-44), but there it will be not protest, but incomprehension and a fear to question him.

The Lucan form of Jesus' saying about the coming passion is derived almost verbatim from Mark 8:31 (save for "on the third day" instead of "after three days"). This saying is the first of three formal announcements that are found in the Lucan Gospel; see 9:43b-45; 18:31-34. These are related because they are found in the Triple Tradition, and form a group in which Jesus' words directly deal with his own violent death. They belong, however, to a larger group of sayings in the Gospels in which Jesus refers to his coming death in one way or another. There are the so-called "veiled" references (to use the terminology of H. Schürmann ["Wie hat Jesus," 329] and V. Howard ["Did Jesus], 518) to his death in Luke 5:33-35; 11:29-32; 13:31-33,34-35; 20:9-18 (with parallels at times in the other Synoptics). There is also a third group of references to Jesus' death in which he comments on the salvific nature of it: Luke 22:19-20; 22:28 (cf. Mark 10:45). Finally, there are other minor announcements in Luke 12:50 ("L"); 17:25 (a Lucan composition, echoing 9:22); 22:22 ("Mk"); 24:7 (Lucan composition recalling previous announcements in this Gospel).

The first group, to which this Lucan verse belongs and which has commonly been called the Synoptic passion-predictions, has, at least since the time of R. Bultmann, been written off simply as *vaticinia ex eventu* (*Theology* 1. 29; cf. *Das Verhältnis der urchristlichen Christusbotschaft zum historischen Jesus* [2d ed.; Heidelberg: C. Winter, 1961]); they are considered as creations of the early Christian community and cannot be ascribed to the historical Jesus in his ministry because of the now well-recognized criterion of dissimilarity (see E. Käsemann, "The Problem of the Historical Jesus," in *Essays on New Testament Themes* [SBT 41; London: SCM, 1964] 37).

When one considers the relatively close position of these three announcements in the Marcan Gospel (8:31; 9:31; 10:32-34), coming as they do in the second half of the Gospel, where they are used to disclose gradually the messianic secret, and when one considers the number of them (why precisely three explicit announcements?), one has to reckon with a studied literary device. There are variations in them, even though one can detect a certain amount of overlapping of detail (in each one "Son of Man" is used, the verb "put to death," and the phrase "rise after three days"; in two of them one finds "hand over," "high priests and scribes"). Attempts to uncover the most original form (J. Jeremias, *NT Theology,* 276-286) have not proved successful. In the third announcement, however, one can clearly see that the formulation is under the influence of the passion narrative itself (see ibid., 277-278). Consequently, it is hard not to admit that there has been literary composition by the evangelists in them, guided by hindsight. To admit that, however, does not immediately mean that we must write them off completely as *vaticinia ex eventu*—and, worse still, lump together with them all the other categories of references to Jesus' violent death found on his lips in the Synoptic Gospels. It is too radical to say with Bultmann that "we can know nothing about *how Jesus understood his end, his death*" (*Das Verhältnis*, 11; *Exegetica*, 452). The pre-Marcan tradition, looking back with hindsight on the Galilean ministry, may well have attributed to some of Jesus' sayings more meaning and more detail—and even read into them a salvific significance which they did not originally have. When all the various sorts of sayings about Jesus' death are considered in and for themselves, one has to reckon with at least a minimal tradition of utterances made by him which reveal that he was gradually realizing that his conflict with the leaders of contemporary Palestinian Judaism would eventually come to a crisis in his own life, in which he could meet with a violent death. John the Baptist had already met with such an end; and the violent deaths of prophets of old (Isaiah [*Asc. Isa.* 5.1-2]; Uriah [Jer 26:20-23]; cf. 2 Chr 24:20-21) would not have been unknown to him. There is enough scattered material in the Synoptic Gospels which should be regarded as snippets of sayings that Jesus uttered about this matter. See further E. Dinkler, "Peter's Confession," 198-200; Howard, "Did Jesus," 525; Schürmann, "Wie hat Jesus," 332-340; cf. V. Taylor, *FGT*, 150.

That such a pre-Marcan tradition eventually found formulation in terms of explicit prediction or announcement as a means to overcome the scandal of the cross is not impossible. That Mark was the first person who so formulated them is not per se evident. That he used them as a threesome in connection with the gradual disclosure of the messianic secret is admissible. From his Gospel the threesome was taken over by both Luke and Matthew.

Intended in this Gospel as a corrective to Peter's confession, Jesus' words provide an answer to Herod's question. They provide, moreover, a background for the beginning of the travel account, where Jesus will set his face toward Jerusalem, the city of destiny. The Lucan Jesus is consciously aware that his destiny is part of the Father's plan; even Peter's recognition of him as God's anointed agent of salvation cannot distract him from a consideration of that destiny at this point in the Gospel. But even Peter (and the rest of the disciples) have to be given an intimation of what lies ahead.

NOTES

9 22. *Then he said.* Lit. "saying," the aor. ptc. *eipōn* modifies the main verb in the preceding v 21. Jesus' words add a clear corrective to Peter's confession and his command of silence.

The Son of Man. This phrase is derived by Luke from Mark 8:31; on its origin and meaning, see NOTE on 5:24. It is used in reference to Jesus himself, and apropos of his passion (a use that is not found in "Q"). *Pace* Dinkler ("Peter's Confession," 184), the identity of the titles "Messiah" and "Son of

Man" is not presupposed in Mark 8:30-31. These titles are of distinct origin in the OT, and they should not be confused; nor should one speak of "Son of Man" as a *messianic* title. It occurs here (and in Mark) precisely as a corrective of a messianic title, of that used by Peter. Note that in Matt 16:21 the pronoun "he" is substituted for it.

must suffer many things. This phrase is again derived from Mark 8:31. The impers. verb *dei,* "must," fits into a larger pattern in Luke's Gospel, where much is made of the necessity incumbent on Jesus in the realization of the Father's plan of salvation (see p. 179 above). Cf. W. Grundmann, *TDNT* 2. 22-25. "Suffering" and the "Son of Man" are joined here in the Synoptic tradition. There is no suffering Son of Man figure in the OT. It has often been asked whether the notion of "suffering" is derived from the Servant of Isa 52:13 - 53:12. There are, of course, allusions to this Servant passage in Lucan writings (Luke 22:37; Acts 3:13; 8:32-33). But the extent to which the "suffering Son of Man" is to be related to that Isaian passage may be debated. It should be noted that "suffering" is not predicated here of the Messiah; and *pace* E. E. Ellis (*Gospel,* 140) and others, there is no evidence that Jews in Jesus' day associated the Isaian Servant texts with the Messiah. The Servant of Isa 52:13 is called *mĕšîḥā'* in *Tg. Isaiah* (see A. Sperber, *The Bible in Aramaic* [Leiden: Brill, 1962] 3. 107), but that targum scarcely antedates the fifth century A.D. See 17:25.

be repudiated. I.e. by the leaders of the Jerusalem populace named in the next phrase. In 17:25 the repudiation is "by this generation."

by the elders, the chief priests, and the Scribes. I.e. by the three groups that made up the Great Sanhedrin in Jerusalem. This threesome is met here for the first time in Luke; see further 20:1; cf. 22:52; Acts 4:5; 23:14; 25:15. The phrase is derived from Mark 8:31. Luke uses the prep. *apo* instead of *hypo* to express agency, a usage that is found elsewhere in Lucan writings (see NOTE on 1:26). He also uses only one article governing the three nouns, thus joining them more closely than in Mark. In Matthew the prep. phrase is joined to "suffer many things" (16:21), where *apo* has rather the sense of "from" or "at the hands of" (BAG, 87; see further J. Carmignac, *RevQ* 9 [1977-1978] 409-427). On elders, see NOTE on 7:3. In Luke 3:2; 22:50,54; Acts 4:6; 5:17, etc. *archiereus* means "high priest," the leader of the priests serving in the Jerusalem Temple, the president of the Great Sanhedrin, and the supreme religious leader of the Jewish people (see Josephus *Ag. Ap.* 2:21 §§ 185-187; G. Schrenk, *TDNT* 3. 269-270). The plural, as used here, does not denote former high priests, but rather "chief priests," those who, coming from priestly families, were members of the Sanhedrin. They controlled the Temple cult, treasury, and priestly discipline. Among them was "the captain of the Temple" (Acts 4:1), the heads of the weekly courses, the leaders of daily service, and Temple proctors (ibid., 270-271). On the Scribes, see NOTE on 5:21. Cf. J. Jeremias, *Jerusalem in the Time of Jesus* (Philadelphia: Fortress, 1969) 223-225.

Josephus, speaking at times of leaders of the Jewish people, has also made a threefold distinction among them: leaders (*dynatoi*), chief priests (*archiereis*), and the council (*boulē;* thus in *J.W.* 2.16,2 § 336); or leaders, chief priests, and "learned Pharisees" (*ton Pharisaiōn gnōrimoi,* apparently = "Scribes"; thus in *J.W.* 2.17,3 § 411). But he does not seem to know the threesome mentioned in the Synoptics. See further J. Blinzler, *Trial of Jesus,* 93-97.

be put to death. It is not said by whom he will be slain. Cf. Acts 2:23,36c.

be raised. I.e. by God (the theological passive, ZBG § 236). Luke here uses the verb *egerthēnai,* as in Matt 16:21, in contrast to Mark 9:31, which has the intrans. *anastēnai,* "rise." For the substitution of it, see the end of the next NOTE. The verb *egeirein* is used here in the same sense as in 7:14,22; 9:7; see NOTE on 7:6. The four infins. thus used with *dei* come to a climax in the resurrection. The fates of suffering, repudiation, and death are not left on the note of defeat, but victory is sounded.

on the third day. This phrase (*tē tritē hēmera*) is further found in Luke 13:32 (without "day"); 18:33; 24:7,21,46; Acts 10:40. In using it here, he departs from Mark 8:31, which rather has "after three days," and creates a minor agreement with Matt 16:21 against Mark. Why Luke has changed this is puzzling, given the phrase "after three days" in 2:46 (see further Acts 25:1; 28:17; cf. 28:11). Is it because he feels that "after three days" would mean "on the fourth day"? So N. Walker, *NovT* 4 (1960) 261-262, appealing to Hos 6:2 where "after two days" is used in parallelism with "the third day." But, apart from Walker's espousal of this meaning in the light of the Jaubert chronology of Holy Week, it is quite unlikely. Josephus uses the Greek phrases synonymously; see *Ant.* 7.11,6 §§ 280-281; 8.8,1-2 §§ 214, 218. It is much more likely that "on the third day" had become a very frequently used expression in Greek pre-Synoptic tradition for dating the resurrection of Jesus in the early church. It is used in 1 Cor 15:4 (a pre-Pauline fragment of the kerygma). Most likely both Matthew and Luke have changed Mark's expression independently to it. (Similarly for *egerthēnai.*) However, J. Kloppenborg (*CBQ* 40 [1978] 363) sees the Lucan/Matthean phrase as an allusion to Hos 6:2, which is possible but not certain. See M. L. Barré, *VT* 28 (1978) 129-141, esp. 138-140.

BIBLIOGRAPHY (9:22)

Feuillet, A. "Les trois grandes prophéties de la passion et de la résurrection des évangiles synoptiques," *RevThom* 67 (1967) 533-560; 68 (1968) 41-74.

Haenchen, E. "Die Komposition von Mk vii 27 - ix 1 und Par.," *NovT* 6 (1963) 81-109.

Hoffmann, P. "Mk 8,31: Zur Herkunft und markinischen Rezeption einer alten Überlieferung," in *Orientierung an Jesus: Zur Theologie der Synoptiker: Für Josef Schmid* (eds. P. Hoffmann et al.; Freiburg im B.: Herder, 1973) 170-204.

Howard, V. "Did Jesus Speak about His Own Death?" *CBQ* 39 (1977) 515-527.

Michel, O. "Der Umbruch: Messianität = Menschensohn: Fragen zu Markus 8,31," in *Tradition und Glaube: Das frühe Christentum in seiner Umwelt:*

Festgabe für Karl Georg Kuhn zum 65. Geburtstag (eds. G. Jeremias et al.; Göttingen: Vandenhoeck und Ruprecht, 1971) 310-316.

Schürmann, H. "Wie hat Jesus seinen Tod bestanden und verstanden? Eine methodenkritische Besinnung," in *Orientierung an Jesus: Zur Theologie der Synoptiker,* 325-363.

Stählin, G. " 'On the Third Day': The Easter Traditions of the Primitive Church," *Int* 10 (1956) 282-299.

Strecker, G. "Die Leidens- und Auferstehungsvoraussagen im Markus-Evangelium," *ZTK* 64 (1967) 16-39.

Tödt, H. E. *The Son of Man in the Synoptic Tradition* (Philadelphia: Westminster, 1965).

Walker, N. " 'After Three Days,' " *NovT* 4 (1960) 261-262.

52. THE FOLLOWING OF JESUS
(9:23-27)

9 23 But to everyone he said, "If anyone wishes to come with me,
let him disregard himself, take up his cross each day, and follow me.
24 Whoever strives to preserve his life shall lose it; but whoever loses
his life for my sake shall really preserve it. 25 For what good does it
do a person to acquire the whole world, if he loses himself or forfeits
his real self. 26 If anyone is ashamed of me and of what I say, the Son
of Man shall be ashamed of him, when he comes with his glory and
with the glory of the Father and of the holy angels. 27 I can tell you
truly, some of these who are standing here shall not taste death before
they see the kingdom of God."

COMMENT

Luke joins to Jesus' first announcement of the passion five other sayings
which deal in general with the loyalty of disciples who would follow him
and their attitude toward life and the kingdom (9:23-27). They were almost certainly distinct sayings of Jesus preserved in the early gospel
tradition (see R. Bultmann, *HST*, 81-82, who regards some of them as
double-stranded meshalim). It is impossible to say whether Mark inherited them as a unit or compiled them himself. Luke has obviously
derived these five sayings from Mark 8:34 - 9:1, as both the sequence and
general wording of them reveal.

The Lucan redactional hand has been at work on them. This is seen,
first of all, in his simplification of the introductory phrase of the first saying, and in his introduction of "each day" into its latter part. The first
saying is the basic one, since the three that follow are all introduced by
gar, "for," which I have at times omitted in the translation. In v. 24 Luke
omits the Marcan phrase, "and the gospel," undoubtedly because of his
general reluctance to use that term (see p. 173 above). In v. 25 Luke improves the Greek style by using three ptcs., but the saying remains substantially the same as in Mark. He must have considered Mark 8:27 to be
repetitious, for he has simply omitted it. In v. 26 he follows Mark 8:38 at
the beginning and the end, but omits the allusion to "this adulterous and

sinful generation." Moreover, he changes the reference to "glory" so that the Son of Man comes with his own glory as well as that of the Father and the angels. Finally, in v. 27 he omits the Marcan introductory phrase and changes *amen* to "truly." He thus joins the last saying more closely to the preceding ones. At the end of the verse, he omits "coming with power" as a description of the kingdom. The overall result of the Lucan redaction is to make the five sayings hang together better as a unit.

Parts of three of the Lucan sayings, 9:23b-d, 24, and 26c, are found in another form in Luke 14:27; 17:33; and 12:9 respectively. These are again Lucan doublets (see p. 81 above), since each of them finds parallels in the Matthean Gospel (10:38-39,33), where they appear in the sermon on the mission of the Twelve. These come to Luke from "Q," and in general seem to represent an older tradition than that in Mark (see E. Dinkler, "Jesu Wort," 111, 124; J. B. Bauer, "Wer sein Leben," 7).

These sayings of Jesus, distinct though they may have been in their original contexts, now assume in the Lucan Gospel the form of another answer given to the question posed by Herod (9:9). Though the answer is only implied in Jesus' own words, it is radical in its demand. For he now appears as one who is to be followed—even to death, if that is what is demanded in a public confrontation with other human beings about him or the kingdom that he announces. Coming immediately after his declaration about his own suffering, repudiation, and death, the sayings reveal how radically Jesus challenges those who would follow him.

In the Lucan Gospel these sayings on discipleship are addressed to "everyone," i.e. to the crowds as well as the disciples. They thus stand in contrast to the question addressed by Jesus to the disciples about what people thought of him and to his own declaration about his passion made only to the disciples. The five sayings intimate that discipleship means a daily share in the fate that eventually will be his. The way that Jesus must go becomes the way that the disciple must follow. The conditions of discipleship that the sayings incorporate are expressed, first of all, in terms of "following," a notion that takes on greater significance in the proximity of the Lucan travel account, i.e. his foreordained journey to the city of destiny. The following is further specified as a carrying of one's cross behind him, as a proper esteem for one's life that cannot be measured by worldly gain, as an attitude toward him that will not falter in the face of public confrontation (shame before others because of him), and as an attitude that may expect a new and better understanding of the mysteries of the kingdom.

The first saying, which demands three things of disciples, self-denial, carrying one's cross, and following, states the basis of Christian loyalty. The first and the third demands are simple enough; but the second one,

involving a metaphor, is problematic. Does it represent an authentic saying of Jesus, uttered in a pre-crucifixion context?

In the Lucan Gospel Jesus does not carry his own cross to the place of
the Skull, as he is depicted in John 19:17. The very metaphor used here
is predicated of Simon of Cyrene in the Lucan Gospel, who is made to
carry Jesus' cross "behind" him (23:26). So Luke has christianized
Simon, who stands in contrast to Jesus' close disciples who are not mentioned (but who are never depicted as defecting in Luke).

The saying becomes intelligible once Jesus had carried "his own cross"
(John 19:17) or simply been crucified (as in the Synoptics), and once
the "story of the cross" (1 Cor 1:18) had taken shape with all its soteriological connotations. The Lucan "following" of Jesus as the mode of
discipleship certainly takes on a specification because of it. But what
meaning would it have had on the lips of Jesus prior to his crucifixion?

One *could,* of course, insist that Jesus did utter exactly these words,
foreseeing his own mode of death; but that is a reassuring answer for
which one has no evidence that the evangelists so intended it to be. See
Dinkler, "Jesu Wort," 112. One could also say (e.g. with V. Taylor,
Mark, 381; C. H. Dodd, *Parables,* 42; or J. M. Creed, *Gospel,* 194) that,
though the figure of carrying one's cross is not found in rabbinic literature
(see Str-B, 1. 587), the sight of criminals on their way to crucifixion was
familiar enough in Roman Palestine to enable Jesus to use it for his radical demand. One will not contest the familiarity of the practice (see
NOTES on 9:23). But the problem is to explain why Jesus would ever use
such an image for *following* him. If, as Plutarch tells us, "Each one of
the criminals carries his own cross" (*Moralia: De sera numinis vindicta,*
9:554A; Teubner ed., 3. 410), what would have prompted the use of
such a metaphor? (Would a modern community leader, seeking to instill
self-denial and dedication to himself in his followers, get his idea across
by telling them to face the firing line or strap themselves into an electric
chair—using a modern mode of execution?)

Since it is only the joining of Jesus' own messiahship with the cross on
which he was crucified that makes the metaphor have any sense, the saying, as we now have it, must come from the early Christian community.
This does not mean that it is fabricated out of whole cloth. Ever since
D. F. Strauss commentators have compared this saying with Matt 11:29,
"take up my yoke upon you," where Matthew uses the same verb *arate*
that is found in the three Synoptic accounts of this saying; it has been
suggested that Jesus more plausibly expressed the following of himself as
a bearing of his yoke. See Dinkler, "Jesu Wort," 115, for references to
commentators. Dinkler himself does not care for this explanation and argues rather that Jesus originally spoke of "bearing his sign" on the fore-

head, arm, or hand, i.e. the *tau*-sign of Ezek 9:4, which was at one time cruciform or like X—which, once Jesus had been crucified, was interpreted in terms of his own cross; and so the saying was shaped in the post-resurrection community. Dinkler's suggestion is ingenious, but his attempt to explain the secondary character of the saying in Matt 11:29, where it is alone attested in the gospel tradition, is unconvincing. It is almost certainly pre-Matthean; see G. Strecker, *Der Weg der Gerechtigkeit* (FRLANT 82; 3d ed.; Göttingen: Vandenhoeck und Ruprecht, 1971) 172-173. Consequently, the reformulation of an original saying of Jesus about carrying his yoke stands the best chance of surviving as the explanation of this enigmatic demand for discipleship.

The second saying, demanding a proper estimate of one's life and its relation to the cause of the kingdom and to Jesus himself, has often been related to the exhortation of a field commander urging on his troops before battle. Bauer ("'Wer sein Leben,'") has related it to many such exhortations in classical Greek and Latin literature and shown how John Chrysostom so interpreted it.

The third saying, expressing an attitude of the Christian disciple toward worldly gain and success, presents a fundamental note in the teaching of Jesus. It is not to be so understood as though Jesus were advocating an opium of the people. This has to be noted especially in the Lucan Gospel, where the attitude toward riches—in reality, quite ambivalent—is often enough negative. The saying here involves rather a question of priorities.

The fourth saying challenges the Christian disciple to face up to the demands of a public allegiance to Jesus and the kingdom's cause.

The final saying, about some who will live to see the kingdom, preserves much of the futurist eschatological nuance of its Marcan counterpart, even though Luke has suppressed the note of its "coming with power." Though he has linked the saying more closely to the four preceding ones and thereby related the kingdom still more closely to following Jesus, he retains the Marcan relationship of this saying to the coming scene of Jesus' transfiguration, which is a partial fulfillment of the final saying (*pace* G. Schneider, *Evangelium nach Lukas,* 213). One cannot help but relate the "seeing of the kingdom" (9:27) by such disciples to their "seeing his glory" (9:32). Thus they are being granted to know the mysteries of the kingdom of God (8:10). Cf. 21:32.

NOTES

9 23. *to everyone.* Contrast 9:18, "the disciples." The word *pantas,* "all (of them)," harks back to the crowds fed by the multiplied loaves and fish (9:17). It is hardly to be restricted to "all" of the disciples, even though vv. 18-22 have intervened. The transition here is not elegant.

to come with me. Lit. "to come after me," in the sense of becoming a disciple; cf. 14:27. The phrase itself is derived from Mark 8:34, but it fits into the larger Lucan motif of discipleship as the following of Jesus along the road. Luke has changed the Marcan aor. infin. to the present (*erchesthai*), which better expresses the continuous nature of the following required and is further explained by the Lucan addition of "each day." The phrase "after me," in the sense of "behind me," used with a different verb (*hypage*) in the rebuke of Peter, stands in contrast to this expression in the Marcan Gospel, but is missing here because of Luke's omission of that rebuke.

let him disregard himself. Lit. "let him deny himself," i.e. adopt an attitude in life that is not self-centered, but that authentically allows one to identify one's conduct with Jesus and his mission. Though the verb *arneisthai* occurred in 8:45 in the sense of "deny, not to admit" (something), this is the first occurrence of it with a personal direct object; see further 12:9; Acts 3:13-14; 7:35. This is usually regarded as a Christian sense of the word (see MM, 78a), an extension of the denial or rejection of Jesus to other persons, oneself included. The word connotes a radical renunciation of self, not merely of one's sinful conduct or sins. See further H. Schlier, *"Arneomai," TDNT* 1. 471. Some mss. (P[75], B*, C, the Koine text-tradition) read the compound *aparnēsasthō*, which scarcely changes the meaning of the saying.

take up his cross. I.e. in imitation of Jesus at his crucifixion. The phrase is derived by Luke from Mark 8:34; that it was already part of the pre-Marcan tradition can be seen from its presence in a slightly different wording in the "Q" parallel (Luke 14:27; Matt 10:38). The image is later applied to Simon of Cyrene (23:26). It presents to the disciple the challenge of readiness for martyrdom, but also of suffering the opposition and hostility met in everyday life. Ms. D and the OL omit this and the following phrase; this omission is almost certainly owing to homoeoarcton (*kai a-* . . . *kai a-*); see B. M. Metzger, *TCGNT,* 147.

It is highly unlikely that there is any connection between this saying of Jesus and Isaac's carrying of the wood for the sacrifice in Gen 22:6, despite attempts to make an allusion to that passage. The wording in the Greek text of Genesis is quite different.

"Cross" is the usual Christian meaning given to the Greek *stauros,* which actually means a "stake," fixed upright. Such an object was used by Persians, Greeks, and Romans as an instrument of torture and death, either for impalement or crucifixion. See M. Hengel, *Crucifixion in the Ancient World and the Folly of the Message of the Cross* (Philadelphia: Fortress, 1977). That *stauros* was used in the sense of "cross," i.e. for crucifixion, in pre-Roman and Roman Palestine is clear from a number of ancient sources: Josephus *Ant.* 13.14,2 § 380; 17.10,10 § 295; *J.W.* 1.4,5-6 §§ 93-98; 2.12,6 § 241; 2.14,9 § 308; 5.11,1 § 451. Sometimes it is spoken of as "being hung on a tree" (Gal 3:13; Acts 5:30) or as "being hanged alive on a tree" (4QpNah 3-4 i 7-8; 11QTemple 64:10-13 [where it is even prescribed as a penalty for crimes in Israel]). See further J. A. Fitzmyer, *CBQ* 40 (1978) 493-513.

each day. This is Luke's redactional addition, which shifts the emphasis of the challenge to daily Christian living. Luke adds this to the saying because he does not envisage readers faced with an imminent persecution, but rather with the realization of what constant loyalty to Jesus means. The phrase is found in 1 Cor 15:31, and because of that some commentators have suspected that it might have been introduced into the text here. But its omission in mss. אᶜ, C, Koine text-tradition, and the OS (in addition to those mentioned in the preceding NOTE) is almost certainly owing to harmonization with the Marcan text.

and follow me. See NOTE on 5:11. In the "Q" parallel (14:27) the saying has a negative formulation: "cannot be my disciple."

24. *strives to preserve his life.* Or, "self." Lit. "wishes to save his *psychē.*" How should one translate *psychē?* In the context of a saying originally uttered in Palestine, it almost certainly does not denote "soul," as opposed to "body" in the understanding of the classical Greek dichotomy. Nor is one to think of it as expressive of the afterlife, in contrast to present life. The emphasis is to be put rather on what one does with one's concrete life or existence; it could mean in this way "the self." The contrast in the two members of the saying is that of "life" in an earthly or earthbound sense, and in a transcendent sense, i.e. not measured merely by material concerns. "To save one's *psychē*" is an expression derived from the Greek OT; see Gen 19:17; 1 Sam 19:11; Jer 48:6 (LXX 31:6). But note that in v. 25, where one has a related saying, joined by the catchword bond *psychē,* Luke has substituted in the latter part the pron. *heauton,* "himself," for the Marcan *tēn psychēn autou,* "his *psychē.*" See further G. Dautzenberg, *Sein Leben bewahren,* 51-82. What the saying demands is a readiness to give up even one's life for Jesus or the kingdom.

shall lose it. I.e. shall let it go to unprofitable waste.

loses his life for my sake. I.e. suffers a loss in the natural, worldly sense of "life," for the cause of Jesus or the kingdom. See Acts 14:22 for another way of putting it.

shall really preserve it. I.e. shall find salvation in such readiness. The verb *sōsei,* a favorite of Luke, is used here, but is really derived from Mark 8:35.

25. *what good does it do a person.* Lit. "in what is a human being profited"? The implication is that the profit amounts to nothing; it is useless and senseless. Jesus' words bear on the earthly striving for gain and success (see 12:16-21).

to acquire the whole world. Lit. "having gained the whole ordered universe (*kosmos*)." The verb *kerdainein* is usually used of the pursuit of wealth, earthly riches, business success.

if he loses himself. Luke uses here the second of three ptcs. *apolesas.*

or forfeits his real self. Lit. "or having been forfeited" (an aor. pass. ptc., "having been damaged," that is not easily translated). The verb *zēmioun,* "lose, forfeit," is often contrasted (as here) with *kerdainein* in documents of business transactions (see MM, 341, 273; cf. Acts 27:21).

26. *If anyone is ashamed of me.* I.e. becomes disenchanted with an identification with or a belonging to Jesus and his cause; it would involve an embarrassment before other human beings, as in the case of Peter (22:56-60). Cf. 12:8-9, where it is put a little more positively in terms of "confessing." The aor. pass. indic. is used in the sense of a middle voice (see BDF § 78), with a direct object. This verse specifies what the cross-carrying of v. 24 could entail in public life. Cf. 2 Tim 2:12b.

and of what I say. Lit. "and of my words." The disciples' relationship to Jesus involves more than an attachment to his person. The phrase is derived by Luke from Mark 8:38.

the Son of Man shall be ashamed of him. In the Lucan Gospel the title refers to Jesus himself, for Luke writes with the clear awareness of Jesus' coming again (see Acts 1:11). One can debate whether it meant this or someone else in the original setting; see NOTE on 5:24. The doublet in 12:9 seems to be an older form of this saying, derived here from Mark 8:38. The Son of Man does not appear here as a judge (contrast Matt 16:27), but rather as an advocate in the public setting of appearance before God and the holy angels. The contrast in the shame has to do with its public character in each part of the saying.

when he comes with his glory. The Lucan redactional modification has changed the Marcan "with his father's glory" into "with his (own) glory and (that) of the Father and of the holy angels." Cf. Luke 21:27. The "glory" belongs not only to the Father, as in Mark, but also to the Son of Man and the angels. *Doxa,* "glory," denotes the status of the risen Christ; see 24:26; it is a quality associated with God himself (see 2:9; Acts 7:2,55). In the present context, in which a saying on the kingdom is juxtaposed, the coming with glory seems to be related to a phase of that kingdom.

and of the holy angels. In Mark 8:38 the angels are the companions of the Son of Man, but here they have become figures that share his glory. Both the Father and they constitute the public before whom the Son of Man will manifest his shame over disciples who manifested their public shame over him. Contrast Mark 13:26-27 and Luke 21:27.

27. *I can tell you truly.* Mark 9:1 used the Semitic word *amēn,* for which Luke has substituted the Greek adv. *alēthōs,* in accord with his usual custom of eliminating such Semitic words. See NOTE on 4:24.

some of these who are standing here. I.e. some among the "all" addressed in v. 23, i.e. those who will really follow him. Luke has substituted the adv. *autou* for Marcan *hōde;* the latter clearly means "here." Usually *autou* means "there," as in Acts 18:19; 21:4. Schneider (*Evangelium nach Lukas,* 210, 213) understands *autou* to mean in this verse, "there," and regards it as a Lucan means to change the eschatological import of the saying; it would make the sight of the kingdom less imminent. But this is not certain. In Matt 26:36 *autou* means "here," being contrasted with *ekei,* "there." See BAG, 123, where it is translated "here" for this verse. Luke himself uses *hōde* (e.g. 4:23; 9:12,33, etc.); it is hard to say why he changed from Mark's use of it.

shall not taste death. The figurative use of *geuesthai* is found in the OT (LXX Job 20:18; Ps 34:9; Prov 31:18), but never in the context of death. Cf. John 8:52. The use of the expression in the Coptic *Gos. Thom.* § 1 is clearly dependent on the Lucan or Johannine usage; cf. OxyP 654, line 5 (*ESBNT,* 365-366).

before they see the kingdom of God. Luke has changed the Marcan source in dropping the phrase, "coming with power." H. Conzelmann (*Theology,* 56) thinks that thereby Luke has shifted the emphasis from its arrival to the state of affairs that the kingdom represents in the Lucan writings. Perhaps. It is more likely (with Schneider, *Evangelium nach Lukas*, 213) that Luke refers to an understanding of the kingdom that will become apparent after the resurrection, when disciples will be given a knowledge of the mysteries of the kingdom (8:10) in a new sense. In any case, the saying preserves a futurist eschatological saying of Jesus, and not one that has to be understood in terms of realized eschatology. See further W. G. Kümmel's discussion of the Marcan text in *Promise and Fulfilment*, 25-29.

BIBLIOGRAPHY (9:23-27)

Bauer, J. B. " 'Wer sein Leben retten will . . .' Mk 8,35 Parr.," in *Neutestamentliche Aufsätze: Festschrift für Prof. Josef Schmid zum. 70. Geburtstag* (eds. J. Blinzler et al., Regensburg: Pustet, 1963) 7-10.

Bornkamm, G. "Das Wort Jesus vom Bekennen," in *Geschichte und Glaube* (BEvT 48; Munich: Kaiser, 1968) 1. 25-36.

Dautzenberg, G. *Sein Leben bewahren:* Psychē *in den Herrenworten der Evangelien* (SANT 14; Munich: Kösel, 1966) 51-82.

Dinkler, E. "Jesu Wort vom Kreuztragen," in *Neutestamentliche Studien für Rudolf Bultmann zu seinem siebzigsten Geburtstag* (BZNW 21; ed. W. Eltester; Berlin: Töpelmann, 1954) 110-129.

Doncoeur, P. "Gagner ou perdre sa *psychē*," *RSR* 35 (1948) 113-119.

Fletcher, D. R. "Condemned to Die: The Logion on Cross-Bearing: What Does It Mean?" *Int* 18 (1964) 156-164.

Fridrichsen, A. " 'Sich selbst verleugnen,' " *ConNT* 2 (1936) 1-8.

Fuller, R. H. "The Clue to Jesus' Self-understanding," *SE III* (TU 88; 1964) 58-66.

George, A. "Qui veut sauver sa vie la perdra; qui perd sa vie la sauvra," *BVC* 83 (1968) 11-24.

Griffiths, J. G. "The Disciple's Cross," *NTS* 16 (1969-1970) 358-364.

Kümmel, W. G. *Promise and Fulfilment*, 25-29.

Perrin, N. "The Composition of Mark ix 1," *NovT* 11 (1969) 67-70.

Riesenfeld, H. "The Meaning of the Verb *arneisthai*," *ConNT* 11 (1947) 207-219.

Schneider, J. "*Stauros*," in *TDNT* 7 (1964) 572-580.

Schulz, A. *Nachfolgen und Nachahmen: Studien über das Verhältnis der neutestamentlichen Jüngerschaft zur urchristlichen Vorbildethik* (SANT 6; Munich: Kösel, 1962) 82-90, 162-165.

Vögtle, A. "Exegetische Erwägungen über das Wissen und Selbstbewusstsein Jesu," in *Das Evangelium und die Evangelien* (Düsseldorf: Patmos, 1971) 296-344.

53. THE TRANSFIGURATION
(9:28-36)

9 28 About eight days after these sayings Jesus took Peter, John, and James along with him and happened to go up on the mountain to pray. 29 While he was at prayer, the appearance of his face suddenly became different, and his garments white and dazzling. 30 Then two men were seen conversing with him. They were Moses and Elijah, 31 who appeared in glory and were speaking of his departure, the one that he was to complete in Jerusalem. 32 But Peter and his companions had been drowsy with sleep; rousing themselves, they saw his glory and the two men who stood beside him. 33 As these gradually withdrew from him, Peter said to Jesus, "Master, it is good that we are here! Let us put up three huts, one for you, one for Moses, and one for Elijah." But he did not know what he was saying. 34 While he was saying this, a cloud formed and cast its shadow over them; and as they passed into the cloud, they became afraid. 35 Then a voice from the cloud spoke out, "This is my Son, *my Chosen One!*[a] *Listen to him!*"[b] 36 Once that voice had spoken, Jesus was found to be alone. And they kept silent, telling no one in those days of what they had seen.

[a] Isa 42:1 [b] Deut 18:15

COMMENT

As in Mark 9:2-8, the episode about the transfiguration of Jesus follows in the Lucan Gospel (9:28-36) immediately on Jesus' saying about discipleship. It presents a heavenly identification of Jesus in contrast to two OT figures and charges Christian disciples to listen to him alone as God's Son and Chosen One.

Though some writers (e.g. E. Dabrowski, *La transfiguration*) have tried to insist that the Matthean form of this episode is the most original, it is clear that, as far as Luke is concerned, he is working with the Marcan form of it. The Lucan passage is replete with his own stylistic expressions (see the NOTES), which have entered into the redaction of the story. That he has a variant tradition on which he is dependent is not clear, despite the attempts of some writers (J. Blinzler, *Die neutes-tamentlichen Berichte,* 57-62; T. Schramm, *Der Markus-Stoff,* 139) to show this. Where his text differs from Mark, the vast majority of the differences can be traced either to Lucan redaction, as H. Conzelmann recognized (*Theology,* 57 n. 1) or to Lucan composition. To the former I should ascribe the following: "about eight days" (9:28) instead of Mark's "six days later"; the *kai egeneto* constructions (9:28,29,30); the *en tō* + infin. construction (9:29,33,34,36); the use of *kai idou* (9:30), *kai autoi* (9:36), and *eipen pros* (9:33). Likewise redactional is the purpose why Jesus goes up on the mountain, "to pray" (9:28), and his experience during prayer (9:29); the better Greek of 9:29, avoiding the connotation of Marcan metamorphosis; the substitution of "Master" for "Rabbi," the word order of v. 33 (to him listen), and the title "my Chosen One" (v. 35). On the other hand, to Lucan composition should be attributed vv. 30-33,34b,36bc.

This might seem like an oversimplification of a very complex problem, for in contrast to what Luke has done with Mark 8:34-9:1, where his wording is closely dependent on the Marcan, he has composed this episode with a great deal of freedom, if he is supposed to be working with Mark 9:2-8. The complexity of the problem in this episode is seen in the number of minor agreements of Matthew and Luke over against Mark. They have been variously counted as fifteen, sixteen, twenty. As a result, a number of commentators have invoked here a variant tradition (in addition to Schramm and Blinzler mentioned above, see Dabrowski, *La transfiguration,* 21; E. E. Ellis, "The Composition of Luke 9," 122-124, etc.). These minor agreements have been studied in detail by F. Neirynck, who has concluded that "the examination of these data enlighten us more about the tendencies of the two gospels than about any source-critical relationship" ("Minor Agreements," 264). See also H. Schürmann, *Lukasevangelium,* 563 (if I understand him correctly). Rather than invoke a separate tradition here, one has to realize that there is a certain curtailment of Marcan material with an independent modification of the common source ("Mk") and the addition of new material (in Matt 17:6-7; in Luke, that mentioned above).

To understand the importance of this episode, one has to take seriously the Lucan context in which it is found, as Conzelmann has insisted (*Theology,* 57-58). But he narrows the context of it too much in saying that the purpose of the heavenly manifestation is the announcement of the passion or even heaven's confirmation of Jesus' announcement of the passion. This connection is found in other writers as well (e.g. J. M. Creed, *Gospel,* 134). What they have said is true, but more is certainly intended in its contextual relationship. For the episode is related to the disciples' "seeing" the kingdom (in v. 27—now they see "his glory"); and again, it is related to the larger context of chap. 9, in providing not only another answer to Herod's crucial question (9:9), but also an important phase in the training of the Galilean witnesses that is prominent in this chapter. As an explicit answer to Herod's question, heaven speaks forth through the voice from the cloud: "This is my Son, my Chosen One!" To the christological answers already given in the chapter, two others are thus added; and another is implicit in the withdrawal of Moses and Elijah, the leaving of Jesus alone, and the heavenly charge, "Listen to him!" viz. he is one to whom human beings must now listen. Whether we are to conclude that Jesus is to be understood in this episode as a new Moses and a new Elijah is problematic. Certainly, Jesus as a new Moses is not a strong motif in the Lucan Gospel, as it is in Matthew; if it is present here, it is inherited from the tradition and finds little development of it in the rest of the Lucan writings. On Jesus as a new Elijah, see p. 213 above.

Yet there is not merely this contextual relationship of the episode that has to be considered, but a special relationship between this episode and the baptism-scene in the Lucan Gospel. The latter has inaugurated the Galilean ministry, with a heavenly voice identifying Jesus as "Son" and showing that ministry as begun under the power of the Spirit (3:21-22). Now that identification is repeated in close conjunction with the journey that is to be taken to the city of destiny (9:51). Jesus goes forth to that city, where prophets are killed (13:34), because his *exodos* (9:31) is related to his being "taken up" (9:51). Conzelmann rightly recognized the connection between these two scenes (*Theology,* 58), but he described the function of neither of them correctly. The baptism was not an introduction of a period of Jesus' messianic awareness (since the scene says nothing about a messiah), and here he limits the scene too much to an awareness of the passion. However one wants to interpret Jesus' *exodos* (see the NOTES), it is clear that in the Lucan Gospel the heavenly identification of him just before that *exodos* begins is clearly parallel to the heavenly identification at the baptism.

To regard the transfiguration (even in its Marcan form) as a "messianic enthronement" is to miss a major point of the episode. It identifies Jesus as more than a messiah; it uses of him "Son" and "Chosen One"— and it would have to be established that "Son" is only intended in a messianic sense (a sense that it never has in the OT and is still to be found in Palestinian Jewish literature prior to or contemporary with the NT). Jesus is not just *Moses redivivus* or *Elias redivivus;* he is God's Son and Chosen One. Here the Synoptic tradition has made use of a title that is pre-Pauline and has connotations other than messiah. See M. Hengel, *The Son of God* (Philadelphia: Fortress, 1976); J. A. Fitzmyer, *NTS* 20 (1973-1974) 391-394. To give "Son" (or even "Son of God") in the Lucan Gospel exclusively the meaning of messiah is simply not convincing.

On the other hand, it is not necessary to load it with the explicit affirmation of divine sonship that it acquires in the patristic writings or in the definition of the Council of Nicaea.

The episode of the transfiguration, coming, as it does in the Synoptics, shortly after Jesus' first announcement of the passion and immediately after Jesus' sayings on discipleship, serves as another corrective about the identification of him. If he is already regarded as one in whom God's power is present, as God's Messiah, as a Son of Man who must suffer, be repudiated, and put to death, as one who is to be followed in all of this, he is, nevertheless, heaven's Son and Chosen One, to whom human beings must now listen for their relation to God's kingdom. The first announcement of the passion did not end on the death of Jesus; it included his being raised on the third day. Now the Lucan form of the transfiguration tells us that the disciples had a glimpse of his "glory" (9:32); the mention of "glory" is found in no other account of the transfiguration in the Synoptics. It is introduced indirectly in 2 Pet 1:17. Given the connotation of "glory" in the NT elsewhere as the status of the risen Christ, it is hard to think that Luke did not intend some connection between this episode and the risen status of Jesus. In fact, he uses "glory" explicitly of that status in 24:26. Just what this means is quite complicated. If one asks the question about Stage III of the gospel tradition, it is easy to say that Luke has related the transfiguration to the resurrection-status of Jesus. If one asks it, however, about Stage I (the ministry of Jesus), one would have to recall that it is introduced by Luke; Mark does not tell us that the metamorphosis of Jesus had anything to do with his "glory" and does not suggest a connection between the transfiguration and the resurrection, save in a most superficial way. Luke is again writing with hindsight.

The real import of the reference to Jesus' glory is not to be missed. Jesus corrected Peter's acknowledgment of him as God's Messiah by announcing his passion and resurrection. This episode now comes along in the Lucan Gospel not so much as a confirmation of the passion, but as a confirmation of the last part of that announcement, viz. that it will not end solely with suffering, repudiation, and death. Luke has sharpened what was in Mark by the introduction of Jesus' "glory."

Moses and Elijah appear in the Marcan form of the scene conversing with Jesus, but the topic of their conversation is not disclosed. Luke depicts them talking about Jesus' *exodos* and appearing "in glory" too. While the mention of *exodos* is related to the Lucan geographical perspective, the very word echoes the Exodus of Israel from Egypt to its promised land, its land of destiny. Yahweh's glory was related to that experience of Israel. The nuances of both these terms in the Lucan account may then have to be considered further. The appearance of Moses would obviously be related to it, but that of Elijah would be puzzling in this consideration, unless one recalls Elijah's journey to Mount Horeb (1 Kgs 19:4-8) and the relation of the latter to the Exodus experience (Exod 3:1; Deut 1:2; 5:2).

Moses and Elijah are, of course, represented in the episode in a more important way, for they are foils to Jesus. Representing the Israel of old, they disappear, leaving Jesus alone; and the heavenly instruction to "listen to him" relates him intimately to the reshaping of Israel as God's people.

The three privileged disciples are said in the Lucan account to have "seen his glory" (v. 32). Luke has thus made of the scene a special vision of an aspect of Jesus not present in the other Synoptics. It is not yet a vision for them of the kingdom (see v. 27); but they behold in him an aspect of the mysteries of the kingdom (8:10).

Luke has preserved this scene in his Gospel because of its presence in his Marcan source, even though he shows little interest in the Marcan sequel to it. I have just tried to set forth the role that the scene plays in the Lucan Gospel but its role in the gospel tradition is another matter.

Form-critically, it is a Story about Jesus; so V. Taylor (*FGT,* 150). Taylor has also well presented the various hypotheses that complicate any decision about the origin of this passage (*Mark,* 386-388). I shall give here only a brief summary of what one can find there in more detail; four interpretations of the scene have been attempted:

a) It has been interpreted as an account of a historical event in the Galilean ministry of Jesus shortly after Peter's confession, a factual experience in which his glory was manifested through his physical condition and seen by the three disciples. Phil 2:6 ("the form of God") has been invoked to explain it. So Origen (*Comm. in Matt.* 12:37; GCS, 40.152); Blinzler, *Die neutestamentlichen Berichte,* 85-89. So explained, it presupposes a Chalcedonian view of Jesus that would be read back into the gospel tradition. Problematic to this view are the appearance of Moses and Elijah (just what were they doing there?) and the voice from the cloud. Also it becomes difficult to explain how, if such an experience were factual, Peter could subsequently have denied Jesus and the disciples have defected (see C. E. Carlston, "Transfiguration," 233).

b) It has been interpreted as a vision-experience accorded to Peter (or the three disciples) akin to those enjoyed by Muhammad or Jeanne d'Arc which were related to religious or political developments. So E. Meyer (who considered the transfiguration as the real basis of historical Christianity), A. von Harnack, J. Schniewind, Taylor (*FGT,* 150). Problematic to this view is the obvious psychologizing of the disciples beyond the literary thrust of the NT accounts. It might be more suitable to the Lucan account than to the others. See Blinzler, *Die neutestamentlichen Berichte,* 97-107.

c) It has been interpreted as an account of an appearance of the risen Christ retrojected into the narrative of the Galilean ministry. So J. Wellhausen, W. Bousset, M. Goguel, R. Bultmann (*HST,* 259); for a longer list, see R. H. Stein, *JBL* 95 (1976) 79 n. 2; cf. Blinzler, *Die neutestamentlichen Berichte,* 116-125. This interpretation is, in fact, widely used today. But it is not without its problems, which have been discussed at length by Stein (ibid., 79-96). The main ones are the following: (1) What would Moses and Elijah be doing in a post-resurrection appearance story? (2) The verb *ōphthē,* "appeared," is not used of Jesus, but only of Moses and Elijah; and it is scarcely restricted to post-resurrection appearances of Jesus in the NT (see Acts 2:3; 7:2,30; 16:9). (3) Jesus' glory is never mentioned in an appearance account. (4) In almost every detail the episode differs form-critically from the appearances of the risen Christ (see C. H. Dodd, "The Appearances of the Risen Christ: An Essay in Form-Criticism of the Gospels," *In Studies in the Gospels: Essays in Memory of R. H. Lightfoot* [ed. D. E. Nineham; Oxford: Blackwell, 1957] 25). See further Blinzler, *Die neutestamentlichen Berichte;* H. Baltensweiler, *Die Verklärung.*

d) It has been interpreted in a purely symbolic way as a means of depicting Jesus as the heavenly Son of Man in the glory of his parousia. So E. Lohmeyer (who further distinguishes in it Jewish eschatological motifs in Mark 9:4-5,[6],7-8 and Hellenistic mystery-ideas in 9:3). This interpretation concentrates on the literary text and the place the episode has in the given Gospel; it is not concerned with the question of historicity.

At the end of his survey V. Taylor remarks, "This . . . suggests that no one explanation can be accepted to the exclusion of the rest" (*Mark,* 388). And again later, "while it is impossible to say exactly what happened upon the mount, we may well believe that the confession of [Mark] viii. 29 was deepened and confirmed in an incommunicable experience of prayer and religious insight." That may be, but it raises the question again about the denial of Peter. Given the diversity of the way in which the incident is reported, no real historical judgment can be made about it; to write it all off as mythical is likewise to go beyond the evidence. Just what sort of an incident in the ministry of Jesus—to which it is clearly related—it was is impossible to say.

The event is referred to in 2 Pet 1:16-18. Though one cannot rule out an independent origin of that reference in the oral tradition of the early church, it cannot be appealed to as an instance of multiple attestation, since to do so one would have to show that it is independent of the

Synoptic tradition. The variety of terminology used there (see the NOTES for details) does not, however, argue for an independent tradition. W. Schmithals (*ZTK* 69 [1972] 396) insists that this passage does not depend on the Marcan story, but rather on a pre-Marcan source. Perhaps. The mention of "honor and glory" (1:17) would seem to relate it rather to the Lucan story. The real reason why reference to the transfiguration is present in 2 Peter is to give authority to the Peter-figure who was being confronted with problems and ideas quoted by people from the writings of his "beloved brother Paul," which were being cited against him. To enhance that authority Peter, who had a post-resurrection vision of Christ (1 Cor 15:5; Luke 24:34) as did Paul (1 Cor 9:1), is made to appeal to a pre-resurrection experience on the holy mountain.

An account of the transfiguration is also found in the Greek and Ethiopic *Apocalypse of Peter* § 15-17 (Hennecke-Schneemelcher, *NTApocrypha* 2. 663-683), which has been dated by some at about A.D. 135. It scarcely represents, however, an independent tradition, being an elaboration of details taken from all three Synoptic accounts (e.g. prayer from Luke 9:28; the indescribability of the dazzling garments, modeled on Mark 9:3; the "holy mountain" from 2 Pet 1:18), mixed with all sorts of standard apocalyptic devices (questions put to an *angelus interpres* [who in this case is "God Jesus Christ"] about the identity of the "two men"). In this account Jesus is actually borne away by the clouds with Moses and Elijah, and the transfiguration is related to the parousia; actually it would be better to say that it becomes a description of Paradise. See further R. H. Stein, *JBL* 95 (1976) 87-88.

NOTES

9 28. *About eight days.* For some reason Luke has changed the Marcan dating, "six days later," to "eight days." This is the only precise dating of any incident in the ministry of Jesus outside of the passion narrative, and some have tried to use it as an indication that the episode is really part of a tradition about a post-resurrection appearance (see the COMMENT). However, the "six days" would not suit the Marcan resurrection narrative nor would the "eight days" suit that of Luke. The "eight days" may be nothing more than a rounded-off way of saying, "about a week later." It is scarcely likely that Luke 2:21 has anything to do with this dating. On the other hand, one cannot exclude an allusion to Lev 23:36, the passage that tells how the Feast of Booths should be celebrated and its indication of time; for an allusion to this feast, see v. 33 below. On the modes of explaining the Marcan "six days," see B. W. Bacon, *HTR* 8 (1915) 94-121; F. R. McCurley, *JBL* 93 (1974) 67-81. Cf. John 20:26.

after these sayings. Or possibly, "after these things." The former translation seems preferable in view of the five sayings that precede in the gospel tradition. The phrase *meta tous logous toutous*, however, is found in the LXX in the sense of "after these events" (1 Macc 7:33 [*RSV*]). It would represent a Semitic use of *logos;* cf. Aramaic *btr ptgmy' 'ln* (1QapGen 22:27), a translation of Hebrew *'ḥr hdbrym h'lh* of Gen 15:1 (where, however, the LXX uses *rēmata*). Cf. Acts 8:21; 15:6.

Peter, John, and James. The same order of names of this threesome is found in 8:51; see NOTES there and on 9:10. Cf. 22:8. In the *Apoc. Peter* only Peter is accorded the vision of the transfigured Christ. Bultmann (*HST*, 260) is inclined to think of this as the more original form of the story. Is it? Note, however, that 2 Pet 1:16-18 mentions no other disciples.

happened to go up. Luke uses here *egeneto de* with the conj. *kai* + finite verb; see p. 119 above. Schramm (*Der Markus-Stoff*, 94 n. 5, 139) identifies this instance as a type without *kai*. The *kai* preceding the ptc. *paralabōn* certainly governs the verb *anebē*. Though it is omitted in some mss. (P⁴⁵, B, א*, H, etc.), it is still the preferable reading (א², A, B, K, L, R, W, etc.).

on the mountain. Jesus leaves the sphere of ordinary events to go to a place of communion with God. In 2 Pet 1:18 it is called "a holy mountain." It is not named here, as it is not in the other Gospels or in 2 Peter. The tradition that associates the transfiguration with Mount Tabor can only be traced back as far as Origen (*Exegetica in Psalmos*, Ps 88:13; PG, 12.1548; possibly Ps.-Origen); cf. D. Baldi, *ELS*, 318-340. Rightly, Conzelmann insists (*Theology*, 57) that the geographical identification of the mountain does not interest Luke, since it is for him "a place of manifestation." But it would be more in line with the Lucan emphasis to view the mountain as a place of prayer, as it is in 6:12; cf. 19:29; 22:39. It is a place where Jesus puts himself in contact with the Father.

to pray. See NOTE on 6:12. Thus Luke describes the purpose of Jesus' going up on the mountain. This is a deliberate Lucan addition (see also v. 29). It excludes the idea that Jesus went up with the three disciples to manifest himself to them. As in 22:39, which it may be foreshadowing, it may be for nocturnal prayer; the nighttime may be suggested from the sleep of the disciples (v. 32).

29. *While he was at prayer.* As often elsewhere in this Gospel, the picture of Jesus at prayer precedes an event of importance. In this case, the Lucan addition of this detail provides a psychological background for the transfiguration, which is not found in the other accounts.

the appearance of his face suddenly became different. Lit. "and it happened, while . . . , (that) the appearance of his face (became) other." Luke here uses *kai egeneto* + an understood finite verb (either *egeneto* or *ēn*, "became," or "was"); see p. 119 above. He has thus expressed the transfiguration of Jesus without the Marcan *metemorphōthē*, "transformed." Many commentators (e.g. A. Plummer, *Gospel*, 251) explain that Luke, writing for Gentile Christians, avoids the Marcan term because of the association it would have with the pagan myths of metamorphosis. For a list of such commentators, see Neirynck, "Minor Agreements," 259 n. 32. For a discussion of the literary evidence, see W. Gerber, "Die Metamorphose Jesu." Strangely enough, Schürmann (*Lukasevangelium*, 556) rejects this explanation as "incredible," suggesting rather that Luke is alluding to Moses' experience in Exod 34:29, where the latter's face was "glorified" on Mount Sinai because of his meeting with Yahweh. But the only phrase that is common to the two verses of Luke and Exodus is *tou prosōpou autou*, "his face." What happened to them is described quite differently; in Exodus the different appearance is caused by something external to Moses. Consequently, it is a question whether Exod 34:29-35 is really an influence here. (If a superficial allusion is being sought, one could point to Bit-Enosh's query in the *Genesis Apocryphon*, "Why is the expression of your face so changed?" [1QapGen 2:16-17; cf. line 11].)

The reason for the sudden difference of expression is suggested in the Lucan addition, "they saw his glory" (v. 32). There *doxa* is understood as an inner quality of Jesus.

and his garments white and dazzling. Luke omits the Marcan comparison of the whiteness of the garments (such as no fuller on earth could whiten, 9:3). For white as an apocalyptic color, one may compare Rev 2:17; 6:2; 20:11. Note its use by Luke in 24:4; Acts 1:10. The ptc. *exastraptōn*, "dazzling," connotes lightning, another apocalyptic stage-prop (see Ezek 1:27-28; Dan 10:6). These details, derived with Lucan redaction from Mark, are used to express the supraterrestrial character of the phenomenon.

30. *Then two men were seen conversing with him.* Lit. "and behold, two men were conversing. . . ." Luke uses *kai idou;* see p. 121 above.

Moses and Elijah. Luke puts Moses before Elijah, as does Matt 17:3; cf. Mark 9:4. These are two OT figures, whose appearance on earth was expected in some way in Jewish beliefs just prior to the Christian era. On Elijah's return, see the NOTES on 1:17; 3:16; 7:19. In the case of Moses, God had promised Israel that he would raise up a prophet like him (Deut 18:15,18). Though this promise was meant in a generic way, it was eventually understood of an eschatological prophet awaited in the future; references to this expectation of "a prophet" or "the prophet" can be found in 1 Macc 4:46; 14:41; cf. 9:27; and in Qumran literature, see 1QS 9:11. It is, however, not always clear that this expected prophet is a specific "prophet like Moses," and some modern commentators have at times explained him rather as one like Elijah. It was probably under the influence of the assumption of Elijah, understood to return to restore things (Mal 3:23 [4:5-6E]; Sir 48:10), that the belief in an expected Moses-like prophet led in time to the assumption of Moses and his return. Even in antiquity the two traditions began to be fused. See further J. Jeremias, *"Mōysēs," TDNT* 4. 856-857 (but use cautiously the references in n. 102); cf. Str-B, 1. 753-758.

Is it possible to specify the role of Moses and Elijah further in this episode? Commentators have often said that Moses and Elijah here represent the Law and the Prophets (see, e.g. Plummer, *Gospel,* 251; Taylor, *Mark,* 390; G. Schneider, *Evangelium nach Lukas,* 216). Schürmann (*Lukasevangelium,* 557) implies the same when he explains the Lucan formula and order of names as dependent on the phrase "Moses and the prophets" (Luke 16:29,31; 24:27; but cf. Acts 26:22). F. Danker (*Jesus,* 116) questions this, saying that in Jewish thought Elijah was not considered a representative of the prophets. But Mal 3:23 [4.5E] clearly gives the returning Elijah the title of prophet, and Moses is implicitly cast in that role by Deut 18:15. Hence, Moses and Elijah

are at least to be understood as two prophetic figures. There is nothing that
really militates against their representing the Law and the Prophets; but in any
case, if this is not certain, then the contrast of the heavenly command at the
end of the episode strikes home just as well, if they are to be regarded merely
as two OT prophetic figures.

31. *who appeared in glory.* This detail is added by Luke, which clearly presents the two as heavenly figures; it appears nowhere in the Marcan (or
Matthean) accounts. The text does not say to whom Moses and Elijah appeared. Jesus at least is certainly meant, since they converse with him.
Schneider (*Evangelium nach Lukas,* 216) believes that because the disciples
sleep, these figures cannot be thought of as having appeared to the disciples.
But this is pressing the text too much and seems to contradict v. 32 itself. In
the OT *doxa* usually expresses the radiance or splendor associated with presence of God (see Exod 24:17; 40:34); in Exod 34:30-35 one reads of the
effect of God's "glory" on the face of Moses. Luke may have this in mind, but
he has extended it also to Elijah.

speaking of his departure. I.e. of his *exodos.* The meaning of this word is
debated. Many commentators, appealing to 2 Pet 1:15; Wisd 3:2; 7:6;
Josephus *Ant.* 4,8,2 § 189 [*exodos tou zēn*], have argued that it means Jesus'
death. So Creed, *Gospel,* 134; Schürmann, *Lukasevangelium,* 558; M.-J. Lagrange, *Luc,* 272. Michaelis (*TDNT* 5. 107) is probably right in refusing to
understand it as a reference to the resurrection, i.e. Jesus' coming out of the
grave. On the other hand, what Jesus is to complete (or fulfill) in Jerusalem
is not just his death (even though Luke 13:33 may hint at that) but also his
analēmpsis, "ascension" (9:51). Hence a number of writers have insisted that
one should rather understand *exodos* not only of Jesus' death, but of his
entire transit to the Father ending in the ascension. Thus J. Mánek, "The New
Exodus"; A. Feuillet, *RevThom* 77 (1977) 189-192; Schneider, *Evangelium
nach Lukas,* 216; E. E. Ellis, *Gospel,* 143. This certainly seems to fit in better
with the geographical perspective of Lucan theology.

to complete in Jerusalem. Or, "to fulfill in Jerusalem" The verb *plēroun* is
used here as in 1:20; 21:24; 22:16, where things are said to come to some
state of completion or fulfillment. It is slightly different from its use with words
or sayings (cf. 4:21; 24:44). The completion or fulfillment has to be understood of the events foreordained in God's salvific plan. Jerusalem is not only
the city where prophets are put to death (13:34), but, as this very phrase intimates, the city of destiny for Jesus. It thus foreshadows the travel account of
9:51.

Moses and Elijah, then, do not appear to Jesus as the consoling angel does in
some mss. of 22:43, strengthening him in view of his death. Nor should they
be understood as informing him about details of his "departure." Their role is
rather to relate that departure to their own prophetic role in the OT, to what
Moses and the prophets have said of him. It is impossible to understand this
exodos to be completed in Jerusalem without some foreshadowing of chap. 24.

32. *drowsy with sleep.* This detail is found only in the Lucan version of the
episode. It may again be an apocalyptic stage-prop (see Dan 10:9); or it may

be Luke's way of indicating that it was night (see 9:37). In any case, it is added to the account to explain the strange suggestion of Peter that three huts be made (v. 33). In 22:45 Luke will excuse the disciples' sleep by "their grief."

they saw his glory. See 9:26,31. As in v. 31, it would suggest some heavenly association of Jesus. This Lucan detail explains the different appearance of his face. Though Paul often refers to *doxa* and the risen Christ (e.g. Rom 6:5), Jesus' *doxa* is never mentioned in any accounts of his post-resurrection appearances.

33. *gradually withdrew from him.* Lit. "in their withdrawing from him." Luke uses *en tō* + infin. (see p. 119 above). The infin. is present, suggesting gradual withdrawal. The detail is likewise Lucan.

Peter said. Lit. "it happened, in their . . . , (that) Peter said." Luke again uses *kai egeneto* + finite verb, without the intervening *kai* (see p. 119 above).

Master. The voc. *epistata* is substituted for the Marcan title *rabbi;* see NOTE on 5:5.

it is good that we are here! Peter seems to think that he can prevent the slipping away of Moses and Elijah.

Let us put up three huts. In both classical and Hellenistic Greek the noun *skēnē* meant a "tent, hut" of nomads, shepherds, or soldiers, i.e. a temporary dwelling. In the LXX it is often used to translate *miškān,* "the (desert) dwelling" of Yahweh, or *sukkāh,* the "hut, booth" associated with *skēnopēgia,* "feast of booths" (Deut 16:13; see W. Michaelis, *TDNT* 7. 369). "Booths" or "Tabernacles" was a joyous harvest feast originally, one of the ancient festivals of Israel, sometimes called that of the ingathering (Exod 23:16; 34:22), "the most sacred and greatest feast among the Hebrews" (Josephus, *Ant.,* 8.4,1 § 100). By the time of Jesus it had become a pilgrimage feast, when Jews traveled to Jerusalem to celebrate it, with a duration of seven days of dwelling in huts or booths (see Lev 23:42-44; cf. R. de Vaux, *Ancient Israel* [New York: McGraw-Hill, 1961] 495-502). Peter seems to liken his experience on the mountain with Jesus transfigured to the joy of this festival. What need heavenly figures like Moses and Elijah would have of huts is precisely why the evangelists have added the last phrase of the verse. On the other hand, the mention of the "three huts" implies that Jesus is something like the other two, i.e. a heavenly figure.

one for you, one for Moses, and one for Elijah. Peter's words reveal that he had not only seen the two men with Jesus, but recognized them. They also put all three figures on the same level.

he did not know what he was saying. This detail is derived from Mark 9:6, but Luke has redacted it by eliminating the fear that Mark uses to explain it. Luke has already provided an explanation in that Peter has been "drowsy with sleep." In its own way it emphasizes Peter's lack of comprehension of the whole vision. The Marcan detail of fear is used below (v. 34).

34. *While he was saying this.* This seems to be, substantially at least, an instance of a minor agreement of Matthew and Luke over against Mark 9:7; but the wording is not the same at all. Lagrange (*Luc,* lxxxi and lxxiii) went so far

as to query whether Matthew had not here borrowed from Luke! See Neirynck, "Minor Agreements," 261. This Lucan phrase is found again in 11:53 (ms. D, with a slight variation) and 13:17.

a cloud formed. The cloud has to be understood in the OT sense of an apocalyptic stage-prop, an instrument of God's presence and glory. See Josephus *Ant.* 3.12,5 § 290; 3.14,4 § 310, where it is explicitly said that the cloud hanging over the desert tabernacle signified "the presence of God" (*tēn eiphaneian tou theou*). The cloud is often found with this meaning in the OT: Exod 16:10; 19:9; 24:15-18; 40:34; 2 Sam 22:12; 1 Kgs 8:10-11; Ezek 10:3-4; Ps 18:11; 2 Macc 2:8. See further H. Riesenfeld, *Jésus transfiguré*, 130-145; G. H. Boobyer, *JTS* 41 (1940) 135-140.

cast its shadow over them. The dir. obj. "them" is unclear. Schürmann (*Lukasevangelium*, 561) says that it surely means over Jesus, Moses, and Elijah; similarly W. Grundmann (*Evangelium nach Lukas*, 193). The trouble is that the following verb, expressing fear, refers to the disciples. But then v. 35 implies that the heavenly voice speaks from the cloud to those outside. If the cloud is meant to overshadow only Jesus, Moses, and Elijah, then it becomes the means of transporting them to God's presence. If it is meant to overshadow the disciples as well, then it is the instrument of his presence to them. The verb *episkiazein* is used here in the literal sense; for a figurative use of it, see 1:35.

as they passed into the cloud. In the Greek text the verb that follows, "they became afraid," actually precedes this phrase. Luke uses here *en tō* + infin.; see p. 119 above. The oldest text of Luke (P75) omits the *autous* which is the subject of the infin. and clearly means that the disciples entered the cloud. Some mss., however, read *ekeinous*, "those" (P45, D, ⊙, and the Koine text-tradition); this solves the problem, since it means that only Jesus, Moses, and Elijah entered the cloud. But the best mss. preserve the ambiguity, which is the *lectio difficilior*. Is there an allusion to Moses' entering the cloud of Exod 24:18?

they became afraid. In Mark 9:6 fear was used to explain Peter's lack of comprehension; here it is created by the cloud's presence and overshadowing. Cf. Dan 10:7, for an apocalyptic use of fear.

35. *a voice from the cloud.* I.e. God's revealing word. See NOTE on 2:22. In 2 Pet 1:18 it is rather "a voice from heaven," no mention being made of the cloud.

This is my Son. The same identification is found in the baptism-scene (3:22). In effect, the heavenly voice refuses Peter's suggestion and corrects his implied identification of his experience with that of the feast of booths. There is more here than that. Note that the voice addresses not Jesus himself, as in the baptism-scene, but the disciples. This is derived, of course, from Mark 9:7, whence Matt 17:4 has also derived it. From there it has crept into the Matthean baptism-scene, where a public proclamation of Jesus' sonship has been substituted for the voice that addressed Jesus himself (3:17; contrast Mark 1:11; Luke 3:22). The words that are addressed to the eyewitness in 2 Pet 1:17 have as their closest parallel in the Synoptics those of the Matthean baptism-scene (3:17). For the sense of the title, see NOTE on 3:22.

my Chosen One! Or possibly, "the Chosen One." The poss. pron. *mou* is so placed in the Greek text that it can be taken with the preceding noun alone or with both titles. The phrase here is *ho eklelegmenos* (pf. ptc. pass. of *eklegein,* "choose"); this is the only place in the NT where it is used. Related to it is *ho eklektos,* "the chosen" (a verbal adj.), of 23:35 (cf. John 1:34 [in some mss.]). It represents a Palestinian Jewish title found in a Qumran Aramaic text, *běḥîr 'ělāhā',* "the Elect of God." See *ESBNT,* 127-160, esp. pp. 151-153. This form, "Elect of God," does not occur in the OT and is not per se a messianic title. "Chosen One" is also found in Hebrew in 1QpHab 9:12 of the Teacher of Righteousness. It is used here, in a Greek form, of him who is the Messiah in the NT, though he is not so called here. It is associated in this text with the title, "my Son," and seems to be an allusion to Isa 42:1 LXX, where Israel is called "my Chosen One," and Jacob, "my Servant/Child" (*ho pais mou*). The wording, however, is not identical with that of the LXX, and *pais* is a translation of Hebrew *'ebed,* "servant." (I italicize the translation at this point with some hesitation.) There is, then, possibly an allusion here to an Isaian Servant passage; but nothing in it is explicitly messianic, *pace* Bultmann (*HST,* 259); Riesenfeld (*Jésus transfiguré*), et al. The heavenly voice calls Jesus clearly "Son" and "Chosen One."

The best mss. (P[45], P[75], ℵ, B, L, etc. read *eklelegmenos,* but some others have *eklektos* (a harmonization with 23:35) or *agapētos,* "beloved" (mss. A, C*, K, P, W, X, etc., a harmonization with Mark 9:7).

Listen to him! Luke writes *autou akouete,* whereas Mark 9:7 has the word order inverted. The Lucan order is closer to the LXX of Deut 18:15 (*autou akousesthe,* "you shall listen to him"). Heaven's word thus substitutes Jesus, its chosen messenger and Son, for the withdrawing heavenly figures of old. Instead of trying to hold on to the figures of old, the heavenly voice charges the disciples to listen to Jesus. The implication is that he now speaks with greater authority than Moses and Elijah. Cf. Acts 3:22.

36. *Once that voice had spoken.* Lit. "in the happening of the voice"; Luke uses *en tō* + infin.; see p. 119 above.

alone. I.e. no longer accompanied by Moses and Elijah. This finding of Jesus alone makes better sense in the Marcan parallel, where there was no mention of the withdrawal of Moses and Elijah before the voice had spoken, as in v. 33 above. The introduction of their beginning to withdraw there creates something of an inconsistency here in Luke. Being found "alone" means that the episode of the transfiguration centers on Jesus; it is not an epiphany of OT figures in and for itself. If the heavenly voice is alluding to Isa 42:1, it casts Jesus in the role of the Servant of Yahweh, who was to be a light to the nations. Now that he is found alone and the OT figures—prophets or representatives of the Law and the prophets—have disappeared, one cannot miss the implication of the scene for the message of Jesus and its universal salvific character.

they kept silent. This notice of the disciples' silence about what had happened on the mountain is not derived from Mark 9:8, but is rather a summary of the following Marcan episode (9:9-13), which Luke omits. In Mark their silence is ordered by Jesus (9:9).

in those days. I.e. during the ministry of Jesus, in contrast to what was recounted later, after the resurrection, and revealed by the evangelist. See NOTE on 4:2.

BIBLIOGRAPHY (9:28-36)

Baltensweiler, H. *Die Verklärung Jesu: Historisches Ereignis und synoptische Berichte* (ATANT 33; Zürich: Zwingli, 1959).

Blinzler, J. *Die neutestamentlichen Berichte über die Verklärung Jesu* (NTAbh 17/4; Münster in W.: Aschendorff, 1937).

Boobyer, G. H. "St. Mark and the Transfiguration," *JTS* 41 (1940) 119-120.

Carlston, C. E. "Transfiguration and Resurrection," *JBL* 80 (1961) 233-240.

Coune, M. "L'Évangile de la transfiguration," *Paroisse et liturgie* 52 (1970) 157-170.

Dabrowski, E. *La transfiguration de Jésus* (Scripta pontificii instituti biblici 85; Rome: Biblical Institute, 1939).

Feuillet, A. "Les perspectives propres à chaque évangéliste dans les récits de la transfiguration," *Bib* 39 (1958) 281-301.

Gerber, W. "Die Metamorphose Jesu, Mark. 9.2f. par.," *TZ* 23 (1967) 385-395.

Kenny, A. "The Transfiguration and the Agony in the Garden," *CBQ* 19 (1957) 444-452.

Léon-Dufour, X. "La transfiguration de Jésus," *Études d'évangile* (Paris: Seuil, 1965) 83-122.

Lohmeyer, E. "Die Verklärung Jesu nach dem Markus-Evangelium," *ZNW* 21 (1922) 185-215.

McCurley, F., Jr. "'And after Six Days' (Mark 9:2): A Semitic Literary Device," *JBL* 93 (1974) 67-81.

Mánek, J. "The New Exodus in the Books of Luke," *NovT* 2 (1958) 8-23.

Masson, C. "La transfiguration de Jésus (Marc 9,2-13)," *RTP* 3/14 (1964) 1-14.

Neirynck, F. "Minor Agreements Matthew-Luke in the Transfiguration Story," in *Orientierung an Jesus: Zur Theologie der Synoptiker: Für Josef Schmid* (eds. P. Hoffmann et al.; Freiburg: Herder, 1973) 253-266.

Ramsey, A. M. *The Glory of God and the Transfiguration of Christ* (London: Longmans, Green & Co., 1949).

Riesenfeld, H. *Jésus transfiguré: L'Arrière-plan du récit évangélique de la transfiguration de Notre-Seigneur* (ASNU 16; Copenhagen: Munksgaard, 1947).

Sabbe, M. "La rédaction du récit de la transfiguration," in *La venue du Messie: Messianisme et eschatologie* (RechBib 6; Bruges: Desclée de Brouwer, 1962) 65-100.

Schmithals, W. "Der Markusschluss, die Verklärungsgeschichte und die Aussendung der Zwölf," *ZTK* 69 (1972) 379-411.

Stein, R. H. "Is the Transfiguration (Mark 9:2-8) a Misplaced Resurrection-Account?" *JBL* 95 (1976) 79-96.

H. Further Miracles and Sayings of Jesus

54. THE CURE OF THE EPILEPTIC BOY
(9:37-43a)

9 37 The next day, when they came down from the mountain, a great crowd of people happened to meet him. 38 Suddenly a man shouted from the crowd, "I beg you, Teacher, look at my son; he is my only child. 39 Often a spirit seizes him, and all of a sudden he screams; it convulses him so that he froths at the mouth; and it leaves him only after a struggle, bruising him badly. 40 I begged your disciples to cast it out, but they were not able." 41 Jesus answered, "What an unbelieving and perverse generation! How long shall I have to be with you and put up with you? Bring your son here." 42 But while the boy was still coming to him, the demon dashed him to the ground and threw him into a convulsion. Jesus charged the unclean spirit, healed the child, and returned him to his father. 43 And all were astounded at God's majestic power.

COMMENT

Though Luke has omitted the Marcan episode about the coming of Elijah before "the rising from the dead" (9:9-13), he continues to follow the Marcan sequence, making the cure of the epileptic boy the sequel to the transfiguration in his account (9:37-43a). Having implied that John the Baptist was the expected Elijah, in applying to him the words of Mal 3:1 (cf. 3:23) in 7:27, he now has no need of Elijah as the forerunner of the resurrection. John has already been presented as the forerunner of Jesus, both in the infancy narrative and in 7:24-30. So there is no further need of Elijah as forerunner in any sense. In the preceding transfiguration scene Elijah has disappeared along with Moses, and Luke capitalizes on that, omitting the entire Marcan episode. Luke has scarcely omitted the Marcan episode simply because Elijah's coming before the resurrection would sound strange to a Gentile Christian audience (see H. Schürmann,

Lukasevangelium, 567). Luke's account stands, then, in contrast to the Matthean Gospel at this point; what was only hinted at in Mark 9:13 becomes an explicit identification of John as Elijah in Matt 17:12-13—a Matthean addition added to clarify Matt 11:10, a clarification for which Luke felt no need.

The episode of the cure of the epileptic boy (Luke 9:37-43a) not only follows the Marcan sequence, but also draws its basic inspiration from Mark 9:14-29. The pericope has been heavily reworked by Luke in the following main ways: (1) The introductory v. 37 is redactional, depending in part on Mark 9:9. (2) Luke omits the notice about Jesus and his three companions meeting the crowd and Scribes in discussion (Mark 9:14-16). (3) Luke more elegantly describes the condition of the boy (9:38-39; =Mark 9:17-18), but omits all the secondary description in Mark 9:20c-25a, though he does retain the saying of Jesus in 9:41 (=Mark 9:19). (4) The rebuking of the unclean spirit is retained in 9:42c (=Mark 9:25b). (5) Luke changes the ending of the story, by omitting Mark 9:25c-29, and substituting his own (typical) ending (9:42d) echoes 7:15b; the Lucan reaction to the miracle in v. 43a). The sixteen Marcan verses have become a mere seven and a half.

Luke is not alone in abridging the Marcan story. Matthew has also done the same, conforming to his own tendency to eliminate needless Marcan details. In this instance, some of his abridgment agrees with Luke's; Matt 17:14-22 likewise omits the discussion of the crowd and Scribes with the disciples (Mark 9:14-16), the secondary description of the boy's condition (=Mark 9:20c-25a), and simplifies the notice of the cure itself, but it retains the disciples' query (=Mark 9:28) why they could not cast out the demon, giving it, however, a typically Matthean answer (17:20, about faith that moves mountains).

At first sight, one might be tempted to think that both Matthew and Luke have substituted a shorter "Q" form of this episode for the Marcan. So B. Weiss. There are indeed minor agreements of Matthew and Luke against the Marcan form of the story: *legōn* (9:38=Matt 17:15); *edynēthēsan* (9:40=Matt 17:16); the addition of *kai diestrammenē* (9:41=Matt 17:17); *hōde* (9:41d=Matt 17:17e). But these are so minor that they cannot be regarded as indicative of anything more than coincidence. Moreover, the wording of Matthew and Luke, in their difference from Mark, is so striking that one cannot appeal to a "Q" form of the story in this case. T. Schramm (*Der Markus-Stoff,* 140) maintains that this episode in Luke "stands clearly under the influence of a tradition-variant." If he is right, then one would have to invoke an "L" form of the story; but is he right? The best solution is to regard the Lucan story as a redaction of Mark 9:14-29 (so Schürmann, *Lukasevangelium,* 571; J. Schmid, et al.).

From the form-critical standpoint, the episode is a miracle-story (see R. Bultmann, *HST,* 211; V. Taylor, *FGT,* 123), specifically an exorcism. The saying of Jesus in v. 41 (=Mark 9:19) seems to be a secondary addition which is more at home in the Marcan form than in the Lucan. Bultmann has suggested that the pre-Marcan tradition had already combined two stories, one a miracle-story (roughly=Mark 9:14-20) and the other a pronouncement-story (roughly=9:21-27); v. 25 may have been the ending of the first, and vv. 28-29 a Marcan redactional addition. In the Lucan form we clearly have a miracle-story, but v. 41 may still be a secondary addition to that part of the Marcan material. For the problem it creates, see the NOTE.

As the miracle-story stands in the Lucan Gospel, it is not a miracle of faith (despite the implication of v. 41). It is a miracle of compassion, similar to that of the raising of the widow's son at Nain (7:11-17). In the Marcan form, faith is clearly an element (9:23-24), and it becomes even more so in the Matthean form (17:19-20). The secondary element of prayer found in the last Marcan verse is omitted by both Matthew and Luke; in the latter case its omission is strange, given all the Lucan emphasis on prayer in the Gospel.

The Lucan form of the story presents Jesus once again making use of his power to heal (recall 4:14; 5:17; 6:19), this time exercised on behalf of an unfortunate boy, an only child (a Lucan motif; cf. 7:12; 8:42). The saying of Jesus criticizes his own generation, but it prepares for the cure itself. In its own way it gives another answer to the question put by Herod in 9:9: Jesus is the one in whom "the power of the Lord" is at work and in whom God's majesty is made manifest. (See NOTE on v. 43a for another possible nuance.)

NOTES

9 37. *The next day.* In contrast to Mark 9:14, which gives the impression that this cure takes place on the same day as the transfiguration, Luke dates it to the following day. This further suggests that for him the transfiguration took place at night; see NOTE on 9:32b. On the other hand, some mss. (e.g. D) and ancient versions (OL, OS) read *dia tēs hēmeras,* "during the day," which has also been preferred by some commentators (e.g. E. Klostermann, *Lukasevangelium,* 109) because of the Jewish mode of reckoning the beginning of the day at sundown. Ms. P45 reads simply *tēs hēmeras,* which probably has the same meaning. On the prep. phrase used here, see NOTE on 7:11; cf. 8:1.

from the mountain. I.e. the unnamed mountain of 9:28. This detail has been borrowed from Mark 9:9a, even though Luke omits the rest of the passage (vv. 9c-13). The silence of Mark 9:9b has already been used in v. 36. From the mountain of communion with God and of transfiguration Jesus descends to the world of human misery. Cf. 6:17.

a great crowd of people happened to meet him. Lit. "and it happened
. . . (that) a great crowd (of people) met him"; Luke uses *egeneto de* + a
finite verb without the intervening *kai* (see p. 119 above). But ms. D uses the
infin. *synelthein,* "came together," one of the alternate constructions. The
crowd must be thought of as awaiting his arrival because the rest of his disciples were there; Luke makes no mention of the scribes in the crowd (see Mark
9:14), or of a debate.

38. *Suddenly.* Lit. "and behold," the Lucan *kai idou* (see p. 121 above). It
occurs again in v. 39, having no counterpart in Mark; it is there translated as
"often."

I beg you. One of the Lucan favorite words, *deisthai* (see p. 110 above).

Teacher. The title is the same as that in Mark 9:17; contrast Matt 17:15
(*kyrie*). See NOTE on 7:40.

look at. Luke uses the verb *epiblepein,* which is predicated of God's compassion in the Magnificat (1:48).

only child. This is a Lucan redactional addition; cf. Mark 9:17 (see COM-
MENT). See NOTE on 7:12.

39. *a spirit.* Luke uses *pneuma* without any of the usual modifiers; perhaps it
is influenced by Mark 9:20. The parallel in Mark 9:17 has *echonta pneuma
alalon,* "having a dumb (*or* mute) spirit." In v. 42 the "spirit" will be referred
to as a "demon" and as an "unclean spirit," the latter being derived from Mark
9:25b. The Matthean story has a noteworthy variant in 17:15, a verb, *sel-
ēniazetai,* "he is moonstruck," but in 17:18 "demon" is used. To any modern
reader who scrutinizes the details in the Marcan description of the boy's condition, it is clear that the child is epileptic (see the *RSV*'s translation of *sel-
ēniazetai,* "he is an epileptic"). "Epilepsy" is derived from Greek *epilēpsia,* "attack, seizure" (<*epilambanein,* "seize"). Lacking the ability to diagnose the
"seizure," the cause was attributed to the moon or a demon/spirit. See NOTE
on 4:33, on protological thinking.

convulses him so that he froths at the mouth. Lit. "pulls him to and fro
with foam." Josephus (*Ant.* 6,12,2 § 245) uses *aphron,* "foam," in his description of David's feigned madness (cf. 1 Sam 21:13). Some Lucan mss. (ℵ, D,
etc.) add another verb, *rēssei kai,* "it tosses and (convulses)." Today epilepsy
is regarded as a chronic nervous disorder involving changes in consciousness
and motion resulting from either an inborn defect which produces convulsions
of greater or lesser severity or an organic lesion of the brain (by tumor, toxic
agents, or injury). The attacks often begin in childhood or at puberty.

after a struggle. Lit. "with difficulty," an adv. expressing the reluctance with
which the demon gives up its control of the child. The adv. is *molis;* but many
good mss. (P45, P75, D, the Koine and Hesychian text-traditions) read *mogis,*
another adv. with, strangely enough, the same meaning.

bruising him badly. Lit. "crushing him together." See J. Wilkinson, *ExpTim*
79 (1967) 39-42.

40. *your disciples.* For another instance in the Gospel in which Jesus is recognized as having disciples in the ministry, see 5:30. A. Plummer (*Gospel,*
254) thinks that they "need not be the Apostles, who were charged to cast out

demons" (9:1). But why exclude them, save for the three who were on the mountain with Jesus? That seems to be the implication of the text. We have not yet been told by Luke that even the demons submit to them (see 10:17). Was the power accorded in 9:1 meant only for the mission?

to cast it out. The best reading is *ekbalōsin auto* (in mss. ℵ, A, B, C, W, the Freer family of minuscules, etc.). But the ms. P⁴⁵ reads, "cast him (*auton*) out," whereas ms. D strangely reads *apallaxōsin auton*, "to reconcile him."

were not able. Luke writes *ouk ēdynēthēsan*, as does Matt 17:16, whereas Mark has *ouk ischysan*, "were not powerful enough," a word which Luke does not otherwise avoid (see 6:48; 8:43; 13:24, etc.). This is one of the minor agreements of Luke and Matthew over against Mark. The thrust of the story suggests that the disciples' inability is stressed in contrast to Jesus' own mighty power. It is a literary contrast of apprentices and the master thaumaturge. Recall Gehazi's inability apart from Elisha in 2 Kgs 4:31.

41. *What an unbelieving and perverse generation!* Jesus' exclamation is more at home in the Marcan context which has mentioned a discussion and debating Scribes as well as the inability of the disciples. It is the first of such explicit, pejorative descriptions of his contemporaries; see another in 11:29. A less pointed reference has already been made to "this generation" in 7:31; see further 11:30,31,32,50,51; 17:25; cf. 21:32. The exclamation is derived from Mark 9:19, but Luke has added to it the second adj. *diestrammenē*, "perverse," as has Matt 17:17. It is another minor agreement of Matthew and Luke against Mark in the Triple Tradition. But, as Schürmann (*Lukasevangelium*, 570 n. 25) notes, it has been added independently, being influenced by the second (verbal) adj. in Deut 32:5 (*genea skolia kai diestrammenē*, "crooked and perverse generation"; cf. Deut. 32:20). Cf. Phil 2:15, where the OT phrase occurs outside the gospel tradition.

To whom do the words refer? For Schürmann (*Lukasevangelium*, 570), E. E. Ellis (*Gospel*, 144), F. W. Danker (*Jesus*, 119), et al., they refer to the disciples. For Plummer (*Gospel*, 255), J. M. Creed (*Gospel*, 136) they are addressed to a larger audience, the father and the crowds. However, the "all" of v. 43b would seem to indicate that Luke was referring to both the disciples and the others. Jesus' words are enigmatic in that they generalize a criticism of "this generation."

shall I have to be with you? Again, this query is more at home in the Marcan context. The words take on an ominous note, when read in the light of the next set of sayings (especially v. 44b). For the prep. *pros* with the verb "to be" in the sense of association, see John 1:1.

put up with you. Jesus' words may allude to Yahweh's putting up with Israel in Isa 46:4 (LXX). Coming shortly after his first announcement of the passion, the querulous exclamation takes on added poignancy. The words may recall Moses' complaint to God about having to act as Israel's nursemaid in the desert (Num 11:12).

Bring your son here. Jesus' compassion stands in contrast to the incomprehension of those about him. Luke uses *prosagage*, a compound of *agein*, whereas Mark 9:19 has *pherete*, "carry"; see NOTE on 4:40.

42. *dashed him to the ground.* I.e. as an effect of the confrontation of Jesus. The verb *errēxen* might appear to be the aor. of *rhēgnymi* and mean "tore (him) to pieces." There is, however, another verb *rhēssein,* which has the same form of the aor. indic., but means "throw down, dash to the ground" (see BAG, 743a).

charged. See NOTE on 4:35. The verb and its object are derived from Mark 9:25.

healed the child. So Luke abridges Mark 9:25cd-27. In most cases the verb *iasthai* is used of healing diseases (as in 5:17; 6:18-19; 7:7; 8:47; 9:2,11; 14:4; 17:15; 22:51; Acts 9:34; 28:8), but here it is said of an exorcism (cf. Acts 10:38). This is another indication of "demon-sickness" or the failure to distinguish clearly between a healing and an exorcism (see NOTE on 4:33).

returned. As he did with the son of the widow of Nain (7:15). The compassionate healer thus answers the father's plea (v. 38b).

43. *at God's majestic power.* Lit. "at the majesty (*or* greatness) of God." The noun *megaleiotēs* is used again in Acts 19:27 (of Artemis of the Ephesians) and in 2 Pet 1:16 (of Christ). This verse records a typically Lucan reaction to the miracle, being present in neither Mark nor Matthew. Cf. 4:32; 8:25; 11:14.

The reaction probably means no more than that the people recognized that what Jesus had done was done as God's agent; God's majesty and power were manifested through him (see W. F. Arndt, *The Gospel,* 266; W. Grundmann, *Evangelium nach Lukas,* 195; Schürmann, *Lukasevangelium,* 570). But in v. 43b no specific subject is mentioned for the verbs in the third sg. (*epoiei, eipen*). In a normal paragraph, that would mean that the last-mentioned person was the subject of them, viz. "God." Normally, *ho theos* in the Synoptics refers to the Father; but the time comes in the NT writings when that title is given to Jesus too (John 1:1; 20:28; Heb 1:8-9; cf. R. E. Brown, *Jesus,* 23-28). Is this another ambiguous verse in the Lucan writings reflecting a similar gradual recognition of Jesus as such? See Luke 8:39; Acts 20:28. If so, it might be another answer to Herod's question.

Luke's omission of Mark 8:28-29 at the end of this story softens the criticism of the disciples (who fail to comprehend that this sort of demon is cast out only by prayer).

BIBLIOGRAPHY (9:37-43a)

Bornkamm, G. "*Pneuma alalon:* Eine Studie zum Markusevangelium," *Geschichte und Glauben* (Munich: Kaiser, 1971) 2. 21-36.

Kertelge, K. *Die Wunder Jesu,* 174-179.

Léon-Dufour, X. "L'Episode de l'enfant épileptique," in *La formation des évangiles* (RechBib 2; Bruges: Desclée de Brouwer, 1957) 85-115.

Schenk, W. "Tradition und Redaktion in der Epileptiker-Perikope Mk 9, 14-29," *ZNW* 63 (1972) 76-94.

Schenke, L. *Die Wundererzählungen des Markusevangeliums* (SBB; Stuttgart: Katholisches Bibelwerk, [1977]) 314-349.

Vaganay, L. "Les accords négatifs de Matthieu-Luc contre Marc: L'Episode de l'enfant épileptique (Mt. 17, 14-21; Mc. 9, 14-29; Lc. 9, 37-43a)," in *Le problème synoptique: Une hypothèse de travail* (Bibliothèque de théologie 3/1; Tournai: Desclée, 1957) 405-425.

Van der Loos, H. *The Miracles of Jesus* (*NovT* 9; Leiden: Brill, 1965) 397-405.

Wilkinson, J. "The Case of the Epileptic Boy," *ExpTim* 79 (1967) 39-42.

55. THE SECOND ANNOUNCEMENT OF THE PASSION
(9:43b-45)

9 43b While all were marveling at all that he was doing, Jesus said to his disciples, 44 "Lay up these words of mine deep within you: The Son of Man is going to be handed over into the hands of men." 45 But they did not understand what he said, and its meaning was hidden from them so that they could not comprehend it. They were even afraid to ask him what he meant.

COMMENT

Immediately after the reaction of the crowd to Jesus' cure of the epileptic boy, Luke, following the sequence of Mark, introduces the second announcement of the passion (9:43b-45=Mark 9:30-32; cf. Matt 17:22-23). Cf. 9:22. Once again, Luke's version depends on the Marcan form, and *pace* T. Schramm (*Der Markus-Stoff,* 136), K. H. Rengstorf (*Evangelium nach Lukas,* 126), the influence of a variant tradition is not certainly evident. See J. Ernst, *Evangelium nach Lukas,* 309; G. Schneider, *Evangelium nach Lukas,* 220.

As usual, Luke has modified what he has taken over from Mark: (1) Verse 43b is a redactional introduction, summing up the reaction of "all" who witnessed his activity. In it Luke omits any notice of Jesus' departure and passage through Galilee (Mark 9:30a). His omission of the detail that Jesus did not want to be recognized fits in with the marveling of all the people. Since Luke had omitted the reference to Caesarea Philippi (Mark 8:27), it is taken for granted that Jesus is still in Galilee. (2) He changes the awkward Marcan present tense, "is being handed over," to an emphatic future, "is going to be handed over," as does Matt 17:22b (with a different word order, which reveals the independent shift). (3) For some reason Luke curtails the announcement, limiting it to the betrayal, and omitting all mention of the death and resurrection after three days. (4) He greatly expands the note about the disciples' incomprehension.

From the viewpoint of form-criticism, the passage belongs to Jesus' sayings. On the problem of the announcement as a *vaticinium ex eventu,* see COMMENT on 9:22.

but also stresses ± taken their v. 45 that of even their incomprehension is not their fault.

Luke chooses this so-called second announcement of the betrayal to stress the incomprehension of Jesus' own disciples. They are explicitly addressed in v. 43b, and their reaction to what Jesus tells them receives explicit Lucan emphasis in v. 45. Joined closely to the preceding episode, as it is, the announcement carries its own poignancy. Jesus has just prescinded from the disbelief and perversity of his own generation to show compassion to an unfortunate human being in the grips of evil, but he himself is now about to be handed over to "human beings" (*eis cheiras anthrōpōn*), and precisely as "the Son of Man." For all its poignancy his announcement falls on deaf ears. It will require the resurrection itself to clarify his words and his destiny (see 24:7, where an allusion is made to this announcement). In another way, one should note the reaction in the passage: marveling and incomprehension, but no faith. Instead of marveling at what he was doing, he seeks to get people to marvel rather at his imminent destiny.

NOTES

9 43b. *While all were marveling.* The reaction to Jesus' majestic deeds is not one of faith, but of wonder. This superficial reaction of the crowd is made the occasion for the announcement of Jesus to his disciples: Attend not to what I have been doing, but to what is my destiny. The Lucan redactional style of this introductory notice is evident in the use of a gen. absol. (*pantōn de thaumazontōn*) and of the expression *eipon pros* + the accus. (see NOTE on 1:13).

said to his disciples. I.e. to those disciples who were accompanying him (see 5:30; 6:1,13,17,20; 7:11; 8:9,22; 9:14,16,18,40). The detail of the passion-announcement being addressed to them is derived from Mark 9:31.

44. *Lay up these words of mine deep within you.* Lit. "store these words in your ears," a solemn and impressive figurative substitute for the simple Marcan statement, "he taught his disciples." The Lucan formula may be an echo of Exod 17:14, "put it in the ears of Joshua" (*wĕśîm bĕʾoznê Yĕhôšûaʿ*), but the LXX translates it rather *dos eis ta ōta Iēsoï*, whereas Luke writes *thesthe*, "put, store." Though *logous* could mean "things" theoretically, in this context it must mean "words," the announcement that is to come. See NOTE on 9:28.

The Son of Man. The title is derived from Mark 9:31b; see NOTES on 5:24; 9:22. Luke has curtailed the Marcan form of the announcement, restricting it only to the betrayal.

is going to be handed over. Instead of the pres. tense, *paradidotai*, "is being handed over," of Mark 9:31b, Luke uses *mellei paradidosthai*, lit. "is about to be handed over," which better suits the announcement. There is an apparent minor agreement of Matthew and Luke in this shift against Mark in the Triple Tradition, but their word order is not the same. No mention is made of who will hand Jesus over; if the passive is to be understood as "theological," then the connotation would be that he is being handed over according to God's plan. But all the details need not be expressed in this obvious literary device.

into the hands of men. There is a play on the use of *anthrōpos* in the saying: the "Son of Man" is to be handed over to "men." For a similar rhetorical parallel, see Acts 3:14 (holy and righteous One vs. a murderer).

45. *did not understand what he said.* Lit. "this saying," or possibly "this thing," since Greek *rhēma* can also mean this (see NOTE on 1:37). But in this context "saying" is preferable. The Lucan curtailment of the announcement brings it about that the disciples' incomprehension focuses on the necessity of Jesus to suffer rather than on his resurrection.

its meaning was hidden from them. Lit. "and it had been hidden from them." The same is said again in 18:34. This clause and the following are added by Luke to the notice of Mark 9:32a. The passive is again the theological (see ZBG § 236).

so that they could not comprehend it. The conj. *hina* is used with consecutive force (see NOTE on 8:10). So W. Grundmann, *Evangelium nach Lukas,* 196; J. M. Creed, *The Gospel,* 138. H. Schürmann (*Lukasevangelium,* 573) prefers to take it in its primitive sense as expressing purpose; so too Ernst, *Evangelium nach Lukas,* 310.

afraid to ask him. Luke follows Mark 9:32b in recording the disciples' fear; but their reaction in Matt 17:23 becomes sadness. Is the fear retained by Luke because he wants to hint that the disciples are beginning to realize that the destiny facing Jesus may have implications for them too?

what he meant. Lit. "about this saying." This is a Lucan addition; contrast Mark 9:32b.

BIBLIOGRAPHY (9:43b-45)
(in addition to that on 9:22 above)

Bastin, M. "L'Annonce de la passion et les critères de l'historicité," *RevScRel* 50 (1976) 289-329; 51 (1977) 187-213.

Gamba, G. "Senso e significato funzionale di Luca, 9, 43b-45," in *Il messianismo: Atti della xviii settimana biblica* (Brescia: Paideia, 1966) 233-267.

56. THE RIVALRY OF THE DISCIPLES
(9:46-48)

9 46 An argument developed among them: Which of them would be greatest? 47 When Jesus realized the thoughts that were in their minds, he took a little child and stood him at his side. 48 "Whoever receives this little child in my name," he said to them, "receives me; and whoever receives me, receives him who sent me. For whoever is the least among you is really great."

COMMENT

The last two episodes of the Lucan account of Jesus' Galilean ministry concentrate on attitudes that are supposed to be found among Christian disciples, humility and openness. The first attitude is inculcated in the story about the rivalry of the disciples (9:46-48); the second in the story of the exorcist who was an outsider (9:49-50). Though Luke is still following the Marcan sequence, in using both of these stories, they are with the foregoing announcement of the passion (9:43b-45) closely related to the transfiguration scene. Not only has Luke omitted the geographical reference to Galilee in v. 43b (see Mark 9:30), but he has also omitted that to Capernaum in v. 46 (see Mark 9:33). The result is that these incidents are more closely related to the episode of the transfiguration. In reading the Lucan account of this first story (the rivalry among the disciples), one sees a better psychological background for it in Jesus' having taken up on the mountain with him three of the apostles, Peter, John, and James (9:28).

The Lucan episode of the rivalry of the disciples is likewise dependent on Mark 9:33-37. At least since the time of J. Wellhausen, commentators have noted the composite character of that Marcan episode; two incidents are topically arranged (9:33-35 and 36-37; see R. Bultmann, *HST*, 149).

Luke has again modified the Marcan source. He omits the first saying of Jesus (=Mark 9:35bc) and composes his own version of it at the end of the story (v. 48c). In introducing, first of all, the illustration of the little child and the saying about it, to which v. 48c is then appended, he

creates a much more unified episode. As mentioned above, he likewise
omits the Capernaum setting for the rivalry debate and the allusion to the
house and the road (Mark 9:33). As usual, he also omits the emotional,
the embrace of the child by Jesus (see Mark 9:36b; cf. p. 95 above).

We also meet here some instances of the doublet tradition. First, v. 48b
may be a doublet form of 10:16 or of 22:26 (see p. 81 above). Second,
the Lucan form of this episode is close to Matt 18:1-2,5. But Matthew
has inserted as v. 3 what parallels Mark 10:15 and Luke 18:17 ("Mk")
and as v. 4 a variant of what he has in 23:12, which is parallel to Luke
14:11 and 18:14. In this complicated matter one notes that the Marcan
Gospel has several sayings of Jesus about the relationship among his disciples or the reception of his kingdom-preaching as a little child. These
have obviously been picked up by Mark from different contexts in the
tradition before him and are used in different ways by him and the later
Synoptic evangelists.

From a form-critical viewpoint, the episode is to be regarded as a
pronouncement-story. Bultmann (*HST,* 27) considered it a biographical
apophthegm. V. Taylor (*FGT,* 148), while admitting that it may have
been a pronouncement-story, thinks that it is now a Story about Jesus.

The episode insists on a rigorous humility in inner-community relationships. The little child taken by Jesus to himself is the sign of Christian greatness, precisely as the least significant and weakest member of
human society. Jesus' saying and the illustration have both a christological and an ecclesiological import. Jesus in his mission as one sent by the
Father can still identify himself with such lowliness; to accept and esteem
God and his emissary one has to be prepared to accept and esteem even
the smallest of human society. Jesus is, therefore, calling for a similar attitude among those who will be his followers in their dealings with one
another.

The episode takes on a further nuance in the context in which it is
found. Following on the preceding passage, in which the disciples fail to
comprehend Jesus' destiny, it suggests that part of that incomprehension
comes from a rivalry among them that obscures their real vision. They do
not comprehend because of the kind of "thoughts" (*dialogismos*) that
they entertain. Again, in the following context, their incomprehension
and rivalry are linked to an attitude about outsiders, non-disciples, who
may chance to invoke the name of their Master.

Verse 48b, "whoever receives me, receives him who sent me," plays an
important role in the Lucan Gospel, aside from the implication of
lowliness in the immediate context. It stresses the origin of Jesus' own
mission, viz. the person of his heavenly Father; in its own way it echoes
Luke 4:18,43. It will find a negative mode of expression in 10:16, "whoever rejects me rejects him who sent me" (see COMMENT there).

NOTES

9   46. *An argument.* Luke uses *dialogismos;* see NOTE on 2:35.

Which one of them would be greatest? Lit. "about: 'Who would be the greater of them?'" The question is introduced by the neuter def. art. *to* (see NOTE on 1:62). The adj. *meizōn* is actually in the comparative degree, but is used here as a superlative (see BDF § 244).

Luke has explicitly formulated the question at issue. Mark 9:33 only hints at it and notes the disciples' embarrassed silence, when Jesus questions them about their discussion on the road to Capernaum. As formulated here, it would refer to greatness within the group of disciples. Matt 18:1 introduces his own nuance with "in the kingdom of heaven."

47. *realized the thoughts that were in their minds.* Lit. "knew the thought (*dialogismon*) of their hearts." See 5:22; 6:8.

took a little child. Jesus does not comment immediately, as in Mark 9:35b; rather, his first reaction is symbolic. He associates with himself the smallest and weakest member of human society, giving him/her a place of honor beside himself. On the identification of the child as Ignatius in later tradition, see A. Plummer, *The Gospel,* 258.

48. *receives this little child.* I.e. accepts with esteem such a person as this. In introducing the dem. pron., Luke makes Jesus call the disciples' attention to one child with whom he identifies himself. Mark 9:37 has a more generic statement, "one of such little children."

in my name. I.e. as a representative of me, or as a type of that for which I stand. Underlying the Greek prep. phrase, *epi tō onomati mou,* is the OT Hebrew phrase, *běšem.* . . . See Exod 5:23; Deut 10:8. Luke uses this expression elsewhere (9:49; 21:8; 24:47; Acts 4:17,18; 5:28,40; 15:14 [sometimes with a different prep.]). The point is not that one has to have a childlike character to enter the kingdom (see 18:17), but rather to accept Jesus himself one has to be prepared to accept and esteem even the lowliest of human society.

whoever receives me, receives him who sent me. I.e. the Father (see 4:43; 10:16). The prons. "me" are in an emphatic position before the verb in the Greek text. The saying reflects a juridical principle; in later rabbinic texts it is formulated thus: "A man's emissary is like the man himself" (*šělûḥô šel 'ādām kěmôtô, m. Berakot* 5:5; see Str-B, 1. 590). Hence deference shown to Jesus is deference shown to God. Related sayings are found in the Johannine tradition (John 17:3,18).

whoever is the least among you is really great. Or possibly, "the greatest," since the positive degree (*megas*) may be used here as a superlative (see NOTE on 5:39). The comparative, *ho mikroteros,* is also used here for the superlative, "least"; see NOTE on v. 46.

This verse contains Jesus' answer to the question in v. 46. Though it corresponds in sense to that given in Mark 9:35b ("If anyone wishes to be first, he will be the last of all and the servant of all"), the Lucan formulation makes practically the same point. Only after Jesus has made this remark in the Marcan Gospel does he introduce the child as an illustration.

BIBLIOGRAPHY (9:46-48)

Black, M. "The Marcan Parable of the Child in the Midst," *ExpTim* 59 (1947-1948) 14-16.

Butler, B. C. "M. Vaganay and the 'Community Discourse,'" *NTS* 1 (1954-1955) 283-290.

Descamps, A. "Du discours de Marc., ix, 33-50 aux paroles de Jésus," *La formation des évangiles* (RechBib 2; Bruges: Desclée de Brouwer, 1957) 152-177.

Leaney, R. "Jesus and the Symbol of the Child (Lc ix. 46-48)," *ExpTim* 66 (1954-1955) 91-92.

Légasse, S. *Jésus et l'enfant: 'Enfants,' 'Petits' et 'Simples' dans la tradition synoptique* (EBib; Paris: Gabalda, 1969).

Lindeskog, G. "Logia-Studien," *ST* 4 (1950) 129-189, esp. pp. 171-177.

Neirynck, F. "The Tradition of the Sayings of Jesus: Mark 9, 33-50," *Concilium* 20 (1966) 62-74.

Schnackenburg, R. "Mk 9, 33-50," *Synoptische Studien: Alfred Wikenhauser zum siebzigsten Geburtstag* (eds. J. Schmid and A. Vögtle; Munich: Zink, 1953) 184-206.

Vaganay, L. "Le schématisme du discours communautaire," in *Le problème synoptique* (Tournai: Desclée, 1954) 361-404; cf. *RB* 60 (1953) 203-244.

57. THE EXORCIST WHO WAS AN OUTSIDER
(9:49-50)

9 49 John then spoke up, "Master, we saw someone using your name to cast out demons and we tried to stop him, because he did not follow along with us." 50 But Jesus said to him, "Do not stop him; for whoever is not against you is for you."

COMMENT

The last episode of Jesus' Galilean ministry in the Lucan Gospel deals with the disciples' attitude toward a non-disciple who sought to cast out demons in Jesus' name (9:49-50). Jesus insists on an attitude of openness toward such outsiders.

Luke has derived this episode from Mark 9:38-41; even T. Schramm (*Der Markus-Stoff*, 140-141) excludes the use here of any variant tradition. What Luke has retained from the Marcan source is almost word-for-word identical, despite the curtailment of the episode. Matthew has no counterpart to this scene, but he does have a saying similar to the pronouncement of v. 50b in 12:30 (=Luke 11:23, "Q").

Luke has modified the Marcan material: (1) He uses his own introductory formula (9:49a) and changes *didaskale*, "Teacher," to *epistata*, "Master." (2) He may have omitted the first rel. cl., "who is not following us," if it were really in the Marcan text that he had (see *app. crit.* on Mark 9:38). (3) He adds "to him" (v. 50). (4) He omits vv. 39b and 41 of Mark. (The last verse is part of a larger section that is omitted, 9:41 - 10:12 at this point; see p. 67 above).

From the form-critical viewpoint, this episode is a pronouncement-story. H. Bultmann (*HST*, 24-25) considered the pronouncement to be in Mark 9:39 and regarded v. 40 as "a secondary addition." If he is right, then Luke has made the equivalent of v. 40 into his pronouncement. The prohibition, "Do not stop him," is the main part of the pronouncement in any case, and, as V. Taylor puts it, "its value for the first Christians needs no argument" (*FGT*, 68).

The pronouncement in v. 50 is clear; it is a contradiction of John's point of view. Though Jesus may have given to the Twelve "power and authority over all demons" (9:1), he does not restrict the use of his powerful name only to them. Hence they must retain an attitude of openness, even of tolerance, toward the outsider who would extend the divine bounty that he was sent to dispense to unfortunate human beings. If the Lucan Jesus is at pains to train his witnesses from Galilee and see that they comprehend his teaching and the power that he would pass on to them, he does not exclude one who "did not follow along with" them from invoking his name and dispensing that bounty too.

Coming on the heels of 9:46-48, with its emphasis on the reception of "the little child" with esteem, this episode implicitly extends that attitude even to those who are outside the group of disciples. The openness called for may mean not only tolerance, but even a respect for such a person who accomplishes something "in Jesus' name"—what disciples were not able to accomplish (9:40).

From a christological point of view, the episode enhances the power that is associated with the name of Jesus, a power that is not only passed on to disciples (9:1), but that even an outsider could share.

For a Pauline reaction to an analogous narrow-mindedness, see Phil 1:15; 1 Cor 3:5-9.

NOTES

9 49. *John.* I.e. the son of Zebedee, brother of James, and one of the Twelve (see NOTES on 5:10; 6:14). He is named here, as in Mark 9:38, as one of the privileged disciples; he poses the question to Jesus implicity: What do we do about this? It reflects a problem in the early Christian community, probably already emergent in the pre-Marcan church. Why John is the spokesman here, and not Peter, is hard to say. He appears again in v. 54 (with James).

spoke up. Luke introduces the episode with *apokritheis eipen* (see p. 114 above).

Master. See NOTE on *epistata*, 5:5.

someone. Luke 11:19 ("Q," see Matt 12:27) reveals that there were Jewish exorcists at work in Jesus' day; cf. Acts 19:13. The implication here is that this non-disciple succeeded in expelling a demon in Jesus' name.

using your name to cast out. Lit. "casting out in your name," i.e. by invoking the power associated with your name. Though the prep. is *en* here, not *epi*, as in 9:48, this phrase is probably the reason for the collocation of the two episodes in the Marcan (or pre-Marcan) tradition—catchword bonding. Underlying the phrase is the Hebrew use of *běšem Yhwh* in the sense of a source of power; see Pss 54:3 [54:1E]; 124:8.

It is possible, of course, that the exorcist is meant to have been using Jesus' name in some sort of abracadabra formula of incantation. For the ancient practice of using the name(s) of renowned religious leader(s) in magical incantations, especially in the exorcism of demons, see the Paris Greek magical papyrus (line 14), which makes "Jesu" into "the god of the Hebrews" and invokes many other deities in an adjuration over "those possessed by demons" (see C. K. Barrett, *NTB*, 31-35 § 27). Christian disciples are depicted using Jesus' name in Acts 3:16; 9:34; 16:18. Cf. Acts 8:9-24 for Simon Peter's reaction to an outsider, even after this injunction of Jesus.

demons. See NOTE on 4:33.

he did not follow along with us. Or possibly, "he did not follow (you) with us." For the use of *akolouthein* in the sense of discipleship, see NOTE on 5:11. Cf. Mark 9:38.

50. *said to him.* The Lucan predilection for *eipen pros* + acc. appears here again (see NOTE on 1:13).

Do not stop him. This and the following statement is derived verbatim from Mark 9:40, save for the shift from the first pl. pronoun to the second pl. Jesus does not try to make the exorcist one of the group.

whoever is not against you is for you. Jesus' answer to John's implied question is given in the form of a proverb. It sounds like a contradiction of the "Q" saying in 11:23a, "Anyone who is not with me is against me" (=Matt 12:30a). In fact, Bultmann (*HST*, 25) considers the latter as the more original and the form used here a product of the early community, because exorcism of demons in Jesus' name would hardly have antedated its use in the early church. The retention of the two sayings may be another instance of Lucan inconsistency. But an explanation for the retention of the two has been given: The saying in 11:23 is a warning to the individual Christian disciple against neutrality and is meant as a test of *oneself*, whereas the form used here is a norm for the attitude of disciples toward *others* who are outsiders. See J. M. Creed, *The Gospel*, 139; A. Plummer, *The Gospel*, 259.

The proverbial form of the sayings can be seen from a similar statement in one of Cicero's speeches, written 46 B.C.: "Though *we* held all to be our opponents but those on our side, *you* [Caesar] counted all as your adherents who were not against you" (*Pro Quinto Ligario* 33). See further Suetonius *Divus Iulius* 75; Plutarch *Solon* 20.1 (89A). Cf. E. Nestle, "'Wer nicht mit mir ist, der ist wider mich,'" *ZNW* 13 (1912) 84-87; A. Fridrichsen, ibid., 273-280.

BIBLIOGRAPHY (9:49-50)

Roloff, J. *Das Kerygma und der irdische Jesus* (Göttingen: Vandenhoeck und Ruprecht, 1970) 185-186.

Wilhelms, E. "Der fremde Exorzist: Eine Studie über Mark. 9,38ff.," *ST* 3 (1949) 162-171.

IV. THE JOURNEY TO JERUSALEM

He Set His Face Resolutely toward Jerusalem

A. THE LUCAN TRAVEL ACCOUNT

a. From the First to the Second Mention of Jerusalem as Destination (9:51 - 13:21)

58. DEPARTURE FOR JERUSALEM AND A SAMARITAN RECEPTION
(9:51-56)

9 51 As the days were drawing near when he was to be taken up to heaven and Jesus had set his face resolutely toward Jerusalem, 52 he happened to send messengers on ahead of him. They went forth and came to a village of the Samaritans to make arrangements for him. 53 But the villagers would not welcome him, seeing that his intention was to proceed to Jerusalem. 54 When the disciples James and John saw this, they said, "Lord, do you want us to *call down fire from heaven to consume*ᵃ these people?" 55 But Jesus turned and rebuked them, 56 and they made their way to another village.

ᵃ 2 Kgs 1:10,12

COMMENT

An important new section of the Lucan Gospel begins at 9:51, the so-called travel account. Since the end of his little interpolation (6:20 - 8:3), Luke has been following Mark's sequence: 8:4 - 9:50=Mark 4:1 - 9:40. Now he omits 9:41 - 10:12, which is the so-called Little Omission, but he will use forms of 9:42-50 later in the travel account (17:1-3; 14:34-35).

The travel account itself is inspired by Mark 10:1-52, where Jesus makes his way with disciples from Galilee to Judea through Perea (cf. Matt 19:1-20:34); notices of his progress to Jerusalem are given only at Mark 10:32-33; 11:1 (cf. Matt 20:17-18; 21:1). The Synoptic tradition knows of only one journey of Jesus to Jerusalem, in contrast to the Johannine (see John 2:13; 5:1; 7:10). Luke refers to the journey indirectly again in Acts 10:39. The counterpart of this Marcan journey is found in Luke 18:15-19:27, but it is prefixed with a lengthy insert that runs for almost nine chapters, the so-called Big Interpolation (9:51-18:14); see p. 67 above. This begins precisely at this point in the Gospel. Most of the material inserted here into the Marcan order is derived from "Q" (see pp. 75-81 above); but no little use is made of "L" material too (see pp. 82-85 above). What is not derived from these two sources is to be ascribed to Lucan composition. The "Q" material that is used is largely the same as that used by Matthew in his great sermons (see the comparative tables in K. Aland, SQE, 562-566).

The reason for making a break at this point in the Gospel is the explicit introduction of the mention of Jerusalem as the goal of Jesus' wanderings with his disciples. Thus far he has been conducting his ministry in Galilee and in the country of the Jews (the last mentioned locales put him in the north: Capernaum, 7:1; Nain, 7:11; Bethsaida, 9:11; even the territory of the Gerasenes, "opposite Galilee," 8:26). Luke's knowledge of Palestinian geography is not what it should be, if one tries to pin it down in any historical sense; but to do so misses the point of his story. At this part of his Gospel he decides to move Jesus to Jerusalem, the city of destiny. It is here explicitly named (9:51), in contradistinction to Mark 10:1 or Matt 19:1. It will be named several times again in the course of this account (9:53; 13:22,33-34; 17:11; 18:31; 19:11 [always *Ierousalēm* save for 13:22, *Hierosolyma*]). That it is crucial to Luke is seen in the way he introduces the mention of it in connection with Jesus' "being taken up" (*analēmpsis,* "assumption") and of fulfillment. In other words, in the Lucan Gospel Jesus goes from Galilee or the country of the Jews to Jerusalem not *via* Perea (as in Mark and Matthew), but he heads instead for the city of destiny through the land that symbolizes opposition, Samaria—or, as Luke puts it at one point, "between Samaria and Galilee" (17:11; see NOTE there on this notorious *crux interpretum*).

Only Luke has such an extended travel account at this point in his Gospel. The trouble with it is that, once Jesus sets out on this (literally) lengthy journey, he seems to be no longer en route. The verb *poreuesthai,* "go, move along," is used frequently at the outset (9:51-53,56-57) and occasionally thereafter (10:38; 13:31,33; 17:11; 19:28) within the travel account. Similarly, the noun *hodos,* "way, road," appears at the beginning (9:57; 10:4), but never again in the travel account referring to Jesus' way or journey. Even though there are at times other vague references to Jesus' movement (see 10:1; 11:53; 18:35; 19:1), the result is that the reader loses sight of the supposed travelogue that he/she is reading. As K. L. Schmidt (*Rahmen,* 269) once put it, "Though Jesus is always traveling to Jerusalem, he never makes any real progress on this journey."

The tension between the matter and the form in the travel account has been the real problem. Though it purports to be the counterpart of Mark 10:1-52, it is for the most part a literary compilation of sayings of Jesus (of various sorts: proverbs, parables, legal and wisdom sayings, criticism of his opponents, eschatological utterances), pronouncement-stories, and a few miracle-stories, all set in the framework of the journey to Jerusalem. The connection between these varied elements is often very loose, and it is impossible to detect a structure in this account or any genetic or logical development. Occasionally, topical arrangement has grouped what were otherwise isolated individual sayings (e.g. those on the conditions of discipleship in vv. 57-62).

In the outline of the Gospel the travel account has been divided into three sections, using the main references to Jesus' moving to Jerusalem (13:22; 17:11 as points of articulation, following other commentators [W. Grundmann, J. Schneider, "Zur Analyse," 226, et al.]). This is, however, a mere convenience, since the division at these points is otherwise insignificant and somewhat arbitrary. At times it has been suggested that this threefold division is really intended and that it reflects the recollection of three journeys of Jesus to Jerusalem, as in the Johannine tradition. But the evidence hardly supports such a suggestion.

The tension between the matter and the form of the travel account, however, has given rise to a debate about the name for this part of the Lucan Gospel. For other names have at times been used of it. It has, for instance, been called "the Perean Section," which is a misnomer in the Lucan Gospel (see B. H. Streeter, *The Four Gospels,* 203), being derived from the Marcan or Matthean counterparts. Streeter himself preferred to call it "the Central Section," which is obviously more neutral, but which is also tied to the Proto-Luke hypothesis, the problems of which at this point in the account have been discussed by H. Conzelmann, *Theology,* 60-61. In imitation of this title, E. E. Ellis, *Gospel of Luke,* 146-150, speaks of "the Central Division," but that is no improvement. Commentators such as A. Schlatter, J. Wellhausen, Schmidt, Ellis think that the Lucan Gospel has no travel account at all. No little part of the reason for denying it is the implication that the historical Jesus did not say or do all these things on the way to Jerusalem.

But, as Conzelmann (*Theology,* 62) has rightly seen, this is an important Lucan "motif," and a "piece of deliberate editorial work." Perhaps the material used by Luke lacks a certain harmony with its insertion into a plan of a journey, but that does not hinder one from recognizing that the journey to Jerusalem is an important framework that Luke has given to this collection of "Q," "L," and other material. Conzelmann has again rightly stressed its christological role in the Gospel; but he is not quite right in restricting it to a way of "progress towards the Passion" (p. 63). It is rather Luke's way of concretizing the *exodos* of Jesus and all that that is supposed to mean in these writings (see NOTE on 9:31). It is a major part of the Lucan geographical perspective (see p. 164 above) and contributes in an important way to his theology as a whole. The artificial expansion of the inherited tradition about Jesus' journey to Jerusalem is a device which serves this christological (and theological) purpose. Coming on the heels of the mention of Jesus' *exodos,* his "being taken up" (9:51) calls for movement to Jerusalem (see 13:33,35b; cf. 19:38) and creates the stage for the dramatic point of that "departure."

It is an important part of the Gospel in the way that it affects Jesus' followers, since he goes up to Jerusalem accompanied by disciples. They will become the authenticated witnesses of all that he has taught and all that he has done. The travel account, therefore, becomes a special device used by Luke for the further training of these Galilean witnesses. If Jesus moves to the city of destiny according to what has been determined, he nevertheless equips his followers for the mission of proclaiming him and his message of salvation after his death and resurrection to "the end of the earth" (Acts 1:8). The travel account becomes, then, a collection of teachings for the young missionary church, in which instruction of disciples alternates with debates with opponents. In playing out his role of teacher in this part of the Gospel, however, he is not depicted by Luke as a "new Moses," *pace* C. F. Evans, "The Central Section."

Departure for Jerusalem

The opening episode of the Lucan travel account describes Jesus setting out for Jerusalem, passing through Samaritan villages, and being refused a welcome in one of them (9:51-56). This scene has no counterpart in any of the other Gospels. If there is any pre-Lucan tradition behind it, it would be limited to vv. 52-55, derived from "L" (see R. Bultmann, *HST,* 26). However, v. 51 is almost certainly Lucan composition, with its characteristic wording (see NOTE) and the markedly christological motif of Jesus fixedly facing his Jerusalem destiny, a note that only Luke has. Verse 56 is also undoubtedly Lucan, being another reference to the journey.

The episode has been related to the form-critical category of pronounce-ment-stories (see Bultmann, *HST,* 25-27, but he has to admit that it contains "no distinctive apophthegm"; see also V. Taylor, *FGT,* 69-70). The lack of a pronouncement was in time remedied in the transmission of the Gospel-text by the addition of a saying in vv. 55-56 (see NOTES). But the absence of this saying in the earliest mss. of the Gospel makes their authenticity suspicious. Hence, as it stands, the passage is better regarded as a Story about Jesus (see Taylor, *FGT,* 153).

The scene stresses Jesus' resolute determination to make his way to Jerusalem, the city of destiny, despite all opposition. Nothing is to dis-tract him from what has been determined. Just as the Galilean ministry was introduced by a rejection-story (4:16-30), so now the next major part of the Gospel, the travel account, will be introduced by a rejection-story. An Elijah motif was introduced into the earlier story (4:25-26); here the Elijah motif will reappear (9:54). This time it will be put to a different use; the suggestion of James and John to call down fire from heaven becomes the occasion of Jesus' rebuke—in effect, a rejection of the identification of himself with the fiery reformer (see p. 664 above).

Taken with the episode that follows about the conditions of dis-cipleship, the two scenes serve to correct wrong ideas of what it means to follow Jesus. Discipleship does not consist in zealous punishment of those who reject Jesus and his mission; nor does it consist in qualified follow-ing. All of this comes from the teacher who walks resolutely toward the goal.

In the two Samaritan episodes to come later on in the travel account, Jesus' dealings with them will be those of kindness and compassion. Here he experiences, on the contrary, a reaction from the inhospitable inhabit-ants of one Samaritan town.

NOTES

9 51. *As the days were drawing near.* Lit. "and it happened, in the filling up of the days of his being-taken-up and he stiffened (his) face to go to Jerusalem, that he sent messengers. . . ." Luke again uses *egeneto de* with the conj. *kai* + finite verb (*apesteilen*); see p. 119 above. Intervening between the introductory *egeneto de* and the *kai* are the articular infin. with *en* and the unstressed *kai autos* (see pp. 119, 120). The verb *symplērousthai,* "being filled up, completed," with "days" occurs only here in the gospel tradition; but see Acts 2:1; in Luke 1:23; 2:6,21,22; 21:22, a similar phrase is used (but with the verb *pimplanai* instead). The expression is Lucan, and the filling up of the days has to be understood of God's plan beginning to move to a new stage of its realization.

when he was to be taken up to heaven. Lit. "(the days) of his assumption."

The Greek noun ~~analēmpsis occurs only here in the whole NT;~~ it is an abstract formation of the verb *analambanein,* used by Luke in Acts 1:2,11,22 of Jesus' so-called ascension (see also Mark 16:19; 1 Tim 3:16). Because the noun occurs only here, some commentators (e.g. J. Schmid, *Evangelium nach Lukas,* 176) appeal to *Ps. Sol.* 4:18 (4:20E [*APOT* 2. 637]), where it seems to be used of death, to restrict it to that meaning here. But the Lucan references in Acts almost certainly give it a larger connotation. J. G. Davies has also stressed the prefigurement of Jesus' ascension in other places of chap. 9 (*JTS* 6 [1955] 229-233). The only question is whether one should restrict it merely to the ascension or understand it in the still broader sense of Jesus' entire transit to the Father (via death, burial, and exaltation). Luke at times speaks of Jesus' "exaltation" (Acts 2:33), thus preserving a primitive formulation (cf. Phil 2:9), but here he prefers to speak of his "assumption" (cf. 24:51b, "carried up"). He never says that Jesus "ascended"; this notion enters the Christian tradition because of Eph 4:8, quoting Ps 68:18, and its interpretation in 4:9-10.

The OT background to the "assumption" of Jesus is to be seen in that of Enoch (Gen 5:24b) and Elijah (2 Kgs 2:11; 1 Macc 2:58; Sir 48:9). In intertestamental literature there is also the *Assumption of Moses* (see 10:12 [*APOT,* 2. 422, esp. n. 12]).

and Jesus had set his face resolutely toward Jerusalem. Lit. "and he stiffened (his) face to go to J." Some mss. (‭א‬, C, D, the Koine text-tradition add "his" before "face." But earlier mss. (P⁴⁵, P⁷⁵, B) omit it. The expression, *to prosōpon estērisen tou poreuesthai . . . ,* is strange. The verb *stērizein,* "harden, stiffen," occurs again in 16:26; 22:32; Acts 18:23, but in no sense that would elucidate its use here with *to prosōpon,* "(his) face." It seems to be a takeoff on Hebrew *śām* (or *nātan*) *pānāyw lĕ-,* "he set his face to . . ." (Gen 31:21; Jer 42:15,17; Dan 9:3), i.e. to head toward. Luke would have substituted a stronger verb, thinking perhaps of the LXX of Ezek 6:2; 13:17; 14:8, *stērizein to prosōpon epi,* "to fix one's face against" (some thing or someone in a hostile or threatening sense). The substitution would express Jesus' resolute determination to face his destiny and any opposition related to it. It has been suggested that the phrase is an echo of Isa 50:7, "I have set my face like flint and know that I shall not be put to shame" (see J. Starcky, *RSR* 39 [1951] 197-202). But the comparison is not perfect in that the Isaian expression uses in the LXX *hōs sterean petran,* "like a hard rock" (*stereos,* with short *e*). Here perhaps one should recall the mission of the prophet Ezekiel to the city of Jerusalem (Ezekiel 8-11).

Jerusalem. Luke uses *Ierousalēm* (see NOTE on 2:22); it is the city of destiny (see p. 164 above).

52. *send messengers on ahead of him.* Perhaps this is another allusion to Mal 3:1 ("I send my messenger to prepare the way before me"), who becomes in Mal 3:23 (4:5E) Elijah.

a village of the Samaritans. Some mss. (‭א‬*, the Freer family of minuscules, Vg) read *polin,* "a town." See v. 56. This is the first mention of the Samaritans in the Gospel. In Matt 10:5 Jesus forbids the disciples he sends out to enter a Samaritan town; otherwise only Luke among the Synoptists depicts Jesus dealing with Samaritans (see 10:30-37; 17:11-19; cf. Acts 1:8;

8:1-13,14,25; 9:31; 15:3). In this he manifests a contact with the Johannine tradition (see John 4:4-42). Luke's interest in Jesus' dealings with such people stems from his emphasis on the universality of salvation now being made available in Jesus (see p. 189 above). Cf. M. S. Enslin, "Luke and the Samaritans," *HiR* 36 (1943) 278-297.

"Samaritan" (Greek *Samaritēs*) was originally a geographic term, an inhabitant of Samaria (Hebrew *šōmĕrôn*), the capital of the northern kingdom, founded by Omri ca. 870 B.C. In time it became an ethnic and religious name for the inhabitants of the area between Judea and Galilee, west of the Jordan. The origin of the split of the Samaritans from the Jews is shrouded in mystery and explained differently in each group (see T. H. Gaster, *IDB* 4. 1910). The split has often been related to the deportation of the Jews of the northern kingdom by the Assyrians after the conquest of 722 B.C. and the importation of non-Jews as colonists of the area (2 Kgs 17:24). The later opposition to the Jewish reconstruction of Jerusalem and its Temple after the Babylonian exile (see Ezra 4:2-24; Neh 2:19; 4:2-9) has often been explained in terms of this split. Whether it goes back to such early times is the problem. In any case, these (half-Jewish?) worshipers of Yahweh, who restricted their Scriptures to the Pentateuch, built a temple on part of Mount Gerizim (Tell er-Râs) in Hellenistic times. It served their needs from the time of Alexander the Great until its destruction under John Hyrcanus (ca. 128 B.C.). From Hellenistic times on the sharp division of Jews and Samaritans is clear; the Samaritans developed their own form of the Pentateuch (redacted in Hasmonean times), their own liturgy (modern Samaritans from Nablus still celebrate the Passover in the open atop Mount Gerizim), and their own liturgical literature in both Hebrew and Aramaic. See further J. Jeremias, *TDNT* 7. 88-94; F. M. Cross, "Aspects of Samaritan and Jewish History in Late Persian and Hellenistic Times," *HTR* 59 (1966) 201-211; J. D. Purvis, "Samaritans," *IDBSup*, 776-777; *The Samaritan Pentateuch and the Origin of the Samaritan Sect* (HSM 2; Cambridge, MA: Harvard University, 1968).

to make arrangements. Lit. "to prepare for him," i.e. a lodging. But see 10:1c, which might give this expression another sense (cf. Mal 3:1). The preferred reading here is *hōs,* following mss. P⁴⁵, P⁷⁵, B, ℵ*, and not *hōste,* even though the latter can have final, not consecutive, sense (BDF § 391.3).

53. *would not welcome him.* The first instance of opposition to Jesus as he proceeds to Jerusalem. Josephus tells of the problems that Galilean pilgrims had "at the time of a festival to pass through Samaritan territory on their way to the Holy City" (*Ant.* 20.6,1 §§ 118-123, incident in the time of the procurator, V. Cumanus, A.D. 48-52; cf. *J.W.* 2.12,3 §§ 232-233). For this reason, Galilean pilgrims often crossed the Jordan and went up to Jerusalem via Perea (see Mark 10:1).

his intention was to proceed to Jerusalem. Lit. "his face was proceeding to Jerusalem." Ms. P⁴⁵ and Latin versions have rather: "his face was of one proceeding to Jerusalem," which is a copyist's correction that eliminates an incongruity. The phrase imitates the LXX of 2 Sam 17:11, "that your face proceed in the midst of them" (*en mesō autōn*), a misunderstanding of the Hebrew *baqĕrāb,* "for battle," for *bĕqereb,* "in the midst of. . . ." Str-B, 2. 165 understands *prosōpon* there as "person" (cf. 2 Cor 1:11; BGD, 721). In any case, the sense is clear: Jesus' destination is the reason for the Samaritan failure to welcome him.

54. *James and John*. The sons of Zebedee (see NOTE on 6:14). In his parallel to the Marcan list of the Twelve (3:17), Luke omitted the epithet given to them, *Boanērges*, i.e. "sons of thunder." Whether that is the reason why the two of them are singled out here we shall never know.

call down fire from heaven to consume these people. Though Luke uses *analōsai* instead of *kataphagein* of the LXX, the words are otherwise a clear allusion to 2 Kgs 1:10 or 12. The disciples want to share Jesus' power to work a punitive miracle. Early copyists, not resisting the temptation to gloss the text, added, "even as Elijah did" (mss. A, C, D, W, Θ, the Koine text-tradition, etc. —a not unimpressive list of witnesses). They noted the allusion. But the gloss is absent in mss. P⁴⁵, P⁷⁵, and the Hesychian text-tradition in general. Most modern critical editions of the Greek NT omit it; but J. M. Ross ("The Rejected Words in Luke 9:54-56," *ExpTim* 84 [1972-1973] 85-88) argues for the retention of them, and also the variants in vv. 55-56.

55. *Jesus turned*. Lit. "having turned," the ptc. *strapheis* occurs again in 10:23; 14:25. He is depicted leading the group of followers.

rebuked them. The rebuke is a correction of disciples who do not yet comprehend what his mission is about (see 9:45). He refuses to be identified with Elijah as the fiery reformer (see p. 664 above). He refuses to have anything to do with this sort of reaction of human beings, even when they are hostile to him. In effect, he is exemplifying a teaching of the sermon on the plain (6:29).

At the end of this verse, some mss. (D, Θ, the Koine text-tradition) add, "and said, You do not know of what spirit you are," and at the beginning of the next verse some add, "(For) the Son of Man has not come to destroy the lives of human beings, but to save (them)." But earlier mss. (P⁴⁵, P⁷⁵, E, and the Hesychian tradition) omit them. Since what is added at the beginning of v. 56 is a variant of 19:10 (cf. John 3:17), it is further suspect. See NOTE at end of v. 54. If the sayings were to be retained in the text, they would constitute Jesus' pronouncement (see COMMENT).

56. *they made their way to another village*. Compare 4:30, where the same verb *poreuesthai*, used in vv. 51,52,53, was also employed for the ending of the rejection-story told there.

BIBLIOGRAPHY (9:51-56)

Travel Account

Benoit, P. "La section IX, 51–XVIII, 14 de saint Luc," *RB* 60 (1953) 446-448.

Bernadicou, P. J. "The Spirituality of Luke's Travel Narrative," *Review for Religious* 36 (1977) 455-466.

Blinzler, J. "Die literarische Eigenart des sogenannten Reiseberichts im Lukas-Evangelium," in *Synoptische Studien: Alfred Wikenhauser zum siebzigsten*

Geburtstag . . . *dargebracht* (eds. J. Schmid and A. Vögtle; Munich: K. Zink, 1953) 20-52.

Conzelmann, H. *Theology*, 60-73.

Davies, J. H. "The Purpose of the Central Section of St. Luke's Gospel," *SE II* (TU 87; 1964) 164-169.

Denaux, A. "Het lucaanse reisverhaal (Lc. 9,51-19,44)," *Collationes brugenses et gandavenses* 14 (1968) 212-242; 15 (1969) 464-501.

Evans, C. F. "The Central Section of St. Luke's Gospel," in *Studies in the Gospels: Essays in Memory of R. H. Lightfoot* (ed. D. E. Nineham; Oxford: Blackwell, 1955) 37-53.

Fransen, I. "Cahier de Bible: La montée vers Jérusalem," *BVC* 11 (1955) 69-87.

Gasse, W. "Zum Reisebericht des Lukas," *ZNW* 34 (1935) 293-299.

Gill, D. "Observations on the Lukan Travel Narrative and Some Related Passages," *HTR* 63 (1970) 199-221.

Girard, L. *L'Évangile des voyages de Jésus: Ou la section 9,51-18,14 de saint Luc* (Paris: Gabalda, 1951).

Goulder, M. D. "The Chiastic Structure of the Lucan Journey," *SE II* (TU 87; 1964) 195-202.

Grundmann, W. "Fragen der Komposition des lukanischen 'Reiseberichts,'" *ZNW* 50 (1959) 252-270.

Lapointe, R. "L'Espace-temps de Lc 9, 51-19, 27," *Église et théologie* 1 (1970) 275-290.

Leal, J. "Los viajes de Jesús a Jerusalén segun San Lucas," in *XIV semana bíblica española (21-26 Sept. 1953)* (Madrid: Consejo superior de investigaciones científicas, 1954) 365-381.

Lohse, E. "Missonarisches Handeln Jesu nach dem Evangelium des Lukas," *TZ* 10 (1954) 1-13.

McCown, C. C. "The Geography of Jesus' Last Journey to Jerusalem," *JBL* 51 (1932) 107-129.

———— "The Geography of Luke's Central Section," *JBL* 57 (1938) 51-66.

Marshall, I. H. *Luke: Historian and Theologian*, 148-153.

Miyoshi, M. *Der Anfang des Reiseberichts Lk 9,51-10,24: Eine redaktionsgeschichtliche Untersuchung* (AnBib 60; Rome: Biblical Institute, 1974).

Ogg, G. "The Central Section of the Gospel according to St Luke," *NTS* 18 (1971-1972) 39-53.

Osten Sacken, P. von der. "Zur Christologie des lukanischen Reiseberichts," *EvT* 33 (1973) 476-496.

Reicke, B. "Instruction and Discussion in the Travel Narrative," *SE I* (TU 73; 1959) 206-216.

Resseguie, J. L. "Interpretation of Luke's Central Section (Luke 9:51 - 19:44) since 1856," *Studia biblica et theologica* 6 (1975) 3-36.

Robinson, W. C., Jr. "The Theological Context for Interpreting Luke's Travel Narrative (9:51ff.)," *JBL* 79 (1960) 20-31.

Schmidt, K. L. *Der Rahmen der Geschichte Jesu: Literarkritische Untersuchungen zur ältesten Jesusüberlieferung* (Berlin: Trowitzsch und Sohn,

1919; reprinted, Darmstadt: Wissenschaftliche Buchgesellschaft, 1964) 246-273.

Schneider, J. "Zur Analyse des lukanischen Reiseberichtes," in *Synoptische Studien: Alfred Wikenhauser, . . . dargebracht* (Munich: Zink, 1953) 207-229.

Sellin, G. "Komposition, Quellen und Funktion des lukanischen Reiseberichtes (Lk. ix 51 - xix 28)," *NovT* 20 (1978) 100-135.

Stagg, F. "The Journey toward Jerusalem in Luke's Gospel: *Luke* 9:51 - 19:27," *RevExp* 64 (1967) 499-512.

Trompf, G. W. "La section médiane de l'évangile de Luc: L'Organisation des documents," *RHPR* 53 (1973) 141-154.

Departure for Jerusalem (9:51-56)

Bouwman, G. "Samaria in Lucas-Handelingen," *Bijdragen* 34 (Nijmegen and Brugge, 1973) 40-59.

Calmet, A. "Il n'est pas digne de moi! Luc 9,51-62," *BVC* 77 (1967) 20-25.

Conzelmann, H. *Theology,* 65-66.

Davies, J. G. "The Prefigurement of the Ascension in the Third Gospel," *JTS* 6 (1955) 229-233.

Dibelius, M. *FTG,* 43-48.

Friedrich, G. "Lk 9,51 und die Entrückungschristologie des Lukas," *Orientierung an Jesus: Zur Theologie der Synoptiker: Für Josef Schmid* (eds. P. Hoffmann et al.; Freiburg: Herder, 1973) 48-77.

Miyoshi, M. *Der Anfang,* 6-32.

Starcky, J. "Obfirmavit faciem suam ut iret Jerusalem: Sens et portée de *Luc,* ix, 51," *RSR* 39 (1951) 197-202.

59. THREE WOULD-BE FOLLOWERS OF JESUS
(9:57-62)

9 ⁵⁷ As they moved along the road, someone said to him, "I will follow you wherever you go." ⁵⁸ But Jesus said to him, "Foxes have holes, and the birds of the sky have nests; but the Son of Man has nowhere to lay his head."

⁵⁹ To another he said, "Follow me." But he replied, "Let me first go and bury my father." ⁶⁰ Jesus said to him, "Leave the dead to bury their dead; rather you go and announce the kingdom of God."

⁶¹ Yet another said to him, "I will follow you, sir; but first let me go and say good-bye to my people at home." ⁶² Jesus said [to him], "No one who puts his hand to the plow and keeps looking back is suited for the kingdom of God."

COMMENT

After the introductory episode of the travel account Luke adds an episode with three sayings of Jesus addressed to would-be followers (9:57-62). They evoke from him attitudes toward those who would become his disciples and follow him on his way.

The first two sayings are derived from "Q," being found in Matt 8:19-22. The third is probably derived from "L," though it could also be the product of Lucan composition, added in either case to make a threesome. They may well stem from entirely independent contexts in the ministry of Jesus.

The Lucan redaction of the "Q" material is seen in the introductory phrase, "as they moved along the road," and in the addition of "to him" (*pros auton;* contrast the "Q" form with the dative in v. 58). Luke also eliminates the reference to the "scribe" (Matt 8:19) and the "disciples" (8:21), which thus casts the sayings as directed to newcomers. In the second saying, "Lord" (Matt 8:21) has been omitted and a final clause has been added, "rather you go and announce the kingdom of God." In v. 59 he has also inserted, "Follow me," which he omits in v. 60 in favor of his own addition.

R. Bultmann (*HST,* 28-29) places the episode in the category of pronouncement-stories, listing the sayings as biographical apophthegms. But he is inclined to think that the settings for the sayings are imaginary —dominical sayings that originally circulated without a framework. Moreover, the first was in reality only a proverb about a human being's lot in comparison with animals, which by the substitution of "son of Man" for *anthrōpos* would have become a saying of Jesus. Perhaps. In any case, V. Taylor (*FGT,* 73) calls attention to the vague descriptions of the candidates for discipleship, which reveals that early Christians were more interested in the sayings of Jesus than the identity of such followers. In each case the narrative framework of the pronouncement is at a minimum.

The pronouncements set forth warnings to those who would identify themselves with Jesus' mission: they must count the costs and reckon with a conflict of loyalties that such an identification might entail. They give a new dimension to the idea of "following Christ," to discipleship. See further p. 241 above.

The first would-be follower makes a spontaneous, enthusiastic offer of unconditioned allegiance. Jesus' sobering answer drives home the gravity of discipleship. The Son of Man is en route; he lives the life of a homeless wanderer, having no shelter, no home, no family—none of the things that people usually consider requisite for ordinary life, "nowhere to lay his head." Even animals are better off.

The second is invited by Jesus himself, but he conditions his willingness to accept the invitation. He begs for a waiting period, time enough to fulfill a filial obligation. Jesus' answer, "Leave the dead to bury their dead" (on its meaning see NOTE), makes it clear that the following of which he speaks may have to transcend even filial ties. Such is the allegiance or loyalty that is asked of a disciple. His answer stresses the element of sacrifice that is involved in every choice. It is not for that reason cruel; it is done in order to announce the kingship of God.

The third follower resembles the first in that he spontaneously offers to be a disciple, but also the second one in that he adds a condition. The condition reminds one of the call of Elisha. In 1 Kgs 19:19-21 Elijah sees the son of Shaphat plowing behind twelve yoke of oxen; Elijah comes and throws his cloak over him, an invitation to be a disciple. But Elisha begs to go first and kiss his father and mother good-bye: "Then I will follow you." Elijah the prophet permits it. Again, Jesus dissociates himself from another form of the Elijah-image that people might have of him. Plowing for the kingdom means sacrifice; it can tolerate no distractions. Following Jesus means devotion to kingdom-work and transcends even ordinary family affection.

Thus, the following of Jesus does not simply mean imitation of him, but entering into the very conditions of his life, ministry, and lot. It calls a person to a sacrifice of security (Case I), filial duty (Case II), and family affection (Case III).

NOTES

9 57. *moved along the road*. Again, the verb *poreuesthai;* see NOTE on 9:55.

58. *Foxes have holes*. . . . Jesus' pronouncement is word-for-word identical to that in Matt 8:20. A form of the same saying is found in *Gos. Thom.* § 86: "[Foxes have] the[ir holes] and birds have [their] nests, but the Son of Man has no place to lay his head and rest." The reference to "rest" is to be understood in the Gnostic sense, as elsewhere in that Gospel. This form of the saying is dependent on the canonical Gospels. See W. Schrage, *Verhältnis,* 168-170; cf. A. Strobel, "Textgeschichtliches zum Thomas-Logion 86 (Mt 8,20/Lk 9,58)," *VC* 17 (1963) 211-224. On the "birds," see NOTE on 8:5.

Son of Man. The title is here used as a surrogate for "I," being applied to Jesus in his ministry, to indicate his lowliness or abasement (as in 6:22; 7:34); see NOTE on 5:24. Bultmann (*HST,* 28 n. 3) is certainly correct in rejecting the title as having meant in the original of this saying "the divine envoy of Gnostic mythology," but it is not evident why this saying has its roots in an old proverb, uttered of a human being, homeless in this world and contrasted with wild beasts. "As a generalization the contrast would be clearly untrue to life: many men have houses" (J. M. Creed, *The Gospel,* 142). A parallel to this saying has been found in Plutarch *Vita Tiberii Gracchi* 9 (828C), but it is considerably developed and not in proverb-form at all.

59. *Follow me*. The invitation, added to the Lucan form of the story, repeats that of 5:27.

bury my father. The willingness to follow Jesus is not denied, but "first" a filial obligation is thought to intervene, as Tob 4:3; 6:15(14E) would suggest. It conditions the immediate following. According to later rabbinic tradition, the obligation of burying the dead parents fell even on Nazirites, priests, and the high priest himself, even though contact with a dead body was normally considered a source of defilement (see Num 6:6-7; Lev 21:11; Philo *De specialibus legibus* 1. 23 §§ 112-116; cf. Str-B, 1. 487-489). In this instance it is not to be assumed that the temporizer would not come back, *pace* G. Schrenk (*TDNT* 5. 982 n. 235). The words could be so read, but that would take the edge off the saying of Jesus. See Luke 14:26.

60. *Leave the dead to bury their dead*. This saying of Jesus has always been regarded as very harsh, and "the apparent harshness and obscurity of the saying is a guarantee for its authenticity" (A. Plummer, *The Gospel,* 267). It stands in opposition to Jewish morals and piety, contains no specifically Christian tenet, and has a certain eschatological implication. For these reasons many have maintained the authenticity of this saying (see N. Perrin, *Rediscovering,* 144). The history of the interpretation of the saying has been traced in large part by K. G. Klemm, "Das Wort von der Selbstbestattung der Toten: Beobachtungen zur Auslegungsgeschichte von Mt. viii. 22 Par.," *NTS* 16

(1969-1970) 60-75. Here we shall cite merely a few examples of the modes of interpretation attempted.

Some commentators (like B. Bauer) denied that Jesus ever uttered such a saying and held that it was really a product of the early community. Some others (like F. A. Fritzsche, T. W. Manson) understood the *nekrous,* "the dead" (the first one) to mean the physically dead: "Let the physically dead bury themselves" (*sine mortuos suos mortuos* [=*suae sortis homines*] *sepelire*)—an interpretation which was eventually laughed off the exegetical stage. Some have maintained that *nekrous* translated a Semitic word *mêtîm,* "the dead," which was actually a title for a society of pallbearers (F. E. Rambach). But no evidence has ever been found to substantiate such a view. A more specific form of it was attempted, however, when F. Perles (*ZNW* 19 [1919-1920] 96) claimed that the Greek saying was a mistranslation of (unvocalized) Aramaic: *šbwq lmyty' lmqbr myty' dylhwn,* in which *lmqbr* was taken as the peal infin., *lĕmiqbar,* "to bury," instead of as the pael ptc., *limĕqabber* [sic], "burier." The original really meant, "Leave the dead to their dead-burier." About this suggestion M.-J. Lagrange commented (*Luc,* 289): "It all becomes clear, but too clear, and banal!" The suggestion, however, was carried further by M. Black (*AAGA*[3], 207-208), who thought that Greek *nekrous* was a mistranslation of Aramaic *mtnyyn,* "waverers" (from *mtn,* "delay, put off"), misunderstood as *mtyn,* "dead." It would have meant: "Let the waverers bury their dead."

All of these interpretations were attempts to avoid the most natural way of understanding the rigorous statement of Jesus, which is still the majority interpretation: The first noun *nekrous* is to be understood in a transferred sense of those who have not followed Jesus and hence are the spiritually dead (so R. Bultmann, *TDNT,* 4. 893: "those who resist the call of Jesus are put on the same level as the dead"; Creed, *The Gospel,* 142; Lagrange, *Luc,* 288; Plummer, *The Gospel,* 267; etc.). The difficulty with the interpretation is the word *heautôn,* "their own," which is reflexive and may suggest that the father himself is regarded by Jesus as among the spiritually dead. But that may be pressing the saying beyond what is necessary. For Jesus' saying does not deny that the follower has a filial obligation, but the next part of it reveals that another consideration is in order. Hence, the sense should be: "Leave the (spiritually) dead to bury their (physically) dead."

rather you go and announce the kingdom of God. Luke omitted the impv. *akolouthei moi,* "follow me," at the beginning of the preceding statement (see Matt 8:22), probably because of this addition which he has made (and also, perhaps, because he inserted it above in v. 59). This has been added to sharpen the urgency put on one who would follow Jesus; it specifies why he must give up even the filial obligation to follow straightaway. The Lucan Jesus does not say this only in a teacher-disciple relationship; he knows, rather, that the demands of the kingdom are bound to rupture even ordinary family life. See 14:26.

On "kingdom," see the NOTE on 4:42. Here Luke uses the impv. *diangelle;* contrast the verbs in 8:1; 9:2.

61. *let me go and say good-bye.* This conditioned offer to follow Jesus has no counterpart in Matthew 8. It may be a Lucan composition, influenced by 1 Kgs 19:19-21. See COMMENT.

62. *[to him].* This phrase, *pros auton* (on which see NOTE on 1:13), is not read with certainty, being omitted in many good mss. (P⁴⁵, P⁷⁵, B, W). Hence the brackets in the translation, following Nestle's text.

puts his hand to the plow. The best reading here is *oudeis epibalōn* (aor. ptc.) *tēn cheira ep' arotron kai blepōn* (pres. ptc.) *eis ta opisō,* "no one putting the hand on the plow and continuing to look toward what is behind." But mss. P⁴⁵, P⁷⁵, D read *eis ta opisō blepōn kai epiballōn tēn cheira autou ep' arotron,* "no one looking to what is behind and putting his hand to the plow." Both ptcs. are present, expressing continuing action. This reading reverses the actions and has a slightly different nuance. The imagery is drawn from 1 Kgs 19:19. See H. J. Blair, *ExpTim* 79 (1967-1968) 342-343; A. Vaccari, *VD* 18 (1938) 308-312. For a discussion of the text-critical problem, see L. Cerfaux, "Variantes de Lc., IX, 62" *ETL* 12 (1955) 326-328; reprinted in his *Recueil* 1. 498-501.

suited for the kingdom of God. The radical claim of the kingdom makes family ties a part of the *ta opisō,* the things that are behind. The one who would follow Jesus and engage in kingdom activity needs a firm hand and eye on the forward-moving plow. In the Elijah story the plow is not the symbol of discipleship; the cloak of the prophet rather is. But a decision to follow Jesus cannot be merely the result of enthusiasm; it calls for resolute determination.

BIBLIOGRAPHY (9:57-62)

Glombitza, O. "Die christologische Aussage des Lukas in seiner Gestaltung der drei Nachfolgeworte Lukas IX 57-62," *NovT* 13 (1971) 14-23.

Hengel, M. *Nachfolge und Charisma: Eine exegetisch-religionsgeschichtliche Studie zu Matt 8:21f. und Jesu Ruf in die Nachfolge* (BZNW 34; Berlin: Töpelmann, 1968) 3-17.

Küven, C. "Weisung für die Nachfolge: Eine Besinnung über Lk 9,57-62," *BibLeb* 2 (1961) 49-53.

Miyoshi, M. *Der Anfang,* 33-58.

Schulz, A. *Nachfolgen und Nachahmen: Studien über das Verhältnis der neutestamentlichen Jüngerschaft zur urchristlichen Vorbildethik* (SANT 6; Munich: Kösel, 1962) 105-108.

Strobel, A. "Die Nachfolge Jesu: Theologische Besinnung zu Lukas 9, 57-62," *TPQ* 98 (1950) 1-8.

Zimmermann, H. *Neutestamentliche Methodenlehre: Darstellung der historischkritischen Methode* (Stuttgart: Katholisches Bibelwerk, 1967) 116-122.